D1516454

Strategic Management

Strategy Formulation and Implementation

Second Edition

The Irwin Series in Management and The Behavioral Sciences
L. L. Cummings and E. Kirby Warren *Consulting Editors*

Strategic Management

Strategy Formulation and Implementation

Second Edition

John A. Pearce II / Richard B. Robinson, Jr.
Both of the College of Business Administration
University of South Carolina

1985 Second Edition

RICHARD D. IRWIN, INC. Homewood, Illinois 60430

ISBN 0-256-03230-0

Library of Congress Catalog Card No. 84–81127

Printed in the United States of America

1 2 3 4 5 6 7 8 9 0 K 2 1 0 9 8 7 6 5

To Susie and Joby

PREFACE

Strategic Management: Strategy Formulation and Implementation, second edition, is a book designed to introduce you to the critical business skills of planning and managing strategic activities. It incorporates three teaching approaches: text, cohesion cases, and business case studies.

The *text* portion of this book attempts to provide you with a readable, up-to-date introduction to the management of strategy in the business enterprise. We have tried to integrate the work of strategic management theorists, practitioners, and researchers with a strong emphasis on real-world applications of strategic management concepts. To further this aim, we have included "Strategy in Action" reports in each chapter that give current examples of the application of key concepts by well-known business firms.

The structure of the text material is guided by a comprehensive model of the strategic management process. The model will help you acquire an executive-level perspective on strategy formulation and implementation. It provides a visual display of the major components of the entire process and shows how they are conceptually related and how they are sequenced through the process.

The major components of the model are each discussed in depth in separate chapters, thereby enabling you to acquire detailed knowledge and specific skills within a broad framework of strategic management. The use of the model is also extended to the cohesion cases and the business case studies, where you will be guided in your case analyses to pursue disciplined, systematic, and comprehensive studies of actual strategic dilemmas.

The *cohesion case* offers a particularly unique feature designed to aid the student and teacher of strategic management and business policy. We have taken a well-known, multiindustry firm—Holiday Inns, Inc.—and used it as the basis of an in-depth case study to illustrate in detail the application of the text material. To do this, we provide a cohesion case section at the end of each chapter which applies the chapter material to the company. The Holiday Inns, Inc., case offers a clear illustration of the corporate, business, and functional levels of strategy—so important to the understanding of strategic management in today's corporate environment.

The cohesion case offers several benefits to the reader:

It provides a continuous illustration of the interdependence of the various parts of the strategic management process by using the same enterprise throughout the chapters.

It can provide a useful aid in understanding the text material when the primary emphasis in the course is to be on case studies or other nontext analysis.

It can provide a useful aid in preparing for the case analysis component of the course, in the event that the instructor prefers to emphasize the conceptual material.

It offers an in-depth basis for class discussion of strategic management concepts, application, and ideas for any classroom pedagogy.

The *business case studies* developed and chosen for the text offer students a wide exposure to a systematically selected cross section of strategic management situations. Among the 33 cases are 3 industry notes which depict broadly framed competitive environments and 9 accompanying cases which detail the strategic posturing of firms operating within those industries. Six businesses are presented as (A) and (B) cases which enable the impacts of their strategic actions to be assessed over time. Twenty of the studied firms are classified as large and 11 as small. Eighteen are in the dynamically growing service sector of our economy, while 13 are in manufacturing. Only 2 of the 33 cases are disguised ("Modern Office Supply" and "Pennsylvania Movie Theatres"), and all of them represent pertinent, relevant, factual, and we hope, interesting and challenging tests of student's skills as strategic managers.

Before preparing this revised edition we surveyed dozens of our first edition adopters and an equal number of "near-adopters." One thing we learned was that they liked the text portion, particularly its systematic and integrative nature. However, they were largely in agreement on four suggested improvements:

1. The book would benefit from a stronger section on industry analysis. We agreed. So in this edition you will find an entirely new Chapter 5 which presents the seminal work of Harvard's Michael E. Porter on how competitive forces shape business strategy.
2. There was widespread interest for an added section on multinational firms. We accommodated this request in a number of ways. First, you will find a major new section on international strategy in Chapter 4. We think you will find it to be among the most enjoyable and thought-provoking material in the book. Second, we increased our offering of cases that include

a major multinational dimension. In particular, you will want to look at "Swiss-Tex" and "Cold-Flo Ammonia Converter."

3. Many students needed more specific direction on the topic of business policies. Near-adopters were especially concerned that we should place greater emphasis on key middle-management aspects of strategy formulation and implementation, namely, policy development and use. In response, we prepared a major new section in Chapter 10 on the role of policies in strategy implementation.
4. Many survey respondents encouraged us to continue our heavy emphasis on strategy implementation. So in this second edition we have further expanded our coverage of the postformulation aspects of strategic management. You will now find three separate, state-of-the-art chapters on the operationalizing, institutionalizing, and monitoring and controlling of strategy.

Our surveys also revealed that professors and their students hoped for a slight reorientation in the cases which we included. They liked the profit-oriented nature of the businesses described, and the qualitative-quantitative components in each of the selections, but they requested a closer balance between service and manufacturing-based cases. They also asked for more industry-related studies and for "current events" cases to which students of the 1980s could more easily relate. As this edition shows, we followed their advice. Only the 13 most popular cases from the first edition were retained, and 4 of those were updated. Of the 20 new cases, 15 are available to students for the first time because of this book. They address such current topics as the restart of Braniff International, the impact on Coca-Cola of Reverend Jesse Jackson's political activities, the personalities and intrigue of the failed attempt to merge Martin Marietta and Bendix, the rise of Wendy's International, and the fall of Merrill Lynch. Other cases help you to take a strategic look at the strategies of manufacturers, like DuPont's decision to produce Kevlar and Georgia Pacific's consideration of a plywood substitute. Other cases describe competition in the grocery, airline, and lodging industries and are accompanied by individual cases on noteworthy competitors like Safeway, Delta Airlines, and Days Inns of America.

From the total selection of 33 cases, six businesses are studied through multiple cases thereby providing you with the opportunity to investigate patterns of strategy formulation and implementation over time and in changing environments. Other cases enable the study of comparative differences between large and small firms, service and manufacturing companies, and retail and wholesale businesses. In addition, the cases share three characteristics that we feel are vitally important: they address strategic management issues, they have been classroom tested to help assure their educational value, and they depict the most modern strategic issues and events offered by any business policy textbook.

The preparation of the new cases in this revised edition of *Strategic Management* was a long and intellectually demanding task. In developing our new materials, we were fortunate to be able to work with a number of noted authors. In particular we are indebted to:

Peter S. Davis, University of Oregon
Timothy S. Mescon, University of Miami, Florida
Benjamin M. Oviatt, Oklahoma State University
Michael S. Smith, University of South Carolina
Tom Van Dyke, Virginia Polytechnic Institute and State University

At the same time that our case development was under way, we were extremely fortunate in identifying several scholars whose own standards of excellence and quality of cases parallel our highest expectations for this second edition. The generous contributions of business case studies by the following authors form what we believe is the real learning core of the book:

Shelia A. Adams, *Arizona State University*
Larry Alexander, *Virginia Polytechnic Institute and State University*
Alan D. Bauerschmidt, *University of South Carolina*
Kenneth Beck, *University of Kansas*
Richard F. Beltramini, *Arizona State University*
Curtis W. Cook, *San Jose State University*
James Graham, *University of Calgary*
Robert D. Hay, *University of Arkansas*
Phillis G. Holland, *Georgia State University*
Neil H. Snyder, *University of Virginia*
A. J. Strickland, *University of Alabama*
Marilyn L. Taylor, *University of Kansas*
John Thiel, *University of Tennessee*
George S. Vozikis, *University of Miami, Florida*

The development of this edition was aided by many friends and colleagues. We are especially grateful to the following people who deserve our special thanks for their helpful and thorough reviews:

Larry Cummings, *Northwestern University*
William Davig, *Auburn University*
Liam Fahey, *Northwestern University*
Don Hambrick, *Columbia University*
Troy Jones, *University of Central Florida*
Cynthia Montgomery, *University of Michigan*

Joseph Paolillo, *University of Wyoming*
Les Rue, *Georgia State University*
Bill Warren, *College of William and Mary*
Kirby Warren, *Columbia University*
Michael White, *Louisiana State University*
Robley Wood, *Virginia Commonwealth University*

The valuable recommendations and the support of these outstanding scholars have added quality to our final product.

The stimulating environment at the University of South Carolina has contributed to the development of this book. Thought-provoking discussions with our business policy colleagues, Alan Bauerschmidt, Carl Clamp, Herb Hand, Clark Holloway, John Logan, and Bob Rosen, gave us many useful ideas. We also want to recognize the important input of doctoral candidates Beth Freeman, Kay Keels, Patricia McDougal, Keith Robbins, and Frank Winfrey in the development, class testing and refinement of selected business case studies. Likewise, we want to thank James F. Kane, dean of the College of Business Administration, James G. Hilton, our associate dean, and Joe Ullman, Program Director in Management, for their interest and support. Our sincere appreciation also goes to the secretaries who helped to prepare our manuscript, Frances Donnelly, Kay Elledge, and Kathy Fine.

In using this text, we hope that you will share our enthusiasm both for the rich subject of strategic management and for the learning approach that we have taken.

Jack Pearce
Richard Robinson

CONTENTS

PART TWO
Strategy Formulation 75

Strategic Management

Strategy Formulation and Implementation

Second Edition

STRATEGIC MANAGEMENT MODEL

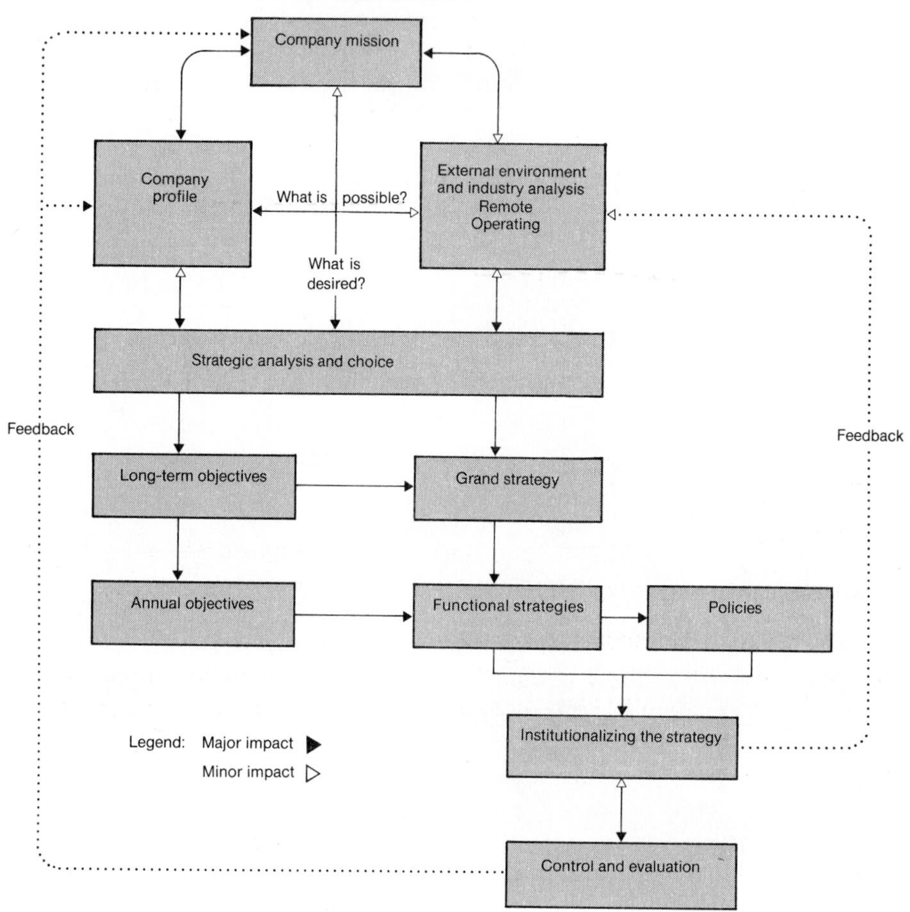
Company mission
Company profile
What is possible?
External environment and industry analysis
Remote
Operating
What is desired?
Strategic analysis and choice
Feedback
Feedback
Long-term objectives
Grand strategy
Annual objectives
Functional strategies
Policies
Institutionalizing the strategy
Legend: Major impact
Minor impact
Control and evaluation

PART ONE

Overview of strategic management

The first two chapters of this text provide a broad introduction to strategic management. They describe the nature, need, benefits, and terminology of the processes for producing and implementing major plans directing business activities. Subsequent chapters then provide greater detail.

Chapter 1, The Nature and Value of Strategic Management, emphasizes the practical value of a strategic management approach for a business organization and reviews the actual benefits for companies that have instituted strategic management. The critical activities of strategic management are then presented as a set of dimensions that can be used to distinguish strategic decisions from other planning tasks of the firm.

Chapter 1 stresses the key point that, in many companies, strategic management activities are undertaken at three levels: corporate, business, and functional. The distinctive characteristics of strategic decision making at each of these levels are discussed; these characteristics will serve as the basis for later observations concerning the impact of activities at different levels on company operations.

The extent to which formality is desirable in strategic management is another key point in Chapter 1, as is the alignment of strategy makers with particular activities in the overall process of strategy formulation and implementation. It is shown that it is possible to assign areas of decision-maker responsibility, and an appropriate degree of formality in strategic activities is suggested. The factors determining these conclusions are discussed in detail.

A final section in Chapter 1 reviews the results of research in business organizations. The studies convincingly demonstrate that companies utilizing strategic management processes often enjoy financial and behavioral benefits that justify the additional costs involved.

Chapter 2 presents a model of the strategic management process. The model is representative of approaches currently used by strategic planners and will serve as an outline for the remainder of the book in that each subsequent chapter is devoted to an in-depth discussion of one of the major components of the model. Each of the individual components is carefully defined and explained in Chapter 2, as is the process by which the components are integrated to produce cohesive and balanced results. The chapter ends with a discussion of the practical limitations of the model and the advisability of tailoring the general recommendations suggested to the unique situations confronted in actual business practice.

CHAPTER 1

The Nature and Value of Strategic Management

The complexity and sophistication of business decision making requires strategic management. Managing various and multifaceted internal activities is only part of the modern executive's responsibilities. The firm's immediate external environment poses a second set of challenging factors. This environment includes competitors whenever profits seem possible, suppliers of increasingly scarce resources, government agencies monitoring adherence to an ever-growing number of regulations, and customers whose often inexplicable preferences must be anticipated. There is also a remote external environment that contributes to the general yet pervasive climate in which a business exists. This environment consists of economic conditions, social change, political priorities, and technological developments, each of which must be anticipated, monitored, assessed, and incorporated in top-level decision making. However, these influences are often subordinated to the fourth major consideration in executive decision making—the multiple and often mutually inconsistent objectives of the stakeholders of the business: owners, top managers, employees, communities, customers, and country.

To deal effectively with all that affects the ability of a company to grow profitably, executives design strategic management processes they feel will facilitate the optimal positioning of the firm in its competitive environment. Such positioning is possible because these strategic processes allow more accurate anticipation of environmental changes and improved preparedness for reacting to unexpected internal or competitive demands.

Broad-scope, large-scale management processes have become dramatically more sophisticated since the end of World War II, principally as a reflection of increases in the size and number of competing firms; of the expanded intervention of government as a buyer, seller, regulator, and competitor in the free-enterprise system; and of greater business involvement in international trade. Perhaps the most significant improvement in management processes came in the 1970s as "long-range planning," "new venture management," "planning, programming, budgeting," and "business policy" were blended with increased emphasis on environmental forecasting and external as well as internal considerations in formulating and implementing plans. This all-encompassing approach is known as *strategic management* or *strategic planning.*[1]

Strategic management is defined as *the set of decisions and actions resulting in formulation and implementation of strategies designed to achieve the objectives of an organization.* It involves attention to no less than nine critical areas.

1. Determining the mission of the company, including broad statements about its purpose, philosophy, and goals.
2. Developing a company profile that reflects internal conditions and capabilities.
3. Assessment of the company's external environment, both in terms of competitive and general contextual factors.
4. Analysis of possible options uncovered in the matching of the company profile with the external environment.
5. Identifying the desired options uncovered when possibilities are considered in light of the company mission.
6. Strategic choice of a particular set of long-term objectives and grand strategies needed to achieve the desired options.
7. Development of annual objectives and short-term strategies compatible with long-term objectives and grand strategies.
8. Implementing strategic choice decisions that are based on budgeted resource allocations and emphasize the matching of tasks, people, structures, technologies, and reward systems.
9. Review and evaluation of the success of the strategic process to serve as a basis for control and as an input for future decision making.

As these nine areas indicate, strategic management involves the planning, directing, organizing, and controlling of the strategy-related decisions and actions of the business. By strategy, managers mean their *large-scale, future-oriented plans for interacting with the competitive environment to optimize achievement of organization objectives.* Thus, a strategy represents a firm's "game plan." Although it does not precisely detail all future deployments (people, financial, and material), it does provide a framework for managerial

[1] In this text the term *strategic management* refers to the broad overall process because to some scholars and practitioners the term *strategic planning* connotes only the formulation phase of total management activities.

decisions. A strategy reflects a company's awareness of how to compete, against whom, when, where, and for what.

Dimensions of Strategic Decisions

What decisions facing a business are strategic and therefore deserve strategic management attention? Typically, strategic issues have six identifiable dimensions.

Strategic Issues Require Top-Management Decisions. Strategic decisions overarch several areas of a firm's operations. Therefore, top management involvement in decision making is imperative. Only at this level is there the perspective for understanding and anticipating broad implications and ramifications, and the power to authorize the resource allocations necessary for implementation.

Strategic Issues Involve the Allocation of Large Amounts of Company Resources. Strategic decisions characteristically involve substantial resource deployment. The people, physical assets, or monies needed must be either redirected from internal sources or secured from outside the firm. In either case, strategic decisions commit a firm to a stream of actions over an extended period of time, thus involving substantial resources.

Strategic Issues Are Likely to Have a Significant Impact on the Long-Term Prosperity of the Firm. Strategic decisions ostensibly commit the firm for a long period of time, typically for five years; however, the time frame of impact is often much longer. Once a firm has committed itself to a particular strategic option in a major way, its competitive image and advantages are usually tied to that strategy. Firms become known in certain markets, for certain products, with certain characteristics. To shift from these markets, products, or technologies by adopting a radically different strategy would jeopardize previous progress. Thus, strategic decisions have enduring effects on the firm—for better or worse.

Strategic Issues Are Future Oriented. Strategic decisions are based upon what managers anticipate or forecast rather than on what they know. Emphasis is on developing projections that will enable the firm to select the most promising strategic options. In the turbulent and competitive free-enterprise environment, a successful firm must take a proactive (anticipatory) stance toward change.

Strategic Issues Usually Have Major Multifunctional or Multibusiness Consequences. A strategic decision is coordinative. Decisions about such factors as customer mix, competitive emphasis, or organizational structure

businesses that constitute approximately 95 percent of all business organizations in the United States.

Alternative 2 is a classical corporate structure comprised of three fully operative levels. The suprastructure is provided at the corporate level, with the superstructure at the business level giving direction and support for functional-level activities.

The approach taken throughout this text is best depicted by alternative 2. Thus, whenever appropriate, topics will be covered from the perspective of each level of strategic management. In this way the text presents one of the most comprehensive and up-to-date discussions of the strategic management process.

Characteristics of Strategic Management Decisions

The characteristics of strategic management decisions vary with the level of strategic activity considered. As shown in Figure 1–2, corporate-level decisions tend to be value oriented, conceptual, and less concrete than are those at the business or functional level of strategy formulation and implementation. Corporate-level decisions are also characterized by greater risk, cost, and profit potential, as well as by longer time horizons and greater needs for flexibility. These characteristics are logical consequences of the more far-reaching futuristic, innovative, and pervasive nature of corporate-level strategic activity. Examples of corporate-level decisions include the choice of business, dividend policies, sources of long-term financing, and priorities for growth.

At the other end of the continuum, functional-level decisions principally

Figure 1–2

Characteristics of strategic management decisions at different levels

	Level of strategy		
Characteristic	***Corporate***	***Business***	***Functional***
Type	Conceptual	Mixed	Operational
Measurability	Value judgments dominant	Semiquantifiable	Usually quantifiable
Frequency	Periodic or sporadic	Periodic or sporadic	Periodic
Adaptability	Low	Medium	High
Relation to present activities	Innovative	Mixed	Supplementary
Risk	Wide range	Moderate	Low
Profit potential	Large	Medium	Small
Cost	Major	Medium	Modest
Time horizon	Long range	Medium range	Short range
Flexibility	High	Medium	Low
Cooperation required	Considerable	Moderate	Little

involve action-oriented operational issues. These decisions are made periodically and lead directly to implementation of some part of the overall strategy formulated at the corporate and business levels. Therefore, functional-level decisions are relatively short range and involve low risk and modest costs because they are dependent on available resources. Functional-level decisions usually determine actions requiring minimal companywide cooperation. These activities supplement the functional area's present activities and are adaptable to ongoing activities so that minimal cooperation is needed for successful implementation. Because functional-level decisions are relatively concrete and quantifiable, they receive critical attention and analysis even though their comparative profit potential is low.

Some common functional-level decisions include generic versus brand-name labeling, basic versus applied R&D, high versus low inventory levels, general-versus specific-purpose production equipment, and close versus loose supervision.

Bridging corporate- and functional-level decisions are those made at the business level. As Figure 1–2 indicates, business-level descriptions of strategic decisions fall between those for the other two levels. For example, business-level decisions are less costly, risky, and potentially profitable than corporate-level decisions, but more costly, risky, and potentially profitable than functional-level decisions. Some common business-level decisions involve plant location, marketing segmentation and geographic coverage, and distribution channels.

Formality in Strategic Management

The formality of strategic management systems varies widely among companies. *Formality* refers to the degree to which membership, responsibilities, authority, and discretion in decision making are specified. It is an important consideration in the study of strategic management because degree of formality is usually positively correlated with the cost, comprehensiveness, accuracy, and success of planning.

A number of forces determine the need for formality in strategic management. As shown in Figure 1–3, the size of the organization, its predominant management styles, the complexity of its environment, its production processes, the nature of its problems, and the purpose of planning system all combine in determining an appropriate degree of formality.

In particular, formality is often associated with two factors: size and stage of development of the company. Methods of evaluating strategic success are also linked to degree of formality. Some firms, especially smaller ones, are *entrepreneurial.* They are basically under the control of a single individual and produce a limited number of products or services. With this mode, evaluation performance is very informal, intuitive, and limited in scope. At the other end of the spectrum, evaluation is part of a comprehensive, formalized,

Figure 1–3

Forces influencing design of strategic management systems

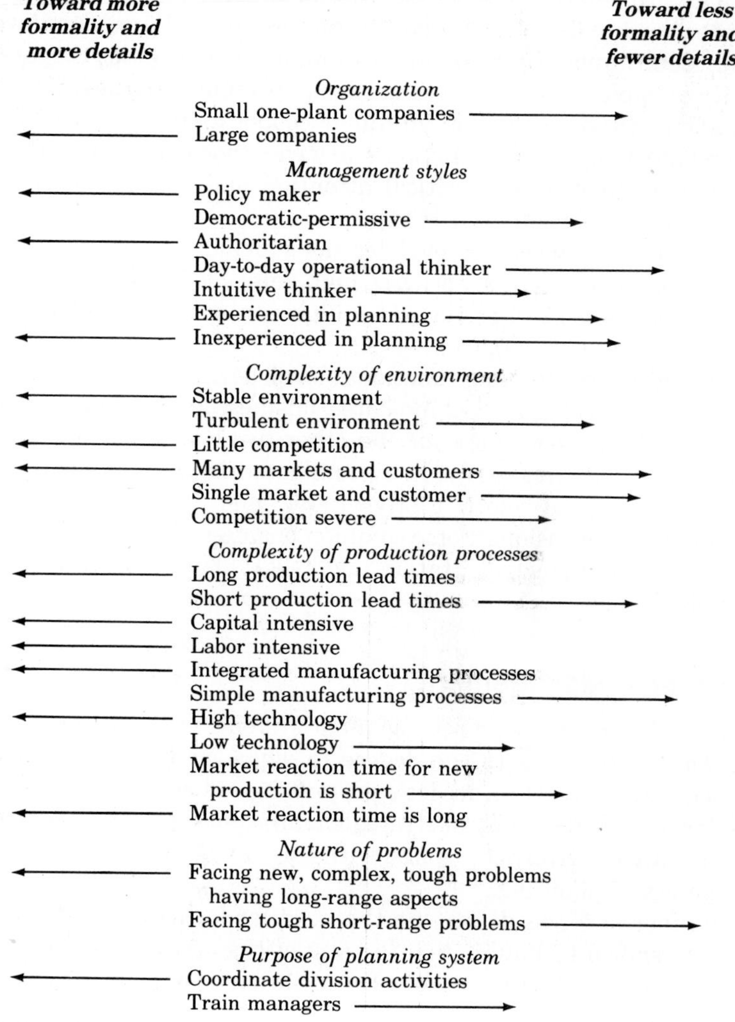

Source: George A. Steiner, *Strategic Planning* (New York: Free Press, 1979), p. 54.

multilevel strategic planning system. This approach, which Henry Mintzberg called the *planning mode,* is used by large firms such as Texas Instruments and General Electric. Mintzberg also identified a third mode (the *adaptive mode*) in the middle of this spectrum which he associated with medium-sized firms in relatively stable environments.[2] For firms in the adaptive mode, identification and evaluation of alternative strategies are closely related to existing strategy. Despite these generalities, it is not unusual to find different modes within the same organization. For example, Exxon might adopt an entrepreneurial mode in the development and evaluation of its solar subsidiary's strategy while the rest of the company follows a planning mode.

The Strategy Makers

The ideal strategic management process is developed and governed by a strategic management team. The team consists principally of decision makers at all three levels (corporate, business, and functional) in the corporation, e.g., the chief executive officer (CEO), the product managers, and the heads of functional areas. The team also relies on input from two types of support personnel: company planning staffs, when they exist, and lower-level managers and supervisors. The latter provide data for strategic decision making and are responsible for implementing strategies.

Because strategic decisions have such a tremendous impact on a firm and because they require large commitments of company resources, they can only be made by top managers in the organizational hierarchy. Figure 1–4 indicates the alignment between levels of strategic decision makers and the kinds of objectives and strategies for which they are typically responsible.

Figure 1–4

Hierarchy of objectives and strategies

		Strategic decision makers			
Ends (What is to be achieved?)	***Means (How it is to be achieved?)***	***Board of directors***	***Corporate managers***	***Business managers***	***Functional managers***
Mission, including goals and philosophy		√√	√√	√	
Long-term objectives	Grand strategy	√	√√	√√	
Annual objectives	Short-term strategy policies		√	√√	√√
Functional objectives	Tactics			√	√√

Note: √√ indicates a principal responsibility; √ indicates a secondary responsibility.

[2] Henry Mintzberg, "Strategy Making in Three Modes," *California Management Review* 16, no. 2 (1973), pp. 44–53.

The use of company planning staffs has increased considerably since the 1960s. In large corporations, the existence of planning departments, often headed by a corporate vice president for planning, is common. Medium-sized firms frequently employ at least one full-time staff member to spearhead strategic data-collection efforts. Even in smaller or less progressive firms, an officer or group of officers designated as a planning committee is often assigned to spearhead the company's strategic planning efforts.

Precisely what are manager's responsibilities in the strategic planning process at the corporate and business levels? Figure 1–5 provides some answers.

Figure 1–5

Responsibility relationships in strategic planning

	Corporate responsibility		*Business responsibility*		*Functional responsibility*
Planning activities	*Top management*	*Corporate planning department*	*General management*	*Staff groups*	*Departmental planning groups*
Establish corporate objectives	△				
Identify performance targets	●	●			
Setting planning horizon	●		●		
Organize and coordinate planning effort		●			●
Make environmental assumptions	△	●	△	●	
Collection information and forecast					
Forecast sales	△		△	●	
Assess firm's strength and weaknesses			△	●	
Evaluate competitive environment			△	●	
Establish business objectives	△		△	●	△
Develop business plans	△	○	△		△
Formulate alternative strategies		○		●	
Select alternative strategies		○	●		
Evaluate and select projects			△	●	
Develop tactics			△	●	
Revise objectives and plans if objectives are not met	△				
Integrate plans		●			
Allocate resources	△				
Review progress against the plan	●		●		
Evaluate plan's effectiveness		●			

Key: △ Approves.
○ Reviews, evaluate, and counsels.
● Does the work.

Source: Adapted from Ronald J. Kudla, "Elements of Effective Corporate Planning," *Long Range Planning,* August 1976, p. 89.

It shows that top management shoulder responsibility for broadly approving each of the six major phases of planning listed. They are assisted in the execution of these responsibilities by the corporate planning department, staff, or personnel, who actually prepare major components of the corporate plan. Top management also review, evaluate, and counsel on most major phases of the plan's preparation.

Figure 1–5 further shows that general managers at the business level have principal responsibilities for approving environmental analysis and forecasting, establishing business objectives, and developing business plans prepared by staff groups. The figure clearly indicates the pervasive and potentially powerful influence of corporate planners in the overall strategic management process.

One final, but perhaps overriding, point must be made about strategic decision makers: a company's president or CEO characteristically plays a dominant role in the process. In many ways this situation is desirable and reasonable. The principal duty of a CEO is often defined as giving long-term direction to the firm. The CEO is ultimately responsible for the success of the business and therefore of its strategy. Additionally, CEO's are typically strong-willed, company-oriented individuals with a high sense of self-esteem. Their personalities often prevent them from delegating substantive authority to others in formulation or approval of strategic decisions.

However, when the dominance of the CEO approaches autocracy, the effectiveness of the firm's strategic planning and management processes are likely to be greatly diminished. The advantages of a team-oriented, participative strategic system are obviously related inversely to the CEO's propensity to make major strategic decisions single-handedly. For these reasons, establishment of a strategic management system carries with it an implicit promise by the CEO to provide managers at all levels with the opportunity to play a role in determining the strategic posture of the firm. The degree to which the CEO fulfills this promise is often parallel to the degree of success enjoyed through the use of the strategic management process.

The Interactive and Iterative Flow of the Strategic Process

The strategic management process is sometimes misperceived as involving a unidirectional flow of objectives, strategies, and decision parameters from corporate- to business- to functional-level managers. In fact, the process is highly interactive, that is, designed to stimulate input from creative, skilled, and knowledgeable people throughout the firm. While the strategic process is certainly overseen by top managers—because they have a broad perspective on the company and its environment—there are multiple opportunities for managers at all levels to participate in various phases of the total process.

Figure 1–6 provides an example of the basic, typical, interactive flow. As indicated by the solid line, strategic management activities tend to follow a

Figure 1–6

Strategic planning process cycle

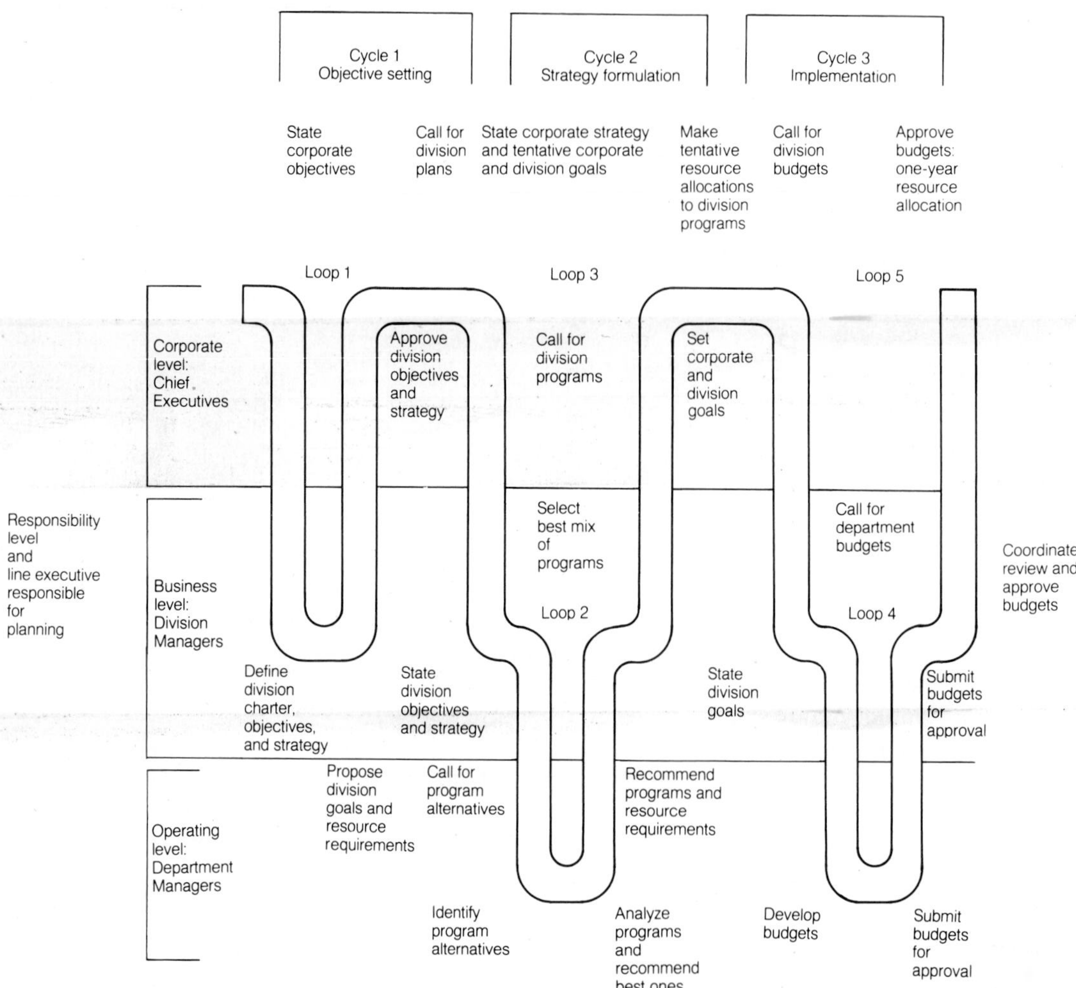

Source: Adapted from Richard F. Vancil and Peter Lorange, "Strategic Planning in Diversified Companies," by permission of the *Harvard Business Review*, January–February 1975.

formalized pattern of top-down/bottom-up interactions involving planners at all three levels.

As indicated by the five loops in Figure 1–6, the strategic management process is also iterative. This means that strategic decisions are usually reached only after trial and error. Management expert Peter Lorange illustrates the five iterative loops as follows:

Loop 1: When the CEO receives inputs indicating where the businesses may be going, he or she may have to reconcile the emerging portfolio pictures with initial tentative objectives. As a result, the CEO may ask one or more of the businesses to revise their inputs, and may change the original tentative objectives, as well. One or more iterations may be necessary before the loop is closed.

Loop 2: In formulating strategy, the business manager may frequently go back to the functional departments and request revisions so that individual programs fit into a more coherent package from the business strategy viewpoint.

Loop 3: When the CEO receives the portfolio of business strategies, he or she may have to recycle one or more of these for revisions to achieve the desired portfolio strategy.

Loop 4: During implementation, a business manager may have to recycle functional proposals so that the overall implementation plan has the desired strategic properties, i.e., becomes a near-term reflection of the longer-term strategy.

Loop 5: Similarly, the CEO might want revisions in one or more of the business implementation plans so that a final overall fit is achieved.[3]

The central point of this discussion is that the team concept is a critical and practiced feature in strategic processes. Managers at various levels have different responsibilities for various parts of the process, but they interact and are interdependent in achieving the final outcome.

Value of Strategic Management

Financial Benefits

The principal appeal of any managerial approach is the expectation that it will lead to increased profit for the firm. This is especially true of a strategic management system with a major impact on both the formulation and implementation of plans.

A series of studies of various business organizations actually measured the impact of strategic management processes on the bottom line. One of the first major studies was conducted by Ansoff, Avner, Brandenburg, Portner, and Radosevich in 1970.[4] In a study of 93 U.S. manufacturing firms, the authors found that formal planners who took a strategic management approach outperformed nonplanners in terms of financial criteria which measured sales, assets,

[3] P. Lorange, *Corporate Planning: An Executive Viewpoint* (Englewood Cliffs, N.J.: Prentice-Hall, 1980), p. 62.

[4] H. I. Ansoff; J. Avner; R. Brandenburg; F. E. Portner; and R. Radosevich, "Does Planning Pay? The Effect of Planning on Success of Acquisitions in American Firms," *Long Range Planning* 3 (1970), pp. 2–7.

sales price, earnings per share, and earnings growth. The planners were also more accurate in predicting the outcome of major strategic actions.

A second pioneering research effort was published in 1970 by Thune and House who studied 36 firms in six different industries.[5] They found that formal planners in the petroleum, food, drug, steel, chemical, and machinery industries significantly outperformed nonplanners in the same fields. Additionally, planners improved their own performance significantly after the formal process had been adopted as compared to their financial performance during the nonplanning years.

Herold later (1972) reported a replication of part of the Thune and House research dealing with drug and chemical companies.[6] His findings supported the earlier study and in fact, suggested that the disparity between the financial performance of planning and nonplanning firms was increasing over time.

In 1974 Fulmer and Rue published a study of the strategic management practices of 386 companies over a three-year period. The authors found that durable-goods manufacturing firms with strategic management were more successful than those without.[7] Their findings did not hold for nondurable and service companies, probably, the authors suspected, because strategic planning among these firms was a recent phenomenon and its effects were not fully realized.

In 1974, Schoeffler, Buzzell, and Heany reported a study designed to measure the profit impact of market studies (PIMS).[8] This PIMS project involved the effects of strategic planning on a firm's return on investment (ROI). The researchers concluded that ROI was most significantly affected by market share, investment intensity, and corporate diversity. The overall PIMS model, which incorporated 37 performance variables, disclosed that up to 80 percent of the improvement possible in a firm's profitability is achieved through changes in the company's strategic direction.

An additional study of widespread impact was reported by Karger and Malik in 1975.[9] In their research involving 90 U.S. companies in five industries, it was found that strategic long-range planners significantly outperformed nonformal planners in terms of generally accepted financial measures.

Finally, while most studies have examined strategic management in large firms, a 1982 report found that strategic planning had a favorable impact on performance in small business. After studying 101 small retail, service,

---

[5] S. S. Thune and R. J. House, "Where Long-Range Planning Pays Off," *Business Horizons,* August 1970, pp. 81–87.

[6] D. M. Herold, "Long-Range Planning and Organizational Performance: A Cross-Validation Study," *Academy of Management Journal,* March 1972, pp. 91–102.

[7] R. M. Fulmer and L. W. Rue, "The Practice and Profitability of Long-Range Planning," *Managerial Planning* 22 (1974), pp. 1–7.

[8] S. Schoeffler, R. D. Buzzell, and D. F. Heany, "Impact of Strategic Planning on Profit Performance," *Harvard Business Review,* March–April 1974, pp. 137–45.

[9] D. W. Karger and Z. A. Malik, "Long-Range Planning and Organizational Performance," *Long-Range Planning,* December 1975, pp. 60–64.

and manufacturing firms over a three-year period, Robinson found a significant improvement in sales, profitability, and productivity among those businesses engaging in strategic planning when compared to firms without systematic planning activities.[10]

The overall pattern of results reported in these seven studies clearly indicates the value of strategic management as gauged by a variety of financial measures.[11] Based on the evidence now available, organizations that adopt a strategic management approach do so with the strong and reasonable expectation that the new system will lead to improved financial performance.

Benefits of Strategic Management[12]

The strategic management approach emphasizes interaction by managers at all levels of the organizational hierarchy in planning and implementation. As a result, strategic management has certain behavioral consequences that are also characteristic of participative decision making. Therefore, an accurate assessment of the impact of strategy formulation on organizational performance also requires a set of nonfinancial evaluation criteria—measures of behavioral-based effects. In fact, it can be argued that the manager trained to promote the positive aspects of these behavioral consequences is also well positioned to meet the financial expectations of the firm. However, regardless of the eventual profitability of particular strategic plans, several behavioral effects can be expected that should improve the welfare of the firm.

1. Strategy formulation activities should enhance the problem prevention capabilities of the firm. As a consequence of encouraging and rewarding subordinate attention to planning considerations, managers are aided in their monitoring and forecasting responsibilities by workers who are alerted to needs of strategic planning.

2. Group-based strategic decisions are most likely to reflect the best available alternatives. There are two reasons that better decisions are probable outcomes of the process. First, generating alternative strategies is facilitated by group interaction. Second, screening options is improved because group members offer forecasts based on their specialized perspectives.

3. Employee motivation should improve as employees better appreciate the productivity-reward relationships inherent in every strategic plan. When employees or their representatives participate in the strategy formulation process, a better understanding of the priorities and operations of the organiza-

[10] R. B. Robinson, Jr., "The Importance of Outsiders in Small Firm Strategic Planning," *Academy of Management Journal,* March 1982, pp. 80–93.

[11] A few additional studies that were not discussed in the chapter reported mixed results. However, only one piece of research has indicated that strategic management might have a negative impact. Refer to Fulmer and Rue, "Practice and Profitability of Long-Range Planning," for details.

[12] This section was adapted in part from J. A. Pearce II and W. A. Randolph, "Improving Strategy Formulation Pedagogies by Recognizing Behavioral Aspects," *Exchange,* December 1980, pp. 7–10, with permission of the authors.

tion's reward system is achieved, thus adding incentives for goal-directed behavior.

4. Gaps and overlaps in activities among diverse individuals and groups should be reduced as participation in strategy formulation leads to a clarification of role differentiations. The group meeting format which is characteristic of several stages of a strategy formulation process promotes an understanding of the delineations of individual and subgroup responsibilities.

5. Resistance to change should be reduced. The participation required helps eliminate the uncertainty associated with change which is at the root of most resistance. While participants may be no more pleased with their own choices then they would be with authoritarian decisions, their acceptance of new plans is more likely if employees are aware of the parameters that limit the available options.

Risks of Strategic Management

While involvement in strategy formulation generates behavior-based benefits for participants and for the firm, managers must be trained to guard against three types of unintended negative consequences. First, while it is readily recognized that the strategic management process is costly in terms of hours invested by participants, the negative effects of managers spending time away from work is considered less often. Managers must be trained to schedule their duties to provide the necessary time for strategic activities while minimizing any negative impact on operational responsibilities.

Second, if the formulators of strategy are not intimately involved in implementation, individual responsibility for input to the decision process and subsequent conclusions can be shirked. Thus, strategic managers must be trained to limit their promises to performance that can be delivered by the decision makers and their subordinates.

Third, strategic managers must be trained to anticipate, minimize, or constructively respond when participating subordinates become disappointed or frustrated over unattained expectations. Frequently, subordinates perceive an implicit guarantee that their involvement in even minor phases of total strategy formulation will result in both acceptance of their preferred plan and an increase in clearly associated rewards. Alternatively, they may erroneously conclude that a strategic manager's solicitation of their input on selected issues will extend to other areas of decision making. Sensitizing managers to these issues and preparing them with effective means of negating or minimizing such negative consequences will greatly enhance the overall potential of any strategic plan.

Summary

Strategic management was defined as the set of decisions and actions resulting in the formulation and implementation of strategies designed to achieve the objectives of an organization. It was shown to involve long-term, future-oriented, complex decision making necessitating top-management action because of the resources required to formulate an environmentally opportunistic plan.

Strategic management was presented as a three-tiered process involving corporate-, business-, and functional-level planners, and support personnel. At each progressively lower level, strategic activities were shown to be more specific, narrow, short term, and action oriented with lower risks but fewer opportunities for dramatic impact.

The value of strategic management was demonstrated in a review of seven large-scale business studies. Using a variety of financial performance measures, each of these studies was able to provide convincing evidence of the profitability of strategy formulation and implementation. In addition, the chapter identified five major behavioral benefits for the team-oriented, strategic-management-directed firm. Despite some noteworthy behavioral costs, the net behavioral gains justify the approach, almost irrespective of the hope of improved financial performance.

Questions for Discussion

1. Find a recent copy of *Business Week* and read the "Corporate Strategies" section. Was the main decision discussed strategic? At what level in the organization was the key decision made?
2. In what ways do you think the subject matter in this strategic management/business policy course will differ from previous courses you have had?
3. Why do you believe that the case method is selected as the best approach for learning the skills needed in strategy formulation and implementation?
4. After graduation you are not likely to move directly into a top-level management position. In fact, most members of your class may never reach that level. Why then is it important for all business majors to study the field of strategic management?
5. Do you expect that outstanding performance in this course will require a great deal of memorization? Why or why not?
6. You have undoubtedly read about individuals who seemingly single-handedly have given direction to their corporations. Is it likely that a participative strategic management approach might stiffle or suppress the contributions of such individuals?

Bibliography

Fulmer, R. M., and L. W. Rue. "The Practice and Profitability of Long-Range Planning." *Managerial Planning* 22 (1974), pp. 1–7.

Herold, D. M. "Long-Range Planning and Organizational Performance: A Cross-Validation Study." *Academy of Management Journal,* March 1972, pp. 91–102.

Hofer, C. W., and D. Schendel. *Strategy Formulation: Analytical Concepts.* St. Paul, Minn.: West Publishing, 1978.

Karger, D. W., and Z. A. Malik. "Long-Range Planning and Organizational Performance." *Long-Range Planning,* December 1975, pp. 60–64.

Kudja, R. J. "Elements of Effective Corporate Planning." *Long-Range Planning,* August 1976, pp. 82–93.

Lorange, P. *Corporate Planning: An Executive Viewpoint.* Englewood Cliffs, N.J.: Prentice-Hall, 1980.

Mintzberg, H. "Strategy Making in Three Modes." *California Management Review* 16, no. 2 (1973), pp. 44–53.

Pearce, J. A., II, and W. A. Randolph. "Improving Strategy Formulation Pedagogies by Recognizing Behavioral Aspects." *Exchange,* December 1980, pp. 7–10.

Robinson, R. B. "The Importance of 'Outsiders' in Small Firm Strategic Planning." *Academy of Management Journal,* March 1982, pp. 80–93.

Schoeffler, S.; R. D. Buzzell; and D. F. Heany. "Impact of Strategic Planning on Profit Performance." *Harvard Business Review,* March 1974, pp. 137–45.

Steiner, G. A. "The Rise of the Corporate Planner." *Harvard Business Review,* September–October 1970, pp. 133–139.

———. *Strategic Planning.* New York: Free Press, 1979.

Thune, S. S., and R. J. House. "Where Long-Range Planning Pays Off." *Business Horizons,* August 1970, pp. 81–87.

Vancil, R. F. ". . . So You're Going to Have a Planning Department!" *Harvard Business Review,* May–June 1967, pp. 88–96.

Introduction to the Cohesion Case: Holiday Inns, Inc.

This section inaugurates a unique feature of this book, the Cohesion Case. Each of the remaining chapters will include an illustration linked to this case. As the word *cohesion* suggests, the objective is to "tie related parts together." Specifically, the objective is to tie together the strategic management concepts discussed in each chapter with an illustration of their practical application in an actual business firm. To ensure continuity across the chapters, the 12 Cohesion Case Illustrations will focus on the same company—Holiday Inns, Inc. This provides the added advantage of illustrating each part of the strategic management process in the same firm, thus offering an integrated, consistent picture of the formulation and implementation of corporate strategy.

Holiday Inns, Inc., is the world's leading hospitality company with interests in hotels/motels, restaurants, transportation, and casino gaming. It was selected for the Cohesion Case for several reasons.

1. It is a highly visible, well-known firm.
2. It is a multibusiness firm, thus providing the opportunity to apply strategic management concepts at three levels—corporate, business, and operational.
3. While Holiday Inns, Inc., is a multibusiness firm, it is still a relatively simple, comprehendable enterprise. As a result, using this firm should

facilitate maximum focus on the application of text material and avoid energy wasted on simply trying to understand what the business is about.

The remainder of this section provides a case study describing Holiday Inns, Inc. This case is the basis for understanding the Cohesion Case Illustrations. This material should be read thoroughly to gain a familiarity with Holiday Inns. As the remaining chapters (and accompanying Cohesion Case Illustrations) are covered, refer to this case material, occasionally rereading it. Doing this will ensure an adequate foundation for understanding how the components of strategic management, discussed in each chapter, are being applied to Holiday Inns in the respective illustrations.

The first objective in dealing with this Cohesion Case is to become more familiar with the total operation of Holiday Inns, Inc., and to think about the relevance of strategic management to this firm. An illustration is provided at the conclusion of the case to aid in applying the Chapter 1 material to Holiday Inns.

One final point: The case covers Holiday Inns, Inc., only through early 1981. This date was chosen because the 1980–81 period represented a key decision point in the strategic posture of the firm. Thus, the Cohesion Case Illustrations allow the reader to assume the role of assistant to the president and executive committee at Holiday Inns with the assignment of formulating and implementing a strategy for the 1980s. An update of key actions at Holiday Inns, Inc. is provided at a later point in this book.

The Cohesion Case

Holiday Inns, Inc.

1 In August 1952, Kemmons Wilson opened his first hotel on the outskirts of Memphis. Wilson entered the business because he was disgruntled by the prices he was forced to pay for cramped lodging on the way to Washington, D.C., while traveling with his wife and five children.

2 From the original, Holiday Inn Hotel Courts, the determined Wilson was able to build what ultimately became the largest hotel/motel chain in the world. Growth was pursued in two primary directions: through company-owned and franchised operations. By 1982 you could make reservations at over 300,000 rooms, in 1,750 Holiday Inns in 60 countries worldwide!

The Businesses of Holiday Inns, Inc.

3 When we think Holiday Inns, we generally are only considering hotels and motels. However, Holiday Inns, Inc., is a $1.2-billion-per-year diversified multinational corporation. In fact, only 54 percent of total corporate revenues results from hotel operations. In 1978, the company structured itself into five divisions:

1. Hotel group
   a. Parent company.
   b. Licensees.
   c. International.
2. Products division.
   a. Inn Keepers Supply.
   b. Innkare.
   c. Dohrmann.
   d. Holiday Press.
   e. HI-Air, Holiday Industrial Park, and other minor businesses.
3. Transportation group.
   a. Trailways, Inc.
   b. Delta Steamship Lines.
4. Restaurant group.
   a. Perkins Cake and Steak.
   b. Good Company.
5. Gaming.
   a. Atlantic City.
   b. Las Vegas.

4 As Holiday Inn moved into the decade of the 1970s, top management sought to broaden its hotel-intensive earnings base. Under the leadership of Kemmons Wilson, Holiday Inns' founder, the mission was redefined from being a food and lodging company to a travel and transportation-related company. This definition led to the five business groups and, until recently, has had Holiday Inns with over 30 unrelated business operations. Most notable in this regard were the acquisitions that created the transportation group and several manufacturing concerns organized within the products group.

5 A reexamination and possible restructuring of the company's operations was being considered as the company's executives devised a strategy for the 1980s. The thrust

This 1985 revised edition of the Holiday Inns, Inc., case was prepared by Richard Robinson, University of South Carolina, and Tim Mescon, University of Miami.

Exhibit 1
Financial information on each business group ($ millions)

	1981	*1980*	*1979*	*1978*	*1977*	*1976*
Revenues:						
Hotel	$ 853	$ 849	$ 784	$ 649	$ 589	$539
Gaming	388	201	1	—	—	—
Restaurant	96	93	30	—	—	—
Transportation	413	377	278	423	324	316
Products and other	13	13	19	130	122	111
	$1,765	$1,533	$1,112	$1,202	$1,035	$966
Operating income						
Hotel	$ 171	$ 155	$ 137	$ 116	$ 90	$ 69
Gaming	56	24	1	—	—	—
Restaurant	6	4	3	—	—	—
Transportation	46	48	17	27	34	33
Products and other	11	7	11	14	7	3
	$ 290	$ 238	$ 169	$ 157	$ 131	$105
Identifiable assets						
Hotel	$ 749	$ 712	$ 651	$ 580	$ 572	$536
Gaming	573	451	30	—	—	—
Restaurant	92	97	98	—	—	—
Transportation	254	268	234	393	335	314
Products and others	147	152	226	224	133	100
	$1,815	$1,680	$1,239	$1,197	$1,040	$950
Capital expenditures						
Hotel	$ 127	$ 122	$ 111	92	74	56
Gaming	29	61	—	—	—	—
Restaurant	2	11	12	—	—	—
Transportation	6	6	2	70	34	13
Products and others	6	7	8	7	4	1
	$ 170	$ 207	$ 133	$ 169	$ 112	$ 70
Depreciation and amortization						
Hotel	$ 53	$ 49	$ 45	$ 41	$ 40	$ 38
Gaming	18	10	—	—	—	—
Restaurant	4	5	1	—	—	—
Transportation	9	8	8	20	16	16
Products and others	3	2	2	2	3	3
	$ 87	$ 74	$ 56	$ 63	$ 59	$ 57

of the reexamination involved both the basic mission of the company and the appropriateness of the above business groups. Exhibit 1 provides some insight into operations at Holiday Inns, Inc. from a financial perspective through 1981. The next several sections briefly describe the operations of the five business groups that make up Holiday Inns, Inc.

The Hotel Group

6 Hotels that are part of the Holiday Inns, Inc., are segregated into two groups. The hotels in the first group are company owned, and those in the second group are franchisee owned and operated. The Holiday Inns system continues to reflect the company's original emphasis on franchising. In 1981, 82 percent of the system was operated by

Exhibit 2

Hotel group

	1981	*1980*	*1979*	*1978*	*1977*	*1976*	*1975*	*1974*	*1973*	*1972*	*1971*	*5-year compound growth rate*	*10-year compound growth rate*
Hotels at year end													
Company owned or managed	229	240	246	270	276	289	305	309	305	297	290	(4.5)%	(2.3)%
Licensed	1,522	1,515	1,495	1,448	1,424	1,424	1,409	1,379	1,286	1,173	1,081	1.3%	3.5%
Total system	1,751	1,755	1,741	1,718	1,700	1,713	1,714	1,688	1,591	1,470	1,371	0.4%	2.5%
Rooms at year end													
Company owned or managed	55,285	56,141	55,821	58,495	58,536	58,332	59,384	59,898	57,940	54,643	51,687	(1.1)%	.7%
Licensed	252,828	247,437	240,430	228,034	220,421	219,732	215,585	207,134	188,973	166,470	148,777	2.8%	5.4%
Total system	308,113	303,578	296,251	286,529	278,957	278,064	274,969	267,032	246,913	221,113	200,464	2.1%	4.4%
Occupancy (company owned)	69.2%	71.5%	73.8%	74.3%	71.2%	68.4%	65.4%	68.3%	70.6%	70.7%	67.4%	—	—
Average rate per occupied-room (company owned)	$40.79	$36.80	$32.65	$27.81	$24.56	$22.17	$20.86	$18.38	$17.63	$16.87	$16.50	13.0%	9.5%

franchisees—independent business people or companies—while Holiday Inns, Inc., operated the remaining 18 percent. The Holiday Inn system has maintained an approximately 80/20 franchised-to-company-owned ratio since the chain was started. Exhibit 2 shows a breakdown of the Holiday Inn system by these two groups.

7 Holiday Inns' commitment to the ownership and operation of properties provides a basis for innovation and leadership in the marketplace; for example, company-operated hotels provide an extensive research base for the development of marketing information, operating procedures, and marketing techniques. The company claims that its 200 plus properties provide a solid, diverse base from which to build and improve operating expertise.

8 As shown in Exhibit 2, the number of company-owned hotels has decreased steadily since 1974. This reflects Holiday Inns emphasis on removing older properties from its system. Commenting on this trend, Roy Winegardner, Chairman of the Board, made the following observation in a December, 1980 interview:

> By 1983, 217,000 rooms or 60 percent of the Holiday Inn hotel system will be new or extensively renovated. A major emphasis for company-owned hotels will be to move into destination and multiuser properties such as airports, suburban, midtown, and downtown locations which are expected to account for over 95 percent of all company-owned or operated rooms.

Franchises

9 The 1,522 inns not operated by the company are owned by independent businesspeople called franchisees. The company carefully screens all applicants for franchises and places a great deal of emphasis on the character, ability, and financial responsibility of the applicant, in addition to the appropriateness of the proposed location. Franchise agreements, which are for a 20-year period, establish standards for service and the quality of accommodations. The company trains franchise management personnel at Holiday Inn University near Memphis, Tennessee; makes inspections three times a year of franchise operations; and provides detailed operational manuals, training films, and instructional aids for franchise personnel. During the initial period of 20 years, most franchises may be terminated in certain circumstances by the franchisee. In the event of a franchisee's violation of the agreement, the company may terminate the franchise. The company's policy in determining whether or not to renew a particular franchise agreement (after the initial 20 years) is in part to evaluate the overall desirability of retaining the franchisee's inn within the system.

10 Since Holiday Inns started franchising in 1955, 20-year renewal activity started becoming a regular issue by the late 1970s. The franchise expiration and renewal activity has been as follows since 1977:

	Franchises expiring	*Number renewed*
1977	5	2
1978	6	2
1979	7	2
1980	34	32
1981	31	?
1982	41	?
1983	34	?

11 The fees required by newly issued or renewed franchise agreements have been increased from time to time. A comparison of 1978 and 1981 requirements for new or renewed domestic franchise agreements is provided below.

1978	*1981*
An initial payment of $5,000.	No initial payment.
A one-time fee of $150 per room ($20,000 minimum).	One-time fee of $300 per room ($30,000 minimum).
A royalty of 4 percent of gross sales paid monthly.	Same 4 percent royalty as in 1978.
Conversion of 2 percent of gross room sales for marketing and reservation services monthly.	Same conversion charge but with a minimum of 14 cents per room per night.

12 **The Legal Status of the Franchise Agreement.**[1] The Holiday Inns franchise agreement has been challenged in recent court actions by an increasing number of licensees (franchisees). The agreement is being challenged on two basic points:

1. Violations of antitrust laws.
2. Fiduciary duties to present franchisees regarding future locations of Holiday Inns properties.

13 Litigation is still pending which involves a class action suit by 412 franchisees that challenges Holiday Inns right to enter into franchise agreements with third parties without giving a first option to established franchises for the operation of a Holiday Inn facility in the same local area where a franchisee's Holiday Inn facility exists. This same litigation asks for damages against Holiday Inns, Inc., by virtue of its franchise agreement prohibiting Holiday Inn franchisees from owning interests in inns, hotels, and motels other than Holiday Inn facilities. This latter issue is challenged as a violation of several sections of the Sherman Antitrust Act, including restraint of trade and unlawful interstate commerce. One franchisee, American Motor Inns, Inc., was awarded $4 million in damages from Holiday Inns on the antitrust issue involving a licensee's right to have non–Holiday Inn facilities. This verdict is still under appeal by Holiday Inns. In 1978, a franchisee of three Holiday Inn facilities in Mobile, Alabama, was awarded in excess of $1 million by a jury only to have the verdict set aside by the court. The right to own non–Holiday Inn facilities was at issue, and the decision is being appealed. Another case is asking $25 million in damages based on Holiday Inns' granting a franchise in Elizabeth, New Jersey. It is claimed that this franchise hurts an existing operation at the Newark Airport in New Jersey. Presently, it is very difficult to ascertain the total impact if Holiday Inns loses the pending court actions.

[1] In addition to challenges to the basic franchise agreement, numerous franchises have raised objections to the quasi-requirement that they buy all furniture, equipment, and supplies through the products group businesses when similar items are available elsewhere at lower costs. These objections are particularly intense during additions, renovations, and construction of additional properties when Holiday Inns' preopening quality inspections try to, among other things, promote the maintenance of high standards in furnishings and equipment while the franchise is trying to reduce initial capital investment.

Multinational Operations

14 Foreseeing possible obstacles in the intensive expansion of hotels/motels in the United States, Holiday Inns, Inc. has been rapidly expanding hotel operations abroad. The company's international development strategy has been to build strong national chains within the country where it now operates, as well as to gradually expand into new markets. Holiday Inns, Inc., argues that this strategy differs from that of its competitors who have but one location in each major city overseas. At the same time, the company has emphasized multiuser, politically stable locations for company-owned hotels. For example, 18 of the 24 hotels in which the company had an ownership interest in 1980 were located in major European cities.

15 By the end of 1978, the Holiday Inn system had 195 international locations in 55 countries (of which 161 were franchised) with well over 40,000 rooms. By early 1981 the number of non–U.S. locations had increased to 226. International operations' performance information is provided below.

	*International operations**		
	1981	*1980*	*1979*
Consolidated assets	$137,641	$134,117	$123,580
Consolidated equity	108,488	98,951	79,896
Revenues	129,219	143,244	129,698
Operating income	21,949	28,049	26,014

* In thousands of dollars.

International projects underway in 1981 nearly equaled domestic activity. By the end of 1981 Holiday Inns maintained an equity interest in only 18 international properties.

Key Operating Systems

16 Holiday Inns operates the Holidex reservation system, which links over 17,000 terminals throughout the world, thus representing the largest reservation system in the hotel industry. The importance of a reservation system such as the Holidex network cannot be overstated. Through 1978, approximately 70 percent of all room-nights at Holiday Inns were sold through advance reservations. The company invested over $20 million in the second generation of this system, Holidex II. It is not only an information system, providing accounting and room inventory services, but it also provides a marketing data base as well as information services at the unit location.

17 In 1980 the new Holidex II network booked about 33 million room-nights, more than a third of all system reservations, and several times more than competing hotel chains. Nonetheless, this number of room-nights booked is down 50 percent from mid-1970 levels.

18 In concert with expanded Holidex II computer capabilities, Holiday Inns' operations management systems (OMS) was developed to improve profits at the hotel level. Consisting of weekly department forecast, energy control, staff scheduling, inventory control, industrial engineering, and quality assurance, the system was fully implemented in

company-owned or -operated properties by 1981. The program helped improve margins on a consistent basis, even where occupancies declined temporarily.

19 Another new internal program—Inn level business planning—calls for careful monitoring of trends in the local market environment, including product competitiveness, rates, opportunities, and competitive developments. This market-by-market monitoring enables each hotel to stay abreast of, and react quickly to, changing competitive situations.

20 Another technological system on which Holiday Inns places major future importance is its HI-NET Satellite Communications Network. The HI-NET system provides low-cost, in-room entertainment that is free to the guest, as well as the capability to hold nationwide teleconferences linking over 150 Holiday Inn facilities. As an example of the capabilities of the HI-NET system for teleconferencing, Holiday Inns, Inc. held a 1981 teleconference meeting for its employees which was aimed at increasing employee involvement and ultimately improving productivity in all of its businesses. They were able to communicate directly with approximately 15,000 employees of Holiday Inns, Harrah's, Perkins, and Delta at over 130 locations throughout the United States.

Competitive Posture

21 President and CEO Mike Rose offered the following summary of the hotel group's mission:

> The mission of the hotel group is to [increase] Holiday Inns' leadership position in the broad midscale segments of the lodging industry. This mission will be achieved by producing superior consumer satisfaction through increased emphasis on the quality of our product and further capitalization on our significant distributional advantages over all other competitors. We also intend to [increase] our consumer recognition as the preferred brand in the lodging industry.

22 The Holiday Inn hotel system leads the lodging industry in terms of number of rooms (see Exhibit 3) as well as customer preference (see Exhibit 4). The sustained leadership of the Holiday Inn brand in the broad midpriced market segment, which accounts for approximately two thirds of all travelers, is attributable to the hotel group's focus on customer satisfaction, according to corporate executives. These executives cite hotel operating systems, extensive training, and emphasis on value for price paid as key elements of this focus. Marketing efforts reinforce this focus. For example, in 1981, the company introduced a "No Excuses" room guarantee program for all

Exhibit 3

Leading lodging firms by number of rooms (in thousands)

	1981	*1977*
Holiday Inns	308	279
Best Western	204	150
Sheraton	109	100
Ramada	98	91
Hilton	76	59

Exhibit 4

Hotel brand preference (percent)

	1981	*1980*	*1979*	*1978*
Holiday Inn	38%	36%	40%	48%
Best Western	7	7	6	—
Hilton	6	5	6	3
Ramada	6	7	6	5
Sheraton	5	5	5	5
Days Inn	4	1	1	1
Hyatt	4	2	2	1
Mariott	3	2	2	1
Howard Johnson	2	3	3	4
Quality Inn	2	1	—	—
Motel 6	2	1	—	—

Source: Ad Track study conducted for Holiday Inns, Inc., among past-year hotel motel lodgers for years 1978 through 1981.

U.S. hotels that promises guests will be satisfied with their rooms, or their room charge for the night's stay will be refunded. The Holiday Inn hotel system is the only hotel chain to offer guests such a guarantee.

23 During the period 1979 to 1983, the hotel group planned to increase the number of company-owned rooms by 72,000 and sell 75,000 new franchise rooms. Riding the crest of steady occupancy growth, the hotel system offered nearly twice as many rooms as its nearest competitor and sold one out of every three hotel chain room-nights in 1978. In the face of mounting competition from both the budget and luxury segments of the lodging industry (see the Note on the U.S. Lodging Industry in the case section for more detail), Holiday Inn executives did not expect occupancy to drop due to price or service competition. As Exhibit 2 shows, occupancy of Holiday Inns' properties declined for the third year in a row to 69.2 percent in 1981, down from 71.5 percent in 1980, 73.8 percent in 1979, and 74.3 percent in 1978. General economic weakness, a decline in family disposable income, and rapidly increasing airline fares were given as primary reasons. Single occupancy, an indicator of business travel, remained virtually unchanged in 1981. Business travel accounts for approximately 60 percent of Holiday Inn hotel room-nights sold. Multiple occupancy, which the company feels reflects personal travel, was down each of these years. Room rates increased 10.8 percent in 1981, compared with 12.7 percent in 1980 and 17.4 percent in 1979 (see Exhibit 2).

24 Some industry forecasters predict that demand for hotel accommodations will grow faster than supply in the 1980s, with the middle-priced segment projected to account for the majority of this growth.[2] Commenting on growth potential in different industry segments, CEO Mike Rose offered the following:

> Holiday Inn® hotels are ideally positioned in the moderate-price market segment to take advantage of the large projected demand growth within this seg-

[2] Other analysts warn of potential overbuilding in this industry. See the Note on the U.S. Lodging Industry in the case section of this book.

ment. In simple terms, the lodging industry could be described in three major segments: the high-price or image segment, the moderate-price segment, and the low-price segment.

While we think the percentage growth of demand will be highest in the high-price or image segment, in absolute terms the demand for rooms in the moderate-price segment will grow three times faster than in either the high-price or low-price segments.

We are further encouraged that new room supply is being focused more and more at the high end of the market, and we can foresee an oversupply of hotel rooms in that segment during this decade. On the other hand, we think that most of our chain competitors in the moderate segment do not have the inherent strength to keep pace with the demand growth in the moderate-price segment, and that we will continue to [increase] our share of that segment during the next decade.

Our domestic parent company development will be predominantly in major metropolitan areas in locations where we serve multiple demand sources. For example, we would like to be in locations that serve both business and leisure travelers, that also serve small group meetings, and that serve people arriving by automobile and air.

25 While Holiday Inn sees enormous growth potential in the middle-priced segment, rumors were beginning to surface in early 1980 that Holiday Inns was considering entry (through acquiring existing chains and/or starting new ones) into both the high-priced and low-priced industry segments.

Products Group

26 In the late 1970s, the products group distributed institutional furnishings, equipment, expendable supplies, and printed products to the lodging, housing, health-care, and food-service markets. The principal businesses within the products group in 1979 were:

Inn Keepers Supply (IKS). IKS accounted for 60 percent of the group's competitive sales in 1978. Distributing furnishings and equipment to the food, lodging, and health-care industries is IKS' principal business. IKS sold its products through 77 salespeople nationwide and four product display centers located across the country. During 1979, the division expanded operations in Great Britain, agreeing to sell furnishings and equipment to the Grand Metropolitan Hotels.

Dohrmann. This distributor of food-service products accounted for almost 16 percent of the group's competitive sales in 1978. Dohrmann, building its reputation for tabletop items (plates, napkins, forks, spoons, condiments, etc.), now carries over 5,000 products and operates in 10 western states through 80 sales representatives.

Innkare. Offering a range of over 4,000 items, including cleaning chemicals, kitchen utensils, and maid supplies, this unit accounted for almost 15 percent of the group's sales in 1978. Operating as a master distributor, the Innkare organization sells to 55 independent distributors nationwide, who sell Innkare products to more than 100,000 motels.

Exhibit 5

Products division financial performance data (in millions of dollars)

	1979	*1978*	*1977*	*1976*
Revenue:				
IKS	NA	$ 89.0	$ 75.3	$ 70.1
Innkare	NA	21.8	19.4	16.8
Dohrmann	NA	23.6	23.8	22.3
Other	NA	13.7	25.1	28.0
Total revenue	$116.0	$148.1	$143.6	$137.2
Operating income	(1)	$ 6.2	$ 6.6	$ 1.7
Operating margin	(0.8%)	4.2%	4.6%	1.2%
Capital expenditures	—	$ 0.8	$ 0.7	$ 0.6
Sales to company	$ 26.0	$ 32.0	$ 28.0	$ 32.0
Assets	29.3	32.3	52.7	54.8

Note: Sales to *company-owned* properties are at cost plus a variable percentage markup which includes handling, administration, and a profit contribution to the selling segment. These are considered noncompetitive sales. Competitive sales are those to franchises and other institutions using a regular pricing structure.

27 These three businesses accounted for over 80 percent of the product groups' annual sales in the late 1970s. Half of the remaining sales were generated through a printing operation called Holiday Press. Two smaller operations—HI-Air, a fixed-base aircraft dealer, and Holiday Industrial Park, a commercial land development project—accounted for the remaining sales in the late 1970s. Exhibit 5 provides financial performance information on this group during the late 1970s.

28 Corporate and products group managers began to seriously question the mission and the strategy of the products group in the late 1970s (the group had become a sprawling set of over 30 businesses in the early 1970s). The initial outcome was a strategy designed to narrow the base of the products group operation to those businesses directly related to services in the lodging, entertainment, and food service industries. By 1979, all but the three major operating businesses mentioned earlier had been divested or liquidated.

29 Holiday Inns sold Dohrmann in mid-1979. This sale reduced the products group to two operating divisions—Inn Keepers Supply (IKS) and Innkare. A major question being addressed by corporate and products group management as the company moved into the 1980s was whether the strategy of the products group should be (1) to build the competitive sales via product and market development at the two divisions or (2) refocus IKS and Innkare more toward supporting company properties and meeting franchisee's product needs. The latter choice would possibly require the restructuring of the product group as simply a division within the hotel group. Proponents of the first option put forward four points: (1) IKS and Innkare had extensive experience in supplying institutional products, (2) institutional supply was a fragmented industry that IKS and Innkare could seek to dominate, (3) buyer groups, particularly hotels/motels, restaurants, and hospitals, were expected to experience continued widespread growth, and (4) IKS and Innkare have the advantage of a large, "captive" customer group in the Holiday Inn system. Proponents of the second option argued that the products group was originally created to serve the institutional needs of members of

the Holiday Inn system. Franchisees in particular had become frustrated with a products group that in their view overpriced numerous products and services.

Transportation Group

30 Entering 1979, the transportation group of Holiday Inns, Inc., consisted of two major units: Trailways (headquartered in Dallas, Texas), the second-largest intercity bus system, and Delta Steamship Lines. The transportation group accounted for 35 percent of Holiday Inns, Inc. revenue, with bus operations producing 22 percent and steamship operations producing 13 percent (see Exhibits 6 and 7).

31 Trailway's fundamental business was to provide intercity passenger service, charter bus service, and express package services. In 1979 the Trailways route system covered 70,000 miles serving 5,000 cities and towns in 43 states.

32 J. Kevin Murphy, formerly president of Purolator Services, Inc., was named president of the bus operations in 1977. Placing primary emphasis on new marketing approaches, Murphy streamlined the company's name from Continental Trailways to Trailways and adopted a sunburst logo. A new marketing program called the Anywhere Program was initiated. It allowed the traveler to go anywhere in the United States—from one origin city to a destination city—with unlimited stopovers for a low, fixed price. Advertising expenditures were increased in the late 1970s on programs stressing the cost-saving aspects of bus travel as opposed to other transportation forms.

33 Greyhound (number one in the bus service industry) and Trailways began to experience increased competition from the newly deregulated airline industry for low-cost intercity travel in the late 1970s. Travelers could often fly and arrive at a destination

Exhibit 6

Transportation group: Bus operations

Bus operating statistics

	1978	*1977*	*1976*	*1975*	*1974*
Bus operating revenues (000)	$ 254,495	$ 240,262	$ 226,568	$ 204,421	$ 195,058
Bus miles (000)	190,770	198,125	207,678	196,682	198,628
Number of intercity buses	2,158	2,203	2,312	2,405	2,271
Passenger miles (000)	2,694,454	2,856,095	2,727,453	2,675,238	2,871,526
Bus occupancy (load factor)	39.5%	40.4%	36.4%	36.6%	39.5%

Bus operations—financial performance ($ millions of dollars)

	1978	*1977*	*1976*
Passenger	$ 145.7	$ 141.9	$ 136.8
Charter	44.7	41.2	38.9
Express	58.8	51.3	44.9
Other	18.9	10.0	14.1
Total revenue	$ 268.1	$ 244.4	$ 234.7
Operating income	$ 19.7	$ 16.4	$ 15.4
Operating margin	7.4%	6.7%	6.5%
Capital expenditures	$ 21.4	$ 10.0	$ 13.1
Assets	177.0	171.3	165.5

Note: More current statistics are not available.

Exhibit 7

Transportation group: Steamship operations

Steamship operating statistics

	1981	1980	1979	1978	1977	1976	1975	Compound growth rates (percent) 5 Year	10 Year
Voyages completed	174	177	162	97	45	51	62	27.8%	11.6%
Tons of cargo (thousands)	3,264.2	3,183.6	2,635.2	1,550.6	793.6	909.0	922.1	29.1	15.3

Steamship operations—Financial performance (in millions of dollars)

	1981	1980	1979	1978	1977	1976
Revenue	$413.2	$377.1	$278.1	$155.0	$ 80.1	$ 81.1
Operating income	46.2	47.8	16.6	7.8	17.3	17.6
Operating margin	15.9%	20.1%	9.8%	5.0%	21.6%	21.7%
Capital expenditures	6.4	5.7	1.4	48.8	24.2	0.2
Assets	258.0	268.4	233.5	215.9	163.3	148.6

from 3 to 10 times faster for a fare only 15 to 25 percent above the cost of a bus ticket. Between 1974 and 1979 the number of scheduled passengers increased by 25 percent for airlines while it declined over 32 percent for buses.

34 In an effort to combat discount fares offered by airlines on selected routes, the Trailways division announced a new series of low fares between major cities in the Northeastern section of the United States. In addition to competing with the airlines, Trailways was trying to counteract Greyhound's discount offerings on interstate routes. These fares represented a reduction of 30 to 50 percent from regular fares and applied primarily to interstate trips averaging 775 miles (one way) or more. An article in *Fortune* concluded that Greyhound and Trailways' price war was hurting only each others' profitability, without producing any additional share of the long-haul business, which was dominated by the airlines at fares only 50 percent above the discount bus fares.

35 Trailways in 1978 became the first intercity bus company to offer a discount to senior citizens, a group which made up 25 percent of its market. The idea was initiated as a result of a recommendation from Trailways' senior citizen advisory council. Holiday Inns corporate executives anticipated that Trailways' senior citizen and charter passengers would provide a convenient customer base for its hotel properties.

36 Two growing segments of bus services are charter operations and package express. Trailways' charter operations served 26 million passengers a year in the late 1970s representing 9 percent of the total charter market. During the last half of the 1970s, charter sales grew at a compounded annual rate of almost 13 percent.

37 Package express, the fastest-growing segment of the Trailways division, accounted for 22 percent of total revenues from bus operations by 1978. Package pickup and delivery were offered in more than 110 major U.S. cities. The package express and

overnight delivery industry was growing at over 60 percent in the late 1970s. Federal Express, the industry leader, virtually created this industry and doubled its volume every six months between 1977 and 1981. The industry has become very competitive and telecommunication technology may become a future basis for the overnight message service.

38 For the 1980s, the company has lobbied vigorously in favor of municipal ownership of bus terminals. Airplane terminals and other public transportation terminals (e.g. trains) are primarily municipally owned. This would also transfer the cost of bus terminal maintenance from the company to the taxpayer—a key savings for Trailways. Unfortunately, this has met with little success to date. The movement in the passenger transportation industry, as evidenced by deregulation of airlines, is toward decreased government involvement. Business analysts have forecast continued hard times for the intercity bus industry, caught between rising energy, labor, and maintenance costs on the one hand and increasing price competition, particularly with airlines, on the other. Toward the end of the 1970s, top management was seriously questioning the strategic fit of Trailways in Holiday Inns, Inc.'s mission and business portfolio.

39 Delta Steamship Lines was acquired by Holiday Inns, Inc. in the 1960s. By 1977, Delta operated a fleet of 24 vessels between Gulf ports, Central America, South America, and Africa (see Exhibit 8).

40 In June 1978, Delta reached an agreement with Prudential Lines, Inc., to acquire 13 vessels and add five new trade routes (from the East and West Coasts of the United States) over the next two years at a cost in excess of $71.5 million. Approximately half of the Prudential acquisition cost was financed using Delta's capital construction fund, and the balance came through Delta assuming low-interest, government-guaranteed mortgages on the vessels.

41 The Prudential acquisition returned Delta to passenger service, an area in which the line had had no involvement since 1968. All four combination passenger/cargo vessels acquired from Prudential have first-class accommodations for 100 passengers.

42 Of greater importance to Holiday Inns' steamship operation, the acquisition doubled the number of Delta's Latin and South American trade routes to Pacific U.S. ports.

43 In 1973, Delta introduced LASH (light aboard ship) cargo containers in its operations. The LASH containers (they are found in all of Delta's fleet) are filled before the arrival of a ship to improve the scheduling of the ship's time in port. For example, the average length of a typical South American voyage was reduced from 84 to 42 days by using LASH containers.

44 While Delta's revenue nearly doubled in 1978, operating income dropped significantly (see Exhibit 7). Captain J. W. Clark, president of the Delta operation in 1978, offered the following reasons:

> For one thing it took longer to absorb the Prudential Lines, Inc. operations than originally thought. This was due to start-up costs connected with the acquisition, the transfer of vessels to new routes, higher-than-anticipated maintenance costs required to bring the new fleet up to Delta standards, and a delay in closing the transaction [that] reduced the revenue base over which expenses could be spread. Unsettled political and economic conditions also affected Delta's West Africa Trade.

45 Though faced with heavy foreign competition, Delta, the major U.S.-flag cargo carrier in its trade routes, anticipated increased market share through effective vessel sched-

Exhibit 8

Delta Line trade routes

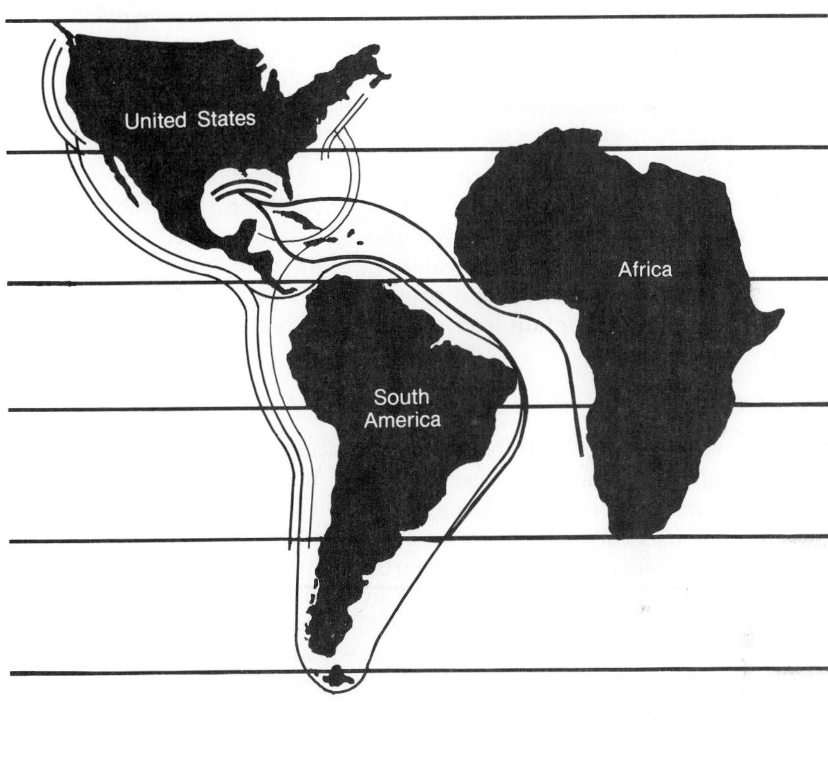

uling, LASH technology, and beneficial government subsidizes of U.S. marine transport operations.[3]

47 By 1980 Delta Steamship Lines, Inc.'s operating income almost tripled to a record $47.8 million on a 35.6 percent revenue increase. (See Exhibit 8.) This dramatic improvement was accompanied by the installation of a new management team. Fifty percent of the subsidiary's top 28 positions were filled by people new to the company. This

[3] Delta operates under differential subsidy agreements (expiring in 1995 and 1997) in which the U.S. Maritime Administration compensates Delta for portions of certain vessel operating expenses that are in excess of those incurred by its foreign competitors. The subsidy recorded in 1980, 1979, 1978, and 1977 amounted to $60,419,000, $52,429,000, $33,666,000 and $15,035,000, respectively.

revitalized management successfully instituted a number of marketing and operational programs in late 1979 which contributed greatly to the 1980 improvement. Cargo tonnage increased by 15.4 percent through fleet deployment to trade routes that best utilized each vessel's capabilities. Better scheduling permitted a 6.8 percent improvement in completed voyages. This increased the frequency of port calls, a factor important to shippers and their customers. Fifty percent more containers for better cargo handling and inexpensive hardware modifications allowed Delta to provide more container equipment to customers while reducing its unit costs through this expanded LASH technology as well as favorable lease arrangements.

48 While Delta's performance has improved dramatically, top management was seriously questioning its fit in Holiday Inns, Inc.'s hospitality-oriented portfolio for the 1980s. Some managers were arguing that Delta should be divested. Others agreed with Winegardner's perspective summarized in the following comment:

> We recognize that Delta might not fit Holiday Inns' long-term objective of being a hospitality company, although it did clearly establish for itself in 1980 an important role in the execution of our hospitality strategy. With its improved performance, Delta provides significant cash flow to fund investment in our hospitality businesses. As a result, Delta has earned an important position in our plans to maintain leadership in the hospitality industry.

Restaurant Group

49 On April 18, 1979, Holiday Inns, Inc. acquired Perkins Cake and Steak, Inc., a privately held restaurant chain headquartered in Minneapolis. The decision to enter the freestanding restaurant business reflects significant research on demographic trends as well as a corporate desire to build a broader earnings base. The 20-to-45-year-old age group will grow to over 50 percent of the U.S. population by 1990. This group eats out frequently—an average of five meals per week. The number of women in the work force is projected to exceed 60 percent in 1990. The number of single households is also steadily increasing. Both trends are associated with more eating out. According to Holiday Inns' research, food away from home is increasingly viewed as a necessary convenience.

50 Based on Holiday Inns' prepurchase market research, two thirds of Perkins' customers were found to be between the ages of 18 and 49 and have annual household incomes in excess of $20,000. Demographically, the Perkins customer profile is similar in many respects to that of a Holiday Inn hotel guest.

51 Perkins is positioned in the marketplace as a family restaurant. It offers a broad menu at moderate prices and table service in "pleasant surroundings." Most Perkins restaurants are open 24 hours a day. A typical Perkins restaurant built since 1977 seats 172 people in a 5,000-square-foot structure. About one third of the restaurants in the Perkins system in 1980 were less than four years old.

52 There were 270 franchised units and 71 company-owned units when Holiday Inns bought the chain in early 1979. By the end of 1979 the number of franchised units remained unchanged while 23 new company-owned units were added. Exhibit 9 highlights Perkins' activity between 1976 and 1981. Commenting on future emphasis for Perkins' growth, one major Holiday Inn executive offered the following in late 1981:

Exhibit 9

Perkins operating data ($ millions of dollars)

	1981	*1980*	*1979**	*1978*	*1977*	*1976*
Revenues	$96.4	$93.2	$81.8	$67.8	$47.0	$35.5
Operating profit	6.5	4.3	10.1	6.8	4.0	2.8
Food and labor cost as percent of sales	56.7%*	55.6%	54.6%	58.0%	57.4%	56.9%
Number of stores:						
Corporate units	101	106	94	71	56	48
Franchise units	242	269	270	270	260	252
Total units	343	375	364	341	316	300

* Estimated.

It is our intent [that] Perkins [grows] primarily through the franchise system, with corporate stores filling in those major markets where we have already established a strong presence. Obviously, Perkins can never become a large part of Holiday Inns, Inc., with such mammoth businesses as the hotel and casino businesses, but we do think it is a vehicle for percentage growth and high return on assets employed.

It is our intention that Perkins will continue to grow using only its own cash flow, so that it will not be competitive with the hotel or casino businesses for capital resources.

53 Perkins' initial performance since being acquired was disappointing. The average customer count at company-owned restaurants dropped annually since the acquisition. This trend and the change in average guest checks are shown below as a percent of change from the previous year:

Average company owned restaurant	*Percent change from previous year*			
	1979	*1980*	*1981*	*1982**
Change in average customer count	(14.9)%	(13.3)%	1.4%	9.0%
Change in average guest check	6.8*	5.4	3.8	0.4

* Estimated.

54 In general, there is no clear nationwide leader among family restaurant chains. In 1980, Perkins system sales represented 10 percent of total sales generated by the five largest family restaurant chains. Perkins was fifth in sales in the family restaurant category in which it competes.

Exhibit 10

Family restaurant industry: 1980

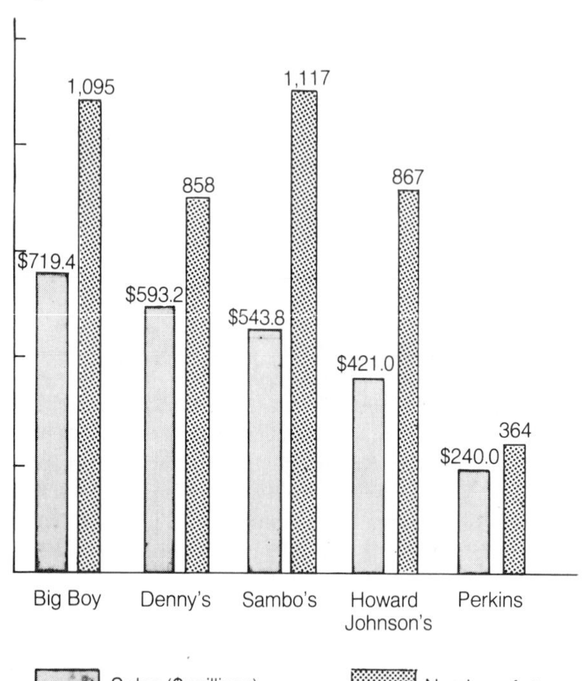

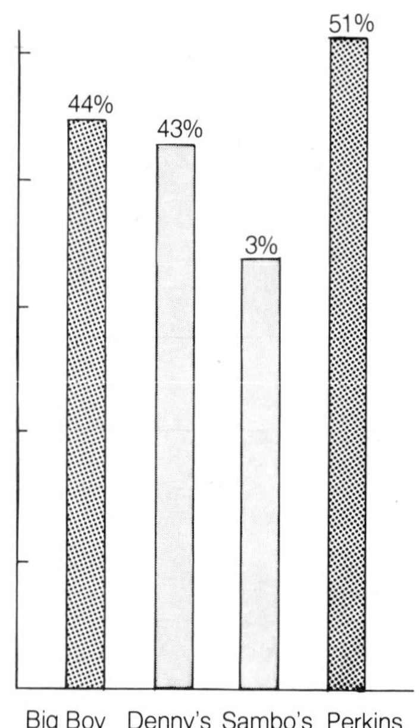

* Percentage giving an "excellent" or "very good" rating.
Source: Institutions Magazine.

55 Overall, the restaurant industry appears to be becoming increasingly competitive. The family restaurant market segment represents about one fourth of total U.S. restaurant sales. Holiday Inns' management expects this segment to have continued growth during the 1980s, with chains expanding at the expense of independent operators.

56 Perkins competes in the large middle market and differentiates itself from the competition, according to company sources, by focusing on consistent high quality, as opposed to low price. Holiday Inns' consumer research shows Perkins' customers prefer a quality dining-out experience in terms of food, service, ambience, and decor. Guest checks at company-owned Perkins restaurants average 10 percent to 25 percent higher than typical competitors' checks.

57 Mike Rose, President and CEO, had the following comment in late 1981: "While Perkins has frankly been a bit of disappointment to us at this stage, we do strongly believe that we can rebuild head counts, continue to control costs, and expand on a regional basis to obtain sufficient market penetration."

58 In response to corporate concerns, Perkins management adopted a back-to-basics philosophy in its approach to operations, especially in service and food preparation, in 1981. The clarity and effectiveness of Perkins' long-term strategy appeared very much in question in late 1981.

Gaming Group

59 In September 1978, the board of directors of Holiday Inns, Inc., announced that it had expanded corporate policy to explore potential opportunities for hotel/casino operations in any area where such operations are legal.[4] While the company stressed that this decision implied no firm commitment toward a new development, it did indeed recognize the fact that the expansion in this area represents a natural extension of its current hotel operations. Previously, corporate policy restricted the expansion of hotel/casino operations to the state of Nevada and areas external to the United States.

60 Just two weeks following this announcement, the company approved a proposal to construct and manage a $75 million hotel/casino in Atlantic City, New Jersey.

61 Gaming was one industry that was examined when the company began researching future growth opportunities in the hospitality industry in 1975. Initial investigation revealed that most successful casino operations include hotels, a business in which the company was an acknowledged leader. Casinos also have sizable food and beverage operations, an area where the Holiday Inn system averages more than $1 billion in annual revenues. Preliminary studies also indicated that the Holiday Inn hotel customer exhibited demographic characteristics similar to those of gaming participants (see the accompanying table). Of greater importance to Holiday Inns, customer surveys indicated that the overwhelming majority of Holiday Inns guests had no objection to the company's becoming involved in the gaming business.

Demographic comparison: 1975

	Las Vegas casino visitor	*Holiday Inn guest*
Age 21–50	66%	66%
Family income: over $20,000	73	69
Occupation: professional, manager, white-collar	40	37

62 Holiday Inns' research showed that 80 percent of adults approve of gambling and 60 percent participate in some form, ranging from casino visits to fund-raising raffles. Their conclusion: gaming is truly a national pastime and is viewed by the public as a leisure activity. Of the 11 million people who visited Las Vegas in 1978, the average guest spent about $200 in nongaming expenditures with $300 budgeted for gaming.

[4] This decision, however, was reached over considerable internal management dissention. Several key managers questioned the inappropriateness of gambling relative to the founding philosophy and mission of Holiday Inns. As evidence of the degree of top-management polarity, this decision triggered the resignation of the company president and chief executive officer, L. M. Clymer. Clymer said that his resignation was incited by personal and religious opposition to this company decision.

63 Traditionally thought of as the exclusive domain of Nevada, the opening of Atlantic City to casino operations has given gaming a whole new outlook, and casino revenues were expected to more than double to between $5 and $7.5 billion nationwide by 1985.

64 Holiday Inns' extensive research led to the conclusion that it "needed outside expertise in gaming and big-name entertainment contracting. Careful control of the large volumes of cash handled requires well-run operations and specialized procedures. Thus, if we [Holiday Inns] were to succeed, we would need seasoned management in place."

65 In 1979, Holiday Inns formed a joint-venture company with Harrah's (of Nevada) to develop, build, and operate all future gaming facilities for both companies. In September 1979, a merger agreement was approved by both firms. Under the merger, Harrah's will maintain its identity as a wholly owned subsidiary and be the gaming operations arm of Holiday Inns, Inc.

66 Commenting on the merger with Harrah's, a Holiday Inn executive said: "We could not have picked a better company than Harrah's, a leader in the hotel/casino and entertainment industry. The control measures developed by Harrah's are now the standards for the industry. They provide seasoned expertise in gaming and big-name entertainment contracting. Their growth record has been superior."

67 U.S. casino gaming industry revenues reached $3 billion in 1980, compared to $2.4 billion in 1979, a 25 percent increase despite the impact of the 1980 recession and escalating transportation costs. In 1980 Atlantic City nearly doubled its 1979 casino revenues, winning more than $600 million. Forecasts made in 1976 when casino gaming was first legalized in New Jersey predicted the Atlantic City market would not reach $800 million in gaming revenues annually until 1988. Many industry experts now expect Atlantic City to gross over $2 billion in gaming revenues in 1985. Part of their prediction is based on Atlantic City's location—one day's drive from one fourth of the U.S. population.

68 Some analysts are less sure about Atlantic City's potential. They point out that many Atlantic City gamblers only stay one day and come back more often rather than staying for an extended period in a hotel facility. Also, Atlantic City has been slow in gaining convention traffic and gambling junkets, partially because of a much more heavily regulated situation than in Nevada.

69 Through its entry into casino gaming operations, Holiday Inns, Inc., has kept pace with the spectacular industry growth. With the November 23, 1980 opening of Harrah's Marina hotel/casino in Atlantic City, Holiday Inns, Inc., became the largest U.S. gaming concern, operating alone or in partnership the most slot machines, 5,656; most table games, 439; and most casino space, 188,200 square feet. Holiday Inns, Inc., is the only company with properties in all four major U.S. gaming centers (see Exhibit 11). Casino gaming accounted for 13 percent of Holiday Inns' revenues in 1980 and 22 percent in 1981 (see Exhibit 11).

70 Commenting on Holiday Inns' rapid success in casino gaming, Mike Rose (HI president) offered management's view of the gaming future:

> Harrah's management depth and the strength of its operating programs and systems place Holiday Inns, Inc., in an excellent position to capitalize on the future growth of gaming. The company is already the largest in terms of facilities and has begun to successfully establish a nationally recognized brand name. These accomplishments, together with innovative marketing and planning, will

Exhibit 11

U.S. gaming industry

A. Largest U.S. gaming companies (1981)

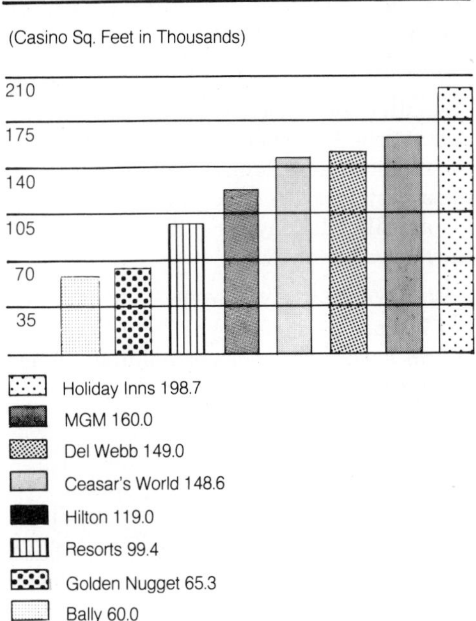

B. Gaming representation in major U.S. markets

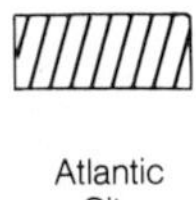

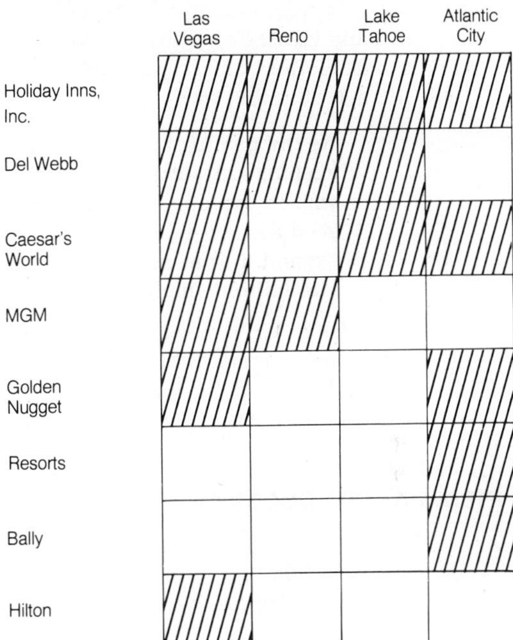

C. U.S. gaming revenues

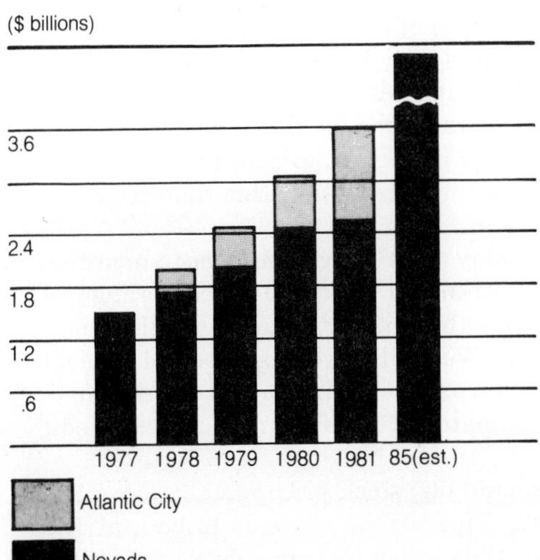

Source: Nevada Gaming Control Board and New Jersey Casino Control Commission.

D. Holiday Inns, Inc.: 1980 gaming group market share by location (in percent of market gaming revenues)

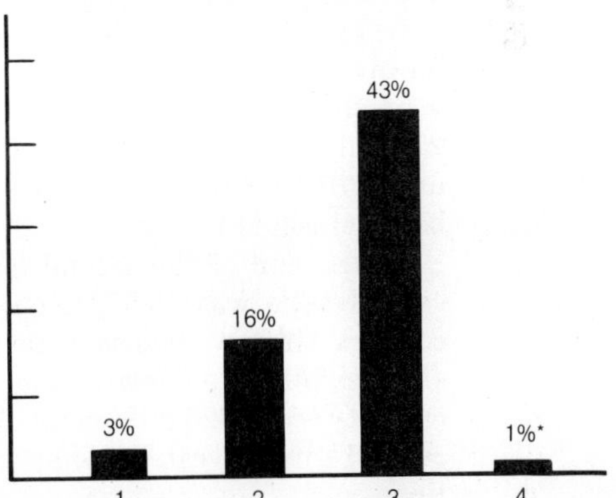

1. Las Vegas.
2. Reno.
3. Lake Tahoe.
4. Atlantic City.

* Facility opened late November. Captured 12 percent of December revenues in Atlantic City.

put the company in the same leadership position in gaming that it enjoys in the lodging industry.

71 Indeed, numerous traditional competitors share the same view. Hilton Hotels Corp. and Hyatt Corporation have already entered the field and are doing quite well. Gerald E. Hollier, chief operating officer at Ramada Inn, echoed Holiday Inns' optimism in a 1980 interview:

> As the gaming industry expands rapidly, smaller companies will have difficulty keeping up with market growth. Even established companies that are doing well in Nevada, such as Del Webb, Caesars World, and Summa, don't have as good a chance as the big companies because they lack the base [from which] to expand. In the long run, it's the big companies like Holiday Inns, Ramada Inns, and Hilton which will do best, because they have the muscle.

72 Only two major lodging competitors, Best Western and Days Inn, are not pursuing casino gaming. Best Western president Robert Hazard sees gaming as "an infatuation that could burst like a bubble," while Days Inn executives consider gaming outside the concept and corporate philosophy underlying Days Inn.

Financial Perspective

73 Exhibits 12 and 13 provide a summary of the financial performance and condition of Holiday Inns, Inc. since 1976. In an August 1981 speech to the New York Society of Security Analysts, Chief Financial Officer Charles Solomonson offered the following comments:

> As part of our strategic planning process, we constantly review our goals and financial policies in light of a rapidly changing business environment. With our recent five-year planning process, we reaffirmed much of our earlier thinking, and where differences arose, they did not represent a radical departure from previous expectations. Let me share the results of our analysis with you.
>
> In the area of capital spending, we have clearly placed increased emphasis on investing for the future growth of our businesses. Capital expenditures this year should be about $175 million and average and in the range of $225 to 275 million between 1982 and 1985. It is also important to note that we expect about 75 percent or more of our investment dollars within this time frame to be hotel related.
>
> At the end of the second quarter, Holiday Inns' long-term debt-to-invested-capital ratio was 43.5 percent. This is within our 40 to 50 percent range of comfort which we believe is necessary to remain competitive and have the financial flexibility to grow and move quickly. We still have a great deal of debt capacity with $325 million in intermediate-term debt facilities available at prime-related interest rates, along with approximately $45 million in unused credit lines.
>
> Flexibility will be further increased should our stock price remain above $22 per share during the early part of 1982. This would allow us to call, at the first opportunity, our 9⅝ percent convertible subordinated debentures issued for the Harrah's acquisition. Such a move, with no other action, would immediately bring our debt-to-capital ratio down by about 10 points to a little over 30

Exhibit 12

Operating results

	1981	1980	1979	1978	1977	1976	5-Year compound growth rate (base 1976)	10-year compound growth rate (base 1971)
Operating results ($ million):								
Revenues	$1,765.1	$1,533.8	$1,112.6	$1,202.2	$1,035.3	$965.6	12.8%	10.3%
Operating income	290.8	238.1	169.3	158.4	131.3	104.7	22.7	11.5
Income before income taxes	196.2	166.6	125.1	111.1	90.8	64.2	25.0	11.2
Pretax margin (percent)	11.1%	10.9%	11.2%	9.2%	8.8%	6.6%	—	—
Tax rate (percent)	30.0%	35.0%	43.0%	44.5%	42.1%	36.6%	—	—
Income	$ 137.4	$ 108.3	$ 71.3	$ 62.8	$ 52.7	$ 39.2	28.5	13.0
Discontinued operations	—	—	(15.4)	—	—	(0.4)	—	—
Net income	$ 137.4	$ 108.3	$ 55.9	$ 62.8	$ 52.7	$ 38.8	28.8%	13.7%
Common stock data:								
Income per share	$3.66	$2.92	$1.76	$2.04	$1.71	$1.27	23.6%	10.7%
Cost Dividends declared per share	0.74	0.70	0.66	0.56	0.465	0.40	13.1	11.5
Book value per share	24.73	21.51	18.93	17.81	16.37	15.22	10.2	8.3
Price range of common	33¼–21⅛	33½–13¾	22⅞–15¼	32¾–14⅛	16⅛–11⅛	20–10⅝	—	—
Average of Number common and outstanding (thousands)	39,449	39,278	31,704	30,854	30,762	30,657	5.2%	2.8%
Financial position ($ million):								
Total assets	$1,815.4	$1,680.1	$1,227.3	$1,196.0	$1,039.6	$960.5	13.6%	59.0%
Property and equipment (net)	1,323.3	1,147.7	737.1	767.1	705.0	679.4	14.3	10.4
Long-term debt	639.6	546.6	311.3	322.2	310.1	299.4	16.4	8.4
Shareholders equity	772.4	708.0	624.5	552.4	504.8	465.8	10.6	8.6
Depreciation and amortization	87.3	74.6	56.3	63.1	58.9	56.2	9.2	n/a
Capital expenditures	170.9	207.1	133.4	169.1	112.1	70.2	19.5	
Current ratio	0.8	0.9	1.4	1.4	1.2	1.3	—	—
Performance measures (percent):								
Return on sales	7.8%	7.1%	6.4%	5.2%	5.1%	4.0%	—	—
Return on average invested capital	12.0	10.6	7.1	8.5	7.8	6.4	—	—
Return on average equity	18.5	16.1	9.5	11.9	10.9	8.6	—	—
Long-term debt to invested capital	41.9	41.3	30.1	n/a	?	?	—	—

Exhibit 13

HOLIDAY INNS, INC.
Balance Sheets
(in thousands of dollars)

	1981	*1980*	*1979*	*1978*	*1977*
Assets					
Current assets:					
Cash	$ 41,347	$ 35,575	$ 23,439	$ 24,216	$ 20,529
Marketable securities, at cost	30,477	85,650	137,774	138,205	70,758
Notes and accounts receivable, net	133,809	131,299	115,987	137,796	87,175
Merchandise and supplies	25,159	26,240	21,728	23,872	27,186
Deferred income tax	14,506	16,104	—	—	—
Prepayments and other deposits to	15,929	16,996	19,490	13,880	11,916
be made to construction	(40,720)	(40,200)	(7,854)	(3,964)	4,258)
Total current assets	220,507	271,664	310,564	334,005	213,306
Construction fund, includes deposits	85,040	50,963	7,958	4,070	26,056
Long-term investments:					
Long-term notes received and other investments	49,705	64,892	55,427	30,974	27,974
	46,535	57,094	62,848	37,895	46,025
Total long-term investments	96,240	121,986	118,275	68,829	73,999
Property and equipment, at cost:					
Land, buildings, and equipment	1,693,082	1,486,298	1,023,983	1,140,843	1,068,118
Accumulated depreciation and amortization	(369,743)	(338,648)	(286,911)	(373,707)	(363,105)
Total property and equipment	1,323,339	1,147,650	737,072	767,136	705,013
Excess of cost over net assets of acquired businesses (amortized)	55,787	56,078	30,595		
Deferred charges and other assets	34,452	31,762	22,888	21,966	21,221
Total assets	$1,815,365	$1,680,103	$1,227,353	$1,196,006	$1,039,595
Liabilities and Shareholders Equity					
Current liabilities:					
Accounts payable	$ 83,205	$ 73,899	$ 73,752	$ 60,010	$ 40,693
Long-term debt due within one year	30,670	45,653	22,708	26,528	28,707
Accrued expenses	175,239	193,521	68,472	80,401	49,985
Federal and state income taxes	—	—	21,159	43,779	30,774
Other	—	—	40,710	36,337	20,996
Total current liabilities	289,114	313,073	226,799	247,055	171,155
Long-term debt*	639,582	564,613	311,302	322,177	310,164
Deferred credits	50,033	59,502	47,026	41,247	10,941
Deferred income taxes	64,259	34,995	15,426	33,139	42,531
Shareholders' Equity:					
Capital stock					
Special stock	648	731	786	803	855
Common stock	49,364	48,767	48,572	45,435	44,999
Capital surplus	161,188	155,704	154,519	118,648	116,028
Retained earnings	626,310	512,802	430,328	395,982	350,995
Capital stock in treasury	(63,170)	(9,669)	(6,943)	(7,492)	(6,705)
Restricted stock	(1,963)	(374)	(463)	(988)	(1,368)
Total equity	772,377	707,961	626,799	552,388	504,804
Total liabilities and shareholders' equity	$1,815,365	$1,680,103	$1,227,352	$1,196,006	$1,039,595

* Long-term debt includes subordinated debentures (9⅝ percent), convertible into common stock at $20 per share which were issued in 1980 with sinking fund payments to run between 1991 and 2005, and subordinated debentures (8 percent), convertible into common stock at $35 per share with sinking fund payments to 1985.

percent. Even without the call, our lenders currently recognize the convertibles as equity for covenant and capacity purposes.

To reduce our reliance on floating rate debt, we would like to issue about $75 million in fixed-rate, long-term debt within the next several months, if market and rate conditions become more favorable.

At year-end 1980, we reassessed our dividend policy to reflect the high costs of capital. We believe that our shareholders will benefit most from an increasing proportion of our earnings being reinvested in our several attractive businesses. While we still expect to increase our dividends each year, they will grow at a slower rate than in the 1970s, unless inflation declines substantially or there is a significant change in federal tax policy on dividends.

On the subject of inflation, we believe Holiday Inns, Inc., is in a unique position to benefit in two major ways from the otherwise insidious effects of inflation. First is our considerable asset base, with real estate holdings all over the world. In our 1980 annual report, we showed the current cost of our net property and equipment at $1.9 billion versus a book value of $1.1 billion. That substantial difference, which would nearly double our reported book value per share, from $21.51 to $42.97, was determined using the current cost methods prescribed by the Financial Accounting Standards Board (FASB). While we do not believe this is the best method, it does give some indication of the differences in value caused by inflation. We are examining the feasibility of having independent appraisals made of our properties. We believe these results could be very enlightening in terms of showing the present market value of our asset base.

Our second unique characteristic is franchising. Using our hotel group as an example, with franchise fees normally tied to room revenues, this provides a "top line" inflation hedge. Our franchise revenues, which include both initial fees and ongoing royalty payments, totaled $63.6 million in 1980 and have grown at a very steady 18.2 percent compound rate since 1975.

The outlook for continued franchise revenue growth is quite positive. Industry supply and demand trends in our segment are favorable and our franchisees have aggressive development plans as well. In addition, starting in the mid-1980s through the end of the century, an average of about 100 franchises a year—or 6 to 7 percent of the currently existing franchise system—will come up for renewal. At renewal time the company not only requires that the units be refurbished to current standards, which helps upgrade the system, but in virtually all cases the new franchise fee will be well in excess of the old rate.

74 Cash flow from operations was $291.8 million in 1981. This provides a sizable source of internally generated funds Holiday Inns, Inc. can use to support future expansion. Capital expenditures were $170.9 million and $207.1 million in 1981 and 1980, respectively. The company had available at year-end 1981 $225 million of prime-related, intermediate-term and $43 million in unused, short-term credit facilities. Only $30 million of the intermediate-term credit was utilized at the end of 1981. Holiday Inns, Inc.'s customers are generally required to pay for the company's products and services at the time they are provided. Consequently, high working capital levels are not necessary. Furthermore, the size and nature of the company's assets offer a number of ways to finance expansion, including fee ownership, leasing, joint ventures, management contracts, and franchising.

75 Corporate management has traditionally been very concerned about maintaining and improving return on shareholder equity. Shareholders' equity rose by $64.4 million or 9.1 percent in 1981, which reflects Holiday Inns, Inc.'s net income less its dividend payments *and* the effect of a 2-million-share repurchase program. Dividends in 1981 increased for the 18th consecutive year. Return on average shareholders' equity increased to 18.5 percent in 1981, up from 16.1 percent in 1980, exceeding near-term corporate objectives.

76 The ratio of long-term debt to invested capital at the end of 1981 was 41.9 percent, up slightly from 1980's 41.3 percent, but still considerably higher than pre-1980 levels (see Exhibit 12). Corporate management considered this debt ratio conservative in view of the company's asset base. Holiday Inns, Inc. engaged an independent firm in 1981 to appraise the appreciated value of the company's tangible assets and certain contract rights. The study indicated a market value of $1.86 billion, or nearly 2.5 times the $.77 billion reported shareholders' equity shown on its 1981 balance sheet. Corporate management believes this information provides a clearer definition of the true financial condition of Holiday Inns, Inc., showing the value of the company's contract income streams as well as the "real" benefits from the appreciation of its substantial real estate assets.

77 Holiday Inns, Inc. had two convertible subordinate debenture issues as a part of its long-term debt. The first, an 8 percent issue for which the company is making sinking fund payments to 1985, is convertible into common stock at $35 per share. The 1981 value of this issue was $5.85 million. The second issue, a 9⅝ percent debenture with sinking fund payments scheduled between 1991 and 2005, was convertible into common stock at $20 per share. This issue represented a $144.2 million long-term debt on Holiday Inns' 1981 balance sheet. The company was considering calling the 9⅝ percent debentures for redemption in 1982 to lower the debt-to-capital ratio (removing $144.2 from debt into capital would lower the ratio to 32.3 percent). The stock price hovered around $22 per share toward the end of 1981.

For the Future

78 Mike Rose, President and CEO, offered the following corporate philosophy to guide Holiday Inns in the 1980s:

> We are operating our businesses under a very simple and straightforward management philosophy. We have shared this philosophy with the entire rank and file of our company and I would like to share it with you because it says a lot about our future success. Our philosophy is:
>
> We are *a forward-looking, innovative industry leader with clearly defined goals, producing superior products, services and consistently high return for our shareholders.*
>
> We will *maintain integrity in both our internal and external relationships, fostering respect for the individual and open, two-way communications.*
>
> We will *promote a climate of enthusiasm, teamwork, and challenge which attracts, motivates, and retains superior personnel and rewards superior performance.*

79 Charles Barnette, director of corporate public relations, succinctly summarized the perspective adopted by Holiday Inns, Inc., for the future. He stated, "We want to

focus business activities on markets and market segments where we can excel, achieve competitive advantage, and be the cost-effective leader."

80 Some of the specifics that emerge from Barnette's statement are: (1) maintain a corporate debt ratio of 35 percent of invested capital; (2) increase corporate return on investment capital (ROIC) to over 13 percent, (3) grow at a rate of 15 percent or more per year; (4) achieve a dividend payment representing 35 percent of net income. While these corporate-wide objectives offer a realistic challenge, the future contribution of different business groups could vary considerably.

81 To summarize their optimism about the future, Kemmons Wilson, founder and retired chairman of the board, placed all corporate objectives for the future in a concise framework. He stated:

> Now it's time to embark on a new era of growth and to continue the very favorable trends for our shareholders that we've seen in the past ten years. The outlook on tourism in this country and worldwide has never been better. We are truly becoming a unified world where people are traveling farther, more frequently, and for more reasons.
>
> Twenty-seven years ago I had a dream. It has been fulfilled. But even in my wildest dreams I could not see the changes that were ahead. I never dreamed that so many people would travel between countries. Or that people would choose to spend a weekend in their own hometown, or that people would begin to eat more meals away from home than at home, or that forms of acceptable entertainment would change so dramatically.
>
> Today we have a better picture of the future, and at Holiday Inns, Inc. I am proud to say we're anticipating change. In fact, we welcome it. And we're determined to be out in front in whatever markets we are able to serve.

82 "Whatever markets we are able to serve" may have a double meaning for Holiday Inns as it moves toward 1990. Is it a challenge for further diversification of this travel-related company or a call for urgent reexamination of what its mission and business strategies should be?

83 Embarking on a new era of growth will be managed, for the first time in over a quarter of a century, without the presence of Kemmons Wilson. As Holiday Inns, Inc., entered the decade of the 1980s, Kemmons Wilson announced his retirement.

At the annual stockholders meeting, held in Memphis, Wilson made this announcement in conjunction with strong words of praise for his business associates and a strong vote of confidence for the company he founded. Wilson stated:

> I have had an opportunity that no one else has had. I have seen the company take my original vision of a standardized lodging concept and turn it into the largest hotel chain in the world.
>
> As I reflect upon what we have accomplished and I study our plans for the future, I am firmly convinced that we are embarking on a new era of growth. My optimism is based upon our management organization and the favorable trends that we see in tourism throughout this country.
>
> It is also important to recognize that more people are moving into the prime lodging customer age, 25 to 45 years old. The baby boom has grown up. This trend will favorably impact Holiday Inns, Inc., for many years to come.

Chapter 1 Cohesion Case Illustration

Strategic Management and Holiday Inns, Inc.

Chapter 1 provided a broad introduction to strategic management. What role does strategic management play (or could it play) at Holiday Inns? Based on the material in Chapter 1, this question can be answered by addressing four issues:

1. Is Holiday Inns facing a strategic decision?
2. What is Holiday Inns' strategy?
3. What value would strategic management offer Holiday Inns?
4. What strategic management structure is appropriate at Holiday Inns?

Is Holiday Inns facing a strategic decision? Yes! The energy crisis in early 1973–74 initiated fundamental changes in the lodging industry. The high cost of gasoline combined with lower-cost air travel (due to deregulation of the airline industry by 1980) led to fundamental changes in the travel practices of the American public. By the beginning of 1980, the lodging industry also had the largest oversupply of rooms since the 1930s. These are but a few key factors that significantly affect Holiday Inn and point out the need for sound strategic decisions.

Other issues foretell a need for strategic decisions. Budget motels are expanding. This threatens the hotel business in the 1980s, and it is the key revenue generator. Holiday Inns is trying to diversify, but the percentage breakdown of revenues shows little change since 1974. Why? Is Holiday Inns' management not seriously pushing diversification? Is the necessary expertise lacking? The recent move into casino gaming represents a potentially major philosophical change for the company, as evidenced by the resignation of President L. M. Clymer. Is this to be a sideline operation or a serious future commitment? What ramifications, in light of Clymer's resignation, does this have for Holiday Inns' top-management structure and cohesion? With Holiday Inns still dependent on hotels/motels for 55 percent of its revenue, is there still room for growth or is the domestic (and international) market becoming saturated? With the departure of Kemmons Wilson, has Holiday Inns completed the evolution from an entrepreneurially run company to a professionally managed one? Clearly, Holiday Inns faces a number of the strategic issues described in Chapter 1.

What is Holiday Inns' strategy? Holiday Inns appears to be pursuing steady growth through gradual, concentric diversification into hospitality- and transportation-related businesses. Its business portfolio is still dominated by the hotel division. But the product and transportation divisions now represent just under 50 percent of Holiday Inns' revenues. And the gaming industry is seen as a strong avenue for growth.

What value does strategic management offer Holiday Inns? With the numerous strategic issues facing Holiday Inns, systematic strategic management would appear essential for survival and prosperity. Holiday Inns' top management team is clearly interested in adopting a proactive rather than reactive strategic orientation. While its nonhotel divisions represent approximately 52 percent of Holiday Inns' revenue, this breakdown has not changed significantly since 1974, raising the question of whether its long-term strategy is just to supplement the hotel core or to actually reduce dependence on the traditional hotel side of its business.

Systematic strategic management clearly is needed to address this issue in looking to the 1990s. Holiday Inns' management also believes the need for strategic management is imperative, based on this comment in the 1981 annual report: "The strategic framework and management team of Holiday Inns, Inc. are in place and we are well positioned for growth and accomplishment."

What strategic management structure is appropriate at Holiday Inns? Clearly, the multibusiness structure presented in Figure 1–1 is called for at Holiday Inns. It could be illustrated as shown in Exhibit 1.

Exhibit 1

Levels of strategy at Holiday Inns, Inc.

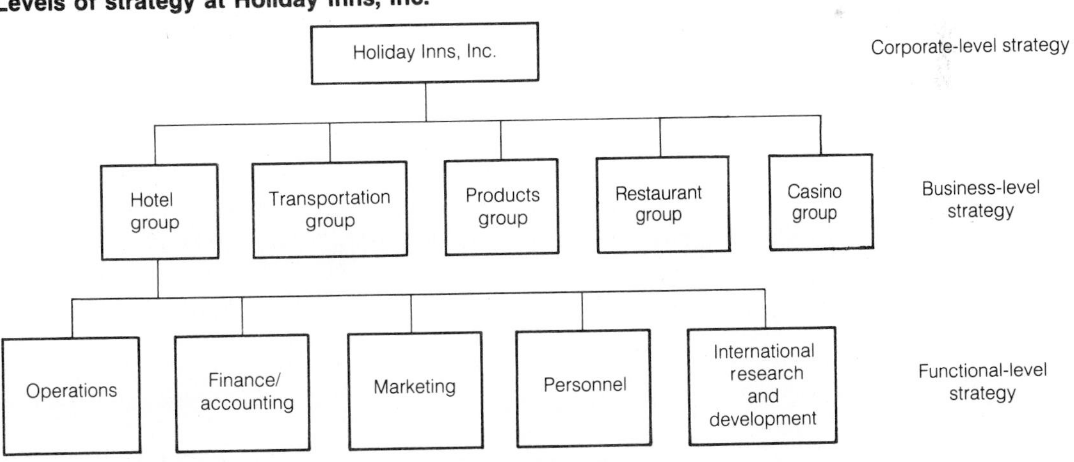

CHAPTER

The Strategic Management Process

Businesses vary in the processes they use to formulate and direct their strategic management activities. Sophisticated planning organizations such as General Electric, Procter & Gamble, and IBM have developed more detailed processes than similarly sized, less formal planners. Small businesses that rely on the strategy formulation skills and limited time of an entrepreneur typically exhibit very basic planning concerns when contrasted with larger firms in their industries. Understandably, firms with diverse operations due to their reliance on multiple products, markets, or technologies also tend to utilize more complex strategic management systems. However, despite differences in detail and degree of formalization, the basic components of the models used to analyze strategic management operations are very similar.[1]

Because of the similarity among general models of the strategic management process it is possible to develop one eclectic model which is representative of the foremost thought in the area. Such a model was developed for this text and is shown in Figure 2–1. This *strategic management model* serves three major functions. First, it provides a visual representation of the major components of the entire strategic management process. The model also shows

Portions of this chapter are from John A. Pearce II, "An Executive-Level Perspective on the Strategic Management Process," *California Management Review*, Spring 1982, pp. 39–48.

[1] Models by academics typically developed from consulting experience and intended either for business or educational use, which reflect such similarity include those of Stevenson (1976), Rogers (1975), King and Cleland (1978), and numerous others. Models recommended for use by small businesses are almost identical to those recommended for larger firms, e.g., those published by Gilmore (1973) and Steiner (1967). Finally models that describe approaches for accomplishing strategic options contain elements similar to those included in general models, see e.g., Pryor (1964) on mergers and Steiner (1964) on diversification. The bibliography at the end of this chapter contains complete citations.

Figure 2–1

Strategic management model

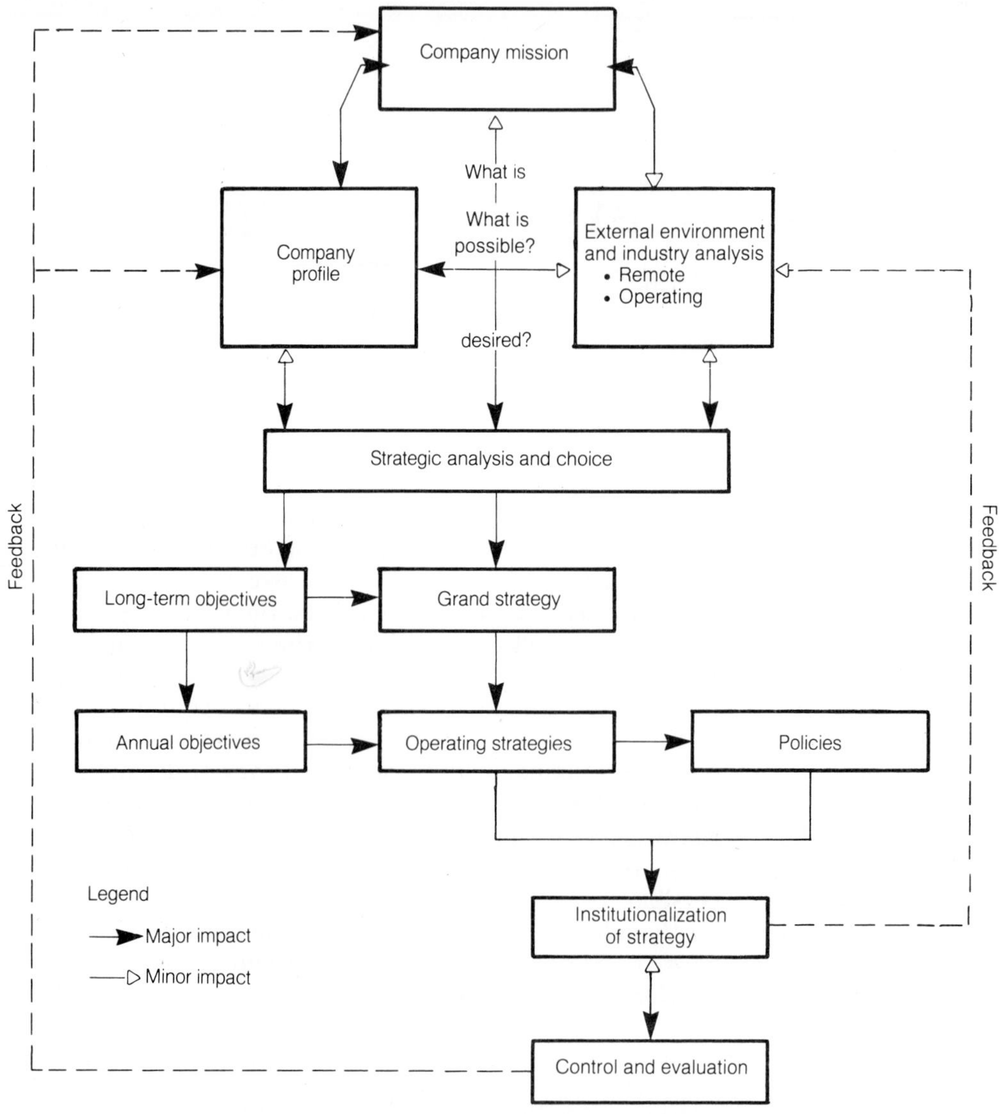
Company mission
What is
What is
possible?
desired?
Company
profile
External environment
and industry analysis
• Remote
• Operating
Strategic analysis and choice
Feedback
Long-term objectives
Grand strategy
Annual objectives
Operating strategies
Policies
Legend
Major impact
Minor impact
Institutionalization
of strategy
Control and evaluation
Feedback

how the components are related and how they are arranged in sequence throughout the process. Second, the model will serve as the outline for this text. After providing a general overview of the strategic management process in this chapter, the major components of the model will be used as the principal theme of subsequent chapters. Finally, the model is suggested for use in analyzing the case studies included in this text. In this context, the model enhances development of strategy formulation skills by guiding the analyst in a systematic and comprehensive study of each business situation.

Components of the Strategic Management Model

In this section the key components of the strategic management model will be defined and briefly described. Each will receive much greater attention in a later chapter. The intention here is simply to provide an introduction to the major concepts.

Company Mission

The mission of a business is the fundamental, unique purpose that sets apart from other firms of its type and identifies the scope of its operations in product and market terms. The mission is a general, enduring statement of company intent. It embodies the business philosophy of strategic decision makers, implies the image the company seeks to project, reflects the firm's self-concept, and indicates the principal product or service areas and primary customer needs the company will attempt to satisfy. In short, the mission describes the product, market, and technological areas of emphasis for the business in a way that reflects the values and priorities of the strategic decision makers.

Because conceptualizing a company mission can be difficult, an excellent example is shown in Figure 2–2, the mission statement of Nicor, Inc., as abstracted from an annual report to its stockholders.

Company Profile

A firm's internal analysis determines its performance capabilities based on existing or accessible resources. From this analysis, a company profile is generated. At any designated point in time, the company profile depicts the quantity and quality of financial, human, and physical resources available to the firm. The profile also assesses the inherent strengths and weaknesses of the firm's management and organizational structure. Finally, it contrasts the historical successes of the firm and the traditional values and concerns of management with the firm's current capabilities in an attempt to identify the future capabilities of the business.

Figure 2–2

Mission statement of Nicor, Inc.

Preamble

We, the management of Nicor, Inc., here set forth our belief as to the purpose for which the company is established and the principles under which it should operate. We pledge our effort to the accomplishment of these purposes within these principles.

Basic purpose

The basic purpose of Nicor, Inc. is to perpetuate an investor-owned company engaging in various phases of the energy business, striving for balance among those phases so as to render needed satisfactory products and services and earn optimum, long-range profits.

What we do

The principal business of the company, through its utility subsidiary, is the provision of energy through a pipe system to meet the needs of ultimate consumers. To accomplish its basic purpose, and to ensure its strength, the company will engage in other energy-related activities, directly or through subsidiaries or in participation with other persons, corporations, firms, or entities.

All activities of the company shall be consistent with its responsibilities to investors, customers, employees, and the public and its concern for the optimum development and utilization of natural resources and for environmental needs.

Where we do it

The company's operations shall be primarily in the United States, but no self-imposed or regulatory geographical limitations are placed upon the acquisition, development, processing, transportation, or storage of energy resources, or upon other energy-related ventures in which the company may engage. The company will engage in such activities in any location where, after careful review, it has determined that such activity is in the best interest of its stockholders.

Utility service will be offered in the territory of the company's utility subsidiary to the best of its ability, in accordance with the requirements of regulatory agencies and pursuant to the subsidiary's purposes and principles.

One kind of analysis used in development of a company profile is the functional-area resource-deployment matrix. As shown in Figure 2–3, this analysis provides the firm with a yearly record of its level of commitment at each functional area. This approach enables the firm to quickly calculate the total investment it has made to each functional area over time as a basis for better understanding comparative and competitive strengths and weaknesses.

External Environment

A firm's external environment consists of all the conditions and forces that affect its strategic options but are typically beyond the firm's control. The strategic management model shows the external environment as consisting of two interactive and interrelated segments: the operating environment and the remote environment.

The operating environment consists of the forces and conditions within a specific industry and a specific competitive operating situation, external to

Figure 2–3

A functional-area resource-deployment matrix

Functional areas	*Resource deployment emphasis*	*Five years ago*	*Four years ago*	*Three years ago*	*Two years ago*	*One year ago*	*This year*
R&D and engineering	Percent strategic development dollars						
	Focus of efforts						
Manufacturing	Percent strategic development dollars						
	Focus of efforts						
Marketing	Percent strategic development dollars						
	Focus of efforts						
Finance	Percent strategic development dollars						
	Focus of efforts						
Management	Percent strategic development dollars						
	Focus of efforts						

Source: William F. Glueck, *Business Policy and Strategic Management* (New York: McGraw-Hill, 1980), p. 169.

the firm, that influence the selection and attainment of alternative objective/strategy combinations. Unlike changes in the remote environment, changes in the operating environment often result from strategic actions taken by the firm or its competitors, consumers, users, suppliers, and/or creditors. Thus, a consumer shift toward greater price consciousness, a loosening of local bank credit restrictions, a new entrant into the marketplace, the development of a substitute product, or the opening of a new wholesale outlet by a competitor are all likely to have direct and intentional positive or negative effects on a firm.

The remote environment refers to forces and conditions which originate beyond and usually irrespective of any single firm's immediate operating environment that provide the general economic, political, social, and technological framework within which competing organizations operate. For example, a company's strategic planners and managers may face spiraling inflation (economic), import restrictions on raw materials (political), demographic swings of population in the geographic areas they serve (social), or revolutionary technological innovations that make their production systems unexpectedly obsolete (technological).

Strategic Analysis and Choice

Simultaneous assessment of the external environment and company profile enables a firm to identify a range of possibly attractive interactive opportunities. These opportunities are *possible* avenues for investment. However, the full list must be screened through the criterion of the company mission before a set of possible and *desired* opportunities is generated. This process results in the selection of a *strategic choice.* It is meant to provide the combination of long-term objectives and grand strategy that will optimally position the firm in the external environment to achieve the company mission.

Consider the case when strategic managers feel that a firm is overly dependent on a single customer group, e.g., a chain of record shops with principal customers 10 to 20 years old. The firm's interactive opportunities might include expanding the product line, heavily emphasizing related products, accepting the status quo, or selling out profitably to a competitor. While each of these options might be possible, a firm with a mission that stressed commitment to continued existence as a growth-oriented, autonomous organization might find that only the first two opportunities are desirable. In that case, these options would be evaluated on the basis of payoff and risk potential, compatibility with or capability for becoming the firm's competitive advantage, and other critical selection criteria.

A complicated subprocess is used to derive the strategic choice. Figure 2–4 shows the strategic analysis and choice components of the strategic management model in greater detail. As the figure shows, strategic analysis involves matching each of the possible and desirable interactive opportunities with

Figure 2–4

Interactive-opportunities analysis and strategic choice

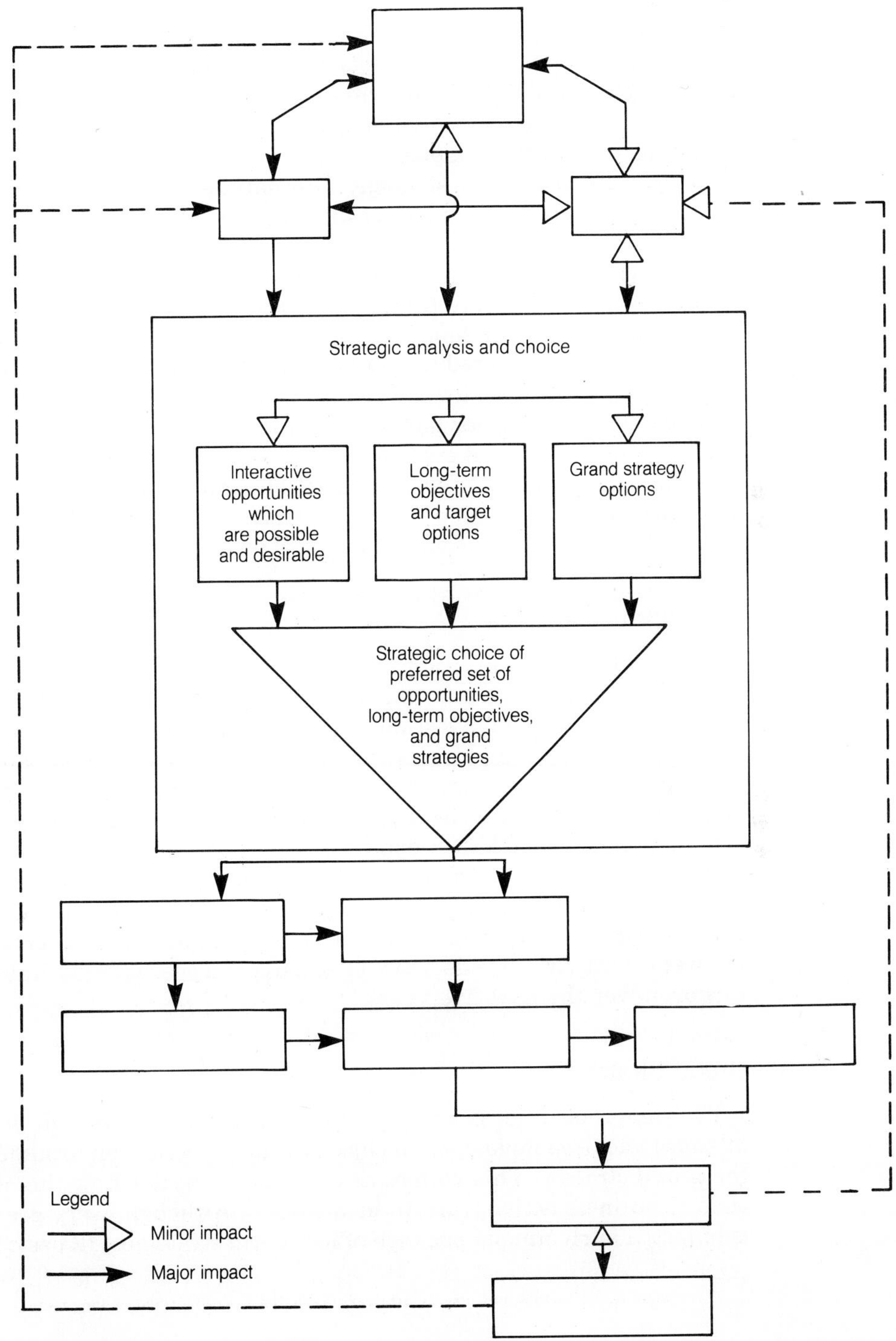

reasonable long-term objectives and targets. In turn, these are matched with the most promising approaches—known as grand strategies—for achieving the desired results. Each of the sets of alternatives is then evaluated individually and comparatively to determine the single set or group of sets that is expected to best achieve the company mission. The chosen set (or sets) is known as the strategic choice.

Critical assessment of strategic alternatives initially involves developing criteria for comparing one set of alternatives with all others. As is the case in making any choice, a company's strategic selection involves evaluating alternatives that are rarely wholly acceptable or wholly unacceptable. The alternatives are therefore compared to determine which option will have the most favorable overall, long-run impact on a firm.

Among the criteria used in assessing strategic choice alternatives are strategic managers' attitudes toward risk, flexibility, stability, growth, profitability, and diversification. Other factors included in the decision-making process are volatility of the external environment, life-cycle stages of the evaluated products, and the company's current level of commitment to its organizational structure, access to needed resources, traditional competitive advantages, as well as the potential reaction of influential external or internal interest groups.

Long-term Objectives

The results an organization seeks over a multiyear period are its *long-term objectives.*[2] Such objectives typically involve some or all of the following areas: profitability, return on investment, competitive position, technological leadership, productivity, employee relations, public responsibility, and employee development. To be of greatest value, each objective must be specific, measurable, achievable, and consistent with other objectives of the firm. Objectives are a statement of *what* is expected from pursuing a given set of business activities. Examples of common company objectives include the following: doubling of earnings per share within five years with increases in each intervening year; moving from third to second as a seller of commercial electrical fixtures in Oregon; and a decrease of 10 percent a year in undesirable employee turnover over the next five years.

Grand Strategy

The comprehensive, general plan of major actions through which a firm intends to achieve its long-term objectives in a dynamic environment is called the *grand strategy.* This *statement of means* indicates how the objectives or ends of business activity are to be achieved. Although every grand strategy is in fact, a fairly unique package of long-term strategies, 12 basic approaches

[2] Five years is the normal, but largely arbitrary, period of time identified as long term.

can be identified: concentration, market development, product development, innovation, horizontal integration, vertical integration, joint venture, concentric diversification, conglomerate diversification, retrenchment/turnaround, divestiture, and liquidation. Each of these grand strategies will be covered in detail in Chapter 8. Any of these grand, master, or business strategies are meant to guide the acquisition and allocation of resources over an extended period of time. Admittedly, no single grand strategy, or even several in combination, can describe in adequate detail the strategic actions a business will undertake over a long period. However, when a firm's strategic managers are committed to a fundamental approach for positioning the business in the competitive marketplace, it provides a galvanizing central focal point for subsequent decision making.

Some brief examples of grand strategies include Hewlett-Packard's technological innovation approach for capturing the high profit margins on new products, First Pennsylvania's retrenchment approach for avoiding bankruptcy despite $75 million in 1980 losses, and General Electric's concentric diversification approach allowing growth through acquisition of related business.

Annual Objectives

The results an organization seeks to achieve within a one-year period are *annual objectives*. Short-term or annual objectives involve areas similar to those entailed in long-term objectives. The differences between them stem principally from the greater specificity possible and necessary in short-term objectives. For example, a long-term objective of increasing companywide sales volume by 20 percent in five years might be translated into a 4 percent growth objective in year one. In addition, it is reasonable that the planning activities of all major functions or divisions of the firm should reflect this companywide, short-run objective. The research and development department might be expected to suggest one major addition to the product line each year, the finance department might set a complementary objective of obtaining the necessary $300,000 in funds for an immediate expansion of production facilities, and the marketing department might establish an objective of reducing turnover of sales representatives by 5 percent per year.

Functional Strategies

Within the general framework of the grand strategy, each distinctive business function or division needs a specific and integrative plan of action. Most strategic managers attempt to develop an operating strategy for each related set of annual objectives, e.g., there will be a functional strategy to indicate how the marketing department's annual objectives will be achieved, one for the production department's objectives, and so on.

Operating strategies are detailed statements of the *means* that will be used to achieve objectives in the following year. The company's budgeting process is usually coordinated with the development of the operating strategies to ensure specificity, practicality, and accountability in the planning process.

Policies

Policies are directives designed to guide the thinking, decisions, and actions of managers and their subordinates in implementing the organization's strategy. Policies provide guidelines for establishing and controlling the ongoing operating processes of the firm consistent with the firm's strategic objectives. Policies are often referred to as *standard operating procedures* and serve to increase managerial effectiveness by standardizing many routine decisions and to limit the discretion of managers and subordinates in implementing operation strategies.

The following are examples of the nature and diversity of company policies:

A requirement that managers have purchase requests for items costing more than $500 cosigned by the controller.

The minimum equity position required for all new McDonald's franchises.

The standard formula used to calculate return on investment for the 43 strategic business units of General Electric.

A companywide decision that employees have their annual performance review on the anniversary of their being hired.

Institutionalizing the Strategy

Annual objectives, functional strategies, and specific policies provide important means of communicating what must be done to implement the overall strategy. By translating long-term intentions into short-term guides to action, they make the strategy operational. But the strategy must also be *institutionalized*—must permeate the very day-to-day life of the company—if it is to be effectively implemented.

Three organizational elements provide the fundamental, long-term means for institutionalizing the firm's strategy: (1) structure, (2) leadership, and (3) culture. Successful implementation requires effective management and integration of these three elements to ensure that the strategy "takes hold" in the daily life of the firm.

Control and Evaluation

An implemented strategy must be monitored to determine the extent to which objectives are achieved. The process of formulating a strategy is largely subjective despite often extensive efforts at objectivity. Thus, the first substantial reality test of a strategy comes only after implementation. Strategic managers must watch for early signs of marketplace response to their strategies. Managers must also provide monitoring and controlling methods to ensure that their strategic plan is followed.

Although early review and evaluation of the strategic process concentrates on market-responsive modifications, the underlying and ultimate test of a strategy is ability to achieve its end—the annual objectives, long-term objectives, and mission. In the final analysis, a firm is only successful when its strategy achieves designated objectives.

Strategic Management as a Process

A *process* is an identifiable flow of information through interrelated stages of analysis directed toward the achievement of an aim. Thus, the strategic management model in Figure 2–1 depicts a process. In the strategic management process, the flow of information involves historical, current, and forecasted data on the business, its operations, and environment, which are evaluated in light of the values and priorities of influential individuals and groups—often called *stakeholders*—who are vitally interested in the actions of the business. The interrelated stages of the process are the 12 components discussed in the last section. Finally, the aim of the process is the formulation and implementation of strategies that result in long-term achievement of the company's mission and near-term achievement of objectives.

There are several important implications of viewing strategic management as a process. First, a change in any component will affect several or all other components. Notice that the majority of arrows in the model point two ways, suggesting that the flow of information or impact is usually reciprocal. For example, forces in the external environment influence the nature of the mission designed by a company's strategic managers and stakeholders. The existence of a given company with a given mission in turn legitimizes the environmental forces and implicitly heightens competition in the firm's realm of operation. A specific example is a power company which is persuaded, in part by governmental incentives, that its mission statement should include a commitment to the development of energy alternatives. The firm might then promise to extend its research and development efforts in the area of coal liquification. Obviously, in this example, the external environment has affected the firm's definition of its mission, and the existence of the revised mission signals a competitive condition in the environment.

A second implication of strategic management as a process is that strategy formulation and implementation are sequential. The process begins with development or reevaluation of the company mission. This step is associated with, but essentially followed by, development of a company profile and assessment of the external environment. Then follow, in order: strategic choice, definition of long-term objectives, design of grand strategy, definition of short-term objectives, design of operating strategies, institutionalization of the strategy, and review and evaluation. However, the apparent rigidity of the process must be qualified.

First, the strategic posture of a firm may have to be reevaluated in terms of any of the principal factors that determine or affect company performance. Entry by a major new competitor, death of a prominent board member, replacement of the chief executive officer, or a downturn in market responsivenesses are among the thousands of changes that can prompt reassessment of a company's strategic plan. However, no matter where the need for a reassessment originates, the strategic management process begins with the mission statement.

Second, not every component of the strategic management process deserves equal attention each time a planning activity takes place. Firms in an extremely stable environment may find that an in-depth assessment is not required every five years.[3] Often companies are satisfied with their original mission statements even after decades of operation and thus need to spend only a minimal amount of time in addressing the subject. In addition, while formal strategic planning may be undertaken only every five years, objectives and strategies are usually updated each year, and rigorous reassessment of the initial stages of strategic planning is rarely undertaken at these points.

A third implication of strategic management as a process is the necessity of feedback from institutionalization, review, and evaluation to the early stages of the process. *Feedback* can be defined as postimplementation results collected as inputs for the enhancement of future decision making. Therefore, as indicated in Figure 2–1, strategic managers should attempt to assess the impact of implemented strategies on external environments. Thus, future planning can reflect any changes precipitated by strategic actions. Strategic managers should also carefully measure and analyze the impact of strategies on the need for possible modifications in the company mission.

A fourth and final implication of strategic management as a process is the need to view it as a dynamic system. *Dynamic* describes the constantly changing conditions that affect interrelated and interdependent strategic activities. Managers should recognize that components of the strategic process are constantly evolving while formal planning artifically freezes the changing conditions and forces in a company's internal and external environments, much as an action photograph freezes the movement of a swimmer. In actuality, change is continuous, and thus, the dynamic strategic planning process must be constantly monitored for significant changes in any components as a precaution against implementing an obsolete strategy.

---

[3] Formal strategic planning is not necessarily done on a rigid five-year schedule, although this is most common. Some planners advocate planning on an irregular timing basis to keep the activity from being overly routine.

Practical Limitations of the Model

It is important to understand the limitations of the strategic management model to gain an awareness of how the model can be properly used. This awareness will help ensure effective strategic management. Thus, in this section, three points will be stressed: the model is holistic, analytical, and nonpolitical.

Holistic. Users of the model believe that strategic planning should be initiated by a company's top management. Thus, because of the broad perspective of these executives, the strategy-formulating process develops from general to specific. The business is first studied as a whole within the context of its competitive environment, then from the standpoint of individual functions or divisions, and eventually specific operational activities of the firm are involved in the process.

Some researchers have argued that in certain circumstances the holistic approach is inferior to a tactical approach in strategic planning.[4] With the tactical approach, strategic managers work "up" through the firm in their study of its potential. After obtaining an operational view of the firm's strengths and weaknesses, managers assess their firm's compatibility with its external environment.

The risk of using the holistic approach implicitly advocated in the strategic management model is that planning might be unrealistic because there is a potential tendency to minimize the difficulties of implementation. The holistic approach can sometimes lead managers to gloss over details that may eventually be critical in making the firm's strategies operational.

On the other hand, the tactical approach poses far greater risks to strategic managers, first because planning may be inflexible. Managers risk emphasizing operational details and overstating the extent to which the firm is locked into the status quo. It is difficult to envision new interactive opportunities when initial planning activities stress narrow operational concerns. Second, the integration of planning activities is more difficult with the tactical approach. Because there is no overall planning framework as is characteristic of the holistic method, the initial phases of planning are often disjointed, complicating development of a unified strategic plan. Third, and most damaging, the tactical approach leads to a concentration on the present rather than on the future while strategic planning is specifically intended to be future oriented. With tactical planning, the emphasis is too often on improving current capabilities instead of on satisfying anticipated needs.

In the final analysis it appears that the holistic approach of the strategic management model is superior to tactical alternatives. However, users of the model should be alert to the shortcomings in planning that the strategic model

[4] For example, see George W. McKinney III, "An Experimental Study of Strategy Formulation Systems" (Ph.D. diss., Graduate School of Business, Stanford University, 1969).

fosters and should guard against them. Specifically, users of the model should continually monitor the data-gathering and implementation phases. In this context, it is important to remember that although middle- and lower-level managers seldom have a voice in the strategic choice process, they are a principal source of the operational data on which the ultimate decisions are largely based. Therefore, their advice and critiques should be actively sought and carefully considered in all phases of strategic management.

Analytic versus Prescriptive. A second major issue of concern in using the strategic management model is that it is analytical rather than prescriptive or procedural. The model generally describes the logical or analytical steps many businesses actually use in their strategic activities. However, it does not describe the procedures or routines necessary to carry out each step. Further, research has not proved that the model is *ideal.* In fact, while there is considerable evidence that firms which have formal strategic planning outperform nonplanners, somewhat different planning models were used by almost every business studied.[5] As a result, no model should be seen as providing a prescription for the way strategic planning should be done. Therefore, when the strategic management model is used it should be remembered that the model builders are recommending the general approach they believe will provide a sound basis for strategic planning, not a model they are certain will lead to the best results. It is important that users of the model are continually alert to the need for occasional additions or deletions. The model will be most valuable if it is treated as a dependable outline for construction of individualized planning systems.

Nonpolitical. The third major limitation of the model is that it is nonpolitical. A naive observer could therefore be misled into seeing strategic management as largely devoid of subjective assessments, biased interpretations, human error, self-serving voting by individual managers, intuitive decision making, favoritism, and other forms of political activity. In reality, most strategic management experts believe the opposite. Strategic management is a behavioral activity and, as such, is vulnerable to the same pitfalls as other "people" processes. It is truly a management process. People involved in all phases of strategy formulation and implementation must be skillfully organized, led, planned about, and controlled. For this reason, the behavioral implications of each phase of the strategic management process will be discussed extensively in this book. However, limitation of the strategic management model per se is it presumes that strategic planners are skilled managers who are sensitive to the people-related issues which continuously arise in every phase of the process.

---

[5] See, for example, Ansoff et al. (1971), Burt (1978), Eastlock and McDonald (1970), Herold (1972), Karger and Malik (1975), Malik and Karger (1975), Rue and Fulmer (1972), Schoeffler et al. (1974), Thune and House (1970), and Wood and LaForge (1979), all listed in the bibliography in this chapter.

The effects of political activity on the strategic management process are critical to its effective functioning and are a principal determinant of the plan's final composition. Effective strategic managers must be attentive to this aspect and attempt to skillfully manage the inevitable people-related concerns.

Summary

This chapter presented an overview of the strategic management process. The model provided will serve as the structure for understanding and integrating all of the major phases of strategy formulation and implementation. Although each of these phases is given extensive individual attention in subsequent chapters, it is important to acquire an early feeling for its nature.

The chapter stressed that the strategic management process centers around the belief that the mission of a firm can best be achieved through a systematic and comprehensive assessment of both a firm's resource capabilities and its external environment. Subsequent evaluation of the company's opportunities leads in turn, to the choice of long-term objectives and grand strategies and, ultimately, to annual objectives and operating strategies that must be implemented, monitored, and controlled.

The holistic approach of strategic management was preferable to a tactical one. However, three potential problems with the holistic method were discussed, as were the means by which their negative impact can be minimized.

Questions for Discussion

1. Think about the courses you have had in functional areas such as marketing, finance, production, personnel, and accounting. What is the importance of each of these areas to the strategic planning process?
2. Discuss with practicing business managers the strategic planning approaches used in their businesses. What are the similarities and differences between their models and the one in the text?
3. In what ways do you believe that the strategic planning approach would differ in profit-oriented and not-for-profit organizations?
4. How do you explain the success of businesses that do not use a formal strategic planning process?
5. Think about your postgraduation job search as a strategic decision. How would the model be helpful to you in identifying and securing the most promising position?
6. Examine the collection of corporate annual reports in your school's library. Can you locate a report that includes a good mission statement? Does it exhibit the characteristics of a company mission described in this chapter?

Bibliography

Ansoff, H. Igor: R. Brandenberg; F. Portner; and R. Radosevich. *Acquisition Behavior of U.S. Manufacturing Firms, 1946–65.* Nashville, Tenn.: Vanderbilt University Press, 1971.

Burt, David. "Planning and Performance in Australian Retailing." *Long-Range Planning,* June 1978, pp. 62–66.

Eastlock, Joseph Jr., and Philip McDonald. "CEO's Role in Corporate Growth." *Harvard Business Review,* May–June 1970, pp. 150–63.

Gilmore, Frank. "Formulating Strategy in Smaller Companies." *Harvard Business Review,* May–June 1973.

Glueck, William F. *Business Policy and Strategic Management.* 3d ed. New York: McGraw-Hill, 1980.

Herold, David. "Long-Range Planning and Organizational Performance: A Cross Validation Study." *Academy of Management Review,* March 1972, pp. 91–102.

Karger, Delmar, and Zafar Malik. "Long-Range Planning and Organizational Performance." *Long-Range Planning,* December 1975, pp. 60–64.

King, William R., and David I. Cleland. *Strategic Planning and Policy.* New York: Van Nostrand Reinhold, 1978.

Malik, Zafar, and Delmar Karger. "Does Long-Range Planning Improve Company Performance?" *Management Review,* September 1975, pp. 27–31.

McKinney, George W. III. "An Experimental Study of Strategy Formulation Systems." Ph.D. dissertation, Graduate School of Business, Stanford University, 1969.

Pearce, John A. II. "An Executive-Level Perspective on the Strategic Management Process." *California Management Review,* Spring 1982, pp. 39–48.

Pryor, Millard H., Jr. "Anatomy of a Merger." *Michigan Business Review,* July 1964, pp. 28–34.

Rogers, David C. D. *Essentials of Business Policy.* New York: Harper & Row, 1975.

Rue, Leslie, and Robert Fulmer. "Is Long-Range Planning Profitable?" *Academy of Management Proceedings,* 1972.

Schoeffler, Sidney, et al. "Impact of Strategic Planning on Profit Performance." *Harvard Business Review,* March–April 1974, pp. 137–45.

Stagner, Ross. "Corporate Decision Making." *Journal of Applied Psychology,* February 1969, pp. 1–13.

Steiner, George A. "Why and How to Diversify." *California Management Review,* Summer 1964, pp. 11–18.

———. "Approaches to Long-Range Planning for Small Business. *California Management Review,* Fall 1967, pp. 3–16.

Stevenson, Howard H. "Defining Corporate Strengths and Weaknesses." *Sloan Management Review,* Spring 1976, pp. 51–68.

Thune, Stanley, and Robert House. "Where Long-Range Planning Pays Off." *Business Horizons,* August 1970, pp. 81–87.

Wood, D. Robley, Jr., and R. Lawrence LaForge. "The Impact of Comprehensive Planning on Financial Performance." *Academy of Management Journal* 22, no. 3 (1979), pp. 516–26.

Chapter 2 Cohesion Case Illustration

Strategic Management Framework for Holiday Inns, Inc.

Chapter 2 presented a framework for the strategic management process. How should it be applied at Holiday Inns, Inc.?

Holiday Inns, Inc., is a multibusiness firm. As such, it must have an overall corporate-level strategy for dealing with decisions involving its portfolio of businesses and for guiding strategic decisions made by key managers within each business group. In addition, *each* business group must formulate and implement a business-level strategy to guide resource deployment and pursuit of opportunity consistent with overall corporate objectives.

The purpose of Chapter 2 was to introduce a logical process for developing and implementing a strategy. Each component was briefly discussed in this chapter; the remaining 10 chapters will deal with each component in greater detail. Thus, the objective at this point is to apply broadly the strategic management paradigm to Holiday Inns, Inc.

As assistant to the president, how would one approach strategy development at Holiday Inns? (Illustrations of two possibilities are provided based on the material in Chapter 2.)

Looking to the 1980s, Holiday Inns must first address its corporate-level strategy. Exhibit 1 shows how to go about this. Strategy at this level is a critical issue for Holiday Inns. What should the company mission be? Is the company a travel business or a hospitality business? How does the current portfolio of business groups fit this overall mission? What do the trends in the competitive environment(s) suggest for each group and the overall mission? What alternative portfolios are available? Which is best? What guidelines must be given to business groups to ensure that their strategy is consistent with and supportive of the corporate strategy chosen? These are some of the issues that must be addressed in designing the corporate-level side of strategic management for Holiday Inns.

Strategies generated for Holiday Inns must also deal with the formulation and implementation of business-level strategy for each business group. Exhibit 2 shows how one might apply the material in Chapter 2 to organize the strategic management of each business group. The mission of the hotel group may be quite different from that of the transportation group or the casino group. Each group has its own strengths and weaknesses. Their respective competitive environments present different opportunities and threats. Alternative strategies, generated through comparison of internal capacity and environmental opportunities, must be evaluated for each business group. And for each business group, a strategy that stakes out the desired competitive position must

Exhibit 1

Corporate-level strategic management process

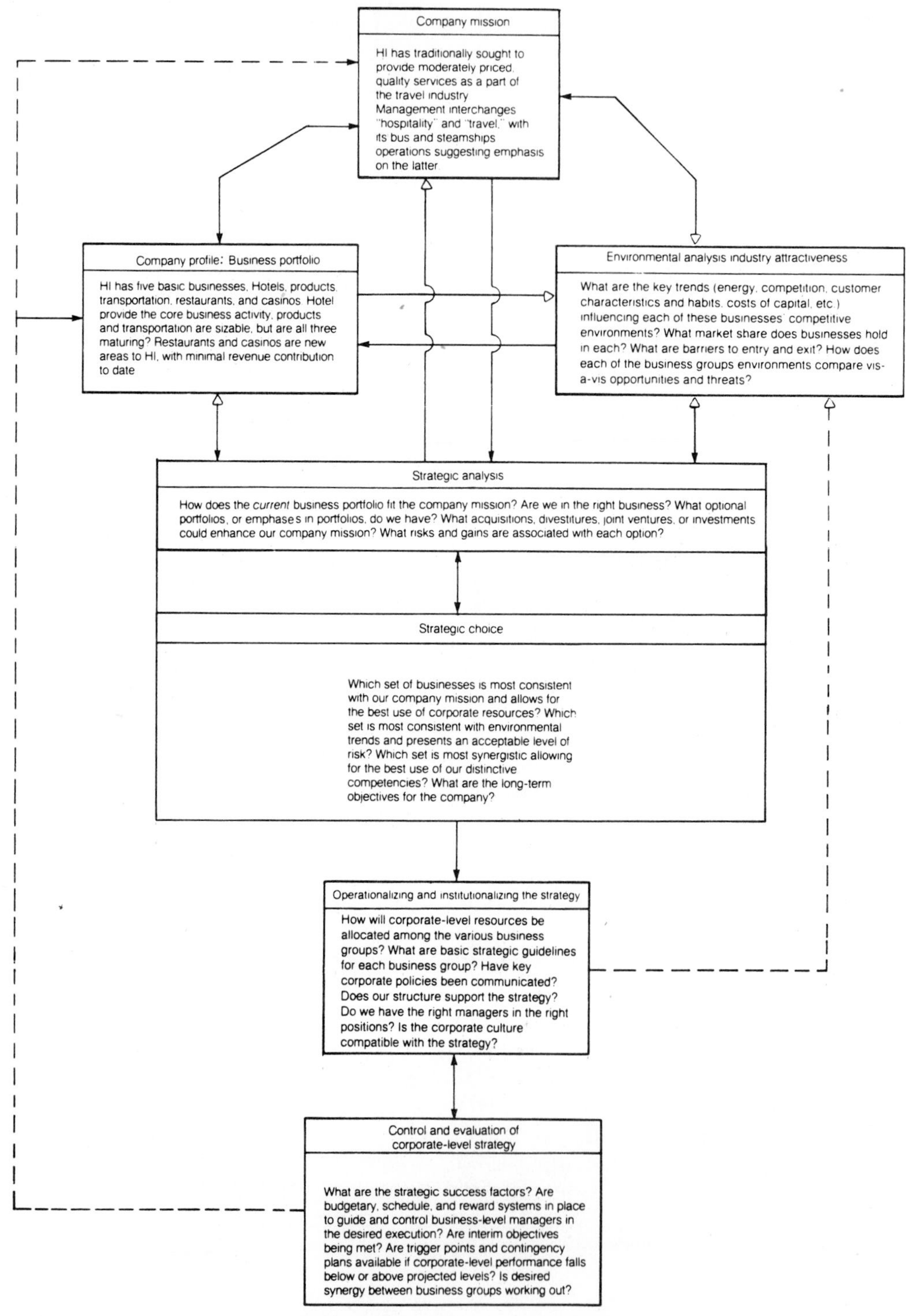

Company mission
HI has traditionally sought to provide moderately priced, quality services as a part of the travel industry. Management interchanges "hospitality" and "travel," with its bus and steamships operations suggesting emphasis on the latter.
Company profile: Business portfolio
HI has five basic businesses. Hotels, products, transportation, restaurants, and casinos. Hotel provide the core business activity, products and transportation are sizable, but are all three maturing? Restaurants and casinos are new areas to HI, with minimal revenue contribution to date.
Environmental analysis industry attractiveness
What are the key trends (energy, competition, customer characteristics and habits, costs of capital, etc.) influencing each of these businesses' competitive environments? What market share does businesses hold in each? What are barriers to entry and exit? How does each of the business groups environments compare vis-a-vis opportunities and threats?
Strategic analysis
How does the current business portfolio fit the company mission? Are we in the right business? What optional portfolios, or emphases in portfolios, do we have? What acquisitions, divestitures, joint ventures, or investments could enhance our company mission? What risks and gains are associated with each option?
Strategic choice
Which set of businesses is most consistent with our company mission and allows for the best use of corporate resources? Which set is most consistent with environmental trends and presents an acceptable level of risk? Which set is most synergistic allowing for the best use of our distinctive competencies? What are the long-term objectives for the company?
Operationalizing and institutionalizing the strategy
How will corporate-level resources be allocated among the various business groups? What are basic strategic guidelines for each business group? Have key corporate policies been communicated? Does our structure support the strategy? Do we have the right managers in the right positions? Is the corporate culture compatible with the strategy?
Control and evaluation of corporate-level strategy
What are the strategic success factors? Are budgetary, schedule, and reward systems in place to guide and control business-level managers in the desired execution? Are interim objectives being met? Are trigger points and contingency plans available if corporate-level performance falls below or above projected levels? Is desired synergy between business groups working out?

Exhibit 2

Business-level strategic management process

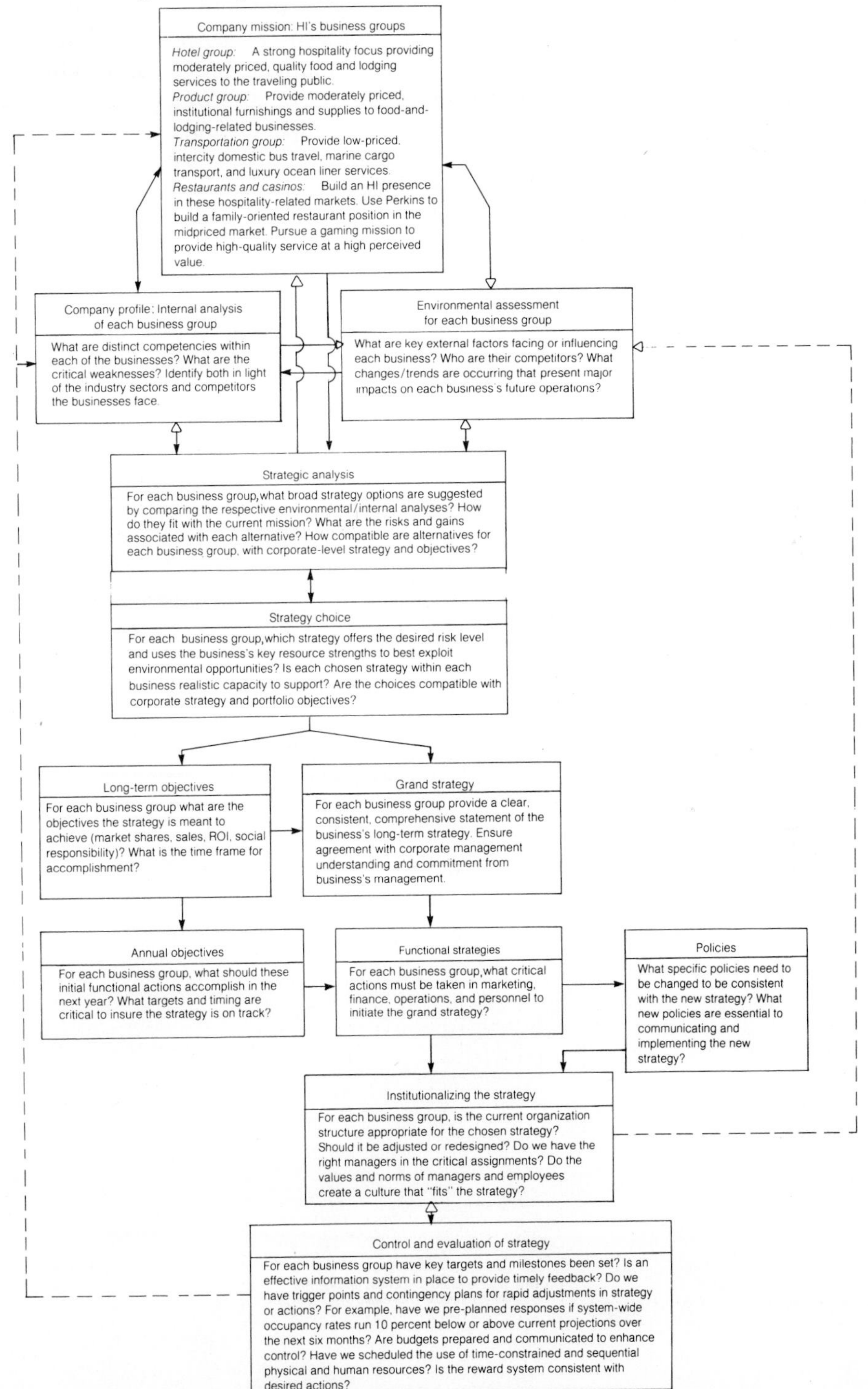

Company mission: HI's business groups
Hotel group: A strong hospitality focus providing moderately priced, quality food and lodging services to the traveling public.
Product group: Provide moderately priced, institutional furnishings and supplies to food-and-lodging-related businesses.
Transportation group: Provide low-priced, intercity domestic bus travel, marine cargo transport, and luxury ocean liner services.
Restaurants and casinos: Build an HI presence in these hospitality-related markets. Use Perkins to build a family-oriented restaurant position in the midpriced market. Pursue a gaming mission to provide high-quality service at a high perceived value.
Company profile: Internal analysis of each business group
What are distinct competencies within each of the businesses? What are the critical weaknesses? Identify both in light of the industry sectors and competitors the businesses face.
Environmental assessment for each business group
What are key external factors facing or influencing each business? Who are their competitors? What changes/trends are occurring that present major impacts on each business's future operations?
Strategic analysis
For each business group, what broad strategy options are suggested by comparing the respective environmental/internal analyses? How do they fit with the current mission? What are the risks and gains associated with each alternative? How compatible are alternatives for each business group, with corporate-level strategy and objectives?
Strategy choice
For each business group, which strategy offers the desired risk level and uses the business's key resource strengths to best exploit environmental opportunities? Is each chosen strategy within each business realistic capacity to support? Are the choices compatible with corporate strategy and portfolio objectives?
Long-term objectives
For each business group what are the objectives the strategy is meant to achieve (market shares, sales, ROI, social responsibility)? What is the time frame for accomplishment?
Grand strategy
For each business group provide a clear, consistent, comprehensive statement of the business's long-term strategy. Ensure agreement with corporate management understanding and commitment from business's management.
Annual objectives
For each business group, what should these initial functional actions accomplish in the next year? What targets and timing are critical to insure the strategy is on track?
Functional strategies
For each business group, what critical actions must be taken in marketing, finance, operations, and personnel to initiate the grand strategy?
Policies
What specific policies need to be changed to be consistent with the new strategy? What new policies are essential to communicating and implementing the new strategy?
Institutionalizing the strategy
For each business group, is the current organization structure appropriate for the chosen strategy? Should it be adjusted or redesigned? Do we have the right managers in the critical assignments? Do the values and norms of managers and employees create a culture that "fits" the strategy?
Control and evaluation of strategy
For each business group have key targets and milestones been set? Is an effective information system in place to provide timely feedback? Do we have trigger points and contingency plans for rapid adjustments in strategy or actions? For example, have we pre-planned responses if system-wide occupancy rates run 10 percent below or above current projections over the next six months? Are budgets prepared and communicated to enhance control? Have we scheduled the use of time-constrained and sequential physical and human resources? Is the reward system consistent with desired actions?

be chosen, implemented, and controlled. This must also be consistent with the role of the business group as expressed in the corporate-level strategy.

The interactive nature of the strategic management process should also be apparent in Exhibits 1 and 2. If the content of one component of the model changes, then the other components will change as well.

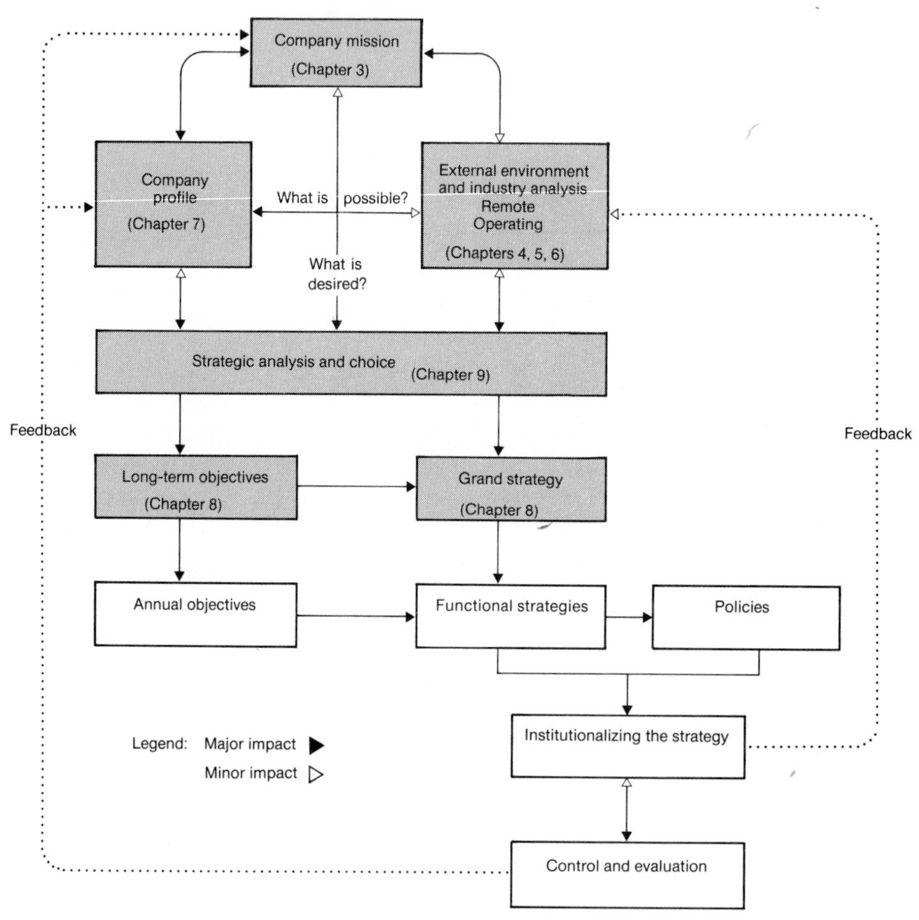

STRATEGIC MANAGEMENT MODEL
Company mission
(Chapter 3)
Company profile
(Chapter 7)
What is possible?
External environment and industry analysis
Remote
Operating
(Chapters 4, 5, 6)
What is desired?
Strategic analysis and choice
(Chapter 9)
Feedback
Feedback
Long-term objectives
(Chapter 8)
Grand strategy
(Chapter 8)
Annual objectives
Functional strategies
Policies
Institutionalizing the strategy
Legend: Major impact
Minor impact
Control and evaluation

PART TWO

Strategy formulation

Strategy formulation is designed to guide executives in defining the business their company is in, the aims it seeks, and the means it will use to accomplish these aims. Strategy formulation involves an improved approach to traditional long-range planning. As discussed the following seven chapters, strategy formulation combines a future-oriented perspective with concern for a firm's internal and external environments in developing its competitive plan of action.

The process of strategy formulation begins with a definition of the company mission as discussed in Chapter 3. In this chapter the purpose of business will be defined to reflect the values of a wide variety of interested parties.

Chapter 4, deals with the principal factors in a firm's external environment that must be assessed by strategic managers so that they can anticipate and take advantage of future business conditions. A recently popular approach to the strategic study of a firm's industry is the focal point of Chapter 5. This chapter systematically outlines and describes a five-forces method of conducting a competitive industry analysis.

Chapter 6 focuses on environmental forecasting—approaches currently used by strategic managers in assessing and anticipating changes in the external environment.

Chapter 7 shows how businesses evaluate their internal strengths and weaknesses to produce a company profile. Such profiles are used by strategic managers to target the competitive advantages they can emphasize and the competitive disadvantages they should correct or minimize.

In Chapter 8 attention turns to the types of long-range objectives set by strategic managers and to the qualities these objectives must have to provide a basis for direction and evaluation. The 12 grand strategies that companies use as broadly defined approaches for achieving long-range objectives are also highlighted.

Detailed comprehensive approaches to evaluation of strategic opportunities and to the final strategic decision are the focus of Chapter 9. The chapter deals with comparing strategic alternatives in a way that allows selection of the best available option for a firm, measured by potential for satisfying the company purpose.

CHAPTER

Defining the Company Mission

What Is a Company Mission?

Whether developing a new business or reformulating direction for an ongoing company, the basic goals, characteristics, and philosophies which will shape a firm's strategic posture must be determined. This *company mission* will guide future executive action. Thus, the company mission is defined as the fundamental, unique purpose that sets a business apart from other firms of its type and identifies the scope of its operations in product and market terms. As discussed in Chapter 2, the mission is a broadly framed but enduring statement of company intent. It embodies the business philosophy strategic decision makers, implies the image the company seeks to project; reflects the firm's self-concept; indicates the principal product or service areas and primary customer needs the company will attempt to satisfy. In short, the mission describes the product, market, and technological areas of emphasis for the business. And it does so in a way that reflects the values and priorities of strategic decision makers.

Figure 3–1 presents an example of a good mission statement because it incorporates major features and provides a broad framework. The statement is from an internal communication of the Zale Corporation, a company with annual sales of $1 billion from four major lines: jewelry ($700 million), sporting

Note: Portions of this chapter are adopted from John A. Pearce II. "The Company Mission as a Strategic Tool." *Sloan Management Review*. Spring 1982, pp. 15–24.

Figure 3–1

Zale Corporation—Summary statement of corporate mission

Our business is specialty retailing. Retailing is a people-oriented business. We recognize that our business existence and continued success is dependent upon how well we meet our responsibilities to several critically important groups of people.

Our first responsibility is to our customers. Without them we would have no reason for being. We strive to appeal to a broad spectrum of consumers, catering in a professional manner to their needs. Our concept of value to the customer includes a wide selection of quality merchandise, competitively priced and delivered with courtesy and professionalism.

Our ultimate responsibility is to our shareholders. Our goal is to earn an optimum return on invested capital through steady profit growth and prudent, aggressive asset management. The attainment of this financial goal, coupled with a record of sound management, represents our approach toward influencing the value placed upon our common stock in the market.

We feel a deep, personal responsibility to our employees. As an equal opportunity employer we seek to create and maintain an environment where every employee is provided the opportunity to develop to his or her maximum potential. We expect to reward employees commensurate with their contribution to the success of the company.

We are committed to honesty and integrity in all relationships with suppliers of goods and services. We are demanding but fair. We evaluate our suppliers on the basis of quality, price, and service.

We recognize community involvement as an important obligation and as a viable business objective. Support of worthwhile community projects in areas where we operate generally accrues to the health and well-being of the community. This makes the community a better place for our employees to live and a better place for us to operate.

We believe in the free enterprise system and in the American democratic form of government under which this superior economic system has been permitted to flourish. We feel an incumbent responsibility to insure that our business operates at a reasonable profit. Profit provides opportunity for growth and job security. We believe growth is necessary to provide opportunities on an ever-increasing scale for our people. Therefore, we are dedicated to profitable growth—growth as a company—and growth as individuals.

goods, footwear, and drugs. Zale is best known for its 769 jewelry stores and enjoys operating profits of approximately $130 million per year.

The Need for an Explicit Mission

Defining the company mission is time-consuming, tedious, and not required by any external body. The mission contains few specific directives, only broadly outlined or implied objectives and strategies. Characteristically it is a statement of attitude, outlook, and orientation rather than of details and measurable targets.

What then is a company mission designed to accomplish? King and Cleland provide seven good answers:

1. To ensure unanimity of purpose within the organization.
2. To provide a basis for motivating the use of organization's resources.
3. To develop a basis, or standard, for allocating organizational resources.

4. To establish a general tone or organizational climate, e.g., to suggest a businesslike operation.
5. To serve as a focal point for those who can identify with the organization's purpose and direction; and to deter those who cannot from participating further in the organization's activities.
6. To facilitate the translation of objectives and goals into a work structure involving the assignment of tasks to responsible elements within the organization.
7. To specify organizational purposes and the translation of these purposes into goals in such a way that cost, time, and performance parameters can be assessed and controlled.[1]

Formulating a Mission

The process of defining the mission for a specific business can perhaps be best understood by thinking about a firm at its inception. The typical business organization begins with the beliefs, desires, and aspirations of a single entrepreneur. The sense of mission for such an owner-manager is usually based on several fundamental elements:

1. Belief that the *product* or *service* can provide benefits at least equal to its price.
2. Belief that the product or service can satisfy a *customer need* currently not met adequately for specific market segments.
3. Belief that the *technology* to be used in production will provide a product or service that is cost and quality competitive.
4. Belief that with hard work and the support of others the business can do better than just *survive,* it can *grow* and be *profitable.*
5. Belief that the *management philosophy* of the business will result in a favorable *public image* and will provide financial and psychological rewards for those willing to invest their labor and money in helping the firm to succeed.
6. Belief that the entrepreneur's *self-concept* of the business can be communicated to and adopted by employees and stockholders.

As the business grows or is forced by competitive pressures to alter its product/market/technology, redefining the company mission may be necessary. If so, the revised mission statement will reflect the same set of elements as the original. It will state the basic type of product or service to be offered, the primary markets or customer groups to be served, the technology to be used in production or delivery; the fundamental concern for survival through growth and profitability; the managerial philosophy of the firm; the public

[1] W. R. King and D. I. Cleland, *Strategic Planning and Policy* (New York: Van Nostrand Reinhold, 1979), p. 124.

image sought; and the self-concept those affiliated with it should have of the firm.

Basic Product or Service; Primary Market; Principal Technology

Three components of a mission statement are indispensable: specification of the basic product or service, primary market, and principal technology for production or delivery. The three components are discussed under one heading because only in combination do they describe the business activity of the company. A good example of these three mission components is to be found in the business plan of ITT Barton, a division of ITT. Under the heading of business mission and area served, the company presents the following information.

> The unit's mission is to serve industry and government with quality instruments used for the primary measurement, analysis, and local control of fluid flow, level, pressure, temperature, and fluid properties. This instrumentation includes flow meters, electronic readouts, indicators, recorders, switches, liquid level systems, analytical instruments such as titrators, integrators, controllers, transmitters, and various instruments for the measurement of fluid properties (density, viscosity, gravity) used for process variable sensing, data collection, control, and transmission. The unit's mission includes fundamental loop-closing control and display devices, when economically justified, but excludes broadline central control room instrumentation, systems design, and turnkey responsibility.
>
> Markets served include instrumentation for oil and gas production, gas transportation, chemical and petrochemical processing, cryogenics, power generation, aerospace, government and marine, as well as other instrument and equipment manufacturers.

This segment of the mission statement clearly indicates to all readers—from company employees to casual observers—the basic products, primary markets, and principal technologies of ITT Barton, and it was accomplished in only 129 words.

Often a company's most referenced public statement of selected products and markets is presented in "silver bullet" form in the mission statement; for example, "Dayton-Hudson Corporation is a diversified retailing company whose business is to serve the American consumer through the retailing of fashion-oriented quality merchandise."[2] Such a statement serves as an abstract of company direction and is particularly helpful to outsiders who value condensed overviews.

[2] See W. Ouchi, *Theory Z* (Reading, Mass.: Addison-Wesley Publishing, 1981). Ouchi presents more complete missions statements of three of the companies discussed in this chapter: Dayton-Hudson, Hewlett-Packard, and Intel.

Company Goals: Survival, Growth, Profitability

Three economic goals guide the strategic direction of almost every viable business organization. Whether or not they are explicitly stated, a company mission statement reflects the firm's intention to secure its *survival* through sustained *growth* and *profitability*.

Unless a firm is able to survive, it will be incapable of satisfying any of its stakeholders' aims. Unfortunately, like growth and profitability, survival is such an assumed goal that it is often neglected as a principal criterion in strategic decision making. When this happens, the firm often focuses on short-term aims at the expense of the long run. Concerns for expediency, a quick fix, or a bargain displace the need for assessing long-term impact. Too often the result is near-term economic failure owing to a lack of resource synergy and sound business practice. For example, Consolidated Foods, makers of Shasta soft drinks and L'Eggs hosiery, sought growth in the 1960s through the acquisition of bargain businesses. However, the erratic sales patterns of their diverse holdings forced the firm to divest itself of more than four dozen of the companies in the late 1970s. The resulting stabilization cost Consolidated Foods millions of dollars and hampered its growth.

Profitability is the mainstay goal of a business organization. No matter how it is measured or defined, profit over the long term is the clearest indication of a firm's ability to satisfy the principal claims and desires of employees and stockholders. The key phrase in the sentence is "over the long term." Obviously, basing decisions on a short-term concern for profitability would lead to a strategic myopia. A firm might overlook the enduring concerns of customers, suppliers, creditors, ecologists, and regulatory agents. In the short term the results may produce profit, but over time the financial consequences are likely to be detrimental.

The following excerpt from the Hewlett-Packard Company's statement of corporate objectives (i.e., mission) ably expresses the importance of an orientation toward long-term profit:

> Objective: To achieve sufficient profit to finance our company growth and to provide the resources we need to achieve our other corporate objectives.
>
> In our economic system, the profit we generate from our operations is the ultimate source of the funds we need to prosper and grow. It is the one absolutely essential measure of our corporate performance over the long term. Only if we continue to meet our profit objective can we achieve our other corporate objectives.

A firm's growth is inextricably tied to its survival and profitability. In this context, the meaning of growth must be broadly defined. While growth in market share has been shown by the product impact market studies (PIMS) studies to be correlated with firm profitability, there are other important forms of growth. For example, growth in the number of markets served, in the variety of products offered, and in the technologies used to provide goods or services frequently leads to improvements in the company's competitive ability. Growth means change, and proactive change is a necessity in a dynamic business environment. Hewlett-Packard's mission statement provides an excellent example of corporate regard for growth:

> Objective: To let our growth be limited only by our profits and our ability to develop and produce technical products that satisfy real customer needs.
>
> We do not believe that large size is important for its own sake: however, for at least two basic reasons continuous growth is essential for us to achieve our other objectives.
>
> In the first place, we serve a rapidly growing and expanding segment of our technological society. To remain static would be to lose ground. We cannot maintain a position of strength and leadership in our field without growth.
>
> In the second place, growth is important in order to attract and hold high-caliber people. These individuals will align their future only with a company that offers them considerable opportunity for personal progress. Opportunities are greater and more challenging in a growing company.

The issue of growth raises a concern about the definition of a company mission. How can a business specify product, market, and technology sufficiently to provide direction without delimiting unanticipated strategic options? How can a company define its mission so opportunistic diversification can be considered while at the same time maintaining parameters that guide growth decisions? Perhaps, such questions are best addressed when a firm outlines its mission conditions under which it might depart from ongoing operations. The growth philosophy of Dayton-Hudson shows this approach:

> The stability and quality of the corporation's financial performance will be developed through the profitable execution of our existing businesses, as well as through the acquisition or development of new businesses. Our growth priorities, in order, are as follows:
>
> 1. Development of the profitable market preeminence of existing companies in existing markets through new store development or new strategies within existing stores;
> 2. Expansion of our companies to feasible new markets;
> 3. Acquisition of other retailing companies that are strategically and financially compatible with Dayton-Hudson;
> 4. Internal development of new retailing strategies.
>
> Capital allocations to fund the expansion of existing operating companies will be based on each company's return on investment, in relationship to its return-on-investment (ROI) objective and its consistency in earnings growth, and on its management capability to perform up to forecasts contained in capital requests.
>
> Expansion via acquisition or new venture will occur when the opportunity promises an acceptable rate of long-term growth and profitability, acceptable degree of risk, and compatibility with the corporation's long-term strategy.

Company Philosophy

The statement of a company's philosophy, often called a company creed, usually accompanies or appears as part of the mission. It reflects or explicitly states basic beliefs, values, aspirations, and philosophical priorities. In turn, strategic decision makers are committed to emphasizing these in managing the firm. Fortunately, company philosophies vary little from one firm to another. Thus, owners and managers implicitly accept a general, unwritten, yet pervasive code of behavior. Through this code, actions in a business setting are governed and largely self-regulated. Unfortunately, statements of philosophy are so similiar and are so full of platitudes, that they look and read more like public relations statements than the commitment to values they are meant to be.

Despite similarities in these philosophies, strategic managers' intentions in developing them do not warrant cynicism. In most cases managers attempt, often successfully, to provide a distinctive and accurate picture of the firm's managerial outlook. One such valuable statement is that of Zale Corporation, whose company mission was presented earlier in this chapter. As shown in Figure 3–2, Zale has subdivided its statement of management's operating philosophy into four key areas: marketing and customer service, management tasks, human resources, and finance and control. These subdivisions allow more refinement than the mission statement itself. As a result, Zale has established especially clear directions for company decision making and action.

The mission statement of the Dayton-Hudson Corporation is at least equally specific in detailing the firm's management philosophy, as shown in Figure 3–3. Perhaps most noteworthy is the delineation of responsibility at both the corporate and business levels. In many ways, the statement could serve as a prototype for the three-tiered approach to strategic management. This new approach argues that the mission statement must address strategic concerns at the corporate, business, and functional levels of the organization. To this end, Dayton-Hudson's management philosophy is a balance of operating autonomy and flexibility on the one hand, and corporate input and direction on the other.

Public Image

Particularly for the growing firm involved in a redefinition of its company mission, public image is important. Both present and potential customers attribute certain qualities to a particular business. Gerber and Johnson & Johnson make safe products; Cross Pen makes high-quality writing instruments. Aigner Etienne makes stylish but affordable leather products; Corvettes are power machines; and Izod Lacoste is for the preppy look. Thus, mission statements often reflect public anticipations, making achieving the firm's goals a more likely consequence. Gerber's mission should not open the possibility

Figure 3–2

Zale Corporation—Operating philosophy

1. Marketing and customer service.
   a. We require that the entire organization be continuously customer oriented. Our future success is dependent on meeting the customers' needs better than our competition.
   b. We expect to maintain a marketing concept and distribution capability to identify changing trends and emerging markets and effectively promote our products.
   c. We strive to provide our customers with continuous offerings of quality merchandise, competitively priced—stressing value and service.
   d. We plan to constantly maintain our facilities as modern, attractive, clean, and orderly stores that are pleasing and exciting places for customers to shop.
2. Management tasks.
   a. We require profitable results from operations—activity does not necessarily equate with accomplishment—results must be measurable.
   b. We recognize there are always better ways to perform many functions. Continuous improvement in operating capability is a daily objective of the entire organization.
   c. We expect all managers to demonstrate capabilities to plan objectives, delegate responsibilities, motivate people, control operations, and achieve results measured against planned objectives.
   d. We must promote a spirit of teamwork. To succeed, a complex business such as ours requires good communication, clearly understood policies, effective controls and, above all, a dedication to "make it happen."
   e. We are highly competitive and dedicated to succeeding. However, as a human organization we will make mistakes. We must openly acknowledge our mistakes, learn from them, and take corrective action.
3. Human resources.
   a. We must develop and maintain a competent, highly motivated, results-oriented organization.
   b. We seek to attract, develop, and motivate people who demonstrate professional competence, courage, and integrity in performing their jobs.
   c. We strive to identify individuals who are outstanding performers, provide them with continuous challenges, and search for new, effective ways to compensate them—utilizing significant incentives.
   d. Promotion from within is our goal. We must have the best talent available and, from time to time, will have to reach outside to meet our ever-improving standards. We heartily endorse and support development programs to prepare individuals for increased responsibility. In like manner, we must promptly advise those who are not geared to the pace, in order that they make the necessary adjustments without delay.
4. Finance and control.
   a. We will maintain a sound financial plan that provides capital for growth of the business and provides optimum return for our stockholders.
   b. We must develop and maintain a system of controls that highlights potential significant failures early for positive corrective action.

for diversification into pesticides, or Cross Pen's into 39-cent brand-named disposables.

On the other hand, a negative public image often prompts firms to reemphasize the beneficial aspects reflected in their mission. For example, as a result of what it saw as a disturbing trend in public opinion, Dow Chemical undertook an aggressive promotional campaign to fortify its credibility particularly

Figure 3–3

Management philosophy of Dayton-Hudson Corporation

The corporation will:
- Set standards for return on investment (ROI) and earnings growth.
- Approve strategic plans.
- Allocate capital.
- Approve goals.
- Monitor, measure, and audit results.
- Reward performance.
- Allocate management resources.

The operating companies will be accorded the freedom and responsibility:
- To manage their own business.
- To develop strategic plans and goals that will optimize their growth.
- To develop an organization that can ensure consistency of results and optimum growth.
- To operate their businesses consistent with the corporation's statement of philosophy.

The corporate staff will provide only those services that are:
- Essential to the protection of the corporation.
- Needed for the growth of the corporation.
- Wanted by operating companies and that provide a significant advantage in quality or cost.

The corporation will insist on:
- Uniform accounting practices by type of business.
- Prompt disclosure of operating results.
- A systematic approach to training and developing people.
- Adherence to appropriately high standards of business conduct and civic responsibility in accordance with the corporation's statement of philosophy.

among "employees and those who live and work in [their] plant communities." Dow's approach was described in their 1980 annual report:

> All around the world today, Dow people are speaking up. People who care deeply about their company, what it stands for, and how it is viewed by others. People who are immensely proud of their company's performance, yet realistic enough to realize it is the public's perception of that performance that counts in the long run.

A firm's concern for its public image is seldom addressed in an intermittent fashion. While public agitation often stimulates greater response, a corporation is concerned about its image even when public concern is not expressed. The following excerpt from the mission statement of Intel Corporation is an example of this attitude:

> We are sensitive to our *image with our customers and the business community.* Commitments to customers are considered sacred, and we are upset with ourselves when we do not meet our commitments. We strive to demonstrate to the business world on a continuing basis that we are credible in describing the state of the corporation, and that we are well organized and in complete control of all things that determine the numbers.

Company Self-Concept

A major determinant of any company's continued success is the extent to which it can relate functionally to the external environment. Finding its place in a competitive situation requires that the firm realistically evaluate its own strengths and weaknesses as a competitor. This idea—that the firm must know itself—is the essence of the company's self-concept. This notion per se is not commonly integrated into theories of strategic management; however, scholars have appreciated its importance to an individual: "Man has struggled to understand himself, for how he thinks of himself will influence both what he chooses to do and what he expects from life. Knowing his identity connects him both with his past and the potentiality of his future."[3]

There is a direct parallel between this view of the importance of an individual's self-concept and the self-concept of a business. Fundamentally, the need for each to know the self is crucial. The ability of a firm or an individual to survive in a dynamic and highly competitive environment would be severely limited if the impact on others and of others is not understood.

In some senses, then, the organization takes on a personality of its own. Hall stated that much behavior in organizations is organizationally based, that is, a business acts on its members in other than individual and interaction ways.[4] Thus businesses are entities that act with a personality that transcends those of particular company members. As such, the firm can be seen as setting decision-making parameters, based on aims different and distinct from the individual aims of its members. The effects of organizational considerations are pervasive.

> Organizations do have policies, do and do not condone violence, and may or may not greet you with a smile. They also manufacture goods, administer policies, and protect the citizenry. These are organizational actions and involve properties of organizations, not individuals. They are carried out by individuals, even in the case of computer-produced letters, which are programmed by individuals—but the genesis of the actions remains in the organization.[5]

The actual role of the corporate self-concept has been summarized as follows:

1. The corporate self-concept is based on management perception of the way others (society) will respond to the corporation.
2. The corporate self-concept will function to direct the behavior of people employed by the company.
3. The actual response of others to the company will in part determine the corporate self-concept.
4. The self-concept is incorporated in statements of corporate mission to

---

[3] J. Kelly, *Organizational Behavior* (Homewood, Ill.: Richard D. Irwin, 1974), p. 258.

[4] R. H. Hall, *Organization—Structure and Process* (Englewood Cliffs, N.J.: Prentice-Hall, 1972), p. 11.

[5] Ibid., p. 13.

Figure 3–4

Abstract of Intel's mission-related information

Management Style: Intel is a company of individuals, each with his or her own personality and characteristics.

Management *is self-critical.* The leaders must be capable of recognizing and accepting their mistakes and learning from them.

Open *(constructive) confrontation is encouraged* at all levels of the corporation and is viewed as a method of problem solving and conflict resolution.

Decision by *consensus* is the rule. Decisions once made are supported. Position in the organization is not the basis for quality of ideas.

A highly communicative open management is part of the style.

A high degree of *organizational skills and discipline* are demanded.

Management must be ethical. Managing by telling the truth and treating all employees equitably has established credibility that is ethical.

Work Ethic/Environment

It is a general objective of Intel to line up individual work assignments with career objectives.

We strive to provide an *opportunity for rapid development.*

Intel is a *results-oriented* company. The focus is on *substance* versus form, *quality* versus quantity.

We believe in the principle that *hard work, high productivity* is something to be proud of.

The concept of *assumed responsibility* is accepted. (If a task needs to be done, assume you have the responsibility to get it done.)

Commitments are long term; if career problems occur at some point, reassignment is a better alternative than termination.

We desire to have *all employees involved and participative* in their relationship with Intel.

be explicitly communicated to individuals inside and outside the company, that is, to be actualized.[6]

A second look at the company mission of the Zale Corporation in Figure 3–1 reveals much about the business's self-concept. The strategic decision makers see the firm as socially responsive, prudent, and fiercely independent.

Characteristically, descriptions of self-concept per se do not appear in company mission statements. Yet, strong impressions of a firm's self-image are often evident. An example from Intel Corporation is given in Figure 3–4.

The Claimant Approach to Company Responsibility

In defining or redefining the company mission, strategic managers must recognize and acknowledge the legitimate claims of other stakeholders of the firm. These include both investors and employees as well as outsiders affected by

[6] E. J. Kelley, *Marketing Planning and Competitive Strategy* (Englewood Cliffs, N.J.: Prentice-Hall, 1972), p. 55.

the company's actions. Such outsiders commonly include customers, suppliers, governments, unions, competitors, local communities, and the general public. Each of these interest groups has justifiable reasons to expect, and often to demand, that the company act in a responsible manner in satisfying their claims. Generalizing, stockholders claim appropriate returns on their investment; employees seek broadly defined job satisfaction; customers want what they pay for; suppliers seek dependable buyers; governments want adherence to legislation; unions seek benefits for members in proportion to contributions to company success; competitors want fair competition; local communities want companies to be responsible citizens; and the general public seeks some improvement in the quality of life resulting from the firm's existence.

However, when a business attempts to define its mission to incorporate the interests of these groups, broad generalizations are insufficient. Thus, four steps need to be taken:

1. Identification of claimants.
2. Understanding of specific claims vis-à-vis the company.
3. Reconciliation of claims and assigning them priorities.
4. Coordination of claims with other elements of the mission.

Identification. The left-hand column of Figure 3–5 lists the commonly encountered claimants, to which the executive officer group is often added. Obviously though, every business faces a slightly different set of claimants who vary in number, size, influence, and importance. In defining a mission, strategic managers must identify all claimant groups and weight their relative ability to affect firm success.

Understanding. The concerns of principal claimants tend to center around the generalities in the right-hand column of Figure 3–5. However, strategic decision makers should understand the specific demands of each group. Then strategic managers will be better able to both appreciate these concerns and initiate clearly defined actions.

Reconciliation and Priorities. Unfortunately, the concerns of various claimants often conflict. For example, the claims of governments and the general public tend to limit profitability, which is the central concern of most creditors and stockholders. Thus, claims must be reconciled. To achieve a unified approach managers must define a mission that resolves the competing, conflicting, and contradictory claims. For objectives and strategies to be internally consistent and precisely focused, mission statements must display a single-minded, though multidimensional, approach to business aims.

There are hundreds, if not thousands of claims on any business—high wages, pure air, job security, product quality, community service, taxes, occupational health and safety and equal opportunity (OSHA, EEOC) regulations, product variety, wide markets, career opportunities, company growth, investment security, high ROI, and many, many more. Although most, if not all, of these claims are desirable ends, they cannot be pursued with equal emphasis. Claims must be assigned priorities that reflect the relative attention the firm will give to each. Such emphasis is reflected by the criteria used in strategic decision

Figure 3–5

A claimant view of company responsibility

Claimant	*Nature of the claim*
Stockholders	Participation in distribution of profits, additional stock offerings, assets on liquidation; vote of stock, inspection of company books, transfer of stock, election of board of directors, and such additional rights as established in the contract with the corporation.
Creditors	Legal proportion of interest payments due and return of principal from the investment. Security of pledged assets; relative priority in event of liquidation. Subsume in some management and owner prerogatives if certain conditions exist within the company (such as default of interest payments).
Employees	Economic, social, and psychological satisfaction in the place of employment. Freedom from arbitrary and capricious behavior on the part of company officials. Share in fringe benefits, freedom to join union and participate in collective bargaining, individual freedom in offering up their services through an employment contract. Adequate working conditions.
Customers	Service provided with the product: technical data to use the product; suitable warranties; spare parts to support the product during customer use; R&D leading to product improvement; facilitation of consumer credit.
Suppliers	Continuing source of business: timely consummation of trade credit obligations; professional relationship in contracting for, purchasing, and receiving goods and services.
Governments	Taxes (income, property, etc.), fair competition, and adherence to the letter and intent of public policy dealing with the requirements of fair and free competition. Legal obligation of businessmen (and business organizations); adherence to antitrust laws.
Unions	Recognition as the negotiating agent for employees. Opportunity to perpetuate the union as a participant in the business organization.
Competitors	Norms established by society and the industry for competitive conduct. Business statesmanship on the part of peers.
Local communities	Place of productive and healthful employment in the community. Participation of company officials in community affairs, regular employment, fair play, purchase of reasonable portion of products of the local community, interest in and support of local government, support of cultural and charity projects.
The general public	Participation in and contribution to society as a whole; creative communications between governmental and business units designed for reciprocal understanding; bear fair proportion of the burden of government and society. Fair price for products and advancement of state of the art technology which the product line involves.

Source: From William R. King and David I. Cleland, *Strategic, Planning and Policy.* © 1978 by Litton Educational Publishing Inc., p. 153. Reprinted by permission of Van Nostrand Reinhold Company.

making; by the company's allocation of human, financial, and physical resources; and by the long-term objectives and strategies developed for the firm.

Coordination with Other Elements. Demands of claimant groups for responsible action by a company constitutes only one set of inputs to the mission. Managerial operating philosophies and determination of the product-market offering are the other principal components considered. The latter factors essentially pose a reality test the accepted claims must pass. The key question is: How can the company satisfy claimants and simultaneously optimize its success in the marketplace?

Social Responsibility

The various claimants on a company can be divided into two categories, as indicated by Figure 3–6. Insiders are individuals and groups who are stockholders or are employed by the firm. Outsiders are all other individuals or groups affected by the actions of the firm. This extremely large and often amorphous set of outsiders makes the general claim that the company be socially responsible.

Questions of social responsibility are perhaps the thorniest of all issues faced in defining a company mission. The claimant approach offers the clearest perspective on the problem. Broadly stated, outsiders often demand that the claims of insiders be subordinated to the greater good of the society, that is, to the greater good of the outsiders. They believe that issues such as elimination of solid and liquid wastes, pollution, and conservation of natural resources should be principal considerations in strategic decision making. Also broadly stated, insiders tend to believe that the competing claims of the outsiders should be balanced against each other in a way that protects the company mission. For example, the consumers' need for a product must be balanced against the water pollution resulting from production, if the company cannot totally afford to eliminate the pollution and remain profitable. Additionally,

Figure 3–6

Inputs to the development of the company mission

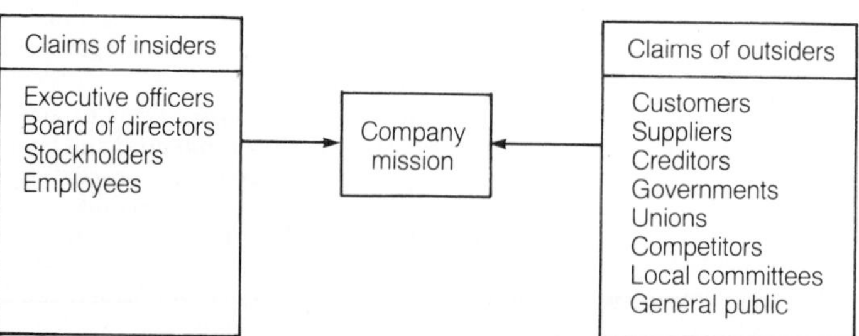

some insiders argue that the claims of society, as activated by government regulation, provide tax money that is more than sufficient to eliminate unwanted business by-products, such as water pollution, if this is truly the wish of the general public.

The issues are numerous and complex, and the problems contingent on the situation. Thus, rigid rules of conduct are not possible. Each business must decide on its approach in trying to meet its perceived social responsibility. Different approaches will reflect differences in competitive position, industry, country, environmental and ecological pressure, and a host of other factors. In other words, they will reflect both situational factors and differing priorities in the acknowledgments of claims.

Despite differences in approaches, most American companies now try to assure outsiders that they attempt to conduct business in a socially responsible manner. Many firms, including Abt Associates, Eastern Gas and Fuel Associates, and the Bank of America, have gone to the effort of conducting and publishing annual social audits. For example, the social audit of Eastern Gas and Fuel, as published in their 1981 annual report is given in Strategy in Action 3–1. These social audits attempt to evaluate the business from the perspective of social responsibility. They are often conducted for the firm by private consultants who offer minimally biased evaluations on what are inherently highly subjective issues.

Strategy in Action 3–1

Social Audit of Eastern Gas and Fuel, 1981

Beyond Financial Concerns

Managing for profit is a common objective of all business, the cornerstone of the free enterprise system. However, business style varies widely. Eastern's philosophy is based on the premise that its performance objectives can be achieved in a manner that is responsive to the needs of Eastern's people—its shareholders, customers, employees, and the general public.

Corporate performance must be in line with shareholder expectations to justify their continued financial support. Service to Eastern's many customers must not be compromised. The selection and development of a highly skilled and motivated work force is essential. The work environment must be safe, healthy, and provide ample opportunity for self-improvement. The needs of the communities in which Eastern has a presence must also be addressed.

In striving to meet all of these objectives, Eastern has established proper business conduct as a top priority.

A. Health and safety

	Number of fatalities		*Incidence rate per 100 full-time workers** Disabling injuries and illnesses		All injuries and illnesses	
	1981	*1980*	*1981*	*1980*	*1981*	*1980*
Coal	1	3	5.9	7.7	6.8	8.6
Coke	0	0	9.3	24.0	60.7	24.4
Gas	0	0	5.7	5.3	6.6	5.8
Marine	0	0	8.0	7.7	13.6	14.0
Total corporate	1	3	6.5	7.4	8.9	9.9

* The incidence rates represent the number of work-related injuries and illnesses × 200,000 (100 employees working 40 hours per week, 50 weeks per year) ÷ total hours worked by employees.

B. Charitable giving

	Total charitable giving 1981	1980
Total contributions (thousands)	$770.3	$679.0
Percent of pretax income*	1.0%	1.0%
Dollar per employee	$82.83	$73.01
Cost per share, after income tax	1.8¢	1.6¢

* Five-year average pretax income.

C. Minority employment

	Minority employment levels (December 31) 1981		1978	
	Number	*Percent of total*	*Number*	*Percent of total*
Officers and managers	35	2.6%	29	2.0%
Professional and technical	36	5.0	37	4.6
Clerical	94	10.2	89	9.6
Skilled	613	13.6	441	9.3
Unskilled	187	9.0	324	16.2
Total Eastern	965	10.0%	920	9.3%

D. Pensions

	Annual cost of pensions and welfare plans ($000) 1981	1980
Company-administered plans for salaried, nonunion, and certain union employees	$ 9,413	$ 8,991
Other union retirement and welfare plans	30,086	27,684
Total cost	$29,509	$36,675

Many other firms periodically report to both insiders and outsiders on their progress to reach self-set social goals. Primarily through their annual reports, companies such as Diamond Shamrock discuss their efforts and achievements in social responsibility. Strategy in Action 3–2 provides the 1980 Diamond Shamrock report.

Strategy in Action 3–2

Social Responsibility Report of Diamond Shamrock (Excerpts from the 1980 Annual Report)

Concern for the safety and well-being of our employees and those communities in which we operate is an integral part of Diamond Shamrock's management philosophy. These concerns are translated into company policies, procedures, and programs, from planning and research to the production, sale, and distribution of our products.

Safety, Health, and the Environment

It is the policy of Diamond Shamrock to manufacture and market our products with care, exercising regard for potential hazards involved in their use and handling by our employees, customers, and the public in general.

During 1980, Diamond Shamrock improved its plant safety record for the 10th consecutive year. Thirty plants and facilities operated without a lost-time accident. Companywide, lost-time injuries were reduced 21 percent from 1979.

The company's highly trained staff of environmental specialists continues to establish an admirable record of meeting or exceeding standards established by local, state, and national regulatory agencies. Diamond Shamrock invested more than $19 million in new and replacement environmental equipment during 1980.

Diamond Shamrock administered 4,626 extensive physical examinations to employees in 1980 at no cost to [the employees]. These served as an integral part of Diamond Shamrock's computer operated health and environmental surveillance system (COHESS). Developed at a cost of more than $2 million, COHESS is designed to compare workplace exposure, employee characteristics, and the results of physical examinations to help ensure that our industrial hygiene programs are effective and to identify unknown risks as quickly as possible. The company has made the program available to other corporations at reasonable cost.

Strategy in Action 3–2 *(concluded)*

In addition to our worker health and environmental control programs, Diamond Shamrock invested more than $4.1 million during 1980 to determine the potential health and environmental effects of our products and to communicate that information to employees and customers. The company not only participates actively in industrywide studies of its products but, through multidisciplinary functions, conducts extensive in-house toxicological and environmental studies through its research center and its health and environmental affairs department.

Human Resources

Company-sponsored employee development spending exceeded $800,000 in 1980, with more than 1,500 individuals attending Diamond Shamrock training programs. These continuing programs have resulted in improved job performance, and have assisted employees in achieving individual career goals.

Diamond Shamrock actively pursues equal opportunity, without regard to religion, race, or sex. In addition, the company participates in and supports programs for the handicapped, Vietnam era veterans, women, and minority students.

Diamond Shamrock's compensation and benefit programs are designed to be not only competitive with [those of] the best of our peer companies but to provide an environment that fosters and gives recognition to excellence. Individual employee compensation is based on performance measured against job goals mutually selected by employee and supervisor.

Public Affairs

Diamond Shamrock maintains a responsive attitude to the needs of those communities in which we operate and considers this an important management responsibility. Several community relations programs assisted us in addressing these concerns during 1980.

The company invested $1,289,005 in philanthropic funds to support public, nonprofit organizations addressing needs of critical importance to the company, our employees, shareholders, and individual communities in 1980, a 26 percent increase from 1979. Plans call for $1,409,000 in philanthropic spending in 1981.

Diamond Shamrock encourages its employees to become involved in community affairs. Through our Citizen-of-the-Year program inaugurated in 1980, the company provides recognition for those employees who unselfishly invest personal time and [funds] for the betterment of their communities. Last year, 40 employees were recognized for their outstanding service to others.

Diamond Shamrock management also plays an important role in other local, state, and national affairs through advice and counsel offered to planning and zoning commissions, cooperation with various regulatory agencies, testimony before congressional review and policymaking committees, and regional task forces addressing significant social challenges.

Guidelines for a Socially Responsible Firm

After decades of debate on the topic of social responsibility, an individual firm still must struggle to determine the orientation reflected in its mission statement. However, public debate and business concern have led to a jelling of perspectives. One excellent summary of guidelines for a socially responsible firm, consistent with the claimant approach, was provided by Sawyer:

1. The purpose of the business is to make a profit; its managers should strive for the optimal profit that can be achieved over the long run.
2. No true profits can be claimed until business costs are paid. This includes all social costs, as determined by detailed analysis of the social balance between the firm and society.
3. If there are social costs in areas where no objective standards for correction yet exists, managers should generate corrective standards. These standards should be based on managers' judgment of what ought to exist, and should simultaneously encourage individual involvement of firm members in developing necessary social standards.
4. Where competitive pressure or economic necessity precludes socially responsible action, the business should recognize that its operation is depleting social capital and, therefore, represents a loss. It should attempt to restore profitable operation through either better management, if the problem is internal, or by advocating corrective legislation, if society is suffering as a result of the way that the rules for business competition have been made.[7]

Summary

Defining a company mission is one of the most easily slighted tasks in strategic management. Emphasizing operational aspects of long-range management activities comes much more easily for most executives. But the critical role of the company mission as the basis of orchestrating managerial action is repeatedly demonstrated by failing firms whose short-run actions are ultimately found to be counterproductive to their long-run purpose.

The principal value of a mission statement is its specification of the ultimate aims of the firm. A company gains a heightened sense of purpose when its managers address the issues of: "What business are we in?" "What customer do we serve?" "Why does this organization exist?" Yet managers can undermine the potential contribution of the company mission when they accept platitudes or ambiguous generalizations in response to these questions. It is not enough to say that Lever Brothers is in the business of "making anything that cleans anything," or that Polaroid is committed to businesses that deal with "the interaction of light and matter." Rather, a firm must clearly articu-

[7] G. E. Sawyer, *Business and Society: Managing Corporate Social Impact* (Boston; Houghton Mifflin, 1979), p. 401.

late its long-term intentions. In this way, its goals can serve as a basis for shared expectations, planning, and performance evaluation.

When a mission statement is developed from this perspective, it provides managers with a unity of direction that transcends individual, parochial, and temporary needs. It promotes a sense of shared expectations among all levels and generations of employees. It consolidates values over time and across individuals and interest groups. It projects a sense of worth and intent that can be identified and assimilated by company outsiders, i.e., customers, suppliers, competitors, local committees, and the general public. Finally, it affirms the company's commitment to responsible action in symbiosis with the firm's needs to preserve and protect the essential claims of insiders—sustained survival, growth, and profitability.

Questions for Discussion

1. Reread the mission statement of the Zale Corporation in Figure 3–1. List five insights into the company you feel you gained as a result of knowing its mission.
2. Locate the mission statement of a company not mentioned in the chapter. Where did you find it? Was it presented as a consolidated statement or were you forced to assemble it yourself from various publications of the firm? How many elements of a mission statement outlined in this chapter did you find discussed or revealed in your company's mission?
3. Prepare a one- or two-page, typewritten mission statement for your school of business or for a company selected by your instructor.
4. List five potentially vulnerable areas for a business without a stated company mission.
5. The social audit shown in Strategy in Action 3–1 included only a few of the possible indicators of a firm's social responsibility performance. Name five additional potentially valuable indicators and describe how company performance in each could be measured.
6. Define the term *social responsibility*. Find an example of a company action which was legal but not socially responsible. Defend your example on the basis of your definition.

Bibliography

Ackoff, R. L. *A Concept of Corporate Planning*. New York: Wiley-Interscience, 1970.

Andrews, K. R. *The Concept of Corporate Strategy*. Homewood, Ill.: Dow Jones-Irwin, 1971.

Ansoff, H. I. *Corporate Strategy*. New York: McGraw-Hill, 1965.

Bender, M. "The Organizational Shrink," *New York Times*, March 5, 1972, p. 3.

Beresford, D., and S. Cowen. "Surveying Social Responsibility Disclosure in Annual Reports," *Business*, March–April 1979, pp. 15–20.

Cleland, D. I., and W. R. King. *Management: A System Approach*, New York: McGraw-Hill, 1972.

"Florida Developer to Refund $17 Million to Buyers," *New York Times,* September 14, 1974.

Hall, R. H. *Organization—Structure and Process.* Englewood Cliffs, N.J.: Prentice-Hall, 1972.

Harrison, R. "Understanding Your Organization's Character." *Harvard Business Review,* May–June 1972, pp. 119–28.

King, W. R., and D. I. Cleland. *Strategic Planning and Policy.* New York: Van Nostrand Reinhold, 1979.

Kelley, E. J. *Marketing Planning and Competitive Strategy.* Englewood Cliffs, N.J.: Prentice-Hall, 1972.

Kelley, J. *Organizational Behavior.* Homewood, Ill., Richard D. Irwin, 1974.

Ouchi, W. *Theory Z.* Reading, Mass.: Addison-Wesley Publishing, 1981.

Rogers, C. R. *Client-Centered Therapy.* New York: Houghton Mifflin, 1965.

Sawyer, G. E. *Business and Society: Managing Corporate Social Impact.* Boston: Houghton Mifflin, 1979.

Chapter 3 Cohesion Case Illustration

The Company Mission at Holiday Inns, Inc.

Chapter 3 described what is necessary for a good mission statement and why such a statement is needed. This Cohesion Case Illustration will first present mission statements of Holiday Inns, Inc., at the corporate and business levels. Afterward, a brief evaluation of the mission statements will be provided, as well as an examination of how these must be readdressed in the strategic management process at Holiday Inns, Inc.

Several observations can be made about Holiday Inns' mission statements. The corporate statement gives a clear overview of products and services offered, primary customer attributes, fundamental concerns, and basic management philosophy. This statement emphasizes the hospitality side of the enterprise when identifying its technology for providing goods and services. This may reflect a lack of in-depth consideration of how parts of the product and transportation businesses fit into the overall corporate mission. With this exception the business group missions otherwise adequately identify the product/market scope of each unit's operations and fit within the umbrella of the corporate mission.

While these mission statements appear adequate and useful, there is an underlying mission-related issue to consider while moving through the strategic management process at Holiday Inns. That issue involves the fundamental purpose of defining company mission: that is, "what businesses are (or should) Holiday Inns be in?" From its beginning in 1954 until the early 1970s, Holiday Inns was in one business—full-service lodging facilities. Seeking a broader earnings base, Kemmons Wilson and senior management redefined the company as a travel- and transportation-related business. This definition is strongly reflected in the current corporate mission statement. That definition led to the Trailways and Delta Steamship acquisitions, as well as to a dual focus (outside the corporation as well as inside) in the products group.

The company mission should provide long-term direction, but that does not mean the mission should be cast in stone. As the strategic management model in Chapter 2 indicated, the mission must be reconsidered in light of environmental analysis, the company profile, and the evaluation of alternative strategies. Thus, the underlying, mission-related issue of whether Holiday Inns should be in a travel- and transportation-related business, a travel-related business, or a hospitality-related business cannot be resolved until strategists begin to evaluate alternative strategies.

Exhibit 1

Holiday Inns, Inc., mission statements

Corporate mission

Holiday Inns, Inc. is a diversified, international corporation providing services in the lodging, food service, entertainment, and transportation industries. Hotel operations consist of both company-managed and franchised Holiday Inn hotels. Transportation operations include Trailways, Inc., the nation's second largest intercity busline, and Delta Steamship Lines, Inc., a major U.S.-flag shipping company. Various product operations market institutional furnishings, design services, equipment, and supplies.

We are a forward-looking, innovative industry leader with clearly defined goals, producing superior products, services, and consistently high returns for our stockholders.

We are committed to leadership in marketing our products and services to the traveling and leisure-time public. Internal growth of our operations will continue to be emphasized. We are also closely monitoring changes in consumer needs and lifestyles so that we can develop or acquire new services to satisfy emerging trends. Pursuing these opportunities will supplement the growth that we anticipate from our existing lines of business.

Five basic tenets form our corporate philosophy. They are:

1. Maintain high ethical standards.
2. Provide above-average growth in earnings.
3. Improve our return on invested capital (ROIC)
4. Maintain a strong balance sheet through prudent financial management.
5. People are our greatest asset. We will promote a climate of enthusiasm, teamwork, and challenge which attracts, motivates, and retains superior personnel and rewards superior performance.

Hotel group mission

The hotel group is committed to maintaining and expanding HI's leadership position in the lodging industry by staying ahead of its competitors in responding to the ever-changing needs of the traveling consumer. Through our company-owned and extensive franchise network, HI will offer moderately priced, full-service facilities in a manner that gives the customer the best price/value in the industry, provides for a superior return on stockholders' equity, and meets our social responsibilities to the communities in which we operate.

Product group mission

The product group is designed to fulfill the needs of HI hotels and restaurants, as well as other lodging and restaurant facilities, for nonfood products and services through three business operations: Inn Keepers Supply (IKS), Innkare, and Dohrmann. As an integral part of the HI system, IKS should provide a total capabilities program including design, engineering, and architecture, as well as furniture, fixtures, and equipment . . . to support hotel development and modernization projects. But many supplies are expendable and need to be replaced daily and weekly. To fulfill this need, the company in 1969 created Innkare to provide a nationwide, one-stop, independent master distribution system for expendable supplies and equipment used within the hotels . . . both Holiday Inn and otherwise. And to focus its attention upon the restaurant side of the business, the company in 1970 acquired and is developing Dohrmann as a major distributor of restaurant equipment and supplies.

Transportation group mission

To provide a solid, profitable base for corporate diversification into travel-related areas. *Trailways:* To position HI as a market leader in providing innovative solutions to transportation (bus) industry problems through quality terminal facilities, better equipment utilization and reversing the industry decline in passenger miles. *Delta Steamships:* Delta is committed to becoming the leading U.S.-flag cargo carrier between U.S. ports and the growing markets of South America, West Africa, and the Caribbean through cost-effective management practices and state-of-the-art technology in cargo vessels.

New developments group mission

To build a broader base for future corporate earnings through diversification into hospitality-related businesses with exceptional growth potential. The customer profiles as well as the necessary operating expertise of these businesses should overlap HI's core capabilities in the food and lodging area. Primary focus in the near future should be on the casino/hotel business and the freestanding restaurant business.

Note: This mission was prominent in 1977-78. By 1980-81, HI's restaurant and gaming operations had become *business groups* with their own distinct missions—see paragraphs 52 and 72.[1] This early mission statement is retained here to give you an example of a "new development" mission statement.

[1] Numbers refer to paragraphs in the Cohesion Case at the end of Chapter 1.

Source: Adapted from Holiday Inns' annual reports: 1977 to 1981.

CHAPTER

4

Assessing the External Environment

A host of external and often largely uncontrollable factors influence a firm's choice of direction and action and, ultimately, its organizational structure and internal processes. These factors, which constitute the *external environment,* can be divided into two interrelated subcategories, those in the *remote* environment and those in the more immediate *operating* environment.[1] The aim of this chapter is to describe the complexities and necessities involved in formulating strategies that optimize a firm's opportunities in a highly competitive market within the overall business environment. Figure 4–1 suggests the interrelationship between the firm and the remote and operating environments.

Remote Environment

The remote environment is composed of a set of forces that originate beyond and usually irrespective of any single firm's operating situation—that is, political, economic, social, technological, and industry factors. It presents opportunities, threats, and constraints for the firm, while the organization rarely exerts any meaningful reciprocal influence. For example, when the economy slows and recession is threatening, an individual housing contractor is likely to suffer a decline in business consistent with an industrywide decrease in construction starts. Yet that same contractor would be unable to reverse the negative economic trend even though he might be successful in stimulating local building activity. As a second example, political forces were operative

[1] Many authors refer to the operating environment as the *task* or *competitive* environment.

Figure 4–1

The firm's external environment

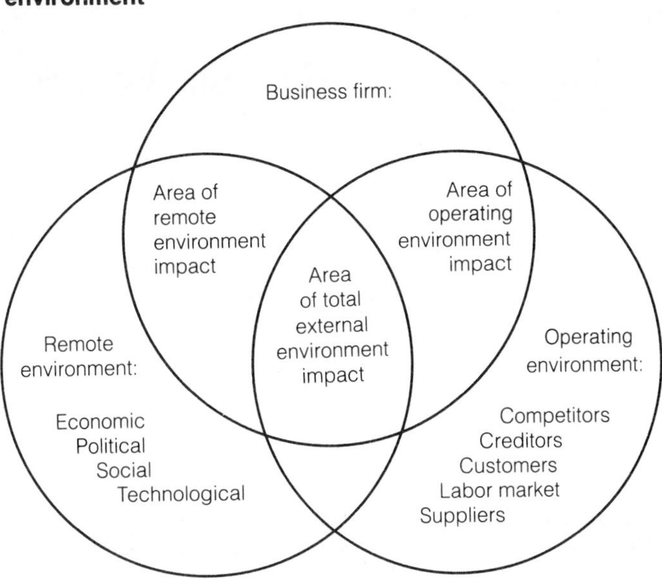

in the trade agreements that resulted in improved relations between America and China in the mid-1970s. These agreements provided opportunities for individual U.S. electronics manufacturers to broaden their international bases of operation.

As a further example, Strategy in Action 4–1 describes the major conclusion of one firm in its pre-1984 assessment of the remote environment.

Economic Considerations

Economic considerations refer to the nature and direction of the economy in which business operates. Because consumption patterns are affected by the relative affluence of various market segments, each firm must understand economic trends in the segments that affect its industry. On both national and international levels, a firm must consider the general availability of credit, the level of disposable income, and the propensity of people to spend. Prime interest rates, rates of inflation, and growth trends of the gross national product are additional economic factors that must be carefully considered in strategic planning.

Until recently, the potential economic impact of international forces appeared to be severely restricted and was largely discounted. However, the

Strategy in Action 4–1

External Factors Affecting the 1984 Strategy of Eastern Air Lines

Before determining its 1984 strategy, Eastern Air Lines conducted an assessment of its remote external environment. The following are the six major conclusions reached by Eastern's strategic planners:

The economic recovery is expected to continue.
GNP: +4.5%

Fuel prices should be stable.

The industry outlook is good:

Domestic passenger miles:	+10.5%
Domestic yield:	+ 6.0%

New, low-cost carriers will continue to exert pressure on prices.
People Express, for example, is expected to take delivery of 18 B-727-200s by April 1984 and to more than double its capacity.

Extensive discounting of daytime fares will continue to limit our ability to establish night coach fare differentials and to increase night coach flying.

Schedule restrictions related to the PATCO (air controllers) strike are being removed.
Slot restrictions at all but four airports will be removed by the end of 1983. Removal of restrictions at Denver and Los Angeles and an increase to at least prestrike levels at La Guardia and O'Hare are expected during the first quarter of 1984. (Quotas at La Guardia and O'Hare were in effect prior to the strike and may be retained.)

emergence of new international power brokers has changed the focus of economic environmental forecasting. Three prominent examples of these new influences are the European Economic Community (EEC), the Organization of Petroleum Exporting Countries (OPEC), and coalitions of lesser-developed countries (LDC).

The EEC or Common Market was established by the Treaty of Rome in 1957, and its members include most Western European countries. Its purposes are elimination of quotas and establishment of a tariff-free trade area for industrial products. This unique example of intra-European cooperation has helped member countries compete more effectively in international markets.

Following the EEC precedent of economic cooperation, the United States, Canada, Japan, the EEC, and other countries conducted multilateral trade negotiations in 1979 to establish rules for international trade and conduct. The outcome of those negotiations had a profound, yet differential, effect on almost every aspect of business activity in the United States.

OPEC is among the most powerful international economic forces in existence today in terms of its impact on the United States. This cartel includes most major world suppliers of oil and gas, and its drastic increases in the price of energy supplied not only impeded U.S. recovery from the recession of the early 1970s, but also fueled inflationary fires the world over. The U.S. automobile industry was particularly affected through an increase in user costs and the legislated redesign of engine sizes and performance standards.

Third World and Fourth World countries have recently assumed a greater role in international commerce, as a source of both threats and opportunities. Following the success of OPEC, these less-developed countries have found it economically beneficial to directly confront the established powers. Since 1974, producers of primary commodities in the LDCs have formed or greatly strengthened their trade organizations to enforce higher prices and achieve larger real incomes for their members. On the other hand, developing countries offer U.S. firms huge new markets for foodstuffs and capital machinery.

Even countries not desiring or unable to form cartels exhibit the new aggressive attitude.

> The intense nationalism of the developing countries, with nearly three fourths of the world's population, represents perhaps the greatest challenge our industrialized society and multinational corporations will face in the next two decades. As one Third World expert puts it . . . "the vastly unequal relationship between the rich and poor nations is fast becoming the central issue of our time."[2]

Each of these international forces has the capacity to affect the U.S. business community's economic well-being—for better or worse, for richer or poorer. Consequently, companies must try to forecast major repercussions of actions taken in both the domestic and international economic arenas. Such forecasts are a critical part of the strategic management process.

Social Considerations

Social considerations involve the beliefs, values, attitudes, opinions, and lifestyles of those in a firm's external environment, as developed from their cultural, ecological, demographic, religious, educational, and ethnic conditioning. As social attitudes change so does demand for various clothing styles, books, leisure activities, and other products and services. As is true of other forces in the remote external environment, social forces are dynamic with

[2] Richard Steade, "Multinational Corporations and the Changing World Economic Order," *California Management Review*, Winter 1978, p. 5.

constant change resulting from individuals' efforts to control and adapt to environmental factors to satisfy their desires and needs.

One of the most profound social changes in recent years is the large number of women entering the labor market. Not only have women affected the hiring and compensation policies and resource capabilities of firms employing them, they have also created or greatly expanded demand for a wide range of products and services necessitated by their absence from the home. Businesses that correctly anticipated or quickly reacted to this social change have profited by offering such products and services as convenience foods, microwave ovens, and day-care centers.

A second accelerating social change is consumer and employee interest in quality-of-life issues, even at the expense of greater affluence. There is evidence of this change in recent contract negotiations in that added to the traditional demand for increased salaries have been worker preferences for such benefits as sabbaticals, flexible hours or four-day workweeks, lump-sum vacation plans, and opportunities for advanced training.

A third important change in the social environment is the shift in national age distribution. Changing social values and increased acceptance of improved birth-control methods have resulted in a rise in the mean age of the population in the United States from 27.9 in 1970 to an expected 34.9 years by the end of the 20th century. This trend will have an increasingly unfavorable impact on most producers of predominantly youth-oriented goods and will necessitate a shift in long-range marketing strategies. For example, producers of hair- and skin-care preparations have already begun to adjust research and development to reflect anticipated changes in the types of products demanded. One company that has recognized the potential impact is Procter & Gamble as discussed in Strategy in Action 4–2.

A consequence of the changing population distribution is sharply increased demands from a growing senior-citizen population. Constrained by fixed incomes, the elderly have demanded that arbitrary and rigid policies on retirement age be modified. They have successfully lobbied for tax exemptions and increases in social security benefits. Such changes have significantly altered the opportunity-risk equations of many firms—often much to the benefit of those businesses that anticipated the social impacts.

Translating social change into forecasts of business effects is a difficult process, at best. Nevertheless, informed estimates of the impact of such alterations as geographic shifts in populations, and changing work values, ethics, and religious orientation can only help a strategizing firm in its attempts to prosper.

Political Considerations

The direction and stability of political factors is a major consideration for managers in formulating company strategy. Political considerations define the legal and otherwise governing parameters in which the firm must or

Strategy in Action 4–2
Procter & Gamble

Procter & Gamble announced a new product on August 7, 1979, symbolizing a revolutionary era at the big Cincinnati company. The product was a medicinal cream for the treatment of skin lesions. Procter & Gamble had just begun a grand invasion of new markets, many of which were institutional and commercial fields well outside of its traditional haven in the nation's supermarkets. The first phalanx of these new products from P&G involved fanning out into such fields as prescription drugs, synthetic foods and food ingredients, and supplies for hospitals and nursing homes. Others, destined for the soft-drink and agriculture-chemicals markets, were laying in wait. These nonsupermarket offerings were forecast to account for as much as 20 percent of the company's business by the mid-80s.

The broad intent of this strategy was clear. With birthrates declining and population growth leveling off, the demographic trends that fueled P&G's ascent over the decades of the 1960s and 1970s were reversing. Given this shift, the company decided to look elsewhere to continue expanding at their previous rate.

The diversification drive also involved huge, unexplored risks. In many of its new fields, such as drugs and chemicals, the company had to take on formidable competitors that were not much impressed by P&G's recognized preeminence in packaged goods. Although the company boasted an unequaled marketing network for consumer products, many rivals doubted its ability to sell to institutions, doctors, and pharmacists.

Still, P&G had clearly decided that the competitive risks did not outweigh the potential rewards of its new-product campaign, nor did they eclipse the company's need to find new avenues of growth.

Based on the article "P&G's New New-Product Onslaught," from the October 1, 1979, issue of *Business Week*.

may wish to operate. Political constraints are placed on each company through fair-trade decisions, antitrust laws, tax programs, minimum-wage legislation, pollution and pricing policies, administrative jawboning, and many other actions aimed at protecting the consumer and the environment. These laws, practices, and regulations are most commonly restrictive, and as a result, they tend to reduce a firm's potential profits. However, other political actions are designed to benefit and protect a company. Examples include patent laws, government subsidies, and product research grants. Thus, political forces are both a limitation and a benefit to the firms they influence.

Political activity may also have a significant impact on three additional governmental functions that influence a firm's remote environment.

Supplier Function. Government decisions regarding creation and accessibility of private businesses to government-owned natural resources and national stockpiles of agricultural products will profoundly affect the viability of some firms' strategies.

Customer Function. Government demand for products and services can create, sustain, enhance, or eliminate many market opportunities. For example, in the same way that the Kennedy administration's emphasis on landing a man on the moon spawned the demand for literally thousands of new products in the 1960s, the Carter administration's emphasis on developing synthetic fuels temporarily created a similar demand for new skills, technologies, and products in the 1980s.

Competitor Function. The government can operate as an almost unbeatable competitor in the marketplace. Thus, knowledge of its strategies gained through assessment of the remote environment can help a firm to avoid unfavorable confrontation with government as a competitor. For example, forecasts that government will increase the number of nuclear power plants or communication facilities might simultaneously serve as a retreat signal to direct private competitors and as an invitation to private producers of services or associated activities.

Businesses are greatly affected by government decisions, as shown in Strategy in Action 4–3. Thus, continual assessment of government strategizing will help individual firms to develop complementary plans that anticipate and optimize environmental opportunities.

Technological Considerations

The final set of considerations in the remote environment involves technological advancements. To avoid obsolescence and promote innovation, a firm must be aware of technological changes that might influence its industry. Creative technological adaptations can affect planning in that new products may be suggested or existing ones improved; manufacturing and marketing techniques may also be improved.

A technological innovation can have a sudden and dramatic effect on the environment of a firm. A breakthrough may spawn sophisticated new markets and products or significantly shorten the anticipated life of a manufacturing facility. Thus, all firms, and most particularly those in turbulent growth industries, must strive for an understanding both of the present state of technological advancement affecting its products and services and of probable future innovations. This quasiscience of attempting to foresee advancements and

Strategy in Action 4–3

A Major Threat in the CPA Firm's Environment

"These are our own ideas and opinions, our private notes," says Robert Hermann, a tax manager with the accounting firm of Deloitte Haskins & Sells. "They are none of the IRS's business."

The Internal Revenue Service disagrees, however, and the result is a bitter controversy.

The notes in question are those in which auditors spell out any doubts they have about a client's tax position. Accountants have always considered these confidential. But now, they say, recent IRS aggressiveness in seeking these papers has undermined their relationships with their corporate clients, and has threatened to damage the quality of financial reports.

Says William Raby, a partner in Touche Ross & Co. "We've seen a drying up of the willingness of clients to discuss or even show data to their auditors. And the bottom line is that it isn't leading to good financial reporting."

When preparing and auditing financial statements, accountants include a reserve for taxes that might be payable if the IRS investigates. A company may take an investment tax credit, for instance, although it realizes that the IRS could disagree. [The company's] memos, and those of its auditors, would spell out the arguments on each side.

But the tax credit likely would be just one of many such items, and the IRS typically sees only the grand total reserve. If [the IRS] had access to the internal documents, it could see a breakdown of all the uncertain areas.

"It's a trail to the sensitive issues on the tax return," says William T. Holloran, a New York City lawyer and accountant. He says accountants try to dream up the worst possible scenarios, but "if the IRS sees that you wondered about something, they may just say 'Gee, there must be something wrong with it.' "

An IRS official takes a different view: "We feel that the information might throw light on the correctness of a taxpayer return." He says the memos are necessary because corporations usually are more open with accountants than with the government, "and we can't stay with a company for an unlimited period of time" ferreting out information. "The tax system shouldn't be viewed as a game of hide and seek. If we can get the papers, we can make a determination [of tax liability] much quicker, and not waste the taxpayers' money."

Most experts say that the only answer may rest with the IRS. "We can only hope that the IRS won't go bananas in this area," says Holloran. "On a normal audit, they have to show restraint."

Source: "Auditors Say IRS Demand for Documents Is Poisoning Relations with Client Firms." Reprinted by permission of *The Wall Street Journal*, © Dow Jones & Company, Inc., January 15, 1981.

estimate their probable impact on an organization's operations is known as *technological forecasting.*

Technological forecasting can help protect and improve the profitability of firms in growing industries. It alerts strategic managers to both impending challenges and promising opportunities. As examples: (1) advances in xerography were a key to Xerox's success but caused major difficulties for carbon-paper manufacturers; and (2) the perfection of transistors changed the nature of competition in the radio and television industry, helping giants like RCA while seriously weakening smaller firms with resource commitments that required products continue to be based on vacuum tubes.

The key to beneficial forecasting of technological advancement lies in accurately predicting future capabilities and probable future impacts. A comprehensive analysis of the effect of technological change involves study of the expected impact of new technologies on the remote environment, on the competitive business situation, and on the business-society interface. In recent years, forecasting in the last area has warranted particular attention. For example, as a consequence of increased concern over the environment, businesses must carefully investigate the probable effect of technological advances on quality-of-life factors such as ecology, aesthetics, and public safety.

Operating Environment

The operating environment involves factors in the immediate competitive situation that provide many of the challenges a particular firm faces in attempting to attract or acquire needed resources or in striving to profitably market its goods and services. Among the most prominent of these factors are a firm's competitive position, customer profile, reputation among suppliers and creditors, and accessible labor market. The operating environment, also called the competitive or task environment, differs from the remote environment in that it is typically subject to much more influence or control by the firm. Thus, when they consider conditions in the operating environment, businesses can be much more proactive as opposed to reactive in strategic planning, than they are when dealing with remote factors.

Competitive Position

By assessing its competitive position, a business improves its chances of designing strategies that optimize environmental opportunities.

Development of competitor profiles enables a firm to more accurately forecast both its short- and long-term growth and profit potentials. Although the exact criteria used in constructing a competitor's profile are largely determined by situational factors in the environment, the following are often included:[3]

1. Market share.
2. Breadth of product line.
3. Effectiveness of sales distribution.
4. Proprietary and key-account advantages.
5. Price competitiveness.
6. Advertising and promotion effectiveness.
7. Location and age of facility.
8. Capacity and productivity.
9. Experience.
10. Raw material costs.
11. Financial position.
12. Relative product quality.
13. R&D advantages/position.
14. Caliber of personnel.
15. General image.

Once appropriate criteria have been selected, they are subjectively weighted to reflect their relative importance to a firm's success. Next, the competitor being evaluated is rated on the criteria. The rankings are multiplied by the weightings and the resulting weighted scores are summed to yield a numerical profile of the competing business, as shown in Figure 4–2.

The type of competitor profile suggested is limited by the subjectivity of the criteria selection, weighting, and evaluation approaches employed. Never-

Figure 4–2

Competitor profile

Key success factors	*Weight*	*Rating†*	*Weighted score*
Market share	.30	4	1.20
Price competitiveness	.20	3	.60
Facilities location	.20	5	1.00
Raw materials cost	.10	3	.30
Caliber of personnel	.20	1	.30
	1.00*		3.30

* The total of the weights must always equal 1.00.

† The rating scale suggested is as follows: very strong competitive position (5 points), strong (4), average (3), weak (2), very weak (1).

[3] These items were selected from a competitive position assessment matrix proposed by Charles W. Hofer and Dan Schendel, *Strategy Formulation: Analytical Concepts* (St. Paul, Minn.: West Publishing, 1978), p. 76.

theless, this process is of considerable value in helping a business to explicitly define its perception of its competitive position. Comparing profiles of the firm and its competitors can further aid managers in identifying specific factors that might make a competitor vulnerable to alternative strategies the firm might choose to implement.

Customer Profiles

Perhaps the most valuable result of analyzing the operating environment is an understanding of the composition of a firm's customers. In developing a profile of present and prospective customers, managers are better able to plan the strategic operations of the firm, anticipate changes in the size of markets, and allocate resources supporting forecast shifts in demand patterns. Four principal types of information are useful in constructing a customer profile: geographic, demographic, psychographic, and buyer behavior, as illustrated in Figure 4–3.

Geographic. It is important to define the geographic area from which customers do or could come. Almost every product or service has some quality that makes it variably attractive to buyers from specific locations. Obviously, a successful regional manufacturer of snow skis in Wisconsin should think twice about investing in a wholesale distribution center in South Carolina. On the other hand, advertising by a major Myrtle Beach (South Carolina) hotel in the Milwaukee *Sun-Times* could significantly expand the hotel's geographically defined customer market.

Demographic. Demographic variables are most commonly used for differentiating groups of customers. The term refers to descriptive characteristics that can be used to identify present or potential customers. Demographic information such as sex, age, marital status, income, and occupation is comparatively easy to collect, quantify, and use in strategic forecasting, and it is the minimum data used as the basis of a customer profile.

Psychographic. Customer personality and lifestyle are often better predictors of purchasing behavior than geographic or demographic variables. In such situations, a psychographic study of customers is an important component of the total profile. Recent soft-drink advertising campaigns by Pepsi-Cola ("the Pepsi generation") and 7UP ("America's turning 7UP") reflect strategic management's attention not only to demographics but also to the psychographic characteristics of their largest customer segment—physically active, group-oriented nonprofessionals.

Buyer Behavior. Buyer-behavior data can also be used in constructing a customer profile. This includes a multifaceted set of factors used to explain

Figure 4–3

Customer profile considerations

Type of information	*Typical breakdowns*
Geographic:	
Region	Pacific; Mountain; West North Central; West South Central; East North Central; East South Central; South Atlantic; Middle Atlantic; New England
County size	A, B, C, D
City or SMSA size*	Under 5,000; 5,000–19,999; 20,000–49,999; 50,000–99,999; 100,000–249,999; 250,000–499,999; 500,000–999,999; 1,000,000–3,999,999; 4 million or over
Density	Urban, suburban, rural
Climate	Northern, Southern
Demographic:	
Age	Under 6, 6–11, 12–17, 18–34, 35–49, 50–64, 65+
Sex	Male/female
Family size	1–2, 3–4, 5+ persons
Family life cycle	Young, single; young, married, no children; young, married, youngest child under 6; young, married, youngest child 6 or over; older, married, with children; older, married, no children under 18; older, single; other
Income	Under $5,000; $5,000–$10,000; etc.
Occupation	Professional and technical; managers, officials and proprietors; clerical, sales; craftsmen, foremen; operatives; farmers; retired; students, homemakers; unemployed
Education	Grade school or less, some high school, graduated from high school, some college, graduated from college
Religion	Catholic, Protestant, Jewish, other
Race	Caucasian, Negro, Oriental, other
Nationality	American, British, French, German, Eastern European, Scandinavian, Italian, Spanish, Latin American, Middle Eastern, Japanese, and so on
Social class	Lower-lower, upper-lower, lower-middle, middle-middle, upper-middle, lower-upper, upper-upper
Psychographic:	
Compulsiveness	Compulsive/noncompulsive
Gregariousness	Extrovert/introvert
Autonomy	Dependent/independent
Conservatism	Conservative/liberal/radical
Authoritarianism	Authoritarian/democratic
Leadership	Leader/follower
Ambitiousness	High achiever/low achiever
Buyer behavior:	
Usage rate	Nonuser, light user, medium user, heavy user
Readiness stage	Unaware, aware, interested, intending to try, trier, regular buyer
Benefits sought	Economy, status, dependability
End use	Varies with the product
Brand loyalty	None, light, strong
Marketing-factor sensibility	Quality, price, service, advertising, sales promotion

* SMSA stands for standard metropolitan statistical area.

Source: Adapted from Philip Kotler, *Marketing Management* (Englewood Cliffs, N.J.: Prentice-Hall, 1972), p. 170.

or predict some aspect of customers' behavior with regard to a product or service. As shown in Figure 4–3, information on buyer behavior such as usage rate, benefits sought, and brand loyalty can aid significantly in designing more accurate and profitably targeted strategies.

Suppliers and Creditors: Sources of Resources

Dependable relationships between a business firm and its suppliers and creditors are essential to the company's long-term survival and growth. A firm regularly relies on its suppliers for financial support, services, materials, and equipment. In addition, a business is occasionally forced to make special requests of its creditors and suppliers for such favors as quick delivery, liberal credit terms, or broken-lot orders. Particularly at these times, it is essential that a business has an ongoing relationship with its suppliers and creditors.

In addition to the strength of a firm's relationships with suppliers and creditors, several other factors should be considered in assessing this aspect of the operating environment. With regard to its competitive position with suppliers, a firm should address the following questions.

1. Are suppliers' prices competitive? Do suppliers offer attractive quantity discounts? How costly are their shipping charges?
2. Are vendors competitive in terms of production standards? In terms of deficiency rates?
3. Are suppliers' abilities, reputation, and services competitive?
4. Are suppliers reciprocally dependent on the firm?

With regard to its position with its creditors, the following questions are among the most important for the strategizing firm:

1. Is stock fairly valued and willingly accepted as collateral?
2. Do potential creditors perceive the firm as having an acceptable record of past payment? A strong working capital position? Little or no leverage?
3. Are creditors' current loan terms compatible with the firm's profitability objectives?
4. Are creditors able to extend the necessary line of credit?

Answers to these and related questions help a business forecast availability of the resources it will need to implement and sustain its competitive strategies. Because quantity, quality, price, and accessibility of financial, human, and material resources are rarely ideal, assessment of suppliers and creditors is critical to an accurate evaluation of the firm's operating environment.

Personnel: Nature of the Labor Market

The ability to attract and hold capable employees is a prerequisite for a firm's success. However, the nature of a business's operating environment most often influences personnel recruitment and selection alternatives. Three factors most affect a firm's access to needed personnel: Reputation as an employer, local employment rates, and ready availability of needed knowledge and skills.

Reputation. A business's reputation within its operating environment is a major element in its long-term ability to satisfy personnel needs. A firm that is seen as permanent in the community, at least competitive in its compensation package, and concerned with employee welfare, as well as being respected for its product or service, and appreciated for its overall contribution to general welfare is more likely to attract and retain valuable employees than is a rival firm which either exhibits fewer of these qualities or emphasizes one factor to the detriment of others.

Employment Rates. Depending principally on the stage of growth of a business community, the readily available supply of skilled and experienced personnel may vary considerably. A new manufacturing firm seeking skilled employees in a vigorous and established industrialized community obviously faces a more difficult problem than would the same firm if it were to locate in an economically depressed area where other similar firms had recently cut back operations.

Availability. Some people's skills are so specialized that they may be forced to relocate to secure appropriate jobs and the impressive compensations their skills commonly command, examples include oil drillers, experienced chefs, technical specialists, and industry executives. A firm seeking to hire such an individual is said to have broad labor-market boundaries. That is, the geographic area within which the firm might reasonably expect to attract qualified candidates is quite large. On the other hand, an individual with more common skills would be less likely to relocate from considerable distance to achieve modest economic or career advancement. Thus, the labor-market boundaries are fairly limited for such occupational groups as unskilled laborers, clerical personnel, and retail clerks.

Strategic Considerations for Multinational Firms

Special complications confront a firm involved in international operations. Multinational corporations (MNCs) headquartered in one country with subsidiaries in others experience difficulties understandably associated with operating in two or more distinctly different competitive arenas.

Awareness of the strategic opportunities and threats posed and faced by MNCs is important to planners in almost every domestic U.S. industry. Among U.S.-headquartered corporations that receive more than 50 percent of their annual profits from foreign operations are Citicorp, the Coca-Cola Company,

Strategy in Action 4–4

Multinational Corporation Ownership Test

In this test, you go down the alphabet and pick out the products that are foreign owned.

A Airwick, Alka-Selzer antacid, Aim toothpaste.
B Baskin Robbins ice cream, Bactine antiseptic, Ball Park Franks.
C Certain-Teed, Capitol records, Castrol oils.
D Deer Park sparkling water, Dove soap, Dunlop tires.
E ENO antacids, Eureka vacuum cleaners, Ehler spices.
F Four Roses whisky, French's mustard, First Love dolls.
G Good Humor ice cream, Garrard turntables, Grand Trunk Railroad.
H Humpty Dumpty magazine, Hires Root Beer, Hills Brothers coffee.
I Imperial margarine, Instant potato mix, Indian Head textiles.
J Juvena cosmetics, Jaeger sportswear, Jade cosmetics.
K Knox gelatine, Kool cigarettes, Keebler cookies.
L Libby's fruits and vegetables, *Look* magazine, Lifebouy soap.
M Magnavox, Massey-Ferguson tractors, Mr. Coffee.
N Norelco appliances, Nescafé coffee, New Yorker hotel.
O Ovaltine drink mix, One-a-Day vitamins.
P Panasonic, Pop Shoppes, Pepsodent toothpaste.
Q Nestlé Quik chocolate mix, Quasar television sets, Quadra-Bar sedatives.
R Ray-O-Vac batteries, Rinso, Rona Barret's gossip magazines.
S Scripto pens, Seven Seas salad dressings, Slazenger tennis balls.
T Tetley tea, Tic Tac Breath fresheners, Taster's Choice instant coffee.
U Underwood typewriters, Urise antiseptics, Ultra Tears eye lotion.
V Valium tranquilizers, Vogue pipe tobacco, Vim detergent.
W Wish-Bone salad dressings, Wisk detergent, White Motor Trucks.
X Xam clock radios, Xylocaine salves, Xylee plastics.
Y Yardley cosmetics, Yale locks, Yashica cameras.
Z Zesta crackers, Zig-Zag cigarette papers, Zestatabs vitamins.

Answer: All of the companies (A through Z) are foreign owned.

Exxon Corporation, the Gillette Company, IBM, Otis Elevator, and Texas Instruments. In fact, according to 1983 statistics, the 100 largest U.S. multinationals earned an average of 37 percent of their operating profits abroad. Equally impressive is the impact of foreign-based multinationals that operate in the United States. Their direct "foreign investment" in America now exceeds $70 billion, with Japanese, West German, and French firms leading the way. The extent of this foreign influence is evident in Strategy in Action 4–4.

Understanding the myriad and sometimes subtle nuances of competing in international markets or against multinational firms is rapidly becoming a prerequisite competency for strategic managers. Therefore, this section will focus on the nature, outlook, and operations of MNCs.

Development of an MNC

The evolution of a multinational company often entails progressively involved strategies. With the first strategy there is export-import activity but minimal effect on existing management orientation or product lines. The second level involves foreign licensing and technology transfer but there is still little change in management or operation. The third level of strategy is characterized by direct investment in overseas operations, including manufacturing plants. This level requires large capital outlays as well as management effort in the development of international skills. At this point, domestic operations continue to dominate company policy, but the firm is commonly categorized as a true MNC. The most involved strategy is indicated by a substantial increase in foreign investment, with foreign assets comprising a significant portion of total assets. The company begins to emerge as a global enterprise with world approaches to production, sales, finance, and control.

While some firms downplay their multinational nature—so as never to appear distracted from their domestic operations—others highlight their international intentions. For example, General Electric's formal statement of mission and business philosophy includes the following commitment:

> "To carry on a diversified, growing, and profitable worldwide manufacturing business in electrical apparatus, appliances, and supplies, and in related materials, products, systems, and services for industry, commerce, agriculture, government, the community, and the home."

A similar worldwide orientation is evident at IBM which operates in 125 countries, conducts business in 30 languages and more than 100 currencies, and has 23 major manufacturing facilities in 14 different countries.

Why Companies Internationalize

In the past 30 years there has been a dramatic decline in the technological advantage once enjoyed by the United States. In the late 1950s, over 80 percent of the world's major innovations were first introduced in the United States. By 1965 this figure had declined to 55 percent, and the decline continues today. On the other hand, France has made impressive advances in electric traction, nuclear power, and aviation. West Germany is a proclaimed leader in chemicals and pharmaceuticals, precision and heavy machinery, heavy electrical goods, metallurgy, and surface transport equipment. Japan leads in optics, solid-state physics, engineering, chemistry, and process metallurgy. Eastern Europe and the Soviet Union, the so-called COMECON (Council for Mutual Economic Assistance) countries, generate 30 percent of annual worldwide patent applications. However, the United States can regain some of the lost competitive advantages. Through internationalization U.S. firms can often reap benefits from emerging industries and evolutionary technologies developed abroad.

Multinational development makes sense as a competitive weapon in many situations. Direct penetration of foreign markets can drain vital cash flows from a foreign competitor's domestic operations. The resulting lost opportunities, reduced income, and limited production can impair the competitor's ability to invade U.S. markets. A case in point is the strategic action of IBM which moved to establish a position of strength in the Japanese mainframe computer industry before two key competitors, Fiyitsue and Hitachi, could gain dominance. Once it had achieved an influential market share, IBM worked to deny its Japanese competitors the vital cash and production experience they needed to invade the U.S. market.[4]

Considerations Prior to Internationalization

To begin their internationalizing activities, businesses are advised to take four steps:[5]

Scan the International Situation. Scanning includes reading journals and patent reports, and checking other printed sources—as well as meeting people at scientific-technical conferences and/or in-house seminars.

Make Connections with Academia and Research Organizations. Enterprises active in overseas R&D often pursue work-related projects with foreign academics and sometimes form consulting agreements with faculty members.

Increase the Company's International Visibility. Common methods of attracting attention include participation in technological trade fairs, circulation of brochures illustrating company products and inventions, and hiring technology-acquisition consultants.

Undertake Cooperative Research Projects. Some multinational enterprises engage in joint research projects to broaden their contacts, reduce ex-

---

[4] C. M. Watson, "Counter Competition Abroad to Protect Home Markets," *Harvard Business Review,* January–February 1982, p. 40.

[5] R. Ronstadt and R. Kramer, "Getting the Most out of Innovation Abroad," *Harvard Business Review,* March–April 1982.

penses, diminish the risk for each partner, or forestall entry of a competitor into the market.

In a similar vein, external and internal assessments may be conducted before a firm enters international markets.[6] External assessment involves careful examination of critical international environmental features with particular attention to the status of the host nation in areas such as economic progress, political control, and nationalism. Expansion of industrial facilities, balance of payments, and improvements in technological capabilities over the past decade should provide some idea of the host nation's economic progress. Political status can be gauged by the host nation's power in and impact on international affairs.

Internal assessment involves identification of the basic strong points of a company's present operations. These strengths are particularly important in international operations because they are often the elements valued most by the host nation and thus offer significant bargaining leverage. Both resource strengths and global capabilities must be analyzed. The resources to be examined in particular include technical and managerial skills, capital, labor, and raw materials. The global capability components include assessing the effectiveness of proposed product-delivery and financial-management systems.

A firm that gives serious consideration to internal and external assessment is Business International Corporation which recommends that seven broad categories of factors be considered. As shown in Strategy in Action 4–5, these categories include economic, political, geographic, labor, tax, capital-source, and business factors.

Strategy in Action 4–5

Checklist of Factors to Consider in Choosing a Foreign Manufacturing Site

The following considerations were drawn from an 88-point checklist developed by Business International Corporation.

Economic factors:

1. Size of GNP and projected rate of growth.
2. Foreign-exchange position.
3. Size of market for the company's products; rate of growth.
4. Current or prospective membership in a customs union.

[6] J. Fayweather and A. Kapoor, *Strategy and Negotiation for the International Corporation* (Cambridge, Mass.: Ballinger, 1976.)

Strategy in Action 4–5 *(concluded)*

Political factors:
5. Form and stability of government.
6. Attitude toward private and foreign investment by government, customers, and competition.
7. Practice of favored versus neutral treatment for state industries.
8. Degree of antiforeign discrimination.

Geographic factors:
9. Efficiency of transport (railways, waterways, highways).
10. Proximity of site to export markets.
11. Availability of local raw materials.
12. Availability of power, water, gas.

Labor factors:
13. Availability of managerial, technical, and office personnel able to speak the language of the parent company.
14. Degree of skill and discipline at all levels.
15. Presence or absence of militant or Communist-dominated unions.
16. Degree and nature of labor voice in management.

Tax factors:
17. Tax-rate trends (corporate and personal income, capital, withholding, turnover, excise, payroll, capital gains, customs, and other indirect and local taxes).
18. Joint tax treaties with home country and others.
19. Duty and tax drawbacks when imported goods are exported.
20. Availability of tariff protection.

Capital-source factors:
21. Cost of local borrowing.
22. Local availability of convertible currencies.
23. Modern banking systems.
24. Government credit aids to new businesses.

Business factors:
25. State of marketing and distribution system.
26. Normal profit margins in the company's industry.
27. Competitive situation in the firm's industry; do cartels exist?
28. Availability of amenities for expatriate executives and families.

Multinational versus Domestic Strategic Planning

Multinational strategic planning is more complex than such purely domestic planning. There are at least five contributing factors:

1. The multinational faces multiple political, economic, legal, social, and cultural environments as well as various rates of change within each of them.

2. Interactions between the national and foreign environments are complex because of national sovereignty issues and widely differing economic and social conditions.
3. Geographical separation, cultural and national differences, and variations in business practices all tend to make communication between headquarters and the overseas affiliates difficult.
4. Multinationals face extreme competition because of differences in industry structures.
5. Multinationals are confronted by various international organizations such as the European Economic Community, the European Free Trade Area, and the Latin American Free Trade Area that restrict a firm's selection of its competitive strategies.

Indications of how these factors contribute to increased complexity in strategic planning and management are provided in Figure 4–4.

Control Problems for the Multinational Firm

An inherent complicating factor for many international firms is that financial policies of the multinational are typically designed to further the goals of the parent company with a minimum of attention paid to the goals of the host countries. This built-in bias creates conflict between the different parts of the organization, between the whole organization and its home and host countries, and between the home and host countries themselves. The conflict is accentuated by various schemes used to shift earnings from one country to another to avoid taxes, minimize risk, or achieve other objectives.

Different financial environments also make normal standards of company behavior concerning disposition of earnings, sources of finance, and the structure of capital more problematic. Thus, the performance of multinational divisions becomes increasingly difficult to measure.

In addition, there are often important differences in measurement and control systems. Fundamental to the concept of planning is a well-conceived, future-oriented approach to decision making based on accepted procedures and methods of analysis. Consistent approaches to planning throughout an organization are needed for effective review and evaluation by corporate headquarters. Such planning is complicated by differences in accounting conventions among countries, by attitudes about work measurement, and by different government requirements for disclosure of information.

Although such problems are more an aspect of the multinational environment than they are consequences of poor management, the problems are often most effectively reduced through increased attention to strategic management. Such planning aids in coordinating and integrating the company's future direction, objectives, and policies around the world. It enables the company to anticipate and better prepare for change. It facilitates the creation of programs

Figure 4–4

Differences between U.S. and multinational operations that affect strategic management

Factor	*U.S. operations*	*International operations*
Language	English used almost universally	Local language must be used in many situations
Culture	Relatively homogeneous	Quite diverse, both between countries and within a country
Politics	Stable and relatively unimportant	Often volatile and of decisive importance
Economy	Relatively uniform	Wide variations among countries and between regions within countries
Government interference	Minimal and reasonably predictable	Extensive and subject to rapid change
Labor	Skilled labor available	Skilled labor often scarce, requiring training or redesign of production methods
Financing	Well-developed financial markets	Poorly developed financial markets. Capital flows subject to government control
Market research	Data easy to collect	Data difficult and expensive to collect
Advertising	Many media available; few restrictions	Media limited; many restrictions; low literacy rates rule out print media in some countries
Money	U.S. dollar used universally	Must change from one currency to another; changing exchange rates and government restrictions are problems
Transportation/ communication	Among the best in the world	Often inadequate
Control	Always a problem. Centralized control will work	A worse problem. Centralized control won't work. Must walk a tightrope between overcentralizing and losing control through too much decentralizing
Contracts	Once signed, are binding on both parties, even if one party makes a bad deal	Can be voided and renegotiated if one party becomes dissatisfied
Labor relations	Collective bargaining; can lay off workers easily	Often cannot lay off workers; may have mandatory worker participation in management; workers may seek change through political process rather than collective bargaining
Trade barriers	Nonexistent	Extensive and very important

Source: R. G. Murdick, R. C. Moor, R. H. Eckhouse, and T. W. Zimmerer, *Business Policy: A Framework for Analysis,* 4th ed. (Columbus, Ohio: Grid 1984).

to deal with worldwide developments. Finally, it helps the management of overseas affiliates to become more actively involved in setting goals and in developing means to more effectively utilize the enterprise's total resources.

Emphasis on Environmental Factors

This chapter has described the remote environment as encompassing four components: economic, political, social, and technological; and the operating environment five factors: competitors, creditors, customers, labor markets, and suppliers. While these descriptions are generally accurate, they may give the false impression that the components and factors are easily identified, mutually exclusive, and equally applicable in all situations. In fact, forces in the external environment are so dynamic and interactive that the impact of any single element cannot be wholly disassociated from the impact of other elements. For example, are increases in OPEC oil prices the result of economic, political, social, or technological changes? Or are a manufacturer's surprisingly good relations with suppliers a result of competitor's, customer's, creditor's, or the supplier's own activities? The answer to both questions is probably that a number of forces in the external environment have combined to create the situation. Such is the case in most studies of the environment.

Strategic managers are frequently frustrated in their attempts to anticipate the environment's changing influences. Different external elements affect different strategies at different times and with varying strengths. The only certainty is that the impact of the remote and operating environment will be uncertain until a strategy is implemented. This disconcerting reality leads many managers, particularly in comparatively less-powerful, smaller firms, to minimize long-term planning which requires a commitment of resources. Instead, they favor more flexibility allowing managers to adapt to new pressures from the environment. While it is true that such a decision has considerable merit for many firms, there is an associated trade-off, namely, that absence of a strong resource and psychological commitment to a proactive strategy effectively bars the firm from assuming a leadership role in its competitive environment.

There is a final difficulty in assessing the probable impact of remote and operating environments on the effectiveness of alternative strategies. This involves collecting information that can be analyzed to disclose predictable effects. Except in rare instances, it is virtually impossible for any single firm to anticipate the consequences of a change in the environment, for example, the precise effect on alternative strategies of a 2 percent increase in the national inflation rate, a 1 percent decrease in statewide unemployment, or the entry of a new competitor in a regional market.

However, there is a real advantage in assessing the potential impact of changes in the external environment. In this way, decision makers are better able to narrow the range of available alternatives and eliminate options that are clearly inconsistent with forecast opportunities. Environmental assessment seldom identifies the best strategy, but it characteristically leads to the elimination of all but the most promising alternatives.

Designing Opportunistic Strategies

The process of designing business strategies is multifaceted, complex, and often principally dependent on fairly subjective and intuitive impact assessments (see Strategy in Action 4–6 for an example). The process is multifaceted because the decision maker must investigate independent and interactive influences from both the remote and operating environments. Such studies must be conducted to prepare any systematic or comprehensive strategic decision. The process is complex because environmental forces have both individual and interactive effects on business generally and variable effects on a given business depending on the unique situation. Finally, most strategies are developed from fairly subjective and intuitive assessments of information gathered on the environment. Limited objectivity is an understandable consequence in that historical trends alone cannot be used to accurately predict future events, given constant changes in competitive external environments.

Designing a strategy to optimize opportunities identified by assessing the business environment is a difficult task:

> It usually means questioning old methods, exploring unfamiliar environmental waters, facing up to an objective evaluation of strengths and weaknesses, forcing important changes on people in the firm and [on] organizational arrangements, and taking high risks with the firm's capital. Moreover, it has to be done in a world of rapid change, and it has to be done continuously.[7]

As a result of the multifaceted, complex, and subjective nature of corporate strategy formulation, strategic managers should give special emphasis to three major design recommendations when developing their firm's plans: selecting forecasting data, conducting environmental impact studies, and planning for flexibility.

Data Selection. Managers gather much of the forecasting information used to design strategies in the regular pursuit of business activities, e.g., reading business and government publications, discussing competitive conditions with sales managers and clients, and serving on community councils and committees. However, such personal data collection is subject to considerable bias in interpretation and its validity is often difficult to document and verify. Therefore, it is beneficial to systematically collect pertinent data from public sources. Such data are readily available, inexpensive, and in general, comparatively reliable. Public data sources include annual reports, business literature indexes, business periodicals and reference services, government publications,

[7] George A. Steiner, *Top Management Planning* (New York: Macmillan, 1969), pp. 238–39.

trade publications, stockbroker reports, and many others. While all of these sources may be examined to detect general environmental trends, managers must carefully select from among them when constructing a strategic data base. Relevance, importance, manageability, accessibility, variability, and cost must be considered in selecting or generating data to be used.

Strategy in Action 4–6

A Coal Industry Perspective

For the coal industry, 1979 was a bleak year. Spare capacity was as high as 20 percent, or 150 million tons. Miners were out of work, and mines were closing. Coal profits were off by more than 50 percent.

However, one segment of the industry appeared on the verge of remarkable gains—coal companies owned by oil companies. Eleven oil companies owned 25 percent of all the coal in the country in 1979, and had the future of coal in their grip. Moreover, oil companies planned to increase the 22 percent production share in 1979 to 50 percent by 1985.

In the past, during periods of slack demand, it was common for small mines to close; when prices firmed up, the mines reopened. In 1978, however, the growing cost and complexity of federal regulations made many such comebacks too expensive for small mines. Approximately 1,000 companies had left the coal business since the mid-1960s—about half of them since 1977.

But if costly regulation and a slack market spelled trouble to the small mines, their impact on big companies was just the opposite. "What oil companies contribute to their coal subsidiaries is staying power," said Hiram E. Bond, president of ARCO Coal Company. In fact, there was little evidence that the industry's slump in 1978 slowed big oil's plan for coal. Most of the country's top oil companies had major coal expansion programs under way. Increasingly, oil company money, technology, and management skills set the pace for coal's growth.

One reason the oil companies were banking on coal was a firmly held belief that utilities, the major coal consumers, had little choice about the fuel they burned in new plants—it had to be coal. The companies also believed that coal would be a major beneficiary of the problems of nuclear energy.

There were some problems. These included environmental laws such as the Clean Air Act and reclamation regulations. In addition, new leasing regulations for federal coal mines slowed the industry's growth. Skyrocketing transportation costs were also a factor. However, the most troubling industry problem was another touchy political issue—the growing tide of sentiment against the oil industry could lead to antitrust action against energy conglomerates.

Based on the article "The Oil Majors Bet on Coal" from the September 24, 1979, issue of *Business Week*.

Impact Studies. The nature and magnitude of the predicted impact of new strategic action is a second important consideration in designing opportunistic strategies. After forecasting data is selected, a business must conduct impact studies to determine the overall consequences of implementing available alternative strategies. In the process, the firm will transform environmental data into situation-specific environmental information. A typical impact study involves a system view in assessing probable effects on the firm's strengths and weaknesses, operating environment, competitive position, and likelihood of achieving corporate objectives, grand strategies, and mission. Although impact studies are predominately subjective and intuitive, businesses attempt to develop objective estimates whenever possible. Firms increasingly employ such techniques as exponential smoothing, time trends, and adaptive forecasting to increase the objectivity of data analysis.

Flexibility. A third important consideration in the design of strategies is the need to incorporate flexibility. Because forecasting environmental conditions, in uncertain decision makers enhance their chances of profitability if they strive for an optimal level of flexibility in their strategic plans. Several approaches to increasing such flexibility can be suggested:

1. State a strategy in general terms so that those implementing it have some discretion in terms of their unique situations.
2. Review strategies frequently.
3. Treat strategies as rules with exceptions so that an aspect of a strategy can be violated if such action can be justified.
4. Keep options open.

While flexibility in a strategic plan will lessen the plan's benefits by increasing costs, shortening planning and action horizons, and increasing internal uncertainty, an overly rigid stance in support of a particular strategy can be devastating to a firm faced with unexpected environmental turbulence.

Summary

The external environment of a business consists of two interrelated sets of variables that play a principal role in determining the opportunities, threats, and constraints a firm faces. Variables originating beyond and usually irrespective of any single firm's operating situation (political, economic, social, and technological forces) form the remote environment. Variables influencing a firm's immediate competitive situation (competitive position, customer profiles, suppliers and creditors, and the accessible labor market) constitute the operating environment. These two sets of forces provide many of the challenges faced by a particular firm in attempting to attract or acquire needed resources, and when striving to profitably market its goods and services. Environmental assessment is more complicated for MNCs because multinationals must evaluate several environments simultaneously.

Designing corporate strategies that will enable a firm to effectively interact with a dynamic external environment is multifaceted, complex, and often principally dependent on fairly subjective and intuitive assessments. Nevertheless, assessments of a firm's external environment can provide a valuable planning base, especially when three major recommendations are followed.

1. Environmental data should be collected for a meaningful range of factors. The personal perceptions of strategic managers should be combined with data from public sources.
2. Impact studies should be undertaken to convert the data into relevant information used in determining the overall consequences for the firm of implementing the available alternative strategies.
3. Flexibility should be incorporated in the strategy to allow for unexpected variations from the environmental forecasts.

Thus, designing opportunistic strategies is based on the conviction that a company which can anticipate future business conditions will improve its performance and profitability. Despite the uncertainty and dynamic nature of the business environment, an assessment process that narrows, if not precisely defines, future expectations is of substantial value to strategic managers.

Questions for Discussion

1. Briefly describe two important recent changes in the remote external environment of U.S business in each of the following areas:
   a. Economic.
   b. Political.
   c. Social.
   d. Technological.
2. Describe two major anticipated environmental changes that you forecast as having a major impact on the wholesale food industry in the next 10 years.
3. Develop a competitor profile for your college and the one geographically closest to it. Next, prepare a brief strategic plan to improve the competitive position of the weaker of the two schools.
4. Assume that a competitively priced synthetic fuel is invented that could supply 25 percent of U.S. energy needs within 20 years. In what major ways might the external environment of U.S. business be changed:
5. With the help of your instructor, identify a local business that has enjoyed great growth in recent years. To what degree and in what ways do you think this firm's success resulted from taking advantage of favorable conditions in its external remote and operating environments?

Bibliography

Capon, N.; Farley, Jr.; and J. Hulbert. "International Diffusion of Corporate and Strategic Planning Practices." *Columbia Journal of World Business,* Fall 1980, pp. 5–13.

Channon, D. F., and M. Jalland. *Multinational Strategic Planning.* New York: AMACOM, 1978.

Conover, Horbart H. "Meeting the New Social Concerns." *Management World,* May 1977, pp. 25–27.

Contractor, F. J. "The Role of Licensing in International Strategy." *Columbia Journal of World Business,* Winter 1981, pp. 73–83.

Cox, Joan G. "Planning for Technological Innovation." *Long-Range Planning,* December 1977, pp. 40–44.

Davidson, W. H. *Global Strategic Management.* New York: John Wiley & Sons, 1982.

Dymsza, W. A. *Multinational Business Strategy.* New York: McGraw-Hill, 1972.

Fayerweather, J., and A. Kapoor. *Strategy and Negotiation for the International Corporation.* Cambridge, Mass.: Ballinger, 1976.

Gerstenfeld, Arthur. "Technological Forecasting." *Journal of Business* 44 (1971), pp. 10–18.

Healey, Dennis F. "Environmental Pressures and Marketing in the 1970s." *Long-Range Planning,* June 1975, pp. 41–45.

Hout, T.; M. Porter; and E. Rudden. "How Global Companies Win Out." *Harvard Business Review,* September–October 1982, pp. 98–108.

Kiser, J. W. "Tapping Eastern Bloc Technology." *Harvard Business Review,* March–April 1982, pp. 85–93.

Neubauer, F. Fredrick, and Norman B. Solomon. "Managerial Approach to Environmental Assessment." *Long-Range Planning,* April 1977, pp. 13–20.

Perry, P. T. "Mechanisms for Environmental Scanning." *Long-Range Planning,* June 1977, pp. 2–9.

Pfeffer, Jeffery, and Gerald Salancik. *The External Control of Organizations.* New York: Harper & Row, 1978.

Preble, John. "Corporate Use of Environmental Scanning." *University of Michigan Business Review,"* September 1978, pp. 12–17.

Ronstadt, R., and R. Kramer. "Getting the Most out of Innovation Abroad." *Harvard Business Review,* March–April 1982, pp. 94–99.

Sadler, Philip. "Management and the Social Environment." *Long-Range Planning,* April 1975, pp. 18–26.

Steade, Richard. "Multinational Corporations and the Changing World Economic Order." *California Management Review,* Winter 1978, pp. 5–12.

Steiner, George A. *Top Management Planning.* New York: Macmillan, 1969.

Turner, Robert C. "Should You Take a Business Forecasting Seriously?" *Business Horizons,* April 1978, pp. 64–72.

Watson, C. M. "Counter Competition Abroad to Protect Home Markets." *Harvard Business Review,* January–February 1982, pp. 40–42.

Chapter 4 Cohesion Case Illustration

Environmental Assessment at Holiday Inns, Inc.

Environmental assessment at Holiday Inns, Inc., must first involve evaluation of the remote and operating environments of each business group. Afterwards, these evaluations would be synthesized to determine the environmental situation facing the overall corporate enterprise. This Cohesion Case Illustration will briefly analyze the remote and operating environments of the key business groups using a tabular format. To aid in this analysis, a scale from +10 to −10 will be used to identify the degree to which each environmental factor represents an opportunity or threat in the business's environment.

Comparing the remote environments in Exhibit 1, Holiday Inns' most favorable opportunities appear in the three hospitality-related businesses: hotels, restaurants, and casinos. Social factors in the remote environment are strongly favorable for all three businesses. The remote environment presents a moderate opportunity for the steamship operation, but is inconsequential for the products group. The major remote-environment threats appear in relations to the Trailways bus operation. Next the operating environments will be evaluated.

Exhibit 2 examines the operating environments of each business group. The operating environments presenting the greatest opportunity are those of the hotel and casino groups. The similarity of their competitive advantages (existing or potential) and favorable opportunities suggest strong synergy between the two groups from a corporate perspective. The operating environment of freestanding restaurants appears favorable, with several dimensions suggesting limited but clearly exploitable opportunities. Delta Steamship encounters selectively favorable opportunities, while Trailways' operating environment presents several formidable threats.

From a corporate perspective, the remote- and operating-environment analyses identify factors suggesting that the greatest opportunities exist in hospitality-related businesses and the most pressing threats face the Trailways bus operation.

Exhibit 1

Assessment of remote environment factors

Business	***Economy***	***Political***	***Social***	***Technology***
Hotels	Reduced vacation travel during recessions/energy costs *(23,24)* (−4)	Legal challenges to franchise agreement/political stability of international locations *(12,14)* (−2)	Increasing leisure time/older population/single travelers and smaller families/baby boom now 25–40 years old *(49)* (+8)	Electronic and computer technology in reservations and control systems/satellite communication/labor-saving technologies *(16,19)* (+6)
Products group	Reduced demand during recession (−2)	? (0)	Changing preferences in furnishings (+3)	Labor-saving technology/obsolescence of current equipment lines (+1)
Trailways	Less travel during recession but bus is a low-priced alternative means of transportation *(33,34)* (+1)	Safety regulations/no government ownership of terminals/deregulation of airline industry (−5)	All of the factors in above hotel block applicable here, though considerably less beneficial *(49)* (−2)	Labor-saving and cost-saving technology only minimal benefits, other transportation areas more affected *(38)* (−3)
Delta Steamship	Recession can hurt exports and imports/energy costs (−3)	Emergence of Third World markets/U.S. subsidies of U.S.-flag carriers and low-interest loans (+5)	Increasing concern for U.S. international trade effectiveness *(44)* (+1)	Labor-saving (LASH) and energy-saving technologies *(43)* (+3)
Freestanding restaurants	Recessions generally have a limited impact on family restaurants/energy costs less severe (+2)	Legal challenges to franchising (−1)	Increasing pattern of eating out/baby boom now 25–40/number of single-member households rising/women in work force *(49)* (+8)	Labor-saving and energy-saving improvements/food preparation technology (+4)
Casino gaming	Recessionary impact on leisure travel/energy costs *(67)* (−2)	Regulation of casino gambling/limited legal gaming markets *(69)* (−2)	All the factors mentioned in the hotel block above/increasing social acceptance of gaming *(49,61,62)* (+8)	Similar to hotel above though with less impact (+3)

Note: Italicized numbers in parentheses at the end of the comments refer to paragraph numbers in the business case study at the end of Chapter 1. Each comment is based on the information provided in the paragraphs identified in italics.

Exhibit 2

Assessment of operating environment factors

Business	*Competition*	*Customers*	*Labor*	*Creditors*	*Suppliers*
Hotel group	Substantial increase in the number of budget-chain competitors/no immediate threat to HI's leadership position but gap is narrowing, especially with budget-conscious traveler *(23)* (+3)	1 out of 6 American travelers stayed at HIs in 1978/research shows HI to be the preference of 40 percent of traveling public—high but declining since 1975/ages 24–49 with +$20,000 incomes most frequent guest/increasing number of single travelers and women travelers (25 percent in 1979)/steady demand for HI franchise with over 60 percent of new franchise locations sought by current franchises *(23)* (+6)	Adequate labor supply although HI's labor-sensitive operating margins hurt by minimum wage increases (+2)	Strong capital structure, undervalued real estate and leadership position make credit readily available *(73)* (+5)	Gasoline cost for customers is rising, which begins to curtail travel (−2)
Products group	Major competition outside the HI customer system/competitors don't operate in captive mode which can allow more freedom/some competitors more price competitive on standardized items (−2)	Large captive market via HI system/limited competitive experience outside this captive market/franchises' resistance to being required to buy through product group businesses certain standardized items *(23)* (+3)	Decreasing labor intensity via mechanization (+2)	Because of low profit margins and sales that come from HI properties (company-owned and franchises) the PG must seek capital resources primarily within corporate structure (−1)	Readily available suppliers; cost of raw materials and other supplies are rapidly escalating. (0)
Trailways	Powerful competition from Greyhound on price, facilities, size, etc./increasing competition from other transportation sectors like airlines, trains, and package delivery services/intensive price-cost squeeze *(33,34)* (−6)	Customer profile quite different from typical HI guest, especially in income/limited gains in passenger miles since 1975/no strong customer loyalty *(32)* (−2)	Labor cost rising though some labor-saving technology improvements (−1)	Weak capital structure in highly competitive industry lessens available credit (−2)	Energy costs, especially fuel, rising significantly (−3)

Exhibit 2 *(concluded)*

Delta Steamship	Stiff competition from foreign cargo vessels in all routes/LASH technology improving relative position/major U.S.-flag carrier *(43,45)* (+2)	Primarily agriculture and manufacturing importers and exporters at both ends of route structure/strong in Gulf ports area *(42)* (+2)	Severely dependent on independent longshore workers/decreasing labor intensity via LASH technology *(43,47)* (−2)	Legislation access to U.S. government low-interest loans and cost subsidies *(45)* (+5)	Energy costs, especially fuel, rising significantly (−3)
Freestanding restaurants	Stiff competition from several nationwide chains, but Perkins' position in northern U.S. rather strong/expanding primary demand which negates, to some extent, competitive impact/opportunities for additional acquisition *(55,56)* (+1)	Customers profile quite similar to typical HI guest/family-oriented image/good brand identity in current geographic locations/trend of increased outside dining and more single households quite favorable/substantial franchise network and interest *(50)* (+5)	Nonskilled labor positions/labor intensive/adequate supply though profit margins sensitive to minimum wage (+1)	Adequate capital structure and operating history for outside credit/HI corporate resources *(73)* (+2)	Rising energy costs in operating units and in food products (−2)
Casino gaming	Growing competition in each of the four legalized gambling markets in U.S./but no dominant competitor overall/rapidly growing primary demand related to increased leisure time and aging population *(69)* (+5)	Customer profile very similar to typical HI guest/HI name, image, and reputation should prove quite beneficial/changing population demographics—baby boom age, single households, increasing leisure time—are strongly favorable *(61)* (+8)	Temporary labor shortages but benefit by HI link in hotel, food, and lodging side/rising labor costs *(61)* (−2)	Impressive profit potential but too early to tell/HI corporate resources *(62,63)* (+1)	Fuel-sensitive business and energy-intensive facilities (−3)

Note: Italicized numbers in parentheses at the end of the comments refer to paragraph numbers in the business case study at the end of Chapter 1.

CHAPTER

5

Industry Analysis

Foreword

In 1980, Professor Michael E. Porter of Harvard University published a book titled *Competitive Strategy.* It propelled the concept of industry analysis into the foreground of strategic thought and business planning. The cornerstone of the book is the following article from the *Harvard Business Review* in which Porter emphasized five forces that shape industry competition. His well-defined analytical framework helps strategic managers to understand industry dynamics and to correctly anticipate the impact of remote factors on a firm's operating environment.

The Authors

Overview

The nature and degree of competition in an industry hinge on five forces: the threat of new entrants, the bargaining power of customers, the bargaining power of suppliers, the threat of substitute products or services (where applicable), and the jockeying among current contestants. To establish a strategic agenda for dealing with these contending currents and to grow despite them, a company must understand how they work in its industry and how they affect the company in its particular situation. This chapter will detail how these forces operate and suggests ways of adjusting to them, and, where possible, of taking advantage of them.

How Competitive Forces Shape Strategy

The essence of strategy formulation is coping with competition. Yet it is easy to view competition too narrowly and too pessimistically. While one sometimes hears executives complaining to the contrary, intense competition in an industry is neither coincidence nor bad luck.

Moreover, in the fight for market share, competition is not manifested only in the other players. Rather, competition in an industry is rooted in its underlying economics, and competitive forces exist that go well beyond the established combatants in a particular industry. Customers, suppliers, potential entrants, and substitute products are all competitors that may be more or less prominent or active depending on the industry.

The state of competition in an industry depends on five basic forces, which are diagramed in Figure 5–1. The collective strength of these forces determines the ultimate profit potential of an industry. It ranges from intense in industries

Figure 5–1

Forces driving industry competition

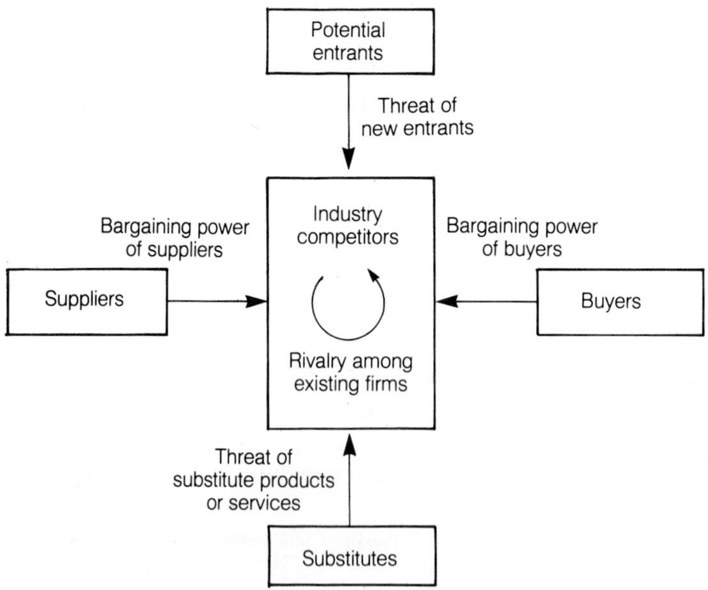

like tires, metal cans, and steel, where no company earns spectacular returns on investment, to mild in industries like oil-field services and equipment, soft drinks, and toiletries, where there is room for quite high returns.

In the economists' "perfectly competitive" industry, jockeying for position is unbridled and entry to the industry very easy. This kind of industry structure, of course, offers the worst prospect for long-run profitability. The weaker the forces collectively, however, the greater the opportunity for superior performance.

Whatever their collective strength, the corporate strategist's goal is to find a position in the industry where his or her company can best defend itself against these forces or can influence them in its favor. The collective strength of the forces may be painfully apparent to all the antagonists; but to cope with them, the strategist must delve below the surface and analyze the sources of competition. For example, what makes the industry vulnerable to entry? What determines the bargaining power of suppliers?

Knowledge of these underlying sources of competitive pressure provides the groundwork for a strategic agenda of action. They highlight the critical strengths and weaknesses of the company, animate the positioning of the company in its industry, clarify the areas where strategic changes may yield the greatest payoff, and highlight the places where industry trends promise to hold the greatest significance as either opportunities or threats.

Understanding these sources also proves to be of help in considering areas for diversification.

Contending Forces

The strongest competitive force or forces determine the profitability of an industry and so are of greatest importance in strategy formulation. For example, even a company with a strong position in an industry unthreatened by potential entrants will earn low returns if it faces a superior or a lower-cost substitute product—as the leading manufacturers of vacuum tubes and coffee percolators have learned to their sorrow. In such a situation, coping with the substitute product becomes the number one strategic priority.

Different forces take on prominence, of course, in shaping competition in each industry. In the ocean-going tanker industry the key force is probably the buyers (the major oil companies), while in tires it is powerful OEM buyers coupled with tough competitors. In the steel industry the key forces are foreign competitors and substitute materials.

Every industry has an underlying structure, or a set of fundamental economic and technical characteristics, that gives rise to these competitive forces. The strategist, wanting to position his company to cope best with its industry environment or to influence that environment in the company's favor, must learn what makes the environment tick.

This view of competition pertains equally to industries dealing in services and to those selling products. To avoid monotony in this article, I refer to both products and services as "products." The same general principles apply to all types of business.

A few characteristics are critical to the strength of each competitive force. They will be discussed in this section.

Threat of Entry

New entrants to an industry bring new capacity, the desire to gain market share, and often substantial resources. Companies diversifying through acquisition into the industry from other markets often leverage their resources to cause a shape-up, as Phillip Morris did with Miller beer.

The seriousness of the threat of entry depends on the barriers present and on the reaction from existing competitors that the entrant can expect. If barriers to entry are high and a newcomer can expect sharp retaliation from the entrenched competitors, obviously he will not pose a serious threat of entering.

There are six major sources of barriers to entry:

1. Economies of Scale. These economies deter entry by forcing the aspirant either to come in on a large scale or to accept a cost disadvantage. Scale economies in production, research, marketing, and service are probably the key barriers to entry in the mainframe computer industry, as Xerox and GE sadly discovered. Economies of scale can also act as hurdles in distribution, utilization of the sales force, financing, and nearly any other part of a business.

2. Product Differentiation. Brand identification creates a barrier by forcing entrants to spend heavily to overcome customer loyalty. Advertising, customer service, being first in the industry, and product differences are among the factors fostering brand identification. It is perhaps the most important entry barrier in soft drinks, over-the-counter drugs, cosmetics, investment banking, and public accounting. To create high fences around their business, brewers couple brand identification with economies of scale in production, distribution, and marketing.

3. Capital Requirements. The need to invest large financial resources in order to compete creates a barrier to entry, particularly if the capital is required for unrecoverable expenditures in up-front advertising or R&D. Capital is necessary not only for fixed facilities but also for customer credit, inventories, and absorbing start-up losses. While major corporations have the financial resources to invade almost any industry, the huge capital requirements in certain fields, such as computer manufacturing and mineral extraction, limit the pool of likely entrants.

4. Cost Disadvantages Independent of Size. Entrenched companies may have cost advantages not available to potential rivals, no matter what their size and attainable economies of scale. These advantages can stem from the effects of the learning curve (and of its first cousin, the experience curve), proprietary technology, access to the best raw materials sources, assets purchased at preinflation prices, government subsidies, or favorable locations. Sometimes cost advantages are legally enforceable, as they are through patents. (For an analysis of the much-discussed experience curve as a barrier to entry, see Strategy in Action 5–1.)

Strategy in Action 5–1

The Experience Curve as an Entry Barrier

In recent years, the experience curve has become widely discussed as a key element of industry structure. According to this concept, unit costs in many manufacturing industries (some dogmatic adherents say in all manufacturing industries) as well as in some service industries decline with "experience," or a particular company's cumulative volume of production. (The experience curve, which encompasses many factors, is a broader concept than the better-known learning curve, which refers to the efficiency achieved over a period of time by workers through much repetition.)

The causes of the decline in unit costs are a combination of elements, including economies of scale, the learning curve for labor, and capital-labor substitution. The cost decline creates a barrier to entry because new competitors with no "experience" face higher costs than established ones, particularly the producer with the largest market share, and have difficulty catching up with the entrenched competitors.

Adherents of the experience curve concept stress the importance of achieving market leadership to maximize this barrier to entry, and they recommend aggressive action to achieve it, such as price cutting in anticipation of falling costs in order to build volume. For the combatant that cannot achieve a healthy market share, the prescription is usually, "Get out."

Is the experience curve an entry barrier on which strategies should be built? The answer is: not in every industry. In fact, in some industries, building a strategy on the experience curve can be potentially disastrous. That costs decline with experience in some industries is not news to corporate executives. The significance of the experience curve for strategy depends on what factors are causing the decline.

A new entrant may well be more efficient than the more experienced competi-

Strategy in Action 5–1 *(concluded)*

tors; if it has built the newest plant, it will face no disadvantage in having to catch up. The strategic prescription, "You must have the largest, most efficient plant," is a lot different from "You must produce the greatest cumulative output of the item to get your costs down."

Whether a drop in costs with cumulative (not absolute) volume erects an entry barrier also depends on the sources of the decline. If costs go down because of technical advances known generally in the industry or because of the development of improved equipment that can be copied or purchased from equipment suppliers, the experience curve is not entry barrier at all—in fact, new or less experienced competitors may actually enjoy a cost advantage over the leaders. Free of the legacy of heavy past investments, the newcomer or less-experienced competitor can purchase or copy the newest and lowest-cost equipment and technology.

If, however, experience can be kept proprietary, the leaders will maintain a cost advantage. But new entrants may require less experience to reduce their costs than the leaders needed. All this suggests that the experience curve can be a shaky entry barrier on which to build a strategy.

While space does not permit a complete treatment here, I want to mention a few other crucial elements in determining the appropriateness of a strategy built on the entry barrier provided by the experience curve:

> The height of the barrier depends on how important costs are to competition compared with other areas like marketing, selling, and innovation.
>
> The barrier can be nullified by product or process innovations leading to a substantially new technology and thereby creating an entirely new experience curve. New entrants can leapfrog the industry leaders and alight on the new experience curve, to which those leaders may be poorly positioned to jump.
>
> If more than one strong company is building its strategy on the experience curve, the consequences can be nearly fatal. By the time only one rival is left pursuing such a strategy, industry growth may have stopped and the prospects of reaping the spoils of victory long since evaporated.

5. Access to Distribution Channels. The new boy on the block must, of course, secure distribution of his product or service. A new food product, for example, must displace others from the supermarket shelf via price breaks, promotions, intense selling efforts, or some other means. The more limited the wholesale or retail channels are and the more that existing competitors have these tied up, obviously the tougher that entry into the industry will be. Sometimes this barrier is so high that, to surmount it, a new contestant must create its own distribution channels, as Timex did in the watch industry in the 1950s.

6. Government Policy. The government can limit or even foreclose entry to industries with such controls as license requirements and limits on access to raw materials. Regulated industries like trucking, liquor retailing, and freight forwarding are noticeable examples; more subtle government restrictions operate in fields like ski-area development and coal mining. The government also can play a major indirect role by affecting entry barriers through controls such as air and water pollution standards and safety regulations.

The potential rival's expectations about the reaction of existing competitors also will influence its decision on whether to enter. The company is likely to have second thoughts if incumbents have previously lashed out at new entrants or if:

The incumbents possess substantial resources to fight back, including excess cash and unused borrowing power, productive capacity, or clout with distribution channels and customers.

The incumbents seem likely to cut prices because of a desire to keep market shares or because of industrywide excess capacity.

Industry growth is slow, affecting its ability to absorb the new arrival and probably causing the financial performance of all the parties involved to decline.

Changing Conditions. From a strategic standpoint there are two important additional points to note about the threat of entry.

First, it changes, of course, as these conditions change. The expiration of Polaroid's basic patents on instant photography, for instance, greatly reduced its absolute cost entry barrier built by proprietary technology. It is not surprising that Kodak plunged into the market. Product differentiation in printing has all but disappeared. Conversely, in the auto industry economies of scale increased enormously with post–World War II automation and vertical integration—virtually stopping successful new entry.

Second, strategic decisions involving a large segment of an industry can have a major impact on the conditions determining the threat of entry. For example, the actions of many U.S. wine producers in the 1960s to step up product introductions, raise advertising levels, and expand distribution nationally surely strengthened the entry roadblocks by raising economies of scale and making access to distribution channels more difficult. Similarly, decisions by members of the recreational vehicle industry to vertically integrate in order to lower costs have greatly increased the economies of scale and raised the capital costs barriers.

Powerful Suppliers and Buyers

Suppliers can exert bargaining power on participants in an industry by raising prices or reducing the quality of purchased goods and services. Powerful suppliers can thereby squeeze profitability out of an industry unable to recover cost increases in its own prices. By raising their prices, soft-drink concentrate producers have contributed to the erosion of profitability of bottling companies because the bottlers, facing intense competition from powdered mixes, fruit drinks, and other beverages, have limited freedom to raise their prices accordingly. Customers likewise can force down prices, demand higher quality or more service, and play competitors off against each other—all at the expense of industry profits.

The power of each important supplier or buyer group depends on a number of characteristics of its market situation and on the relative importance of its sales or purchases to the industry compared with its overall business.

A *supplier* group is powerful if:

It is dominated by a few companies and is more concentrated than the industry it sells to.

Its product is unique or at least differentiated, or if it has built up switching costs. Switching costs are fixed costs buyers face in changing suppliers. These arise because, among other things, a buyer's product specifications tie it to particular suppliers, it has invested heavily in specialized ancillary equipment or in learning how to operate a supplier's equipment (as in computer software), or its production lines are connected to the supplier's manufacturing facilities (as in some manufacture of beverage containers).

It is not obliged to contend with other products for sale to the industry. For instance, the competition between the steel companies and the aluminum companies to sell to the can industry checks the power of each supplier.

It poses a credible threat of integrating forward into the industry's business. This provides a check against the industry's ability to improve the terms on which it purchases.

The industry is not an important customer of the supplier group. If the industry is an important customer, suppliers' fortunes will be closely tied to the industry, and they will want to protect the industry through reasonable pricing and assistance in activities like R&D and lobbying.

A *buyer* group is powerful if:

It is concentrated or purchases in large volumes. Large-volume buyers are particularly potent forces if heavy fixed costs characterize the industry—as they do in metal containers, corn refining, and bulk chemicals, for example—which raise the stakes to keep capacity filled.

The products it purchases from the industry are standard or undifferentiated. The buyers, sure that they can always find alternative suppliers, may play one company against another, as they do in aluminum extrusion.

The products it purchases from the industry form a component of its product and represent a significant fraction of its cost. The buyers are likely to shop for a favorable price and purchase selectively. Where the product sold by the industry in question is a small fraction of buyers' costs, buyers are usually much less price sensitive.

It earns low profits, which create great incentive to lower its purchasing costs. Highly profitable buyers, however, are generally less price sensitive (that is, of course, if the item does not represent a large fraction of their costs).

The industry's product is unimportant to the quality of the buyers' products or services. Where the quality of the buyers' products is very much affected by the industry's product, buyers are generally less price sensitive. Industries in which this situation obtains include oil-field equipment, where a malfunction can lead to large losses; and enclosures for electronic medical and test instruments, where the quality of the enclosure can influence the user's impression about the quality of the equipment inside.

The industry's product does not save the buyer money. Where the industry's product or service can pay for itself many times over, the buyer is rarely price sensitive; rather, he is interested in quality. This is true in services like investment banking and public accounting, where errors in judgment can be costly and embarrassing, and in businesses like the logging of oil wells, where an accurate survey can save thousands of dollars in drilling costs.

The buyers pose a credible threat of integrating backward to make the industry's product. The Big Three auto producers and major buyers of cars have often used the threat of self-manufacture as a bargaining lever. But sometimes an industry engenders a threat to buyers that its members may integrate forward.

Most of these sources of buyer power can be attributed to consumers as a group as well as to industrial and commercial buyers; only a modification of the frame of reference is necessary. Consumers tend to be more price sensitive if they are purchasing products that are undifferentiated, expensive relative to their incomes, and of a sort where quality is not particularly important.

The buying power of retailers is determined by the same rules, with one important addition. Retailers can gain significant bargaining power over manufacturers when they can influence consumers' purchasing decisions, as they do in audio components, jewelry, appliances, sporting goods, and other goods.

Strategic Action. A company's choice of suppliers to buy from or buyer groups to sell to should be viewed as a crucial strategic decision. A company can improve its strategic posture by finding suppliers or buyers who possess the least power to influence it adversely.

Most common is the situation of a company being able to choose whom it will sell to—in other words, buyer selection. Rarely do all the buyer groups a company sells to enjoy equal power. Even if a company sells to a single industry, segments usually exist within that industry that exercise less power (and that are therefore less price sensitive) than others. For example, the replacement market for most products is less price sensitive than the overall market.

As a rule, a company can sell to powerful buyers and still come away with above-average profitability only if it is a low-cost producer in its industry or if its product enjoys some unusual, if not unique, features. In supplying large customers with electric motors, Emerson Electric earns high returns because its low cost position permits the company to meet or undercut competitors' prices.

If the company lacks a low cost position or a unique product, selling to everyone is self-defeating because the more sales it achieves, the more vulnerable it becomes. The company may have to muster the courage to turn away business and sell only to less potent customers.

Buyer selection has been a key to the success of National Can and Crown, Cork and Seal. They focus on the segments of the can industry where they can create product differentiation, minimize the threat of backward integration, and otherwise mitigate the awesome power of their customers. Of course, some industries do not enjoy the luxury of selecting "good" buyers.

As the factors creating supplier and buyer power change with time or as a result of a company's strategic decisions, naturally the power of these groups rises or declines. In the ready-to-wear clothing industry, as the buyers (department stores and clothing stores) have become more concentrated and control has passed to large chains, the industry has come under increasing pressure and suffered falling margins. The industry has been unable to differentiate its product or engender switching costs that lock in its buyers enough to neutralize these trends.

Substitute Products

By placing a ceiling on prices it can charge, substitute products or services limit the potential of an industry. Unless it can upgrade the quality of the product or differentiate it somehow (as via marketing), the industry will suffer in earnings and possibly in growth.

Manifestly, the more attractive the price-performance trade-off offered by substitute products, the firmer the lid placed on the industry's profit potential. Sugar producers confronted with the large-scale commercialization of high-fructose corn syrup, a sugar substitute, are learning this lesson today.

Substitutes not only limit profits in normal times, they also reduce the bonanza an industry can reap in boom times. In 1978 the producers of fiberglass insulation enjoyed unprecedented demand as a result of high energy costs and severe winter weather. But the industry's ability to raise prices was tempered by the plethora of insulation substitutes, including cellulose, rock wool, and styrofoam. These substitutes are bound to become an even stronger force once the current round of plant additions by fiberglass insulation producers has boosted capacity enough to meet demand (and then some).

Substitute products that deserve the most attention strategically are those that *(a)* are subject to trends improving their price-performance trade-off with the industry's product or *(b)* are produced by industries earning high profits. Substitutes often come rapidly into play if some development increases competition in their industries and causes price reduction or performance improvement.

Jockeying for Position

Rivalry among existing competitors takes the familiar form of jockeying for position—using tactics like price competition, product introduction, and advertising slugfests. Intense rivalry is related to the presence of a number of factors:

Competitors are numerous or are roughly equal in size and power. In many U.S. industries in recent years foreign contenders, of course, have become part of the competitive picture.

Industry growth is slow, precipitating fights for market share that involve expansion-minded members.

The product or service lacks differentiation or switching costs, which lock in buyers and protect one combatant from raids on its customers by another.

Fixed costs are high or the product is perishable, creating strong temptation to cut prices. Many basic materials businesses, like paper and aluminum, suffer from this problem when demand slackens.

Capacity is normally augmented in large increments. Such additions, as in the chlorine and vinyl chloride businesses, disrupt the industry's supply-demand balance and often lead to periods of overcapacity and price cutting.

Exit barriers are high. Exit barriers, like very specialized assets or management's loyalty to a particular business, keep companies competing even though they may be earning low or even negative returns on investment. Excess capacity remains functioning, and the profitability of the healthy competitors suffers as the sick ones hang on. If the entire industry suffers from overcapacity, it may seek government help—particularly if foreign competition is present.

The rivals are diverse in strategies, origins, and "personalities." They have different ideas about how to compete and continually run head-on into each other in the process.

As an industry matures, its growth rate changes, resulting in declining profits and (often) a shakeout. In the booming recreational vehicle industry of the early 1970s, nearly every producer did well; but slow growth since then has eliminated the high returns, except for the strongest members, not to mention many of the weaker companies. The same profit story has been played out in industry after industry—snowmobiles, aerosol packaging, and sports equipment are just a few examples.

An acquisition can introduce a very different personality to an industry, as has been the case with Black & Decker's takeover of McCullough, the producer of chain saws. Technological innovation can boost the level of fixed costs in the production process, as it did in the shift from batch to continuous-line photo finishing in the 1960s.

While a company must live with many of these factors—because they are built into industry economics—it may have some latitude for improving matters through strategic shifts. For example, it may try to raise buyer's switching costs or increase product differentiation. A focus on selling efforts in the fastest-growing segments of the industry or on market areas with the lowest fixed costs can reduce the impact of industry rivalry. If it is feasible, a company can try to avoid confrontation with competitors having high exit barriers and can thus sidestep involvement in bitter price cutting.

Formulation of Strategy

Once the corporate strategist has assessed the forces affecting competition in his industry and their underlying causes, he can identify his company's strengths and weaknesses. The crucial strengths and weaknesses from a strategic standpoint are the company's posture vis-à-vis the underlying causes of each force. Where does it stand against substitutes? Against the sources of entry barriers?

Then the strategist can devise a plan of action that may include (1) positioning the company so that its capabilities provide the best defense against the competitive force; and/or (2) influencing the balance of the forces through strategic moves, thereby improving the company's position; and/or (3) anticipating shifts in the factors underlying the forces and responding to them, with the hope of exploiting change by choosing a strategy appropriate for the new competitive balance before opponents recognize it. Each strategic approach will now be considered in turn.

Positioning the Company

The first approach takes the structure of the industry as given and matches the company's strengths and weaknesses to it. Strategy can be viewed as building defenses against the competitive forces or as finding positions in the industry where the forces are weakest.

Knowledge of the company's capabilities and of the causes of the competitive forces will highlight the areas where the company should confront competition and where to avoid it. If the company is a low-cost producer, it may choose to confront powerful buyers while it takes care to sell them only products not vulnerable to competition from substitutes.

The success of Dr Pepper in the soft-drink industry illustrates the coupling of realistic knowledge of corporate strengths with sound industry analysis to yield a superior strategy. Coca-Cola and Pepsi-Cola dominate Dr Pepper's industry, where many small concentrate producers compete for a piece of the action. Dr Pepper chose a strategy of avoiding the largest-selling drink segment, maintaining a narrow flavor line, forgoing the development of a captive bottler network, and marketing heavily. The company positioned itself so as to be least vulnerable to its competitive forces while it exploited its small size.

In the $11.5 billion soft-drink industry, barriers to entry in the form of brand identification, large-scale marketing, and access to a bottler network are enormous. Rather than accept the formidable costs and scale economies in having its own bottler network—that, following the lead of the Big Two and of 7UP—Dr Pepper took advantage of the different flavor of its drink to "piggyback" on Coke and Pepsi bottlers who wanted a full line to sell to customers. Dr Pepper coped with the power of these buyers through extraordinary service and other efforts to distinguish its treatment of them from that of Coke and Pepsi.

Many small companies in the soft-drink business offer cola drinks that thrust them into head-to-head competition against the majors. Dr Pepper, however, maximized product differentiation by maintaining a narrow line of beverages built around an unusual flavor.

Finally, Dr Pepper met Coke and Pepsi with an advertising onslaught emphasizing the alleged uniqueness of its single flavor. This campaign built strong brand identification and great customer loyalty. Helping its efforts was the fact that Dr Pepper's formula involved lower raw-materials cost, which gave the company an absolute cost advantage over its major competitors.

There are no economies of scale in soft-drink concentrate production, so Dr Pepper could prosper despite its small share of the business (6 percent). Thus, Dr Pepper confronted competition in marketing but avoided it in product line and in distribution. This artful positioning combined with good implementation has led to an enviable record in earnings and in the stock market.

Influencing the Balance

When dealing with the forces that drive industry competition, a company can devise a strategy that takes the offensive. This posture is designed to do more than merely cope with the forces themselves; it is meant to alter their causes.

Innovations in marketing can raise brand identification or otherwise differentiate the product. Capital investments in large-scale facilities or vertical integration affect entry barriers. The balance of forces is partly a result of external factors and partly in the company's control.

Exploiting Industry Change

Industry evolution is important strategically because evolution, of course, brings with it changes in the sources of competition. In the familiar product life-cycle pattern, for example, growth rates change, product differentiation is said to decline as the business becomes more mature, and the companies tend to integrate vertically.

These trends are not so important in themselves; what is critical is whether they affect the sources of competition. Consider vertical integration. In the maturing minicomputer industry, extensive vertical integration, both in manufacturing and in software development, is taking place. This very significant trend is greatly raising economies of scale as well as the amount of capital necessary to compete in the industry. This is turn is raising barriers to entry and may drive some smaller competitors out of the industry once growth levels off.

Obviously, the trends carrying the highest priority from a strategic standpoint are those that affect the most important sources of competition in the industry and those that elevate new causes to the forefront. In contract aerosol packaging, for example, the trend toward less product differentiation is now dominant. It has increased buyers' power, lowered the barriers to entry, and intensified competition.

The framework for analyzing competition can also be used to predict the eventual profitability of an industry. In long-range planning the task is to examine each competitive force, forecast the magnitude of each underlying cause, and then construct a composite picture of the likely profit potential of the industry.

The outcome of such an exercise may differ a great deal from the existing industry structure. Today, for example, the solar heating business is populated by dozens and perhaps hundreds of companies, none with a major market position. Entry is easy, and competitors are battling to establish solar heating as a superior substitute for conventional methods.

The potential of this industry will depend largely on the shape of future barriers to entry, the improvement of the industry's position relative to substitutes, the ultimate intensity of competition, and the power captured by buyers and suppliers. These characteristics will in turn, be influenced by such factors as the establishment of brand identities, significant economies of scale or experience curves in equipment manufacture wrought by technological change, the ultimate capital costs to compete, and the extent of overhead in production facilities.

The framework for analyzing industry competition has direct benefits in setting diversification strategy. It provides a road map for answering the extremely difficult question inherent in diversification decisions: "What is the potential of this business?" Combining the framework with judgment in its application, a company may be able to spot an industry with a good future before this good future is reflected in the prices of acquisition candidates.

Multifaceted Rivalry

Corporate managers have directed a great deal of attention to defining their businesses as a crucial step in strategy formulation. Numerous authorities have stressed the need to look beyond product to function in defining a business, beyond national boundaries to potential international competition, and beyond the ranks of one's competitors today to those that may become competitors tomorrow. As a result of these urgings, the proper definition of a company's industry or industries has become an endlessly debated subject.

One motive behind this debate is the desire to exploit new markets. Another, perhaps more important motive is the fear of overlooking latent sources of competition that someday may threaten the industry. Many managers concentrate so single-mindedly on their direct antagonists in the fight for market share that they fail to realize that they are also competing with their customers and their suppliers for bargaining power. Meanwhile, they also neglect to keep a wary eye out for new entrants to the contest or fail to recognize the subtle threat of substitute products.

The key to growth—even survival—is to stake out a position that is less vulnerable to attack from head-to-head opponents, whether established or new, and less vulnerable to erosion from the direction of buyers, suppliers, and substitute goods. Establishing such a position can take many forms—solidifying relationships with favorable customers, differentiating the product either substantively or psychologically through marketing, integrating forward or backward, or establishing technological leadership.

Questions for Discussion

1. Choose a specific industry and, relying solely on your impressions, evaluate the impact of the five forces that drive competition in that industry.
2. Repeat your analysis in question 1 but this time refer to published sources to provide more objective information on which to base your conclusions. (Hint: The appendix to Chapter 6 provides a helpful list of sources.)
3. Choose an industry in which you would like to compete. Use the five-forces methods of analysis to explain why that industry is attractive to you.
4. Many businesses neglect industry analysis. When does this hurt them; when does it not?
5. The model below depicts industry forces analysis as a funnel that focuses on remote-factor analysis as a means of better understanding the impact of factors in the

operating environment. Do you agree with this model? If not, how would you improve it?

6. Who in an organization should be responsible for industry analysis? Suppose that there is no strategic planning department.

Bibliography

Caves, R. E., and M. E. Porter. "From Entry Barriers to Mobility Barriers: Conjectural Decisions and Contrived Deterrence to New Competition." *Quarterly Journal of Economics* 91 (1976), pp. 421–34.

Elzinga, K. G. "The Restructuring of the U.S. Brewing Industry." *Industrial Organization Review* 1 (1973), pp. 101–14.

Koch, J. V. "Industry Market Structure and Industry Price-Cost Margins." *Industrial Organization Review* 2 (1974), pp. 186–93.

Porter, M. E. "The Structure within Industries' and Companies' Performance." *Review of Economics and Statistics* 61 (1979), pp. 214–27.

Scherer, F. M. *Industrial Market Structure and Economic Performance,* 2d ed. Skokie, Ill.: Rand McNally, 1980.

Weber, J. A. "Market Structure Profile Analysis and Strategic Growth Opportunities." *California Management Review* 20 (1977), pp. 34–46.

Chapter 5 Cohesion Case Illustration

Industry Analysis at Holiday Inns, Inc.

Industry analysis is a useful aid to the strategic management process at Holiday Inns, Inc. Each of Holiday Inns' business units must understand how the five basic competitive forces work in their industries and how they affect the business in its particular situation. In doing this, strategists are better prepared to establish an agenda for dealing with these contending forces. One business group—hotels—will be used to illustrate industry analysis at Holiday Inns Inc. The technique is also necessary for the strategic management of each of Holiday Inns' remaining groups. Readers are encouraged to apply industry analysis to one or more of the other business groups.

Exhibit 1 is a diagram of basic forces driving competition in the lodging industry. It is useful to assess these forces to understand their relative influence on the lodging industry and ultimately to provide a basis for charting Holiday Inns' strategic course.

Threats of/barriers to entry. The lodging industry has created several strong barriers to entry. *Economies of scale* have been built via the existence of large, franchised networks for each of the major chains. This allows cost sharing in marketing, research, training, and technological services (like reservation systems). Interestingly, these networks have also facilitated the emergence of *product differentiation* as a barrier to entry. Brand identity and customer loyalty, particularly for firms like Holiday Inns, has been strongly established within the lodging industry. *Capital requirements,* particularly when the need for a network of locations is so important, is a substantial barrier to entry. Franchising has been one way to overcome this barrier, although the proliferation of franchises has lessened the viability of this strategy for newcomers to the industry. *Knowledge* of how to operate in the industry has become increasingly important as operating complexity increases. This in turn is becoming an entry barrier. *Access to distribution channels,* particularly in the sense of controlling prime locations (such as proximity to airports, downtown business centers, resorts, etc.) can create a substantial barrier to entry in several specific locations.

While entry barriers are increasing in this industry, the 1970s witnessed several entrants that overcame the barriers, particularly in the budget segment of the industry (e.g., Days Inn, La Quinta). Numerous individual investors aided this entrance as franchises. In the 1980s there appear to be potentially successful entrance strategies in the high-priced end of the industry. Predominantly located in large cities or resort locations, these "destination" entrants

Exhibit 1

Forces driving lodging-industry competition

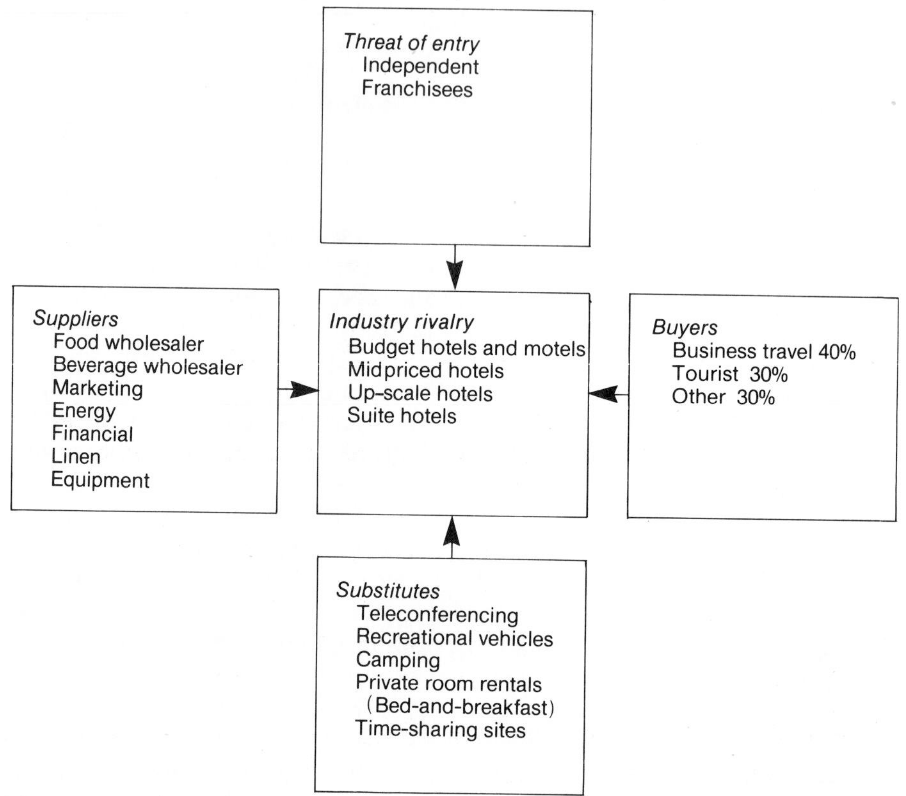

are successfully building positions in the industry by offering elaborate, expensive service to a narrow clientele.

Suppliers. Typical *suppliers* to the lodging industry include equipment manufacturers, linen suppliers, food and beverage wholesalers, energy sources, financial suppliers and "people" resources. Generally, these suppliers are rather fragmented and do not offer unique products. Overall, there is very little threat of forward integration. Labor sources are generally not unionized and the skill level required for entry positions is minimal. Training is provided by the industry. Finally, the lodging industry is usually an important, steady customer for most products and services offered by these suppliers. Therefore, the lodging industry is generally quite powerful relative to its suppliers.

Buyers. The lodging industry is relatively powerful in relation to its *buyers.* First, buyers are primarily individuals, relatively small groups, and organizations—there is limited *concentration* of buying power. In some ways the service offered—bed, shower, TV, phone, food and beverage—can be seen as undifferentiated. Realistically, however, lodging services *are differentiated* by level of service, location of facilities, marketing efforts, brand identification, and the capacity of facilities (banquets, etc.). There is very little threat of backward integration. While buyers are fragmented, buyer power has manifest itself to some extent via the emergence of greater industry segmentation. To a sizable buyer segment—family businesses, salespeople on fixed allowances, families on limited budgets—lodging accommodations can represent a significant part of their "cost." Standard accommodation, not excess quality, is the key to the needs of these groups. Their "collective" power has led to the emergence of numerous chains providing budget accommodations.

Substitutes. The services deserving the greatest strategic attention as potential *substitute products* are improving their price-performance trade-off with current lodging services, particularly when the services are produced by industries earning high profits. Teleconferencing and telecommunication are examples of this type of emerging potential substitute. Business and government employees, a major component of the lodging industry's customer base, have frequent travel needs (e.g. to attend meetings, call on people, demonstrate products, etc.). As satellite-based teleconferencing and telecommunications technology become steadily less expensive, they represent potentially cost-effective alternatives to travel and lodging services in some situations. Several major lodging firms, most notably Holiday Inns, have made significant commitments to expanding their teleconferencing capability so that this threat actually becomes a service advantage for their lodging network.

Competitive rivalry. There are several factors associated with intense *rivalry among competitors* in the lodging industry. Competitors have become numerous in virtually every segment of the lodging industry. While Holiday Inns is still recognized as the industry leader and has the largest number of rooms, other competitors have grown much more rapidly in the last 10 years. For example, Best Western actually has more locations in its system than does Holiday Inns.

Industry growth has slowed, particularly during the recession of 1981–82. Yet expansion-minded competitors are quite active which should rapidly precipitate major market-share fights. The services offered, while somewhat differentiated, generally do not involve "switching costs" that tie buyers to one particular competitor.

Fixed costs (debt service and overhead) are high in the lodging industry and the product ("one room-night") is *very* perishable in that it cannot be retained in inventory if it is not rented. This could create a strong temptation to cut prices if the capacity of lodging facilities expands too fast. Exit barriers can intensify the problem—who wants to buy a poorly performing motel? Industry participants have increasingly built their properties to purposely plan for office or condominum conversion so that exit options are greater.

The five-forces analysis suggests that industry rivalry is the critical force shaping industry competition. Teleconferencing is emerging as the most important *potential* substitute. Neither suppliers nor buyers are very powerful, and barriers to entry are generally high. Increasing segmentation of buyers has increased industry rivalry and in some ways allowed selected entrants to successfully overcome entry barriers.

CHAPTER

Environmental Forecasting[1]

Importance of Forecasting

Change was rapid in the 1970s and first half of the 80s, with even greater changes and challenges forecast as the 80s come to a close. The crucial responsibility for managers will be ensuring their firm's capacity for survival. This will be done by anticipating and adapting to environmental changes in ways that provide new opportunities for growth and profitability. The impact of changes in the remote industry and task environments must be understood and predicted.

Even large firms in established industries will be actively involved in transitions. The $5.5 billion loss in the U.S. auto industry during 1980 and 1981 shows what can happen when firms fail to place a priority on environmental forecasting. In the preceding decade there was a 20 percent penetration of the U.S. new-car market by foreign competition; the oil embargo in 1973; rapidly climbing fuel prices; and uncertain future supplies of crude oil. Yet the long-term implications of these predictable factors on future auto sales were largely ignored by U.S. automakers. Because it was not open to changes in technology, Detroit was left without viable, fuel-efficient, quality-made alternatives for the American market. On the other hand, the Japanese anticipated the future need for fuel efficiency, quality, and service through careful market research and environmental forecasting. As a result, the Japanese gained

[1] Portions of this chapter are adopted from John A. Pearce II and Richard B. Robinson, Jr., "Environmental Forecasting: Key to Strategic Management," *Business*, July–September 1983, pp. 3–12.

additional market share at Detroit's expense. However, in the early 1980s, American automakers spent $80 billion on product and capital-investment strategies meant to recapture their lost market share. They realized that success in strategic decisions rests not solely on dollar amounts but also on anticipation of and preparation for the future.

Accurate forecasting of changing elements in the environment is an essential part of strategic management. One specific example is the case of National Intergroup described in Strategy in Action 6–1.

Forecasting the business environment for the second half of the 1980s has led some firms, such as Sears, Roebuck, to expand. From 1980 to 1985, Sears opened new financial centers in 250 retail stores.

Other corporations have forecast a need for massive retrenchment. One such firm is the Weyerhauser Company, which laid off 2,000 employees in 1982 to streamline its cost of doing business. Still other companies have cut back in one area of operations to underwrite growth in another. In 1984 General Electric decided to close 10 plants and reduce its work force by 1,600 employees while simultaneously making a commitment to spend $250 million by 1986 to upgrade its facilities.

From these and many other examples, it is evident that strategic managers need to develop skill in predicting significant environmental changes. To aid in the search for future opportunities and constraints the following steps should be taken:

1. Select those environmental variables that are critical to the firm.
2. Select the sources of significant environmental information.
3. Evaluate forecasting approaches or techniques.
4. Integrate forecast results into the strategic management process.
5. Monitor the critical aspects of managing forecasts.

Select Critical Environmental Variables

Management experts have argued that the most important cause of the turbulent business environment is the change in population structure and dynamics. This change, in turn, produces other major changes in the economic, social, and political environments.

Historically, population shifts tended to occur over 40- to 50-year periods and, therefore, had little relevance to business decisions. However, during the second half of the 20th century, population changes have become radical, erratic, contradictory, and therefore of great importance.

For example, the U.S. baby boom between 1945 and the mid-1960s has had and will have a dramatic impact on all parts of society—from maternity wards and schools to the labor force and the marketplace. This population bulge is facing heavy competition for jobs, promotions, and housing, despite a highest-ever education level. Compounding this dilemma are the heightened

Strategy in Action 6–1

National Intergroup

In 1982 National Steel's sales dropped 26 percent to $3 billion, while the previous year's $86 million profit disintegrated into a massive $463 million loss. But long before the company reached this abyss, Chairman Howard M. Love, perplexed by the historically poor returns on steel, began to take a "cold, ungilded look" at every aspect of the company. This three-year analysis asked why the company's management did not perform better and culminated with the adoption of a new name that does not mention steel: National Intergroup Inc. (NII).

As the 1980s began National seemed mired, and its efforts to change were fizzling. Attempts to establish then-unproved quality circles at its Weirton, West Virginia steel mill foundered because middle management—not labor—was unresponsive. With the help of Responsive Organizations, an Arlington, Virginia consulting firm, National's top management came to realize that its managers lacked commonly held goals. To remedy that, 250 executives were involved for over a year in meetings meant to seek a consensus on the company's mission and to outline its financial, marketing, personnel, and social goals.

The company also set up task forces to study its strategic-planning process and the system by which one unit, such as coal, charged another unit, such as steel, for its products. But the discussions "all began running up against a stone wall," said John A. McCreary, NII's vice president for human resources. The barrier, "an inappropriate organizational structure," focused too much on steel production.

So in 1982 the corporation was restructured into six autonomous business groups—steel, financial services, aluminum, distribution, energy, and diversified business. Each was a profit center with its own group president, and the new corporate name reflected this change.

National's studies showed that its two biggest markets—autos and cans—were irrevocably reducing their use of steel. "The size of the steel company we have now matches the markets we want to participate in," said Love. Future capital investment could be concentrated on improving smaller plants. Consequently, Love believed, "we'll be significantly more profitable with less tons." In early 1983 National showed this was no idle boast: It reported an operating profit of $2 for each ton of steel it produced, while other major steel makers lost from $17 to $32 per ton. The company's mills were running at 82 percent of capacity, while industry as a whole was sputtering along at 56 percent.

National's balance sheet was in much better shape than it had been in the previous year. As of June 30, 1983, the company had $74 million in cash, three times its holdings at year end. Long-term debt was knocked down to $600 million by September 30, 1983, or 36 percent of capitalization versus 41 percent the previous year, and its stock had more than doubled in price in the same year. "They've got their act together," said John C. Tumazos, an industry analyst with Oppenheimer & Company, who in 1982 listed National as one of the steel industry's financially weakest companies.

Source: Adapted from *Business Week*, September 26, 1983, p. 82.

Figure 6–1

Population growth by age group (millions)

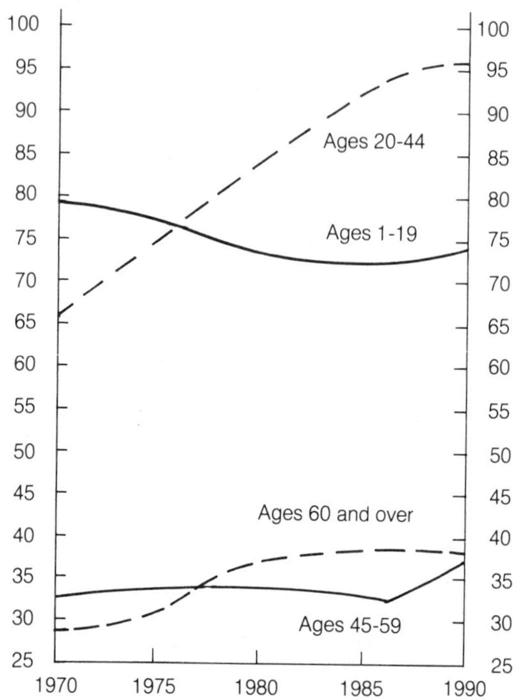

Source: Bureau of the Census. U.S. Department of Commerce, 1980.

demands of women and racial minorities. The lack of high-status jobs to fit the expectations of this large, educated labor force poses a potential for major social and economic changes. In addition, these workers encounter an increasing aging labor force that find it difficult to give up status, power, and employment when retirement programs are either not financially attractive or not available at the traditional age of 65. (See Figure 6–1 for comparative population growth projections.)

Obviously, the demands of these groups will have important effects on social and political changes in terms of lifestyle, consumption patterns, and political decisions. In economic terms, the size and potential affluence of these groups suggest increasing markets for housing, consumer products, and leisure goods and services.

Interestingly, the same shifts in population, life expectancy, and education have occurred in many developed nations. However, developing nations face the opposite population configurations. Although birthrates have declined, survival rates, because of medical improvements, have created a large population of people reaching adulthood in the 1980s. Jobs and food are expected to be in short supply. Therefore, many developing countries will face severe social and political instability unless they can find appropriate work for their surplus labor.[2]

The rates of population increase can obviously be of great importance, as indicated by the contrasting effects forecast above. If a growing population has sufficient purchasing power, new markets will be developed to satisfy their needs. However, too much growth in a country with a limited amount or a drastic inequity in distribution of resources may result in major social and political upheavals and may pose substantial risks for businesses.

If forecasting were as simple as predicting population trends, strategic managers would only need to examine census data to predict future markets. But economic interpretations are more complex. Migration rates, mobility trends, birth, marriage, and death rates, and racial, ethnic, and religious structures complicate population statistics. In addition, resource development and its political use in this interdependent world further confuse the problem—as evidenced by the actions of some of the oil states like Saudi Arabia, Iraq, Libya, and Kuwait. Changes in political situations, technology, or culture add further complications.

Domestically, the turbulence is no less severe. Continually changing products and services, changing competitors, uncertain government priorities, rapid social change, and major technological innovations all add to the complexity of planning for the future. To grow, be profitable, at times, even to survive in this turbulent world, a firm needs sensitivity, commitment, and skill in recognizing and predicting those variables that will most profoundly affect its future.

Who Selects the Key Variables? Although executives or committees in charge of planning may assist in obtaining forecast data, responsibility for environmental forecasting usually lies with top management. This is the case at the Sun (oil) Company where responsibility for the long-range future of the corporation is assigned to the chairman and vice chairman of the board of directors. One of the key duties of the vice chairman is environmental assessment. In this context, *environment* refers not to air, water, and land but rather to the general business setting created by the economic, technological, political, and social forces in which Sun plans to operate.

---

[2] Peter Drucker (*Managing in Turbulent Times,* New York: Harper & Row, 1980) suggests that the practice of production sharing between developed and developing nations can be the economic integration needed by both groups of countries. Production sharing will include bringing together the abundant labor resources of the developing countries with the management, technology, educated people, markets, and purchasing power of the developed countries.

The environmental assessment group consists of Sun's chief economist, a specialist in technological assessment, and a public issues consultant—all reporting to the vice president of environmental assessment. The chief economist evaluates and forecasts the state of the economy; the technological assessment specialist covers technology and science; and the public issues consultant concentrates on politics and society.[3]

However, headquarter's capability and proficiency may be limited in analyzing political, economic, and social variables around the world. Therefore, on-the-spot personnel, outside consultants, or company task forces may be assigned to assist in forecasting.

What Variables Should Be Selected? A list of key variables that will have make-or-break consequences for the firm must be developed. Some may have been crucial in the past and others may appear to be important in the future. This list can be kept to manageable size by limiting key variables in the following ways:

1. Include all variables that would have a significant impact although their probability of occurrence is low, e.g., trucking deregulation. Also include highly probable variables regardless of impact, e.g., a minimal price increase by a major supplier. Delete others with little impact and low probabilities.
2. Disregard major disasters such as nuclear war.
3. Aggregate when possible into gross variables, e.g., a bank loan is based on the dependability of a company's cash flow more so than on the flow's component sources.
4. If the value of one variable is based upon the value of the other, separate the dependent variable for future planning.[4]

Limits of money, time, and skill in forecasting prevent a firm from predicting many variables in the environment. The task of predicting even a dozen variables is substantial. Often firms try to select a set of key variables by analyzing the environmental factors in the industry that are most likely to force sharp growth or decline in the marketplace. For the furniture, appliance, and textiles industries, housing starts are significant. Housing, in turn, is greatly affected by high interest rates.

Figure 6–2 identifies some of the key issues that may have critical impacts on a firm's future success. Examples of the importance of a few of these variables are also presented.

[3] Eric Weiss, "Future Public Opinion of Business," *Management Review,* March 1978, p. 9.

[4] Robert E. Linneman and John D. Kennell. "Shirt-Sleeve Approach to Long-Range Plans," *Harvard Business Review,* March–April 1977, p. 145.

Figure 6–2

Strategic forecasting issues

Key issues in the remote environment.

Economy.

Purchasing power depends on current income, savings, prices, and credit availability. The economic trends to be forecast often attempt to answer the following questions.

What are the probable future directions of the economies in the corporation's regional, national, and international markets? What changes in economic growth, inflation, interest rates, capital availability, credit availability, and consumer purchasing power can be expected?

What income differences can be expected between the wealthy upper-middle class, working class, and underclass in various regions?

What shifts in relative demand for different categories of goods and services can be expected?

Example. The record-setting high interest rates of 1980 and 1981 resulted in a general economic washout in the United States. Industries that depend upon long- and short-term credit for their sales, such as housing and automobiles, were most severely affected. Despite the possibility that higher interest rates would be used to curtail the increasing inflation, little effort was made by loan institutions to develop innovative loan programs such as variable interest loans.

Society.

In the rapidly changing social environment of the highly interdependent spaceship earth, businesses feel great pressure to respond to the expectations of society more effectively.

What effect do changes in social values and attitudes regarding childbearing, marriage, lifestyle, work, ethics, sex roles, racial equality, education, retirement, pollution, energy, and so on have on the firm's development? What effect will population changes have on major social and political expectations—at home and abroad? What constraints or opportunities will develop? What pressure groups will increase in power?

Example. The declining birthrate of the United States is a threat to some industries producing children's food, toys, clothes, and furniture. However, forecasting by trend extrapolation of birthrates in the late 1950s was so inaccurate that it created a severe threat to firms such as the Gerber Company. The six firms that survived or prospered into the 1980s were those that learned to recognize sociocultural value changes and to incorporate such changes in their strategic forecasts.

Politics.

Although political forecasts are usually based on "soft" data, as compared to hard—attitudes and opinions—the impact of political issues and trends, as shown below, is frequently as important as economic or technological variables.

What changes in government policy can be expected regarding industry cooperation, antitrust activities, foreign trade, taxation, depreciation, environmental protection, deregulation, defense, foreign trade barriers, and other governing parameters? What success will a new administration have in achieving its stated goals? What effect will that success have on the firm?

Example. After the 1980 presidential election major forecast adjustments were made to reflect the Reagan administration's new priorities in military defense, private sector growth, and reduced government spending.

Will specific international climates be hostile or favorable? Is there a tendency toward instability, corruption, or violence? What is the level of political risk in each foreign market? What other political or legal constraints or support can be expected in international business (e.g., trade barriers, equity requirements, nationalism, patent protection, etc.)?

Figure 6–2 *(continued)*

Example. Despite the low political risk involved several major U.S. firms discovered the importance of in-depth environmental forecasting when investing in Canada. Although aware of the Quebec separatist movement, ITT Rayonier dismissed its potential effect on construction of a $120-million pulp mill. ITT's use of English-speaking supervisors, supervisor conflict with the separatists, a power struggle between two labor federations, and a shortage of skilled labor more than doubled the construction cost to $250 million. Asbestos Corporation of America was also surprised when the province of Quebec nationalized their asbestos mines. Both firms underestimated the significance of growing nationalism.

Technology.

Technological innovations can give the firm a special competitive advantage. Without continued product or service improvement, profitability and survival are often jeopardized.

What is the current state of the art? How will it change? What pertinent new products or services are likely to become technically feasible in the foreseeable future? What is the future impact of technological breakthroughs in related product areas? How will they interface with other remote considerations such as economic issues, social values, public safety, regulations, and court interpretations?

Example. Recent applications to telephone interconnections of sophisticated computer technology such as PBX units have developed an entire new industry that is seen as a first step toward the integrated electronic office of the future. In addition, decisions by the Federal Communications Commission curtailed previous monopolistic practices of AT&T that excluded the use of equipment from other than AT&T sources. The result has been the spin-off from AT&T of a marketing-oriented unit that will compete head-on with firms seeking to relate computers to communication systems. Among the announced competitors are Xerox, IBM, Exxon, Volkswagen, ROLM Corporation, Northern Telecom, Mitel Corporation, and Nippon Electric Company.

Industry.

At any given time in its life cycle, certain underlying forces in an industry operate to broadly define the potential for a company's success.

What is the degree of integration of major competitors? What is the industry's average percentage utilization of production capacity? What is the industry's vulnerability to new or substitute products? What, and how great, are the barriers to entry? What is the number and concentration of suppliers? What is the nature of the industry's customer base?

Example. Head Ski began in 1967 with a concentration strategy targeted at the high-quality/high-price niche of the snow ski market. With a quickly achieved 50 percent market share, the company faced only four major competitors. However, by 1971 industry competition had changed dramatically. Head had diversified into new product-markets, such as ski clothing, accessories, and archery equipment. It had also diversified geographically into Europe. Competitors had buttressed their resource bases through mergers with conglomerates such as Beatrice Foods. Then, in 1972, Head Ski followed suit when it was acquired by AMF. Thus, in just five years, the competitive industry composition had shifted from nondiversified, relatively small, single industry businesses to large, multinational, multi-industry, diversified conglomerates.

Key issues in the operating environment.

Competitive position.

How probable is the entrance of important new competitors into the industry? Will they offer substitute or competing products? What strategic moves are expected by existing rivals—inside and outside the United States? What competitive advantage is necessary in selected foreign markets? What will be the competitor's priorities and their ability to change? Is their behavior predictable?

Figure 6–2 *(concluded)*

Example. Employing a penetration strategy similar to that used in the auto, steel, shipbuilding, and television markets. Japanese medical-electronics makers are gaining a niche with low-cost, stripped-down versions of competitor's equipment. American firms, like General Electric, dismissed the Japanese strategy by insisting that users of medical electronic equipment are concerned not with price but quality. However, as in past entry strategies, the Japanese researched the needs of the market. They then began development of a three-dimensional scanner-monitor that was a major technical breakthrough and may eventually give them a competitive edge in the marketplace.

Customer profiles and market changes.

What is and will be considered as needed value by our customers? Is market research done, or do managers talk to each other to discover what the customer wants? Which customer needs are not being met by existing products? Why? Are R&D activities underway to develop means for fulfilling these needs and what is their status? What marketing and distribution channels should be used?

Example. The Japanese research future customer needs and wants by interviewing those who own products of their major competitor, thereby identifying desired improvements. As an example, in the 1970s Japanese researchers identified Volkswagen's shortcomings by interviewing owners in the United States. They then designed Toyotas and Datsuns accordingly and consequently overcame the Beetles' dominance in the United States.

What demographic and population changes can be anticipated? What do they portend for the size of the market and sales potential? What new market segment or product might develop as a result of these changes? What will be our customer groups' buying power?

Example. Because 95 percent of its $3.5 billion in revenues are generated from soft drinks and other beverages. Coca-Cola has become concerned about the aging of the prime soft-drink population, 13- to 24-year-olds. Because Coke can identify the key population variables that will have make-or-break consequences for their product lines, it can more accurately forecast future market potential. As a result, Coke has decided to pursue the aging population bulge in the United States by diversifying into wines. By further expanding internationally with their soft-drink products, Coke is also tapping growing youth markets in foreign countries.

Suppliers and creditors.

What is the likelihood of major cost increases because of a dwindling supplies of needed natural resource? Will sources of supply, especially of energy, be reliable? Are there reasons to expect major changes in cost and availability of inputs as a result of money, people, or subassembly problems? Which suppliers and creditors can be expected to respond to special emergency requests?

Example. As short-term interest rates skyrocketed to 20 percent in late 1979, hundreds of small firms fell into the marginal or money-losing categories. Often officers of their banks became alarmed and called in the loans. The resulting squeeze forced many of these businesses into bankruptcy.

Labor market.

Are potential employees with desired skills and abilities available in the geographic areas involved? Are colleges and vocational-technical schools located near plant or store sites to aid in meeting training needs? Are labor relations in the industry conducive to expanding needs for employees?

Example. The 1950s and 1960s were periods of business expansion into the southern states where labor was plentiful and unions were comparatively weak. In the 1970s northern states regained a measure of attractiveness because they were able to offer unemployed or underemployed skilled workers and attractively priced industrial sites.

Select Sources of Significant Environmental Information

Before forecasting can begin in a formal way, appropriate sources of environmental information should be identified. Casual gathering of strategic information is part of the normal course of executive actions—reading, interactions, and meetings—but is subject to bias and must be balanced with alternative viewpoints. Although *The Wall Street Journal, Business Week, Fortune, Harvard Business Review, Forbes,* and other popular trade and scholarly journals are important sources of forecasting information, formal, deliberate, and structured searches are desirable. A special feature of this chapter is a supplement which appears immediately after the Bibliography. It lists published sources that can be used in forecasting. A review of these will help strategic managers to identify sources that can help meet specific forecasting needs. If the firm can afford the time and expense, primary data should also be gathered in such areas as market factors, technological changes, and competitive and supplier strategies.

Evaluate Forecasting Techniques

Debate exists over the accuracy of quantitative versus qualitative approaches to forecasting (see Figure 6–3), with most research supporting quantitative models. However, the difference in predictions made using each type of approach is often minimal. Additionally, subjective or judgmental approaches may often be the only practical method of forecasting political, legal, social, and technological trends in the remote external environment. The same is true of several factors in the task environment, especially customer and competitive considerations.

Ultimately, the choice of technique depends not on the environmental factor under review, but on such considerations as the nature of the forecast decision, the amount and accuracy of available information, the accuracy required, the time available, the importance of the forecast, the cost, and the competence and interpersonal relationships of the managers and forecasters involved.[5] Frequently, assessment of these factors leads to the selection of a combination of quantitative and qualitative techniques, thereby strengthening the accuracy of the ultimate forecast.

Techniques Available

Economic Forecasts. At one time, only forecasts of economic variables were used in strategic management. These forecasts were primarily concerned with remote factors such as general economic conditions, disposable personal income, the consumer price index, wage rates, and productivity. Derived from

[5] Steven C. Wheelwright and Darral G. Clarke, "Corporate Forecasting: Promise and Reality," *Harvard Business Review,* November–December 1976, p. 42.

Figure 6–3

Popular approaches to forecasting

*Technique**	*Short description†*	*Cost*	*Popularity***	*Complexity*	*Association with life-cycle stage‡*
Quantitative:					
Causal					
Econometric models	Simultaneous systems of multiple regression equations	High	High	High	Steady state
Single and multiple regression	Variations in dependent variables are explained by variations in the independent one(s)	High/ Medium	High	Medium	Steady state
Time series					
Trend extrapolation	Linear, exponential, S-curve, or other types of projections	Medium	High	Medium	Steady state
	Forecasts are obtained by linear or exponential smoothing or averaging of past actual values	Medium	High	Medium	Steady state
Qualitative or judgmental					
Sales force estimate[5]	A bottom-up approach aggregating salespersons' forecasts	Low	High	Low	All stages
Juries of executive opinion	Marketing, production, finance, and purchasing executives jointly prepare forecasts	Low	High	Low	Product development
Customer surveys; market research	Learning abut intentions of potential customers or plans of businesses	Medium	Medium	Medium	Market testing and early introduction
Scenario	Forecasters imagine the impacts of anticipated conditions	Low	Medium	Low	All stages
Delphi	Experts are guided toward a consensus	Low	Medium	Medium	Product development
Brainstorming	Idea generation in a noncritical group situation	Low	Medium	Medium	Product development

* Only techniques discussed in this chapter are listed.

† Adapted in part from S. C. Wheelwright and S. Makridakis, *Forecasting Methods for Management,* 3d ed. (New York: John Wiley & Sons, 1980), pp. 34–35.

** Adapted in part from S. C. Wheelwright and D. C. Clark, "Corporate Forecasting: Promise and Reality," *Harvard Business Review,* November–December 1976.

‡ Adapted in part from J. C. Chambers, J. K. Mullick, and D. D. Smith, "How to Choose the Right Forecasting Technique," *Harvard Business Review,* July–August 1971. The associations shown are "most common," but most techniques can be used at most stages.

For details see N. C. Mohn and L. C. Sartorius, "Sales Forecasting: A Manager's Primer." *Business,* May–June 1981 and July–August 1981.

government and private sources, the economic forecasts served as the framework for industry and company forecasts. The latter forecasts dealt with task-environment concerns such as sales, market share, and other pertinent economic trends.

Econometric Models. With the advent of sophisticated computers, the government and some wealthy companies contracted with private consulting firms to develop "causal models," especially those involving *econometrics.* These models utilize complex simultaneous regression equations to relate economic occurrences to areas of corporate activity. They are especially useful when information is available on causal relationships and when large changes are anticipated. During the relatively stable decade of the 1960s and on into the 1970s econometrics became one of the nation's fastest growing industries. However, since early in 1979 the big three econometric firms—Data Resources (McGraw-Hill), Chase Econometrics (Chase Manhattan Bank), and Wharton Econometric Forecasting Associates (Ziff-Davis Publishing)—have fallen on hard times. The explosion of oil prices, inflation, and the growing interdependence of the world economy have created problems beyond the inherent limits of econometric models. And despite enormous technological resources, these models still depend on the judgment of the model builders. Recently, that judgment has not been dependable.[6]

Two more widely used and less expensive approaches to forecasting are *time-series models, and judgmental models.* Time-series models attempt to identify patterns based on combinations of historical trend, seasonal, and cyclical factors. This technique assumes that the past is a prologue to the future. Time-series techniques, such as exponential smoothing and linear projections, are relatively simple, well-known, inexpensive, and accurate.

Of the time-series models, *trend analysis* is the most frequently used. This model assumes that the future will be a continuation of the past following some long-range trend. If sufficient historical data, such as annual sales, are readily available, a trend analysis can be done quickly and inexpensively.

In the trend analysis depicted in Figure 6–4, concern should focus on long-term trends, such as Trend C, which represents 10 years of fluctuating sales. Trend A, where three excellent years were used in the trend analysis, is too optimistic. Similarly, the four bad years depicted in Trend B represent a much too pessimistic outlook.

The major limitation of trend analysis is the assumption that all relevant conditions will remain relatively constant in the future. Sudden changes in the conditions upset the trend prediction.

Judgmental models are useful when historical data are not available or when they are hard to use. Examples of judgmental or qualitative approaches are *sales force estimates* and *juries of exeuctive opinion.* Sales force estimates

[6] "Where the Big Econometric Models Go Wrong," *Business Week,* March 30, 1981, pp. 70–73.

Figure 6–4

Interpretations in trend analysis

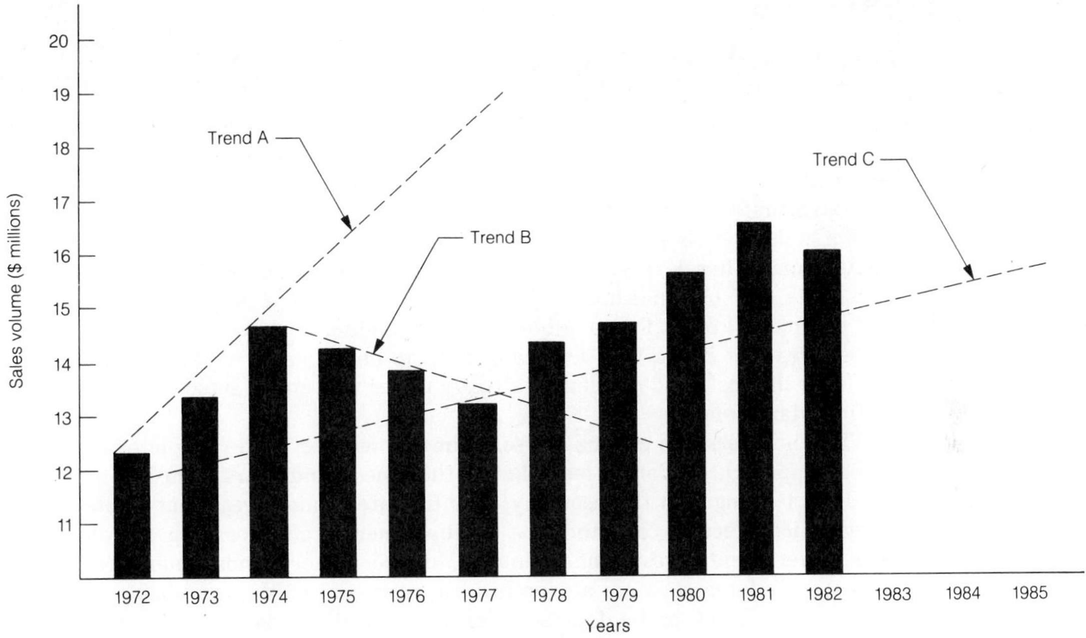

consolidate salespersons' opinions of customer intentions and opinions regarding specific products. These can be relevant if customers respond honestly and remain consistent in their intentions. Juries of executive opinion combine estimates made by executives from marketing, production, finance, and purchasing and then average their views. No elaborate math or statistics are required.

Customer surveys may involve personal interviews or telephone questionnaires. The questions must be well stated and easily understood. Respondents are a random sample of the relevant population. Surveys can provide valuable in-depth information. They are often difficult to construct and time-consuming to administer, but many market research firms use such surveys. One strong advocate of judgmental approaches is a senior partner of Lord, Abbett Investment, as is discussed in Strategy in Action 6–2.

Social Forecasts. Relying only on economic indicators for strategic forecasting neglects many important social trends that can have a profound impact. Some firms have recognized this and forecast social issues as part of their environmental scanning to identify social trends and underlying attitudes.

Strategy in Action 6–2
Lord, Abbett Investment

Development of investment strategies usually involves sophisticated econometric and mathematical models to forecast future investment values. However, John M. McCarthy, senior partner of Lord, Abbett Investment, a $3.6 billion investment company, has developed his own qualitative forecasting approach. As president of its $1.7 billion Affiliated Fund, McCarthy uses a subjective approach that examines events for tangible signs of pending changes in the economy. He believes that if you wait for the obvious to be discussed on TV, the process of solving the economic problem is already under way and it is too late to invest for important gains.

While numbers and graphs are sometimes combined in the jury of executive opinion approach, McCarthy feels that by the time the numbers of the key indicators reflect changes in the economy, it is too late to aid investment strategies. Instead, his forecasts tend to focus on fundamental changes such as interest rates, government investment incentives, and consumer trends. Among McCarthy's specific forecasts were a drop in interest rates in 1981, a probable return to the bond market, and a depressed consumer goods market until the mid 80s. He believes that President Reagan's savings and investment incentives will break the American habit of borrow and spend. Company and personal investment strategies will need to be fine tuned, as these and other forecasts do or do not become reality.

Generally, McCarthy looks for the mainly unpopular investments. Often these are undervalued. An illustration of his unique but commonsense approach resulted in investment strategies of purchasing stocks that declined in price while interest rates climbed in 1980. Interest-sensitive issues, such as AT&T, utilities, and banks, account for about 18 percent of Affiliated's current portfolio.

Although this conservative strategy caused Lord, Abbett's growth rate to be below the averages of the Dow Jones Industrial Average and Standard & Poor's 500 during the brief bull market in 1980, McCarthy has focused on long-term results. This forecasting approach and investment strategy enabled Affiliated to grow 173.1 percent compared to 105.5 percent for the Dow during the period January 1975 through September 1980.

Lord, Abbett follows the same forecast method and investment strategy in managing its $1.5 billion of pension fund money.

Source: "Lord, Abbett Senior Partner Weaves Theology into His Investment Credo." Reprinted by permission of *The Wall Street Journal*, © December 9, 1980. All rights reserved.

Social forecasting is very complex. Recent efforts have involved analyzing such major social areas as: population, housing, social security and welfare, health and nutrition, education and training, income, and wealth and expenditures.

A variety of approaches is used in social forecasting, including time-series analysis and the judgmental techniques described earlier. However, a fourth approach called *scenario development,* is probably the most popular of all techniques. Scenarios are imagined stories that integrate objective and subjective parts of other forecasts. They are designed to help managers anticipate changes. Because scenarios can be presented in an easily understood form, they have gained popularity in social-forecast situations. Scenarios can be developed by the following process:

1. Prepare the background by assessing the overall social environment under investigation (such as social legislation).
2. Select critical indicators and search for future events that may affect the key trends (e.g., growing distrust of business).
3. Analyze reasons for past behavior for each trend (e.g., perceived disregard for air and water quality).
4. Forecast each indicator in at least three scenarios, showing the least favorable environment, the likely environment, and the most favorable environment.
5. Write the scenario from the viewpoint of someone in the future and describe conditions then and how they developed.
6. Condense the scenario for each trend to a few paragraphs.

Figure 6–5 presents an example of a "most likely" scenario for the future of business-government relations on social issues. Scenarios prepare strategic managers for alternative possibilities if certain trends continue, thus enabling them to develop contingency plans.

Political Forecasts. Some strategic planners want to treat political forecasts with the same seriousness and consideration given to economic forecasts. They believe that shifts toward or against a broad range of political factors—such as the size of government budgets, tariffs, tax rates, defense spending, the growth of regulatory bodies, and the extent of business-leader participation in government planning can have profound effects on business success.

Political forecasts for foreign countries are also important. Political risks increase the threat to businesses in any way dependent upon international subsidiaries or suppliers for customers or critical resources. Increasing world interdependence makes it imperative for firms of all sizes to consider the international political implications of their strategies.

Because of the billions of U.S. dollars lost in the 1970s as a result of revolu-

Figure 6–5

Scenario on the future of business-government regulations: Social issues

The government-corporate relationship in the 1978–1987 period continued to develop along patterns established in previous decades, with no major discontinuities or radical surprises. The most far-reaching and substantial change occurred late in the period when Congress enlarged the planning authority of its budget office, setting 5- and 10-year national manpower, natural resource, and other economic goals. This legislation primarily affected federal fiscal policies and contained no authority to compel action on the part of the private sector to meet the indicated goals.

Nevertheless, following the lead of West Germany, the federal government did offer some incentives to companies that acted to meet certain national objectives—for example, locating new industrial facilities in certain areas for social reasons (such as environmental or employment reasons). During the decade the government made a commitment to guaranteed jobs rather than guaranteed income.

In the environmental arena, economic incentives and penalties became the government's major tools for compliance. Effluent charges were established to internalize the costs of pollution. Other tax incentives and loans were made available to companies for the installation of pollution-control equipment. Congress also legislated a time limit for legal actions to block a construction project on environmental grounds.

In other regulatory areas, the government moved selectively, increasing requirements on some industries while reducing controls on others. For example, while moving to deregulate much of the air transport business, Congress at the same time passed a full-disclosure labeling act for prepared foods that requires the listing of all ingredients and the percentage of each ingredient. Congress also set a rule requiring that every proposal for new regulation be accompanied by a regulatory impact statement detailing the probable effects of the proposal on the economy.

Turning down proposals for federal chartering of corporations, Congress nevertheless acted to influence the internal governance of large corporations: it passed a full-disclosure law concerning most corporate activities and established a limit on the number of inside directors permitted to serve on the boards of directors. Legislation established due process and protection for whistle blowers (employees who report legal violations). The government placed stringent safeguards on corporate data banks containing information about employees and customers.

In the domain of social legislation affecting business, the minimum wage was indexed to the cost of living and Congress passed a comprehensive national health plan in which employers pay a significant portion.

Source: James O'Toole, "What's Ahead for Business-Government Relationships," *Harvard Business Review*, March–April 1979, p. 100.

tions, nationalization, and other manifestations of political instability, multinational firms and consultants have developed a variety of approaches to international forecast. Among the better known are:

Haner's Business Environmental Risk Index which monitors 15 economic and political variables in 42 countries.

Frost & Sullivan's World Political Risks Forecasts which predicts the likelihood of various catastrophes befalling an individual company.

Probe International's custom reports for specific companies which examine broad social trends.

Arthur D. Little's (ADL) developmental forecasts which examine a country's progress from the Stone Age to the computer age.[7]

Of all the approaches, ADL's forecasting techniques may be the most ambitious and sophisticated. With computer assistance, they follow the progress of each country by looking at five criteria: social development, technological advancement, abundance of natural resources, level of domestic tranquility, and type of political system. When a country's development in any one of these areas gets too far ahead of the others, tension builds and violence often follows. Using this system, political turbulence was forecast in Iran as early as 1972. ADL foresees that uneven development will likely produce similar turmoil in 20 other countries such as Peru, Chile, Malaysia, and the Phillipines. ADL believes that the world is highly predictable if one asks the right questions. Unfortunately, too many executives fail to use the same logic in analyzing political affairs that they use in other strategic areas. Political analysis should be routinely incorporated into economic analyses. Ford, General Motors, Pepsi, Singer, DuPont, and United Technologies are among the many companies that follow ADL's advice.

Technological Forecasts. Such rapidly developed and revolutionary technological innovations as lasers, nuclear energy, satellites and other communication devices, desalination of water, electric cars, and miracle drugs have prompted many firms to invest in technological forecasts. Knowledge of probable technological development helps strategic managers prepare their firms to benefit from change. To make technological forecasts, all of the previously described techniques, except econometrics, can be used. However, uncertainty of information favors use of scenarios and two additional forecasting approaches: brainstorming and the Delphi technique.

Brainstorming is used to help a group generate new ideas and forecasts. With this technique analysis or criticism of contributions made by participants is postponed so that creative thinking is not stifled or restricted. Because there are no interruptions, group members are encouraged to offer original ideas and build on the innovative thoughts of other participants. The most promising ideas generated by this means are thoroughly evaluated at a later time.

The *Delphi* technique involves a systematic procedure for obtaining a consensus from a group of experts. The procedure includes:

1. A detailed survey of expert opinion, usually obtained through a mail questionnaire.

[7] Niles Howard, "Doing Business in Unstable Countries," *Dun's Review,* March 1980, pp. 49–55.

2. Anonymous evaluation of the responses by the experts involved.
3. One or more revisions of answers until convergence is achieved.

The Delphi technique, although expensive and time-consuming, can also be successful for social and political forecasting.

Integrate Forecast Results into the Strategic Management Process

Once the techniques are selected and the forecasts made, the results must be tied into the strategic management process. For example, the economic forecast must be related to analyses of the industry, suppliers, the competition, and key resources. Figure 6–6 presents a format for displaying interrelationships between forecast remote-environment variables and the influential task-environment variables. The resulting predictions become part of the assumed environment in formulating strategy.

It is critical that strategic decision makers understand the assumptions on which environmental forecasts are based. An example is the experience of Itel, a computer-leasing firm. In 1978, Itel was able to lease 200 plug-in computers made by Advanced Systems and by Hitachi largely because IBM was unable to deliver its newest systems. Consequently, Itel made a bullish sales forecast for 1979, that it would place 430 of its systems—despite the rumor that IBM would launch a new line of aggressively priced systems in the first quarter of that year. Even Itel's competitors felt that customers would hold off their purchasing decisions until IBM made the announcement. However, Itel signed long-term purchase contracts with its suppliers and increased its marketing staff by 80 percent. This forecasting mistake and the failure to examine sales forecasts in relationship to actions of competitors and suppliers was nearly disastrous. Itel slipped close to bankruptcy within less than a year.

Forecasting external events enables a firm to identify the probable requirements for future success, to formulate or reformulate its basic mission, and to design strategies to achieve goals and objectives. If the forecast identifies any gaps or inconsistencies between the firm's desired position and its present position, strategic managers can respond with plans and actions.

Dealing with the uncertainty of the future is a major function of the strategic manager. The forecasting task requires systematic information gathering coupled with the ability to utilize a variety of forecasting approaches. A high level of intuitive insight is also needed to integrate risks and opportunities in formulating strategy. However, intentional or unintentional delays or lack of understanding of certain issues may prevent an organization from using insights gained in assessing the impact of broader environmental trends. Consistent sensitivity and constant openness to new and better approaches and opportunities are therefore essential.

Figure 6–6

Task and remote environment impact matrix

Remote environments	*Task environments*			
	Key customer trends	*Key competitor trends*	*Key supplier trends*	*Key labor market trends*
Economic	*Examples:* Trends in inflation and unemployment rates		*Example:* Annual domestic oil demand and worldwide sulfur demand through 1987	
Social	*Example:* Increasing numbers of single-parent homes			*Example:* Increasing education level of U.S. population
Political	*Example:* Increasing numbers of punitive damage awards in product liability cases		*Example:* Possibility of Arab oil boycotts	
Technological		*Example:* Increasing use of superchips and computer-based instrumentation for synthesizing genes	*Example:* Use of Cobalt 60 gamma irradiation to extend shelf life of perishables	
Industry		*Example:* Disenchantment with vertical integration; increases in large horizontal mergers		*Example:* Increasing availability of mature workers with experience in "smokestack" industries

Monitor the Critical Aspects of Managing Forecasts

Although almost all aspects of forecasting can be considered as critical in specific situations, three aspects stand out over the lifetime of a business.

The first is identification of factors that deserve forecasting. Although there are literally hundreds of different factors that might affect a firm, often a few factors of immediate concern such as sales forecasts and competitive trends are most important. Unfortunately, seldom are enough time and resources available for complete understanding of all environmental factors that might be critical to the success of a strategy. Therefore, executives must depend on their collective experience and perception of what is important in identifying factors worthy of the expense of forecasting.

The second critical aspect is whether there are reputable, cost-efficient sources outside the firm that can expand the company's forecasting data base. Strategic managers should locate federal and state governments, trade and industry associations, and other groups or individuals that can provide data forecasts at reasonable costs.

The third critical aspect of forecast management arises with the decision to handle forecasting tasks in-house. Given the great credence often given formally developed forecasts—despite the inherent uncertainty of the data base—the selection of forecasting techniques is indeed critical. A firm beginning its forecasting efforts is well advised to start with less technical methods, such as sales force estimates and the jury of executive opinion, rather than highly sophisticated forecasting techniques such as econometrics. With added exprience and understanding, the firm can add approaches that require greater analytical sophistication. In this way, managers learn to cope with the inherent weaknesses as well as the variable strengths of forecasting techniques.

Summary

Environmental forecasting starts with identification of factors external to the firm that might provide critical opportunities or pose threats in the future. Both quantitative and qualitative strategic-forecasting techniques are used to project the long-range direction and impact of these critical remote- and task-environment factors. The strengths and weaknesses of the various techniques must be understood in evaluating and selecting the most appropriate forecasting approaches for the firm. Usually employing more than one technique is advised to balance the potential bias or errors individual techniques involve.

Critical aspects in the management of forecasting include the selection of key factors to forecast, the selection of forecast sources outside the firm, the selection of forecasting activities to be done in-house, and understanding between developers and users of the environmental forecasts.

Questions for Discussion

1. Identify five anticipated changes in the remote environment which you believe will affect major industries in the United States over the next decade. What forecasting techniques could be used to assess the probable impact of these changes?

2. Construct a matrix with forecasting techniques on the horizontal axis and at least five qualities of forecasting techniques across the vertical axis. Next, indicate the relative strengths and weaknesses of each technique.
3. Develop three *heuristics* (rules of thumb) to guide strategic managers in using forecasting.
4. Develop a two-page, typewritten forecast of a variable which you believe will affect the prosperity of your business school over the next 10 years.
5. Using prominent business journals, find two examples of firms which either profited or suffered from environmental forecasts.
6. Describe the background, skills, and abilities of the individual you would hire as the environmental forecaster for your $500-million-in-annual-sales firm. How would the qualifications differ for a smaller or larger business?

Bibliography

Drucker, P. M. *Managing in Turbulent Times.* New York: Harper & Row, 1980.

Fahey, L., and W. R. King. "Environmental Scanning for Corporate Planning." *Business Horizons.* August 1977, pp. 61–71.

Howard, Niles. "Doing Business in Unstable Countries," *Dun's Review.* March 1980, pp. 49–55.

Kast, F. "Scanning the Future Environment: Social Indications." *California Management Review.* Fall 1980, pp. 22–32.

La Bell, D., and O. J. Krasner. "Selecting Environmental Forecasting Techniques from Business Planning Requirements." *Academy of Management Review.* July 1977, pp. 373–83.

Linneman, R. E. *Shirt-Sleeve Approach to Long-Range Planning: For the Smaller, Growing Corporation.* Englewood Cliffs, N.J.: Prentice-Hall, 1980.

Linneman, R. E., and J. D. Kennell. "Shirt-Sleeve Approach to Long-Range Plans." *Harvard Business Review.* March–April 1977, pp. 141–150.

Madridakis. S., and S. Wheelwright, eds. *Forecasting.* New York: North Holland Publishing, 1979.

________. "Forecasting: Issues and Challenges for Marketing Management." *Journal of Marketing.* October 1977, pp. 24–38.

Weiss, E. "Future Public Opinion of Business." *Management Review.* March 1978, pp. 8–15.

Wheelwright, S. C., and D. G. Clarke. "Corporate Forecasting: Promise and Reality." *Harvard Business Review.* November–December 1976, pp. 40–64.

"Where the Big Econometric Models Go Wrong." *Business Week.* 30 March 1981, pp. 70–3.

Chapter supplement:

Sources for remote environmental and operating forecasts

Remote environment

A. Economic considerations.
1. *Predicasts* (most complete and up-to-date review of forecasts).
2. National Bureau of Economic Research.
3. Handbook of Basic Economic Statistics.
4. *Statistical Abstract of the United States* (also includes industrial, social, and political statistics).
5. Publications by the Department of Commerce agencies:
   a. Office of Business Economics (e.g., *Survey of Business*).
   b. Bureau of Economic Analysis (e.g., *Business Conditions Digest*).
   c. Bureau of the Census (e.g., *Survey of Manufacturers* and various reports of population, housing, and industries).
   d. Business and Defense Service Administration (e.g., *United States Industrial Outlook*).
6. Securities and Exchange Commission (various quarterly reports on plant and equipment, financial reports, working capital of corporations).
7. The Conference Board.
8. *Survey of Buying Power.*
9. *Marketing Economic Guide.*
10. *Industrial Arts Index.*
11. U.S. and National chambers of commerce.
12. American Manufacturers Association.
13. *Federal Reserve Bulletin.*
14. *Economic Indicators,* annual report.
15. *Kiplinger Newsletter.*
16. International economic sources:
    a. *Worldcasts.*
    b. Master key index for business international publications.
    c. Department of Commerce.
       (1) Overseas business reports.
       (2) Industry and Trade Administration.
       (3) Bureau of the Census—*Guide to Foreign Trade Statistics.*
17. Business Periodicals Index.

Sources: Adapted with numerous additions from C. R. Goeldner and L. M. Kirks, "Business Facts: Where to Find Them." *MSU Business Topics,* Summer 1976, pp. 23–76, reprinted by permission of the publisher. Division of Research, Graduate School of Business Administration, MSU: F. E. deCarbonnel and R. G. Donance, "Information Source for Planning Decisions," *California Management Review,* Summer 1973, pp. 42–53; and A. B. Nun, R. C. Lenz, Jr., H. W. Landford, and M. J. Cleary, "Data Sources for Trend Extrapolation in Technological Forecasting," *Long-Range Planning,* February 1972, pp. 72–76.

B. Social considerations.
   1. Public opinion polls.
   2. Surveys such as *Social Indicators and Social Reporting,* the annals of the American Academy of Political and Social Sciences.
   3. Current controls: Social and behavioral sciences.
   4. Abstract services and indexes for articles in sociological, psychological, and political journals.
   5. Indexes for *The Wall Street Journal, New York Times,* and other newspapers.
   6. Bureau of the Census reports on population, housing, manufacturers, selected services, construction, retail trade, wholesale trade, and enterprise statistics.
   7. Various reports from groups such as the Brookings Institute and the Ford Foundation.
   8. World Bank Atlas (population growth and GNP data).
   9. World Bank-World Development Report.

C. Political considerations.
   1. *Public Affairs Information Services Bulletin.*
   2. CIS Index (Congressional Information Index).
   3. Business periodicals.
   4. Funk & Scott (regulations by product breakdown).
   5. Weekly compilation of presidential documents.
   6. *Monthly Catalog of Government Publications.*
   7. *Federal Register* (daily announcements of pending regulations).
   8. *Code of Federal Regulations* (final listing of regulations).
   9. Business International Master Key Index (regulations, tariffs).
   10. Various state publications.
   11. Various information services (Bureau of National Affairs, Commerce Clearing House, Prentice-Hall).

D. Technological considerations.
   1. *Applied Science and Technology Index.*
   2. *Statistical Abstract of the United States.*
   3. Scientific and Technical Information Service.
   4. University reports, congressional reports.
   5. Department of Defense and military purchasing publishers.
   6. Trade journals and industrial reports.
   7. Industry contacts, professional meetings.
   8. Computer-assisted information searches.
   9. National Science Foundation annual report.
   10. *Research and Development Directory* patent records.

E. Industry considerations
   1. *Concentration Ratios in Manufacturing* (U.S. Bureau of the Census).
   2. *Input-Output Survey* (productivity ratios).
   3. *Monthly Labor Review* (productivity ratios).
   4. *Quarterly Failure Report* (Dun & Bradstreet).
   5. *Federal Reserve Bulletin* (capacity utilization).

6. *Report on Industrial Concentration and Product Diversification in the 1,000 Largest Manufacturing Companies* (Federal Trade Commission).
7. Industry trade publications.
8. Bureau of Economic Analysis, U.S. Department of Commerce (specialization ratios).

Operating environment

A. Competition and supplier considerations.
   1. Target Group Index.
   2. U.S. Industrial Outlook.
   3. Robert Morris annual statement studies.
   4. Troy, Leo Almanac of Business & Industrial Financial Ratios.
   5. Census of Enterprise Statistics.
   6. Securities and Exchange Commission (10-K reports).
   7. Annual reports of specific companies.
   8. *Fortune 500 Directory, The Wall Street Journal, Barrons, Forbes, Dun's Review.*
   9. Investment services and directories: Moody's, Dun & Bradstreet, Standard & Poor's, Starch Marketing, Funk & Scott Index.
   10. Trade association surveys.
   11. Industry surveys.
   12. Market research surveys.
   13. *County Business Patterns.*
   14. *County and City Data Book.*
   15. Industry contacts, professional meetings, salespeople.
   16. *NF1B Quarterly Economic Report for Small Business.*

B. Customer profile.
   1. *Statistical Abstract of the U.S.,* first source of statistics.
   2. *Statistical Sources* by Paul Wasserman (a subject guide to data—both domestic and international)
   3. *American Statistics Index* (Congressional Information Service Guide to statistical publications of U.S. government—monthly).
   4. Office of the Department of Commerce.
      a. Bureau of the Census reports on population, housing, and industries.
      b. *U.S. Census of Manufacturers* (statistics by industry, area, and products).
      c. *Survey of Current Business* (analysis of business trends, especially February and July issues).
   5. Market research studies (*A Basic Bibliography on Market Review,* compiled by Robert Ferber et al., American Marketing Association).
   6. *Current Sources of Marketing Information: A Bibliography of Primary Marketing Data* by Gunther & Goldstein, AMA.
   7. *Guide to Consumer Markets.* Conference Board (provides statistical information with demographic, social, and economic data—annual).
   8. *Survey of Buying Power.*
   9. *Predicasts* (abstracts of publishing forecasts of all industries, detailed products, and end-use data).

10. *Predicasts Basebook* (historical data from 1960 to present, covering subjects ranging from population and GNP to specific products and services. Series are coded by Standard Industrial Classifications).
11. *Market Guide* (individual market surveys of over 1,500 U.S. and Canadian cities. Data includes population, location, trade area, banks, principal industries, colleges and universities, department and chain stores, newspapers, retail outlets, and sales).
12. *County and City Data Book* (includes bank deposits, birth and death rates, business firms, education, employment, income of families, manufacturers, population, savings, wholesale, and retail trade).
13. *Yearbook of International Trade Statistics* (UN).
14. *Yearbook of National Accounts Statistics* (UN).
15. *Statistical Yearbook* (UN—covers population, national income, agricultural and industrial production, energy, external trade and transport).
16. *Statistics of (Continents): Sources for Market Research* (includes separate books on Africa, America, Europe).

C. Key natural resources.
   1. *Minerals Yearbook, Geological Survey* (Bureau of Mines, Department of the Interior).
   2. *Agricultural Abstract* (U.S. Department of Agriculture).
   3. Statistics of electric utilities and gas pipeline companies. Federal Power Commission.
   4. Publications of various institutions: American Petroleum Institute, U.S. Atomic Energy Commission, Coal Mining Institute of America, American Steel Institute, and Brookings Institution.

Chapter 6 Cohesion Case Illustration

Environmental Forecasting at Holiday Inns, Inc.

Holiday Inns, Inc., uses several of the forecasting techniques discussed in Chapter 6 to project changes in its remote and operating environments that are of major importance to the firm's future strategic position. The greatest emphasis, even at the corporate level, is on environmental forecasting for hospitality-related factors. The primary environmental variables emphasized include the following factors.

1. Customer.
2. Social.
3. Technological.
4. Competition.

Exhibit 1 summarizes some of the forcasting techniques in terms of what they focus on relative to these key environmental factors.

To help understand these forecasts and how they might be useful, a few of the items that are particularly relevant to the hotel business in Exhibit 1 are illustrated below.

In better managing properties on a weekly basis to ensure operating margins are maintained, projected occupancy cycles based on historical trends can be quite helpful from the corporate level (planning cash flows) to the individual hotel level (budgeting and scheduling). Exhibit 2 shows systemwide occupancy projections for 1982 relative to actual 1981 levels. The widely fluctuating, yet historically consistent pattern can clearly accommodate weekly scheduling and budgeting of resources.

Trend analysis, surveys, and judgmental scenarios about changing customer profiles and social characteristics constitute the major forecasting emphasis at Holiday Inns. Using these techniques, the following forecasts have been made about customer and social characteristics:

Fewer and later marriages mean that HI's customer base has broadened to include a greater concentration of single persons, couples, and business people with greater freedom to travel (49).[1]

The demographic characteristics of the typical hotel, restaurant, and casino guest are virtually identical: age 24 to 49, income over $25,000, with a preference for reliable and quality service instead of the lowest price (49, 62).

[1] Numbers in parentheses refer to the appropriate paragraphs in the Cohesion Case at the end of Chapter 1.

Exhibit 1

Environmental forecasting at Holiday Inns, Inc.

Main environmental factors	*Forecasting techniques*		
	Trend analysis	*Surveys*	*Judgment/scenarios*
Customers	Changing demographic profile Specific HI guest characteristics Historical occupancy-rate cycles	Changing consumer preferences Perceptions and brand recognition of HI	Future travel patterns and destination areas
Social	Baby-boom generation Household composition Women's changing role Use of leisure time	(little use)	Worldwide status of the travel industry
Technology	Energy-saving technology, especially in terms of automobile and hotel operation Gas prices and impact on vacation travel	(little use)	Future travel modes Computer usage in property management Communication, especially satellite, developments
Competition	Size and growth of competitors Location emphasis (regions? type of location?), key price/value available from competition	Level of consumer name recognition Consumer image and brand preference	Which competitors represent key threats to aspects of HI operations

In three out of four instances, HI guests were male, but the trend to more women travelers is steadily growing (49, 83).

The movement of the baby-boom generation through the prime traveling age (25 to 45) over the next 15 years suggests unprecedented growth opportunity in the hospitality business (49, 83).

There are predictions that by the end of the century, as larger numbers of people pursue business and travel, the travel industry will have become the world's largest (81).

Exhibit 2

Company-owned properties monthly domestic occupancy comparison 1982 versus 1981 (percent)

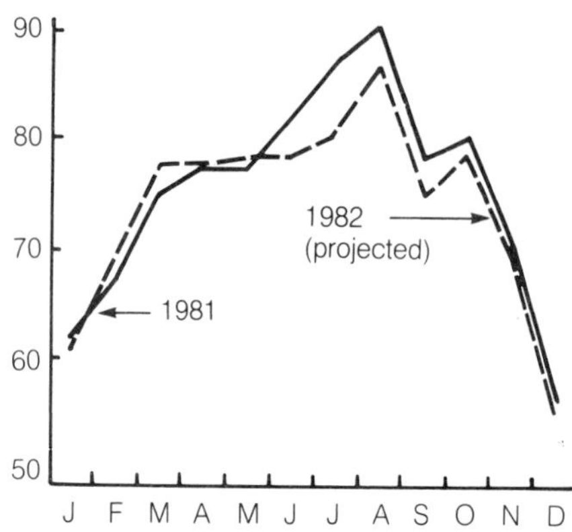

Using similar techniques regarding competition and technology, Holiday Inns, Inc. has developed such forecasts as:

Holiday Inn hotels will remain the brand preference of over one third of the traveling public through the 1980s (23).

Hospitality facilities located in multiuser locations will dominate industry growth and development in the 1980s (24).

Even with gasoline at $2 a gallon, highway driving habits will not change appreciably.

About 80 percent of U.S. adults, approve of gambling and 60 percent participate in some form. Gaming is fast becoming a national pastime and is viewed by the public as a leisure activity (62).

Most countries served by Delta Steamships are undergoing continued development and industrial expansion. This thrust provides a market for imports of high-value goods—of which U.S. industry is a major supplier (39, 40).

Are these forecasts accurate? Most seem plausible, although some have been previously questioned. At Best Western International, for example, a 17 percent cutback in auto travel as gas prices hit $2 a gallon is predicted. This view is shared by the American Petroleum Institute.

Holiday Inn executives disagree. They offer the following summary of their forecasts relative to the hospitality core of HI's business for the 1980s:

> The decade of the 1980s offers excellent potential for the hospitality industry. Business analysts see continued growth for travel through the end of the century.

While temporary gasoline shortages have been a short-term negative factor in our operations twice in the past six years, we remain quite optimistic about gasoline availability for our customers. We expect occasional brief shortages, but by and large, we believe that adequate supplies will be available.

Our optimism is fostered by a significantly more efficient car fleet and rising energy prices. The 1980 auto fleet is 55 percent more fuel efficient than its 1974 counterpart. In 1985, the average car will travel 27.5 miles per gallon of gas, a 37.5 percent increase over 1980. As gasoline prices rise, we believe the consumer will be more selective. Conservation is already becoming the rule and needless intracity travel is being curtailed. Our research tells us that our customers will continue to use their automobiles for intercity travel and vacations. Thus, we believe we are strongly positioned for the coming decade, especially as demand for our facilities will continue to outgrow supply.

Our research shows us that the hospitality business is a good business, and will remain so for as far as we can see. We look forward to the future and see continued growth, development, and profitability.

Two interesting factors that may receive increased attention in Holiday Inns for future forecasts are economic and political aspects. In the economical area, 1974 and 1981 recessions were associated with poor performance years in Holiday Inns hotel, restaurant, casino gambling, and transportation businesses. Although traditionally seen as somewhat "recession proof," these businesses are proving to be sensitive to economic cycles. Politically, as Holiday Inns concentrates on internal development, it will become more sensitive to political factors such as the situation in other countries and in terms of concerns such as currency exchange, regulation (of shipping, for example), and ownership restrictions.

CHAPTER

7

The Company Profile: Internal Analysis of the Firm

Formulation of an effective strategy is based on a clear definition of company mission, an accurate appraisal of the external environment, and a thorough internal analysis of the firm. For a strategy to succeed, at least three ingredients are critical. First, the strategy must be *consistent* with conditions in the competitive environment. Specifically, it must take advantage of existing and/or projected opportunities and minimize the impact of major threats. Second, the strategy must place *realistic* requirements on the firm's internal resources and capabilities. In other words, pursuit of market opportunities must be based on key internal strengths and not only on the existence of such opportunity. Finally, the strategy must be *carefully executed.* The focus of this chapter is on the second ingredient for strategic success: realistic analysis of the firm's internal capabilities.

Internal analysis is difficult and challenging. An internal analysis that leads to a realistic company profile frequently involves trade-offs, value judgments, and educated guesses as well as objective, standardized analysis. Unfortunately, this dichotomy can lead managers to slight internal analysis by emphasizing personal opinion. But systematic internal analysis leading to an objective company profile is essential in the development of a realistic, effective strategy.

Internal analysis must identify the strategically important strengths and weaknesses on which a firm should ultimately base its strategy. Ideally, this purpose can be achieved by first identifying key internal factors (e.g., distribution channels, cash flow, locations, technology, and organizational structure) and second by evaluating these factors. In actual practice, the process is neither linear nor simple.[1] The steps tend to overlap, and managers in different positions and levels approach internal analysis in different ways. One major study found that managers even use different criteria for evaluating apparent strengths and potential weaknesses.[2] These findings will be examined in more detail later in this chapter.

While the process of internal analysis in most firms is not necessarily systematic, it is nonetheless recognized as a critical ingredient in strategy development. If only on an intuitive basis, managers develop judgments about what the firm does particularly well—its key strengths or distinct competencies. And based on the match between these strengths and defined or projected market opportunities, the firm ultimately charts its strategic course.

The Value of Systematic Internal Assessment

Before the components of internal analysis are discussed in greater detail, the impact of systematic internal analysis will be illustrated. The experiences of business firms, both large and small, suggest that thorough internal assessment is critical in developing a successful business strategy. Regardless of the favorable opportunities in the environment, a strategy must be based on a thorough consideration of internal strengths and weaknesses of the firm if such opportunities are to be maximized. Kalso Earth® Shoes and American Motors Corporation (AMC) illustrate the value of systematic internal analysis in shaping future strategies (see Figures 7–1, 7–2).

Kalso Earth® Shoes was a U.S. company that in the early 1970s, began making shoes based upon the patented "negative-heel" design developed in Denmark by Ann Kalso. Earth® Shoes were manufactured in Massachusetts and retailed by independent franchises throughout the United States.

Kalso Earth® Shoes faced an impressive opportunity in the demand for its shoes by the mid-1970s. Kalso's pursuit of this opportunity took precedence over *objective* internal analysis of production logistics, financial capacities, and dealer organization. The firm's single, large production facility in Massachusetts encountered difficulty in managing production runs and distribution to a nationwide network of small, franchised outlets. Each outlet ordered directly from the factory. Frequently, styles requested by outlets differed because of local market preferences. Therefore, the Kalso plant was constantly faced with the trade-off between small, inefficient production runs or, by holding orders until efficient runs were feasible, a slow response to consumer demand. Each outlet was an autonomous distributor/retailer linked directly to the Massachusetts production facility.

Kalso's financial structure presented additional difficulties. The company

[1] Howard H. Stevenson, "Defining Strengths and Weaknesses," *Sloan Management Review*, Spring 1976, pp. 51–68.

[2] Ibid., p. 65.

Figure 7–1

Kalso Earth Shoe Company

We walk in a tough world. A world made of steel and concrete. A world without sympathy for our feet!

That's why Anne Kalso invented Earth® Shoes. They're designed to create underfoot the same natural terrain that existed before the earth was paved.

Patterned in the form of a healthy footprint in soft earth, the Earth® Shoe promises unsurpassed comfort and a new way of walking.

Meet Anne Kalso . . .

During her studies and experiments, Anne Kalso observed that by flexing the foot or lowering the heel, one could achieve a physical feeling similar to that attained in the Lotus or Buddah position of Yoga. Her further observations of foot imprints in sand, confirmed to her that nature intended people to walk with the weight of their bodies sunk low into the heels.

---

about the EARTH® natural heel shoe.

Wearing the EARTH® Shoe, you will experience a completely new way of walking that might take some getting used to. Initially, you may feel off-balance because of the natural heel. This is normal so don't be alarmed. Young people adapt very quickly, older people take a little longer...

In effect, you are walking barefoot on the beach . . . or across summer fields . . . wherever you go. Because walking in EARTH® Shoes is a form of exercise, some may at first experience stiffness in the calves or thighs; some may find our unique arch may take getting used to; so moderate wear is advised in the beginning.

The uniquely contoured sole will allow you to walk in a gentle rolling motion. This helps to develop a more natural, graceful walk. There is no reason why you cannot interchange the use of other shoes with the EARTH® Shoes.

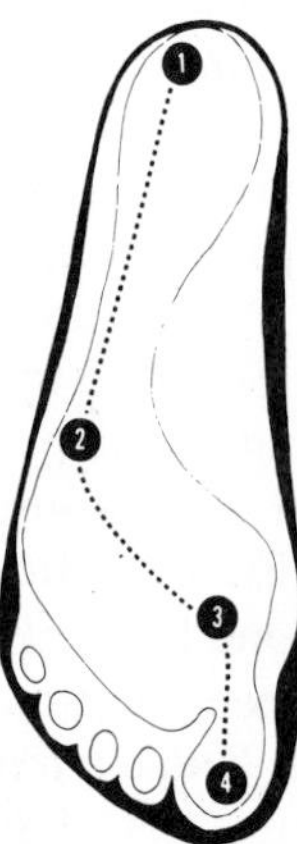

The human foot carries the entire weight load of our bodies and as we walk, this weight is constantly shifting.

The first point of contact, the heel ❶, takes the brunt of the load which then shifts to the outside of the foot ❷, and then across the metatarsal area to the ball ❸, and finally onto the large toe ❹ from which we spring into our next step.

The EARTH® Shoe is specifically designed to accommodate the shifting of weight load on our feet with the greatest ease and comfort.

Another feature of the EARTH® Shoe is the unique arch support.

Style 110 is the classic walking shoe. Our most popular all-around casual shoe. Available in sizes 6½ - 11 for women, and 7 - 11½ for men. Colors are Almond (medium brown) and Syrup (light tan).

Style 150 is a rugged, moccasin-toe oxford featuring an attractive closed-stitched design. Available in sizes 6½ - 11 for women, and 7 - 11½ for men. Colors are Almond and Sand Suede.

Figure 7–2

AMC products, 1950s through 1980s

A. 1954 Nash Hudson.

B. 1957 Rambler.

C. 1970 Hornet Pacer.

D. 1973 Jeep.

E. 1980 Renault LeCar.

F. 1984 Renault Alliance.

sought to finance increasing demand through short-term borrowing and the leveraging available through franchising. Kalso management wanted to maintain tight control over ownership of the firm, which they considered critical to maintaining the quality associated with their patented, negative-heel design. The popularity of their product and demand for franchises increased, but Kalso's pressed financial structure could not support such rapid growth.

As a result of Kalso's production logistics, distribution system, and emphasis on short-term debt, Kalso became overextended and failed. This happened even as the demand for its negative-heel design was escalating. Kalso Earth® Shoes' strategy, even given an enviable market opportunity, was not based on a systematic objective analysis of its internal strengths and weaknesses.

AMC is the number four automaker in the United States. At three crucial times since 1954, AMC has seen its market share drop below 2 percent as it found itself competing head-on with General Motors and Ford. In 1954, AMC's outdated Hudson and Nash lines were not competitive with the bigger, more ornate GM and Ford models. The sales volume of GM and Ford provided unmatched cost advantages through economies of scale. AMC, on the verge of extinction, concentrated on a small, unserved market niche for economic cars. Identifying its internal resourcefulness, low capital investment, and a sizable (yet concerned) dealer network, AMC offered the Rambler based on these limited internal strengths (see Figure 7–2). In the early 1970s, again outmaneuvered by GM, Ford, and now foreign competition, AMC examined its internal capabilities. AMC had acquired Kaiser Jeep in early 1970, and its ultimate strategy was to become a "Jeep" company. This successful strategy was based upon limited, but critical internal competence in the production and distribution of four-wheel-drive vehicles. Finally, a long-term R&D relationship with Regir Nationale des Usines Renault became a major internal strength on which, in response to the energy crisis, AMC's 1980 turnaround strategy was based. By 1982, Renault LeCar compacts were rolling off AMC assembly lines. And by 1984, AMC's domestically produced auto line was exclusively small, Renault cars.

American Motors Corporation faced massive environmental threats to its continued survival at three critical times since 1954. Each time, AMC management focused objectively and intensively upon rather limited internal strengths as a basis for its subsequent strategy. In each instance, AMC developed a successful strategy just as industry experts were finalizing AMC's obituary.

Systematic internal analysis is particularly essential in small business firms. Small firms are continually faced with limited resources and markets. At the same time, these firms are flexible and capable of making specialized, uniquely catered responses to selected market needs. To effectively channel their limited resources in directions that maximize these limited market opportunities, small firms must frequently make objective internal analyses.

Given these brief illustrations of the value of systematic internal analysis, it is appropriate to examine the process in more detail.

Developing the Company Profile

A company profile is the determination of a firm's strategic competencies and weaknesses. This is accomplished by identifying and then evaluating strategic internal factors.

What are strategic internal factors? Where do they originate? How do we decide which are truly strategic factors that must be carefully evaluated? These questions might be raised by managers in identifying and evaluating key internal factors as strengths or weaknesses on which to base the firm's future strategy.

Identification of Strategic Internal Factors

Strategic internal factors are a firm's basic capabilities, limitations, and characteristics. Figure 7–3 provides a list of typical factors, some of which would be the focus of internal analysis in most business firms. This list of factors is broken down along functional lines.

Firms are not likely to consider all of the factors in Figure 7–3 as potential strengths or weaknesses. To develop or revise a strategy, managers would rather identify the few factors on which success will most likely depend. Equally important, reliance on different internal factors will vary by industry, market segment, product life cycle, and the firm's current position. Managers are looking for what Chester Barnard calls "the strategic factors," those internal capabilities that appear most critical for success in a particular competitive area.[3] For example, strategic factors for firms in the oil industry will be quite different from those of firms in the construction or hospitality industries. Strategic factors can also vary between firms within the same industry. In the mechanical writing industry, for example, the strategies of BIC and Cross, both successful, are based on different internal strengths: BIC's on its strengths in mass production, extensive advertising, and mass distribution channels. Cross's on high quality, image, and selective distribution channels.

Strategists examine past performance to isolate key internal contributors to favorable (or unfavorable) results. What did we do well, or poorly, in marketing, operations, and financial management that had a major influence on past results? Was the sales force effectively organized? Were we in the right channels of distribution? Did we have the financial resources to support the past strategy? The same examination and questions can be applied to a firm's current situation, with particular emphasis on changes in the importance of key dimensions over time. For example, heavy advertising along with mass production and mass distribution were strategic internal factors in BIC's initial strategy for ball-point pens and disposable lighters. With the product life cycle fast reaching maturity, BIC has currently determined that cost-conscious mass production is a strategic factor, while heavy advertising is not.

---

[3] Chester Barnard, *Functions of the Executive* (Cambridge, Mass.: Harvard University Press, 1939), chapter 14.

Figure 7–3

Key internal factors: Potential strengths and weaknesses

Marketing:

Firm's products/services; breadth of product line.

Concentration of sales in a few products or to a few customers.

Ability to gather needed information about markets.

Market share or submarket shares.

Product/service mix and expansion potential: life cycle of key products; profit/sales balance in product/service.

Channels of distribution: number, coverage, and control.

Effective sales organization; knowledge of customer needs.

Product/service image, reputation, and quality.

Imaginative, efficient, and effective sales promotion and advertising.

Pricing strategy and pricing flexibility.

Procedures for digesting market feedback and developing new products, services, or markets.

After sale service and follow-up.

Goodwill/brand loyalty.

Finance and accounting:

Ability to raise short-term capital.

Ability to raise long-term capital: debt/equity.

Corporate-level resources (multibusiness firm).

Cost of capital relative to industry and competitors.

Tax considerations.

Relations with owners, investors, and stockholders.

Leverage position: Capacity to utilize alternative financial strategies such as lease or sale and leaseback.

Cost of entry and barriers to entry.

Price-earnings ratio.

Working capital; flexibility of capital structure.

Effective cost control; ability to reduce cost.

Financial size.

Efficient and effective accounting system for cost, budget, and profit planning.

Production/operations/technical:

Raw materials cost and availability; supplier relationships.

Inventory control systems; inventory turnover.

Location of facilities; layout and utilization of facilities.

Economies of scale.

Technical efficiency of facilities and utilization of capacity.

Effective use of subcontracting.

Degree of vertical integration; value added and profit margin.

Efficiency and cost/benefit of equipment.

Effective operation control procedures; design, scheduling, purchasing, quality control, and efficiency.

Costs and technological competencies relative to industry and competitors.

Research and development/technology/innovation.

Patents, trademarks, and similar legal protection.

Figure 7–3 *(concluded)*

Personnel:
- Management personnel.
- Employee's skill and morale.
- Labor relations costs compared to industry and competition.
- Efficient and effective personnel policies.
- Effective use of incentives to motivate performance.
- Ability to level peaks and valleys of employment.
- Employee turnover and absenteeism.
- Specialized skills.
- Experience.

Organization of general management:
- Organizational structure.
- Firm's image and prestige.
- Firm's record for achieving objectives.
- Organization of communication system.
- Overall organizational control system (effectiveness and utilization).
- Organizational climate; culture.
- Use of systematic procedures and techniques in decision making.
- Top management skill, capabilities, and interest.
- Strategic planning system.
- Intraorganizational synergy (multibusiness firms).

Analysis of past trends in sales, costs, and profitability is of major importance in identifying strategic internal factors. And this identification should be based on a clear picture of the nature of the firm's sales. An anatomy of past trends broken down by product lines, channels of distribution, key customers or types of customers, geographic region, and sales approach should be developed in detail. A similar anatomy should focus on costs and profitability. Detailed investigation of the firm's performance history helps isolate internal factors influencing sales, costs, profitability, or their interrelationships. These factors are of major importance to future strategy decisions. For example, one firm may find that 83 percent of its sales result from 25 percent of its products. Another firm may find that 30 percent of its products (or services) contribute 78 percent of its profitability. To understand such results, a firm may determine that certain key internal factors (for example, experience in particular distribution channels, pricing policies, warehouse location, technology) deserve major attention in formulating future strategy.

Identifying strategic factors requires an external focus, as well. When a strategist isolates key internal factors through analysis of past and present performance, industry conditions/trends and comparisons with competitors also provide insight. BIC's identification of mass production and advertising as key internal factors is based as much on analysis of industry and competitive characteristics as on past performance of BIC itself. Changing industry conditions can lead to the need to re-examine internal strengths and weaknesses in light of newly emerging determinants of success in the industry. Strategy in Action 7–1 illustrates a strategic shift in Merrill Lynch's internal strengths and weaknesses based on changing determinants of success in the financial services industry. Furthermore, strategic internal factors are often chosen for in-depth evaluation because firms are contemplating expansion of products or markets, diversification, and so forth. Clearly, scrutinizing the industry under consideration and current competitors are key means of identifying strategic factors if a firm is evaluating its capability to move into unfamiliar markets.

Strategy in Action 7–1

Merrill Lynch's Strategic Dilemma

As deregulation melds together the once-segmented financial service industries, Merrill Lynch faces increasing direct competition from Sears, Roebuck; American Express; Citicorp; and other formidable companies outside the securities industry. While Merrill Lynch has proved itself the equal of anyone in innovating financial products and services, in the way it delivers them to consumers, in its compensation methods, and in its corporate culture, Merrill Lynch remains quintessentially a brokerage house.

Merrill Lynch's attempt to strike a balance between old Wall Street and the emergence of one-stop financial shopping has trapped it in a truly nasty dilemma. The company's greatest strength—its retail system of 431 branch offices and 8,763 brokers—may have become its greatest weakness. By funneling nearly all of its growing number of financial products through its brokers, Merrill Lynch generates huge sales volume. But because its brokers get a cut of all they sell, this approach is very expensive. And its inflexibility makes Merrill Lynch vulnerable at a time when discount brokering and other low-cost distribution methods are gaining market share.

But any attempt to tamper with Merrill Lynch's retail sales organization is perilous because the broker—not the company—typically commands customer loyalty. "My customers are my blanket," said one veteran Merrill Lynch broker. "I can just pick them up and walk away." Merrill Lynch has gingerly begun to walk a fine line between remaking its vaunted broker system and destroying it. The company has raised its performance standards for brokers and is beginning to weed out the laggards. It has also begun the delicate task of converting the broker into a financial adviser at the hub of a network of salaried sales assistants and professionals who specialize in insurance, lending, and tax matters.

Some veteran brokers are disillusioned by the trend toward one-stop financial shopping, while the performance crackdown stirs resentment among the newcomers. "Merrill Lynch is losing touch with its distribution system," claims a senior executive of a major Wall Street firm. "It's become a case of the home office proposing and the field disposing." The erosion of Merrill Lynch's legendary morale has made it easier for his company to lure away brokers, he says.

Merrill's vice president for human resources insists that the turnover rate among Merrill Lynch's sales force is "trending sideways at an acceptable level" and that most of those brokers who do leave are not top performers. Still, Merrill Lynch was one of the first firms to sue former brokers who allegedly violated pledges not to take their customers with them to other firms.

Especially at a time of internal tension, Merrill Lynch's monolithic retail distribution system is a cumbersome way of serving an unsettled market. Discount brokers, which do not pay commissions to their brokers, have doubled their share of equity trading volume to 16 percent in 1983.

Meanwhile, many full-service brokers are expanding their branch systems at a furious pace. "The name of the game in the 1980s is distribution," said James Settel, a senior vice president at Prudential Bache. "The more good distribution points you have, the better are your chances of picking up all the marbles."

Dean Witter Reynolds Inc., now part of Sears, Roebuck & Company, plans to nearly double its branches and to increase its corps of brokers from 4,900 to 11,000 by 1988. About 280 of the offices will be in Sears stores.

Roger Birk, Merrill Lynch board chairman in 1984, recognized the difficulty in first identifying and acting on the brokerage firm's strengths and weaknesses in the changing financial services industry. Birk seems undaunted. "Who ever said it would be easy? It's not," he says. "This is a tough business—a very difficult business to manage."

Based on the article "Merrill Lynch's Big Dilemma," from the January 6, 1984, issue of *Business Week*.

Evaluation of Internal Strategic Factors

Identification and evaluation of key internal factors have been separated for discussion, but in practice they are not separate, distinct steps. The objective of internal analysis is a careful determination of a firm's strategic strengths and weaknesses. An internal analysis that generates a long list of resources and capabilities has provided little to help in strategy formulation. Instead, internal analysis must identify and evaluate a limited number of strengths and weaknesses relative to the opportunities targeted in the firm's current and future competitive environment.

What are potential strengths and weaknesses? A factor is considered a strength if it is a distinct competency or competitive advantage. It is more than merely what the firm has the competence to do. It is something the firm does (or has the future capacity to do) particularly well relative to abilities of existing or potential competitors. A distinctive competence (strength) is important because it gives an organization a comparative advantage in the marketplace.[4] For example, Kalso Earth[R] Shoe's product image and patented design were two distinct competencies for that firm.

A factor is considered a weakness if it is something the firm does poorly, or doesn't have the capacity to do although key rivals have the capacity. Centralized production facilities and lack of capital resources were major weaknesses for Kalso Earth® Shoes in trying to compete with other shoe manufacturers on a nationwide basis. Scripto's outdated production facilities and lack of financial resources to support mass advertising were major weaknesses. The firm's management had to weigh these factors deciding to challenge BIC in the ball-point segment of the writing implement industry.

How should strategists evaluate key internal factors as strengths or weaknesses? There are four basic perspectives: (1) comparison with competitors, (2) comparison with the firm's past performance, (3) stages in the evolution of product/markets, and (4) comparison with factors in the firm's industry that appear to lead to success.

Comparison with Competitors. A major focus in determining a firm's strengths and weaknesses is comparison with existing (and potential) competitors. Firms in the same industry often have different marketing skills, financial resources, operating facilities and locations, technical know-how, brand image, levels of integration, managerial talent, and so on. These different internal capabilities can become relative strengths (or weaknesses) depending upon the strategy the firm chooses. In choosing strategy, a manager should compare the company's key internal capabilities with those of its rivals, thereby isolating key strengths or weaknesses.

In the major home appliance industry, for example, Sears and General Electric are major rivals. Sears' major strength is its retail network. For GE, distribution—through independent franchised dealers—has traditionally been a relative weakness. With the financial resources to support modernized mass production, GE has maintained both a cost and technological advantage over its rivals, particularly Sears. This major strength for GE is a relative weakness for Sears which depends solely on subcontracting to produce its Kenmore brand applicances. On the other hand, maintenance and repair service are important in the applicance industry. Historically, Sears has strength in this area because it maintains a fully staffed service component and spreads the costs over numerous departments at each retail location. GE, on the other hand, has had to depend on regional service centers and local contracting with independent service firms by its local, independent dealers.

In ultimately developing a strategy, distribution network, technological capabilities, operating costs, and service facilities are a few of the internal factors Sears and GE must consider. To ascertain whether their internal capabilities on these and other factors are strengths or weaknesses, comparison to key competitors can prove useful. Significant favorable differences (existing or

[4] A. A. Thompson, Jr., and A. J. Strickland III, *Strategy Formulation and Implementation* (Plano, Tex.: Business Publications, 1983), p. 277.

expected) are potential cornerstones of the firm's strategy. Likewise, through comparison to major competitors, a firm may avoid strategic commitments it cannot competitively support.

Comparison with Past Performance. Strategists also use the historical experience of the firm as a basis for evaluating internal factors. Managers are most familiar with their firm, its internal capabilities and problems, because they have been immersed over time in managing the firm's financial, marketing, production, and R&D activities. Not surprisingly, a manager's assessment of whether certain internal factors—such as production facilities, sales organization, financial capacity, control systems, and key personnel—are strengths or weaknesses will be strongly influenced by his or her internal experience. In the capital-intensive airline industry, for example, debt capacity is a strategic internal factor. Delta Airlines has a debt/equity ratio of less than 0.6, while Braniff's was 5.2 shortly before the carrier declared bankruptcy in 1983. Frank Borman, president of Eastern Air Lines, considered Eastern's ratio of 2.1 to be an emerging strength for the firm in the early 1980s. While he was obviously aware of competitive comparisons, Borman based this evaluation on the historical experience of Eastern—on the fact that the ratio had improved from 4.1 to 2.1 since he joined the firm in 1975. Unfortunately for Borman, debt capacity has worsened in recent years[5] and is now considered a major weakness, as discussed in Strategy in Action 7–2.

While historical experience can provide a relevant evaluation framework, strategists must avoid tunnel vision. Texaco management, for example, had long considered its large number of service stations (27,000 in 1980) a key

Strategy in Action 7–2

Eastern Air Lines Searches for Key Strengths to Support Its 1984–1985 Strategy

Deregulation of the airline industry in the early 1980s introduced major changes for participating airlines. Where routes and fares had been stringently controlled, deregulation meant that both setting fares and the decision to serve a particular location were open to each airline based on competitive market conditions or other priorities. This new freedom led to intense fare competition on the 200 most popular intercity routes in the United States in the early 1980s.

Braniff Airways was one of the first casualities of this intensified competition. Using debt to rapidly increase its fleet so that it could enter several of the newly

[5] Eastern Air Lines, Inc., 1983 Annual Report.

Strategy in Action 7–2 *(concluded)*

deregulated routes, Braniff found itself caught between decreasing fares and increasing interest rates. Bankruptcy quickly followed in 1982. By 1983, bankruptcy was likely for Continental Air Lines and rumored a possibility at Eastern Air Lines.

Eastern, seeking to calm nervous investors and employees, went to unusual lengths to communicate the basis for its 1984–85 corporate strategy. One key ingredient was its assessment of internal capabilities. Six key points were presented by Eastern management:

1. We will have the resources to substantially expand our operation.
   a. An average of 13 additional aircraft, primarily B-757s delivered in 1983, will be available for scheduled service.
   b. The pilot agreement permits additional hours to be flown with the existing work force. Similar productivity improvements are expected to limit the required increase in other personnel.
2. There are identified schedule opportunities at our established hubs for using the additional aircraft.
   a. Restoration of daytime service to the levels that preceded the air traffic controllers' (PATCO) strike at Atlanta and LaGuardia alone would effectively use the 13 aircraft.
3. Our position in the marketplace has been strong and improving.
   a. As measured by revenue per airplane seat mile (ASM), we led all major airlines in 1982 and continued to outperform the industry in the first quarter of 1983.
4. Committed increases in employee compensation require increases in productivity that realistically can be achieved through both normal attrition and basic airline expansion.
   a. The pilot agreement includes improvements in productivity that are fundamental to our success. Similar improvements must be made elsewhere in the corporation.
5. In the aftermath of recent negotiations with the airline mechanics union, employee attitudes—morale and the willingness of different groups to work together—clearly are a major concern. Effectively addressing this issue is a major challenge for 1984.
6. Our balance sheet and cash situation require constant attention.

Eastern's management has identified excess capacity in its fleet and routes as key strengths. Revenue per ASM is interpreted as an indicator of strong customer demand. Eastern clearly sees its financial position as a major weakness and morale/productivity as a pivotal factor that must become a clear strength for Eastern to succeed.

strength. This strength (along with other perceived strengths) had "worked so well for so long [at Texaco] that even the thought of changing them was heretical to management."[6] But Shell, with just over 6,280 service stations, sold slightly more gasoline than Texaco.[7] Clearly, using only historical experience as a basis for identifying strengths and weaknesses can prove dangerously inaccurate.

Stages in Product/Market Evolution. The requirements for success in product/market segments evolve and change over time. As a result, strategists can use these changing patterns associated with different stages in product/market evolution as a framework for identifying and evaluating the firm's strengths and weaknesses.

Figure 7–4 depicts four general stages of product/market evolution and the typical changes in functional capabilities that are often associated with business success at each stage. In the early development of a product/market, for example, there are minimal growth in sales, major R&D emphasis, rapid technological change in the product, operating losses, and a need for sufficient resources or slack to support a temporarily unprofitable operation. Success at this stage may be associated with technical skill with being first in new markets, or with having a marketing advantage that creates widespread awareness. Radio Shack's initial success with its TRS-80 home computer was based in part on its ability to gain widespread exposure and acceptance in the ill-defined home computer market via the large number of existing Radio Shack outlets throughout the country.

The strengths necessary for success change in the growth stage. Rapid growth brings new competitors into the market. Factors such as brand recognition, product/market differentiation, and the financial resources to support both heavy marketing expenses and the effect of price competition on cash flow can be key strengths at this stage. IBM entered the personal computer market in the growth stage and was able to rapidly become the market leader with a strategy based on key strengths in brand awareness and the financial resources to support consumer advertising.

As the product/market moves through a "shakeout" phase and into the maturity stage, market growth continues, but at a decreasing rate. The number of market segments begins to expand, while technological change in product design slows considerably. The result is usually more intense competition, and promotional or pricing advantages, or differentiation become key internal strengths. Technological change in process design becomes intense as the many competitors seek to provide the product in the most efficient manner. Where R&D was critical in the development stage, efficient production has now become crucial to a business's continued success in the broader market segments. General Motors has found efficiency a key strength in the auto industry.

[6] "Texaco: Restoring Luster to the Star," *Business Week*, December 22, 1980, p. 54; and "Inside the Shell Oil Company," *Newsweek*, June 15, 1981, p. 74.

[7] "Texaco," p. 60.

Figure 7–4

Sources of distinctive competence at different stages of product/market evolution

Takeoff
Growth rate ≈ GNP
Unit sales
Market growth rate ≈ Population growth rate
Profits (dollars)
Growth rate <0

Functional area	*Introduction*	*Growth*	*Maturity*	*Decline*
Marketing	Resources/skill to create widespread awareness and find acceptance from customers; advantageous access to distribution channels	Ability to establish brand recognition; find niche; reduce price; solidify strong distribution relations and develop new channels	Skill in agressively promoting products to new markets and holding existing markets; pricing flexibility; skills in differentiating products and holding customer loyalty	Cost-effective means of efficient access to selected channels and markets; strong customer loyalty or dependence; strong company image
Production/operations	Ability to expand capacity effectively; limit number of designs; develop standards	Ability to add product variants; centralize production or otherwise lower costs; improve product quality; seasonal subcontracting capacity	Improve product and reduce costs; ability to share or reduce capacity; advantageous supplier relationships; subcontracting	Ability to prune product line; cost advantage in production, location, or distribution; simplified inventory control; subcontracting or long production runs
Finance	Resources to support high net cash overflow and initial losses; ability to use leverage effectively	Ability to finance rapid expansion; still have net cash outflows but increasing profits; need resources to support product improvements	Ability to generate and redistribute increasing net cash inflows; effective cost control systems	Ability to reuse or liquidate unneeded equipment; advantage in cost of facilities; control system accuracy; streamlined management control
Personnel	Flexibility in staffing and training new management; existence of employee with key skills in new products or markets	Existence of and ability to add skilled personnel; motivated and loyal work force	Ability to cost effectively reduce work force; increase efficiency	Capacity to reduce and reallocate personnel; cost advantage
Engineering and research and development	Ability to make engineering changes; have technical bugs in product and process resolved	Skill in quality and new feature development; start developing successor product	Reduce costs; develop variants to differentiate products	Support other growth areas or apply to unique customer needs
Key functional area and strategy focus	Sales; consumer loyalty; market share	Engineering; market penetration	Production efficiency; successor products	Finance; maximum investment recovery

Source: Adapted from Peter Doyle, "The Realities of the Product Life Cycle," *Quarterly Review of Marketing,* Summer 1976, pp. 1–6; Harold Fox, "A Framework for Functional Coordination," *Atlantic Ecomonic Review,* November–December 1973; Charles W. Hofer, *Conceptual Constructs for Formulating Corporate and Business Strategy* (Boston: Intercollegiate Case Clearing House, 1977), p. 7; Philip Kotler, *Marketing Management* (Englewood Cliffs, N.J.: Prentice-Hall, 1980); and Charles Wasson, *Dynamic Competitive Strategy and Product Life Cycles* (Austin, Tex.: Austin Press, 1978).

When products/markets move toward a saturation/decline stage, strengths and weaknesses center on cost advantages, superior supplier or customer relationships, and financial control. Competitive advantage can exist at this stage, at least temporarily, if a firm serves gradually shrinking markets that competitors are choosing to leave. Strategy in Action 7–3 describes Firestone's efforts to re-examine its strengths and weaknesses in the rapidly maturing tire market.

Figure 7–4 is a rather simple model of the stages of product/market evolution. These stages can and do vary. But it is important to realize, especially as illustrated in the preceding discussion, that the relative importance of various determinants of success differs across stages of product/market evolution. Thus, stage of evolution must be considered in internal analysis. Figure 7–4 suggests different dimensions that are particularly deserving of in-depth consideration when developing a company profile.

Success Factors in the Industry. Industry analysis involves identifying factors associated with successful participation in a given industry. As was true of the evaluation methods discussed above, the key determinants of success in an industry may be used to identify the internal strengths and weaknesses of a firm. By scrutinizing industry competitors, as well as customer needs, vertical industry structure, channels of distribution, costs, barriers to entry, availability of substitutes, and suppliers, a strategist seeks to determine whether a firm's current internal capabilities represent strengths or weaknesses in new competitive arenas. The previous discussion in Chapter 6 provides a useful framework—five industry forces—against which to examine potential strengths and weaknesses. General Cinema Corporation, the nation's largest movie theater operator, determined that its internal skills in marketing, site analysis, creative financing, and management of geographically dispersed operations provided key strengths relative to major success factors in the soft-drink bottling industry. This assessment proved to be accurate. Since entering the soft drink bottling industry in 1968, General Cinema has become the largest franchised bottler of soft drinks in the United States, handling Pepsi, 7up, Dr Pepper, and Sunkist.

Use of industry-level analysis to evaluate a firm's capacity for success and to help devise future strategy has become a popular technique in the 1980s.[8] Its relevance as an aid to comprehensive internal analysis is discussed more fully in a subsequent section of this chapter.

Quantitative versus Qualitative Approaches in Evaluating Internal Factors

Numerous quantitative tools are available for evaluating selected internal capabilities of a firm. These entail measurement of a firm's effectiveness vis-

[8] Michael E. Porter, *Competitive Strategy: Techniques for Analyzing Industries and Competitors* (New York: Free Press, 1980) offers broad, in-depth coverage of numerous techniques for evaluating the strengths and weaknesses of a firm and its competitors. Chapter 6 presents key aspects underlying Professor Porter's analytical approaches.

Strategy in Action 7–3

Firestone Examines Its Strengths and Weaknesses

The Firestone Tire & Rubber Company has finally turned around. Or so John J. Nevin, the company's president, believes. Recruited from Zenith to get the troubled number two tire maker back on track, Nevin was alarmed by "the terrible load of excess and obsolescent plant capacity we were carrying." He saw Firestone suffocating in a glut of unsold tires that [the firm] had used all its cash and much of its credit to produce. Firestone's trauma was just one of those visited upon American industry by sharply higher energy costs.

In Nevin's view, Firestone management had acted as though the tire industry had suffered only a temporary slump. Instead, he says, the industry and its market was becoming permanently smaller. He observes that smaller, lighter new cars need only 75 pounds of tires each, instead of 150 pounds. Imported cars, each equipped with five foreign tires, are taking a growing share of the U.S. market. People are driving less because gasoline costs more and because smaller cars are less comfortable on long trips. New cars come equipped with radial tires, which will run twice as far as bias tires, the old industry standard.

While tire demand was falling, Firestone had kept its unused capacity for producing bias tires expecting to exploit the market when competitors dropped out. But the new forecasts meant that Firestone's overcapacity would become an enormous burden. Nevin presented a drastic remedy: shutdown of six tire plants that together accounted for one third of Firestone's car-tire and truck-tire capacity.

Shutting down the plants automatically cut inventory. Nevin decided to go further and reduce the number of products from 7,289 different types of tires—5,472 of them for private-label customers that accounted for only 35 percent of tire sales—to 4,895.

That action restored some of the glow to Firestone's pallid balance sheet. The reduction in tire inventories has freed $280 million to reduce debt from 80 to 64 percent of the shareholders' equity. Nevin still intends to bring debt down to the 50-percent-of-equity target.

Meanwhile, Firestone's remaining plants are expected to operate far more profitably at 90 percent or more of capacity.

"The improved balance sheet becomes a stepping-stone to the future," Nevin said. "We have an objective of diversifying, but there isn't any sense in talking about diversifying if you don't have the internal strengths."

Source: "Firestone Becomes Leaner and Stronger by Cutting Capacity, Jobs, Product Lines." Reprinted by permission of *The Wall Street Journal,*

à-vis each relevant factor and comparative analysis of this measurement against both competitors (directly or through industry averages) and the historical experience of the firm. Ratio analysis is one example that is useful for evaluating selected financial, marketing, and operating factors. The firm's balance sheet and income statement are important sources from which to derive meaningful ratios. The appendix at the end of the text section of this book (p. 399) illustrates the use of these techniques for internal analysis.

Dun & Bradstreet and Robert Morris Associates regularly publish sets of ratios for a variety of industries.[9] Trade publications for specific types of firms are another source of comparative information. Information from these sources and the firm's past performance are useful if ratio analysis is used to evaluate an internal factor. Examples of other quantitative or analytical tools include cash-flow analysis, sensitivity analysis, and elasticity and variability analysis.[10]

Quantitative tools cannot be applied to all internal factors, and the normative judgments of key planning participants may be used in evaluation. Company or product image and prestige are examples of internal factors more amenable to qualitative evaluation. But, even though qualitative and judgmental criteria are used, identification and serious evaluation of this type of factor is a necessary and important aspect of a thorough internal analysis. Research by Harold Stevenson found this to be particularly true in evaluating weaknesses.[11] Stevenson interviewed 50 executives in six medium-to-large firms and found the following criteria used to identify and evaluate strengths and weaknesses:

Type of criteria	*Degree of use (percent)*	
	Strengths	***Weaknesses***
Historical experience	90	10
Industry/competitor comparison	67	33
Normative judgment	21	79

While managers used past performance and competitive comparison in evaluating tentative strengths, they relied heavily on normative judgment (qualitative assessment and opinion) in evaluating probable weaknesses. Stevenson suggested that this was true because weaknesses often reflect competencies or areas in which the firm (and its managers) lack experience. And because they have no experience in these areas, managers must use qualitative assess-

[9] *Dun's Review,* published monthly by Dun & Bradstreet, N.Y. RMA: *Annual Statement Studies* published annually by Robert Morris Associates, Philadelphia.

[10] O. M. Joy, *Introduction to Financial Management* (Homewood, Ill. Richard D. Irwin, 1980), pp. 119–28, 207–9, provides a useful discussion of cash-flow analysis and sensitivity analysis; C. W. Hofer and D. Schendel, *Strategy Formulation: Analytical Concepts* (St. Paul, Minn.; West Publishing, 1978), especially chapter 2, provides a discussion of sensitivity analysis, elasticity analysis, variability analysis, and the product life-cycle concept as tools for evaluating a business's strengths and weaknesses.

[11] Stevenson, "Defining Strengths," pp. 64–68.

ment and opinion to evaluate the weakness. Stevenson's research probably does not reflect how all business firms evaluate strengths and weaknesses, but it provides a vivid illustration of how often typical managers employ normative judgments in internal analysis.

Linking the Company Profile to the Overall Strategic Management Process

Internal analysis does not take place in a vacuum. It is dependent upon other aspects of the strategic management process. Perhaps most critical is the relationship between internal analysis and environmental assessment. Environmental assessment, particularly as it focuses on competitors, product/market trends, consumer preferences, technological changes, and changing industry forces, provides a critical basis for evaluating internal factors and identifying key strengths and weaknesses. And this relationship is important for another reason: Matching internal strengths and weaknesses in the assessment of environmental/industry conditions is an essential step for generating viable alternative strategies. Figure 7–5 illustrates the fundamental dynamics of this process.

Systematic comparison of the environmental/industry analysis and the profile of business strengths and weaknesses is the basis for any approach to strategic management. Industry analysis has narrowed the focus to the relative importance of selected, critical factors (or competencies) for successful participation in an industry and its various market segments. The company profile identifies key strengths and weaknesses and distinct competencies, particularly relative to the key factors identified in the industry analysis.

The four situations in Figure 7–5 illustrate potential outcomes of comparing an industry analysis and a company profile. Obviously, many additional outcomes are possible.

Situation 1. The firm in situation 1 has a strong competitive position. Its distinctive competencies match the determinants of industry (or product/market segment) success. A firm in this position should pursue an aggressive strategy exploiting its key strengths. Several characteristics of an appropriate strategy in this situation would include: grow, seek dominance, maximize investment, expand market share, diversify, and reinforce distinct competencies. Situation 1 would support strategies that challenge rival firms head on, even where competitors are strong. Following the analogy of the airline industry suggested in Figure 7–5, a firm in situation 1 would be Delta Airlines. With its strong financial position, hub location, relatively efficient aircraft, low labor costs, and improving market share, Delta strategists narrow the alternatives to growth-oriented, share increasing strategies that exploit the carrier's cost advantages.

Figure 7–5

Matching internal analysis and environment/industry assessment

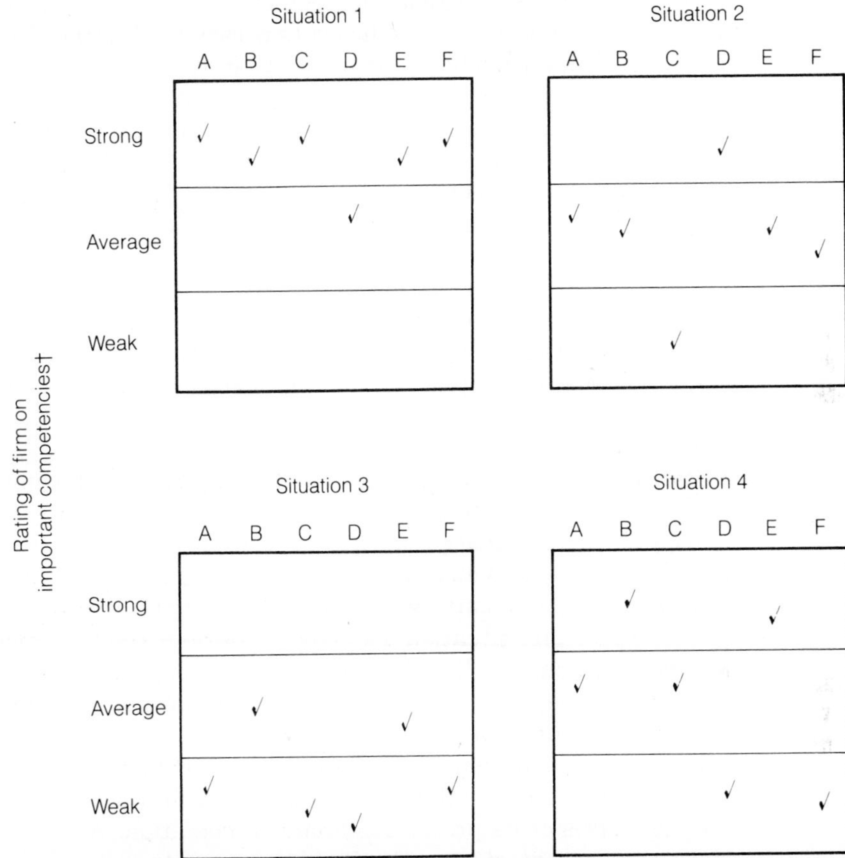

* A, B, C, D, E, and F represent key determinants of success in an industry or, where the industry is not dominated by one major product market, key determinants of success in a particular segment. Using the domestic airline passenger industry as an example, A–F would represent high-density routes, energy-efficient aircraft, hub location, market share, debt capacity, and labor-cost relations, respectively.

† This dimension represents the internal analysis of a business's competencies in light of the key determinants of success in the industry or product market segment. Four typical business situations are represented here. Each check (√) shows the strength of a business's competency relative to a key determinant of success in the industry.

Situation 2. The firm in situation 2 has moderate competence in terms of the key factors associated with industry (or product/market) success. Firms in this situation might be inclined toward stable growth strategies, seeking to maintain position and minimize risk and the firm's dependence on weaker competencies. Specialization, selected growth via segmentation, and functional strategies to improve critical competencies would be characteristic of appropriate strategies for situation 2 firms. Contrary to situation 1, situation 2 firms would be unlikely to choose strategies that attack rival firms where the latter are strong. Rather, strategies should be sought that attack rival's weaknesses and less-emphasized market segments. Again, using the airline analogy, American Airlines is a situation 2 firm. It serves selected high-density routes, yet American's overall fleet is not energy efficient. Its hub location, market share, financial/debt capacity, and labor costs/relations, though adequate, are not nearly as strong as Delta's. American strategists logically prefer to protect key (profitable) routes, maintain current position, selectively seek new segments for limited growth, and try to improve their competence in such factors as aircraft efficiency and financial strength. More aggressive strategies might call for greater competence than American can muster, spelling future disaster.

Situation 3. The firm in situation 3 occupies a weak competitive position. Its level of competence relative to key determinants of industry (or product/market) success is marginal to poor on each factor. A firm in this situation is rather limited and appropriately narrows its choices to defensive strategies. Retrenchment, cost cutting, and maintenance of minor market-segment positions characterize situation 3 strategies. Serious consideration must be given to divestiture and/or liquidation where the potential for improvement is unrealistic. Turnaround strategies may be appropriate if one or more competencies might be improved.

Eastern is a situation 3 competitor in the airline industry. Eastern is consistently weak in terms of the key success factors for the airline industry, particularly in terms of its precarious financial condition. As a result, Eastern has chosen to concentrate on a limited route structure, to gradually divest itself of an inefficient portion of its fleet, to cut costs via labor and pilot concessions, and to stabilize profitability around a smaller market share.

Situation 4. For the firm in situation 4, the match of its competencies with industry (or product/market) success requirements is dispersed. It is strong in some areas and weak in others. Such a position lends itself to the strategy evaluation axiom: maximize opportunities and strengths while minimizing threats and weaknesses. In other words, firms in this situation should seek strategies in which success depends upon its competencies and not on the areas in which the firm is weak. Realistically, for a firm to pursue an aggressive, growth-oriented strategy based upon key strengths (e.g., reputation and technology) it often must assume higher levels of risk with a necessary dependence upon weaker competencies (like location or financial capacity) if the strategy is to be successful.

USAir might well be a situation 4 firm in the airline industry. When airlines were deregulated, USAir was basically a regional airline. In terms of the domestic passenger airline industry, USAir was strong in energy-efficient aircraft and low labor costs, weak in financial/debt capacity and hub location, and moderate-to-poor in market share and high-density routes. USAir adopted a strategy of selective, stable growth. The carrier pursued shorter, secondary routes that major airlines abandoned due to cost considerations. As USAir built its market share, it selectively moved into more popular (high-density) routes. USAir adopted a selective growth strategy based upon maximizing strengths and minimizing weaknesses in circumstances similar to those in situation 4.

Figure 7–5 and the accompanying discussion illustrate the important contribution of an accurate company profile in designing an effective strategy. Different patterns of internal strengths and weaknesses lead to very different strategy options for the firm, as you can see in Figure 7–5. Clearly accuracy of internal analysis in identifying key strengths and weaknesses is critical in ultimately identifying the best strategy for a firm. The next chapter describes the strategy alternatives a firm may consider.

Summary

Generating a company profile is critical in the strategic management process. This profile is developed through thorough internal analysis of the firm, starting with identification of strategic internal factors that determine the firm's effectiveness. Key internal factors are identified through in-depth analysis of performance history, current involvements, and the firm's existing or potential competitive environment.

The second phase of internal analysis is thorough evaluation of these key factors. Here, historical experience and industry/competitor comparison can provide key frameworks. Technical or quantitative tools, such as ratio analysis and product life cycle, are often used in this comparative evaluation. Normative judgments are frequently called for, particularly if strategists lack the technical capacity or comparative knowledge for evaluation.

Internal analysis is critically dependent on environmental assessment for relevance and accuracy. The ultimate purpose of internal analysis is to isolate strategic strengths and weaknesses around which a firm's future strategy is built.

Reminder: An appendix at the end of this book illustrates the use of ratio analysis and other financial analysis techniques. See page 399.

Questions for Discussion

1. Describe the process used to identify key internal factors in a firm's strategic management process. Why does this appear to be an important part of the strategic management process?
2. Apply the two broad steps of internal analysis to yourself and your career aspirations. What are your major strengths and weaknesses? How might these be used to develop your future career plans?
3. Select one business in your area that appears to be doing well and another that appears to be doing poorly. Form two small teams with the help of your instructor. Have each team take one of the businesses and schedule a brief interview with a key manager. Obtain a *specific* assessment of each firm's internal strengths and weaknesses. Compare the results in a subsequent class. Are there substantial differences? Is one more comprehensive and specific than the other? Do strengths and weaknesses vary by type of business?
4. Explain why a firm might emphasize historical experience over competitor comparison in evaluating its strengths and weaknesses. When would the reverse emphasis be more relevant?

Bibliography

Barnard, Chester. *Functions of the Executive.* Cambridge, Mass.: Harvard University Press, 1939, chapter 14.

Buchele, Robert B. "How to Evaluate a Firm." *California Management Review,* Fall 1962, pp. 5–17.

Cooper, A. C., and Dan Schendel. "Strategic Responses to Technological Threats." *Business Horizons* 19 (1976), pp. 61–69.

"Corporate Culture: The Hard-to-Change Values That Spell Success or Failure." *Business Week,* October 27, 1980, pp. 148–60.

Doyle, Peter. "The Realities of the Product Life Cycle." *Quarterly Review of Marketing,* Summer 1976, pp. 1–6.

Dun's Review. New York: Dun & Bradstreet, published monthly.

Fox, Harold. "A Framework for Functional Coordination." *Atlantic Economic Review,* November–December 1973.

Gilmore, Frank. "Formulating Strategy in Smaller Companies." *Harvard Business Review,* May–June 1971, pp. 71–81.

Glueck, William F. *Business Policy and Strategic Management.* New York: McGraw-Hill, 1980, chapter 4.

Henry, Harold W. "Appraising a Company's Strengths and Weaknesses." *Managerial Planning,* July–August 1980, pp. 31–36.

Hofer, Charles W., and Dan Schendel. *Strategy Formulation: Analytical Concepts.* St. Paul, Minn.: West Publishing, 1978, chapter 2.

"Inside the Shell Oil Company." *Newsweek,* June 15, 1981, p. 74.

Joy, O. M. *Introduction to Financial Management.* Homewood, Ill.: Richard D. Irwin, 1980, pp. 119–28 and 207–9.

Kotler, Philip. *Marketing Management.* Englewood Cliffs, N.J.: Prentice-Hall, 1980.

Mintzberg, Henry. "Strategy Making in Three Modes." *California Management Review* 16, no. 2 (1973), pp. 44–53.

Porter, Michael E. *Competitive Strategy: Techniques for Analyzing Industries and Competitors.* New York: Free Press, 1980.

RMA: *Annual Statement Studies.* Philadelphia: Robert Morris Associates, published annually.

Schendel, Dan; G. Richard Patton; and James Riggs. "Corporate Turnaround Strategies: A Study of Profit Decline and Recovery." *Journal of General Management* 3, no. 3 (Spring 1976), pp. 3–11.

South, Stephen E. "Competitive Advantage: The Cornerstone to Strategic Thinking." *Journal of Business Strategy* 1, no. 4 (1981), pp. 15–25.

Stevenson, Howard H. "Defining Strengths and Weaknesses." *Sloan Management Review,* Winter 1976, pp. 1–8.

"Texaco: Restoring Luster to the Star." *Business Week,* December 22, 1980, p. 54.

Thompson, A. A., Jr., and A. J. Strickland III. *Strategy Formulation and Implementation.* Plano, Tex.: Business Publications, 1983, p. 277.

Vancil, Richard R. "Strategy Formulation in Complex Organizations." *Sloan Management Review,* Winter 1976, pp. 1–18.

Wasson, Charles. *Dynamic Competitive Strategy and Product Life Cycles.* Austin, Tex.: Austin Press, 1978.

Chapter 7 Cohesion Case Illustration

Internal Analysis at Holiday Inns, Inc.

At Holiday Inns internal analysis must be conducted at both the business and corporate levels. To do this, strengths and weaknesses within each business group should be examined first. After these analyses have been completed, they should be pulled together in an integrated overview of the strengths and weaknesses of Holiday Inns as a multibusiness firm.

Hotel Group. Clearly, this is the key business group for internal analysis. The hotel group is the core of Holiday Inns' diversified operations. It provides over 48 percent of total corporate revenues and over 59 percent of corporate income before taxes. Based on the case material and the lodging industry note in the case section, the strengths and weaknesses of the hotel group are shown in Exhibit 1.

Transportation Group. This is a growing segment of Holiday Inns, Inc.'s overall corporate endeavor. Two rather different businesses make up the transportation group—Continental Trailways bus system and Delta Steamship. Trailways seeks to provide moderate- to low-priced domestic intercity travel, while Delta provides marine cargo service and, increasingly, ocean pleasure cruises. Based on the case material, the strengths and weaknesses of this business group are outlined in Exhibit 2.

Products Group. The products group originated as an ancillary to parent-owned and franchised hotels/motels, ensuring standardization of furnishings and equipment and helping to recoup the overhead paid out to independent suppliers. It has grown to be the leading supplier of institutional products and related design services in the hospitality industry, primarily because the hotel group had a heretofore captive market. Its strengths and weaknesses are shown in Exhibit 3.

Restaurant Group. In late 1979 Holiday Inns, Inc., moved into the free-standing restaurant market with its purchase of Perkins Cake and Steak, Inc., and its joint venture into casino operations in Atlantic City and Las Vegas. Because these are relatively new business groups, the case material is rather limited. You are encouraged to seek outside information from such sources as *Moody's* and *Standard & Poor's Industry Surveys* to round out the assessment of strengths and weaknesses provided here. Tentative strengths and weaknesses are listed in Exhibit 4.

Exhibit 1

Hotel group: Internal analysis*

Strengths

HI dominates the industry in number of rooms available. It has the largest market share of lodging revenue dollars. (Exhibit 3) *(20)*

Name, image, and customer awareness. *(19, 22)*

Extensive and steadily growing franchise network (80 percent of all units) with franchise revenues inflation-immune because they are based on a percentage of gross revenues. (Exhibit 2) *(6)*

Massive real estate holdings rising steadily in value providing an expanding asset base. Also, older mortgage rates provide a relative advantage against the cost newer competitors must encounter. (Exhibit 13 & 14) *(76)*

Accumulated lodging experience both domestically and abroad. Extensive managerial talent and resources as evidenced by franchisee Winegardner's move to the top. *(22)*

Generally stable occupancy rate, revenues per room, gross revenue, and profit margin. *(73)*

Well-balanced locations for interstate, airport, resort, and downtown traveler needs. *(8, 22, 23, 83)*

Quality control system. *(19)*

Food and lounge facilities at every location.

Weaknesses

Increasing average age of the typical property suggests increased maintenance and renovation expense. *(8, 9)*

Dependent on the traveling public, which faces increased gasoline prices. *(23, 24)*

Hotels/motels are energy wasters that can disturb margins in an era of rapidly increasing energy costs. *(18)*

HI has become the moderate-to high-priced accommodation relative to the rapidly expanding budget chains. *(25)*

A maturing domestic lodging industry with limited expansion opportunities as evidenced by the net decline in the number of company-owned facilities over the last five years. (Exhibit 2) *(8)*

Sensitivity to economic downturns as people curtail pleasure travel. *(23, 24)*

Rapidly escalating price competition on the one end (Days Inn, Best Western) and quality competition (Hilton, Marriott, Hyatt) on the other cuts at HI's large middle market. Also, relative to price competition, HI's built-in overhead—like 16-hour restaurants, big lobbies, room service—limits flexibility in lowering operating margins. (Exhibit 3) *(23, 24)*

Cash drain on hotel group to support corporate-level overhead and ventures into new areas. Related attitude of franchisees regarding use of their fees to support this versus occupancy-enhancing activities. *(73)*

Challenges to the franchise agreement and relative dependence on franchisees. *(12, 13)*

* Exhibit numbers in parentheses in this and following exhibits refer to exhibits in the Holiday Inns, Inc., Cohesion Case in Chapter 1. Italicized numbers in parentheses refer to appropriate paragraphs of the Cohesion Case in Chapter 1.

Having completed a basic internal analysis of each business group, Holiday Inns, Inc.'s strengths and weaknesses must be examined from an overall corporate standpoint. The focus in Exhibit 5 is on the overall business portfolio and the strengths and weaknesses it provides as corporate management views internal corporate capabilities.

These are some of the key strengths and weaknesses facing Holiday Inns, Inc., at the business and corporate level. Compared with the environment analyses in Chapters 4, 5, and 6, this internal analysis provides the basis for generating alternative strategies. The Chapter 9 Cohesion Case will look at this comparison. Before leaving internal analysis, however, do you agree with the strengths and weaknesses identified? Are any key factors missing? Are any factors identified as strengths that could be weaknesses or vice versa?

Exhibit 2

Transportation group: Internal analysis

Strengths

Increasing cost of auto travel should bolster ridership on Trailways. Some executives feel that Trailways' riders could complement hotel operations, especially tour and charter services. *(35, 38)*

Second largest domestic bus service. *(33)*

Steady increase in transportation group revenues, particularly package express services. *(37)*

Steady increase in net bus income, although no improvement in income as percent of revenues and a major drop within the steamship component. (Exhibit 1)

Growing revenue in package express services and the existence of Trailway's already established, intercity bus network to provide these services. *(37)*

Delta Steamship (cargo) represents an operating base not directly tied to vacation and business travel. *(41)*

Cargo business, with strong presence in South American and African routes, suggests a solid presence serving U.S. exports to Third World countries. *(41, 42)*

LASH technology is a distinct cargo cost advantage. *(43)*

Cruise ship passenger service is a high-margin business. *(43)*

Weaknesses

Major competition from Greyhound, the number one bus line, as well as from air and train transportation. *(33, 34)*

Unsure whether the typical Trailways passenger is the typical HI motel/hotel customer. *(35, 38)*

Rising maintenance and energy-related costs while at the same time engaging in a price war with Greyhound. *(33, 34)*

Privately owned and maintained terminal facilities instead of the municipally owned terminals airlines enjoy. *(38)*

Condition and rising maintenance/replacement costs of Trailways bus terminals. *(38)*

Growing popularity of airlines for both leisure and business travel based on a price/time in transit comparison. *(33)*

Growing number and variety of companies providing package express services. The questionable ability of Trailways to deliver *anywhere* within 24 hours. *(37)*

Extent of managerial expertise in transportation—bus and marine cargo—is rather limited. *(32, 44)*

Heavy capital investment in marine cargo and ocean passenger business. (Exhibit 8) *(73)*

Small market share in marine transport and ocean passenger markets. *(45)*

Lack of clear synergy between Delta operations and Trailways or both and the hotel group. *(38)*

Exhibit 3

Products group: Internal analysis

Strengths	*Weaknesses*
Vast company-owned and franchisee captive market, especially to the extent franchisees can be required to purchase from Inn Keepers, Dohrmann, and Innkare. *(29)*	Resistance from franchisees to being forced to buy from Inn Keepers, Dohrmann, and Innkare. *(12, 13, 29)*
Stable institutional market with growth potential in health-care segment. (Exhibit 5)	A captive, intracompany business more than an independent, competitive, institutional supplier. *(27, 29)*
Long-term experience in the design and supply of food and lodging equipment and furnishings. *(28)*	Consistently low profit margins. (Exhibit 5)
Logical synergy with the hotel group. *(28)*	Revenue has not increased significantly in over five years. (Exhibit 5)

Exhibit 4

Restaurant and gaming groups: Internal analysis

Strengths

Restaurants:

Perkins provides an immediate presence in the freestanding restaurant business via 360 company-owned and franchised operations in 30 states.

HI is expèrienced in restaurant operation.

Perkins is positioned as a family restaurant with a customer profile quite similar to that of the HI hotel guest. *(50)*

It is a franchise-based business, again deriving synergy from past experiences and hotel expertise at HI. *(49)*

Provides economy of scale advantage in purchasing and advertising with restaurant business. *(52)*

Casinos:

Most casinos include hotels and sizable food and beverage operations, a natural synergy with HI's core expertise. *(61)*

Casino gaming revenue is fast growing and profitability is quite high. *(63)*

The demographic profile of the typical casino customer is quite similar to that of the typical HI hotel guest. *(61)*

Weaknesses

Restaurants:

Must be integrated into a growingly complex and diversely focused corporate management.

Faces stiff competition from similar firms like Sambo's, Shoney's, Denny's, and fast-food firms like McDonald's, Burger King, and Wendy's. (Exhibit 10) *(55)*

Limited geographic emphasis—northern United States. *(49)*

Casinos:

Philosophical contradiction with founding principles at HI, such as family environment. *(59)*

While HI has hospitality experience, it has little gambling experience. *(64)*

Gambling is only legal in a few areas. *(59)*

Because of lack of experience, the cost of entry (real estate, etc.) is quite high. *(60)*

Compatibility with corporate image and organized crime inference. *(59)*

Exhibit 5

Corporate-level internal analysis

Strengths	*Weaknesses*
The hotel business provides an excellent cash generator to support growth areas.	Management capability to absorb a rapidly increasing number of businesses may be severely challenged, especially in the short term.
Substantial and appreciating real estate holdings enhance corporatewide debt capacity.	Hotels and now restaurants represent a major dependence of outside franchisees—with several threatening legal challenges in progress.
Synergy between the hotel core and restaurant (Perkins) and casino operations should produce a distinct advantage.	Questionable whether some operations, especially Trailways buses, ocean cruises, and to some extent, institutional products, clearly fit with other businesses in a related diversification strategy.
Casino gaming and increasing resort emphasis within company-owned expansion provide a logical synergy.	Severity of the budget-chain threat and eventual price/cost squeeze on the essential cash generator—the hotel group—during a time of rapid cash outflows to gain positions in other business arenas.
Delta Steamship provides an avenue for lessening the travel-based, cyclical exposure of other HI businesses.	Philosophical divisions among long-time managers over certain diversifications, especially casinos, and restaurants have corporatewide effect.
Restaurants, casinos, and possibly marine transport provide reasonable growth avenues as the lodging industry matures.	Revenues in the restaurant and gaming groups in 1980–81 indicate that these businesses may be more sensitive to recessionary business cycles than originally thought.
Franchising and marketing expertise across multiple businesses.	The debt/total capitalization ratio, at a 10-year low in 1978 (34.6 percent), stood at a comparative high (over 42 percent) in 1981.
The 9⅝ percent convertible subordinate debentures represent $144 million of potential equity if they can be converted. Management estimates a stock price of over $22 (in 1982) would be necessary to issue a successful call.	

CHAPTER

Formulating Long-Term Objectives and Grand Strategies

The company mission was described (in Chapter 3) as encompassing the broad aims of the organization. The most specific statement of wants appeared as the goals of the firm. However, these goals, which commonly dealt with profitability, growth, and survival, were stated without specific targets or time frames. They were always to be pursued but could never be fully attained. So while they gave a general sense of direction, goals were not intended to provide specific benchmarks for evaluating the company's progress in achieving its aims. That is the function of objectives.[1]

In the first part of this chapter, the focus will be on long-term objectives. These are statements of the results a business seeks to achieve over a specified period of time, typically five years. In the second part of the chapter, focus will shift to formulation of grand strategies. These provide a comprehensive general approach guiding major actions designed to accomplish long-term business objectives.

The chapter has two major aims: (1) to discuss in detail the concept of long-term objectives, the topics they cover, and the qualities they should exhibit; and (2) to discuss in detail the concept of grand strategies, the 12 principal options available, and two approaches to grand strategy selection.

Long-Term Objectives

Strategic managers recognize that short-run profit maximization is rarely the best approach to achieving sustained corporate growth and profitability.

[1] Throughout this text the terms *goals* and *objectives* are each used to convey a special meaning, with *goals* being the less specific and more encompassing concept. Most writers agree with this usage of the terms. However, some authors use the two words interchangeably while others reverse the definitions.

An often-repeated adage states that if impoverished people are given food they will enjoy eating it but will continue to be impoverished. However, if they are given seeds and tools and shown how to grow crops, they will be able to permanently improve their condition. A parallel situation confronts strategic decision makers:

1. Should they eat the seeds by planning for large dividend payments, by selling off inventories, and by cutting back on research and development to improve the near-term profit picture, or by laying off workers during periods of slack demand?
2. Or should they sow the seeds by reinvesting profits in growth opportunities, by committing existing resources to employee training in the hope of improving performance and reducing turnover, or by increasing advertising expenditures to further penetrate a market?

For most strategic managers the solution is clear—enjoy a small amount of profit now to maintain vitality, but sow the majority to increase the likelihood of a long-term supply. This is the most frequently used rationale in selecting objectives.

To achieve long-term prosperity, strategic planners commonly establish long-term objectives in seven areas:

Profitability. The ability of any business to operate in the long run depends on attaining an acceptable level of profits. Strategically managed firms characteristically have a profit objective usually expressed in earning per share or return on equity.

Productivity. Strategic managers constantly try to improve the productivity of their systems. Companies that can improve the input-output relationship normally increase profitability. Thus, businesses almost always state an objective for productivity. Commonly number of items produced or the number of services rendered per unit of input are used. However, productivity objectives are sometimes stated in terms of desired decreases in cost. This is an equally effective way to increase profitability if unit output is maintained. For example, objectives may be set for reducing defective items, customer complaints leading to litigation, or overtime.

Competitive Position. One measure of corporate success is relative dominance in the marketplace. Larger firms often establish an objective in terms of competitive position to gauge their comparative ability for growth and profitability. Total sales or market share are often used; and an objective describing competitive position may indicate a corporation's priorities in the long term. For example, in 1975 Gulf Oil set an objective of moving by 1981 from third to second place as a producer of high-density polyproplylene. Total sales was to be their measure.

Employee Development. Employees value growth and career opportunities in an organization. With such opportunities, productivity is often increased and expensive turnover decreased. Therefore, strategic decision makers frequently include an employee development objective in their long-range plans. For example, PPG has declared an objective of developing highly skilled and flexible employees thereby providing steady employment for a reduced number of workers.

Employee Relations. Companies actively seek good employee relations, whether or not they are bound by union contracts. In fact, a characteristic concern of strategic managers is taking proactive steps in anticipation of employee needs and expectations. Strategic managers believe that productivity is partially tied to employee loyalty and perceived management interest in worker welfare. Therefore, strategic managers set objectives to improve employee relations. For example, safety programs, worker representation on management committees, and employee stock option plans are all normal outgrowths of employee-relations objectives.

Technological Leadership. Businesses must decide whether to lead or follow in the marketplace. While either can be a successful approach, each requires a different strategic posture. Therefore, many businesses state an objective in terms of technological leadership. For example, Caterpillar Tractor Company, which manufactures large earth movers, established its early reputation and dominant position in the industry on being a forerunner in technological innovation.

Public Responsibility. Businesses recognize their responsibilities to customers and society at large. In fact, many actively seek to exceed the minimum demands made by government. Not only do they work to develop reputations for fairly priced products and services, but they also attempt to establish themselves as responsible corporate citizens. For example, they may establish objectives for charitable and educational contributions, minority training, public or political activity, community welfare, and urban renewal.

Qualities of Long-Term Objectives

What distinguishes a good objective from a bad one? What qualities of an objective improve its chances of being attained?

Perhaps the best answer to these questions is found in relation to seven criteria that should be used in preparing long-term objectives: acceptable, flexible, measurable over time, motivating, suitable, understandable, and achievable.

Acceptable. Managers are most likely to pursue objectives that are consistent with perceptions and preferences. If managers are offended by the objectives (e.g., promoting a non-nutritional food product) or believe them to be inappropriate or unfair (e.g., reducing spoilage to offset a disproportionate fixed overhead allocation), they may ignore or even obstruct achievement. In addition, certain long-term corporate objectives are frequently designed to be acceptable to major interest groups external to the firm. An example might involve air-pollution abatement efforts undertaken at the insistence of the Environmental Protection Agency.

Flexible. Objectives should be capable of modification in the event of unforeseen or extraordinary changes in the firm's competitive or environmental forecasts. At the same time flexibility is usually increased at the expense of specificity. Likewise, employee confidence may be tempered because adjustment of a flexible objective may affect their job. One recommendation for providing flexibility while minimizing associated negative effects is to allow for adjustments in the level rather than the nature of an objective. For example, an objective for a personnel department "to provide managerial development training for 15 supervisors per year over the next five-year period" can easily be adjusted by changing the number of people to be trained. In contrast, changing the personnel department's objective after three months to "assisting production supervisors in reducing job-related injuries by 10 percent per year" would understandably create dissatisfaction.

Measurable. Objectives must clearly and concretely state what will be achieved and within what time frame. Numerical specificity minimizes misunderstandings; thus, objectives should be measurable over time. For example, an objective to "substantially improve our return on investment" would be better stated as "increase the return on investment on our line of paper products by a minimum of 1 percent a year and a total of 5 percent over the next three years."

Motivating. Studies have shown that people are most productive when objectives are set at a motivating level—one high enough to challenge but not so high as to frustrate or so low as to be easily attained. The problem is that individuals and groups differ in their perceptions of high enough. A broad objective that challenges one group frustrates another and minimally interests a third. One valuable recommendation is develop multiple objectives, some aimed at specific groups. More sweeping statements are usually seen as lacking appreciation for individual and somewhat unique situations. Such tailor-made objectives require time and involvement from the decision maker, but are more likely to serve as motivational forces.

Suitable. Objectives must be suited to the broad aims of the organization, which are expressed in the statement of company mission. Each objective should be a step toward attainment of overall goals. In fact, objectives that do not coincide with company or corporate missions can subvert the aims of the firm. For example, if the mission is growth oriented, an objective of reducing the debt-to-equity ratio to 1.00 to improve stability would probably be unsuitable and counterproductive.

Understandable. Strategic managers at all levels must have a clear understanding of what is to be achieved. They must also understand the major criteria by which their performance will be evaluated. Thus, objectives must be stated so that they are understandable to the recipient as they are to the giver. Consider the potential misunderstandings over an objective "to increase the productivity of the credit card department by 20 percent within five years." Does this mean: Increase the number of cards outstanding? Increase the use of outstanding cards? Increase the employee workload? Make productivity gains each year? Or hope that the new computer-assisted system which should automatically improve productivity is approved by year five? As this simple example illustrates, objectives must be prepared in clear, meaningful, and unambiguous fashion.

Achievable. Finally, objectives must be possible to achieve. This is easier said than done. Turbulence in the remote and operating environments adds to the dynamic nature of a business's internal operations. This creates uncertainty, limiting strategic management's accuracy in setting feasible objectives. For example, the wildly fluctuating prime interest rates in 1980 made objective setting extremely difficult for 1981 to 1985, particularly in such areas as sales projections for consumer durable goods companies like General Motors and General Electric.

An especially fine example of long-term strategic objectives is provided in the 1981 to 1986 plan of Hawkeye Savings and Loan, a prominent financial organization in Iowa. Shown in Strategy in Action 8–1 are five of Hawkeye's major objectives for the period, specific performance targets for 1981 and 1982, and results from 1981. Other material from the 23-page planning document, such as post-1982 performance figures and forecasts, could not be presented for security reasons. However, it is evident that Hawkeye's approach is wholly consistent with the list of desired qualities for long-term objectives. In particular, Hawkeye's objectives are flexible, measurable over time, suitable, and understandable.

Strategy in Action 8–1

Long-Range Objectives of Hawkeye Savings and Loan 1981–1985

Objective 1. Hawkeye should earn, after taxes, not less than 15 percent on average stockholder equity annually and by December 31, 1985, be earning up to 20 percent on average stockholder equity. Per-share earnings should increase 10 percent annually.

	1981 objectives	*1981 results*	*1982 objectives*
Average stockholder equity	$84.5 million	$86.3 million	$110.0 million
Return on equity	16.3%	15.5%	14.6%
Earnings per share	2.75	2.50	2.56

Objective 2. Hawkeye will grow from $1 billion in assets to $2 billion by December 31, 1985. This will be accomplished by: *(a)* acquiring $100 million in assets annually. And *(b)* internal growth of 8 percent per annum.

	1981 objectives	*1981 results*	*1982 objectives*
Beginning assets	$1,100 million	$1,153 million	$1,408 million
Acquisitions	100	146	100
Internal growth	80	109	112
Ending assets	$1,280 million	$1,408 million	$1,620 million

Objective 3. Hawkeye will maintain capital and reserves in subsidiary banks in an amount not less than 7 percent of assets, realizing regulatory authorities may require amounts in excess of that amount. The parent company will maintain a debt ratio under 35 percent of total capitalization and 40 percent of stockholders' equity.

	1981 objectives	*1981 results*	*1982 objectives*
Year-end stockholders' equity	$97.0 million	$105.2 million	$115.0 million
Parent company debt	39.0 million	39.6 million	46.0 million
Average subsidiary bank capital and reserves-to-asset ratio	8.0%	8.7%	8.0%

Objective 4. Hawkeye's basic mission of "helping Iowans achieve their financial goals" requires that member banks are willing to loan funds. The willingness of Hawkeye's banks to loan funds also requires the bank to collect funds loaned.

	1981 objectives	*1981 results*	*1982 objectives*
Total loans	$650 million	$696 million	$708 million
Of the average total loans, total loan loss not to exceed	0.15%	0.242%	0.15%
Classified loans not to exceed	2.00%	1.750%	2.00%
Credit card delinquences not to exceed	10.00%	6.790%	10.00%
Loan-to-deposit ratio not to exceed	73.50%	62.900%	73.50%

Objective 5. The Financial Services Group will expand the number and variety of financial services offered in keeping with Hawkeye Bancorporation's mission to build a regional financial corporation. These activities will account for an increasing share of Hawkeye profits.

	After-tax earnings objectives		
	1981 Estimate	*1981 Actual*	*1982 Estimate*
Hawkeye Insurance Services, Inc.	$260,000	$169,000	$ 217,000
Central Hawkeye Life Insurance Company	137,000	171,000	480,000
Hawkeye Investment Management, Inc.	26,000	33,000	1,000
Hawkeye Farm Management	13,000	13,000	19,000
Iowa Higher Education Loan Program	80,000	145,000	196,000
Credit Card Center (service fees only)	34,000	47,000	187,000
Hawkeye Mortgage Company	16,000	(68,000)	87,000
STFIT	0	180,000	360,000
	$566,000	$690,000	$1,547,000

Grand Strategies[2]

Despite variations in implementing the strategic management approach, designers of planning systems generally agree about the critical role of *grand strategies.*[3] Grand strategies, which are often called master or *business* strategies, are intended to provide basic direction for strategic actions. Thus, they are seen as the basis of coordinated and sustained efforts directed toward achieving long-term business objectives.

[2] Portions of this section are adapted from John A. Pearce II, "Selecting among Alternative Grand Strategies," *California Management Review,* Spring 1982, pp. 23–31.

[3] Among recent such models or theories of strategic management are those of Pearce (1981), Steiner (1979), Higgins (1979), Ansoff (1979). King and Cleland (1978), and Steiner and Miner (1977), all listed in the bibliography to this chapter.

As theoretically and conceptually attractive as the idea of grand strategies has proved to be, two problems have limited use of this approach in practice. First, decision makers often do not recognize the range of alternative grand strategies available. Strategic managers tend to build incrementally from the status quo. This often limits their search for ways to improve corporate performance unnecessarily. Other executives have simply never considered the options available as attractive grand strategies.

Second, strategic decision makers may generate lists of promising grand strategies but lack a logical and systematic approach to selecting an alternative. Few planning experts have attempted to proffer viable evaluative criteria and selection tools.

The purpose of this section is therefore twofold: (1) to list, describe, and discuss 12 business-level grand strategies that should be considered by strategic planners; and (2) to present approaches to the selection of an optimal grand strategy from available alternatives.

Grand strategies indicate how long-range objectives will be achieved. Thus, a grand strategy can be defined as a comprehensive general approach that guides major actions. As an example, Strategy in Action 8–2 presents a form of the grand strategy of Eastern Airlines.

There are 12 principal grand strategies, any one of which could serve as the basis for achieving major long-term objectives of a single business: concentration, market development, product development, innovation, horizontal integration, vertical integration, joint venture, concentric diversification, conglomerate diversification, retrenchment/turnaround, divestiture, and liquidation. When a company is involved with multiple industries, businesses, product lines, or customer groups—as many firms are—several grand strategies are usually combined. However, for clarity, each of these grand strategies is described independently in this section with examples to indicate some of their relative strengths and weaknesses.

Concentration

The most common grand strategy is *concentration* on the current business. The firm directs its resources to the profitable growth of a single product, in a single market, and with a single technology. Some of America's largest and most successful companies have traditionally adopted the concentration approach. Examples include W. K. Kellogg and Gerber Foods which are known for their product, Shaklee which concentrates on geographic expansion, and Lincoln Electric which bases its growth on technological advances.

The reasons for selecting a concentration grand strategy are easy to understand. Concentration is typically lowest in risk and in additional resources required. It is also based on the known competencies of the firm. On the negative side, for most companies concentration tends to result in steady but slow increases in growth and profitability and a narrow range of investment options. Further, because of their narrow base of competition, concen-

Strategy in Action 8–2
The 1984 Grand Strategy of Eastern Air Lines*

The past five years have been turbulent for the airline industry. Deregulation was quickly followed by a dramatic increase in oil prices; high inflation; skyrocketing interest rates; the most severe and prolonged recession since the Great Depression; the formation of new, low-cost airlines; and the PATCO strike resulting in imposition of new government controls on operations. Under these circumstances, it should not be surprising that one trunk carrier has gone bankrupt and that others are in perilous financial condition.

During this period, Eastern's basic strategy has remained consistent:

A commitment to a modern, efficient fleet and support facilities, necessarily accompanied by some financial risk.

Growth through productivity

Protection of job security to the maximum extent possible.

Protection of yields by selectively and carefully offering competitive prices in our markets.

Formation of a route structure which permits efficient development of our marketing strength at our primary traffic hubs.

Protection of our traditional major markets.

Development of new market opportunities.

A commitment to quality.

While Eastern's financial results have been unsatisfactory, the success of this strategy can be measured by Eastern's performance relative to that of other major carriers. In 1982, Eastern ranked first among the trunk carriers in operating margin; and, as measured by Merrill Lynch's "Passenger Profitability Index," Eastern ranks behind only Southwest and USAir.

Thus, our strategy will remain essentially intact. There will be changes in emphasis to reflect an improving external environment, our financial structure, and the employee productivity improvements we are anticipating. However, the basic direction remains unchanged.

* The details of a company's grand strategy are among its most closely guarded secrets. Since this statement of Eastern Air Line's grand strategy was *intended* for public consumption, it necessarily omitted the huge volumes of detailed analysis that preceded this extremely abbreviated and superficial overview.

trated firms are especially susceptible to performance variations resulting from industry trends.

Concentration strategies succeed for so many businesses—including the vast majority of smaller firms—because of the advantages of business-level specialization. By concentrating on one product, in one market, and with one technology, a firm can gain competitive advantages over its more diversified competitors in production skill, marketing know-how, customer sensitivity, and reputation in the marketplace.

A grand strategy of concentration allows for a considerable range of action. Broadly speaking, the business can attempt to capture a larger market share by increasing present customers' rate of usage, by attracting competitors' customers, or by interesting nonusers in the product or service. In turn, each of these actions suggests a more specific set of alternatives. Some of these options are listed in the top section of Figure 8–1.

When strategic managers forecast that the combination of their current products and their markets will not provide the basis for achieving the company mission, they have two options that involve moderate cost and risk: market development and product development.

Market Development

Market development commonly ranks second only to concentration as the least costly and least risky of the 12 grand strategies. It consists of marketing present products, often with only cosmetic modifications, to customers in related market areas by adding different channels of distribution or by changing the content of advertising or the promotional media. Several specific approaches are listed under this heading in Figure 8–1. Thus, as suggested by the figure, businesses that open branch offices in new cities, states, or countries are practicing market development. Likewise, companies that switch from advertising in trade publications to newspapers or add jobbers to supplement their mail-order sales efforts are using a market development approach.

Product Development

Product development involves substantial modification of existing products or creation of new but related items that can be marketed to current customers through established channels. The product development strategy is often adopted either to prolong the life cycle of current products or to take advantage of favorable reputation and brand name. The idea is to attract satisfied customers to new products as a result of their positive experience with the company's initial offering. The bottom section of Figure 8–1, lists some of the many specific options available to businesses that undertake product development. Thus, a revised edition of a college textbook, a new car style, and a second formula of shampoo for oily hair each represents a product development strategy.

Figure 8–1

Specific options under the grand strategies of concentration, market development, and product development

Concentration (increasing use of present products in present markets):
1. Increasing present customers' rate of usage.
   a. Increasing the size of purchase.
   b. Increasing the rate of product obsolescence.
   c. Advertising other uses.
   d. Giving price incentives for increased use.
2. Attracting competitors' customers.
   a. Establishing sharper brand differentiation.
   b. Increasing promotional effort.
   c. Initiating price cuts.
3. Attracting nonusers to buy the product.
   a. Inducing trial use through sampling, price incentives, and so on.
   b. Pricing up or down.
   c. Advertising new uses.

Market development (selling present products in new markets):
1. Opening additional geographical markets.
   a. Regional expansion.
   b. National expansion.
   c. International expansion.
2. Attracting other market segments.
   a. Developing product versions to appeal to other segments.
   b. Entering other channels of distribution.
   c. Advertising in other media.

Product development (developing new products for present markets):
1. Developing new product features.
   a. Adapt (to other ideas, developments).
   b. Modify (change color, motion, sound, odor, form, shape).
   c. Magnify (stronger, longer, thicker, extra value).
   d. Minify (smaller, shorter, lighter).
   e. Substitute (other ingredients, process, power).
   f. Rearrange (other patterns, layout, sequence, components).
   g. Reverse (inside out).
   h. Combine (blend, alloy, assortment, ensemble; combine units, purposes, appeals, ideas).
2. Developing quality variations.
3. Developing additional models and sizes (product proliferation).

Source: Adapted from Philip Kotler, *Marketing Management: Analysis, Planning, and Control,* 2d ed., © 1972, pp. 170, 237. Reprinted by permission of Prentice-Hall, Inc., Englewood Cliffs, N.J.

Strategy in Action 8–3 shows how Kohler Company was able to combine market and product development into an extremely effective grand strategy.

Innovation

In many industries it is increasingly risky not to innovate. Consumer as well as industrial markets have come to expect periodic changes and improve-

Strategy in Action 8–3
A Tub-and-Toilet Dynasty

In 1983, with the home-building industry in a long-running slump, profits in the plumbing fixtures business were swirling down the drain. For companies that made tubs, toilets, sinks, and showers, it seemed a time to retrench.

Not, however, for the privately held Kohler Company of Kohler, Wisconsin, creator of the Infinity Bath, the Super Spa, and other exotica for people who want their bathrooms to be fun as well as functional. Even though Kohler had to lay off 300 of its 6,000 workers because of slow sales of some products, the company was going ahead with its most ambitious capital spending program ever. In 1983 Kohler invested $50 million, more than 10 percent of its expected sales of $400 million. The plan included a big expansion of its factories in Brownwood, Texas.

Unlike most American executives, who were often criticized for trying to boost short-run profits at the expense of long-range investment, Chairman Herbert Kohler could afford to disregard the short-term bottom line. His family and relatives owned or controlled 90 percent of the Kohler stock. While the typical U.S. company reinvested 60 percent of its earnings, Chairman Kohler claimed to put 90 percent of his profits back into the firm.

Kohler viewed a recession as a grand opportunity to increase his share of the kitchen and bathroom business. Because of the slump, he pointed out, some building materials cost less than they did in 1980, and thus the construction of new factories was comparatively inexpensive. During the recession in 1973–75, Kohler expanded its facilities enough to overtake American Standard as the largest manufacturer of luxury plumbing fixtures in the United States.

When Herbert Kohler became chairman in 1972, he decided that plumbing had not reached its potential. Said he, "I felt we could innovate with shapes and colors to change the whole function of the bathroom and make it something stimulating, possibly even social."

The company has since introduced the Infinity Bath, a kidney-shaped tub for two (price: $2,000), and the Super Spa, a giant whirlpool ($4,000) that can come with a built-in table for those who, for example, want to play poker as they soak. Kohler's masterpiece is the $12,500 Environment, a pleasure chamber that pampers bathers with "tropic rain, jungle steam, chinook winds, and Baja sun," all accompanied by soothing stereo music.

Though plumbing fixtures are rarely mentioned in the same breath with computers or robots, Kohler was convinced that the bathroom business had considerable growth potential. He expected to see the day when whirlpools were virtually standard in middle-class homes.

Source: "Rub-a-Dub-Dub," *Time,* July 26, 1982, p. 37.

ments in the products offered. As a result, some businesses find it profitable to base their grand strategy on *innovation.* They seek to reap the initially high profits associated with customer acceptance of a new or greatly improved product. Then, rather than face stiffening competition as the basis of profitability shifts from innovation to production or marketing competence, they move on to search for other original or novel ideas. The underlying philosophy of a grand strategy of innovation is creating a new-product life cycle, thereby making any similar existing products obsolete. Thus, this approach differs from the product development strategy of extending an existing product's life cycle. The automobile industry provides many excellent examples. Ford Motor Company's 1981 introduction of the sporty, economical, two-seater EXP was an effort to interest a segment of American drivers who traditionally bought foreign-made sports cars in trying a Ford product. This was an innovation strategy because a new life cycle had been started for Ford. At the same time, Ford modified the Fairmont to make it lighter and more fuel efficient. This was a product-development strategy since the Fairmont life cycle was extended.

While most growth-oriented firms appreciate the need to be innovative occasionally, a few companies use it as their fundamental way of relating to their markets. An outstanding example is Polaroid which heavily promotes each of its new cameras until competitors are able to match their technological innovation. By this time, Polaroid is normally prepared to introduce a dramatically new or improved product. For example, in short succession consumers were introduced to the Swinger, the SX-70, the One Step, and the Sun Camera 660.

Few innovative ideas prove to be profitable because research, development, and premarketing costs incurred in converting a promising idea into a profitable product are extremely high. A study by the management research department of Booz, Allen and Hamilton provides some understanding of the risks. As shown in Figure 8–2, Booz, Allen and Hamilton studied 51 companies and found that less than 2 percent of the innovative projects initially considered eventually reached the marketplace. Specifically, out of every 58 new product ideas, only 12 pass an initial screening test which finds them to be compatible with the company's mission and long-term objectives. Only seven of these remain after an evaluation of their product potential, and only three survive actual attempts to develop the product. Two of these still appear to have profit potential after test marketing but, on the average, only one will be commercially successful. In fact, other studies show this success rate to be overly optimistic. For example, the results of one research project disclosed failure rates for commercial products to be as high as 89 percent.[4]

[4] Burt Schorr, "Many New Products Fizzle, Despite Careful Planning, Publicity," *The Wall Street Journal*, April 5, 1961.

Figure 8–2

Decay of new product ideas (51 companies)

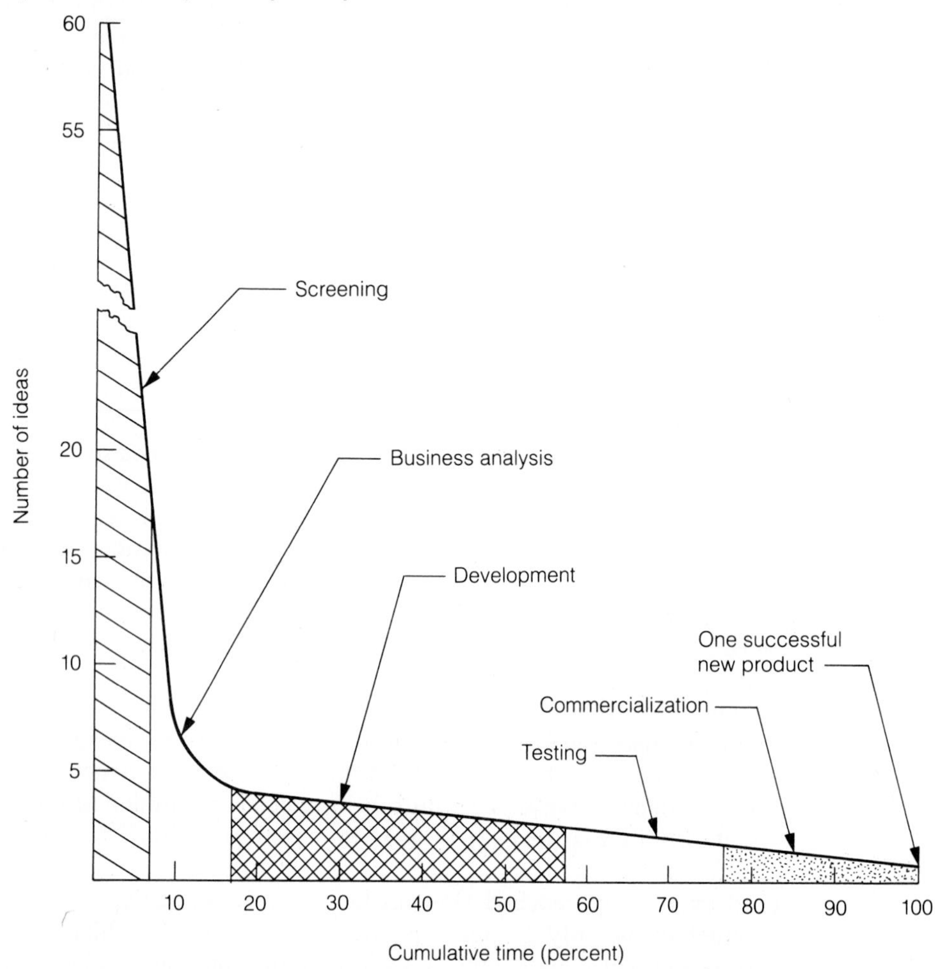

Horizontal Integration

When the long-term strategy of a firm is based on growth through the acquisition of one or more similar business operating at the same stage of the production-marketing chain, its grand strategy is called *horizontal integration.* Such acquisitions provide access to new markets for the acquiring firm and eliminate competitors. For example, Warner-Lambert Pharmaceutical Company's acquisition of Parke Davis reduced competition in the ethical drugs field for Chilcott Laboratories, a company Warner-Lambert had previously acquired. A second example is the long-range acquisition pattern of White Consolidated Industries, which expanded in the refrigerator and freezer market through a grand strategy of horizontal integration. In 1967 it acquired the Franklin Appliance Division of Studebaker, in 1978 it bought the Kelvinator Appliance Division of American Motors, in 1971 it acquired the Refrigerator Products Division of Bendix Westinghouse Automotive Air Brake, and finally in 1979 it bought Frigidaire Appliance from General Motors. For yet another example of a successful horizontal integration grand strategy read the case the Santa Fe and Southern Pacific railroads in Strategy in Action 8–4. Thus, the combinations of two textile producers, two shirt manufacturers, or two clothing store chains would be classified as horizontal integrations.

Strategy in Action 8–4

Merging to Build a New Empire

In 1983 the Santa Fe and Southern Pacific railroads joined forces to form the third largest railroad in the United States, with 26,000 miles of track. Due to the $6.3 billion merger, only the Burlington Northern railroad (28,900 miles) and CSX (26,400) were bigger. The combined Santa Fe–Southern Pacific network stretched from Chicago in the North to New Orleans in the South to Portland in the West.

The new company was to be not just a railroad, but a business empire. Chicago-based Santa Fe Industries (1982 revenues: $3.16 billion) has gas wells, coal and uranium mines, and a forest-products division. The company was one of the largest U.S. producers of heavy crude oil. San Francisco–based Southern Pacific (1982 revenues: $3.1 billion) operated petroleum pipelines and leased executive aircraft, truck fleets, computers, mining machinery, and communications equipment. With huge holdings of farm land, timberland, and urban real estate, Southern Pacific was the largest private landlord in California.

[Southern Pacific] also owned the nation's only operational coal-slurry pipeline, which ran 273 miles between Arizona and Nevada. The pipeline allowed coal that has been mixed with water to be transported swiftly and cheaply.

Santa Fe and Southern Pacific saw their union as the best way to compete with two other big Western railroads that were built up through mergers: Burlington Northern and Union Pacific. Santa Fe and Southern Pacific intended to become more efficient by abandoning duplicate routes and pooling equipment. The combined 57,000-member work force of the two railroads would shrink but through attrition rather than layoffs.

Source: "Merging to Build New Empires," *Time*, October 10, 1983, p. 50.

Figure 8–3

Vertical and horizontal integrations

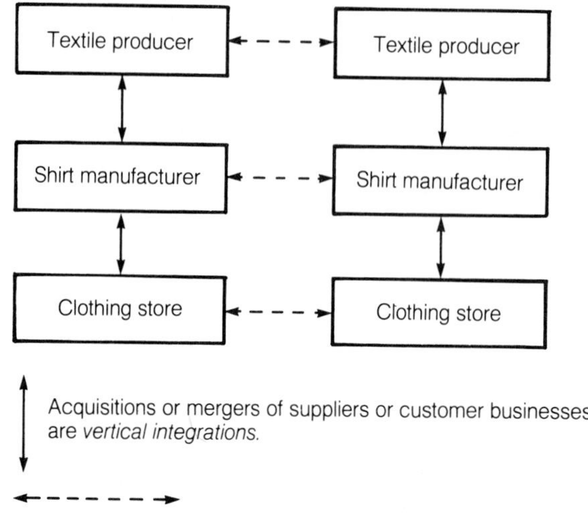
Textile producer
Textile producer
Shirt manufacturer
Shirt manufacturer
Clothing store
Clothing store
Acquisitions or mergers of suppliers or customer businesses are *vertical integrations.*
Acquisitions or mergers of competing businesses are *horizontal integrations.*

Vertical Integration

When the grand strategy of a firm involves the acquisition of businesses that either supply the firm with inputs such as raw materials, or serve as a customer for the firm's outputs, such as warehousers for finished products, *vertical integration* is involved. For example, if a shirt manufacturer acquires a textile producer—by purchasing its common stock, buying its assets, or through an exchange of ownership interests—the strategy is a vertical integration. In this case it is a *backward* vertical integration since the business acquired operates at an earlier stage of the production/marketing process. If the shirt manufacturer had merged with a clothing store, it would have been an example of *forward* vertical integration involving the acquisition of a business nearer to the ultimate consumer.

Figure 8–3 depicts both horizontal and vertical integration. The principal attractions of a horizontal integration grand strategy are readily apparent. The acquiring firm is able to greatly expand its operations, thereby achieving greater market share, improving economies of scale, and increasing efficiency of capital usage. Additionally, these benefits are achieved with only moderately increased risk, since the success of the expansion is principally dependent upon proven abilities.

The reasons for choosing a vertical integration grand strategy are more varied and sometimes less obvious. The main reason for backward integration is the desire to increase the dependability of supply or quality of raw materials or production inputs. The concern is particularly great when the number of suppliers is small and the number of competitors is large. In this situation, the vertically integrating firm can better control its costs and thereby improve the profit margin of the expanded production/marketing system. Forward integration is a preferred grand strategy if the advantages of stable production are particularly high. A business can increase the predictability of demand for its output through forward integration, that is, through ownership of the next stage of its production/marketing chain.

There are also some increased risks associated with both types of integration grand strategies. For horizontally integrated firms the risks stem from the increased commitment to one type of business. For vertically integrated firms the risks result from expansion of the company into areas requiring strategic managers to broaden the base of their competencies and assume additional responsibilities.

Joint Venture

Occasionally two or more capable companies lack a necessary component for success in a particular competitive environment. For example, no single petroleum firm controlled sufficient resources to construct the Alaskan pipeline. Nor was any single firm capable of processing and marketing the volume of oil that would flow through the pipeline. The solution was a set of *joint ventures.* As shown in Figure 8–4, these cooperative arrangements could provide both the necessary funds to build the pipeline and the processing and marketing capacity to profitably handle the oil flow.

The particular form of joint venture discussed above is joint ownership.[5] In recent years it has become increasingly appealing for domestic firms to join foreign businesses through this form. For example, Bethlehem Steel acquired an interest in a Brazilian mining venture to secure a raw-material source. The stimulus for this joint ownership venture was grand strategy, but such is not always the case. Certain countries virtually mandate that foreign companies entering their markets do so on a joint-ownership basis. India and Mexico are good examples. The rationale of these countries is that joint ventures minimize the threat of foreign domination and enhance the skills, employment, growth, and profits of local businesses.

One final note: Strategic managers in the typical firm rarely seek joint ventures. This approach admittedly presents new opportunities with risks that can be shared. On the other hand, joint ventures often limit partner

[5] Other forms of joint ventures such as leasing, contract manufacturing, and management contracting offer valuable support strategies. However, because they are seldom employed as grand strategies, they are not included in the categorization.

Figure 8–4

Typical joint ventures in the oil pipeline industry

Pipeline company (assets in $ millions)	*Co-owners*	*Percent held by each*
Colonial Pipeline Co. ($480.2)	Amoco	14.3
	Atlantic Richfield	1.6
	Cities Service	14.0
	Continental	7.5
	Phillips	7.1
	Texaco	14.3
	Gulf	16.8
	Sohio	9.0
	Mobil	11.5
	Union Oil	4.0
Olympic Pipeline Co. ($30.7)	Shell	43.5
	Mobil	29.5
	Texaco	27.0
West Texas Gulf Pipeline Co. ($19.8) . .	Gulf	57.7
	Cities Service	11.4
	Sun	12.6
	Union Oil	9.0
	Sohio	9.2
Texas-New Mexico Pipeline Co. ($30.5)	Texaco	45.0
	Atlantic Richfield	35.0
	Cities Service	10.0
	Getty	10.0

Source: Testimony of Walter Adams in *Horizontal Integration of the Energy Industry,* hearings before the Subcommittee on Energy of the Joint Economic Committee, 94th Congress, 1st sess. (1975), p. 112.

discretion, control, and profit potential while demanding managerial attention and other resources that might otherwise be directed toward the mainstream activities of the firm. Nevertheless, increasing nationalism in many foreign markets may require greater consideration of the joint venture approach if a firm intends to diversify internationally.

Concentric Diversification

Grand strategies involving diversification represent distinctive departures from a firm's existing base of operations, typically the acquisition or internal generation (spin-off) of a separate business with synergistic possibilities counterbalancing the two businesses' strengths and weaknesses. For example, Head Ski initially sought to diversify into summer sporting goods and clothing to offset the seasonality of its snow business. However, diversifications are occasionally undertaken as unrelated investments because of their otherwise minimal resource demands and high profit potential.

Regardless of the approach taken, the motivations of the acquiring firms are the same:

Increase the firm's stock value. Often in the past, mergers have led to increases in the stock price and/or price-earnings ratio.

Increase the growth rate of the firm.

Make an investment that represents better use of funds than plowing them into internal growth.

Improve the stability of earnings and sales by acquiring firms whose earnings and sales complement the firm's peaks and valleys.

Balance or fill out the product line.

Diversify the product line when the life cycle of current products has peaked.

Acquire a needed resource quickly; for example, high-quality technology or highly innovative management.

Tax reasons, purchasing a firm with tax losses that will offset current or future earnings.

Increase efficiency and profitability, especially if there is synergy between the two companies.[6]

When diversification involves the addition of a business related to the firm in terms of technology, markets, or products, it is a *concentric diversification.* With this type of grand strategy, the new businesses selected possess a high degree of compatability with the current businesses. The ideal concentric diversification occurs when the combined company profits increase strengths and opportunities, as well as decrease weaknesses and exposure to risk. Thus, the acquiring company searches for new businesses with products, markets, distribution channels, technologies, and resource requirements that are familiar but not identical, synergistic but not wholly interdependent.

Conglomerate Diversification

Occasionally a firm, particularly a very large one, plans to acquire a business because it represents the most promising investment opportunity available. This type of grand strategy is commonly known as *conglomerate diversification.* The principal and often sole concern of the acquiring firm is the profit pattern of the venture. There is little concern given to creating product/market synergy with existing businesses, unlike the approach taken in concentric diversification. Financial synergy is what is sought by conglomerate diversifiers such as ITT, Textron, American Brands, Litton, U.S. Industries, Fuqua, and I.C. Industries. For example, they may seek a balance in their portfolios between current businesses with cyclical sales and acquired businesses with counter-

[6] William F. Glueck, *Business Policy and Strategic Management* (New York: McGraw-Hill, 1980), p. 213.

cyclical sales, between high-cash/low-opportunity and low-cash/high-opportunity businesses, or between debt-free and highly leveraged businesses.

The principal difference between the two types of diversification is that concentric acquisitions emphasize some commonality in markets, products, or technology, whereas conglomerate acquisitions are based principally on profit considerations.

Retrenchment/Turnaround

For any of a large number of reasons a business can find itself with declining profits. Economic recessions, production inefficiencies, and innovative breakthroughs by competitors are only three causes. In many cases strategic managers believe the firm can survive and eventually recover if a concerted effort is made over a period of a few years to fortify basic distinctive competencies. This type of grand strategy is known as *retrenchment.* It is typically accomplished in one of two ways, employed singly or in combination:

1. Cost reduction. Examples include decreasing the work force through employee attrition, leasing rather than purchasing equipment, extending the life of machinery, and eliminating elaborate promotional activities.
2. Asset reduction. Examples include the sale of land, buildings, and equipment not essential to the basic activity of the business, and elimination of "perks" like the company airplane and executive cars.

If these initial approaches fail to achieve the required reductions, more drastic action may be necessary. It is sometimes essential to lay off employees, drop items from a production line, and even eliminate low-margin customers.

Since the underlying purpose of retrenchment is to reverse current negative trends, the method is often referred to as a *turnaround* strategy. Interestingly, the turnaround most commonly associated with this approach is in management positions. In a study of 58 large firms, researchers Schendel, Patton, and Riggs found that turnaround was almost always associated with changes in top management.[7] Bringing in new managers was believed to introduce needed new perspectives of the firm's situation, to raise employee morale, and to facilitate drastic actions such as deep budgetary cuts in established programs.

Divestiture

A *divestiture strategy* involves the sale of a business or a major business component. When retrenchment fails to accomplish the desired turnaround,

[7] Dan Schendel, G. Richard Patton, and James Riggs, "Corporate Turnaround Strategies: A Study of Profit Decline and Recovery," *Journal of General Management* 3 (1976), pp. 3–11.

strategic managers often decide to sell the business. However, because the intent is to find a buyer willing to pay a premium above the value of fixed assets for a going concern, the term *marketing for sale* is more appropriate. Prospective buyers must be convinced that because of their skills and resources, or the synergy with their existing businesses, they will be able to profit from the acquisition.

The reasons for divestiture vary. Often they arise because of partial mismatches between the acquired business and the parent corporation. Some of the mismatched parts cannot be integrated into the corporation's mainstream and thus must be spun off. A second reason is corporation financial needs. sometimes the cash flow or financial stability of the corporation as a whole can be greatly improved if businesses with high market value can be sacrificed. A third, less frequent reason for divestiture is government antitrust action when a corporation is believed to monopolize or unfairly dominate a particular market.

Although examples of grand strategies of divestiture are numerous, an outstanding example in the last decade is Chrysler Corporation, which in quick succession divested itself of several major businesses to protect its mission as a domestic automobile manufacturer. Among major Chrysler sales were its Airtempt air-conditioning business to Fedders and its automotive subsidiaries in France, Spain, and England to Peugeot-Citroen. These divestitures yielded Chrysler a total of almost $500 million in cash, notes, and stock, and thus, in the relatively short term, improved its financial stability. Other corporations which have recently pursued this type of grand strategy include Esmark, which divested Swift and Company, and White Motors, which divested White Farm.

An example of the value of divestiture is shown in Strategy in Action 8–5. As discussed, Gulf & Western used the proceeds of divestitures together with savings from selective retrenchments to create tax write-offs and reduce the firm's huge level of long-term debt.

Liquidation

When the grand strategy is that of *liquidation,* the business is typically sold in parts, only occasionally as a whole, but for its tangible asset value and not as a going concern. In selecting liquidation, owners and strategic managers of a business are admitting failure and recognize that this action is likely to result in great hardships to themselves and their employees. For these reasons liquidation is usually seen as the least attractive of all grand strategies. However, as a long-term strategy it minimizes the loss to all stakeholders of the firm. Usually faced with bankruptcy, the liquidating business tries to develop a planned and orderly system which will result in the greatest

Strategy in Action 8–5

Gulf & Western Slims Down

Charles Bluhdorn was one of the earliest and flashiest conglomerateurs, a master of the unfriendly takeover. Starting with a small auto-parts company in 1958, he assembled an incredible array of disparate businesses into Gulf & Western Industries (1982 sales: $5.3 billion). Bluhdorn eventually bought some 100 companies large and small, ranging from Paramount Pictures to publisher Simon & Schuster to New York City's Madison Square Garden. In one six-year period, he brought 80 firms into what became jokingly known as "Engulf and Devour." Bluhdorn died in February 1983, at 56 after a heart attack, and his successors were in no mood to keep up that pace. They contracted Gulf & Western almost as fast as Bluhdorn had expanded it.

In 1983, a new management team headed by Vice Chairman and Chief Executive Martin Davis, 56, announced a major streamlining program to rid the company of low-profit operations. Among the cast-offs: Arlington Park race track near Chicago and Roosevelt Raceway in New York, manufacturer E. W. Bliss, and Sega's video-game unit. The moves saved the company about $470 million in tax write-offs, but produced a loss of $215 million in the first year.

The divestitures were just the latest ordered by Davis, who went to Gulf & Western from Paramount in 1969 and took over immediately after Bluhdorn's death. Davis had earlier moved to sell off $650 million of company-owned stock in 30 companies, leaving the conglomerate with some $150 million in such holdings. The money was used to bring down the company's mountain of debt to $1.2 billion. Davis then also sold Gulf & Western's 21.4 percent stake in Brunswick, the sports-equipment manufacturer, for $97 million. Davis likewise chopped away at the company's work force, reducing it by about 10,000 to 47,000.

Pointless mixing of dissimilar firms seemed finished at Gulf & Western. Said Shearson/American Express Analyst Scott Merlis: "Few of their businesses were related to their other businesses." Instead, the company now seemed determined to focus sharply on a few areas: consumer products (apparel, Kayser-Roth; home furnishings, Simmons), entertainment (Paramount), and financial services (Associates Corp.).

Gulf & Western was only one of several companies to follow the newly fashionable divestiture route. Such firms as Beatrice Foods, Quaker Oats, and General Electric all sold off major holdings during 1982–1983.

Source: "The Big Sell-Off," *Time*, August 29, 1983, p. 45.

possible return and cash conversion as the business slowly relinquishes its market share.

Planned liquidation can be worthwhile. For example, the Columbia Corporation, a $130-million diversified firm, liquidated its assets for more cash per share than the market value of its stock.

Selection of Long-term Objectives and Grand Strategy Sets

At first glance the strategic management model, which provides the framework for study throughout this book, seems to suggest that strategic choice decision making leads to the *sequential* selections of long-term objectives and grand strategy. In fact, however, strategic choice is the *simultaneous* selection of long-range objectives and grand strategy. Figure 8–5, which first appeared as Figure 2–2, depicts the actual process. When strategic planners study their opportunities, they try to determine which are most likely to result in achieving various long-range objectives. Almost simultaneously they try to forecast whether an available grand strategy can take advantage of preferred opportunities so that the tentative objectives can be met. In essence then, three distinct but highly interdependent choices are being made at one time. Usually several triads or sets of possible decisions are considered.

A simplified example of this process is shown in Figure 8–6. In this example the business has determined that six strategic choice options are available. These options stem from three different interactive opportunities, e.g., West Coast markets which present little competition. Because each of these interactive opportunities can be approached through different grand strategies—in options 1 and 2 they are horizontal integration and market development—each offers the potential for achieving long-range objectives to varying degrees. Thus, a business can rarely make a strategic choice only on the basis of its preferred opportunities, long-range objectives, or grand strategy. Instead, the three elements must be considered simultaneously because only in combination do they constitute a strategic choice.

In an actual decision situation the strategic choice would be complicated by a wider variety of interactive opportunities, feasible company objectives, promising grand strategy options, and evaluative criteria. Nevertheless, Figure 8–6 does partially reflect the nature and complexity of the process by which long-term objectives and grand strategy are selected.

In the next chapter, the strategic choice process will be fully explained. However, knowledge of long-term objectives and grand strategies is essential to understanding that process. Thus, the topics were presented here first, even though a company's specific selections of long-term objectives and grand strategies are actually outputs based on choice, as the strategic-management-process model shows.

Figure 8–5

Detailed component: Interactive opportunities analysis and strategic choice

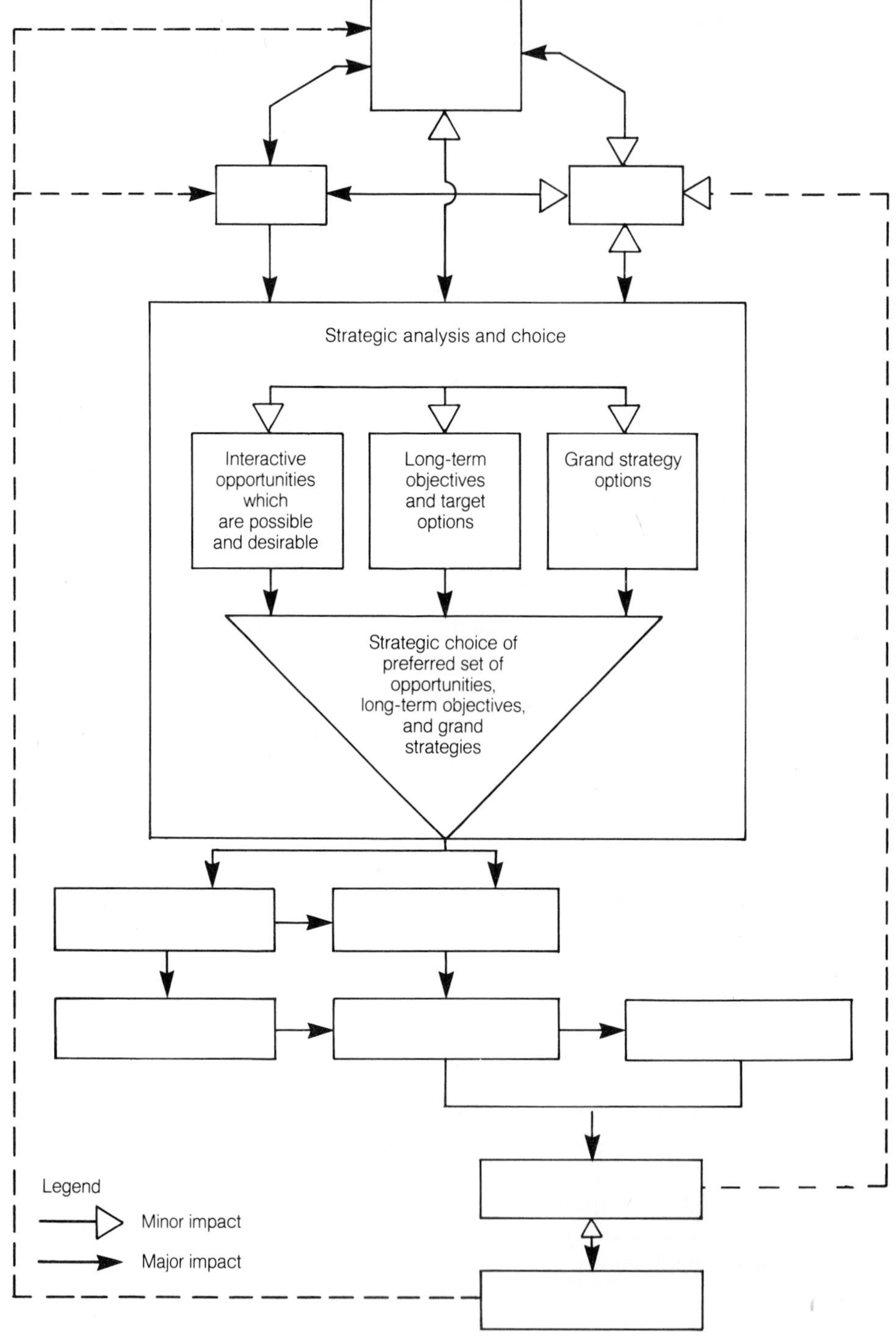

Figure 8–6

A profile of strategic choice options

	Six strategic choice options					
	1	*2*	*3*	*4*	*5*	*6*
Interactive opportunities	West Coast markets present little competition		Current markets sensitive to price competition		Current industry product lines after too narrow a range of markets	
Appropriate long-range objectives (limited sample): Average 5-year ROI Company sales by year 5 Risk of negative profit	 15% +50% .30	 19% +40% .25	 13% +20% .10	 17% +0% .15	 23% +35% .20	 15% +25% .05
Grand strategies	Horizontal integration	Market development	Concentration	Selective retrenchment	Product development	Concentration

Sequence of Objectives and Strategy Selection

The selection of long-term objectives and grand strategies involves simultaneous rather than sequential decisions. While it is true that objectives are needed so that the company's direction and progress are not determined by random forces, it is equally true that objectives are valuable only if strategies can be implemented, making achievement of objectives realistic. In fact, the selection of long-term objectives and grand strategies is so interdependent that until the 1970s most business consultants and academicians did not stress the need to distinguish between them. Most popular business literature and practicing executives still combine long-term objectives and grand strategies under the heading of company strategy.

However, the distinction has merit. Objectives indicate what strategic managers *want* but provide few insights as to *how* this will be achieved. Conversely, strategies indicate what type of *actions* will be taken but do not define what *ends* will be pursued or what criteria will serve as contraints in refining the strategic plan.

The latter view of objectives as constraints on strategy formulation rather than as ends toward which strategies are directed is stressed by several prominent management experts.[8] They argue that strategic decisions are designed (1) to satisfy the minimum requirements of different company groups, e.g., the production department's need for more inventory capacity, or the marketing department's need to increase the sales force and (2) to create synergistic profit potential given these constraints.

Does it matter whether strategic decisions are made to achieve objectives or to satisfy constraints? No, because constraints are objectives themselves. The constraint of increased inventory capacity is a desire (an objective) not a certainty. Likewise, the constraint of a larger sales force does not assure that it will be achieved given such factors as other company priorities, labor market conditions, and the firm's profit performance.

Summary

Before learning how strategic decisions are made, it was important to understand the two principal components of any strategic choice, namely, long-term objectives and grand strategy. Such understanding was the purpose of the chapter.

Long-term objectives were defined as the results a business seeks to achieve

[8] See, for example, P. F. Drucker, *The Practice of Management* (New York: Harper & Row, 1954); R. M. Cyert, and J. G. March, *A Behavioral Theory of the Firm* (Englewood Cliffs, N.J.: Prentice-Hall, 1963); H. A. Simon, "On the Concept of Organizational Goals," *Administrative Science Quarterly* 9 (1964), pp. 1–22; and M. D. Richards, *Organizational Goal Structures* (St. Paul: West Publishing, 1978).

over a specified period of time, typically five years. Seven common long-term objectives were discussed: profitability, productivity, competitive position, employee development, employee relations, technological leadership, and public responsibility. These, or any other long-term objectives, should be acceptable, flexible, measurable over time, motivating, suitable, understandable, and achievable.

Grand strategies were defined as comprehensive approaches guiding major actions designed to achieve long-term business objectives. Twelve specific grand strategy options were discussed. They included concentration, market development, product development, innovation, horizontal integration, vertical integration, joint ventures, concentric diversification, conglomerate diversification, retrenchment/turnaround, divestiture, and liquidation.

Questions for Discussion

1. Think of the business community nearest to your college or university. Identify businesses you believe are using each of the 12 grand strategies.
2. Try to identify businesses in your community that appear to rely principally on 1 of the 12 grand strategies. What kind of information did you use to classify the firms?
3. Write a long-term objective for your school of business that exhibits the seven qualities of long-term objectives described in this chapter.
4. Distinguish between the following pairs of grand strategies:
   a. Horizontal and vertical integration.
   b. Conglomerate and concentric diversification.
   c. Product development and innovation.
5. Rank each of the 12 grand strategy options on the following three scales:

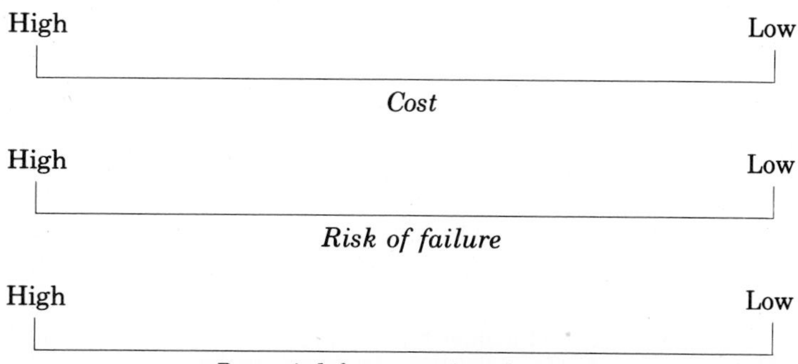

6. Identify companies that use one of the eight specific options shown in Figure 8–1 under the grand strategies of concentration, market development, and product development.

Bibliography

Ansoff, H. I. "Strategies for Diversification." Harvard Business Review, September–October 1957, pp. 113–124.

________. *Corporate Strategy.* New York: McGraw-Hill, 1965.

________. *Strategic Management.* New York: John Wiley & Sons, 1979.

Cyert, R. M., and J. G. March. *A Behavioral Theory of the Firm.* Englewood Cliffs, N.J.: Prentice-Hall, 1963.

Drucker, P. F. *The Practice of Management.* New York: Harper & Row, 1954.

Glueck, W. F. *Business Policy and Strategic Management.* New York: McGraw-Hill, 1980.

Higgins, J. M. *Organizational Policy and Strategic Management.* Hinsdale, Ill.: Dryden Press, 1979.

King, R., and D. I. Cleland. *Strategic Planning and Policy.* New York: Van Nostrand Reinhold, 1978.

Kotler, P. *Marketing Management.* Englewood Cliffs, N.J.: Prentice-Hall, 1972.

Luck, D. J., and A. E. Prell. *Market Strategy.* New York: Appleton-Century-Crofts, 1968.

Osborn, A. F. *Applied Imagination.* 3d rev. ed. New York: Charles Scribner's Sons, 1968.

Pearce, J. A. H. II. "An Executive-Level Perspective on the Strategic Management Process." *California Management Review,* Summer 1981, pp. 39–48.

________. "Selecting among Alternative Grand Strategies." *California Management Review,* Spring 1982.

Richards, M. D. *Organizational Goal Structures.* St. Paul, Minn.: West Publishing, 1978.

Schendel, Dan G.; G. R. Patton; and J. Riggs. "Corporate Turnaround Strategies: A Study of Profit Decline and Recovery." *Journal of General Management* 3 (1976), pp. 3–11.

Schoor, B. "Many New Products Fizzle, Despite Careful Planning, Publicity." *The Wall Street Journal,* April 5, 1961.

Simon, H. A. "On the Concept of Organizational Goals." *Administrative Science Quarterly,* 1964, pp. 1–22.

Steiner, G. A. *Strategic Planning.* New York: Free Press, 1979.

Steiner, G. A., and J. B. Miner. *Management Policy and Strategy.* New York: Macmillan, 1977.

Chapter 8 Cohesion Case Illustration

Long-Term Objectives and Grand Strategies at Holiday Inns, Inc.

Long-term objectives at Holiday Inns, Inc., exist at both the corporate and business level. Selected examples of long-term objectives are provided below:

Corporate long-term objectives:

Increase corporatewide return on equity to 17.5 percent by 1984.

Achieve and maintain a debt-to-invested-capital ratio that does not exceed a 40 to 50 percent range.

Improve the corporatewide after-tax margin to a minimum of 7 percent by 1984.

Ensure a corporationwide sales growth that will maintain hotel group contribution at less than 60 percent of sales by 1984.

Business group long-term objectives:

Increase the number of rooms in the HI system by 70,000 between 1982 and 1987. *(Hotel group)*

Improve hotel operating margins to 20 percent by 1984. *(Hotel group)*

Triple the number of company-owned properties in multiuser locations by 1987. *(Hotel group)*

Increase the cash flow generated by Delta for corporatewide use from $25 million in 1980 to $60 million in 1985. *(Transportation group)*

Increase the ROI from gaming operations to 15 percent by 1987. *(Casino group)*

Increase the average daily customer count at Perkins Restaurants to 1,000 people per day by 1987. *(Restaurant group)*

Decrease the capital invested in institutional products manufacturing capacity by 70 percent by 1985. *(Products group)*

These objectives provide examples of the strategic focus that long-term objectives can provide the firm. Strategic direction is further clarified through grand strategies.

Twelve fundamental grand strategies were discussed in Chapter 8. Each grand strategy is illustrated below as it might apply to a particular business group:

Concentration. The *hotel group* might consider that continued emphasis on expansion of selected company-owned and franchised Holiday Inn properties has sufficient potential to achieve long-term objectives. This would call for a concentration on growth via the group's current approach with emphasis on maintaining and improving operating advantages and effectiveness.

Market Development. The *hotel group* might determine that domestic growth potential is decreasing. If so, it might pursue a strategy that emphasizes major international expansion of the Holiday Inns network.

Product Development. *Perkins* might determine that inadequate menu selection is one reason for its mediocre performance. A product development strategy would therefore pursue growth via systematic development and expansion of menu items.

Innovation. The *products group* might consider pursuing growth via the systematic development of revolutionary new institutional equipment for hotel operations. This innovation-based strategy would be one option (probably a remote one) for the products group.

Horizontal Integration. One way for the *gaming group* to grow rapidly would be to acquire casinos in key markets where the group currently competes or desires to compete.

Vertical Integration. Vertical integration can be either *forward* or *backward.* For example, *Delta Steamships* might see growth via route expansion as fairly limited. As a result it might seek manufacturing capacity for LASH containers *(backward integration)* to serve its needs and those of other shippers. Another alternative is involvement in warehousing or brokering *(forward integration),* as a basis for shipping-related growth.

Joint Ventures. The *hotel group* may project faster growth in the high-priced and budget-priced lodging segments than in the broad middle segment. It may seek joint ventures with chains in one or both of these segments to get a foothold and a possible expansion base.

Retrenchment. Profits of the *transportation group* declined for several years in the late 1970s. A retrenchment strategy cutting out unprofitable routes, unnecessary overhead, and level of terminal services was a possible grand strategy for this group.

Divestiture. The *restaurant group* may determine that the best way to achieve long-term ROI objectives is to sell several subpar restaurant locations. Selling these as going concerns would represent a divestiture strategy if it represented the group's key orientation.

Liquidation. The *products group* expanded rapidly in the 1960s acquiring 30 businesses. Several of these businesses solely supplied Holiday Inns' institutional and printing needs. The product group might choose to sell the equipment used by some of these businesses if sale of the business as a going concern is not realistic. This would be a liquidation strategy.

Concentric Diversification. The best way to view this grand strategy at Holiday Inns, Inc., is to look at selected decisions made at Holiday Inns when it was predominantly a hotel chain. Holiday Inns' expansion into the freestanding restaurant business and the casino-gaming business is a concentric diversification strategy in relation to Holiday Inns, Inc.'s dominant core business.

Conglomerate Diversification. From the same perspective, Holiday Inns, Inc.'s acquisition of Trailways, Delta Steamships, and some of the manufacturing businesses in the products group represent a conglomerate diversification strategy in that these businesses were essentially unrelated to Holiday Inns' core businesses.

These examples illustrate each grand strategy concept. As you can see, each grand strategy is a possible alternative for at least one of Holiday Inns, Inc.'s businesses.

CHAPTER

Strategic Analysis and Choice

The previous chapter described basic characteristics of major strategic alternatives that a firm might consider. Several questions remain. How does a company identify alternative strategies? What are some of the diagnostic tools used to identify and evaluate realistic alternative strategies in multibusiness companies? What factors influence the ultimate choice of strategy?

This chapter will examine possible answers to these questions. Techniques used to aid strategic choice at the corporate and business levels will be explored. Managerial, political, and behavioral factors affecting the choice of strategy will also be discussed.

The search for alternative strategies is both incremental and creative in that strategists begin by considering alternatives they are familiar with and think will work. These are usually incremental alterations of past strategies. Systematic comparison of external and internal factors is often used to search for alternative strategies. Creativity can be important in this internal/external comparison. The search for multiple alternatives depends on systematic comparison of the strengths, weaknesses, risks, and trade-offs of each alternative. Several alternatives are generated and systematically evaluated in a comparative framework. The quality of the ultimate choice is thereby logically enchanced. Evaluation of alternative strategies is much the same whether new alternatives or the old strategy is considered. The focus is the future. Both old and new strategies must be subjected to the same systematic evaluation if a logical choice is to be made.

The process of strategic analysis and choice involves five incremental phases. Figure 9–1 identifies these phases at the business and corporate levels. Because strategic choice is a judgmental/analytical process meant to ascertain the

Figure 9–1

The process of strategic analysis

Time	*Corporate-level strategy*	*Business-level strategy*
↓	Analysis of the overall company *portfolio* of businesses in terms of relative business-unit strength *matched* with relative industry attractiveness and stage of development.	Analysis of the *match* between the business's current strategic position (company profile) and the major strategic opportunities and threats (environmental analysis) that exist or will exist in the planning time period.
	Identification of probable corporate performance if the current business-unit portfolio is maintained with respective strategies.	Examining the probable results of pursuing the current strategy in light of the new business-environment match.
	Comparison of this projected corporate performance with tentative corporate objectives to identify major performance gaps.	Comparison of these results with tentative business objectives to identify major performance gaps and strategic concerns.
	Identification of alternative portfolios (including different strategy combinations at the business-unit level) to close performance gaps.	Identification of alternative strategies to close performance gaps and confront (or avoid) strategic concerns.
	Evaluation of the alternatives and strategic choice.	Evaluation of the alternatives and strategic choice.

future impact of one or more strategies on corporate (and/or business-unit) performance, the answers to three basic questions are sought:

1. How effective has the existing strategy been?
2. How effective will that strategy be in the future?
3. What will be the effectiveness of selected alternative strategies (or changes in the existing strategy) in the future?

Strategic Analysis at the Corporate Level

A fundamental method of corporate strategic analysis in diversified, multi-industry companies is the business portfolio approach. General Electric, for example, has over 40 strategic business units (SBUs).[1] Thus, General Electric must decide how this portfolio of businesses should be managed to achieve corporate objectives. A corporate strategy is sought that sets the basic "strate-

[1] General Electric combined selected businesses or operations, regardless of organizational level, into SBUs for planning purposes.

An SBU is generally created when the following requirements are met by the component:

1. It has a unique business mission.
2. It has an identifiable set of competitors.
3. It is a viable competitor.
4. The SBU strategic manager can make or implement a strategic decision relatively independent of other SBUs.
5. Crucial operating decisions can be made within the SBU.

gic thrust" for each business unit in a manner consistent with the resource capabilities of the overall company.

The *portfolio approach,* with analysis of corporate-level strategy distinct from business-level strategy, is adaptable to multiproduct market firms in which each product/market is managed as a separate business or profit center and the firm is not dominated by one product/market. The approach involves examining each business as a separate entity and as a contributor to the corporation's total *portfolio* of businesses. In dominant product/market companies and single product/market firms corporate strategy considerations are not separate and distinct from business-level considerations.

In a broad sense, corporate strategy is concerned with generation and allocation of corporate resources. The firm's portfolio of businesses are, to varying degrees, the generators and recipients of these resources. The portfolio approach provides a simple, visual way of identifying and evaluating alternative strategies for the generation and allocation of corporate resources.

The BCG Growth/Share Matrix

One of the most widely used portfolio approaches to corporate strategic analysis has been the growth/share matrix pioneered by the Boston Consulting Group (BCG), and illustrated in Figure 9–2. This matrix facilitates corporate strategic analysis of likely "generators" and optimum "users" of corporate resources.

To use the BCG matrix, each of the company's businesses is plotted according to market growth rate (percentage growth in sales) and relative competitive position (market share). Market growth rate is the projected rate of sales growth for the market to be served by a particular business. It is usually measured as the percentage increase in a market's sales or unit volume over the two most recent years. Market growth rate provides an indicator of the relative attractiveness of the markets served by each of the businesses in the corporation's portfolio of businesses. Relative competitive position is usually expressed as the ratio of a business' market share divided by the market share of the largest competitor in that market. Relative competitive position thus provides a basis for comparing the relative strength of different businesses in the business portfolio in terms of the "strength" of their position in each business' respective market.

Business are plotted on the matrix once their market growth rate and relative competitive positions have been computed. Figure 9–2 represents the BCG matrix for a company with nine businesses. Each circle represents a business unit. The size of the circle represents the proportion of corporate revenue generated by that business unit. This provides visualization of the current importance of each business as a revenue generator.

Market growth rate is frequently separated into "high" and "low" areas by an arbitrary 10 percent growth line. Relative competitive position is usually divided at a relative market share between 1.0 and 1.5, so that a "high"

Figure 9–2

BCG's growth/share matrix

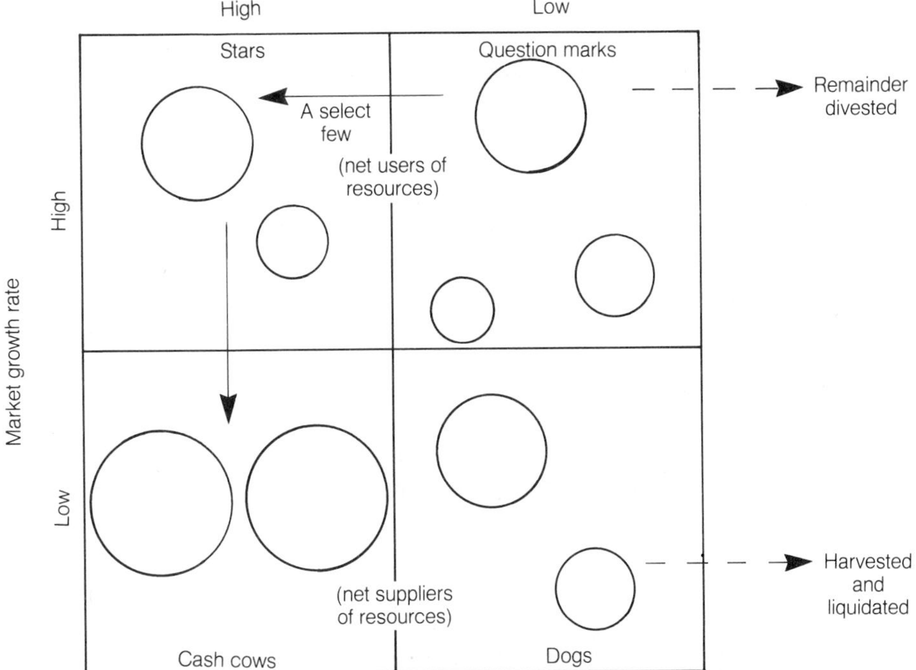

Source: Adapted from Barry Hedley, "Strategy and the Business Portfolio," *Long-Range Planning*, February 1977, p. 10.

position signifies market leadership. Once plotted, businesses in the BCG matrix will be in one of four cells with differing implications for their role in an overall corporate-level strategy.

High Growth/High Competitive Position. The *stars,* as the BCG matrix labeled them, are businesses in rapidly growing markets with large market shares. Stars represent the best long-run opportunities (growth and profitability) in the firm's portfolio. These businesses require substantial investment to maintain (and expand) their dominant position in a growing market. This investment requirement is often in excess of what can be generated internally. Therefore, these businesses are short-term, priority consumers of corporate resources within the overall business portfolio.

Low Growth/High Competitive Position. *Cash cows* are high-market-share businesses in maturing, low-growth markets or industries. Because of their strong position and minimal reinvestment requirements for growth, these businesses often generate cash in excess of their needs. Therefore, these businesses are selectively "milked" as a source of corporate resources for deployment elsewhere (to stars and question marks). Cash cows are yesterday's stars and remain the current foundation of their corporate portfolios. They provide the cash to pay corporate overhead and dividends, and provide debt capacity. They are managed to maintain their strong market share while efficiently generating excess resources for corporatewide use.

Low Growth/Low Competitive Position. The BCG matrix calls businesses with low market share and low market growth the *dogs* in the firm's portfolio. These businesses are in saturated, mature markets with intense competition and low profit margins. Because of their weak position, these businesses are managed for short-term cash flow (through ruthless cost cutting, for example) to supplement corporate-level resource needs. According to the original BCG prescription, they are eventually divested or liquidated once the short-term harvesting is maximized.

Recent research has questioned the notion that all *dogs* should be destined for divestiture/liquidation.[2] The thrust of this research suggests that *well-managed dogs* turn out to be positive, highly reliable resource generators (although still far less resource-rich than cows). The well-managed dogs, according to these studies, combine a narrow business focus, emphasis on high product quality and moderate prices, strenuous cost cutting and cost control and limited advertising. While suggesting that well-managed dogs can be a useful component of a business portfolio, these studies warn that ineffective dogs should still be considered prime candidates for harvesting, divestiture, or liquidation.

High Growth/Low Competitive Position. *Question mark* businesses have considerable appeal because of their high growth rate, yet present questionable profit potential because of low market share. Question mark businesses are known as cash guzzlers because their cash needs are high as a result of rapid growth, while their cash generation is low due to a small market share. Because market growth rate is high, a favorable market share (competitive position) should be easier to obtain than with the dogs in the portfolio. At the corporate level the concern is identifying the question marks that would most benefit from extra corporate resources resulting in increased market share and movement into the star group. When this long-run shift in a business' position from question mark to star is unlikely, the BCG matrix suggests divesting the business to reposition the resources more effectively in the remaining portfolio.

The BCG matrix was a valuable initial development in the portfolio ap-

---

[2] Carlyn Y. Woo and Arnold C. Cooper, "Strategies of Effective Low Market Share Businesses," *Harvard Business Review* November–December 1982, pp. 106–13. Donald Hambrick and Ian MacMillan, "Dogs," *Boardroom Reports,* October 15, 1981, pp. 5–6.

Strategy in Action 9–1
Portfolio Management at Mead Corporation

Mead Corporation, under the direction of Chairman and CEO J. W. McSwiney, was one of the pioneers in the use of a portfolio approach in the strategic management of its numerous forest-products-related businesses. The following is excerpted from a presentation by J. W. McSwiney, President Warren L. Batts, and Vice Chairman William W. Wommack to Paper and Forest Products Analysts at the Princeton Club in New York about Mead's early experience using portfolio planning:

> As the first step toward achieving Mead's corporate goals, Mr. McSwiney assigned Bill Wommack full-time responsibility for developing a new strategic philosophy, a planning system, and then a strategy for each of Mead's businesses. The strategic concept he developed was straightforward and very effective:
>
> Obtain market leadership in markets we serve.
>
> If market leadership is not possible, redeploy our assets to markets where leadership potential exists.
>
> This concept can be translated into a matrix as follows:

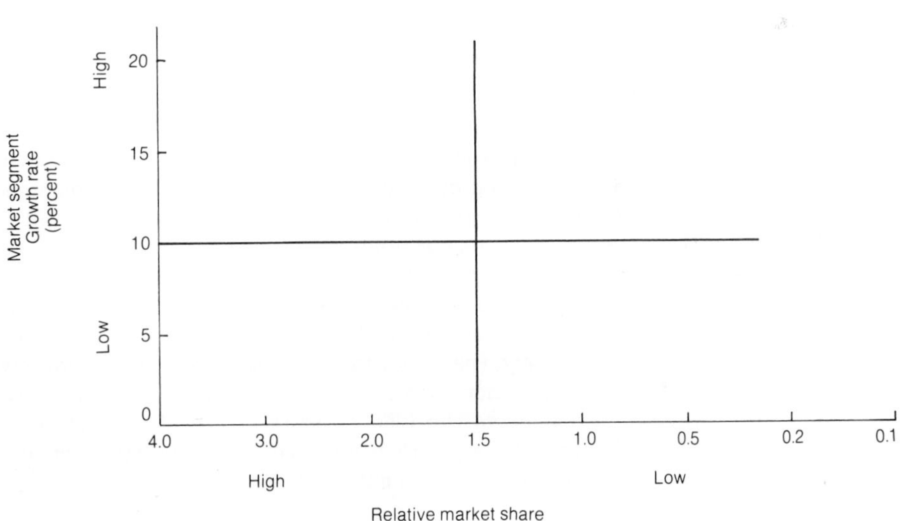

Strategy in Action 9–1 *(continued)*

We consider a high-growth market to be one that is growing by at least 10 percent in real terms. To us, relative market share is what counts. We consider a leadership position exists when a business has a market share that is at least 1.5 times the share of its next largest competitor, as shown by the vertical line at 1.5 in the figure above.

Starting with the upper right-hand quadrant:

For a business in a high-growth market with a low market share, we assess our chances for leadership, and either grow our share aggressively or get out.

In a high-growth market with a high market share, we grow our share as rapidly as we can and invest to become the most cost-effective producer.

In a low-growth market with a high market share, we maintain our market share and cost effectiveness. We also generate cash for the balance of the company.

In a low-growth market with low market share, we operate to generate cash—we have generally found this means we get out.

When we classified our businesses on this matrix, we found many were competing in low-growth segments with low market share. We decided that within five years we should eliminate those low-growth and low-market-share businesses and allocate capital to the remaining businesses so that they could attain greater market share and grow larger.

Our first step was to dispose of 15 businesses where it was not practical to become a leader. They were essentially the low-growth, low-market-share businesses. This step generated $80 million in cash, plus it saved $25 million we would have had to invest if we'd kept them. Especially important, these actions immediately improved our mix of businesses and the total return from our assets.

Second, we had to change the way our managers managed; plus we all had to operate in a more highly focused manner. We started with formal in-house training programs for some 300 Mead managers. [Our strategy] would not be carried out unless key managers truly understood the new . . . philosophy . . . and how to use the underlying analytical techniques. But even when managers understood what we were trying to do, some were unable to accept the discipline required. We had to reorganize several businesses and change a number of managers. Five of our six operating group vice presidents were changed, as well as 19 of our 24 division presidents. Fortunately, the talent to effect these changes was largely in-house.

Finally, we put increased emphasis on managing our assets. We consider return on net assets the true measure of operating performance, so we tied each general manager's compensation to a balance between his business unit's earnings and its net assets.

We categorized and managed our businesses from a strategic point of view as follows:

Poor businesses.

Those businesses which had good strategies in place.

Those business which needed a change in strategy.

Examining these categories demonstrates how we improved our results by:

Shifting assets.

Improving performance.

Carefully investing.

	Asset mix (percent)		*Return on net assets (percent)*	
Category	***Year 1***	***Year 5***	***Year 1***	***Year 5***
Poor businesses	13.2%	2.1%	2.4%	4.2%
No change	38.5	53.4	8.8	9.6
Change	48.3	44.5	2.8	11.8
Total corporate	100.0%	100.0%	4.7%	10.4%

In Year 1 our sales totaled $1.1 billion. Four years later sales totaled $1.6 billion. This was a 9 percent compound growth rate, even though we had disposed of businesses having sales of $180 million. It is worth noting that sales of our Forest Products category increased at a 15 percent rate, so that percentage of the total rose to 56 percent.

Pretax earnings during this period increased from about $39 million to $167 million, or a 34 percent compound growth rate. Again, earnings in our Forest Products category increased sixfold.

We continually review our businesses, and we will reclassify a business and change its strategy when it's prudent to do so.

I believe we now have the fundamentals for long-term success firmly in place—both in the physical sense of good businesses serving growing markets, and in the management sense of realistic objectives, sound strategies—and the internal discipline to carry them out.

Source: Mead executive management presentation to Paper and Forest Product Analysts at the Princeton Club, New York, New York, February 8, 1977. Reprinted with permission.

proach to corporate-level strategy evaluation. The goal of the BCG approach is to determine the corporate strategy that best provides a balanced portfolio of business units. BCG's ideal, balanced portfolio would have the largest sales in cash cows and stars, with only a few question marks and very few dogs (the latter with favorable cash flow).

The BCG matrix makes two major contributions to corporate strategic choice: the assignment of a specific role or mission for each business unit, and the integration of multiple business units into a total corporate strategy. By focusing simultaneously on comparative growth/share positions, the underlying premise of corporate strategy becomes exploitation of competitive advantage.

While the BCG matrix is an important visual tool with which to analyze corporate (business-portfolio) strategy, strategists must recognize six limitations.

1. Clearly defining a *market* is often difficult. As a result, accurately measuring *share* and *growth rate* can be a problem. This in turn, creates the potential for distortion or manipulation.
2. Dividing the matrix into four cells based on a *high/low* classification scheme is somewhat simplistic. It does not recognize the markets with *average* growth rates or the businesses with *average* market shares.
3. The relationship between market share and profitability underlying the BCG matrix—the *experience curve* effect—varies across industries and market segments. In some industries a large market share creates major advantages in unit costs; in others it does not. Furthermore, some companies with low market share can generate superior profitability and cash flow with careful strategies based on differentiation, innovation, or market segmentation. Mercedes and Polaroid are two examples.
4. The BCG matrix is not particularly helpful in comparing relative investment opportunities across different business units in the corporate portfolio. For example, is every star better than a cash cow? How should one question mark be compared to another in terms of whether it should be built into a star or divested?[3]
5. Strategic evaluation of a set of businesses requires examination of more than relative market shares and market growth. The attractiveness of an industry may increase based on technological, seasonal, competitive, or other considerations as much as on growth rate. Likewise, the value of a business within a corporate portfolio is often linked to considerations other than market share.[4]
6. The four colorful classifications in the BCG matrix somewhat oversimplify the types of businesses in a corporate portfolio. Likewise, the simple strategic missions recommended by the BCG matrix often don't reflect the diversity of options available, as shown earlier in discussing dogs.

---

[3] Dereck F. Abell and John S. Hammond, *Strategic Market Planning* (Englewood Cliffs, N.J.: Prentice-Hall, 1979), p. 212.

[4] For an interesting elaboration of this point, see Walter E. Ketchell III, "Oh Where Oh Where Has My Little Dog Gone? Or My Cash Cow? Or My Star?" *Fortune*, November 2, 1981, pp. 148–52.

Before leaving the BCG matrix, the use of labels associated with this matrix deserves further comment. A recent survey of numerous executives in large firms using portfolio-planning techniques found widespread dislike of the *dog, question mark, cash cow,* and *star* terminology. Typical executive comments were as follows:[5]

> To the extent that a division manager was to see a chart and see the word "dog" written next to his division, it's bound to create motivational problems. It's much easier to say that your mission is to reduce investment and you will be paid for achieving that objective and not for maximizing sales growth than to say you are a cash cow or a dog.
>
> We try to avoid the use of words such as cash cow or dog like the plague. If you call a business a dog, it'll respond like one. It's one thing to know that you are an ugly duckling much worse to be told explicitly that you are.

While criticism was widespread regarding BCG labels, there was strong support for use of more meaningful labels associated with positions in the BCG matrix or the GE planning grid (see Figure 9–3). Typical comments were as follows:[6]

> In our company, the business unit labels are made explicit. In fact, the business unit managers are the ones who recommend what the strategy for their businesses should be. If we did not use explicit strategy labels such as "build," "hold," and "harvest," the room for confusion over exactly what a business unit's strategy is would be very high. At the same time, it is important to remember that a business that's harvest today might need to have a build strategy tomorrow.
>
> Our business units know their strategies in terms such as "grow," "maintain," and "shrink." Only "withdraw" is not made explicit. Making strategy explicit helps in implementation; for example, it ensures that harvest managers won't ask for resources. . . . We don't label managers, but only their businesses; we keep moving people around since the idea is to develop well-rounded managers.

This study suggests a preference for strategy labels such as *build, hold, harvest,* and *withdraw* rather than *star, cash cow, question mark,* and *dog* in the strategic planning activities of major multibusiness firms. The reasons are apparently threefold:

1. Some of the BCG terms are seen as negative and unnecessarily graphic.
2. The BCG terms are somewhat "static" while "build/hold/harvest" are more dynamic and action oriented.
3. Terms like "dog/star/cash cow" have meaning only within a BCG context, while "build/hold/harvest" have universal validity and clarity of strategic intent even without a portfolio planning approach.

---

[5] Anil K. Gupta and V. Govindarajan, "Build, Hold, Harvest: Converting Strategic Intentions into Reality," *Journal of Business Strategy,* March 1984, pp. 34–47.

[6] Ibid., p. 40.

Figure 9–3

General Electric's nine-cell planning grid

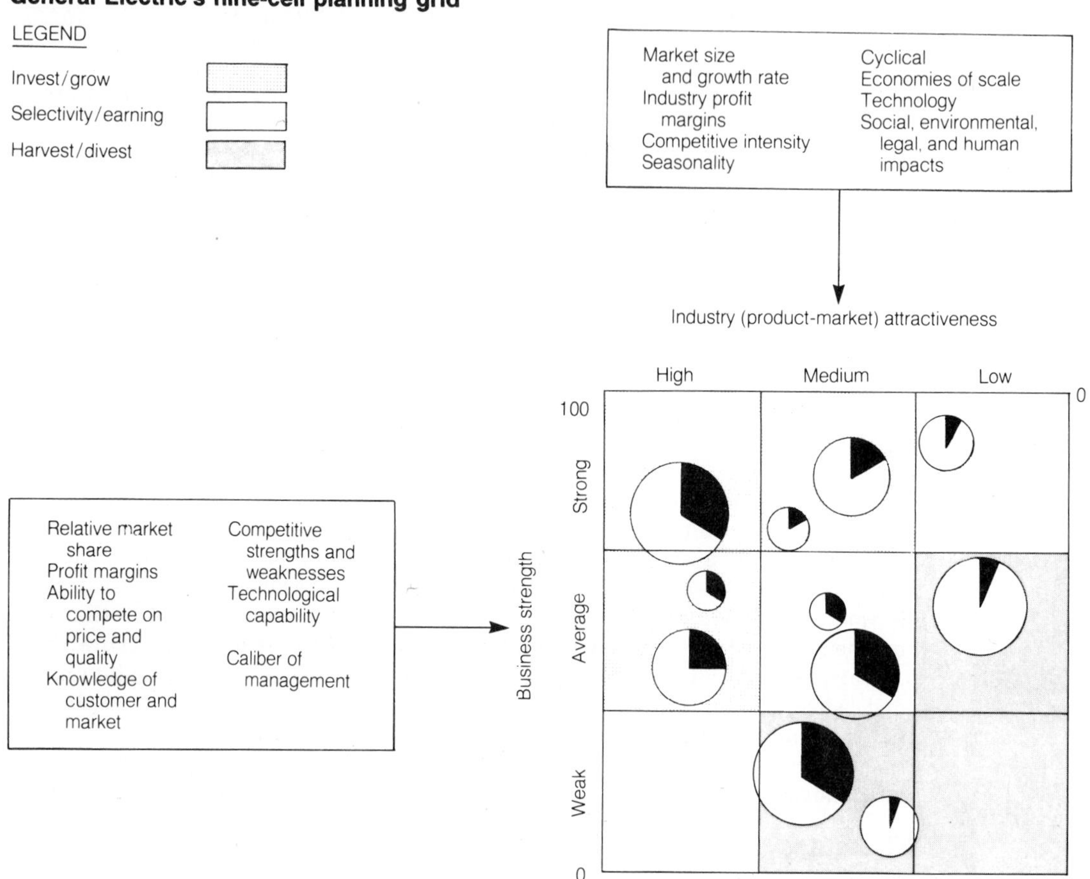

One executive's comment perhaps best illustrates the value of the preferred set of strategy labels:

> We have [generally] shied away from using any portfolio model. Yet we recognize that different businesses may need to have different strategic missions. In fact, our strategy documents require business unit managers to indicate explicity the strategies for their units in terms such as "build," "hold," "harvest," "withdraw," and "explore."[7]

[7] Gupta and Govindarajan, "Build, Hold, Harvest," p. 35.

The GE Nine-Cell Planning Grid[8]

General Electric popularized an adaptation of the BCG approach (Figure 9–3) that attempts to overcome some of the matrix limitations mentioned above. First, the GE grid uses multiple factors to assess industry attractiveness and business strength, rather than the single measures (market share and market growth, respectively) employed in the BCG matrix. Second, GE expanded the matrix from four cells to nine—replacing the high/low axes with high/medium/low axes to make finer distinction between business portfolio positions.

To use the GE planning grid, each of the company's business units is rated on multiple sets of strategic factors within each axis of the grid:

Business Strength Factors: Market share, profit margin, ability to compete, customer and market knowledge, competitive position, technology, and management caliber are the factors contributing to business strength.

Industry Attractiveness Factors: Market growth, size and industry profitability, competition, seasonality and cyclical qualities, economies of scale, technology, and social/environmental/legal/human factors are identified as enhancing industry attractiveness.

A business's position within the planning grid is then calculated by "subjectively" quantifying the two dimensions of the grid.

To measure industry attractiveness, the strategist first selects those factors contributing to this aspect. The procedure then involves assigning each industry attractiveness factor a weight that reflects its perceived importance relative to the other attractiveness factors. Favorable to unfavorable future conditions for those factors are forecasted and rated based on some scale (a 0 to 1 scale is illustrated below). A weighted composite score is then obtained for a business' overall industry attractiveness as show below.

Industry attractiveness factor	*Weight*	*Rating**	Score
Market size	20	0.5	10.0
Project market growth	35	1.0	35.0
Technological requirements	15	0.5	7.5
Concentration (a few large competitors)	30	0	0
Political and regulatory factors	Must be nonrestrictive	—	—
Total	100	—	52.5

* High = 1.0, Medium = 0.5, Low = 0.0.

[8] Label terminology in the GE planning grid is more consistent with executives' preferences. The discussion of the GE labels is cross-referenced to BCG terminology to show the overlap between the two sets of labels.

To assess business strength, a similar procedure is followed in selecting factors, assigning weights to them, and then rating the business on these dimensions, as illustrated below.

Business strength factor	*Weight*	*Rating**	*Score*
Relative market share	20	0.5	10
Production			
Capacity	10	1.0	10
Efficiency	10	1.0	10
Location	20	0	—
Technological capability ...	20	0.5	10
Marketing			
Sales organization	15	1.0	15
Promotion advantage	5	0	—
	100		55

* High = 1.0, Medium = 0.5, Low = 0.0.

These examples illustrate how one business within a corporate portfolio might be assessed using the GE planning grid. It is important to remember that what should be included or excluded as a factor, as well as how it should be rated and weighted, is primarily a matter of managerial judgment; and usually several managers are involved during the planning process. The result of such ratings is a high, medium, or low classification in terms of both the projected strength of the business and the projected attractiveness of the industry, as shown in Figure 9–3.

Three basic strategic approaches are suggested for any business in the corporate portfolio depending on its location within the grid: (1) invest to grow, (2) invest selectively and manage for earnings, or (3) harvest or divest for resources. The resource allocation decisions remain quite similar to those in the BCG approach. Businesses classified as *invest to grow* would be treated like the *stars* in the BCG matrix. These businesses would be accorded resources to pursue growth-oriented strategies. Businesses classified in the *harvest/divest* category would be managed like the *dogs* in the BCG matrix. They would follow strategies that provided net resources for use in other business units. Businesses classified in the *selectivity/earnings* category would either be managed as *cash cows* providing maximum earnings for corporatewide use or as *question marks* (selectivity chosen for investment or divestment).

While the strategic recommendations generated by the GE planning grid are similar to those from the BCG matrix, the GE nine-cell grid improves on the BCG matrix in three fundamental ways. First, as research discussed earlier pointed out, the terminology associated with the GE grid is preferable because it is less offensive and more universally understood. Second, the multiple measures associated with each dimension of the GE grid tap more factors relevant to business strength and market attractiveness than simply market share and market growth. This provides (or even forces) broader assessment during the planning process; considerations of strategic importance both in strategy formulation *and* in strategy implementation are brought to light. Finally, the nine-cell format obviously allows finer distinction between portfolio positions (most notably for "average" businesses) than does the four-cell BCG format.

The Product/Market–Evolution Matrix

Charles Hofer has made further improvements in the portfolio approach to corporate strategic analysis.[9] Concerned that the GE matrix did not clearly depict the position of new businesses about to emerge as winners in new industries, Hofer proposed a 15-cell matrix to evaluate corporate portfolios. Figure 9–4 illustrates Hofer's product/market–evolution matrix in which businesses are plotted in terms of their *competitive position* and their *stage of product/market evolution.* The circles represent the size of industries (or product/market segments), and the wedges represent the market share of the business unit. Looking at Figure 9–4, several strategic considerations regarding the business portfolio become apparent.

1. Business A appears to be an emerging star, and thus a target for excess resource allocation—especially to strengthen its competitive position in light of its strong market share.
2. Business B presents much the same scenario as business A but corporate resource allocation would probably be contingent on determining why B has been unable to obtain a higher market share, given its strong competitive position, and on the presentation of sound plans to rectify this deficiency.
3. Business F and, to a lesser extent, business E represent cash cows within the corporate portfolio and would be key targets for corporate resource generation.
4. Business G appears to be an emerging dog, managed to generate short-term cash flow and for eventual divestiture or liquidation.

The product/market–evolution continuum adds a useful dimension to the identification, analysis, and evaluation of corporate–level portfolio strategies. Stage of product/market evolution was discussed earlier in Chapter 7.

While the variety of alternative portfolios could be infinite, Hofer and Schendel suggest that most corporate-level portfolio strategies are variations of one of three ideal portfolios: (1) growth portfolios, (2) profit portfolios, and (3) balanced portfolios.[10] Figure 9–5 illustrates these ideal portfolios which

---

[9] C. W. Hofer, "Conceptual Constructs for Formulating Corporate and Business Strategies" (Boston: Intercollegiate Case Clearing House, 9–378–754, 1977), p. 3.

[10] Charles Hofer and Dan Schendel, *Strategy Formulation: Analytical Concepts* (St. Paul, Minn.: West Publishing, 1978).

Figure 9–4

Product/market–evolution matrix

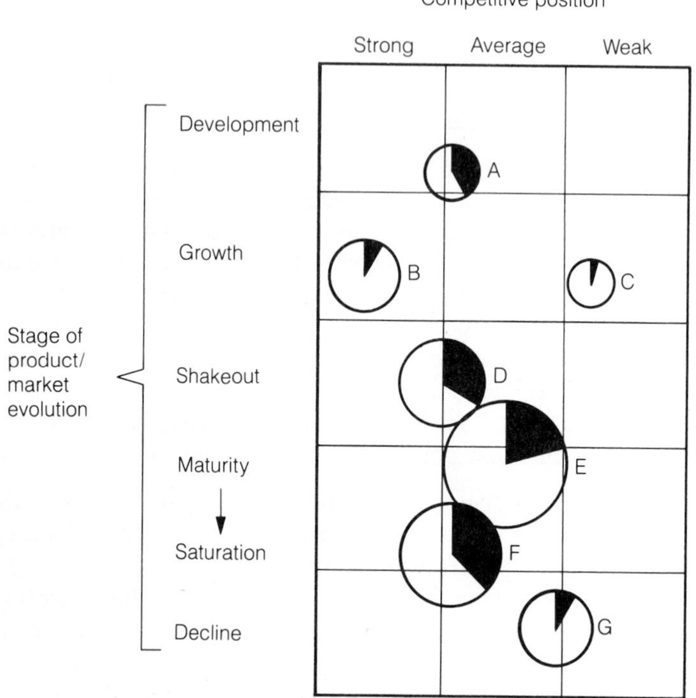

Source: Adapted from C. W. Hofer, "Conceptual Constructs for Formulating Corporate and Business Strategies" (Boston: Intercollegiate Case Clearing House, 9–378–754, 1977), p. 3.

represent different goals a company might pursue through strategic allocation of corporate resources. In the last two decades, for example, large cigarette companies (like R. J. Reynolds or Phillip Morris) sought profit portfolios to maximize generation of excess corporate resources; these resources would eventually be used to acquire (and sustain) new businesses in early product/market evolution or turnaround candidates in existing products/markets. Phillip Morris' acquisition and successful development of Miller beer is an example. With oil revenues generating substantial corporate resources, large oil companies (such as Exxon and Gulf) have become "energy" companies seeking growth portfolios of businesses in alternative, emerging energy technologies. Most multi-industry firms want corporate-level portfolio strategies that are close to the balanced model. They seek a balance of sufficient resource generators and short-term cash-flow maximizers with a small number of stars

Figure 9–5

Three types of ideal corporate portfolios

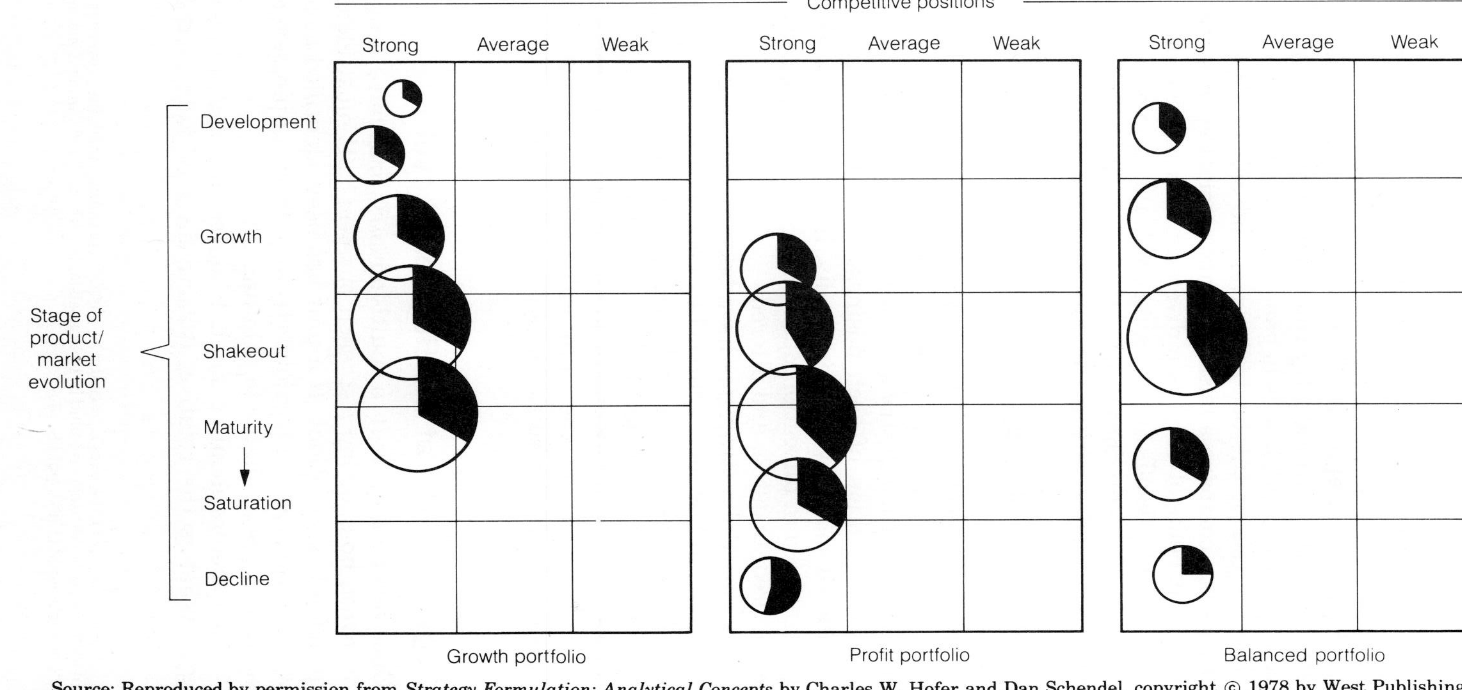

Source: Reproduced by permission from *Strategy Formulation: Analytical Concepts* by Charles W. Hofer and Dan Schendel, copyright © 1978 by West Publishing Company.

and developing winners to maximize internal control of resource needs. GE is a good example of a balanced-portfolio pursuer.

The portfolio approach is useful for examining alternative corporate-level strategies in multi-industry companies. Portfolio planning offers three potential benefits. First, it aids in generating good strategies by promoting competitive analysis at the business level and substantive, comparative discussion across the company's business units, resulting in a strategy that capitalizes on the benefits of corporate diversity. Second, it promotes selective resource allocation trade-offs by providing a visualization of the corporatewide strategic issues and a standardized, "neutral" basis for resource negotiation. Thus, power struggles within the company can be more objectively focused and channeled. Third, some users feel portfolio approaches help in implementation of corporate strategy because increased focus and objectivity enhance commitment.[11]

Its visual appeal notwithstanding, the portfolio approach is useful in evaluation because it allows a thorough and comparative analysis of market share, market growth, industry attractiveness, competitive position, and/or product/market evolution of each business unit. This portfolio evaluation must be conducted routinely and repeatedly. In this way, the effectiveness of resource generation and allocation decisions in achieving corporate objectives can be monitored, updated, and altered.

Once portfolio strategies have been identified, business strategies must be determined. Portfolio approaches help clarify and determine broad strategic intent. But this is not enough. Basic decisions involving allocation of corporate resources and the general manner in which a business unit will be managed (invest to grow, for example) do not complete the process of strategic analysis and choice. Each business unit must examine and select a specific grand strategy to guide its pursuit of long-term objectives.

Grand Strategy Selection at the Business Level

Once business units in a multi-industry firm have been identified in terms of invest, hold, or harvest, each business unit must identify and evaluate its grand strategy options. If a unit has been identified as a resource generator within the corporate portfolio strategy, for example, several alternative grand strategies are available in fulfilling this role.

What factors should a single business consider in selecting its grand strategy? What is the relative attractiveness of each of the 12 grand strategy

[11] A discussion of the uses and limits of portfolio planning, including coverage of companies and industries in terms of portfolio usage, is found in P. Haspelslagh's "Portfolio Planning: Uses and Limits," *Harvard Business Review* 60, no. 2 (1982), pp. 58–73.

options discussed in Chapter 8 for a single business? Three approaches to answering these questions are the focus of this section.

SWOT Analysis

SWOT is an acronym for the internal *S*trengths and *W*eaknesses of a business and environmental *O*pportunities and *T*hreats facing that business. SWOT analysis is a systematic identification of these factors and the strategy that reflects the best match between them. It is based on the logic that an effective strategy maximizes a business's strengths and opportunities while at the same time minimizing its weaknesses and threats. This simple assumption, if accurately applied, has powerful implications for successfully choosing and designing an effective strategy.

Environmental/industry analysis (Chapters 4, 5, and 6) provides the information with which key opportunities and threats in the firm's environment can be identified. These can be defined as follows.

Opportunities. An *opportunity* is *a major favorable situation in the firm's environment.* Key trends represent one source of opportunity. Identification of a previously overlooked market segment, changes in competitive or regulatory circumstances, technological changes, and improved buyer or supplier relationships could represent opportunities for the firm.

Threats. A *threat* is *a major unfavorable situation in the firm's environment.* It is a key impediment to the firm's current and/or desired future position. The entrance of a new competitor, slow market growth, increased bargaining power of key buyers or suppliers, major technological change, and changing regulations could represent major threats to a firm's future success.

Consumer acceptance of home computers was a major opportunity for IBM. Deregulation of the airline industry was a major opportunity for regional carriers such as USAir to serve routes that were previously closed to additional service. Some traditional carriers, such as Eastern, saw deregulation as a major threat and credit deregulation with a rapid decline in profitability in high-traffic routes. So opportunity for one firm can be a strategic threat to another. And the same factor can be seen as both a potential opportunity and a potential threat. For example, as the baby boom generation moves into the prime earning years, there is a major opportunity for financial service firms such as Merrill Lynch.[12] However, this group wants convenient financial services, which is a major threat to Merrill Lynch's established broker network.

Understanding the key opportunities and threats facing a firm helps manag-

[12] "Merrill Lynch's Dilemma," *Business Week,* January 6, 1984, p. 60.

ers identify realistic options from which to choose an appropriate strategy. Such understanding clarifies the most effective niche for the firm.

The second fundamental focus in SWOT analysis is identifying key *strengths* and *weaknesses* based on examination of the company profile (Chapter 7). Strengths and weaknesses can be defined as follows:

Strengths. A *strength* is *a resource, skill, or other advantage* relative to competitors and the needs of markets a firm serves or anticipates serving. A strength is *a distinctive competence* that gives the firm a comparative advantage in the marketplace. Financial resources, image, market leadership, and buyer/supplier relations, are examples.

Weaknesses. A *weakness* is *a limitation or deficiency in resources, skills, and capabilities* that seriously impedes effective performance. Facilities, financial resources, management capabilities, marketing skills, and brand image could be sources of weaknesses.

Sheer size and level of customer acceptance proved to be key strengths around which IBM built its successful strategy in the personal computer market. Braniff's limited financial capacity was a weakness that management did not sufficiently acknowledge, leading to an unsuccessful route-expansion strategy and eventual bankruptcy after deregulation. Relative financial capacity was a weakness recognized by Piedmont Airlines which charted a selective route-expansion strategy that has been quite successful in a deregulated airline industry.

Understanding the key strengths and weaknesses of the firm further aids in narrowing the choice of alternatives and selecting a strategy. Distinct competence and critical weakness are identified in relation to key determinants of success for different market segments; this provides a useful framework for making the best strategic choice.

SWOT analysis can be used in at least three ways in strategic choice decisions. The most common application provides a logical framework guiding systematic discussions of the business's situation, alternative strategies, and ultimately, the choice of strategy. What one manager sees as an opportunity, another may see a potential threat. Likewise, a strength to one manager may be a weakness from another perspective. Different assessments may reflect underlying power considerations within the organization, as well as differing factual perspectives. The key point is that systematic SWOT analysis ranges across all aspects of a firm's situation. As a result, it provides a dynamic and useful framework for choosing a strategy.

A second application of SWOT analysis is illustrated in Figure 9–6. Key external opportunities and threats are systematically compared to internal strengths and weaknesses in a structured approach. The objective is identification of one of four distinct patterns in the match between the firm's internal and external situation. These patterns are represented by the four cells in Figure 9–6. *Cell 1* is the most favorable situation; the firm faces several envi-

Figure 9–6

SWOT analysis diagram

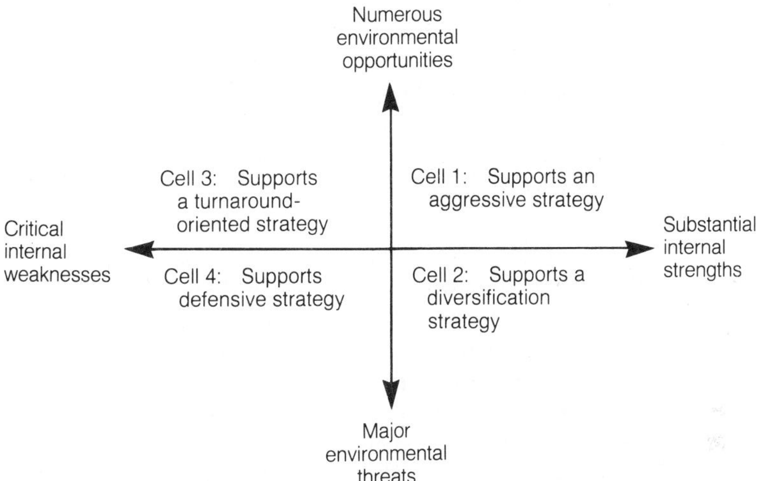

ronmental opportunities and has numerous strengths that encourage pursuit of such opportunities. This condition suggests growth-oriented strategies to exploit the favorable match. IBM's intensive market development strategy in the personal computer market was the result of a favorable match between strengths in reputation and resources and the opportunity for impressive market growth. *Cell 4* is the least favorable situation, with the firm facing major environmental threats from a position of relative weakness. This condition clearly calls for strategies that reduce or redirect involvement in the products/markets examined using SWOT analysis. Chrysler Corporation's successful turnaround from the verge of bankruptcy in the early 1980s is an example of such a successful strategy developed from a SWOT analysis that revealed mainly environmental threats and internal weaknesses.

In *Cell 2* a firm with key strengths faces an unfavorable environment. In this situation, strategies would use current strengths to build long-term opportunities in other products/markets. Greyhound, possessing many strengths in intercity bus transportation, still faces an environment predominated by fundamental, long-term threats such as airline competition and labor costs. The result was product development into nonpassenger (freight) services followed by diversification into other businesses (e.g., financial services). A business in *Cell 3* faces impressive market opportunity but is constrained by several internal weaknesses. Businesses in this predicament are like the question marks in the BCG matrix. The focus of strategy for such firms is eliminating internal weaknesses to more effectively pursue market opportunity. Apple's redirection of its "Lisa" technology to multiple products was an attempt to reformulate the company's technology-based strategy across several new product offerings in the microcomputer industry.

A major challenge in using SWOT analysis lies in identifying the position the business is actually in. A business that faces major opportunities may likewise face some key threats in its environment. It may have numerous internal weaknesses but also have one or two major strengths relative to key competitors. Fortunately, the value of SWOT analysis does not rest solely on careful placement of a firm in one particular cell. Rather, it lets the strategist visualize the overall position of the firm in terms of the product/market conditions for which a strategy is being considered. Does the SWOT analysis suggest that the firm is dealing from a position of major strength? Or must the firm overcome numerous weaknesses in the match of external and internal conditions? In answering these questions, SWOT analysis helps resolve one fundamental concern in selecting a strategy: *What will be the principal purpose of the grand strategy?* Is it to take advantage of a strong position or to overcome a weak one?[13] SWOT analysis provides a means of answering this fundamental question. And this answer is input to one dimension in a second, more specific tool for selecting grand strategies: the *grand strategy selection matrix.*

Grand Strategy Selection Matrix

A second valuable guide to the selection of a promising grand strategy is the matrix shown in Figure 9–7. The basic idea underlying the matrix is that two variables are of central concern in the selection process: (1) the principal purpose of the grand strategy and (2) the choice of an internal or external emphasis for growth and/or profitability.

In the 1950s and 1960s planners were advised to follow certain rules or prescriptions in their choice of strategies. Most experts now agree that strategy selection is better guided by the unique set of conditions that exist for the planning period and by company strengths and weaknesses. It is valuable to note, however, that even early approaches to strategy selection were based on matching a concern for internal versus external growth with a principal desire to either overcome weakness or maximize strength.

The same concerns led to the development of the grand strategy selection matrix. A firm in *Quadrant I* often views itself as overly committed to a particular business with limited growth opportunities or involving high risks because the company has "all its eggs in one basket." One reasonable solution

[13] A recent broad-based empirical study (L. G. Hrebiniak and C. Snow, "Top-Management Agreement and Organizational Performance," *Human Relations* 35, no. 12 (1982), pp. 1139–58) offers strong support that using SWOT analysis in this manner contributes to effective strategic choice. Examining 247 top-level managers in 88 organizations *and* eliminating the effects of other variables (types of planning, prior performance, industry), this study found strong, positive relationships between top management's agreement on the firm's strengths and weaknesses in relation to its environmental context, and the measure of organizational performance—return on assets—used in the study. In other words, a comprehensive SWOT analysis, agreed upon by top management, provided one key input in the selection of an appropriate, effective strategy for the firm.

Figure 9–7

Grand strategy selection matrix

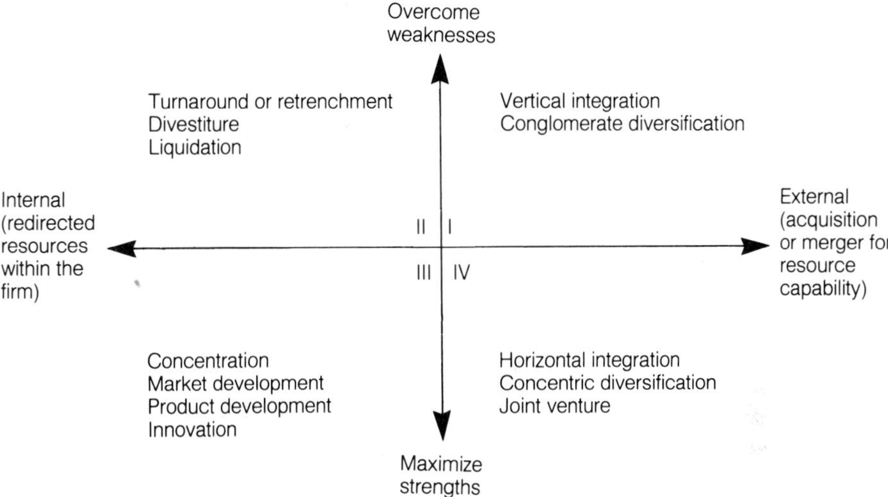

is *vertical integration,* which enables the firm to reduce risk by reducing uncertainty either about inputs or about access to customers. Alternatively, a firm may choose *conglomerate diversification,* which provides a profitable alternative for investment without diverting management attention from the original business. However, the external orientation to overcoming weaknesses usually results in the most costly grand strategies. The decision to acquire a second business demands both large initial time investments and sizable financial resources. Thus, strategic managers considering these approaches must guard against exchanging one set of weaknesses for another.

A more conservative approach to overcoming weakness is found in *Quadrant II.* Firms often choose to redirect resources from one business activity to another within the company. While this approach does not reduce the company's commitment to its basic mission, it does reward success and enables further development of proven competitive advantages. The least disruptive of the quadrant II strategies is *retrenchment,* the pruning of a current business's activities. If weaknesses arose from inefficiencies, retrenchment can actually serve as a *turnaround* strategy, meaning that the business gains new strength by streamlining its operations and eliminating waste. However, when the weaknesses are a major obstruction to success in the industry, and when the costs of overcoming the weaknesses are unaffordable or are not justified by a cost-benefit analysis, then eliminating the business must be considered. *Divestiture* offers the best possibility for recouping the company's investment, but even *liquidation* can be an attractive option when the alternatives are an unwarranted drain on organizational resources or bankruptcy.

A common business adage states that a company should build from strength. The premise is that growth and survival depend on an ability to capture a market share that is large enough for essential economies of scale. If a firm believes that profitability will derive from this approach and prefers an internal emphasis for maximizing strengths, four alternative grand strategies hold considerable promise. As shown in *Quadrant III,* the most common approach is *concentration* on the business, i.e., market penetration. The business that selects this strategy is strongly committed to its current products and markets. It will strive to solidify its position by reinvesting resources to fortify its strength.

Two alternative approaches are *market* and *product development.* With either of these strategies the business attempts to broaden its operations. Market development is chosen if strategic managers feel that existing products would be well received by new customer groups. Product development is preferred when existing customers are believed to have an interest in products related to the firm's current lines. This approach may also be based on special technological or other competitive advantages. A final alternative for quadrant III firms is *innovation.* When the business's strengths are in creative product design or unique production technologies, sales can be stimulated by accelerating perceived obsolescence. This is the principle underlying an innovative grand strategy.

Maximizing a business's strength by aggressively expanding its basis of operations usually requires an external emphasis in selecting a grand strategy. Preferred options here are shown in *Quadrant IV. Horizontal integration* is attractive because it enables a firm to quickly increase output capability. The skills of the original business's managers are often critical in converting new facilities into profitable contributors to the parent company; this expands a fundamental competitive advantage of the firm, management.

Concentric diversification is a good second choice for similar reasons. Because the original and newly acquired businesses are related, the distinctive competencies of the diversifying firm are likely to facilitate a smooth, synergistic, and profitable expansion.

The final option for increasing resource capability through external emphasis is a *joint venture.* This alternative allows a business to extend its strengths into competitive arenas that it would be hesitant to enter alone. A partner's production, technological, financial, or marketing capabilities can significantly reduce financial investment and increase the probability of success to the point that formidable ventures become attractive growth alternatives.

Model of Grand Strategy Clusters

A third guide to selecting a promising grand strategy involves Thompson and Strickland's modifications of the BCG growth share portfolio matrix.[14]

As shown in Figure 9–8, a business's situation is defined in terms of the growth rate of the general market and the company's competitive position in that market. When these factors are considered simultaneously, a business can be broadly categorized in one of four quadrants: (I) strong competitive position in a rapidly growing market, (II) weak position in a rapidly growing market, (III) weak position in a slow-growth market, or (IV) strong position in a slow-growth market. Each of these quadrants suggests a set of promising possibilities for selection of a grand strategy.

Firms in quadrant I are in an excellent strategic position. One obvious grand strategy for such firms is continued concentration on their current business as it is presently defined. Because consumers seem satisfied with the firm's current strategy, it would be dangerous to shift notably from the established competitive advantages. However, if the business has resources that exceed the demands of a concentration strategy, it should consider vertical integration. Either forward or backward integration helps a business protect its profit margins and market share by ensuring either better access to consumers or to material inputs. Finally, a quadrant I firm might be wise to consider concentric diversification to diminish the risks associated with a narrow product or service line; with this strategy, heavy investment in the company's basic area of proven ability continues.

Firms in quadrant II must seriously evaluate maintaining their present approach to the marketplace. If a firm has competed long enough to accurately assess the merits of its current grand strategy, it must determine (1) the reasons its approach is ineffectual, and (2) whether the company has the capability to compete effectively. Depending on the answers to these questions, the firm should choose one of four grand strategy options: formulation or reformulation of a concentration strategy, horizontal integration, divestiture, or liquidation.

In a rapidly growing market, even a small or relatively weak business is often able to find a profitable niche. Thus, formulation or reformulation of a concentration strategy is usually the first option to consider. However, if the firm lacks either a critical competitive element or sufficient economies of scale to achieve competitive cost efficiencies, then a grand strategy that directs company efforts toward horizontal integration is often a desirable alternative. A final pair of options involve deciding to stop competing in the market or product area. A multiproduct firm may conclude that the goals of its mission are most likely to be achieved if this one business is dropped through divestiture. Not only does this grand strategy eliminate a drain on resources, it may also provide additional funds to promote other business activities. As an option of last resort, a firm may decide to liquidate the business. In practical terms this means that the business cannot be sold as a going concern and

---

[14] Arthur A. Thompson, Jr., and A. J. Strickland, III, *Strategic Management: Concepts and Cases* (Plano, Tex.: Business Publications, 1984), p. 99. The BCG matrix was discussed earlier in this chapter.

Figure 9–8

Model of grand strategy clusters

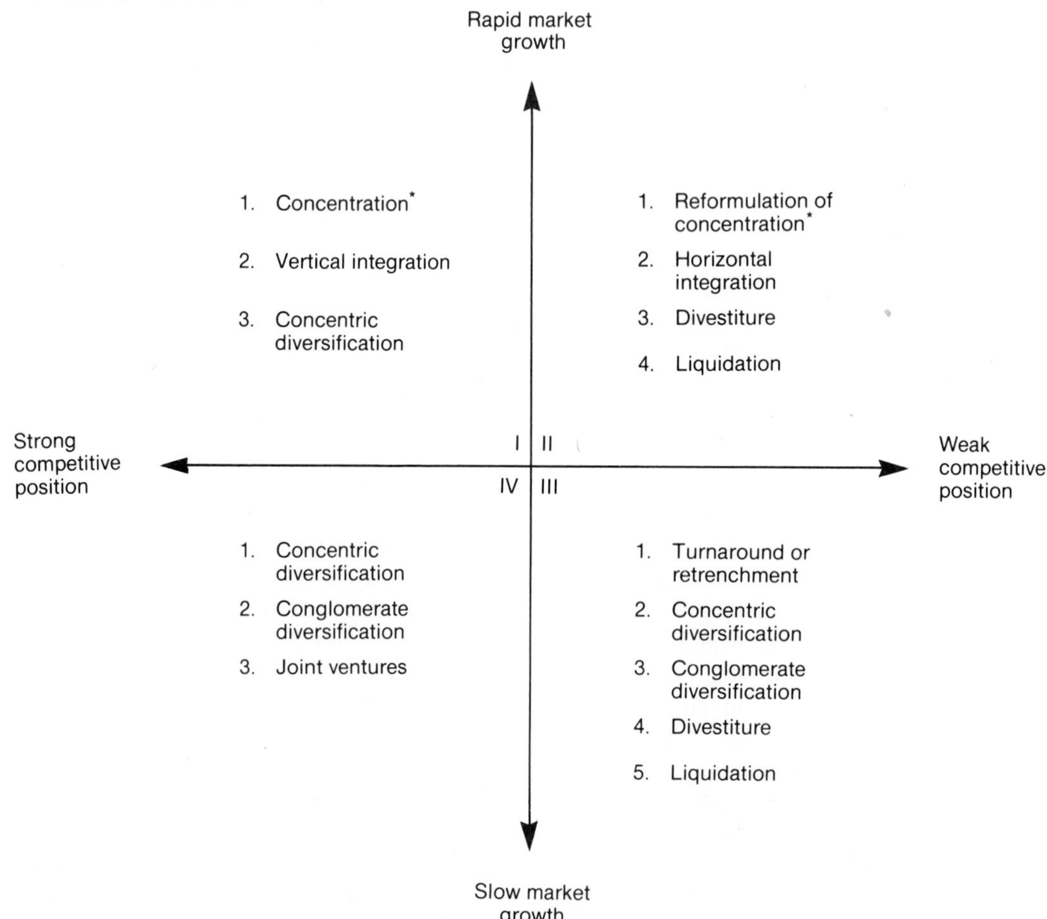

The grand strategy of innovation was omitted from this model. Apparently the authors felt that the notion of market growth was incompatible with the assumptions underlying the innovation approach.

Grand strategies are listed in probable order of attractiveness.

* In this model the grand strategy of concentration was meant to encompass market development and product development.

Source: Adapted from Arthur A. Thompson, Jr., and A. J. Strickland, III, *Strategic Management: Concepts and Cases* (Plano, Tex.: Business Publications, 1984), p. 210.

is at best worth only the value of its tangible assets. The decision to liquidate is an undeniable admission of failure by a firm's strategic management and is thus often delayed—to the further detriment of the company.

Strategic managers tend to resist divestiture because it is likely to jeopardize their control of the firm and perhaps even their jobs. By the time that the desirability of divestiture is acknowledged, the business has often deteriorated to the point of failing to attract potential buyers as a business. The consequences of such delays are financially disastrous for the owners of the firm, because the value of a going concern is many times greater than simple asset value.

Strategic managers who have a business in the position of quadrant III and feel that continued slow market growth and a relatively weak competitive position will usually attempt to decrease their resource commitment to that business. Minimal withdrawal is accomplished through retrenchment; this strategy has the side benefits of making resources available for other investments and of motivating employees to increase their operating efficiency. An alternative strategy is to divert resources for expansion through investment in other businesses. This approach typically involves either concentric or conglomerate diversification, because the firm usually wants to enter more promising arenas of competition than forms of integration or development would allow. The final options for quadrant III businesses are divestiture, if an optimistic buyer can be found, and liquidation.

Quadrant IV businesses (strong competitive position in a slow-growth market) have a basis of strength from which to diversify into more promising growth areas. These businesses have characteristically high cash-flow levels and limited internal growth needs. Thus, they are in an excellent position for concentric diversification into ventures that utilize their proven business acumen. A second choice is conglomerate diversification, which spreads investment risk and does not divert managerial attention from the present business. The final option is joint ventures which are especially attractive to multinational firms. Through joint ventures a domestic business can gain competitive advantages in promising new fields while exposing itself to limited risks. Strategy in Action 9–2 describes Anheuser-Busch's approach to strategy analysis and choice under quadrant IV circumstances.

Behavioral Considerations Affecting Strategic Choice

Strategic choice is a decision. At both the corporate and the business level, this decision determines the future strategy of the firm.

After alternative strategies are examined, strategic choice is made. This is a decision to adopt one of the alternatives scruntinized. If the examination identified a clearly superior strategy, or if the current strategy will clearly

Strategy in Action 9–2

Anheuser-Busch's Choice of Strategy for the 1980s

In 1985 Anheuser-Busch will have completed a $2 billion, five-year expansion program that will increase its capacity 40 percent and add significantly to its 29 percent share of the beer market.

The St. Louis brewer is evaluating three options for post-1985 growth:

1. Diversification.
2. Overseas expansion.
3. A combination of both.

To evaluate and ultimately choose its strategy, Anheuser-Busch is using what its managers call learning probes—miniventures or experiments relative to each alternative strategy.

Anheuser-Busch's first learning probe was into the soft-drink business. From the start, the test was the subject of considerable second-guessing. "Would Coke and Pepsi enter the beer industry from scratch and go up against Anheuser-Busch and Miller?" asks a skeptical rival brewer. "I think the answer would be no."

Anheuser-Busch's answer, after two years of testing, also may be no. "We've learned it's a competitive jungle out there," says August Busch III, chairman, "just like us and Miller in the brewing industry."

Root 66 beer and its sugar-free version—sold in five cities since 1980—have a respectable market share, but competitors contend it was achieved mostly through cents-off discounts offered to consumers. Chelsea, a citrus beverage that could have had the snob appeal and profit margin of Perrier, was hooted off the market by nurses and others who objected to the alcoholic content (0.4 percent) and beer-like appearance of the "not-so-soft drink."

Beer distributors were used for the soft-drink test and also for a look at the snack business, where Anheuser-Busch is selling its new Eagle line in bars. One sign of success: distribution is being widened to 24 cities from a handful.

The third learning probe, less prominent than snacks or soda but more encouraging to several followers of Anheuser-Busch, is the company's development of Sesame Place educational parks in conjunction with Children's Television Workshop, producers of "Sesame Street."

The other alternative strategy, which requires even less capital and could pay off sooner than the others, is overseas expansion of the brewing business. International sales account for less than 1 percent of Anheuser-Busch's beer volume.

Company officials, reluctant to disclose much about the prospects for their learning probes, acknowledged that "beer earnings and share growth may slow as we approach our long-term 40 percent market share goal." The brewer is planning for that day by "getting our feet wet in new business areas, not massive diversification efforts."

Source: "If Anheuser-Busch Gets Its Way, Saying 'Bud' Won't Say It All." Reprinted by permission of *The Wall Street Journal,*

meet future company objectives, then the decision is relatively simple. Such clarity is the exception however, making the decision judgmental and difficult. Strategic decision makers, after comprehensive strategy examination, are often confronted with several viable alternatives rather than the luxury of a clear-cut, obvious choice. Under these circumstances, several factors influence the strategic choice decision. Some of the more important are:

1. Role of past strategy.
2. Degree of the firm's external dependence.
3. Attitudes toward risk.
4. Internal political considerations and the CEO.
5. Timing.
6. Competitive reaction.

Role of Past Strategy

A review of past strategy is the point at which the process of strategic choice begins. As such, past strategy exerts considerable influence upon the final strategic choice.

Current strategists are often the architects of past strategies. Because they have invested substantial time, resources, and interest in these strategies, the strategists would logically be more comfortable with a choice that closely parallels past strategy or represents only incremental alterations.

This familiarity and commitment to past strategy permeate the organization. Thus, lower-level management reinforces the top manager's inclination toward continuity with past strategy during the choice process. In one study, during the planning process, lower-level managers suggested strategic choices that were consistent with current strategy and likely to be accepted while withholding suggestions with less probability of approval.[15]

Research by Henry Mintzberg suggests that the past strategy strongly influ-

[15] Eugene Carter, "The Behavioral Theory of the Firm and Top Level Corporate Decisions," *Administrative Science Quarterly* 16, no. 4 (1971), pp. 413–28.

ences current strategic choice.[16] The older and more successful a strategy has been, the harder it is to replace. Similarly, a strategy, once initiated, is very difficult to change because organizational momentum keeps it going.

Mintzberg's work and research by Barry Staw found that even as the strategy begins to fail due to changing conditions, strategists often increase their commitment to the past strategy.[17] Firms may thus replace key executives when performance has been inadequate for an extended period because replacing top executives lessens the influence of unsuccessful past strategy on future strategic choice.

Degree of the Firm's External Dependence

A comprehensive strategy is meant to effectively guide a firm's performance in the larger external environment. Owners, suppliers, customers, government, competitors, and unions are a few of the elements in a firm's external environment, as elaborated on in Chapter 4. A major constraint on strategic choice is the power of environmental elements in supporting this decision. If a firm is highly dependent on one or more environmental factors, its strategic alternatives and ultimate choice must accommodate this dependence. The greater a firm's external dependence, the lower its range and flexibility in strategic choice.

Two examples highlight the influence of external dependence on strategic choice. For many years Whirlpool sold most of its major appliance output to one customer, Sears. With its massive retail coverage and access to alternate suppliers, Sears was a major external dependence for Whirlpool. Whirlpool's strategic alternatives and ultimate choice of strategy were limited and strongly influenced by Sears' demands. Whirlpool's grand strategy and important related decisions in areas such as research and development, pricing, distribution, and product design were carefully narrowed and chosen with the firm's critical dependence on Sears in mind. Chrysler Corporation's dependence on federal loan guarantees and financial concessions by labor considerably limited the strategic choices available in the early 1980s. The decision of Chrysler's Lee Iaccoca to pay off several federal obligations before they were due was partially meant to increase Chrysler's flexibility by reducing one restrictive external dependence.

These examples show that a firm's flexibility in strategic choice is lessened when environmental dependence increases. If external dependence is critical, firms may include representatives of the external factor (government, union, supplier, bank) in the strategic choice process. In 1979, Chrysler, for example,

---

[16] Henry Mintzberg, "Research on Strategy Making," *Proceedings of the Academy of Management,* Minneapolis, 1972.

[17] Barry Staw, "Knee-Deep in the Big Muddy: A Study of Escalating Commitment to a Chosen Course of Action," *Organizational Behavior and Human Performance,* June 1976, pp. 27–44; Mintzberg, "Research on Strategy."

took the unprecedented action of including Leonard Woodcock, president of the United Auto Workers, on its board of directors.

Attitudes toward Risk

Attitudes toward risk exert considerable influence on strategic choice. This may vary from eager risk taking to strong aversion to risk, and influences the range of available strategic choices. Where attitudes favor risk, the range and diversity of strategic choices expand. High-risk strategies are acceptable and desirable. Where management is risk-averse, the diversity of choices is limited and risky alternatives are eliminated before strategic choices are made. Risk-oriented managers prefer offensive, opportunistic strategies. Risk-averse managers prefer defensive, safe strategies. Past strategy is quite influential in the strategic choices made by risk-averse managers, but is less of a factor for risk-oriented managers. Figure 9–9 illustrates the relationship between attitudes toward risk and strategic choice.

Industry volatility influences managerial propensity toward risk. In highly volatile industries, top managers must absorb and operate with greater amounts of risk than their counterparts in stable industries. Therefore, managers in volatile industries consider a broader, more diverse range of strategies in the strategic choice process.

Product/market evolution is another determinant of managerial risk propensity. If a firm is in the early stages of product/market evolution, it must

Figure 9–9
Managerial risk propensity and strategic choices

Risk averse		*Risk prone*
Decrease choices	←→	Expand choices
Defensive strategies	←→	Offensive strategies
Stability	←→	Growth
Incremental	←→	Innovation
Minimize company weaknesses	←→	Maximize company strengths
Strong ties to past strategy	←→	Fewer ties to past strategy
Stable industry	←→	Volatile industry
Maturing product/market evolution	←→	Early product/market evolution

operate with considerably greater risk than a firm later in the product/market evolution cycle.

In making a strategic choice, risk-oriented managers lean toward opportunistic strategies with higher payoffs. They are drawn to offensive strategies based on innovation, company strengths, and operating potential. Risk-averse managers lean toward safe, conservative strategies with reasonable, highly probable returns. The latter are drawn to defensive strategies to minimize a firm's weaknesses and external threats, as well as the uncertainty associated with innovation-based strategies.

A recent study examined the relationship between the willingness of strategic business unit (SBU) managers to take risks and SBU performance. The study found a link between risk taking and strategic choice. Looking first at SBUs assigned build or star strategic missions within a corporate portfolio, researchers found that the general managers of higher performing SBUs had *greater willingness to take risks* than did their counterparts in lower performing build or star SBUs. Looking next at SBUs assigned harvest strategies, successful units had general managers *less willing to take risks* than general managers in lower performing harvest SBUs.[18]

This study supports the idea that managers make different decisions depending on their willingness to take risks. Perhaps most important, the study suggests that being either risk-prone or risk-averse is not inherently good or bad. Rather, SBU performance is more effective when the risk orientation of the general manager is consistent with the SBU's strategic mission (build or harvest). While this is only one study and not a final determination of the influence of risk orientation on strategic choice, it helps illustrate the importance of risk orientation on the process of making and implementing strategic decisions.

Internal Political Considerations

Power/political factors influence strategic choice. The existence and use of power to further individual or group interests is common in organizational life. An early study by Ross Stagner found that strategic decisions in business organizations were frequently settled by power rather than by analytical maximization procedures.[19]

A major source of power in most organizations is the chief executive officer (CEO). In smaller enterprises, the CEO is consistently the dominant force in strategic choice and this is also often true in large firms, particularly those with a strong or dominant CEO. When the CEO begins to favor a particular choice, it is often unanimously selected.

Cyert and March identified another power source that influences strategic

---

[18] Gupta and Govindarajan, "Build, Hold, Harvest."

[19] Ross Stagner, "Corporate Decision Making," *Journal of Applied Psychology* 53, no. 1 (1969), pp. 1–13.

Figure 9–10

Political activities in phases of strategic decision making

Phases of strategic decision making	*Focus of political action*	*Examples of political activity*
Identification and diagnosis of strategic issues	Control of: Issues to be discussed Cause-and-effect relationships to be examined	Control of agenda Interpretation of past events and future trends
Narrowing the alternative strategies for serious consideration	Control of alternatives	Mobilization Coalition formation Resource commitment for information search
Examining and choosing the strategy	Control of choice	Selective advocacy of criteria Search and representation of information to justify choice
Initiating implementation of the strategy	Interaction between winners and losers	Winners attempt to "sell" or co-opt losers Losers attempt to thwart decisions and trigger fresh strategic issues
Designing procedures for evaluation of results	Representing oneself as successful	Selective advocacy of criteria

Source: Adapted from Liam Fahey and V. K. Naroyanan, "The Politics of Strategic Decision Making," in *The Strategic Management Handbook,* ed. Kenneth J. Albert (New York: McGraw-Hill, 1983), p. 21–20.

choice, particularly in larger firms.[20] They called this the *coalition* phenomenon. In large organizations, subunits and individuals (particularly key managers) have reason to support some alternatives and oppose others. Mutual interest often draws certain groups together in coalitions to enhance their position on major strategic issues. These coalitions, particularly the more powerful ones (often called *dominant coalitions*), exert considerable influence in the strategic choice process. Numerous studies confirm the use of power and coalitions on a frequent basis in strategic decision making. Interestingly, one study found that managers occasionally try to hide the fact that they prefer judgmental/political bargaining over systematic analysis and that when politics was a factor, it slowed decision-making.[21]

Figure 9–10 illustrates the focus of political activity across phases of strategic decision making. It illustrates how the *content* of strategic decisions and

[20] Richard M. Cyert and James G. March, *A Behavorial Theory of the Firm* (Englewood Cliffs, N.J.: Prentice-Hall, 1963).

[21] See for example: H. Mintzberg; D. Raisinghani; and Andre Theoret, "The Structure of Unstructured Decision Process," *Administrative Science Quarterly,* June 1976, pp. 246–75; and William Guth, "Toward a Social System Theory of Corporate Strategy," *Journal of Business,* July 1976, pp. 374–88.

the *processes* of arriving at such decisions are politically intertwined. Each phase in the process of strategic choice presents a real opportunity for political action intended to influence the outcome. The challenge to strategists is in recognizing and managing this political influence. If such processes are not carefully overseen various managers can bias the content of strategic decisions in the direction of their own interests.[22] For example, selecting the criteria used to compare alternative strategies or collecting and appraising information regarding these criteria may be particularly susceptible to political influence. This must be recognized and, where critical, "managed" to avoid dysfunctional political bias. Reliance on different sources for obtaining *and* appraising information might be effective in this context.

Rather than simply being denoted as "bad" or inefficient, organizational politics must be viewed as an inevitable dimension of organizational decision making that must be accommodated in strategic management. Some authors argue that politics are a key ingredient in the "glue" that holds an organization together. Formal and informal negotiating and bargaining between individuals, subunits, and coalitions are indispensable mechanisms for organizational coordination.[23] Recognizing and accommodating this in choosing future strategy will result in greater commitment and more realistic strategy. The costs are likely to be increased time spent on decision making and incremental as opposed to drastic change.

Timing Considerations

The time element can have considerable influence on strategic choice. Consider the case of Mech-Tran, a small manufacturer of fiberglass piping that found itself in financial difficulty in early 1980. At the same time it was seeking a loan guarantee through the Small Business Administration (SBA), it was approached by KOCH Industries (a Kansas City–based supplier of oil field supplies) with a merger offer. The offer involved 100 percent sale of Mech-Tran stock and a two-week response deadline, while the SBA loan procedure could take three months. Obviously, management's strategic decision was heavily influenced by external time constraints, which limited analysis and evaluation. Research by Peter Wright indicates that under such a time constraint, managers put greater weight on negative than on positive information and prefer defensive strategies.[24] The Mech-Tran owners decided to accept the KOCH offer rather than risk losing the opportunity and subsequently being turned down by the SBA. Thus, faced with time constraints, management opted for a defensive strategy consistent with Wright's findings.

---

[22] Liam Fahey and V. K. Naroyanan, "The Politics of Strategic Decision Making," in *The Strategic Management Handbook*, ed. Kenneth J. Albert (New York: McGraw-Hill, 1983), p. 21–18.

[23] Ibid.

[24] Peter Wright, "The Harrassed Decision Maker," *Journal of Applied Psychology* 59, no. 5 (1974), pp. 555–61.

There is another side to the time issue—the timing of a strategic decision. A good strategy may be disastrous if it is undertaken at the wrong time. Winnebago was the darling of Wall Street in 1970, with its stock rising from $3 to $44 per share in one year. Winnebago's 1972 strategic choice, focusing on increasing its large, centralized production facility, was a continuation of the strategy that had successfully differentiated Winnebago in the recreational vehicle industry. The 1973 Arab oil embargo with subsequent rises in gasoline prices and overall transportation costs had dismal effects on Winnebago. The strategy was good, but the timing proved disastrous. On the other hand, IBM's decision to hold off entering the rapidly growing personal computer market until 1982 appeared to be perfectly timed. Welcomed by Apple with a full-page advertisement in *The Wall Street Journal,* IBM assumed the market share lead by early 1983.

A final aspect of the time dimension involves the lead time required for alternative choices and the time horizon management is contemplating. Management's primary attention may be on the short or long run depending upon current circumstances. Logically, strategic choice will be strongly influenced by the match between management's current time horizon and the lead time (or payoff time) associated with different choices. As a move toward vertical integration, Du Pont went heavily into debt to acquire Conoco in a 1982 bidding war. By 1983, the worldwide oil glut meant that Du Pont could have bought raw materials on more favorable terms in the open market. This short-term perspective was not of great concern to Du Pont management, however, because the acquisition was part of a strategy to stabilize Du Pont's long-term position as a producer of numerous petroleum-based products.

Competitive Reaction

In weighing strategic choices, top management frequently incorporates perceptions of likely competitor reactions to different options. For example, if management chooses an aggressive strategy that directly challenges a key competitor, that competitor can be expected to mount an aggressive counterstrategy. Management of the initiating firm must consider such reactions, the capacity of the competitor to react, and the probable impact on the chosen strategy's success.

The beer industry provides a good illustration. In the early 1970s, Anheuser-Busch dominated the industry. Miller Brewing Company, recently acquired by Phillip Morris, was a weak and declining competitor. Miller's management, contemplating alternative strategies, made the decision to adopt an expensive, advertising-oriented strategy. While this strategy challenged the big three (Anheuser-Busch, Pabst, and Schlitz) head-on, Miller anticipated that the reaction of the other brewers would be delayed due to Miller's current declining status in the industry. Miller proved correct, and was able to reverse its trend in market share before Anheuser-Busch countered with an equally intense advertising strategy.

Miller's management took another approach in their next major strategic decision. In the mid-1970s they introduced (and heavily advertised) a low-calorie beer—Miller Lite. Other industry members had introduced such products without much success. Miller chose a strategy that did not directly challenge key competitors and, Miller anticipated, would not elicit immediate and strong counterattacks. This choice proved highly successful, because Miller was able to establish a dominant share of the low-calorie market before major competitors decided to react. In both cases, Miller's expectation of competitor reaction was a key determinant of strategic choice.

Contingency Approach to Strategic Choice

Ultimate strategic choices often depend upon various assumptions about future conditions. The success of the strategy chosen is contingent, to varying degrees, upon future conditions. And changes in the industry and environment may differ from forecasts and assumptions.

For example, Winnebago's 1972 strategy of centralized, economy-of-scale production and extensive inventories of large recreational vehicles (RVs) was contingent upon a continued supply of plentiful, inexpensive gasoline for future customer use. With the 1973 Arab oil embargo, this contingency changed dramatically. Winnebago was left with extensive inventories of large RVs and high break-even–oriented production facilities for large RVs. As a result, Winnebago is still trying to recover in the mid-1980s.

To improve their ability to cope in similar circumstances, an increasing number of firms has adopted a contingency approach to strategic choice. The critical assumptions on which success of the chosen strategy depends are identified. Conditions that may turn out to be different from the basic forecast or assumptions for these critical contingencies are identified, particularly negative ones.[25] A downturn in the economy, a labor strike, an increase in the prime rate, a technological breakthrough, or a shortage of critical material are examples of such contingencies. Once these scenarios are identified, managers develop alternative, contingency strategies for the firm. Such contingency strategies can be short and/or long term and are appropriate at the corporate-, business- and/or functional-levels. Firms which use this contingency approach often identify trigger points to alert management that a contingency strategy should be considered. The trigger points are specific deviations in key forecasts of industry or environmental conditions (like the supply and price of gasoline) and are set to alert management to the need to consider the alternative strategy and allow sufficient lead time for implementation of the contingency response.

[25] Positive as well as negative alternatives should be considered. If circumstances are unusually positive, the firm may not be in a position to exploit the favorable circumstances. However, most firms are primarily concerned with negative deviation in key contingencies.

Summary

This chapter has presented and examined several considerations in strategic analysis and choice. The form of strategic analysis and choice varies considerably according to the stage of development of the firm, and the focus differs at the corporate and business levels.

For multi-industry and multiproduct-market firms, strategic analysis begins at the corporate level. Different strategies are examined in terms of generating and allocating corporate resources. The portfolio approach is one method of strategy examination at the corporate level. Portfolio matrixes and stage of product/market evolution are conceptual tools guiding the portfolio approach.

Strategic analysis and choice do not end with corporate-level strategy. Alternative business-level strategies must be examined within the context of each business unit in multi-industry firms, much as strategy is evaluated in single–product/service firms. Three approaches that facilitate grand strategy selection at the business level were discussed.

Strategic analysis often limits alternatives to several viable choices. Strategic choice seldom involves the luxury of making an obvious choice. Nonetheless, a choice must be made. Several factors influence strategic choice, such as propensity for risk, past strategy, and coalitions, which are outside the realm of purely analytical consideration. Some firms attempt a contingency approach to strategic choice by incorporating the flexibility to alter a chosen strategy if underlying assumptions change.

Choosing corporate-and business-level strategies is not the end of the strategic management process. Functional strategies must be identified and implemented to initiate and control daily business activities in a manner consistent with business strategy, as must organizational systems and processes to implement and control the strategy. The next section of this book examines the implementation phase of the strategic management process.

Questions for Discussion

1. How is strategic analysis at the corporate level different from strategic analysis at the business level? How are they related?
2. Why would multi-industry companies find the portfolio approach to strategy evaluation useful?
3. Explain the role of SWOT analysis as a tool facilitating strategic choice at the business level. How is it similar/dissimilar to the grand strategy selection matrix and the model of grand strategy clusters?
4. What role does politics play in the development and evaluation of alternative strategies? Please explain.
5. Explain and illustrate the role of three behavioral considerations in strategy examination and choice.

Bibliography

Abell, Derik F. "Strategic Windows." *Journal of Marketing,* July 1978, pp. 21–26.

Buzzell, Robert D.; T. G. Bradley; and Ralph Sultan. "Market Share: A Key to Profitability." *Harvard Business Review,* January–February 1975, pp. 97–106.

Christensen, H. K.; A. C. Cooper; and C. A. DeKluyver. "The 'Dog' Business: A Reexamination." *Proceedings of the Academy of Management* (1981), pp. 26–30.

Cyert, Richard M., and James G. March. *A Behavioral Theory of the Firm.* Englewood Cliffs, N.J.: Prentice-Hall, 1963.

Gupta, Anil K., and V. Govindarajan. "Build, Hold, and Harvest: Converting Strategic Intentions into Reality." *Journal of Business Strategy,* no. 4, March 1984, pp. 34–47.

————. "Business Unit Strategy, Managerial Characteristics, and Business Unit Effectiveness at Strategy Implementation." *Academy of Management Journal* 27, no. 1 (1984).

Guth, William. "Toward a Social System Theory of Corporate Strategy." *Journal of Business,* July 1976, pp. 374–88.

Hall, William K. "SBUs: Hot, New Topic in the Management of Diversification." *Business Horizons,* February 1978, pp. 17–25.

Hambrick, D. C.; I. C. MacMillan; and D. L. Day. "Strategic Attributes and Performance in the MCG Matrix—A PIMS Based Analysis of Industrial-Product Businesses." *Academy of Management Journal* 25, no. 3 (1982), pp. 510–31.

Haspeslagh, P. "Portfolio Planning: Uses and Limits." *Harvard Business Review,* January–February 1982, p. 58.

Hax, Arnoldo C.; and Nicolas S. Majluf. "The Use of the Growth-Share Matrix in Strategic Planning." *Interfaces* 13, no. 1 (1983), pp. 8–21.

————. "The Use of the Industry Attractiveness-Business Strength Matrix in Strategic Planning." *Interfaces* 13, no. 2 (1983), pp. 54–71.

Hedley, Barry. "Strategy and the Business Portfolio." *Long-Range Planning,* February 1977, pp. 8–15.

Hofer, Charles W. "Toward a Contingency Theory of Business Strategy." *Academy of Management Journal,* December 1975, pp. 784–810.

Hofer, Charles, and Dan Schendel. *Strategy Formulation: Analytical Concepts.* St. Paul, Minn.: West Publishing, 1978.

Macmillan, I. *Strategy Formulation: Political Concepts.* St. Paul, Minn.: West Publishing, 1978.

Mintzberg, Henry. "Research on Strategy Making." *Proceedings of the Academy of Management,* 1972, pp. 218–22.

————. "Strategy Making in Three Modes." *California Management Review,* Winter 1973, pp. 44–53.

Mintzberg, Henry; D. Raisinghani; and Andre Theoret. "The Structure of Unstructured Decision Process." *Administrative Science Quarterly,* June 1976, pp. 246–75.

Murray, E., Jr. "Strategic Choice as a Negotiated Outcome." *Management Science,* 24, no. 9 (1978), pp. 960–72.

Schoeffler, Sidney; Robert Buzzell; and Donald Heany. "Impact of Strategic Planning on Profit Performance." *Harvard Business Review,* March–April 1974, pp. 137–45.

Stagner, Ross. "Corporate Decision Making." *Journal of Applied Psychology,* February 1969, pp. 1–13.

Staw, Barry M. "Knee-Deep in the Big Muddy: A Study of Escalating Commitment to a Chosen Course of Action." *Organizational Behavior and Human Performance,* June 1976, pp. 27–44.

"Wanted: A Manager to Fit Each Strategy," *Business Week,* February 25, 1980, p. 166.

Chapter 9 Cohesion Case Illustration

Strategic Analysis and Choice at Holiday Inns, Inc.

Before evaluating alternatives and choosing a strategy for the 1980s at Holiday Inns Inc., take a few minutes to review what has been done in the cohesion case sections up to this point. First, the company mission was examined. An essential issue that surfaced was whether Holiday Inns is in the travel business, hospitality business, or some broader combination of the two. Holiday Inns' executives have traditionally used the travel definition, although the mission must be readdressed as you evaluate and choose a strategy. Second, consecutive sections have examined the present and projected environment of Holiday Inns, as well as analyzing the internal strengths and weaknesses of Holiday Inns at the corporate and business-group levels. Comparing these external and internal analyses is a key basis for generating, evaluating, and choosing corporate- and business-level strategies. Finally, different possible grand strategies for each business group were examined. Now, realistic alternative strategies for Holiday Inns must be identified, evaluated, and the strategies chosen that will guide Holiday Inns through the 1980s.

How is strategy analyzed and chosen at Holiday Inns? To begin, the distinction between corporate- and business-level strategy must be recognized. With both levels applicable at Holiday Inns, this illustration will concentrate initial identification at the business level. In other words, alternative grand strategies for each of Holiday Inns' business units will be identified. Subsequent evaluation and choice of business-level strategies will follow evaluation and choice of corporate-level strategy.

For each business group at Holiday Inns, what are the most appropriate grand strategy options? Exhibit 1 provides an answer. It places each business in its appropriate cell on the grand strategy selection matrix, which was discussed in this chapter (Figure 9–7). This helps identify the more appropriate grand strategies for each Holiday Inns business. At Trailways, for example, the key grand strategies to be evaluated are turnaround/retrenchment or divestiture (quadrant II). In the restaurant group, quadrants III and IV must be evaluated because there are attractive possibilities in both areas. Thus, it is important to look at market development or joint venture and concentration or horizontal integration.

How is the business placed in an appropriate quadrant? This cohesion case section will illustrate the placement of two of Holiday Inns' businesses and leave to you the assignment of fitting the other businesses in the two matrix dimensions.

Exhibit 1

Grand strategy selection matrix for Holiday Inns, Inc.

Purpose of the grand strategy	Areas of emphasis — Internal: Redirect resources within the firm	Areas of emphasis — External: Acquisition of the resource capacity
Overcome weakness and threats	Quadrant II • Turnaround or retrenchment • Divestiture • Liquidation Trailways	Quadrant I • Vertical integration • Conglomerate diversification
Maximize strengths and opportunities	Quadrant III • Concentation • Market development • Product development • Innovation Products Hotels Delta Restaurants	Quadrant IV • Horizontal integration • Concentric diversification • Joint venture Casinos

Trailways. Trailways faced numerous environmental threats (heavy competition, rising energy costs, lack of subsidies for terminals and significant internal weaknesses (price/cost squeeze, aging terminals, inferior image). The primary focus of its ultimate strategy will necessarily have to overcome these weaknesses and threats. To pursue its ultimate strategy, Trailways will depend on and emphasize internal operating capabilities—it already has buses, terminals, and so on—rather than develop operating capacity through external acquisitions. Combining these two assessments, Trailways logically fits in quadrant II of the grand strategy selection matrix.

Restaurant Group. The restaurant group faces key enviromental opportunities (eating-out, age, and single-household trends) and significant internal strengths (franchising expertise, synergy with the core hotel business, Perkins' northern U.S. position). Logically, the purpose of its grand strategy is to maximize strengths and opportunities. The area of emphasis for anticipated growth is both internal and external. The company is positioned to carry out company-owned growth (internal emphasis). But the underlying rationales of the restaurant group are seeking external operating capacity through franchising and possible acquisition of additional chains. Thus, the restaurant group logically fits within quadrants III and IV.

Other Groups. It should now be possible to surmise why the other Holiday Inns businesses were placed as shown in Exhibit 1. These decisions can be briefly summarized. The hotel group has attractive strengths and environmental opportunities while it (like restaurants) must emphasize both company-owned (internal) and franchise (external) growth. Delta Steamship has limited but important opportunities (growing Third World markets) and strengths (major U.S.–flag carrier), while depending primarily on internal resource capability. The products group has limited but key strengths/opportunities (captive hotel group) and must emphasize its internal capabilities in pursuit of the chosen strategy. The casinos group, while facing impressive opportunities, must look outside for operational capabilities in the near future, thus, its placement in quadrant IV.

This analysis suggests that the key grand strategy options for each of Holiday Inns' businesses are as shown in Exhibit 2.

Several specific grand strategy alternatives could be generated for subsequent analysis. To illustrate, the discussion in Chapter 9, a limited range of strategy alternatives for subsequent analysis and choice will be presented.

Exhibits 3 through 6 show a limited range of alternative strategies within

Exhibit 2

Grand Strategy Options at Each of Holiday Inns' Businesses

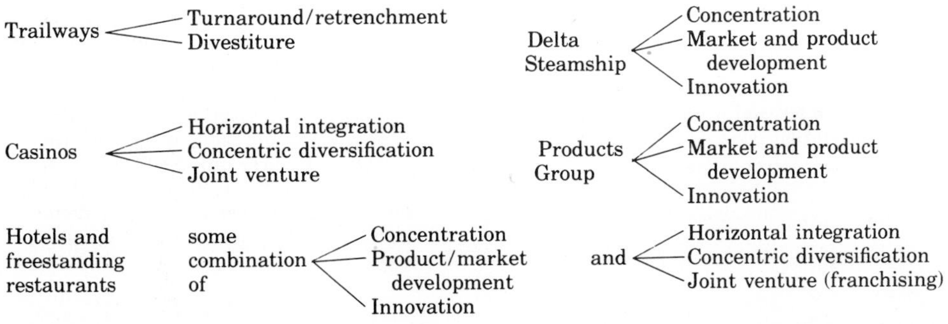

Exhibit 3

Hotel group

Strategy alternatives	*Strategy analysis*
Pursue rapid growth through domestic and international expansion while seeking to become increasingly price competitive with quality budget chains. (Market development and joint-venture franchising)	Hotels are HI's core business, the major profit contributor, and its greatest distinctive competencies. Rapid growth can only be achieved by taking on the lower-priced competitors because available locations are limited. But with markets maturing, and either increased financing or dependence on franchisees required, this alternative is risky.
Selective growth with company-owned movement into multi-user properties (resorts, airports, downtown) and gradual franchise expansion while maintaining the traditional upper-medium focus in price with high-quality service. (Concentration and joint-venture franchising)	Consistent with changing travel patterns and shorter vacations for business and family travelers. Allows company-owned positioning in the more lucrative markets. Maintains favorable profit margins and positive cash generator role for corporate activity. Risks continual threat from quality budget chains, especially for the broad franchise base.

Exhibit 4

Products group

Strategy alternatives	*Strategy analysis*
Aggressive expansion into new markets for institutional furnishings and equipment to lessen dependence of HI network and gain pricing autonomy. (Market development)	Not clear that the products group has the experience and competitive edge to compete in an open market. Would necessitate greater autonomy in pricing, product designs, and so on from the hotel group.
Stable growth continuing with the current operational makeup. (Concentration)	The products group has evolved into a large operation, primarily as an ancillary to the hotel. Its organization, mission, and strategy are not competitively derived. May have gotten too big to continue as an afterthought, given its low contribution to corporate earnings.
Retrench to streamline operations as strictly an institution service to the hotel group. (Concentration/retrenchment)	There is a large institutional market the products group would be ignoring with this strategy. However, this could clarify the exact role of the products group as strictly an ancillary service and provide better structure for future operating decisions.

Exhibit 5

Transportation group

Strategy alternatives	*Strategy analysis*
Trailways: Stabilize market share and profitability through a combination of price competition, improved image, elimination of inefficient routes and equipment, more efficient terminals, and linking with motel network. (Retrenchment/turnaround)	Transportation market is quite competitive, with Greyhound as well as the deregulated airline industry. Could increase ridership, but lowering prices in face of rising energy costs would threaten profit margins. Questionable whether Trailways' ridership is compatible with HI guest profile.
Divestiture of the Trailways bus operation. (Divestiture)	Possibly extreme and even detrimental because the bus operation has contributed at a steadily growing rate of approximately 23 percent of corporate revenue since 1974. However, profitability has steadily declined and the bus operation is not compatible with all other groups in terms of customer profile. Managerial and financial resources might be better used elsewhere.
Delta Steamship: Steady growth in new LASH cargo services seeking to exploit and expand market share in South American routes. (Concentration/market development)	Delta has competitive start with LASH technology and a strong South American/West African route structure. Ships provide useful tax shelter and government subsidies against foreign competition. Cargo emphasis, however, is getting way outside.
Divestiture of Delta Steamship (Typical strategy consideration that would be introduced at the corporate level)	Drastic improvement in sales and profits in 1978 makes Delta quite marketable. Steamship cargo and passenger services are increasingly removed from HI's core competencies, suggesting divestiture. But, as of now, an increasingly profitable unit to harvest until the right buyer appears.

each of Holiday Inns' business groups. This set of alternative business strategies will then be used to generate a limited range of alternative corporate-level strategies. Each alternative will provide a brief analysis, which both illustrates the analysis of strategy and gives a basis for strategic choice.

When the analysis of each business group's alternative strategies is complete, a choice must be made. To ensure that the business-level choices are consistent, this choice must be made at the corporate level and finalized at each business level.

The critical issue at the corporate level for Holiday Inns Inc., returns to its overall mission. Which of the following does it see as its mission?

1. Diversified firm in travel- and transportation-related industries.
2. Diversified firm in the travel-related industry.
3. Diversified firm in the hospitality industry.

Exhibit 6

Other groups: Restaurants and casinos

Strategy alternatives	*Strategy analysis*
Restaurants: Rapid expansion into freestanding restaurant business through additional acquisition as well as geographic expansion with Perkins franchises. (Market development, joint-venture franchising, and horizontal intergration)	A growing primary market, but strong competition nationwide. Organizational capacity of HI to absorb and manage rapid acquisition of additional regional chains is doubtful. Risk of a market shakeout with heavy level of competition is a real possibility.
Concentration and steady growth via the Perkins chain above. (Concentration and joint-venture franchising)	Perkins provides an established, competitive base and competent management to guide its stable growth, backed as necessary by corporate resources. Allows HI to evaluate this new operating area before making additional acquisition or resource commitments.
Casinos: Rapid expansion into the four major U.S. areas for legalized gambling via direct investment and particularly joint ventures or acquisition. (Horizontal integration, joint ventures)	A rapidly expanding market that offers exceptional profit potential. A logical extension of HI's lodging and restaurant expertise, particularly when matched with another firm's gaming expertise. Limited U.S. areas having legalized gambling, so should move rapidly to secure a foothold in each area. Offers a natural international spin-off and ultimate lessening of corporate dependence on roadside travel accommodations and franchisees.
Stabilize with current endeavors into gaming and only gradually commit further resources. (Joint-venture holding pattern)	Lets HI make sure gaming is an area it should be in before committing sizable resources. However, with limited areas available, could fall behind competition or newcomers (like Ramada Inns) in establishing a foothold.

Clearly, Holiday Inns' current business portfolio would align itself with the first mission statement. However, Holiday Inns has traditionally perceived itself within mission statement 2. Its corporatewide expertise and distinctive competence are strongest relative to statement 3. So to choose a strategy, Holiday Inns, Inc., must also clarify its overall mission.

To illustrate corporate-level strategic choice, we have placed HI businesses in a business portfolio matrix in Exhibit 7. This matrix gives several insights into corporate-level strategy evaluation and choice.

HI's strongest position is in the hospitality-related area, with hotels providing stable growth and strong cash flow, while casinos and, to a lesser extent, Perkins restaurants represent key areas for corporate growth.

Exhibit 7

Business portfolio matrix for Holiday Inns

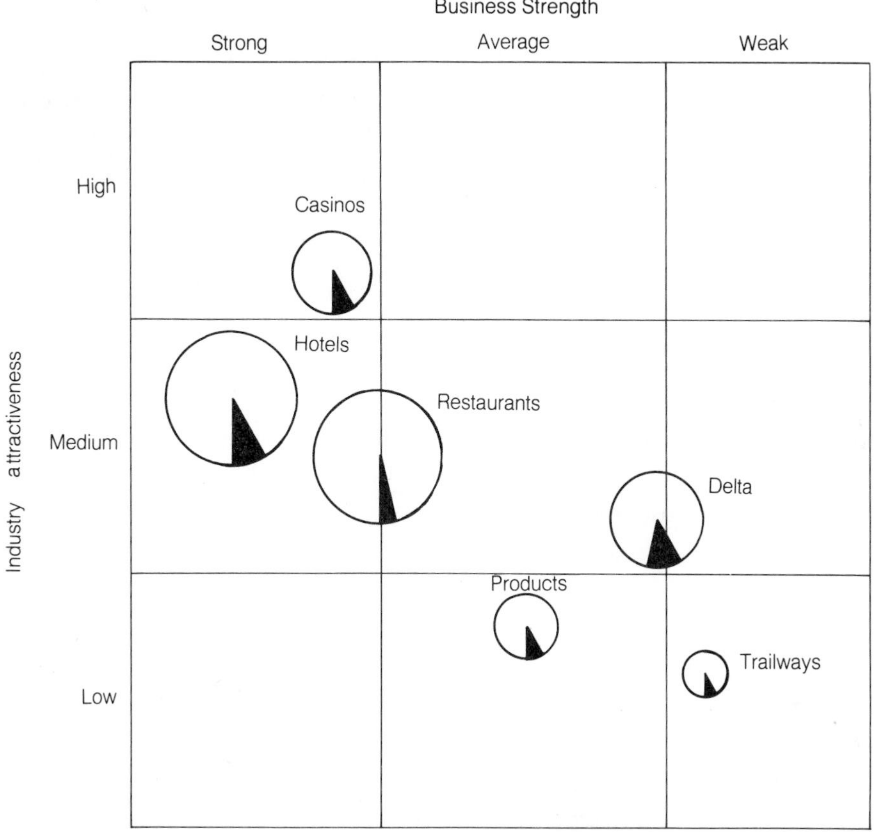

Institutional products and bus operations are the weakest portfolio members, with Trailways of questionable long-term value to the firm. The products group is of questionable value in other than a captive service role to the hotel (and other food and lodging) groups.

Delta provides a steadily profitable business, though without the potential of the hospitality group and clearly unrelated to that group.

The portfolio matrix suggests two basic corporate strategy choices for Holiday Inns, Inc.

1. Stabilize and improve the current business portfolio.
2. Concentrate on the hospitality part of the portfolio with major growth emphasis (particularly) in casinos.

The choice is related to the need for clarification of the company mission mentioned earlier, so that two points must be dealt with: the mission must be clarified and the corporate strategy chosen. This will set the parameters for business-level strategic choices. The choice actually made is described in an appendix at the end of the Chapter 12 Cohesion Case Illustration. Holiday Inns' decision for the 1980s can be summarized as follows:

Company mission and corporate strategy: "Our strategy for the coming decade will be to grow consistently from our leadership base in *the hospitality industry* seeking major positions in the closely related fields of hotels, casino gaming, and restaurants."

Business group strategies (refer to the earlier discussion):

Hotel group—option 2, concentration with selective company-owned growth.

Products group—option 3, retrenchment and pruning.

Trailways—option 2, divestiture with a $15 million loss.

Delta—combination of options 1 and 2, continued cargo service expansion until profitable divestiture can be made.

Restaurants—option 2, concentrated, steady growth at Perkins.

Casinos—option 1, rapid growth into four major regions.

And the long-term objectives associated with the corporate strategy are as follows:

"The primary goal of HI management is to maximize the value of HI stock to its shareholders."

Dividend payout of 25 to 30 percent of normalized earnings.

Maintain a debt/capital ratio under 40 percent.

Return on equity to exceed 17 percent annually.

Develop a favorable climate for the company in the communities in which it conducts its business through corporate philanthrophy with an annual goal of $1.5 million in 1981.

STRATEGIC MANAGEMENT MODEL

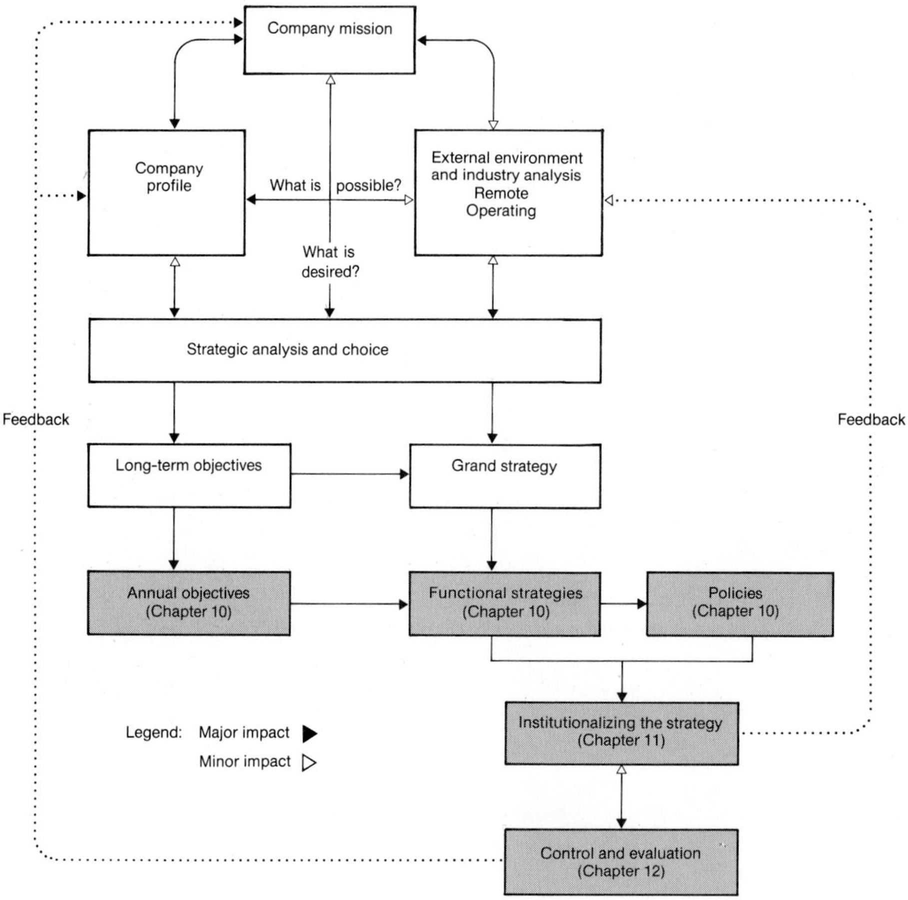

PART THREE

Strategy implementation

The last part of this book examines what is often called the action phase of the strategic management process: implementation of the chosen strategy. Up to this point, three major phases have been covered: strategy formulation, analysis of alternative strategies, and strategic choice. While these phases are important, they alone cannot ensure success. The strategy must be translated into concrete action, and that action must be carefully implemented. Otherwise, accomplishment is left to chance. The three chapters in this section discuss key aspects of the implementation phase of strategic management.

Implementation is successfully initiated in three interrelated stages:

1. Identification of measurable, mutually determined *annual objectives.*
2. Development of specific *functional strategies.*
3. Development and communication of concise *policies* to guide decisions.

Annual objectives guide implementation by converting long-term objectives into specific, short-term ends. Functional strategies translate grand strategy at the business level into current action plans for subunits of the company. Policies provide specific guidelines for operating managers and their subordinates in executing strategies. Chapter 10 examines how to maximize the use of annual objectives, operating strategies, and policies to operationalize a strategy.

A new strategy must be institutionalized—permeate the very day-to-day life of the company—to be effectively implemented. In Chapter 11, three organizational elements providing fundamental, long-term means of institutionalizing the company's strategy are discussed:

1. *Structure* of the organization.
2. *Leadership* of the CEO and key managers.
3. The fit between the strategy and the company's *culture.*

Strategy is implemented in a changing environment. Thus, execution must be controlled and evaluated if the strategy is to be successfully implemented and adjusted to changing conditions. The control and evaluation process must include at least three fundamental dimensions:

1. *Establishing control systems* based on performance standards that are linked to annual objectives.
2. *Monitoring* performance and evaluating deviations.
3. *Motivating* control and evaluation.

In addition to a focus on internal operations, this control and evaluation process must monitor the key external factors on which the success of the strategy depends. Likewise, a reward system that provides both the motivation for evaluation and the feedback to encourage effective control is an integral aspect of strategic control. Chapter 12 examines each dimension of the control and evaluation process.

CHAPTER

10

Operationalizing the Strategy: Annual Objectives, Functional Strategies, and Business Policies

Even after the grand strategies are determined and long-term objectives tentatively set, the strategic management process is far from complete. The tasks of operationalizing, institutionalizing, and controlling the strategy still remain. These tasks signal a critical new phase in the strategic management process: translating strategic thought into strategic action. There are three interrelated concerns in shifting from formulation to implementation:

1. Identification of measurable, mutually determined annual objectives.
2. Development of specific functional strategies.
3. Communication of concise policies to guide decisions.

Annual objectives translate long-range aspirations into this year's budget. If annual objectives are well developed, they provide clarity that is a powerful, motivating facilitator of effective strategy implementation. This chapter looks at how to develop annual objectives that maximize implementation-related payoffs.

Functional strategies translate grand strategy at the business level into action plans for subunits of the company. Operating managers assist in developing these strategies which, in turn, helps clarify what the managers' units are expected to do in implementing the grand strategy. This chapter examines the value and characteristics of functional strategies and the key areas in an organization for which operating strategies enhance implementation of the grand strategy.

Policies are specific guides for operating managers and their subordinates. Policies, often misunderstood and misused, can provide a powerful tool for strategy implementation if they are clearly linked to operating strategies and long-term objectives. This chapter explains how to use policies in the implementation and control of a company's strategies.

Annual Objectives

Chapter 8 dealt with the importance of long-term objectives as benchmarks for corporate and business strategies. Measures like market share, ROI, return on equity (ROE), stock price, and new-market penetration provide guidance in assessing the ultimate effectiveness of a chosen strategy. While such objectives clarify the long-range purpose of a grand strategy and the basis for judging its success, they are less useful in guiding the operating strategies and immediate actions necessary to implement a grand strategy.

A critical step in successful implementation of grand strategy is the identification and communication of annual operating objectives that relate logically to the strategy's long-term objectives.[1] Accomplishment of these annual objectives adds up to successful execution of the business's overall long-term plan. A comprehensive set of annual objectives also provides a specific basis for monitoring and controlling organizational performance. Such objectives can aid in the development of "trigger points" that alert top management to variations in key performance areas that might have serious ramifications for the ultimate success of a strategy.

Qualities of Effective Annual Objectives

Annual objectives are specific, measurable statements of what an organization subunit is expected to achieve in contributing to the accomplishment of the business's grand strategy. Although this seems rather obvious, problems in strategy implementation often stem from poorly conceived or stated annual objectives. To maximize their contribution, certain basic qualities must be incorporated in developing and communicating these objectives.

Linkage to Long-Term Objectives. An annual objective must be clearly linked to one or more long-term objectives of the business's grand strategy. However, to accomplish this, it is essential to understand how the two types of objectives differ. Four basic dimensions distinguish annual and long-term objectives:

1. *Time frame.* Long-term objectives are focused usually five years or more in the future. Annual objectives are more immediate, usually involving one year.

[1] An *annual* time frame is the most popular short-term planning horizon in most firms. Short-term objectives, particularly for a key project, program, or activity, may involve a shorter time horizon, e.g. a three- or six-month horizon. The discussion in this section accommodates such shorter horizons.

2. *Focus.* Long-term objectives focus on the future position of the firm in its competitive environment. Annual objectives identify specific accomplishments for the company, functional areas or other subunits over the next year.
3. *Specificity.* Long-term objectives are broadly stated. Annual objectives are very specific and directly linked to the company, a functional area, or other subunit.
4. *Measurement.* While both long-term and annual objectives are quantifiable, long-term objectives are measured in broad, relative terms; for example, 20 percent market share. Annual objectives are stated in absolute terms, such as a 15 percent increase in sales in the next year.

Annual objectives add breadth and specificity in identifying *what* must be accomplished if the long-term objective is to be achieved. For example, the long-term objective "to obtain 20 percent market share in five years" clarifies where the business wants to be. But achieving that objective can be greatly enhanced if a series of specific annual objectives identify what must be accomplished each year to achieve that objective. If market share is now 10 percent, then one likely annual objective would be "to achieve a minimum 2 percent increase in relative market share in the next year."

Specific annual objectives should provide targets for performance of operating areas if the long-term objective is to be achieved. "Open two regional distribution centers in the southeast in 1987" might be one annual objective that marketing and production managers agree is essential in achieving a 20 percent market share in five years. "Conclude arrangements for a $10 million line of credit at 1 percent above prime in 1986" might be the annual objective of financial managers to support the operation of new distribution centers and the additional purchases necessary to increase output in reaching the long-term objective.

The link between short-term and long-term objectives should resemble cascades through the business from basic long-term objectives to numerous specific annual objectives in key operating areas. Thus, long-term objectives are segmented and reduced to short-term (annual) objectives. The cascading effect has the added advantage of providing a clear reference for vertical communication and negotiation that may be necessary to ensure integrated objectives and plans at the operating level.[2]

Integrated and Coordinated Objectives. Implementation of grand strategies requires objectives that are *integrated and coordinated.* However, subunit managers (e.g., vice president of finance, vice president of marketing, vice president of production) may not consider such a "superordinate" purpose in setting annual objectives. Consider the example in Figure 10–1. As can

[2] Lawrence G. Hrebiniak and William F. Joyce, *Implementing Strategy* (New York: Macmillan, 1984), p. 110.

Figure 10–1

Logistic priorities in a manufacturing firm

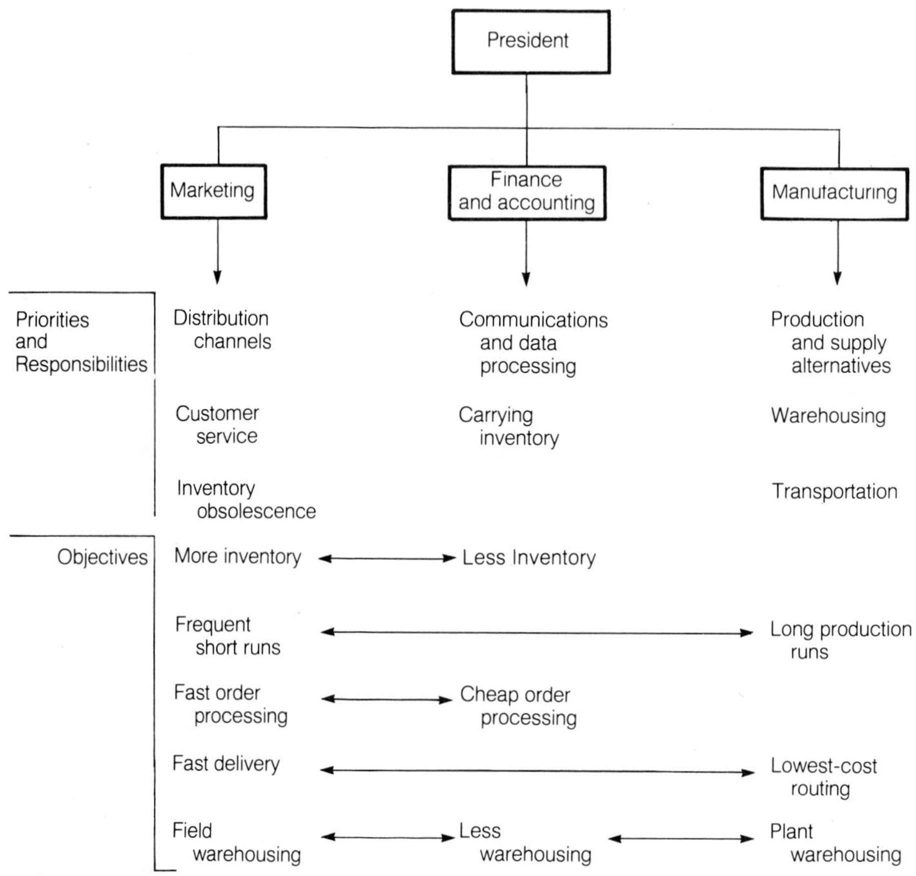

Source: Adapted from John F. Stolle, "How to Manage Physical Distribution," *Harvard Business Review*, July–August 1967, p. 95.

be seen, priorities of the marketing function can easily conflict with those of manufacturing or finance/accounting. For example, manufacturing might logically prefer long production runs and plant warehousing to maximize efficiency. On the other hand, marketing might be better served by frequent, short production runs and field warehousing to maximize customer convenience. Other functional conflicts are evident in Figure 10–1. Without concerted effort to integrate and coordinate annual objectives, these natural conflicts can contribute to the failure of long-term objectives (and the grand strategy), even though the separate annual objectives are well designed.

Successful implementation of strategy depends on coordination and integration of operating units. This is encouraged through the development of short-term (annual) objectives. Expressed another way, annual objectives provide a focal point for raising and resolving conflicts between organizational subunits that might otherwise impede strategic performance.

Managers should be involved at key points in the planning process so that annual objectives are integrated and coordinated. These managers are brought together to discuss important data, assumptions, and performance requirements. This promotes discussion of key interdependencies and a clearer, possibly negotiated determination of annual objectives in key performance areas. Particularly if major strategic change is involved, participation is essential both to establish the relationship of short-term operating activities and long-term strategy, *and* to integrate and coordinate operating plans and programs.

Consistency in Annual Objectives

Experience indicates that managers in the same organization will have different ways of developing objectives. For example, managers in different functions, departments, or other subunits will often emphasize different criteria. Due to this lack of consistency units may not be comparable, commitment to objectives may differ, and the interdependence of units may be dysfunctional. For example, if the marketing area of the firm in Figure 10–1 had very clear, specific objectives regarding delivery time to customers while the manufacturing area's objectives in this regard were ill defined, conflict might be frequent and counterproductive to the strategic success of the firm.

Annual objectives are more consistent when each objective clearly states *what* is to be accomplished, *when* it will be done, and *how* accomplishment will be *measured*. Objectives can then be used to monitor both the effectiveness of an operating unit and, collectively, progress toward the business's long-term objectives. Figure 10–2 illustrates several effective and ineffective annual objectives. If objectives are measurable and state what is to be done and when it will be achieved in a clear, understandable manner, there is less likelihood of misunderstanding between the interdependent operating managers who must implement the grand strategy.

Measurable. *Measurability* cannot be overemphasized as a key quality of annual objectives. Unfortunately, some key results are easier to measure than others. For example, *line* units (e.g. production) may easily be assessed by clear, quantifiable measures, while criteria for certain *staff* areas (e.g. personnel) are more difficult to measure. However, successful implementation requires setting measurable annual objectives in these difficult areas, as well. This is usually accomplished by initially focusing on *measurable activity* followed by the identification of acceptable, measurable *outcomes*.

Other qualities of good objectives discussed in Chapter 8—acceptable, flexi-

Figure 10–2

Operationalizing measurable annual objectives

Examples of deficient annual objectives	*Examples of annual objectives with measurable criteria for performance*
To improve morale in the divisions (plant, department, etc.).	To reduce turnover (absenteeism, number of rejects, etc.) among sales managers, by 10 percent by January 1, 1987. *Assumption:* Morale is related to measurable outcomes (i.e., high and low morale are associated with different results.)
To improve support of the sales effort.	To reduce the time lapse between order date and delivery by 8 percent (two days) by June 1, 1987. To reduce the cost of goods produced by 6 percent to support a product price decrease of 2 percent by December 1, 1987. To increase the rate of before- or on-schedule delivery by 5 percent by June 1, 1987.
To develop a terminal version of the SAP computer program.	To develop a terminal version of SAP capable of processing X bits of information in time Y at cost not to exceed Z per 1,000 bits by December 1, 1987. *Assumption:* There virtually is an infinite number of "terminal" or operational versions. Greater detail or specificity defines the objective more precisely.
To enhance or improve the training effort.	To increase the number of individuals capable of performing X operation in manufacturing by 20 percent by April 15, 1987. To increase the number of functional heads capable of assuming general management responsibility at the division level by 10 percent by July 15, 1987. To provide sales training to X number of individuals, resulting in an average increase in sales of 4 percent within six months after the training session.
To improve the business's image.	To conduct a public opinion poll using random samples in the five largest U.S. metropolitan markets and determine average scores on 10 dimensions of corporate responsibility by May 15, 1987. To increase our score on those 10 items by an average of 7.5 percent by May 1, 1988.

Source: Adapted from Laurence G. Hrebiniak and William F. Joyce, *Implementing Strategy* (New York: Macmillan, 1984), p. 116.

ble, suitable, motivating, understandable, and achievable—also apply to annual objectives. While these will not be discussed here, the reader should review the earlier discussion to appreciate the qualities common to all objectives.

Priorities. Another critical quality of annual objectives involves the need to prioritize short-term objectives. Due to timing considerations and relative impact on strategic success, annual objectives often have *relative* priorities.

Timing considerations often necessitate initiating or completing one activity before another is started. Figure 10–3 shows how this became a problem for Citibank in implementing a program designed to expand its credit card base as part of an ambitious market development strategy in the financial services industry. Citibank's objective for establishing the accounting procedures needed to support the marketing program was not given sufficient priority.

While all annual objectives are important, some deserve additional attention because of their particular impact on the success of a strategy. If such priorities are not discussed and indicated, conflicting assumptions about the relative importance of annual objectives might inhibit progress toward strategic effectiveness.[3] Facing the real possibility of bankruptcy in 1983, Eastern Air Lines formulated a retrenchment strategy with several important annual objectives in labor relations, routes, fleet, and financial condition. But its highest priority involved maintaining the integrity of selected debt-related measures which would satisfy key creditors who could otherwise move to force bankruptcy.

Priorities are usually established in one of several ways. A simple *ranking* may be based on discussion and negotiation during the planning process. However, this does not necessarily communicate the *real* difference in the importance of objectives, so terms such as "primary," "top," or "secondary" may be used to indicate priority. Some businesses assign weights (for example, 0–100 percent) to establish and communicate the relative priority of each objective. Whatever the method, recognizing the priorities of annual objectives is an important dimension in implementing the strategy.

Benefits of Annual Objectives

Systematic development of annual objectives provides a tangible, meaningful focus through which managers can translate long-term objectives and grand strategies into specific action. Annual objectives give operating managers and personnel a better understanding of their role in the business's mission.

[3] Ibid., p. 119.

Figure 10–3

A case of misplaced priorities

CITIBANK

Citibank (New York State), N.A.
P.O. Box 227
Cheektowaga, New York 14225

January 18, 1984

Dear Silver Card Customer:

Several months ago we at Citibank began issuing The Silver Card to Goodyear customers.

The Silver Card revolving loan plan was established and offered by Citibank to provide a more effective nationwide tire and auto service credit card for customers of Goodyear's retail outlets.

As a national credit card, The Silver Card will offer you far more convenience than previously available. Our objective is to make The Silver Card the best credit card available anywhere.

Providing The Silver Card to over a million customers was an ambitious and complex effort and it resulted in account processing problems for some account holders. We understand how frustrating these types of problems can be for you. We are working around the clock to assure that any problems will be corrected promptly.

In the meantime, we trust that you will continue to patronize your Goodyear retail outlet as they will render you the finest products and service available anywhere.

We apologize for any inconvenience we may have caused you and we thank you for your patience and understanding.

Sincerely,

CITIBANK

Source: Mailed to the author, a Goodyear credit customer.

This *clarity of purpose* can be a major force in effectively mobilizing the "people assets" of a business.[4]

A second benefit involves the process required to derive annual objectives. If these objectives have been developed through the participation of managers responsible for their accomplishment, they provide an "objective" basis for

[4] One recent book that supports this point is Thomas J. Peters and R. H. Waterman, Jr., *In Search of Excellence* (New York: Harper & Row, 1982). There is extensive literature on one of the best-known management techniques, management by objectives (MBO), that supports the value of objective setting in achieving desired performance. For a useful discussion of MBO, see Karl Albrecht, *Successful Management by Objectives* (Englewood Cliffs, N.J.: Prentice-Hall, 1978).

addressing and accommodating conflicting political concerns that might interfere with strategic effectiveness. Effective annual objectives become the essential link between strategic intentions and operating reality.

Well-developed annual objectives provide another major benefit: *a basis for strategic control.* The question of controlling strategy will be examined in greater detail in Chapter 12. But it is important to recognize here the simple yet powerful benefit of annual objectives in developing budgets, schedules, trigger points, and other mechanisms for controlling strategy implementation.

Annual objectives can provide motivational payoffs in strategy implementation. If objectives clarify personal and group roles in a business's strategies and are also measurable, realistic, and challenging, they can be powerful motivators of managerial performance—particularly when they are linked to the business's reward structure.

While annual objectives provide a powerful tool in operationalizing business strategy, they aren't sufficient in themselves. Functional strategies, the *means* to accomplished these objectives, must be clearly identified to encourage successful implementation.

Developing Functional Strategies

A *functional strategy* is the short-term game plan for a key functional area *within* a company. Such strategies clarify grand strategy by providing more specific details about how key functional areas are to be managed in the near future.

Functional strategies must be developed in the key areas of marketing, finance, production/operations, R&D, and personnel. They must be consistent with long-term objectives and grand strategy. Functional strategies help in implementation of grand strategy by organizing and activating specific subunits of the company (marketing, finance, production, and so forth) to pursue the business strategy in daily activities. In a sense, functional strategies translate thought (grand strategy) into action designed to accomplish specific annual objectives. For every major subunit of a company, functional strategies identify and coordinate actions that support the grand strategy and improve the likelihood of accomplishing annual objectives. Strategy in Action 10–1 illustrates key functional strategies used to implement Eastern Airlines' grand strategy (retrenchment/turnaround) in the early 1980s.

Figure 10–4 illustrates the important role of functional strategies in implementing corporate and business strategy. The corporate strategy defined General Cinema Corporation's general posture in the broad economy. The business strategy outlined the competitive posture of its operations within the domestic movie exhibition industry. But to increase the likelihood that these strategies will be successful, more specific guidelines are needed for the business's operating components. Thus, functional strategies are derived that clarify the business strategy, giving specific, short-term guidance to operating managers. The

Strategy in Action 10–1

1984 Annual Objectives and Functional Strategies at Eastern Air Lines

Eastern Air Lines moved precariously close to bankruptcy during the recession in 1981 and 1982. Charting a turnaround strategy in 1983, Eastern management sought to solidify that turnaround as economic conditions continued to improve in 1984. Below are selected 1984 annual objectives and functional strategies presented by Eastern in late 1983.

Annual Objective for 1984. The level of flying in 1984, as measured in both block hours and airplane seat miles (ASMs), will be 12 percent above 1983 levels. As shown below, the capacity growth will be primarily in daytime flying.

Fleet growth	9%
Increased daytime utilization	1%
Increased night coach utilization	2%

Schedule Strategy. Eastern's primary emphasis in 1984 will be on consolidating our position in existing markets. A key element will be the restoration of service cancelled because of slot restrictions at major airports, particularly Atlanta, that were related to the PATCO (air traffic controllers') strike.

Atlanta	Will be the main focus of the service increase. Twenty departures are being added in July 1983; and, as slot restrictions are removed at key northern airports and control centers, additional Atlanta flights will be scheduled.
New York (La Guardia)	Will have increased service. With Piedmont and Northwest moving to other facilities at La Guardia, the gate constraint on our schedules has been removed. As we obtain additional slots, service will be added.
New York–Florida	Will be served primarily by widebodies and B-757s. With the increased presence of People Express, other carriers have reduced their New York–Florida service. Pricing has become a primary competitive tool, with the need for schedule frequency somewhat reduced. The A300s, L-1011s, and B-757s give us the seat-mile costs needed to economically compete.
Miami	Will have added service as slot restrictions in northern airports are removed.
South America	Service is essentially in place and will not change significantly until the area's economy improves. With our current service pattern, we have established a solid competitive position in South America.

Houston	Service levels and patterns will be refined based on traffic and financial performance. It is premature to make any judgment on Houston's performance. Because of slot restrictions, it was not until May (1984) that necessary connecting complexes could be constructed. Further, yields have been depressed by Continental's cut-rate pricing.
Charlotte	Service will be adjusted to reflect changing competitive conditions.
Philadelphia	Is receiving additional emphasis as a secondary hub. As the results of the May additions to Boston, Buffalo, and Toronto are evaluated, the schedule will be refined.

Marketing and Pricing Strategy. No significant strategic changes are indicated. Eastern's revenue performance relative to the industry has been excellent.

Productivity Strategy. Minimally acceptable profit levels in 1984 require a substantial increase in productivity. We plan to increase our level of operations while maintaining current employment levels to meet that need.

Financial Strategy. A basic objective over the next several years must be to dramatically improve Eastern's balance sheet, preserving sufficient liquidity to see us through periods of unfavorable business conditions. Consistent profitability is the key to Eastern's financial future. We will limit capital spending to what is absolutely necessary or has an immediate financial payback.

Management Process. Employee involvement represents a fundamental change in the way the company is managed. Its objective is to make us a more efficient company while also enhancing our employee's job satisfaction. It is a process that has worked in American industry and, given our commitment, will work at Eastern. This represents a long-term commitment. We will not see results overnight, but, in the long run, we will be a better company.

example in Figure 10–4 shows possible functional strategies in the functional areas of operations, marketing, and finance. Additional functional strategies are necessary, most notably in the personnel area.

Differences between Business and Functional Strategies

To better understand the role of functional strategies within the strategic management process, they must be differentiated from grand strategies. Three basic characteristics differentiate functional and grand strategies:

1. Time horizon covered.
2. Specificity.
3. Participation in the development.

Figure 10–4

Role of functional strategies at General Cinema Corporation

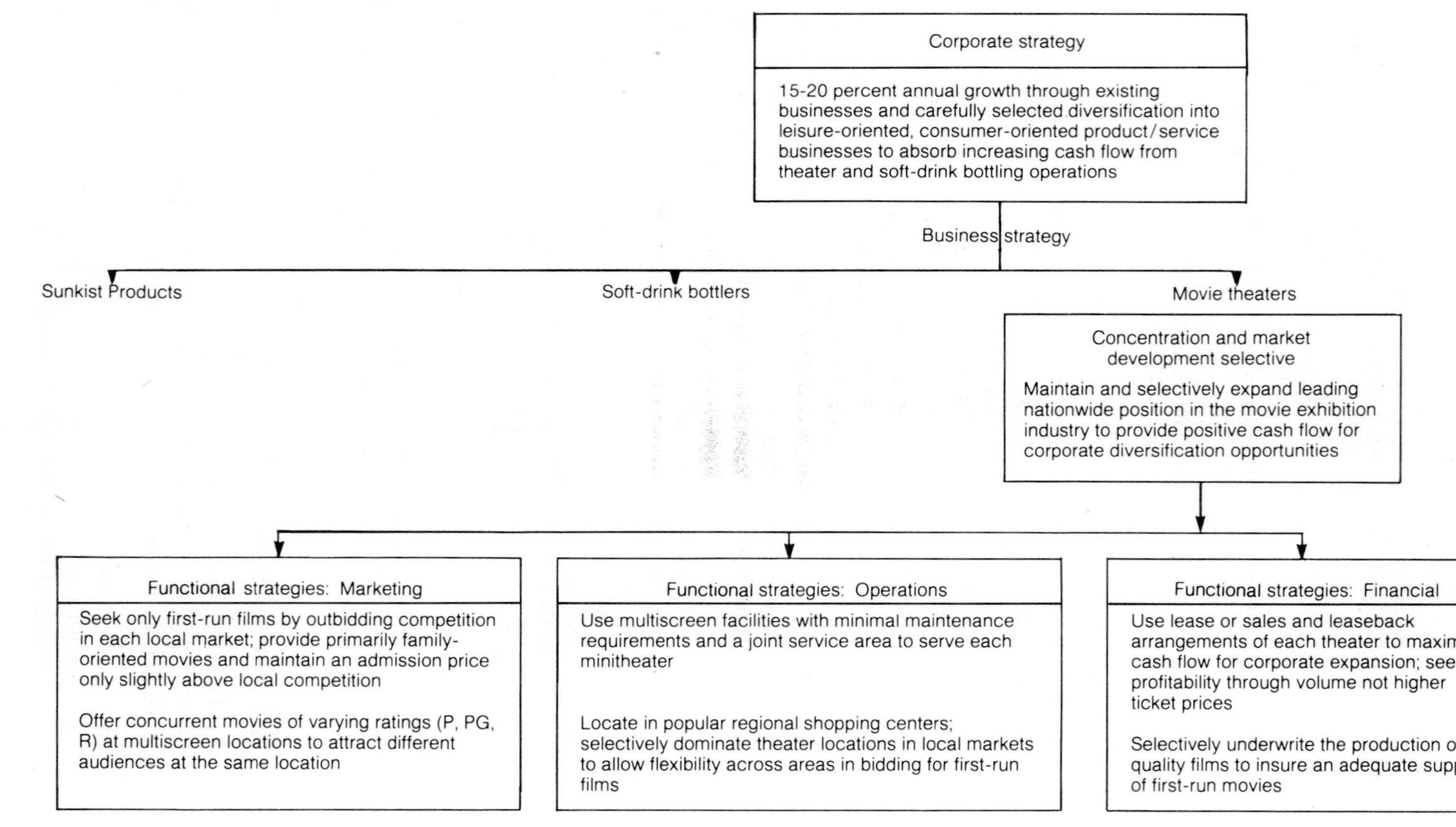

Time Horizon. The time horizon of a functional strategy is usually comparatively short. Functional strategies identify and coordinate short-term actions, usually undertaken in a year or less. Sears, for example, might implement a marketing strategy of increasing price discounts and sales bonuses in its appliance division to reduce excess appliance inventory over the next year. This functional strategy would be designed to achieve a short-range (annual) objective that ultimately contributes to the goal of Sears' grand strategy in its retail division over the next five years.

This shorter time horizon is critical to successfully implementing a grand strategy for two reasons. First, it focuses functional managers' attention on what needs to be done *now* to make the grand strategy work. Second, the shorter time horizon allows functional managers to recognize current conditions and adjust to changing conditions in developing functional strategies.

Specificity. A functional strategy is more specific than a grand strategy. Functional strategies guide functional actions taken in key parts of the company to implement grand strategy. The grand strategy provides general direction. Functional strategies give specific guidance to managers responsible for accomplishing annual objectives. Such strategies are meant to ensure that managers know *how* to meet annual objectives. It is not enough to identify a general grand strategy at the business level. There must also be strategies that outline what should be done in each functional area if the annual (and ultimately long-term) objectives of the company are to be achieved. Specific functional strategies improve the willingness (and ability) of operating managers to implement strategic decisions, particularly when those decisions represent major changes in the current strategy of the firm.

Figure 10–4 illustrates the difference in specificity of grand and operating strategies. General Cinema's grand strategy for its movie theater division gives broad direction on how the division should pursue a concentration and selective-market-development strategy. Two functional strategies are illustrated in the marketing area that give specific direction to managers on what types of movies (first-run, primarily family-oriented, P, PG, R) and what pricing strategy (competitive in the local area) should be followed.

Specificity in functional strategies contributes to successful implementation for several reasons. First, it adds substance, completeness, and meaning to what a specific subunit of the business must do. The existence of numerous functional strategies helps ensure that managers know what needs to be done and can focus on accomplishing results.[5] Second, specific functional strategies clarify for top management how functional managers intend to accomplish the grand strategy. This increases top management's confidence in and sense

[5] While a company typically has one grand strategy, it should have a functional strategy for each major subunit and several operating strategies within the subunit. For example, a business may specify distinct pricing, promotion, and distribution strategies as well as an overall strategy to guide marketing operations.

of control over the grand strategy. Third, specific functional strategies facilitate coordination between operating units *within* the company by clarifying areas of interdependence and potential conflict.

Participants. Different people participate in strategy development at the functional and business levels. Business strategy is the responsibility of the general manager of a business unit. Development of functional strategy is typically delegated by the business-level manager to principal subordinates charged with running the operating areas of the business. The business manager must establish long-term objectives and a strategy that corporate management feels contributes corporate-level goals. Key operating managers similarly establish annual objectives and operating strategies that help accomplish business objectives and strategies. Just as business strategies and objectives are approved through negotiation between corporate managers and business managers, the business manager typically ratifys the annual objectives and functional strategies developed by operating managers.[6]

The involvement of operating managers in developing functional strategies contributes to successful implementation because understanding of what needs to be done to achieve annual objectives is thereby improved. And perhaps most critical, active involvement increases commitment to the strategies developed.

It is difficult to generalize about the development of strategies across functional areas. For example, key variables in marketing, finance, and production are different. Furthermore, within each functional area, the importance of key variables varies across business situations. Thus, in the next several sections we will not exhaustively treat each functional area, but attempt to indicate the key decision variables that should receive attention in the functional strategies of typical areas.

Functional Strategies in the Marketing Area

The role of the marketing function is to profitably bring about the sale of products/services in target markets for the purpose of achieving the business's goals. Functional strategies in the marketing area should guide this endeavor in a manner consistent with the grand strategy and other functional strategies. Effective marketing strategies guide marketing managers in determining who will sell what, where, when, to whom, in what quantity, and how. Marketing strategies must therefore entail four components: product, price, place, and promotion. Figure 10–5 illustrates the types of questions that operating strategies must address in terms of these four components.

A functional strategy for the *product component* of the marketing function

[6] A. A. Thompson, Jr., and A. J. Strickland III, *Strategy Formulation and Implementation* (Plano, Tex.: Business Publications, 1983), p. 77.

Figure 10–5

Functional strategies in marketing

Key functional strategies	*Typical questions that should be answered by the functional strategy*
Product (or service)	Which products do we emphasize? Which products/services contribute most to profitability? What is the product/service image we seek to project? What consumer needs does the product/service seek to meet? What changes should be influencing our customer orientation?
Price	Are we primarily competing on price? Can we offer discounts or other pricing modifications? Are pricing policies standard nationally or is there regional control? What price segments are we targeting (high, medium, low, etc.)? What is the gross profit margin? Do we emphasize cost/demand or competition-oriented pricing?
Place	What level of market coverage is necessary? Are there priority geographic areas? What channels of distribution are key? What are the channel objectives, structure, and management? Should the marketing managers change their degree of reliance on distributors, sales reps, and direct selling? What sales organization do we want? Is the sales force organized around territory, market, or product?
Promotion	What are key promotion priorities and approaches? Which advertising/communication priorities and approaches are linked to different products, markets, and territories? Which media would be most consistent with the total marketing strategy?

should clearly identify the customer needs the firm seeks to meet with its product and/or service. An effective functional strategy for this component should guide marketing managers in decisions regarding features, product lines, packaging, accessories, warranty, quality, and new-product development. This strategy should provide a comprehensive statement of the product/service concept and the target market(s) the firm is seeking to serve. This in turn, fosters consistency and continuity in the daily activity of the marketing area.

A product or service is not much good to a customer if it is not available when and where it is wanted. So the functional strategy for the *place compo-*

nent identifies where, when, and by whom the product/services are to be offered for sale. The primary concern here is the channel(s) of distribution—the combination of marketing institutions through which the products/services flow to the final user. This component of marketing strategy guides decisions regarding channels, e.g., single versus multiple channels, to ensure consistency with the total marketing effort.

The *promotion component* of marketing strategy defines how the firm will communicate with the target market. Functional strategy for the promotion component should provide marketing managers with basic guides for the use and mix of advertising, personal selling, sales promotion, and media selection. It must be consistent with other marketing strategy components and, due to cost requirements, closely integrated with financial strategy.

Functional strategy regarding the *price component* is perhaps the single most important consideration in marketing. It directly influences demand and supply, profitability, consumer perception, and regulatory response. The approach to pricing strategy may be cost oriented, market oriented, or competition (industry) oriented. With a cost-oriented approach, pricing decisions center on total cost and usually involve an acceptable mark-up or target price ranges. Pricing is based on consumer demand, e.g., gasoline pricing in a deregulated oil industry, when the approach is market oriented. With the third approach, pricing decisions center around those of the firm's competitors. The discount pricing that occurred in the U.S. automobile industry in the early 1980s, with several domestic and foreign producers following Chrysler's discount pricing initiatives, is an example of competitor-based pricing. While one approach, e.g., market demand, may predominate a firm's pricing strategy, the strategy is always influenced to some degree by the other orientations.

Functional Strategies in Finance/Accounting

While most operating strategies guide implementation in the immediate future, the time frame for financial functional strategies varies because strategies in this area direct the use of financial resources in support of the business strategy, long-term goals, and annual objectives. Financial operating strategies with longer time perspectives guide financial managers regarding long-term capital investment, use of debt financing, dividend allocation, and the leveraging posture of the firm. Operating strategies designed to manage working capital and short-term assets have a much more immediate focus. Figure 10–6 highlights some key questions financial strategies must answer for successful implementation.

Long-term financial strategies usually guide capital acquisition in the sense that priorities change infrequently over time. The desired level of debt versus equity versus internal long-term financing of business activities is a common issue in capital acquisition strategy. For example, Delta Airlines has a long-standing operating strategy that seeks to minimize the level of debt in propor-

Figure 10–6

Functional strategies in finance

Key functional strategies	*Typical questions that should be answered by the functional strategy*
Capital acquisition	What is an acceptable cost of capital? What is the desired proportion of short- and long-term debt, preferred and common equity? What balance is between internal and external funding? What risk and ownership restrictions are appropriate? What level and forms of leasing should be used in providing assets?
Capital allocation	What are the priorities for capital allocation projects? On what basis is final selection of projects to be made? What level of capital allocation can be made by operating managers without higher approval?
Dividend and working capital management	What portion of earnings should be paid out as dividends? How important is dividend stability? Are things other than cash appropriate as dividends? What are the cash-flow requirements; minimum and maximum cash balances? How liberal/conservative should credit policies be? What limits, payment terms, and collection procedures are necessary? What payment timing and procedure should be followed?

tion to equity and internal funding of capital needs. General Cinema Corporation has a long-standing strategy of long-term leasing to expand its theater and soft-drink bottling facilities. The debt-to-equity ratios for these two firms are approximately 0.50 to 2.0, respectively. Both have similar records of steady profitable growth over the last 20 years and represent two different yet equally effective operating strategies for capital acquisition.

Another financial strategy of major importance is capital allocation. Growth-oriented grand strategies generally require numerous major investments in facilities, projects, acquisitions, and/or people. These investments cannot generally be made immediately (nor are they desired to be). Rather, a capital allocation strategy sets priorities and timing for these investments. This also helps manage conflicting priorities among operating managers competing for capital resources.

Retrenchment or stability often require a financial strategy that focuses on the reallocation of existing capital resources. This could necessitate pruning product lines, production facilities, or personnel to be reallocated elsewhere in the firm. Clearly the overlapping careers and aspirations of key operating managers create an emotional setting. Even with retrenchment (perhaps even

Strategy in Action 10–2

K mart Operationalizes a New Business Strategy

Not long ago, employees in K mart discount department stores began shuffling shelves, replacing racks, moving whole departments, and blazing new aisles. When they finished, the stores had a new look, and K mart Corp., the world's second largest retailer, had started on a new merchandising tack.

The trouble is that K mart can no longer rely entirely on its old strategy of growth through building new stores. Since the first K mart opened in 1962, offering everything from baby oil to motor oil at cut-rate prices, the stores have proliferated, turning the former S. S. Kresge Company from a so-so five-and-dime chain into the biggest retailer next to Sears, Roebuck & Co.

Now, with stores in nearly all the 300 top metropolitan areas in the country, some of which are saturated, K mart's growth through expansion is increasingly limited. The answer is to try for more volume, and more profitable volume per store, from the cost-conscious consumers attracted by K mart's low prices. K mart can't risk losing its discount appeal, but at the same time it must move more and higher-quality goods. To achieve this new business strategy, K mart is relying heavily on a sophisticated operating strategy in merchandising. The standard K mart—a cavernous building of plain design filled with racks, bins, and metal shelves—has been changed here to emphasize the merchandise at least as much as the price tags and signs. Displays of clothing and other goods are being altered to stimulate impulse buying. In addition, higher-quality goods are being offered.

K mart's heavy advertising consistently has attracted customers, especially cost-conscious middle- and upper-income customers. "But too often we fail to merchandise all of the items that customers would buy from us after we get them into the store," said K mart's CEO. "We simply aren't getting enough of their spendable dollars."

Although the changes in K marts seem subtle, they're designed to create an atmosphere conducive to free spending. In women's apparel, rows and rows of long piperacks have been replaced by multilevel, circular, and honeycomb racks that allow customers to see whole garments. Higher-quality, more fashionable soft goods hang on the new racks. Delicatessen and snack counters have moved to a wall from their front-and-center position. Now, jewelry greets shoppers inside the entrances. "We wanted to get the popcorn out from in front of the door," said a K mart Vice President. The jewelry includes higher-quality pieces and more brand-name items. Sales of women's wear and jewelry have increased in the redesigned stores, K mart managers say.

Source: "K mart Stores Try New Look to Invite More Spending." Reprinted by permission of *The Wall Street Journal,* © Dow Jones & Company, Inc., November 26, 1980, p. 29. All rights reserved.

more so!), a clear operating strategy that delineates capital allocation priorities is important for effective implementation in a politically charged organizational setting.

Capital allocation strategy frequently includes one additional dimension—level of capital expenditure delegated to operating managers. If a business is pursuing rapid growth, flexibility in making capital expenditures at the operating level may enable timely responses to an evolving market. On the other hand, capital expenditures may be carefully controlled if retrenchment is the strategy.

Dividend management is an integral part of a firm's internal financing. Because dividends are paid on earnings, lower dividends increase the internal funds available for growth, and internal financing reduces the need for external, often debt, financing. However, stability of earnings and dividends often make a positive contribution to the market price of a firm's stock. Therefore, a strategy guiding dividend management must support the business's posture toward equity markets.

Working capital is critical to the daily operation of the firm, and capital requirements are directly influenced by seasonal and cylical fluctuations, firm size, and the pattern of receipts and disbursements. The working capital component of financial strategy is built on an accurate projection of cash flow and must provide cash-management guidelines for conserving and rebuilding the cash balances required for daily operation.

Functional Strategies in Research and Development

With the increasing rate of technological change in most competitive industries, research and development (R&D) has assumed a key functional role in many organizations. In the technology-intense computer and pharmaceutical industries, for example, firms typically spend between 4 and 6 percent of their sales dollars on R&D. In other industries, such as the hotel/motel and construction industries, R&D spending is less than 1 percent of sales. Thus, R&D may be a vital function—a key instrument of business strategy—although in stable, less innovative industries, R&D is less critical as a functional strategy than is marketing or finance.

Figure 10–7 illustrates the types of questions addressed by an R&D operating strategy. First, R&D strategy should clarify whether basic research or product development research will be emphasized. Several major oil companies now have solar energy subsidiaries with R&D strategy emphasis on basic research, while smaller competitors emphasize product development research.

Directly related to the choice of emphasis between basic research and product development is the time orientation for these efforts mandated by R&D strategy. Should efforts be focused on the near or the long term? The solar subsidiaries of the major oil companies have long-term perspectives, while their smaller competitors appear to be focusing on the immediate future.

Figure 10–7

Functional strategies in R&D

R&D decision area	*Typical questions that should be answered by the functional strategy*
Basic research versus commercial development	To what extent should innovation and break-through research be emphasized? In relation to the emphasis on product development, refinement, and modification? What new projects are necessary to support growth?
Time horizon	Is the emphasis short term or long term? Which orientation best supports the business strategy? marketing and production strategy?
Organizational fit	Should R&D be done in-house or contracted out? Should it be centralized or decentralized? What should be the relationship between the R&D unit(s) and product managers? marketing managers? production managers?
Basic R&D posture	Should the firm maintain an offensive posture, seeking to lead innovation and development in the industry? Should the firm adapt a defensive posture, responding quickly to competitors' developments?

These orientations are consistent with each business's strategy if the major oil companies want to ensure their long-term position in the energy field, while the smaller companies want to establish a competitive niche in the growing solar industry.

R&D strategy should also guide organization of the R&D function. For example, should R&D efforts be conducted solely within the firm or should portions of the work be contracted outside? A closely related issue is whether R&D should be a centralized or decentralized function.

The basic R&D posture of the firm influences each of these decisions because strategy in this area can be offensive, defensive, or a combination of these. If the R&D strategy is offensive, technological innovation and new product development are emphasized as the basis for the firm's future success, as is true for small, high-technology firms. However, this orientation entails high risk (and high payoff) and demands considerable technological skill, forecasting expertise, and the ability to quickly transform basic innovations into commercial products.

A defensive R&D strategy emphasizes product modification and the ability to copy or acquire new technology to maintain a firm's position in the industry. American Motors (AMC) is a good example. Faced with the massive R&D budgets of General Motors, Ford, and foreign competitors, AMC has placed R&D emphasis on bolstering the product life cycle of its prime products (particularly Jeeps) and acquiring small car technology through a partnership arrangement with Renault of France.

A combination of offensive and defensive R & D strategy is often used by large companies with some degree of technological leadership. GE in the electrical industry, IBM in the computer industry, and Du Pont in the chemical industry all have defensive R&D strategies for currently available products *and* emphasis on an offensive R&D posture in basic, long-term research.

Functional Strategies in Production/Operations

Production/operations management (POM) is the core function in the business firm. POM is the process of converting inputs (raw material, supplies, people, and machines) into value-enhanced output. This function is most easily associated with manufacturing firms. However, it applies equally to all other types of businesses (including service and retail firms, for example).

Functional strategies in POM must guide decisions regarding: (1) the basic nature of the firm's POM system, seeking an optimum balance between investment input and production/operations output and (2) location, facilities design, and process planning on a short-term basis. Figure 10–8 illustrates these concerns by highlighting key decision areas in which the POM strategies should provide guidance.

The facilities and equipment component of POM strategy involves decisions

Figure 10–8

Functional strategies in POM

Key operating strategies	*Typical questions that should be answered by the functional strategy*
Facilities and equipment	How centralized should the facilities be? (One big facility or several small facilities?) How integrated should the separate processes be? To what extent will further mechanization or automation be pursued? Should size and capacity be oriented toward peak or normal operating levels?
Purchasing	How many sources are needed? How do we select suppliers and manage relationships over time? What level of forward buying (hedging) is appropriate?
Operations planning and control	Should work be scheduled to order or to stock? What level of inventory is appropriate? How should inventory be used (FIFO/LIFO), controlled, and replenished? What are the key foci for control efforts (quality, labor cost, downtime, product usage, other)? Should maintenance efforts be preventive or breakdown oriented? What emphasis should be placed on job specialization? plant safety? use of standards?

regarding plant location, size, equipment replacement, and facilities utilization that should be consistent with grand strategy and other operating strategies. In the mobile-home industry, for example, Winnebago's plant and equipment strategy entailed one large, centralized production center (in Iowa) located near its raw materials with modernized equipment and a highly integrated production process. Fleetwood, Inc., a California-based competitor, opted for dispersed, decentralized production facilities located near markets. Fleetwood emphasizes maximum equipment life and less integrated, labor-intensive production processes. Both are leaders in the mobile home industry.

The purchasing function is another area that should be addressed in the POM strategy. From a cost perspective, are a few suppliers an advantage or risky because of overdependence? What criteria (for example, payment requirements) should be used in selecting vendors? How should purchases be made in terms of volume and delivery requirements to support operations? If such questions are critical to the success of a grand strategy, functional strategy guidelines improve implementation.

Functional strategies for the planning and control component of POM provide guidelines for ongoing production operations. They are meant to encourage efficient organization of production/operations resources to match long-range, overall demand. Often this component dictates whether production/operations will be demand oriented, inventory oriented, or subcontracting oriented. If demand is cyclical or seasonal, then POM strategy must ensure that production/operations processes are efficiently geared to this pattern. A bathing suit manufacturer would prefer inventories to be at their highest in the early spring, for example, not the early fall. If demand is less cyclical, a firm might emphasize producing to inventory, wanting a steady level of production and inventories. When demand fluctuations are less predictable, many firms subcontract to handle sudden increases in demand while avoiding idle capacity and excess capital investment. Thus, a POM strategy should aid in such decisions as:

What are the appropriate inventory level? purchasing procedures? level of quality control?

What is the trade-off in emphasizing cost versus quality in production/operations? What level of productivity is critical?

How far ahead should we schedule production? guarantee delivery? hire personnel?

What criteria should be followed in adding or deleting equipment, facilities, shifts, and people?

POM operating strategies must be coordinated with marketing strategy if the firm is to succeed. Careful integration with financial strategy components (such as capital budgeting and investment decisions) and the personnel function are also necessary.

Functional Strategies in Personnel

The strategic importance of functional strategies in the personnel area has become more widely accepted in recent years. Personnel management aids in accomplishing grand strategy by ensuring the development of managerial talent, the presence of systems to manage compensation and regulatory concerns, and the development of competent, well-motivated employees. Functional strategies in personnel should guide the effective utilization of human resources to achieve both the annual objectives of the firm and the satisfaction and development of employees. These strategies involve the following areas:

Employee recruitment, selection, and orientation.

Career development and counseling, performance evaluation, and training and development.

Compensation.

Labor/union relations and Equal Employment Opportunity Commission (EEOC) requirements.

Discipline, control, and evaluation.

Operating strategy for recruitment, selection, and orientation guides personnel management decisions for attracting and retaining motivated, productive employees. This involves such questions as: What are the key human resource needs to support a chosen strategy? How do we recruit for these needs? How sophisticated should the selection process be? How should new employees be introduced to the organization? The recruitment, selection, and orientation component of personnel strategy should provide basic parameters for answering these questions.

The development and training component should guide personnel actions taken to meet future human resource needs of the grand strategy. Merrill Lynch, a major brokerage firm, has a long-term corporate strategy of becoming a diversified financial-service institution. In addition to handling stock transactions, Merrill Lynch is actively moving into areas such as investment banking, consumer credit, and venture capital. In support of these far-reaching, long-term objectives, Merrill Lynch has incorporated extensive early-career training and ongoing career development programs to meet its expanding need for personnel with multiple competencies.

Functional strategies in the personnel area are needed to guide decisions regarding compensation, labor relations, EEOC, discipline, and control to enhance the productivity and motivation of the work force. Involved are concerns such as: What are the standards for promotion? How should payment, incentive plans, benefits, and seniority policies be interpreted? Should there be hiring preference? What are appropriate disciplinary steps? These are specific personnel decisions that operating managers frequently encounter. Functional strategies in the personnel area should guide such decisions in a way that is compatible with business strategy, strategies for other functional areas and the achievement of annual objectives.

To summarize, functional strategies are important because they provide specifics on *how* each major subactivity contributes to the implementation of the grand strategy. This specificity, and the involvement of operating managers in its development, help ensure understanding of and commitment to the chosen strategy. Annual objectives, linked to both long-term objectives and functional strategies, reinforce this understanding and commitment by providing measurable targets that operating managers have agreed upon. The next step in implementing a strategy involves the identification of *policies* that guide and control decisions by operating managers and their subordinates.

Developing and Communicating Concise Policies

Policies are directives designed to guide the thinking, decisions, and actions of managers and their subordinates in implementing an organization's strategy. Policies provide guidelines for establishing and controlling ongoing operations in a manner consistent with the firm's strategic objectives. Often referred to as "standard operating procedures," policies serve to increase managerial effectiveness by standardizing many routine decisions and controlling the discretion of managers and subordinates in implementing operational strategies. Logically, policies should be derived from functional strategies (and in some instances, from corporate or business strategies) with the key purpose of aiding in strategy execution.[7] Strategy in Action 10–3 illustrates selected policies from several well-known companies.

The Purpose of Policies. Policies communicate specific guides to decisions. They are designed to control and reinforce the implementation of functional strategies and the grand strategy, and fulfill this role in several ways:[8]

1. *Policies establish indirect control over independent action* by making a clear statement about how things are *now* to be done. By limiting discretion, policies in effect control decisions and the conduct of activities without direct intervention by top management.

[7] The term *policy* has various definitions in management literature. Some authors and practitioners equate policy with strategy. Others do this inadvertently by using "policy" as a synonym for company mission, purpose, or culture. Still other authors and practitioners differentiate policy in terms of "levels" associated respectively with purpose, mission, and strategy. "Our policy is to make a positive contribution to the communities and societies we live in" and "our policy is not to diversify out of the hamburger business" are two examples of the breadth of what some call policies. This book defines *policy* much more narrowly as specific guides to managerial action and decisions in the implementation of strategy. This definition permits a sharper distinction between the formulation and implementation of functional strategies. And of even greater importance, it focuses the tangible value of the policy concept where it can be most useful—as a key administrative tool to enhance effective implementation and execution of strategy.

[8] These eight points are adapted from related discussions by Richard H. Buskirk, *Business and Administrative Policy* (New York: John Wiley & Sons, 1971), pp. 145–55; Thompson and Strickland, *Strategy Formulation*, pp. 377–79; Milton J. Alexander, *Business Strategy and Policy* (Atlanta, Ga.: University Publications, 1983), Chapter 3.

Strategy in Action 10–3

Selected Policies that Aid Strategy Implementation

Wendy's has a *purchasing policy* to give local store managers the authority to buy fresh meat and produce locally rather than from regionally designated or company-owned sources.

(This policy supports Wendy's functional strategy of having fresh, unfrozen hamburgers daily)

General Cinema has a *financial policy* that requires annual capital investment in movie theatres not exceed annual depreciation.

(By keeping capital investment no greater than depreciation, this policy supports General Cinema's financial strategy of maximizing cash flow—in this case all profit—to growth areas of the company. It also reinforces General Cinema's financial strategy of leasing as much as possible.)

Holiday Inns has a *personnel policy* that every new innkeeper attend Holiday Inns University's three-week innkeeper program within one year of being hired.

(This policy supports Holiday Inns' functional (POM) strategy of strict compliance with specific standards at every HI location by ensuring standardized training of every new innkeeper at every Holiday Inn whether company owned or franchised.)

IBM originally had a *marketing policy* not to give free IBM personal computers (PCs) to any person or organization.

(This policy attempted to support IBM's image strategy as a professional, high-value, service business and its effort to retain that image as it seeks to dominate the PC market.)

Crown, Cork and Seal Company has a *R&D policy* not to invest any financial or people resources in basic research.

(This policy supports Crown, Cork and Seal's functional strategy that emphasizes customer service, not technical leadership.)

First National Bank of South Carolina has an *operating policy* that requires annual renewal of the financial statement of all personal borrowers.

(This policy supports First National's financial strategy that seeks to maintain a loan/loss ratio below the industry norm.)

2. *Policies promote uniform handling of similar activities.* This facilitates coordination of work tasks and helps reduce friction arising from favoritism, discrimination, and disparate handling of common functions.
3. *Policies ensure quicker decisions* by standardizing answers to previously answered questions that would otherwise recur and be pushed up the management hierarchy again and again.
4. *Policies help institutionalize basic aspects of organization behavior.* This minimizes conflicting practices and establishes consistent patterns of action in terms of how organizational members attempt to make the strategy work.
5. *Policies reduce uncertainty in repetitive and day-to-day decision making* thereby providing a necessary foundation for coordinated, efficient efforts.
6. *Policies can counteract resistance to or rejection of chosen strategies by organization members.* When major strategic change is undertaken, unambiguous operating policies help clarify what is expected and facilitate acceptance, particularly when operating managers participate in policy development.
7. *Policies offer a predetermined answer to routine problems,* giving managers more time to cope with nonroutine matters; dealing with ordinary and extraordinary problems is greatly expedited—the former by referring to established policy and the latter by drawing upon a portion of the manager's time.
8. *Policies afford managers a mechanism for avoiding hasty and ill-conceived decisions in changing operations.* Prevailing policy can always be used as a reason for not yielding to emotion-based, expedient, or temporarily valid arguments for altering procedures and practices.

Policies may be written and formal or unwritten and informal. The positive reasons for informal, unwritten policies are usually associated with some strategic need for competitive secrecy. Some unwritten policies, such as "promotion from within," are widely known (or expected) by employees and implicitly sanctioned by management. However, unwritten, informal policies may be contrary to the long-term success of a strategy. Still, managers and employees often like the latitude "granted" when policies are unwritten and informal. There are at least seven advantages to formal written policies:[9]

1. Managers are required to think through the policy's meaning, content, and intended use.
2. The policy is explicit so misunderstandings are reduced.
3. Equitable and consistent treatment of problems is more likely.
4. Unalterable transmission of policies is ensured.

---

[9] Adapted from Robert G. Murdick, R. Carl Moor, Richard H. Eckhouse, and Thomas W. Zimmerer, *Business Policy: A Framework for Analysis* (Columbus, Ohio: Grid, 1984), p. 65.

5. Authorization or sanction of the policy is more clearly communicated when the policy is written. This can be helpful in many cases.
6. A convenient and authoritative reference can be supplied to all concerned with the policy.
7. Indirect control and organizationwide coordination, key purposes of policies, are systematically enhanced.

Policies can vary in their level of strategic significance. Some, such as travel reimbursement procedures, are really work rules that are not necessarily linked to the implementation of a specific strategy. At the other extreme, organizationwide policies such as Wendy's requirement that every location invest 1 percent of gross revenue in local advertising is virtually a functional strategy.

Policies can be externally imposed or internally derived. Policies regarding EEOC practices are often developed in compliance with external (government) requirements. Likewise, policies regarding leasing or depreciation may be strongly influenced by current tax regulations.

Regardless of the origin, formality, and nature of the policy, the key point to bear in mind is the valuable role policies can play in strategy implementation. Carefully constructed policies enhance strategy implementation in several ways. Obviously, it is imperative to examine existing policies and ensure the existence of policies necessary to guide and control operating activities consistent with current business and functional strategies. Ensuring communication of specific policies will help overcome resistance to strategic change and foster greater organizational commitment for successful strategy implementation.

Summary

The first concern in the implementation of a grand strategy is to operationalize that strategy throughout the organization. This chapter discussed three important tools to accomplish this: annual objectives, functional strategies, and policies.

Annual objectives guide implementation by translating long-term objectives into current targets. Annual objectives are derived from long-term objectives, but differ in time frame, focus, specificity, and measurement. For annual objectives to be effective in strategy implementation, they must be integrated and coordinated. They must also be consistent, measurable, and prioritized.

Functional strategies are a second important tool for effective implementation of a grand strategy. Functional strategies are derived from business strategy and provide specific, immediate direction to key functional areas within the business in terms of what must be done to implement the grand strategy.

Policies provide another means of directing and controlling decisions and actions at operating levels of the firm in a manner that is consistent with business and functional strategies. Effective policies channel actions, behavior, decisions, and practices to promote strategic accomplishment.

While annual objectives, functional strategies, and policies represent the start of implementation, much more remains. The strategy must be institutionalized—must permeate the basic foundation of the company. The next chapter examines the institutionalization phase of strategy implementation.

Questions for Discussion

1. Explain the phrase "translate thought into action." How does this relate to the relationship between grand strategy and operating strategy? between long-term and short-term objectives?
2. How do functional strategies differ from corporate and business strategies?
3. What are the key concerns that must be addressed by functional strategies in marketing? finance? POM? personnel?
4. How do policies aid strategy implementation? Illustrate your answer.
5. Illustrate a policy, an objective, and an operating strategy in your personal career strategy.
6. Why are annual objectives needed when long-term objectives are already available? What function do they serve?

Bibliography

Albrecht, Karl. *Successful Management by Objectives.* Englewood Cliffs, N.J.: Prentice-Hall, 1978.

Alexander, Milton J. *Business Strategy and Policy.* Atlanta, Ga.: University Publications, 1983, chapter 3.

Bales, Carter. "Strategic Control: The President's Paradox." *Business Horizons,* August 1977, pp. 17–28.

Buffa, E. S. *Basic Production Management,* 3d ed. New York: John Wiley & Sons, 1979.

Buskirk, Richard H. *Business and Administrative Policy.* New York: John Wiley & Sons, 1971, pp. 145–155.

Fox, Harold. "A Framework for Functional Coordination." *Atlanta Economic Review,* November–December 1973, pp. 10–11.

Friend, J. K. "The Dynamics of Policy Changes." *Long-Range Planning,* February 1977, pp. 40–47.

Glueck, W. F. *Personnel: A Diagnostic Approach,* 2d ed. Plano, Tex.: Business Publications, 1978.

Helfert, E. A. *Techniques of Financial Analysis,* 4th ed. Homewood, Ill.: Richard D. Irwin, 1978.

Heskett, James L. "Logistics—Essential to Strategy." *Harvard Business Review,* November–December 1977, pp. 85–96.

Hobbs, John, and Donald Heany. "Coupling Strategy to Operating Plans." Harvard Business Review, May–June 1977, pp. 119–26.

Hofer, Charles. "Conceptual Scheme for the Implementation of Organizational Strategy." Boston: Intercollegiate Case Clearing House 9–378–737, 1977.

Hrebiniak, Lawrence G., an William F. Joyce. *Implementing Strategy.* New York: Macmillan, 1984, p. 110.

Ingrasia, Paul. "McDonald's Seek to Boost Dinner Sales to Offset Surge in Costs and Competition." *The Wall Street Journal,* October 16, 1978.

Kotler, Phillip. *Marketing Management: Analysis, Planning, and Control,* 3d ed. Englewood Cliffs, N.J.: Prentice-Hall, 1976.

MacMillan, Ian C. "Strategy and Flexibility in the Smaller Business." *Long-Range Planning,* June 1975, pp. 62–63.

McCarthy, E. J. *Basic Marketing,* 7th ed. Homewood, Ill.: Richard D. Irwin, 1981.

Murdick, Robert G.; R. Carl Moor; Richard H. Eckhouse; and Thomas W. Zimmerer. *Business Policy: A Framework for Analysis.* Columbus, Ohio: Grid, 1984, p. 65.

Peters, Thomas J., and R. H. Waterman, Jr. *In Search of Excellence.* New York: Harper & Row, 1982.

Shapiro, Benson P. "Can Marketing Manufacturing Coexist." *Harvard Business Review,* September–October, 1977, pp. 105–14.

Shirley, R. C.; M. H. Perers; and A. I. El-Ansary. *Strategy and Policy Formation: A Multifunctional Orientation,* 2d ed. New York: John Wiley & Sons, 1981.

Stolle, John F. "How to Manage Physical Distribution." *Harvard Business Review,* July–August 1967, p. 95.

Tellier, Richard. *Operations Management: Fundamental Concepts and Methods.* New York: Harper & Row, 1978.

Thompson, A. A., Jr., and A. J. Strickland III. *Strategy Formulation and Implementation.* Plano, Tex.: Business Publications, 1983, p. 77.

Vancil, Richard. "Strategy Formulation in Complex Organizations." *Sloan Management Review,* Winter 1976, pp. 2–5.

Weston, J. F., and E. F. Brigham. *Essentials of Managerial Finance,* 3d ed. Hinsdale, Ill.: Dryden Press, 1978.

Chapter 10 Cohesion Case Illustration

Functional Strategies at Holiday Inns, Inc.

The cohesion case in Chapter 9 dealt with strategy analysis and choice. It concluded with the identification of Holiday Inns' choice of corporate-level and business-level strategies. But choice of strategies is not the end of the strategic management process. The strategies must be implemented–translated into appropriate organizational action. The first step in implementation is making the strategy operational. This requires identification of annual objectives, functional strategies, and key policies.

Illustrating the process for each business group at Holiday Inns, Inc. would require extensive text. Instead, this section will isolate one business group—hotels—to identify annual objectives, operating strategies, and policies as discussed in this chapter. It should ke kept in mind, however, that a similar effort would be required for each business group at Holiday Inns to effectively implement corporate-wide and business-level strategies.

Exhibit 1 highlights key long-term objectives and the business-level strategy (concentration and market development) the hotel group seeks to pursue in its five-year plan.

Annual objectives, functional strategies, and policies must be linked to the grand strategy and long-term objectives in Exhibit 1 if the strategy is to be effectively implemented. Exhibit 2 briefly summarizes key annual objectives and the functional strategies used to implement the hotel group's strategy.

Annual objectives help clarify long-term objectives. For example, Holiday Inns' annual objective of at least 50 new franchised properties feeds directly into the five-year objective of 70,000 rooms in the system. With the average property consisting of approximately 225 rooms, 50 properties would add 11,250 rooms per year. The balance needed would be just under 14,000 (or 2,750 per year), well within the stated preferences for 80 percent franchisee and 20 percent company-owned hotels in the system. Five years at this rate would mean 56,250 franchised rooms.

Functional strategies guide managers, while attempting to ensure synergy with the grand strategy. For example, Holiday Inns' quality control strategy of two unannounced visits annually with expulsion from the system if both are failed clarifies for quality control managers, property managers, and franchisees the implicit priorities of the grand strategy.

Finally, organizational policies help guide strategy implementation at Holiday Inns. For example, Holiday Inns has a systemwide policy that every new managerial or supervisory employee at a hotel property—inkeeper, restaurant manager, etc.—must attend Holiday Inns University's course (usually two

Exhibit 1

Long-term objectives and business-level strategy in the hotel group

Long-term objectives (5 years)	*Business-level strategy*
Net addition of 70,000 new rooms by 1987 217,000 new and extensively renovated rooms in HI system by 1985 95 percent of all HI-owned properties in multiuser areas 50 new franchised properties per year 17 percent return on investment 40 percent debt-to-capitalization ratio Best price/value ratio in industry	Maintain and expand HI's leadership position in the lodging industry by providing the largest number of high-quality, moderately priced, full-service lodging facilities worldwide with emphasis on selective, company-owned expansion into multiuser-oriented properties and steady expansion through franchising with continuous updating or elimination of older properties. Maintain the leadership position as the Number 1 brand preference among lodging customers.

or three weeks) for that position. This policy helps instill the "Holiday Inns way" and ensures that service standards related to the firm's leadership strategy are consistently implemented at the day-to-day operating level.

This section has highlighted annual objectives, functional strategies, and policies in the hotel group. Are other necessary areas that were not mentioned here useful in implementing the hotel group's strategy? Apply the vehicles for operationalizing grand strategies to each of Holiday Inns' other business units.

Exhibit 2

Operationalizing the hotel-business strategy: Annual objectives and functional strategies

Annual objectives

Maintain a 70 percent systemwide occupancy rate annually.

Clear identification of customer profile and changes in same on an annual basis.

Maintain 33 percent or greater customer preference for Holiday Inns in 1984.

Lead the industry in the number of reservations each year.

Prebook over one third of systemwide room nights each year.

Average 50 new franchised properties per year between 1982 and 1985.

Have 50 percent or higher of new franchised units built by existing franchises in 1984.

Have every managerial or supervisory employee at both company-owned and franchised properties trained at HI University by 1984.

35 percent debt-to-capitalization ratio by 1984.

17 percent operating margin (before taxes) each year.

17 percent average return on equity each year.

Ensure that every property failing two consecutive inspections is out of the HI system within one year.

Functional strategies

Marketing. Clearly identify the typical HI guest, provide superior price/value lodging services desired, and ensure customer awareness that these services exist.

Marketing research. Make sure HI knows clearly who their customers are, what they want, and when and where to provide it via a continuous $1.2 million annually budgeted consumer-research program.

Advertising. Extensive magazine and TV advertising with largest industry budget and most recognized campaign—No Excuses—in the industry.

Sales. Offer the most advanced reservation system in the industry.

Franchising. Maintain high level of franchise satisfaction and gradual expansion of franchise units systemwide.

Personnel. Ensure highly skilled operating personnel for all hotel properties. To accomplish this, HI University offers one- to three-week courses for all new hotel managers, assistant managers, food and beverage managers, front office, sales, maintenance, and housekeeping supervisors with mandatory attendance.

Financial. Maintain a financially sound capital structure relative to industry averages by using 50 percent internal and/or equity financing of company-owned expansion. Maintain profitability and stable growth by improving operating margins and a steady return on equity. Call the $9\frac{5}{8}$ percent convertible subordinate debentures as soon as the stock price exceeds $22 per share.

Operations. Ensure high-quality, standardized, superior-service lodging facilities throughout the HI network. Emphasize quality control, particularly at existing facilities, and update services offered systemwide to match changing customer profile and needs.

Quality control. At least one unannounced quality control inspection at every property twice annually. Also, achieve 50 percent of all systemwide rooms being either new or substantially renovated every five years.

Up-to-date services. Continuous improvement of services/facilities offered to match customer preferences. For example: HI-NET satellite communications network for multicity meetings and more king-sized beds for increasing number of single and business guests.

CHAPTER

Institutionalizing the Strategy

Annual objectives, functional strategies, and specific policies provide important means of communicating what must be done to implement the overall strategy. By translating long-term intentions into short-term guides to action, they make the strategy operational. But the strategy must also be *institutionalized*—permeate the very day-to-day life of the company—if it is to be effectively implemented. Three organizational elements provide the fundamental, long-term means for institutionalizing the firm's strategy: (1) structure, (2) leadership, and (3) culture.

In the first part of this chapter, the focus will be on organizational structure, the formal reporting relationships and responsibilities within a company. In the second part, focus will shift to the leadership of top management in the accomplishment of strategic objectives. The final part of this chapter will focus on organizational culture—the shared values, norms, and beliefs of organization members.

The chapter has three major aims: (1) to present structural alternatives, their advantages and disadvantages, and their role in strategy implementation, (2) to discuss the key dimensions of leadership that are important in strategy implementation, and (3) to discuss the concept of organizational culture, illustrate its impact, and examine ways to improve the strategy-culture relationship.

Structural Considerations

An organization is necessary if strategic purpose is to be accomplished. Thus, organizational structure is a major priority in implementing a carefully formulated strategy. If activities, responsibilities, and interrelationships are not organized in a manner that is consistent with the strategy chosen, the structure is left to evolve on its own. If structure and strategy are not coordinated, the result will probably be inefficiencies, misdirection, and fragmented efforts.

The need for structure becomes apparent as a business evolves. In a small firm where one person manages current operations and plans for the future, organizational structure is relatively simple. Owner-manager's have no organizational problem until their hurried trips to the plant, late-night sessions assimilating financial information for their CPA, and pressed calls on potential customers are inadequate to meet the demands of a business's increasing volume. As the magnitude of business activity increases, the need to subdivide activities, assign responsibilities, and provide for the integration and coordination of the new organizational parts becomes imperative. Thus, how to structure the organization to effectively execute the business's strategy has become a major concern.

What is structure? A basically simple concept: the division of tasks for efficiency and clarity of purpose, and coordination between the interdependent parts of the organization to ensure organizational effectiveness. Structure balances the need for specialization with the need for integration. It provides a formal means of decentralizing *and* centralizing consistent with the organizational and control needs of the strategy.

Structure is not the only means for getting "organized" to implement the strategy. Reward systems, planning procedures, and information and budgetary systems are other examples that should be employed. In the day-to-day implementation of strategy, these elements operate *inter*dependently with the formal organizational structure to shape how things are done. These other means may also be important, but it is through structure that strategists attempt to balance internal efficiency and overall effectiveness within a broader environment.

What are the structural choices? There are five basic types currently used by most business firms.

1. Simple.
2. Functional.
3. Divisional.
4. Strategic business unit.
5. Matrix.

Diversity and size create unique structural needs for each firm, but these five structural choices involve basic underlying features common to most business organizations.

Structure is not an end in itself, but a means to an end. It is a tool for managing the size and diversity of a business to enhance the success of its strategy. This section identifies structural options and examines the role of structure in strategy implementation.

Simple and Functional Organizational Structures

Figure 11–1 is a model of simple and functional organizational structures. In the smallest business enterprise, the simple structure prevails. All strategic and operating decisions are centralized in the owner-manager's domain. With the strategic concern primarily survival, and the likelihood that one bad decision could seriously threaten continued existence, this structure maximizes the owner's control. It also allows rapid response to product/market shifts and the ability to accommodate unique customer demands without coordination difficulties. Simple structures encourage employee involvement in more than one activity and are efficacious in businesses that serve a localized, simple

Figure 11–1

Simple and functional organizational structures

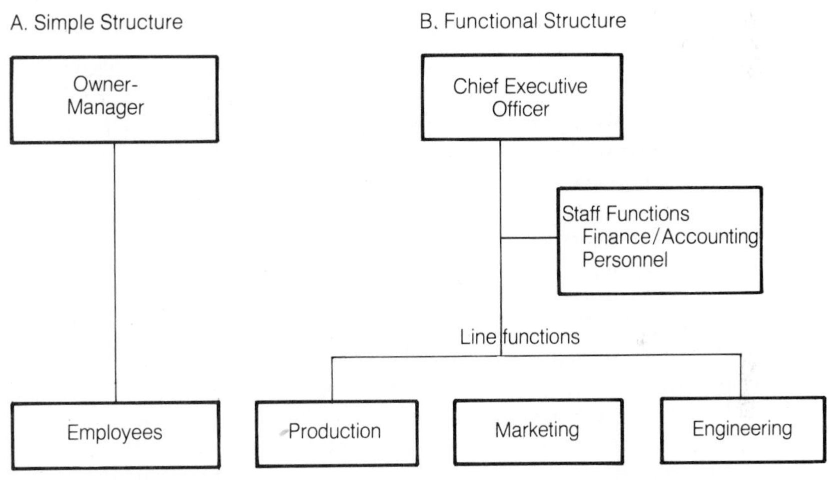

Advantages

1. Facilitates control of all the businesses's activities.
2. Rapid decision making and ability to change with market signals.
3. Simple and informal motivation/reward/control systems.

Disadvantages

1. Very demanding on the owner-manager.
2. Increasingly inadequate as volume expands.
3. Does not facilitate development of future managers.
4. Tends to focus owner-manager on day-to-day matters and not on future strategy.

Advantates

1. Efficiency through specialization.
2. Improved development of functional expertise.
3. Differentiates and delegates day-to-day operating decisions.
4. Retains centralized control of strategic decisions.

Disadvantages

1. Promotes narrow specialization and potential functional rivalry or conflict.
2. Difficulty in functional coordination and interfunctional decision making.
3. Staff-line conflict.
4. Limits internal development of general managers.

product/market. This structure can be very demanding on the owner-manager and, as volume increases, can pressure the owner-manager to give increased attention to day-to-day concerns at the expense of time invested in strategic management activities.

Functional structure predominates in firms that concentrate on one or a few related products/markets. Functional structures group similar tasks and

Strategy in Action 11–1

From Divisional to Functional Structure at Crown, Cork and Seal

John Connelly became chief executive officer at Crown, Cork and Seal (CCS), a major company in the metal container industry, when CCS had fallen on hard times. In trying to compete on all fronts with much larger competitors like American Can and Continental Can, CCS had become overextended and was on the verge of bankruptcy. It had a product-oriented, divisional structure, similar to that of its larger competitors, which had been adopted to facilitate decentralized competition.

Connelly formulated a desperate retrenchment strategy to turn CCS around. The strategy focused CCS on the production of cans for hard-to-hold products, aerosol cans, and evolving international markets. The emphasis was to sell to large purchasers and provide extensive service in purchaser's canning operations. Thus, Connelly's strategy was to narrow CCS's scope to the most profitable product/market segments, build a service-related competitive advantage, and maintain tight fiscal control to overcome the imminent threat of bankruptcy.

Connelly quickly realized that the existing divisional structure was not consistent with the needs of the new strategy. Corporate-level overhead was both costly and unnecessary given the narrowed scope of CCS operations under the new strategy. To accommodate its narrow product/market scope and the need for tight fiscal control, Connelly reorganized CCS along functional lines with three vice presidents—manufacturing, sales, and finance—reporting directly to him. This provided the centralized control needed for the retrenchment strategy and cut the managerial labor force by 24 percent. By making plant managers responsible for the profitability of their operations, he accommodated the strategy's need for tight control of geographically dispersed units within an efficient, streamlined functional structure.

CCS's strategy has been quite effective with the company consistently leading the industry in return on equity, profitability, and return on investment. And the success of this strategy was clearly linked to an appropriate organizational structure and the strong, forceful leadership of John Connelly.

activities (usually production/operations, marketing, finance/accounting, research and development, personnel) as separate functional units within the organization. This specialization encourages greater efficiency and refinement of particular expertise, and allows the firm to seek and foster distinct competencies in one or more functional areas. Expertise is critical to single product/market companies and to firms that are vertically integrated. Strategy in Action 11–1 illustrates Crown, Cork and Seal's shift from a divisional structure to the centralized functional structure that was more consistent with its strategy. The functional structure allowed Crown, Cork and Seal to fine tune its competitive advantage in understanding and responding to the technical needs of customers for "hard-to-hold" beverage containers.

The strategic challenge in the functional structure is effective coordination of the separate functional units. The narrow technical expertise sought through specialization can lead to limited perspectives and different priorities across different functional units. Specialists may not understand problems in other functional areas and may begin to see the firm's strategic issues primarily as "marketing" problems or "production" problems. This potential conflict makes the coordinating role of the chief executive critical if a strategy is to be effectively implemented using the functional structure. Integrating devices such as project teams or planning committees are frequently used in functionally organized businesses to enhance coordination and to facilitate understanding across functional areas.

Divisional Organizational Structure

When a firm diversifies its product/service lines, covers broad geographic areas, utilizes unrelated market channels, or begins to serve distinctly different customer groups, a functional structure rapidly becomes inadequate. For example, functional managers may wind up overseeing the production or marketing of numerous and different products or services. And coordination demands on top management are beyond the capacity of a functional structure. Some form of divisional structure is necessary to meet the coordination and decision-making requirements resulting from increased diversity and size. Such a structure is illustrated in Figure 11–2.

Days Inn's strategy to expand via new geographic markets in the 1970s required it to move from a functional structure to a divisional structure with three geographic divisions. Each division manager had major operating responsibility for company-owned properties in a particular geographic region of the United States. IBM has adopted a divisional organization based on different customer groups. For many years, Ford and General Motors adopted classic divisional structures organized based on product groups.

A divisional structure allows corporate management to delegate authority for the strategic management of a distinct business entity. This can expedite critical decision making within each division in response to varied competitive environments, and it forces corporate management to concentrate on corpo-

Figure 11–2

Divisional organization structure

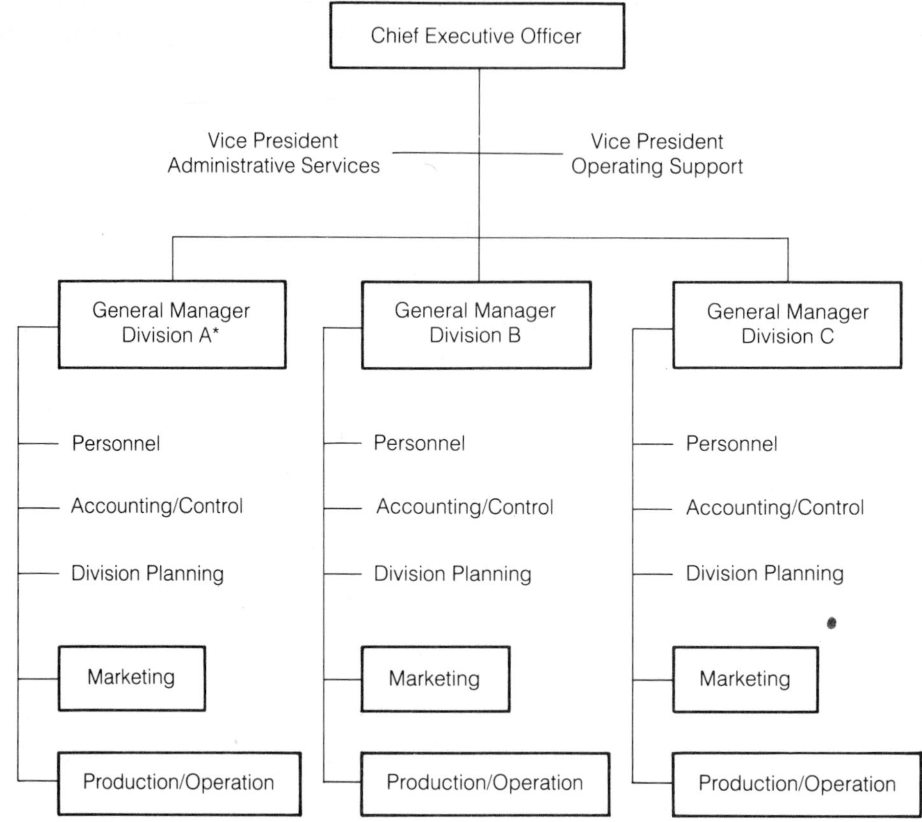

Advantages

1. Forces coordination and necessary authority down to the appropriate level for rapid response.
2. Places strategy development and implementation in closer proximity to the divisions' unique environment.
3. Frees chief executive officer for broader strategic decision making.
4. Sharply focuses accountability for performance.
5. Retains functional specialization within each division.
6. Good training ground for strategic managers.

Disadvantages

1. Fosters potentially dysfunctional competition for corporate-level resources.
2. Problem with the extent of authority given to division managers.
3. Potential for policy inconsistencies between divisions.
4. Problem of arriving at a method to distribute corporate overhead costs that is acceptable to different division managers with profit responsibility.

* The divisions might be for different product lines, geographic segments, distinctly different market channels, or customer groups. The functions included under the manager's domain would then vary depending on how the divisions were defined. For example, divisions based on market channels might not include the manufacturing function which might still be centralized. The same could hold for customer-based divisions. The figure is typical for a manufacturing firm with diverse product lines and/or geographic locations.

rate-level strategic decisions. The semiautonomous divisions are usually given profit responsibility. The divisional structure thus seeks to facilitate accurate assessment of profit and loss.

Strategic Business Units

Some firms encounter difficulty in controlling their divisional operations as the diversity, size, and number of these units continues to increase. And corporate management may encounter difficulty in evaluating and controlling its numerous, often multi-industry divisions. Under these conditions, it may become necessary to add another layer of management, in order to improve strategy implementation, promote synergy, and gain greater control over the diverse business interests. This can be accomplished by grouping various divisions (or parts of some divisions) in terms of common strategic elements. These groups, commonly called strategic business units (SBUs), are usually structured based on the independent product/market segments served by the firm.

Figure 11–3 illustrates an SBU organizational structure. General Electric, faced with massive sales growth but little profit growth in the 1960s, was a pioneer in the SBU organization. GE restructured over 48 divisions into six (sector) SBUs. For example, three separate divisions making food preparation appliances were merged into a single SBU serving the housewares market.[1] General Foods, after originally defining SBUs along product lines (which served overlapping markets), restructured along menu lines. SBUs for breakfast foods, beverages, main meals, desserts, and pet foods allowed General Foods to target specific markets.[2]

Matrix Organization

In large companies, increased diversity leads to numerous product and project efforts, *all with major strategic significance.* The result is a need for an organizational form that provides and controls skills and resources where and when they are most useful. The *matrix organization,* pioneered by firms like defense contractors, construction companies, and large CPA firms, has increasingly been used to meet this need. The list of companies now using some form of matrix organization includes Citicorp, Digital Equipment, General Electric, Shell Oil, Dow Chemical, and Texas Instruments.

The matrix organization provides for dual channels of authority, performance responsibility, evaluation, and control, as shown in Figure 11–4. Essentially, subordinates are assigned to both a basic functional area and a project or product manager. The matrix form is included to combine the advantages

[1] William K. Hall, "SBUs: Hot, New Topic in the Management of Diversification," *Business Horizons,* February 1978, p. 19.

[2] Ibid., p. 19.

Figure 11–3

Strategic business unit organizational structure

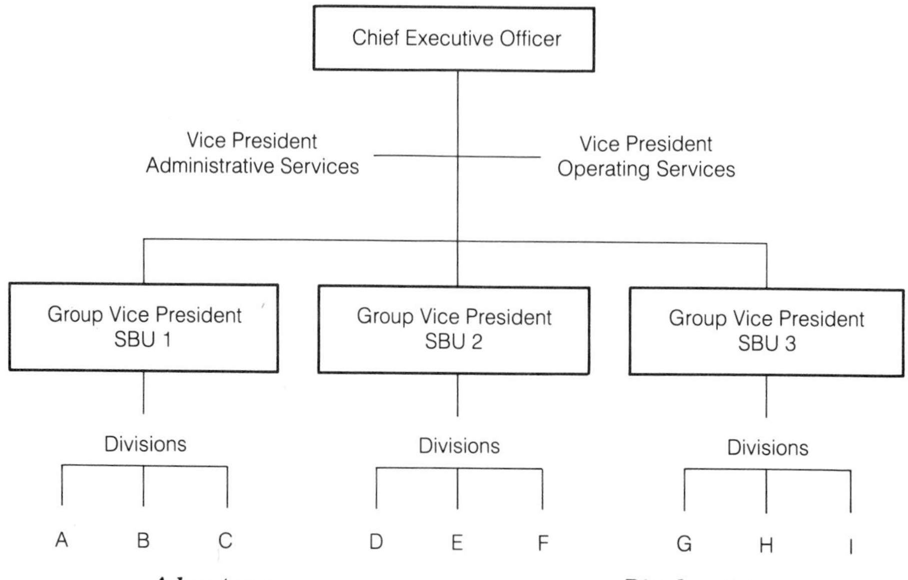

Advantages

1. Improves coordination between divisions with similar strategic concerns and product/market environments.
2. Tightens the strategic management and control of large, diverse business enterprises.
3. Facilitates distinct and in-depth business planning at the corporate and business levels.
4. Channels accountability to distinct business units.

Disadvantages

1. Places another layer of management between the divisions and corporate management.
2. Dysfunctional competition for corporate resources may increase.
3. The role of the group vice president can be difficult to define.
4. Difficulty in defining the degree of autonomy for the group vice presidents and division managers.

of functional specialization and product/project specialization. In theory, the matrix is a conflict resolution system through which strategic and operating priorities are negotiated, power is shared, and resources are allocated internally on a "strongest case for what is best overall for the unit" basis.[3]

The matrix structure increases the number of middle managers exercising general management responsibilities and broadens their exposure to organizationwide strategic concerns. Thus, it can accommodate a varied and changing

[3] Arthur A. Thompson, Jr. and A. J. Strickland III, *Strategy Formulation and Implementation* (Plano, Tex.: Business Publications, 1983), p. 335.

Figure 11–4

Matrix organizational structure

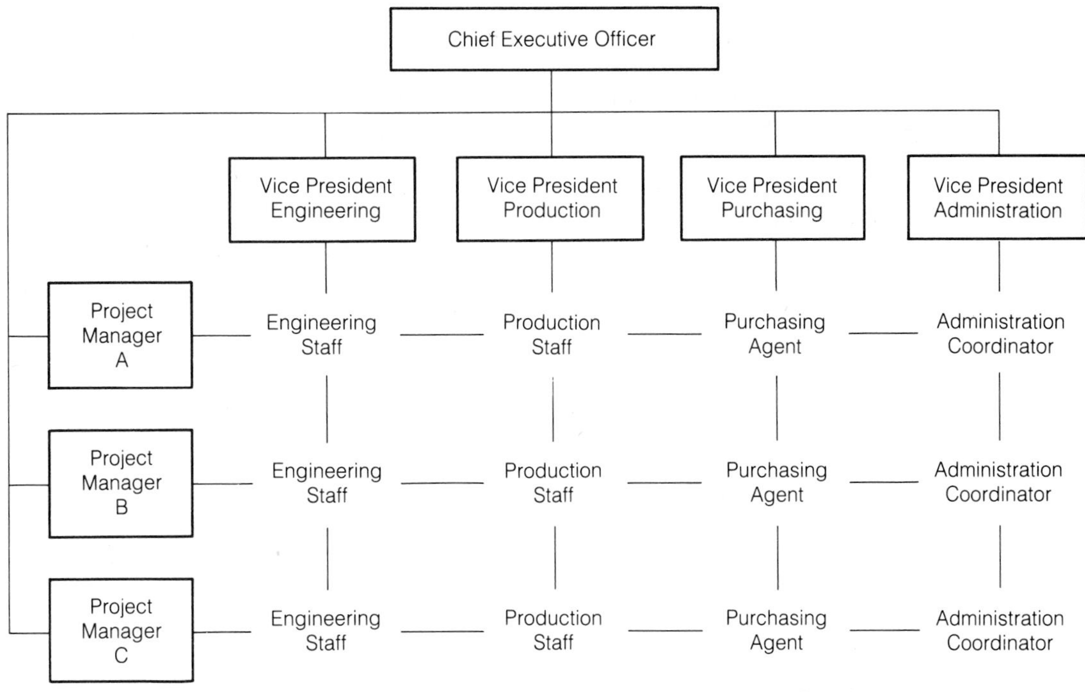

Advantages

1. Accommodates a wide variety of project-orieted business activity.
2. Good training ground for strategic managers.
3. Maximizes efficient use of functional managers.
4. Fosters creativity and multiple sources of diversity.
5. Broader middle-management exposure to strategic issues for the business.

Disadvantages

1. Dual accountability can create confusion and contradictory policies.
2. Necessitates tremendous horizontal and vertical coordination.

project, product/market, or technology focus and increase the efficient use of functional specialists who otherwise might be idle.

Citicorp used the matrix organization to implement an international expansion strategy focusing on both geographically different financial service requirements and at the same time targeting the multinational-corporation market segment. The change was designed to increase the priority given to large, international organizations. Ultimately the strategy gave Citicorp a better understanding of the worldwide financial needs and activities of multinational corporations than even the chief financial officers of these corporations had. Matrix structure was a strategic tool that allowed Citicorp to gain a competitive advantage with this important segment.[4]

While the matrix structure is easy to design, it is difficult to implement. Dual chains of command challenge fundamental organizational orientations. Negotiating shared responsibilities, use of resources, and priorities can create misunderstanding or confusion among subordinates. Strategy in Action 11–2 illustrates the varied reactions in Shell Oil's move to a matrix structure.

To overcome the deficiencies that might be associated with a permanent matrix structure, some firms are using a "temporary" or "flexible" *overlay structure* to accomplish a particular strategic task. This approach, used recently by firms like General Motors, IBM, and Texas Instruments, is meant to take *temporary* advantage of a matrix-type team while preserving the shape and spirit of the underlying divisional structure.[5] Thus, the basic idea of the matrix structure, to *simplify and amplify the focus of resources on a narrow but strategically important product, project, or market,* appears to be an important structural alternative within large, diverse organizations.

The Role of Structure: Linking Structure to Strategy

Which structure is best? Considerable research has been done on this question and the collective answer is that it depends on the strategy of the firm. The structural design ties together key activities and resources of the firm. Therefore, it must be closely aligned with the needs/demands of the firm's strategy.

Alfred Chandler provided a landmark study in understanding the choice of structure as a function of strategy.[6] Chandler studied 70 large corporations over an extended time period and found a common strategy-structure sequence:

1. Choice of a new strategy.
2. Emergence of administrative problems; decline in performance.
3. A shift to an organizational structure more in line with the strategy's needs.
4. Improved profitability and strategy execution.

General Electric's recent history supports Chandler's thesis. Operating with a simple divisional structure in the late 1950s, GE embarked on a broad diversification strategy. In the 1960s, GE experienced impressive sales growth. However, GE also experienced administrative difficulties in trying to control and improve the corresponding lack of increase in profitability. In the early

[4] Paul J. Stonich, *Implementing Strategy* (Cambridge, Mass.: Ballinger, 1982), p. 60.

[5] Robert H. Waterman, T. J. Peter, and J. R. Phillips, "Structure Is Not Organization," *Business Horizons,* June 1980, p. 20.

[6] Alfred D. Chandler, *Strategy and Structure* (Cambridge, Mass.: MIT Press, 1962).

Strategy in Action 11–2

Shell Oil: Matrix Structure to Implement Strategy

Fifteen miles off the coast of Louisiana, a giant platform called Cognac rattles and shakes under the ceaseless activity. Hard-hatted roughnecks are spudding a new well, sending drilling bits twisting 1,200 feet through the choppy waters to reach rich reservoirs of crude oil beneath the Gulf of Mexico's floor. Meanwhile, 60 other wells drilled from the massive midsea factory shoot crude through a ganglion of pipe to onshore refineries. Everything about the Cognac field is imposing. It represents a capital investment of about $800 million and every 24 hours it gushes out an awesome return: 16,000 barrels of oil worth $576,000 at current prices. Cognac, a mere blip on the Shell balance sheets, is a microcosmic example of the stupefying risks and rewards of the modern oil business. Shell, which analysts consider one of the best-run companies in the industry, employs a strategy different from that of competitors. Shell's corporate strategy focuses almost exclusively on the development of energy resources and petrochemicals.

Managing by Matrix. To make and implement the far-reaching decisions this strategy requires, Shell management relies on a matrix system to structure its organization. Like most large corporations, Shell has managers who report to general managers who report to vice presidents. But it also has a network of interlevel, interdivisional teams that try to coordinate the activities of everyone from petroleum engineers to public relations specialists. As a result, more employees participate in decision making and understand the reasons for policies before they are dictated. And in theory, at least, the system helps guard against redundant activities. Instead of maintaining separate research projects for exploration and production, oil products, and chemicals, Shell has a single research division that serves the entire company.

The matrix can be exasperating at times. "We meet ourselves to death," complains Ken Spauling, manager of chemical-products plans. But it reinforces Shell's policy of delegating responsibility to "the level of maximum knowledge." J. B. Henderson, the president of Shell Chemical Co., for instance, doesn't decide whether or not to buy a certain cargo of crude oil for his facilities. "I can't make the decision intelligently," he says. "Someone in the buying department can."

Source: "Inside the Shell Oil Company," *Newsweek*, June 15, 1981, pp. 72–77. Condensed from *Newsweek*.

Figure 11–5

Corporate stages of development

Stage	*Characteristics of the firm*	*Typical structure*
I	Simple, small business. Offering one product/service or one line of products, services to a small, distinct local or regionalized market.	Simple to functional
II	Singular or closely related line of products/services but to a larger and sometimes more diverse market in (geography, channels, or customers)	Functional to divisional
III	Expanded but related lines of products/services to diverse, large markets.	Divisional to matrix
IV	Diverse, unrelated lines of products/services to large, diverse markets.	Divisional to SBUs

1970s, GE executives redesigned its organizational structure to accommodate the administrative needs of strategy (ultimately choosing the strategic-business-unit structure), subsequently improving profitability of and control over the diversification strategy.

Chandler's research and the GE example allow us to make four important observations. First, all forms of organizational structure are not equally effective in implementing a strategy. Second, structures seem to have a life of their own, particularly in larger organizations. As a result, the need for immediate and radical changes in structure is not immediately perceived. Once the need is perceived, lagging performance may be necessary before politically sensitive structure is changed or organizational power redistributed. Third, sheer growth can make restructuring necessary. Finally, as firms diversify into numerous related or unrelated products and markets, structural change appears to be essential if the firm is to perform effectively.

Research on corporate stages of development provides further understanding of the structure-strategy relationship.[7] After studying numerous business firms, these researchers concluded that companies move through several stages as size and diversity increase. Figure 11–5 is a synthesis of these stage-of-development theories. The figure shows that a firm moves through each stage, size, diversity, and competitive environment change.
To compete effectively at different stages requires, among other things, different structures. Again, the choice of structure appears to be contingent upon the strategy of the firm in terms of size, diversity of the products/services offered, and markets served. Two firms in the metal container industry help

[7] Several authors have dealt with stage of development. Some of the more frequently cited include J. T. Cannon, *Business Strategy and Policy* (New York: Harcourt Brace Jovanovich, 1968), pp. 525–28; Malcomb Salter, "Stages of Corporate Development," *Journal of Business Policy* 1, no. 1 (1970), pp. 23–37; Bruce Scott, "Stages of Corporate Development—Part I and II," mimeographed (Boston: Harvard Business School, 1970); and Donald H. Thain, "Stages of Corporate Development," *Business Quarterly,* Winter 1969, pp. 33–45.

illustrate this point. Continental Can, the industry leader, employs a divisional structure. This is used to implement a diversification strategy intended to serve virtually every user of metal containers, as well as to compete in unrelated markets like forest products. Crown, Cork and Seal, the industry's fourth largest company, employs a modified functional structure to serve a limited domestic and international market of users with specialized container needs. Both firms are successful. Both derive their greatest revenues from the same industry. But each employs a different organizational structure because their strategies (narrow versus broad product/market scope) are different.

The choice of structure must be determined by the firm's strategy. And the structure must segment key activities and/or strategic operating units to improve efficiency through specialization, response to a competitive environment, and freedom to act. At the same time, the structure must effectively integrate and coordinate these activities and units to accommodate interdependence of activities and overall control. The choice of structure reflects strategy in terms of the firm's (1) size, (2) product/service diversity, (3) competitive environment and volatility, (4) internal political considerations, and (5) information/coordination needs for each component.

Even a change in strategy, with its accompanying alteration of administrative needs, does not lead to an immediate change in structure. The research of Chandler and others suggests that commitment to a structure lingers even when its become inappropriate for a current strategy.[8] Whether this is due to inertia, organizational politics, or a realistic assessment of the relative costs of immediate structural change, historical evidence suggests that the existing structure will be maintained and not radically redesigned until a strategy's profitability is increasingly disproportionate with increasing sales.[9]

Organizational Leadership

While organizational structure provides the overall framework for strategy implementation, it is not in itself sufficient to ensure successful execution. Within the organizational structure, individuals, groups, and units are the mechanisms of organizational action. And the effectiveness of their actions is a major determinant of successful implementation. In this context, two basic factors encourage or discourage effective action—leadership and culture.[10] This section examines the leadership dimension as a key element

[8] Chandler, *Strategy and Structure;* and J. R. Galbraith and D. A. Nathanson, *Strategy Implementation: The Role of Structure and Process* (St. Paul, Minn.: West Publishing, 1978).

[9] C. W. Hofer; E. A. Murray, Jr.; R. Charan; R. A. Pitts, *Strategic Management* (St. Paul, Minn.: West Publishing, 1984) p. 20.

[10] Leadership and organizational culture are interdependent phenomena. Each aspect of leadership ultimately helps shape organizational culture. Conversely, the prevailing organizational culture can profoundly influence a leader's effectiveness. The richness of this interdependence will become apparent. The topics are addressed in separate sections because it is important to develop an appreciation of the role of each in strategy implementation. Strategy in Action 11–3 gives a vivid illustration of the interdependence of leadership, cultural, and structural considerations in strategy implementation.

Strategy in Action 11–3
Leadership Practices at Intel Corporation

Andrew Grove, founder and president of Intel Corporation, has made a conscious effort to foster informality in the management and decision-making practices of the highly successful microelectronics company he started in 1968. Visible examples of informality are many: no reserved parking, no executive dining rooms, no corporate jets (*everyone* flies coach), rather than offices every manager from the chairman of the board and president on down operates out of a maze of cubicles separated by five-foot-high sound-proofed partitions. A journalist, puzzled by this, once asked Andrew Grove if his company's emphasis on visible signs of egalitarianism was just so much affectation. Grove replied that it was not affectation but a matter of survival and offered the following explanation:

> In traditional industries where the chain of command is precisely defined, a person making a certain kind of decision is a person occupying a particular position on an organization chart. As the saying goes, authority (to make decisions) goes with responsibility (position in the management hierarchy). In businesses that deal mostly with information and know-how, however, a manager has to cope with a new phenomenon. Here a rapid divergence develops between power based on position and power based on knowledge. The divergence occurs because the base of knowledge that constitutes the foundation of the business changes rapidly.
>
> What do I mean? When someone graduates from college with a technical education, at that time and for the next several years that person will be very up-to-date in the technology of the time. Hence, he possesses a good deal of knowledge-based power in the organization that hires him. If he does well, he will be promoted, and as the years pass his position power will grow. At the same time, his intimate familarity with current technology will fade. Put another way, even if today's veteran manager was once an outstanding engineer, he is not now the technical expert he once was. At high-technology firms, we managers get a little more obsolete every day.
>
> So a business like ours has to employ a management process unlike that used in more conventional industries. If we had people at the top making all the decisions, then these decisions would be made by those unfamiliar with the technology of the day. In general, the faster the change in the know-how on which a business depends, the greater the divergence between knowledge and position power is likely to be.
>
> Since our business depends on what it knows to survive, we mix "knowledge-power people" with "position-power people" daily, so that together they make the decisions that will affect us for years to come. We at Intel

frequently ask junior members of the organization to participate jointly in a decision-making meeting with senior managers. This only works if everybody at the meeting voices opinions and beliefs as equals, forgetting or ignoring status differentials. And it is much easier to achieve this if the organization doesn't separate its senior and junior people with limousines, plush offices, and private dining rooms. Status symbols do not promote the flow of ideas, facts, and points of view. So while our egalitarian environment may appear to be a matter of style, it is really a matter of necessity, a matter of long-term survival.

This idea of mixing knowledge-based and position-based power underlines the quality circle movement and the participative management concept. The real benefit of the quality circle movement, the participative management concept, and our informality at work is not cosmetic, nor is it really to make people feel better (although that is not a bad consequence, either). It is to team up people with hands-on knowledge with those in positions of power to create the best solutions in the interest of both.

Source: "Breaking the Chains of Command," *Newsweek,* October 3, 1983, p. 23. Condensed from *Newsweek.*

in strategy implementation. In the next section, the importance of organizational culture in effectively executing strategy will be illustrated and discussed.

Leadership, while seemingly vague and esoteric, is an essential element in effective strategy implementation. And two leadership issues are of fundamental importance here: (1) the role of the chief executive officer (CEO), and (2) the assignment of key managers.

Role of the CEO

The chief executive officer is the catalyst in strategic management. This individual is most closely identified with and ultimately accountable for a strategy's success. In most firms, particularly larger ones, CEOs spend up to 80 percent of their time developing and guiding strategy.

The nature of the CEO's role is both *symbolic* and *substantive* in strategy implementation. First, the CEO is a symbol of the new strategy. This individual's actions and the perceived seriousness of his or her commitment to a chosen strategy, particularly if the strategy represents a major change, exert a significant influence on the intensity of subordinate managers' commitment to implementation. Lee Iaccoca's highly visible role in the early 1980s as spokesperson for the "New Chrysler Corporation" on television, in Chrysler factories and offices, and before securities analysts was intended to provide a strong symbol that Chrysler's desperate turnaround strategy could work.

Second, the firm's mission, strategy, and key long-term objectives are strongly influenced by the personal goals and values of its CEO. To the extent that the CEO invests time and personal values in the chosen strategy, he or she represents an important source for clarification, guidance, and adjustment during implementation.

Major changes in strategy are often preceded or quickly followed by a change in CEO. The timing suggests that different strategies require different CEOs if they are to succeed. The resignation of L. M. Clymer as CEO at Holiday Inns clearly illustrates this point. Holiday Inns' executive group was convinced that casinos provide a key growth area for the company. Clymer chose to resign because his personal values and perception of what Holiday Inns should be were not consistent with this change. Research has concluded that a successful turnaround stragegy "will require almost without exception either a change in top management or a substantial change in the behavior of the existing management team."[11] Clearly, successful strategy implementation is directly linked to the unique characteristics, orientation, and actions of the CEO.

Assignments of Key Managers

A major concern of top management in implementing a strategy, particularly if it involves a major change, is that the right managers are in the right positions for the new strategy. Of all the tools for ensuring successful implementation, this is the one CEOs mention first. Confidence in the individuals occupying pivotal managerial positions is directly and positively correlated with top-management expectations that a strategy can be successfully executed.

This confidence is based on the answers to two fundamental questions:

1. Who holds the current leadership positions that are especially critical to strategy execution?
2. Do they have the right characteristics to ensure that the strategy will be effectively implemented?[12]

What characteristics are most important in this context? It would be impossible to specify this precisely, but probable characteristics include: (1) ability and education, (2) previous track record and experience, and (3) personality and temperament.[13] These, combined with gut feeling and top managers' confidence in the individual, provide the basis for this key decision.

Recently, numerous attempts have been made to match "preferred" manage-

---

[11] Charles W. Hofer, "Turnaround Strategies," *Journal of Business Strategy* 1, no. 1 (1980), p. 25.

[12] William F. Glueck, *Business Policy and Strategic Management* (New York: McGraw-Hill, 1980), pp. 306–7.

[13] Ibid., p. 307.

rial characteristics with different grand strategies.[14] These efforts are meant to capsulize, for example, the behavioral characteristics appropriate for a manager responsible for implementing an "invest to grow" strategy in contrast to those for a manager implementing a "harvest" strategy. Despite widespread theoretical discussion of this idea, two recent studies covering a broad sample of companies did not find a single firm that matched managerial characteristics to strategic mission in a formal manner. However, they did find several firms addressing such considerations in an informal, intuitive manner.[15] The following comment summarizes these findings:

> Despite the near unanimity of belief that, for effective implementation, different strategies require different skills . . . many corporate executives avoid too rigid an approach to matching managerial characteristics and strategy [for three reasons]: (1) exposure to and experience at managing different kinds of strategies and businesses is viewed as an essential component of managerial development; (2) too rigid a differentiation is viewed as much more likely to result in some managers being typecast as "good builders" and some others as "good harvesters," thereby creating motivational problems for the latter; and (3) a "perfect match" between managerial characteristics and strategy is viewed as more likely to result in overcommitment [or] self-fulfilling prophecies (a harvester becoming *only* a harvester) as compared with a situation where there was some mismatch.[16]

One practical consideration in making key managerial assignments when implementing strategy is whether to emphasize current (or promotable) executives or bring in new personnel. This is obviously a difficult, sensitive, and strategic issue. Figure 11–6 highlights major advantages and disadvantages associated with either alternative.

While key advantages and disadvantages can be clearly outlined, actual assignment varies with the situation and the decision maker. Two fundamental aspects of the strategic situation strongly influence the managerial assignment decision: (1) the changes required to implement the new strategy, and (2) the effectiveness of past organizational performance. Figure 11–7 and the following discussion illustrate how these aspects might affect managerial assignments.

Turnover Situation. A company's performance has been ineffective for several years. The new strategy and the organizational requirements necessary

---

[14] See, for example, J. G. Wisseman, H. W. Van der Pol, and H. M. Messer, "Strategic Management Archtypes," *Strategic Management Journal* 1, no. 1 (1980), pp. 37–45; William F. Glueck and Lawrence R. Jauch, *Strategic Management and Business Policy* (New York: McGraw-Hill, 1984), p. 365; Boris Yavitz and William H. Newman, *Strategy in Action* (New York: Free Press, 1982), p. 167; and "Wanted, A Manager to Fit Each Strategy," *Business Week*, February 25, 1980, p. 166.

[15] Anil Gupta and V. Govindarajan, "Build, Hold, Harvest: Converting Strategic Intentions Into Reality," *Journal of Business Strategy*, Winter, 1984, p. 41; Peter Lorange, "The Human Resource Dimension in the Strategic Planning Process," mimeographed Sloan School, M.I.T. 1983, p. 13.

[16] Gupta and Govindarajan, "Build, Hold, Harvest," p. 41.

Figure 11–6

Key considerations in managerial assignments to implement strategy

	Advantages	Disadvantages
Using existing executives to implement a new strategy	Already know key people, practices, and conditions Personal qualities better known and understood by associates Have established relationships with peers, subordinates, suppliers, buyers, etc. Symbolizes organizational commitment to individual careers	Less adaptable to major strategic changes because of knowledge, attitudes, and values Past commitments may hamper hard decisions required in executing a new strategy Less ability to become inspired and credibly convey the need for change
Bringing in outsiders to implement a new strategy	Outsider may already believe in and have "lived" the new strategy. Outsider is unemcumbered by internal commitments to people. Outsider comes to the new assignment with heightened commitment and enthusiasm. Bringing in an outsider can send powerful signals throughout the organization that change is expected.	Often costly, both in terms of compensation and "learning-to-work-together" time Candidates suitable in all respects (i.e., exact experience) may not be available, leading to compromise choices Uncertainty in selecting the right person The "morale" costs when an outsider takes a job several insiders wanted "What to do with poor ol' Fred" problem

Source: Adapted from Boris Yavitz and William H. Newman, *Strategy in Action* (New York: Free Press, 1982), Chapter 10; and Paul J. Stonich, *Implementing Strategy* (Cambridge, Mass.: Ballinger, 1982), Chapter 4.

Figure 11–7

Four managerial assignment situations

Changes required to implement the new strategy		Effective	Ineffective
	Many	"Selective blend" *Current executives* via promotion and transfer where skills match new roles; otherwise, seek skills and experience via *outsiders*	"Turnover" *Outsiders* should be a high priority to provide new skills, motivation, and enthusiasm.
	Few	"Stability" *Current executives* and internal promotions should be a major emphasis in order to reward, retain, and develop managerial talent.	"Reorientation" *Outsiders* are important to replace weaknesses and "communication seriousness." *Current executives* should be a priority where possible via promotion, transfer, or role clarification.

Assessment of past organizational performance

to implement it represent major changes from the "way things have been done in the past." In this situation, the advantages of bringing in outside managers can be maximized. Because the experience necessary to implement the new strategy is unavailable or ineffective internally, outsiders are sought. Current executives may react defensively when faced with major changes, while outsiders generally undertake a new assignment with a positive commitment to the new direction and are not encumbered by internal commitments to people. Widespread changes will also be taken more seriously by employees if outsiders are brought in who possess skills that match the changes and supplement well-known inadequacies in current management.

Chrysler Corporation's situation in the early 1980s is a case in point. Following several years of ineffective, declining performance, Chrysler's board went outside the organization to recruit a new CEO (Lee Iaccoca) who was capable of redirecting Chrysler into a small-car-oriented strategy. Iacocca eventually brought in outsiders to fill over 80 percent of Chrysler's top management positions because they had the new skills and commitment necessary to quickly and decisively implement Chrysler's new strategy.

Selective Blend. A different emphasis in key managerial assignments is needed when a company's new strategy requires major changes but the need for change is not based on poor performance. The company has been an effective performer with its previous strategy yet changing market, competitive, technological, or other environmental factors necessitate a change in the company's strategic posture. IBM's move into the personal computer industry is a good illustration.

The advantages and disadvantages associated with either source of managerial talent are applicable in this situation. Using existing executives rewards past effectiveness and takes advantage of the knowledge of "people practices" and relationships necessary to integrate changes into a previously successful system. It also reinforces the company's commitment to individual careers and facilitates executive development. On the other hand, the outsider brings all the advantages described in Figure 11–6, especially skill and experience in one or more of the key change areas. But there is a critical difference—the past performance of this company. Thus, the advantage of the outsider as a "change agent" is much less important than his or her value as a provider of the key skills needed to *supplement* current management talent. Emphasis in this situation is a selective blend using current or promotable executives while objectively incorporating outsiders to provide needed knowledge and skill that is not available internally.

IBM's move into personal computers required major changes in the firm's past, highly successful market-development strategy. IBM needed to sell and service a small computer primarily for numerous individual and small-business users. This was quite different from what was needed to lease or sell expensive computer systems and office equipment to large public and private organizations. IBM used existing talent to implement this small-computer strategy. Use of outsiders was primarily related to the development of direct retail outlets, a sales approach not used with past IBM products, but critical to ensure IBM's long-term, profitable access to a broad, fragmented, and individualized market. So IBM sought to selectively blend its "inside/outside" emphasis in new managerial assignments consistent with the key advantages of each approach.

Stability. A stability situation is generally attractive in managing executive assignments. The company's past performance has been effective and implementation requires only minor deviation from "the ways things were done in the past." The advantages associated with using current and promotable existing executives are maximized. These executives are familiar with people, practices, and the ways to get things done. They have established relationships with suppliers, buyers, peers, and subordinates. Past performance indicates that the managers have achieved assigned results. This is recognized through assignment to new responsibilities associated with the new strategy. In this situation, junior-level managers can be developed because there is an effective performance environment within which they will observe and acquire managerial and technical skills. The risk in this situation is that there are fewer opportunities to advance talented personnel who contributed to past effectiveness because change was minor and retaining the current executive teams was emphasized.

Wendy's hamburger chain was a firm facing this situation in the early 1980s. The firm had been quite effective carving a profitable niche in the fast-food industry. Its new strategy for the 1980s sought to emphasize three things: market penetration, product development, and diversification via Sister's Chicken 'n Biscuits. While this was an aggressive new strategy, the changes required were relatively minor: market penetration necessitated a slight shift in Wendy's franchising approach; product development efforts were well underway; and the Sister's chicken implementation plan would be modeled exactly after the Wendy's approach in the hamburger segment. Wendy's assignment of managerial positions emphasized the use of current management. The Sister's venture was seen as an ideal way to open up career opportunities for talented operating personnel. By 1984, 30 of the 37 members of Wendy's executive committee (its "top management team") were new, but only 2 of the 30 new members can from outside the Wendy's organization.

Reorientation. Some companies face a situation in which the fundamental changes required to implement a new strategy are minor—the basic strategy appears appropriate—yet past performance has been ineffective. With IBM at the top of the personal computer market in early 1984, the former leader Apple, was in just such a situation. Its new strategy was an attempt to refocus on its formerly successful product development strategy by making key (yet relative few) organizational changes. For example, Steven Jobs (Apple's cofounder) sought to reinvigorate research and development efforts by personal involvement. Key managerial assignments in marketing and finance were filled from outside the company to systematically reorient Apple's competitive posture against IBM. Apple added a new CEO from outside the organization to oversee this effort. At the same time, Apple sought to transfer and clarify the roles of several current managers, particularly younger managers with product development skills, to aid in reinvigorating Apple's technological reputation.

Apple is an example of a company with a sound strategy but ineffective implemention. A key issue in this context is whether the ineffectiveness can be linked to inadequate skills or capabilities of the management team. If such inadequacies are found, outsiders could play a key role in reorienting or refocusing organizational efforts toward an otherwise sound strategy.

Organizational Culture

Every organization has its own culture. Organizational culture is similar to an individual's personality—an intangible yet ever-present theme that provides meaning, direction, and the basis for action. Culture is the shared values, beliefs, expectations, and norms learned by becoming a part of and working in a company over time. Much as personality influences the behavior of an individual, shared values and beliefs within a company set a pattern for activities, opinions, and actions within that firm. A company's culture influences how employees and managers approach problems, serve customers, deal with suppliers, react to competitors, and otherwise conduct activities *now and in the future.* Comparing the success of Japanese and American automakers, Robert Waterman vividly illustrated the importance of culture:

> It has not been just strategy that led to big Japanese wins in the American auto market. It is a culture that enspirits workers to excel at fits and finishes, to produce moldings that match and doors that don't sag. It is a culture in which Toyota can use that most sophisticated of management tools, the suggestion box, and in two years increase the number of worker suggestions from under 10,000 to over 1 million with resultant savings of $250 million.[17]

The Strategy-Culture Connection

Culture gives employees a sense of how to behave, what they should do, and where to place priorities in getting the job done. Culture helps employees *fill in the gaps* between what is formally decreed and what actually takes place. As such, culture is of critical importance in the implementation of strategy.

A company's culture can be a major strength when it is consistent with strategy and thus can be a powerful driving force in implementation. The following examples at IBM and Delta Airlines illustrate how a supportive culture enhances employee efforts in implementing strategy:

> Delta Airlines has emphasized a market development strategy with a focus on customer service that requires a high degree of teamwork. Employees have become very receptive to substituting in other jobs to keep planes flying, baggage moving, and reservations confirmed. A simple story told in a recent book illustrates the degree to which these values are [inculcated] at Delta: A woman inadvertently missed out on a "Super Saver" ticket because the family had moved and, owing to a technicality, the ticket price was no longer valid. She called to complain. Delta's president intervened personally and, being there at the time, met her at the gate to give her the new ticket.[18]

> IBM's strategy in business machines has had as its basic premise offering unparalleled service to customers. A customer's explanation of his decision to choose IBM in a major computer system purchase for a hospital illustrates how values reinforcing this strategy permeate IBM employees: "Many of the others were ahead of IBM in technological wizardry. And heaven knows their software is easier to use. But IBM alone took the trouble to get to know us. They interviewed

---

[17] Robert H. Waterman, Jr., "The Seven Elements of Strategic Fit," *Journal of Business Strategy* 2, no. 3 (1982), p. 70.

[18] Thomas J. Peters and Robert H. Waterman, Jr., *In Search of Excellence* (New York: Harper & Row, 1982), p. xxi.

> extensively up and down the line. They talked our language, no mumbo jumbo on computer innards. Their price was fully 25 percent higher. But they provided unparalleled guarantees of reliability and service. They even went so far as to arrange a backup connection with a local steel company in case our system crashed. Their presentations were to the point. Everything about them smacked of assurance and success. Our decision, even with severe budget pressure, was really easy.[19]

At both IBM and Delta Airlines, the values *(culture)* that drive employee behavior are fully consistent with the "service-driven" strategies of the companies.

The opposite can occur. A culture can prevent a company from meeting competitive threats or adapting to changing economic or social environments that a new strategy is designed to overcome. One widely cited example is AT&T. AT&T adopted a marketing-oriented strategy for the 1980s to replace its service- and public-utility-oriented strategy. This new strategy was chosen in response to antitrust pressures, the Federal Communications Commission's decision to allow other companies to sell products in AT&T's once-captive markets, and the unregulated competition in the emerging telecommunications industry. AT&T has now labored for several years to behave like a marketing company, but with marginal success. Efforts to serve different market segments in different ways have run afoul of the strong values, beliefs, and norms managers have imbibed since the turn of the century—that it's important to furnish telephone service to everybody, and that you do so by not discriminating too much among different kinds of customers.[20] The solution seems obvious: change the culture. Changing the orientation of approximately 1 million employees is not easy.

A similar experience in the oil industry was reported in *Business Week:*

> Five years ago the chief executives of two major oil companies determined that they would have to diversify out of oil because their current business could not support long-term growth and faced serious political threats. Not only did they announce their new long-range strategies to employees and the public, but they established elaborate plans to implement them. Each of the CEOs was unable to implement his strategy, not because it was theoretically wrong or bad, but because neither had understood that his company's culture was so entrenched in the traditions and values of doing business as oilmen that employees resisted (and sabotaged) the radical changes that the CEOs tried to impose. Oil operations require long-term investments for long-term rewards; but the new businesses needed short-term views and an emphasis on current returns. Successes had come from hitting it big in wildcatting, but the new success was to be based on such abstractions as market share or numbers growth—all seemingly nebulous concepts to them.[21]

---

[19] Ibid., p. xx.

[20] "The Corporate Culture Vultures," *Fortune,* October 17, 1983, p. 66.

[21] "Corporate Culture," *Business Week,* October 27, 1980, p. 148.

After several years of pursuing diversification strategies, both companies are firmly back in the oil business and the two CEOs have been replaced. *Business Week* analysts attributed each strategy's failure to the idea that "implementing them violated employees' basic beliefs about their roles in the company and the traditions that underlie the companies' cultures."[22]

These examples help demonstrate the important role of culture in institutionalizing a company's strategy. As a consequence, managing culture to successfully implement a strategy is critical. The issue is simple to state yet exceedingly difficult to effect. Strategy in Action 11–4 illustrates this difficulty at Apple Computer. Efforts to understand culture and improve strategy-culture consistency are enhanced if the factors that shape culture are identified. Managing those factors to improve the match between strategy and culture should also be examined.

Factors that Shape Culture

Defining culture as the shared values of organizational members may effectively communicate the concept. But this definition does not provide a measurable basis from which managers can assess the need for adjusting, changing, or reinforcing a company's culture. And in the 1980s, numerous consulting firms pay a great deal of attention to the need for an operational basis to assess a company's culture. All approaches seem to have one thing in common: rather than trying to assess culture directly, culture is best "measured" if viewed as the product of selected factors common to all organizations.

The consulting firm of McKinsey & Co. has popularized what it calls the "7-S® Framework" which suggests that an organization's culture is the product of seven broad factors: (1) *strategy,* (2) *structure,* (3) the *systems* (information, manufacturing processes, budgeting, and performance measurement are examples) that involve how things get done from day to day, (4) the *styles* as evidenced by the behavior of management, (5) *staffing,* the people demographics of the company (engineers versus skilled technicians versus blue collar, labor versus office and clerical employees, age, male versus female, length of service, and so on), (6) the degree to which people in the organization have (or don't have) *shared values* both organizational and personal such that there are bonds of compatibility and a spirit of who they are and where they are headed, and (7) the main *skills,* capabilities, and distinctive competence of the organization as a whole.[23] Management Analysis Center, Inc., another consulting firm that deals extensively with corporate culture, has tried to simplify the cultural equation by linking culture to three broad factors: structure, systems, and people.[24]

---

[22] Ibid., p. 148.

[23] Waterman, "Seven Elements of Strategic Fit," p. 71; Thompson and Strickland, *Strategy Formulation,* p. 384. The alliteration (strategy, structure, systems, style, staff, shared values, and skills) is an intentional aid to memory.

[24] Stonich, *Implementing Strategy,* p. 32.

Strategy in Action 11–4

Can Corporate Counterculture Survive at Apple?

The great success of Apple Computer Inc. is due to more than just having the right product at the right time. It is also the result of the company's homespun, entrepreneurial corporate culture. And as the personal computer maker launches its counterattack on market leader IBM, Apple management recognizes that its most important challenge will be to retain that small-company culture even though its sales rate has zoomed past $1 billion annually.

"What we don't want to lose is the special culture Apple has, even though Apple is going to look a lot different over the next year," says President John Sculley. "Failure for us doesn't mean going out of business," he says, but rather finding that Apple is not "a great place to work anymore." The informal attire of Apple's youthful staff reflects an underlying attitude that gives far more weight to doing an interesting, important job than to possessing the trappings of power. At Apple, Sculley explains, "small teams doing great things have a higher priority than the hierarchy of management."

The spirit of Apple is mostly a reflection of Steven P. Jobs, the company's mercurial 28-year-old chairman and cofounder. Jobs, a college dropout, brought to Apple a blunt style of communication, a dislike for hierarchy and rules, and a bias in favor of "a small, madcap group of brilliant guys producing something in a corner on a very tight deadline," says former Apple executive John D. Couch. Adds William "Trip" Hawkins, now president of software publisher Electronic Arts Inc.: "Steve used to say that the reason we're going to blow IBM away is because we're unprofessional. 'Professional' was a word he used to spit out like an insult." Such unconventionality attracted other bright, young people who felt stifled in more traditional computer companies.

Scully says that he is determined not to sacrifice the attractive aspects of the culture as he imposes more control and structure on the company. He hopes to strike the delicate balance between creative ferment and discipline "by making the product divisions smaller." But seasoned observers of corporate culture warn that Sculley's task will not be easy. "A billion-dollar corporation trying to act like a $30-million company is just plain contradictory," says one consultant. "But," he added, "I hope Sculley succeeds."

Based on the article "Can Apple's Corporate Counterculture Survive?" from the January 16, 1984, issue of *Business Week*.

Shifting the emphasis from the broad concept to these seven (or three) determinants focuses attention on the specific factors that shape culture. These factors are also the central elements a business must use in implementing strategy. Structural adjustments, management systems, core skills, and people resources are key factors in strategy implementation and provide the basis for managing the strategy-culture relationship. The question that must be dealt with is whether the "fit" between these factors is consistent with the implementation requirements of the chosen strategy, as discussed below.

Managing the Strategy-Culture Relationship

Managers have a difficult time thinking through the relationship between culture and the critical factors on which strategy depends. They quickly recognize, however, that key components of the company—structure, staff, systems, people, style—influence the way key managerial tasks are executed and critical management relationships are formed. Culture is the product of these components. And strategy implementation is largely concerned with adjustments in these components to accommodate the perceived needs of the new strategy. So managing the strategy-culture relationship requires sensitivity to the interaction between the changes necessary to implement strategy and the compatibility or "fit" between those changes and the organization's culture. Figure 11–8 provides a simple but useful framework for managing the strategy-culture relationship by identifying four basic situations a company might face.

Figure 11–8

Managing the strategy-culture relationship

Changes in key organizational factors that are necessary to implement the new strategy	High	Low
Many	Link changes to basic mission and fundamental organizational norms (1)	Reformulate strategy or prepare carefully for long-term, difficult change (4)
Few	(2) Synergistic—Focus on reinforcing culture	(3) Manage around the culture

Potential compatibility of changes with existing culture

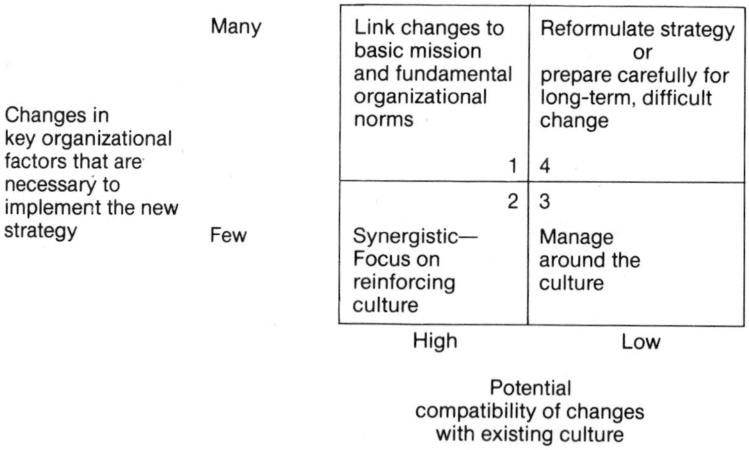

Link to Mission. A company in *cell 1* faces implementing a new strategy that requires several changes in structure, systems, managerial assignments, operating procedures, or other fundamental aspects of the organization. At the same time, most of the changes are potentially compatible with the existing organizational culture. Companies in this situation are usually those with a tradition of effective performance that are either seeking to take advantage of a major opportunity or attempting to redirect major product/market operations consistent with core, proven capabilities. Such companies are in a very promising position: they can pursue a strategy requiring major changes but still benefit from the power of cultural reinforcement.

Companies seeking to manage a strategy—culture relationship in this context need to emphasize four basic considerations. First, *key changes must be visibly linked to the basic company mission.* The mission provides a broad official foundation for the organizational culture. Therefore, top executives should use every internal and external forum available to reinforce the message that the changes are inextricably linked to the fundamental company mission. Second, *emphasis should be placed on using existing personnel* where possible to fill positions created in implementing the strategy. Existing personnel carry with them the shared values and norms that help ensure cultural compatibility as major changes are implemented. Third, *care must be taken if adjustments are needed in the reward system.* These should be consistent with currently rewarded behavior. If, for example, a new product/market thrust requires significant changes in the way sales are made and therefore in incentive compensation, common themes (e.g., incentive-oriented) must be emphasized. In this way, current and future approaches are related and the changes are justified (encourage development of less familiar markets). Fourth, *key attention should be paid to changes that are least compatible with current culture* so that current norms are not disrupted. For example, a company may choose to subcontract an important step in a production process because the process would be incompatible with current culture.

IBM's strategy in entering the personal computer market is an illustration. The strategy required numerous organizational changes to serve a radically different market. To maintain maximum compatibility with its existing culture, IBM went to considerable public and internal effort to link its new with PC's the corporation's long-standing mission. The message relating the PC to IBM's tradition of top-quality service appeared almost daily on television and in magazines. Internally, every IBM manager was given PC. The corporation also emphasized the use of IBM personnel where feasible to fill new positions. But because production requirements were not compatible with current operations, IBM subcontracted virtually all manufacturing for the PC.

Maximize Synergy. A company in *cell 2* is in the enviable position of needing only a few organizational changes to implement a new strategy; and those changes are potentially quite compatible with the current culture. A company in this position should emphasize two broad themes: (1) *take advantage of this situation to reinforce and solidify the company's culture;* and (2) *use this time of relative stability to remove organizational roadblocks to the desired culture.* Holiday Inns' move into casino gambling required few major organizational changes for the parent company. Casinos were seen as resort locations requiring lodging, dining, and gambling/entertainment services. Holiday Inns had only to incorporate gambling/entertainment expertise into its management team which otherwise had the complete capability to manage the lodging and dining requirements of casino (or any other) resort locations. This single, major change was successfully inculcated in part by selling it internally as completely compatible with Holiday Inns' mission to provide high-quality accommodations for business and leisure travelers. The resignation of then CEO Roy Clymer removed one final organization roadblock, legitimizing a culture that prided itself on quality service to the middle-to-upper income business traveler rather than one that placed its highest priority on family-oriented service. The latter value was fast disappearing from the Holiday Inns' culture with the encouragement of most of Holiday Inns' top management, but was not yet fully sanctioned because of personal beliefs shared by Clymer. His voluntary departure helped solidify the new values top management wanted.

Manage around the Culture. A company in *cell 3* must make a few major organizational changes to implement its new strategy. At the same time, these changes are potentially inconsistent with current organizational culture. The critical question for this firm is whether these changes can be made with a reasonable chance for success.

Consider, for example, a multibillion-dollar industry leader facing several major threats to its record of outstanding growth and profitability. To meet these threats, considerable effort is made to design a new organizational structure around major markets. After formally assessing the "cultural risks" of such a change, the proposal is rejected as too radical and too inconsistent with the company's functional culture. A positive alternative is available. Planning and coordination personnel can be increased to *manage around the culture* in implementing the strategy.[25] This can be an important means of implementation if a company faces changing a factor (like structure) that is inextricably linked to the organization's culture.

Several alternatives can facilitate managing around culture: create a separate company or division; use task forces, teams, or program coordinators; subcontract; bring in an outsider; or sell out. These are a few of the alternatives available, but the key idea is to create an alternative method of achieving

[25] Howard Schwartz and Stanley M. Davis, "Matching Corporate Culture and Business Strategy," *Organizational Dynamics,* Summer 1981, p. 43.

the change desired without directly confronting the incompatible cultural norms. As cultural resistance diminishes, the change may be absorbed into the organization.

Rich's is a highly successful, quality-oriented department store serving higher-income customers in several southeastern locations. With Sears and K mart experiencing rapid growth in mid-to-lower-priced merchandise in the 1970s, Rich's decided to serve this market as well. Finding such merchandise inconsistent with the successful values and norms (a quality-merchandise, customer-service-oriented culture) of its traditional business, Rich's created a separate business called Richway to tap this growth area in retailing. Rich's found it necessary and appropriate to create an entire new store network to *manage around its culture.* Both businesses have since flourished, based in part on radically different cultures.

Reformulate. A company in *cell 4* faces the most difficult challenge in managing the strategy-culture relationship. The company must make numerous organizational changes to implement its new strategy. But the number and nature of the changes are incompatible with the current, usually entrenched, values and norms. AT&T, discussed earlier in this chapter, illustrates the substantial dilemma faced by a firm in this situation. Like AT&T, the company in this situation faces the awesome challenge of changing its culture—a complex, expensive, often long-term proposition. It is a challenge numerous organizational culture consultants say borders on an impossibility.[26] Strategy in Action 11–5 describes the decade-long experience at PepsiCo that was necessary to change its culture.

When faced with massive change and cultural resistance, a company should first examine whether strategy reformulation is appropriate. Is it really necessary to change many of the fundamental organizational factors? Can the changes be made with any real expectation that they will be acceptable and successful? If the answer to these questions is no, the business should seriously reconsider and reformulate its strategic plan. In other words, the strategy that the firm can realistically implement must be one that is more consistent with established organizational norms and practices. Merrill Lynch & Co. provides a recent example of a firm that faced this dilemma. Seeking to remain number one in the newly deregulated financial services industry, Merrill Lynch chose to pursue a new, product development strategy in its brokerage business. The success of this strategy depends on Merrill Lynch's traditional, service-oriented brokerage network becoming sales and marketing oriented in order to sell a broader range of investment products to a more diverse customer base. Initial efforts to implement this strategy generated substantial resistance from Merrill Lynch's highly successful brokerage network. The

[26] "Corporate Culture Vultures," p. 72.

Strategy in Action 11–5

The Pepsi Challenge: Creating an Aggressive Culture to Match an Aggressive Strategy

For decades, Coke's unchallenged position in the cola market was so complete that the brand name Coke became synonymous with cola drinks. It attained this distinction under Robert W. Woodruff, who served as chief executive for 32 years and was still chairman of the company's finance committee at age 90. Woodruff had an "almost messianic drive to get Coca-Cola [distributed] all over the world," according to Harvey Z. Yazijian, coauthor of *The Cola Wars*. So successful was Coke in accomplishing this under Woodruff and later J. Paul Austin, that Coca-Cola became known as "America's second State Department." Its trademark became a symbol of American life itself.

"A real problem in the past," said Yazijian, "was that they had a lot of deadwood" among employees. Nevertheless, Coke's marketing and advertising were extremely effective in expanding consumption of the product. But the lack of serious competition and the company's relative isolation in its hometown of Atlanta allowed it to become "fat, dumb, and happy," according to one consultant. Coke executives are known to be extremely loyal to the company and circumspect to the point of secrecy in their dealings with the outside world.

In the mid-1950s, Pepsi, once a sleepy, New York–based bottler with a lame slogan, "Twice as much for a nickel too," began to develop into a serious threat under the leadership of Chairman Alfred N. Steele. The movement gathered momentum, and by the early 1970s, the company had become a ferocious competitor under chairman Donald M. Kendall and President Andrall E. Pearson, a former director of [the consulting firm] McKinsey & Co. The culture that these two executives determined to create was based on the goal of becoming the number one marketer of soft drinks.

Severe pressure was put on managers to show continual improvement in market share, product volume, and profits. "Careers ride on tenths of a market share point," offered John Sculley, a Pepsi vice president. This atmosphere pervades the company's nonbeverage units as well. "Everyone knows that if the results aren't there, you had better have your resume up-to-date," says a former snack-food manager.

To keep everyone on their toes, a "creative tension" is continually nurtured among departments at Pepsi, says another former executive. The staff is kept lean and managers are moved to new jobs constantly, which results in people working long hours and engaging in political maneuvering "just to keep their jobs from being reorganized out from under them," says a headhunter.

Kendall himself sets a constant example. He once resorted to using a snowmobile to get to work in a blizzard, demonstrating the ingenuity and dedication to work he expects from his staff. This type of pressure has pushed many managers out. But a recent company survey shows that others thrive under such conditions. "Most of our guys are having fun," Pearson insists. They are the kind of people, elaborates Scully, who "would rather be in the marines than in the army."

Like marines, Pepsi executives are expected to be physically fit as well as mentally alert: Pepsi employs four physical-fitness instructors at its headquarters, and a former executive says it is an unwritten rule that to get ahead in the company a manager must stay in shape. The company encourages one-on-one sports as well as interdepartmental competition in such games as soccer and basketball. In company team contests or business dealings, says Sculley, "the more competitive it becomes, the more we enjoy it." In such a culture, less-competitive managers are deliberately weeded out. Even suppliers notice a difference today. "They are smart, sharp negotiators who take advantage of all opportunities," says one.

While Pepsi steadily gained market share in the 1970s, Coke was reluctant to admit that a threat existed, Yazijian says. Pepsi now has bested Coke in the domestic take-home market, and it is mounting a challenge overseas. At the moment, the odds are in favor of Coke, which sells one third of the world's soft drinks and has had Western Europe locked up for years. But Pepsi has been making inroads: Besides monopolizing the Soviet market, it has dominated the Arab Middle East ever since Coke was ousted in 1967, when it granted a bottling franchise in Israel. Still, Coke showed that it was not giving up. It cornered a potentially vast new market—China.

With Pepsi gaining domestic market share faster than Coke—in the last five years it has gained 7.5 percent to Coke's 5 percent—observers believe that Coke will turn more to foreign sales or food sales for growth. Roberto C. Goizueta, Coke's chairman, will not reveal Coke's strategy. But one tactic the company has already used is hiring away some of Pepsi's "tigers." Coke has lured Donald Breen, Jr., who payed a major role in developing the "Pepsi Challenge"—the consumer taste test—as well as five other marketing and sales executives associated with Pepsi. Pepsi won its court battle to prevent Breen from revealing confidential information over the next 12 months.

The company's current culture may be unlikely to build loyalty. Pepsi may well have to examine the dangers of cultivating ruthlessness in its managers, say former executives.

Only time can tell if these comments are accurate or simply "sour grapes." Regardless, Pepsi has clearly sought to ensure consistency in every aspect of changing its culture from a passive to an aggressive one over the last 20 years.

Based on the article "Corporate Culture: The Hard to Change Values that Spell Success or Failure," from the October 27, 1980, issue of *Business Week*.

strategy is fundamentally inconsistent with long standing cultural norms at Merrill Lynch that emphasize personalized service and very close broker-client relationships. Following the 1984 resignation of Merrill Lynch's CEO, numerous analysts reported serious reconsideration of this product development strategy toward one that was more consistent with traditional values and norms inculcated in the brokerage network.

For many businesses facing this dilemma, reformulation is not in the long-term interests of the firm. Oftentimes, as illustrated in Strategy in Action 11–6, major external changes necessitate a new strategy that requires difficult changes in the fundamental culture of the organization. In the situation where the culture must be changed, several basic managerial actions—both symbolic and substantive—should be considered as the bases for cultural change. Five types of basic managerial actions that will aid in the difficult process of changing organizational culture are discussed below.

Strategy in Action 11–6

Texaco Tries to Change Its Culture to Fit a New Strategy

John McKinley, a chemical engineer who became Texaco's chairman on November 1, 1980, is attempting to implement a major new strategy for the firm. While the oil business supplies the cash, the plan counts heavily on synthetic fuels and other high-technology, alternative-energy products to provide the earnings base for the company in the 1990s. "People can still find oil and gas at lower cost than any of the alternate energy schemes," says McKinley, "but I see great movement toward alternate energy."

Texaco is putting into place new management systems to streamline decision making, open lines of communication among middle managers, and decentralize power to make the company more responsive to changes in the economic and political environments. Such systems have been in place at most oil companies for most of the decade, but they represent a drastic change for Texaco. They include these arrangements: (1) a totally revised organizational structure, setting up geographic profit centers with responsibility for financial and operating decisions; (2) basing bonuses mainly on performance instead of largely on seniority; (3) recruiting at all levels rather than only at the entry level; (4) opening communications among line managers and between top managers and the public; and (5) encouraging and rewarding entrepreneurship at staff levels.

An important goal of the restructuring is to push decision making down into the ranks—to make the people on the front lines more responsive and more responsible. Nevertheless, say Texaco observers, the success of that effort will depend more on the style of the people than on the structure of the company. McKinley realizes that implementation will depend on an entirely new Texaco employee, one with an attitude vastly different from that of the employees who preceded him.

People who have followed Texaco or worked for it assign the blame for lack of flexibility to the corporate culture set by Augustus C. Long, the domineering Texas oilman who was Texaco's chairman for 10 years. Long, says a Wall Street analyst, "tended to surround himself with yes men. What you've seen in the 1970s is a logical consequence of that." Decisions on even minor expenditure, such as remodeling service stations or replacing rusted storage tanks, required his approval. A former staffer charges that "Texaco treated its middle managers like peons, and the managers came to believe they were."

Commenting on his efforts to change Texaco's culture, McKinley concluded: "Nobody can assure you that any one organizational structure can do any specific thing. It's the people, the systems, the establishment of realistic strategic goals. But with all that," he adds, "you have to have an organization that is capable of reacting promptly, and you have to have aggressive leaders. We're moving in that direction."

Based on the article "Texaco: Restoring Luster to the Star" from the December 22, 1980, issue of *Business Week*.

Chief Executive's Role. The CEO has to visibly lead the organization in *each* fundamental change. This is a symbolic role in communicating the need for change and recognizing initial successes; and a substantive role in making hard decisions. The top-management team must create the pressure for change and set an example that unequivocably demonstrates the seriousness of the new direction.

Who Is Hired and Promoted. One key way to begin the process of changing values and norms is to bring in new people who share the desired values. Likewise, indoctrination of new personnel into the company is a key time for clarifying and inculcating desired values. Companies can also remove employees that strongly resist or blunt efforts to revamp the old culture. In extreme cases, this can mean changing top management.

Change the Reward Structure. A powerful way of changing values and behavior is to link the reward structure and the desired change. This can be done individually and with subunits of the organization. Compensation is the most obvious reward, but resource allocation, perks, and other visible "rewards" help positively reinforce desired change.

Clarify Desired Behavior. Unless managers are fully aware of the behavior required to get things done in the new culture, they will not change how they approach tasks and relationships. So planning teams and other educational vehicles must clarify what the "new rules" are and how the new behavior will enhance development and advancement in the company.[27]

Foster Consistency between Desired Changes and Rewards. One element appears to be certain in changing culture: employees cannot be fooled. They understand the "real" priorities in the company. At the first inconsistency they will become confused, then reluctant to change, and eventually intransigent. So consistency between what is said to be important and what is rewarded as such is critical in cultural change. Indeed, consistency in every aspect of a culture is essential to its success, as PepsiCo's transformation into an archrival of Coke shows in Strategy in Action 10–5.

Changing an organizational culture takes time. Strategy in Action 10–6 describes efforts at Texaco that have been underway since 1980. Executives who have succeeded in fundamentally transforming a culture estimate that the process requires from 6 to 15 years.[28] So in trying to change underlying organizational factors, strategists must recognize that reshaping "the way things are done" in a company is often an incremental process. Small opportunities should be sought for making a change or initiating an action that visibly reinforces the spirit and direction of the new culture. Top management should continually try (and urge their subordinates to try, as well) to gradually build and nurture the company's shared psychological and attitudinal commitment to the new strategy so that the fit between shared employee values and the new strategic mission continually improves.

Summary

This chapter examined the idea that a key aspect of implementing strategy is the need to *institutionalize* that strategy so that it permeates daily decisions and actions in a manner consistent with long-term strategic success. Three fundamental elements must be managed to "fit" the strategy if that strategy is to be effectively institutionalized: organizational *structure, leadership,* and *culture.*

Five fundamental organizational structures were examined and the advantages and disadvantages of each were identified. Institutionalizing the strategy requires a good strategy-structure fit. This chapter dealt with how this need is often overlooked until performance becomes inadequate, and examined conditions under which alternative structures would be more appropriate.

---

[27] Schwartz and Davis, "Matching Corporate Culture," p. 44.

[28] "Corporate Culture Vultures," p. 70.

Organizational leadership is essential to effective strategy implementation. The CEO plays a critical role in this regard. Assignment of key managers, particularly within the top management team, is an important aspect of organizational leadership. The question of promoting insiders versus hiring outsiders is often a central leadership issue in strategy implementation. This chapter provided a situational approach to making this decision in a manner that best institutionalizes the new strategy.

In recent years, organization culture has been recognized as a pervasive force influencing strategy implementation. Culture is described as the shared values of organizational members, and is shaped by key organizational factors that must ultimately be used in implementing strategy. An approach to managing the strategy-culture fit was discussed in this chapter. We identified four fundamentally different strategy-culture situations based on the changes necessary to implement the strategy and the "fit" of these changes with the company's culture. Recommendations for managing the strategy-culture fit vary across the four situations.

Questions for Discussion

1. What key structural considerations must be incorporated into strategy implementation? Why does structural change often lag a change in strategy?
2. Which structure is most appropriate for successful strategy implementation? Explain how stage of development affects your answer.
3. Why is leadership an important element in strategy implementation? Find an example in a major business periodical of the CEO's key role in strategy implementation.
4. Under what conditions would it be more appropriate to fill a key management position with someone from outside the company when a qualified insider is available?
5. What is organizational culture? Why is it important? Explain two different situations a firm might face in managing the strategy-culture relationship.

Bibliography

Adizes, Ichak. "Mismanagement Styles." *California Management Review,* Winter 1976, pp. 5–20.

"Corporate Culture." *Business Week,* October 27, 1980, pp. 148–60.

"Corporate Culture Vultures." *Fortune,* October 17, 1983, pp. 66–73.

Deal, Terrence E., and Allan A. Kennedy. *Corporate Cultures.* Reading, Mass: Addison-Wesley Publishing, 1982.

Fenton, Noel J. "Managing the Adolescent Company." *Management Review,* December 1976, pp. 12–19.

Galbraith, Jay R., and Daniel A. Nathanson. *Strategy Implementation: The Role of Structure and Process.* St. Paul, Minn.: West Publishing, 1978.

"GE's New Billion Dollar Small Businesses." *Business Week,* December 19, 1977.

Hall, Jay. "To Achieve or Not: The Manager's Choice." *California Management Review,* Summer 1976, pp. 5–18.

Hrebiniak, Lawrence G., and William F. Joyce. *Implementing Strategy.* New York: Macmillan, 1984.

Leontiades, Milton. *Strategies for Diversification and Change.* Boston: Little, Brown, 1980, Chapters 2, 3, 6.

———. "Choosing the Right Manager to Fit the Strategy." *Journal of Business Strategy,* Fall 1982, pp. 58–69.

MacMillan, Ian C. "Strategy and Flexibility in the Smaller Business." *Long-Range Planning,* June 1975, pp. 62–63.

"Matsushita: A Nontraditional Youth Movement in Management." *Business Week,* April 17, 1978, p. 102.

Miles, R. E., and C. C. Snow. *Organizational Strategy, Structure, and Process.* New York: McGraw-Hill, 1978.

Peters, Thomas J. "Beyond the Matrix Organization." *Business Horizons,* October 1979, pp. 15–27.

Peters, Thomas J., and Robert Waterman. *In Search of Excellence.* New York: Harper & Row, 1982.

Salter, Malcolm S. "Stages of Corporate Development." *Journal of Business Policy* 1, no. 1 (1970), pp. 23–37.

Slocum, John W., Jr., and Don Hellriegel. "Using Organizational Designs to Cope with Change." *Business Horizons,* December 1979, pp. 65–76.

Stonich, Paul J. *Implementing Strategy.* Cambridge, Mass.: Ballinger, 1982.

Tichy, N. M., C. J. Fombrun; and M. A. Devanna. "Strategic Human Resource Management." *Sloan Management Review,* Winter 1982, p. 47.

"Wanted: A Manager to Fit Each Strategy." *Business Week,* Febuary 25, 1980, p. 166.

Webber, Ross A. "Career Problems of Young Managers." *California Management Review,* Summer 1976, pp. 19–33.

Yavitz, Boris, and William H. Newman. *Strategy in Action.* New York: Free Press, 1982.

Chapter 11 Cohesion Case Illustration

Institutionalizing the Strategy at Holiday Inns, Inc.

Holidays Inns has emphasized three key elements to institutionalize its strategy for the 1980s: structure, selection and assignment of key managers, and organizational culture.

Organizational Structure. Exhibit 1 provides an abbreviated look at the organizational structure of Holiday Inns, Inc. As you can see, Holiday Inns has a divisional structure with four rather autonomous business groups. This clearly reflects the needs of its corporate diversification strategy by providing each business group with its own functional support and broad decision-making capability. Second, the formerly separate products group has been reorganized within the hotel group. This clearly reflects the strategy of retrenchment and divestiture within the products group limiting it primarily to a service role for the hotel group's furnishing and equipment needs. Finally, Delta Steamship has been organized as a fully independent and autonomous unit. This distinguishes Delta from the hospitality businesses and facilitates rapid divestiture should Holiday Inns find the right opportunity to do so (which it did in December 1982).

Assignment of Key Managers. Several key managerial assignments reflect a deliberate choice at the corporate level to effectively implement Holiday Inns'diversification strategy. Holiday Inns's three nonhotel divisions have as their presidents the former CEOs at Harrah's, Perkins, and Delta, respectively. Instead of putting a Holiday Inns-trained executive in charge, corporate management deliberately chose to maintain autonomy and leadership to meet the unique needs of these new groups. Finally, reflecting a corporate portfolio strategy that emphasizes casinos as a key growth area, gaming is the only business group other than hotels to have representation on the board of directors and of the corporate management level.

Mile Rose (CEO) and Roy Winegardner (chairman of the board) were initially successful franchisees before becoming involved with Holiday Inns' top management team in the mid-1970s. Thus, they understand franchisees—an attribute critical to the franchise-dominated hotel and restaurant businesses. They also (particularly Rose) had less of a tie to Holiday Inns' previous family-oriented hotel philosophy and widespread, transportation-related diversification. This made them more objective and effective in addressing and implementing the casino decision and several major divestitures (product group and transportation businesses).

Exhibit 1

Organizational structure at Holiday Inns, Inc.

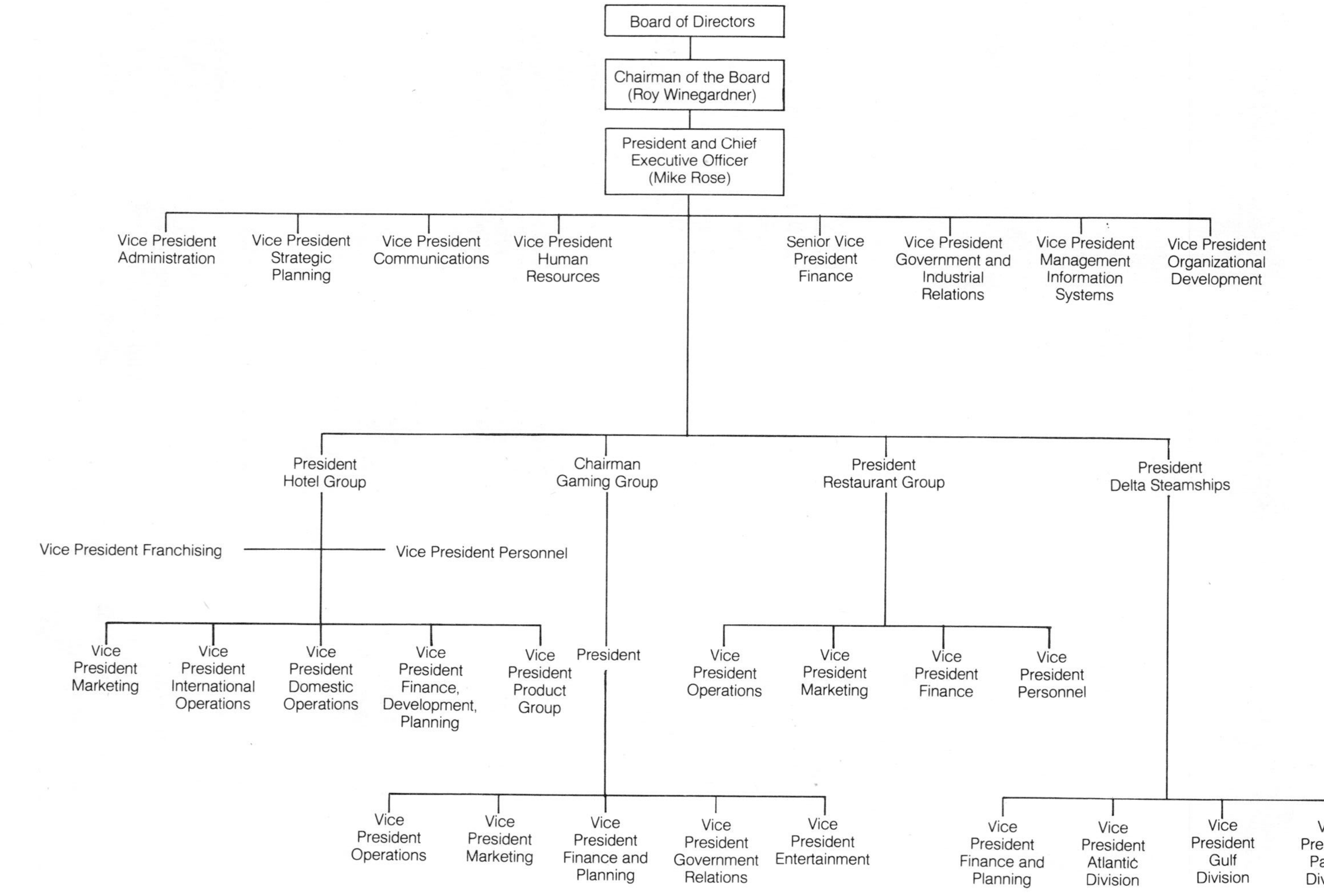

Two additions to the board reflect Holiday Inn's institutionalization of its hospitality strategy. Donald Smith, senior vice president with PepsiCo and president of its Food Service Division, brings well-respected food service experience to Holiday Inns' top management team. Smith was credited with turning Burger King into a viable competitor with McDonald's in fast foods. James Farley, chairman and CEO of Booz, Allen and Hamilton (a worldwide consulting firm) reflects a serious commitment to systematic strategic planning for Holiday Inns' future.

Organization Culture. The structural and key managerial changes reflect a steady shift from an entrepreneurial to a professionally managed company. Refocusing on being a *hospitality* company in three industries—hotels, gaming, and restaurants—has been repeatedly presented as the "new Holiday Inns." The common threat for each operation is a strong service orientation that encourages and rewards superior individual performance. The "new" Holiday Inns sees its people assets as key to its service success as reflected by its corporate philosophy and statements by Roy Winegardner, shown below:

> *Corporate Philosophy Statement:*
>
> We are a forward-looking innovative industry leader with clearly defined goals, producing superior products services and consistently high return for our shareholders.
>
> We will maintain integrity in both our internal and external relationsips, fostering respect for the individual and open two-way communications.
>
> We will promote a climate of enthusiasm, teamwork, and challenge which attracts, motivates, and retains superior personnel and rewards superior performance.
>
> Our employees give us our greatest competitive advantage. We employ and develop high-quality people because they are the key to our continued leadership and growth. (Roy E. Winegardner, chairman, Holiday Inns, Inc.)

CHAPTER

12

Controlling and Evaluating the Strategy

The fundamental purpose of strategic management is to effectively position and guide the firm within a changing environment. For most firms, the rate of change in its environment has accelerated in recent years. Therefore, a process for controlling and evaluating strategy execution is essential if the strategy is to be successfully implemented and adjusted to changing conditions. The management team must be able to measure performance, evaluate deviations from planned standards, and initiate actions to both reinforce success and take corrective actions. In addition to a focus on internal operations, this process must monitor the key external factors on which the success of the strategy depends. Integral to this control and evaluation is the need for a reward system providing the motivation for evaluation and the feedback to encourage effective control. The process of controlling and evaluating strategy must include at least three fundamental dimensions: (1) establishing control systems based on performance standards that are linked to annual objectives; (2) a way of monitoring performance and evaluating deviations; and (3) a means for motivating control and evaluation. This chapter discusses ways a manager can ensure that a firm's strategic management process includes control and evaluation.

Establishing Control Systems Linked to Annual Objectives

There are two basic control systems for controlling and evaluating new-strategy implementation: strategic control and operational control. *Strategic control* is the concern of the firm's top executives; it focuses on factors related to external forces and internal performance that are essential to the success of a strategy. *Operational control* is the concern of a company's operating managers; it involves allocation and use of a firm's financial, physical, and human resources.

Before we examine each system in detail, it is important to understand basic features common to both. First, there is a necessary link to annual and long-term objectives. Long-term objectives indicate the strategic ends for the company in five or more years. Annual objectives break down these broad goals into specific, short-term targets. Fundamental to effective control and evaluation is the need to link these targets to specific performance standards, resource allocation guidelines, and strategic assumptions about the external forces influencing accomplishment of key objectives. Linking annual and long-term objectives to performance standards and other measures of each control system clarifies the relationship between strategic plans and what people do.

A second feature common to both control systems is derived from a very basic idea of motivation: behavior is affected by the means used to measure it. Managers, generally, are highly motivated and want to meet or exceed the expectations of their superiors. However, a key obstacle is that these expectations are often either unclear or are not linked to what "really counts" in many companies. Effective control clarifies expectations, provides specific performance feedback, and clearly communicates "what counts" through relationship to strategic objectives. In this way, control and evaluation become a positive, motivational force encouraging effective strategy implementation.

The third feature common to both strategic and operating control is the need for an "early warning system" that alerts management to deviations that signal potential problems (or opportunities) in the strategy or in the way it is being implemented. Objectives are expressed as concrete performance standards, resource allocation guides, and major external assumptions. This gives management a basis for recognizing deviations and examining their significance in terms of implications for the successful execution of strategies.

In addition to these similarities, there are two fundamental differences between strategic and operational control systems. First, strategic control systems are necessary to meet the needs of top managers, while operational control systems focus on the needs of subunit managers. Second, strategic control has both external and internal focuses, monitoring both assumptions about external factors and key internal performance. Operational control systems focus on internal factors, evaluating use of the firm's strategic resources.

Strategic Control[1]

Top management's understanding of the marketplace and expectations for the company form the basis for long-term objectives. To reach these objectives,

[1] This section draws on ideas underlying Arthur Andersen & Company's "Information for Motivation" program.

a strategy must be not only developed, but successfully implemented. In this context, a control and evaluation system bridges the gap between strategy development and strategy execution. This control system must focus on limited, strategic information that indicates whether a company is progressing in the desired direction. The information concerned involves the key factors that determine the success of the strategy.

These success factors are essential to a company's strategy. They are activities or events that will have a major impact on how effective the company will be in implementing its strategy. Success factors can be strategic or operational, and can reflect key assumptions about environmental factors as well as critical internal performance standards. There are four basic categories of success factors.

Environmental Factors. A company has little or no control over environmental success factors, but they exercise considerable influence over the success of the strategy. Inflation, technology, interest rates, regulation, and demographic/social changes are examples of such factors.

Industry Factors. These factors affect the performance of companies in a given industry. They differ among industries, and a company should be aware of the factors that influence success in its particular industry. Competitors, suppliers, substitutes, and barriers to entry are a few such factors about which strategic assumptions are made.

Strategy-Specific Factors. The company's strategy is always dependent on several critical features. Customer service, cost control, market share, new distribution channels, completion of a new plant, and rolling out a new product or promotional effort are examples of strategy-related success factors.

Company-Specific Factors. Strategy choice involves difficult decisions about dependence on company strengths and weaknesses in implementation. Issues considered might include managerial succession, capacity utilization, employee morale, product-line changes, debt, or current asset utilization—all key internal considerations linked to the ultimate success of the new strategy.

Based on these sources, top management must identify the *strategic* success factors on which to base a strategic control process.

Strategic Success Factors. These are the factors that are of greatest importance in implementing the company's strategies. Strategic success factors identify performance areas that must receive continuous management attention and critical assumptions about key environmental and industry factors. Examples of typical strategic success factors focused on internal performance include: (1) improved productivity, (2) high employee morale, (3) improved product/service quality, (4) increased earnings per share, (5) growth in market share, and (6) completion of new facilities. Strategic success factors concerned with key environmental/industry assumptions might include: (1) increasing disposable income, (2) decrease in interest rates, (3) stability of product/market emphasis of current competitors, (4) cost of raw materials, and (5) strengthening of key barriers to entry in the industry. Strategy in Action 12–1 illustrates the strategic success factors monitored by top management at Chrysler to control and evaluate its turnaround strategy in the 1980s.

Strategic success factors succinctly communicate the critical elements of strategy to the organization. Because their achievement requires the successful performance of several key individuals, these factors can be a foundation for teamwork among managers in meeting the company's strategic objectives.

Some strategic success factors apply to the company as a whole, while others apply only to major operating units or specific product lines. Regardless of the organizational level at which they apply, all strategic success factors facilitate control and evaluation most effectively if they are clearly defined, controlled (or if, like environmental factors, they cannot be controlled, then monitored) and converted into measurable information.

There must be measurable performance indicators for each success factor. A software company's management, for example, may have identified product quality, customer service, employee morale, and competition as the four key determinants of strategy success. These are four clear, controllable or monitorable variables, but specific indicators must be used to measure each factor. Key performance indicators might include the following:

For product quality:
- Performance data versus specifications.
- Percentage of product returns.
- Number of customer complaints.

For customer service:
- Delivery cycle in days.
- Percentage of orders shipped complete.
- Field service delays.

For employee morale:
- Trends in employee attitude survey.
- Absenteeism versus plan.
- Employee turnover trends.

For competition:
- Number of firms competing directly.
- Number of new products introduced.
- Percentage of bids awarded versus standard.

Strategy in Action 12–1

Strategic Success Factors in Chrysler's Turnaround Strategy

When Lee Iacocca came to Chrysler in 1979, the Michigan State Fairgrounds were jammed with thousands of unsold, unwanted, rusting Chryslers, Dodges, and Plymouths. Foreign operations were leeching the lifeblood out of the company. And worst of all, cars were coming off the assembly line with loose doors, chipped paint, and crooked moldings.

According to Iacocca, the Chrysler experience highlighted four painful realities:

The quality of our products had declined.

Work practices had shortchanged productivity.

The government had become an enemy instead of an ally.

Foreign countries that the United States had defeated in war and rebuilt in peace were beating this country in its own markets.

Chrysler was faced with a choice. The company could go under—the suggestion of not a few—or efforts could be made to save the company, and with it, according to Iacocca, "the American way of doing business—with honesty, pride, ingenuity, and good old-fashioned hard work."

In charting Chrysler's turnaround strategy, Iacocca identified six strategic success factors essential to a successful turnaround. Chrysler executives used these six factors as the basis for their *strategic* control of the turnaround strategy. Careful, systematic attention was given to monitoring progress on each factor as a key indicator of desired execution of the turnaround strategy.

1. Reduce wage and salary expenses by half the 1980 level. (Chrysler ultimately reduced its work force from 160,000 to 80,000 and received over $1.2 billion in wage and benefit sacrifices.)
2. Reduce fixed cost by over $4 billion. (Chrysler closed 20 plants and modernized the remaining 40 with state-of-the art robot and computer technology.)
3. Reduce the number of different parts by one third. (Chrylser reduced the number of parts from 75,000 to 40,000, shaking $1 billion out of inventory in the process.)
4. Improve its weak balance sheet. (Chrysler retired its U.S. bank debt by converting $1.3 billion into preferred stock, and some preferred into common stock.)
5. Improve the quality of its components and finished products. (Chrysler reduced warranty costs by 25 percent in 1982; it reduced scheduled maintenance costs to a level $20 to $200 below that of the competition.)
6. Implement a $6 billion product improvement program. (Chrysler has a lead in front-wheel-drive technology; it has the best fuel economy in the industry; it offers the industry's most extensive 50,000-mile warranty.)

Source: Based on Lee A. Iacocca, "The Rescue and Resuscitation of Chrysler," *Journal of Business Strategy* 4, no. 3, (1983), pp. 67–69.

Once key performance indicators are identified, strategic success factors can be monitored by senior management. This provides a basis for *strategic* control and evaluation that focuses on a very limited number of key indicators rather than on the flood of information often endured by many senior managers.

There are several questions that must be addressed in setting the guidelines for monitoring key indicators. For example, will key performance indicators measure a single period, year to date, or a moving average of several periods? Will key individuals be responsible for a few or many indicators? Will achievement relative to key indicators be communicated broadly to the organization? The answer to these questions must be related to the needs of each company and its strategy. And each answer should recognize the role of strategic success factors, allowing senior managers to focus on a very limited set of factors that indicate the progress of the strategy and key reasons behind its likely success or failure.

Strategic success factors are useful to top management in monitoring, controlling, and evaluating strategy implementation. But operating managers also need control and evaluation methods appropriate to their level of strategy implementation. The primary concern at the operating level is allocation and use of the company's resources.

Operational Control Systems

Operational control systems guide, monitor, and evaluate progress in meeting a strategy's objectives. To be effective, operational control systems must incorporate standards of performance, measurement of performance, comparison/evaluation of performance, and the impetus for corrective action. These components control use of the firm's financial, human, and physical resources for effective strategy execution. The key mechanisms for operational control are budgets and schedules.

Budgeting Systems. The budgetary process was the forerunner of strategic planning. Capital budgeting in particular provided the means for strategic resource allocations. With the growing use of strategic management, such allocations are now based on strategic assessment and priorities, and not solely on capital budgeting.[2] Yet capital and expenditure budgeting, as well as sales budgeting, remain important control mechanisms in strategy implementation.

A budget is simply a resource allocation plan that helps managers coordinate operations and facilitates managerial control of performance. Budgets themselves do not control anything. Rather, they set standards against which action

---

[2] Peter Lorange, *Corporate Planning* (Englewood Cliffs, N.J.: Prentice-Hall, 1980), p. 155.

can be measured. They also provide a basis for negotiating short-term resource requirements to implement strategy at the operating level.

Historically, budgets were devices for limiting expenditures. Currently, budgets are viewed as tools for obtaining the most profitable and productive use of a company's resources.[3] Budgeting cuts across all organizational resources—financial, physical, and human—as a control tool. Budgets are typically developed for one-year periods, but budgets covering from one month to five years are not uncommon.

Budgets require a set of performance or resource-utilization standards. But to enhance strategy implementation, a budget must be more than a set of standards or targets. The standards in a budget are a detailed extrapolation of the firm's broader objectives. Thus, the budget itself should be used for monitoring and evaluating performance with reference to those standards. Most firms employ a budgeting system, not a singular budget, in controlling strategy implementation Figure 12–1 represents a typical budgeting system for a manufacturing business. A budgeting system incorporates a series of different budgets fitted to the organization's unique characteristics. Because organizations differ, so do their budgets. Yet most firms include three general types of budgets—sales, capital, and expenditure—in their budgetary control system.

Sales Budgets. If a firm is seen as a generator and user of funds, sales revenue is critical. Most firms employ some form of sales/revenue budget to monitor their sales projections (or expectations), because this reflects a key objective of the chosen strategy. The sales budget provides important information for the daily management of financial resources and key feedback as to whether the strategy is working. For evaluative purposes, the sales budget may be derived from sales forecasts arrived at in the planning process or it may be linked to past sales patterns. For example, most hotel/motel operators emphasize daily revenue compared to revenue for the same day in the previous year as a monitor of sales effectiveness.

A sales budget is particularly important as a tool for control of strategy implementation. Sales budgets provide an early warning system about the effectiveness of the firm's strategy. And if the deviation is considerably below or above expectations, this budgetary tool should initiate managerial action to reevaluate and possibly adjust the firm's operational or strategic posture.

Capital Budgets. The phrase "capital budgeting" is often synonomous with net present value, discounted cash flow, risk-adjusted discount rate, and numerous other techniques for evaluating capital investment decisions. These

[3] J. F. Weston and E. F. Brigham, *Essentials of Managerial Finance* (Hinsdale, Ill.: Dryden Press, 1977), p. 116.

Figure 12–1

A typical budgeting system for controlling strategy implementation

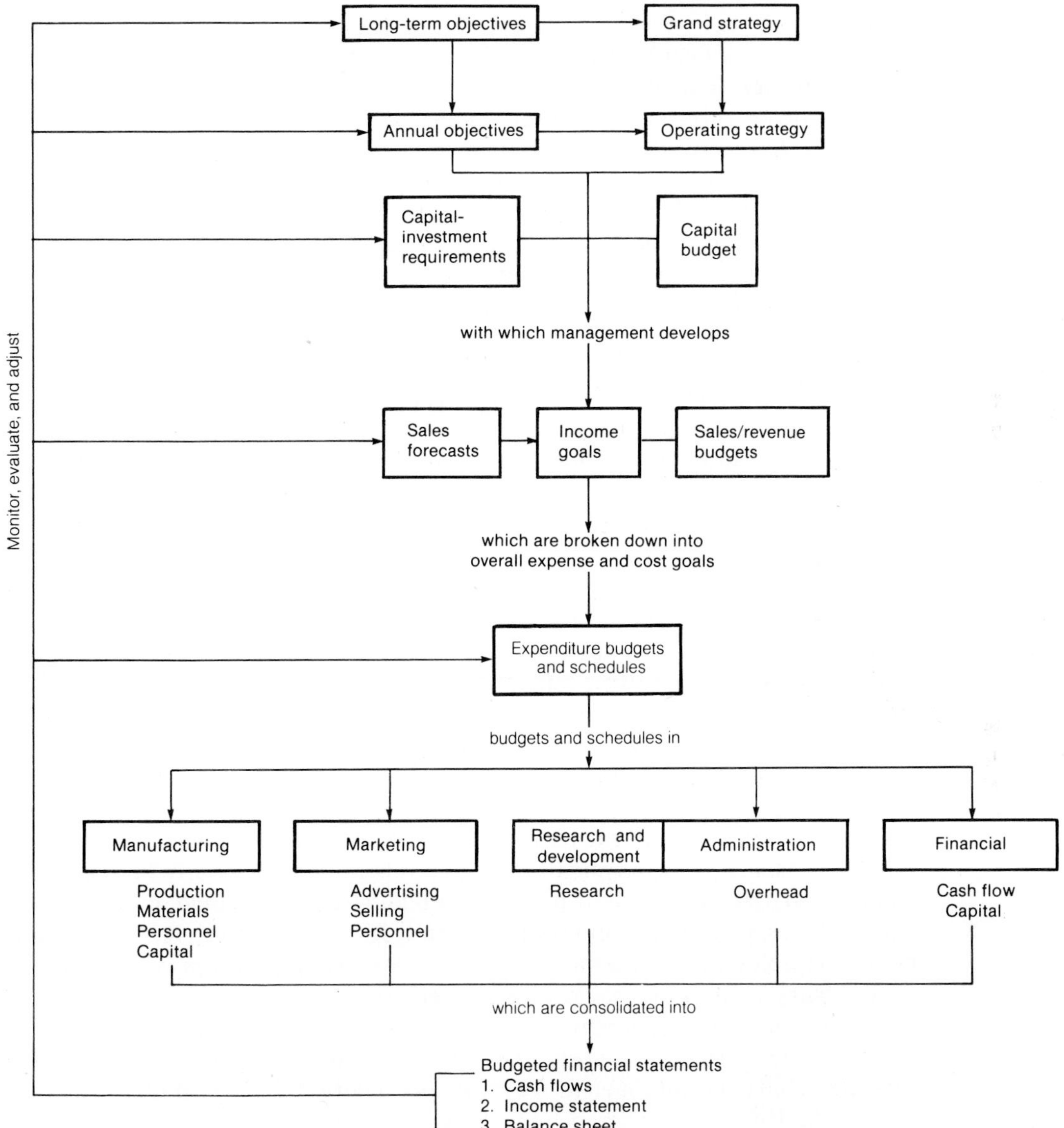

are important techniques, but the concern here is with the budgetary tool used to implement the capital investment decisions. Thus, the *capital budget* is the mechanism for allocating financial resources in implementing major capital investment decisions.

To support their strategic choice, many firms require capital investment or divestiture. A firm committed to a strong growth strategy may need additional capacity or facilities to support increased sales. On the other hand, a firm intent on retrenchment may have to divest major parts of its current operations to reach a desired activity level. In both cases, the firm is concerned with management of significant financial resources, probably over an extended time period. For effective control, a capital budget that carefully plans the acquisition and expenditure of funds, as well as the timing, is essential.

Capital budgeting affects the use of both financial and physical resources in implementing the firm's strategy. Operating plans, schedules, and budgets of operational subunits (e.g., production and/or marketing) are tied to capital investment decisions and the subsequent capital budget to accommodate the acquisition or divestiture of operating capacity. Thus, if the capital investment decisions are poorly conceived or poorly implemented, performance throughout the organization can suffer. In the extreme case, particularly considering the financial dimension, the firm's very existence could be threatened. Clearly, the capital budget is an important tool in implementation and control of the capital investment requirements of a firm's strategic choice.

Expenditure Budgets. Numerous expense/cost budgets will be necessary for budgetary control in implementation of strategy in various operating units of the firm. An expenditures budget for each functional unit and for subfunctional activities can guide and control unit/individual execution of strategy, increasing the likelihood of profitable performance. For example, a firm might have an expenditure budget for the marketing department and another for advertising activities.

In such budgets, dollar variables will be the predominant measure, although nondollar measures of physical activity levels may occasionally be used as a supplement.[4] For example, a production budget might include standards for expenditures as well as standards for output level or productivity. These nondollar variables might also include targets or milestones that provide evidence of necessary progress in particular strategic programs.

An expenditure or operating budget is meant to provide concrete standards against which operational costs and activities can be measured and, if necessary, adjusted to maintain effective strategy execution. The expenditure budget is perhaps the most common budgetary tool in strategy implementation. If its standards are soundly linked to strategic objectives, then it can provide an effective communication link between top management and operating man-

[4] Lorange, *Corporate Planning,* p. 158.

agers about what is necessary for a strategy to succeed. It provides another warning system alerting management to problems in the implementation of the firm's strategy.

The budgeting system (see Figure 12–2) provides an integrated picture of the firm's operation as a whole. The effect on overall performance of a production decision to alter the level of work-in-process inventories or of a marketing decision to change sales organization procedures can be traced through the entire budget system. Thus, coordinating these decisions becomes an important consideration for the control of strategy implementation.

Figure 12–2 provides an illustration of how budgets can be coordinated to aid in coordinating operations. In this chart, production, raw material purchases, and direct labor requirements are coordinated with anticipated sales. In more comprehensive systems, other budgets may be included: manufacturing expense, inventories, building services, advertising, maintenance, cash flow, administrative overhead, and so on, as suggested earlier in this section.

Scheduling. Timing is often a key factor in the success of a strategy. Simply stated, strategic success means being at the right place and doing the right things at the right time. If a strategy is to work, timing its implementation must be carefully planned and controlled. And this must be done by those aware of strategic direction. Otherwise, subtle shifts in past operating practices may not be initiated.

At the corporate or business level of strategy, timing can be critical in relation to product/market evolution. Abell has suggested that there are "strategic windows" in many industries (products/markets), that is, limited periods of time during which a firm may successfully adopt and implement a completely new strategy.[5] Thus, timing seems critical in a firm that is radically changing its strategy. And scheduling is useful in controlling the timing of activities and resource deployments in new-strategy implementation.

Scheduling is simply a planning tool for allocating the use of a time-constrained resource or arranging the sequence of interdependent activities. The success of strategy implementation is quite dependent on both. So scheduling offers a mechanism with which to plan for, monitor, and control these dependencies. For example, a firm committed to a vertical integration strategy must carefully absorb expanded operations into its existing core. Such expansion, whether involving forward or backward integration, will require numerous changes in the operational practices of some of the firm's organizational units. Scheduling through techniques like the critical path method (CPM) and program evaluation and review technique (PERT) can aid and control the effective introduction of a new organizational unit into the firm's operating structure. Coors Brewery, for example, made the decision in early 1970 to integrate backward by producing its own beer cans. A comprehensive, two-

[5] Derek F. Abell, "Strategic Windows," *Journal of Marketing*, July 1978, pp, 21–26.

Figure 12–2

Illustration of budget coordination

Sales Budget for Year

Product	*Units*	*Price*	*Total sales*
1	20,000	$20.00	$ 400,000
2	30,000	30.00	900,000
3	50,000	15.00	750,000
4	5,000	50.00	250,000
	105,000		$2,300,000

Production Budget

	Products			
Description	*1*	*2*	*3*	*4*
Quantity	20,000	30,000	50,000	5,000
Ending inventory	5,000			
Total required	25,000	etc.		
Less:				
Beginning inventory	3,000			
Required production	22,000			

Raw Materials Unit

	Products				
Material	*1*	*2*	*3*	*4*	*Total*
St. (lbs.)	10,000	5,000	2,000	1,000	18,000
Cu. (lbs.)					
Al. (lbs.)		etc.			

Raw Materials Purchases Budget

Material	*Production*	*Ending Inventory*	*Total*	*Less beginning inventory*	*To be purchased*	*Price*	*Cost*
St. (lbs.)	18,000	8,000	26,000	6,000	20,000	$150	$3,000,000
Cu. (lbs.)			etc.				
Al. (lbs.)							

Direct Labor Budget

Product	*Quantity to be produced*	*Standard labor-hours per unit*	*Total standard labor-hours*	*Budget at $5 per standard labor-hour*
1	22,000	2	44,000	$220,000
2				
3		etc.		
4				

Source: Adapted from George A. Steiner, *Strategic Planning* (New York: Free Press, 1979), p. 219.

year schedule of actions and targets for incorporating manufacture of beer cans and bottles into the product chain contributed to the success of this strategy. Major changes in purchasing, production scheduling, machinery, and production systems were but a few of the critical operating areas that Coors' scheduling efforts were meant to accommodate and control.

Managers in critical areas and other key human resources are often major determinants of the success of strategic programs. A diversified firm may have numerous business units and/or strategic projects that need the services of a limited group of key managers. Obviously, for strategy implementation to have the greatest chance of succeeding, these managerial resources must be carefully allocated. Scheduling is one way to plan and subsequently control this resource. The method can also be used with other human resources, particularly those in short supply. Since the deregulation of oil prices, major oil firms have greatly expanded their search for new domestic supplies. The result has been a lack of competent petroleum geologists within the industry, which has raised compensation for petroleum geologists as oil firms fight to retain such critical expertise. It has also necessitated careful scheduling or "petroleum-geologist budgeting" within most oil firms to carefully allocate this valuable human resource across numerous exploration projects critical to the success of a firm's strategy.

Like budgeting, scheduling is an important tool at the operating level of an organization in controlling execution of a chosen strategy. Whenever time-constrained resources or interdependent activities exist, whether in a business unit or a district sales office, scheduling can provide identifiable targets to guide and control implementation.

Monitoring Performance and Evaluating Deviations

Strategic and operating control systems require the establishment of performance standards. In addition, progress must be monitored and deviations from standards evaluated as the strategy is implemented. Timely information must be obtained so that deviations can be identified, the underlying cause determined, and actions taken to correct *or* exploit them.

Figure 12–3 illustrates a simplified report to senior management on the current status of key performance indicators linked to the firm's strategy. These strategic success factors and key indicators represent progress after two years of a five-year plan intended to differentiate the firm as a customer-service-oriented provider of high-quality products. Senior managements' concern is comparing *progress to date* with *expected progress* at this point in the plan. Of particular interest is the *current deviation* because it provides a basis for examining *suggested actions* (usually from subordinate managers) and finalizing decisions on any necessary changes or adjustments in the strategy.

Figure 12–3

Monitoring and evaluating performance deviations

Strategic success factors	*Objective, assumption or budget*	*Forecast performance at this time*	*Current performance*	*Current deviation*	*Analysis*
Cost control:					
Ratio of indirect overhead to direct field and labor costs	10%	15%	12%	+3 (ahead)	Are we moving too fast or is there more unnecessary overhead than originally thought?
Gross profit	39%	40%	40%	0%	
Customer service:					
Installation cycle in days	2.5 days	3.2 days	2.7 days	+0.5 (ahead)	Can this progress be maintained?
Ratio of service to sales personnel	3.2	2.7	2.1	−0.6 (behind)	Why are we behind here? How can we maintain the installation cycle progress?
Product quality:					
Percentage of products returned	1.0%	2.0%	2.1%	−0.1% (behind)	Why are we behind here? Ramifications for other operations?
Product performance versus specification	100%	92%	80%	−12% (behind)	
Marketing:					
Sales per employee monthly	$12,500	$11,500	$12,100	+$600 (ahead)	Good progress. Is it creating any problems to support?
Expansion of product line	6	3	5	+2 products (ahead)	Are the products ready? Are the perfect standards met?
Employee morale in service area:					
Absenteeism rate	2.5%	3.0%	3.0%	(on target)	
Turnover rate	5%	10%	15%	−8% (behind)	Looks like a problem! Why are we so far behind?
Competition:					
New product introductions (average number)	6	3	6	−3 (behind)	Did we underestimate timing? Implications for our basic assumptions?

In Figure 12–3, the company appears to be maintaining control of its cost structure. Indeed, it is ahead of schedule on reducing overhead. The company is well ahead of its delivery cycle target, while slightly below its service-to-sales-personnel ratio objective. Product returns look OK, although product performance against specification is below standard. Sales per employee and expansion of the product line are ahead of schedule. Absenteeism in the service area is meeting projections, but turnover is higher than planned. Competitors appear to be introducing products more rapidly than expected.

After deviations and the underlying reasons for them are identified, the implications of these deviations for the ultimate success of the strategy must be seriously considered. For example, the rapid product-line expansion indicated in Figure 12–3 may be in response to competitors' increased rate of product expansion. At the same time, product performance is still low and while the installation cycle is slightly above standard (improving customer service), the ratio of service to sales personnel is below its target. Contributing to this substandard ratio (and perhaps reflecting a lack of organizational commitment to customer service) is the exceptionally high turnover in customer service personnel. The rapid reduction in indirect overhead costs might mean that administrative integration of customer-service and product-development requirements has been reduced too quickly.

As a result of this information, senior management faces several options. The deviations observed may be attributed primarily to internal factors or discrepancies. In this case, priorities can be scaled up or down. For example, greater emphasis might be placed on retaining customer-service personnel while deemphasizing overhead reduction and reducing the emphasis on new-product development. On the other hand, the management team could decide to continue as planned in the face of increasing competition and decide to accept or gradually improve the customer-service situation. Another possibility is reformulating the strategy or a component of the strategy in the face of rapidly increasing competition. For example, the firm might decide to shift emphasis toward more standardized or lower-priced products to overcome customer-service problems and take advantage of an apparently ambitious sales force.

This interpretation of Figure 12–3 is but one of many possible explanations. The important point is the critical need to monitor progress against standards and give serious, in-depth attention to both the reasons underlying observed deviations and the most appropriate responses to them.

Evaluations such as this are appropriate for organizational subunits, product groups, and operating units in a firm. Budgets, schedules, and other operating control systems with performance targets and standards that are linked to the strategic plan deserve this type of attention in detecting and evaluating deviations. The time frame is more compressed—usually quarterly or even monthly during the budgeted year. The operating manager typically reviews year-to-date progress against budgeted figures. After deviations are evaluated, slight adjustments may be necessary to keep progress, expenditures, or other factors in line with programmed needs of the strategy. In the unusual event that deviations are extreme—usually because of unforeseen changes—management is alerted to the possible need for revising the budget, reconsidering certain functional plans related to budgeted expenditures, or examining the units and effectiveness of the managers responsible. Variable budgets, with cost figures or other budgeted amounts "varying" in relation to a specific item like output or sales, are used increasingly to ensure that deviations and reactions to them are consistent with the fundamental budgeted performance relationships.

If budget deviations are observed, care must be taken to ensure that short-term adjustments resulting from control and evaluation do not alter strategic plans. Thus, top management usually must approve significant budgetary alterations so the strategic implications of such adjustments can be assessed.

An acceptable level of deviation should be allowed before action is taken or the control process will become an administrative overload. Standards should not be regarded as absolute because the estimates used to formulate them are typically based on historical data, which, by definition, are "after the fact." Furthermore, absolute standards (keep equipment busy 100 percent of the time, or meet 100 percent of quota) are often used with no provision for variability. Standards are also often derived from averages, which by definition, ignore variability. These difficulties suggest the need for defining acceptable *ranges* of deviation in budgetary figures or key indicators of strategic success. This approach helps in avoiding administrative difficulties, recognizing measurement variability, delegating more realistic authority to operating managers in making short-term decisions, and hopefully improves motivation.

Some companies use trigger points for clarification of standards, particularly in monitoring strategic success factors. A *trigger point* is a level of deviation of a key indicator or figure (such as a competitor's actions or a critical cost category) that management identifies in the planning process as representing either a major threat or an unusual opportunity. When that point is "hit," management is immediately alerted ("triggered") to consider necessary adjustments in the firm's strategy. Some companies take this idea a major step forward and develop one or more *contingency plans* to be implemented once predetermined trigger points are reached. These contingency plans redirect priorities and actions rapidly so that valuable reaction time is not "wasted" on administrative assessment and deliberation of the extreme deviation.

Correcting deviations in performance brings the entire management task into focus. Managers can correct performance by changing measures. Perhaps deviations can be resolved by changing plans. Management can eliminate poor performance by reorganizing the company, by hiring new people, by retraining present workers, by changing job assignments, and so on. To correct deviations from plans, therefore, can involve all of the functions, tasks, and responsibilities of managers in the strategic management process.[6] To return to points made in the second chapter, control and evaluation are inextricably interwoven into the entire strategic management process. Control and evaluation provide essential feedback in developing future plans as well as in efforts to implement the current strategy.

Motivating Control and Evaluation

Control and evaluation of strategy ultimately depend on individual organizational members, particularly key managers. And motivating and rewarding good performance by individuals and organizational units are key ingredients in effective strategy implementation. While positive reinforcements are given primary emphasis, sanctions or negative reinforcements are important tools for controlling and adjusting poor performance. Motivating and controlling individual efforts, particularly those of managerial personnel, in execution of strategy is accomplished through a firm's reward-sanction mechanisms—compensation, raises, bonuses, stock options, incentives, benefits, promotions, demotions, recognition, praise, criticism, more (or less) responsibility, group norms, performance appraisal, tension, and fear. These mechanisms are positive and negative, short run and long run.

Control mechanisms align personal and subunit actions and objectives with the objectives and needs of the firm's strategy. This is not easy and reward-sanction structures controlling strategy execution vary greatly across different firms. For example, Harold Geneen, former CEO of ITT, purportedly used an interesting combination of money (compensation and incentives), tension (strict accountability for results), and fear to control individual manager's efforts toward strategy implementation. According to one author:

> Geneen provides his managers with enough incentives to make them tolerate the system. Salaries all the way through ITT are higher than average—Geneen reckons 10 percent higher—so that few people can leave without taking a drop. As one employee put it: "We're all paid just a bit more than we think we're worth." At the very top, where the demands are greatest, the salaries and stock options are sufficient to compensate for the rigors. As someone said, "He's got them by their limousines."
>
> Having bound his men to him with chains of gold, Geneen can induce the tension that drives the machine. "The key to the system," one of his men explained, "is the profit forecast. Once the forecast has been gone over, revised, and agreed on, the managing director has a personal commitment to Geneen to carry it out. That's how he produces the tension on which the success depends." The tension goes through the company, inducing ambition, perhaps exhilaration, but always with some sense of fear: what happens if the target is missed?[7]

[6] George A. Steiner, *Strategic Planning* (New York: Free Press, 1979), p. 283.

[7] Anthony Sampson, *The Sovereign State of ITT* (New York: Steig & Day, 1973), p. 132.

BIC Pen Company takes a different approach. Its reward structure involves incentive systems, wide latitude for operating managers, and clearly specified objectives to motivate and control individual initiative. All employees are invited to participate in a stock purchase plan whereby up to 10 percent of their salary can be used to purchase stock at a 10 percent discount from the market price. Functional managers are given wide rein in operational decisions while being strictly accountable for results. The director of manufacturing, for example, is free to spend up to $500,000 for a cost-saving machine, as long as profit margin objectives are maintained. Commenting on his approach to rewarding executives, BIC's president, Robert Adler, said:

> We have a unique bonus system which I'm sure the Harvard Business School would think is crazy. Each year I take a percentage of profits before tax and give 40 percent to sales, 40 percent to manufacturing, and 20 percent to the treasurer to be divided up among executives in each area. Each department head keeps some for himself and gives the rest away. We never want bonuses to be thought of as salaries because they would lose their effect. So we change the bonus day each year so that it always comes as a pleasant surprise, something to look forward to.[8]

These two examples highlight several generalizations about the use of rewards and sanctions to control individuals, and particularly managers, in strategy execution. Financial incentives are important reward mechanisms. They are particularly useful in controlling performance when they are directly linked to specific activities and results. Intrinsic, nonfinancial rewards, such as flexibility and autonomy in the job and visible control over performance, are important managerial motivators. And negative sanctions, such as withholding financial and intrinsic rewards or the tensions emanating from possible consequences of substandard performance, are necessary ingredients in directing and controlling manager's efforts.

The time horizon on which rewards are based is a major consideration in linking rewards and sanctions to strategically important activities and results. Numerous authors and business leaders have expressed concern with incentive systems based on short-term (typically annual) performance. They fear that short-term reward structures can result in actions and decisions which undermine the long-term position of a firm. A marketing director who is rewarded based on the cost effectiveness and sales generated by the marketing staff might place significantly greater emphasis on established distribution channels than on "inefficient" nurturing and development of channels that the firm has not previously used. A reward system based on maximizing current profitability can potentially shortchange the future in terms of current investments (time, people, and money) from which the primary return will be in

[8] C. R. Christensen, K. R. Andrews, and J. L. Bower, *Business Policy: Text and Cases* (Homewood, Ill.: Richard D. Irwin, 1978), p. 318.

the future.[9] If the firm's grand strategy is growth through, among other means, horizontal integration of current products into new channels and markets, the reward structure could be directing the manager's efforts in a way that penalizes the ultimate success of the strategy. And the marketing director, having performed notably within the current reward structure, may have moved on to other responsibilities before the shortcomings emerge.

Short-term executive incentive schemes typically focus on last year's (or last quarter's) profits. This exclusive concentration on the bottom line has four weaknesses in terms of promoting a new strategy:[10]

1. It is backward looking. Reported results reflect past events and, to some extent, past strategy.
2. The focus is short term, even though many of the recorded transactions have effects over longer periods.
3. Strategic gains or losses are not considered due, among other things, to basic accounting methods.
4. Investment of time and money in future strategy can have a negative impact. Since such outlays and efforts are usually intermingled with other expenses, a manager can improve his or her bonus by *not* preparing for the future.

While there are clear dangers in incentive systems that encourage decidedly short-run thinking and neglect the longer term, there is real danger in hastily condemning short-term measures. It is easy to argue that managers must be concerned with long-run performance; it also may be too easy to make the mistake of concluding that short-term concerns are not important or that they are necessarily counterproductive to the strategic needs of the organization. Such a simplistic and quick conclusion can be dangerous. In an effectively implemented strategy, short-term objectives or aims support and are critical to the achievement of long-term strategic goals. The real problem is not the short- versus long-term concerns of management; it is the lack of integration of and consistency between long- and short-term plans and objectives in the control system that is vital to the successful implementation of strategy.[11] The critical ingredients for the achievement of this consistency are appropriate rewards and incentives.

To integrate long- and short-term concerns, it is necessary to base reward systems on the assessment and control of both the short-run and long-run (strategic) contributions of key managers. An effective reward system should provide payoffs that control and evaluate the creation of *potential* future

[9] W. R. King and D. I. Cleland, *Strategic Planning and Policy* (New York: Van Nostrand Reinhold, 1978), p. 364.

[10] Boris Yavitz and William H. Newman, *Strategy in Action* (New York: Macmillan, 1984), pp. 204–9.

[11] Lawrence G. Hrebiniak and William F. Joyce, *Implementing Strategy* (New York: Macmillan, 1984), pp. 204–9.

performances as well as last year's results. Figure 12–4 illustrates a management reward system tied to a five-year cycle of strategy implementation. Review and evaluation in a specific year include *both* an assessment of performance during that year *and* an evaluation of progress toward the five-year strategic objectives. The annual objectives and incentives in each year can reflect adjustments necessary for successful implementation of the strategy. This helps integrate short- and long-term considerations in strategy implementation by linking adjustments necessary in supporting revised, long-term considerations to next year's reward structure. The second component in the management reward system in Figure 12–4 is an incentive based on cumulative progress toward strategic objectives. It is shown as increasing in size or amount over time which reinforces a long-term, strategic perspective. Incentives such as stock options, deferred bonuses, or cumulative compensation indexed to future performance indicators are ways this reward component could be structured. The key ingredient is an incentive system linked to longer-term progress toward strategic goals. This approach reinforces the interdependence of performance over the five-year period rather than the importance of any one year.

Figure 12–4

Annual incentive system with long-term perspective

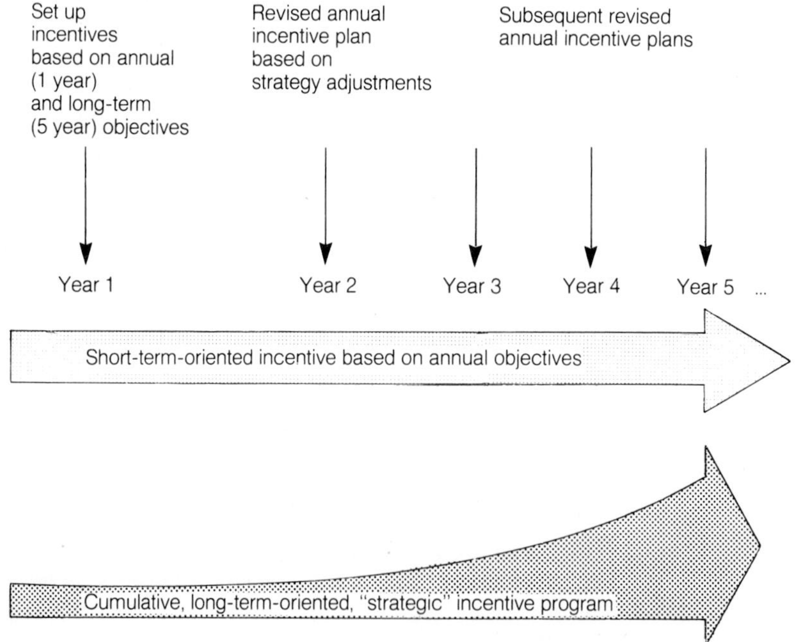

These incentive priorities (long-term versus short-term) should vary depending upon the basic nature of the strategy. Figure 12–5 provides the results of a recent study that illustrates this point. Comparing the importance of 11 criteria used in determining bonuses for SBU managers, the researchers found that long-term criteria were more important determinants of bonuses in SBUs with "build-oriented" strategies than in SBUs with "harvest-oriented" strategies. Short-term criteria were important in both types of SBUs although these criteria were much more important than long-term criteria for determining incentive structures in "harvest-oriented" SBUs. Strategy in Action 12–2 illustrates how top executives at two multibusiness companies that participated in this research link reward structures for their SBUs to each SBU's basic strategy.

Another refinement that has been suggested in constructing incentive systems that reward long-term (strategic) as well as short-term thinking is the

Figure 12–5

Perceived importance of various performance dimensions in determination of SBU general manager's incentive bonus

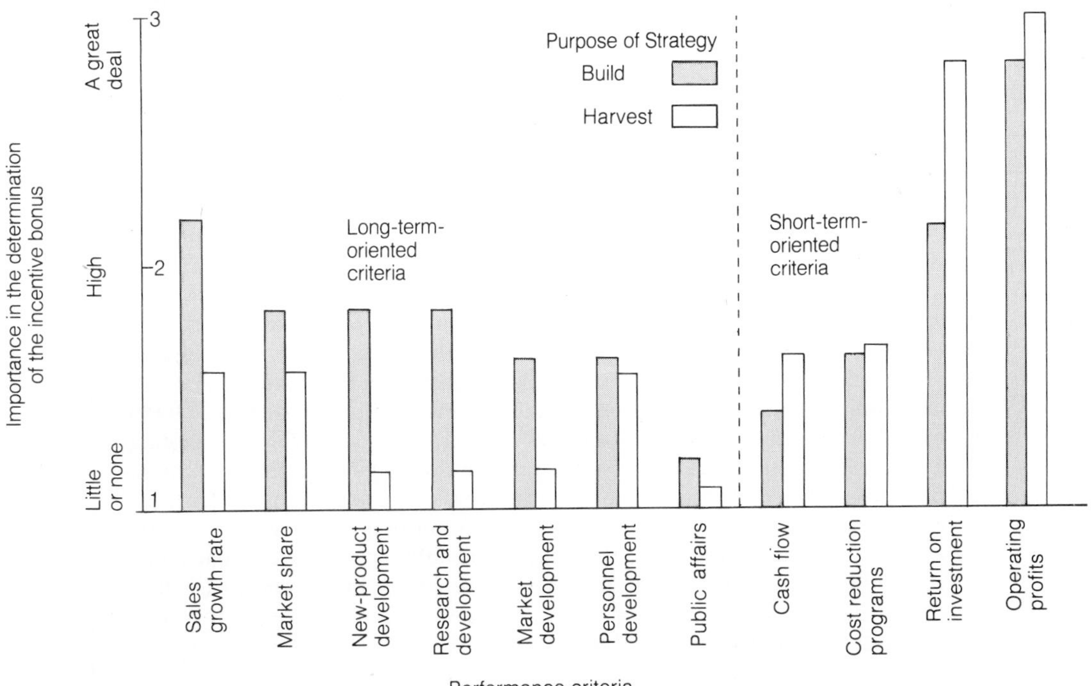

Source: Anil K. Gupta and V. Govindarajan, "Build, Hold, Harvest: Converting Strategic Intentions into Reality," *Journal of Business Strategy,* Winter 1984, p. 43.

Strategy in Action 12–2

Linking Incentive Compensation to Strategy in Large Multibusiness Firms

Recent research suggests that large firms are moving away from uniform (usually "bottom-line") profit criteria to determine incentives in favor of multiple criteria linked in some way to business-unit strategy. Below are reports from two multi-business firms:

At a $5 billion producer of specialty chemicals and metal alloys, the strategic plan for each business is prepared before the annual budgeting process. The objective of the annual budgeting process, however, is not just to prepare an operating budget but also what executives in this firm refer to as a *strategic budget.* The latter "budget" lists specific strategic actions that the business-unit manager would, in line with the long-range strategic plan, need to undertake during the coming year. Examples of items in such a strategic budget are: "increase market share from *x* percent to *y* percent," "prepare a strategic plan to reposition product P by such and such date," "find a buyer for subunit A," and so on. Managers are required to submit progress reports on a quarterly basis on accomplishments vis-à-vis this strategic budget. On a yearly basis, these accomplishments are evaluated for the purposes of determining the second half of a manager's incentive bonus. The link between the strategic mission and the incentive system then becomes a straightforward task—one part of the bonus is linked to certain items in the annual operating budget and the other part to certain other items in the annual strategic budget.

At a $5 billion producer of electronics components and equipment, 25 percent of every SBU manager's bonus is based on corporate performance ("we want them to take a broader, corporatewide perspective") and the remaining 75 percent is split equally between the SBU's bottom-line and nonfinancial objectives. A group vice president detailed how this incentive system operates: "I have three units. I essentially get the same data on each. But in the nonfinancial objectives—more so than in the financial ones—I try to evaluate the three units against their strategic missions. For instance, for [business with a build strategy], I look for acquisitions planned, progress on capital projects, market share, and so forth. For my other two units [with maintain and harvest strategies], I focus on pricing, elimination of low-margin items, cost control, and the line. It is in these nonfinancial objectives where you can differentiate the performance criteria by strategy."

In firms that appear to have made the maximum progress toward matching the incentive system to strategy, the bonus is usually split into two parts: one based on financial figures—such as earnings, return on investment, cash flow, etc.—and the other based on the manager's accomplishments with regard to certain "strategic milestones" derived from the long-range strategic plan.

Adapted from Avil K. Gupta and V. Govindarajan, "Build, Hold, Harvest: Converting Strategic Intentions into Reality," *Journal of Business Strategy,* Winter 1984.

Strategy in Action 12–3

Linking Bonus Compensation to Strategy: What the INC. 100 Fastest-Growing Companies Grant

Type of long-term compensation	*Definition*	*Number of INC 100 companies*	
Investment:			
Incentive stock option	Right to purchase company stock at a set price over period not to exceed 10 years; price must equal 100 percent of fair market value at grant with optionee limited to $100,000 (plus unused carry overs) per year in aggregate exercise cost, must be exercised in order of grant; capital gains at sale if acquired shares held at least one year after exercise and two years after grant.	New plan (1982) Continuing plan Total	29 54 83
Nonqualified stock options	Rights to purchase company stock at a set price over a stated period, often years, typically, price is 100 percent of market value at grant, but can be less. Gain at exercise is taxable income.	New plan (1982) Continuing plan Total	2 55 57
Stock purchases	Short-term rights to purchase company stock, typically at a discount from market value and/or with financing assistance from the company. Shares may be subject to transfer restrictions.	New plan (1982) Continuing plan Total	2 7 9
Noninvestment:			
Stock appreciation rights	Right to receive in stock and/or cash appreciation the gain in market value of specified number of shares since grant, typically granted in conjunction with stock options.	New plan (1982) Continuing plan Total	1 8 9
Stock grants (restricted stock)	Grants of stock, typically subject to transfer restrictions and risk of forfeiture until earned by continued employment with the company.	New plan (1982) Continuing plan Total	— 1 1

Source: "Beyond the Paycheck: Compensating for Growth," *INC*, September 1983, p. 110.

use of *strategic budgets.*[12] In this approach, strategic budgets are employed simultaneously with operating budgets, but the objectives and plans associated with each budget vary a great deal. The focus of the operating budget is control and evaluation of business as usual. The strategic budget specifies resources (and targets) for key programs or activities linked to major initiatives that are integral to the long-term strategy. Concerned that executive incentive plans can and should give more explicit weight to strategic activities, proponents of a strategic budget approach suggest three basic steps:[13]

1. Measure progress toward strategic targets separately from results of established operations.
2. Determine incentive awards separately for established operations and for progress toward strategic targets.
3. Devise a long-term, stock-option equivalent to encourage revisions of strategy and entrepreneurial risk taking.

Common to each of these reward and sanction approaches is growing recognition of the need for a two-tiered incentive system linked to short-run and long-term considerations. The relative emphasis in terms of reward linkages should be determined by the focus of the strategy. For businesses with growth-oriented strategies, for example, incentive systems weighted toward long-term payoffs are more appropriate. Strategy in Action 12–3 illustrates a clear emphasis on this type of executive reward system among *INC* magazine's top 100 growth firms in 1982. Each of these incentives emphasizes long-term value based upon either stock appreciation, length of the option, or a combination of both considerations. While this emphasis is appropriate, short-term operating objectives deserve attention so that short-term performance is geared toward long-term objectives. For businesses pursuing more immediate strategic goals, the incentive emphasis should shift accordingly. In *harvest* business units of large firms, for example, there appears to be greater emphasis on short-term, easily quantified performance indicators as the basis for reward systems designed to evaluate strategic results.

Summary

Essential elements of the strategic management process are control and evaluation of strategy implementation. Three basic considerations are fundamental in this context: (1) the need to identify performance standards, (2) the need to monitor performance and evaluate deviations, and (3) the need to motivate control and evaluation.

---

[12] Peter Lorange, *Implementation of Strategic Planning* (Englewood Cliffs, N.J.: Prentice-Hall, 1982), and "Strategic Control: Some Issues in Making It Operationally More Useful," in *Latest Advances in Strategic Management,* ed. R. Lamb Warren (Englewood Cliffs, N.J.: Prentice-Hall, in press).

[13] Yavitz and Newman, *Strategy in Action,* p. 179.

There are two fundamental perspectives—strategic and operational control—that provide the basis for designing necessary control systems. Strategic control systems involve identifying and monitoring the essential building blocks for the strategy's success. They are designed to meet top-management control needs and require identification of strategic success factors that are linked to the environmental assumptions and key operating requirements necessary for successful strategy implementation.

Operational control systems identify the performance standards associated with allocation and use of the company's financial, physical, and human resources in pursuit of the strategy. Budgets and schedules linked to annual objectives and operating strategies provide the key means for operational control.

Control systems, linked to the firm's objectives and strategies, require systematic evaluation of performance against predetermined standards or targets to maximize the contribution of the control system in strategic management. A critical concern here is identification and evaluation of performance deviations, with careful attention paid to determining the underlying reasons and strategic implications for observed deviations before management reacts. Some companies use trigger points and contingency plans in this phase.

The reward system is a key ingredient in motivating managers to emphasize control and evaluation in steering the business toward strategic success. Companies should emphasize incentive systems that ensure adequate attention to strategic thrusts. This usually requires a concerted effort to emphasize long-term performance indicators rather than solely emphasizing short-term measures of performance. Short- and long-term performance considerations must be integrated to ensure performance consistent with the company's strategy and provide a basis for monitoring future short-run performance against objectives incrementally linked to long-term strategic outcomes.

Questions for Discussion

1. Distinguish strategic control from operating control. Give an example of each.
2. Select a business that has a strategy you are familiar with. Identify what you think are its strategic success factors. Then select the key indicators you would use to monitor each strategic success factor.
3. Why are operating budgets and schedules essential to strategic control and evaluation?
4. What are key considerations in monitoring deviations from performance standards?
5. How would you vary an incentive system for a growth-oriented versus a harvest-oriented business?
6. Why do strategists prefer reward systems similar to that shown in Figure 12–4? What are the advantages and disadvantages of such a system?

Bibliography

Bales, Carter. "Strategic Control: The President's Paradox." *Business Horizons,* August 1977, pp. 17–28.

Bower, Joseph. "Planning and Control." *Journal of General Management* 1, no. 3 (1974), pp. 20–31.

Camillus, J. C. "Six Approaches to Preventive Management Control." *Financial Executive,* December 1980, pp. 28–31.

Christopher, W. "Achievement Reporting—Controlling Performance against Objectives." *Long-Range Planning,* October 1977, pp. 14–24.

Diffenbach, J. "Finding the Right Strategic Combination." *Journal of Business Strategy,* Fall 1981, pp. 47–58.

Hobbs, John, and Donald Heany. "Coupling Strategy to Operating Plans." *Harvard Business Review,* May–June 1977, pp. 119–26.

Horovits, J. N. "Strategic Control: A New Task for Top Management." *Long-Range Planning,* June 1979, pp. 2–7.

Lenz, R. T. "Determinants of Organizational Performance: An Interdisciplinary Review." *Strategic Management Journal* 2 (1981), pp. 131–54.

Merchant, Kenneth A. "The Control Function of Management." *Sloan Management Review* 23, no. 4 (1982), pp. 43–55.

Newman, W. H. *Constructive Control: Design and Use of Control Systems.* Englewood Cliffs, N.J.: Prentice-Hall, 1975.

Rappaport, Alfred. "Executive Incentives versus Corporate Growth." *Harvard Business Review,* July–August 1978, pp. 81–88.

Rockart, J. F. "Chief Executives Define Their Own Data Needs." *Harvard Business Review,* March–April 1979, pp, 85–94.

Chapter 12 Cohesion Case Illustration

Control and Evaluation at Holiday Inns, Inc.

With four distinct business groups, there are a wide range of control issues across the business level at Holiday Inns, Inc. Rather than discuss each group we will identify several control and evaluation issues within the hotel business to illustrate the material in Chapter 12.

Strategic Control

The identification of strategic success factors, key performance indicators or other measures that should be used to monitor those factors, and a determination of guidelines for decision making where deviations occur are essential to control of the hotel group's strategy. Top management must be concerned with identifying and monitoring key environmental factors, industry forces, strategy-specific requirements, and company-related capabilities that are critical to the ultimate success of the strategy.

Examples of strategic success factors that Holiday Inns' hotel group would consider critical to the success of its strategy are shown below. Accompanying the factors are possible measures that should provide an accurate basis for monitoring the hotel group's performance with regard to each strategic success factor. Also included below are abbreviated control guidelines that might exist to guide reaction to deviations from expectations in each success factor.

Operational Control

The hotel group must seek to compliment strategic control by ensuring the presence of an adequate operational control systems link to short-term resource usage and performance objectives. We will briefly describe two operational control systems within the hotel group that serve this purpose: expenditure budgeting and quality control.

Holiday Inns has an *expenditure budgeting system,* which is called operations management systems (OMS), that has been implemented at the individual inn level. The purpose of this system is monitoring and controlling profitability by providing weekly budgets for the use of hotel resources that reflect the cyclical nature of occupancy patterns throughout the year. This OMS budget projects staff scheduling, energy control, departmental (inn, restaurant, and lounge) expenditures and usage, inventory control, and quality assurance needs for each week throughout the year to help control profitability and the level of service the customer expects.

Strategic success factors	*Key performance indicators or measures*	*Strategic control guidelines*
Environmental:		
Interest rates	Prime rate; trends in near term t-bills	Need to stabilize long-term financing costs: look for opportunity to call 9⅝ percent debentures to establish a broader equity base.
Level of overall business activity	GNP; Airline passenger miles	Prepare to accelerate or decelerate expansion depending on rise or fall in business travel activity.
Industrywide:		
Competitive intensity	Industrywide occupancy trends; supply of rooms and announced openings; level of industry segmentation	Holiday Inn's occupancy targets are influenced by industrywide supply and demand. As competition increases in the broad middle segment, HI must look to more rapid growth in other lodging segments.
Strategy specific:		
Systemwide occupancy of 68 percent plus.	Daily, weekly, and monthly occupancy results compared to projected trends and assumptions.	Prepare to accelerate, (if occupancy is above 70 percent) or decelerate (if occupancy is below 65 percent), expansion efforts. Use to guide franchise renewal decisions by eliminating weaker franchises.
Opening of new locations	Planned (scheduled) versus actual openings	Ensure immediate follow-up where behind schedule, particularly in key markets; coordinate with demand sensitive indicators of need to accelerate/decelerate expansion.
Company specific:		
Financial capacity	Long-term debt to invested capital ratio	Ensure that this ratio does not exceed 35 percent on an annual basis.
Quality standards	Number of units cited as sub-par by HI inspectors each quarter	Enforce stringent quality standards and eliminate sub-par units from the system.

The hotel group puts major emphasis on its *quality control system* to ensure that the strategy of standardized, high-quality accommodations is being implemented. The heart of the quality control system is 25 full-time inspectors who travel over 1 million miles during the year performing over 4,300 property reviews. Most properties are inspected three times a year on an unannounced basis during which some 1,100 different items are checked. Hotels failing to meet standards (after two inspections) are removed from the system.

Reward System

Holiday Inns' *reward system* is multifaceted in its approach to guiding desired strategy implementation. First, the hotel group monitors industry-wide compensation packages to ensure that Holiday Inns' basic package is comparable to or greater than the industry norm. They also provide an incentive cash bonus plan for officers and key employees whereby these individuals can earn up to 81 percent of their annual salary if implementation targets are met. Recognizing the key corporate objective of enhancing stock value, Holiday Inns provides key management personnel with long-term cash or stock bonuses based on appreciation in the price of the company's publicly traded stock.

Appendix—Cohesion Case Conclusion: Update of Key Strategic Decisions and Actions at Holiday Inns, Inc., in the Early 1980s

Up until now, the Cohesion Case Illustrations have demonstrated the application of strategic management concepts to the situation at Holiday Inns as it sought to design its strategies for the 1980s. This appendix provides a brief summary of the key strategic decisions actually made to guide Holiday Inns, Inc. through the 1980s.

Holiday Inns, Inc., entered the mid-1980s as quite a different company from the Holiday Inns, Inc., of the 1970s. Under founder Kemmons Wilson, who retired in 1979, Holiday Inns' executives defined their operations as part of the travel business, seeking to rationalize a broad-based diversification program. Under this definition, Holiday Inns eventually enter over 30 different businesses from furniture manufacturing to the operation of buses that the company anticipated would funnel some customers to its inns. This rapid diversification taxed management capabilities at Holiday Inns. In addition, the underlying travel-related assumptions proved to be unrealistic in several instances. Corporate strategists initially failed to foresee, for example, that few bus passengers were likely to stay at medium- to high-priced hotels, or that hotel franchisees might balk because Holiday Inn produced furniture was more expensive than the products of alternative sources. Since assuming the chief executive officer (CEO) position in 1978, and the chairmanship one year later, Roy Winegardner recognized the failure of the travel-related philosophy and has sought to change it. Commenting on this change in an interview with *Business Week* in 1980, Winegardner said:

> We are in the process of reshaping Holiday Inns into a different company. Holiday Inns is actually a "hospitality" company—a concept that will limit its scope to food, lodging, and entertainment. . . . In the future the company will get into as few businesses as possible, and only those that have good growth, high returns, and are synergistic with our main business—hotels.

On August 13, 1981, the management of Holiday Inns, Inc., made a presentation before the New York Society of Security Analysts, outlining the company's businesses, strategies, and financial goals for the 1980s.

The following remarks provide an edited version that shows the strategic choices made by Holiday Inns' management team.

Roy E. Winegardner, Chairman of the Board

We are pleased to have the opportunity to discuss what we term "the new Holiday Inns, Inc.," for our company today is much different from what it was when I joined it in 1974.

At that time we were the world's largest lodging company, but we were also a company with interests in some 30 nonrelated businesses.[1] Additionally, seven years ago, the way our industry conducted its business began to change rapidly. The business environment was unpredictable—we were in the middle of an oil embargo, we were facing one of the worst recessions ever, and the lodging industry had the largest oversupply of rooms since the 1930s.

Obviously, we needed to adapt to these changes, but we also realized that to succeed in the coming years we would have to develop a management team and a management style that would allow us to successfully run our businesses in a constantly changing environment. So we started building an organization with emphasis on strategy planning. Beginning with Mike Rose, we assembled a first-rate management team which started to examine, and then to reshape the direction of our company. We decided to concentrate on the area that we knew best, *the hospitality industry,* so we set a plan in motion to strengthen and grow our leadership position.

---

[1] The majority of these businesses, 26 in the early 1970s, were part of Holiday Inns' sprawling products group. In August 1979, Holiday Inns sold its Trailways bus operations to a private investment group for $94 million. The divestiture of Trailways reduced 1979 net income by $15.4 million, reflecting a small operating loss ($270,000) to the date of sale, plus a loss of $15.2 million on disposition. Although taking a loss on the sale, Holiday Inns removed an unrelated, poorly performing business from its corporate portfolio. Of equal importance to Holiday Inns, the sale generated over $90 million in cash to partially underwrite its rapid movement into casino gaming. In 1980, management decided to narrow the scope of the Product Services Division of the Hotel Group, which had marketed a wide range of supplies, special items, furnishings and equipment to food, lodging, and other institutional customers. The division now serves as a hotel procurement vehicle for the company and the Holiday Inn system and also provides planning and design services to the company and the system. In 1981, the company discontinued operations of its InnKare unit, which had provided consumable items to the hotel and restaurant industries.

As part of that plan, we concluded that we simply could not provide the right kind of management to the wide variety of businesses we were in at the time, so we set about divesting ourselves of those that did not fit with our hospitality strategy.

Hospitality Focus. We are now clearly focused on three hospitality-oriented businesses that have excellent long-range growth potential—hotels, gaming, and restaurants. Additionally, we have defined the function and relationship of our fourth business, Delta Steamship Lines. Delta is a good company with strong management serving profitable growth markets.

We have long-range plans in place for each of our businesses—through which we continuously review present and future economic and social trends, so that we can anticipate and proact, rather than react, to changes in our operating environment. During the process of change in the past seven years, we became a professionally managed hospitality company without losing our heritage of a strong entrepreneurial spirit.

In 1974, we experienced the worst year in the company's history. By contrast, 1980 was the best, despite a soft economy and high inflation. In 1974, income from continuing operations was $12.7 million. In 1980, it was $108.3 million, up a compound annual rate of 43 percent.

Income per share from continuing operations was $.41 in 1974. Last year 1980 income per share was $2.92, up a compound annual rate of 39 percent, which includes a substantial increase in the number of shares outstanding. The after-tax margin in 1974 was only 1.8 percent. By 1980 it had nearly quadrupled to a very acceptable 7.1 percent. Return on equity (ROE) has improved steadily from 6.7 percent in 1974 to 16.1 percent in 1980.

1980 was our best year ever, and 1981 is shaping up to be even better. I believe that this is a clear indication of things to come for Holiday Inns, Inc.

We have the businesses in place and are making the necessary investments to ensure their continued successful growth. We have the programs in place to direct our businesses in periods of high inflation and in difficult and turbulent economic times. And we have the people in place to successfully manage our businesses in the face of whatever changes this decade may produce.

Michael D. Rose, President and Chief Executive Officer

Roy's remarks focused on the evolution of the company from an entrepreneurial, high-growth situation without a clear focus, into a company with very clear direction to be the hospitality industry leader in the 1980s. The evolution of our hospitality strategy has been very straightforward.

We wanted to build from our core hotel business where we are the industry leader, and utilize the management skills and techniques that we have developed over the years in the hotel business to apply to other hospitality businesses where a degree of synergy existed. We also wanted to be in businesses that offer growth opportunities and high returns on capital investment at least equal to or potentially higher than the hotel business.

The key to our long-term direction is the fact that our hotel business will be our core business for the future. Hotel Group operating income accounted for more than 60 percent of total operating income during the first half of 1981, and we expect this percentage to reamin relatively constant over the next five years.

The mission of the Hotel Group is to grow Holiday Inns' leadership position in the broad midscale segments of the lodging industry. This mission will be achieved by producing superior consumer satisfaction through increased emphasis on the quality of our product and further capitalization on our significant distributional advantages over all other competitors. We also intend to grow our consumer recognition as the preferred brand in the lodging industry.

Margins Nearly Doubled. At the same time that we have set our mission in clear terms of consumer satisfaction, we also have been concentrating on improved profitability and productivity. Over the last five years we have nearly doubled operating margins in our hotel business from 10.8 percent in 1976 to more than 21 percent for the first half of 1981. It is particularly pleasing to me that we have been able to improve our margins in 1980 and 1981 despite industrywide occupancy declines due to the soft economy during that period.

We can continue to see significant opportunities for unit growth in our hotel business, both domestically and abroad. Our intent is to develop through a combination of franchisee growth and parent company investment. We would expect over the next decade that the current relationship of four franchise units for each parent unit would generally be maintained.

Holiday Inn hotels are ideally positioned in the moderate-price market segment to take advantage of the large projected demand growth within this segment. In simple terms, the lodging industry could be described in three major segments: the high-price or image segment, the moderate-price segment, and the low-price segment.

Demand Growth. While we think the percentage growth of demand will be highest in the high-price or image segment, in absolute terms the demand for rooms in the moderate-price segment will grow three times faster than in either the high-price or low-price segments.

We are further encouraged that new room supply is being focused more and more at the high end of the market, and we can foresee an oversupply of hotel rooms in that segment during this decade. On the other hand, we think that most of our chain competitors in the moderate segment do not have the inherent strength to keep pace with the demand growth in the moderate-price segment, and that we will continue to grow our share of that segment during the next decade.

Our domestic parent company development will be predominantly in major metropolitan areas in locations where we serve multiple demand sources. For example, we would like to be in locations that serve both business and leisure travelers, that also serve small group meetings, and that serve people arriving by automobile and air.

Two good examples of this type of development are our two newest parent company hotels, one located between the airport and Opryland in Nashville, Tennessee, and another located at the San Antonio, Texas, airport in an area that is experiencing great commercial growth. Although these hotels have been open less than six months, in July they were both running occupancies in excess of 93 percent with rates well above $40. These kinds of properties in these kinds of locations will provide a significant amount of the absolute dollar growth in profits for Holiday Inns out into the future.

In addition to the development of new hotels, we have been consolidating our base of hotels over the last seven years. Our mix of property types has changed over this period of time (see table). Particular emphasis should be on the fact that we have moved away from the roadside or oasistype location into areas with multiple sources of demand such as downtown, midtown, and airport locations.

Room mix by location type (company owned or managed percent)

	1974	*1981*
Roadside	21	7
Downtown	26	32
Airport	5	8
Suburban	35	37
Resort	12	14
Small towns	3	2
	100%	100%

In terms of number of rooms, our current plan is to add to the Holiday Inn system on a gross basis between 60,000 and 70,000 rooms over the next five years. This would translate into approximately 40,000 to 50,000 net new rooms as we continue to remove rooms from our system that do not maintain our increasingly more demanding quality standards.

International Development. On the international front, development will be pursued with limited parent company capital investment. We will continue to expand aggressively through management contracts and franchising, with some minority equity positions in areas that we believe to be politically and economically stable. Our strategy is to develop in the major gateway cities of the world, and then to fill in behind these locations to develop regional and national chains with strong brand identification in the local areas.

Technological Development. As we look ahead into the decade of the 1980s, the ability to manage technological change will play a large part in the success, or lack of it, for many companies. We have attempted to stay on the leading edge of technology as applied to the hotel business throughout our history. The best example of this is our Holidex® reservations system, which was developed in 1964 and revolutionized the way reservations were made in the hotel industry.

During 1981 we will be completing the implementation of the second generation of Holidex, which is the culmination of a meticulously planned and executed effort stretching over a five-year period. Holidex II℠ will continue to be the most cost-effective reservations system in the industry, but will have significantly expanded capability to provide inventory control, advance guest registration, the storage and retrieval of significant marketing information, and the ability ultimately to transmit management data in addition to reservations on a timely basis.

Another technological first for Holiday Inns is our HI-NET℠ satellite communications network. The HI-NET system provides low-cost, in-room entertainment that is free to the guest, as well as the capability to hold nationwide teleconferences using Holiday Inn facilities.

To give you an example of the capabilities of the HI-NET system for teleconferencing, we recently held a teleconference meeting for our own employees which was aimed at increasing employee involvement and ultimately improving productivity in all of our businesses. We were able to communicate directly with approximately 15,000 employees of Holiday Inns, Harrah's, Perkins, and Delta at over 130 locations throughout the United States.

Outlook Bright. The future outlook for our hotel business has never been brighter. With demand projected to grow at a faster rate than supply, we have the assets in place, the most recognized and preferred brand, and the strongest franchise organization in the lodging industry. We have the financial strength, and our franchisees have the financial strength, to attract new capital for hotel development. While financing has been extremely difficult to obtain recently for hotel development in general, I think it is important for you to note that during 1981 we project that the Holiday Inn hotel system will open 65 new properties with 13,200 rooms. Further, 52 new Holiday Inn hotels will go under construction in 1981, representing an estimated 10,800 rooms.

With this level of development at a time when financing has been as difficult as in any period in our history, we are confident that we can aggressively grow our business when the financial markets return to some level of stability.

Having strategically identified the hotel business as the core around which we intend to build our future, we began several years ago to look for other businesses which had synergy with the hotel business. One of the obvious industries was the casino/hotel business, which we entered in 1979. In early 1980 we acquired Harrah's, and at the end of 1980 we opened our Harrah's® Marina hotel/casino in Atlantic City.

As a result of this major thrust into the gaming business, Holiday Inns, Inc., through Harrah's, has become the largest gaming company in the country and is the only company represented in all four of the major gaming markets: Las Vegas, Reno, Lake Tahoe, and Atlantic City. Our Gaming Group currently operates 457 table games and 5,736 slot machines in more than 188,000 square feet of gaming space.

The mission of the Gaming Group is to provide high-quality customer service at a high perceived value. In acquiring Harrah's, we also acquired the best casino management team in the gaming industry, one that is dedicated to delivering superior levels of product and service to the gaming customer. And as the song goes, "Nobody does it better."

This year we have placed increasing emphasis on the control and reduction of overhead costs and on human resource development. It is our intent to develop people and management systems that can be transferred to new locations as we see gaming expand both domestically and internationally.

We expect margins to improve at Harrah's with this increased emphasis on cost control and streamlined management systems. We also are focusing on improving ROI through the sale of some of the unproductive assets which we acquired in the acquisition of Harrah's. You may be aware that we are currently negotiating for the sale of Harrah's auto collection, and we expect that a transaction may be consummated before the end of this year which will free up a significant amount of capital for reinvestment in income-producing assets.

Nevada Expansions. Both of our northern Nevada casinos in Reno and Lake Tahoe have been expanded since the acquisition, and both properties continue to gain market share due to their outstanding positioning in the marketplace. We are also expanding in Las Vegas with completion scheduled for this fall.

Much of our optimism about growth and profits in our Gaming Group in the near term comes from the results that we are currently experiencing in Atlantic City. Despite the ongoing regulatory difficulties which make Atlantic City a very high-cost place [in which] to operate when compared with other jurisdictions, the market remains extremely strong, and we believe that we have found a very good position with our Marina property.

We are building a reputation for quality service and qualtiy facilities in Atlantic City similar to that which we enjoy in northern Nevada. It is our intention to increase our emphasis on attracting the higher-limit casino players through a more flexible use of credit facilities, while continuing to have the most productive slot machines in the Atlantic City market.

At the end of the second quarter, we increased our ownership in Harrah's Marina to 99 percent, and you will begin to see the impact of that move in our third-quarter results.

We think there is a great deal of opportunity for growth in the gaming business, both domestically and internationally. We have very strong market positions in each of the markets where we currently do business, and we believe that we can continue to either grow our share or benefit from the ongoing growth in these markets. While we do not see legalization in other jurisdictions in the United States in the near term, we do anticipate that tax revenue from casino gaming will continue to get the attention of politicians around the country as other sources of tax revenue become more difficult to obtain.

On the other hand, we were delighted to see the demise of gaming legislation in New York because we felt that our company and the rest of the industry were not ready, from either a people or capital standpoint, to make a major new thrust into a heavily populated state like New York. With the quasimonopoly positions of New Jersey and Nevada, and significant assets in place in both areas, we will not be pressing other jurisdictions to legalize gaming.

The third element of our hospitality business is our Perkins® restaurant chain. Acquired in 1979, Perkins has 358 stores in 29 states; of these, 102 are company owned and the remaining are franchised.

Perkins Improvement. After extremely fast growth over several years, Perkins suffered from declining customer counts and lower margins last year, as did the restaurant industry as a whole. We have slowed the growth of Perkins and focused the attention of an aggressive young management team on improving operations and rebuilding headcounts. While Perkins has frankly been a bit of a disappointment to us at this stage, we do strongly believe that we can rebuild headcounts, continue to control costs, and expand on a regional basis to obtain sufficient market penetration.

It is our intent to grow Perkins primarily through the franchise system, with corporate stores filling in those major markets where we have already established a strong presence. Obviously, Perkins can never become a large part of Holiday Inns, Inc., with such mammoth businesses as the hotel and casino businesses, but we do think it is a vehicle for percentage growth and high return on assets employed.

It is our intention that Perkins will continue to grow using only its own cash flow, so that it will not be competitive with the hotel or casino businesses for capital resources.

The fourth major business under the Holiday Inns banner is Delta Steamship Lines. Delta is a highly profitable market leader in providing cargo transportation service between the United States and South America and West Africa.

Delta operates as a U.S. flag carrier from major port facilities in San Francisco, New Orleans, and New York.

In 1978, we doubled the number of routes and ships operated by Delta with the acquisition of Prudential Lines. In 1979, we began to substantially change our management team to handle the level of expanded business, bringing Andy Gibson in as chief executive. This new management organization produced earnings of almost $48 million in 1980, nearly tripling the operating income of $16.5 million in 1979. While 1980 results will be difficult to match, we are pleased that for the first half of 1981 we are slightly ahead of our record pace in 1980.

Although Delta is obviously not a hospitality company, despite the fact that four of its ships do serve cruise passengers, it does have a fit in our long-term hospitality strategy by providing significant free cash flow for reinvestment into the hospitality businesses. Just this month, for example, Delta paid dividends of $28 million to Holiday Inns, Inc., for unrestricted corporate use. It also has provided an additional $40 million in cash advances year to date.

Delta Well Positioned. Delta is well positioned in the trade routes in which it operates and has a broad base of customers in the countries it serves. With a flexible fleet and a highly skilled management team in place, we expect solid profit performance for Delta in the future.

For those of you who have followed our company over the years, you have heard us talk a lot about our planning process and the pride that we have taken in both planning our future and achieving our plans. We have just completed our most recent five-year plan, incorporating our new businesses for the first time in a comprehensive manner.

One of the key focuses of our planning process is on the ever-increasing need to improve productivity in each of our businesses through greater involvement and utilization of our human resources. In service industries such as ours, the ongoing key to our success will be our ability to attract, motivate, retain and fully challenge superior people.

Additional Comments by Rose

By early 1983, Rose offered these additional comments about Holiday Inn's strategic efforts for the 1980s: We celebrated our 30th anniversary as a company in 1982, and during the year we took many important steps to assure our long-term growth and vitality.

The most important of these steps was the completion of the sale of Delta Steamship Lines, Inc.[2] With the disposition of our steamship subsidiary, Holi-

---

[2] In December 1982, the Company sold Delta Steamship Lines to a subsidiary of Crowley Maritime Corporation for $96 million in cash.

day Inns, Inc., is now strategically focused on the hospitality industry. The Delta sale represents the culmination of more than seven years of planning and execution aimed at positioning our company as the worldwide leader in the hospitality business.

We also introduced a new sign and logo for our Holiday Inn hotel system in 1982. The Great Sign has become a symbol of Americana, and it was difficult to say goodbye to an old friend. However, we feel that our new sign projects a more contemporary image, better reflecting the range of property types and level of product quality that will characterize the Holiday Inn hotel system in the decades ahead.

Recognizing the increasing segmentation of the lodging market, we also began construction on two new hotel products in 1982 that will be marketed under new brand names and are designed to meet the needs of growing market segments. Holiday Inn Crowne Plaza hotels will be located in major metropolitan areas and aimed at the upper end of the Holiday Inn hotel customer profile. These hotels will deliver higher levels of product quality and service than our more moderately priced Holiday Inn hotels. The second concept, our new Embassy Suite hotel product, will provide expanded room accomodations in high-quality hotels targeted primarily to the business traveler at the upper end of the lodging market.

At the end of 1982, eight Holiday Inn Crowne Plaza brand hotels were under construction. Some 30 existing Holiday Inn hotels worldwide also are expected to be converted to meet the top-of-the-line specifications for this group. We intend to have under construction or to have acquired for conversion at least 10 Embassy Suite hotels by year-end 1983.

We also embarked on an aggressive expansion plan for our core Holiday Inn hotel brand in 1982. At year end, we had seven company-owned or managed core brand Holiday Inn hotels under construction worldwide and our franchisees had 41 of these hotels under way. This represents the most aggressive company hotel development effort in recent years, and reflects our continuing belief in the long-term strength of the lodging market and of our Holiday Inn brand within the large moderate-priced segment of that market.

We have moved forward with the expansion of our gaming business over the past year. On January 4, 1983, we acquired the remaining 60 percent of the Holiday Casino in Las Vegas. This 31,000-square-foot casino, in combination with the recently expanded 1,000-room Holiday Inn-Center Strip hotel, gives us a major presence on the world famous "Strip" in Las Vegas.

Atlantic City has established itself as the number one tourist destination in America, attracting more visitors in 1982 than either Las Vegas or Disney World in Orlando. Our company has prospered with the growth of Atlantic City, as our Harrah's Marina facility there has proven to be the most profitable hotel/casino in that market on a pretax, preinterest basis. To capitalize on Atlantic City's continuing market growth, we entered into a joint venture to build a new 600-room hotel and 60,000-square-foot casino on the Boardwalk.

Scheduled to open in the spring of 1984, this facility will be connected to the Atlantic City Convention Center, which is in the initial phases of an extensive renovation. We believe this is the premier location on the Atlantic City Boardwalk, and it should contribute to Harrah's ability to achieve the same brand leadership position in Atlantic City that it now enjoys in northern Nevada.

During 1982 we made other more difficult decisions that we believe will benefit the company over the long term, but which had a negative impact on our 1982 earnings. One of these was the decision to restrain price increase in both our hotel and restaurant businesses. As a result of this pricing strategy, operating margins suffered in our hotel business. However, this approach enabled us to maintain 1981 occupancy levels in 1982, despite the fact that occupancies declined throughout the rest of the hotel industry. At Perkins Restaurants, Inc., our restaurant subsidiary, this pricing strategy paid off, contributing to substantially higher customer count and improved unit profitability.

We also made the decision to dispose of a number of restaurants and hotels which were not performing to our financial standards, resulting in a provision for loss on disposition for hotels and for Perkins restaurants in 1982. We believe this step puts us in a better position for future growth and improved return on investment in the years ahead.

We continue to be impressed by Perkins' progress and expect to resume a modest company-owned unit expansion program in 1983 to complement franchise expansion activity. We also will be testing new facilities and menu designs in 1983, aimed at increasing our dinner business while maintaining Perkins' strong image as a high-quality breakfast and luncheon restaurant chain.

In addition to strengthening our market position, we also strengthened our balance sheet in 1982. The company's 9⅝ percent convertible subordinated debentures were called for redemption on March 2, 1982. The result was conversion to $143 million of additional equity, which provides the basis for significant new debt capacity to fund our future expansion.

Consistent with our stated intention to reduce floating rate debt, we issued $75 million in fixed-rate, 10-year notes in August 1982.

Our funds flow from continuing operations has nearly doubled over the past three years, and we expect a healthy improvement in funds flow again in 1983. Given that, and the receipt of $96 million in cash proceeds from the sale of Delta, we are well positioned to meet our capital needs for our aggressive expansion efforts.

In 1982 we commissioned an update of an independent study of the appreciated value of the company's tangible assets and certain contract rights. This study indicated that the net market value of these assets approximated $2.5 billion, nearly three times the $0.9 billion shareholders equity shown on our balance sheet. The information provided by this study gives lenders, investors, and rating agencies a clearer picture of the financial condition of our company, since the appraisal reflects the value of the company's franchise and management contract income streams as well as the appreciation of our real estate assets.

As we look ahead to the remainder of the 1980s, the economic picture remains clouded. We cannot accurately predict the impact of unprecedented massive federal budget deficits on our economy. That introduces an element of uncertainty which affects our ability to set our goals for a return on equity, determine the appropriate amount of leverage, and establish our dividend policy. While we believe our objectives in each of these areas remain appropriate, given the unpredictability of the economic environment, we must continue to monitor all of our performance standards for potential revision in the future.

Summary

Holiday Inns, Inc.'s strategy for the 1980s is clearly to emphasize existing businesses that have a hospitality (food, lodging and/or entertainment) orientation. The hotel group will be the core of this overall corporate strategy. Expected to generate approximately 60 percent of overall revenues, the hotel group has chosen to pursue both market and product development strategies in an effort to expand their leadership position. The market development is focused on identifying new, multiuser locations and stable international markets. The product development strategy has the hotel group, with the introduction of the Hampton Inns budget chain (no restaurants or lounges) in late 1983, offering four different hotel chains focused on distinct segments of the lodging market.

The gaming group is pursuing concentration strategies to rapidly gain even larger positions in the key legalized gambling markets in Nevada and New Jersey. Perhaps the greatest long-term growth potential is viewed by HI management to rest with this group.

The Perkins group is still emphasizing a concentration strategy centered on consolidating and clarifying Perkins' niche in the restaurant industry. Interestingly, Perkins was not mentioned in Mike Rose's March, 1984 "Letter to Shareholders" that summarized the condition and future priorities of Holiday Inns, Inc.

Consistent with this hospitality orientation and the need to generate or redirect resources to support it, Trailways was divested in late 1979. Delta Steamships, clearly a "cash cow," was eventually divested once the right buyer was found in late 1982.

APPENDIX

Using Financial Analysis*

One of the most important tools for assessing the strength of an organization within its industry is financial analysis. Managers, investors, and creditors all employ some form of this analysis as the beginning point for their financial decision making. Investors use financial analyses in making decisions about whether to buy or sell stock, and creditors use them in deciding whether or not to lend. They provide managers with a measurement of how the company is doing in comparison with its performance in past years and with the performance of competitors in the industry.

Although financial analysis is useful for decision making, there are some weaknesses that should be noted. Any picture that it provides of the company is based on past data. Although trends may be noteworthy, this picture should not automatically be assumed to be applicable to the future. In addition, the analysis is only as good as the accounting procedures that have provided the information. When making comparisons between companies, one should keep in mind the variability of accounting procedures from firm to firm.

There are four basic groups of financial ratios: liquidity, leverage, activity, and profitability.

Depicted in Exhibit 1 are the specific ratios calculated for each of the basic groups. Liquidity and leverage ratios represent an assessment of the risk of the firm. Activity and profitability ratios are measures of the return generated

---

* Prepared by Elizabeth Gatewood, University of Georgia.

Exhibit 1

Financial ratios

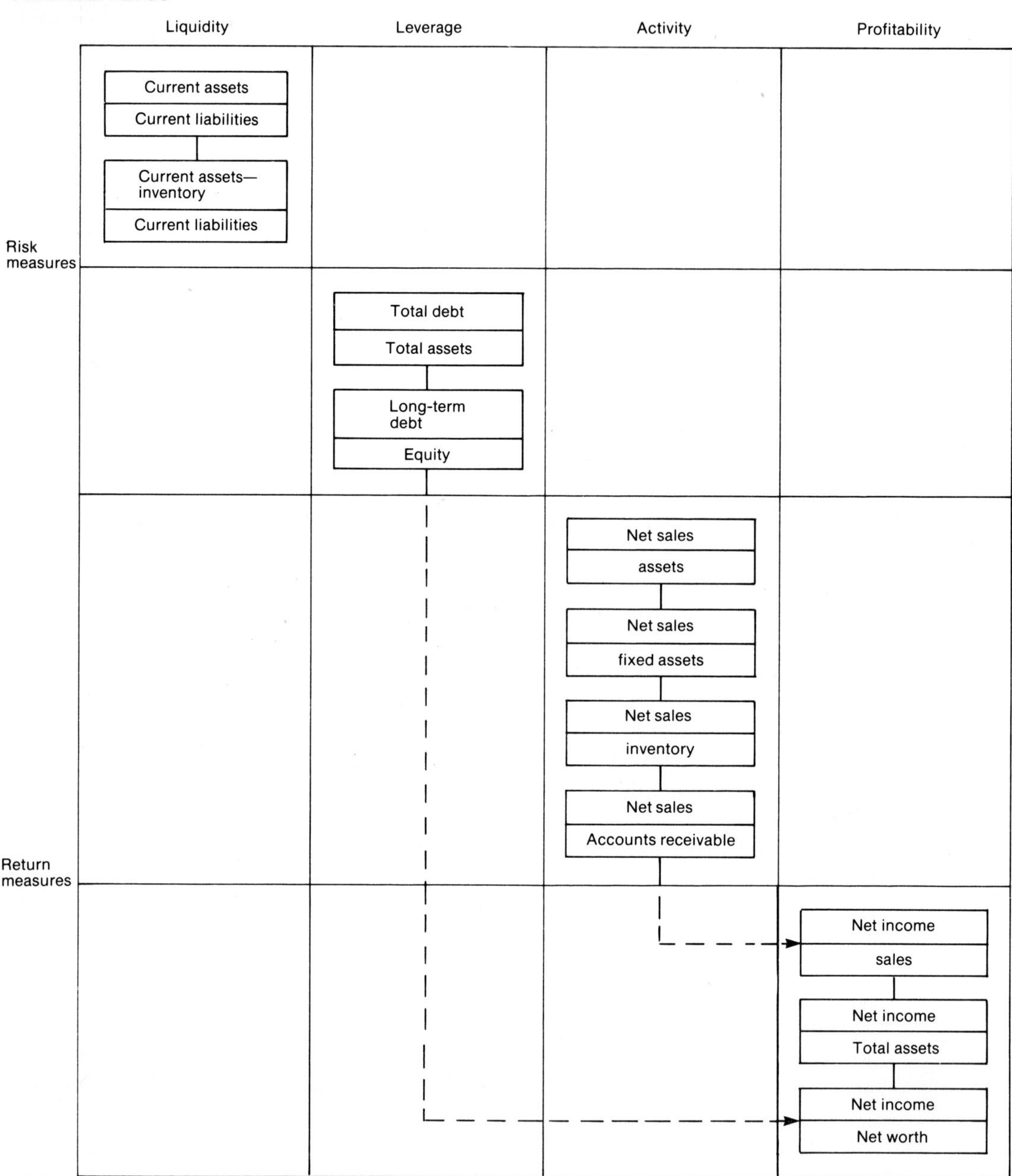

by the assets of the firm. The interaction between certain groups of ratios is indicated by arrows.

Typically two common financial statements are used in financial analyses: the balance sheet and the income statement. Exhibit 2 is a balance sheet and Exhibit 3 an income statement for the ABC Company. These statements will be used to illustrate the financial analyses.

Exhibit 2

ABC COMPANY
Balance Sheet
As of December 31

		1985		*1984*
Assets				
Current assets:				
Cash		$ 140,000		$ 115,000
Accounts receivable		1,760,000		1,440,000
Inventory		2,175,000		2,000,000
Prepaid expenses		50,000		63,000
Total current assets		4,125,000		3,618,000
Fixed assets:				
Long-term receivables		1,255,000		1,090,000
Property and plant	$2,037,000		$2,015,000	
Less: Accumulated depreciation	862,000		860,000	
Net property and plant		1,175,000		1,155,000
Other fixed assets		550,000		530,000
Total fixed assets		2,980,000		2,775,000
Total assets		$7,105,000		$6,393,000
Liabilities and Stockholders' Equity				
Current liabilities:				
Accounts payable		$1,325,000		$1,225,000
Bank loans payable		475,000		550,000
Accrued federal taxes		675,000		425,000
Current maturities (long-term debt)		17,500		26,000
Dividends payable		20,000		16,250
Total current liabilities		2,512,500		2,242,250
Long-term liabilities		1,350,000		1,425,000
Total liabilities		3,862,500		3,667,250
Stockholders' equity:				
Common stock (104,046 shares outstanding in 1985; 101,204 shares outstanding in 1984)		44,500		43,300
Additional paid-in capital		568,000		372,450
Retained earnings		2,630,000		2,310,000
Total stockholders' equity		3,242,500		2,725,750
Total liabilities and stockholders' equity		$7,105,000		$6,393,000

Exhibit 3

ABC COMPANY
Income Statement
For the Years Ending December 31

		1985		*1984*
Net sales		$8,250,000		$8,000,000
Less: Cost of goods sold	$5,100,000		$5,000,000	
Administrative expenses	1,750,000		1,680,000	
Other expenses	420,000		390,000	
Total		7,270,000		7,070,000
Earnings before interest and taxes		980,000		930,000
Less: Interest expense		210,000		210,000
Earnings before taxes		770,000		720,000
Less: Federal income taxes		360,000		325,000
Earnings after taxes (net income)		$ 410,000		$ 395,000
Common-stock cash dividends		$ 90,000		$ 84,000
Addition to retained earnings		$ 320,000		$ 311,000
Earnings per common share		$ 3.940		$ 3.90
Dividends per common share		$ 0.865		$ 0.83

Liquidity Ratios

Liquidity ratios are used as indicators of a firm's ability to meet its short-term obligations. These obligations include any current liabilities, including currently maturing long-term debt. Current assets move through a normal cash cycle of inventories—sales—accounts receivable—cash. The firm then uses cash to pay off or reduce its current liabilities. The best-known liquidity ratio is the current ratio: current assets divided by current liabilities. For the ABC Company the current ratio is calculated as follows:

$$\frac{\text{Current assets}}{\text{Current liabilities}} = \frac{\$4,125,000}{\$2,512,500} = 1.64\ (1985)$$

$$= \frac{\$3,618,000}{\$2,242,250} = 1.61\ (1984)$$

Most analysts suggest a current ratio of 2 to 3. A large current ratio is not necessarily a good sign; it may mean that an organization is not making the most efficient use of assets. The optimum current ratio will vary from industry to industry, with the more volatile industries requiring higher ratios.

Since slow-moving or obsolescent inventories could overstate a firm's ability to meet short-term demands, the quick ratio is sometimes preferred to assess a firm's liquidity. The quick ratio is current assets minus inventories, divided by current liabilities. The quick ratio for the ABC Company is calculated as follows:

$$\frac{\text{Current assets} - \text{inventories}}{\text{Current liabilities}} = \frac{\$1{,}950{,}000}{\$2{,}512{,}500} = 0.78\ (1985)$$

$$= \frac{\$1{,}618{,}000}{\$2{,}242{,}250} = 0.72\ (1984)$$

A quick ratio of approximately 1 would be typical for American industries. Although there is less variability in the quick ratio than in the current ratio, stable industries would be able to safely operate with a lower ratio.

Leverage Ratios

Leverage ratios identify the source of a firm's capital—owners or outside creditors. The term "leverage" refers to the fact that using capital with a fixed interest charge will "amplify" either profits or losses in relation to the equity of holders of common stock. The most commonly used ratio is total debt divided by total assets. Total debt includes current liabilities and long-term liabilities. This ratio is a measure of the percentage of total funds provided by debt. A total debt-total assets ratio higher than 0.5 is usually considered safe only for firms in stable industries.

$$\frac{\text{Total debt}}{\text{Total assets}} = \frac{\$3{,}862{,}500}{\$7{,}105{,}000} = 0.54\ (1985)$$

$$= \frac{\$3{,}667{,}250}{\$6{,}393{,}000} = 0.57\ (1984)$$

The ratio of long-term debt to equity is a measure of the extent to which sources of long-term financing are provided by creditors. It is computed by dividing long-term debt by the stockholders' equity.

$$\frac{\text{Long-term debt}}{\text{Equity}} = \frac{\$1{,}350{,}000}{\$3{,}242{,}500} = 0.42\ (1985)$$

$$= \frac{\$1{,}425{,}000}{\$2{,}725{,}750} = 0.52\ (1984)$$

Activity Ratios

Activity ratios indicate how effectively a firm is using its resources. By comparing revenues with the resources used to generate them, it is possible to establish an efficiency of operation. The asset turnover ratio indicates how efficiently management is employing total assets. Asset turnover is calculated by dividing sales by total assets. For the ABC Company, asset turnover is calculated as follows:

$$\text{Asset turnover} = \frac{\text{Sales}}{\text{Total assets}} = \frac{\$8{,}250{,}000}{\$7{,}105{,}000} = 1.16\ (1985)$$

$$= \frac{\$8{,}000{,}000}{\$6{,}393{,}000} = 1.25\ (1984)$$

The ratio of sales to fixed assets is a measure of the turnover on plant and equipment. It is calculated by dividing sales by net fixed assets.

$$\text{Fixed asset turnover} = \frac{\text{Sales}}{\text{Net fixed assets}} = \frac{\$8{,}250{,}000}{\$2{,}980{,}000} = 2.77\ (1985)$$

$$= \frac{\$8{,}000{,}000}{\$2{,}775{,}000} = 2.88\ (1984)$$

Industry figures for asset turnover will vary with capital-intensive industries, and those requiring large inventories will have much smaller ratios.

Another activity ratio is inventory turnover, estimated by dividing sales by average inventory. The norm for American industries is 9, but whether the ratio for a particular firm is higher or lower normally depends upon the product sold. Small, inexpensive items usually turn over at a much higher rate than larger, expensive ones. Since inventories are normally carried at cost, it would be more accurate to use the cost of goods sold in place of sales in the numerator of this ratio. Established compilers of industry ratios such as Dun and Bradstreet, however, use the ratio of sales to inventory.

$$\text{Inventory turnover} = \frac{\text{Sales}}{\text{Inventory}} = \frac{\$8{,}250{,}000}{\$2{,}175{,}000} = 3.79\ (1985)$$

$$= \frac{\$8{,}000{,}000}{\$2{,}000{,}000} = 4\ (1984)$$

The accounts receivable turnover is a measure of the average collection period on sales. If the average number of days varies widely from the industry norm, it may be an indication of poor management. A too low ratio could indicate the loss of sales because of a too restrictive credit policy. If the ratio is too high, too much capital is being tied up in accounts receivable, and management may be increasing the chance of bad debts. Because of varying industry credit policies, a comparison for the firm over time or within an industry is the only useful analysis. Because information on credit sales for other firms is generally unavailable, total sales must be used. Since not all firms have the same percentage of credit sales, there is only approximate comparability among firms.

$$\text{Accounts receivable turnover} = \frac{\text{Sales}}{\text{Accounts receivable}} = \frac{\$8{,}250{,}000}{\$1{,}760{,}000} = 4.69\ (1985)$$

$$= \frac{\$8{,}000{,}000}{\$1{,}440{,}000} = 5.56\ (1984)$$

$$\text{Average collection period} = \frac{360}{\text{Accounts receivable turnover}}$$

$$= \frac{360}{4.69} = 77 \text{ days (1985)}$$

$$= \frac{360}{5.56} = 65 \text{ days (1984)}$$

Profitability Ratios

Profitability is the net result of a large number of policies and decisions chosen by an organization's management. Profitability ratios indicate how effectively the total firm is being managed. The profit margin for a firm is calculated by dividing net earnings by sales. This ratio is often called return on sales (ROS). There is wide variation among industries, but the average for American firms is approximately 5 percent.

$$\frac{\text{Net earnings}}{\text{Sales}} = \frac{\$410{,}000}{\$8{,}250{,}000} = 0.0497 \text{ (1985)}$$

$$= \frac{\$395{,}000}{\$8{,}000{,}000} = 0.0494 \text{ (1984)}$$

A second useful ratio for evaluating profitability is the return on investment—or ROI, as it is frequently called—found by dividing net earnings by total assets. The ABC Company's ROI is calculated as follows:

$$\frac{\text{Net earnings}}{\text{Total assets}} = \frac{\$410{,}000}{\$7{,}105{,}000} = 0.0577 \text{ (1985)}$$

$$= \frac{\$395{,}000}{\$6{,}393{,}000} = 0.0618 \text{ (1984)}$$

The ratio of net earnings to net worth is a measure of the rate of return or profitability of the stockholders' investment. It is calculated by dividing net earnings by net worth, the common-stock equity and retained-earnings account. ABC Company's return on net worth, also called ROE, is calculated as follows:

$$\frac{\text{Net earnings}}{\text{Net worth}} = \frac{\$410{,}000}{\$3{,}242{,}500} = 0.1264 \text{ (1985)}$$

$$= \frac{\$395{,}000}{\$2{,}725{,}750} = 0.1449 \text{ (1984)}$$

It is often difficult to determine causes for lack of profitability. The Du Pont system of financial analysis provides management with clues to the lack of success of a firm. This financial tool brings together activity, profitabil-

Exhibit 4

Du Pont's financial analysis

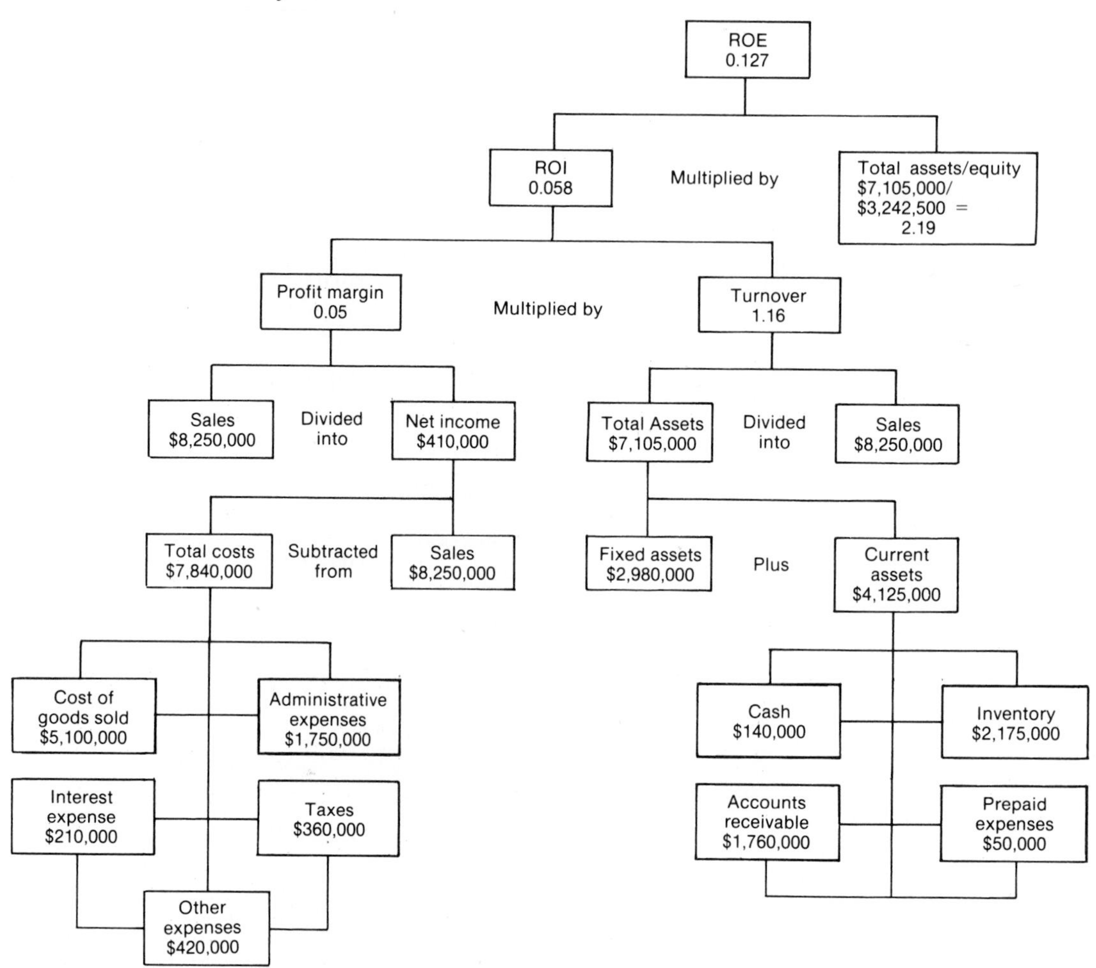

ity, and leverage measures and shows how these ratios interact to determine the overall profitability of the firm. A depiction of the system is set forth in Exhibit 4.

The right side of the figure develops the turnover ratio. This section breaks down total assets into current assets (cash, marketable securities, accounts receivable, and inventories) and fixed assets. Sales divided by these total assets gives the turnover on assets.

The left side of the figure develops the profit margin on sales. The individual expense items plus income taxes are subtracted from sales to produce net profits after taxes. Net profits divided by sales gives the profit margin on sales. When the asset turnover ratio on the right side of Exhibit 4 is multiplied by the profit margin on sales developed on the left side of the figure, the product is the return on assets (ROI) for the firm. This can be shown by the following formula:

$$\frac{\text{Sales}}{\text{Total assets}} \times \frac{\text{Net earnings}}{\text{Sales}} = \frac{\text{Net earnings}}{\text{Total assets}} = \text{ROI}$$

The last step in the Du Pont analysis is to multiply the rate of return on assets (ROI) by the equity multiplier, which is the ratio of assets to common equity, to obtain the rate of return on equity (ROE). This percentage rate of return could, of course, be calculated directly by dividing net income by common equity. However, the Du Pont analysis demonstrates how the return on assets and the use of debt interact to determine the return on equity.

The Du Pont system can be used to analyze and improve the performance of a firm. On the left, or profit, side of the figure, attempts to increase profits and sales could be investigated. The possibilities of raising prices to improve profits (or lowering prices to improve volume) or seeking new products or markets, for example, could be studied. Cost accountants and production engineers could investigate ways to reduce costs. On the right, or turnover, side, financial officers could analyze the effect of reducing investment in various assets as well as the effect of alternative financial structures.

There are two basic approaches to using financial ratios. One approach is to evaluate the corporation's performance over several years. Financial ratios are computed for different years, and then an assessment is made as to whether there has been an improvement or deterioration over time. Financial ratios can also be computed for projected, or pro forma, statements and compared with present and past ratios.

The other approach is to evaluate a firm's financial condition and compare it with the financial conditions of similar firms or with industry averages in the same period. Such a comparison gives insight into the firm's relative financial condition and performance. Financial ratios for industries are provided by Robert Morris Associates, Dun and Bradstreet, and various trade association publications. (Associations and their addresses are listed in the *Encyclopedia of Associations* or the *Directory of National Trade Associations*.) Information about individual firms is available through *Moody's Manual,* Standard and Poor's manuals and surveys, annual reports to stockholders, and the major brokerage houses.

To the extent possible, accounting data from different companies must be standardized so that companies can be compared or so that a specific company can be compared with an industry average. It is important to read any footnotes of financial statements, since various accounting or management practices can have an effect on the financial picture of the company. For example, firms using sale-leaseback methods may have leverage pictures that are quite different from what is shown as debts or assets on the balance sheet.

Analysis of the Sources and Uses of Funds

The purpose of this analysis is to determine how the company is using its financial resources from year to year. By comparing balance sheets from one year to the next, one may determine how funds were obtained and the way in which these funds were employed during the year.

To prepare a statement of the sources and uses of funds it is necessary to (1) classify balance sheet changes that increase cash and changes that decrease cash, (2) classify from the income statement those factors that increase or decrease cash, and (3) consolidate this information on a sources and uses of funds statement form.

Sources of funds that increase cash are as follows:

1. A net decrease in any asset other than a depreciable fixed asset.
2. A gross decrease in a depreciable fixed asset.
3. A net increase in any liability.
4. Proceeds from the sale of stock.
5. The operation of the company (net income, and depreciation if the company is profitable).

Uses of funds include:

1. A net increase in any asset other than a depreciable fixed asset.
2. A gross increase in depreciable fixed assets.
3. A net decrease in any liability.
4. A retirement or purchase of stock.
5. Payment of cash dividends.

We compute gross changes to depreciable fixed assets by adding depreciation from the income statement for the period to net fixed assets at the end of the period and then subtracting from the total the net fixed assets at the beginning of the period. The residual represents the change in depreciable fixed assets for the period.

For the ABC Company the following change would be calculated:

Net property and plant (1985)	$1,175,000
Depreciation for 1985	+ 80,000
	$1,255,000
Net property and plant (1984)	−1,155,000
	$ 100,000

To avoid double counting, the change in retained earnings is not shown directly in the funds statement. When the funds statement is prepared, this account is replaced by the earnings after taxes, or net income, as a source of funds and dividends paid during the year as a use of funds. The difference between net income and the change in the retained-earnings account will equal the amount of dividends paid during the year. The accompanying sources and uses of funds statement was prepared for the ABC Company.

A funds analysis is useful for determining trends in working-capital positions and for demonstrating how the firm has acquired and employed its funds during some period.

ABC COMPANY
Sources and Uses of Funds Statement
For 1985

Sources:	
Prepaid expenses	$ 13,000
Accounts payable	100,000
Accrued federal taxes	250,000
Dividends payable	3,750
Common stock	1,200
Additional paid-in capital	195,500
Earnings after taxes (net income)	410,000
Depreciation	80,000
Total sources	1,053,500
Uses:	
Cash	25,000
Accounts receivable	320,000
Inventory	175,000
Long-term receivables	165,000
Property and plant	100,000
Other fixed assets	20,000
Bank loans payable	75,000
Current maturities of long-term debt	8,500
Long-term liabilities	75,000
Dividends paid	90,000
Total uses	1,053,500

Conclusion

It is recommended that you prepare a chart such as Exhibit 5 so that you can develop a useful portrayal of these financial analyses. The chart allows a display of the ratios over time. The Trend column could be used to indicate your evaluation of the ratios over time (for example, "favorable," "neutral," or "unfavorable"). The "Industry Average" column could include recent industry averages on these ratios or those of key competitors. These would provide information to aid interpretation of the analyses. The Interpretation column can be used to describe your interpretation of the ratios for this firm. Overall, this chart gives a basic display of the ratios that provides a convenient format for examining the firm's financial condition.

Exhibit 5

A summary of the financial position of a firm

Ratios and working capital	*1981*	*1982*	*1983*	*1984*	*1985*	*Trend*	*Industry average*	*Interpretation*
Liquidity: Current								
Quick								
Leverage: Debt/Assets								
Debt/Equity								
Activity: Asset turnover								
Fixed asset ratio								
Inventory turnover								
Accounts receivable turnover								
Average collection period								
Profitability: ROS								
ROI								
ROE								
Working-capital position								

PART FOUR

Cases

SECTION

Strategy Formulation

case 1 Wendy's International, Incorporated (A)

1 In just 11 years, Wendy's International grew from one store to over 1,800 company-owned and franchised outlets. Between 1974 and 1979, Wendy's growth was explosive with sales, including company-owned and franchised units, growing 4,200 percent ($24 million to $1 billion). In the same period, revenues from company-owned store sales and from franchise royalties grew 726 percent ($38 million to $274 million). Net income increased 2,091 percent in this period from $1.1 million to $23 million. Earnings per share made substantial gains from $.12 in 1974 to $1.54 in 1979, a 1,283 percent rise. Wendy's grew to a position of being the third-largest fast-food hamburger restaurant chain in the United States, ranking behind Burger King and McDonald's, the leading U.S. hamburger chain.

2 Wendy's entry and amazing growth in the hamburger segment of the fast-food industry shocked the industry and forced competitors within it to realize that their market positions are potentially vulnerable. Wendy's flourished in the face of adversities plaguing the industry. Throughout the 70s, experts said the fast-food industry was rapidly maturing. Analysts for *The Wall Street Journal* and *Business Week,* citing a "competitively saturated fast-food hamburger industry," predicted in the early 1970s that the Wendy's venture would not succeed. As they saw it, market saturation, rising commodity prices, fuel costs, and labor costs were already plaguing the fast-food industry.

3 Clearly unconcerned about such commentary, R. David Thomas pushed Wendy's relentlessly. It opened an average of one restaurant every two days through 1979 and became the first hamburger chain to top $1 billion in sales in its first 10 years.

This case was prepared by Richard Robinson of the University of South Carolina and William C. Craver, attorney-at-law.

History

4 R. David Thomas had an idea. He knew Americans love hamburgers. If he could develop a hamburger better than those currently offered, he believed he could use it to establish a leadership position in the competitive fast-food hamburger market.

5 In November 1969, Thomas, an experienced restaurant operator and Kentucky Fried Chicken franchisee, began to put his idea into reality when he opened Wendy's first unit in downtown Columbus, Ohio. A year later, in November 1970, Wendy's opened its second unit in Columbus, this one with a drive-through pickup window. In August 1972, Wendy's sold L. S. Hartzog the franchise for the Indianapolis, Indiana, market, kicking off Wendy's rapid expansion into the chain hamburger business. Later the same year, Wendy's Management Institute was formed to develop management skills in managers, supervisors, area directors, and franchise owners. After five years, company revenues exceeded $13 million with net income in excess of $1 million. Sales for both company-owned and franchised units topped $24 million for the same period. In June 1975, the 100th Wendy's opened in Louisville, Kentucky. Three months later, Wendy's went public. December 1976 saw Wendy's 500th open in Toronto, Canada. In 1977, Wendy's went national with its first network television commercial, making it the first restaurant chain with less than 1,000 units to mount a national advertising campaign. Eleven months later, Wendy's broke yet another record by opening its 1,000th restaurant in Springfield, Tennessee, within 100 months of opening the first Wendy's in Columbus. In 1979, Wendy's signed franchise agreements for eight European countries and Japan and opened the first European restaurant, company-owned, in Munich, West Germany. Also 1979 saw test marketing of a limited breakfast menu, a children's menu, and salad bars.

Wendy's Developmental Concept: The Last 10 Years

The Menu

6 Wendy's management team believes that its limited menu has been a key factor contributing to Wendy's success. The idea was to concentrate on doing only a few things, but to do them better than anyone else. As a result, the aim was to provide the customer with a Cadillac hamburger that could be custom-made to meet individual preferences.

7 The basic menu item was the quarter-pound hamburger made of only fresh, 100 percent beef hamburger meat converted into patties daily. This kept Wendy's out of head-on competition with McDonald's and Burger King's 1/10 pound hamburger. If people desired a bigger hamburger, they could order a double (two patties on a bun) or a triple (three patties on a bun). Besides having just one basic menu item, the hamburger, Wendy's also decided to differentiate itself by changing their hamburger's design. Instead of the traditional round patty found in competing fast-food outlets, Wendy's patty was square and sized so its edges would stick out over the edge of the round bun. The unique design alleviated the frequent complaint by most people that they were eating a breadburger. Other menu decisions included the following.

1. To offer different condiments to the customers—cheese, tomato, catsup, onion, lettuce, mustard, mayonnaise, and relish.
2. To provide a unique dairy product, the frosty—a cross between chocolate and vanilla flavors which borders between soft ice cream and a thick milk shake.
3. To serve a product that was unique in the fast-food market—chili.
4. To sell french fries because the public expected a hamburger outlet to offer them.

Facilities

8 Under Thomas's direction, the exterior style and interior decor of all Wendy's restaurants conformed to company specifications. The typical outlet was a freestanding one-story brick building constructed on a 25,000-square-foot site that provided parking for 35 to 40 cars (see Exhibits 1 and 2). There were some downtown storefront-type restaurants which generally adhered to the standard red, yellow, and white decor and design. Most of the freestanding restaurants contained 2,100 square feet, had a cooking area, dining room capacity for 92 persons, and a pickup window for drive-in service (see Exhibit 3). The interior decor featured table tops printed with reproductions

Exhibit 1

Typical freestanding building design

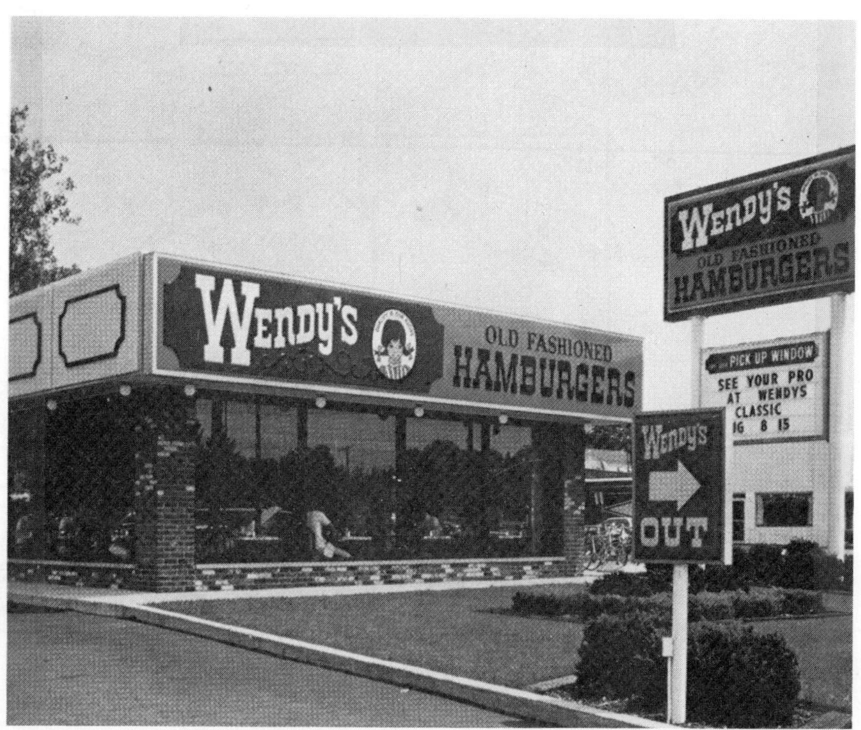

Exhibit 2

Wendy's typical site 1—typical lot layout for freestanding unit

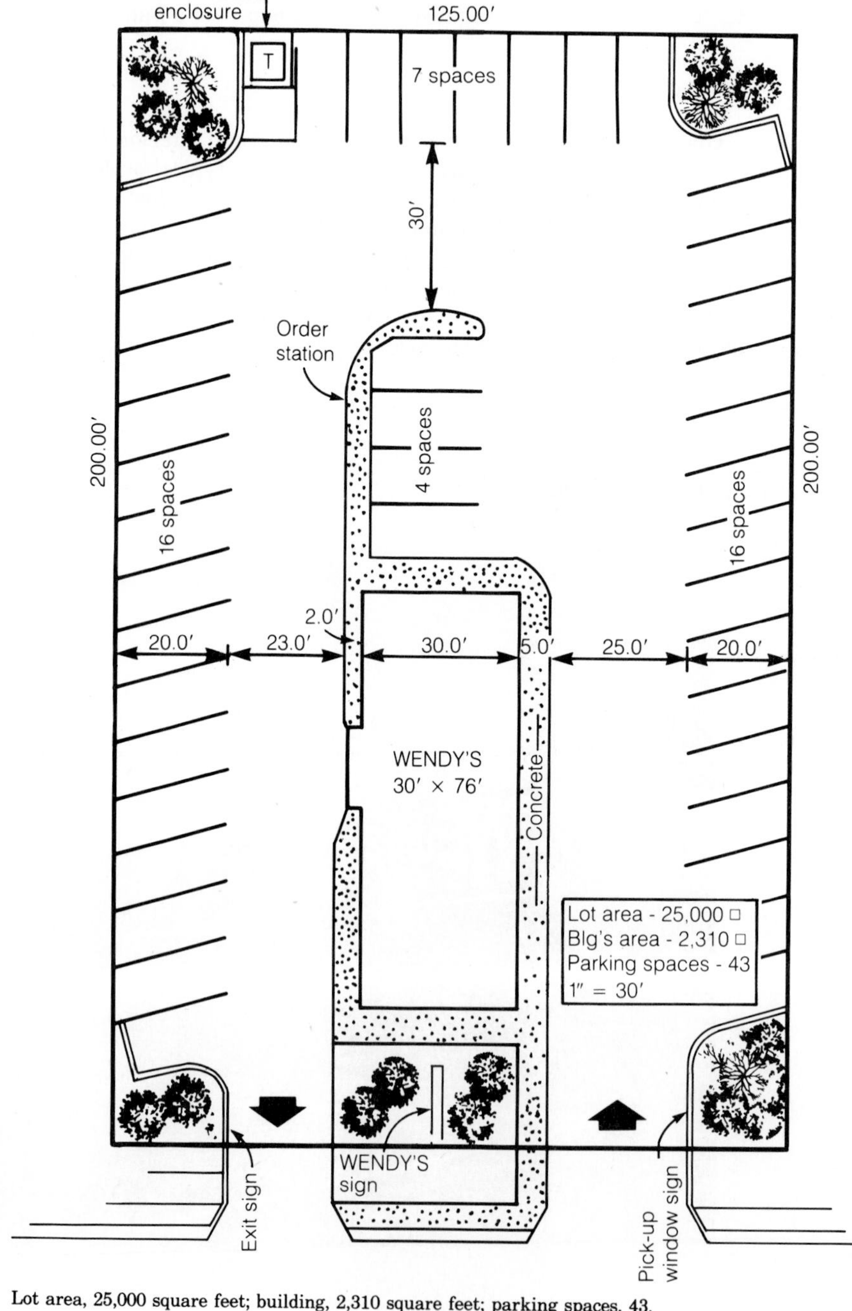

Lot area, 25,000 square feet; building, 2,310 square feet; parking spaces, 43.

of 19th century advertising, Tiffany-styled lamps, bentwood chairs, colorful beads, and carpeting.

9 Generally, the strategy was to build a functionally modern building that would reflect the old-fashioned theme. Another plus for their building design was its flexibility. With only minor changes, they could sell almost any type of food in the building. It would also be possible to change from the Gay 90s theme to any other theme in just a matter of days.

10 The most unique feature in their building design was the addition of the pickup window, and Wendy's was the first major restaurant chain to successfully implement the use of one. Here, Wendy's was able to gain an advantage because their units could be smaller and at the same time handle the larger amount of business volume generated by using the pickup window. The logic for implementing the use of the pickup window was that people in their cars don't fill up tables or take up a parking space. The result showed that on a square-foot basis, Wendy's units did more business than any other chain.

11 The building design also contributed to what Michael J. Esposito, an investments analyst for Oppenheimer & Company, has called the most impressive part of the company's operation: the delivery system. In a report recommending Wendy's as an investment, Esposito wrote:

> In our judgment, the transaction time (time elapsed from when order is placed to its delivery to the customer) is the lowest in the industry, generally averaging about one minute. Utilizing a grill system where a constant flow of hamburgers is cooked at a relatively low temperature, a worker takes the hamburger off the grill, places it on a bun, adds the condiments ordered by the customer, assembles and wraps the sandwich. Another crew member supplies chili, french fries, beverage, and a frosty dessert, and another reviews the order and releases it to the customer.

The Marketing Strategy

12 In their book, *The Chain-Restaurant Industry,* Earl Sasser and Daryl Wycoff stated:

> The Wendy's strategy was described by one analyst as "selling better hamburgers than McDonald's or Burger King at a cheaper price per ounce." As he commented, it takes no more labor to prepare a large hamburger at a higher price.

13 To support the higher-priced hamburger, Wendy's marketing strategy has been to stress the freshness and quality of their product. The objective of this strategy is to target Wendy's for the world's fastest-growing market segment. By offering a freshly ground, made-to-order hamburger as well as stylish, comfortable decor, Wendy's was aiming squarely at a key segment of the population: young adults with a taste for better food. With the post-World War II babies reaching their 20s and 30s, those young adults have been expanding faster than any other age group. As a result, it is thought that Wendy's success is coming not so much at the expense of the other burger chains but from having selected a special niche in the otherwise crowded market. Most agree that Wendy's basically expanded the market, and statistics from customer surveys bear out the claim. Fully 82 percent of all Wendy's business comes from customers over 25, an unusually old market for any fast-food chain. By contrast, McDonald's generated 35 percent of its revenues from youngsters under 19.

Exhibit 3

Restaurant interior layout

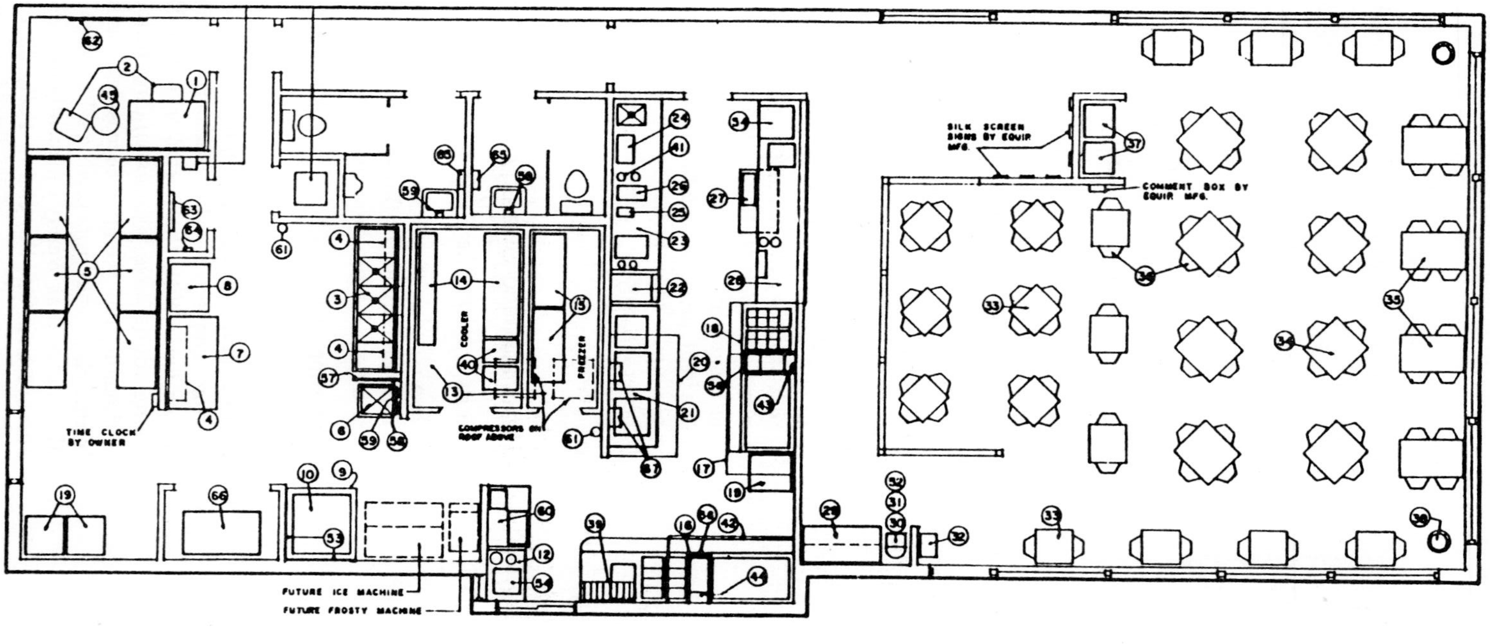

TIME CLOCK BY OWNER

COOLER

FREEZER

COMPRESSORS ON ROOF ABOVE

SILK SCREEN SIGNS BY EQUIP MFG.

COMMENT BOX BY EQUIP MFG.

FUTURE ICE MACHINE

FUTURE FROSTY MACHINE

Key:

1. Desk.
2. Chair.
3. Sink unit.
4. Wall shelving.
5. Wall shelving.
6. Sink unit.
7. Work table.
8. Hamburger patty-making machine.
9. Exhaust canopy system.
10. Range top.
11. Open number.
12. Cashier counter assembly.
13. Walk-in cooler/freezer.
14. Wire shelving.
15. Frozen french fry storage platform.
16. Custom cooks counter assembly.
17. Exhaust canopy system.
18. Custom cook.
19. Bun rack.
20. Exhaust canopy system.
21. Custom fry station assembly.
22. Frosty machine.
23. Rear counter assembly.
24. Coffee maker.
25. Tea machine.
26. Hot chocolate machine.
27. Ice and drink machine.
28. Front counter assembly.
29. Condiment station.
30. High chair.
31. Booster chairs.
32. Water fountain.
33. Pedestal tables.
34. Pedestal tables.
35. Pedestal tables.
36. Side chairs.
37. Waste containers.
38. Costumers.
39. Condiment holder.
40. Meat racks.
41. Marshmallow holder.
42. Exhaust canopy system (fire protection).
43. Custom paper holder.
44. Custom paper holder.
45. Floor safe.
46. Litter receptacle.
47. Tiffany-style light fixtures.
48. Carpet.
49. Wall covering.
50. Beads.
51. Installation package.
52. Booster chair hanger.
53. Stainless wall panel.
54. Cash registers.
55. Open number.
56. Bun cabinet.
57. Stainless partition.
58. Towel dispenser.
59. Soap dispenser.
60. Ice and drink machine.
61. Fire extinguishers.
62. Coat hook bar.
63. Broom holder.
64. Hose holder.
65. Hand dryers.
66. Syrup tank rack.
67. French fry computers.

14 Wendy's advertising efforts have emphasized nationwide television advertising to attract this young adult market. Since 1974, Wendy's "Hot 'n' Juicy" advertising theme has been central to this effort. In the late 1970s, with its position established, Wendy's national advertising started focusing on new market segments like dinner after 4 P.M. after family meals on weekends. Apparently feeling the Hot 'n' Juicy theme had served its purpose, Wendy's adopted a new advertising theme: "There ain't no reason to go anyplace else."[1] This theme has sparked considerable attention, particularly a negative reaction to the word *ain't* and the phrase's double negative.

Franchising

15 In 1972, Wendy's management made the decision to become a national chain as quickly as possible, which meant growing through franchising. The franchises were awarded on an area basis rather than single-store franchises. As a result, Wendy's 10 largest franchise owners operated a total of 406 restaurants by 1979. The franchise agreements were among the most straightforward in the restaurant industry and are deliberately designed to establish a fair business relationship. They specify the number of units to be opened within a certain time frame, the area to be developed, a technical assistance fee, and a royalty of 4 percent of gross sales. They also stipulate that 4 percent of gross sales be spent for local and national advertising. Wendy's operated no commissaries and sold no food, fixtures, or supplies to franchise owners.

16 To support their growing network of franchised restaurants, Wendy's franchise operations department maintained a staff of 50 franchise area supervisors who are the company's operations advisors to the franchise owners. They are charged with ensuring that Wendy's quality standards are met throughout the entire franchise network.

17 Wendy's also provided the following services to their franchisees:

1. Site approval procedures for locations.
2. On-site inspection and evaluation by a staff representative.
3. Counseling in business planning.
4. Drawings and specifications for buildings.
5. Training for franchisees at Wendy's headquarters.
6. Advice on supplies from suppliers selected by Wendy's and assistance in establishing quality-control standards and procedures for supplies.
7. Staff representatives to help in the opening of each restaurant.
8. Assistance in planning opening promotion and continuing advertising, public relations, and promotion.
9. Operations manual with information necessary to operate a Wendy's restaurant.
10. Research and development in production and methods of operations.
11. Information on policies, developments, and activities by means of bulletins, brochures, reports, and visits of Wendy's representatives.
12. Paper-goods standards.
13. National and regional meetings.

[1] A recent article in *The Wall Street Journal* offered another explanation: "Wendy's ads showed diners biting into its hot and juicy hamburgers and then mopping juice from their chins. But some people thought the image projected by the ads was hot and greasy. Many franchises quit advertising, in effect voting no confidence in the company's marketing plan." (July 8, 1980, p. 29.)

18 The criteria used by Wendy's for franchisee selection is basically simple but strictly adhered to. They look for good proven business ability. The applicant must demonstrate that he or she is interested in making profits and does not mind getting involved. Wendy's did not make their profits by selling goods and services to their franchisees. Their income came from the restaurants' sales volume. Therefore, the franchisee must be able to build sales.

19 Wendy's operates company-owned restaurants in 26 markets around the following cities:

Columbus, Ohio	33	Indianapolis, Indiana	15
Cincinnati, Ohio	20	Dallas/Ft. Worth, Texas	26
Dayton, Ohio	26	Houston, Texas	25
Toledo, Ohio	12	Oklahoma City, Oklahoma	12
Atlanta, Georgia	35	Tulsa, Oklahoma	12
Tampa, Sarasota, St. Petersburg, Clearwater, Florida	22	Memphis, Tennessee	13
		Louisville, Kentucky	14
		Syracuse, New York	10
Jacksonville, Florida	15	Harrisburg, Pennsylvania	22
Daytona Beach, Florida	4	Philadelphia, Pennsylvania	20
Detroit, Michigan	20	Virginia Beach, Virginia	15
Portland, Oregon	10	Charleston, West Virginia	14
Reno, Nevada	6	Parkersburg, West Virginia	20
Greensboro, North Carolina	10	Munich, West Germany	2

Other than Detroit, no franchises exist in these markets.

20 At the end of 1979, there were 1,385 franchised restaurants operated by 161 franchise owners in 47 states and 3 foreign countries.

21 In a report to the Securities and Exchange Commission, Wendy's discussed the current state of its franchise program and described the franchise owners' relationship with the company:

> Although franchised areas exist in all states except three, areas of some states remain unfranchised. In addition, most franchise owners have the right to build more units in their franchised areas than had been constructed at December 31, 1979. At that date, no franchise owner had more than 88 stores in operation. Several franchise owners operate restaurants in more than one state.
>
> The rights and franchise offered by the company are contained in two basic documents. A franchise owner first executes a development agreement. This document gives the franchise owner the exclusive right to select proposed sites on which to construct Wendy's Old Fashioned Hamburgers restaurants within a certain geographic area (the franchised area), requires the submission of sites to the company for its acceptance, and upon acceptance of a proposed site by the company, provides for the execution of a unit franchise agreement with the company to enable the franchise owner to construct, own, and operate a Wendy's Old Fashioned Hamburgers restaurant upon the site. The development agreement provides for the construction and opening of a fixed number of restaurants within the franchised area in accordance with a development or perfor-

mance schedule. Both the number of restaurants and the development and performance schedules are agreed upon by the franchise owner and the company prior to the execution of the development agreement. The development agreement also grants a right of first refusal to the franchise owner with respect to the construction of any additional restaurants in the franchised area beyond the initially agreed-to number.

The development agreement requires that the franchise owner pay the company a technical assistance fee. The technical assistance fee required by newly executed development agreement is currently $15,000 for each franchise restaurant which the franchise owner has agreed to construct. Under earlier forms of the development agreement or franchise agreements, this fee was either $5,000, $7,500, or $10,000. However, approximately 12 existing franchise owners have the right under certain circumstances to receive additional franchise areas on the basis of the earlier $10,000 fee.

The technical assistance fee is used to defray the cost to the company of providing to its franchise owners site selection assistance; standard construction plans, specifications and layouts; company review of specific restaurant site plans; initial training in the company's restaurant systems; and such bulletins, brochures, and reports as are from time to time published regarding the company's plans, policies, research, and other business activities.

22 From time to time, the company has reacquired franchised operations. A summary of these acquisitions is presented in Exhibit 4. In 1979, the company adopted a rather aggressive approach to franchise acquisition. Of 145 new company-owned operations in 1979 (representing a 50 percent increase during the year), 84 were acquired from franchisees. This major shift to company-owned restaurant growth away from franchised growth reflects the concern for systemwide control of quality as well as the increasing competition for available locations. Exhibit 5 illustrates the emphasis on company-owned growth since 1974. Granting large territorial franchises rather than single-outlet franchises was similarly practiced by Burger King in its formative stages. At Burger King, this led to franchise empires that were bigger than parent-company operations. Wendy's emphasis on company-owned growth may well be intended to avoid the problem that led to Burger King's decline in the late 1960s.

Finances

23 Wendy's revenues (see Exhibit 6) increased steadily between 1975 and 1980. Net income dropped in 1979 compared to 1978, but Thomas explains:

> During 1979, we were informed by the U.S. Department of Labor that a review of company labor practices for a three-year period indicated that certain company policies had not been uniformly adhered to, and as a result, the company was not in full compliance with the Fair Labor Standards Act.
>
> Based on this review and the company's own investigation, we have determined that $3,800,000 should be accrued and charged against 1979 pretax income. Had this charge not been made, 1979 net income would have been $25,096,000, an increase of 8 percent over the $23,215,000 originally reported a year earlier. We believe company labor practices now comply with both company policy and the act, and in addition, future compliance will not materially affect net income in 1980 and ensuing years.

Exhibit 4

Acquisition date	*Company acquired*	*Restaurants in operation*	*Location*	*Accounting treatment*	*Common shares issued/ purchase price*
1. 7/31/76	Wendy's Management, Inc., and subsidiaries	40	Atlanta, Georgia Indianapolis, Indiana Louisville, Kentucky Jacksonville, Florida	Purchase	733,195
2. 10/1/77	Wendy's Old Fashioned Hamburgers of New York, Inc.	5	Syracuse, New York	Purchase	Immaterial
3. 6/30/78	Wendy's of West Virginia, Inc.	33	West Virginia Eastern Kentucky Southeast Ohio	Pooling	535,000
4. 9/30/78	Springfield Management Company, Inc., and Dakota Land Corp.	6	Springfield, Ohio Richmond, Indiana	Pooling	39,294
5. 5/26/59	1620 South Atlantic, Inc. Forsyth, Inc. RR&WW, Inc. Reaves & Reaves Restaurants, Inc.	14	Greensboro, North Carolina Winston-Salem, North Carolina Daytona Beach, Florida	Pooling	268,900
6. 5/30/79	Wendcorp of Nevada, Inc. Wendcorp of Portland, Inc.	16	Reno, Nevada Portland, Oregon	Pooling	245,815
7. 8/31/79	Susquehanna Food Services, Inc.	40	Southeastern Pennsylvania and northern Delaware	Pooling	508,861
8. 11/30/79	Wendy's of Virginia, Inc.	14	Southeastern Virginia	Purchase	$5,520,000

Exhibit 5

Growth in company-operated restaurants

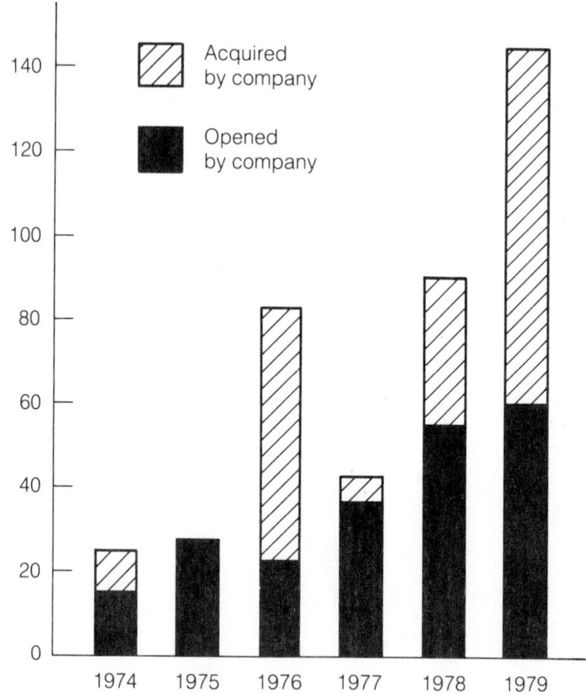

24 Whether the cost of labor compliance was the only cause of the abrupt slowdown in Wendy's steady increase in revenue and profit is questionable. Several factors suggest that Wendy's, after a decade of rapid growth, was reaching the limits of its current capabilities.

25 The heart of Wendy's success has been its streamlined, limited menu with primary emphasis on a quality hamburger. Since 1977, beef prices have soared, as shown in Exhibit 7. And while Wendy's has responded with tighter controls and a series of price increases just under 15 percent for 1979 alone (see Exhibit 8), this has still contributed to a decline in profitability.

26 Further evidence suggests that Wendy's may have been reaching a plateau in its historical pattern of growth. The average sales per restaurant, which climbed steadily from $230,000 in 1970 to $688,800 in 1978, declined significantly in 1979 at both company-owned and franchised restaurants as shown in Exhibit 9. The impact on the parent company was felt in every revenue category as shown in Exhibit 10. Wendy's continued to experience increased retail revenue (company-owned stores) and royalties (from franchises based on a percent of sales), but at a drastically slower rate. And for the first time, Wendy's experienced a decrease in technical assistance (franchise) fees.

Exhibit 6

WENDY'S INTERNATIONAL, INCORPORATED
Consolidated Statement of Income
For the Years Ended December 31, 1975–1979

	1979	*1978*	*1977*	*1976*	*1975*
Revenue:					
Retail operations	$237,753,097	$198,529,130	$130,667,377	$71,336,626	$35,340,665
Royalties	30,564,613	23,396,211	11,810,277	4,655,432	1,567,008
Technical assistance fees	2,822,500	3,540,000	2,510,000	1,560,000	622,500
Other, principally interest	2,903,261	2,685,909	1,802,691	965,521	246,901
Total revenues	274,043,471	228,151,250	146,790,345	78,517,579	37,777,074
Costs and expenses:					
Cost of sales	146,346,806	113,812,874	72,482,010	40,509,285	19,629,179
Company restaurant operating costs	51,193,050	43,289,285	28,088,460	14,348,150	7,292,391
Department of labor compliance review	3,800,000				
Salaries, travel, and associated expenses of franchise personnel	4,187,399	3,148,532	1,936,877	1,156,493	622,879
General and administrative expenses	15,741,592	13,292,845	8,191,394	4,137,226	2,581,166
Depreciation and amortization of property and equipment	7,355,818	5,444,092	3,767,259	2,240,215	799,876
Interest	4,357,973	3,771,878	3,215,432	2,583,876	995,410
Total expenses	232,982,638	182,759,506	117,681,432	64,975,245	31,920,901
Income before income taxes	41,060,833	45,391,744	29,108,913	13,542,334	5,856,173
Income taxes:					
Federal:					
Current	15,583,700	18,324,600	12,052,200	5,784,600	2,926,700
Deferred	1,303,200	1,020,800	323,700	(19,600)	(501,900)
	16,886,900	19,345,400	12,375,900	5,765,000	2,424,800
State and local taxes	1,077,500	1,559,700	1,296,200	694,400	298,800
Total income taxes	17,964,400	20,905,100	13,672,100	6,459,400	2,723,600
Net income	$ 23,096,433	$ 24,486,644	$ 15,436,813	$ 7,082,934	$ 3,132,373
Net income per share	$1.54	$1.63	$1.04	$.57	$.29
Weighted average number of common shares outstanding	14,970,526	15,017,708	14,855,503	12,525,294	10,645,694
Dividends per common share	$.40	$.14	$.125	$.004	$.001

Source: Wendy's International, Form 10-K, 1979.

Exhibit 7

Yearly average meat price per pound for company-owned stores

Year	Price	Year	Price
1969	$.59	1975	$ .69
1970	.62	1976	.72
1971	.64	1977	.72
1972	.67	1978	1.02
1973	.90	1979	1.29
1974	.74		

Exhibit 8

Percentage price increases for hamburgers

Date	Increase	Date	Increase
1/1/77	0.6%	10/22/78	0.15%
3/1/77	0.3	10/29/78	0.10
12/10/77	6.0	12/17/78	3.40
3/19/78	3.0	1/14/79	3.06
4/16/78	2.5	2/25/79	3.60
5/21/78	1.8	4/8/79	0.10
7/23/78	1.2	4/15/79	0.03
10/1/78	1.7	12/16/79	4.45

Exhibit 9

Average sales per restaurant

	1979		*1978*	
	Amount	*Percent change**	*Amount*	*Percent change**
Company	$624,000	(2.9)%	$642,900	14.3%
Franchise	618,800	(12.4)	706,000	11.7
Systemwide	620,000	(10.0)	688,800	13.0

* Percent increase (or decrease) over the same figure for the previous year.

27 Other evidence of a slowdown in Wendy's growth can be seen in the rate of new store openings. For the first time in its history, Wendy's experienced a decline in the rate of new store openings, as shown in Exhibit 11.

28 While revenue and profitability growth slowed in 1979, Thomas was confident this was only temporary. Feeling strongly that Wendy's was in a good position to finance continued growth, Thomas offered the following observation:

> While construction money is more difficult to obtain than in the last few years, lines of credit already arranged guarantee financing of 1980 company plans to

Exhibit 10

Changes in revenue from 1978 to 1979

	1979		*1978*	
	Amount*	***Percent*** †	***Amount***	***Percent***
Retail operations	$39,224,000	19.8%	$67,862,000	51.9%
Royalties	7,168,000	30.6	11,586,000	98.1
Technical assistance fees	(718,000)	(20.3)	1,030,000	41.0
Other, principally interest	(217,000)	(8.1)	883,000	49.0

* Absolute dollar increase (or decrease) over the previous year.
† Percent increase (or decrease) over the previous year.

Exhibit 11

New restaurant openings: 1979 versus 1978

	*Company**		*Franchise*		*Systemwide*	
	1979	*1978*	*1979*	*1978*	*1979*	*1978*
Open at beginning of year	348	271	1059	634	1407	905
Opened during the year	71	77	340	425	411	502
Purchased from franchise owners	14	—	(14)	—	—	—
Total open at end of year	433	348	1385	1059	1818	1407
Average open during year	381	309	1235	828	1616	1137

* Restaurants acquired from franchise owners in poolings of interest have been included since date of opening.

open 60 or more restaurants. We also anticipate exploring avenues of long-term debt to finance our growth beyond 1980. We believe that with $25 million of long-term debt, exclusive of capitalized lease obligations, and over $100 million in shareholders' equity, we have substantial untapped borrowing power.

Exhibit 12 summarizes Wendy's balance sheet for 1978 and 1979.

Wendy's Future

29 Addressing Wendy's stockholders in early 1980, R. David Thomas offered the following assessment of Wendy's first 10 years:

We are proud to be marking the 10th anniversary of Wendy's International, Inc. Just 10 years ago, in November 1969, we opened the first Wendy's Old Fashioned Hamburgers restaurant in downtown Columbus, Ohio. Now, after a decade of explosive growth, there are Wendy's quick-service restaurants in 49 of the 50 states and in Canada, Puerto Rico, Germany, and Switzerland.

At year-end 1979, there were 1,818 Wendy's restaurants in operation, 411

Exhibit 12

WENDY'S INTERNATIONAL, INCORPORATED
Consolidated Balance Sheets
For the Years Ended December 31, 1978, and 1979

	1979	*1978*
Assets		
Current assets:		
Cash	$ 2,285,180	$ 1,021,957
Short-term investments, at cost, which approximates market, including accrued interest	12,656,352	27,664,531
Accounts receivable	4,902,746	3,248,789
Inventories and other	2,581,528	1,855,313
Total current assets	22,425,806	33,790,590
Property and equipment, at cost Schedule 5:		
Land	30,916,049	23,906,365
Buildings	40,784,581	30,049,552
Leasehold improvements	16,581,947	8,954,392
Restaurant equipment	34,052,952	24,461,860
Other equipment	9,722,666	8,413,363
Construction in progress	1,751,788	2,027,570
Capitalized leases	21,865,829	18,246,427
Total property and equipment before depreciation	155,675,812	116,059,529
Less: Accumulated depreciation and amortization	(20,961,702)	(13,543,473)
Total property and equipment	134,714,110	102,516,056
Cost in excess of net assets acquired, less amortization of $699,410 and $481,162, respectively	8,408,788	5,207,942
Other assets	7,152,131	2,377,648
Total cost over net assets and other assets	15,560,919	7,585,590
Total assets	$172,700,835	$143,892,236

more than at the close of 1978. Of the 433 company-operated restaurants, 84 were acquired from franchise owners during 1979. It was a year of progress for our international expansion program as we opened our first restaurants in Europe and entered into agreements for development of Japan, France, Belgium, Luxembourg, the Netherlands, Switzerland, Spain, Germany, and the United Kingdom.

During 1979, the company established a research and development department which is testing a number of potential menu items. The salad bar, which was tested in our Columbus, Ohio, market, had been introduced into 171 restaurants by year-end.

In 1979, our industry was faced with major challenges, such as inflation and energy problems. Higher labor costs and rising beef prices affected Wendy's profitability and depressed profits for our entire industry. The minimum wage, which

Exhibit 12 *(concluded)*

	1979	*1978*
Liabilities and Shareholders' Equity		
Current liabilities:		
Accounts payable, trade	$ 10,174,980	$ 11,666,272
Federal, state, and local income taxes		7,839,586
Accrued expenses:		
Administrative fee		664,770
Salaries and wages	2,368,244	1,970,977
Interest	433,540	369,603
Taxes	1,932,192	1,498,521
Department of Labor compliance review	3,800,000	
Other	1,576,851	739,588
Current portion, term debt, and capitalized lease obligations	3,891,247	2,781,671
Total current liabilities	24,177,054	27,530,988
Term debt, net of current portion	25,097,688	15,308,276
Capital lease obligations, net of current portion	18,707,838	15,130,617
	43,805,526	30,438,893
Deferred technical assistance fees	1,995,000	2,117,500
Deferred federal income taxes	2,027,604	664,300
Shareholders' equity:		
Common stock, $.10 stated value; authorized: 40,000,000 shares; issued and outstanding: 14,882,614 and 14,861,877 shares, respectively	1,488,261	1,486,188
Capital in excess of stated value	34,113,173	33,962,916
Retained earnings	65,094,217	47,691,451
Total shareholders' equity	100,695,651	83,140,555
Total liabilities and shareholders' equity	$172,700,835	$143,892,236

Source: Wendy's International, Form 10-K, 1979.

affects 90 percent of our employees, increased in January 1979 and January 1980. Ground beef prices increased to an average of $1.29 per pound in 1979, 79 percent higher than the 1977 average price. During 1979, we minimized our retail price increases, with the goal of increasing our market share. This strategy, coupled with more aggressive marketing, helped rebuild customer traffic in the latter part of the year. Although holding back on price increases affected our margins, we believe it was appropriate and that margins benefited by our cost efficiencies, especially in purchasing and distribution.

During 1979, we remained flexible and open to changing customer needs and attitudes, and we continued to take the steps necessary to achieve and support future growth and profitability as we—

Tested and implemented a highly successful salad bar concept.

Tested a breakfast concept and other menu items.

Began development of the European and Japanese markets.

Initiated a new marketing program designed to increase dinner and weekend business.

Prepared to open another 250 to 300 Wendy's restaurants systemwide in 1980.

30 And setting the tone for Wendy's in the 1980s, Thomas said:

> We are aware, as we enter our second decade, that we have achieved a unique position in a highly competitive industry. It was no less difficult and competitive 10 years ago than it is today, we believe, than it will be 10 years from now. We intend to build further on our achievement of being recognized as a chain of high-quality, quick-service restaurants. We will continue to produce fresh, appealing, high-quality food; price it competitively; and serve it in a clean, attractive setting with employees who are carefully selected, well-trained, and responsive to our customers.

31 Similar to the way they questioned R. David Thomas's venture into the hamburger jungle in 1970, several business writers once again began to question Wendy's future. Illustrative of this is the following article that appeared in *The Wall Street Journal:*

> Wendy's International, Inc., is making changes it once considered unthinkable.
>
> Wendy's faced the choice confronting many companies when the initial burst of entrepreneurial brilliance dims: Should it stick with the original concept and be content with a niche in a bigger market, or should it change and attempt to keep growing? Wendy's chose to revamp its operations. It is adding salad bars, chicken and fish sandwiches, and a children's meal to its menu, adopting a new advertising strategy, and considering whether to alter the appearance of its restaurants.
>
> Some observers predict Wendy's will regret the quick changes. "This is a company that was able to convince a certain segment of the country it had a different taste in hamburgers," says Carl De Biase, an analyst with Sanford C. Bernstein & Co. in New York. "They've achieved their mandate, and anything they do now is just going to screw up the concept."
>
> But Robert Barney, Wendy's president and chief executive officer, says the company is "in some very difficult times right now." Among the problems: discontented franchise holders and the likelihood that beef prices will rise sharply again in the second half. Barney says Wendy's doesn't even "have the luxury of waiting to see" how each change works before moving to the next one.
>
> This spring, shortly after the changes began, Thomas resigned as chief executive saying he wanted more time for public relations work and community affairs. Thomas, who is 47 years old and will continue as chairman, had been closely identified with the old ad campaign and with company resistance to broadening the menu.
>
> The company has been doing a little better so far this year, and franchisees say they're much more optimistic. The menu changes, they say, were long overdue. "It had been suggested to everyone in the company," says Raymond Schoen-

baum, who operates 33 Wendy's outlets in Alabama and Georgia. "But the mentality wouldn't allow menu diversification before. It had to be forced on them."

Barney concedes that prior to last year "we never did a lot of planning." But that has been remedied, he says, partly with a "research and development department" that will examine new menu prospects.

Not everyone believes that tinkering with the menu will bring back customers and profits. Edward H. Schmitt, president of McDonald's, predicts an image problem for Wendy's and maintains that the company will lose the labor advantage it held over other fast-food outlets. He adds that McDonald's tried and abandoned salad bars. "It's practically a no-profit item," he says, "and it's a high-waste item."

Some franchises complain that the new children's meal, called Fun Feast, will draw the company into a can't-win competition with McDonald's and Burger King for the children's market, which Wendy's has avoided so far. "Every survey we have says we shouldn't go after that market," a franchisee reports. "Our chairs aren't designed for kids to climb on, and our carpet isn't designed for kids to spill ketchup on."

But Barney insists that Fun Feast isn't intended to attract children. He says Wendy's is trying to remove the adults' reason for not coming to the restaurant. "Where we tested it," he says, "we didn't sell so many of them but we did see an increase in adult traffic."

Wendy's may evolve from a sandwich shop into a more generalized quick-service restaurant that doesn't compete as directly with McDonald's and Burger King. "We're going to be between" McDonald's and quick-service steakhouses, says Schoenbaum, the Georgia and Alabama franchise holder.

To this end, Schoenbaum says, Wendy's will reduce the abundance of plastic fixtures in its restaurants and perhaps cut down on the amount of glass. He says the glass makes Wendy's a pleasant, brightly lit lunch spot but doesn't create a good atmosphere for dinner.

Wendy's officials confirm that they are considering altering the appearance of their restaurants, but they aren't specific. And as for whom Wendy's competes with, Barney says: "We're in competition with anywhere food is served, including the home."[2]

---

[2] "It's Vigor Lost, Wendy's Seeks a New Niche," *The Wall Street Journal,* July 8, 1980, p. 29.

case 2 Wendy's International, Incorporated (B)

1 Wendy's opened its first store in 1969; by 1983, it had 2,460 stores. Early on, the company made the decision to be a large national chain, rather than a small regional one, and to grow as rapidly as possible. Wendy's early mission adhered to a limited menu, resisting product additions to protect the restaurants' assembly-line delivery system.

2 In the late 1970s, Wendy's was a typical emerging young company with entrepreneurial leadership and entrepreneurial management. Everything went fine until beef prices soared in 1978. Wendy's limited menu (mainly hamburgers) made the company extremely vulnerable when the price of beef rose.

3 At this time, Wendy's created its Research and Development Department and quickly began testing new products: the salad bar, a chicken sandwich, and breakfast. R&D was playing catch-up.

4 Recognizing that the customers who supported Wendy's early growth might not be the same people who could maintain its growth rate into the future, Wendy's sought to identify new growth opportunities while simultaneously beginning the process of transforming itself from an entrepreneurial company to a professionally managed business.

5 Focusing on a long-term growth strategy of continued U.S. penetration, international growth, and concentric diversification into the chicken segment, Wendy's management team plans to have 4,000 Wendy's restaurants by 1990. This case examines Wendy's strategic initiatives during the period between 1979 and 1983.

Product/Market Development

6 Committed to the idea that a restaurant was better off doing a few things well rather than many things poorly, Wendy's founder, R. David Thomas, originally limited Wendy's menu to hamburgers, chili, french fries, soft drinks, and a frosty dessert. But in 1979, the soaring price of beef, together with a decline in traffic, lowered profits for the first time since the company was organized.

7 Wendy's did not have a Research and Development Department until 1978. The department quickly began to test new products, and one year later, Wendy's became the first fast-food chain to introduce a salad bar. Accounting for 7 to 8 percent of

This case was prepared by Richard Robinson and Patricia McDougall, both of the University of South Carolina.

the typical Wendy's sales within a year, the salad bar lessened the company's dependence on beef and appealed to people in new market segments. It was credited with boosting the female customer base from 10 percent to 50 percent of the total. Explaining this success, Thomas said, "Women, weight-conscious people, and customers with smaller appetites are finding the salad bar an attractive and welcome addition to their neighborhood Wendy's."

8 The chicken sandwich was another R&D-derived response to high beef prices. "The filet of chicken breast sandwich supports our high quality image," remarked Mr. Thomas, "and provides another opportunity for our existing customers to eat in our restaurants." The chicken sandwich averages about 6 percent of sales in the typical Wendy's.

9 Commenting on Wendy's future product development focus, Joseph Madigan, executive vice president and chief financial officer, offered the following in early 1981:

> Quality has always been the rule for Wendy's products. During 1980, we took several steps which will enable us to continue as the quality leader in the industry and which we are confident will ensure our future growth.
>
> Our Research and Development Department, now over two years old, has helped develop quality products that will keep us growing in the future.
>
> The department develops new products within these guidelines:
>
> 1. Any product additions must reinforce our quality image.
> 2. They must be profitable.
> 3. They must expand a market base.
> 4. They must increase frequency of visits.
> 5. They must merge easily into our system of operations.
> 6. They must help reduce vulnerability to beef prices.

10 Commenting further on product/market developments, Mr. Madigan offered the following summary of a perspective quite different from the founding Wendy's philosophy:

> Another new product we are introducing is a children's menu item. The Wendy's Kids' Fun Pak gives us the child-size portion we've needed and gives parents the reason they've wanted to make Wendy's their lunch or dinner choice.
>
> Each of the new menu items expands our customer base by appealing to more market segments than was possible with our original menu. At the same time, each new item gives us the chance to increase the frequency of visits of our existing customer base.
>
> We are now testing several different breakfast menus and combinations of items. Our aim is to build that part of the day, but we will not move beyond the test stage until we have the product we are sure is the best in the business. Research and development will continue to play an important role in our future as we develop the products that satisfy our customers and meet the needs of our business.
>
> We are constantly aware of the changing environment in which we do business. To keep pace with these changes, we continually evaluate our products, our restaurants, and other key elements of our business. In 1980, we built a restaurant in which we are testing several variations on the basic Wendy's style and appear-

ance. This restaurant is providing us with valuable insights, and what we are learning is being incorporated into the plans for our future restaurants.

11 With the salad bar, chicken sandwich, and Wendy's Kids' Fun Pak representing approximately 18 percent of company store sales, taco salad was introduced in 1982 with the company's first national market support for a new menu item.

12 Taco salad is marketed as a complete meal of less than 400 calories. It has several virtues for Wendy's. It is preferred by women, thereby helping to further expand the chain's traditional male-oriented customer base. Taco salad is a low-cost item as most of its ingredients are already available at Wendy's restaurants. This helps to hold down the introduction cost to a mere $45 per store. Sales of taco salad will also help reduce the amount of chili that must be thrown away at the end of each day.

13 As a focal point in reaching Wendy's stated goal of increasing average sales per restaurant to $1 million a year within five years,[1] product testing and development has become a high priority in the 1980s. Recipes, procedures, and kitchen equipment are tested in the company's new research and development laboratory.

14 The core of the strategic role of R&D in achieving the objectives of higher unit sales and better margins is not just menu diversification but developing new products that increase both incremental sales and profitability. Each new product is designed to accomplish a specific sales-building task. For example, one product might be designed to target a specific demographic group or a particular consumer trend such as the shift toward dinner, while another product might be aimed at boosting volume in a specific day part. In a presentation to security analysts, Fay outlined Wendy's R&D program to build sales into four sharply defined objectives—"higher check averages, more frequent visits, increased party size, and a far broader customer base."

15 After moving cautiously during the 1981–82 recession, Wendy's introduced four major product changes in 1983: the bacon cheeseburger; improved french fries; an upgraded "Garden Spot" salad bar with eight additional food items; and its hot stuffed baked potatoes. In what appears to be Wendy's most significant new product since the salad bar, the baked potatoes were offered plain or with a choice of five toppings: cheese, broccoli and cheese, bacon and cheese, chili and cheese, and sour cream and chives. The company expects to serve about 225 million baked potatoes annually, thus further lessening Wendy's dependence on beef and providing another alternative to consumers who prefer lighter meals. Spot checks of franchisees following the introduction revealed that many units have experienced average weekly sales gains in excess of 10 percent since the baked potatoes' introduction.

16 Wendy's president, Ronald Fay, touts the plain potato as 99 percent fat free and a good source of vitamin C. He points to its versatility as "something better for Wendy's kind of people." Barney added his expectation that "the baked potato should have as much impact as the salad bar had on the fast-service food industry."

17 Products introduced by Wendy's since 1978 now produce between 25 and 30 percent of total store sales, reducing burger sales in the typical Wendy's from 60 percent to 40 percent of total store revenue within the past four or five years. The company is testing gourmet hamburgers, chicken club sandwiches, BLTs, and dessert items and is expanding its test of the fish sandwich and dinner items.

18 Breakfast will soon be offered at all company-operated and most franchised Wendy's. The chain is trying to crack the breakfast market by attacking McDonald's lack of

[1] The $1 million average sales goal represents a 40 percent increase from its 1982 base.

variety.[2] The breakfast features four made-to-order omelets, French toast, a scrambled egg platter, and an egg sandwich with a choice of toppings. Part of the slowness in moving into breakfast is due to concern over maintaining consistent quality—for example, how to make a good omelet in 30 seconds.

19 Wendy's officials seem more enthusiastic about the potential of dinner items. Dinner entrees such as chicken parmesan, country beef and gravy, and chopped beef with mushroom sauce are being tested. "Our biggest obstacle is getting people to think of us as a fast-service restaurant that offers a superior dining experience," stated William Welter, senior vice president for marketing. Company officials concede there is a lot of new ground to break in attracting the dinner crowd but point to success in a recent promotional program featuring Sunday as a family day.

20 McDonald's also appears eager to cultivate a dinner business. Like Wendy's, McDonald's is finding it difficult to persuade the customer who was in earlier for a quick lunch to come back for the evening meal. McDonald's may be further handicapped by its close association with the "sandbox" set. McDonald's president and CEO, Fred Turner, insists, "we want to move toward the adult user." He cites McNuggets, just 310 calories for six pieces, as a move to appeal to adults and speculates on the possibility that modified table service at the dinner meal time may be helpful.

21 Wendy's expenditures for R&D in 1983 were almost five times greater than in 1980 as menu management became a top priority. While new products can create excitement, incremental sales, and better profits, Wendy's officials recognize that the menu cannot be expanded indefinitely. The company is prepared to offer some items on a seasonal basis, offer products with a strong regional appeal only in certain areas, and replace some products on the menu.

22 Besides meeting the criteria of higher check averages, more frequent visits, increased party size, and a broader customer base, new products must also fit smoothly into Wendy's assembly-line delivery system. Fay emphasizes the commitment to superior speed and service and places the preservation of the integrity of the delivery system as paramount as the company strives toward its $1 million per unit sales goal.

Financial

23 Wendy's revenues result primarily from sales by company-operated restaurants (see Exhibit 1). Royalties and technical-assistance fees from franchisees make up the other

Exhibit 1

Changes in revenues from 1978 to 1982

	1982	*1981*	*1980*	*1979*	*1978*
Revenues:					
Retail operations	92.2%	91.4%	89.0%	86.8%	87.0%
Royalties	6.9	7.9	10.2	11.2	10.3
Technical assistance fee	.3	.3	.4	1.0	1.5
Other	.6	.4	.4	1.0	1.2
	100.0%	100.0%	100.0%	100.0%	100.0%

[2] In 1982, McDonald's generated $780 million (10 percent of its total revenue) from breakfast sales. That translates into approximately $120,000 annually at the typical McDonald's location.

major sources of revenue. The franchise agreement requires that the franchise owner pay a royalty equivalent to 4 percent of sales. It also calls for a technical-assistance fee to defray such costs as site-selection assistance, specifications and layouts, initial training, and so on. Currently, the fee is $15,000 for each franchise restaurant the franchise owner has agreed to construct. This compares to McDonald's $12,500 franchise fee and 3 percent royalty and Burger King's $40,000 franchise fee and 3.5 percent royalty.

24 With the exception of the buns sold by New Bakery Company of Ohio, Inc., Wendy's does not sell fixtures, food, or supplies to the franchise owners. The New Bakery Company of Ohio, Inc., a wholly owned subsidiary of Wendy's, supplies buns for 450 company-operated restaurants and for 478 franchise restaurants. It was acquired in 1981.

25 Royalty income from franchised restaurants increased 9 percent in both 1982 and 1981. However, royalties as a percent of total revenue declined in both years, largely as a result of the company's acquisition of 161 formerly franchised restaurants.

26 Total revenues increased 24 percent in 1982 (compared to 1981) to $608 million (see Exhibit 2). After the 1979 dip, net income continued on its upward growth track into 1982, up 20 percent from 1981, on top of a 22 percent increase in 1981, and a 30 percent increase in 1980. (See Exhibit 3.) Net income's five year growth rate was 23 percent per year since 1977.

27 Earnings per share increased 12 percent in 1982 to $1.13. (See Exhibit 4.) The five-year data reflect 3-for-2 stock splits in both 1981 and 1982. The debt-to-equity ratio declined to 39 percent at the end of 1982 from 49 percent (see Exhibit 5), reflecting increased borrowing capacity available to the company. In addition, $25 million in

Exhibit 2

Revenue ($ millions): Five-year compounded annual growth, 33 percent

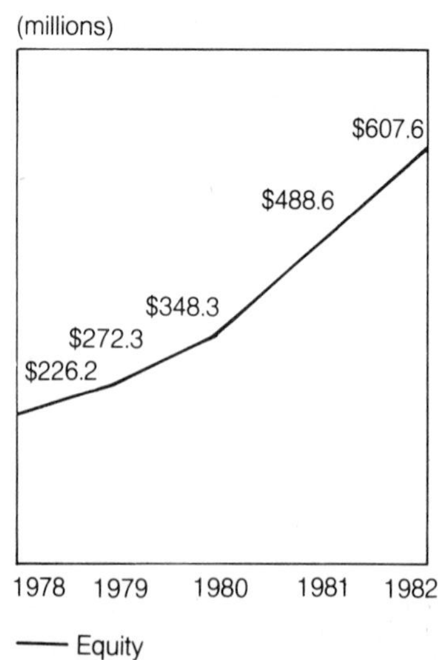

Exhibit 3

Net income ($ millions): Five-year compounded annual growth, 23 percent

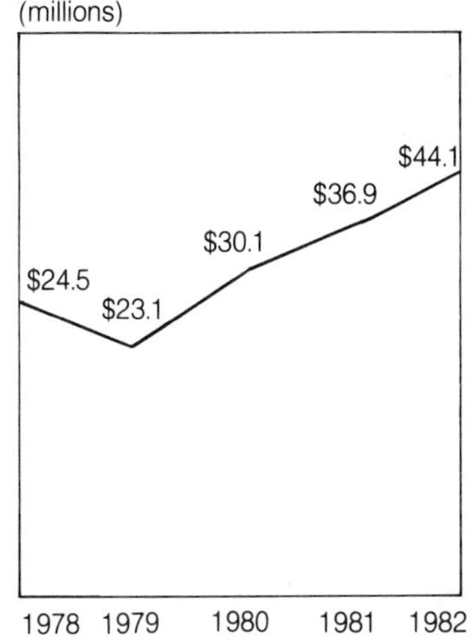

unused contractual lines of credit were available to the company at the end of 1982.

28 Of the $70.6 million in 1982 capital expenditures, $38.9 million was for new domestic Wendy's restaurants, $12.3 million for new Sisters and international restaurants, and $19.4 million principally for costs associated with the image enhancement program, restaurant refurbishings, and computerized registers (see Exhibit 6).

Exhibit 4

Earnings per share (dollars): Five-year compounded annual growth, 20 percent

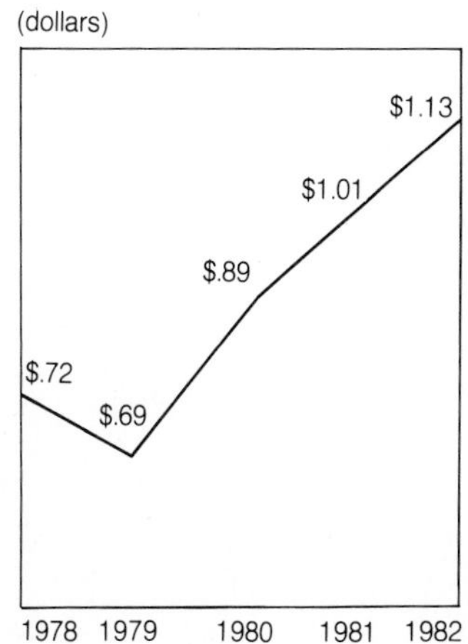

Exhibit 5

Debt to equity ($ millions)

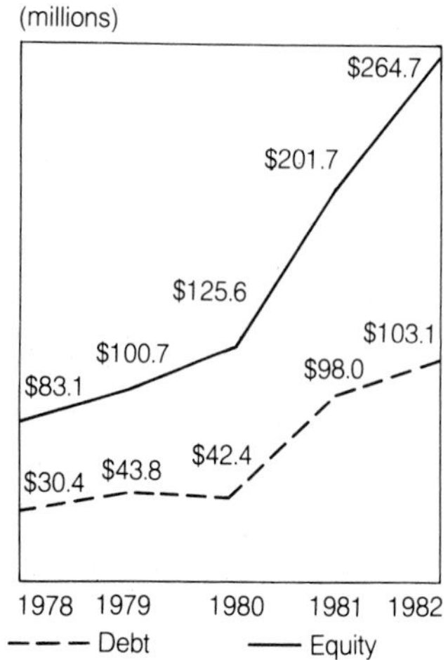

29 For Wendy's company-operated restaurants, profit margins at the store level improved to 18.1 percent from 16.7 percent in 1981 and 17.5 percent in 1980. In Wendy's 1982 annual report, this improvement was attributed to lower overall food costs (primarily beef—see Exhibit 7), more efficient product usage and reduction of food waste, and a reduction in couponing.

Exhibit 6

Capital expenditures ($ millions)

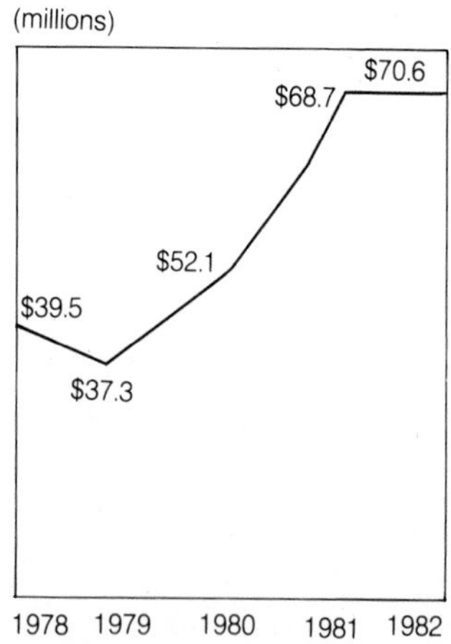

Exhibit 7

Yearly average beef price per pound for company-owned stores

1977	$ .72	1980	$1.23
1978	1.02	1981	1.14
1979	1.29	1982	1.11

Exhibit 8

Average sales per restaurant (in thousands of dollars)

	1982	*Percent change*	*1981*	*Percent change*	*1980*	*Percent change*	*1979*	*Percent change*	*1978*	*Percent change*
Company	$706	1%	$702	6%	$665	7%	$624	(3)%	$643	14%
Franchise	701	6	662	8	615	(1)	619	(12)	706	12
Systemwide ..	703	4	674	7	627	1	620	(10)	689	13

30 Retail prices have benefited from price increases. Average price increases were 3 percent and 8 percent in 1982 and 1981, respectively. Average 1982 sales per restaurant systemwide rose 4 percent to $703,000 (see Exhibit 8). Wendy's goal of increasing annual sales per store to $1 million within five years will require a sales increase of 40 percent from the current base.

31 Exhibits 9–11 contain 1978–1982 selected financial ratios, balance sheets, and statements of income.

Exhibit 9

Selected financial data (percent)

	1982	*1981*	*1980*	*1979*	*1978*
Return on average equity ...	19.50%	22.00%	26.60%	25.10%	34.20%
Return on average assets ...	14.00	15.20	18.20	18.60	22.30
Current ratio	.80	.58	.55	.93	1.23
Ratio of debt to equity	39.00	49.00	34.00	44.00	37.00
Ratio of debt to total capitalization	28.00	33.00	25.00	30.00	27.00

Exhibit 10

WENDY'S INTERNATIONAL, INCORPORATED, AND SUBSIDIARIES
Consolidated Balance Sheet
For the Years Ended December 31, 1978–1983
(in thousands of dollars)

	1983	*1982*	*1981*	*1980*	*1979*	*1978*
Assets						
Current assets:						
Cash	$ 8,177	$ 8,098	$ 9,210	$ 5,876	$ 2,285	$ 1,022
Short-term investments, at cost which approximates market	24,257	30,410	12,877	7,012	12,656	27,665
Notes receivable	8,781	2,026	2,713	186	—	—
Accounts receivable	1,990	7,180	7,841	5,328	4,903	3,249
Inventories and other	14,481	8,581	5,967	6,305	2,582	1,855
Total current assets	57,686	56,295	38,608	24,707	22,426	33,791
Property and equipment, at cost:						
Land	75,420	66,349	54,121	40,410	30,916	23,906
Buildings	126,246	103,765	82,212	56,920	40,785	30,050
Leasehold improvements	67,337	57,699	45,881	21,787	16,582	8,954
Restaurant equipment	113,597	92,735	75,317	48,853	34,053	24,462
Other equipment	29,367	22,495	19,016	10,808	9,723	8,413
Construction in progress	2,445	1,540	1,300	2,895	1,752	2,028
Capitalized leases	52,281	50,301	51,975	22,286	21,866	18,246
Total property and equipment before depreciation	466,693	394,884	329,822	203,960	155,676	116,060
Less: Accumulated depreciation and amortization	(88,782)	(67,442)	(48,814)	(29,725)	(20,962)	(13,543)
	377,911	327,442	281,008	174,235	134,714	102,516
Other assets:						
Unexpended construction funds	539	5,973	7,067	—	—	—
Cost in excess of net assets acquired, net	20,325	18,631	19,408	8,648	8,409	5,208
Investment in and advances to equity subsidiaries	27,553	23,931	14,410	—	—	—
Other	22,699	23,686	15,728	11,278	7,152	2,378
Total cost over net assets and other assets	71,116	72,221	56,613	19,926	15,561	7,586
Total assets	$506,713	$455,958	$376,229	$218,868	$172,701	$143,892

Operations

32 Wendy's marketing strategy has been to target the high-quality end of the quick-service market with primary appeal among young and middle-age adults, and its philosophy of quality, service, cleanliness, and value was aimed at this key segment of the population. With post-World War II babies reaching their 30s, these young adults have been expanding faster than any other age group. Wendy's success has come not so much at the expense of the other burger chains, but has tended to expand the market.

Exhibit 10 ***(concluded)***

	1983	1982	1981	1980	1979	1978
Liabilities and Shareholders' Equity						
Current liabilities:						
Accounts payable, trade	$ 41,739	$ 30,224	$ 36,899	$ 24,685	$ 10,175	11,666
Federal, state, and local income taxes	10,924	13,959	4,074	6,256	—	7,840
Accrued expenses:						
Salaries and wages	7,035	4,715	3,486	3,440	6,168	1,971
Taxes	9,883	8,032	6,228	3,100	1,932	1,499
Other	8,107	6,498	5,853	3,220	2,010	1,774
Current portion of long-term obligations	11,001	7,102	9,836	4,340	3,891	2,782
Total current liabilities	88,689	70,530	66,376	45,042	24,177	27,531
Long-term obligations, net of current portion:						
Term debt	42,514	59,913	52,242	22,458	25,098	15,308
Capitalized lease obligations	44,157	43,157	45,714	19,960	18,708	15,131
	86,671	103,070	97,956	42,418	43,806	30,439
Deferred technical assistance fees	1,270	1,105	1,433	1,644	1,995	2,118
Deferred income taxes	21,801	16,520	8,726	4,168	2,028	664
Shareholders' equity:						
Common stock, $.10 stated value						
Authorized: 60,000,000 and 40,000,000 shares, respectively						
Issued and outstanding: 40,746,000 and 38,322,000 shares, respectively	4,079	4,075	3,832	1,496	1,488	1,486
Capital in excess of stated value	107,727	107,345	78,550	34,875	34,113	33,963
Retained earnings	200,271	155,648	119,356	89,226	65,094	47,691
Translation adjustments	(3,795)	(2,335)				
Total shareholders' equity	308,282	264,733	201,738	125,596	100,696	83,141
Total liabilities and shareholders' equity	$506,713	$455,958	$376,229	$218,868	$172,701	$143,892

33 Other demographic trends, such as the increase in working women, greater frequency of eating out, and the heightened interest in nutrition and health have all had a favorable impact.

34 A "new image" exterior design is in keeping with Wendy's market niche. Moving further away from the brightly colored, plastic fast-food atmosphere, restaurants with the new upgraded image feature copper-colored roof panels and decorative awnings and lighting. Interior changes emphasize quality and comfort.

35 To expand at sites that may not accomodate a full-sized restaurant, the company has built and is testing 11 more-compact and less costly to build units and is also testing a drive-through-only restaurant.

36 Advertising spending has been increased. Franchise owners in addition to spending 3 percent of their gross receipts for local advertising, and promotions have increased their contribution to Wendy's national advertising program (WNAP) from 1 percent

Exhibit 11

WENDY'S INTERNATIONAL, INCORPORATED, AND SUBSIDIARIES
Consolidated Statement of Revenue and Earnings
For the Years Ended December 31, 1978–1983
(in thousands of dollars)

	1983	*1982*	*1981*	*1980*	*1979*	*1978*
Revenue:						
Retail operations	$665,591	$560,516	$446,800	$310,067	$237,753	$ 198,529
Royalties	49,505	41,918	38,619	35,555	30,565	23,396
Technical assistance fees	*	1,856	1,223	1,406	2,823	3,540
Other	5,287	3,350	1,938	1,280	2,903	2,686
Total revenue	720,383	607,640	488,580	348,308	274,044	228,151
Costs and expenses:						
Cost of sales	371,176	315,473	257,735	187,968	146,347	113,813
Company restaurant operating costs	168,048	143,326	114,233	67,714	54,993	43,289
Direct expenses of franchise personnel	7,674	6,023	5,061	4,544	4,187	3,149
General and administrative expenses	42,318	31,686	24,521	19,831	15,742	13,293
Depreciation and amortization of property and equipment	24,892	20,906	15,308	9,782	7,356	5,444
Interest net	6,799	9,519	7,070	3,748	4,358	3,772
Total costs and expenses	620,907	526,933	423,928	293,587	232,983	182,760
Income before income taxes	99,476	80,707	64,652	54,721	41,061	45,391
Income taxes	44,756	36,605	27,800	24,625	17,964	20,905
Net income	54,720	44,102	36,852	30,096	23,097	24,486
Retained earnings—beginning of year	155,648	119,356	89,226	65,094	47,691	25,234
Cash dividends		(7,810)	(6,722)	(5,964)	(5,694)	(1,943)
Pooled Subchapter S corporations' reclassifications	—	—	—	—	—	(283)
Effect of conforming fiscal year end of pooled corporation	—	—	—	—	—	196
Retained earnings—end of year	$210,868	$155,648	$119,356	$ 89,226	$ 65,094	$ 47,690
Per share data:						
Net income per share	$1.00	$1.13	$1.01	$.89	$1.54	$1.63
Weighted average shares outstanding	54,701†	39,165	36,445	33,774	14,971	15,018
Dividends per share	$.20	$.20	$.19	$.18	$.38	$.13

* Reported as part of other Revenue.
† Reflects 4-for-3 stock split in 1984.

Exhibit 12

Advertising and promotion expenses

	1982	*1981*	*1980*
Company expenses	$25,201,000	$21,429,000	$12,778,000
WNAP	$16,000,000	$13,000,000	$11,000,000
Franchise	In addition to WNAP contributions, each franchise owner must spend 3 percent of gross receipts for local advertising and promotions.		

to 1.5 percent of gross sales (see Exhibit 12). The total amount spent on advertising and promotions in 1983 came to about $75 million. While other competitors have been increasing couponing, Wendy's has reduced it from the 1981 level of 3.1 percent of sales to a 1.3 percent level.

37 Advertising in the fast-food burger chain industry has become more fierce since Burger King launched its now famous and controversial comparative advertising campaign. The "Battle of the Burgers" claimed that the Whopper beat the Big Mac and Wendy's hamburger and also claimed that Burger King's hamburgers were flame broiled while McDonald's and Wendy's fried their hamburgers. Wendy's and McDonald's filed lawsuits leading to out-of-court settlements in which Burger King agreed to phase out the campaign.

38 In March 1983, Burger King introduced its "Project BIB" or "Broiling Is Better" campaign. This modified version of its earlier ads singles out McDonald's, but not Wendy's, by name. Burger King has posted an average 10 percent monthly sales gain since the campaign began. With pugnacious Burger King and with McDonald's $300 million ad budget, Wendy's has changed to harder-hitting campaigns than such previous campaigns as "Hot 'n' Juicy," and "Ain't No Reason to Go Anyplace Else."

39 Unlike Burger King's controversial comparative ad campaign, Wendy's has opted to make its point of supposed differences between itself and its two main rivals without actually naming either Burger King or McDonald's though the commercials make it clear who Wendy's targets are. They are referred to as "two famous hamburger places" or as "some hamburger places." The five 30-second spots proclaim in a humorous way that Wendy's, unlike some other chains, makes its burgers with fresh, not frozen, ground beef; that its burgers are served hot off the grill; and that customers don't have to step aside or park for special orders. The "Wendy's Kind of People" campaign was rumored to be in response to pressure from franchisees demanding a more-aggressive marketing stance, but Wendy's executives denied the published report.

40 Kicking off 1984 was the nationally televised commercial with three elderly ladies shown standing at a Brand X hamburger counter. Pointing to the idea that Wendy's single hamburger has more beef "despite its modest name" than some bigger-named competitors, one elderly woman demands, "Where's the beef?" The commercial has prompted fan clubs for one of the actresses, inspired a taunt at high school basketball games, and spawned a complaint from the Michigan State Office of Services to the Aging that the commercial is demeaning to the elderly. Wendy's officials responded

that the commercial is actually a positive portrayal of an elderly woman demanding her rights as a consumer.

41 Wendy's delivery system—its drive-in window and single order and pickup line—has been one of the most-impressive segments of the company's operations. With its goal of 15 seconds to fill an order inside the restaurant and 25 seconds for the pickup window (from the time the order is given), speed of service is recognized as essential. For its basic snake-line system to work, order takers get customers' requests before they get to the cash register during peak lunch periods. Outside order takers and change takers even have been initiated near the pickup window (the pickup window accounts for over 40 percent of Wendy's sales).

42 The sight of a jammed-up line may cause potential customers to forego eating at Wendy's. The company has already found it necessary in some instances to depart from its single-line concept and has launched multilines in downtown Manhattan, Chicago, and Columbus. But Chairman Barney has indicated a preference to opening new units if suburban single lines get jammed up, rather than changing to multilines in the suburban restaurants.

43 A variety of management programs have been initiated to improve restaurant efficiency. Since 1981, the ratio of management at all operating levels has increased. Management turnover has been reduced with a five-day workweek aimed at removing some of the work burden. A co-manager, assistant manager, and, in busier restaurants, a trainee-manager, are being utilized. Trainees or assistants can now move up to manager within a year and a half rather than waiting two or three years as was the case previously. A computerized cash register data system was installed to increase managers' productivity, and over 300 restaurants were using the system by late 1982. The technology can eliminate as much as 20 hours of administrative work per month, thus freeing managers to devote more attention to customers and crew personnel.

Franchising

44 Two main thrusts appear to characterize Wendy's franchising emphasis for the 1980s: (1) enhanced operational control and support of domestic franchises and (2) expansion through international locations.

45 Commenting on domestic emphasis, Ronald Fay, president and chief operating officer, offered the following overview in early 1983:

> 46 Over the last two years in units where franchisees have not kept up with development plans, such as Los Angeles, we have withdrawn development rights and involved new franchisees in those markets. We refranchised that area last year, and our present franchisees now are committed to add 20 new stores each year in L.A. for the next several years.
>
> 47 Now we are laying the groundwork to further stimulate franchised growth—especially in high-density areas. Wendy's will begin to franchise individual units in certain markets to augment our area franchise approach of the past 13 years.[3] During the next three years, we may award several hundred such unit franchises.

[3] To foster its initial development, Wendy's pursued an area franchising strategy in which franchise contracts were awarded for cities and parts of states with the average franchise owner operating nine restaurants. Area franchising strategy was instrumental in Wendy's achieving its record growth.

48 In early 1980, Wendy's established a new regional structure for managing company-owned and franchise outlets. It increased the number of personnel in regional operating centers by 25 percent with each of them supervising fewer restaurants than in the past, placing major emphasis on having more company personnel to assist the franchise organization in maintaining operational excellence. A key emphasis in this regard was to improve communications and cooperation between management and franchisees. Wendy's established a Franchise Advisory Council to provide a formal communication link between the company and the franchisees. It was comprised of key company personnel and franchisees selected on a regional basis by their peers. Touted to be the most-important element in strengthening the company-franchisee relationship during 1980 was the introduction of Wendy's new senior management to the franchise system. Beginning in August 1980, Wendy's senior management group traveled to every region of the country and conducted a series of "town hall meetings" with its franchisees. This process has continued, according to Ray, because "the exchange of information and philosophy at such sessions contributes significantly to Wendy's future development."

49 When interest rates hit historical highs in 1981 and 1982, many potential franchisees could not find funds locally. To encourage franchise restaurant expansion and to generate additional royalty revenues, a financial assistance program was arranged for qualified franchise owners. Under the "Wenequity" program, franchise owners lease the land and building while owning their business. The company formed a wholly owned subsidiary to purchase newly constructed stores and lease them back to franchisees. Wendy's packaged the restaurants in groups of 20 or more and marketed them to investors, primarily insurance companies. The finance subsidiaries received 25 percent of their capital from Wendy's and 75 percent from privately placed debt, with the rent paid by the franchisees being more than adequate to service the debt. By early 1983, the Wenequity program had helped franchisees build 87 stores. Currently, the program is winding down.

50 To accelerate the growth of the Wendy's system through the development of minority markets and to provide opportunities for minorities through franchise ownership, the company established a minority franchise program. Since its inception in 1979, 12 restaurants have opened under the program.

51 In 1981, Wendy's acquired 161 franchise restaurants in Denver, Phoenix, Seattle, suburban Atlanta, Chicago, Milwaukee, and Lakeland, Florida. The company has withdrawn development rights and involved new franchisees in markets where franchisees have not kept up with development plans. Combined with the 81 company stores opened in 1981, the percent of company-owned stores increased from 25 percent at the end of 1980 to 34 percent in 1981.

52 The expansion of company-operated stores has also accelerated. Sixty-six stores were added in 1982 with about 80 to be added in 1983. Plans for the following two years are to increase company operations to about 100 additions per year. The growth rate of company-owned stores from 1980 to 1983 has been 41%, contrasted with the growth rate in franchised stores of 4.5 percent (see Exhibit 13).

53 Wendy's has identified 200 markets as underrepresented. For example, in Wendy's hometown of Columbus, there are 48 Wendy's, while Chicago has only 41 in operation, Philadelphia, only 29, and Houston, only 18. The population in Columbus numbers only 37,000 people per Wendy's restaurant. In contrast, in Chicago there are 140,000 people per unit, in Los Angeles, 221,000, and in New York, 370,000 people per unit.

Exhibit 13

	1980–1983 growth rate	*Mid-1983*	*1982*	*1981*	*1980*
Company	41%	860 (35%)	827 (34%)	748 (34%)	506 (25%)
Franchised	4½%	1,600 (65%)	1,603 (66%)	1,481 (66%)	1,528 (75%)
Total		2,460	2,430	2,229	2,034

In Los Angeles, where company analysts feel that the market can support four times the number of Wendy's there now, the area has already been refranchised as noted earlier.

54 In a stated effort to stimulate growth, especially in high-density areas, the company announced a unit franchise strategy to augment its area franchise approach of the past 13 years. This concept (unit franchise strategy) enables individuals who could not develop a multiunit franchise to join the Wendy's family, Ronald Fay explained. "Additionally, single-unit franchising gives Wendy's the opportunity to develop each market to its maximum potential."

55 The major shift to company-owned restaurants and unit franchising, away from large-area franchising, reflects the concern for systemwide control of quality. This move may well be intended to avoid the problem that led to Burger King's decline in the late 1960s—franchise empires were bigger than parent company operations.[4]

International

56 Wendy's established an international division in 1979, and by 1983, there were 125 Wendy's operating outside the United States. Franchised restaurants numbered 100: 70 in Canada, 15 in Japan, 8 in Puerto Rico, 3 each in Switzerland and Australia, and 1 in Malaysia. In addition, there are 14 company operations in Germany, 6 in Spain, and 5 in the United Kingdom. Openings were slated for the first Wendy's in Italy, Hong Kong, Singapore, and Mexico. Company development is expected to focus on the United Kingdom, Spain, and Germany, with franchisees being most active in Japan.

57 Of the fast-food hamburger chains, McDonald's is the best established internationally with approximately 1,500 units in 32 countries. Those units are heavily concentrated in Canada (335), Japan (212), Australia (107), and various parts of Europe. McDonald's is expected to accelerate its development of the international market, where it has been adding 150 units a year. Burger King presently has 224 overseas units in 18 countries, 58 of which were added in 1982. The company is expected to begin rapid international expansion in 1986.

58 With concern that the American fast-food market may be approaching the saturation point, some fast-food chains have turned to overseas markets to meet growth goals. *Nation's Restaurant News* reports the market potential in western Europe is enticing

[4] In 1981, over 80 percent of the Burger King restaurants were franchise operations.

because fast food currently represents less than 3 percent of all meals consumed away from home. Further reinforcing the contention that this market is still largely untapped, European per-capita spending on fast food is only $3.50 a year compared to approximately $150 for each American in 1982.

59 However, there are numerous pitfalls and high risks to overseas expansion. Investment in land, buildings, and equipment for a new McDonald's in Germany is at least $1 million, compared with less than $750,000 at home. Labor may run 40 percent of revenues in that same West German store, while labor consumes only about 20 to 25 percent of the typical domestic unit's revenue. These higher fixed and variable costs result in lower per-unit profit margins overseas. While 1981 operating profits at U.S. McDonald's units were 17.5 percent, European McDonald's units ranged between only 7 to 9 percent.

60 With the recognition that international development is both a slow and costly undertaking, Wendy's officials project that it takes about 26 trips to establish the first store in each country. Aside from the language problems, there is distribution to set up, finding products that meet specifications, and construction site approval, among others.

61 Wendy's international activity has accelerated with 22 restaurants opened in 1982 and 32 openings scheduled for 1983. Citing the need to increase penetration, Wendy's officials have indicated that the major thrust of international operations will be on the franchise side. International management has been strengthened through the creation of a European zone office in London and a Far East zone office in Honolulu. From these bases, senior Wendy's personnel will support the worldwide franchises and company operation in such staff functions as quality assurance, construction, marketing, and purchasing.

62 Second only to Canada in number of restaurants, Japan has become a primary market for Wendy's. In developing this market, Wendy's associated itself with the Daiei Group, Japan's largest retailer with annual sales of $4 billion. This allowed Wendy's to take advantage of profitable opportunities while limiting development costs and currency risks to acceptable levels. Plans in 1983 were to add 12 more restaurants to the 15 already operating there. Of those 15, only 8 were in operation prior to 1982. A training center was established in 1982 in Japan, as well as in England and Germany, to develop local managers and crew people.

63 Besides Japan, Wendy's is making inroads on other continents. In Madrid, the company advertised on commercial television for the first time outside of North America. The Australian licensees opened the first three Australian Wendy's in Melbourne in 1982. The company is especially excited about the potential of the Australian market since the lifestyle there is so similar to that in the United States.

64 In 1982, company operations in Spain and the United Kingdom were profitable at the store level. Industry analysts project profitability of overseas operations in late 1985 or early 1986.

65 Reflecting on the international sphere as Wendy's future arena for franchising (and licensing) growth, Edward Lifmann, international director, offered the following:

66 We've developed the flexibility necessary to be successful overseas in the face of differing eating habits and tastes. Eating times vary so we've changed our hours. Living and shopping habits vary from the American style of suburban development, so we're mainly basing in-line units in urban centers. New product sizes and offerings have been developed to meet local tastes and dietary needs.

Competitors

67 In 1983, Wendy's laid claim to approximately 5 percent of the fast-food industry's total sales of $38 billion, accounted for 9.4 percent of the $18 billion hamburger segment and claimed the position of the third-largest hamburger chain behind direct competitors, McDonald's and Burger King (see Exhibit 14).[5]

Exhibit 14

How the three hamburger giants slice the market (estimated 1983 sales—$ billions)

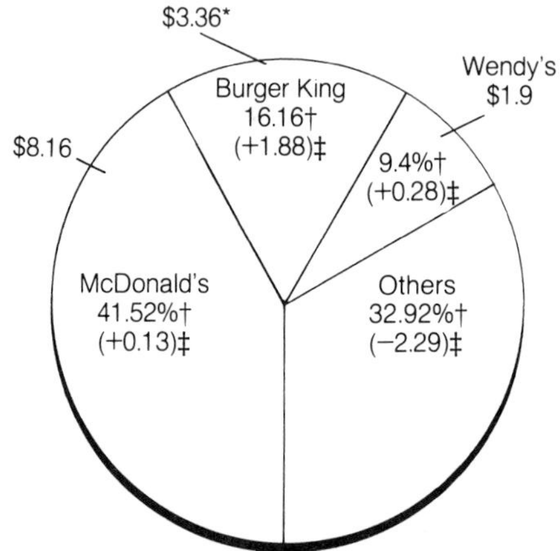

Note: Fiscal years ended december 1983 for McDonald's and Wendy's; May 1984 for Burger King.
* Market share.
† Percent of market.
‡ Percentage-point change in market share since 1981.
Source: "The Fast-Food War: Big Mac under Attack," *Business Week*, January 30, 1984, p. 46.

68 Having originally left the adult market to Wendy's, Burger King is now going after it with a vengeance. Burger King has oriented its advertising to adults and is appealing to health-conscious consumers with its salad bar. Its newest menu entree is a salad sandwich in pita bread.

69 Burger King recently developed the Whopper Express, a tiny outlet in the Wall Street area of New York City, where the customer can walk in, be served, and walk out again in 2½ minutes. With a slimmed-down menu, this unit is about one third the size of a normal Burger King and is designed to penetrate high-volume urban areas where rent costs would normally make it impossible to locate.

70 Although McDonald's has been injured by the battle of the burgers campaign and has had problems with the perception of its burgers' quality, the company holds a

[5] With Hardee's 1982 acquisition of 380 Burger Chef restaurants, Hardee's moved slightly above Wendy's in sales and number of units.

staggering 42 percent of the hamburger market share. As an early entrant into the industry, McDonald's has premium site locations and mammoth size. With 6,000 domestic units and about 1,500 overseas units, McDonald's is more than twice the size of Pillsbury's Burger King and triple that of Wendy's. Its return on equity is more than 20 percent and its growth is expected to center on international focus. McDonald's is also said to be testing smaller, limited-menu stores (McSnacks) and looking at such previously neglected markets as schools, parks, and military installations.

71 After failing with the McChicken and McRib Sandwich, McDonald's introduced Chicken McNuggets, which accounted for 12 percent of sales by 1983, and it is reviewing a low-calorie Big Mac, a McFeast sandwich, a Mexican product, caramel rolls, and biscuits. McDonald's has not been definitive on the major challenges: developing new products, getting dinner business, and advertising.

72 With the average American household spending nearly one in three food dollars away from home, nearly twice the proportion of two decades ago, ethnic and upscale outlets are trying to lure more of the fast-food industry's $38 billion in sales by pecking away at the hamburger customer base.[6] Mexican food sales increased 21 percent in 1983 to become a $1.6 billion market. Barbecue has gained popularity as modern cooking machines have made it possible to mass produce this food.

73 With customers' interest in anything fresh perceived as healthy, gourmet pizza with fresh ingredients is gaining customer attention. Fresh pasta with a variety of sauces is another Italian entree grabbing customers. Small bakeries with croissants, quiche, muffins, and so forth may be making a comeback. Chicken chains are also doing well, and Japanese food may be ready to take off.

74 With the fast-food customer becoming more sophisticated, numerous restaurants are positioning themselves one step above typical fast-food outlets and one step below the typical full-service restaurant. For example, Atlanta-based D'Lites, which specializes in light fast food, offers a typical fast-food meal at half the calories of other outlets (498 calories versus 1,066 calories). Gourmet hamburgers, costing from $3 to $5, are also doing well.

75 Some of the fast-food restaurants have recently expanded menus and upgraded decor such as A&W's new "Good Food." The A&W outlet serves a broad menu with such dishes as shrimp tempura, pasta with a variety of sauces, and hamburgers and hotdogs with a "dress-your-own" bar, but they serve the food very fast and use disposables.

76 Wendy's former director of franchising, Graydon Webb, has founded the upscale fast-food restaurant G. D. Ritzy's, which serves extravagant peanut butter and jelly sandwiches, spicy chili, hotdogs, hamburgers, and gourmet ice cream, among other fast-food items.

77 Fast-food prices have generally risen more quickly over the past few years than have table-service restaurant menu prices, and the price differential has narrowed, although the sit-down restaurants are still more expensive.

78 As the baby-boom generation (see Exhibit 15) who fueled fast-food's growth in the 1970s are moving into their more sedate 30s, the baby boomers are beginning to trade up to medium-priced, full-service restaurants, because with their maturing tastes in food, they perceive greater value for their food dollars.

---

[6] U.S. Bureau of Labor Statistics' Consumer Expenditure Surveys indicate that in 1980–81, 33 percent of the food budget was spent on food away from home. In 1960–61, it was 17 percent.

Exhibit 15

The baby boom matures (age distribution of the U.S. population)

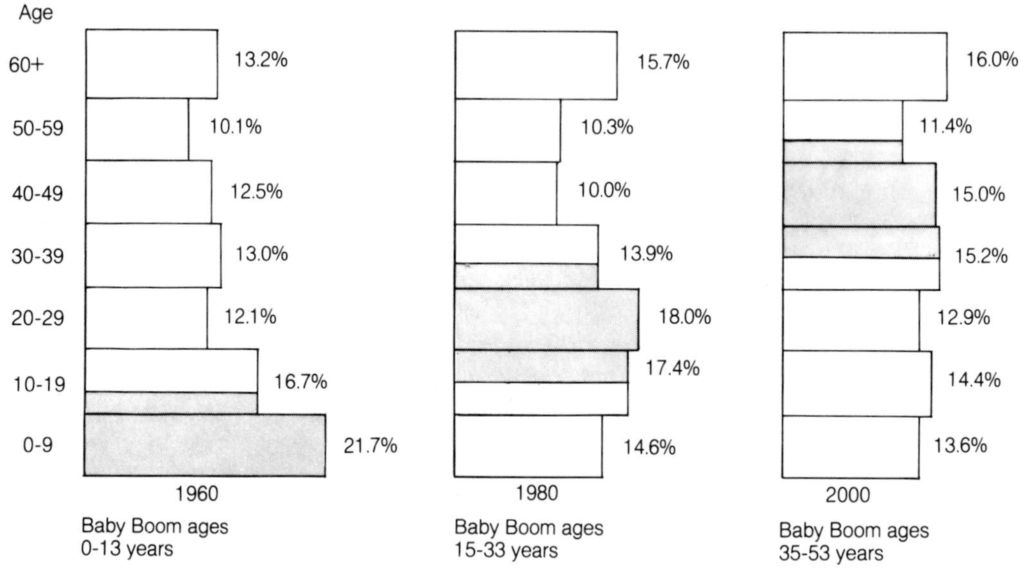

Sisters' Development

79 Scoffing at reports that the fast-food burger industry may be oversaturated, Wendy's officials portray the company's recent move into the chicken restaurant industry as an avenue in which to apply the principles that built its success to other segments of the industry and as an opportunity for further growth.

80 Before investing in hamburgers, Wendy's founder made his first million in chicken. R. David Thomas, who named his 65-foot houseboat *The Colonel* after Colonel Harland Sanders, Kentucky Fried Chicken's founder, was admittedly strongly influenced by the "Chicken King." At the age of 32, Thomas obtained an interest in four nearly bankrupt Kentucky Fried Chicken carryouts in Columbus, Ohio. For $65, Thomas was promised 45 percent of the Columbus franchise if he could turn the carryouts around, pay off a $200,000 deficit, and make a profit. The restaurants began to prosper, and four more Columbus locations were added. In 1968, Thomas sold the restaurants back to the parent company for $1.5 million.

81 After selling his interest in the Columbus Kentucky Fried Chicken franchise, Thomas became regional operations director for the parent company. In working and traveling with Colonel Sanders, he had the opportunity to observe and to learn from Sanders's mistakes.

82 A decade later, when CEO Robert Barney thought there was a void in the chicken industry that could be filled by an upscale restaurant serving quality food, Barney and Thomas asked James Near, an experienced restaurateur and former Wendy's franchisee, to develop this concept. With the conviction that the same principles which

built its success could be applied to other segments of the industry, Wendy's initially owned 20 percent of Sisters International and, in 1981, exercised its option to purchase the remaining 80 percent.

83 In a Wendy's press release announcing the nationwide expansion of Sisters, Near, president and chief operating officer of Sisters International, Inc., indicated that Wendy's corporate muscle would greatly enhance Sisters' growth. He said, "We can take advantage of Wendy's financial strength as well as their extensive knowledge of the marketplace. Additionally, we have a ready-made franchising network of successful operators who know what quality is."

84 As the first major diversification by Wendy's, company officials are excited about the future prospects of Sisters. Near predicts that Sisters will "continue the tradition of quality, service, and value which is Wendy's hallmark." The Sisters' concept, to combine the self-service of the quick-food industry with the full menu and warmth of comfortable dining facilities of the traditional family restaurant, is designed to appeal specifically to the maturing, value-conscious consumer.

85 Principal in this target group are the baby boomers, who are producing, although belatedly, a baby boom echo. Exhibit 16 gives comparative age data between 1970 and 1980. By 1990, 45 percent of all Americans will be between 20 and 49 years of age, compared with 32 percent in 1960.

Exhibit 16

Age structure of the resident population of the United States: April 1, 1980, and April 1, 1970

	Population		*Percent distribution*		*Population change, 1970–80*	
Age	*April 1, 1980*	*April 1, 1970*	*April 1, 1980*	*April 1, 1970*	*Number*	*Percent*
All ages	226,504,825	203,235,298	100.0%	100.0%	23,269,527	11.4%
Under 5 years	16,344,407	17,162,836	7.2	8.4	−818,429	−4.8
5–9 years	16,697,134	19,969,056	7.4	9.8	−3,271,922	−16.4
10–14 years	18,240,919	20,804,063	8.1	10.2	−2,563,144	−12.3
15–19 years	21,161,667	19,083,971	9.3	9.4	2,077,696	10.9
20–24 years	21,312,557	16,382,893	9.4	8.1	4,929,664	30.1
25–34 years	37,075,629	24,922,511	16.4	12.3	12,153,118	48.8
35–44 years	25,631,247	23,101,173	11.3	11.4	2,530,074	11.0
45–54 years	22,797,367	23,234,790	10.1	11.4	−437,423	−1.9
55–64 years	21,699,765	18,601,669	9.6	9.2	3,098,096	16.7
65–74 years	15,577,586	12,442,573	6.9	6.1	3,135,013	25.2
75–84 years	7,726,826	6,121,627	3.4	3.0	1,605,199	26.2
85 years and over	2,239,721	1,408,136	1.0	0.7	831,585	59.1
Median age	30.0	28.0	(x)	(x)	(x)	(x)

Source: U.S. Census, 1980 and 1970.

86 As one of the best-performing categories in 1983, chicken chains saw growth of 19.7 percent in the previous year to become a $4 billion segment of the fast-food industry (see Exhibit 17). U.S. per capita consumption of chicken grew at more than twice the rate for hamburgers during the last decade.

Exhibit 17

Fast-food industry total sales—$38 billion

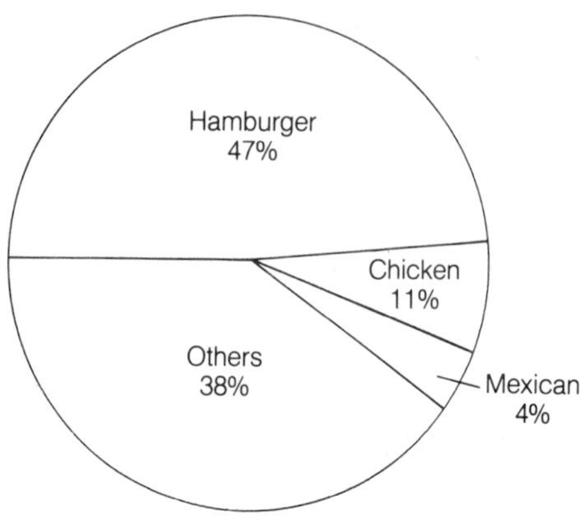

87 With its country classic decor, the Sisters chicken and biscuits building (Exhibit 18) is styled as a turn-of-the-century home, framed with a picket fence and flower beds. The interior design is accented with antique china, collector glassware, and gaslight-style lighting projecting a warm country feeling. The restaurant design also includes carryout and drive-through service.

88 Sisters has a breakfast menu, as well as a lunch and dinner menu. Breakfast includes fresh buttermilk biscuits with pork sausage, ham, beef steak, and scrambled eggs. The lunch and dinner menu features fresh, never frozen, spicy or mild fried chicken, buttermilk biscuits, creamed chicken (an innovative way to control food cost), cole slaw, baked beans, fried potato wedges, Sisters' spicy rice, corn on the cob, and strawberry shortcake. Salad bars, dessert bars, and baked-potato bars are being added. Dining-room customers receive their meals on plates, rather than the traditional chicken boxes of most chains.

89 According to industry analysts, new Sisters units are producing $850,000 in annual revenue per location on an average $500,000 capital investment (see Exhibit 19). This compares with average sales of $468,000 per store for Kentucky Fried Chicken's 837 company stores and average sales of $355,000 per store for Kentucky's 3,641 franchised stores. Church's 1,137 company-owned stores averaged $413,100, and Church's reported a $378,860 per-store average for its 242 licensed stores. The average cost of a new Church's restaurant was $350,000 in 1983.

90 Franchising will follow the same path that led to Wendy's rapid growth. Franchises will be awarded by counties or metropolitan areas to enable the franchise owner to have a number of restaurants and build an organization. All current Wendy's franchise owners will be considered first for their existing territories, with some Wendy's company markets to be available to new prospective franchisers for Sisters. Contracts have been signed with 45 franchise groups and call for the opening of 470 franchised Sisters by 1988.

91 By late 1983, 42 Sisters were operating in 15 markets. Between 150 and 250 restau-

Exhibit 18

SISTERS INTERNATIONAL, INC.
167 South State St., P.O. Box 111, Westerville, Ohio 43081
Phone 614/891-9303

Making Chicken Special Again!

Exhibit 19

1982 Comparison of a typical Wendy's and Sisters restaurant

	Building size	*Seating*	*Needed capitalization*	*Revenue per store*	*Sales-to-investment ratio*	*Margins*
Sisters	2,100 sq. ft.	84	$500,000	$850,000	1.70	10–11% (E)*
Wendy's	2,100 sq. ft.	92	$613,000	$703,000	1.15	15%

* Estimated.

rants are expected to be operating at the end of 1985. Enthusiastic over the initial success, Barney hopes "to make Sisters the Wendy's of the chicken restaurant industry by making chicken special again." Wendy's competitors are watching with interest. Burger King is hinting that it may try its hand at a new chain. McDonald's, who is expected to accumulate an excess cash flow of $1 billion between 1984 and 1990, is thought to be considering acquiring something in the food-service area.

Management Reorganization

92 For the first 11 years of its history, Wendy's was guided by an entrepreneurial spirit that gave the company the fastest growth record in the history of the food-service industry. This accelerated growth from one restaurant into a franchised worldwide system employing approximately 29,000 people demanded a restructuring of management. With sales of over $1 billion a year, and with continued growth in sales and earnings becoming increasingly difficult to achieve, the consensus that a shift in philosophy from an entrepreneurial to a more professionally managed firm was necessary had become evident by the late 1970s. At the end of 1982, Wendy's management had changed substantially with only 7 of its present 37 officers having been officers in 1979.

93 With the pressure of soaring beef prices, inflation, and recession, founder and former Chairman R. David Thomas, who presently serves as senior chairman of the board, took the first step in April 1980 when he recommended to the board that President Robert L. Barney be named chief executive officer. Mr. Barney, who has since been named chairman of the board in addition to being chief executive officer, implemented the remainder of the management reorganization plan.

94 Rounding out Wendy's top management team is President Ronald P. Faye, a former franchisee with 32 years of experience in the industry at all levels of restaurant operations and management. Wendy's top executive trio has combined restaurant industry experience of more than 90 years.

95 The marketing department was reorganized under the direction of Darrough Diamond. Bringing more than 15 years of marketing experience to his new position as senior vice president of marketing, Mr. Diamond consolidated Wendy's field marketing programs into a regional marketing concept. He grouped company-owned and franchise restaurants into regions by geographical location and market penetration, with field

marketing supervisors assigned to coordinate national and local marketing programs in each region. In addition, Dancer Sample was named Wendy's new national advertising agency.

96 A new regional structure was also instituted for the Company Operations and Franchising Department. The department was given more personnel, with each supervising fewer restaurants than in the past. In response to an emphasis in 1980 on improving communications and cooperation between company management and franchisees, the Franchise Advisory Council was created (see the discussion of the council in the earlier section on franchising).

97 In addition to revamping marketing and operations, a senior management group was formed to provide improved direction and control for achieving the company's goals and objectives and implementing management's strategies for future growth.

98 The 1981 acquisition of 161 franchisees forced the company to again increase its operations management staff, in keeping with the company's strategy of increasing the ratio of supervisory personnel to number of stores. Along with the enlarged marketing effort, this pushed 1981 company restaurant operating costs to 25.6 percent of retail sales, compared with 21.8 percent in 1980 and 23.1 percent in 1979. The rise continued in 1982, escalating to 26 percent of sales.

99 Although now a more professionally managed company, the entrepreneurial spirit is still alive at Wendy's.

case 3
The Bendix-Martin Marietta Acquisition Attempt*

Introduction

1 Bendix Corporation had been poised for a major new business acquisition for over a year and a half, and speculation in the business community over what firm would be its target had continued through the summer of 1982. William Agee, 44, the chairman and chief executive officer of Bendix, encouraged the guessing game by indicating only that his firm was looking at candidates possessing sophisticated technology. Bendix was already considered a "high-tech" firm with 33 percent of its $4.4 billion sales coming from aerospace and electronics during 1981. But Agee seemed aimed at lessening Bendix's dependence on the unhealthy U.S. automotive industry—49 percent of 1981 sales.

2 The speculation about Bendix's acquisition plan continued until August 24, when the price of the common shares of the Martin Marietta Corporation rose $2.50, and Wall Street rumors indicated that Mr. Agee had found his target! The next day Bendix Corporation announced an offer of $1.5 billion of cash and stock to acquire Martin Marietta, a diversified manufacturing enterprise. The directors and managers of Martin Marietta valued their independence and responded with their own attempt to acquire Bendix. This unusual move, actually aimed at avoiding acquisition entirely, was named the "Pac-Man Defense" because each company was trying to gobble up the other's shares and gain control. And it ignited one of the most complex acquisition battles in history.

3 The battle highlighted several unsettling questions concerning U.S. business practices. Some observers found the battle to be a disgusting waste of resources, driven only by the egos of the participants and involving little thought to corporate or business strategy. Others believed it was an unfortunate but inevitable part of the U.S. capitalistic system. Still others said a mismanaged economy made such acquisition activity necessary (see Exhibits 1 and 2). Mr. Agee made a strong argument that growth through

---

* The case writers made extensive use of many publicly available documents to prepare this case. Sources include *Business Week, The Chicago Tribune, Fortune, Moody's Industrial Manual, The Wall Street Journal,* the *Washington Post,* and others. Two articles by Peter W. Bernstein, "Upheaval at Bendix" and "Things the Business School Never Taught," which appeared in the November 3, 1980, issue of *Fortune* magazine were quoted extensively with permission: © 1980 Time, Inc. All rights reserved. *The Wall Street Journal* was the main source for the section of "Pac-Man Corporation Style," and Exhibits 1, 2, and 4 are reprinted by permission of *The Wall Street Journal,* © Dow Jones & Company, Inc., 1982. All rights reserved.

Exhibit 1

Four-Way Takeover Fight Amuses Some Spectators, Disturbs Others

On Wall Street, they call it the Pac-Man Takeover.

Speculators and traders watch it like Pac-Man, too, on video terminals flashing news and stock prices that signal gainers and losers, and create and decimate large paper fortunes. Two big defense contractors, Bendix Corp. and Martin Marietta Corp., were trying to gobble each other up. Then United Technologies Corp. and later, Allied Corp., joined in, each apparently eager to swallow, in whole or in part, the juiciest and most vulnerable of the contenders.

For businessmen and others on the sidelines, the boardroom battles of the past few weeks at times have seemed amusing—but also disturbing. A steel company executive puts it this way: "Maybe there's something wrong with our system when these four companies can line up large amounts of money in order to purchase stock, when it doesn't help build one new factory, buy one more piece of equipment, or provide even one more new job.

"In fact, some consolidation will probably take place, eliminating some jobs—whereas we in the steel industry have lots of trouble with banks obtaining financing to modernize. We're trying to reindustrialize America, while these other companies want to deindustrialize America."

Many business people were willing to express themselves on the subject, and in talks with reporters for *The Wall Street Journal,* they did. A sampling of their views follows:

This takeover battle has the makings of a beautiful business school exercise. It puts me in mind of the phalarope syndrome—you know, the African bird that spends its entire life chasing its own tail. Does it really matter, and will it result in a more efficient operating unit? I doubt it.

—Fred C. Yeager, professor of finance, School of Business and Administration, St. Louis University, St. Louis

You don't see these things in closely held companies when the president is spending his own money.

—Max Dillard, chairman and president, Drillers Inc., Houston

It has all the drama and excitement of a good football game, which maybe is a good thing with the pro football players out on strike now. Allied Corp. kicked a 48-yard field goal with 15 seconds left on behalf of Bendix. I admire Martin Marietta for their spunk. They just simply refused to roll over and play dead. That's part of the drama. . . . I wouldn't characterize it as constructive or destructive, but consistent with free enterprise.

—Joseph E. Hall, president and chief executive officer, Flow General Inc., Philadelphia

It's a much easier path to buy a Bendix or a Martin Marietta than it is to create one. I assure you that the chief executives think the battle is for real. One or two of them will wish the battle hadn't happened. We are a very large shareholder in Allied. We own 507,000 shares of its preferred. We are delighted

Exhibit 1 *(continued)*

to see Allied get into the fight, because we are going to come out a winner no matter how you slice it.

—*Joseph S. Gaziano, president and chief executive officer, Tyco Laboratories Inc., Exeter, N.H.*

It's not a merger. It's a three-ring circus. If they're really concerned about America, they'd stop it right now. It's no good for the economy. It wrecks it. If I were in the banking system, I'd say no more (money) for conglomerations for one year.

—*Lee Iacocca, chairman, Chrysler Corp., Detroit*

I don't care what they do. Whatever it is, it won't do any good for the workers.

—*Douglas Fraser, president, United Auto Workers of America, Detroit*

It's cheaper to buy than to make. I wouldn't accuse anyone of setting new standards of corporate statesmanship. (But) competition takes many forms, and competition is to be encouraged. It's a lot more fascinating than watching fluctuations in M1, M2, and M3.

—*Murray Weidenbaum, economist and former chairman of the Council of Economic Advisers, St. Louis.*

I frankly confess that I am confused, and I'm an attorney. I do think the legal profession will be enhanced greatly by all this.

—*Nelson G. Harris, president and chief executive officer, Tasty Baking Co., Philadelphia*

What do you tell your son to do when a bully picks on him in school? When somebody hits you, you react in kind. But sometimes these fights aren't productive, whether it's kids in school or corporate management. Shareholder and customer interest often isn't best served by takeover fights. To the extent that management allows itself to be distracted from its job, it's abdicating its responsibility. We managers need to keep our heads screwed on right. Sometimes our egos get in the way.

—*Cal Turner, Jr., president and chief executive officer, Dollar General Corp., Chicago*

What I can't understand is, are they doing it all with a straight face? Are they really serious? The frightening thing we're seeing in the last couple of years is everybody thinks the way to expand is to go out and buy a big company. From a corporate strategy (viewpoint), they're all nuts.

—*D. E. (Ned) Mundell, president and chief executive officer, U.S. Leasing International, Inc., San Francisco*

What the hell are those (Bendix) directors thinking of? Why would they let management go out and attack a corporation like Martin Marietta?

—*William C. Norris, chairman and chief executive officer, Control Data Corp., Minneapolis*

I think it's a shame. It's the kind of thing corporate America ought not to do because the poor stockholder is the one whose interest is being ignored in favor of the egos of directors and executives.

Exhibit 1 ***(continued)***

And who the hell is running the show—the business of making brakes and aerospace equipment—while all this is going on? I think Martin Marietta has conducted itself well. They haven't dragged the Mary Cunningham business into it, and all of their actions have been taken in quiet dignity in defense of the corporation. I don't think anybody wants to be taken over by Bill Agee.

—*Robert W. Purcell, retired business consultant and former Bendix Corp. director, Detroit*

A chief executive officer is just like anyone else. Once you start something, you don't like to be thwarted. Your personal ego gets caught up in the thing. Now Agee's fighting for his life. He bit off more than he can chew. I would have conducted myself differently if I were in Agee's shoes. But then, I don't have his ego. Or his money. It would be a lot better for Corporate America if this had never started, because it's made the group seem to be avaricious power-hunters.

—*Charles Haverty, president and chief executive officer, Xonics, Inc., Des Plaines, Ill.*

One has the sense of capitalism gone mad. Has each of these companies had adequate time to consider what they're getting, the quality of assets, etc.? People are spending too much money too quickly without adequate thought.

—*Harvey Goldschmid, professor of law, Columbia University School of Law, New York*

Frankly, we've seen so many of these in the last two years, they're becoming a bore. They're little wars. They're almost like Latin American revolutions. Unless you're one of the generals involved, it's hard to get interested.

—*Arthur D. Austin, professor of law, Case Western Reserve University Law School, Cleveland*

Agee perceived a value in Martin Marietta, and the rest is a response to what he did. Martin Marietta should be complimented for its resolve. It strapped itself to the masthead during a hurricane. I don't think there's a moral question here. Business is business. People do the things they feel are in their best interest at the time.

—*Salim B. Lewis, chief executive officer, S.B. Lewis & Co., New York*

These aren't gunslingers or crapshooters. They are responsible businessmen. They're attempting to find value for their shareholders. In the meantime, of course, some of them are protecting themselves, too.

—*Edward I. O'Brien, president, Securities Industry Association, New York*

Fifty percent of it's ego, and 50 percent of it's they probably believe they're doing a good job for their shareholders. (But) it's a waste of shareholders' money, and that's not right.

—*John Lemke, secretary and counsel, Amalgamated Sugar Co., Ogden, Utah*

I bet you Bill Agee and the rest of them haven't spent 10 minutes thinking about running their companies, making better

Exhibit 1 *(concluded)*

products, or serving the public in the past two weeks. Who's minding the store? I have nothing but contempt for the speculators and manipulators. (Agee) started it all, and this whole idea of feathering his nest (with salary guarantees) whether Bendix wins or gets swallowed up, that's the most despicable thing yet. He's taking no risks.

—*David L. Lewis, professor of business history, University of Michigan Graduate School of Business and Administration, Ann Arbor*

Source: *The Wall Street Journal,* September 24, 1982, p. 37.

Exhibit 2

Review and Outlook (Pac-Man Economics)

Everyone likes a good show, and the Bendix-Marietta-United Technologies-Allied shoot-out has been one of the best Wall Street has seen in years. The pace was fast. The stake-your-company risk-taking was bold and forceful. And the characters! Young Bill Agee and his beautiful wife Mary taking on Marietta's Tom Pownall, a man we're told who once arm-wrestled ex-footballer Jack Kemp to a draw at the cost of several torn ligaments; cagey old Harry Gray, whose United Technologies is the corporate equivalent of "Jaws," edging in to help Mr. Pownall avoid more torn ligaments; and finally Mr. Gray's estranged former associate, Ed Hennessy, maneuvering to gain mastery over Mr. Agee.

Bankers and arbitragers were more than casual bystanders. Then there was the Pac-Man question: When two companies swallow each other, what's left? A black hole? Double acute indigestion? One theorist suggests the little old lady in Dubuque, with 100 shares of the right company and enough stubbornness to resist the juicy offers, could have ended up controlling the whole conglomerate. More serious was the fear that the only winners would be the investment bankers, who collected very large fees.

But as the roundup of corporate opinion on the *Journal's* second front page last Friday made clear, some folks were not amused. A steel company executive said, "We're trying to industrialize America while other companies want to deindustrialize America."

We are deindustrializing America whether we like it or not, and it may not be an altogether bad thing. Services account for a large and rising share of the gross national product. In manufacturing, the growth is in high-tech, high-value-added products for the most

Exhibit 2 ***(concluded)***

part. Yet the steel man has a point. Something seems amiss when highly talented executives of four companies that are not low-tech are committing their brains and company resources to corporate cannibalism. Did this Wall Street drama have any redeeming social value?

Perhaps it did, if you believe in morality plays. It may well be true that this whole thing came about because supercharged managerial egos were seeking self-expression, but that would only be part of the story, and not necessarily the most important part in an economic sense. Mr. Agee and his former strategist, Mary Cunningham, did not look toward acquisitions—as opposed to building new plants in Illinois—for no reason. Mr. Gray did not assemble his conglomerate because he loves the ups and downs of Otis elevators. Mr. Hennessy is not on the merger and acquisitions prowl for lack of imagination. They all are simply among that sizable number of executives who, in recent years, have consulted their computers and decided the best place to apply their cash and leverage—and maximize returns for their shareholders—was in the acquisition of existing assets.

In some cases this has involved deindustrializing, as the acquiring management closed old plants and devoted talents and energies to different kinds of enterprises better suited to the needs of consumers and the markets. That process is part of the adaptive and accommodative character of private industry.

But there obviously is something amiss in an economy where corporate assets look more attractive to the investment strategists of other corporations than they look to ordinary investors. The reasons why are fairly complex, but inflation has been at the heart of the problem. Not only has it discouraged personal saving and thus stretched very thin the supply of capital, but it also has attracted the available supply of capital to high-yielding debt rather than equities. Corporate assets have been on the bargain counter for anyone who might be able to put them to more profitable use.

The interesting thing about the Bendix attempt, however, is that it proved to be far more difficult than some we were seeing a year or so ago. Martin Marietta did not turn out to be a sitting duck for a company with ready cash. Indeed, the whole pace of merger and acquisitions activity has slowed this year, despite the fact that corporations have been generating liquidity. And as anyone can see, the stock market—that is, the value of existing assets—has been rising. Martin Marietta was an attractive quest, but Mr. Agee may have moved a bit too late.

Those who have been decrying the great tender offer fights should note the lesson. The urge to merge is merely one symptom of a mismanaged economy, and the roots of inflation lie with the likes of Lyndon Johnson and Richard Nixon, not with William Agee or Harry Gray. When the economic environment comes under control, our corporate chieftains will quite naturally start to vent their egos not in buying up old assets but in creating new ones.

Source: *The Wall Street Journal,* September 27, 1982, p. 22 (editorial page).

acquisitions had benefited his firm greatly. However, opponents argued that Bendix's vast liquid assets could be more beneficially invested in internal growth.

4 An important side issue in the fray involved Mary Cunningham, the developer of Bendix's strategic plan. *Fortune* magazine reported that Ms. Cunningham, 30, resigned from Bendix in late 1980 because of prurient speculations about how she rose in only a year and a half from Harvard Business School graduate to vice president for strategic planning and close advisor to Mr. Agee. Within four months after her resignation, and after sorting through numerous job offers, Ms. Cunningham joined Joseph E. Seagram and Sons, Inc., as vice president for strategic planning with an annual salary reportedly exceeding $100,000. Later she and Mr. Agee married, and the devoutly Catholic Ms. Cunningham and her husband sought annulments of their previous marriages. She became a close advisor to her husband during his attempt to acquire Martin Marietta, but many participants in the negotiations resented her presence and advice, pointing out that she was an employee of Seagram, not Bendix. Ms. Cunningham was quoted by the *Washington Post* as arguing that she was a continuing victim of sexist attitudes, and she saw herself as a knowledgeable advisor simply bringing her strategic plan for Bendix Corporation to fruition.

Mary Cunningham

5 The previously mentioned *Fortune* articles provided some details of Mary Cunningham's background. She was reported to have been raised in Hanover, New Hampshire, the fourth of five children. When she was six years old, she said she took an IQ test that revealed she was a genius with a score of over 160. Her parents divorced when she was five, and she was raised by her mother and a Catholic priest who was curate of the local church and who later became a chaplain at Dartmouth College. Ms. Cunningham believes this platonic relationship between her mother and their priest was misunderstood in the community at that time.

6 Ms. Cunningham attended Wellesley College in Massachusetts, and the *Fortune* articles indicated that when she was a senior she courted a black man, 11 years older than she, who was attending the Harvard Business School. They were married within a year and moved to New York where she worked for a year as a paralegal and for three years as a junior officer at the Chase Manhattan Bank. She was the youngest assistant treasurer in the history of the bank. Ms. Cunningham has acknowledged that she and her husband at the time "were much more focused on the message we were sending to society than our marriage." After she began commuting to the Harvard Business School in 1977, their marriage began to dissolve, and they were soon separated. At Harvard, she built an excellent academic record which won the admiration of her fellow students, although they saw her as making few friends and being somewhat calculating and manipulative of associates.

7 In June 1979, after a three-hour interview with William Agee, she joined Bendix as Agee's executive assistant. In June 1980, she was promoted to vice president for corporate and public affairs. Gossip about the relationship between Agee and Cunningham gained momentum during that summer, and their references to each other emphasized a close relationship. In August, Agee and his wife of 23 years abruptly divorced. Although Bendix employees complained that Agee was less accessible, Cunningham seemed to be constantly with him. They traveled together, and they stayed in the

same two-bedroom suite at the Waldorf Towers. By September, Cunningham had been promoted to vice president for strategic planning. *Fortune* magazine indicated that to some people it seemed that Agee and Cunningham had to be having an affair; it seemed the only explanation for her rapid promotions. However, in private meetings with members of the board and top management, the two denied that there was an affair. Cunningham offered to resign at one point but noted that it would seem to confirm the rumors, would send a frustrating signal to other potential female executives, and would seem to let rumor dictate decision at Bendix. Then at an employee assembly, Agee and Cunningham leaped into the public eye when Agee announced that Cunningham's promotions were justified, while admitting their "very, very close" friendship. A wave of publicity swept over the situation during September and October 1980. The public criticism damaged Cunningham's credibility within Bendix, and after some initial vacillation, both she and the Bendix board agreed she should resign. Four months later, Ms. Cunningham secured the position of vice president of strategic planning at Seagram.

William Agee and the Bendix Corporation

8 As the *Fortune* articles indicated, that fall was an eventful time for Bendix Corporation. Not only was there publicity about Mary Cunningham but Bendix president and chief operating officer, William Panny, resigned, apparently because of disagreements with Agee. At the same time, Jerome Jacobson, executive vice president for strategic planning, resigned, opening the strategic planning position for Mary Cunningham. A week later, Bendix announced the sale of its forest products division for $425 million and the desire to sell its 20 percent share of Asarco, a nonferrous metals mining and production operation. Eventually, Asarco bought its own shares back from Bendix for about $336 million. A week after those announcements, Bendix unveiled the details of a major program of decentralization involving termination or transfer of almost one third of the corporate staff.

9 *Business Week* and *Fortune* articles revealed certain aspects of William Agee's background and actions in the Bendix Corporation which help in understanding the strategy of the firm. After graduating from the Harvard Business School in 1963, Agee took a position with Boise Cascade in his native Idaho. By 1967, at the age of 32, he was chief financial officer for Boise. When the real estate investments at the firm soured in 1969 and 1970, Agee says he went through a very difficult period in his life, and in 1972, W. Michael Blumenthal, then chairman of Bendix, hired him away. Four years later, when Blumenthal joined the Carter administration, Agee became Bendix's chairman.

10 As the *Fortune* articles indicated, the atmosphere at Bendix began to change almost immediately. Agee removed the boardroom table, and directors found themselves meeting in a circle. Some status symbols such as reserved parking and executive dining privileges were attenuated. Agee invited speakers such as Vernon Jordan and Gloria Steinem to address the board and top management on controversial social topics. Agee served as cochair of the National Business Council for the Equal Rights Amendment.

11 Mr. Agee and Mr. Panny also slowly began changing the businesses at Bendix. They turned around a large French subsidiary that made electrical and mechanical

parts by selling substantial assets and cutting the work force. By 1978, Bendix businesses of forest products, machine tools, and auto parts were viewed as satisfactorily countercyclical. Also in 1978, Agee bought 20 percent of Asarco for $127.7 million, viewing it as a turnaround candidate with mineral resources which would quickly appreciate in value. *Fortune* reported he wanted to acquire the whole firm and to move into minerals generally, but Panny and others argued against it, wanting only a limited investment, a board seat, and an opportunity for a quick exit. In 1979, Agee sold a domestic mobile-home subsidiary that had performed poorly, and acquired three other businesses.

12 Bendix served in the capacity of a "white knight" when in 1980 it acquired Warner & Swasey, a machine tool manufacturer, for $300 million in cash and convertible securities worth $83 per share, for shares with a book value of $45. However, the acquired company had $65 million in liquid assets, some $40 million of which Agee sold. Warner & Swasey was approximately equal in size to Bendix's own machine tool business, but the two made different products for different customers, and the combination became the second-largest business in that industry, topped only by Cincinnati-Milacron.

13 In 1978, Agee had talked of strengthening Bendix's forest products business. In fact, two of the acquisitions made in 1979 had been small wood products marketers. Bendix originally had acquired the forest products business in 1969 with the hope of successfully using Bendix's technological expertise in machine tools to achieve efficiencies unique to the lumber industry. But the effort had been a failure. By spring 1980, Agee was considering the sale of the division.

14 According to *Fortune* articles, Agee also indicated he might consider having the firm sell its automotive division—the original basic business of the company—if it did not measure up to expectations. Insiders were reported to be in agreement that the automotive division should be trimmed, and one plant had been sold. But Mr. Panny and others disagreed with Mr. Agee on the amount of trimming needed. The chief operating officer argued that the corporation should not leave a business it knew in order to acquire a business it did not know. In June 1980, Agee asked Cunningham and a staff of seven to prepare a report on Bendix's North American automotive operations. A three-volume study was prepared within 40 days. Bendix's managers resented the newcomer's report on their industry, discounted the value of its results, and objected to Cunningham's unwillingness to coordinate her investigation with them. Eventually, Mr. Agee's desire to emphasize the aerospace operation at the expense of the automotive division contributed to the resignation of Mr. Panny and Mr. Jacobson.

15 *Fortune* reported that the reorganization which Mr. Agee wanted was another issue that contributed to the resignations. The difference in Panny's measured pace of action and Agee's impatience for completion of tasks had always caused them some difficulties. Mr. Panny was particularly critical of the speed with which the chief executive officer wanted to create organizational decentralization. Within two weeks after the Panny and Jacobson resignations, Agee announced the reorganization.

16 Some people viewed the eventful September of 1980 as continuing evidence of Agee's lack of strategic thinking and said that Agee's change of heart regarding the importance of minerals and forest products was a good example of this problem. When Agee said he was accumulating liquid assets through divestitures and was planning to use these assets for acquisitions, critics accused him of inconsistency in spending $265

million of his cash to repurchase 17 percent of Bendix's common stock. When Agee pointed to the $75 million in aftertax profit made on the Asarco sale and to twice that profit level from the sale of the forest products division, the critics accused him of legerdemain with Bendix's assets. But Agee noted the 14 percent increase in Bendix's share price during two days in late September 1980—the month when several major actions were announced and when the Cunningham "affair" became public.

17 By 1981, the business press characterized Bendix as a one-man show. Former Bendix managers claimed that Agee was advised by only a small circle of confidants, and suspicion that Agee lacked a strategy for Bendix continued. But some outlines of a strategy seemed to emerge. Agee stressed publicly that Bendix would make investments in high technology. Company officials said that in 1981, R&D spending would be at least $100 million, up from $79.2 million in 1980, and an advanced technology center was opened. In 1981, Agee made it clear that he was out for an acquisition involved in high technology. But he would not identify any target industries, and the 1981 annual report provided only vague acquisition guidelines: "small ventures to open up new opportunities . . . extensions of present businesses to improve market position, increase competitive effectiveness, and expand long-range potential . . . major new businesses which are sound values in the areas where Bendix skills and marketing capabilities can be fully utilized." Agee stressed that he was in no hurry. Indeed, the liquid assets which Bendix had accumulated in preparation for an acquisition contributed 17 percent of the company's profits in 1981. Then in September 1981 and again in March 1982, Bendix moved to acquire significant blocks of RCA stock until it owned 7.2 percent of all that company's outstanding shares. However, when the RCA chairman made it very clear that he did not approve of Mr. Agee's stock purchases, the Bendix chief retreated and agreed to buy no more RCA stock for the time being.

Pac-Man Corporation Style

18 The press reported that by April of 1982, Mr. Agee had identified Martin Marietta as an acquisition target. *The Wall Street Journal* indicated that Martin Marietta was originally identified during Ms. Cunningham's tenure as Bendix's chief strategic planner. Mr. Agee seemed attracted by the synergies which might be achieved in a merger of Bendix's and Martin Marietta's aerospace divisions. Agee believed that some of their products and services were complementary and that some of Bendix's technology could be used by Martin Marietta. Agee seemed only interested in the Martin Marietta aerospace division, and it is generally believed that Agee planned to divest the other Martin Marietta divisions.

19 From April through July 1982, Bendix quietly acquired 4.5 percent of Martin Marietta's stock—once 5 percent of a firm is accumulated, public disclosure is required by the SEC. Yet Bendix managers were apparently unaware that Martin Marietta closely followed movements of its own shares and had detected Bendix's accumulation. Martin Marietta managers could not mistake Agee's intention, and desiring to avoid a takeover, they quietly began arranging a $1 billion credit line to finance a defense.

20 During August, the financial and stock markets suddenly experienced enormous changes as shown in Exhibits 3 through 5, and Agee decided to make his move. His friendly merger offers were rebuffed by Thomas Pownall, CEO of Martin Marietta

Exhibit 3

Daily closing stock prices and price-earnings ratios

Date	Bendix Price	Bendix P/E	Martin Marietta Price	Martin Marietta P/E	United Technologies Price	United Technologies P/E	Allied Price	Allied P/E
Aug. 2	$48.75	9	$24.50	6	$42.375	5	$35.25	5
3	49.875	9	24.375	6	42.25	5	35.25	5
4	49.00	9	24.50	6	41.625	5	x33.875	4
5	48.75	9	25.00	6	40.875	5	33.875	4
6	48.625	9	24.875	6	39.875	5	33.625	4
9	48.00	9	24.75	6	39.375	5	33.625	4
10	47.75	9	24.625	6	39.375	5	32.00	4
11	47.50	9	25.00	6	39.375	5	31.125	4
12	47.75	9	24.50	6	39.625	5	31.00	4
13	47.75	9	24.625	6	39.875	5	32.25	4
16	48.00	9	25.50	6	39.875	5	32.25	4
17	48.25	9	27.50	6	42.00	5	32.25	4
18	49.00	9	25.625	6	43.125	5	32.125	4
19	48.875	9	28.25	7	43.75	5	32.625	4
20	50.25	9	30.625	7	45.50	6	33.25	4
23	51.00	10	30.625	7	x46.50	6	34.625	4
24	52.50	10	33.125	8	45.25	6	34.00	4
BC 25	50.00	9	39.25	9	46.00	6	34.75	4
26	51.125	10	42.25	10	46.625	6	35.00	4
27	54.375	10	41.00	10	47.25	6	34.00	4
MM 30	57.00	11	—		47.50	6	34.50	4
31	56.125	11	x40.00	9	47.875	6	34.875	4
Sept. 1	53.00	10	39.875	9	47.25	6	34.25	4
2	55.875	10	37.00	9	48.50	6	34.25	4
3	x58.50	11	37.125	9	50.25	6	34.50	4
UT 7	56.50	11	36.125	8	47.375	6	34.875	4
8	62.75	12	35.875	8	48.50	6	35.25	5
9	61.00	11	35.625	8	48.875	6	36.00	5
10	59.00	11	37.25	9	48.25	6	36.25	5
13	59.25	11	33.625	8	48.625	6	36.00	5
14	57.25	11	35.50	8	50.00	6	34.75	4
15	59.75	11	35.625	8	49.25	6	34.625	4
16	57.625	11	37.625	9	49.00	6	35.125	4
17	54.125	10	46.00	11	48.625	6	34.75	4
20	56.875	11	44.875	11	48.00	6	35.125	4
21	54.25	10	43.875	10	48.75	6	35.625	5
AC 22	57.50	11	43.50	10	49.00	6	34.875	4
23	—		—		49.00	6	—	
24	—		—		48.50	6	—	
27	74.25	14	35.125	8	48.00	6	32.125	4
28	75.25	14	35.25	8	47.875	6	32.625	4
29	73.75	14	36.625	9	47.00	6	31.375	4
30	73.25	14	36.25	8	47.00	6	31.25	4
Oct. 4	72.125	13	37.375	9	46.00	6	30.625	4
5	72.625	14	37.875	9	46.50	6	30.625	4
6	73.625	14	38.00	9	48.75	6	32.00	4
7	74.50	14	38.25	9	50.375	6	33.00	4
8	74.75	14	39.25	9	50.375	6	34.00	4

x = Ex dividend date.
— = Trading of these shares halted because of imbalance of supply and demand or because of price discontinuity.
BC = Bendix announces its initial offer for Martin Marietta.
MM = Martin Marietta announces its initial offer for Bendix.
UT = United Technologies announces its initial offer for Bendix.
AC = Allied Corporation announces its initial offer for Bendix.
Source: *The Wall Street Journal.*

Exhibit 4

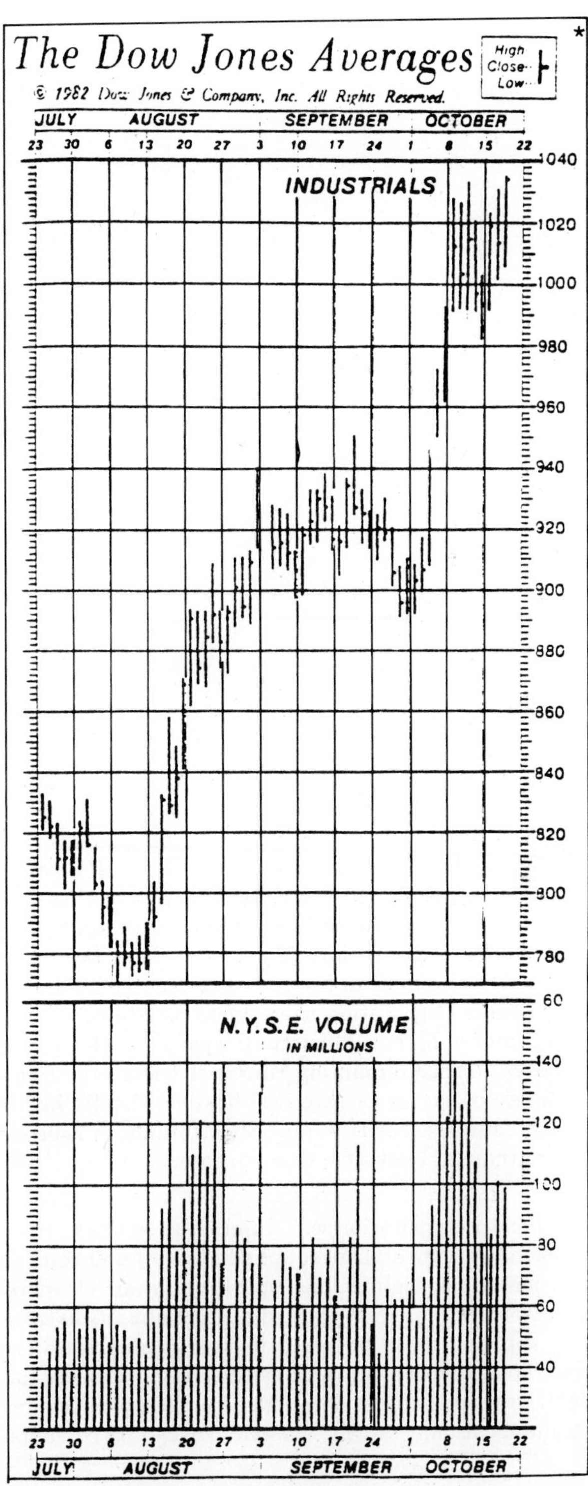

Source: *The Wall Street Journal,* October 21, 1982.

Exhibit 5

Prime Rate

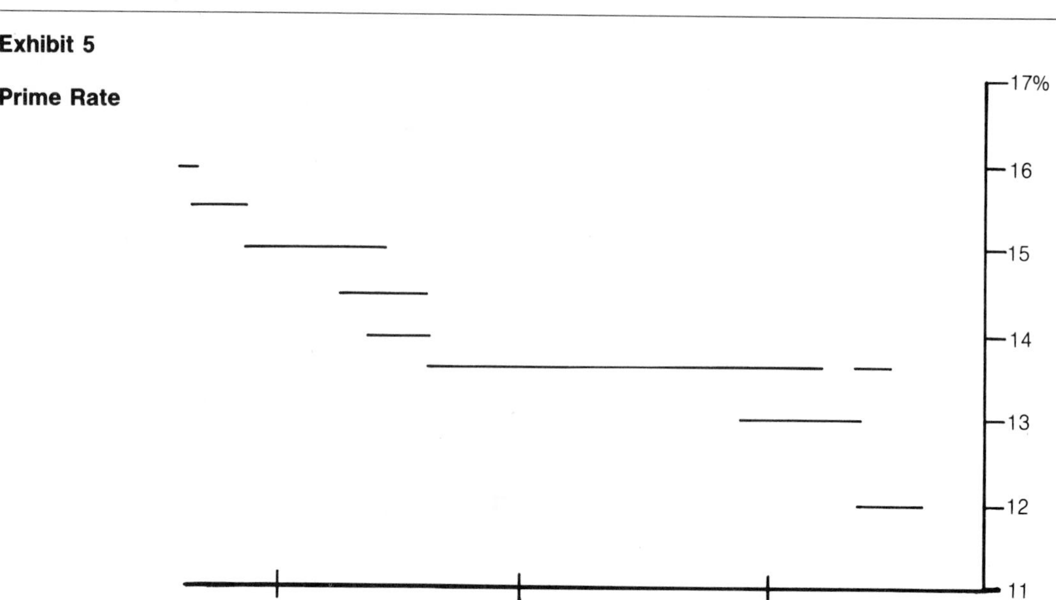

Note: On July 19, the prime rate declined from 16.5 percent to 16 percent. Prior to that date, the prime rate had been 16.5 percent for most of the first half of 1982.
Source: *The Wall Street Journal.*

according to the September articles in *The Wall Street Journal.* Pownall was reported to be very leery of Mr. Agee's personality and methods; also the board and top managers of Martin Marietta wanted very much to retain their independence. On August 25, 1982, Bendix's offer to buy Martin Marietta began a month-long merger battle in which new and significant skirmishes occurred almost daily.

21 The Bendix Corporation offered $43 per share for up to 45 percent, or 15.8 million, of the shares of Martin Marietta Corporation. Bendix anticipated exchanging .82 Bendix shares for each remaining Martin share in a tax-free swap once Bendix took control, but the exact exchange rate was flexible. Bendix had $350 million available in cash and marketable securities, plus $675 million in short-term and revolving-credit lines at more than 20 banks for this purpose.

22 The Bendix Corporation was number 86 on the Fortune 500 in 1982. Its automotive division (Fram, Autolite) supplied systems and components, especially brakes, friction materials, cooling fans, spark plugs, air cleaners, and other filters to foreign and domestic manufacturers of autos, light trucks, and heavy vehicles. The division also supplied these products to the automobile aftermarket. The aerospace and electronics division provided products and services for commercial, military, space programs, and general aviation. The main products included brakes, wheels, radar, communication, controls, electric power, instruments, and electromechanical and

hydraulic systems. Also, Bendix produced electrical connectors, cables, meteorological equipment, and pollution monitoring equipment. Bendix's industrial division supplied the metalworking industry with machine tools and accessories.

23 The $43 offer contained a requirement that promises to deliver the Martin shares (tenders) reach the Bendix agents by midnight, September 4, 1982 (the proration deadline). If, at that time, more than 15.8 million shares were tendered, each investor would be allowed to sell to Bendix only a prorated amount of his Martin shares, so that a maximum of 15.8 million shares would be sold to Bendix at the offer price, $43. If less than 15.8 million shares were tendered by the proration deadline, Bendix might withdraw its offer and not purchase any Martin shares, or Bendix might extend its offer. The offer also had a withdrawal deadline of midnight, September 16, which meant that investors might change their mind and withdraw their tenders through that date. At that point, Bendix could be expected to actually purchase the tendered shares at $43 and complete the transaction by midnight, September 23, when the offer expired. After Bendix acquired what it believed were sufficient shares to use as votes in a shareholder meeting, it could then take operating control of Martin Marietta.

24 Bendix also began litigation in federal court to block state laws which might hamper or thwart the acquisition. Later this erupted into a number of suits in at least seven state and federal courts prompting one judge to condemn the actions as a "seven-ring circus." Meanwhile, the Justice Department and the Federal Trade Commission began their routine and antitrust investigations.

25 In the beginning, Mr. Agee seemed convinced that he could obtain a genuinely friendly takeover, although it appeared unlikely that he would be able to induce this by offering a higher price because Bendix earnings per share would be diluted. However, by the next day, it became known that Martin Marietta had retained Kidder, Peabody, and Company, an investment banking firm experienced in protecting clients from takeovers.

26 The day after that, Standard & Poor's bond rating service placed Bendix and Martin on their "credit watch" for possible rating changes. It was estimated that the merger would create a debt/equity ratio for the combined companies of 44 percent. However, the increased revenue base of the unified company could offset the undesirable increase in debt.

27 On August 30, the Martin Marietta board of directors unanimously rejected Bendix's offer as inadequate. They countered with an offer of $75 per share for just over 50 percent of Bendix stock (11.9 million of Bendix's total of 23.7 million shares). Martin would exchange some of its shares valued at $55 for each of the remaining Bendix shares. Martin arranged for a $1 billion credit line without saying how it would be repaid.

28 Martin Marietta was number 108 on the Fortune 500 in 1982. The firm's most important business was the aerospace division. It designed, developed, and produced space systems, launch vehicles, missiles, weapons, electronic and communications systems, and aircraft components. It was a primary systems manager and contractor for the Defense Department. In addition, the division was involved in solar energy research and data processing. The cement division produced portland and masonry cements for the construction industry. The aggregates division made crushed stone,

sand, and gravel for the construction, agricultural, glass, and foundry industries. Martin Marietta chemicals produced dyes, organic chemicals, concrete admixtures, grout compounds, floor hardeners, magnesite refractories, and chemical magnesia. The aluminum division produced aluminum ingots, sheets, plates, extrusions, and forgings. It also produced ingredients used in the production of aluminum and titanium. In addition, it managed a U.S. government ordnance plant in Tennessee for a contracted fee.

29 Mr. Pownall said that the merger would be better if led by Martin Marietta. This relatively new method of resisting hostile takeover attempts was dubbed the "Pac-Man Defense," since each company was trying simultaneously to swallow the other. This tactic had never been used in an acquisition of this size, and the legal conundrum of which company controls operations when two corporations own each other had never been settled. Taken to the limit, the tactic, could cause both firms to be financially crippled in bidding fights for each other's shares.

30 The proration deadline for the Martin offer was September 9, the withdrawal deadline was September 21, and the offer expired on September 28. These later deadlines seemed to put Bendix ahead in the Pac-Man race. However, Martin was headquartered in Maryland, where state law required a 10-day waiting period before a special meeting of stockholders could be called to vote on a change of directors. Under Delaware law, where Bendix was headquartered, Martin could take control of Bendix almost immediately after acquiring enough Bendix shares. Bendix representatives, however, said that its lawyers would take care of that problem.

31 The next day, the Bendix board of directors rejected the Martin offer as inadequate. It reiterated its own offer for Martin and announced the establishment of a "golden parachute," which would provide long-term contracts and financial protection for 27 top employees in case Bendix was acquired by another firm. Bendix representatives seemed surprised that Martin was able to raise the money so quickly to make its counteroffer.

32 The same day, Martin threatened discussions with a "white knight"—a firm that would make a higher and acceptable offer to acquire Martin Marietta. Sometimes such an offer is used to get the original firm to increase its offer, and sometimes it is a genuine attempt to avoid takeover by the original firm.

33 On September 5, Bendix announced that it held tenders for 58 percent of Martin Marietta shares at the proration deadline. But experts said that Bendix might need to increase its offer to more than $43 per share for Martin in order to avoid too many withdrawals of its tenders. Bendix also announced a special meeting of Bendix stockholders for September 21 to gain approval of a change in the Bendix charter which would make a hostile acquisition of Bendix much more difficult. This was interpreted to mean that Bendix was truly concerned that the Maryland laws might thwart its takeover attempts.

34 On September 7, United Technologies entered the contest with an offer of $75 per share for 50.3 percent of Bendix stock and proposed a one-for-one stock swap for the remaining shares. Proration and withdrawal deadlines were both September 28, and the offer expired October 5. United insisted that Bendix terminate its offer for Martin and stop the September 21 stockholders' meeting. United agreed to buy Bendix only

if Martin failed in its own efforts. Martin and United agreed to split up the Bendix divisions between them if they were successful.

35 United Technologies was number 20 in the Fortune 500 in 1982. The power division manufactured aircraft engines and spare parts (Pratt and Whitney), turbo chargers, compressors, steam turbines (Elliot), large electric motors (Ideal), and as a joint venture, it ran two electric power plants. The flight systems products included helicopters and propellers (Sikorsky), rocket motors, radar (Norden), and sophisticated electronic and electrical measurement and control systems for aircraft and spacecraft (Hamilton Standard). Building systems included air conditioning (Carrier), elevators and escalators (Otis). Industrial products included automotive, electrical, and electronic parts and motors, diesel parts, and varied industrial and military machinery and instruments.

36 With this announcement, Martin said it would not seek help from a white knight. With the aid of United, Martin had reduced its cost in taking over Bendix and had put Bendix under a constant threat of takeover unless Bendix dropped its own takeover efforts. If Bendix acquired Martin, it could then be acquired by United. Martin would then be "regurgitated," and Bendix would be split up between Martin and United. Reports in the press indicated the earnings per share of United Technologies would be reduced by its acquisition of Bendix, and thus, its stock price declined.

37 On the same day, Bendix increased its offer for Martin stock to $48 per share. Bendix's managers were not surprised that United had become involved, but they had expected the firm to make an offer for Martin. They were surprised by United's unusual offer for Bendix, and this surprise was also evident throughout the business community. By the following day, advisors of United Technologies reported that its earnings per share would not be reduced by the acquisition of Bendix.

38 Two days later, it became known that Martin Marietta had written U.S. congressmen portraying Bendix managers as finance specialists without the ability to manage Martin's defense contracts which were vital to the nation. The press later noted this as one of many small dirty tricks which the firms played on each other throughout the acquisition battle.

39 By September 10, it became known that Martin was having trouble getting the Bendix tenders it needed, partially because nearly 4.5 million of Bendix's shares, or 23 percent of the total shares outstanding, were deposited in an employee stock ownership plan (ESOP). These shares could only be withdrawn on the last day of the month, after 15 days' notice—too late for the acquisition effort. Martin, however, convinced the ESOP trustee, Citibank, that it had a fiduciary responsibility to Bendix stockholders to submit its tenders to Martin, since the Martin offer was significantly above the current market price for Bendix shares. Thus, Martin obtained tenders for 63.5 percent (fully diluted) of Bendix's shares by the proration deadline.

40 Bendix angrily objected to Citibank's move and pointed to possible conflicts of interest—three managers of United Technologies served on the board of Citibank, and the Citibank president was on the United board. Bendix sued Citibank in an effort to get the ESOP tenders out of Martin's hands. Citibank responded with the statement that it had merely maintained all available options for the ESOP, its participants, and Bendix.

41 Also on September 10, Bendix increased the number of Martin shares it sought to

18.5 million in order to gain 55 percent control. They also added First Boston, an investment banking firm, to their list of advisors. With Solomon Brothers, Inc., already advising them, Bendix was estimated to be paying at least $7.2 million in fees during the acquisition effort. United and Martin's fees were only slightly lower.

42 On September 13, Martin had increased its credit line by $700 million. Two days later, the Justice Department cleared the Martin Marietta and Bendix merger, but it continued its routine antitrust investigation of the other possible business combinations involved. On that same day, United Technologies increased its offer to $85 per share for Bendix stock, but this price would only apply if a merger could be negotiated on a friendly basis. Meanwhile, rumors were flying of a new offer for Martin Marietta by a white knight. By SEC rules, this would force a 10-day delay of any purchases of Martin stock by Bendix.

43 On September 16, a federal Judge extended the withdrawal deadlines by 10 days for each firm. The judge expressed apprehension that the Pac-Man tactics might cause the firms and their investors irrevocable damage, and he urged a negotiated agreement between the firms. Bendix, fearing it would miss its first chance to actually purchase tendered shares, successfully appealed the judge's ruling.

44 On September 17, Bendix rejected the new United offer, bought 19.3 million Martin shares, and offered $48 per share for up to 70 percent of Martin's shares. Bendix viewed this increased ownership of Martin as strengthening its legal position. It was speculated that Bendix might also try to gain ownership of 90 percent of Martin's stock, then ask for a court-ordered merger without the need to change Martin's board of directors. Experts believed the latter move might be beyond Bendix's financial means. There already were concerns that Bendix was experiencing severe financial strain in trying to consummate the Martin Marietta acquisition.

45 Martin Marietta was still relying on the difference in the Maryland and Delaware laws to give it the time it needed to win. However, if Bendix won its legal efforts to remove the ESOP shares from Martin's pool of tenders, Martin would probably have less than 50 percent of Bendix stock. Despite this, the United and Martin combination was still considered in a superior position. Although United must have been concerned that Bendix had already spent millions of its assets to buy Martin shares, some Wall Street sources indicated that United could force Bendix's shareholders to pay for this by reducing its offer below the present $75 per share. A lower offer might still be attractive to Bendix investors since the current share price was only about $54.

46 By September 20, Bendix owned 70 percent of Martin. Federal Judge Edelstein delayed the hearing on whether Citibank could tender the Bendix shares it held in trust. Bendix postponed the special stockholders' meeting called to change the Bendix charter.

47 On the following day, Bendix's representatives argued before Federal Judge Joseph Young that Martin should be required to hold a special stockholders' meeting on September 30, at which time Bendix would vote its Martin stock to replace the present Martin board of directors with its own nominees. However, Judge Young indicated that he was inclined to deny the motion and to let the battle continue. At the same time, he condemned the actions of both Martin and Bendix, saying that individual stockholders might be injured by the acquisition attempts. He urged a negotiated settlement.

48 Actually, the top managers of Bendix and Martin or their advisors had held discus-

sions throughout the merger battle in an unsuccessful attempt to achieve an agreement. On September 21, Mr. Agee and his advisors, which included Mary Cunningham, traveled to the Maryland headquarters of Martin Marietta in a final attempt to reach an agreement. Agee offered to relieve Martin's management and directors of all potential legal liabilities and to buy the remaining 30 percent of Martin's stock for securities that Mr. Agee valued at $55 per share. Mr. Pownall reported that his top management and advisors did not believe it was possible to be relieved of legal liabilities by Bendix. Furthermore, they seemed to doubt that the securities which Mr. Agee offered were truly worth $55 per share. Thus, last-minute efforts to reach an agreement were a failure.

49 *The Wall Street Journal* reported (and Martin Marietta denied) that Ms. Cunningham's presence infuriated the Martin Marietta top management. It was further reported that her involvement was apparently a factor contributing to the desire of Martin Marietta to remain independent. Later, Ms. Cunningham revealed to the press that she had been intensely involved in the decisions made concerning that merger throughout the month-long battle. She maintained she had an important hand in shaping the Bendix strategy and in choosing Martin Marietta as an acquisition target, and therefore, she had unique expertise.

50 Also on September 21, Judge Edelstein denied the Bendix suit against Citibank; however, almost all of the ESOP tenders were withdrawn by Bendix employees before the midnight withdrawal deadline. This meant that Martin Marietta had only 42.4 percent of Bendix stock in its tender pool.

51 Some attorneys were surprised that the federal judges were reluctant to intervene in this merger battle. The results could have led to legal battles lasting years with little settled, while the firms continued to deplete their assets in attempts to control each other. It was even possible that a minority of independent stockholders would decide the final outcome. This was because state laws in Delaware and Maryland said that if the stock of a company is owned by a majority-controlled subsidiary, that stock could not be voted. If Bendix and Martin were deemed subsidiaries of each other, neither could vote the other's stock. It was assumed that there would then be a proxy contest between Bendix and Martin to solicit the shares of the minority of shareholders still eligible to vote.

52 By September 22, concern had increased that Bendix would be under severe financial strain to complete its acquisition of Martin. Earnings per share would be reduced, and its debt might be tripled.

53 On that day, Allied Corporation announced an offer of $85 for each of 13.1 million shares of the Bendix Corporation, and if this 51 percent of the outstanding shares of Bendix were tendered, Allied would offer 1.3 of its own shares plus an additional $27.50 in Allied securities (possibly convertible to common shares) for the remaining Bendix shares. This surprising announcement was a friendly takeover sought by Bendix. Under the terms of the proposal, Mr. Agee would become a member of the board and president of the Allied Corporation and would remain chief executive officer of Bendix. The announcement also included a separate agreement that Bendix would sell its aerospace and electronics group to Allied if another company topped Allied's bid for Bendix. This latter provision was designed to deny United Technologies and Martin Marietta the most-attractive portion of Bendix if they did not stop their own acquisition efforts.

54 The Allied Corporation was number 49 in the Fortune 500 in 1982. It was a major producer of chemicals such as sulphuric acid and fluorocarbons used for industrial processes. Agricultural chemicals were also an important segment. Allied was an important manufacturer of man-made fibers, polyurethane plastics, and nylon plastics. Most of the oil and gas Allied produced was sold to companies for further processing, for fuel, or for transmission, but it used some for its own processes and its own retail sales (Texgas). The major electrical and electronic businesses were acquired in 1979 and 1981 (Eltra and Bunker Ramo) and supplied parts, motors, and batteries for a wide variety of industrial, automotive, marine, and communication uses. The business also supplied typesetting equipment (Mergenthaler Linotype), electronic and electrical connectors (including fiber optics, microwave, and cable), and electronic transaction systems for banks, insurance companies, and savings and loan associations. Fisher Scientific supplied scientific laboratory equipment. Allied was the world's largest producer of automotive seat belts.

55 Although the announcement took the business world by surprise, it was revealed that Allied and Bendix had explored the possibilities of some sort of combination for almost two weeks. Mr. Agee agreed to the merger about midday on the 22d, and the public announcement was made on that date. However, the actual filing with the SEC did not occur until the 23d because board approval and document preparation could not be completed on the 22d. This single day of delay allowed Martin Marietta to purchase its first share of Bendix stock shortly after midnight on the 23d. Had Bendix and Allied been able to file their merger plans with the SEC on the 22d, SEC regulations would have forced Martin to wait at least 10 days before purchasing Bendix stock.

56 Four outside directors at Bendix quit, apparently because they questioned the wisdom of the merger with Allied and the haste with which the decision was made.

57 Martin Marietta and United Technologies were initially uncertain how the proposed merger between Bendix and Allied would affect their own acquisition efforts and their ownership of Bendix stock. Therefore, they did not immediately change their publicly stated intentions.

58 On September 23, Martin Marietta bought the 42.4 percent of Bendix stock in its tender pool and offered to continue buying Bendix shares at $75 each on a first-come, first-serve basis. By the end of the day, Martin had acquired 46 percent of Bendix. At the same time, however, Allied and Martin were discussing terms for the exchange of Bendix and Martin stock. Also on that day, Allied and Bendix continued to haggle over the details of the terms of their own agreement. United Technologies appeared to be waiting for guidance from its ally, Martin Marietta. Exhibits 6 through 8 provide consolidated financial information on all the companies.

Mr. Agee and Ms. Cunningham

59 Agee and Cunningham appear to have been the targets of most of the criticism generated by this merger contest. Their relative youth and brash style caused them to be considered outsiders in the business community. Their prominence and previous suc-

cess in business in the state of Michigan, where business activity was generally poor at the time, may have caused some prejudice. Mr. Agee was accused of allowing his ego to dominate his business judgment in trying to build a large, high-tech, prestigious company through the acquisition of a tenaciously reluctant Martin Marietta. Observers said he misjudged the Martin managers' resolve and strength to resist and should have withdrawn when this became apparent. Ms. Cunningham was criticized for her lack of insight into the emotional reaction which her presence would cause among the opposing negotiators.

60 Prior to the announcement of his resignation, Mr. Agee implied that he was very pleased with the end result, although he acknowledged that the history of the month-long battle "isn't very pretty." He criticized other managers who had failed to strengthen their firms through acquisition and accused them of ignoring shareholder value. He noted that share prices were depressed in mid-1982 and that Bendix and Martin Marietta had an opportunity for technological synergy. Agee accepted the label of portfolio manager and pointed to the dangers of diminishing demand in single-business, vertically integrated firms such as existed in the auto and steel industries.

Mr. Hennessy

61 Hennessy and his advisors were criticized for acquiring Bendix with too little study. Mr. Hennessy, it was suspected, failed to look far enough beyond personal reasons for entering the Pac-Man game. An investment banker, noting that Allied had tried and failed at a few mergers in recent years, felt that they "needed to do a deal," so they would not be seen as a failure in this area. It was also speculated that Mr. Hennessy wanted revenge against his former boss, Harry Gray, CEO of United Technologies. From 1962 to 1979, he was the senior vice president for finance and administration at United Technologies and was considered a possible successor to Mr. Gray, but they disagreed often on business matters and their personal styles were very different. Mr. Hennessy was a devout Catholic and lived in a conservative and reserved manner. Mr. Gray was fond of motorcycles, travel, and had been married three times. Mr. Gray may have been close to firing Mr. Hennessy when the latter accepted the position of CEO at Allied in 1979.

62 Mr. Hennessy soon changed his new firm's name from Allied Chemical and began acquisitions aimed at diversifying away from chemicals. He indicated he was still shopping for new businesses with high technology when he found a good opportunity in Bendix. In his opinion, Bendix's aerospace electronics division fit well with the Allied electronics businesses. In addition, the Bendix acquisition offered an opportunity to reduce the percentage of Allied's portfolio devoted to oil and gas and to vulnerable commodity products. Furthermore, Mr. Hennessy said that the acquisition would lower Allied's corporate tax rate by increasing domestic income. He admitted that it might seem odd to some that Allied should incur large debts to buy another business when Allied had very recently cut its own production and personnel. He said that the acquisition of Bendix was an investment in the future and was consistent with his increased spending on R&D in recent years. He promised to look for ways of reducing Allied's debt while preserving and creating jobs.

63 Mr. Hennessy also made it clear that with a 39 percent ownership of Martin and two board seats, Martin Marietta would not be a passive investment for Allied.

Mr. Pownall

64 Mr. Thomas Pownall, 60, was CEO of a low-profile firm that had in the past stressed operations management, not portfolio management. He had only been CEO since April 1982, and Mr. J. Donald Rauth, 65, the immediate past CEO, was chairman at the time. Mr. Pownall had joined Martin Marietta in 1963. He had held several top positions for a number of years in the aerospace division, and he served a short stint as executive vice president of the corporation before his promotion to CEO. Neither Mr. Pownall nor Mr. Rauth were experienced with mergers, and Mr. Rauth shied from publicity. It is believed that they relied heavily on the advice of their consultants during the contest in September.

65 Mr. Pownall was described as urbane, aggressive, and extroverted, and he commanded respect from his employees. He was generally praised by the business community for his determined desire for independence from Mr. Agee.

66 Although Martin Marietta was not taken over by Bendix, the managers of Martin Marietta could expect Allied to be looking over their shoulder, and their firm had taken on a huge burden of debt. Martin had borrowed $892 million to buy Bendix shares and could expect interest payments on that to be $30 million in 1982 and

Exhibit 6

Consolidated statements of income ($ millions except per share data)

	Bendix Corporation September 30			*Martin Marietta December 31*		
	1982	*1981*	*1980*	*1982*	*1981*	*1980*
Net sales	$ 4,092	$ 4,393	$ 3,838	$ 3,527	$ 3,294	$ 2,619
Cost of goods sold	3,229	3,509	3,033	3,120	2,792	2,145
Selling, general, and administrative expenses	551	557	468	238	15	111
Noncash expenses	108	75	81	96	265	133
Other income	129	242	57	87	71	55
Total income	333	494	313	160	293	285
Interest and financing charges	100	110	83	68	10	7
Domestic and foreign tax	95	179	95	1	83	90
Net income before extraordinary item	138	205	135	91	200	188
Extraordinary item	(5)	248	57	0	0	0
Net income	133	453	192	91	200	188
Preferred dividend	$ 17	$ 17	$ 9	$ 0	$ 0	$ 0
Net income applicable to common shares*	$ 133	$ 453	$ 192	$ 91	$ 200	$ 188
Number of common shares	22,907,000	24,482,000	24,952,000	31,397,890	37,099,456	37,364,662
Earnings per share	$5.80	$18.49	$7.68	$2.92	$5.39	$5.03
Dividends per share	$3.32	$ 3.00	$2.84	$1.92	$1.80	$1.55

* Bendix does not subtract preferred dividends from net income to compute earnings per share.

$120 million in 1983. Mr. Pownall predicted his firm would regain its financial strength within a year, but Moody's rating service lowered Martin's commercial paper from "prime-2" to "not prime" and senior debt from Baa2 to Baa3.

67 In an effort to solve these problems, Martin Marietta swapped stock for $10 million of one of its subsidiaries' debt securities in January 1983. In March, Martin sold $2 million shares at $42.75 and avoided spending precious cash by making the required pension fund contribution in $19.2 million worth of shares, also valued at $42.75 per share. Additionally, some of Martin Marietta's assets—the aluminum and cement businesses—were put up for sale. A cement plant, some bauxite holdings, and a chemicals venture had been sold off by March 1983. Unfortunately, the cement and aluminum businesses had suffered recent losses so severe that Martin expected its first losing quarter in 22 years during the initial period of 1983. Still, Mr. Pownall won praise from Wall Street for chopping his debt by $450 million in such a short time. Martin Marietta's stock appreciated to nearly $44 per share in mid-March.

Exhibit 6 ***(concluded)***

	United Technologies December 31			*Allied Corporation December 31*		
	1982	*1981*	*1980*	*1982*	*1981*	*1980*
Net sales	$ 13,577	$ 13,668	$ 12,324	$ 6,167	$ 6,407	$ 5,519
Cost of goods sold	10,790	10,817	9,698	4,743	4,802	4,095
Selling, general, and administrative expenses	1,674	1,475	1,231	376	198	115
Noncash expenses	256	367	473	263	336	319
Other income	139	97	75	89	21	45
Total income	996	1,106	997	874	1,092	1,035
Interest and financing charges	251	254	230	84	88	81
Domestic and foreign tax	318	403	374	507	685	637
Net income before extraordinary item	427	458	393	283	319	317
Extraordinary item	107	0	0	(11)	29	(28)
Net income	534	458	393	272	348	289
Preferred dividend	$ 70	$ 77	$ 81	$ 68	$ 38	$ 23
Net income applicable to common shares*	$ 464	$ 381	$ 312	$ 204	$ 310	$ 266
Number of common shares	53,104,845	49,402,486	42,855,312	32,810,044	33,840,648	32,610,944
Earnings per share	$8.74	$7.71	$7.28	$6.22	$9.17	$8.15
Dividends per share	$2.40	$2.40	$2.20	$2.40	$2.35	$2.15

Exhibit 7

Consolidated balance sheets ($ millions)

	Bendix Corporation September 30			*Martin Marietta December 31*			*United Technologies December 31*			*Allied Corporation December 31*		
Assets	*1982*	*1981*	*1980*	*1982*	*1981*	*1980*	*1982*	*1981*	*1980*	*1982*	*1981*	*1980*
Current assets:												
Cash and marketable securities	$ 148	$ 572	$ 44	$ 26	$ 84	$ 103	$ 121	$ 168	$ 147	$ 176	$ 181	$ 189
Accounts receivable	576	622	648	361	292	334	1,552	1,507	1,586	728	933	785
Inventories	765	902	890	507	461	338	2,866	2,732	2,778	647	841	601
Prepaid expenses, other	39	43	71	44	47	24	64	82	66	73	56	74
Total current assets	1,528	2,139	1,653	938	884	799	4,603	4,489	4,577	1,624	2,011	1,649
Investments	1,347	98	34	92	67	53	298	166	151	1,570†	226	388
Plant, equipment, land, minerals—net	776	780	706	1,659	1,439	1,078	2,386	2,203	1,963	2,858	2,866	2,384
Goodwill and intangibles	93	89	91	59	60	61	532	563	—	132	139	60
Other	127	115	440	90	96	78	174	134	645	88	102	57
Total assets	$3,871	$3,221	$2,924	$2,838	$2,546	$2,069	$7,993	$7,555	$7,336	$6,272	$5,344	$4,538

Liabilities and Owners' Equity												
Current liabilities:												
Accounts payable	$ 387	$ 370	$ 411	$ 297	$ 251	$ 219	$ 871	$ 870	$ 913	$ 769	$ 974	$ 673
Short-term borrowing and current long-term debt	585	104	143	79	14	4	505	467	689	38	53	33
Accrued liabilities	514	481	382	161	126	106	1,368	1,228	1,237	302	286	430
Other	2	211	24	159	74	123	306	350	379	99	60	46
Total current liabilities	1,488	1,166	960	696	465	452	3,050	2,915	3,218	1,208	1,373	1,182
Long-term debt and capital leases	832	520	549	1,235	360	163	927	832	867	700	857	885
Deferred taxes	43	49	37	445	494	330	246	284	204	287	335	311
Other liabilities	27	33	37	25	27	21	288	311	312	284	288	236
Total liabilities	2,390	1,768	1,583	2,401	1,346	966	4,511	4,342	4,601	2,479	2,853	2,614
Common equity:												
Preferred stock	71	172	171	115	0	0	698	751	855	1,780†	591	260
Stock*	107	97	115	41	41	27	1,144	1,059	678	669	629	616
Additional paid-in capital	141	43	47	220	222	221	—	—	—	—	—	—
Retained earnings	1,166	1,145	1,012	1,066	1,034	915	1,640	1,403	1,202	1,354	1,290	1,057
Treasury stock	(4)	(4)	(4)	(1,005)	(97)	(60)	—	—	—	(10)	(19)	(9)
Total equity	1,481	1,453	1,341	437	1,200	1,103	3,842	3,213	2,735	3,793	2,491	1,924
Total liabilities and owner's equity	$3,871	$3,221	$2,924	$2,838	$2,546	$2,069	$7,993	$7,555	$7,336	$6,272	$5,344	$4,538

* Par values: Bendix and United Technologies = $5; Martin Marietta and Allied = $1.

† Includes $893 million investment in Bendix Corporation and $301 million investment in Martin Marietta Corporation.

‡ Includes $1,194 million in adjustable rate cumulative preferred stock held by Bendix Corporation during the interim period until the merger was approved in January 1983. Does not show up in Bendix statements because of differences in the dates of the fiscal years.

Mr. Gray

68 Mr. Harry Gray, 62, was CEO of United Technologies, a conglomerate much larger than any of the other three firms involved. It appeared that an important motivation for his entering the battle was a friendship with Mr. Pownall of Martin Marietta and a desire to make progress toward his stated goal of making United Technologies a $20 billion firm by the time he retired. Although he is described as easygoing in manner, Mr. Gray was regarded as one of Wall Street's shrewdest and most hard driving business professionals. Once the Pac-Man game ended, United Technologies escaped with little apparent damage.

Exhibit 8

Composition of revenues and income, 1981

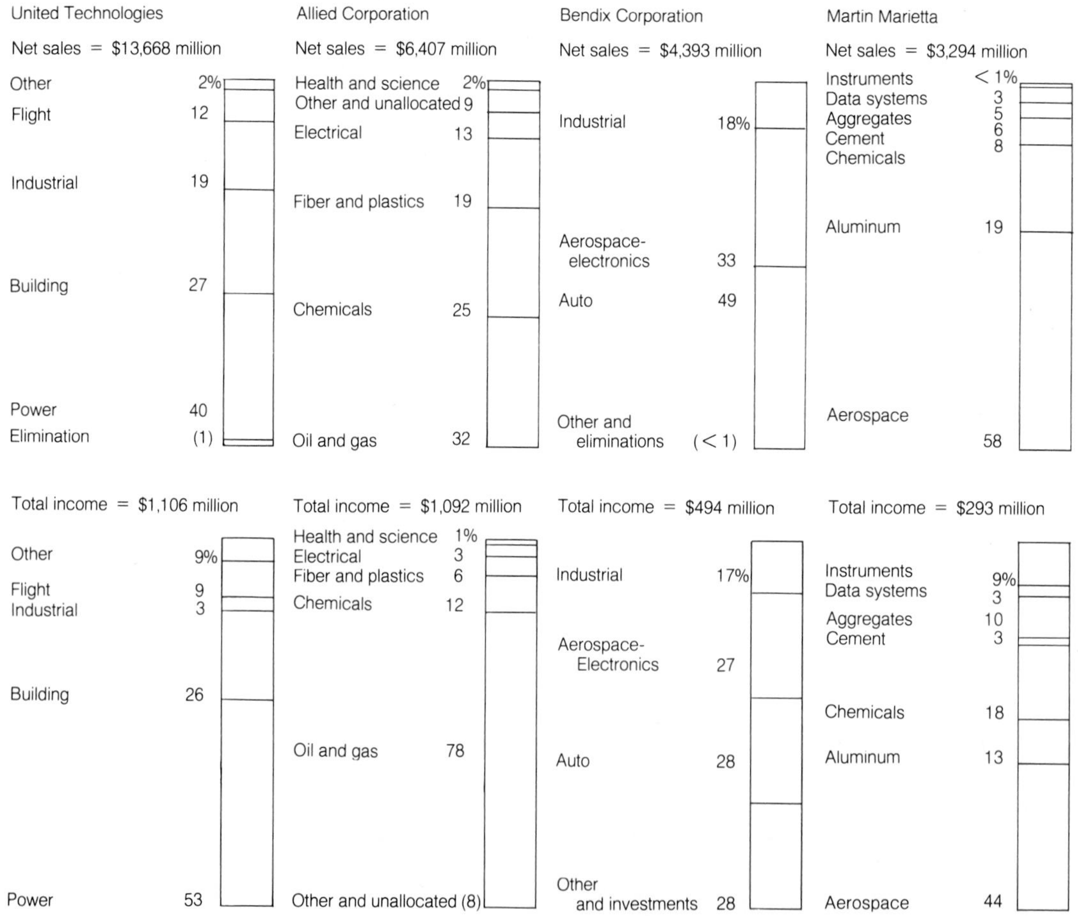

United Technologies

Net sales = $13,668 million

Other	2%
Flight	12
Industrial	19
Building	27
Power	40
Elimination	(1)

Total income = $1,106 million

Other	9%
Flight	9
Industrial	3
Building	26
Power	53

Allied Corporation

Net sales = $6,407 million

Health and science	2%
Other and unallocated	9
Electrical	13
Fiber and plastics	19
Chemicals	25
Oil and gas	32

Total income = $1,092 million

Health and science	1%
Electrical	3
Fiber and plastics	6
Chemicals	12
Oil and gas	78
Other and unallocated	(8)

Bendix Corporation

Net sales = $4,393 million

Industrial	18%
Aerospace-electronics	33
Auto	49
Other and eliminations	(<1)

Total income = $494 million

Industrial	17%
Aerospace-Electronics	27
Auto	28
Other and investments	28

Martin Marietta

Net sales = $3,294 million

Instruments	< 1%
Data systems	3
Aggregates	5
Cement	6
Chemicals	8
Aluminum	19
Aerospace	58

Total income = $293 million

Instruments	9%
Data systems	3
Aggregates	10
Cement	3
Chemicals	18
Aluminum	13
Aerospace	44

case 4
Pennsylvania Movie Theatres, Inc.

The Corporate Perspective

1 Pennsylvania Movie Theatres, Inc. (PMT), was an organization of largely autonomous and previously independent theatres located throughout Pennsylvania. Seven years ago, 28 manager-owners of privately held operations exchanged their theatre ownership for PMT stock and the right to continue as theatre managers with the newly formed corporation. At their first annual meeting, the managers voted to select a five-member board of directors from their ranks to coordinate theatre operations and to oversee all corporate activities. Further, they determined that one new director would be elected each year to fill a scheduled vacancy. Each director would serve in a part-time capacity for a four-year term at $3,000 per year.

2 The PMT managers believed that as a corporation they have better opportunities and capabilities than were available to them when they owned their theatres separately. Because of their system of cooperative exchange, they would be able to minimize film rental and advertising costs. They could also offer better opportunities for advancement to their assistant managers. Additionally, the corporate form enabled the managers to provide support to weaker member theatres because of their collective managerial experience and collective financial strength. Taking a long-term perspective, the managers believed that this consolidation arrangement would result in a more profitable operation for all theatres.

3 The PMT managers wished to offer their communities a safe, inexpensive, and pleasurable leisure-time activity. By satisfying these and other societal needs, they believed that they can achieve their basic corporate objectives of survival and profitability. Among other pertinent societal needs, the managers saw the desire for:

1. A safe, inexpensive form of entertainment.
2. A wholesome, imaginative, and stimulating children's diversion.
3. A forum for social debate.
4. An opportunity for family activity.
5. A source for employment of local manpower.
6. An escape from demanding realities.
7. An opportunity for educational and cultural enhancement.

4 Because of their concern for satisfying these needs, the managers chose their films carefully, attempting to offer high-quality movies at the peak of their popularity. They

This case was prepared by John A. Pearce II of the University of South Carolina.

were also concerned with appealing to an audience which included people of all ages and descriptions. The managers saw the corporation as a group of family theatres, so they wanted to ensure that, with few exceptions, a family unit could attend any show at a PMT theatre without totally sacrificing the enjoyment of any single member. Since their incorporation, PMT theatres had, therefore, restricted their film offerings primarily to those movies rated G (general audience), PG (parental guidance suggested), and R (restricted to persons over 18). With rare exceptions, X-rated, but never hard-core pornographic, films had been shown.

5 The managers also wanted to ensure that the family could enjoy a movie in pleasant surroundings. They attempted to maintain a future-oriented perspective in supervising the daily operations of the theatres as well as when selecting films to be shown. Theatre facilities were periodically renovated, and employees were well trained. All of these efforts were expended in order to provide the most comfortable of theatre experiences and to ensure continued audience patronage.

6 PMT gauged its corporate performance in a number of different ways, among which were ticket sales by type, show time, and movie rating; quarterly revenues; and quarterly profits. Last year, PMT's seventh in operation, the net profits of the PMT theatres dropped almost 7 percent from the year before, even though during the same period, the theatre industry at large had reached all-time, high-profit levels. Two years ago, the return on investment achieved by PMT had been 11.7 percent, while the industry average was 11.3 percent. Last year, the return on investment for PMT was down to 10.1 percent, while the industry average climbed to 11.8 percent. The industry average return on investment for the past five years was 10.9 percent.

7 In reviewing the performance of individual films shown during the past year, the PMT directors found that the few X-rated films they had offered far and away resulted in the greatest profit per film, followed by those rated R. They also noted that on dates when their competitors had shown pornographic-type films, they had appeared to outdraw PMT theatres. Further, since adult ticket sales were the most profitable, the loss of these customers probably represented an associated loss in net income.

An Alternative

8 A major film distributor recently approached the PMT directors with an offer to supply them with a selection of good-quality X-rated and pornographic-type films for the minimum contract period of 12 months. If ordered, these films would constitute approximately one third of the movies shown at any single theatre during the year, with the remaining two thirds being supplied by the corporation's present distributor.

9 While a revised movie offering would not require any major technological changes for PMT (for example, the present projection screens and sound system would be adequate), there is a potentially strong psychological impact upon both the PMT employees and their audiences.

10 Thus, the directors realized that a large and varied set of factors needed to be taken into consideration prior to any contractual commitment to the second distributor.

11 One such factor was the possible consequence of a bill currently before the Pennsylvania state legislature which would ban the showing of pornographic films within the state. Although the bill was being hotly debated, it was given only a 10 percent chance

of being passed. The directors were also watching the upcoming gubernatorial election in the state with particular interest. One of the declared candidates was running as a morality candidate, and a major plank in his platform was the banning of all X-rated films in Pennsylvania theatres. While he was given only a 5 percent chance of being elected, the news media had given great attention to the morality issues raised by this candidate, as they had to the pending legislation.

12 On the other hand, the directors perceived a widespread belief among the general population that sexual explicitness in any medium had some value. They also sensed growing support for the individual's right to decide what did or did not possess redeeming social value.

13 Another factor which the directors considered was that as the nation's affluence increased, so does its leisure time and its demand for leisure-time activities such as movie theatre entertainment. They were uncertain, however, about the effects which current economic conditions would have on their operations. They expected an economic recession but were unsure whether the accompanying period of tight money would bring more people to the theatre in lieu of more-expensive forms of entertainment or, alternatively, whether all entertainment businesses would suffer.

14 Another consideration affecting the directors' decision was the fact that the majority of PMT theatres were located in small- to medium-sized towns with an average population of 23,569 people. All of the theatres were in downtown business districts, and all theatre fronts opened onto main shopping streets. In nearly every case, however, the PMT theatres had a competitor within two city blocks. These facts concerned the directors, since they believed that trends toward liberalism were relatively slow to develop in small towns and that any failure on their part would be to the immediate advantage of their competitors.

15 The possible impact on price policies and theatre hours was also considered. The average price for an adult movie ticket at a PMT theatre in the past year was $3.68, while the average price for PMT competitors was estimated at $3.83. Should the second contract be approved, PMT estimated that its average could rise to $3.77, reflecting the corporation's ability to increase its rates for the X-rated movie audiences.

16 Although show hours varied slightly among PMT theatres, the pattern for weekdays includes a matinee at 2 P.M. and two evening shows at 7:30 P.M. and 9:30 P.M. On weekends, a late-afternoon performance at 5:30 P.M. was added. On Saturdays, the matinee was often reserved for the showing of children's films which were scheduled by the individual managers especially for this purpose. Although these films contributed no profit to the corporation—because of their low ticket prices—the managers felt that this policy developed goodwill between the theatre and the community. No change in the theatre hours was anticipated by the directors in the event the second supplier contract was signed.

17 In addition to price policies (selective rate increases needed) and modifications in theatre hours (no changes required), the directors considered the possible effects of showing X-rated films on other facets of the theatres' operations, for example, media advertising and in-theatre promotion.

18 PMT theatres advertised through the radio and newspaper media. Whether the new contract with the supplier of the X-rated films was signed, these two media would continue to be used, with the expectation that neither costs nor potential audiences would change significantly.

19 Concession-stand operations were not expected to be affected, since on previous occa-

sions when X-rated movies were shown, managers did not notice any changes in concession volume or item preference. The directors believed the concession stand would continue to yield approximately 93 cents (gross) per customer regardless of the movie being shown.

20 PMT's distribution channels should be unaffected in the event that a contract with the second film supplier was approved. No additional distribution costs were expected, therefore, but some inventory control changes would be necessary. The main change would be that the two brands of film would need to be kept separate in the film depository, which would be possible through the initiation of a second numerical filing system. The PMT managers recognized the difficulties commonly associated with such a new system but felt that the required adjustments could be quickly overcome.

21 No attempt had yet been made to determine how nonmanagerial PMT employees would feel about an increase in the number of X-rated films being shown in their theatres. Of central concern was the impact which the change might have upon the employees' interest in union membership. To management's knowledge, no attempt had ever been made by its employees to bring in a union. The directors attributed this desired situation to its employee relations effort and to the high turnover rate among its teen-age employees. To date, there had been only one incident, involving a 55-year-old female street booth ticket clerk who objected to "dirty films," to indicate that the employees might react negatively to any increase in X-rated offerings.

Consolidated Projections

22 After conducting the broad-based assessment of the impact that offering X-rated and pornographic films might have upon PMT's profits, the directors reached the following projection for three years from now, assuming that the second contract was signed:

Likelihood of reaching or exceeding industry average	30%
Likelihood of equaling their own performance of last year	30
Likelihood of a 10 percent decrease in the PMT return on investment from the previous year	20
Likelihood of a 20 percent (or greater) decrease in the PMT return on investment from the previous year	20

23 Overall, the directors foresaw an opportunity to increase business by attracting a new segment of moviegoers. Additionally, the prospective new supplier argued that regular adult PMT customers would attend the theatre more often. Thus, the directors believed that a revised film offering would enable them to better meet the interests of an enlarged segment of the population and that, in return, these customers would help ensure PMT's long-term survival.

24 Should they contract with the second supplier, the directors planned to monitor the corporate performance carefully. Among their targets would be the following:

1. Adult ticket sales per movie for all but X-rated films should remain stable or increase slightly.
2. Children's ticket sales should remain stable or increase slightly.
3. Adult ticket sales per movie on X-rated films should exceed adult ticket sales per movie for films of any other rating.
4. Quarterly profits, adjusted for seasonal variations, should reflect an upward trend.

In the event any of these targets were not being met, it would signal a need to reassess the wisdom of the revised film offering.

25 Although the PMT directors had the responsibility of proposing corporate strategy, the success of the strategy rested on the commitment of the managers in carrying it out. The question arose for the directors as to the extent to which the managers would give the films of the second supplier a real chance. Although, or since, a manager's bonus reflected the degree of profit of his theatre, he may be reluctant to fully implement a new strategy regardless of the directors' judgment. A recent straw vote of managers to the question "Do you favor an increased offering of X-rated and pornographic-type films?" showed 12 in favor, 5 against, and 11 undecided.

26 It appeared that the results of the straw vote somewhat paralleled the performance of the voting managers' theatres. Managers who were experiencing increasing revenues tended to vote against the second supplier, those with relatively level sales seemed to be undecided, while those with decreasing or typically low sales favored the proposal. Such voting tendencies might have been a reflection of the managers' bonus system. Each manager-owner received an annual bonus equal to 60 percent of the pretax net income of their individual theatre and a $\frac{1}{28}$ share of a pool composed of 25 percent of the pretax net income of all theatres.

27 In two months, the annual stockholders' meeting would take place. The managers all anticipated that the main order of business would be a discussion of the directors' proposal regarding a contract with the second distributor.

case 5 Anheuser-Busch Companies, Inc. (A)

Background of the Firm

1 In 1852, George Schneider opened the Bavarian Brewery on the south side of St. Louis, Missouri. Five years later, the brewery faced insolvency. In 1857, it was sold to competitors who renamed it Hammer and Urban. The new owners launched an expansion program with the help of a loan from Eberhard Anheuser, a successful soap manufacturer at the time. By 1860, the brewery had faltered once again, and Anheuser assumed control. Four years later, his son-in-law, Adolphus Busch, joined the brewery as a salesman. Later Adolphus became a partner and finally president of the company. Busch was the driving force behind the company's success, and in 1879, the company name was changed to Anheuser-Busch Brewing Association.

2 An important reason for the brewery's success was Adolphus Busch's innovative attempt to establish and maintain a national beer market. In 1877, he launched the industry's first fleet of refrigerated freight cars. He also pioneered the application of a new pasteurization process. Busch's talents were not limited to technology alone; he concurrently developed merchandising techniques to complement his technological innovations. By 1901, annual sales had surpassed the million-barrel mark for the first time.

3 August A. Busch succeeded his father as president of Anheuser-Busch in 1913. With the advent of Prohibition, he was forced to harness the company's expertise and energies into new directions (corn products, bakers' yeast, ice cream, commercial refrigeration units, truck bodies, and nonalcoholic beverages). These efforts kept the company from collapsing during the dry era. With the passage of the 21st Amendment, Anheuser-Busch was back in the beer business. To celebrate, a team of Clydesdale horses was acquired in 1933—the Budweiser Clydesdales.

4 In 1946, August A. Busch, Jr., became president and chief executive officer. During his tenure, the company's beer operation flourished. Eight breweries were constructed, and annual sales increased from 3 million barrels in 1946 to more than 34 million in 1974. The corporation also diversified extensively, adding family entertainment centers, real estate, can manufacturing, transportation, and a major league baseball franchise.

5 August A. Busch III was elected president in 1974 and chief executive officer the following year, making him the fifth Busch to serve in that capacity. Thus far under

---

This case was prepared by Douglas J. Workman, Neil H. Snyder, Rich Bonaventura, John Cary, Scott McMasters, and Karen Cook of the McIntire School of Commerce of the University of Virginia.

his direction, Anheuser-Busch has accomplished the following: opened its 10th brewery; introduced Michelob Light, Anheuser-Busch Natural Light, and Würzburger Hofbräu; opened a new Busch Gardens theme park; launched the largest brewery expansion projects in the company's history; vertically integrated into new can manufacturing and malt production facilities; and diversified into container recovery, soft drinks, and snack foods.

The Industry and Competition

6 Ninety percent of Anheuser-Busch's sales come from their beer products. (Generically, the term *beer* refers to any beverage brewed from a farinaceous grain.) The type of beer consumed in America today originated in the 1840s with the introduction of lager beer. Lager beer is bottom fermented (meaning yeast settles to the bottom during fermentation). The beer is then aged (or lagered) to mellow, resulting in a lighter, more-effervescent potation. Prior to 1840, Americans' tastes closely resembled British tastes (that is, heavily oriented toward ale, porter, and stout). The influx of German immigrants in the 1840s initially increased the importance of lager beer because of the influence of German tastes and brewing skills.

7 By 1850, there were 430 brewers in the United States producing a total of 750,000 barrels per year, and by the end of the decade, there were 1,269 brewers producing over 1 million barrels per year. At that time, brewers served relatively small local areas. In the latter half of the 19th century, several significant technological advances were adapted to the beer industry, including artificial refrigeration, mechanized bottling equipment, and pasteurization. The latter innovation enabled brewers to ship warm beer and store it for a longer period of time without refermentation. With developments in transportation technology, the 20th century saw the rise of the national brewer. The combined impact of these technological advances resulted in greater emphasis on marketing as the primary instrument of competition.

8 The modern era of the brewing industry begins with the end of World War II. Prior to that time, only a few brewers sold beer nationally, and they primarily operated out of a single plant. To offset additional transportation costs not incurred by local or even regional brewers, the national firms advertised their beers as being of premium quality and charged a premium price. This structural change in the industry (from predominantly local or regional to national producers) in the post-World War II time period has resulted in a steady decline in the number of brewers and plants and an increase in the market concentration of the large national brewers. Exhibit 1 shows the number of breweries and brewery firms for 1946–1976. Exhibit 2 shows concentration ratios for 1935–1977.

9 In the period following World War II, annual beer sales hit a record high in 1947 and then declined and stagnated until 1959. Exhibit 3 shows per-capita demand trends in total beer, packaged beer, and draft beer for this time period.

10 Many analysts blamed the lack of growth in demand upon demographic factors. According to *Brewers Almanac 1976* (p. 82), past industry surveys have shown that persons in the 21–44 age group account for about 69 percent of beer consumption. Since this age group exhibited little growth during 1948–1959, population demographics offer a good explanation for stagnated demand during this period. However, other factors must be introduced to account for post-59 growth, because beer sales grew more than twice as fast as the number of people in this age group.

Exhibit 1

Number of breweries and brewery firms: 1946–1976

Year	*Plants*	*Firms*
1946	471	
1947	465	404
1948	466	
1949	440	
1950	407	
1951	386	
1952	357	
1953	329	
1954	310	263
1955	292	
1956	281	
1957	264	
1958	252	211
1959	244	
1960	229	
1961	229	
1962	220	
1963	211	171
1964	190	
1965	179	
1966	170	
1967	154	125
1968	149	
1969	146	
1970	137	
1971	134	
1972	131	108
1973	114	
1974 (June)	108	
1976	94	49

Source: For the years 1946–74: *Brewing Industry Survey* (New York: Research Company of America, 1973, 1974); 1947–72 (for number of firms): U.S. Bureau of the Census, *Census of Manufactures;* and 1976: *Brewers Digest Brewery Directory, 1977.*

Economies of Scale

11 A major reason for the growth of national firms is the economies of scale obtained in their plant operations. Economies of scale in plant size enable brewers to obtain the lowest possible unit cost. According to Dr. Kenneth G. Elzinga of the University of Virginia (an authority on the brewing industry), the minimum efficient size (MES) plant capacity for the brewing industry is 1.25 million barrels per year. Cost savings accrue from water-processing equipment, sewage facilities, refrigeration equipment, management, laboratories, and custodial cost reductions. Scale economies from most of these sources continue to plant capacities of 10 million barrels per year, but beyond the size of 4.5 million barrels, cost savings are negligible. Exhibit 4 shows one method used to estimate the extent of economies of scale: the survivor test.

Exhibit 2

National beer sales concentration ratios: 1935–1977 (percent)

Year	*Four firm*	*Eight firm*
1935	11	17
1947	21	30
1954	27	41
1958	28	44
1963	34	52
1966	39	56
1967	40	59
1970	46	64
1972	52	70
1973	54	70
1974	58	74
1975	59	78
1976	59	80
1977	63	83

Source: For the years 1935–72: U.S. Bureau of the Census, *Census of Manufactures* (based on value of shipments, establishment basis); 1973: based on share of total sales of U.S. brewers in *Brewing Industry Survey* (New York: Research Company of America, 1974); 1974–75: based on sales data in *Advertising Age,* November 3, 1975, and December 27, 1976; and 1976–77: based on sales data in *Modern Brewery Age,* February 14, 1977, and February 13, 1978, by permission.

12 Economies of scale played a central role in the restructuring of the brewing industry which led to the demise of hundreds of breweries between 1945 and 1970. Moreover, according to Charles F. Keithahn of the Bureau of Economics of the Federal Trade Commission, an analysis based solely on economies of scale would indicate a decline in firm concentration over the 1970s (in a world in which all plants are of minimum efficient size but no larger). Exhibit 5 shows the minimum market share a firm with a MES plant would need for survival.

The Effects of Mergers on Industry Concentration

13 Leonard Weiss of the University of Wisconsin at Madison developed a means of delineating the impact of mergers on an industry's structure. Using his methodology, Dr. Elzinga found that mergers accounted for a negligible amount of the concentration occurring in the brewing industry. In fact, concentration trends in the brewing industry are rather unique in that most of the increased concentration was brought about by internal expansion rather than by merger or acquisition. Strict enforcement of the antitrust laws by the Justice Department (DOJ) is the reason mergers have accounted for such a small share of the increase in concentration. But the DOJ, through its rigid enforcement of the antitrust laws, may have promoted the end result it was seeking to prevent—increased national concentration. With the elimination of the merger route, the national brewers were forced to expand internally. They built large

Exhibit 3

Analysis of per capita beer demand in the United States, 1935–1963

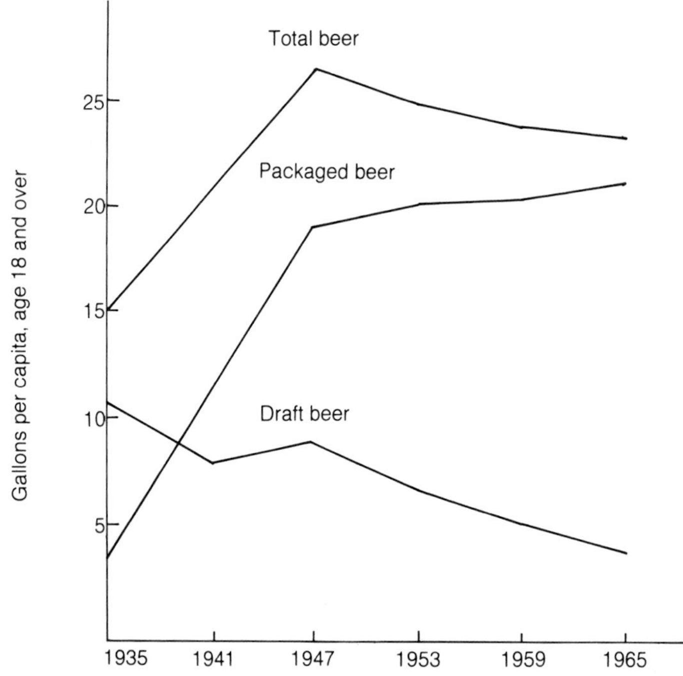

Source: John G. Keane (Ph.D. diss., University of Pittsburgh).

new breweries, which were more efficient than the older, smaller ones. If mergers had been permitted, the national firms might have acquired old, small breweries and might have grown slower than they actually did.

The Effect of Advertising

14 Forced to expand internally in a capital-intensive industry (it costs between $25 and $45 for each additional barrel of capacity), the national firms sought to ensure a steady demand for their products. The need for larger markets resulting from increased capacity coincided with the development of television which led to an increase in the firm's desired level of product identification. Advertising, particularly television spots, became the key to product differentiation in an industry where studies have shown that under test conditions, beer drinkers cannot distinguish between brands. Exhibit 6 shows comparative advertising expenditures for 10 brewers. Exhibit 7 shows relative advertising effectiveness.

15 In the last decade, a new rivalry has developed among major national brewers (this time at the instigation of Miller Brewing Company). In 1970, Philip Morris completed

Exhibit 4

Surviving breweries by capacity: 1959–1973

Listed capacity (thousands of barrels)	*1959*	*1961*	*1963*	*1965*	*1967*	*1969*	*1971*	*1973*
0–25	11	9	8	7	3	3	2	2
26–100	57	51	46	44	33	23	19	11
101–250	51	44	39	30	26	23	19	11
251–500	40	37	33	24	18	14	14	10
501–750	14	15	13	12	13	15	12	5
751–1,000	16	19	20	20	22	20	20	15
1,001–1,500	14	14	12	13	15	13	13	13
1,501–2,000	4	5	5	3	3	8	8	7
2,001–3,000	5	6	6	7	5	6	9	9
3,001–4,000	3	3	4	5	5	3	3	3
4,001+	2	2	3	3	4	7	7	11

Source: Compiled from plant capacity figures listed in the *Modern Brewery Age Book* (Stamford, Conn.: Modern Brewery Age Publishing Co., various years), and from industry trade sources. These figures do not include plants listed only on a company-consolidated basis (in the case of multiplant firms) or single-plant firms not reporting capacity in the *Blue Book*. Most plants list their capacity.

Exhibit 5

Economies of plant scale expressed as a percentage of total industry production for 1970, 1975, 1980

	Production (millions of barrels)	*MES plant as a percent of production*
1970	134.7	.9%
1975	150.3	.8
1980 (estimated)	176.8	.7

Source: Dr. Willard Mueller, from testimony before the Subcommittee on Antitrust and Monopoly of the Committee of the Judiciary, United States Senate, 95th Congress, 2d sess. (1978).

an acquisition of Miller, and according to Dr. Willard F. Mueller of the University of Wisconsin, Philip Morris's multiproduct and multinational operations in highly concentrated industries enabled it to engage in cross-subsidization of its brewing subsidiary. This capacity, coupled with the relatedness of the marketing function between Philip Morris and Miller, provided a powerful vehicle for industry restructuring. Miller adopted aggressive market segmentation and expansion strategies, thus increasing their capacity fivefold between 1970 and 1977. According to Dr. Mueller, a doubling of 1977 capacity was planned by 1981. Exhibit 8 shows comparative financial data on Philip Morris and the rest of the leading brewers.

16 In 1975, Miller found a successful method for promoting a low-calorie beer, Lite, which they had purchased from Meister Brau, Inc., of Chicago in 1972. They spent heavily, around $6.00 per barrel, to introduce it nationwide. However, Lite's success

Exhibit 6

Barrelage sold, measured media advertising expenditures, and advertising expenditures per barrel, 10 leading brewers, 1972–1977

	Philip Morris-Miller			*Anheuser-Busch*		
Year	*Barrels (000)*	*Advertising* ($000)*	*A/B†*	*Barrels (000)*	*Advertising* ($000)*	*A/B†*
1977	24,410	$42,473	$1.74	36,640	$44,984	$1.23
1976	18,232	29,117	1.60	29,051	25,772	.89
1975	12,862	20,894	1.62	35,200	19,237	.55
1974	9,066	12,140	1.34	34,100	12,359	.36
1973	6,919	10,002	1.45	29,887	12,936	.43
1972	5,353	8,400	1.57	26,522	14,808	.56

	Schlitz			*Pabst*		
Year	*Barrels (000)*	*Advertising* ($000)*	*A/B†*	*Barrels (000)*	*Advertising* ($000)*	*A/B†*
1977	22,130	$40,830	$1.85	16,300	$10,843	$ .67
1976	24,162	33,756	1.40	17,037	9,112	.53
1975	23,279	23,173	1.00	15,700	9,007	.57
1974	22,661	17,977	.79	14,297	7,711	.54
1973	21,343	16,615	.78	13,128	6,422	.49
1972	18,906	17,782	.94	12,600	6,142	.49

	Coors			*Olympia (Hamm 1975)*		
Year	*Barrels (000)*	*Advertising* ($000)*	*A/B†*	*Barrels (000)*	*Advertising* ($000)*	*A/B†*
1977	12,824	$ 3,966	$ .25	6,831	$ 8,470	$1.24
1976	13,665	1,626	.12	6,370	5,430	.85
1975	11,950	1,093	.09	5,770	5,555	.96
1974	12,400	801	.06	4,300	2,764	.64
1973	10,950	699	.06	3,636	2,323	.64
1972	9,785	1,332	.14	3,330	2,491	.75

	Heileman (Grain Belt 1975)			*Stroh*		
Year	*Barrels (000)*	*Advertising* ($000)*	*A/B†*	*Barrels (000)*	*Advertising* ($000)*	*A/B†*
1977	6,245	$ 4,636	$ .74	6,114	$ 7,212	$1.18
1976	5,210	3,616	.69	5,765	5,017	.87
1975	4,535	2,864	.63	5,133	3,950	.77
1974	4,300	2,329	.54	4,364	3,477	.80
1973	4,420	2,243	.51	4,645	3,145	.68
1972	3,675	2,260	.61	4,231	3,567	.84

	Schaefer			*C. Schmidt*		
Year	*Barrels (000)*	*Advertising* ($000)*	*A/B†*	*Barrels (000)*	*Advertising* ($000)*	*A/B†*
1977	4,700	$ 4,219	$ .90	3,571	$ 3,912	$1.10
1976	5,300	2,516	.47	3,450	2,703	.78
1975	5,881	2,637	.45	3,330	2,269	.68
1974	5,712†	2,308	.40	3,490	3,035	.87
1973	5,500	2,438	.44	3,520	2,916	.83
1972	5,530	2,994	.54	3,194	2,104	.66

* Advertising expenditures in six measured media as reported in *Leading National Advertisers,* various issues.

† Advertising per barrel.

Source: Company sales for 1970–77 from *Advertising Age,* various issues.

Exhibit 7

Relative media advertising effectiveness by beer brand, 1975–1978

	Media advertising expense ($ million)	*Total barrels (millions)*	*Advertising expense per barrel*	*Barrel change 1978 versus 1974*	*Advertising expense per incremental million barrels*
Premium category					
Budweiser	$71.5	100.2	$ .71	1.1	$65.00
Miller High Life	60.5	61.3	.99	13.5	4.48
Schlitz	70.4	59.3	1.18	(5.2)	n.a.
Light category					
Lite	63.8	22.9	2.79	8.4	7.60
Anheuser-Busch					
Natural Light	24.0	3.8	6.32	2.3	10.43
Michelob Light	6.5	0.9	7.22	0.9	7.22
Schlitz Light	30.3	3.6	8.42	0.7	43.29
Super premium category					
Michelob	35.9	23.0	1.56	4.3	8.35
Lowenbrau	29.4	1.7	17.29	1.2	24.50

n.a. = Not available.
Source: C. James Walker III, *Competition in the U.S. Brewing Industry: A Basic Analysis* (New York: Shearson Hayden Stone, September 26, 1979).

Exhibit 8

Assets, sales, net profit, net income on stockholders' investment, and total advertising expenditures, 1977 ($ millions)

Company	*Assets*	*Sales*	*Net profit*	*Total profit on equity*	*Total advertising*
Philip Morris (Miller)	$4,048	$3,849*	$335	19.8%	$277
Anheuser-Busch	1,404	1,838	92	13.5	79
Joseph Schlitz	727	937	20	5.5	55
Pabst Brewing	396	583	22	8.1	27
Adolph Coors	692	593	68	12.2	12‡
Total 2d to 5th	3,219	3,951	202	9.8†	176
Philip Morris as a percent of 2d to 5th	126%	97%	166%	202%	157%

* Excludes U.S. and foreign excise taxes.
† Unweighted average.
‡ Estimate.
Source: "500 Largest Industrials," *Fortune,* May 1977; advertising data reported in individual company Security and Exchange Commission's Form 10-K reports for 1977.

was not wholly attributable to heavy advertising. Low-calorie beers were promoted in the past with a notable lack of success. Through marketing research, Miller discovered that a significant portion of the beer market is comprised of young and middle-aged men who are sports fans with dreams of athletic prowess. In advertising Lite, Miller relied predominantly on retired athletes renowned for their speed and agility. The message was that one could drink a lot of Lite and still be fast, not that one should drink Lite to keep from getting fat.

17 By 1975, Schlitz and, to some extent, Anheuser-Busch began to increase their own advertising expenditures and made plans to enter the low-calorie beer market. This was done not only as a response to Miller's aggressiveness but also because of a general lack of growth in demand in the face of increasing industry capacity. By 1978, 9 of the 10 largest brewers had light brands on the market. Exhibits 9 through 11 show brand shipment breakdowns for the three major brewers.

18 Currently, the only company with the financial resources to battle Miller and its multinational conglomerate backer is Anheuser-Busch, the industry leader, and Anheuser-Busch responded aggressively to Miller's program. In 1977, Anheuser-Busch surpassed Miller and Schlitz in advertising expenditures by spending over $44 million.

19 Exhibit 12 shows market share performance for the top five brewers and all others in the 1974–1978 period.

20 Clearly, Anheuser-Busch's and Miller's growth have been at the expense of the regional brewers and the faltering national brewers (Schlitz and Pabst). C. James Walker III, an industry analyst for Shearson Hayden Stone, Inc., estimates only 2.7 percent per year industry growth for the early 1980s. The capital-intensive nature of the industry, coupled with huge advertising outlays, make it very unlikely that any firm will be able to challenge the two leaders. To quote August Busch III, "This business is now a two-horse race."

Organization of Anheuser-Busch

21 Effective October 1, 1979, Anheuser-Busch, Inc., became a wholly owned subsidiary of a new holding company, Anheuser-Busch Companies, Inc., and the outstanding shares of Anheuser-Busch, Inc., were exchanged for an equal number of shares of the holding company. Concerning this change, August A. Busch III said,

Exhibit 9

Estimated Anheuser-Busch brand breakdown: 1974–1978; shipments in barrels (millions)

	1978	*1977*	*1976*	*1975*	*1974*
Budweiser	27.5	25.4	21.1	26.2	26.4
Michelob	7.4	6.4	5.0	4.2	3.1
Michelob Light	0.9	—	—	—	—
Busch	3.5	3.3	3.0	4.8	4.6
Natural	2.3	1.5	—	—	—
Total	41.6	36.6	29.1	35.2	34.1

Source: C. James Walker III. *Competition in the U.S. Brewing Industry: A Basic Analysis* (New York: Shearson Hayden Stone, September 26, 1979).

Exhibit 10

Estimated Miller brewing brand breakdown: 1974–1978; shipments in barrels (millions)

	1978	*1977*	*1976*	*1975*	*1974*
High Life	21.3	17.3	13.5	9.2	7.8
Lite	8.8	6.4	4.6	3.1	0.4
Lowenbrau	1.2	0.5	0.1	0.0	—
Other	0.0	0.0	0.2	0.5	0.9
Total	31.3	24.2	18.4	12.8	9.1

Source: C. James Walker III. *Competition in the U.S. Brewing Industry: A Basic Analysis* (New York: Shearson Hayden Stone, September 26, 1979).

The holding company's name and structure will more clearly communicate the increasingly diversified nature of our business, thereby reflecting not only our position of leadership in the brewing industry but also our substantial activities in yeast and specialty corn products, family entertainment, transportation, can manufacturing, real estate, and other businesses. The new structure will also provide management with increased organizational and operational flexibility.

Each of our businesses can eventually be operated as separate companies under Anheuser-Busch Companies, Inc., with responsibilities divided among management personnel.

This reorganization will help facilitate our long-range plan to not only continue to grow in production and sales of beer but also to continue to expand and diversify into other areas which offer significant opportunities for growth.

22 Additionally, Busch announced that Fred L. Kuhlmann, executive vice president, had been elected vice chairman of the board of Anheuser-Busch Companies, Inc., and that Dennis P. Long had been elected president and chief operating officer of Anheuser-Busch, Inc., a subsidiary of the holding company. Long has overall responsibility for the conduct of the company's beer business, and he reports to Busch. (Busch is chairman and chief executive officer of Anheuser-Busch, Inc.)

23 Also, Long was elected a member of the corporate office of Anheuser-Busch Companies, Inc. Three individuals comprise the corporate office. They are Busch, Kuhlmann,

Exhibit 11

Estimated Schlitz brewing brand breakdown: 1974–1978; shipments in barrels (millions)

	1978	*1977*	*1976*	*1975*	*1974*
Schlitz	12.7	14.3	15.9	16.8	17.9
Old Milwaukee	4.3	4.9	5.5	5.2	3.9
Schlitz Light	0.7	1.3	1.4	0.2	—
Malt Liquor	1.7	1.4	1.3	1.0	0.8
Primo	0.2	0.2	0.1	0.1	0.1
Total	19.6	22.1	24.2	23.3	22.7

Source: C. James Walker III. *Competition in the U.S. Brewing Industry: A Basic Analysis* (New York: Shearson Hayden Stone, September 26, 1979).

Exhibit 12

Market share performance

	1978				1977			
	Barrel shipments (millions)	*Market share*	*Barrel increment (millions)*	*Percent increase (decrease)*	*Barrel shipments (millions)*	*Market share*	*Barrel increment (millions)*	*Percent increase (decrease)*
Anheuser	41.6	25.1%	5.0	13.7%	36.6	22.9%	7.5	25.8%
Miller	31.3	18.9	7.1	29.3	24.2	15.2	5.8	31.5
Schlitz	19.6	11.8	(2.5)	(11.3)	22.1	13.9	(2.1)	(8.7)
Pabst	15.4	9.3	(0.6)	(3.8)	16.0	10.0	(1.0)	(5.9)
Coors	12.6	7.6	(0.2)	(1.6)	12.8	8.0	(0.7)	(5.2)
Top 5	120.5	72.7	8.8	7.9	111.7	70.0	9.5	9.3
All others	41.7	25.2	(3.5)	(7.7)	45.2	28.3	(3.0)	(6.2)
U.S. industry	162.2	97.9	5.3	3.4	156.9	98.4	6.5	4.4
Imports	3.45	2.1	0.8	30.8	2.6	1.6	0.2	8.3
All beer	165.6	100.0	6.1	3.8	159.5	100.0	6.7	4.5

	1976				1975			
	Barrel shipments (millions)	*Market share*	*Barrel increment (millions)*	*Percent increase (decrease)*	*Barrel shipments (millions)*	*Market share*	*Barrel increment (millions)*	*Percent increase (decrease)*
Anheuser	29.1	19.0%	(6.1)	(17.3)%	35.2	23.4%	1.1	3.2%
Miller	18.4	12.0	5.6	43.8	12.8	8.5	3.7	40.7
Schlitz	24.2	15.8	0.9	3.9	23.3	15.5	0.6	2.6
Pabst	17.0	11.1	1.3	8.3	15.7	10.4	1.4	9.8
Coors	13.5	8.8	1.6	13.4	11.9	7.9	(0.4)	(3.3)
Top 5	102.2	66.9	3.3	3.3	98.9	65.8	6.4	6.9
All others	48.2	31.5	(1.5)	(3.0)	49.7	33.1	(3.3)	(6.2)
U.S. industry	150.4	98.4	1.8	1.2	148.6	98.9	3.1	2.1
Imports	2.4	1.6	0.7	41.2	1.7	1.1	0.3	21.4
All beer	152.8	100.0	2.5	1.7	150.3	100.0	3.4	2.3

	1974		*1974–1978*		
	Barrel shipments (millions)	***Market share***	***Increased barrel shipments (millions)***	***Market share point change***	***Compounded annual shipment growth***
Anheuser	34.1	23.2%	7.5	+ 1.9	5.1%
Miller	9.1	6.2	22.2	+12.7	36.2
Schlitz	22.7	15.4	(3.1)	− 3.6	(3.3)
Pabst	14.3	9.7	1.1	− 0.4	1.9
Coors	12.3	8.4	0.3	− 0.8	0.4
Top 5	92.5	63.0	28.0	+ 9.7	6.8
All others	53.0	36.0	11.3	−10.8	(4.9)
U.S. industry	145.5	99.0	16.7	− 1.1	2.7
Imports	1.4	1.0	2.0	+ 1.1	24.9
All beer	146.9	100.0	18.7	0.0	3.1

Source: C. James Walker III, *Competition in the U.S. Brewing Industry: A Basic Analysis* (New York: Shearson Hayden Stone, September 26, 1979).

and Long. Kuhlmann and Long consult with Busch on major corporate matters and assist him in implementing corporate policy.

24 Busch announced that the operating executives of two other divisions and subsidiaries have been named presidents of their respective operating units. W. Robert Harrington was named president of Industrial Products, and W. Randolph Baker was named president of Busch Gardens.

Key Executives[1]

25 August A. Busch III was born June 16, 1937, and attended public and private schools in St. Louis, the University of Arizona, and the Siebel Institute of Technology, a school for brewers in Chicago. Chairman of the board and president of Anheuser-Busch Companies, Inc., he began his career with the company in 1957 in the St. Louis Malt House. Since that time, he has worked in practically every department of both the brewing and operations divisions. In 1962, he moved into marketing, working in the field with wholesalers as well as in company-owned branches in all areas of the country. Returning to St. Louis, he was promoted to assistant sales manager—regional brands and later was named sales manager for regional brands where he was responsible for the marketing of Busch throughout the product's marketing area.

26 Busch was named a member of the company's board of directors and appointed vice president—marketing operations in 1963. He became general manager in July 1965, executive vice president and general manager in April 1971, president in February 1974, chief executive officer in May 1975, and chairman of the board in April 1977.

27 Fred L. Kuhlmann, a native of St. Louis, is vice chairman of the board of directors and executive vice president of Anheuser-Busch Companies, Inc. He joined Anheuser-Busch, Inc., in August 1967 as general counsel and was elected a vice president in January 1971, senior vice president—administration and services and member of the board of directors in February 1974, and executive vice president—administration in June 1977. He was elected to his present position in October 1979.

28 Kuhlmann received his A.B. degree from Washington University in St. Louis and his LL.B. from that institution's school of law. He also has an LL.M. degree from Columbia University School of Law in New York. He has been active in a number of business and civic groups and serves as a director of the St. Louis National Baseball Club, Inc., and Manufacturers Railway Company. He is also a director of Boatmen's National Bank of St. Louis, Civic Center Redevelopment Corporation, and St. Louis Regional Commerce and Growth Association.

29 Dennis P. Long, 44, president of Anheuser-Busch, Inc., attended Washington University in St. Louis, Missouri. He has extensive experience spanning more than 25 years at Anheuser-Busch in both brewing and nonbrewing areas. After serving as national price administrator in beer marketing from 1960 to 1964, he was promoted to assistant to the vice president of beer marketing operations and worked in the field with the nationwide beer wholesaler network as well as with the company-owned branch distribution centers. He was promoted to assistant to the vice president and general manager in 1965.

[1] The information presented in this section was obtained from the corporate headquarters of Anheuser-Busch Companies, Inc.

30 In 1972, Long was elected group vice president responsible for the Busch Gardens and industrial products division and Busch Properties, Inc. Under his leadership, the industrial products division became the nation's leading producer of bakers' yeast; the division's sales of both yeast and corn products and profitability increased to record proportions. He also headed the transition of Busch Gardens from beer promotional facilities to a separate profit center. Since then, a new Busch Gardens has been opened in Williamsburg, Virginia, and that division also operates profitably. Since he took charge of Busch Properties, Inc., the real estate subsidiary has embarked further into residential and resort development in addition to the commercial-industrial field, and the performance of Busch Properties has improved markedly.

31 In June 1977, Long became vice president and general manager of the beer division and since that time, has embarked upon a strong effort to increase beer sales volume and profitability. His efforts include new and expanded marketing efforts, increased productivity in brewing and packaging, and a strong cost control and cost reduction effort.

Products Offered by Anheuser-Busch

32 Over the past five years, Anheuser-Busch's beer division has accounted for approximately 90 percent of consolidated net sales. It produces Budweiser, Michelob, Busch, Michelob Light, Classic Dark, and Anheuser-Busch Natural Light. The remaining 10 percent of the consolidated net sales come from family entertainment (Busch Gardens Division), can manufacturing, container recycling, transportation services (St. Louis Refrigerator Car Company and Manufacturers Railway Company), major league baseball (St. Louis Cardinals), real estate development (Busch Properties, Inc.), and the manufacture and sale of corn products, brewer's yeast, and bakers' yeast (industrial products division). Anheuser-Busch is the nation's leading producer of bakers' yeast with a market share of well over 40 percent. Exhibit 13 presents data by product line.

33 During 1978, Anheuser-Busch made significant progress in redefining its diversifica-

Exhibit 13

Revenue generated by product class (in thousands of dollars)

	1978	*1977*	*1976*	*1975*	*1974*
Consolidated sales	$2,701,611	$2,231,230	$1,752,998	$2,036,687	$1,791,863
Federal and state beer taxes	441,978	393,182	311,852	391,708	378,772
Consolidated net sales	$2,259,633	$1,838,048	$1,441,146	$1,644,979	$1,413,091
Beer division	2,056,754	1,691,004	1,282,620	1,480,481	1,271,782
Percent of consolidated net sales	91%	92%	89%	90%	90%
Other divisions*	$ 202,879	$ 147,044	$ 158,526	$ 164,498	$ 141,309
Percent of consolidated net sales	9%	8%	11%	10%	10%

* All other divisions include: industrial products division, Busch Gardens division, Busch Properties, Inc., transportation, and the St. Louis Cardinals.

Source: Anheuser-Busch Company, Inc., annual reports, 1974–1978.

tion objectives as a means of building for the future. A corporate policy was established to concentrate initially on developing new food and beverage products which are compatible with the existing capabilities and, where possible, on distributing these products through the company's existing wholesaler network. The company is presently working on developing a line of snack foods, reportedly called Eagle Snacks, which would also be compatible with existing production and distribution facilities.

34 The company began test marketing Würzburger Hofbräu beer in the United States early in 1979. This full-bodied, premium, German beer will be brewed in Wurzburg, West Germany, and shipped in large insulated barrels to the United States where it will be bottled by Anheuser-Busch and distributed through the company's wholesaler network.

35 Anheuser-Busch has a new installation in St. Louis, Missouri, which annually produces 1.8 million pounds of autolyzed yeast extract, a flavoring agent for processed foods. As the only producer of the extract in the United States with its own captive supply of brewer's yeast, Anheuser-Busch entered this new venture with a decided competitive advantage.

36 Anheuser-Busch's well-known family of quality beers includes products in every market segment. Budweiser has been brewed and sold for more than 100 years. Premium Bud, available in bottles, cans, and on draught nationwide, is the company's principal product and the largest selling beer in the world. Michelob was developed in 1896 as a "draught beer for connoisseurs." Superpremium Michelob is sold nationally in bottles, cans, and on draught.

37 With a greater percentage of the population entering the weight-conscious 25–39-year-old range, Anheuser-Busch has introduced Michelob Light. It has 20 percent fewer calories than regular Michelob, and when introduced in 1978, it was the first superpremium light beer. In order to capitalize on this by transferring the consumer appeal for Michelob to Michelob Light, Anheuser-Busch communicates "the heritage of Michelob and the taste of Michelob Light" in its advertising. Michelob Light is available nationwide in cans, bottles, and on draught. Anheuser-Busch also offers Natural Light for weight-conscious beer drinkers.

38 Busch Bavarian beer was introduced in 1955 as a low-priced beer in direct competition with subpremium regional beers. In April 1978, a smoother, sweeter, and lighter Busch beer was successfully test marketed in New England as a premium-priced brand to capitalize on anticipated growth of the premium segment of the market in future years. In 1979, with new package graphics and advertising, premium Busch was introduced in areas where the company previously marketed Busch Bavarian.

39 Anheuser-Busch's expanding corporate programs of vertical integration into can manufacturing and barley malting play an important role in overall beer division activities and profitability. The company's various vertically integrated enterprises provide an added advantage in controlling the cost and supply of containers and ingredients. Vertical integration helps to reduce cost pressures in brewing operations and to ensure continuity and quality of supply.

40 Metal Container Corporation, a wholly owned subsidiary of Anheuser-Busch Companies, produces two-piece aluminum beer cans at facilities in Florida, Ohio, and Missouri. Container Recovery Corporation, another wholly owned subsidiary of Anheuser-Busch Companies, operates container recovery facilities in Ohio and New Hampshire which are actively involved in collecting and recycling aluminum cans.

41 The company's materials acquisition division is responsible for purchasing all agricul-

tural commodities, packaging materials, supplies, and fuel. Its objective is to increase stability and flexibility in the procurement of commodities and materials. This division investigates alternative methods of supply, analyzes vertical integration opportunities available, and monitors the supply and cost of all commodities purchased by the company.

42 Anheuser-Busch processes barley into brewer's malt at plants in Manitowoc, Wisconsin (total capacity of 8.5 million bushels annually), and Moorhead, Minnesota (annual capacity of 6.4 million bushels). These two malt production facilities provide the company with the capability to self-manufacture approximately one third of its malt requirements.

43 The industrial products division produces corn syrup and starch for numerous food applications, including the processing of canned frozen foods and the manufacture of ice cream and candy. Additionally, the division markets starch and resin products used in the manufacture of paper, corrugated containers, and textiles. The company's corn processing plant in Lafayette, Indiana, currently has a grind capacity of 11 billion bushels of corn yearly.

44 The company's brewer's yeast food plant in Jacksonville, Florida, has a yearly capacity of 3 million pounds. The debitterized brewer's food yeast is sold to health food manufacturers for use in a variety of nutritional supplements. Busch Entertainment Corporation, the company's family entertainment subsidiary, operates theme parks in Florida and Virginia. Unique blends of natural beauty and family entertainment activities and attractions are featured in both locations. Busch Properties, Inc., is the company's real estate development subsidiary. It is currently involved in the development of both residential and commercial properties at sites in Virginia and Ohio. St. Louis Refrigerator Car Company, Manufacturers Railway Company, and five other companies compose Anheuser-Busch's transportation subsidiaries. They provide commercial repair, rebuilding, maintenance, and inspection of railroad cars, terminal railroad switching services, and truck cartage and warehousing services.

Marketing

45 Anheuser-Busch has a coast-to-coast network of 11 breweries which are selectively situated in major population and beer-consumption regions. Once the beers leave the breweries, distribution to the consumer becomes the responsibility of 959 wholesale distribution operations and 11 company-owned beer branches which provide the company with its own profit centers within the distribution system. The beer branches perform sales, merchandising, and delivery services in their respective areas of primary responsibility. The company's beer branches are located in Sylmar and Riverside, California; Denver, Colorado; Chicago, Illinois; Louisville, Kentucky; New Orleans, Louisiana; Cambridge, Massachusetts; Kansas City, Missouri; Newark, New Jersey; Tulsa, Oklahoma; and Washington, D.C.

46 The beer industry has always been a highly competitive industry. Success depends on volume, and sales by the nation's top five brewers account for an estimated 70 percent of the total market. There is intense competition between the industry leaders. According to *Value Line,* it was expected that by 1980, the top five brewers would account for approximately 80 percent of the market.

47 Competitive pressures have led Anheuser-Busch to take an aggressive stance in its marketing strategy. It is the country's largest brewer in terms of barrel sales per

year and the 34th largest national advertiser. The 1978 annual report of Anheuser-Busch said their marketing efforts were "the most extensive and aggressive in company history," stressing product and packaging innovations, brand identity, and off-premise merchandising. The company entered the 1980s with new packaging innovations and new marketing programs. The aggressive packaging is aimed at further market segmentation and penetration. Presently, the company sells more than 80 basic packages.

48 Anheuser-Busch's advertisements have traditionally been aimed at communicating the quality of the company's beer products which appeal to virtually every taste and price range. Television advertisements and sports sponsorships continue to be the major focal point for marketing the company's beer brands. Television advertisements focus on prime-time programming and sports. To increase its presence on college campuses, Anheuser-Busch utilizes a unique marketing team of 400 student representatives at major colleges and universities across the country.

49 Anheuser-Busch has enlarged its marketing staff in the beer division. A field sales task force has been established to provide immediate and concentrated assistance in markets needing a sales boost. The national accounts sales department was created to provide better marketing coordination and communication between the company's sales staff and large national chain accounts such as grocery stores, convenience stores, fast-food outlets, hotels, motels, liquor chains, and athletic stadiums. The marketing services department coordinates and expands activities in the areas of sales promotion, merchandising, special markets, point-of-sale, and incentive programs.

Production Facilities

50 Reviewing the production facilities utilized by Anheuser-Busch provides insight into the growth pattern of the organization. Devotion to investment in plant capacity has been extensive in the past decade, and the future capital expenditure program allows for future expansion and modernization of facilities (annual report, 1978).

51 The largest subsidiary of Anheuser-Busch Companies is the beer production sector. Exhibit 14 is a listing of the geographically dispersed breweries with their corresponding annual capacity in millions of barrels and dates of first shipments.

52 As can be seen from this exhibit, many of the beer production facilities are quite new. Plants in St. Louis and Newark have undergone extensive modernization programs to upgrade older plants and equipment and ensure consistent quality regardless of brewery location. In 1980, Anheuser-Busch purchased a brewery formerly owned and operated by Schlitz. The seller was forced to close the plant because of declining sales due to competitive pressures.

53 Commitments to plant expansion have been extensive in the past few years. For example, capital expenditures will approach $2 billion for the five years ending 1983, with 93 percent for beer-related activities, according to industry analyst Robert S. Weinberg. Expansion is currently being undertaken at several of the 11 breweries. At the Los Angeles plant, the largest expansion project, capacity is being increased by more than 6 million barrels. Capacity in Williamsburg, Virginia, is being increased threefold.

54 Plant expansion in the areas of can manufacturing and industrial products manufacturing is being conducted at rapid rates. Vertical integration into can manufacturing and malt production is requiring substantial increases in plant investment. Can-production facilities were completed in Jacksonville, Florida, in 1974, Columbus, Ohio, in

Exhibit 14

Production facility locations and capacities

	Millions of barrels	*Beginning of shipment*
St. Louis, Missouri	11.6	1880
Los Angeles, California	10.0	1954
Newark, New Jersey	4.7	1951
Tampa, Florida	2.2	1959
Houston, Texas	2.6	1966
Columbus, Ohio	6.2	1968
Jacksonville, Florida	6.5	1969
Merrimack, New Hampshire	2.8	1970
Williamburg, Virginia	7.5	1972
Fairfield, California	3.5	1976
Baldwinsville, New York	6.0	1982

Source: Anheuser-Busch annual reports.

1977, and Arnold, Missouri, in 1980. Nearly 40 percent of cans used were provided internally by 1980. In addition, two can recycling facilities are currently in operation.

Research and Development

55 According to the 1978 Securities and Exchange Commission's Form 10-K report, Anheuser-Busch

> does not consider to be material the dollar amounts expended by it during the last two fiscal years on research activities relating to the development of new products or services or the improvement of existing products or services. In addition, the company does not consider the number of employees engaged full time in such research activities to be material.

56 The company is, however, extensively involved in research and development. R&D funds are currently being used to develop new food and beverage products which are consistent with the company's production and distribution capabilities. The organization has a corn products research group which recently developed a number of new and very profitable modified food starches. In addition to these, Anheuser-Busch's research on possible new beer products helped to place Michelob Light and Anheuser-Busch Natural Light beers on the market.

57 Along with research on new and profitable products, the company is striving to cut packaging costs by doing research in the production of aluminum. Anheuser-Busch paid $6 million in 1978 to a major international aluminum company, Swiss Aluminum, Ltd., for access and participation rights in this company's ongoing research in the development of certain new technologies in aluminum casting. This area should greatly reduce costs in the future.

58 Besides product and container research, Anheuser-Busch's R&D departments are studying matters of social concern. The reasons for this type of research are so the company can remain active in its social responsibility as a public corporation and

also to strengthen its influence in reducing government regulations and thus avoid possible costly restrictions to its operations. Research to determine the causes of alcoholism and develop effective treatment and prevention programs, in cooperation with the United States Brewers Association, is one example of the company's effort here. Other examples relate to environmental matters. In an independent effort toward developing and utilizing alternative energy systems, other than scarce natural gas and oil, Anheuser-Busch is researching solar energy. In 1978, the company installed a new pilot project at its Jacksonville, Florida, brewery. At this plant, solar energy is being tested in pasteurizing bottled beers. In addition, the company is developing new land application programs aimed at soil enrichment and energy conservation. Under these programs, rich soil nutrients are taken from the breweries' liquid wastes and used to grow various crops, primarily sod, grass, and grains.

Money Matters at Anheuser-Busch

59 Exhibits 15, 16, 17, and 18 contain relevant financial data on Anheuser-Busch.

Future

60 In his letter to the shareholders in the 1978 annual report, August A. Busch III discussed Anheuser-Busch's expansion and diversification plans. He wrote:

> We continue to commit substantial resources to provide the capacity necessary to support our planned sales growth and to maintain our industry leadership. Furture growth and profitability also depend, however, on our willingness to commit funds and energies to the development of new products and new areas of business activity.
>
> For a number of years, we have been investing considerable sums of money

Exhibit 15

Per share data ($)

	Year-end December 31									
	1978	*1977*	*1976*	*1975*	*1974*	*1973*	*1972*	*1971*	*1970*	*1969*
Book value	16.71	15.07	13.72	13.17	11.93	11.11	10.25	9.20	8.02	7.03
Earnings*	2.46	2.04	1.23	1.88	1.42	1.46	1.70	1.60	1.40	1.01
Dividends	0.82	0.71	0.68	0.64	0.06	0.60	0.58	0.53	0.42½	0.40
Payout ratio	33%	35%	55%	34%	42%	41%	34%	33%	30%	39%
Prices—High	27¾	25¼	38⅝	39⅝	38	55	69	57½	39⅝	36⅞
Low	17½	18¾	20¾	24½	21	28⅝	51	37	27⅛	28½
Price-earnings ratio	11–7	12–9	31–17	21–13	27–15	38–20	41–30	36–23	28–19	36–28

Data as originally reported. Adjusted for stock dividends of 100 percent April 1971.
* Before results of discontinued opertions of—0.09 in 1972.
Source: *Standard OTC Stock Reports* 46, no. 125, sec. 5 (October 31, 1979). Copyright © 1979 Standard & Poor's Corporation. All rights reserved.

Exhibit 16

Income data ($ millions)

Year ended December 31	Revenues	Operating income	Percent operating income of revenues	Capital expend-itures	Depreci-ation	Interest expense	Net before taxes†	Effective tax rate	Net income	Percent net income of revenues
1978	2,260	288	12.8%	229	66.0	28.9	206	46.0%	111	4.9%
1977	1,838	246	13.4	157	61.2	26.7	170	45.9	92	5.0
1976	1,441	181	12.6	199	53.1	26.9	103	46.4	55	3.8
1975	1,645	226	13.8	155	51.1	22.6	165	48.7	85	5.2
1974	1,413	164	11.6	126	45.0	11.9	122	47.3	64	4.5
1973	1,110	162	14.6	92	41.1	5.3	126	48.1	66	5.9
1972*	978	184	18.8	84	39.0	6.0	147	48.0	76	7.8
1971	902	170	18.9	73	35.0	6.6	136	47.3	72	7.9
1970	793	155	19.5	65	33.8	7.1	121	48.2	63	7.9
1969	667	122	18.2	71	30.1	7.4	93	51.2	45	6.8

* Before results of discontinued operations of—0.09 in 1972.
Source: *Standard OTC Stock Reports* 46, no. 125, sec. 5 (October 31, 1979).

Exhibit 17

Balance sheet data ($ million)

December 31	Cash	Current			Total assets	Return on assets	Long-term debt	Com-mon equity	Total capital	Percent long-term debt of capital	Return on equity
		Assets	Liabilities	Ratio							
1978	196	492	255	1.9	1,648	7.3%	427	754	1,393	30.7%	15.5%
1977	154	400	212	1.9	1,404	6.9	337	680	1,191	28.3	14.0
1976	135	347	167	2.1	1,268	4.5	341	618	1,101	30.9	9.1
1975	224	420	161	2.6	1,202	7.9	342	594	1,041	32.9	15.0
1974	89	252	113	2.2	931	7.5	193	538	818	23.6	12.3
1973	60	176	100	1.8	765	9.0	93	501	666	14.0	13.6
1972*	69	166	81	2.0	698	11.3	99	462	617	16.1	17.4
1971	69	163	75	2.2	654	11.3	117	414	579	20.1	18.5
1970	61	158	78	2.0	605	10.8	128	358	527	24.3	18.6
1969	45	142	65	2.2	550	8.4	135	314	485	27.8	15.1

* Before results of discontinued operations of—0.09 in 1972.
Source: *Standard OTC Stock Reports* 46, no. 125, sec. 5 (October 31, 1979).

Exhibit 18

Ten-year financial summary (thousands of dollars, except per share and statistical data)

Consolidated summary of operations:	*1978*	*1979*	*1976*
Barrels sold	41,610	36,640	29,051
Sales	$2,701,611	$2,231,230	$1,752,998
Less federal and state beer taxes	441,978	393,182	311,852
Net sales	2,259,633	1,838,048	1,441,146
Cost of products sold	1,762,410	1,462,801	1,175,055
Gross profits	497,223	375,247	266,091
Less marketing, administrative, and research expenses	274,961	190,470	137,797
Operating income	222,262	184,777	128,294
Interest income	11,693	7,724	10,304
Interest expense	(28,894)	(26,708)	(26,941)
Other income net	751	4,193	1,748
Loss on partial closing of Los Angeles Busch Gardens (1)			10,020
Income before income taxes	205,812	169,986	103,385
Income taxes	94,772	78,041	47,952
Income before extraordinary item	111,040	91,945	55,433
Extraordinary item (2)			
Net income	$ 111,040	$ 91,945	$ 55,433
Per share (3) income before extraordinary item	2.46	2.04	1.23
Net income	2.46	2.04	1.23
Cash dividends paid	37,013	32,036	30,646
Per share (3)	.82	.71	.68
Dividend payout ratio	33.3%	34.8%	55.3%
Average number of shares outstanding (3)	45,138	45,115	45,068
Book value per share	16.71	15.07	13.72
Balance sheet information:			
Working capital	236,396	188,069	194,814
Current ratio	1.9	1.9	2.2
Plant and equipment, net	1,109,243	951,965	857,073
Long-term debt	427,250	337,492	340,737
Debt to debt plus total equity	34.5%	31.7%	34.0%
Deferred income taxes	153,080	125,221	99,119
Deferred investment tax credit	58,053	48,371	43,174
Shareholders' equity	754,423	680,396	618,429
Return on shareholders' equity	15.1%	14.2%	9.2%
Other information:			
Capital expenditures	228,727	156,745	198,735
Depreciation	66,032	61,163	53,105
Total payroll cost	421,806	338,933	271,403
Effective tax rate	46.0%	45.9%	46.4%

Notes to 10-year financial summary:

(1) In December 1976, the company decided to close a portion of the Los Angeles Busch Gardens and convert the remainder to a sales promotion facility. Closing a portion of the Gardens resulted in a nonoperating charge of $10,020,000 (before reduction for income tax benefits of approximately $5 million). This nonoperating charge, which reduced earnings per share by 11 cents, has been reported in accordance with *Accounting Principles Board Opinion No. 39* which was effective September 30, 1973.

Exhibit 18 ***(concluded)***

1975	1974	1973	1972	1971	1970	1969
35,196	34,097	29,887	26,522	24,309	22,202	18,712
$2,036,687	$1,791,863	$1,442,720	$1,273,093	$1,173,476	$1,036,272	$871,904
391,708	378,772	333,013	295,593	271,023	243,495	205,295
1,644,979	1,413,091	1,109,707	977,500	902,453	792,777	666,609
1,343,784	1,187,816	875,361	724,718	658,886	579,372	490,932
301,195	225,275	234,346	252,782	243,567	213,405	175,677
126,053	106,653	112,928	108,008	108,087	92,660	84,113
175,142	118,622	121,418	144,774	135,480	120,745	91,564
10,944	9,925	4,818	3,299	3,102	3,715	3,604
(22,602)	(11,851)	(5,288)	(6,041)	(6,597)	(7,104)	(7,401)
1,816	4,840	5,287	4,855	4,065	3,420	5,171
165,300	121,536	126,235	146,887	136,050	120,776	92,938
80,577	57,517	60,658	70,487	64,412	58,227	47,627
84,723	64,019	65,577	76,400	71,638	62,549	45,311
			4,093			
$ 84,723	$ 64,019	$ 65,577	$ 72,307	$ 71,638	$ 62,549	$ 45,311
1.88	1.42	1.46	1.70	1.60	1.40	1.02
1.88	1.42	1.46	1.61	1.60	1.40	1.02
28,843	27,041	27,037	26,109	23,784	18,991	17,843
.64	.60	.60	.58	.53	.425	.40
34.0%	42.3%	41.1%	36.0%	33.1%	30.4%	39.2%
45,068	45,068	45,063	45,020	44,887	44,686	44,616
13.17	11.93	11.11	10.25	9.20	8.02	7.03
268,099	145,107	82,352	88,711	92,447	85,102	80,963
2.7	2.3	1.8	2.1	2.2	2.1	2.3
724,914	622,876	541,236	491,671	453,647	416,660	387,422
342,167	193,240	93,414	99,107	116,571	128,080	134,925
35.6%	25.7%	15.3%	17.2%	21.4%	25.6%	29.2%
80,748	66,264	54,281	41,456	34,103	27,274	23,212
24,293	21,157	17,225	14,370	14,276	13,563	12,577
593,642	537,762	500,784	461,980	413,974	358,476	314,121
15.0%	12.3%	13.6%	16.5%	18.6%	18.6%	15.1%
155,436	126,463	91,801	84,217	73,214	65,069	66,396
51,089	45,042	41,059	38,970	34,948	33,795	30,063
268,306	244,437	221,049	190,517	176,196	156,576	133,872
48.7%	47.3%	48.1%	48.0%	47.3%	48.2%	51.2%

(2) In December 1972, the company decided to close a portion of the Houston Busch Gardens and convert the remainder to a sales promotion facility. Closing a portion of the Gardens resulted in an extraordinary aftertax charge against 1972 earnings of $4,093,000, or 9 cents per share, net of applicable income tax benefits of $4,006,000.

(3) Per share statistics have been adjusted to give effect to the two-for-one stock split in 1971.

Source: Anheuser-Busch Companies annual reports, 1969–1978.

and a great deal of effort in the area of vertical integration of our beer business . . . new can and malt plants and, more recently, in exploring the possibility of producing our own aluminum sheet used in the manufacture of cans. These activities have proved to be successful in controlling costs, and we will continue to pay close attention to vertical integration.

We are also exploring opportunities to diversify into other business ventures which are not beer related. We can do this either through acquisitions or through internal development of new products. At the present time, we are emphasizing a program aimed at maximizing use of existing capabilities. We are in the process of developing internally a line of soft drinks and other consumer products which can be distributed through our wholesale network. We recognize from the outset that we may not achieve success in every one of these new ventures. However, the financial risks are relatively small, and the potential rewards are considerable.

61 C. James Walker III, an industry analyst, predicted a 1981 shipment level of 55 million barrels indicating a 9.2 million barrel growth in the 1979–1981 period. This is comparable to that achieved in 1977–1979. However, without the presence of a visible new major category similar to "Light" in size, Walker doubts that growth in the 1980s can match the expansion of the late 1970s. According to Walker, new brands such as Würzburger and Busch Premium seem unlikely to garner the growth that Natural Light and Michelob Light may attain. Exhibit 19 shows Walker's estimate for 1981, which would make Anheuser-Busch fall 6 percent shy of its goal of 98 percent capacity utilization.

Exhibit 19

Estimated volume by brewer 1978 and 1981

	1978		*1981**		*1978–1981*	
	Barrel shipments (millions)	*Market share*	*Barrel shipments (millions)*	*Market share*	*Barrel increment (millions)*	*Compounded annual rate of growth*
Anheuser-Busch	41.6	25.1%	51.5	28.7%	+ 9.9	7.4%
Miller	31.3	18.9	44.9	25.0	+13.6	12.6
Schlitz	19.6	11.8	17.2	9.6	− 2.4	(3.8)
Pabst	15.4	9.3	14.7	8.2	− 0.7	(1.2)
Coors†	12.6	7.6	17.2	9.6	+ 4.6	11.1
Top 5	120.5	72.8	145.5	81.1	+25.0	6.6
All others‡	41.7	25.2	28.4	15.8	−13.3	(9.7)
U.S. industry	162.2	97.9	173.9	97.0	+11.7	2.3%
Imports	3.4	2.1	5.4	3.0	+ 2.0	16.5
All beer	165.6	100.0%	179.3	100.0%	+13.7	2.7%

* Estimated.

† Coors was in a 16-state market in 1978 and an estimated 19-state market in 1981 (additions: Arkansas, Louisiana, and Minnesota).

‡ In 1981, the operations of Blitz-Weinhard are included with Pabst; in 1978, about 600,000 barrels of Blitz are in the all-other group.

Source: C. James Walker III, *Competition in the U.S. Brewing Industry: A Basic Analysis* (New York: Shearson Hayden Stone, September 26, 1979).

62 Busch, on the other hand, was more optimistic. He wrote:

> In anticipation of what we can expect to encounter in the marketplace, we have developed strong and aggressive marketing and promotion programs to enhance our position as industry leader. We will be introducing more new products and new packages to keep Anheuser-Busch in the forefront of market segmentation. And we will be intensifying our emphasis on the quality of our products.
>
> Competitive pressures will demand the most dedicated and creative efforts that we can muster, but we are confident that with our strong sales momentum, our quality products, our great wholesaler family, and the team effort of our employees, we will have another successful year and will continue to build a solid corporate foundation for future growth and profits.

case 6 Anheuser-Busch Companies, Inc. (B)

1 1982 represented a banner year for Anheuser-Busch Companies, Inc. The company savored both the best financial performance in its history and the World Series victory of its St. Louis Cardinals. Anheuser-Busch successfully weathered its competitive duel with Miller Brewing Company to maintain its position as the "King of Beers," and it enhanced its dominant market position through the successful introduction of Budweiser Light in 1982 and its entry into several international markets. During 1982, the company aggressively pursued its diversification strategy into consumer products by acquiring Campbell Taggart, Inc., the second-largest manufacturer of fresh-baked goods in the United States. Commenting about the acquisition in a letter to stockholders, August A. Busch III, chairman of the board and president of Anheuser-Busch Companies, Inc., stated:

> Anheuser-Busch Companies decided that its first major acquisition should have a relatively low down-side risk, while at the same time providing up-side growth potential. Campbell Taggart met that objective. The combination of Campbell Taggart with Anheuser-Busch Companies will allow us to capitalize on our strengths within our organization and benefit from synergies between the business operations of the two companies.

2 Campbell-Taggart represented Anheuser-Busch's first major externally generated diversification effort. Prior to this acquisition, Anheuser-Busch had concentrated on internally generated diversification efforts in the 1977–1982 time period. By 1982, Anheuser-Busch was still solidly a beer brewer with over 90 percent of its total revenue coming from the sale of beer.

The Brewing Industry

3 The brewing industry in the United States was populated by hundreds of small local and regional brewers prior to the 20th century. Following World War II, there was a structural transformation of the industry. The pressure for national advertising and national distribution at low-shipping costs combined with increased price competition necessitated increased size and geographic dispersion in order to remain competitive. As economies of scale became a major key to success in brewing, large national brewers increased their market share while the attrition rate among small competitors skyrocketed. By 1970, the number of breweries had dropped from over 300 to just

92 American breweries. The eight-firm concentration ratio increased from 21 percent in 1947 to 63 percent in 1977.[1] Only 43 brewers remained in business in 1982. Ten of these brewers accounted for 95 percent of all beer sold, with Anheuser-Busch and Miller controlling 56 percent of the market (see Exhibit 1). Analysts expect the trend toward industry concentration to continue and predict the two giant brewers, Anheuser-Busch and Miller, will grab an estimated 70 percent of the market by 1990.

4 In the face of increasing competition, many of the remaining rival firms are expected to merge or look for acquisitions to maintain their viability as industry participants. For example, Stroh acquired Schlitz after the Justice Department barred Heileman from acquiring the troubled Schlitz in late 1981 on the grounds it would produce too heavy a concentration in the Midwest. Heileman has been the most-effective challenger for Anheuser-Busch on a regional basis, using a strategy of acquiring and reviving local brands, keeping production costs low, and employing aggressive (some say "cutthroat") marketing techniques. Its strategy has been to revitalize the acquired regional brands, gradually introduce other Heileman brands to the region, and then saturate the new market with highly promoted products. Heileman's base is the Midwest, and a Schlitz acquisition would have provided plants in the West, South, and Southeast—markets Anheuser-Busch has targeted as its major sources of future growth. Reacting to the Justice Department's decision, an Anheuser-Busch spokesman said, "Stroh-Schlitz is a lesser competitive threat than Heileman-Schlitz." Russell Cleary, Heileman chairman, offered a different opinion: "We are the only company Anheuser-Busch does not do well against. The prospect of our entry into the South scared them." Unfortunately for Heileman, the Justice Department also rejected a Heileman bid for Pabst while clearing the way for an Olympia-Pabst merger.

5 As Anheuser-Busch and Miller bring their fight into local and regional markets, a widely recognized industry analyst argues that there is no room in the industry for brewers of under 20 million barrels because of the economies of scale needed to compete in production and marketing.

6 In 1982, industrywide beer sales were up less than 1 percent over 1981—the result of a sluggish economy and lower beer prices. Domestic brewers actually suffered a slight profit decline, the first in 25 years, although Anheuser-Busch and G. Heileman Brewing Company posted significant volume gains among domestic brewers. Imported beers sold 5.7 million barrels in the United States in 1982, a 10 percent increase from 1981. Representing 3 percent of the market by volume, imports (because of their higher prices) accounted for approximately 5 percent of total 1982 retail dollar beer sales in the United States.

7 From 1975 to 1980, imports expanded at an average annual rate of 22 percent, while the industry as a whole expanded at approximately 4 percent annually. Import beers are expected to continue as the fastest-growing segment of the beer industry—pegged at between 5 and 10 percent by industry analysts—culminating with a projected 5.6 percent market share (dollars) and annual sales of 12 million barrels. Overall industry growth is projected to run at 1.7 percent annually through the remainder of the 1980s.

8 Through 1982, the heaviest import consumption centered in the nation's largest metropolitan or regional markets (New York, Florida, Chicago, and California). In 1982, one in every four imported beers was consumed by a New Yorker.

[1] Concentration ratio refers to the percent of total industry sales accounted for by one or several firms. In this case, the sales of eight firms represent 63 percent of total beer sales in the United States.

Exhibit 1

The brewing industry

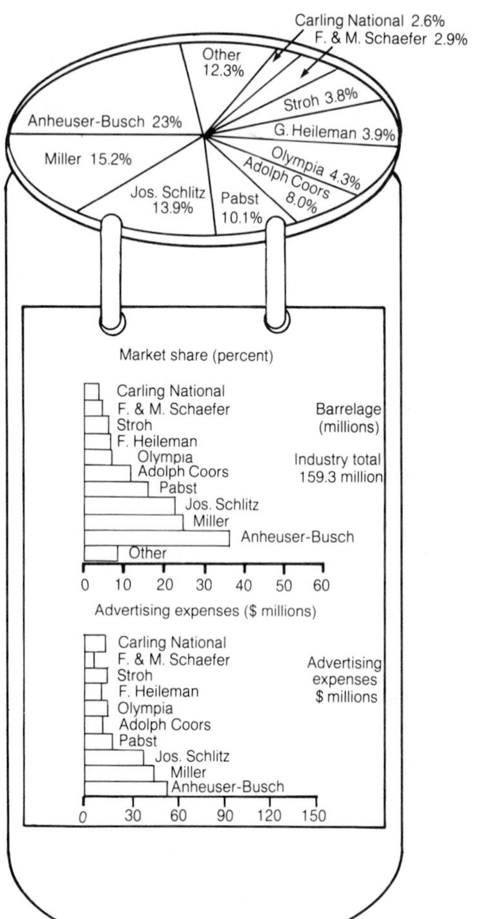

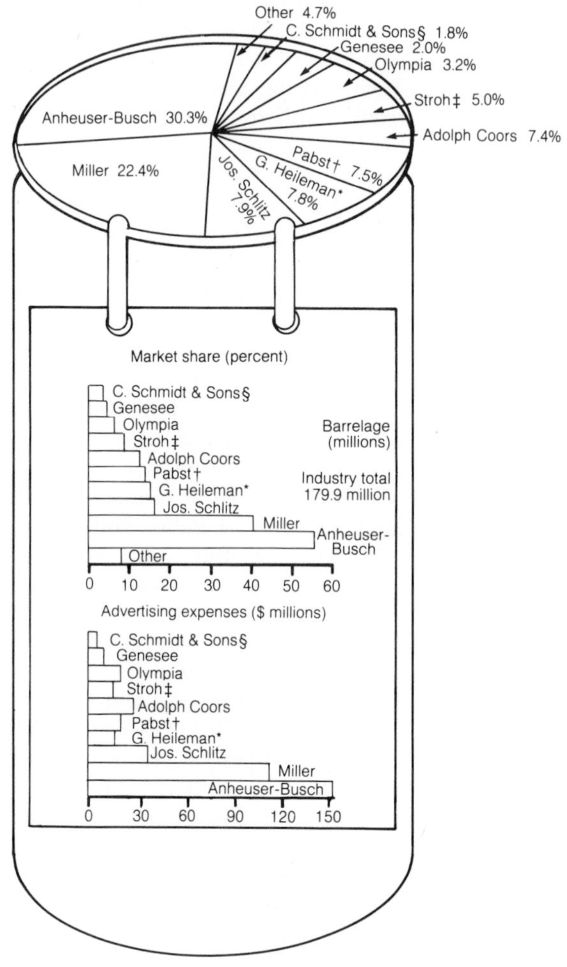

* Includes acquisition of Falls City, Carling National, Rainier.
† Includes acquisition of Blitz-Weinhard Co.
‡ Includes acquisition of F. & M. Schaefer.
§ Includes acquisition of Henry F. Ortieb Brewing.
Source: *Business Week,* July 12, 1982, p. 51.

9 Distribution is much easier and volume is concentrated in large urban areas. Imports, moreover, are primarily consumed in restaurants and other food-service institutions—two thirds of all imports are consumed "on premises" according to 1982 industry figures. For domestic beers, it's just the opposite—two thirds are purchased for home consumption. So imports have grown to date primarily in urban centers with high restaurant concentrations.

10 Three fourths of the import volume comes from two countries—the Netherlands (Heineken) and Canada (Molson, Moosehead, and Labatt's). Germany and Mexico supply the next-largest group of import offerings.

11 Several factors that should have a major impact on the beer industry are summarized below.

The 20 percent expansion of the adult population in the 1970s will trickle to half that rate in the 1980s. The 18–34-year-old group, which accounts for more than half of all beer consumed, will increase by less than 2 percent by 1990. The 18–24-year-old group, historically the most important single beer consuming group (approximately 29 to 30 percent), will decline in size by 1990 to three fourths its 1980 size (see Exhibit 2).

Fueling the contraction of demand in the 18-to-24 age group is a push by many states to raise their legal drinking ages—6 in 1982, 12 in 1983, and 25 with such legislation in the 1984–85 agenda—to 20 or 21 years.

State and federal governments are increasing attempts to raise excise taxes on alcoholic beverages. Relatedly, trends in some states are to require the

Exhibit 2

Age distribution of the U.S. population

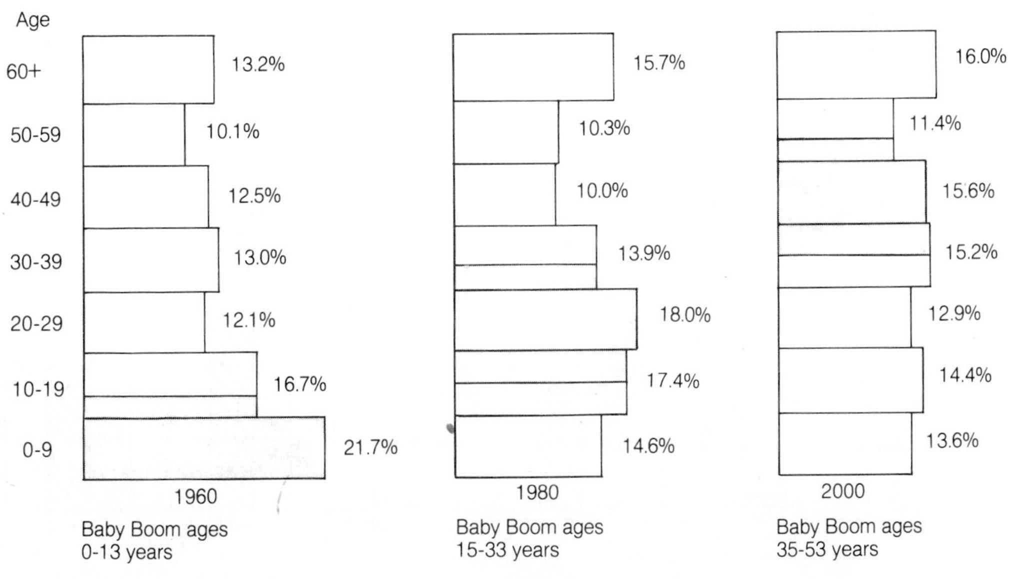

use of expensive, market-disrupting packaging like returnable bottles and nonpenetrable (from the Tylenol poisoning experience) packaging.

Social and legislative concern with the problems of alcoholism is growing. Thirty-two states passed increasingly stringent drinking-and-driving penalties between 1980 and 1984. Powerful organizations such as MADD (Mothers against Drunken Drivers) have become vocal and prominent in the 1980s.

Overcapacity (estimated to be 181 million barrels in 1983) looms heavily over the industry. Volume projections for industry growth noted earlier project a 1.7 percent annualized growth rate in beer consumption through 1990. Yet several brewers, most notably Pabst and Schlitz, are producing at approximately 70 percent of capacity in 1984. Anheuser-Busch is scheduled to complete a $2 billion, 27 percent increase in capacity by 1987. This would boost its current 63-million-barrel capacity to over 80 million barrels. On the other hand, Miller indefinitely delayed (in 1984) opening a new, 8-million-barrel plant in Ohio that was ready to produce at the end of 1983. The top U.S. brewers and their 1982 sales and market share are as follows:

No. 1—Anheuser-Busch, Inc. (59.1 million barrels/32.0 percent).
No. 2—Miller Brewing Co. (39.3 million barrels/21.3 percent).
No. 3—Stroh Brewing Co. (22.9 million barrels/12.4 percent).

Exhibit 3

Population growth by region

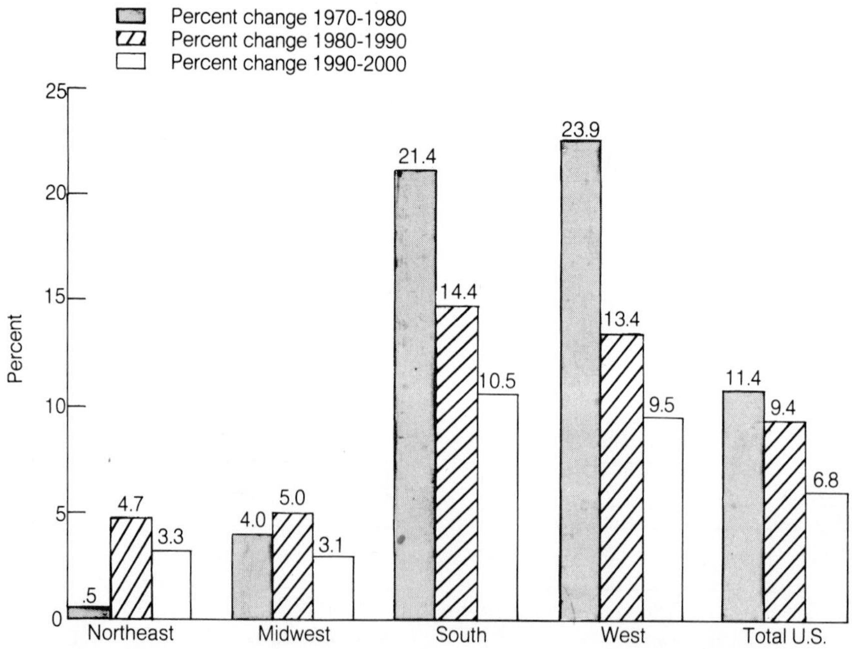

Source: Census Bureau, 1981.

No. 4—G. Heileman Brewing Co. (14.5 million barrels/7.9 percent).
No. 5—Pabst Brewing Co. (12.3 million barrels/6.7 percent).
No. 6—Adolph Coors Co. (11.9 million barrels/6.5 percent).
No. 7—Olympia Brewing Co. (5.2 million barrels/2.8 percent).
No. 8—Genesee Brewing Co. (3.4 million barrels/1.8 percent).
No. 9—Falstaff/General Brewing Co. (3.2 million barrels/1.7 percent).
No. 10—C. Schmidt & Sons (3.2 million barrels/1.7 percent).

The region population growth rates are highest in the South. At the same time, the rate of growth is dropping in the areas as shown in Exhibit 3.

Anheuser-Busch Brewery

12 Founded in 1852 on the south side of St. Louis, Missouri, Anheuser-Busch has enjoyed a position of preeminence in the brewing industry since the late 19th century. Under the leadership of successive generations of the Busch family, the company has continued to maintain the dominant position in the U.S. brewing industry.

13 Anheuser-Busch's primary business has always been brewing with the brief exception of their successful diversification into the production of bakers' yeast during the Prohibition era. Today, Busch Industrial Products produces 50 percent of all the baker's yeast sold in the United States.

14 For 30 years following World War II, Anheuser-Busch concentrated on building a dominant position in the brewing industry. Between 1946 and 1974, the company increased its brewery capacity from 3 million barrels to 34 million barrels annually. It was also during this time that Anheuser-Busch diversified on a limited basis. When August A. Busch III was elected CEO in 1975, the corporation had limited interests in real estate, family entertainment centers, can manufacturing, transportation, and a major league baseball franchise—the St. Louis Cardinals. However, revenue from these nonbrewing interests comprised less than 10 percent of total corporate receipts.

15 Despite Anheuser-Busch's previous success and its position as the market-share leader in the brewing industry, the mid-1970s represented a critical juncture in the company's history. A formerly lackluster Miller Brewing Co., acquired by Philip Morris Incorporated in 1970, rose from seventh place to the No. 2 market-share position in the brewing industry by 1977. Miller created a virtual revolution in the brewing industry through the introduction of sophisticated marketing techniques. As a subsidiary of Philip Morris, Miller Brewing was transformed into an aggressive effective marketing firm through its ability to draw on both the marketing and financial resources of its parent company. Miller's successful strategy included market segmentation, innovative promotion and advertising, and improved production efficiency. Miller was not content with its No. 2 position, however. Its announced goal by 1976 was to wrest the No. 1 position from Anheuser-Busch .

16 Initially, Anheuser ignored Miller's challenge and was caught off guard by Miller's huge success in the low-calorie segment of the beer market in 1976. Concurrently, Anheuser-Busch was hit with a devastating 95-day labor strike in 1976. These factors precipitated the company's worst financial performance since the Depression. The firm's inability to meet deliveries during the strike left its traditionally powerful marketing network in a shambles and its executives unable to meet the Miller challenge.

Industry analyst Donald Rice reflected the view of many industry observers when he stated: "A lot of people thought Miller would end up on top."

17 Faced with this formidable challenge, August C. Busch III (the fifth-generation Busch to lead Anheuser) initiated a massive reorganization designed to transform the lumbering giant into an efficient and effective modern brewery. He totally revamped the corporation's strategy in his efforts to fend off Miller's attack and regain the market share Anheuser-Busch lost during the 95-day strike.

18 In order to overhaul the company's marketing strategy, Busch recruited experienced executives from major marketing-oriented firms such as Procter & Gamble and General Mills. Management teams composed of merchandising, advertising, and planning specialists were established to both spearhead an aggressive new marketing posture and determine where Miller had made its most damaging inroads. To increase sales and reestablish its traditionally strong relationship with its wholesalers, Anheuser-Busch developed extensive training seminars for its wholesalers in 1980.

19 The training program emphasizes such topics as financial management, warehousing, and aggressive marketing—operating topics designed to support and shore up Anheuser-Busch's extensive wholesaler network. The company further helped its network by developing a computerized shelf-space management program for retailers that audits sales, margins, and turnover by brand, package, and promotion. This system also facilitates Anheuser-Busch's monitoring of wholesaler performance and marketing (account-call frequency, weekly and monthly sales, and so forth) activity. This detailed attention is critical, says CEO Busch, "because much of this decade's fight will be waged at the wholesale and field level."

20 Promotional emphasis has been considered a key component of Anheuser-Busch's overall strategy. The company almost doubled its media advertising budget between 1976 and 1981 to over $145 million. It allocated approximately $45 million in 1982 to support one brand—Budweiser Light. It has chosen to dominate sponsorship of sporting events—98 professional and 310 collegiate sports events in 1982 versus 12 and 7, respectively, in 1976. Anheuser-Busch has also emphasized market segmentation by expanding from three brands in 1976 to eight in 1982—Busch and Natural Light in the popular price range; Bud and Bud Light in premium; and Michelob, Michelob Light, Michelob Dark, and Würzburger (an import) in superpremium.

21 Historically, Anheuser-Busch had always operated at very high capacity levels, and it was not unheard of for sales to exceed capacity during the peak selling season in the summer months. It was critical, therefore, that the company seriously consider increasing its production capabilities to meet the volume increases expected from its aggressive marketing thrust. Otherwise, it might stimulate demand and encourage a distribution network it couldn't support. Confronted with this risky, capital-intensive decision, Busch decided to undertake an extensive program of expansion and modernization of Anheuser-Busch's beer production facilities. Capacity was increased by 60 percent in five years (1976–1981) at a total cost of $1.8 billion. To further enhance operating efficiency and lower production costs (one of the key ingredients for long-term success in the increasingly competitive brewing industry), Anheuser-Busch vertically integrated into can, labeling, and malt production (see Exhibit 4).

22 The final leg of Anheuser-Busch's strategy was to upgrade and expand its distribution system by employing more personnel and building a network of modern refrigerated warehouses (see Exhibit 5). This tactic not only improved delivery but also enhanced the maintenance of product quality from production to delivery.

Exhibit 4

Anheuser-Busch's vertical integration

Bush Agricultural Resources, Inc.

Busch Agricultural Resources processes barley into brewer's malt at plants in Wisconsin and Minnesota. These plants, with a combined annual capacity of more than 15 million bushels, provide Anheuser-Busch, Inc., with a dependable supply of high-quality malt. During 1981, they supplied the company's brewing operations with approximately 28 percent of its malt requirements. In addition, the subsidiary operates rice handling and storage facilities in Arkansas and Missouri in connection with its rice acquisition program. A rice milling facility is under construction in Arkansas.

Metal Label Corporation

Metal Label Corporation was formed in 1979 to extend the company's capabilities into the production of beer labels and other printed materials. Metal Label formed a partnership with Illochroma International, S.A., an integrated metalizing and printing firm based in Brussels, Belgium. This joint venture is known as International Label Company.

Clarksville, Tennessee: International Label Company constructed the first fully integrated paper metalizing and printing plant in the United States. The 100,000-square-foot plant began some phases of production in late 1980.

Metal Container Corporation

Metal Container Corporation, the company's can manufacturing subsidiary, is a significant factor both in company brewing operations and the U.S. can industry. During 1981, Metal Container produced 3.6 billion cans, providing approximately 40 percent of Anheuser-Busch, Inc.'s total can requirements and representing more than 10 percent of all the beer cans produced in the United States.

Brewery Production

Anheuser-Busch, Inc.'s strategically located network of 11 operating breweries provides the company with the most extensive production network in the world.

The company's operating breweries provide a combined estimated shipping capacity of 60 million barrels, equivalent to 827 million cases of beer. By the mid-80s, the company plans to expand its brewing capacity to more than 70 million barrels.

Brewing Facilities (year established)

St. Louis, Missouri: (1870) In 1946, annual shipping capacity of approximately 13.0 million barrels.

Newark, New Jersey: (1951) Shipping capacity of approximately 5 million barrels.

Los Angeles, California: (1954) An expansion, the largest in company history, was completed in early 1982. It nearly tripled the brewery's capacity to approximately 10.5 million barrels.

Exhibit 4 ***(continued)***

Tampa, Florida: (1959) Approximate annual shipping capacity of 1.8 million barrels.

Houston, Texas: (1966) Shipping capacity of approximately 3.7 million barrels.

Columbus, Ohio: (1968) Shipping capacity of 6.3 million barrels.

Jacksonville, Florida: (1969) Annual shipping capacity of approximately 6.7 million barrels.

Merrimack, New Hampshire: (1970) Approximate shipping capacity of 2.8 million barrels.

Williamsburg, Virginia: (1972) A major expansion project, completed in 1980, increased the plant's shipping capacity to 8.3 million barrels.

Fairfield, California: (1976) Annual shipping capacity of approximately 3.9 million barrels.

Baldwinsville, New York: (1980) The company purchased the former Jos. Schlitz Brewing Co. Capacity of approximately 6 million barrels.

Beer Distribution System

Once Anheuser-Busch, Inc.'s beers leave the breweries, distribution to the consumer becomes the responsibility of its more than 960 independent beer wholesalers and 16 company-owned wholesale operations. Together, they provide the company with the most extensive and effective beer distribution system in the brewing industry.

St. Louis Refrigerator Car Company

St. Louis Refrigerator Car Company, one of the company's transportation subsidiaries, has been in existence since 1878. This operation provides commercial repair, rebuilding, maintenance, and inspection of railroad cars at facilities in Missouri, Illinois, and Texas. In addition, St. Louis Refrigerator Car operates a fleet of 900 specially insulated and cushioned railroad cars used exclusively for the transportation of Anheuser-Busch, Inc.'s beer products and a 17,000-ton molasses terminal on the Mississippi River to receive barge shipments of molasses for the St. Louis yeast plant.

Manufacturers Railway Company

Manufacturers Railway Company, the company's other transportation subsidiary, provides terminal rail switching services to industries in St. Louis, Missouri, over its 42 miles of company-owned and operated rail track. In addition, Manufacturers operates a fleet of 50 hopper cars and 270 general service box cars utilized by the company and outside firms. Manufacturers' four trucking subsidiaries, utilizing a fleet of 200 specially designed trailers, furnish cartage and warehousing service at six Anheuser-Busch, Inc., brewery locations—Fairfield, California; St. Louis, Missouri; Houston, Texas; Williamsburg, Virginia; Newark, New Jersey; and Merrimack, New Hampshire. The subsidiary will also serve the Baldwinsville, New York, brewery when it opens.

Busch Creative Services Corporation

Busch Creative Services, the company's multimedia and creative design subsidiary, was formed in early 1980 to produce a variety of multimedia, print, videotape, film,

Exhibit 4 ***(concluded)***

and other corporate and marketing communications materials and programs. The subsidiary is a full-service business and marketing communications company, selling its products and creative services to both Anheuser-Busch and clients outside the company. New services include theatrical services, consisting of stage and scenic design, lighting design, special effects, live entertainment, and theme party production.

Container Recovery Corporation

Container Recovery Corporation, the company's can reclamation and recycling subsidiary, was established in 1978. The creation of the subsidiary reflects growing corporate concerns for reducing litter, reclaiming vital raw materials and conserving energy while, at the same time, providing a positive alternative to mandatory deposit legislation and reducing container costs for Anheuser-Busch, Inc.

To meet these goals, Container Recovery functions in two different ways—by collecting aluminum cans for recycling at the consumer level and by operating container recycling process plants in Ohio, New Hampshire, and Florida. This program, operating in 35 states by the end of 1981, collected more than 100 million pounds of scrap aluminum during 1981.

Source: *Anheuser-Busch Fact Book,* 1982.

23 By 1982, Budweiser was recognized by most industry observers as having the best distribution system in the country.

24 In 1980, Emanuel Goldman, a respected brewing-industry analyst, predicted that Miller wouldn't be able to overtake Anheuser-Busch's top market share, even with the 95-day strike because, "Anheuser has taken the right marketing steps." Goldman's prediction proved to be insightful. By 1982, Anheuser-Busch had not only halted Miller's attack but had solidified its once precarious No. 1 ranking by garnering a 32.0 percent market share in the $10.5 billion beer industry. This represented an 8.5 percent increase in sales volume over 1981 and translated into a record high 19.8 million-barrel-margin over Miller. Miller's market share was 21.3 percent in 1982, down from its 22.3 percent in 1981. "We are working hard to stay humble," insisted Chairman Busch in commenting on Anheuser-Busch's victory.

Strategic Management at Anheuser-Busch

25 In 1982, *Dun's Business Month* selected Anheuser-Busch Companies, Inc., as one of the five best-managed companies of the year. In making the selection, the edition stated, "excellent management is more than an ability to make money in difficult times. It is the mark of companies smartly led, prudently financed, and sure of their direction. This year's winners had all that and something else—a carefully worked strategy to wrest greater market shares from their competitors."

26 Anheuser-Busch is managed on three basic principles as set forth by Chairman Busch: planning, teamwork, and communications. The 10-member Policy Committee, composed of senior executives from every major function within the organization, is involved in all decisions on strategies, planning, policies, and other major issues con-

Exhibit 5

Major operations

Corporate offices:
1. St. Louis

Breweries:
1. St. Louis
2. Newark
3. Los Angeles
4. Tampa
5. Houston
6. Columbus
7. Jacksonville
8. Merrimack
9. Williamsburg
10. Fairfield
11. Baldwinsville

Wholesale operations:
12. Sylmar
13. Riverside
14. Denver
15. Chicago (2)
16. Louisville
17. New Orleans
18. Boston
19. Kansas City
2. Newark
20. Tulsa
21. Washington, D.C.
22. Addison
23. Joliet
24. Waukegan
25. Liverpool

Can/lid manufacturing:
7. Jacksonville
6. Columbus
26. Arnold
27. Gainesville

Container recycling/processing:
28. Marion
29. Nashua
30. Cocoa

Malt production:
31. Manitowoc
32. Moorhead

Rice storage:
33. Jonesboro
34. Springfield
35. Brinkley

Label production:
36. Clarksville

Yeast production:
1. St. Louis
37. Old Bridge
38. Bakersfield

Family entertainment:
4. Tampa
9. Williamsburg
39. Langhome
40. Dallas/Fort Worth

Real estate development:
9. Williamsburg
6. Columbus
10. Fairfield

Rail car repair:
1. St. Louis
41. Wood River
42. Saginaw

Transportation services:
10. Fairfield
1. St. Louis
5. Houston
9. Williamsburg
43. Saratoga Springs, N.Y.

Baseball:
1. St. Louis

Tourist attractions:
1. St. Louis
8. Merrimack
4. Tampa
6. Columbus
7. Jacksonville
9. Williamsburg

Source: *Anheuser-Busch Fact Book,* 1982.

cerning the company. Busch claims that the high level of teamwork and open communications on the Policy Committee have been the catalyst for Anheuser-Busch's outstanding performance. The committee approves and reviews each subsidiary's annual budget and also formulates a five-year plan of company goals and strategy. Busch believes this detailed, continuous planning process has created a predictable climate in which to operate. In fact, according to Busch, the company's beer production in 1982 was within 300,000 barrels of the amount planned for seven years ago. (See Exhibits 6 and 7.)

27 Commenting on future strategic priorities, CEO Busch said in 1982:

> The company's primary objective is well-planned and well-managed growth. In addition to continued volume and profit increases in the beer and beer-related

Exhibit 6

ANHEUSER-BUSCH COMPANIES, INC., AND SUBSIDIARIES
1978–83 Financial Summary—Operations
(millions, except per share data)

	1982	*1981*	*1980*	*1979*	*1978*
Barrels sold	59.1	54.5	50.2	46.2	41.6
Sales	$5,185.7	$4,409.6	$3,822.4	$3,263.7	$2,701.6
Federal and state beer taxes	609.1	562.4	527.0	487.8	442.0
Net sales	4,576.6	3,847.2	3,295.4	2,775.9	2,259.6
Cost of products sold	3,331.7	2,975.5	2,553.9	2,172.1	1,762.4
Gross profit	1,244.9	871.7	741.5	603.8	497.2
Marketing, administrative, and research expenses	752.0	515.0	428.6	356.7	274.9
Operating income:	492.9	356.7	312.9	247.1	222.3
Interest expense	(89.2)	(89.6)	(75.6)	(40.3)	(28.9)
Interest capitalized	41.2	64.1	41.7	—	—
Interest income	17.0	6.2	2.4	8.4	11.7
Other income (expense), net	(8.1)	(12.2)	(9.9)	5.4	.7
Gain on sale of Lafayette plant	20.4	—	—	—	—
Income before income taxes	474.2	325.2	271.5	220.6	205.8
Income taxes	186.9	107.8	99.7	76.3	94.8
Net income	$ 287.3	$ 217.4	$ 171.8	$ 144.3	$ 111.0
Per share—net income	$ 5.97	$ 4.79	$ 3.80	$ 3.19	$ 2.46
Per share—fully diluted	$ 5.88	$ 4.61	$ 3.80	$ 4.34	$ 2.46
Cash dividends paid	$ 65.80	$ 51.2	$ 44.8	$ 40.7	$ 37.0
Per share	$ 1.38	$ 1.13	$ .99	$ .90	$ .82
Average number of shares outstanding (millions)	48.1	45.4	45.2	45.2	45.1

Notes to consolidated financial statements:

The following summarizes the company's business segment information for 1982. Segment information is not presented for 1981 and 1980, because the company's beer operations represented dominant industry segment.

	Beer and beer-related	*Food products*	*Other diversified operations*	*Eliminations*	*Consolidated*
Net sales	$4,488.1	$282.8	$145.1	$339.4	$4,576.6
Operating income	464.1	23.5	5.3		492.9
Identifiable assets	2,758.1	779.3	365.4		3,902.8
Depreciation and amortization expense	110.8	8.8	14.0		133.6
Capital expenditures	310.1	23.4	22.3		355.8

Exhibit 7

ANHEUSER-BUSCH COMPANIES, INC., AND SUBSIDIARIES
1978–1983 Financial Summary—Balance Sheet and Other Information
(millions, except per share and statistical data)

	1982	*1981*	*1980*	*1979*	*1978*
Balance sheet information:					
Working capital	$ 45.8	$ 45.9	$ 26.3	$ 88.1	$ 223.7
Current ratio	1.1	1.1	1.1	1.3	1.8
Plant and equipment, net	$2,988.9	$2,257.6	$1,947.4	$1,461.8	$1,109.2
Long-term debt	$ 969.0	$ 817.3	$ 743.8	$ 507.9	$ 427.3
Total debt to total debt plus equity	35.4% (1)	42.4%	43.4%	36.0%	36.4%
Deferred income taxes	$ 455.1	$ 357.7	$ 261.6	$ 193.8	$ 146.9
Common stock and other shareholders' equity	$1,526.6	$1,206.8	$1,031.4	$ 904.3	$ 747.9
Return on shareholders' equity	19.9%	19.3%	17.8%	16.9% (2)	15.6%
Total assets	$3,902.8	$2,875.2	$2,449.7	$1,926.0	$1,648.0
Other information:					
Capital expenditures	$ 355.8	$ 421.3	$ 590.0	$ 432.3	$ 228.7
Depreciation and amortization	133.6	108.7	99.4	75.4	66.0
Total payroll cost	853.3	686.7	594.1	529.1	421.8
Effective tax rate	39.4%	33.1%	36.7%	34.6%	46.0%
Pro forma information assuming retroactive application of the flow-through method of accounting for the investment tax credit (3):					
Net income (4)	$ 287.3	$ 217.4	$ 171.8	$ 144.3	$ 121.9
Net income per share (4)					
Primary	5.97	4.79	3.80	3.19	2.70
Fully diluted	5.88	4.61	3.80	3.19	2.70
Common stock and other shareholders' equity	1,526.6	1,206.8	1,031.4	904.3	800.1
Return on shareholders' equity	19.9%	19.3%	17.8%	16.9%	16.1%
Book value per share	$ 31.61	$ 26.57	$ 22.83	$ 19.98	$ 17.72
Effective tax rate	39.4%	33.1%	36.7%	34.6%	40.8%

Notes to 10-year financial summary—balance sheet and other information:

(1) This percentage has been calculated by including redeemable preferred stock as part of equity because it is convertible into common stock and is trading primarily on its equity characteristics.

(2) This percentage has been adjusted to reflect the change in the method of accounting for the investment tax credit in 1979 but excludes the cumulative effect.

(3) Effective January 1, 1979, the company adopted the flowthrough method of accounting for the investment tax credit. In prior years, the company followed the practice of adding investment tax credit to income over the productive lives of the assets generating such credit, rather than in the year in which the assets were placed in service. Accordingly, such benefits deferred in prior years are being added to income in the current year.

(4) Includes the capitalization of interest effective January 1, 1980, that relates to the capital cost of acquiring certain fixed assets.

businesses, Anheuser-Busch Companies is pursuing its strategy through diversification, vertical integration activities, and the development of new business areas internally which have constituted the major diversification thrust in the past.

Diversification Strategy

28 As the premier beer producer in the world, what do you do for an encore? Jerry E. Ritter, vice president-finance and treasurer, acknowledged in 1980 that "beer earn-

ings and share growth may slow as we approach our long-term 40 percent market share goal." Anheuser-Busch is planning for the future, he said "by getting our feet wet in new business areas, not massive diversification efforts." The company has coined the term *learning probe* to describe its incremental approach to diversification.

29 Hoping to trade on its established strength in producing and marketing packaged beverages, the company extended its first learning probe into the soft-drink industry. Root 66 root beer was test marketed in five major cities in 1979. After two years of testing in the industry dominated by Coca-Cola and Pepsi, President Busch remarked, "We've learned it's a competitive jungle out there, just like us and Miller in the brewing industry." On October 7, 1981, Anheuser-Busch quietly announced it was suspending further test marketing of Root 66.

30 A second learning probe for Anheuser-Busch has been salted snack foods with their Eagle snacks. Initially the superpremium snack line was sold through on-premise outlets in market testing. The company's powerful distribution system of 950 beer wholesalers which has fleets of trucks and established relationships with bars, restaurants, and supermarkets was deemed a key strength for entry into this market. The size of the salted-snack market was more than $6.5 billion at the retail level—unit volume growth was over 6 percent in 1981.

31 Frito-Lay, a PepsiCo division, which dominates in salted snack foods, claims 35 percent of the potato chip market. Otherwise, the salted-snack market is very fragmented. Supermarkets account for about 60 percent of salted-snack sales, and convenience stores represent another 9 percent of sales.

32 Eagle snacks sales have been encouraging in ½-ounce bags and 1¾-ounce tins—primarily in airport lounges, in Amtrak train bars, and on several airlines. These lines carry sizable profit margins.[2] But competing with Frito-Lay at retail outlets is much more difficult. Frito-Lay has a substantial delivery system bolstered by its Pepsi network, and a steady stream of new products, resulting in fast turnover—a considerable enticement for retailers. And other big snack companies, such as the recently merged Standard Brands and Nabisco, Inc., have invested substantial resources without visible inroads into Frito-Lay's turf.

33 Anheuser-Busch's third major diversification arena is its entertainment division. The company has operated Busch Gardens in Tampa, Florida, since 1959. The 300-acre African theme park has consistently been one of the most popular family attractions in Florida with approximately 3 million visitors each year. In 1975, the Old Country was opened in Williamsburg, Virginia. This 17th-century European theme park occupies 360 acres and entertains approximately 2 million guests annually.

34 Building on its expertise developed through the operation of these parks, Anheuser-Busch established a joint venture with Children's Television Workshop, the creator of "Sesame Street" educational television programs. In the summer of 1980, the result of this collaboration was unveiled with the opening of the first Sesame Place park just north of Philadelphia. This innovative entertainment concept features contemporary entertainment for families, including science exhibits, computer games, and outdoor play elements instead of the traditional theme-park concept. The primary advantage of this new approach to family entertainment is its relative cost advantage: The parks require only a small fraction of land compared to the theme parks (15 acres

[2] The Eagle line has over 11 products, including honey-roasted peanuts, lattice-style potato chips, tortilla chips with nacho cheese flavor, and pretzels.

in Philadelphia), and elaborate amusement rides are not included. A 30.3 acre Sesame Place was opened in Dallas/Ft. Worth in the summer of 1982.

35 In 1982, Anheuser-Busch Entertainment Corporation played host to 6.3 million guests, but profits were down from previous years. Company representatives considered the decline a temporal one caused by a sluggish economy.

36 Anheuser-Busch plans to continue expansion of its entertainment division in order to benefit from the demographic changes predicted for the 1980s. The company believes the theme parks and Sesame Place parks have a relatively strong appeal among the adult and preteen segments of the population. These segments are expected to be among the fastest-growing age groups for the remainder of the decade.

International Expansion

37 The final probe in Anheuser-Busch's diversification strategy, one requiring less capital than the others, was international expansion. Industry experts were not optimistic about Anheuser-Busch's prospects as an international brewer. Foreign protective tariffs and laws would make exported beers or brews produced in an Anheuser-Busch plant overseas prohibitively expensive to consumers. "Besides," remarked one beer marketing expert, "what makes them think foreigners crave American beer?"

38 Despite the experts' pessimism, Anheuser-Busch entered the Canadian market in 1980, aligning itself with John LaBatt, Ltd., the second-largest brewer in that country. Although most foreign beers tend to be heavier than American brews, market research by the company indicated Budweiser could be sold on its own merits, one of which was that it was well known to Canadians. In retrospect, one competitor said, "They've got to have stressed the overflow of U.S. television advertising (into Canadian markets) in their planning." By 1981, Budweiser was pulling close to 7 percent of the market in Ontario, surpassing even the most-optimistic predictions of their marketing executives.

39 In discussing Anheuser-Busch's interest in international diversification, industry analysts maintain that the company's preeminent market position in the United States allows and even compels it to diversify abroad. Andrew Melvick, an analyst at Drexel Burnham Lambert, Inc., noted, "They're running out of space here; its as simple as that."

40 As the first American brewer to enter the world beer market, Anheuser-Busch is positioning itself in a market four times larger than the U.S. market. The company's strategy for market entry has been to enter into licensing agreements with foreign brewers, allowing the company to circumvent import and tariff regulations to keep the price of their product within a feasible range and utilize the existing distribution system of its overseas affiliates. Exhibit 8 lists the current foreign markets and licenses for Anheuser-Busch products. Other licensing arrangements are pending with several Third World countries, Sweden, and the People's Republic of China.

Campbell Taggart, Inc.

41 In October 1982, Anheuser-Busch made its first major diversification away from beer with the acquisition of Campbell Taggart, Inc., the nation's second-largest bakery firm. This represented a significant strategic shift for Anheuser-Busch as all its previous diversification efforts had focused on internally generated new products.

42 Anheuser-Busch paid $36 each for about half of Campbell Taggart's 15 million shares

Exhibit 8

Anheuser-Busch around the world

Market	*Licensee*	*Date introduced*	*Name of product*
Canada	Labatt's, Ltd.	June 1980	Budweiser
France	SEB (BSN sub.)	March 1982	Busch
Japan	Suntory, Ltd.	1984 (1980 import)	Budweiser
Israel	General Brewing	1984	Name not determined.

Import market	*Product*
Japan	Budweiser
Trust territories (including Guam)	Budweiser, Budweiser Light, Michelob, Michelob Light, Natural Light
American Samoa	Budweiser, Budweiser Light, Michelob, Michelob Light, Natural Light
England	Budweiser
Chile	Budweiser
Sweden	Budweiser
New Zealand	Budweiser

Source: "Anheuser-Busch Goes Flat in Europe but Scores in Canada, Japan," *Advertising Age,* February 14, 1983, p. 12+.

and converted the rest into a new Anheuser-Busch convertible preferred stock. Including the assigned redemption value, the acquisition cost Anheuser-Busch approximately $570 million.

43 Wall Street's initial reaction to the merger of the two premier companies in their fields was mixed. Although both are considered the low-cost producers in their industries, the profit margins for Campbell Taggart are only about 3.6 percent compared to the 5.6 percent margin Anheuser-Busch gets from beer, and the acquisition was expected to dilute 1983 earnings. However, some industry analysts deemed the acquisition a "tremendous fit." Emanuel Goldman of Sanford C. Bernstein & Co. stated "this makes sense." As the nation's largest yeast supplier, Anheuser-Busch "knows Campbell Taggart and the baking industry extremely well, and they are well positioned to handle a major acquisition."

44 Several of Campbell Taggart's strengths may have attracted Anheuser-Busch. The bakery company has invested heavily in the last five years (approximately $50 million annually) to maintain modern plants and equipment and has a strong distribution system, particularly in the healthy Sun Belt market. This strength may aid Anheuser-Busch in marketing its new Eagle line of snack foods.

45 In 1981, Campbell Taggart's net income was $41.7 million ($2.50 per share) on sales of $1.26 billion, while Anheuser-Busch earnings per share were $4.79 on net income of $217.4 million. The Dallas-based Campbell Taggart has been averaging a 17 percent return on equity for the past five years—the same as Anheuser-Busch.

46 The baking industry is fragmented and highly competitive. Campbell Taggart's strategy has been market segmentation and product diversification while avoiding entry into the more highly competitive and saturated New York and Chicago markets. The company offers a wide array of baked products under such labels as Rainbow, Earth Grains, and Honey Grain in addition to refrigerated dough products, frozen foods,

refrigerated salad dressings, snack dips and toppings, and prepared sandwiches for retail and food-service customers.

47 The future of the food-processing industry is promising. The cost of raw materials has leveled off, and growth is expected in the 12 percent to 14 percent range in the near future. Higher rates of growth are expected for expensive products due to changing consumer tastes. The rising number of women in the work force is also expected to produce a positive impact on industry sales.

48 Industry analysts now claim that Anheuser-Busch may have struck a bargain in their purchase of Campbell Taggart, because they paid only a 15 percent premium over the market price. From the standpoint of Anheuser-Busch's goal of diversification, this acquisition will decrease their level of dependence on beer alone. Corporate earnings from nonbeer operations were expected to rise from 10 percent to 20 percent by the end of 1983 as a result of the acquisition.

Future Directions

49 Anheuser-Busch plans to continue looking for growth opportunities beyond its primary line of business, the domestic beer market. American's beer consumption is expected to decline as the population ages, and Anheuser-Busch is planning to expand its diversification efforts through further acquisitions and internal expansion. Although the company's international beer operations and snack-food line are still a "drop in the barrel," Busch believes their growth potential is greater than that for domestic beer sales.

50 Anheuser-Busch's primary objective is well-planned and well-managed growth. Its strategy for achieving this goal is to make other sizable acquisitions while continuing to excel in its primary line of business—beer. President Busch has stressed that Anheuser-Busch will continue to search for acquisitions in recession-resistant segments of the consumer products area which are based on a sound business strategy and fit the corporation's standards for quality products and services.

case 7
KSM/Beefalo Breeding Company: Entrepreneurial Strategies in Diversified Markets

1 "It seems that every week brings a new dimension to our business," mused George Schweiger, president of KSM Enterprises. "I wonder where we will be a year from now?" Schweiger sat reflectively at his desk gazing out the window of the log home that served as the sales office for the Beaver Log Home distributorship that KSM acquired late in the summer of 1977. He was looking across a snow-covered pasture toward the barns and livestock pens of the Clarence Korte farm. It was on this Illinois farm that Schweiger and Korte launched the Beefalo Breeding Company in April 1977 with the importation of 40 head of half-blooded beefalo from California. After less than a year of operation in their two businesses, the management team of Schweiger and Korte were considering diversification into yet another distinct enterprise—fast-food restaurants.

Events Leading to the New Businesses

2 The business experience of George Schweiger, which spans 30 years, has been primarily that of a salesman, promoter, and entrepreneur. For 13 years, he was in the insurance business, for 7 years, in the construction business, part of which involved site location/acquisition, contractor negotiations, and equipment installations for the Bonanza Steak House chain of restaurants in the Seattle region. About 11 years ago, he relocated in Illinois as the national marketing director for a new firm specializing in outdoor lighting systems. From this position, he spun off a new firm involved in custom plastic packaging. Eventually, this enterprise diversified toward end products by manufacturing nonprescription pharmaceuticals and cosmetics. Schweiger's function in the above two businesses was in *sales management.* Five years ago, he switched into brokerage consulting, specializing in diamonds and bulk Scotch whiskey. After two years in the brokerage business, he organized a company to develop an organic fertilizer produced from a bacterial blend of decomposing sawdust. It was through this agricultural venture that he developed a working relationship with Clarence Korte, an experienced organic farmer and dairy rancher.

This case was prepared by Curtis W. Cook of San Jose State University.

3 Clarence Korte, after retiring from military service in 1956, joined his brother Ralph to start the Korte Construction Company. Currently this construction firm is one of the largest in southern Illinois with several multimillion dollar contracts for industrial and commercial buildings. However, in 1962, Clarence decided to leave management involvement in Korte Construction and return to his family's tradition in farming. In partnership with his brother, Clarence developed a large Holstein dairy herd and converted to all-organic farming on the 520-acre farm near Pocahontas, about 40 miles east of St. Louis. In November 1976, fire destroyed most of the physical plant of the dairy operation, causing an estimated $350,000 loss. Rather than rebuild for dairy production, the Kortes liquidated all dairy assets in February 1977. Clarence was intrigued by the economic and nutritional superiorities of beefalo (a bison-bovine hybrid) over conventional beef cattle. In conjunction with George Schweiger, the Kortes decided to venture into this new breed of livestock. Thus, Beefalo Breeding Company was formed as the start of a herd buildup in the spring of 1977.

4 While the calamity of a fire provided the circumstances that cleared the way for entry into beefalo production, the log home business began more as a marketing outgrowth of another product line sold through KSM Enterprises. KSM was also established in 1977 when Schweiger, who has a penchant for novel products, brought to the new firm the distributorship for a European-produced, low-temperature radiant heating system. The product is a system of conductive foil sealed in sheet plastic that is stapled to ceiling framing prior to installation of drywall, plasterboard, or acoustical tile. Out of a desire to have a means of displaying and demonstrating the product, the possibility of selling and/or constructing homes was considered. Management quickly narrowed the search to becoming a distributor for some manufacturer of precut log homes, and Beaver Log Homes of Grand Island, Nebraska, was selected.

5 Thus, by the end of their first year of investment/management association, Schweiger and Korte had established their two principal businesses as log home sales and beefalo breeding/production. Yet serious challenges remained as to the desired direction and rate of future growth, with capital availability a chronic constraint.

Managerial Roles

6 In seeking to define alternatives relative to these challenges, the two principals in these joint enterprises have informally evolved specialized roles. Clarence Korte, with experience in construction and livestock/farming management, concentrates on production-related tasks. This involves not only management of the livestock operation but also supervision of erecting log structures and constructing whatever finishing touches are desired by the purchaser of a log home or barn.

7 George Schweiger tends to the sales and financial side of the business. Included in his role are direct selling/merchandising of both log homes and beefalo as well as promoting investments in beefalo under a variety of tax-sheltered programs. Schweiger acknowledges that he is a dreamer and promoter of ideas and novel concepts:

> Probably the greatest problem I have is going from one thing to another. I am looking for the new products, the different ideas. I have always maintained that talent is the cheapest commodity that can be obtained. Sure, good talent is expensive, but in relationship to its performance, it is a value. My feeling has always been that if I can get it together, so to speak, then I'll find somebody

> else more qualified than I to manage it. . . . So I tend to be a dreamer. If a potential product is there, it can be made to work given the proper infusion of capital and management expertise. If I have any expertise at all, I think it is in the field of taking ideas and converting them into different types of presentations for development of a business.

KSM Enterprises and the Beaver Log Home Contract

8 KSM Enterprises, Inc., was incorporated on March 1, 1977, with 300,000 no-par shares authorized (although franchise taxes were paid on only 100,000 shares). An initial equity capitalization of approximately $87,000 was obtained with investments from Korte equal to 29.2 percent of the total, Schweiger with 26.5 percent, one silent investor with 32 percent, and six others totaling 12.3 percent. As of December 31, 1977, book value was 87 cents per share. During its formative period, KSM relied on borrowed funds to provide partial financing of physical facilities and periodically to supply working capital. One year from date of incorporation, debt financing totaled approximately $35,000.

9 Schweiger brought to KSM the radiant heating system with which he had been involved for about eight months prior to incorporation. In deciding to expand the product line to include the home in which the heating system could be installed, he did not want the newly established KSM to compete directly with more-experienced companies. Speaking in February 1978, Schweiger explained:

> We just didn't want to go out and start building stick-built homes, so we started to explore the log home market and found that everything indicated that it was probably the fastest-growing segment of the building market. We felt that there was an opportunity here. Three years ago, there probably wasn't a log home—other than Abe Lincoln's cabin up at Salem—within a 50-mile radius of here. Today there are probably a dozen.

10 With a determination to enter into a distinctly different segment of the construction industry, after researching the product, production methods, and financial capabilites of 15 log home manufacturers, management decided to negotiate with Beaver Log Homes. When asked why Beaver Log Homes was selected over other manufacturers, Schweiger stated:

> Principally, because our studies of other companies indicated to us that both from the standpoint of the finished product as well as the overall financial strength and capabilities of the firm, Beaver offered to us and to the consumer the best log home on the market today for the price. There is a log home superior to Beaver, cut from Michigan white cedar, but it is not the home for the average buyer. So we just felt that Beaver was by far the best company to deal with.

11 The contract gave KSM dealership rights to all of southern Illinois, including the right for KSM to contract for subdealers in communities throughout that part of the state. One contract provision required KSM to build either a log home or log office building to serve as a demonstration model. Since the Korte farmland was adjacent to I-70 (a major interstate connecting the St. Louis metropolitan region to points east), management decided to erect a log office facility adjacent to the interstate where

it would be clearly visible from both directions, even though exits and the closest commercial activities are approximately two miles from the site. The nearest community with light industrial firms is Highland, about five miles to the southwest.

12 Under terms of the contract with Beaver, KSM will receive a 27.5 percent discount from list price if they equal or exceed the purchase of 50,000 lineal feet of logs annually. Additionally, quarterly quotas are to be met or the margin will be reduced. For each quarter that quotas are met, an additional 2 percent production bonus (beyond 27.5 percent) is awarded.

Marketing of Log Homes

13 Beaver sells log homes principally on the basis of logs precut for several types of basic floor plans, both one- and two-story homes. The design of an average-sized Beaver Log Home requires 2,359 lineal feet of logs, with the suggested retail price for logs about $8,300. Custom design is possible as log construction is not limited to size or shape of floor design, although height is limited without cross-tie structural support. Clarence Korte, for example, built and custom designed a 3,100-square-foot home for his family. Logs are cut and number coded (to match blueprint designs) at the mill in Claremore, Oklahoma, and transported directly by truck to the building site.

14 KSM sells on a cash basis with 30 percent down payment required either from the individual purchaser or the subdealer at the time the contract is signed. The remainder is due at the time logs are delivered. KSM will help prospective customers work with local banks or S&Ls to arrange mortgage financing. For individuals purchasing within about a 100-mile radius of Highland, Illinois, KSM will erect the log home shell on the owner's foundation if the owner/builder so desires. Clarence Korte assembles and supervises a crew of laborers for this purpose on an as-needed basis. KSM will also provide whatever finishing the customer desires. Once a contract is signed, the normal delivery schedule is 45 days for delivery, with 15 days variance according to the mill's cutting schedule.

15 KSM engages in little newspaper advertising. The parent does advertise in some trade magazines and popular home-related magazines (for example, *Better Homes and Gardens*). KSM primarily relies on local home shows as a means of achieving exposure and creating interest. For such purposes, an 8-foot by 10-foot display booth (constructed of Beaver logs) is erected at the show site. The principal costs of such promotional activity is the show promotional fee and the labor cost of someone to work at the booth distributing free brochures, talking to those who pass by, and selling to interested parties a $3 book of Beaver plans and specifications for standard model homes. Promotional fees are for advertising of the home show, typically for radio spots which might run from $280 to $560 for 40 to 120 spots that promote both the show and the sponsor (in this case KSM's Beaver Homes).

16 Because of the vastness of the franchised sales territory, KSM management intends to sell primarily through contracts with builders/dealers who represent one to three county areas. KSM will discount logs to subdealers or contract builders from 5 percent to 22.5 percent off list price, depending on expected sales volume of the dealer. Such a practice would reduce the pressures on Schweiger to personally be responsible for direct selling to individual home owners.

17 For KSM to qualify for the 27.5 percent operating margin discount, approximately 24 average-size homes of 2,050 lineal feet need to be sold annually with about 20

per year necessary to break even. Such an average size (based on Beaver sales statistics) represents a value of $7–$8,000 each. Logs represent 18–25 percent of the total cost of the house, with 20 percent considered a rule of thumb. Other cost factors include foundation or basement, plumbing, heating systems, electrical, doors and windows, and so on.

18 After the first six months of the Beaver dealership, KSM had sold three homes. By February 1979 (after 1½ years), a total of 18 log buildings had been sold, and bids were out on 15 additional plans.

Beefalo as a New Meat Source

19 Beefalo are a hybrid bison/bovine cross-developed to impart the growth advantages of bison (buffalo) into meat production animals that would have color, confirmation (shape), and edible characteristics similar to beef cattle. A successful breed was first announced in 1973 by developer D. C. "Bud" Basolo, after years of experimentation and breeding up to arrive at a pureblood sire. A pureblood beefalo is defined as three eights American bison and five eights domestic bovine (typically three eights Charolais and two eights Hereford). Several production advantages are claimed for beefalo over beef.

20 1. Beefalo calves are smaller at birth (approximately 45–65 pounds compared to 80–105 pounds for cattle). Thus, less assistance and care are necessary at birth resulting in lower losses (deaths), especially on open ranges.

21 2. Beefalo are believed heartier than cattle, able to withstand greater temperature extremes and less prone to sickness. Historically, buffalo herds roamed from Canada to Mexico, and prior to man, their principal adversary was the predator (wolves, coyotes, and so forth). Calves are able to run approximately four hours after birth regardless of weather conditions.

22 3. Beefalo mature more quickly than beef. Animals mature to a slaughter weight (approximately 1,000–1,100 pounds) in about 12 months compared to about 18 months for beef.

23 4. Beefalo convert feed to flesh more efficiently than beef and require less grain for finishing. A test conducted by Dr. Gary C. Smith at Texas A&M University in 1976 statistically confirmed the superior productive efficiency of 486 head of beefalo compared to bovine control groups. Among some of Dr. Smith's findings, one pen of cattle on a feed ration of 14 percent roughage and 86 percent concentrate (corn, rolled oats, soy meal, and so on), over a 120-day period for finishing prior to slaughter, gained an average 2.55 pounds per day at a feed cost of 47 cents per pound. Beefalo which were on a 26 percent roughage ration averaged a gain of 2.71 pounds per day at the same 47 cents cost. Those beefalo on a 36 percent roughage produced an average daily gain of .5 to .7 of a pound more (3.21 to 3.41) at a cost of 37 cents per pound.

24 5. Buffalo yield a proportionately higher percentage of meat to live weight. This results from more energy being converted into muscle tissue rather than fat. In the A&M study, all beefalo carcasses were federally graded in yield grade 2, the most-favored yield grade of producers since excess fat is minimal yet the meat tissue is bright in color and well conformed (blocky rather than thin and rangy). As a percentage of dressed carcass to live weight, the beefalo averaged 63 percent compared to a typical 59–61 percent yield for steers or English-bred cattle. Dr. Smith commented, "Based on my experience of 15 years' work in this field, they (beefalo) have remarkable dressing

percentages, and it is due to the fact that they are muscular, extremely muscular in relation to other cattle."

25 Considered as food for human consumption, beefalo test out favorably in terms of nutritional value relative to beef. The following data from Certified Labs, Inc., 19 Hudson St., New York, (USDA Certified Laboratory #3677) are representative of comparative analysis of beefalo (ground) and ground beef as purchased in supermarkets:

	Lot Dec 484 ground beefalo	*Lot Dec 483 ground beef*
Protein	20.35%	16.67%
Fat	3.65%	24.80%
Calories	32.4/ounce	82.4/ounce
Cholesterol	5.19 mg./ounce	150.5 mg./ounce

Beefalo Breeding Company's Production Operations

26 Within one year of its inception, Beefalo Breeding company developed the largest herd of beefalo in the Midwest. Most of the 520 acres on the Korte brothers farm are devoted to organic farming of feed grains for feed fattening and finishing of livestock. Since 1970, the farm has been entirely organic, eliminating the use of chemical fertilizers, herbicides, and pesticides. The farm carries organic certification and is one of two selected by Dr. Barry Commoner of Washington University for comparative studies between chemical and ecological farming. This farm has a capacity for producing grain and alfalfa capable of finishing approximately 800 head per year on the basis of a quarterly turnover (90-day finishing). The Korte farm itself is not intended for extensive grazing, as all but about 65 acres is cultivated farmland. Currently, there are four grain storage tanks adjacent to the feedlot, each capable of holding approximately 65 tons of feed.

27 The company is incorporated separate from KSM with Schweiger and the Korte brothers as the stockholders. It is a member of both the World Beefalo Association (California) and the American Beefalo Association (Kentucky), organizations concerned with registering breeders and developing performance data on the various beefalo blood lines. Beefalo Breeding Company is under a management/feeding contract with the Korte farm for the feeding and care of the herd. Under terms of the arrangement, the corporation pays Korte 27.5 cents per pound of weight gain which provides an adequate return to the Korte farm. If Holsteins or Herefords were being fattened instead of beefalo, a fee of at least 35 cents per pound would be necessary for the farm to obtain a similar return. This difference is because of the genetic advantage of beefalo which have the same digestive tract as buffalo, a more efficient converter of feed.

28 Beefalo Breeding Company prefers to place 800- to 850-pound beefalo (after grass feeding) into the feedlot for 60–90 days. A 12- to 15-bushel hot feed ration (of rolled oats, corn, crushed wheat, soy meal, and so forth) will produce white marbling and exterior fat suitable to yield a choice quality grade (the most-used grade in major supermarkets) and a quantity-yield grade of 2.

29 To accommodate grassland feeding, Beefalo Breeding Company bought a 670-acre ranch located in south-central Missouri, near Salem (valued at $300,000). The 540 acres of pastureland in this ranch, once improved, will be capable of supporting a 300–350-head beefalo cow-calf operation. While the first year of business saw a buildup to 130 animals at the Illinois facility, in April 1978, the first 124 head were delivered to the Missouri ranch. This herd was purchased from a breeder in Pauls Valley, Oklahoma, at a cost of $38,000 delivered, financed through an open-end bank note.

Marketing Beefalo

30 While beefalo is subject to the same grading process as beef, in February 1978, the meat division of the USDA issued basic guidelines to their field graders that would certify beefalo as a separate class of animals from beef. Having this classification enables beefalo to be marketed as distinct from beef, although in practice, it can be sold through supermarkets as beef since the consumer would not discern the difference.

31 Since beefalo are a relatively new breed of livestock, on a national basis herd sizes remain small. To build up herds, most breeders retain heifers for calf production and sell off as slaughter animals young bulls/bullocks (most breeding is through artificial insemination from registered pureblood bulls). This scarcity of slaughter animals enables beefalo producers generally to command a premium price for their meat, usually about 10 cents per pound over comparable beef carcass grades. Organically produced and certified meat of any kind also usually commands a higher price because of presumed health advantages.

32 By late March 1978, Beefalo Breeding Company had 30 head ready for slaughter (1,100–1,200 pounds each), the first in any quantity for retail sale. At this time, the Chicago Board of Trade price quote for choice beef was in the $46–48 range, liveweight basis. Schweiger and Korte both expressed disillusion with conventional meat distribution systems, since the producer essentially is a price taker. For this reason, they explored alternative marketing approaches. Schweiger remarked:

> We are not in accord with the current marketing methods of the agricultural industry. We think they are controlled too much by speculators. If we can control our production cost and go directly to the consumer with the finished product, we can reap the profits currently enjoyed by the speculators as opposed to the producers.

33 Since Beefalo Breeding had not previously slaughtered more than one or two animals at a time, they had no regular clientele or distribution procedures. Several alternatives were thus explored. Schweiger phoned Nelson Name Service in Minneapolis to see if they could compile lists of all of the health food stores and Weight Watchers Clubs in Illinois. Packages of frozen select retail cuts (steaks, roasts, ground beefalo) could be sold to health food stores. To Weight Watchers, the intent would be to sell halves or quarters of beefalo, either in fresh carcass form or cut and frozen. Beefalo Breeding Company also was contacted by a New York beefalo firm asking if it would be possible to purchase slaughter-ready livestock. Although the New York firm was smaller in actual numbers of beefalo, they had an established promotional and distribution system (selling direct to consumers in halves and quarters).

34 Schweiger also contacted area supermarket chains to explore the feasibility of a

special beefalo promotion. In talking with the manager of meat operations with the National Supermarket chain (which had a large share of the market in the St. Louis area), the idea was readily acceptable. However, to be able to use beefalo as a promotional item, National would require at least 300 head since they followed a policy of uniform advertising within a metropolitan market.

35 Another option was to have approximately 80 percent of the carcass ground into hamburger patties to build up a supply pending the opening of Beefalo Barns restaurants (details noted in future section). The remaining 20 percent (steaks only) would be packaged in 10-pound units, frozen, and sold through local promotion.

36 However, because these animals had to go to slaughter (additional feeding would result in minimal salable weight gain), Schweiger in April made arrangements to supply five IGA markets (local independents) in Peoria, Illinois, with 14 head for a special sale. The price was 10 cents per pound dressed weight over choice beef. Additionally, in a reciprocal arrangement with a Springfield, Illinois, radio station, Beefalo Breeding Company sold livestock directly to a Springfield packer with the radio station advertising the availability of beefalo halves and quarters. The advertising was at no direct cost to the company since Clarence Korte had supplied an electrical power generator to the radio station when an ice storm in late March knocked out their power source and forced them off the air. Schweiger saw these market sources more as temporary, although he recognized residual value in *(a)* exposing the public to beefalo, *(b)* possibly attracting some wealthy investors into tax-sheltered partnerships of herds under management contract to Beefalo Breeding Company, or *(c)* attracting potential investors to the fast-foods concept of Beefalo Barns.

The Need for Outside Capital

37 While developing markets (at a premium price) for fattened livestock consumed part of Schweiger's time, most of his energy during 1978 was devoted to developing a variety of prospecti for attracting equity investors or debt capital. Additional capital was desired for three purposes: *(a)* to build up herd size to fully utilize the feedlot capacity and/or provide adequate meat supply for six restaurants, *(b)* to launch a fast-food restaurant operation through general partnerships, franchising, and/or stock placement, and *(c)* to lease and/or purchase additional pastureland where beefalo could graze until reaching an appropriate feedlot weight.

38 Schweiger worked with two firms that might be able to attract investors interested in the tax-sheltering prospects of livestock. He held several meetings during 1978 with the St. Louis office senior tax partner of Peat, Marwick, Mitchell and with a principal in the Investment Planning Group of Clayton, Missouri. The intent of working with these firms was to pull together a group of investors with sufficient capital for one or more large herds of beefalo. Schweiger explained the basics of one of his proposals:

> If we had 100 per herd, we would sell an absentee owner group the animals and manage the herd under the contract. With this arrangement we would not need anyone's money (for working capital). We would have all our own. The basic annual fee would be $350 per year per cow. There would be a $300 maintenance cost on the cow plus a $50 breeding fee. We would maintain the cow with her calf until the calf was weaned and then prorate the remaining number

of months (to anniversary date of contract) against the $300 maintenance fee for the offspring. We would assume all feeding costs and charge outside veterinarian fees. If the investing group wanted insurance, it would be their responsibility. The annual management-maintenance fees would be paid in advance.

A 100-head partnership program would require a total capital investment of $204,000. If we had one partner in a 40–50 percent tax bracket, let's say with a 5 percent participation, he would initially invest $10,200. In the first year, he would write off 85 percent of his capital contribution against his income tax (for paper losses since there is no revenue inflow). In the second year, against his cash contribution, he will write off 188 percent against his taxes; the fourth year, 444 percent; and from the fourth year on, the partnership is actually in an income-producing position. But from an investor's viewpoint, the front-end years provide a tremendous write-off against personal income tax. The net result of a seven-year program, based on current prices of animals, would be a net cash accumulation in excess of $2 million if the herd is liquidated. Although programmed to terminate at the end of the seventh year, in reality there would be no good reason to liquidate unless the limited partners wanted their capital to invest in another program that would have an accelerated depreciation schedule.

39 Finding it difficult to put together tax-sheltered partnerships in the magnitude mentioned above, Schweiger toward year-end 1978 began promoting smaller programs, based on a minimum of 10 head. Such programs would involve a first-year cash outlay of approximately $11,000 for 10 heifer (female) beefalo. This proposal included many of the features of previous ones (that is, describing beefalo, the principle of breeding up, advantages of starting with half-blood heifers, risk factors, and management), although in less detail. Exhibits 1–A through 1–D present some of the agreement forms and financial projections for this type of program.

The Beefalo Barns (Fast-Food) Concept

40 Most of the conventional marketing alternatives available to Beefalo Breeding Company represent variations of the beef distribution system. The company is committed to breed and produce beefalo, but it seeks a market outlet that preserves the identity of beefalo and provides a premium price. When asked if his proposed development of a new fast-food chain was viewed as a means of controlling disposition of the end

No, I see the restaurant alternative as a completely separate program, with beefalo as a catalyst for a restaurant chain—for a franchised chain—as opposed to setting up one or two restaurants just to get into the restaurant business. The ultimate limitation with the restaurant concept is that it cannot enjoy the accelerated growth that potentially might be there because there simply are not the animals to support it. This year we wouldn't assemble more than 50,000 head of beefalo even if we contacted every breeder in the country. But we can put together a sufficient number of animals to supply six restaurants over the next 12–18 months.

Exhibit 1–A

Sample pages of tax-shelter beefalo proposal

BEEFALO PURCHASE AGREEMENT

THIS AGREEMENT made and entered into on the ________________ day of ________________ 197__, by and between Clarence A. Korte and George D. Schweiger, d/b/a Beefalo Breeding Company, (Seller) R.R. #1, Pocahontas, Illinois 62275, and ________________________________ ("Buyer") whose mailing address is ________________________________

____

WITNESSETH:

In consideration of the mutual covenants, terms and conditions contained herein, the parties hereto do hereby agree as follows:

1. Seller agrees to sell to Buyer ________ head of one-half (½) blood registered Beefalo Breeding cattle (hereinafter referred to as the Breeding Herd) which animals are more particularly described in Exhibit A attached hereto and made a part hereof. All animals purchased shall be subject to the approval of Buyer at the time of delivery.

2. Buyer and Seller are entering into a certain Management and Marketing Agreement of even date herewith, relating to the management, maintenance and breeding of the Breeding Herd and all progeny resulting therefrom.

3. The animals in the Breeding Herd are represented and warranted to be breeders capable of being registered in either or both the World Beefalo Association (WBA) or the American Beefalo Association (ABA) and, at the option of Buyer, shall be registered in the association elected by Buyer.

4. Seller shall successfully breed each female in the Breeding Herd with semen from a pureblood Beefalo bull. Should any animal fail, after a reasonable time to settle, Seller shall replace it with a comparable animal. Any replacement or substitution of animals in the Breeding Herd shall carry the same warranties as setforth herein.

5. Buyer agrees to pay a total purchase price of one thousand five hundred ($1,500) dollars for each female in the Breeding Herd for a total purchase price of $ ________________________ .

a. The sum of six hundred ($600) dollars per female in the Breeding Herd shall be paid on the date hereof:

b. The balance of nine hundred ($900) dollars per female in the Breeding Herd shall be paid on or before January 1, 197__, provided, however, that Buyer may have the option, in lieu of making such payment, to execute and deliver to Seller a Promissory Note in the form attached hereto as Exhibit ______ in the principal amount of such balance. The Promissory Note, until the balance of the purchase price is paid, shall accrue interest at the rate of nine percent (9%) per annum, and such principal shall be paid upon the earlier of:

(1) Sale, with the consent of Buyer, of female animals (except culls) from

Exhibit 1–A *(concluded)*

Buyer's herd which are the animals purchased hereunder or their progeny (or sale of any animals in liquidation of the herd), such payment to be limited to the proceeds of such sale.

(2) Seven years from date of the execution hereof.

6. The outstanding balance of principal and interest thereon shall be secured by a security interest in all animals purchased hereunder and their progeny. Buyer agrees to execute from time to time such Financing Statements or other documents as Seller may request to perfect such security interest in the State of Illinois, Missouri and elsewhere; including, without limitation, any Uniform Commercial Code Financing Statements or renewals thereof. Buyer appoints Seller as Buyer's attorney-in-fact to execute and file any such documents.

7. In the event Seller shall default under the Management and Marketing Agreement and as a result of such default Buyer as Owner terminates said Agreement, Buyer shall nevertheless remain obligated to satisfy the Note.

8. In the event that Buyer terminates this Agreement during the first three calendar years, he will pay to the Company 50% of the progeny value as additional fees. Determination of the value of the progeny shall be made by an independent third party selected and mutually agreed upon by both parties hereto.

9. All representations, conditions, warranties and agreements setforth herein shall survive delivery of title and Buyer acknowledges that there have been no representations, expressed or implied, except as setforth herein.

10. This Purchase Agreement, the Management and Marketing Agreement, the Security Agreement and the Note constitute the entire understanding between the parties hereto with respect to the subject matter hereof. Any changes, amendments or deletions must be in writing and signed by the parties to this Agreement.

This Agreement shall be interpreted in accordance with the laws of the State of Illinois.

IN WITNESS WHEREOF the parties have set their hands and seals this ____________ day of ______________ 197______.

Buyer ________________________ Seller ____________________________

41 The concept that Schweiger began exploring early in 1978 was to develop distinctiveness in fast foods both through product and building design. His idea was to extend the log home concept into a restaurant building structure constructed of Beaver logs. The menu would feature beefalo burgers in several sizes as a means of achieving product differentiation. The integration of the product and the structure would build promotion and furnishings around a western theme. Schweiger did not, however, foresee thrusting a marketing appeal to specific segments, such as the health-conscious consumer. He commented, "Anyone who stops at a fast-food restaurant is a market

Exhibit 1–B

MANAGEMENT AND MARKETING AGREEMENT

THIS AGREEMENT is made and entered into on this ________ day of ____________ 197_____, by and between Clarence A. Korte and George D. Schweiger, d/b/a Beefalo Breeding Company, hereinafter referred to as Company and ____________________
whose mailing address is ____________________
__________ hereinafter referred to as "Owner."

WITNESSETH:

WHEREAS, Owner is the sole owner and operator of the Beefalo breeding livestock, hereinafter referred to as "livestock" or "animals" described in Exhibit A, which is attached hereto and made a part hereof, and,

WHEREAS, The Company is presently operating Beefalo breeding ranches in Illinois and Missouri and is experienced in the breeding management and marketing of Beefalo livestock, and,

WHEREAS, Owner desires Company to manage, breed and sell said Livestock under the terms and conditions of this Management and Marketing Agreement.

NOW THEREFORE, in consideration of the mutual promises and covenants contained here, the parties agree as follows/

1. Owner represents that he is the sole owner of the Livestock (Exh. A), subject only to the terms of the Beefalo Purchase Agreement, and a promissory note and Security Agreement referred to therein.

2. Company shall provide all management and shall maintain, care for, feed and take whatever other steps are reasonably necessary for the well-being of the Livestock and their progeny. The maintenance of the Livestock under this Agreement shall include the breeding, feeding, calving, normal veterinarian services, raising and growing out of progeny, and the keeping of breeding and identification records in connection with the Livestock. Company agrees to maintain, care for and breed the Livestock in accordance with the standard practices for a purebred Beefalo operation and in accordance with the instruction of Owner.

3. Company shall furnish owners semiannual reports regarding the status of the Livestock subject to this Agreement. In addition Company will furnish Owner, as soon as reasonably possible, data concerning any accident, illness or sickness causing the death of any of the Livestock, and a postmortem report with regard to such animal.

4. At the option of Owner and at Owner expense, Company will prepare applications for registration in Owner's name of all progeny complying with the regulations covering said registration in either or both the World Beefalo Association (WBA) or the American Beefalo Association (ABA) and shall use its best efforts to obtain a lifetime membership in the Association of Owner's choosing. Fees for membership in or the registration of progeny shall be paid by Owner and are not included in the fee due Company described in paragraph 8.

Exhibit 1–B *(continued)*

5. In order to assist Owner in its operation of its Livestock, Company shall be available periodically to consult with Owner in connection with the maintenance, care, and growth of the animals subject to this Agreement. Such advice and counsel shall be in connection with the general and special maintenance of the Livestock, the sale of progeny, the retention of progeny, the selling, culling and replacement of Livestock in the Herd, and such other matters which are incident to the husbandry of Beefalo Livestock.

6. All Livestock subject to this Agreement shall be kept and maintained at such place or places as Company determines in its sole discretion, and during the term of this Agreement, Company shall, at all times, maintain control and jurisdiction over said animals; provided Company shall advise Owner of the location thereof and they shall be available for Owner's inspection at reasonable times.

7. Company shall not be responsible or liable for any loss or damage to any of the Beefalo Livestock subject to this Agreement, on account of any accident, disease, or death, or by reason of any acts of any employee, servant, or agent of the Company, except in the event of gross negligence or willful misconduct by Company or its employees, servants or agents. However, Company shall have the right to replace or substitute any animal lost for any reason from the original Beefalo Breeding Herd, said replacement or substitution to be of comparable quality to animal(s) replaced or substituted.

8. In consideration of the Company's responsibilities, obligations and warranties hereunder, as a fee for the management of the Breeding Herd, Owner agrees to pay the Company as follows:

(1) The sum of four hundred ($400) dollars for each breeding female in the herd, said sum payable upon the date first set forth above.

(2) The sum of four hundred ($400) dollars for each breeding female in the herd, said sum payable on the date of the first anniversary of this Agreement.

(3) The sum of four hundred ($400) dollars for each breeding female in the herd, said sum payable on the date of the second anniversary of this Agreement.

(4) In addition to the fees set forth above, [para. 8 one, two & three], the Company shall receive fifty percent (50%) of all net proceeds (gross sales less expenses) derived from the sale of any animals or other income from Owners Herd during the term of this Agreement and the Beefalo Purchase Agreement as full payment for management, maintenance, breeding and other services provided by the Company.

Company and Owner agree that the net proceeds realized from the sale of animals from the Herd, income from semen sales or other income, shall be distributed between the parties as setforth below:

a. Company shall receive fifty percent (50%) of all net income as provided in paragraph 8, Art. 4 above.

Exhibit 1–B *(continued)*

b. Owner shall receive fifty percent (50%) of all net income, provided, however, that from such amount Owner shall pay to Company any interest due on the Note for the current or prior years.

9. The Company may collect and sell semen obtained from bulls in the Owners Breeding Herd. Bulls and semen from Owners Breeding Herd may be used by Company on all cattle owned or managed by Company at no cost to Company.

10. This Management Agreement shall be effective commencing the date of execution and shall continue for a period of seven years from said date, provided however, that this Agreement shall be renewed at then prevailing rates being charged new Herd owners and, otherwise, on the same terms and conditions for one additional seven-year period from and after such termination date unless either party notifies the other, in writing, prior to 90 days preceding the termination date, of its intent to terminate this Agreement. Notwithstanding the foregoing, Owner may at any time cancel this contract by 90 days' written notice to Company. Upon termination of this Agreement for any reason, all amounts owing to either party in accordance with the terms of this Agreement shall be paid on the same basis as if the Agreement were continued to the end of the quarter following the quarter in which notice is given. Owner shall be responsible for the removal of the Livestock from the place or places in which they are maintained as of the effective date of the termination, and as of such date Company shall have no further responsibilities in connection with such Livestock.

11. All notices required or permitted under the terms of this Agreement shall be delivered in person or by certified mail, postage prepaid, addressed as follows:

If to Company:

BEEFALO BREEDING COMPANY
R.R. 1
Pocahontas, Illinois 62275

If to Owner:

____

____

12. This Agreement shall be binding upon the parties hereto, their heirs, executors and administrators.

13. Any insurance with regard to the Livestock subject to this Agreement shall be paid by Owner, provided however, the Company shall use its best efforts to secure such coverage as requested by Owner.

14. The obligations of Owner under this Agreement are secured by a Security Agreement of even date herewith, and a default hereunder shall constitute a default under the Security Agreement.

Exhibit 1–B *(concluded)*

15. Company shall not be required to advance any sums on behalf of Owner, but if it does, Owner shall repay the same promptly on demand and repayment thereof shall be secured by the security interest in the livestock.

16. Owner is fully aware of the speculative nature of purchasing and managing breeding cattle and represents that his or its financial circumstances are consistent with this investment and that he or it is a sophisticated investor and by reason of his or its business and financial experience, he or it has the capacity to protect his or its own interests in connection with his or its investment.

17. This Agreement constitutes the entire agreement of the parties hereto.

IN WITNESS WHEREOF, the parties hereto have set their hands on the date and year first above written.

OWNER (s) BEEFALO BREEDING COMPANY

By ______________________ By ______________________

for us. We're not after only the teenage market, the older-age market, the afterhours disco crowd, or anything like that." However he later noted that the health aspects of beefalo might be a major selling point. "This is the message we want to get to the American people. If you're going to eat red meat, then why not eat something that's good for you."

42 To identify his project, Schweiger initially used the name Beefalo Inns, then later changed to Beefalo Barns. He spoke of the need to approach the naming of the restaurant from a scientific view but suggested that tentatively the barn concept captured the architectural style with its gabled roof atop the log structure. He was further thinking about freeway locations for the first Beefalo Barns in order to quickly expose people to the idea. "If we use freeway locations, people are adventuresome, so they're going to try it. The type of building housing our restaurant is a totally new concept in fast-food buildings. We also have a meat product that probably 99 percent of the American public still have not tasted. But it is being more widely known and advertised every day."

43 The principal feature of Beefalo Barns would be a variety of burgers. Schweiger would prefer to use all fresh meat, to achieve further product distinctiveness similar to Wendy's. He would use the Burger Chef concept of a condiment bar to allow customers to add what they like. Steaks might possibly be offered; if so, the selections probably would be a 6-ounce ground beefalo steak and an 8-ounce rib eye. Prices would be competitive but probably 10 percent over McDonald's or Burger Chef. "Basically what we want to shoot for is a $1.70 average ticket covering patties, fries, drink, and apple turnover."

44 Schweiger estimated that at least two restaurants would be necessary to test the feasibility of continued expansion. Although the first facility probably would be wholly owned, he projected moving quickly to joint venturing or franchising. "I would see

Exhibit 1–C

Three-year cash investment

Purchase of 10 beefalo breeding heifers:		
Down payment		$ 6,000.00
Management expense		4,000.00
Interest (prepaid)		810.00
Cash paid out 197__		$10,810.00
Tax effects:		
Depreciation (seven-year life–half year)	$2,142.90	
Management expense	4,000.00	
Interest expense	810.00	
Investment tax credit (10%)*	3,000.00	
Total equivalent deductions		$ 9,952.90
Second year:		
Management expense		
Interest expense		
Cash paid out 197_		$ 4,810.00
Tax effect:		
Depreciation†	$3,673.50	
Management expense	4,000.00	
Interest expense	810.00	
Total deductions		$ 8,483.50
Third year:‡		
Management expense		$ 7,000.00
Interest expense		810.00
		$ 7,810.00
Income (estimated sales $6,000 ÷ 50%)		3,000.00
Cash paid out 197_		$ 4,810.00
Tax effect:		
Depreciation	$2,623.90	
Management expense	4,000.00	
Interest expense	810.00	
Total deductions		$ 7,633.90

* Investment tax credit assumes a 50 percent tax bracket and a tax credit being the equivalent to $3,000 of standard deductions.

† Balance of depreciation is $6,559.70.

‡ No direct cash investment after third year.

getting into the fast-food business as a vehicle for a national franchise. To me, who needs the hassle of operating simply one restaurant." Six facilities were seen as a feasible target for the first year, with additional facilities limited only by the number of animals available for slaughter. He thought that one way of assuring adequate meat supply would be to involve other breeders as limited partners, stockholders, or franchisees. Schweiger noted that there are approximately 50 beefalo breeders in Kentucky and Tennessee, so that might be a natural area in which to expand. Nationally, there are breeders in the 48 continental states. (Two pages of a 10-page proposal

Exhibit 1–D

Economic projection seven-year program*

	Ordinary income	*Capital gains*	*Total*
Total sales	$90,000	$136,800	$226,800
Expenses:			
Cost of herd	15,000		15,000
Management and marketing			
Original fees	14,000		14,000
50 percent of sales	45,000	68,400	113,400
Interest	5,670		5,670
Total expenses	79,670	68,400	148,070
Net profit before taxes	10,330	68,400	78,730
Net tax liability below†			17,345
Net aftertax profit			$ 61,385
Taxes:			
Net profit before tax	$10,330	$ 68,400	$ 78,730
60 percent capital gain exclusion		41,040	41,040
Total taxable	10,330	27,360	37,690
Tax on above at 50 percent			18,845
Investment tax credit			1,500
Net tax liability (above)			$ 17,345

* Assumptions:

1. An expected 100 percent live calf crop in the first year and an 80 percent calf crop thereafter. That 50 percent are male and 50 percent are female and all females are bred and calve annually.
2. The original herd increases to 126 head, the average price is $1,800 per head, and herd liquidation takes place at the end of seven years.
3. That 40 percent of sales is ordinary income and 60 percent is capital gains.

† For the purposes of this computation, it has been assumed that the 50 percent management fee would be deducted against the proceeds to which they relate. Accordingly, a substantial portion ($68,400) has been deducted against capital gains income. Had this instead been reflected as an ordinary deduction, the net tax liability of $17,345 would have been a net refund of $3,175 or additional net aftertax profits of $20,620.

The analysis of economic benefits are based on assumptions concerning future events and present tax laws (which may be changed). Some assumptions may not occur which could have substantial effect. Therefore the actual results obtained may vary considerably from the projections.

circulated to interested breeders and parties are reproduced as Exhibits 2–A and 2–B, which include the introduction and pro forma income statement.)

45 During 1978, Schweiger entered into negotiations with property holders of several potential sites. (See map in Exhibit 3.) One site was the Pocahontas exit off I-70, about two miles from the KSM sales office and Korte farm. Preliminary studies indicated a year-round average traffic count under the interstate overpass at 11,000 cars per day in 1976 with a summer average of 13,900. The exit traffic (coming off the interstate) was 4,000 cars per day of which 20 percent was considered to be local traffic. Year-round passenger count per vehicle was 1.7, while during the months of May through September, it was 2.5. Based on these figures, Schweiger calculated that roughly 3,700 persons per day might be looking for food or other services such as gasoline. He commented: "If we can tap 15 percent of the potential traffic May through

Exhibit 2–A

Sample pages of Beefalo Barn proposal

Introduction

Beefalo Barns offers a new and exciting approach to the fast-food industry. The serving of beefalo exclusively in the atmosphere of early American log buildings combine to offer a unique dining experience for the consumer.

The format of the Beefalo Barns will combine the features of several fast-food-type restaurants and will offer both eat-in and carryout service.

The success of the so-called fast-food industry and the forecast for future growth are a phenomenon in the business world. When one considers that in 1960, just 18 years ago, there were virtually no fast-food chains, it is difficult to realize the tremendous impact these outlets have had and the amount of the consumers' food dollar that is going into their cash registers.

Most people are familiar with the golden archs of McDonald's or the goatee of Colonel Sanders, but few realize the true magnitude of their operations. McDonald's alone uses the hamburger from 20,000 head of cattle per week, Kentucky Fried Chicken uses about 7 percent of our total poultry production, and these are but two of a long and growing list of chains, that is, Wendy's, A&W, French's, Taco Bell, Zantigo, Burger Chef, Dairy Queen, Burger King, Pizza Hut, and so on.

Combined annual sales of the fast-food industry today exceed $20 million and represent about 35 percent of all food dollars.

We, at Beefalo Barns, strongly believe that there is room for one more, one that is built around a new meat called beefalo. We hope as you evaluate the balance of the material in this brochure that you will come to the same conclusion and will join with us in this new venture.

September, we can pay all our bills, gross $150,000, and lock up the place for six months if need be (the nontourist season)."

46 Negotiations were entered into for a second site, also adjacent to I-70, but several miles to the west at the Illinois 143 exit. This property is owned by King Oil Company who operates a truck stop at the off-ramp location (the only commercial establishment at the exit). The oil company tentatively would be willing to construct the building with site improvements (exclusive of interior equipment) and lease the facility to Beefalo Barns for a 10 percent return to King (lease payments estimated $6–$7,000 annually). Schweiger thought such terms to be advantageous:

> I don't see how we can go wrong in putting in the equipment and opening this location because it certainly reduces the sales volume necessary to meet the lease obligation. The other advantage obviously is that it eliminates a lot of front-end cash requirements on our part. Where we were nominally looking at probably $60–$100,000 cash up front, we are probably looking at $25–$40,000 maximum with this type of arrangement. As a pilot program, obviously the lower you can keep your cash requirements, the better off you are going to be.

Exhibit 2–B

BEEFALO BARN
Pro Forma Income and Expense
(in thousands of dollars)

	%		%		%	
Gross sales	100%	$200,000		$300,000		$400,000
Food costs	32	64,000		96,000		128,000
Gross profit	68	136,000		204,000		272,000
Operating expenses:						
Labor	22.0%	44,000	21.0%	63,000	20.0%	80,000
Employee taxes, benefits	3.0	6,000	3.0	9,000	3.0	12,000
Paper goods	4.0	8,000	4.0	12,000	4.0	16,000
Utilities	2.0	4,000	2.2	6,600	2.5	10,000
Laundry	.5	1,000	.6	1,800	.7	2,800
Advertising	1.5	3,000	1.8	5,400	2.0	8,000
Office supplies	.3	600	.4	1,200	.5	2,000
Telephone	.6	1,200	.6	1,800	.6	2,400
Legal and accounting	.5	1,000	.8	2,400	.7	2,800
Insurance	1.5	3,000	1.5	4,500	1.5	6,000
Maintenance and repairs	1.0	2,000	1.0	3,000	1.0	4,000
Miscellaneous	1.0	2,000	1.0	3,000	1.0	4,000
Total operating expenses	38.4	75,000	37.9	113,700	37.5	160,000
Fixed costs:						
Land and building		16,000		16,000		16,000
Equipment and fixtures		14,000		14,000		14,000
Total fixed costs	15.0	30,000	10.0	30,000	7.5	30,000
Total costs	85.4	169,000	79.9	239,700	77.0	318,000
Net income	14.6%	$ 31,000	20.1%	$ 60,300	23.0%	$ 82,000

Note: land and building costs can vary substantially from unit to unit. Equipment and fixtures are assuming five-year lease.

47 The King Oil site probably would be operated year-round because of the steady flow of trucks and cars that normally stop for refueling. Among other sites where investor contact had been made was one in conjunction with a sports complex at Rend Lake (seasonal resort area) and a downtown location in Mt. Vernon (year-round). (See Exhibit 3.) Schweiger indicated that a group of Illinois and St. Louis investors expressed an interest in owning the Beefalo Barn at the Mt. Vernon site:

> Tentatively we would set up ownership on a limited partnership basis, and we (Beefalo Barns, Inc.) would be the general partners. We would probably establish 50 units at $2,100 per unit, with a two-unit minimum to comply with Illinois security statutes of limiting the partnership to 25 or fewer investors. Of the $105,000 we would raise, $100,000 would be applied to the partnership capital account, and $5,000 would cover organizational expenses. We would then as a partnership acquire the land, build the facility, lease the equipment, and provide the operating capital. With such an arrangement, we would probably go in as general partners at 30–40 percent participation, with no capital contributions. The limited partners would pick up 60–70 percent with their capital contribution. As general partners, we would not participate in any partnership profits until

Exhibit 3

Proposed Beefalo Barn locations

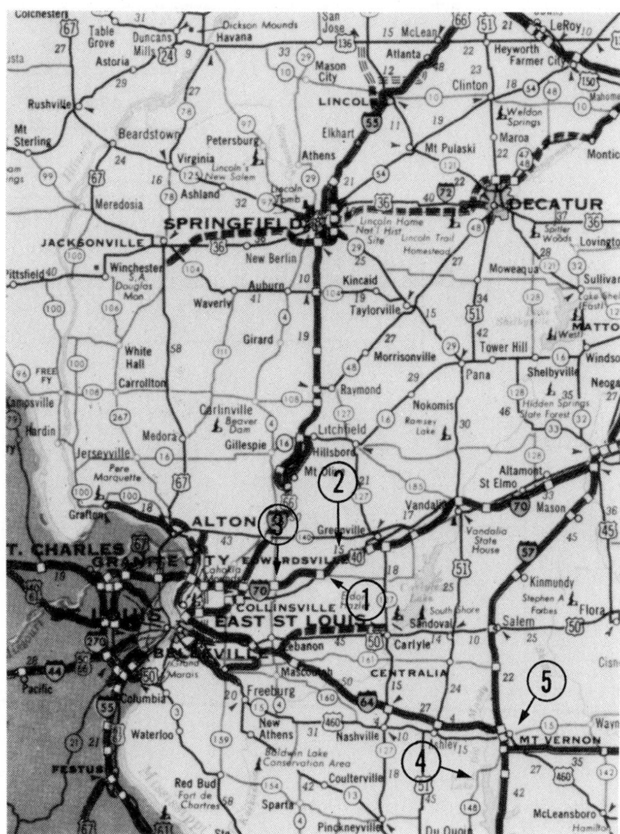

Key:
1—KSM/BBC.
2—Pocahontas.
3—King Oil.
4—Rend Lake.
5—Mt. Vernon.

all limited partners had received back their capital contributions. Once they have 100 percent return, then we participate on a proportional basis.

48 Management believes they would be unable to require large franchise fees should this be the direction of expansion. In the absence of an established record, they are considering not charging a franchise fee, per se, but charging a predetermined fee based on franchise performance. A tentative front-end fee of $5,000 was discussed to cover Beefalo Barn's expenses for assistance in site location, building design, equipment lineup, and so forth. The franchisee would have total obligation for purchasing equip-

Exhibit 4

Beefalo Barn restaurant layout (seating = 66)

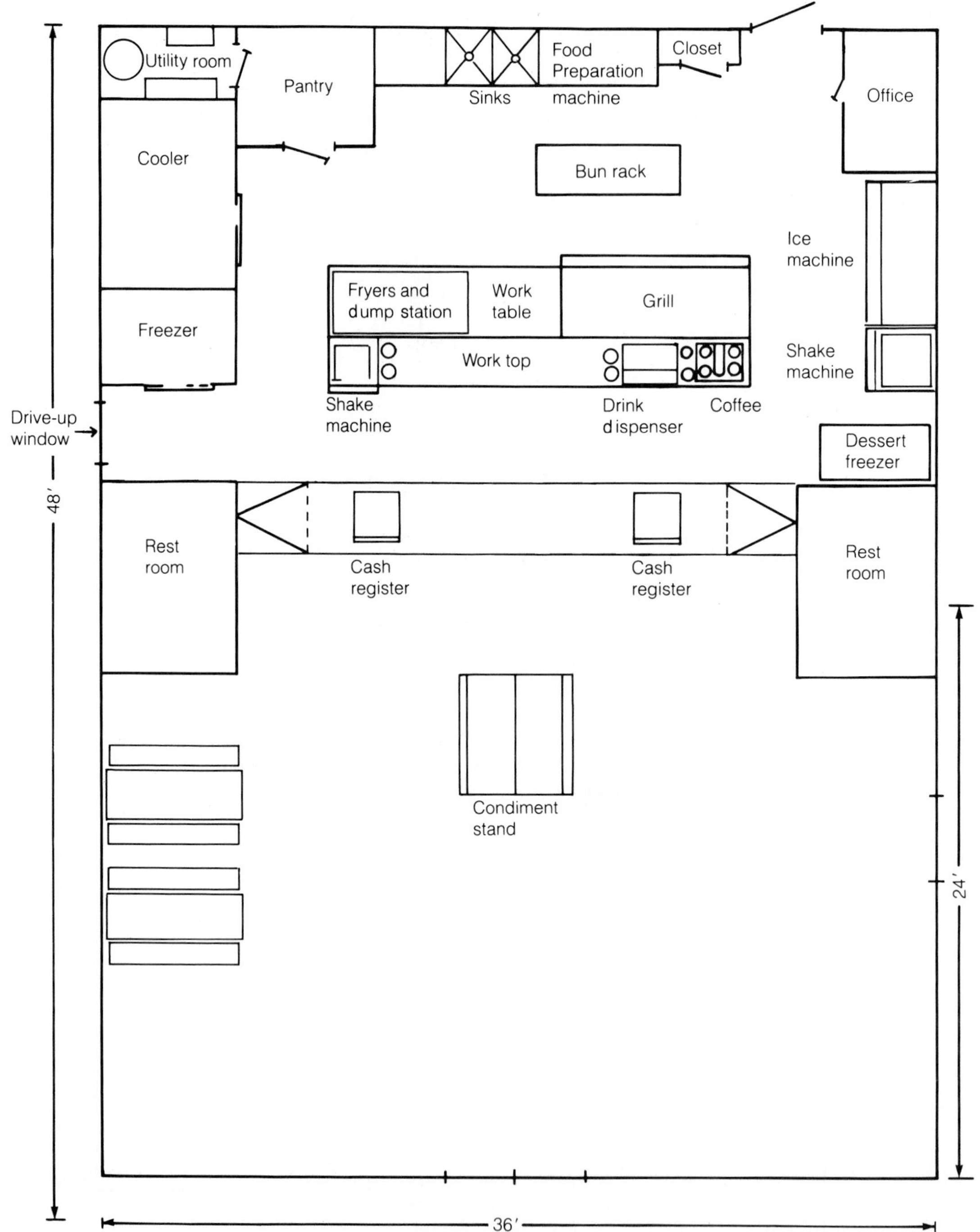

ment, land, and building. Beefalo Barns would then charge a royalty fee based on dollar sales of beefalo purchased through the parent firm.

49 The Beefalo Barn restaurant would use a 36-by-48-foot Beaver log building, with seating capacity for 66 people (see Exhibit 4). Decor would be in a western motif with wooden tables, wagon-wheel light fixtures, cattle brand displays, and so on. Service equipment would use standard models (not customized), with a gas-fired fry grill used for cooking. Schweiger anticipated relying heavily on experienced managers (or formally trained food-service managers from one of the special schools in Dallas, Las Vegas, or Purdue) for operation of the restaurants. Some standards would be established regarding personnel, sanitation, and food storage/preparation. But largely, individual restaurant managers would have responsibility and authority to manage their operation in response to local conditions. For example, deciding whether to open for breakfast and the specification of breakfast menu items would be the manager's prerogative.

50 Schweiger emphasized that quality control is the primary factor on which success is dependent:

> To me, the most critical factor in the whole thing is the movement of meat from the feedlot, through the slaughterhouse, to the retail outlet. To start out, we're only going to have one to three stores, and we're going to be starting from scratch. So we've got two things to worry about initially—to control the quality of that meat and keep spoilage down and, yet, to maintain adequate supplies at the restaurant, because the last thing you need to do is to run out.

The Future

51 By early 1979, the future direction for KSM and Beefalo Breeding Company remained uncertain. During mid-1978, the Beefalo Barns idea was very central to the thinking of Schweiger. It presented not only an outlet for beefalo in which maximum value could be added to the product but also an opportunity to branch out into another business. Six months later, however, no commitments had been made to start the first restaurant. In the interim, Schweiger had been closely involved with a group of investors in southern California, who were considering not only the tax-sheltering possibilities of beefalo but who also expressed interest in the concept of marketing beefalo through restaurants (tentatively located either in California or Colorado). This group potentially could assemble a multimillion dollar capital investment fund within 72 hours. Their major reservation to date about starting a restaurant chain was concern over the availability of a guaranteed supply of beefalo. They estimated at least 1,000 cows producing calves for meat would be necessary to sustain the scale of operation they felt necessary to make attractive a major investment.

52 In the first year in which beefalo were available for meat production, about $50,000 was generated through red meat sales. The most recent sale involved 4,200 pounds of ground beefalo to an Oklahoma public school system for institutional feeding (cafeterias). By February 1979, Beefalo Breeding Company was caring for approximately 500 head of beefalo, about two thirds of which involved herd management contracts for outside investors. Seventy-five head had recently arrived at the Missouri ranch from a prominent California beefalo producer. It was expected that a management contract for another 250-head herd would be finalized within 60 days. In anticipation of herd expansion, on February 15, Schweiger was meeting with representatives of

property east of Jefferson City, Missouri, to work out terms for a 15-year lease of 600–880 acres of pastureland capable of supporting 400 head.

53 Schweiger continued to feel himself stretched thin in terms of being able to devote ample time to his various programs. Much of his time was involved in negotiating and attempting to persuade various individuals and groups in one or more facets of his existing or proposed businesses. He talked at one time of taking on an assistant, but finding a relatively young person who could function as a jack-of-all-trades with high tolerance for uncertainty was difficult. Hiring such a person at this time also was complicated by limited cash flow, since herd buildup required keeping cows out of the marketing stream for breeding purposes.

54 In discussing his dilemma with a class of M.B.A. students, Schweiger remarked:

> I'm not reasonably sure at this time which of our business activities ought to be emphasized. Which way do I go? Should I spend most of my time raising capital for buying beefalo herds and in finding high-paying outlets for carcass beefalo? If so, what would be my best approach to marketing? What do I do with the Beefalo Barns idea, or with Beaver Homes? What are the trade-offs and payoffs? I'm open to your suggestions.

case 8
The Proposed Cox-GE Merger

Introduction

1 On October 5, 1978, Cox Broadcasting Corporation and General Electric (GE) announced publicly that an agreement in principle had been reached regarding a proposed merger between the two companies. Representatives of both companies were authorized to begin negotiations on a definitive agreement. Acceptance of the proposal would have made it the second-largest broadcasting merger and the largest media property exchange to date.

2 Cox had begun to consider a merger because of increased pressure about its cross-media ownership. Suits had been filed against Cox to deny license renewals to two of its Atlanta stations, alleging Cox had exhibited anticompetitive practices and held an unlawful concentration of control in that market.

3 Although Cox's existing media combinations were not barred under FCC cross-media ownership rules at that time, the company was concerned about its vulnerability to future allegations. The most-attractive method management considered for alleviating this vulnerability was merger with another large company that also had broadcasting interests. Such an arrangement was seen as necessary to dilute ownership by the Cox family (the FCC ruling was that primary ownership be no more than 51 percent.)

4 General Electric seemed to meet both these criteria, but Cox management had to analyze other important factors as well as to determine the ultimate value of the merger. Among the salient factors for analysis were: the possible strategic fit of Cox and GE, future trends in industry regulation, and possible benefits of the merger to the general public. To aid in predicting future trends in regulation and in determining possible benefits to the public, the broadcasting industry had to be examined in detail.

The Broadcasting Industry

History of Regulation of Television and Radio

5 Commercial broadcasting in the United States began in 1921 when radio stations KDKA (Pittsburgh) and WBZ (Springfield, Massachusetts) were issued broadcast licenses by the secretary of commerce. During the rest of that decade, the rapid prolifera-

This case was prepared by John A. Pearce II of the University of South Carolina with the assistance of Katherine L. Moore, Elizabeth L. Newell, Barbara A. Rivers, and Rebecca Sims. It has been accepted for publication in the *Journal of Management Case Studies.*

tion of amplitude-modulated (AM) stations caused so much airwave interference that Congress passed the Dill-White Radio Act in 1927. The act authorized a five-member commission to assign frequencies to stations and control station power.

6 A few years later, the Communications Act of 1934 was passed establishing a single agency to regulate all interstate communications by wire and radio. This act created the seven-member Federal Communications Commission (FCC) whose functions were to:

1. Allocate space among the airways for broadcast and nonbroadcast services.
2. Assign stations a specific location, frequency, and power to avoid interference among stations with the same channel (frequency).
3. Regulate existing stations.

A broadcast license was granted to a station for a period of three years, after which time an application had to be filed for renewal of the license for an additional three-year period. Applications for license renewals offered the commission an opportunity to evaluate the station's record to ensure that it had been operating in the public interest. If there were competing applications or petitions from outside groups to deny licensure, the FCC had to order a full hearing.

7 From its inception in 1934, the FCC encouraged local ownership of stations, believing it would result in station managements more responsive to local interests and community needs. However, the FCC had no power to enforce its preference. As a result, many newspapers and other groups acquired both radio and television stations.

8 Newspaper owners became involved to protect their existing interests in advertising dollars and in news coverage. In many cases, the newspaper companies were the only investors willing to assume the risks of the new industry. By 1953, newspaper groups owned 79 percent of the television stations in the United States. The most popular acquisitions were very high frequency (VHF) stations located in the larger cities.

9 Between 1953 and 1955, the total number of stations doubled. After that time, very few newspaper groups applied for station licenses. The choice VHF stations were already taken, and the FCC was trying to discourage new newspaper/broadcast cross-ownership arrangements. Since that time, the actual number of stations owned by newspapers has remained fairly stable. However, due to the increased number of television stations in the 1960s and 1970s, the percentage of newspaper-owned stations declined, as shown in Exhibit 1.

10 In 1975, after two decades of indecision regarding the cross-ownership issue, the FCC banned new joint arrangements between newspapers and broadcast stations located in the same city. At the time, newspaper/broadcast cross-ownership existed in over half of the 20 largest U.S. cities. Eighty television-newspaper combinations operated in 74 cities, and 406 radio-newspaper combinations operated in 196 cities.

11 The 1975 cross-ownership pronouncement was appealed not only by newspaper and broadcast groups but also by the National Citizens Committee for Broadcasting, NCCB, led by former FCC Chairman Nicholas Johnson. The latter organization questioned the ban's application to future cross-ownership and not to existing ones.

Exhibit 1

Newspaper cross-ownership of television stations

Year	*Stations broadcasting*	*Newspaper-owned stations (percent)*
1950	96	43%
1955	419	36
1960	533	30
1971	683	24
1974	693	24

12 In 1977 a federal appeals court struck down the FCC's 1975 ruling, stating that the ban on new cross-ownership was inconsistent with the commission's efforts to encourage diversified ownership of media sources. In effect, the 1977 appeals court ruling prohibited most existing as well as new cross-ownership arrangements within the same city between the two industries. Although the FCC had taken no action to enforce this ban, many newspaper and station owners, including Cox Broadcasting, experienced increased pressure from both the courts and citizens' groups and made plans to divest their cross-ownership interests before they were forced to do so.

13 In 1979, the Supreme Court reversed the 1977 federal appeals decision banning existing cross-ownerships. Therefore, the 1975 FCC ruling was upheld: New cross-ownerships were not allowed, but existing newspaper/broadcast arrangements in the same market were permitted. This decision was reinforced by the unanimous passage of a bill offered in 1980 by the House Communications Subcommittee (H.R. 6228) which prohibited the FCC from considering cross-ownership as a factor in determining whether licenses should be renewed. Thus, the FCC regulations regarding station acquisitions were as follows:

1. No entity could own more than seven stations in each service (AM, FM, or TV). Of the TV holdings, no more than five could be VHF.
2. No owner of three VHFs in the top 50 markets could purchase other VHFs in the top 50 without proving compelling public interest.
3. Newspaper owners could no longer acquire broadcast stations in the same market, nor could radio station owners acquire television stations there, nor TV owners, radio stations.
4. Owners of a broadcasting company could no longer have more than a 1 percent controlling interest in the stock.

14 **Self-Regulation.** In general, the broadcasting industry tended toward self-regulation regarding station programming and advertising practices. The National Association of Broadcasters (NAB) issued guidelines to its 470 commercial television and 2,000 commercial radio station members pertaining to programming and advertising policies. For instance, the NAB codes for radio and television limited the amount of commercial time to 18 and 16 minutes per hour, respectively.

15 Along with federal and industry regulation, pressures from political and minority groups, consumer advocates, and other organizations had markedly increased through-

out the 1970s. Until about 1981, license-renewal applications were granted almost automatically. After that time, stations began to experience increasing numbers of conflicting applications and/or petitions by various citizen groups to deny license renewals. The large volume of challenges caused considerable concern among broadcasters. For many stations, the value of the franchise to broadcast was worth up to one-half the value of the station, so the denial of a license could have resulted in a considerable financial loss. Also, the time and expense required to contest challenges was prohibitive. Between 1969 and 1973, the average time for the resolution of a challenge was 18 months. By 1974, the situation was worse, with action pending on over 200 petitions to deny. In 1975, decisions on 215 petitions were awaiting decision.

16 By 1978, Congress was considering several bills which would have increased station renewal periods from three to five years. In addition, the FCC, faced with its backlog of petitions, had encouraged negotiations between challengers and stations, lessening the involvement of the commission. In the meantime, the broadcasting industry was increasing its efforts to forecast the direction of regulation and to participate in more self-regulating activities.

Financial Aspects of Broadcasting

17 Although educational and other noncommercial television and radio stations had been increasing in numbers throughout the 70s, the American broadcasting system was commercial in nature (see Exhibit 2). Television and radio stations have been supported by revenues from those who advertised products and services to the audience. Television stations competed with other TV stations and with radio, newspapers, magazines, and other media for advertising dollars. Advertising rates varied from station to station depending on the market size and the station's share of the audience at a particular time of day. These rates were influenced by demand, the economy, and rating-service estimates.

18 Advertising revenue for television in the 1970s came from three groupings: (1) the sale of network time to national advertisers, which accounted for about 45 percent of the television total; (2) the sale of time by individual stations to national or regional advertisers, that is, national spots, which made up about 8 percent of the total; and (3) the sale of time by individual stations to local advertisers—local spots, with 27 percent of the total. In contrast, radio's advertising revenues were approximately 75 percent from local spots, 20 percent from national and regional spots, and only 5 percent from network radio.

19 During the 1960s, television advertising revenues outpaced the country's total advertising receipts, helped along by the increased penetration of households. However, in 1971, following a two-year recession, this pattern was interrupted. Although the drop in revenues was only 2 percent, many felt the television industry was becoming sensitive to the business cycle and that market share might be stabilizing. However, the drop was due to several forces. At that time, cigarette advertising on television was banned. Also, the standard commerical length changed from 60 to 30 seconds, which in effect doubled the number of commercial spots. As a result, the demand for ad time dropped, the supply of commerical periods increased, and a buyer's market emerged. This buyer's market put a great pressure on prices of ads since air time was a perishable item. According to the percentages in Exhibit 3, the television industry regained its 1970 share of the advertising revenues (18.4 percent) by 1975.

Exhibit 2

Growth of broadcast service

	Commercial radios in operation		*Commercial TV stations in operation*			*Noncommercial FMs in operation*	*Noncommerical TVs in operation*		
Year	***AM***	***FM***	***Total***	***VHF***	***UHF***		***Total***	***VHF***	***UHF***
1950	2,086	733	97	97	—	48	—	—	—
1955	2,669	522	439	294	117	122	9	—	—
1960	3,456	678	573	441	76	162	44	—	—
1965	4,012	1,270	586	487	99	255	88	54	34
1970	4,319	2,184	690	508	182	396	182	77	105
1975	4,432	2,636	711	513	198	717	241	95	146
1978	4,513	3,001	727	516	211	926	259	101	158

Source: *Broadcasting Yearbook.*

Exhibit 3

Advertising media: Shares of the market (percent)

Media	*1970*	*1971*	*1972*	*1973*	*1974*	*1975*	*1976*	*1977*	*1978*
Newspapers	29.2%	29.9%	30.1%	30.2%	29.9%	29.9%	27.4%	29.2%	29.0%
Television	18.4	17.0	17.6	17.8	18.2	18.6	19.9	20.0	20.2
Radio	6.7	7.0	6.9	6.9	6.9	7.0	6.9	6.8	6.8
Magazines	6.6	6.6	6.2	5.8	5.6	5.2	5.3	5.7	5.9
All other	39.1	39.5	39.2	29.3	39.4	39.3	38.5	38.3	38.1
Total	100%	100%	100%	100%	100%	100%	100%	100%	100%

20 Demand for television time caught up with the supply in the mid-1970s. By then, advertisers had realized that television appealed to mass audiences and was the most-efficient medium for reaching numbers of potential customers. The growth of advertising revenues was strong and fairly steady throughout the 70s, as seen in Exhibit 4.

21 Radio revenues from advertising experienced a steady growth in the 1970s in spite of competition from other media (see Exhibit 4). Part of this growth was due to the increasing automobile commuting market and to the growth of FM radio. Also, unlike television which appealed to mass media, radio targeted its market with specialized programming. Although ad revenues increased in the 1970s, radio lost a share of the total advertising market due to increased competition from television and newspapers.

22 In the late 1970s, FM had experienced a steady increase in the share of the listening audience, while AM's share declined. By 1979, FM's audience share was over 46 percent in the daytime and 53 percent during the evening. However, the share of total advertising revenues attributed to FM stations was only 30 percent, much less than its share of the audience. This gap was due to less commercial time available on FM, lower AM rates, and fewer cars equipped with FM. This discrepancy was expected to disappear by the early 1980s when total radio advertising revenues would be split between AM and FM.

23 Growth in radio advertising also resulted from its viability as an alternate form;

Exhibit 4

Advertising volume by media ($ millions)

Media	*1970*	*1971*	*1972*	*1973*	*1974*	*1975*	*1976*	*1977*	*1978*
Television	3,596	3,534	4,091	4,460	4,854	5,263	6,721	7,612	10,880
Radio	1,308	1,445	1,612	1,723	1,837	1,980	2,330	2,586	2,955
Newspapers	5,704	6,198	7,008	7,595	8,001	8,442	9,910	11,132	12,690
Direct mail	2,766	3,067	3,420	3,698	3,986	4,181	4,813	5,333	6,030
General and farm magazines	1,354	1,427	1,499	1,513	1,576	1,539	1,875	2,252	2,700
Outdoor	234	261	292	308	309	335	383	418	465
Other	4,588	4,808	5,378	5,823	6,172	6,490	7,688	8,727	10,050
All media	19,550	20,740	23,300	25,120	26,740	28,230	33,720	38,060	43,740

advertising on television has expensive, limited air time. Since radio was basically a local advertising form, it benefited from favorable, local economic health.

24 Both radio and television were capital-intensive industries characterized by a high ratio of fixed to variable costs and therefore a ratio of substantial operating leverage to profit. Once the relatively fixed overhead costs had been met, much of the incremental revenues passed through to profit. As a result, broadcasting profits advanced at a greater rate than general economic activity, although the opposite tended to occur in periods of economic downturn.

25 The industry was also characterized by a high rate of return on invested capital and sizable cash flows. However, due to the FCCs limitation on the number of broadcast interests an entity could own, broadcasters had problems finding other investments with a rate of return comparable to broadcasting.

26 Those entities who purchased more broadcast holdings encountered marked increases in the prices of broadcast interests by the late 1970s, when demand exceeded supply. By 1980, the average television station sold for 10 times its cash flow; the average AM radio station sold for 7 times its cash flow, and a well-established FM radio station with potential for growth sold for 10 times its cash flow.

Future Trends for the Industry

27 By 1979, the broadcasting industry was entrenched in the American lifestyle. Over 700 television stations broadcast to 98 percent of all U.S. households. Approximately 93 percent received UHF stations, and 16 percent were connected to a cable system. In the same year, 7,662 U.S. radio stations broadcast over 444 million radios, 328 million (74 percent) of them in homes and 116 million (26 percent) outside homes.

28 The future was expected to depend on the strength of the economy, advertising revenues, government regulations, and technological advances. Revenue projections through 1985 looked favorable for broadcasting. Television advertising revenues were expected to grow at an average annual rate of 11.5 percent, radio's at 9.4 percent. All media advertising expenditures were forecast to increase 8.4 percent annually during the same period. Industry revenues in 1981 were projected as follows: television revenues, 69 percent; radio, 21 percent; cable television, 10 percent.

29 Several economic factors were expected to affect the future of television earnings. Due to the movement in the population from the cities to the suburbs, television was expected to take some of newspaper's retail advertising revenues. A larger suburban population would benefit from the wider coverage area television offered. Also, the advertising expenditures by national advertisers and local retailers is consistent. Even in a recession, these advertisers were expected to continue to spend large amounts of advertising money to maintain their products' position in the market.

30 Radio's future growth was forecast to be affected by increased local retail advertising and its advantage of wider coverage as the population continued to move from the city to the suburbs.

31 The increased use of communication satellites and other technological advances was predicted to change the nature of broadcasting, and competition among the different media was predicted to increase. The market was also expected to be more fragmented. Cable television and other newly developed media forms were expected to provide traditional broadcasters with an outlet for their excess cash that would offer a sizable return.

The Development of Community Antenna Television

32 Community Television Systems (CATV) began in the late 1940s. These systems received television and FM radio signals with the use of high antennas or by microwave or satellite transmission, amplified the signals, and distributed them to the homes of subscribers via coaxial cable. The subscribers paid a fee for the service and received a greater choice of program offerings with improved reception.

33 Later, CATV systems moved into larger cities where subscribers were interested in the diversity of progamming available through cable. At the time, cable systems were not broadcasting and did not fall under FCC jurisdiction. As a result, the regulation of CATV was left up to local governments which issued the local franchises. Requirements for a franchise varied from state to state, and hundreds of cable systems spread haphazardly throughout the United States.

34 Regulation of cable television began in 1965 when the FCC established rules for microwave-served systems. CATV systems were required to carry the signals of local stations and were prohibited from televising the same programs on imported stations within 15 days of the program's local broadcast. Although CATV served only a small percentage of the population, its rapid growth threatened the viability of the UHF stations that the FCC so heavily promoted in the 1960s.

35 As a result, the commission placed a freeze on CATV systems located in the top 100 U.S. cities. The freeze was lifted in 1972 and replaced by restrictions on the number of imported stations that could be carried and on the programs that could be aired by the imported stations. Lifting of the freeze led to a marked increase in local CATV franchises (as shown in Exhibit 5). By 1973, at least one fourth of the top 100 cities had CATV or had made plans for the system.

36 By 1980, over one fifth of all U.S. households subscribed to CATV, whereas in 1970, only 1 in every 25 was a subscriber. Projections indicated that by 1981, every third home would be using a cable service. At that level of service, CATV became a viable national advertising medium, and significant increases in cable advertising dollars were expected to occur. More advertising revenues were translated into more attractive programming followed by an increase in subscriptions and more advertising dollars.

37 By the late 70s, the cable industry had increased its revenues and its number of subscribers. In 1974, CATV industry revenues were approximately $600 million, less than half the industry revenues for 1980. The fastest growing cable service was Pay-TV, which was offered to almost half the cable subscribers. Pay-TV was generally distributed through a cable system to a subscriber who paid a per-program or monthly charge. Between 1975 and 1979, the number of Pay-TV subscribers soared from 50,000 to 2.6 million. Through 1983, expected annual rate of growth for Pay-TV was 24 percent, compared to 7.5 percent for basic cable. Annual revenue growth was expected to be 15 percent.

38 Pay-TV had enabled cable system operators to improve profitability with a minimum of additional capital investment. Suppliers of Pay-TV programs simply leased a channel from CATV operators and installed a special decoder device in the subscriber's home. Pay-TV also helped increase the number of homes using cable by offering even greater diversification of programming.

39 CATV created much concern among TV broadcasters regarding competition for audiences and as an entertainment vehicle. Two sources in the industry seemed to indicate

Exhibit 5

Growth of the cable industry in the United States

Year	*Total homes (in thousands)*	*TV homes (in thousands)*	*CATV systems*	*CATV homes (in thousands)*	*CATV saturation of TV homes (percent)*
1952	44,760	15,300	70	14	0.1%
1953	45,640	20,400	150	30	0.2
1954	46,660	26,000	300	65	0.3
1955	47,620	30,700	400	150	0.5
1956	48,600	34,900	450	300	0.9
1957	49,500	38,900	500	350	0.9
1958	50,370	41,925	525	450	1.1
1959	51,150	43,950	560	550	1.3
1960	52,500	45,750	640	650	1.4
1961	53,170	47,200	700	725	1.5
1962	54,300	48,855	800	850	1.7
1963	55,100	50,300	1,000	950	1.9
1964	55,900	51,600	1,200	1,085	2.1
1965	56,900	52,700	1,325	1,275	2.4
1966	57,900	53,850	1,570	1,575	2.9
1967	58,900	55,130	1,770	2,100	3.8
1968	59,900	56,670	2,000	2,800	4.9
1969	61,300	58,250	2,260	3,600	6.2
1970	62,700	59,700	2,490	4,500	7.5
1971	64,500	61,600	2,639	5,300	8.6
1972	66,280	63,500	2,841	6,000	9.4
1973	68,330	65,600	2,991	7,300	11.1
1974	69,859	69,400	3,158	8,700	12.5
1975	n.a.	70,837	3,200	10,000	14.1

n.a. = not available.
Source: *Broadcasting and Cable Television.*

that cable would become a bigger challenge to TV broadcasters in the 1980s. First, it appeared that the government supported the increased competition since the almost-monopoly power of TV would be diminished under such competition. Second, increased technology in the CATV industry seemed to indicate that cable systems would no longer be as fragmented as they were during the 1970s.

Backgrounds of the Companies

40 In addition to surveying the broadcasting industry, management at Cox felt it necessary to determine the possibility for strategic fit between Cox and GE. To make this determination, profiles of both companies had to be developed.

Profile of Cox Broadcasting Company

41 Cox Broadcasting Company (CBC) was formed in 1964 by former Ohio Governor and prominent newspaper publisher and politician James M. Cox. Although its begin-

nings were in newspapers, by the late 1970s, the company had expanded into five divisions, (1) broadcasting, (2) cable television, (3) Bing Crosby Productions, (4) services, and (5) publishing.

42 The broadcasting division was made up of six very high frequency (VHF) television stations (in Atlanta, Dayton, San Francisco, Oakland, Pittsburgh, and Charlotte) and five standard AM and seven FM radio systems (in Atlanta, Philadelphia, Baltimore, Dayton, Charlotte, Los Angeles, and Miami). Cox Cable Communications operated 44 community antenna television (CATV) stations in 17 states. Bing Crosby Productions consists of a film production house producing motion pictures for theatrical and television exhibitions. CBC service division operated 13 automobile auction centers which provided services and facilities where automobile manufacturers, new and used dealers, and rental and leasing companies could buy and sell automobiles to regulate and balance their inventories. Included in this division was a data processing service which provided computer software for each of Cox's divisions. Cox's publishing division published trade magazines for the machinery, photographic, floor covering, and electronic fields.

History of Cox Broadcasting and CATV

43 In the early 1960s, the communications industry began to grow rapidly, and governmental and regulatory problems were more prevalent. Due to this increased regulation, James M. Cox, Jr., Governor Cox's son, and Leonard Beinsch, managing director of the broadcasting operations, reorganized the Cox operations. On February 6, 1964, after 30 years of separate ownership, Cox Broadcasting Corporation was formed to operate the 12 stations and 4 CATV systems which had been acquired from the various Cox interests. On July 17, 1964, the stock was admitted for trading on the New York Stock Exchange (NYSE). The Cox family maintained control over the company by holding 63.8 percent of the stock and by having five family members serving on the board of directors. Since Cox's incorporation, expansion in broadcasting and diversification into related areas were given top priority. This expansionary philosophy was exemplified by Clifford M. Kirkland, Jr., secretary-treasurer of the corporation. He once stated that Cox did not intend to become a conglomerate but that the company was seeking investments outside the broadcasting industry that had some fit.

44 With this philosophy in mind, Cox not only began to acquire more broadcasting stations but diversified into related fields, particularly the cable television and the service and leisure-time areas.

45 Cox's cable communications division had been successful in fulfilling both the company's mission and its expansionary philosophy. Cox Cablevision grew rapidly during the early years of the new corporation. It acquired additional franchises and formed joint-venture companies with local newspapers in such cities as Toledo, Cleveland, San Diego, Bakersfield, and Atlanta.

46 During the early years of cable, many broadcasters felt threatened by cable's growth into the television audience. During this time, the FCC put a freeze on cable expansion into major markets. This freeze was lifted in 1972. Although most of the broadcasting industry held an anti-CATV posture, management at Cox believed the public would demand continued growth of the product; therefore, Cox remained in the CATV market and profited by it. Cox cable continued its expansion philosophy and in 1968 consolidated Cox's cable TV interests by incorporating into Cox Cable Communications, Inc.

47 By 1967, Cox Cable had contributed over $373,000 to Cox's total net income, and 10 years later, its contribution had increased to over $2 million (see Exhibit 6). Due to the acquisition of Telesystems, by 1969, Cox was recognized as the second-largest cable complex in the United States. Revenues for CATV had increased from 1968 to 1972 at an average annual rate of 17 percent. After the FCC lifted the freeze into major markets in 1972, Cox Cable revenues increased by 28 percent. Also from 1972 to 1977, revenues increased at an average rate of 26 percent.

48 In 1977, Cox Cable merged with Cox Broadcasting. In that same year, Cox management saw several trends that could improve the potential for CATV to provide substantial returns on investment. For example, a clearing away of several regulatory hurdles which had barred cable's growth was expected to create the best business and regulatory climate for cable since the early 1960s. Additionally, the rapid development and use of satellite technology to distribute programming to cable systems nationwide was expected to increase the diversity of programming, such as the Home Box Office (HBO) network, sports and special events, and premium service movies. This technology was also forecast to contribute substantially to viewer awareness of cable TV nationwide. With cable TV's predicted capabilities to deliver more and more product each year, new opportunities would arise in terms of bidding on franchises in cities that had not yet granted a CATV franchise.

49 Cox's estimates for the future seemed to be on target. From 1977 to 1978, CATV revenues increased by 33 percent and from 1978 to 1979, 38 percent. Also, cable television subscriptions went from 489,900 in 1977 to 706,900 in 1979. CATV revenues were the second major contributor to CBC's total operating revenues (see Exhibit 7). Thus, Cox Cable Communication's history stood as evidence of how efficiently CBC had carried on its expansionary mission. A comparison of Cox to the industry is shown in Exhibit 8.

Commitment to Broadcasting

50 Although Cox had expanded into cable, its main business continued to be broadcasting. In the 1971 annual report, management at Cox highlighted their belief in the vitality of the broadcasting media and its ability to serve the public interest and, at the same time, generate financial rewards.

51 CBC believed the vitality of the broadcasting division was proven by its history of acquisitions of television stations and AM and FM radio stations. According to the 1971 annual report, CBC intended to expand radio operations as soon as properties became available that met investment criteria. The company believed that as long as radio and television stations continued to recognize needs and preferences of the communities they are licensed to serve, broadcasting would be assured a healthy future.

52 Cox saw its ownership of radio and TV stations as a key to its future success in the broadcasting field. The company measured its broadcasting division not only in terms of financial performance but by the extent to which stations constructively involved themselves in the lives of total communities.

53 Commitment to news and public affairs programming was evidenced by analysis of FCC data collected in the 1970s. The analysis revealed that CBC devoted more time to local news each day than any other broadcasting group in the survey. Further evidence of this commitment was found in 1976–1979, when stations were providing

Exhibit 6

Comparative financial data for Cox Broadcasting (in dollars)

	For the year ended December 31					
	1964	*1965*	*1966*	*1967*	*1968*	*1969*
Operating revenues	$ 20,083	$ 28,111	$ 35,919	$ 45,190	$ 51,368	$ 61,071
Operating, selling, general, and administrative expenses		16,052	20,717	27,742	33,010	41,864
Income before income taxes	6,643	9,152	11,867	13,829	14,783	14,848
Income taxes	3,507	4,595	6,115	7,057	8,597	8,483
Income of consolidated companies	3,136	4,557	4,606	6,772	6,186	6,366
Share of net income of Cox Cable Communications, Inc.	(29)	(26)	(230)	373	669	736
Net income	3,107	4,531	4,376	7,145	6,855	7,102
Net income per common share	.59	.80	.77	1.23	1.19	1.23
Depreciation and amortization	921	1,388	1,769	2,121	2,373	3,088
Interest expense		1,637	1,684	1,745	1,785	1,977
Other income—net		118	118	247	583	707
Dividends per common share	.15	.20	.21¼	.25	.25	.26¼
At December 31:						
Net current assets	5,913	8,153	7,652	12,637	11,234	10,670
Plant and equipment—net	11,689	13,842	15,164	16,201	19,230	20,774
Long-term liabilities	29,664	29,903	32,745	31,332	32,088	30,747
Shareholders' equity	18,557	22,631	25,899	33,961	43,996	49,838
Number of common shares outstanding	5,670,162	5,675,702	5,678,302	5,788,362	5,767,000	5,789,000

	For the year ended December 31				
	1970	*1971*	*1972*	*1973*	*1974*
Operating revenues	$ 74,533	$ 79,555	$ 92,911	$ 108,650	$ 123,381
Operating, selling, general, and administrative expenses	50,444	52,822	61,308	73,452	83,014
Income before income taxes and minority interest	17,203	18,442	22,303	24,245	28,518
Income taxes	9,041	9,731	11,461	12,788	14,852
Minority interest in earnings of Cox Cable	526	558	740	822	930
Income before extraordinary item and cumulative effect of accounting change					
Income per common share before extraordinary item and cumulative effect of accounting change					
Net income	7,636	8,153	10,102	10,635	12,736

Exhibit 6 *(concluded)*

Income per common share before extraordinary item and cumulative effect of accounting change					
Net income per common share	1.32	2.40	1.73	1.82	2.18
Depreciation and amortization	5,375	6,189	7,064	8,035	8,705
Interest expense	2,399	2,356	2,475	3,224	4,276
Other income—net	888	254	239	306	1,132
Dividends per common share	.30	.30	.30	.35	.36¼
At December 31:					
Net current assets	18,906	21,438	15,983	17,318	15,761
Plant and equipment	34,914	37,717	42,617	53,126	66,491
Intangible assets	43,576	52,075	53,483	64,713	72,029
Long-term notes payable	31,724	38,574	36,910	52,289	57,469
Shareholders' equity	55,726	62,873	71,874	80,693	91,708
Number of common shares outstanding	5,789,000	5,827,000	5,826,379	5,831,179	5,806,179

	For the year ended December 31				
	1975	***1976***	***1977***	***1978***	***1979***
Operating revenues	$ 139,251	$ 167,461	$ 186,430	$ 230,444	$ 271,187
Operating, selling, general, and administrative expenses	94,297	108,015	117,330	140,150	168,196
Income before income taxes and minority interest	31,947	44,011	49,871	67,172	77,258
Income taxes	16,395	22,623	24,753	33,324	35,468
Minority interest in earnings of Cox Cable	1,248	1,629	1,429		
Income before extraordinary item and cumulative effect of accounting change			23,689		41,790
Extraordinary item					
Cumulative effect of change in accounting method			1,767		
Net income	14,304	19,759	25,456	33,847	43,767
Income per common share before extraordinary item and cumulative effect of accounting change			3.82		6.20
Net income per common share	2.45	3.36	4.11	5.07	6.50
Depreciation and amortization	9,922	11,793	14,698	18,132	22,619
Interest expense	4,286	4,650	5,433	5,791	5,111
Other income—net	1,201	1,008	902	801	1,997
Dividends per common share	.41¼	.50	.60	.67½	.77½
At December 31:					
Net current assets	21,496	29,348	30,197	24,017	8,611
Plant and equipment	76,525	85,049	95,334	117,176	160,853
Intangible assets	73,066	73,423	104,402	112,634	116,848
Long-term notes payable	59,807	57,240	69,451	59,086	51,665
Shareholders' equity	104,452	121,631	164,375	195,038	234,924
Number of common shares outstanding	5,857,178	5,875,062	6,617,971	6,684,199	6,741,743

Source: CBC annual reports.

Exhibit 7

CBC operating revenues by division (in thousands of dollars)

					Services		
	Broadcasting	*CATV*	*Publishing*	*Bing Crosby Productions*	*Auto auctions*		*Data processing*
1967	$ 32,206	$ 4,410	$ 5,600	$7,384			
1968	35,904	8,358	7,059	8,405			
1969	40,372	9,781	8,606	7,349		$4,744	
1970	41,715	10,806	9,073	6,292		7,018	
1971	42,453	13,561	9,853	4,299	$ 8,371		$ 381
1972	48,945	15,823	11,998	4,673	11,138		527
1973	57,237	18,249	13,888	7,362	11,447		682
1974	63,708	23,416	15,662	6,266	14,012		759
1975	68,656	29,435	15,189	9,629	15,745		1,027
1976	87,965	37,878	17,019	4,486	18,078		2,542
1977	94,813	47,532	20,421	4,694	18,920		*
1978	115,659	65,901	23,234	4,122	21,528		
1979	133,678	90,869	22,375	2,152	22,113		

* The data processing service became primarily a support organization for Cox stations and cable systems.
Source: CBC annual reports.

the sports, special events, miniseries, and made-for-television movies that were the trend for this period.

54 Broadcasting also provided CBC with a great deal of financial support. Broadcasting revenues had consistently been the major contributor to CBC's total revenues. Even in 1971, when the industry lost 8 percent of its revenues because of the ban on cigarette advertising, Cox broadcasting revenues increased from $41,715,000 in 1970 to $42,453,000. Also, despite the energy crisis and the many economic questions it raised in 1973, revenues increased from $48,945,000 in 1972 to $57,237,000 in 1973 (see Exhibit 7).

55 From 1970 to 1973, the number of television homes in markets served by CBC stations grew by 12 percent. During the same period, TV homes watching the CBC stations in those markets increased over 36 percent. In 1974, CBC controlled 6.5 percent of TV audiences. While broadcasting revenues only increased by 8 percent in the 1974–1975 recession, they still showed considerable resiliency against the recession.

Exhibit 8

Comparative ratios: Cox versus industry (1978)

	Cox			Industry		
Ratio	*High*		*Low*	*High*		*Low*
P/E	12		6	9.3		5.89
Net income to sales		14.7			10.68	
Net profit to sales		38.8			22.65	
Debt to total capitalization		24.9			34.13	

56 In 1975, Cox completed a study on the future of broadcasting. This study predicted a strong growth in advertising expenditures in broadcast media, particularly for local television and local radio. Cox's predictions seemed to be holding up through 1979. For example, while local television revenues remained at 33 percent from 1974 to 1976 (see Exhibit 9), they increased to 37 percent in 1977 and 38 percent in 1979.

57 In 1975–1978, local radio revenues increased. For example, in 1975, local radio advertising increased to 65 percent of total broadcasting revenues. These revenues continued

Exhibit 9

Broadcasting revenues by source ($ millions)

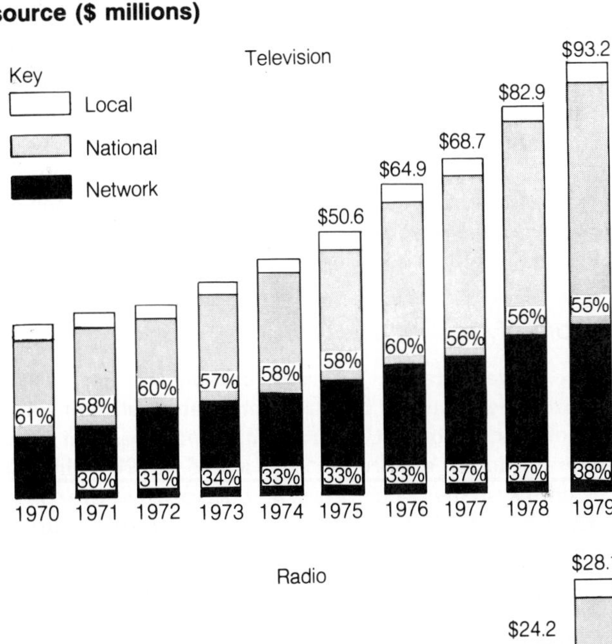

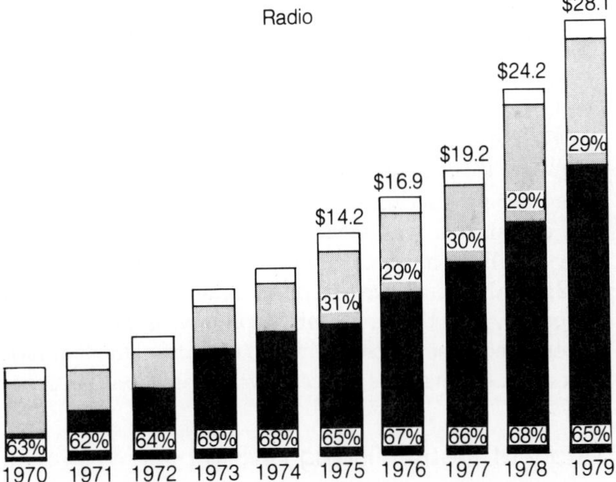

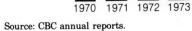

Source: CBC annual reports.

to increase in 1976–1979 at an average annual rate of 15 percent. Thus, over the years, broadcasting had proven to be a major strength of CBC.

History of Bing Crosby Productions

58 Consistent with its expansion philosophy of seeking investments outside the broadcasting industry that had some fit, CBC purchased Bing Crosby Productions in 1967. From 1967 to 1978, the division averaged approximately one feature-length motion picture a year. Some of the most successful ones were the *Walking Tall* trilogy, *The Reincarnation of Peter Proud, Willard,* and its sequel *Ben.*

59 In 1976–1979, however, revenues declined in the motion picture division. The decrease in 1976 was due largely to the movie *Special Delivery,* which did poorly at the box office. In 1978, *Mean Dog Blues* was also unsuccessfully received at the box office, contributing to the decrease in revenues in 1977–1978.

60 Cox experienced a decline in revenues due to the high degree of risk in the motion picture area. However, it tried to curb these risks by having several markets (television being one) for the movies so its investment could be recouped over the life of the film. CBC movies were also produced at low-to-medium budgets of $1.5 to $3 million, with partners who shared the costs. Finally, a factor which CBC considered critical to a movie's success and which it continued to maintain was control over the marketing function.

History of the Service Division

61 Cox's diversification program took on another aspect in December 1968 when it acquired the Manheim Services Corporation of Pennsylvania. This firm, which became the cornerstone of CBC's service division, operated a chain of 13 automobile auction centers. Another service unit was added in 1969 when Cox Data Systems was formed. The data systems segment was an outgrowth of the company's computer center. Originally it served not only CBC's divisions but also a limited number of outside customers. However, service to outsiders was discontinued in 1979.

62 Revenues for the service division increased each year, especially in 1975–1976. In 1976, automobile auctions made a substantial contribution to consolidated revenues. In the same year, Cox data systems limited its marketing effort until it had further developed the broadcast minicomputer system. In 1977, Data Systems introduced a new computerized billing and accounting service for cable television, and in the same year, new U.S. car sales increased 11 percent from 1976.

63 New car production and sales are influencing factors in the growth of auto auctions. This correlation was evidenced by an increase in revenues in 1977. In 1978, there were 3 million more cars on the road. Revenues in 1977–1978 increased from $18.9 to $21.5 million. However, in 1979, as a result of the gasoline shortages, higher new car prices, and the uncertain economy, growth in revenues slowed. There was a 10 percent decrease in the number of cars sold at auctions from 1978 to 1979. Yet of the cars registered, 54 percent were sold—only 4 percent less than 1978 sales.

History of the Publishing Division

64 In 1965, CBC purchased 80 percent of United Technical Publications, which became its basic strength in the publishing division. UTP, which published magazines, catalogs,

and loose-leaf services for the electronics, medical electronics, and office equipment fields, was purchased for $4.4 million.

65 In 1971, CBC acquired an additional 18 percent of UTP's stock, and by 1976, with UTP's publications and services positioned in a broad range of fields, it became Cox's second-largest division. However, revenues ranked behind broadcasting, CATV, and services.

66 The drop in profits in the 1974–1975 period was not caused totally by the economic slump. While the principal reasons for the decline were the depressed condition of the electronics industry and the escalating costs of advertising, the publication profits were also held down by the cost of developing several new publications. The decline in profits in 1978 and 1979 was largely due to the development costs of a new publication, *High Technology*.

Competition

67 CBC competed for listeners' and viewers' time with various broadcasting stations and leisure-time activities. In each of the market areas of Cox television stations, for example, there were three or more other television stations. In the market served by Cox radio stations, there was a range of 14–57 other significant radio stations. Other sources of competition included CATV, Pay Cable, and subscription television operations. CATV systems generally did not compete with other CATV systems but with the direct reception of television signals by the viewer's own antenna. CATV systems operated in most of the market areas served by Cox's broadcasting stations. Possible competitors to Cox's CATV systems were other companies that had or were about to obtain franchises in areas where Cox had them. Cox competed with a number of large companies with some broadcasting interests.

68 The production of motion pictures was a highly competitive business, and Cox competed with a large number of these companies. The principal competition to Cox's auto auctions were similar auctions within a 150- to 200-mile radius of the auction site. Although other auctions were located within the market areas of each of Cox's auctions, Cox owned one of the leading auctions in each of these areas. Cox's principal publications competed with two to six comparable publications and services.

69 Cox also faced competition from a number of large companies with diverse broadcasting interests. General Electric was one of these competitors. To determine the desirability of a Cox-GE merger, management at Cox studied corporate information from GE.

General Electric Company

History

70 A number of pioneer companies in the electrical field incorporated in Schenectady, New York, on April 15, 1892, to become the General Electric Company (GE). Originally, GE was in the business of supplying electricity. Through concentric diversification, GE acquired interests in other electric companies. As its size and strength grew, General Electric diversified into other businesses and ultimately became an international conglomerate.

Operations

71 The company has been viewed as one of the finest-managed corporations in the world. One reason for its managerial success is its use of the strategic business unit (SBU) concept of management. Its operations are highly decentralized and organized into six sectors with each sector containing a number of SBUs. These sectors are shown in Exhibit 10 along with their contribution to total corporate profits.

Exhibit 10

General Electric earnings by operating sector

Operating sector	*Included in sector*	*1979 profits (percent of company total)*
Industrial Products and Components	Electrical components; industrial and capital equipment; electronic components.	19%
Power Systems	Nuclear fuel assemblies and power reactors; fossil-fuel turbines; installation and service engineering.	8
Technical Systems and Materials	Jet engines; medical and communication equipment; aerospace electronic and high-technology products, materials, time sharing, computing, and remote data processing.	25
Natural Resources	Utah International, Inc., a miner of uranium, coking coal, steam coal, iron ore, and copper; also oil and gas production; ocean shipping; and land acquisition and development.	15
Foreign Multiindustry	Foreign manufacturing affiliates.	5
Consumer Products and Services	Major appliances; lighting products; A/C equipment; TV receivers; broadcasting and CATV services; and GE Credit Corporation	28

Outlook for Operating Sectors

72 The overall outlook for GE's operating sectors was promising in the late 1970s, with the Technical Systems and Foreign Multiindustry operations expected to experience strong growth. The Natural Resources Sector was expected to grow in spite of increased competition. Growth in the Industrial Products and Power Systems divisions was predicted to be moderate, due to a slowdown in the economy. The Consumer Products sector, of which broadcasting was a part, was forecast to have continued success in its markets throughout the 1980s.

Exhibit 11

General Electric's broadcasting stations

Station	*Location*
Television:	
WRGB	Schenectady, New York
WNGE	Nashville, Tennessee
KOA-TV	Denver, Colorado
AM radio:	
WGY	Schenectady, New York
WSIX-AM	Nashville, Tennessee
KOA	Denver, Colorado
FM radio:	
WGFM	Schenectady, New York
WSIX-FM	Nashville, Tennessee
KOAQ	Denver, Colorado
WJIB	Boston, Massachusetts
KFOG	San Francisco, California

GE's Broadcast Interests

73 General Electric had held broadcast interests since the earliest days of the industry, operating under General Electric Broadcasting Company and General Electric Cablevision. The company ranked number 1 in the top 100 companies in electronic communications. A summary of the stations owned by GE is included in Exhibit 11. In addition to these stations, General Electric operated 13 CATV systems with approximately 170,000 subscribers. About 800 employees were engaged in GE's broadcasting interests.

Financial Situation

74 With an average annual sales growth of 10 percent since 1970, GE's growth was well ahead of the U.S. economy. The company had paid dividends every year since 1922, and its common stock ranged in price from 45 to 55⅛ in 1979. Stock price information and other financial data pertaining to GE has been included in Exhibits 12 and 13.

Exhibit 12

General Electric common stock information

	1979	*1978*	*1977*	*1976*
Par value	$2.50	$2.50	$2.50	$—
Earnings per share	6.20	5.39	4.79	4.12
Dividends per share	2.70	2.40	2.00	1.70
Price range	55⅛–45	57⅝–43⅝	57¼–47¾	58¾–46

Source: *Moody's Industrial Manual.*

Exhibit 13

GENERAL ELECTRIC COMPANY
Comparative Balance Sheet
For the years ended December 31, 1976–1979
($ millions)

Assets	***1979***	***1978***	***1977***	***1976***
Current assets:				
Cash and cash items	$ 1,904.3	$ 1,992.8	$ 1,717.9	$ 1,059.0
Marketable securities	672.3	470.3	560.3	554.3
AR & NR, net	3,646.6	3,288.5	2,982.7	2,717.3
Inventories	3,161.3	3,003.4	2,604.3	2,354.4
Total current assets	9,384.5	8,755.0	7,865.2	6,685.0
Investments:				
Securities of affil. not cons.	981.5	770.3	691.9	639.6
Miscellaneous investments	380.6	360.5	375.1	320.4
Mkt. eg. sec. & assoc. cos., net	329.4	279.7	366.3	326.3
Total investments	1,691.5	1,410.5	1,433.3	1,286.3
Property and equipment:				
Property, plant, and equipment	9,365.2	8,328.2	7,514.5	6,954.8
Less: Depreciation reserve	4,752.4	4,305.6	3,930.4	3,598.4
Net property account	4,612.8	4,022.6	3,584.1	3,356.4
Other assets	955.7	847.9	814.2	722.0
Total assets	$16,644.5	$15,036.0	$13,696.8	$12,049.7
Liabilities and Stockholders Equity				
Current liabilities:				
Short-term borrowings	$ 871.0	$ 960.3	$ 722.1	$ 611.1
A. P.	1,476.7	1,217.2	1,021.4	879.7
Taxes accrued	655.6	532.6	619.9	554.9
Other costs and expenses accrued	1,752.7	1,650.2	1,508.8	1,287.8
Prog. coll. & price adj. accrued	1,957.0	1,667.3	1,369.7	1,169.7
Dividends payable	158.8	147.6	125.1	101.7
Total current liabilities	6,871.8	6,175.2	5,417.0	4,604.9
Stockholders' equity:				
Debenture, 1992	80.5	100.9	113.3	123.3
Debenture, 1996	149.3	156.5	171.0	179.2
Debenture, 1999	—	—	125.0	125.0
Debenture, 2004	295.0	300.0	300.0	300.0
Other long-term debt	422.0	436.4	575.0	594.8
Other liabilities	1,311.9	1,129.5	921.2	750.6
Minority interests	151.7	150.8	131.4	119.0
Common stock ($2.50)	578.7	578.7	578.7	575.9
Amounts received for stock in excess of par	656.3	658.0	668.4	618.3
Retained earnings	6,307.6	5,522.4	4,862.5	4,251.2
Total stockholders' equity	7,362.3	6,586.7	5,942.9	5,252.9
Total liabilities and stockholders' equity	$16,644.5	$15,036.0	$13,696.8	$12,049.7

Source: *Moody's Industrial Manual.*

Exhibit 13 *(concluded)*

GENERAL ELECTRIC COMPANY
Comparative Consolidated Income
For the Years Ended December 31, 1976–1979
($ millions)

Net sales	$22,460.6	$19,653.8	$17,518.6	$15,697.3
Cost and expenses:				
GGS	15,990.7	13,915.1	12,744.4	11,481.2
Selling and administrative expenses	3,715.9	3,204.4	3,076.2	2,688.2
Depreciation, depletion, and amortization	624.1	576.4	—	—
Operating margin	2,129.9	1,957.9	1,698.0	1,527.9
Other income	519.4	419.0	390.3	274.3
Interest and finance charges	258.6	224.4	199.5	174.7
EBIT	2,390.7	2,152.5	1,888.8	1,627.5
Provision—income taxes	953.4	893.9	773.1	668.6
Minority interest	28.5	28.9	27.5	28.3
Net earnings	1,408.8	1,229.7	1,088.2	930.6
Retained earnings: 1/1	5,522.4	4,862.5	4,521.2	3,681.4
Dividends declared	623.6	569.8	476.9	332.5
Other changes	—	—	—	28.3
Retained earnings: 12/31	$ 6,307.6	$ 5,522.4	$ 4,862.5	$ 4,251.2

Source: *Moody's Industrial Manual.*

Definitive Agreement

75 In February of 1979, GE and Cox executed a definitive agreement concerning the merger. Several factors had been considered by each corporation.

76 **Financial.** One of the prime considerations was the exchange ratio between GE and Cox stock. Depending upon the exact common stock price ratio of GE common stock, the exchange ratio would have been 1.3 shares of GE common for each share of Cox. The common stock price ratio used was the average closing price of GE common stock during the 20 consecutive trading days immediately prior to the date of the first public announcement by the FCC of its approval of the merger. Cox shareholders, therefore, were to receive between $65 and $75 worth of GE stock for each Cox share. The value of the merger was placed between $460.5 million and $507.9 million, provided that the transaction closed on or before September 30, 1979. If the closing was after September 30, 1979, the exchange ratio would have been some fraction of the common stock price ratio, depending upon the price of General Electric stock. In addition to common stock, GE was to purchase a number of shares of Cox Broadcasting Corporation's special preferred stock with a par value of $1,000 per share. Exhibit 14 shows the pro forma financial situation of General Electric and Cox and their consolidated affiliates and subsidiaries as of December 31, 1978. Included in Exhibit 15 are the comparative market prices for the two securities. For pro forma accounting purposes, adjustments for the purchase method of accounting were made.

Exhibit 14

GENERAL ELECTRIC COMPANY AND COX BROADCASTING CORPORATION
Pro Forma Debt and Capitalization
($ millions)

	General Electric	*Cox*	*Pro forma adjust-ments*	*Pro forma combined*
Long-term borrowings (excluding current portion):				
5¾% notes due 1991	$ 75.0	—	—	$ 75.0
5.30% debentures due 1992	100.9	—	—	100.9
7½% debentures due 1996	157.5	—	—	156.5
8½% debentures due 2004	300.0	—	—	300.0
Notes with banks due in installments to 1981 at varying interest rates	22.7	—	—	22.7
8% guaranteed sinking fund debentures due 1987	17.8	—	—	17.8
7.6% notes due 1988	36.0	—	—	36.0
4¼% bonds due 1985	26.9	—	—	26.9
4¼% debentures due 1987	50.0	—	—	50.0
5½% Sterling/Dollar Guaranteed Loan Stock due 1993	7.4	—	—	7.4
6½% note due in installments to 1987		$ 18.4	—	18.4
7¾% note due in installments to 1982		8.4	—	8.4
Senior promissory notes at 8¾% due in installments to 1988		13.5		13.5
Senior promissory notes at 10⅞% due in installments to 1991		14.5		14.5
Other	200.6	4.3	—	209.4
Total long-term borrowings	993.8	59.1	—	1,052.9
Minority interest in equity of consolidated affiliates	150.8	1.5	—	152.3
Shareowners' equity:				
General Electric preferred stock par value $1.00 Authorized—2,000,000 shares	—	—	—	—
Cox special preferred stock, par value $1,000		1.0	$ (1.0)	
Cox preferred stock, par value $1.00 Authorized—1,000,000 shares	—	—	—	—
GE common stock, par value $2.50	587.7	—	—	578.7
Cox common stock, par value $1.00		6.7	(6.7)	—
Amounts received for stock in excess of par value	658.0	39.1	(39.1)	658.0
Retained earnings	5,522.4	148.2	(148.2)	5,522.4
Gain recognized on disposition of GE stations	—	—	24.4	24.4
Treasury stock	(172.4)	—	—	(172.4)
Total shareowners' equity	6,586.7	195.0	(170.6)	6,611.1
Total long-term borrowings, minority interest, and shareowners' equity	$7,731.3	$255.6	$(170.6)	$7,816.3

Exhibit 14 ***(concluded)***

GENERAL ELECTRIC COMPANY AND COX BROADCASTING CORPORATION
Condensed Pro Forma Combined Statement of Financial Position
(unaudited, $ millions)

Assets	***General Electric***	***Cox***	***For Pur. Accounting***	***Est. Disps.***	***Pro forma combined***
Current assets:					
Cash and marketable securities	$ 2,463.1	$ 20.7	$(455.5)	$109.8	$ 2,138.1
Current receivables	3,288.5	33.0	—	—	3,321.5
Inventories	3,003.4	—	—	—	3,003.4
Other current assets	—	—	—	—	—
Total current assets	8,755.0	75.3	(477.1)	109.8	8,463.0
Property, plant and equipment less accumulated depreciation, depletion, and amortization	4,022.6	115.0	21.0	(7.1)	4,151.5
Investments	1,410.5	—	—	—	1,410.5
Intangible assets less accumulated amortization	—	112.6	232.3	(47.0)	297.9
Other assets	847.9	20.1	21.0	2.2	890.7
				3.9	
Total assets	$15,036.0	$323.0	$(202.8)	$ 57.4	15,213.6
Liabilities and Equity					
Current liabilities:					
Short-term borrowings	$ 960.3	$ 8.2	—	—	$ 968.5
Accounts payable	1,217.2	18.7	—	—	1,235.9
Progress collections and price adjustments accrued	1,667.3	—	—	—	1,667.3
Dividends payable	147.6	1.3	—	—	148.9
Taxes accrued	532.6	9.9	—	$ 34.1	576.6
Other current liabilities	1,650.2	13.2	—	—	1,663.4
Total current liabilities	6,175.2	51.3	—	34.1	6,260.6
Long-term borrowings	993.8	59.1	—	—	1,052.9
Other long-term liabilities	1,129.5	8.3	—	(1.1)	1,136.7
Deferred credits	—	7.8	$ (7.3)	—	—
Total liabilities	8,298.5	126.5	(7.8)	33.0	8,450.2
Shareowners' equity:					
Minority interest in equity of consolidated affiliates	150.8	1.5	—	—	152.3
Preferred stock	—	1.0	(1.0)	—	—
Common stock par value	587.7	6.7	(6.7)		578.7
Amounts received for stock in excess of par value	658.0	39.1	(39.1)	—	658.0
Retained earnings	5,522.4	148.2	(148.2)	24.4	5,546.8
	6,759.1	195.0	(195.0)	24.4	6,783.5
Deduct common stock held in treasury	(172.4)	—	—	—	172.4
Total share owners' equity	6,586.7	195.0	(195.0)	24.4	6,611.1
Total liabilities, minority, interest, and equity	$15,036.0	$323.0	$(202.8	$ 57.4	$15,213.6

Exhibit 15

Comparative market prices

	Cox		*General Electric*	
	High	*Low*	*High*	*Low*
1977:				
1st quarter	$33⅝	$28	$55⅞	$49
2d quarter	29⅞	26¼	57¼	47⅞
3d quarter	29⅜	25½	56½	50⅜
4th quarter	36¾	26⅝	52¾	47⅜
1978:				
1st quarter	36½	32	49⅝	43⅝
2d quarter	44	35½	54⅞	45⅞
3d quarter	49⅛	40½	57⅝	49⅞
4th quarter	59⅞	47⅞	53⅞	45¾
1979:				
1st quarter	50¾	55	50⅜	45½
2d quarter (to June 14)	62¾	59	51⅝	46⅞

Source: Cox Broadcasting Corporation, proxy statement.

77 Solomon Brothers and Lazard Freres and Company issued opinions regarding the fairness of the proposed basis of exchange between the two securities. Both investment bankers issued opinions stating that the merger was fair to Cox shareholders from a financial point of view.

78 **Divestiture of Assets.** Another factor considered in drawing up the merger agreement was the divestiture of certain television and radio stations. The FCC had rules barring the ownership of more than 21 broadcast properties by one licensee. The combined holdings of General Electric and Cox were 8 VHF television stations, 8 AM radio stations, and 12 FM ratio stations at the time.

79 To comply with FCC rules and the merger agreement, three television stations, two AM radio stations, and four FM radio stations would have to be sold. Those stations which were agreed to be disposed of are listed in Exhibit 16. General Electric would sell five stations, while Cox would dispose of four.

80 **Minorities.** Many factors were considered in the disposition of General Electric and Cox stations besides the dollar value offered by the prospective purchasers. One of these factors was the FCC's policies encouraging new entrants into broadcasting and minority and local ownership of broadcast stations. John F. Welch, senior vice president and sector executive of General Electric's consumer products and services sector, stated the entire approach to the divestiture program was to help meet the

81 More than two thirds of the stations would be acquired by new entrants into the broadcasting business. (Exhibit 16 shows the prospective purchasers of the dispositions.) Seven of the proposed purchasers of the spin-offs included substantial, if not majority, black ownership (more than two thirds).

Exhibit 16

General Electric and Cox stations to be sold

Station	*Location*	*Seller*	*Purchaser*	*Price*
WHIO-TV	Dayton, Ohio	Cox	Ohio Valley Broadcasting Company, Inc.	$47,500,000
WSOC-AM/FM	Charlotte, North Carolina	Cox	Charlotte Broadcasting Company	$2,080,000 plus 20 percent of the capital stock of the purchaser.
WSB-AM	Atlanta, Georgia	Cox	Metromedia, Inc.	Traded for WCBM-AM Baltimore, Maryland, plus $8,650,000 by Metromedia
WSB-FM	Atlanta, Georgia	Cox	BENI Broadcasting of Georgia, Inc.	$4,400,000 plus a $1,100,000 9.5 percent convertible subordinated note
WRGB-TV	Schenectady, New York	GE	Group Six Broadcasting, Inc.	$4,400,000 plus a $2,000,000 9.5 to 11.5 percent convertible subordinated note
WGFM	Schenectady, New York	GE	Mountain Radio, Inc.	$1,600,000
WSIX-AM/FM	Nashville, Tennessee	GE	The Kate Agency, Inc.	$3,000,000
WNGE-TV	Nashville, Tennessee	GE	Nashville Television, Inc.	$20,000,000 plus a $5,000,000 9.5 percent convertible subordinated note
KFOG-FM	San Francisco, California	GE	Under negotiation	

82 General Electric would also set up an autonomous foundation for minority broadcasting development. The foundation was to have aided minority program development in Atlanta.

83 **Management.** General Electric and Cox also considered management of the new organization. General Electric operated its broadcast holdings under the direction of Reid L. Shaw, president of General Electric Broadcasting Company and General Electric Cablevision. Clifford M. Kirkland was Cox's president and chief executive officer. The merger agreement stated that General Electric would retain Cox's present management. It was assumed that Shaw would retain his position.

FCC Position on the Cox-GE Merger

84 On May 31, 1979, General Electric and Cox Broadcasting filed their application with the FCC for approval of the proposed merger.

85 According to GE, FCC approval would significantly diversify ownership of mass media. Because of the sale of some stations to new entrants to broadcasting, co-located newspaper/television and television/radio ownerships would be broken up.

86 The approval would also serve as a vehicle to provide assistance for minorities interested in careers in communications. Minority assistance would be conducted through the independent foundation that GE would set up with the proceeds of the sale of some stations.

87 One other result of FCC approval would be improved programming of the stations that General Electric owned. GE would accomplish this through broadcasting 160 television and 85 radio public service announcements.

Cox Approval

88 On July 18, 1979, the stockholders of Cox Broadcasting approved the proposed merger. At that time, it was not expected the merger would be completed before early 1980 since the companies had to wait for FCC approval.

Problems with Public Interest

89 Two principal petitions to block the proposed merger were filed with the FCC. One was made by VBTC, Virginia Beach Telecommunications Corporation and the other was submitted by the National Citizens Committee for Broadcasting, NCCB.

90 The petitions contended that Cox and GE lacked the character qualifications to be licensees. They further stated that Cox and GE had failed to show the "compelling public interest" required of a broadcaster seeking to own more than two VHF stations in the top 50 markets. The merger, NCCB and VBTC believed, would result in an undue concentration of control.

91 General Electric and Cox promptly requested that the petitions be dismissed, reiterating the benefits the public would receive as a result of the merger. Cox and GE received support from the National Black Media Coalition who stated that the benefits of the proposed merger were monumental.

The Decision

92 Because the merger had not been approved by September 30, 1979, negotiations were reopened regarding the exchange ratio. General Electric was willing to increase the value of the merger to $600 million.

93 By April 1980, sharp increases had taken place in the price of cable television properties. Wall Street analysts stated that a system was worth $1,000 per connection. If Cox, with 775,000 connections, sold its cable operations at only $750 a connection, the value would have been almost $600 million. The value of FM radio and television stations were also on the rise. Because of these sharp increases in broadcasting property values, the stipulated merger price was far below the company's worth. Cox officials said they now wanted at least $700 million (around $95 a share) for the corporation.

94 On April 28, 1980, the FCC approved the proposed merger between Cox Broadcasting Corporation and General Electric Company.

case 9
The Cold-flo™ Ammonia Converter—Imperial Oil Limited

1 In Edmonton in May 1978, John Singer was considering an offer for the exclusive distributorship of an innovative fertilizer applicator called the Cold-flo Converter. As field services coordinator of agricultural chemicals for Imperial Oil (the Exxon Canadian affiliate), he felt that the converter would be an improved method for applying the popular fertilizer, anhydrous ammonia. John wondered if prairie farmers would accept the new applicator and if Imperial Oil should be directly involved in selling the applicator.

Background Information

2 Imperial Oil entered the fertilizer market in 1963 with Engro fertilizer in granular form. This was done for two reasons. First, a major competitor, Federated Co-op Ltd. of Saskatchewan, sold both petroleum and fertilizer while Imperial Oil distributed only petroleum. As a defensive move, Imperial Oil entered the fertilizer market with fertilizer purchased from Cominco. Second, Imperial Oil entered the fertilizer market to provide increased earning opportunities for its independent Esso agents. Prior to the introduction of fertilizer, Esso agents had depended on bulk petroleum and lubricants for their income.

3 In 1965, Imperial Oil realized that service demands for fertilizer had changed. A more-efficient distribution system was needed. The company commenced a test building program for fertilizer warehouses and a manufacturing feasibility study.

4 In 1966 and 1967, Imperial Oil completed construction of the field warehouse network at a cost of $7 million.

5 In 1969, the company built a $57 million fertilizer plant in Redwater, Alberta, with an annual capacity of 500,000 tons. Several bottlenecks in the plant had been worked out since 1969, and the plant's present capacity was about 700,000 tons.

6 In 1971, Imperial Oil added anhydrous ammonia (NH_3) to the Engro family of fertilizers. NH_3 was a big success. The total market for this product had grown from 20,000 tons in 1971 to about 155,000 tons in 1978. In 1978, the average ammonia customer purchased 13 tons. The total NH_3 market was expected to grow for many years at an annual rate of 10 to 11 percent. Imperial Oil's gross margin on NH_3 was more than twice the gross margin for granular fertilizers, which was approximately 5 percent.

This case was prepared by James Graham with the assistance of Denise Palock and Michael Fuller, all of the University of Calgary. Reprinted with permission of the Case Research Association.

7 The total prairie market for fertilizer was 1.5 million tons in the 1977–78 crop year. Imperial Oil presently held about 21 percent of this market. In Alberta, Imperial Oil's severest competition came from Sherritt-Gordon, a large mining company, and Western Co-ops Ltd.[1] Sherritt-Gordon had a plant in Alberta and marketed aggressively through a network of independent dealers and wholesaled through the United Grain Growers (UGG) elevator chain. Another major competitor in Alberta was Cominco. Cominco, owned by one of Canada's largest firms, CP Investments, had a network of independent dealers who sold Elephant Brand fertilizer. In Saskatchewan, the Saskatchewan Wheat Pool had a major chunk of the market. The Prairie Wheat Pools, UGG, and Federated Co-op all depended heavily on the "co-op doctrinaire" segments of the Prairie population (about 40 percent). John Singer estimated that half of the cooperative segment always patronized the wheat pools. The other half, primarily larger farmers, could be lured away by Imperial Oil if Esso agents offered equally attractive prices and better service. Compared to the wheat pools, Esso agents were more likely to have application equipment and products available when needed and were more willing to work after hours to supply service to customers. The wheat pools, as farmer owned cooperatives, repatriated profits to customers at the end of the crop year. The dividends returned on fertilizer sales had been as high as 10 percent of the purchase price.

Anhydrous Ammonia and Other Fertilizers

8 There are three types of fertilizer: granular (crystals and pellets of fertilizer), solution (fertilizer mixed with water), and gas (NH_3). Imperial Oil did not sell solutions although two of its competitors, Manitoba Wheat Pool and Simplot, did. John Singer knew that Imperial Oil had not found solutions profitable. Solutions were also the most-expensive form of fertilizer to the farmer.

9 Consumption (in tons) of the best-selling nitrogen fertilizers is shown in Exhibit 1.

Exhibit 1

Name	*1974–1975 season*	*1975–1976 season*	*1976–1977 season*
Anhydrous ammonia	81,585	127,309	145,872
Ammonium nitrate	207,687	239,673	202,394
Ammonium sulphate	54,499	64,891	44,194
Urea	86,843	105,416	144,161
Urea ammonium nitrate solution	20,266	24,504	40,084
Total	450,880	561,793	576,705

10 Granular fertilizer was used across the Prairies. Anhydrous ammonia was used primarily in Alberta, although it was expanding rapidly into Saskatchewan and Manitoba. Solutions were prevalent in Saskatchewan and Manitoba.

11 These fertilizers could be distinguished from one another by the percentages they contained of the nutrients nitrogen (N), phosphate (P_2O_5), potash (K_2O), and sulphur

[1] Western Co-ops Ltd. was owned by the Alberta, Manitoba, and Saskatchewan wheat pools and Federated Co-op. Western Co-ops and Cominco had both completed major expansions to their fertilizer production facilities in the last two years.

(S). For instance, 21–0–0–24 indicated a fertilizer that contained 21 percent N, 0 percent P_2O_5, 0 percent K_2O, and 24 percent S. While all crops were physiologically indifferent to their source of nutrients, different crops used varying amounts of nutrients. Also, soil types affected the form and amount of fertilizer required.

12 Granular fertilizers were applied by spreading them over the surface of the soil (top dressing) or by drilling them into the soil with seed. Solution fertilizers was sprayed on the soil. Anhydrous ammonia was injected into the soil as a liquid using a specially equipped tillage tool that plowed the liquid into the ground.

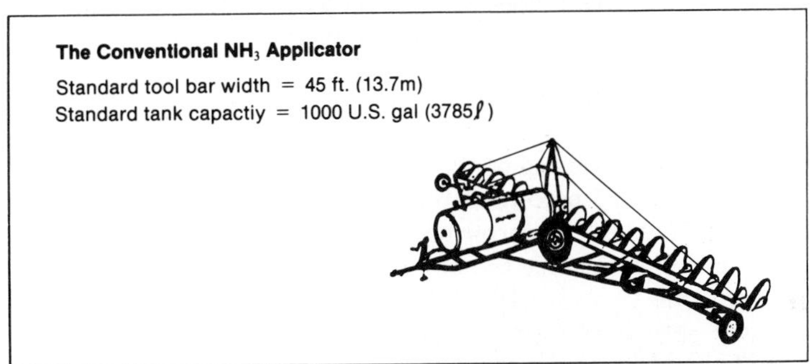

The Conventional NH_3 Applicator
Standard tool bar width = 45 ft. (13.7m)
Standard tank capactiy = 1000 U.S. gal (3785ℓ)

13 Anhydrous ammonia application presently required an NH_3 tank and truck (for agent-to-farm delivery) and an NH_3 applicator (see above). Conversion kits could be installed on conventional tillage equipment as well. These were less costly but less efficient than a standard NH_3 applicator. Presently, 90 percent of Prairie ammonia customers used the conventional applicators, and 10 percent used the conversion kits.

14 Regardless of the application method used, it was important that the NH_3 be injected at least 6–3 inches (15–20cm) in the soil. If the NH_3 was injected too shallowly or under adverse soil or mositure conditions, the liquid NH_3 quickly vaporized with the reduction of pressure and temperature increase and the gaseous NH_3 would escape from the soil.

15 Anhydrous ammonia could be applied in the fall or spring. In the fall, cooler soil temperatures reduced the loss of NH_3 due to evaporation. However, spring application was more popular. In the spring, farmers were more certain of their cropping plans and could judge accurately the amount of nitrogen the soil required. Also, for sandy soils, spring NH_3 application reduced the risk of leaching loss. The seasonal demand for fertilizers had resulted in dealers being unable to supply fertilizer and application equipment in sufficient quantities to meet demand during peak periods.

16 Anhydrous ammonia had to be carefully handled since it could burn exposed skin by freezing. Exposure to high concentrations of NH_3 vapor or liquid could be fatal. However, NH_3 was easily detected by its pungent odor, and first aid was very simple: apply lots of water.

The Cold-flo Ammonia Converter

17 The Cold-flo Converter was developed by United States Steel (USS) in conjunction with researchers at Pennsylvania State University. USS had marketed the converter as part of its "conserve America's energy resources" advertising strategy. The offer

by USS for exclusive distributorship of the Cold-flo system was made to Imperial Oil by accident: representatives of the two companies had met during rock phosphate negotiations in April 1977. A tentative verbal agreement giving Imperial Oil exclusive distribution rights for three years was made in June 1977. John Singer had to present his recommendations to the field services manager, Doug Mackenzie, late in June 1978. A final decision had to be made at that time.

18 The Cold-flo Converter consisted of a small cylindrical chamber that changed NH_3 to a liquid at atmospheric pressure. The conventional application applied NH_3 as a gas under slight pressure. The converter had two basic functions—it served as an expansion chamber for pressure release and separated liquid ammonia from ammonia vapor. Ammonia was metered into the converter from a nurse tank by means of a regulator. After conversion, the liquid ammonia flowed by gravity from the bottom of the converter through a manifold and hose system into the soil. Vaporized ammonia exited from the top of the converter to a second manifold and hose system into the soil. About 85 percent of the NH_3 was liquid and 15 percent vapor.

19 The Cold-flo Converter had several advantages. It was a low-cost method of fertilizer application because the ammonia could be applied as the soil was tilled. This meant that one trip over the field was eliminated and time, equipment wear, labor, and fuel were saved.[2] Also, herbicides could be incorporated into the application procedure. The Cold-flo system could be used on soil too heavy for use of a conventional applicator for NH_3.

20 Since the Cold-flo Converter applied NH_3 to the soil as a liquid, sealing problems (holding the gaseous NH_3 in the soil) were minimized, and shallower application was possible. Ammonia could be applied to the soil as shallow as four inches (10cm) deep near the feeder roots of most crops. Deeper placement was recommended for coarse textured soils.

21 The Cold-flo Converter could be mounted on most standard field cultivators, chisel plows, or disc harrows. A farmer could purchase the mount or make one himself. In the United States, the Cold-flo Converter had been most widely used on field cultivators. The procedure for setting up the system varied only slightly for chisel plows and disc harrows.

22 The successful operation of the converter with any tillage equipment depended on four factors. First, there had to be proper calibration of the NH_3 regulator to the rate of application per acre to ensure proper rate of application. Second, liquid and vapor hoses had to be properly arranged so the NH_3 flowed in a uniform and unrestricted fashion to ensure even application. Liquid hoses had to be downward sloping. Third, liquid and vapor attachments had to be properly placed to ensure complete coverage of the ammonia. Finally, the correct number of liquid and vapor outlets had to be used. United States Steel had developed tables for determining the proper number of outlets and the best application rates per hour per acre.

Some considerations

23 The Cold-flo Converter had been tested by the Department of Land Resource Science at the University of Guelph. The results of the testing had been published by the

[2] In the United States, the savings had been estimated at \$1–\$2 per acre.

Ontario Ministry of Agriculture and Food in May 1978. The report found the converter to be simple and safe but also raised a number of questions.

24 The Ontario ministry warned that heavy crop residues, wet soil conditions, or fine soil texture could increase the escape of vaporized NH_3 from the soil. Also, ammonia losses could result when the converter was used with a disc harrow because disc penetration was uneven and varied between two and six inches (5 and 15cm). Further, the ministry thought that the gravity flow system might be hampered when driving over sloped land. There was also a danger that the NH_3 would damage germinating seed if improperly applied. The ministry acknowledged, however, that no published data existed that compared the Cold-flo system to other methods of nitrogen fertilizer application.

25 John Singer said any fertilizer was capable of damaging seed if improperly applied. He felt that the problem of seed damage had been satisfactorily solved by three methods used by American farmers familiar with Cold-flo. One method consisted of applying NH_3 at an angle or opposite to the direction of planting. Another method was simply to ensure that the NH_3 was applied at least four inches below the soil surface. Finally, a farmer could wait about a week after NH_3 application before planting.

26 It was possible that farmers, like the Ontario ministry, might overestimate the loss of vaporized NH_3 from the soil. This was because a white cloud could sometimes be observed rising from the soil where NH_3 had been applied. While some of this cloud could be gaseous ammonia, most of the vapor was water that condensed upon contact with the cold NH_3 liquid. Also, any loss of ammonia could be smelled around the tillage equipment.

27 Another aspect of Cold-flo merited consideration. If Imperial Oil marketed the system, the company would be able to associate itself with an innovative product. There was nothing to stop competitors from supplying NH_3 for the Cold-flo converter because the pressurized NH_3 tanks were standardized. Further, the demand for NH_3 exceeded supply in the Prairie market. In the short term, Imperial Oil was unwilling to invest in storage and transportation equipment sufficient to supply all the present markets in any one location because customers who shopped around for NH_3 would leave Esso agents once competitors had a local supply of NH_3 and were able to satisfy the customers in the area. John believed the NH_3 market to be dislocated due to these growing pains, especially in Alberta.

28 An alternative existed to the Cold-flo system. A Nebraska firm had developed a "Can Converter" system that operated on the same principle as Cold-flo except that the canister-like converters were small and mounted on each shank of the tillage equipment. USS had viewed the system as an infringement on its patient and had purchased the rights to the system, although the Can Converter system did not work nearly as efficiently as the Cold-flo system.

The Cold-flo Converter and Esso Agents

29 Imperial Oil had 450 Esso agents in the Prairies, 70 of whom sold anhydrous ammonia. These agents were independent businessmen who sold Imperial Oil products on a commission basis. They were serviced and supervised by 28 sales representatives in three areas.

30 Esso agents were encouraged by Imperial Oil to sell both petroleum and fertilizer products. Many agents, particularly in the small rural communities, had combined

incomes. Along with Imperial Oil products they sold everything from herbicides to insurance and equipment. Sometimes an agent was related to the farmers that he sold to.

31 Imperial Oil's best agent, located in Lacombe, sold 6,000 tons of granular fertilizer a year. Two other Esso agents sold 5,000 tons yearly. The vast majority of Esso agents sold between 1,000 and 4,000 tons yearly. Esso agents received a commission of $65 per ton of NH_3 sold and $10 per ton of bulk granular fertilizer sold. About 70 percent of the granular fertilizer sold by Esso agents was in bulk, rather than bagged.

32 Fertilizer sales were becoming an increasingly significant portion of agents' total income, due largely to the growth of NH_3 sales. An agent just starting to sell NH_3 could be virtually guaranteed $25,000 in gross commissions in the first year with a $50,000 investment in equipment. Petroleum products did not have this growth factor. An agent earned between 4 and 6 cents per gallon on fuels and lubricants and had to work all year to sell them. On both petroleum and fertilizer sales, agents would net about one third of their commissions.

33 In addition to selling Imperial Oil products, Esso agents rented fertilizer application equipment.[3] This service saved farmers from investing in little-used application equipment. Esso agents, along with farm radio and newspapers, were also a source of information. When fertilizer shortages occurred in 1974 and 1978, the agents had advised farmers of the impending shortages and price increases.

34 This information service provided by agents could have a variety of effects. During fertilizer shortages, agents received a strict allocation of product. Naturally, the Esso agents wanted to ensure that their regular customers received fertilizer and so told them to order early. The agents hoped that this action would encourage their regular customers to remember them in the future, if fertilizer prices dropped and the agents faced stiff competition. However, news of shortages caused farmers to shop around in an effort to obtain fertilizer. This behavior heightened apparent demand.

35 As the price of fertilizer rose in a shortage situation, farmers often purchased more rather than less fertilizer. This was due in part to hoarding, but the major reason seemed to be the general economic outlook. In 1974 and 1978, the price of grain had risen; farmers believed they could afford to purchase fertilizer, and fertilizer purchases reduced their taxable income. The increase in yield resulting from the use of fertilizer more than offset the cost of buying and applying the product.

36 Esso agents also provided farmers with information concerning the safe handling of anhydrous ammonia. The agents could supply 20-minute audiovisual cassettes that explained NH_3 characteristics and handling procedures.

37 If Imperial Oil adopted the Cold-flo system, the agents would have to fulfill several requirements. These would be:

1. Supplying the NH_3 to existing nurse tanks and continuing to provide delivery of NH_3 to existing nurse tanks.
2. Using a Cold-flo installer from Esso Chemical to set up the initial unit at the agency and for troubleshooting thereafter. (Once the setup of the system was demonstrated, farmers would be able to install the equipment themselves.)

[3] Esso agents owned and financed all mobile equipment (for example, fertilizer applicators, NH_3 nurse tank trailers, trucks). Imperial Oil owned all fixed equipment (for example, warehouses and fertilizer tanks) and paid the depreciation and interest on mobile equipment. The pay-out period for mobile equipment was five years.

3. Encouraging farmers to request the installer early, since its availability would be limited prior to and during the fertilizer season.
4. Providing farmers Cold-flo Converter kits composed of: 1 Cold-flo Converter, liquid and vapor manifolds, and hoses.
5. Providing liquid and vapor dispensers designed for Cold-flo to be attached to the shanks of tillage tools.
6. Providing converter mounting stands.
7. Providing Cold-flo splitters and extra manifolds for extrawide tillage equipment.

38 Esso agents would obtain Cold-flo equipment from Esso Chemical, and they would be invoiced on their 30-day merchandise accounts. Parts for Cold-flo equipment would be ordered by telephone. Delivery of parts from inventories held in Calgary and Winnipeg would normally take two to five days.

39 The selling price for the Cold-flo equipment could be kept under $1,000. If the price was more than $1,000, the agents would have to be licensed under the Provincial Farm Implement Act to sell farm equipment. Licensed dealers were controlled in that they were required to service equipment sold and meet other requirements such as keeping repair parts for as long as one year after the sale of the equipment.

40 Customers would be aware that Imperial Oil was willing to refund the price of any Cold-flo unit found to be unsatisfactory with normal use. This guarantee would be good for 12 months after the date of purchase.

The Cold-flo Converter and Farmers

41 The rural areas of the prairies had undergone some major changes. Farms had decreased dramatically in number and increased in size. (See Exhibits 2 and 3.) There was an accelerating movement away from ownership of farmland and towards tenancy and part tenancy and ownership.

42 The Prairie farmer's investment in equipment was significant. A heavy-duty chisel plow (33-foot cultivator) could cost about $8,600, and a 30-foot disc harrow could cost about $13,000. Four-wheel-drive tractors cost between $40,000 and $125,000, and harvesters could cost as much as $65,000. Farmers easily have $250,000 to $500,000 worth of equipment. A complete Cold-flo unit would cost a farmer about as much as the tires for his combine (see Exhibit 4).

43 Fertilizer demand over certain periods was also strongly correlated to farm incomes. Increases in fertilizer demand typically lagged one year behind increases in farm income. Small farmers especially were often reticent about purchasing new equipment. They tended to purchase equipment when they could pay cash because a poor year could leave them with bills that could not be paid. For many Alberta farmers, owning modern equipment was a point of pride rather than a pure economic decision.

44 In order to convert a tillage tool to Cold-flo, a farmer would have to obtain Cold-flo equipment from an Esso agent. Some of this equipment could be made by the farmer (for example, the converter mounting stand) or purchased from other suppliers (for example, liquid and vapor dispensers). The Cold-flo system also required other ammonia equipment that was not normally supplied by Esso agents. This equipment included:

One ammonia flow regulator.

One breakaway quick couple for the pressurized ammonia line from the nurse tank.

Exhibit 2

Number of farms in Canada

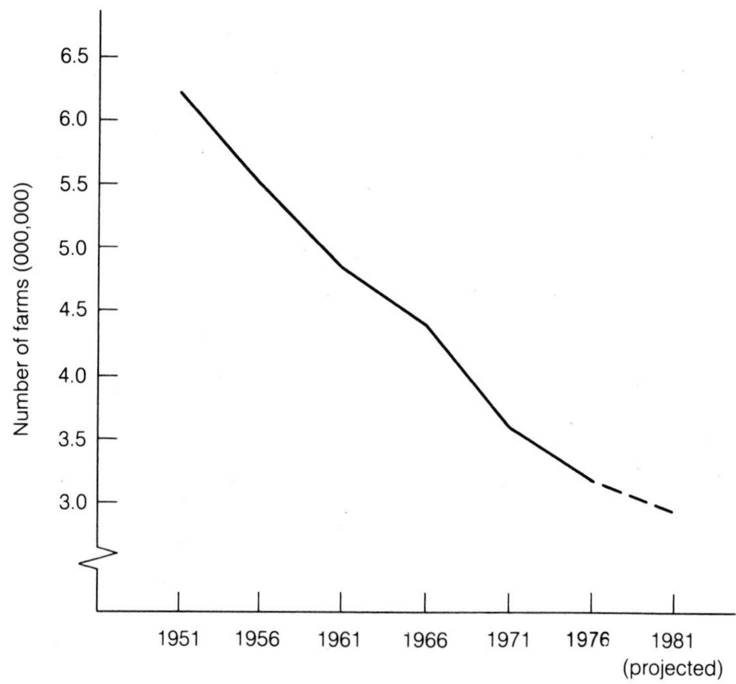

Vapor hose.
Vapor system hose clamps (two per vapor line).
Liquid system hose clamps (two per liquid line).
Four U-bolts for mounting vapor manifolds to the implement frame.
Two ammonia pressure hoses.
One hitch.

45 Other Prairie companies such as Agwest, Westeel, Rosco, and Norwesco supplied hoses, regulators, and quick couples. Hose clamps and bolts were available from any hardware store.

46 The cost per ton of NH_3 would be reduced by $10 to Cold-flo users since the agent would not have to supply a conventional applicator. If a farmer already happened to own a nurse tank trailer as well, his cost per ton of NH_3 would be reduced by $20. In addition to the reduced cost of fertilizer, farmers with their own applicators would be less affected by shortages in equipment during peak application periods. (See Exhibit 5.)

Exhibit 3

Size of farms in Canada

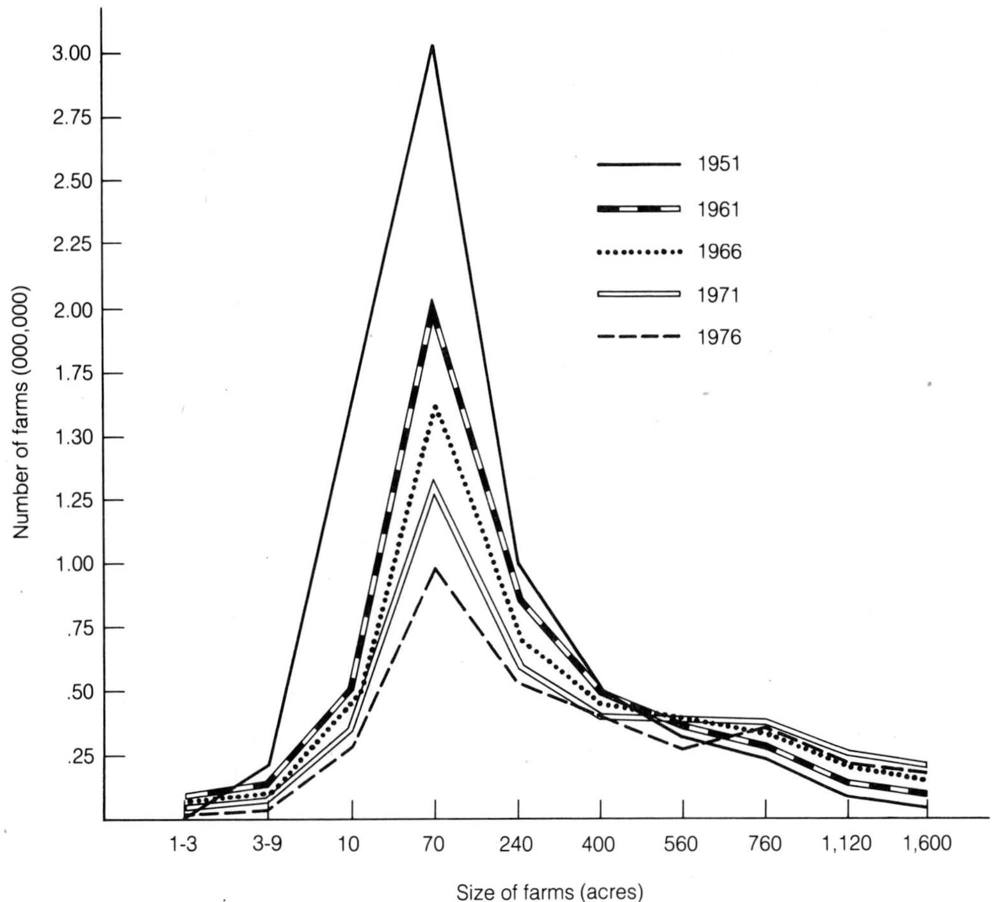

The Current Situation

47 USS had sold about 3,000 units since the Cold-flo Converter had been introduced two years ago. USS had encountered some production constraints and claimed that an additional 4,000 units could have been sold. Imperial had four alternatives with regard to Cold-flo:

1. Exclusive distribution through Esso agencies.
2. Marketing by Esso Chemical on a wholesale basis through the Esso agency system.
3. Nonexclusive distribution through Esso agencies.
4. Nonparticipation.

Exhibit 4

Pricing of the Cold-flo system

	Price delivered to agent	*Suggested retail price*
System 16—Converter package with 16 liquid outlets	$500.00	$560.00
System 24—Converter package with 24 liquid outlets	530.00	595.00
System 32—Converter package with 32 liquid outlets. (This is a system 16 plus a flow splitter and an extra 16-outlet liquid manifold.)	660.00	745.00
System 48—Converter package with 48 liquid outlets. (This is a system 24 plus a flow splitter and an extra 24-outlet liquid manifold.)	750.00	845.00
Type 1—Liquid dispenser for field cultivator	3.25	3.65
Type 2—Combination dispenser for chisel plow	9.25	10.40
Type 3—Combination dispenser for cultivator with trailing hose (for use in difficult soil conditions)	5.65	6.35
Type 4—Vapor dispenser for field cultivator	3.25	3.65
Converter mounting stand	84.00	94.50

48 A preliminary testing of the Cold-flo system was done in the fall of 1977. Two units had been installed on a farm near Beiseker, Alberta. The units were reported to be running well after some modifications to the dispensers.

49 Three units had been tested in Manitoba near Portage, Winkler (a heavy soil area that restricted the use of conventional application equipment), and Brandon. The farmers were pleased with the performance of Cold-flo. Several inquiries about the Cold-flo system were generated, including inquiries by a co-op and an Agwest dealer. A Hutterite colony near Beiseker requested two units for the spring of 1978. In total, 3,000 acres were tested. Twenty-five to 50 units had been sold for the spring of 1978.

50 The distribution of the Cold-flo system in the Prairie could have the following benefits:

1. Increased ammonia volume for Esso agents.
   a. Diversified approach (conventional applicators and Cold-flo) to serve a wider range of customer needs.
   b. Sales of Cold-flo to customers whose needs do not justify tying up the agent's applicator.
   c. Cold-flo sales may draw in potential ammonia customers.
2. Enhancement of profitable ammonia sales versus less-profitable granular fertilizer sales.
3. Reduction of the required agent investment per ton of fertilizer sales.
   a. Agent could build sales volume quickly.
4. Promotion of Imperial Oil's image of progress and leadership.
   a. Innovative product.
   b. Energy and labor saving.

Exhibit 5

Engro posted price history—Alberta bulk ($/ton)

Date	*82-0-0*	*34-0-0*	*46-0-0*	*21-0-0-24*
1971				
March	$150.00	$ 71.00	$ 91.50	$41.00
June	150.00	71.00	99.50	41.00
September	150.00	75.00	94.00	39.00
December	150.00	75.00	94.00	39.00
1972				
March	155.00	75.00	94.00	39.00
June	155.00	75.00	94.00	39.00
September	155.00	76.00	92.00	42.00
December	155.00	76.00	92.00	45.00
1973				
March	155.00	76.00	92.00	45.00
June	155.00	76.00	92.00	45.00
September	170.00	82.00	103.00	54.50
December	185.00	89.00	113.00	59.50
1974				
March	185.00	89.00	113.00	59.50
June	185.00	89.00	113.00	59.50
September	215.00	100.00	135.00	75.00
December	285.00	100.00	182.00	95.00
1975				
March	255.00	135.00	169.00	95.00
June	255.00	120.00	169.00	95.00
September	265.00	132.00	175.00	93.00
December	265.00	119.50	159.00	87.00
1976				
March	280.00	122.00	159.00	75.00
June	280.00	132.00	164.00	83.00
September	260.00	122.00	159.00	74.00
December	250.00	122.00	159.00	74.00
1977				
March	270.00	125.00	159.00	79.00
June	255.00	128.00	157.00	78.00
September	240.00	122.00	152.00	78.00
December	240.00	125.00	155.00	82.00
1978				
March	260.00	136.00	169.00	85.00

51 Singer wasn't certain that all of the factors involving the Cold-flo decision had been considered. Basically, he wanted to know: should Imperial Oil market the Cold-flo Converter, and if so, how?

case 10
Iowa Beef Processors, Inc. (A)

1 Iowa Beef Processors, Inc. (IBP) celebrated the 20th anniversary of its founding in 1981. The founders, Currier J. Holman and Andrew Anderson, borrowed $300,000 from the Small Business Administration and sold stock to local farmers to finance the beef slaughtering operation. Located in Denison, Iowa, the plant was close to the farms and feedlots of the Midwest and designed to operate with unskilled labor. Cattle were brought to slaughter before they began to lose weight ("shrink") as they were transported to distant slaughterhouses. This increased the yield and provided more beef for its dollars to Iowa Beef. The assembly-line operations at IBP lowered labor costs so IBP's early success was based on controlling shrink and costs.

2 In operation for only seven months of 1961, IBP generated sales of about $35 million and earnings after taxes and bonuses of $232,382. Earnings increased 100 percent each of the next two years and have continued to grow. In 1980, the company earned $53.1 million on sales of $4.6 billion. These earnings represented better than an 18 percent return on capital and 22.3 percent on stockholders' equity. This was the 11th consecutive year of increased earnings. For the previous decade, sales had grown at an annual compound rate of 23.6 percent while earnings growth for the same period was 25.5 percent.

3 IBP's growth has come at the expense of older meatpackers who were saddled with inefficient and labor-intensive operations. By performing more of the butchering operations at the slaughterhouse, IBP perfected the shipping of packaged beef cuts in boxes to customers. Efficient operations, lower labor costs, better use of by-products, and lower transportation costs for boxed beef as opposed to carcasses gave IBP a cost advantage which has made IBP the nation's largest meatpacker.

4 Having established dominance in beef processing, IBP managers had begun to evaluate opportunities for long-term growth. The pork segment of the red meat industry had generated the most support. The major question to be answered was whether IBP's unquestionably successful strategy in beef would work as well in the pork industry.

5 Another issue which management of IBP faced in its 20th anniversary year was quickly resolved. Occidental Petroleum purchased IBP in a stock swap valued at $800 million. Negotiations were initiated by IBP's largest stockholder in June, and the merger was approved by stockholders of both companies in August. The rationale

This case was prepared by Phyllis G. Holland as the basis for class discussion rather than to illustrate either effective or ineffective handling of an administrative situation.

for the merger as well as the possible long-term effects on IBP were the subject of much inconclusive debate among observers.

6 This case will provide information on the beef and pork sectors of the red meat industry, strategy and operations of IBP, and the terms of the merger.

The Beef Industry

7 The provision of beef for American tables begins in the Plains areas where breeding cows and calves are pastured.

8 Calves are sold or moved to better pastures when they reach six to eight months of age and at about one to one and a half years are ready for dry-lot feeding. The purpose of dry-lot feeding is to produce USDA Choice and USDA Prime carcasses.[1] Physical activity of the animals is restricted, and feed mixtures are calculated to produce the maximum weight gain per dollar of feed. Growth hormones are typically used. At the conclusion of the feeding period (three months is considered the minimum time period to produce USDA Choice), the cattle are shipped to major livestock centers

Exhibit 1

Selected expenses of Corn Belt cattle feeding

Expenses	*Dollars per head*	*Dollars per head*	*Dollars per head*
Purchased during *Marketed during*	*July 1975* *January 1976*	*July 1980* *January 1981*	*July 1981* *January 1982*
600-lb. feeder steer	$208.20	$439.92	$375.32
Transportation to feedlot (400 miles)	5.28	5.26	5.28
Corn (45 bu.)	122.40	122.85	141.75
Silage (1.7 tons)	35.12	36.47	42.84
30 percent soy protein supplement (270 lbs.)	22.82	31.55	35.78
Hay (400 lbs.)	8.70	9.45	11.45
Labor (4 hours)	8.76	12.92	14.80
Vet medicine	2.99	4.47	4.87
Interest on purchase (6 months)	10.41	30.75	34.66
Power, equipment, fuel, shelter, depreciation	13.94	20.87	22.73
Death loss (1 percent of purchase)	2.08	4.40	3.79
Transportation (100 miles)	2.31	2.31	2.31
Marketing expenses	3.35	3.35	3.35
Miscellaneous and indirect costs	10.41	15.48	17.23
Total	$456.77	$740.11	$720.16

Source: *Federal Livestock Marketing Survey.*

[1] Other grades in descending order of quality are USDA Good and Ungraded. Lower grades have different cooking requirements for producing a tender, flavorful result. Three other grades, Utility, Cutter, and Canner, are used in processed meat products and rarely sold in retail stores.

Exhibit 2

Commercial cattle slaughter (1971–1980)

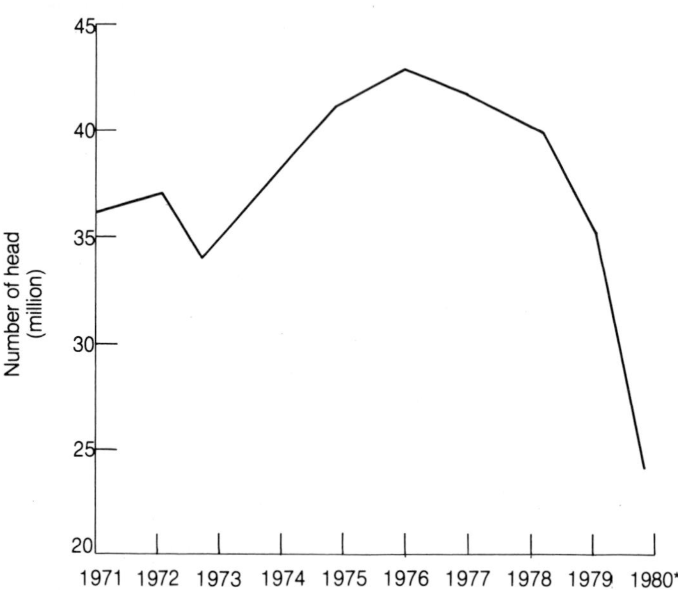

* First three quarters.

Source: *Federal Livestock Marketing Survey.*

for sale or sold in the "country" to buyers representing the packers. Country sales accounted for about 60 percent of dry-lot feeding sales in the late 70s as the industry moved toward decentralization.

9 The supply of feeder cattle depends on such factors as the weather, the price of grain, and the management of breeding and feeding operations. Exhibit 1 shows the breakdown of expenses for fed cattle while Exhibit 2 indicates the fluctuations in the number of cattle slaughtered during the 70s.

Slaughter and Processing

10 The killing of cattle is done according to a procedure established by the Humane Society to ensure humane treatment. The carcass is drained of blood and various organs, and other parts are removed. The hide is also removed. The remaining carcass is stored in large coolers until it is ready for shipment or further processing. This process is frequently referred to as a "kill and chill" operation.

11 Further processing of carcasses results in products and by-products which include:

Meat, fresh and frozen.

Meat, canned and cooked.

Hides and skins for leather.

Edible fats and inedible fats for soap.

Bones for buttons, knife handles, and bone meal.

Blood meal and fertilizer.

Glycerin with industrial uses.

Hair for brushes, felt, rugs, upholstering, and baseball gloves.

Intestines for sausage casing, violin strings, and surgical ligatures.

Gelatin, glue, sandpaper, pet food, and neat's-foot oil.

Pharmaceuticals.

The by-products of slaughter are called the drop. Dressed beef is usually sold for less total dollars than the initial total dollar cost of the live animal. The drop makes up the difference and provides the profits. And profit margins are small, usually under 1 percent.

12 Traditionally, packers supplied carcass beef to local butchers for further processing in a complex distribution system. In the mid-60s, boxed beef was introduced, and by 1981, more than half of the nation's meat was supplied to retailers in boxed form. The transition from carcass to boxed beef has had a profound—some say revolutionary—effect on the structure of the industry. Exhibit 3 compares the two systems on some important dimensions. The channel of boxed beef is significantly shorter than for the traditional carcass method.

13 Although boxed beef was introduced by some retail grocery chains, its most vigorous and successful proponents have been newcomers to the industry—IBP and MBPXL, formerly Missouri Beef Packers and now a subsidiary of Cargill. The newcomers set up operations in new, efficient plants in rural areas close to the supply of beef. Plants were designed to eliminate the need for costly union labor. The older packers were saddled with 50-year-old, multistory plants in central locations. They employed skilled butchers to perform breaking and processing operations. Their operations were inherently more costly, and their yields were lower because of these factors. Exhibit 4 traces the recent history of some of the major traditional meatpackers. All of the former giants in the industry have been purchased by conglomerates and are undergoing significant changes.

Price

14 Beef processing is essentially a commodity business. Much fresh meat sold is unbranded so meat packers have had little control over selling price. In addition, the price of cattle fluctuates according to supply, which in turn is dependent on the price and availability of feed grain and on the weather. What the packer does control is the cost of processing and this, along with volume, is the key to profitability in the industry.

Federal Regulation

15 Federal regulation of the meat industry began in 1906 with the Meat Inspection Act. This legislation requires inspection of live animals before slaughter and of the carcass to ensure that no diseased animals are used for food. There are around 70 known diseases that are transmittable from animal to man. Federal meat inspectors also check for clean and sanitary handling and/or preparation of food, for adulteration

Exhibit 3

Production and distribution of carcass beef (traditional) compared with production and distribution of boxed beef

Steps:	*Traditional*	*Boxed*
Slaughter	Live cattle are killed; carcass is bled; hide, vital organs, other by-products are removed; carcass is chilled in cooler.	Slaughtering, breaking, and boning performed by processor. Beef is trimmed and boxed ready for final sale or fabrication.
Breaking	"Breaker" buys carcasses for breaking into primal cuts (rounds, chucks, ribs, and loins).	
Boning	"Boner" buys cuts for boning and some processing.	
Processing and fabricating	Chain, foodservice supplyhouse, or other processor buys meat to prepare for final sale. Fresh meat is further trimmed and packaged or meat is processed into portions and frozen or partially cooked and frozen.	Meat prepared in individual portions; usually involves cooking and/or freezing.
Labor	Each step requires skilled labor (butcher) paid by union scale.	Facilities and process designed for unskilled labor; high capital investment.
Location of facilities	Slaughter houses located for convenience of shipping live cattle by rail, usually in urban centers.	Located for minimal shipping of live animals; truck access to markets.
Shrink	Live cattle subject to shrink in transport to slaughter house; carcass subject to further shrink in transport.	Minimal shrink of live cattle; no shrink of cuts when packaged and shipped.
Drop	By-products collected at every stage.	All by-products collected before boxing.

of meat, and for proper labeling of meat and meat products. Meat is stamped by inspectors for identification purposes.

16 The Wholesome Meat Act of 1967 had the effect of extending the regulations under which the large meatpackers engaged in interstate commerce to smaller, predominantly interstate, meatpackers. The smaller operations had been subject to inspection by local authorities and were eligible to obtain a certificate of exemption from federal inspection for interstate shipping if their operations satisfied local inspectors. This eligibility was discontinued by the act, and these packers were given until the end of 1970 to reach compliance. Many marginal firms failed to comply and discontinued operations.

Exhibit 4

Acquisitions and divestitures of large meatpackers (1967–1981)

Packer	*Acquired by*	*1981 status*
Wilson and Co.	LTV in 1967 for $81 million	Parent spinning off by offering 1 share of Wilson for 10 of LTV
Armour and Co.	Greyhound in 1970 for $400 million	Restructuring organization and management
Cudahy Co.	General Host in 1971 for $70 million	Negotiating agreement to sell to current management
Swift	Esmark in 1972	Divested fresh meat segment (now SIPCO) to public and concentrated on branded products
Oscar Mayer	General Foods in 1981	Being restructured to stress food-service and branded products
MBPXL (originally Missouri Beef)	Cargill	Slaughter and pack boxed beef

17 The Federal Grading Service was instituted in 1927, and grading is done by employees of the U.S. Department of Agriculture. Use of this service is voluntary, and a little over half of all beef is graded. Since 1964, federal law requires that packers pay for cattle within 48 hours of purchase. Packers, on the other hand, generally wait at least two weeks for payment from their own accounts. The cost per animal of federal inspection was estimated at $1.24 in 1978, and the cost of grading in that year was $20 per hour. The 48-hour payment requirement requires extra working capital.

18 Individual meatpackers and the industry as a whole have periodically received scrutiny from a variety of government bodies including Congress, the Justice Department, the USDA, and state and local investigators. Charges have included price-fixing, monopolistic practices, and conspiracy.[2]

19 The industry uses large quantities of water and produces significant waste in spite of the practice of "using everything but the squeal" and thus is subject to regulation by the Environmental Protection Agency.

Industry Outlook

20 The per capita consumption of beef is declining (see Exhibit 5) as demand shifts to poultry, pork, and fish. Polls indicated that 20 percent of beef eaters were concerned about their health, but only 9 percent reduced consumption because of that concern. On the other hand, 73 percent objected to the price of beef. A farm management specialist described the industry outlook for beef producers compared to other sectors of the meat industry:

> All these people (pork and chicken producers) have done a good job of promotion. And they have better feed converters in chickens and hogs. A chicken will have

[2] A widely distributed industry handbook contains a chapter on "Commercial Bribery" in which various forms of kickbacks are described and the legal and ethical implications of doing business on such a basis are explained.

Exhibit 5

Per capita consumption of beef and pork (1973–1980)

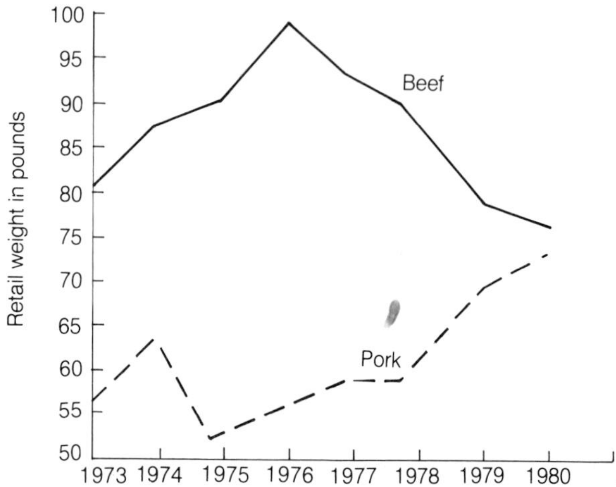

Source: USDA Economic Research Division, *Livestock and Meat Situation and Outlook.*

a pound of gain for 2½ pounds of feed. A hog will make the same gain with 4½ pounds of feed, while it takes 8 pounds to add a pound of weight to a steer.

The one big advantage the cattle raiser has, and perhaps the only one, is that he can grow cattle on land unfit for cultivation. This is not true for poultry and hogs, because they must be confined to smaller areas and given some kinds of prepared farm-grown feed from infancy.

Getting people to eat more beef is a serious problem, and it may get worse before it improves. Back in 1975, we were consuming 130 pounds of beef per person in the United States. By 1981, it was projected at 105 pounds, and indications are that before long it may drop below 100 pounds per person.

I don't think this is because people no longer prefer beef. Rather it is a matter of economics. Eventually people may get tired of eating pork, fish, and poultry and return to beef, but it doesn't seem likely within the near future.[3]

Vertical Integration

21 Vertical integration has been suggested and attempted as a means of smoothing out the fluctuations in price and supply of cattle. One proposal is for packers to forward contract with producers to assure a constant supply of finished cattle of the desired grade. Feeders and packers could also form cooperatives to make the supply and quality more consistent. Another proposal is for three-way cooperatives of producer-feeders, packers, and retailers—presumably chain stores. The feeder would charge a cost-plus

[3] Jess F. Blair, "Another tough year predicted for cattlemen in 1982," *Feedstuffs* 53 (November 24, 1981).

management fee. The feeder would charge a cost-plus per head fee for slaughter and/or fabrication. The retailer would be assured a supply of beef of the desired quality and quantity.

Capacity Utilization

22 Increased capacity utilization is another concern of the industry which is operating at an estimated 70–75 percent capacity. Modernization and double shifts are offered as options to increase utilization.

Boxed Beef and Packaging

23 The boxed beef concept was intended to improve efficiency in the distribution of beef by breaking the carcass at the slaughter house rather than locally. Less waste fat and bone were shipped and retailers could choose the cuts they wanted. Meat marketing researchers at Michigan State University say that 65–70 percent of beef sold to retail stores in 1981 was boxed beef, and the figure is expected to rise to 80 percent by 1985, "The trend is for the processor to do more of the work in some way," according to a chain store executive. "There may even come a time when there is no cutting at the store level at all."

24 The National Live Stock and Meat Board listed the following packaging systems that rely on the boxed beef concept:

A Detroit, Michigan, supermarket chain is test-marketing retail cuts that have been centrally cut and packaged in transparent, vacuum-sealed packages. The package allows 100 percent visibility and extends marketing life to 15 days at 28–32 degrees F.

About 91 percent of the U.S. meat merchandisers now offer a "family pack" of meat cuts, and 79 percent see greater use of them in the future.

Some retailers are offering wholesale subprimal meat cuts in bags directly to the consumer saving consumers 20 to 30 cents per pound.[4]

A continuing packaging concern is the development of packaging systems which will not discolor red meat.

The Pork Industry

25 Pork is a $20 billion industry. Per capita consumption is shown in Exhibit 5. Hogs are bred to yield over 50 percent of the carcass weight in trimmed hams, loins, picnics, and Boston butts. The process of breeding, feeding, and selling hogs is very similar to that of beef cattle with the exception that hogs cannot be initially pastured as cattle can.

26 Hogs yield a variety of products which include:

Meat, fresh and frozen.

Meat, smoked, cured, canned, and cooked.

[4] "Retail packaging will direct industry future: Meat Board," *Feedstuffs* 53 (July 13, 1981), p. 5.

Sausage and variety meats.
Hides and skins for leather.
Edible fats (lard) and inedible fats.
Pork fat by-product used for truck tires, insecticides, and germicides.
Hair for brushes, felt, rugs, upholstering.
Gelatin.
Pharmaceuticals.

Volume can be an important factor in the production of by-products. The pancreas of about 100,000 hogs must be saved to produce one pound of dry insulin, for example.

Characteristics

27 Although some have compared the pork industry of the 80s to the beef industry of the 60s citing old plants, high labor costs, and locations far from current hog-growing regions, others disagree. Pork, they point out, is less labor intensive than beef and some pork slaughterhouses have already adopted the boxed beef concept. Furthermore, more pork is sold branded. While most beef is sold as a commodity, an estimated 50–70 percent of the hog is processed into products such as bacon, hot dogs, and cured hams and sold under brand names which are frequently heavily advertised.

28 Local processors are more significant in pork because of their ability to match their products to regional tastes. These brands are also well advertised in their areas and may outsell national brands. These processors may or may not also slaughter; many found that their slaughtering facilities could not be brought up to the national standards as required by the Wholesome Meat Act of 1967 and were forced to stop slaughtering operations and become customers of former competitors. The number of pork processing plants in the United States dropped 15 percent from 1974 to 1978, while the number of hogs slaughtered remained constant.

29 The pork industry is unionized with the bulk of its workers organized by the United Food and Commercial Workers Union. The industry is governed by nationwide master agreements with the UFCW which have a common expiration date.

Government Regulation

30 Pork slaughter and processing is regulated by the federal government under the Meat Inspection Act and the Wholesome Meat Act to ensure slaughtered animals are free from disease and that meat is handled properly, unadulterated, and accurately labeled. Grade standards were established in 1952 and are based on yield and quality of meat. There are three grades, Choice, Medium, and Cull, with three further divisions within the Choice grade.

Goals and Objectives of IBP

31 In 1968, IBP management identified four phases of development for the company. These four phases represent the general direction the company followed in the ensuing years. Phase 1 was slaughter; Phase 2 was breaking and fabricating; Phase 3 was

variety meats; and Phase 4 was portion cutting, cooked and frozen foods. Management has indicated that it would consider the company "mature" when it has entered the portion-control segment of the meat industry.

32 As the company seeks extension of operations in meat processing, management has reiterated the means of accomplishing growth should be primarily internal. A 1978 statement emphasizes this philosophy and includes other goals and objectives:

> We seek to render values and to provide ourselves and our shareholders with controlled growth and a return on their investment consistent with reasonable risks; to serve real needs and to help feed a hungry world; to be a responsible member of our society; to provide the best of markets to our producers, the finest products to our customers, and excel in our service to both; and finally, to provide a part of the jobs that are so necessary to the economic health of our home communities.[5]

IPB executives have stated their aims in even more simple language: "We are only out to be the lowest cost producer in the industry."

Slaughter Operations

33 IBP's original name, Iowa Beef Packers, reflected the emphasis on slaughter operations (Phase 1) in the early years of the company. The old, established meatpackers had located their facilities based on the system of rail transportation which brought cattle to stockyard towns—Chicago, Des Moines, Los Angeles, Omaha, among others. As a newcomer to the industry, IBP was free to build in new locations which were close to the large feedlots and still accessible to the nation's large markets by the interstate highway system and trucks.

34 IBP's cattle buyers were sent to local feedlots in radio-equipped cars to buy directly from the farmers while coordinating their buying with the needs of the plant. The price paid the farmer was roughly the same offered in Chicago or Kansas City but saved them transportation, yard costs, and commissions. On the IBP side, the yield was better because the cattle were slaughtered before the shrink could begin. According to IBP President Robert Peterson, "If you lose even a pound, not 10 pounds, but a pound—on today's (1981) market, that's $1 a head, and when we make only $5 or $6 a head out of the entire system, you've got to be careful."

35 In addition to using new criteria for choosing plant location, the founders of Iowa Beef Processors also approached the actual slaughtering operations differently with large, single-story plants in which cattle were stunned, lifted by one hoof onto a moving chain, killed, halved and quartered, all on a moving line. The processing was done, not by skilled butchers, but by a succession of relatively unskilled workers performing a number of elementary tasks—removing the hoofs or tail, slitting open the abdomen or halving a carcass, making a single cut with an electric saw.

36 The first plant Holman designed had a kill cost of $10 a head, versus $15 to $20 for conventional plants. Although absolute costs have risen, the advantage has been maintained. Slaughter on the assembly line is labor-intensive, but by breaking the work down into its simplest elements, IBP was able to replace the highly skilled and

[5] Iowa Beef Processors, Annual Report, 1978.

high-cost packing-house butcher with relatively low-cost assembly-line labor. So labor made part of the difference in cost. The rest came from the economies of scale offered by plants capable of killing 300,000 or 500,000 or a million cattle a year. IBP diligently pursued these scale economies.

37 Some of the most notable economies come from making more efficient use of the drop—the by-products of the meat-packing process—tongues, liver, hearts for the export market, ingredients for sausage and pet food. Urban butchers shipped fat to tallowmakers for shortening, bone to glue factories. But IBP with its large-scale plant could collect these products for conversion into edible animal feeds, gather the glands for use in pharmaceuticals, prepare the hides for tanning, even collect the gallstones for aphrodisiacs. "Our drop can get as high as $50 a head," Peterson says, "and our kill costs are less than that." A lot less, in fact—less than $20 a head. IBP slaughters about 6 million cattle a year.[6]

Breaking and Fabricating Operations

38 In 1967, Iowa Beef moved into the second phase of its development program with the addition of breaking and fabricating to its operations and utilization of the boxed beef concept. While IBP did not originate the idea of boxed beef, the name of the company has become virtually synonymous with the concept because of their persistent promotion of boxed beef and their ultimate success. The development of the concept and the problems which the company encountered in gaining entrance into major markets are reported in the following excerpt from an article which appeared in the June 22, 1981, issue of *Forbes:*

> 39 The usual procedure (for processing beef) involved shipping carcasses in halves or quarters to the wholesaler, food chain, or retail butcher, who then broke the carcass down into the various primal and subprimal cuts—loins, ribs, rounds and chucks; top sirloin, strip, and tenderloin. IBP was prepared to do that itself, to take out the unneeded fat and bone, as well as to wrap the primal cuts in cryovac film, box them, and ship them to market. Putting the beef in a vacuum-packed plastic bag not only added 21 days to the normal 3- to 7-day shelf life of the carcass, it also sharply reduced the shrink that refrigeration exposed the carcasses to, and it expanded the beef packers' marketing area.
>
> 40 In boxed beef, a concept pioneered by Safeway and Armour, IBP found it necessary to reorganize the market, and that took some doing. The only market big enough to absorb the output of the great new plant Holman built at Dakota City, Nebraska, was metropolitan New York, which consumes maybe a quarter of the nation's meat production. Though IBP's executives may have been barefoot boys from the cornfields of Iowa, they weren't born yesterday, and they could hardly have been unaware that getting boxed beef into the New York market was going to take some heavy payoffs in the right places. As one IBP executive admitted later, "It was a common practice that people paid off other people to do business in New York City."
>
> 41 For IBP's boxed beef to prevail, the supermarkets were going to have to scrap their traditional butchering methods, and the unions were going to have to accept

[6] Iowa Beef Processors. Annual Report, 1978.

> the fact that a lot of their member butchers would lose their jobs. The situation was especially touchy insofar as the union that controlled the New York market, the Amalgamated Meat Cutters—now the UFCW—was also the union that had just organized IBP's new Dakota City plant and gone out on strike. When that happened, the New York meatcutters had an excuse to lend their support and banned boxed beef from the New York market.
>
> 42 IBP was prepared to make a deal with New York mob associate Moe Steinman, a labor consultant who had influence both with the local meatcutters union and the beef buyers of most of the New York supermarkets. If the Dakota City strike went on, the IBP could not find a market for its beef; the company's very existence would be endangered. In April 1970, Steinman brought Holman together with union officials in New York, and the problem was solved. Holman was told, as he later confided to *Forbes,* that IBP could get the beef into New York if it agreed to settle the strike in Dakota City. The strike ended. IBP agreed to suspend a $4.5 million damage suit against the union, and the union agreed to suspend its boycott of IBP's boxed beef.
>
> 43 But the mediation had its price. Soon thereafter Steinman set up a sales agency known as C.P. Sales, into which IBP paid a cent on average for every pound of beef it sold in New York. The courts concluded that those funds were intended to bribe both union executives and supermarket buyers to let IBP's beef into New York City and found both Holman and IBP guilty of conspiracy to bribe union and supermarket officials.

44 Although Holman and the company were found guilty, Mr. Holman was granted an unconditional discharge, and the company was fined $7,000. The charges were appealed, but the conviction upheld. Federal charges resulting from the investigation were dropped. In the aftermath of the investigation, rumors of mob involvement persisted as reported in the 1975 annual report.

> Mr. Bodenstein has managed on a contract basis IBP's most successful sales agency, C.P. Sales, Inc., serving the New York City area, and was the logical choice (for group vice president of) the Processing Division and its marketing reorganization program. The drawback was that his wife's father had been convicted of admitted bribery in the meat business prior to 1970 and was alleged to have underworld connections. The press played up the association. We believe that Mr. Bodenstein was victimized and is not guilty of any wrongdoing. Nevertheless, inferences made led the New York Stock Exchange to temporarily halt trading in IBP stock for five days, and some members of Congress spoke out. The board of directors felt obliged to authorize a full-page statement of the company's position in the Midwest newspapers and *The Wall Street Journal* on December 1 and 2. The lesson learned by IBP from this encounter with misperceptions, on the part of several important audiences, is that better anticipation of likely public reaction, however baseless in fact, must be given greater consideration in decision making. Public opinion ran the gamut—from fears that outside forces were taking over IBP to alarms that we were unwisely trying to manipulate such forces—all somewhat baffling to Midwestern naivete and to our native self-reliant sense. One IBP vice president said that the Bodenstein appointment was "the wrongest right decision" we have made.

45 With New York penetrated by boxed beef, the company turned its marketing attention to cities within the Chicago/Houston/Denver triangle. Although labor contracts between meatcutters' locals and retailers slowed the entry of boxed beef, they were opened up, one by one. By 1981, only St. Louis remained closed to boxed beef. The only other really large market remaining was Los Angeles (second to New York in beef consumption and supplied by local packers). By 1981, demand for boxed beef exceeded IBP's capacity to supply, and it was estimated that well over half of all beef moved in boxes with 40 percent of those boxes originating in IBP plants. Boxed beef's share of the market by 1983 was expected to exceed 80 percent.

IBP's attack on what is called the "closed cities" depended on price and service as well as dealings with the unions. Cost advantages in the factory could be translated into lower prices for the retailer. The company claimed to be able to process and deliver boxed beef to a retail store for \$23 to \$36 a head less than the retailer could buy and process the carcass for himself. The company also emphasized service centers as part of their sales efforts.

46 Chains are also turning to boxed beef. Some of the converts include Grand Union, Stop and Shop, Safeway, and Albertson's. Of the large chains, only Kroger and Winn-Dixie are committed to carcass beef with their own multimillion dollar breaking facilities. It would be difficult for chains to return to doing their own slaughtering and breaking once they stop because of the increasing capital investments required to obtain the efficiency and volume of an IBP plant. Packers who once sold carcass beef to chains are also unable to build their own breaking facilities and are either going out of business or selling premium carcasses to other breakers and boxers. Dubuque Packing, a large slaughterer, is becoming an important IBP supplier.

47 IBP's real competition is the packers who are also providing boxed beef to meet the demand which IBP has generated but since 1976 has not been able to meet. MBPXL (a subsidiary of Cargill), Swift Independent, and Spencer Beef (subsidiary of the Land O' Lakes farm cooperative) are following similar strategies to that of IBP with success.

Current Operations

Scope and Capacity

48 IBP operates beef slaughter, beef processing, and pork slaughter plants (see Exhibit 6: Plant locations and principal activities). All of the production of the pork plant was sold to Armour in 1981. Plant activities are described in detail in the prospectus prepared in connection with the Occidental Petroleum–IBP merger proposal:

> IBP's slaughter plants reduce cattle to dressed carcass form and process certain by-products. After stunning, the cattle move by conveyor systems through the plants until, in the form of dressed carcasses, they are placed in coolers, graded by the U.S. Department of Agriculture, and held for shipment or further processing.
>
> IBP's processing plants at Dakota City, Emporia, Finney County, Amarillo, and Pasco conduct breaking and fabricating operations to reduce dressed carcasses to bone-in or boneless primal and subprimal cuts of beef. In these plants,

Exhibit 6

Plant locations and principal activities

Plant	*Activities*
Amarillo, Texas	Slaughter; breaking and fabricating; hide treatment; metal fabrication
Boise, Idaho	Slaughter
Dakota City, Nebraska	Slaughter; breaking and fabricating, hide treatment, executive and administrative offices
Denison, Iowa	Slaughter; hide treatment; confined feedlot
Emporia, Kansas	Slaughter; breaking and fabricating; hide treatment
Finney County, Kansas	Slaughter; breaking and fabricating; hide treatment
Fort Dodge, Iowa	Slaughter
Irvington, Iowa	Farming
Duverne, Minnesota	Kosher slaughter
Madison, Nebraska	Pork slaughter and processing
Pasco, Washington	Slaughter, breaking and fabricating; tallow refining; hide treatment
Salix, Iowa	Farming
Sioux City, Iowa	Ground beef and related products (not operating in 1980); aviation
West Point, Nebraska	Slaughter

production employees work at either side of fabricating tables having conveyor tops. The primal and subprimal cuts are channeled along the production lines, cut and trimmed to specifications, packaged in plastic film, boxed, and moved by a complex of continuous conveyors to cooled inventory storage areas where they are held to await loading for delivery. IBP's production process requires a minimum of production handling and eliminates the shipping of surplus fat and bone. In both the slaughter and processing plants, each employee is assigned specified tasks, which facilitates the training and use of unskilled labor, promotes a high degree of work proficiency, and thus enhances production capacity.

The approximate capacity of all the IBP's beef slaughter plants is 21,400 head of cattle per day. The approximate capacity of all of IBP's beef processing plants is 16,800 head per day. IBP sells to others carcasses not meeting the specifications of its processing plants and, when necessary, purchases carcasses from others for its processing plants. The processing division currently purchases approximately 8 percent of the beef carcasses used in its operations from outside sources. These purchases are subject to significant fluctuations resulting from live cattle supplies, customer demand, and the quality of slaughtered cattle. Through the first six months of fiscal 1981, IBP's various slaughter facilities operated at approximately 88 percent of capacity, and the processing facilities operated at approximately 89 percent of capacity.

By-products are handled in bulk with the exception of butcher products, sausage, pet food, and pharmaceutical commodities which are trimmed, boxed, and frozen in small lots. Facilities for curing hides are located at six plants and use modern, automated equipment for brine curing.

Supplies

49 The cattle supply is a variable which is given to uncertainty as an agricultural commodity. IBP does not enter long-term cattle buying agreements, preferring the vicissitudes of the open market to the fluctuations of the cattle futures market. Cattle costs are always close to current market levels.

50 Most of IBP's cattle are purchased from farmers and feeders in Kansas, Iowa, Texas, Nebraska, Colorado, Oklahoma, Washington, South Dakota, Minnesota, Idaho, and Oregon. Cattle are purchased for immediate slaughter, and the company has no facilities for holding cattle over an extended period of time. Coordination of cattle purchases and production schedules of plants is achieved by radio communication between buyers and production schedulers. Generally purchases are sufficient for operations of a week or less.

51 Long-term difficulties with this system are described in the prospectus:

> Cattle supplies or prices may be adversely affected if a lack of moisture in major grain-producing areas increases the cost of feeding operations. Permanent or long-term water shortages could make operation of certain plants less economical. However, IBP believes it has located its plants in areas least likely to be adversely affected by water shortages.

52 The exception to IBP's policy of not entering into long-term cattle buying agreements was their agreement with a marketing cooperative which operated feedyards that provide cattle for slaughter and processing in the Northwest. This agreement was investigated by the Justice Department and ended on June 22, 1982, after five years.

Products

53 IBP's principal product categories are carcasses; broken, fabricated, and other processed products; and by-products and pork. Exhibit 7 (percentage of sales revenue by principal product category) indicates how sales are distributed among these products.

Customers

54 The merger prospectus described IBP's customers as follows:

> IBP currently has approximately 3,000 active customers which include grocery chains, meat distributors, wholesalers, purveyors, and restaurant and hotel chains. Approximately 2,200 customers purchase broken and fabricated cuts of beef which are boxed and shipped in vacuum packages from the Amarillo, Dakota City, Emporia, Finney County, and Pasco plants. Purchasers of carcass beef shipped from all slaughtering units total approximately 200 accounts.
>
> Approximately 45 percent of all sales are made directly by IBP's employees. Approximately 53 percent of all sales are made through offers to buy from customers solicited by nine IBP Service Centers located in Atlanta, Boston, Chicago, Columbus (Ohio), Dallas, Fairfax (Virginia), Los Angeles, Lyndhurst (New Jersey), and Vancouver (Washington). The balance of about 2 percent is sold through brokers. Normally, IBP's largest single customer accounts for less than 4 percent

Exhibit 7

Percentage of sales revenues by products

Product	Percent of sales during fiscal year				
	1976	*1977*	*1978*	*1979*	*1980*
Carcasses	22%	27%	22%	20%	20%
Broken, fabricated, and other products	67	60	66	66	69
By-products and pork	11	13	12	14	11
	100%	100%	100%	100%	100%

of its total sales volume. Approximately 88 percent of sales are on open account and the balance on secured terms.

IBP operates a training program for customers and prospective customers at its Center for Modern Meat Management at Dakota City. In addition to the center's programs, IBP and the service centers each maintain a staff of field consultants who service customers using IBP boxed beef.

Facilities

55 One of the original founders of IBP, Mr. Andrew Anderson, had as his major responsibility the construction of the facilities. Until 1970, this was accomplished in-house with planning, design, and actual construction performed by IBP's Construction Division. During that time, 44 separate patent claims were allowed on breaking and fabrication facilities. Plant construction crews became an important source of employees according to the 1980 annual report:

> That first plant at Denison was built by a crew of young farmers who wanted the construction work because farm income was declining. When the plant was completed, many of the young farmers stayed on as production workers or in supervisory capacities. To this day, construction crews at new IBP plants are given the first opportunity at production jobs when the project is finished because they have first-hand knowledge of how the equipment has been set up and how it should operate. A number of present IBP production management personnel, including several plant managers, started their careers at the company as members of a plant construction crew.

56 The construction division continued to design and supervise the construction of plants after Mr. Anderson's retirement in 1970. IBP management feels that this practice has decreased shake-down periods and start-up costs. The division is also responsible for renovation, expansion, and updating of existing facilities with the goal of remaining the low-cost producer in the meat industry. A sampling of such projects in 1980 included installation of a new processing floor and material handling system in the Dakota City plant, a new waste treatment system for the Pasco, Washington, plant, and "a major improvement in the processing of edible oil."

57 The division supervised construction of the world's largest slaughter plant in Finney County, Kansas. The following information provides some perspective on the size of the operation:

> Its refrigeration capacity is approximately 6,000 tons. That would air condition almost 1,500 private homes the year round. About 1,140 miles of copper wiring are contained in the plant. That's enough to completely wire 3,000 homes.
>
> The total electrical capacity compares to that of a city with a population of 9,000. If the 50,000 yards of prestressed concrete in the plant were used to construct a 3-inch-thick, 3-foot sidewalk, that walk would stretch 4,328 city blocks.

When processing at capacity, the plant will be capable of slaughtering and processing 1.2 million head of cattle a year. The $100 million facility is expected to be in full operation by 1984.

Financial Performance Policies

58 Exhibits 8 and 9 contain financial information for the company.

59 Financial policy has been conservative with most growth generated through retained earnings. The 1975 annual report explained the rationale for this and the evolution of IBP's dividend policy:

> We tend to think of growth in terms of physical expansion or what is needed to furnish the means of performance growth in a later day. Capital resources are the key at a time of severe national shortage. In a recent study by the New York Stock Exchange, it was estimated that America faces a capital shortfall of $650 billion over the next decade. In choosing among the equity market, long-term debt, and retained earnings, we have historically favored the latter as the most prudent and feasible source of capital, partly because our debt equity ratio as reported in *Forbes* rose to 0.8 compared with an all-industry average of 0.4. We have resisted pressures to compromise growth, because we believe such policy to be in the best long-term interest of shareowners who have invested in our success.
>
> It is appreciated, of course, that the wants of stockholders vary, with some preferring a spendable return sooner rather than later.
>
> . . . To make a meaningful beginning, the board of directors on January 17, 1976, decided to adopt a cash dividend policy of approximately 7.5 percent of aftertax earnings, payable semiannually. The actual declaration—exact amounts—and timing of payment will be determined by the board and announced at the annual meeting of shareholders on March 13, 1976, at Sioux City, Iowa.

The dividend payout record of IBP is shown in Exhibit 8.

Accounting Policy

60 The company has supplied information on financial results on current cost and equivalent dollar bases since 1976. Also to better state performance, the company adopted the LIFO (changing from FIFO) method of accounting for inventories in 1977.

Exhibit 8

IOWA BEEF PROCESSORS, INC.
Ten-Year Summary of Operations, 1971–1980
(in thousands of dollars except per share data)

	1980	*1979*	*1978*	*1977*	*1976*	*1975*	*1974*	*1973*	*1972*	*1971*
For the fiscal year:										
Net sales	$4,639,454	$4,216,370	$2,968,099	$2,023,765	$2,077,158	$1,805,340	$1,537,198	$1,422,271	$1,244,595	$979,718
Cost of products sold	4,506,150	4,105,533	2,872,214	1,937,823	1,990,176	1,735,592	1,483,262	1,377,686	1,212,206	956,239
Selling, general, and administrative expense	42,924	34,326	31,864	27,787	24,374	22,992	19,820	16,442	12,832	11,641
Interest income (expense)—net	3,724	(2,038)	(3,138)	(3,281)	(3,666)	(3,740)	(2,906)	(4,468)	(5,612)	(5,526)
Earnings before income taxes	94,104	74,473	60,883	54,874	58,942	43,016	31,210	23,675	13,945	6,312
Income taxes	40,940	31,726	27,296	24,909	30,164	19,779	14,672	11,427	6,578	2,539
Net earnings	53,164	42,747	33,587*	29,965	28,778	23,237	16,538	12,248	7,367	3,773
Average common and common-equivalent shares outstanding	10,289	9,995	9,722	9,528	9,320	8,718	8,532	8,262	8,025	7,821
Net earnings per common and common-equivalent share	5.17	4.28	3.46*	3.14	3.09	2.68	1.98	1.51	.92	.48
Cash dividends paid per common share	.60	.52	.26	.25	.20	—	—	—	—	—
Earnings on beginning common stockholders' equity	22.3%	21.8%	20.7%	22.3%	26.8%	29.9%	27.0%	25.0%	18.3%	10.4%
At yearend:										
Common stockholders' equity	$290,480	$238,831	$196,095	$162,631	$134,292	$107,557	$ 77,617	$ 61,180	$ 48,926	$ 40,174
Property, plant, and equipment, at cost	280,884	208,998	187,522	166,270	141,695	122,600	99,839	77,786	73,823	68,803
Total assets	509,492	416,789	354,778	277,527	253,437	229,684	189,246	152,913	160,726	130,370
Working capital	164,598	173,412	142,535	107,538	89,502	79,823	69,152	40,968	28,428	22,762
Current ratio	2.2 to 1	2.9 to 1	3.0 to 1	3.6 to 1	2.7 to 1	2.6 to 1	2.8 to 1	1.8 to 1	1.4 to 1	1.5 to 1

* Effective October 30, 1977, the company adopted the last-in, first-out (LIFO) method of valuing product and certain supplies inventories, the effect of which was to reduce net earnings for the year 1978 by $5,924,000 (61 cents per share) from amounts which would otherwise have been reported. The net earnings for 1977 and prior years are not comparable to those of any subsequent year as a result of this change.

Exhibit 9

IOWA BEEF PROCESSORS, INC.
Consolidated Balance Sheets

	November 1, 1980	*November 3, 1979*
Assets		
Current assets:		
Cash	$ 23,334,000	$ 27,138,000
Marketable debt securities at cost	4,000,000	—
Accounts receivable, net	170,941,000	155,107,000
Inventories	97,113,000	80,164,000
Deferred tax benefit	3,419,000	3,557,000
Prepaid expenses	1,891,000	1,135,000
Total current assets	300,698,000	267,101,000
Property, plant, and equipment, at cost		
Land and land improvements	22,058,000	17,051,000
Buildings and stockyards	62,665,000	56,188,000
Equipment	140,462,000	128,166,000
	225,185,000	201,405,000
Less accumulated depreciation	74,228,000	62,085,000
	150,957,000	139,320,000
Construction in progress	55,699,000	7,593,000
Total property, plant, and equipment	206,656,000	146,913,000
Other assets	2,138,000	2,775,000
Total assets	$509,492,000	$416,789,000
Liabilities and Stockholders' Equity		
Current liabilities:		
Note payable	$ 15,000,000	$ 20,000,000
Accounts payable and accrued expenses	102,501,000	60,182,000
Federal and state income taxes	15,096,000	10,559,000
Current maturities on long-term obligations	3,503,000	2,948,000
Total current liabilities	136,100,000	93,689,000
Deferred income taxes	20,535,000	17,410,000
Long-term debt and capital lease obligations	61,300,000	66,859,000
Other liabilities	1,077,000	
Commitments and contingencies:		
Stockholders' equity:		
Common stock, par value $1.50 a share:		
Authorized—24,000,000 shares		
Issued—9,905,189	14,858,000	14,537,000
Additional paid-in capital	22,000,000	18,221,000
Retained earnings	253,622,000	206,369,000
Total stockholders' equity	290,480,000	239,127,000
Less common stock in treasury, at cost—16 shares	—	296,000
Stockholders' equity, net shares outstanding—9,905,173	290,480,000	238,831,000
Total liabilities and stockholders' equity	$509,492,000	$416,789,000

Management, Organization, and Administration

61 IBP recruits many (but not all) of its top management internally. The CEO in 1981 began his career with IBP as a cattle buyer when the company opened in 1961. Pertinent information concerning top management is contained in Exhibit 10.

Exhibit 10

IBP top management

Name	*Age**	*Office*	*Background*
Robert L. Peterson	48	Co-chairman of board, president, and CEO	Group vice president at IBP, president and chief operating officer
Dale C. Tinstman	62	Co-chairman of board, chief financial officer	Financial consultant to IBP, president and chief operating officer
Perry V. Haines	37	Executive vice president	Group vice president at IBP

* As of May 1981.

62 The company is organized along functional lines with divisions of Processing, Physical Distribution, Administration, Finance, Custom Products, Research and Engineering, and a Carcass Division. The current organization is the result of a reorganization in the early 70s to better prepare the company to manage its increased size and more-complex activities.

Employees and Labor Relations

63 Approximately 8,750 plant and production workers were employed by IBP in 1981. In addition, there were 80 cattle buyers, a sales staff of 100, and 2,500 other management and management support personnel. Hourly workers are usually locally recruited and trained by IBP. Because of the design of the jobs, less skill is involved than required for traditional breaking and meat processing. Consequently IBP's wage rates have been lower than the other meatpackers who have employed skilled butchers under union master agreements which set wages industrywide. In 1981, John Morrell and Co. paid $10.02 an hour at its Sioux Falls, South Dakota, beef plant while the comparable wage at the Dakota City plant of IBP was $8.20. Fringe benefits for the unionized plant were also greater than the IBP employees. Armour reported its average labor costs were 40 percent to 60 percent higher than IBP and others. The higher labor costs also prevented older companies from entering the market with boxed beef according to Swift President John Copeland. "When you're at a noncompetitive cost," he said, "the more you do to the animal, the more noncompetitive you get."

64 IBP has achieved its low labor costs at a price that was sometimes high. Seven strikes stopped work in various IBP plants between 1970 and 1980. Some of these involved violence ranging from sabotage to shootings, and several stretched into months of decreased production which were reflected in financial performance drops. IBP executives expressed their determination to maintain the unskilled status and thus the lower wages of their operations. It was reported that founder and former CEO Currier

Holman expressed a readiness to have one out of every three plants out on strike at any given time. Current CEO Peterson says:

> People who blame the labor unions for this nation's sliding productivity are barking up the wrong tree. Put the blame where it really belongs—on management, which has, by default, forfeited its right to manage.

Of 11 plants operated by the company in 1981, six were not organized by any union. The organization and contract expiration date of the remaining five are listed below:

1. Madison, Nebraska (United Food and Commercial Workers, Int'l. AFL-CIO), February 1982.
2. Dakota City, Nebraska (UFCW), May 1982.
3. Fort Dodge, Iowa (UFCW), October 1982.
4. Pasco, Washington (Teamsters), November 1982.
5. Amarillo, Texas (Teamsters), March 1985.

The United Food and Commercial Workers were formerly the Amalgamated Meatcutters Union and the Retail Food Workers Union. The new group represents 80 percent of the industry's 158,000 employees.

Legal Proceedings

65 IBP has been the subject of investigations and legal proceedings throughout its history. A list of these proceedings and their status as of 1981 is presented in Exhibit 11.

Exhibit 11

IBP involvement in legal actions (1981)

Action	*Status*	*IBP Position*
Price-fixing by IBP and others alleged by a group of cattle producers.	Several suits against IBP and other defendants consolidated; damages requested for triple amount of actual damages.	"Without factual foundation."
IBP and union involved in suits and countersuits; IBP claims harassment by false suits and union claiming interference with employment among other things.	Cases were consolidated; IBP seeks $15 million in damages; union and others seeking total of $35 million.	"Suits totally without merit."
Jury in New York found IBP guilty of price-fixing but could not determine injury to plaintiff (a supermarket chain).	Possibility of retrial to determine damages.	"No violation if no damage" but "any resulting damage verdict will not be material."
Various suits totalling $3 million concerning cattle buying practices of IBP dating from 1974.	Two thirds have been settled.	

66 Whether IBP's alleged mob connections, chronic labor problems, or conservative dividend policy or some combination of these factors was responsible for sluggish stock market performance can be debated. IBP management noted stock prices not in keeping with the company's earnings record in 1975 as did a market analyst for Mid-America, Inc., writing in 1980:

> IBP shares, currently selling at 4.9 times our 1980 earnings estimate and at a slight discount to book value, are undervalued in our opinion. Purchase is recommended.[7]

One of the major effects of the merger with Occidental Petroleum was short-term gains for the stockholders. IBP stockholders received 1.3 shares of OP common and .4 shares of OP voting nonconvertible preferred for each IBP share. The value of the offer was roughly $77 per share. The last IBP price before the merger offer was announced was $58.50 per share.

Merger with Occidental Petroleum

67 David H. Murdock, a Los Angeles developer and investor and the largest single IBP stockholder with 19 percent of the outstanding stock, served as a go-between in the negotiations between Occidental Petroleum and IBP. The merger was friendly although two board members expressed reservations about the price and the desirability of losing independence. Both were outside directors. *Fortune* calculated the gains of Murdock and three officers as follows:[8]

	Gain ($ million)	*Value of holdings ($ million)*
David H. Murdock	35.2	146.6
Robert L. Peterson	3.0	12.7
Dale C. Tinstman	1.2	4.9
Perry V. Haines	1.4	5.8

Peterson and Haines also received employment contracts for 10 years and 5 years, respectively, and significant raises. Peterson's salary increased from $124,583 to $250,000 with bonuses of up to 80 percent of salary in cash and stock. Haines's salary went from $65,974 to $200,000 with a similar bonus arrangement. Peterson's bonus for the year ended in 1980 had been $200,000, while Haines had earned $93,400.

68 The merger made Mr. Murdock the largest single stockholder in Occidental with 2.8 percent of the stock. The next largest stockholder, Chairman of Board Armand Hammer, owns 1.2 percent.

69 Occidental is a diversified energy and natural resources and chemical concern and was ranked as the 13th largest energy company in 1980. OP revenues in 1980 were $12.5 billion compared with $4.6 billion for IBP (see Exhibits 12 and 13 for other

[7] "Iowa Beef Processors, Inc.," *Wall Street Transcript,* April 21, 1980, p. 57569.

[8] Alexander Stuart, "Meatpackers in stampede," *Fortune,* June 29, 1981, p. 68.

Exhibit 12

OCCIDENTAL PETROLEUM CORPORATION
Consolidated Statements of Operations
For the Years Ended December 31, 1978–1980
(in thousands of dollars except per share amounts)

	1980	*1979*	*1978*
Revenues:			
Net sales	$12,476,125	$9,554,795	$6,252,574
Interest and other income	110,995	75,763	61,566
Equity in net income of unconsolidated subsidiaries and affiliates	15,577	7,689	1,483
Gain on futures contracts	123,615	—	—
Total revenues	12,726,312	9,638,247	6,315,623
Costs and other deductions:			
Cost of sales	9,057,175	6,862,503	4,668,169
Selling, general, and administrative and other operating expenses	832,816	723,656	562,776
(Gain) change related to European refining investments	—	(31,400)	122,100
Interest and debt expense, net	129,438	137,826	112,749
Minority interest in net income of subsidiaries and partnerships	11,644	11,564	8,757
Total costs	10,031,073	7,704,149	5,474,551
Income before taxes	2,695,239	1,934,098	841,072
Provision for domestic and foreign income, franchise and other taxes	1,984,454	1,372,452	834,372
Net income	$ 710,785	$ 561,646	$ 6,700
Earnings (loss) per common share	$ 8.82	$ 7.30	$ (.39)
Fully diluted earnings per share	$ 8.31	$ 6.66	$ *

* Not applicable as the effect of the calculation is antidilutive.

Exhibit 13

OCCIDENTAL PETROLEUM CORPORATION
Consolidated Balance Sheets
For the year ended December 31, 1979, 1980

Assets	*1980*	*1979*
	(in thousands of dollars)	
Current assets:		
Cash	$ 274,615	$ 246,498
Receivables—		
Trade, net	1,481,098	1,265,121
Other	17,094	33,879
Inventories	629,595	496,511
Prepaid expenses and other	34,323	28,158
Total current assets	2,433,725	2,070,167
Long-term receivables, net	31,013	27,043

Exhibit 13 *(concluded)*

Assets	*1980*	*1979*
	(in thousands of dollars)	
Investment in, net of advances from, Occidental Land, Inc.	41,050	63,467
Investments in and advances to, net of advances from, subsidiaries and affiliates	56,942	49,754
Property, plant, and equipment, at cost, net	3,931,417	3,182,475
Other assets:		
Deferred financing costs, net of amortization	19,736	27,710
Capital project expenditures	2,806	68,800
Other	113,200	70,914
Total other assets	135,742	167,424
Total assets	$6,629,889	$5,560,330
Liabilities and Equity		
Current liabilities:		
Current maturities of senior funded debt and capital lease liability	$ 131,396	$ 79,560
Notes payable to banks	51,547	62,995
Accounts payable	1,007,381	904,957
Accrued liabilities	392,455	305,602
Domestic and foreign income, franchise, and other taxes	549,957	477,910
Dividends payable	43,854	27,099
Total current liabilities	2,176,590	1,858,123
Senior funded debt, net of current maturities	925,422	1,044,074
Capital lease liability, net of current portion	76,482	51,905
Deferred credits and other liabilities:		
Deferred and other domestic and foreign income taxes	511,319	292,052
Revenue from sale of future production	165,280	170,000
Coal workers compensation reserve, net of current portion	109,617	102,265
Other	267,978	206,993
Total other liabilities	1,054,194	771,310
Minority equity in subsidiaries and partnerships	117,190	133,066
Redeemable preferred stocks, $1.00 par value	225,734	238,690
Nonredeemable preferred stocks, common shares, and other shareholders' equity:		
Nonredeemable preferred stocks, $1.00 par value; stated at liquidation value	103,273	213,331
Common shares, $20 par value; authorized 100 million shares; issued 79,765,778 shares in 1980 and 72,775,613 shares in 1979 (including treasury shares of 141,446 in 1980 and 450,454 in 1979)	15,954	14,555
Other shareholders' equity:		
Additional paid-in capital (net of amounts applicable to preferred stocks)	605,260	442,057
Retained earnings	1,332,679	802,418
Treasury shares, at cost	(2,889)	(9,199)
Total other shareholders' equity	2,054,277	1,463,162
Total liabilities and equity	$6,629,889	$5,560,330

financial data). Its earnings base in 1981 was concentrated in foreign sources such as Libya and Peru. OP brought to the merger enough investment tax credits to shelter two years of IBP income. OP's president, A. Robert Abboud, explained the strategic background of the merger offer:

> Our strategy for the 1990s is to be prominent in the food area. We're going to be running into a food scarcity situation in the 1990s in the same way that we have an energy shortage in the 1980s. We will continue to build in this area.[9]

The merger was not expected to change IBP's operations which were to continue to be autonomous. Most analysts agreed that the short-term gains for IBP stockholders were the most significant foreseeable results of the deal.

THE FUTURE OF IBP

70 IBP's growth has been based on taking market share from competitors rather than developing new markets. Complaints of monopoly have been heard, and Rep. Neal Smith (D-Iowa) has unsuccessfully introduced legislation to limit a meatpacker's share of the market to 25 percent. Whether growth in meatpacking is limited by legislation or by competition, other avenues of growth will be needed to maintain current growth rates. Some possibilities which have been explored include applying the IBP system to pork slaughter and processing, increasing exports, and adding portion-control products.

Pork

71 IBP's involvement in pork at the time of the merger was limited to one plant which operated as a custom slaughter facility for Armour. While inefficiencies exist in pork slaughter and processing, the gap between current costs and possible efficiencies may not be as great in pork as it was in beef when IBP entered the industry. Another difference is the absence of large-scale hog feeding operations comparable to beef feed lots. There are, however, thousands of small farms in Iowa, Illinois, and Minnesota which could supply a massive centrally located plant. Peterson has said, "We'll come big (in pork) with a couple of hundred million dollar plants."

72 If IBP continues the pattern of taking a new position in an old market rather than developing a new market, several approaches are possible. One would be to follow the boxed beef concept while the other would involve more emphasis on processing and branding. Most pork plants produce 60 percent processed meats (hams, bacon, sausage, and so forth) and 30 percent fresh pork. IBP could produce mainly fresh pork and sell most of its output to pork producers currently slaughtering in-house for further processing. Production efficiencies and economies of scale would presumably make it possible for IBP to supply fresh pork to processors more cheaply than they could slaughter for themselves. A second possible approach would be to strive for brand identification for pork products processed by IBP. Margins for processed pork are three times that of fresh pork, but in this segment, there are many well-established brands already.

[9] "Occidental Plans to Buy Iowa Beef for $800 million," *The Wall Street Journal,* June 2, 1981, p. 2.

73 Late in 1981, the company was investigating possible sites for construction of a pork processing plant. Of four sites under consideration, the smallest number of hogs marketed within a 150-mile radius of a site was 7.4 million, while the largest number for a site was 17.4 million.

Export

74 Most of IBP's exports have been by-products and hides. Between 1976 and 1980, the company exported 1.3 billion pounds of various meat products, generating a sales volume of over $745 million. In 1980, IBP began selling boxed beef in Europe and Japan.

75 Shortly after the merger, Dr. Hammer of Occidental Petroleum announced that arrangements were in progress for an exchange of technical information in the field of meat processing with the possibility of construction of a processing plant in the Soviet Union.

Portion Control

76 IBP's primary competitor in boxed beef, MBPXL, has already moved into the marketing of prepackaged retail-style cuts of beef, steaks, and roasts. IBP considers these products to be Phase 4 of its development but does not foresee their addition to the product line before the end of the 80s.

77 IBP entered the 80s as the largest, most successful meat packer in the United States. The challenges of the decade will require determining how and where its resources can be utilized to maintain its position.

case 11
Iowa Beef Processors (B) and Meatpacking in the 1980s

1 From the National Cattlemen's Association convention in New Orleans, to the feature pages of *Hog Farm Management,* to executive offices of poultry firms—the same question was asked in the winter of 1983–84: "What is happening in the meatpacking industry?" As raw materials suppliers to the meatpackers, the cattlemen, hog farmers, and poultry producers were concerned about the demand and consumption patterns for various types of meat, the changing structure of the meatpacking industry, and specific plans of leading companies like IBP, Inc.[1]

Meat Consumption

2 While consumption of red meat (beef and pork) in 1984 was close to the all-time high, Exhibit 1 indicates that the trend toward increased consumption for most of this century was being reversed. Exhibit 2 reports the results of a study by Oscar Mayer of changes in consumption habits. Exhibit 3, from the same study, reports consumers' reactions to pork specifically. These changes reflect, in part, health concerns of consumers. Red meat is generally viewed as high in fat (although hogs are bred to be 50 percent leaner than 25 years ago) and cholesterol. Red meat is also more expensive than the lower-calorie white meats, and the gap is widening. In the 1950s, a pound of poultry cost about 80 percent as much as a pound of beef. By 1980, poultry cost about 30 percent of the cost of beef. In the 1960s, poultry cost 75 percent as much as pork; by 1980, it cost 50 percent as much.

3 Companies like IBP, Inc., and Excel (subsidiary of Cargil, formerly known as MBPXL) have increased efficiency in meatpacking by cutting processing costs, but they are limited in the ability to cut raw materials costs by the commodity nature of the business and by some inherent inefficiencies of red meat animals as breeders and food processors. The situation was exacerbated in 1983 by drought and a government program. (Payment in Kind) which was intended to reduce grain stockpiles but which also resulted in high feed costs. *Forbes* described the commodity cycle:

> When feed prices are low, costs decline and herd sizes increase. This sends more cattle to market, which reduces prices. Reduced prices spark consumption, which in turn starts pushing prices back up as demand equals supply. Farmers

Case prepared by Phyllis G. Holland, Georgia State University. Carol A. Reeves served as Research Assistant.

[1] Iowa Beef Processors, Inc., became IBP, Inc., in 1982, a year after its acquisition by Occidental Petroleum. For details of IBP's rise to leadership in the beef industry, see the case, "Iowa Beef Processors (A)."

Exhibit 1

Food consumption in the United States (1981–1984)

	Pounds per Person			
	1981	*1982*	*1983*	*1984**
Animal products				
Red meat†	157	151	155	149
Beef and veal	79	79	80	76
Pork	65	59	62	60
Other	13	13	14	13
Poultry	63	64	65	66
Eggs	34	33	34	33
Dairy products	304	302	305	305
Other	24	24	24	25
Total animal products	582	574	584	578
Crop products (vegetables, sugar, grain, and so forth)	814	811	814	819
Total food consumption	1,396	1,385	1,398	1,397

* Estimated.
† Red meat consumption was 122 pounds per person in 1922, 134 pounds per person in 1940, and 157 pounds per person in 1980.
Source: Economic Research Service, USDA, *Agricultural Outlook*, December 1983.

then increase their herds, and the process begins again. Because it takes at least two years for a cow to grow to market size, the production curve is seldom smooth. Now (January 1984), there is an oversupply of red meat at high prices. But the PIK program is also driving up grain costs. So packers of fresh meat are in a squeeze. "Our costs are rising while prices are dropping," said John Copeland, chairman of Swift Independent Packing Corporation.

Beefpackers, of course, don't operate in isolation. At some point, consumers get their fill of expensive steaks, and demand shifts to pork and chicken. "With enough time, high grain prices are better for chicken than they are for other meats," explained Don Tyson of Tyson Foods.

Exhibit 2

Meat usage in 1982—responses to question: "How does your family's meat consumption compare to five years ago?"

	Turkey	*Chicken*	*Fish*	*Beef*	*Pork*
Eating more	28%	45%	23%	15%	18%
About the same	57	51	55	52	48
Eating less	15	4	22	33	34
Change	+13	+41	+1	−18	−16

Source: *The National Provisioner*, February 4, 1984, p. 10. (Based on 1,000 U.S. households.)

Exhibit 3

Consumer reactions to pork—responses to question: "Which phrases describe your feelings about pork?"

	1983	*1982*	*1981*
Preservatives	13%	14%	13%
Freshness	12	11	8
Costs too much	9	9	11
Additives	8	9	9
Salt	7	7	5
Fat/cholesterol	6	6	6
Taste	4	5	5
Not good for you	1	2	2
Nothing to change	27	26	27

Source: *The National Provisioner,* February 4, 1984, p. 10. (Based on 1,000 U.S. households.)

That's because chickens require less feed. Thanks to breeding, better-controlled chicken farming, and computer-formulated feeds, broilers grow to a bigger market weight faster (eight weeks) than they did 20 years ago. Result: It takes only two pounds of feed to produce one pound of chicken, half the conversion ratio of the 1950's.

Beef and pork producers are not so lucky, and progress is slow because of longer breeding cycles. Three and a half pounds of feed go into a pound of pork and seven pounds into a pound of good steak on the hoof. Thus, every penny rise in the price of feed widens the cost advantage of chicken and pork over beef.[2]

In the view of one pessimistic observer, beef "may be at or past a ceiling on total per capita meat supplies which can be marketed at a profit to producers."[3] Others are more optimistic, citing the development of "light" beef, the continuing domination by beef of the away-from-home market, and industrywide advertising efforts as hopes of stabilizing consumption patterns. The proportion of red meat currently exported is about 1 percent. "The potential [for export] is enormous," according to Kenneth Monfort, president of Monfort of Colorado. "We have to find places affluent enough to eat meat but which don't have their own production."[4] Japan and Europe fit the bill, but trade restrictions have limited exploitation of foreign markets.

4 While breeders expressed their concern about the shifts in ultimate demand for their products, they were also watching carefully the changing fortunes of their immediate customers, the packers.

Evolution of an Industry

5 It is difficult to imagine that the "Big Four" meatpackers, Swift, Wilson, Armour, and Cudahy, were once a target for those who attacked monopolistic practices of big

[2] Jeff Blysbal, "Food Processors," *Forbes,* January 2, 1984, pp. 206–7.

[3] "Beef Consumption Patterns," *Beef Digest,* July 1981, p. 12.

[4] Blysbal, "Food Processors," p. 207.

business earlier in the century. The Big Four were tamed in the 30s and 40s and had been swallowed up in the 60s and 70s by conglomerates. The fresh meat market was large (approximately $50 billion in1984), which made it attractive to companies seeking growth, but the new owners found the opportunities evaporating because of net margins of less than 1 percent and vulnerability to agricultural cycles. For the former Big Four, another kind of cycle began. As subsidiaries competing for resources with other subsidiaries, the meatpackers couldn't meet the return-on-investment criteria for capital allocation set up by their corporate owners and did not receive new capital. Their facilities became obsolete and, according to many observers, their management lethargic. The unions were able to negotiate industrywide master contracts which further sliced margins.

6 Into this situation came the "new" packers led by IBP. The IBP approach was based on new packing locations close to feedlots; large, modern, efficient plants; a new distribution system called boxed beef; and either nonunion labor or a policy of tough negotiations with unions to maintain low labor costs. Other companies followed IBP's lead, and the lessons of freedom from conglomerate decision making and cost control were not lost on the Big Four. Exhibit 4 summarizes the important changes in the affiliation and approach of industry competitors.

7 IBP's performance was spectacular in sales growth as well as earnings [see Iowa Beef Processors (A) case], and the industry experienced some dramatic changes. The number of packing plants has declined since 1971 (see Exhibit 4), with the decline centered in plants slaughtering less than 50,000 head annually. The 28 large plants accounted for more than half of the 1980 slaughter. Four-firm concentration ratios are shown in Exhibits 5, 6, and 7. In terms of profitability, the upper quartile aftertax return on equity for the industry moved from 11.4 to 17.6 during the period, indicating a greater spread in profit performance. This payoff has generated conglomerate interest in the new packers as indicated by the acquisition of IBP, Inc., (by Occidental Petroleum) and Excel (by Cargill).

8 While these shifts in beef packing were occurring, hog packing experienced only minor changes in ownership and plant location. In the late 1970s and early 1980s, the pace of change began to accelerate. IBP entered the industry with plans to create the same kinds of efficiencies in pork that had been so successful in beef. Other competitors have fought to cut costs with varying degrees of success.

9 One result of the changes in beef has been opposition of smaller operators to the large producers. For the first time since the early part of the century, the words *monopoly* and *concentration* have become a rallying cry. To explain Monfort of Colorado's legal efforts to stop the purchase of Spencer Beef by Excel, Kenneth Monfort said:

> The theory of our lawsuit was very clear. As they expand those plants and put in boxed beef facilities and double shifts, we would end up with two packers in our industry with something like 70 to 80 percent of the boxed beef market. We thought that concentration was too much.
>
> We don't believe such concentration would cause collusion, however. On the contrary, we thought there would be a very tough aggressive fight for market share that would eventually chase many of the smaller packers—even this one—out of business. Once we were out of business, the largest survivors could then go back to increasing their margins.
>
> We used to view competition in the packing industry as a fair fight—survival

Exhibit 4

Status of major competitors in meatpacking

Company	*Sales (in $ billions)* 1983	1982	*Ownership*	*Current status*
IBP, Inc.	$6	$5	Wholly owned by Occidental Petroleum.	Expanding into pork production after building world's largest beef slaughtering facility.
Excel (formerly MBPXL)	n.a.	n.a.	Owned by Cargill, an agricultural conglomerate.	Planned acquisition of Land o'Lakes' Spencer Beef subsidiary blocked by courts; acquired only one of the three plants instead.
SIPCO (Swift Independent Packpendent Packing Company)	2.5	1.8	Spun off to public by Esmark which retained 35 percent ownership, assumed $135 million pension liability, and provided $35 million working capital.	Closed and subsequently reopened two plants, cutting labor costs in plants by 50 percent; planning expansion of pork slaughtering by acquisition of three plants with combined revenue of $500 million.
Armour	2.4	2.5	Closed by owner Greyhound in hopes of sale without burden of master contract.	ConAgra has purchased some of the closed plants.
Wilson	2.2	2.2	LTV spun-off Wilson Foods to stockholders, absorbing $23 million in plant-closing costs.	In Chapter 11 reorganization. High labor costs cited as reason for losses.
Hormel	1.4	1.4	Public.	$225 million in capital improvements in recent years, including new plant; inefficient plant closed.
Monfort of Colorado	.995	.820	75 percent family owned.	Vertically integrated into cattle feeding; labor costs have been a problem in older of two plants.
Dubuque Packing Company	.800	1.85	Sold meat plants to executives for $30.5 million.	Reopened as FDL Foods, Inc., with $4/hour reduction in wages and work rules.
Morrell	n.a.	1.2	United Brands.	Five of company's seven slaughter plants have been closed; turnaround may be underway with subcontracting of slaughtering.
Rath	n.a. ($455 million in 1981)	n.a.	Employee owned.	Bankrupt.
Bar S Foods	n.a.	n.a.	Spun-off from General Foods' Cudahy Co. in leveraged buy-out by officers.	Operating.

n.a. = not available.

Exhibit 5

Comparison of numbers of cows and bulls slaughtered annually by region and size group—1971, 1976, and 1981 (number of plants)

		Slaughter per year			
Region	***Year***	***Less than 5,000***	***5,000–49,999***	***50,000 and more***	***Total***
North Atlantic	1971	62	39	0	101
	1976	50	28	5	83
	1981	59	19	2	80
East North Central	1971	118	24	6	148
	1976	83	28	10	121
	1981	64	14	6	84
West North Central	1971	62	42	9	113
	1976	44	37	18	99
	1981	40	25	13	78
South Atlantic	1971	67	16	1	84
	1976	50	26	4	80
	1981	44	13	3	60
South Central	1971	60	30	2	92
	1976	43	31	8	82
	1981	36	13	2	51
Southern Plains	1971	70	28	3	101
	1976	62	33	10	105
	1981	53	23	4	80
Mountain	1971	53	17	1	71
	1976	43	21	4	68
	1981	35	14	2	51
Pacific	1971	59	30	0	89
	1976	44	34	1	79
	1981	28	18	5	51

Source: Packers and Stockyards Administration. Includes plants reporting to P&SA.

of the fittest. But things have changed, when two giant companies with the wherewithal to do with the beef market whatever they decided to do acquired the two largest packing companies—Occidental's acquisition of IBP, the nation's largest packer, and Cargill's acquisition of Excel.[5]

10 Some have urged cattlemen to support the strengthening of antitrust legislation, to support administrative or civil lawsuits where there is evidence of anticompetitive practices, and to support legislation such as the Smith proposal to limit the size of packers. This legislation would put a cap on market share for individual packers. Others maintain there is no evidence of noncompetitive behavior. One observer has pointed out that meatpackers have not done well as subsidiaries of other organizations

[5] Warren Kester, "Are We Heading for Monopoly in the Beef Packing Business?" *Beef*, March 1984, pp. 86–94.

Exhibit 6

Percentage of total slaughter of cows and bulls accounted for by top four firms—1971, 1976, 1981

State	*1971*	*1976*	*1981*	*Change 1971–76*	*Change 1976–81*
California	42.8%	35.1%	56.5%	−7.7%	21.4%
Florida	80.0	72.9	86.7	−7.1	13.8
Georgia	82.7	72.7	97.1	−10.0	24.4
Iowa	71.8	82.7	97.3	10.9	14.6
Kentucky	88.9	90.5	97.9	1.6	7.4
Michigan	79.2	78.5	87.9	−.7	9.4
Minnesota	74.7	84.2	90.8	9.5	6.6
Mississippi	86.7	81.6	97.3	−5.1	15.7
Nebraska	69.5	71.4	81.8	1.9	10.4
New York	41.0	64.2	66.1	23.2	1.9
Oklahoma	69.4	60.8	78.5	−8.6	17.7
Pennsylvania	37.6	62.5	77.0	24.9	14.5
South Dakota	100.0	93.2	92.8	−6.8	−.4
Tennessee	59.1	59.4	85.3	.3	25.9
Texas	40.8	36.8	42.6	−4.0	5.8
Wisconsin	73.5	67.8	89.7	−5.7	21.9
Simple average	68.6%	69.6%	82.8%	1.0%	13.1%

Source: Packers and Stockyards Administration. Includes plants reporting to P&SA.

Exhibit 7

Four-firm concentration ratio (1969–1981)

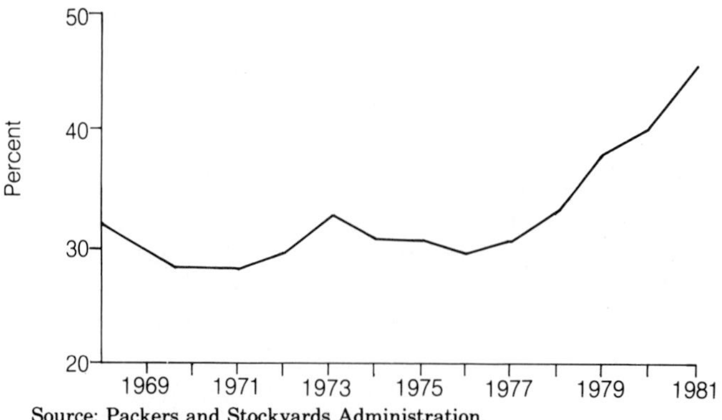

Source: Packers and Stockyards Administration.

and that there may be some surprises with the Big Four finally independent again and the new packers under conglomerate ownership.

11 There are also some definite predictions about the evolution of pork. One industry observer made the following predictions:

> Most old-time pork packers will be out of the hog slaughtering business by the end of the 1980s.
>
> New firms or organizations will be slaughtering hogs.
>
> Few master labor contracts will survive, and the cost of labor will decrease.
>
> More automation will occur in pork slaughtering and processing.
>
> Rather than large firms, most slaughtering firms will own only one or two plants.
>
> Plants will be larger.
>
> More plants will only slaughter, with processing at other sites.
>
> The major pork brands will survive but will buy meat and process only.[6]

Clearly, IBP intends to be the moving force behind several of these trends.

IBP

12 Acknowledged as the number 1 U.S. meatpacker for several years, IBP was ranked number 5 in sales of all food processors in 1983. This ranking compared with number 6 in 1982. While all packers suffered lower margins in 1983, IBP continued to set the industry standards in profitability. See Exhibit 8 for comparative performance data.

Exhibit 8

Performance data for selected meatpackers, 1982

Company	*Revenues ($ millions)*	*Net income ($ millions)*	*Return on sales*	*Return on stockholders' equity*
IBP	$4,900*	$49*	1.0%*	n.a.
Swift Independent	$2,488	$25	1.0	26.1%
Wilson Foods	$2,233	$17	0.7	20.0
Geo. A. Hormel	$1,427	$28	2.0	11.4
Monfort of Colorado	$0.996	$19	1.9	34.5

n.a. = not available.
* Estimate.
Source: *Fortune,* May 2, 1983.

13 While IBP's activities in beef have included the acquisition and renovation of a plant in Joslin, Illinois, in 1982 and several suspensions and one closing in 1983 because of capacity problems, most of the excitement was in the new pork business.

14 IBP's entry into pork processing came with the acquisition of a facility in Storm

[6] Marvin Skadberg, "Who Will Slaughter the Hogs?" *Hog Farm Management,* February 1984, p. 54.

Lake, Iowa, in 1982. It underwent extensive renovation and opened the following September with one shift operating. With the addition of a second shift in 1983, capacity increased to 3 million hogs per year. Meanwhile, the company announced it would build the nation's largest hog slaughtering facility, setting off competition for the site among several towns in the Midwest. The field was narrowed to Sheffield, Illinois, and Stanwood, Iowa, both small towns with depressed agricultural economies. After stiff competition, marked by significant concessions to IBP by both sites, Stanwood was chosen to receive the plant. Reasons given were the location in the heart of hog-raising country, the cost advantage of a federal grant Stanwood had agreed to apply for, and the uncertain corporate tax situation in Illinois (Illinois would tax on the basis of Occidental Petroleum's worldwide earnings, although a proposed change would have based the tax only on IBP's nationwide operations.)

15 The federal grant for which Stanwood had agreed to apply (and upon the receipt of which the site selection was contingent) was to finance a pipeline from a nearby river to the proposed plant. The grant was for $10 million although some claimed the cost of the pipeline would only be about a third of that amount. The request was rejected in January of 1983, but IBP continued its plans to build. The plant will have a capacity of 4 million hogs per year and will cost $45 million. When this plant is completed, IBP's hog slaughtering capacity will be approximately 7 million hogs per year. Some competitors have complained such plans will add new capacity to an industry where there is already considerable excess.

16 By early 1984, there were several indications that IBP was interested in acquiring existing capacity rather than creating any more new capacity. Occidental Petroleum offered $162 million ($95 million plus assumption of $67 million in notes, debentures, and lease obligations) for troubled Wilson Foods. The offer, which was not accepted, provoked a storm of criticism. Competitors predicted the purchase would mean further slashing of labor costs and speed the shakeout in pork packing. The combination would also increase IBP's domination of both suppliers and customers, critics maintained. Possible antitrust violations from such a merger also caused concern.

17 Another possible acquisition candidate was John Morrell and Company, the nation's third-largest pork packer and a subsidiary of United Brands. Acquisition and rehabilitation of existing facilities would, if pursued, constitute a departure from IBP's successful practice of building facilities and then hiring the construction workers as employees in the finished plant. Acquisition of existing facilities would involve union workers as well.

18 The relationship between IBP and the Food and Commercial Workers Union (FCWU), which claims to represent 85 percent of the 130,000 U.S. meatpacking workers, has been marked by strife since IBP entered the industry 1961. IBP rejected the union's master contract, which set industrywide wages, and hired and trained local workers for less-skilled jobs created by their new processing techniques. The resultant lower wages helped IBP gain a strong foothold in an industry saddled with expensive wage and benefit contracts.

19 IBP's gains in labor costs have not come without a price. Several strikes have resulted in lengthy work stoppages and violence.[7] The most-recent strike at the Dakota City

[7] There were nine strikes, several marked by violence, against IBP between 1969 and 1982. One of the most-violent strikes occurred in 1969 at the Dakota City plant, where a company executive's home was burned and a 16-year-old girl was fatally shot. IBP executives, determined to hold down production costs, have refused to grant major concessions to the labor union, causing what is, at best, a strained relationship between them.

plant was marked by violence after 2,000 union members walked out on June 7, 1982. The workers had overwhelmingly rejected IBP's offer of a four-year freeze of $9.27 per hour average wage for slaughterhouse workers and $8.97 per hour average for processing employees. The company had also demanded a clause that would allow it to reduce wages if any other local of the union signed a contract at a lower wage rate. The violence escalated when IBP reopened the plant in July with 1,400 workers, several hundred of whom were union members.

20 The walkout ended in October without an agreed-upon contract. In July 1983, Local 222 accepted a 42-month agreement that cut wages by $1.07 per hour. IBP claimed the cuts were necessary to ensure profitability, especially given the fact that other meatpackers had recently won wage concessions or freezes from their workers. The union contended IBP was trying to destroy it and vowed to regain concessions at future contract talks.

21 The meatpacking industry in the mid-1980s had come a long way from its beginnings when salt was the only preservative and barrels the principle means of transport. The most-recent changes were begun by IBP in the 1960s. Cattlemen, hog farmers, and poultry producers who watched and depended on the industry could only agree on the fact that these effects had not yet been completely felt.

SECTION

Strategy Implementation, Monitoring, and Control

case 12 The Coca-Cola Company and Operation PUSH

1 In hot Atlanta on August 10, 1981, at a press conference at Coca-Cola's headquarters, the working press was reminded of the turbulent 1960s when the civil rights movement came of age. There was Coretta Scott King, soft-spoken, refined, very strong, the widow of the slain leader and Nobel Peace Prize laureate Martin Luther King, Jr. Over there was the Reverend Jesse L. Jackson, older certainly than in the days when he marched to Selma with the Reverend King but, at 39, still brash, enigmatic, controversial, charismatic. He had grown to power through the Chicago-based activist organization People United to Save Humanity (PUSH), which he founded in the early 1970s, and had sought to extend black unity beyond the boundaries of the United States. Talking with him was the Reverend Joseph Lowery, another King protege, who was president of the Southern Christian Leadership Conference (SCLC), which was holding its annual convention in New Orleans this week. Present also was the Honorable Maynard Jackson, no longer simply an attorney but the seasoned mayor of Atlanta, Georgia, which had a metropolitan area population of almost 2 million, who was retiring after two terms in office.

2 The dusty roads near Selma, the marble steps of the capitol, the streets of Birmingham were a far cry from the paneled conference room of a corporate giant where the group gathered today. Trying to get a word in and announce his company's expanded minority participation program was Donald R. Keough, president and chief operating officer of the Coca-Cola Company.

3 Coke and PUSH had invited the black leaders to the historic press conference, called for August 10, 1981, at the multinational company's headquarters in Atlanta. The purpose of the conference was to announce expansion of the company's entire minority

This case was prepared by Robert D. Hay, University of Arkansas, with the assistance of Jane Lobell.

participation program, a "moral covenant" which would channel $34 million from Coca-Cola's general system into black economic development. President Keough addressed the press.

Good morning. First, I want to acknowledge the presence today of so many of America's prominent black leaders, especially the mayor of our city, the Honorable Maynard Jackson. I am happy to be part of this historic occasion for the company, Reverend Jackson, and the black leadership assembled here. As an employee of the Coca-Cola Company, I am proud for many reasons, not the least of which is that the company, through its decades under the guidance of Mr. Woodruff and other outstanding leaders, has always merited a place in the forefront of social justice.

Over the years, the Coca-Cola Company has maintained a high level of involvement in the black community through corporate gifts, scholarships, and executive time devoted to such organizations as United Negro College Fund, Atlanta University, Morris Brown, Spelman College, and Morehouse Medical School. In addition, the company has provided financial aid to the Martin Luther King Center and to many civil rights organizations, created career development films for black youth, and been involved in other endeavors too numerous to tick off here.

As a result, when we were approached by Reverend Jackson and his associates in Operation PUSH last November, we had no reason to hesitate to enter into discussions with them to hear their views on minority participation in the company's system.

Over the months, we listened very carefully, and we matched their comments, suggestions, and concerns with our own agenda for the black community, which we recognize as a significant segment of our society in the decade of the 1980s.

From the beginning, however, we listened on a broader scope than just across the conference table or over a telephone line. We had self-imposed tests to apply to the discussions—and the ideas arising out of them—to determine whether what we are now doing, and plan to do, is *what we ought to do.*

Several months ago, the chairman of the Coca-Cola Company, Roberto Goizueta, set forth his strategy for the company for the decade of the 80s. This strategy statement has been shared with all our employees and stockholders. In it, Mr. Goizueta states, and I am quoting from the document: "All employees will have equal opportunities to grow, develop, and advance within the company. Their progress will depend only on their abilities, ambition, and achievements." In addition, it is a focal point of Mr. Goizueta's strategy to nurture the sensitivity to adapt to change and to manage our enterprise in such a way that we will always be considered a welcomed and important part of the communities in which we operate.

Those are not idle words but the essence of what we fully intend to be. With nearly a century of operation behind us and our strategy for the 80s as a guideline, it was indeed easy for my associates to move forward in discussions with Reverend Jackson. In any human endeavor of this kind, there are inevitable periods of misconception which interrupt discussions. However, throughout the process, our discussions have maintained the integrity of forthrightness, courtesy, and respect.

Let me pause here to say that special words of gratitude are due to Mrs.

Coretta Scott King, Rev. Joseph Lowery, and his associates at the SCLC, and others in this room whose counsel, advice, and friendship were valuable to our discussions with Operation PUSH.

One point is critical to understanding the initiatives we are announcing here today. Since his election last November, President Reagan has been sending the business community a message which we at the Coca-Cola Company have heard very clearly. His philosophy on the subject we are discussing today was probably best presented in his June 29 speech to the NAACP.

In that speech, he noted the changing federal philosophy toward less interference by government in business and appealed to "business and industry to bring about an economic emancipation of blacks and the poor." Economic revitalization, the president said, is the "surest, most-equitable way to ease the pressures on all the segments of our society."

Given this new direction and the new economic policy as recommended by President Reagan and as enacted by the Congress, the force of the free enterprise system is being unleashed. In direct response to this new direction, we are accelerating and enlarging our programs already in place. And the black community, as an integral part of our system and society, will benefit with dignity and will receive a well-deserved piece of the action.

We wholeheartedly endorse the potential of free enterprise. We believe that our understanding developed with Reverend Jackson is a clear indication on the part of a major American company that business can listen and respond to presidential and congressional actions for tax-cut relief to business and also to the message and the promise that the free enterprise system can do more to develop opportunity for all elements of society.

We are willing to put more than rhetoric behind this belief. We have defined our future plans and will aid black entrepreneurs who seek to enter the beverage industry in the bottling and fountain wholesaling business. We have outlined programs in eight areas:

Bottler franchises.

Fountain wholesaling and wine distributorships.

Minority business development opportunities.

Advertising.

Banking opportunities.

Management opportunities and employment.

Corporate contributions.

Professional service contracts and minority purchasing programs.

Details about each of these areas are contained in the information handed out today.

In order to make sure we move expeditiously, we are engaging a research consulting firm which will help us select appropriate candidates.

In closing, I want to thank you, Reverend Jackson, and your associates for your patience and cooperation throughout our discussions. Personally, I am pleased to be the spokesman for a company that continues to demonstrate that it does *what it ought to do.*

4 Upon finishing his remarks, Mr. Keough passed out a news release.

5 Reverend Jackson, acknowledging the program announced by the Coca-Cola Company, said, "This program will indeed become a model for American industry. President Reagan has put the ball squarely in the court of the private sector, and the Coca-Cola Company has responded. It is the intention of Operation PUSH to see that other leading companies in the private sector follow this intiative by the Coca-Cola Company."

6 The plan was designed to increase black involvement in eight areas of the company's business system:

1. Bottler franchises: Recognizing the need for black Americans to share in ownership and wealth, the company will identify bottling franchises which may become available and refer such opportunities to a pool of black prospective investors.
2. Fountain wholesalers/wine distributorships: The company will appoint 32 black-owned distributors across the country within the next 12 months and has committed to provide specialized training, lists of prospective customers, and future advice and counsel as necessary to assist these businesses' success. The company is also researching opportunities for black participation in the distribution of its wine products. The estimated value of these programs is $1.3 million for over 100 new jobs, plus ownership.
3. Business development: The company will establish a venture capital fund of $1.8 million for the funding of black participation in the areas associated with and serviced by the company and the soft drink industry.
4. Advertising: The company will double the amount of its advertising dollars in black-owned newspapers and magazines and increase its advertising expenditures with black-owned radio. The estimated value of this advertising is over $2 million. In addition, a black-owned advertising agency will be given "agency-of-record" responsibility for a company brand with an estimated budget of $8 million.
5. Banking: The company will substantially increase its deposits and borrowing activities with black-owned banks and increase the number of black-owned financial institutions utilized by the company. The total commitment in this area represents $2 million.
6. Management and employment: The company is actively searching for a black to join its board of directors and expects to have selected that person within six months. The company is also committed to continue its hiring and promotion of blacks to management positions toward the goal of 12.5 percent of the management force. At least 100 of the blue-collar openings during the next year will be filled by blacks. The value of the jobs contained in these goals is approximately $5.2 million.
7. Corporate contributions: The company will continue to designate a significant portion of its corporate contributions to black organizations and institutions. The initial annual value of these contributions is $250,000. In the area of education, additional scholarships and chairs will be endowed at black colleges and universities.
8. Goods and services: The company will continue its active minority purchasing program and expand it in terms of numbers of minority vendors and dollars spent. This year, the level of this minority purchasing will increase to an estimated $14 million through over 800 suppliers.

Reverend Jackson said, "Operation PUSH is now ending its national withdrawal of enthusiasm campaign and will take affirmative steps to promote and publicize the new relationship that has been established between Black America and the Coca-Cola Company."

Background Information

7 A background of events might help explain what led to Coke's press conference.

8 In November of 1980, the Reverend Jackson of Operation PUSH approached Coca-Cola and suggested they talk about Coke's minority participation program. Jackson took the initiative, and Coke's executives listened.

9 Mr. Keough later said the decision to talk about Jackson was not a "huge decision" since it had been the philosophy of Coca-Cola "from time immemorial" to discuss its relationship with minorities.

10 Talks with Jackson were approved by himself, Keough said, and Roberto C. Goizueta, chairman and chief executive officer. He and Goizueta were kept informed of all talks with Jackson and PUSH, and the board was routinely informed. Keough said the negotiations and final program did not require the formal approval of the board, as the decisions were "in the purview of the chief executive officer."[1]

11 During the next nine months, the discussions between Jackson's PUSH executives and Coke's executives continued. Jackson's basic philosophy during those discussions became evident.

12 Reverend Jackson called his concept a development formula and stated:

> Black America, as an *underdeveloped nation,* must renegotiate the *relationship with corporate America* around three critical economic principles.
>
> 1. Reciprocity. No longer is generosity alone enough. Black America must demand its fair share in a mutually beneficial relationship. Jobs are not enough. Full employment with no pay is slavery, and employment without ownership is colonialism. The reinvestment of a rightful portion of black consumer dollars in the development of our economic institutions and community is the new demand.
>
> 2. Development plans and formulae. Black America, as an underdeveloped nation, requires a development plan and formula. Development requires new rules—not just new rulers—that are designed for national development. All other such underdeveloped nations have development plans and formulae that must be complied with to do business in their community. Black America can settle for nothing less.
>
> 3. Supply-side economics. There must be a concentrated focus on institutional economic development by Black America. Basic black economic institutions—banks, savings and loans, insurance companies, newspapers, radio and television stations, advertising agencies, and more—must be built. We must focus on the supply side as well as the demand side of the economic ledger. It is not enough to have affirmative action on the demand side—jobs and consumer protection. We must have affirmative action on the supply side—our share of ownership, wealth, and control."[2]

---

[1] Thomas Oliver, "Coca-Cola Admits It Mishandled PUSH Pact," *Atlanta Journal and Constitution,* September 3, 1981, p. 16A.

[2] Jesse L. Jackson, "Metropolitan Washington PUSH and Mid-Atlantic Coca-Cola Reach Agreement," PUSH news release, August 25, 1981, p. 3.

13 Other significant external events which affected the discussions occurred during the nine months. For example, in January 1981, President Reagan was sworn into office. He started to loosen regulations on business and suggested that private business take on the obligations of governing its own affairs in social responsibilities. In fact, in June 1981, President Reagan addressed the NAACP and called for the private sectors of the economy to develop minority programs on their own without governmental prodding.

14 The new president of Coca-Cola, Roberto C. Goizueta, elected in March 1981, took over the reins from Paul Austin and became the CEO and chairman of the board. He agreed with President Reagan's assessment and was ready to push harder for minority programs with PUSH. In fact, by early July 1981, Coca-Cola's agreements with operation PUSH were 95 percent complete.

15 On July 7, 1981, the Reverend B. W. Smith delivered an address at the convention of Operation PUSH. There was no mention of a boycott. Four days later, the Reverend Jesse Jackson, however, called for blacks to "withdraw their enthusiasm" from Coca-Cola products. He asked black ministers to urge their congregations to boycott Coke.

16 Mr. Keough explained what happened: "Another misjudgement by Coca-Cola brought about the withdrawal of enthusiasm." PUSH had invited Keough to Chicago prior to the group's annual convention in early July. Jackson and Keough were to put the finishing touches on the minority participation program, and Jackson would then have the agreement in hand when the convention convened. But Keough didn't go to Chicago; instead he sent William Allison, a black who head Coca-Cola's community affairs program.

17 Jackson interpreted the substitution of Allison, whom Jackson described as a "messenger with no authority," as a sign that Coca-Cola was pulling back in its commitment to the program. "We had to declare the withdrawal to get their attention," Jackson said.

18 But Keough said PUSH misunderstood Coca-Cola's intentions. He had not gone to Chicago, Keough said, because "the trip just didn't fit my calendar." Keough speculated that had he gone to Chicago, the boycott might have been avoided.[3]

19 Coca-Cola was caught unaware when Jackson called the boycott on July 11. The company was close to announcing a major expansion of its minority program which is updated annually as part of the firm's agreement with the federal EEOC.

20 Keough went so far as to say that PUSH President Jesse Jackson called the boycott only because the final agreement could not be reached in time for Jackson to announce it at PUSH's annual convention in early July.[4]

21 The Reverend Jesse Jackson, on the other hand, said: "When negotiations with Coke failed to get the company to beef up its economic support of black businesses, the 'demonstration stage' began—the last stage before asking store owners to take Coke off their shelves. I asked black ministers to preach on July 19 against drinking Coke."[5]

22 Syndicated columnist William Raspberry reported:

---

[3] Oliver, "Coca-Cola Admits It Mishandled PUSH Pact," p. 16A, footnote 1.

[4] Thomas Oliver, "Coke-PUSH Pact No Danger to Firm's Finances, Analysts Declare," *Atlanta Journal and Constitution*, August 13, 1981, p. 8B.

[5] Emily F. Rubin, "Jackson an Activist Turned Economist in Battle with Coke," *Atlanta Journal and Constitution*, August 2, 1981, p. 4K.

When the initial talks floundered, PUSH called its 50-city network into play, using ministers, politicians, and others to implement a "withdrawal of enthusiasm" for Coke products. Shortly thereafter, Coca-Cola was taken off the shelves in four black-owned 7-Eleven franchises in Washington, D.C., alone and was followed by similar action in white-owned stores. Gary's Mayor Richard Hatcher, chairman of the Black Mayor's Conference, started a move to remove Coke machines from the 194 city halls under black control. Coke came off the shelves in 100 Chicago stores.

Coke got the message, and Keough himself got involved in the renewed talks.[6]

23 For the next month, the boycott was proceeding while negotiations were going forward. The Reverend Jackson credited the civil rights leaders Reverend Joseph Lowery, Coretta Scott King, and Hosea Williams, businessman Jesse Hill, Atlanta Chamber of Commerce President Herman Russell, and Atlanta City Council President Marvin Arrington as being instrumental in getting Coca-Cola and PUSH to the bargaining table.

24 In August, the newspapers reported: "We are still hammering out some critical details," the Reverend Jackson said in a telephone interview from his Chicago office to Thomas Oliver of the *Atlanta Journal and Constitution,* "but the negotiations are going well, and if completed on schedule, we hope to be able to make a joint announcement Monday."[7]

25 Finally on August 10, 1981, the press conference was held.

Why PUSH Targeted Coca-Cola

26 The rationale behind the campaign, the Reverend Jackson later said, was that blacks consumed a lot of Coke—more Coke than Coke's margin of profit, he claimed. In exchange for that, Coke was supposed to initiate some economic development in the black community. Coke was to contribute back to the black community what it had taken out.

27 PUSH's research showed that in the top 50 markets where blacks lived, they spent $100 billion a year and bought 25 percent of the Coke consumed in those markets, according to the Reverend Jackson.

28 A financial analyst interviewed by the *Atlanta Journal and Constitution* said that Coca-Cola was targeted not so much because of a record of shortchanging minorities but because Coca-Cola was the "biggest name consumer product" in the world and was vulnerable to a boycott. One reason for Coke's vulnerability was the competitive nature of the beverage industry, which Coca-Cola once dominated with little thought of its rivals. Also, the company, under new leadership, had been launched on a new "entrepreneurial" course, which didn't allow for any diversion of management's time and energy.

29 "The boycott was a problem they wanted to go away, and the cost to them was nothing," said the analyst. The $34 million agreement pales next to the $470 million in after-tax profits the company should earn this year," he added.

---

[6] William Raspberry, "Jesse Jackson and the Coca-Cola Co.," syndicated column, late August.

[7] Thomas Oliver, "Coke and PUSH Accord Claimed," *Atlanta Journal and Constitution,* August 8, 1981, p. 1.

30 He pointed out that part of the $34 million is in the form of loans which must be paid back to Coke. Other parts of the settlement apparently require only a shifting of budgeted funds, not an increase in the overall budget of the company.[8]

31 Coke's chief financial officer, Sam Ayoub, emphasized that the program was not a giveaway.

32 Another reason Operation PUSH targeted Coca-Cola, some say, was the company's reputation for promoting minority participation, a record which made it open to further demands from civil rights organizations.

Coke's History of Social Responsibility

33 One example of Coke's exercise of its social responsibility was its response to migrant farm workers in its Minute Maid Corporation of Orlando, Florida, in 1968; its hiring and promotion of blacks; and its corporate financial contributions.

34 After it acquired Minute Maid, Coca-Cola, under the direction of former Chairman Paul Austin, investigated living conditions of its inherited 1,200 agricultural workers. (Seventy percent of the workers were black, 20 percent were white, and 10 percent were Mexican.) Subsequently, Coke put workers on the payroll instead of paying a piece rate and sought to involve workers in seeking solutions to housing, educational, medical, and other problems. At the time, the company was criticized on national television as "the culprit" of the poor conditions, although other businesses were looking at Coke's program as a model of social responsibility.[9]

35 Mr. Austin was active in national associations of businesses to promote the hiring, training, and promoting of minorities. The company had previously had black representation on its board of directors. A black served on the board from 1973 to 1977 when he resigned to accept a key position in the federal government. When he left Washington in March, he chose to accept an executive position with the company and, therefore, did not return to the board.

36 Even when the boycott was in effect, Mr. Woodruff, the former CEO, was honored by a predominantly black college. Morris Brown College bestowed upon Mr. Woodruff its "Centennial Man of the Year in Georgia" award, the *Atlanta Journal and Constitution* reported on August 2, 1981. Morris Brown president, Dr. Robert Threatt, called the Coca-Cola Company a "good friend," and said that Coke's leadership had meant a great deal to the college. Dr. Threatt cited financial gifts from the Woodruff family foundation of an endowment of Coca-Cola stock worth more than $500,000; a $100,000 donation for the recent renovation of Fountain Hall on the campus; and a $10 million donation to build the new Atlanta University Center library complex which Morris Brown would use.

Administrative Philosophy of Coca-Cola

37 In March 1981, Chief Executive Officer and Board Chairman Paul Austin was succeeded by Cuban-born Roberto C. Goizueta. Before his election in May 1980, Mr. Goi-

---

[8] Oliver, "Coke-PUSH No Danger to Firm's Finances, Analysts Declare," p. 1B.

[9] Cecil G. Howard and Lynn E. Dellenbarger, Jr., "Case 3–2: The Coca-Cola Company Foods Divisions and the Migrant Worker," in *Business and Society: Cases and Text* by Robert D. Hay, Edmund R. Gray, and James E. Gates (Cincinnati: South-Western Publishing, 1976), pp. 224–35.

zueta, the second highest paid officer of Coke (next to Mr. Austin) had not even made some of the lists of dark-horse candidates for the job. Immediately prior to his election, Mr. Goizueta was executive vice president responsible for administration, external relations, legal, and technical divisions.

38 Mr. Goizueta commented on the company's business behavior in a formal statement adopted by the board of directors in March 1981 and sent to the company's 41,000 employees in 135 countries and its shareholders.

> I have previously referred to the *courage and commitment* that will be indispensable as we move through the 1980s. To this I wish to add *integrity and fairness* and to insist that the combination of these four ethics be permeated from top to bottom throughout our organization so that our behavior will produce leaders and good managers who are—most importantly—opposed to being only reactive and that we *encourage intelligent individual risk taking.*

39 Mr. Goizueta's philosophy and his objectives for the company were contained in various speeches and interviews.

> For the first time in years, the government is listening to business and trying new ideas. This state's [California's] favorite son has given American business a window in time—one clear chance to prove that business *unfettered* will be business *unflagging* in the service to American society. For the first time in years, the overall psychological mood of the nation is becoming more favorable to business. . . . We have, for all the years I can recall, asked government to get off our backs—to free us from punitive taxes, from burdensome regulations and costs, from mountains of red tape and forests of paperwork. Today, we are beginning to get the opportunity that we have wanted for so long . . . the opportunity to prove that when private enterprise is relatively free, it can be the primary agent of response to human need.[10]
>
> Thus, I commend to all of us that the war on the economy is ours, that the war on inequality is ours, that the war on social injustice is ours.
>
> If we are realistic in our expectations . . . if we are willing, as a people, to live with the consequences of some difficult decisions now . . . then I am convinced that the underlying strength of this society will carry us through the full realization of what is known as the American dream.
>
> I can only add that I want to join today's pioneers in the new corporate citizenship to reach heights of achievement for this country like this country has never seen before. The ball is surely on our side of the court.[11]

40 A Coca-Cola executive sent the following letter to the case researcher:

41 It is unfortunate that some accounts have portrayed our program as a "cave-in" to the "withdrawal of enthusiasm" for our products announced by PUSH. That is not the case. The PUSH activities had no adverse economic impact on

[10] Roberto C. Goizueta, "Reflection on Corporate Citizenship in Today's Business Climate" (Speech presented at *Los Angeles Times* dinner, September 28, 1981, p. 7.

[11] Ibid., p. 12.

the company. And it should be clearly understood that the plan announced does not channel any funds to the Reverend Jesse Jackson or PUSH.

42 However, special-interest groups do offer insight that is sometimes useful in the refinement of our programs, and we are always willing to listen to their views, as well as to those of any consumer.

43 The Coca-Cola Company has a proud tradition of bringing blacks and other minorities into our business system through employment, advertising, educational opportunities, and other means. The question in this instance was whether we were doing enough in light of the current message to the free-enterprise system from the federal government.

44 Factoring in the views and perspectives of PUSH and many others, we decided that we were not and took steps to augment our minority participation programs. We believe that this is the right thing to do, both for the benefit of the Coca-Cola Company and society. As I am sure you realize, the Coca-Cola Company has long had a minority participation program. Under the new program, we will simply be accelerating and extending existing activities to bring more minorities into our business system.

45 Professor Hay, I hope this information is helpful and that it is responsive to your inquiry. We appreciate your continued interest.

46 Thank you for getting back in touch with me about Operation PUSH as it gives me the opportunity to share with you the philosophy and rationale behind our current program to bring more minorities into the Coca-Cola Company's business system. It also provides an opportunity to clear up some misconceptions about the action we have taken.

47 The point that is critical to understanding our program is that both President Reagan and the Congress, by their action regarding federal budget cuts and lower individual and corporate taxes, have set a new economic policy designed to unleash the force of the free-enterprise system in this country. A portion of the corporate tax burden has been reduced. Some social welfare programs have been reduced as well. In these circumstances, the free-enterprise system is being called on to utilize some of its resources, so that more segments of our society have not only an opportunity to purchase and consume but an opportunity to become producers of our products.

48 Those of us in the business sector must do more than merely applaud the new direction from the federal government. We must assume new responsibilities as a result of it. The Coca-Cola Company's program to enlist more minorities as business partners is aimed at meeting that responsibility.

49 It is unfortunate that some accounts have portrayed our program as a "giveaway" activity. That clearly is not the case. The initiatives announced on August 10 are designed to bring more blacks into our business system for the purpose of investing in, and contributing to, the production, marketing, and distribution of our products. These businesses and investments would be subject to the usual risks of the free-enterprise system.

50 As mentioned in the fact sheet I sent to you, there are some 4,000 fountain wholesalers of Coca-Cola in the United States, but only two are black owned. Under our recently announced program, it is our hope that we will encourage more black entrepreneurs to go into the fountain wholesaling business, thereby creating profit for themselves and for us and creating jobs. There is no "giveaway"

in this transaction. It's merely an opportunity to expand, concurrently, the business of the Coca-Cola Company and minority participation.

51 As another example, these initiatives include a minority purchasing program which the company established several years ago, but for which the current goal has been set at $14 million. This is not a "giveaway" but a plan to purchase necessary goods and services from minority vendors.

Coke's View of the Boycott's Impact

52 Mr. Keough later told a reporter from the *Atlanta Journal and Constitution* that the boycott didn't receive "two minutes' attention here because we just never considered it a real issue. We felt absolutely no impact from it and didn't think we would."[12]

53 Another spokesman said that because of the short duration of the PUSH boycott, Coke had been unable to accurately estimate any impact the boycott had.

54 Mr. Keough said that the company viewed the "withdrawal of enthusiasm" as insignificant compared to the "real barnburners" and "honest-to-God boycotts" it had experienced in Florida, Guatemala, and throughout the Arab world.

55 "We really kind of brushed it aside as a typical ploy. We flat didn't consider it to be a significant issue, so maybe from a public relations viewpoint, we made a misjudgment," he said.

56 "We were 95 percent completed with our discussions [with Jackson] when the boycott issue was raised, but it obviously gave the people the mistaken belief we were bowing to pressure," he said.[13]

57 No substantive concessions were made because of the boycott, Coca-Cola officials said. In discussions with the Reverend Jackson during the boycott, these officials said, some timetables were added to the minority program, and dollar values were assigned to a number of provisions. In a separate interview, the Reverend Jackson agreed with this assessment.

58 Operation PUSH studies indicated that black consumer sales with the Coca-Cola Company totaled more than $296 million. PUSH estimates of black sales with other companies were: $348 million, Procter & Gamble; $317 million, General Foods; $476 million, Philip Morris; $306 million, McDonald's; $278 million, Pepsi-Cola; $462 million, Sears, Roebuck & Co.; $117 million, Revlon; $200 million, Toyota. In addition, some PUSH estimates of the blacks' market share with companies were: 32 percent of Gillette's razor blade market, 11–12 percent of Nabisco sales, 15.2 percent of the Listerine mouthwash market, 11 percent of the total Pillsbury Hungry Jack biscuit market, 10 percent of the Pillsbury frosting mix market, 7 percent of the Pillsbury cake mix market, 23 percent of the Johnny Walker Red market, 12 percent of the Chivas Regal market, 16 percent of the J & B market, 27.8 percent of the Old Forrester market, and 24.4 percent of the Old Taylor market. PUSH also said the leading products—Jim Beam, Old Crow, Old Forrester, and Old Taylor—have a total of more than 1.5 million black customers and that blacks spent more than $6 billion on liquor in 1979 alone.

---

[12] Oliver, "Coca-Cola Admits It Mishandled PUSH Pact," p. 1A.

[13] Ibid., p. 16A.

59 The Reverend B. W. Smith, in an address entitled "Awakening a Sleeping Giant: The Black Church—A Major Economic Force," delivered at the 10th annual convention of Operation PUSH at the Hyatt Regency in Chicago on July 7, 1981, (before the boycott) said, "Coca-Cola had gross sales of $4.9 billion in 1979 and made a profit of $420.1 million. In addition to Coca-Cola, this company markets Fresca, Sunkist, Dr Pepper, Minute Maid Orange Juice, and Hi-C, and they are the fifth largest wine producer in the nation. Black consumer sales with this company total over $296 million.

60 "Coca-Cola is getting too much of our money, and there is not too much difference between the profit/loss margin and between Coke and Pepsi for us to let them off without being exactly where we think they ought to be," the Baptist minister exhorted. (See Exhibit 1.)

The Coca-Cola Company

61 The foundation of the Coca-Cola Company was the soft drink, Coca-Cola, which in 1980 accounted for 76 percent of the company's $5.9 billion in sales.

62 The company's origin dates to 1886 when an Atlanta, Georgia, pharmacist Dr. John Smyth Pemberton, according to legend, cooked up the first syrup for Coca-Cola in a three-legged brass pot in his backyard. The first glass of the new soda fountain drink went on sale for 5 cents a glass on May 8, 1886, in an Atlanta pharmacy where, by design or accident, carbonated water was teamed with the new syrup to produce the drink. In 1888, rights to the product were purchased by Asa G. Candler, a businessman, who became the "sole proprietor of Coca-Cola," at a cost of $2,300. Sales grew, and in 1892, the company was formally incorporated as a Georgia corporation, named the Coca-Cola Company, with a capital stock of $100,000.

63 In 1919, Candler sold out to Atlanta banker Ernest Woodruff and an investor group he had organized. Sale price was $25 million. Soon after the sale, the business was incorporated as a Delaware corporation and its common stock put on public sale for $40 a share. Its current financial position is shown in the financial statements (see Exhibit 2).

Exhibit 1

930 E. 50TH ST. - CHICAGO 60615 - 312:373-3366

Remarks by
REVEREND B. W. SMITH

before
The Tenth Annual Convention
of Operation PUSH
Hyatt Regency Chicago
Chicago, Illinois
July 7, 1981

"AWAKENING A SLEEPING GIANT:
The Black Church—A Major Economic Force"

EXODUS 4:2 AND THE LORD SAID UNTO HIM, WHAT IS THAT IN THINE HAND? AND HE SAID A ROD.

EXODUS 14:15 AND THE LORD SAID UNTO MOSES, WHEREFORE CRIEST YOU UNTO ME? SPEAK UNTO THE CHILDREN OF ISRAEL THAT THEY GO FORWARD.

Somewhere in the scripture there, it says there arose a Pharoah in Egypt, and without recalling that entire story of how Joseph went there as a friend of the Pharoah and friended himself to the Pharoah, there were a series of incidents. Now, there was a spiral on the throne, and they put the children of Israel in bondage. As they grew old, their spirits waxed cold. And somewhere, it said that they refused to sing the song of Zion in a strange land. They lost their desire to think.

The blues grew out of our community because of us being down and feeling low—the song, "Don't Let the Sun Catch You Crying"; and the other song, "The Sun's Gon' Shine in My Back Door Someday." Well, they refused to sing; they lost their desire to sing. They were desolate, they were depressed. And in one place it says that they hung their hearts on the willows and wept by the waters as they remembered Zion. Crying is sometimes a release, expressing impotence, the inability to do anything about the situation you're in, and you weep because it sometimes typifies helplessness. And they wept. Many of us in the community are weeping because of the Reaganomics that is sweeping this country. Many of us now are refusing to sing because of Reaganomics.

But I want to tell you today, that the National Black Church Congress numbers better than 20 million persons. More than 11 million are Baptist. Twenty million consumers making up a major part of the $125 billion dollars spent by Black Americans each year. Many of us as church leaders have begun to look pessimistically at the future. We have accepted the fact that Reaganomics will destroy us all.

Exhibit 1 *(continued)*

The Lord is speaking to us (ministers) like he did to Moses. *"Wherefore Criest Thou unto me? Speak unto the children that they go forward."* If Black Americans were a separate nation, we would be the ninth richest in the free world. We are not impotent; we are not helpless. All we need is to be sensitized to our resources.

It was the Black church leaders that led the Montgomery bus boycott and brought an end to segregated bus service in Montgomery, Alabama. It was the Black church that formed the vanguard for the struggle in the South under the leadership of Martin Luther King in the 60s. It was the Black church leaders that made Operation Breadbasket work under the leadership of our own Rev. Jesse Jackson. The Black church must come back and the Black church leaders, the preacher/prophet must once again take his rightful place in the leadership of this movement. Who better than the Black preacher is qualified to challenge the big insensitive corporations to do what is right. We will encourage our people to "withdraw their enthusiasm," as Mr. Daryl Grisham puts it.

Coca-Cola had gross sales of $4.9 billion in 1979 and made a profit of $420.1 million. In addition to Coca-Cola, this company markets Fresca, Sprite, Sunkist, Dr Pepper, Minute Maid Orange Juice, and HI-C, and they are the fifth largest wine producer in the nation. Black consumer sales with this company total over $296 million. Blacks consume 49 percent of all the grape soda produced in the United States. *WHY CRIEST THOU UNTO ME?* is the question, *WHAT IS THAT THAT'S IN YOUR HAND?*

A $125 billion rod. Use it! Use what you have in your hand. Coke has had to change its mind. They have with us today their top Black executive, who is here with a mess of porridge to make a peace pact. We thought we were about ready to accept it, but we're looking at it again a little closer. I told them wait. Let their consumer patronage council look at that a little closer before we sign, or our good friend may have to go back to Atlanta with that and come back to us again. Coca-Cola is getting too much of our money, and there is not too much difference between the profit/loss margin and between Coke and Pepsi for us to let them off without being exactly where we think they ought to be.

Our Survival Plan

Since we (Black people) are concentrated in mostly urban areas, we've got to have a survival plan. Seventy-five percent of us live in urban areas. And since four fifths of our population attend some form of the Black church—the Black preacher/prophet becomes a real authentic leader, a 21-carat-gold leader. The clergy speaks on a regular basis to more people than any person in our community. We cannot allow our people to continue to dissipate their resources like they are. Pastors must give their members direction. I'm a pastor. I refuse to pastor 3,000 members at St. John and let the politician tell them how to vote. I'm going to tell 'em how to vote! I refuse to pastor 3,000 folk and let the business people in the community tell them where to shop and what to buy. I'll tell them what to do about that. I refuse to turn my congregation over to the community leaders who know nothing about God or care less, for I lead a called-out people who have come ye out from among them and have decided to be also

Exhibit 1 *(continued)*

separated. So since they have come out from the world, then their instructions will come from me! "My sheep"—Lord I wish I could say—"They know my voice and a stranger, they will not follow." My sheep will hear my voice and when politicians come calling, no sense in talkin'. They're going to say, "What does Reverend say?" I'll make sure that the politicians are accountable because before I give a member the right hand of fellowship, I register them to vote right in the lobby.

And every time a politician comes there, I say, "All of the registered voters stand up." And the whole house goes up. We see three or four people. And that says to them that this is a fella' we're going to have to deal with a little bit differently than is our usual technique, e.g. to bring Reverend a free ticket to Church's Chicken.

Operation PUSH is targetting these 50 cities in the United States for action based on their population. Some of these cities are Chicago, Boston, Buffalo, Newark, New York City, Philadelphia, Cincinnati, Cleveland, Kansas City, St. Louis, Detroit, Los Angeles, Baltimore, New Orleans, Memphis, Dallas, Houston, San Francisco, Oakland, Miami, Gary, Washington, D.C., and other cities. The 50 markets contain 65 percent of the Black population and sustain 75 percent of the income of Blacks, or $98.7 billion. In each of these cities, we need a council of clergy that are on the alert and have their congregations sensitized to the call for a selective buying campaign against any company that is unfair to the Black community in their hiring practices—advertising in Black media, investments in Black banks and savings and loans, contributions to Black colleges (UNCF—United Negro College Fund), scholarships to needy Blacks in the community, etc. We must insist upon our share of the franchises and the corporate positions.

We want a Black from the boiler room to the board room. We must get our share of the legal, advertising, and public relations contracts, also in an amount commensurate to our spending power.

There are approximately 25 major companies that we have zeroed in on for action, and others we are looking at closely. These are companies that get the largest portion of our consumer dollar. Some of them are Kellogg's, Church's Chicken, Pillsbury, R. J. Reynolds, General Mills, Scott Towels, Green Giant, Gallo Wines, National Distillers, K mart, Nissan Datsun, Toyota, Texaco, Oscar Mayer, Pizza Huts, Nehi, Royal Crown, Hilton Hotels, Marriott Hotels, Standard Oil, Carnation, Bob Evans Sausage, Cannon Towels, Del Monte, Colgate-Palmolive, Wrigley Chewing Gum, Mobil Oil (Montgomery Ward), General Foods, Holly Farms, Procter & Gamble, Sky Chief, Campbell Soup, Honda, Winn-Dixie, Eastman Kodak, and Revlon. *"AND GOD SAID, WHAT IS THAT THAT'S IN YOUR HAND?"*

My response to you is IT IS *MONEY!* IT'S *LONG* AND IT'S *GREEN,* $125 billion. We cannot afford to spend that kind of money foolishly. The dollar changes hands in the white community 2 to 3 times, in the Chinese community, 10 to 12 times. That same dollar stays in the Black community about 6 to 7 hours. We must organize consumer clubs within our churches and in our community. These clubs will monitor the behavior of leading consumer companies, particularly the chain grocery or drug companies and the retail clothing industries.

A clergy representative from each of the target cities will form a national selective

Exhibit 1 *(continued)*

patronage council, of which I chair, and we will go over these companies' records. This council, with the aid of national staff, will contact companies targeted for review. Each company will receive an approach letter indicating our concern and identifying who we are. The letter will also call for a meeting wherein we can further detail our concerns and reasons for seeking an economic argument with that particular company. In that letter or one subsequent to it, a questionnaire covering the areas of concern will be submitted.

If the company is responsive, the negotiations will continue. We will present proposals based upon our research and the information they have submitted in the questionnaire and in the meetings. If the company chooses to evade negotiations to resist our objectives, we will report this to our local communities along with information about its sales and economic impact upon our community. At that time, we will prepare a selective patronage campaign (boycott) withdrawing our enthusiasm.

If the company chooses to return to the table (we call that reconciliation), the proposal will be restated and refined for further discussion and reflect the additional loss suffered by the Black community due to the company's recalcitrance, while we were waiting on them to make up their mind. We will *up the ante,* as you would say, in some areas. The *minister,* the *preacher* is the force that must make this happen. The moral authority of mankind has been entrusted to the preacher/prophet. We have the power and the authority to use it! We are the only ones who can tell corporate America that it is sinful—what you are doing to Black people.

WHAT IS THAT YOU HAVE IN YOUR HAND? YOU HAVE A ROD IN YOUR HAND, USE IT! You can build the Black business community, and you can tear down corrupt corporate entities. You can challenge schools, and tear down corrupt corporate entities. You can challenge school teachers to teach, and you can challenge young people to learn—*WHAT IS THAT THAT'S IN YOUR HAND?*

If you will speak unto the children and command them to go forward, the waters of the corporate Red Sea will back up. If you speak, the winds of selective buying will blow, and Black people can pass over on dry land. If you speak and command the people to march, the walls of injustice and discrimination in hiring will crumble. If you speak, crippled ghetto dwellers living below a decent level will rise up and walk to a job we have for them. If you speak, the blinded eyes of an insensitive media will open and see us in a different light and better understand our dissatisfaction.

If you speak, the jangling discords of our disunity will be transformed into a beautiful symphony. The multitudes that are basking in the economic valley of dry bones can be resurrected into a great army marching to independence and liberation. Therefore, I charge you to leave this place with a message to corporate America, that we demand respect commensurate to the $125 billion we spend. I charge you to meticulously examine the records of the target companies in the geographical area in which you live.

I charge you to mobilize your congregation, mobilize your community, the PTAs, the fraternal organizations, the civic clubs, the block clubs, yes, and even go into the streets and to the neighborhoods and knock on doors and ring door bells. We must let this country know we mean business.

Exhibit 1 ***(concluded)***

Finally, my brethern, we must trust in God. When Moses trusted God, the Red Sea parted. When He said, "Why I speaked thou unto me? Cry I speak to the children that they might go forward." When they stepped forward, the Red Sea backed up. Moses trusted God. When Joshua trusted God, Jericho fell. When Abraham trusted God, Sarah bore a son. When Jacob trusted God, his cattle outnumbered Laban's. When Shadrach, Meshach, and Abednego trusted God, Nebuchadnezzar's fiery furnace could do them no harm. When Gideon trusted God, he defeated the Midianites with 300 men. When the widow at Zarephath trusted God and the man of God, her meal barrel ran over and her oil never failed. When Naaman trusted God and the man of God, when he dipped in the Jordan seven times, he lost his leprosy.

Mr. Reagan can do what he likes. He can cut out food stamps. We made it without them. He can cut out CETA. We made it without it. He can cut out medicare. We made it without it. He can cut out social security. We made it without it. But, let me tell you something. I know somebody that sits high and looks low. *HE PROMISED NEVER TO LEAVE ME, NEVER TO LEAVE ME ALONE!*

I've seen the lightning flashing. I've heard the thunder roar. I've felt sin breakers dashing, trying to conquer my soul. BUT I'VE HEARD THE VOICE OF JESUS TELLING ME STILL FIGHT ON. HE PROMISED (you don't hear me!) HE PROMISED, HE PROMISED NEVER, NEVER, NEVER TO LEAVE ME, NEVER TO LEAVE ME ALONE! The song writer says, "He walks with me, He talks with me and tells me I am His own." Let me tell you, preachers, go back to your churches, go back to your congregations. Tell them if they rise up and walk, trust in God, and follow your leadership, He'll bring things out alright. Ain't He alright? Ain't He alright? Have you tried Him? Ain't He alright? Won't he fix it if you trust him? Ain't He alright? Ain't He alright. Ain't He alright? Ain't He alright?

Exhibit 2

THE COCA-COLA COMPANY AND SUBSIDIARIES
Consolidated Balance Sheets
For the Years Ended December 31, 1979 and 1980

	1980	*1979*
Assets		
Current assets:		
Cash	$ 129,685	$ 106,686
Marketable securities, at cost (approximates market)	101,401	41,685
Trade accounts receivable, less allowance of $8,594 in 1980 and $8,113 in 1979	523,123	435,079
Inventories	810,235	669,614
Prepaid expenses	57,809	52,339
Total current assets	1,622,253	1,305,603
Investments and other assets	302,184	206,975
Property, plant, and equipment:		
Land and improvements	96,567	97,906
Buildings	537,235	518,517
Machinery and equipment	1,183,438	1,092,882
Containers	314,349	292,085
	2,131,589	2,001,390
Less allowance for depreciation	790,749	717,212
Total property, plant, and equipment	1,340,840	1,284,178
Formulae, trademarks, goodwill, and contract rights	140,681	141,285
Total assets	$3,405,958	$2,938,041
Liabilities and Stockholders' Equity		
Current liabilities:		
Notes payable	$ 87,587	$ 103,816
Current maturities of long-term debt	7,528	4,384
Accounts payable and accrued expenses	733,023	576,862
Accrued taxes—including income taxes	233,442	199,099
Total current liabilities	1,061,580	884,161
Long-term debt	133,221	30,989
Deferred income taxes	136,419	104,187
Stockholders' equity:		
Common stock, no par value—authorized 140,000,000 shares; issued 123,989,854 shares in 1980 and 123,960,295 shares in 1979	62,372	62,357
Capital surplus	113,172	112,333
Retained earnings	1,914,547	1,759,367
	2,090,091	1,934,057
Less 401,338 shares of stock held in treasury at cost	15,353	15,353
Total stockholders' equity	2,074,738	1,918,704
Total liabilities and stockholders' equity	$3,405,958	$2,938,041

Exhibit 2 ***(concluded)***

THE COCA-COLA COMPANY AND SUBSIDIARIES
Consolidated Statements of Income
For the Years Ended December 31, 1978–1980
(in thousands of dollars except per share data)

	1980	*1979*	*1978*
Net sales	$5,912,595	$4,961,402	$4,337,917
Cost of goods sold	3,425,889	2,794,026	2,438,188
Gross profit	2,486,706	2,167,376	1,899,729
Selling, administrative, and general expenses	1,713,426	1,448,022	1,221,643
Operating income	768,280	719,354	678,086
Interest income	40,774	37,048	34,718
Interest expense	(35,218)	10,676	7,762
Other income (deductions)—net	(9,537)	(3,534)	(13,646)
Income before income taxes	764,299	742,192	691,396
Income taxes	342,191	322,072	316,704
Net income	$ 422,108	$ 420,120	$ 374,692
Net income per share	$ 3.42	$ 3.40	$ 3.03

THE COCA-COLA COMPANY
Consolidated Statements of Retained Earnings
For the Years Ended December 31, 1978–1980
(in thousands of dollars except per share data)

	1980	*1979*	*1978*
Balance at January 1	$1,759,367	$1,581,406	$1,421,356
Net income for the year	422,108	420,120	374,692
Dividends paid in cash:			
The Coca-Cola Company (per share—1980, $2.16; 1979, $1.96; 1978, $1.74)	266,928	242,159	214,344
Presto Products, Incorporated, prior to combination	—	—	298
Balance at December 31	$1,914,547	$1,759,367	$1,581,406

case 13
Modern Office Supply, Inc. (revised)*

1 In July 1959, two experienced retail managers in their early 30s pooled their resources and purchased Greentree Stationery and Supply, Inc. This retail firm was a specialty-type store carrying high-quality lines of office supplies. The store was located on the main street in the downtown shopping area of Greentree, Ohio, an industrial community of 40,000 people located 20 miles east of Columbus.

2 Under its previous owner, the company had enjoyed 23 years of successful growth and profitability. Although it was small for its type, the company was financially sound and was well established as a reputable business.

3 Immediately after the purchase, the new owner-managers, Martin Hersh and Paul Dixon, ceased operations for a 10-week period in order to renovate and redecorate the store. Then, on January 10, 1960, under the new name of Modern Office Supply, Inc., the firm reopened to the public.

4 In its abbreviated first year of operations, Modern Office Supply had a sales volume of $74,160, a decrease of $10,630 from the previous year. This downturn was quickly reversed, however, and in the next 18 years of operation, the firm never again suffered a decrease in sales, as is shown in Exhibit 1.

5 The growth of the business necessitated an increase in inventory storage space and a larger sales area. Thus, in 1972, Modern Office Supply relocated across the street in a newly remodeled building which offered double the square footage of their first store. The new store provided 11,000 square feet of shopping space on two levels and an equal amount of inventory space.

6 There was also a steady need for additional employees. By 1977 the managers were supervising 12 full-time salesclerks. All the clerks were women, although men were also actively sought when positions were available. Ten of the 12 were married, and in 1978, they averaged 45.2 years of age, with a range of 32 to 62 years. Modern Office Supply also regularly employed four high-school students on a part-time basis to perform stockroom, janitorial, and delivery duties.

7 That Modern Office Supply had experienced an exceptionally low turnover rate throughout its history is shown by the fact that in 1978, seven full-time employees had been with the firm for over 10 years. To a large degree, the appeal of the company as an employer was due to a fringe benefit program which was far superior to those offered by other local businesses. The Modern Office Supply plan included the following features:

---

* This case is disguised to protect the privacy of the firm.

Exhibit 1

Sales and income figures, 1960–1978

Year	*Sales volume**	*Percentage change for the year*	*Taxable income*
1960	$ 74,160	−13	$ (3,640)
1961	111,240	50	3,340
1962	127,920	15	5,240
1963	143,360	12	6,020
1964	163,460	14	6,200
1965	181,460	11	5,980
1966	197,780	9	5,140
1967	215,600	9	6,900
1968	230,680	7	5,300
1969	258,400	12	11,360
1970	286,820	11	12,900
1971	318,360	11	11,140
1972	347,020	9	10,760
1973	388,660	12	20,600
1974	443,060	14	21,700
1975	487,400	10	17,060
1976	531,240	9	13,920
1977	562,320	6	10,680
1978	574,380	2	3,460

* All figures have been rounded.

1. Six paid holidays were given to all full-time employees.[1]
2. A Christmas bonus of $10 for every year of full-time employment and $5 for every year of part-time employment was paid on an individual basis to employees at the annual company-sponsored Christmas party.
3. Five paid but noncumulative sick days were available to full-time employees each year.
4. Paid vacations were given to full-time employees according to the following schedule: one week after 1 year, two weeks after 5 years, and three weeks after 10 years or more with the firm.

8 In addition to the attractive benefit program, Modern Office Supply paid a wage which was competitive for the industry and the locale. Further, merit raises, based on the employee's individual performance, were awarded annually to deserving full-time salespeople.[2] The hourly wages were also updated each year by an automatic raise of 4 cents. This minimum adjustment was seen by the managers as a protection for the employees against either economic inflation or unfair bias affecting the individual manager's decision on merit raises. Exhibit 2 illustrates the effect of raises on the wage payroll for the full- and part-time sales personnel as of December 1978.

[1] Holiday pay was calculated by dividing the average workweek by five and then multiplying this number by the individual's hourly wage rate.

[2] *Full-time* was defined as 30 hours a week even though the average workweek of full-time employees had always exceeded this number of hours.

Exhibit 2

Current wage structure

Employee	*Date hired*	*Years of employment*	*Base rate*	*Accumulated automatic raises (4 cents/ year)*	*Accumulated merit raises*	*Hourly rate before January 1, 1979*
Full time*						
Gardner	01/09/60	19	$2.65	76¢	80¢	$4.21
Ulrich	04/09/63	16	2.65	64	44	3.73
Mockin	07/07/64	15	2.65	60	40	3.65
Gould	02/10/65	14	2.65	56	40	3.61
Butler	04/05/68	11	2.65	44	30	3.39
Bliss	05/20/68	11	2.65	44	24	3.33
Schoaf	07/14/68	11	2.65	44	24	3.33
Meyers	01/04/70	9	2.65	36	36	3.37
Liston	02/18/71	8	2.65	43	16	3.13
Freeman	03/15/73	6	2.65	24	16	3.05
Cline	03/15/73	6	2.65	24	10	2.99
Alloway	09/01/74	5	2.65	20	10	2.95
Part time†						
Fenton	10/22/74	5	2.25			2.75
Barbour	04/30/75	4	2.25			2.65
Kyle	09/01/75	4	2.25			2.65
Hinning	05/02/77	2	2.25			2.45

* Thirty hours a week or more.
† Less than 30 hours a week.

8 Throughout Modern Office Supply's history, the management philosophy had been to maintain an image as merchandisers of high-quality products. This philosophy was an important factor in the rapid growth of Modern Office Supply, primarily because sales to industrial firms in the area, which constituted approximately 30 percent of the company's business, were mainly of high-quality materials and equipment. In late 1976, however, a change in the industrial segment's purchasing behavior became evident, as an increasing inflationary trend and predicted recession in the economy caused business firms to begin cutting back on expenses. Companies were forgoing the purchase of new, expensive, high-quality equipment and materials and tended toward the purchase of medium-quality items. However, due to inventory and space limitations, and the management philosophy of offering quality products at a moderate price, Modern Office Supply chose not to compete on medium-quality lines. Perhaps as a result, the company experienced a leveling off in its yearly sales volume in 1977.

Recent Difficulties

10 In 1978, Modern Office Supply was confronted with a difficult situation. The firm's yearly sales had bettered those of the previous 12 months by a scant 2 percent, with sales in the industrial market most adversely affected. Area businesses had initiated harsh expense-cutting policies, and many had shifted a significant percentage of their

purchases to low-priced, low-quality items, such as those carried by discount and department stores. The problem was amplified by the opening of a shopping mall in a location three miles from the Modern Office Supply facility. In addition to 23 other stores, this new shopping center housed a Murphy Mary, a Sears department store, and a locally owned and operated Cut-Rite outlet. These three stores in particular posed competitive challenges to Modern Office Supply sales in both the consumer and business markets. Items such as typewriters, office furniture, paper, and writing instruments could be purchased at a somewhat lower price from the mall stores, and thus they increasingly appealed to budget-constrained purchasers in spite of the fact that the apparent quality of these items was inferior.

11 The demand of furniture customers for the interior design service offered by Modern Office Supply dropped precipitously. Consumers considered this service expendable since, to the degree it was needed, this service could be performed by the purchaser. By so doing, the consumer saved the cost of the interior decorator and was spared any feeling of obligation to buy the high-priced furniture supplied by Modern Office Supply.

12 Faced with these conditions, Hersh and Dixon found it essential to cut back on their own expenses. This objective was accomplished by reducing the store's weekly hours. After a thorough analysis of the store's sales patterns, the managers decided to eliminate the Thursday night store hours of 5 P.M. to 9 P.M.[3] The reason for this step was twofold. First, it cut back on various operating overhead expenses. Second, it reduced the weekly hourly payroll by 36 hours, since nine full-time clerks were kept on the floor during these four evening business hours. Consequently, the average full-time week was reduced from 37.5 hours to 34.5 hours.

13 The minimum wage law amendment of 1978 presented Hersh and Dixon with an additional dilemma. This legislation had the effect of offsetting the decrease in expenses achieved by the reduction in store hours. The law required companies the size of Modern Office Supply to increase their minimum wage in progressive steps from the current level of $2.65 an hour to $3.35 an hour by 1981. Workers were to begin earning $2.90 an hour on January 1, 1979, $3.10 an hour on January 1, 1980, and $3.35 an hour on January 1, 1981. The effect of these hourly wage changes is shown in Exhibit 3.[4]

14 The owners of Modern Office Supply saw this new law as potentially devastating to their profitable operations. The recent economic downturn, coupled with new competition from the mall stores, had caused such a significant decrease in the firm's sales volume that Hersh and Dixon had recently been finding it difficult to justify objectively even the current hourly payroll. Since the new wage legislation would force the amount of the payroll to rise if the total employee hours remained unchanged, the managers decided they would have to reduce the payroll hours in order to stabilize the payroll. However, rather than cut back on individual weekly hours, the managers decided to lay off the full-time employees with the least seniority. They reasoned it was better to provide 11 workers with the opportunity to earn a respectable income that in was

---

[3] The remaining business hours were Monday through Friday from 9 A.M. to 5 P.M., Monday night from 5 P.M. to 9 P.M., and Saturday from 9 A.M. to 12 noon. With the exception of the Thursday night hours, these remaining hours were identical to those kept by the majority of retail stores located in downtown Greentree.

[4] The reported profit figures of Modern Office Supply, Inc. (Exhibit 1) are misleading due to the impact of a bonus system which was designed to keep the firm's yearly taxable income below $25,000. Under this plan, both Hersh and Dixon received a yearly bonus of 25 percent of the company's pretax income.

Exhibit 3

Planned wages

Employee	*1979 ($2.90 base)*	*1980 ($3.10 base)*	*1981 ($3.35 base)*
Full time:			
Gardner	$4.56	$4.76	$5.01
Ulrich	4.08	4.28	4.53
Mockin	4.00	4.20	4.45
Gould	3.96	4.16	4.41
Butler	3.74	3.94	4.19
Bliss	3.68	3.88	4.13
School	3.68	3.88	4.13
Meyers	3.72	3.92	4.17
Liston	3.48	3.68	3.93
Freeman	3.40	3.60	3.85
Cline	3.34	3.54	3.79
Alloway	3.30	3.50	3.75
Part time:			
Fenton	2.77	2.99	3.25
Barbour	2.72	2.94	3.20
Kyle	2.72	2.94	3.20
Hinning	2.62	2.84	3.10

to place 12 full-time employees at an income level approaching unemployment compensation.

15 Although this approach was not appealing, no other viable alternatives seemed available under the prevailing conditions. Before this action was initiated, however, several employees approached the managers with a proposal to avoid the layoff of their co-workers. The clerks had held a private meeting at which they had unanimously agreed to take whatever cuts were necessary in their individual weekly hours in order to maintain the present sales force. The managers were pleased and readily accepted the proposal, for it allowed them to achieve their goal of reduced payroll hours while also enabling them to retain a valued salesperson.

16 One major issue still required resolution. The minimum wage legislation mandated a rate of pay substantially greater than that which would normally be paid at Modern Office Supply. When the new wage adjustments were added to the fringe-benefit program currently offered by the firm, the payment to employees in real dollar terms far exceeded both the individual and local averages and the level which Hersh and Dixon felt was reasonable. Therefore, the managers decided to try to offset the future wage increases in other areas of the employees' total compensation package. This goal was achieved through modifications of the fringe-benefit program which were made effective on January 1, 1979:

1. The Christmas bonus plan was eliminated for all employees.
2. The number of paid holidays was reduced to three; namely, Christmas, Thanksgiving, and New Year's Day.

Two further changes pertained only to the fringes provided for employees hired on or after January 1, 1979:

3. The sick pay allowance was discontinued.
4. Paid vacations were given to full-time employees according to the following schedule: one week after one year and two weeks after five or more years with the firm.

Although these four modifications substantially decreased the worth of fringe benefits, the managers believed the benefits had only been reduced to the level that was considered average for local retail stores.

17 The more difficult problem, however, from the perspective of the Modern Office Supply managers, was the proper means by which to administer the new wage legislation. A quick analysis of the net changes in the employees' compensation package for 1979 disclosed that if the present workweek remained the same, and the hourly rates for all full-time employees were raised by 25-cent increments, the net change in the employee payroll would result in an increase of 11 percent over 1978. Again, excluding the traditional merit and automatic raises, these same calculations extrapolated to 1980 showed an expected increase of 33 percent over 1978.

18 A careful study of their firm's financial statements, shown in Exhibits 4 and 5, convinced Hersh and Dixon that the net dollar impact of the new wage legislation must be further blunted. In formulating their strategy to accomplish this objective, the managers stressed consideration of five key elements of the total compensation package: (1) the fringe benefit program, (2) the minimum wage law changes in the hourly base, (3) the automatic yearly 4-cent-an-hour raise, (4) the annual merit wage adjustments, and (5) the current status of several employees who were paid substantially above the minimum wage as a result of length of service.

19 The fringe benefit program, which was about to be severely cut, and the wage law changes were considered unalterable. However, Hersh and Dixon believed that, in effect, the new wage law required them to increase Modern Office Supply's annual

Exhibit 4

MODERN OFFICE SUPPLY, INC.
Income Statement
For the Year Ended December 31, 1978

Net sales	$574,380
Cost of goods sold	318,200
Gross margin on sales	256,180
Managers' salaries	100,000
Depreciation	6,500
Other general/administrative expenses	140,280
Operating income	9,400
Interest expenses	2,480
Income before bonus and taxes	920
Managers' bonus	3,460
Taxable income	$ 3,460

Exhibit 5

MODERN OFFICE SUPPLY, INC.
Statement of Financial Position
As of December 31, 1978

Assets		
Current assets:		
Cash	$20,202.12	
Accounts receivable	36,462.84	
Inventories	96,116.08	
Fixed assets:		
Equipment	22,677.88	
Total assets		$175,458.92
Liabilities		
Current liabilities:		
Accounts payable/trade	11,448.10	
Other current debt	5,897.46	
Long-term debt:		
Long-term bank loans	24,184,36	
Total liabilities		$ 41,529.92
Stockholders' Equity		
Capital stock	65,000.00	
Retained earnings	68,929.00	
Total stockholders' equity		133,929.00
Total liabilities and stockholders' equity		$175,458.92

4-cent an hour automatic raises by a total of 58 cents an hour over the next three years. Thus, they decided to eliminate the traditional automatic raises.

20 The issue of whether to continue the policy of annual merit wage adjustments posed a more difficult dilemma. The managers thought that because of the required increases in the wage base, any merit raises would be unaffordable. On the other hand, the perceived motivational benefits of the merit system would be lost if the plan were discontinued.

21 Closely related to the merit wage issue was the case of several senior employees who might be considered overpaid as a result of their long years of service. Although the $2.90 figure was intended by law as the lowest amount to be paid to clerks, it could also be viewed as the level at which clerks were to be paid. Since all of modern office's full-time employees were already paid above $2.90 per hour, it would be possible to make no immediate upward wage adjustments. This strategy would greatly reduce the financial burden of the minimum wage legislation. However, the managers feared that such action might eliminate much of the motivational impact of previous merit and automatic raises. In addition, the higher hourly rates of the senior salesclerks often reflected their greater-than-average contributions to the operation of the firm. Senior clerks were often given responsibilities far in excess of those assigned to new, less-experienced personnel. Therefore, their overpayment really represented fair compensation for services rendered. Thus, by narrowing the wage gap between the higher-

Exhibit 6

MODERN OFFICE SUPPLY, INC.

Dear

Recently President Carter signed into a law an amendment raising the minimum wage for workers in our size business in stages from $2.65 an hour to $3.35 an hour by 1981.

The wage scale provides that the workers in our category are to begin earning $2.90 an hour on January, 1979, $3.16 on January, 1980, and $3.35 on January, 1981.

It also provides that not more than four students may be employed at 85 percent of the regular full-time rate.

We are in agreement with this law as a protection of workers. Unfortunately it has not been designed to take into consideration the side benefits of any job, and therefore we now find it necessary to convert some of the company programs into "direct-pay" dollars which you are assured of receiving pay by pay.

For new employees hired *after* January 1, 1979, paid vacation earned after one full year of full-time employment will be one week until five years full-time employment, when paid vacation will be two weeks annually thereafter. *Present employees are not affected.*

Our company sick-pay policy will remain in force until attainment of 65th birthday for full-time employees hired *prior* to January 1, 1979. For persons hired *after* January 1, 1979, sick-pay benefits will go into effect on the anniversary of five years' employment.

The following will be paid holidays effective January 1, 1979: New Year's Day, Thanksgiving, and Christmas.

Although the monetary Christmas gift has been a happy tradition for many years, with the newly imposed hourly direct-pay regulations, this tradition must, regretfully, be discontinued.

On Monday, January 2, 1979, your hourly rate has been increased by $________ to $________ per hour and is $________ above the $2.90 wage law minimum.

We have always tried to offer better-than-average hourly rates to our experienced employees and hope you will be pleased with this arrangement.

Sincerely,

Martin Hersh, Paul Dixon

and lower-paid employees, the managers believed they would be taking the risk of alienating clerks who performed special functions for the organization.

22 Having carefully considered several different alternatives, the managers decided that in the years 1979 through 1981, the amount of the legislatively mandated wage base increases would be added to all full-time employees' rates across the board. Essentially then, in 1979, all full-time employees received a 25-cents-an-hour wage increase. In 1980, their wages were to be increased by 20 cents, and in 1981, by 25 cents. Part-time workers also received upward adjustments based on the governmentally legislated minimum of 85 percent of the base pay of full-time employees. Thus, in 1979, part-time employees' minimum wage jumped from $2.65 to $2.90 an hour, while their average workweek remained at 25.5 hours.

23 On the morning of December 19, 1978, at a weekly Monday morning sales meeting, both full-time and part-time employees were informed of general changes in the company's wage-compensation program. That afternoon copies of a carefully prepared announcement letter (Exhibit 6) were mailed to each of Modern Office Supply's 16 sales personnel, detailing how their wages, in specific, would be affected by the minimum wage law and the changes in the firm's fringe-benefit program.

case 14
Merrill Lynch & Co.: The Movement toward Full Financial Service

1 In 1978, Merrill Lynch & Co., Inc., was a leading financial services company. Through its subsidiaries, Merrill Lynch offered a broad range of services that were tailored to the varying financial and investment needs of individuals, corporations, institutions, and governments. While Merrill Lynch strived to expand its position as leader in the securities business, in recent years it had also expanded beyond that industry to fulfill its commitment to better serve the financial needs of its customers. Merrill Lynch was considering the "Cash Management Account" to give customers full financial service and to help offset the cyclical nature of their commissions earnings. The Cash Management Account would represent a further move into the banking industry by providing bill-paying, record-keeping, checking, and credit-transactions services.

Historical Background

2 Charles Merrill began the firm of Charles E. Merrill & Co. in January 1914. Initially, the firm occupied a space sublet from Eastman, Dillon, but by May 1914, had moved to 7 Wall Street. In July of that year, Merrill persuaded Edmund Calvert Lynch to join him in a co-partnership agreement, and the firm became known as Merrill Lynch & Co. The new firm followed through on Merrill's and Lynch's personal philosophy for success: there are many potential investors, beyond the elite, which Merrill Lynch could cater to. These small investors represented a segment which the old brokerage houses had ignored.

3 During the early years, Merrill and Lynch emphasized the importance of developing their clients' trust of the partners as financial advisors. Merrill Lynch's first newspaper ads, inviting the public to invest in stocks and bonds, were also designed for maximum credibility. One of the first Merrill Lynch ads was a full-page spread in a newspaper, running eight columns of small type, explaining the fundamentals of stocks and bonds. The Merrill Lynch monthly investment plan was one of the first marketing campaigns on Wall Street to appeal directly to the small investor, and the firm was also one of the first proponents on Wall Street of lower commission rates.

4 Merrill Lynch & Co.'s first big deal, completed in 1915, was an offering of McCrory Stores. Through the 1920s, Merrill Lynch introduced the investing public to some

This case was prepared by John A. Pearce II of the University of South Carolina with the assistance of Russell Furtick, Larry Keele, and Richard Mathis.

up-and-coming retail enterprises, including J. C. Penney, National Tea, Western Auto Supply, First National Stores, People's Drug, and a couple of retailers that would become today's Winn-Dixie.

5 Merrill Lynch also played a major role in bringing several industrial companies to market. Many of these were in areas not then accepted by the financial establishment, such as automobiles, movies, and oil. As the Great Depression began in the late 1920s, Charles Merrill foresaw a prolonged period of suffering for Wall Street, and he decided to retrench and withdraw from the retail commission business and concentrate on investment banking. He sold the firm's retail business and branches to E. A. Pierce and Co. in early 1930, thus transferring many of Merrill Lynch's employees to Pierce. At the time, Pierce was the nation's largest wire house with extensive branch networks connected by private telegraph wires.

6 E. A. Pierce and Company survived the Depression. The return on partners' capital was small, however, and with the 10-year partnership agreement due to run out at the end of 1939, there was growing doubt that enough partners were willing to renew.

7 At this time Winthrop Hiram Smith, who ran Pierce's Chicago office, was extremely concerned whether the E. A. Pierce and Co. partnership would be renewed. Smith, who had previously been employed by Merrill, approached Merrill about resuming work with him, bringing together Merrill Lynch and E. A. Pierce.

8 Merrill knew that brokerage firms were experiencing a slump in activity. There was a large amount of distrust, disinterest, and misunderstanding of the financial markets, and stockbrokers were widely regarded as dishonest. In 1936, Merrill met Ted Braun, a leading public relations expert who had done several studies on public attitude. One of Braun's studies outlined what people wanted in a securities firm. Merrill used this study as the organizational blueprint for a new company which would cater to a mass of investors and would be guided by the principles of scientific management. The new firm was ready for business on April 1, 1940, as Merrill Lynch, E. A. Pierce & Cassatt. Cassatt was the long-established Philadelphia firm of Cassatt and Co., which had been sold to E. A. Pierce in 1935.

9 The new company made itself known to the public through attention-drawing advertisements, with the initial announcement stating Merrill's policy. Referred to as the "Ten Commandments," the first stated: "The interests of our customers MUST come first."

10 By 1941, Merrill Lynch wanted not to be known merely as the nation's largest wire house, but also wanted acceptance of itself and Wall Street as essential public institutions. Its new policies and ideas caused a large response nationwide. More than 12,000 new accounts were opened before the end of 1940, which is impressive considering total customers at year-end totaled only 50,000. Then, completely unprecedented, Merrill Lynch published an annual report. This move was even more surprising, for it showed a loss of $309,000 for the nine months the company operated in 1940. Since 1941, however, the company has been profitable each year.

11 In August 1941, there was a major addition to Merrill Lynch, and the firm became known as Merrill Lynch, Pierce, Fenner & Beane. Fenner was the founder of Fenner and Solari, which teamed with Alpheus C. Beane, Sr., in 1905. Fenner and Beane had been a large cotton house and had developed a large network of branch offices specializing in commodity futures. Fenner and Beane, upon deciding to handle its own stock business, became the second-largest wire house behind Pierce. The merger of Fenner and Beane with Merrill greatly strengthened Merrill's commodities trading.

12 Merrill Lynch continued to be innovative, and in 1945, they initiated the first training program for brokers. Merrill and Smith felt that training their own young executives would enable them to make a broker's career more inviting and would therefore attract top-flight candidates. Since the first training school class in 1945, Merrill Lynch has graduated more than 20,300 account executives from its program.

13 In addition to educating his employees, Charles Merrill believed strongly in educating the public. He wanted to show people how to become investors, to teach them to invest intelligently, and to supply them with data and analysis of specific investments. Merrill's long-time advertising director, Lou Hengel, put out a series of famous educational ads and pamphlets. In addition, Hengel wrote the best seller, *How to Buy Stocks,* which had more than 4 million copies in print.

14 Charles Merrill also emphasized the importance of providing meaningful research information to all investors. In further serving investors, Merrill made certain that their business was properly processed. This was known as the backstage function. To help in the proper processing of business, Merrill brought in an administrator, Michael W. McCarthy, who had previously worked with Merrill. McCarthy worked to establish procedures and installed the machines, systems, and people needed for Merrill Lynch to continue progressing. The progress McCarthy achieved since the mid-1940s is well illustrated by the following incident. In 1947, the U.S. Department of Justice filed antitrust charges against 17 major investment-banking firms, but Merrill Lynch was not even mentioned in these cases.

15 Upon Charles Merrill's death in 1956, McCarthy was appointed as the new managing partner. Alpheus C. Beane, Jr., son of the late cofounder of Fenner and Beane, decided to withdraw from the firm because of his disapproval of McCarthy, and so in early 1958, the company became Merrill, Lynch, Pierce, Fenner & Smith.

16 Not until 1953, did the New York Stock Exchange permit brokers to incorporate. Five years later, in 1958, only 51 (mostly small) of 655 brokerage firms had done so. The 119 partners of Merrill Lynch were planning to become incorporated, again showing Merrill's leadership in the industry, for at that time, they were already the world's largest brokerage firm (see Exhibit 1). Merrill Lynch's reason for incorporating in January 1959 was "to assure continuity of the firm because each partner cannot add to his capital in the firm until after individual income taxes are paid; and because each is liable for the debts or lawsuits of the others, the threat of a capital drain is always present."[1]

17 After much early success, Merrill Lynch continued to remain at the top by actively pursuing new ideas. In 1964, Merrill Lynch acquired the business of C. J. Devine, a leading government securities dealer, forming the base of Merrill Lynch Government Securities, Inc. "We the People" or "The Thundering Herd," as Merrill Lynch was called, continued expansion through further acquisitions. In 1968, Merrill Lynch entered real estate financing by acquiring Hubbard, Westervelt, and Mottelay. Through this acquisition, Merrill Lynch became a major dealer in Ginnie Maes and helped develop such financing innovations as mortgage-backed pass-throughs.

18 A major development took place in 1968 when Donald Regan became president of Merrill Lynch. He became chief executive officer in 1971. With Regan in power, the company grew a great deal. Some of his innovations included putting internally trained financial managers at the top and putting the "business getters," who traditionally

[1] "The Herd, Inc.," *Business Week,* October 4, 1958, p. 30.

Exhibit 1

1959 brokerage and underwriting standings

	Fifteen biggest brokers—gross income ($ millions)		Fifteen leading underwriters—corporate underwritings managed or co-managed ($ millions)	
1.	Merrill Lynch	$136.0	First Boston	$1,042
2.	Bache	38.0	Morgan Stanley	965
3.	Francis I. du Pont	31.2	Lehman	880
4.	E. F. Hutton	30.0	Blyth	868
5.	Paine, Webber, Jackson & Curtis	29.1	White, Weld	833
6.	Dean Witter	*	Merrill Lynch	815
7.	Walston	27.2	Kuhn, Loeb	696
8.	Goodbody	24.8	Halsey, Stuart	650
9.	Shearson, Hammill	24.0	Eastman Dillon	456
10.	Loeb, Rhoades	23.0	Stone & Webster	388
11.	Harris, Upham	22.0	Goldman, Sachs	366
12.	Reynolds	21.6	Dillon, Read	363
13.	Hayden, Stone	21.5	Smith, Barney	358
14.	Eastman, Dillon, Union Securities	*	Kidder, Peabody	275
15.	Thomson & McKinnon	18.0	Harriman Ripley	245

* Gross income figure not available.
Source: "The Biggest Broker in the World," *Fortune*, August 1960, p. 98.

filled the top positions in partnerships, farther down the corporate structure. This arrangement was a radical innovation on Wall Street. He also increased computer capacity to upgrade the firm's efficiency and instituted a diversification program.

19 In 1969, Merrill Lynch changed its strategy from seeking small clients to trying to attract large accounts. This change in strategy was made possible by the acquisition of Lionel D. Edie & Co., a large investment management and consulting firm.

20 At that time, while Merrill Lynch continued their expansion, many Wall Street firms were entering a disastrous era. Other firms overextended, resulting in their losing track of the trades they made, the whereabouts of the certificates they represented, and the status of their customers' accounts. Many Wall Street firms were unable to meet their obligations and subsequently collapsed, taking their customers' accounts with them. In 1970, the New York Stock Exchange requested Merrill Lynch to take over the fifth-largest retail broker, Goodbody & Co., which was sinking fast. This was a high-risk job for Merrill Lynch even though there were some reimbursement provisions from the total New York Stock Exchange community. The Wall Street crisis which forced Merrill Lynch to take over Goodbody threw Merrill Lynch's long-range plans for greater involvement in the financial services industry off schedule. Merrill Lynch, however, was able to set up important underpinnings of a sound diversification effort by establishing a holding company. This holding company, known as Merrill Lynch & Co., had Merrill Lynch, Pierce, Fenner & Smith as the principal subsidiary. Under this new format, Merrill Lynch, which had already expanded into such areas as government securities, real estate, financing, and economic consulting, diversified farther into specialty insurance, relocation services, and asset management.

21 Throughout the 1970s, Merrill Lynch campaigned for a national market system. Merrill Lynch managers felt that the national market system would greatly help their business. If another brokerage firm handled the other side of the transaction, Merrill Lynch wanted that member of the industry to handle the transaction efficiently, thereby making Merrill Lynch more efficient.

22 In 1974, Merrill Lynch acquired Family Life Insurance, a Seattle-based company which specialized in mortgage-protection insurance for homeowners. Also during that year, Merrill Lynch added AMIC, which offered mortgage-default insurance to the institutions that issue mortgages. Merrill Lynch had also become the top-ranked U.S. investment banking house internationally by 1974.

23 In early 1977, Merrill Lynch acquired a company that became Merrill Lynch Relocation Management. This subsidiary, which contracted corporations to help their employees who needed to transfer, also provided Merrill Lynch with the executive expertise to form Merrill Lynch Realty Associates. In June 1977, Merrill Lynch launched a national weekly stock option guide, *Options Alert,* representing a major entry into the publishing business for Merrill Lynch. It was the result of Merrill Lynch's corporate planning unit, which had been established in May 1975 to further the firm's continuing diversification program into areas not subjected to the market's cyclical nature.

The Managerial Philosophy of Merrill Lynch

24 To gain and keep its competitive advantage in the financial services field, Merrill Lynch had developed a unique managerial personality for a brokerage house.

The Merrill Lynch Concept of Management

25 Merrill Lynch worked toward financial diversification through the process of management by objectives, a process rarely attempted on Wall Street. The process involved setting specific long-term and short-term goals—in a continuous succession of one-year, three-year, and five-year plans—for every operating unit and every executive in the company. Also, management by objectives meant having a periodic critical review to see that each unit and manager was on target.

26 Merrill Lynch first brought its strategic planning to life in 1973. The company had until then been product-sales oriented. It had only a few products and services that it sold. The new plan called for Merrill Lynch to be market oriented, that is, organized around the needs of potential customers. These customers fell into four groups: individuals, corporations, institutions, and governments.

Concentration in Financial Services

27 By going public in 1971, Merrill Lynch acquired enough capital to undertake a wide range of new ventures. Company officials continually stressed, however, that all diversification efforts would be within the realm of financial services. Merrill Lynch's size gave it the opportunity to try out a variety of new businesses at once. It learned these businesses and either expanded or divested them. It had the ability to experiment,

Exhibit 2

Merrill Lynch's fast-branching family tree

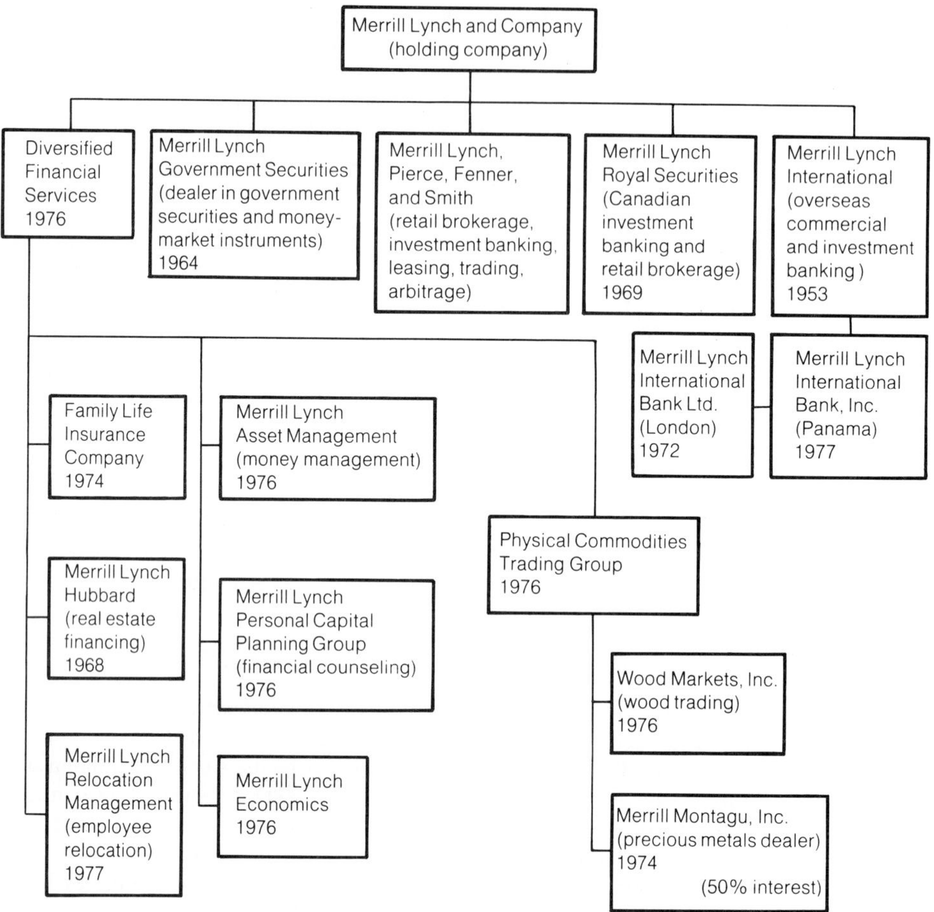

Dates represent years when units were acquired or established by Merrill Lynch.
Source: "Merrill Lynch: The Bull in Banking's Shop," *Business Week,* August 8, 1977, p. 51.

and a single failure did not pose as grave a problem for them as it would have for some smaller firms. For example, Merrill Lynch's move from a broker-oriented stock-exchange system to one of dealer markets, where brokers trade with customers from their own inventories, made capital a vital factor.

28 Merrill Lynch was divided into five separate units, as shown in Exhibit 2. These units were (1) the Merrill Lynch, Pierce, Fenner, & Smith brokerage unit; (2) Merrill Lynch International; (3) Merrill Lynch Government Securities; (4) Merrill Lynch Royal Securities (a Canadian subsidiary); and (5) Merrill Lynch Diversified Financial Services.

Services Offered by Merrill Lynch

29 Merrill Lynch offered many services, including corporate securities trading, options and commodity futures, equity trading and arbitrage, and investment banking.

Corporate Securities Trading

30 According to the 1977 Form 10-K of Merrill Lynch, the major source of Merrill Lynch, Pierce, Fenner & Smith's (MLPF&S) revenues was from commissions earned as broker, or agent, for its customers in the purchase or sale of common and preferred stocks. MLPF&S had traditionally emphasized its services to individual investors, but in recent years, the institutional investor had taken on greater importance. On May 1, 1975, fixed minimum commission rates for brokerage transactions were eliminated by the Securities and Exchange Commission. It became the policy of MLPF&S to negotiate commissions for accounts that were actively traded, including both individual and institutional accounts. Under the MLPF&S Sharebuilder Plan, which involved mass processing of orders, individual customers received discounts on commission rates on transactions of $5,000 or less.

31 Securities transactions made by MLPF&S were executed on either a cash or margin basis. Under the margin transactions, MLPF&S extended credit to customers based on the market value of the securities in the customer's account. To finance customers' margin account borrowings, MLPF&S used its own capital, bank borrowings, and borrowings provided by free credit balances in customer accounts.

Options and Commodity Futures

32 MLPF&S was licensed to buy and sell options on the Chicago Board Options Exchange, the American Stock Exchange, and in the over-the-counter market. MLPF&S bought and also wrote options for its customers.

33 MLPF&S was a dealer and broker in the purchase and sale of futures contracts in substantially all commodities and held memberships on all major commodity exchanges in the United States and Canada. Since substantially all buying of commodity futures was done on margin, the required margin was significantly lower than that required of common-stock customers. Commodity trading was a high-risk, speculative business, and MLPF&S was exposed to a large amount of financial risk due to the market volatility of commodities.

Equity Trading and Arbitrage

34 MLPF&S regularly made a market in approximately 650 domestic common stocks and more than 100 foreign securities. Its market-making activities were conducted with other dealers in the interdealer market and in the retail market. As part of its trading activities, MLPF&S engaged in both riskless and risk arbitrage. Whereas riskless arbitrage typically involved the simultaneous purchase and sale of securities, risk arbitrage depended upon the ability to rapidly assess certain market conditions. At Merrill Lynch, all positions were liquidated as soon as possible, and positions in arbitrage were not taken without an analysis of the security's marketability. Merrill

Lynch also made a market in municipal obligations and corporate fixed-income securities.

Investment Banking and Research

35 MLPF&S was a major investment banking firm which was active in every aspect of investment banking in a principal, agency, or advisory capacity. They underwrote the sale of securities themselves or arranged for a private placement with investors. They also provided a broad range of financial and advisory services for clients, including mergers and acquisitions, mortgage and lease financing, and advice on specific financing problems.

36 To provide its customers with current information on investments and securities markets, MLPF&S maintained Wall Street's largest securities research division, which performed technical market analysis as well as fundamental analysis of fixed-income securities and analysis of the municipal and corporate bond markets. MLPF&S had a computer-based opinion retrieval system that published current information and research opinions on approximately 1,400 foreign and domestic corporations.

Other Activities

37 MLPF&S sold shares of 191 income, growth, and money market funds, 13 of which were advised by Merrill Lynch Asset Management, Inc. In the money market area, MLPF&S also sponsored municipal investment trust funds, corporate income funds, and government securities income funds. These were all closed-end unit investment trusts which were registered under the Investment Company Act of 1940.

38 MLPF&S also provided transaction clearing services to broker-dealers on a basis which was fully disclosed to the broker-dealers' customers. While the original firm retained all sales functions, MLPF&S handled all settlement and credit aspects of the transaction.

Competition

39 All aspects of MLPF&S's financial services business were extremely competitive. MLPF&S was in direct competition with firms such as Dean Witter, Bache & Co., and E. F. Hutton. MLPF&S also competed for investment funds with banks, insurance companies, and mutual fund management companies. Since the elimination of fixed commissions on May 1, 1975, the security brokerage industry had become intensely competitive. In addition to commissions charged, MLPF&S also competed on the basis of its services to investors, both individual and institutional. The establishment of a national market system, which MLPF&S supported, was intended to provide investors with the benefits of competing market places. Many firms had merged on Wall Street, resulting in securities firms with strengthened financial resources. In turn, these firms provided increased competition to the MLPF&S network of financial services.

40 The life insurance business of Merrill Lynch was also highly competitive. Many companies, like Prudential and Metropolitan, were older and larger than Family Life and provided strong competition because of their strong financial base and large agency organization. However, Family Life did have an advantage, as it specialized in mortgage-cancellation life insurance.

41 Merrill Lynch's operations in the real estate area were divided into two parts: (1) employee relocation and (2) real estate financing, mortgage banking, and real estate management. There were approximately eight companies which provided employee relocation services, with Merrill Lynch Relocation Management, Inc., and Homequity, Inc., being predominant in the industry. Of course, numerous organizations were involved in real estate and mortgage banking.

Regulation

42 The securities business of MLPF&S was regulated by several different agencies. Although the SEC provided the bulk of the regulations, the company was also regulated by the National Association of Securities Dealers, Inc. The securities industry was more highly regulated than many other industries; and violations of applicable regulations could result in the suspension of broker licenses, fines, or suspension or expulsion of a firm, its officers, or employees.

43 As a brokerage firm registered with the SEC and as a NYSE firm, MLPF&S was subject to the Uniform Net Capital Rule which was designed to measure the general financial integrity and liquidity of a broker-dealer. Under this rule, MLPF&S was required to maintain "net capital" equal to 4 percent of the total dollar amount of customer-related assets. Under NYSE rules, MLPF&S had to reduce its business if its net capital was less than 6 percent of its total customer-related assets. Compliance with these net capital rules tended to limit their operation, especially in underwriting and maintaining the securities inventory required for trading.

The Brokerage Industry in 1976

44 The after-tax earnings of all New York Stock Exchange brokerage firms increased about 22 percent from 1975, to a total of about $508 million. The total revenues rose 18 percent to $6.9 billion. Profits for the 12 large publicly held brokerage firms showed a 16 percent increase to $230 million and an 18 percent increase in revenues to $2.9 billion.

45 The trading volume also increased in 1976, with the daily trading average up 14 percent to 21.2 million shares. The total dollar value of New York Stock Exchange share volume increased 16 percent to $152 billion.

46 Brokerage firms were depending less on securities commissions and more on other products and services. For the past several years, most of the leading firms had increased their diversification and strengthened their activities not dealing with security commissions. Firms were entering the insurance business, going into foreign brokerage operations, developing new services, and increasing marketing efforts. Investment banking, principal transactions, and commodity trading were being emphasized. Exhibit 3 summarizes some of the effects of diversification on brokerage firms' revenues. In 1976, revenues from securities commissions were about 46 percent of total revenues, as compared to 52 percent in 1975.

47 The number of brokerage firms had been decreasing since 1962 because of closings or mergers of member firms. In the 1970s, several large, respected institutional firms had closed or sought mergers because of the unprofitability of keeping large research staffs while the commission rates for the larger accounts had been cut back. Major

Exhibit 3

Diversification of the major brokers

	Merrill Lynch	*E. F. Hutton*	*Bache Group**	*Paine Webber*
Brokerage commissions	39%	60%	53%	50%
Trading government, municipal, corporate, and money-market securities	23	10	9	17
Interests on margin balances and securities owned	21	13	17	18
Investment banking	10	14	17	13
Other business	6	3	4	2
Total 1976 revenues ($ millions)	$1,125	$315	$248	$225

* Year ended July 31.
Source: "Merrill Lynch: The Bull in Banking's Shop," *Business Week*, August 8, 1977, p. 52.

moves in 1976 were the merger of William D. Witter into Drexel Burnham and the Reynolds Securities International acquisition of Baker, Weeks, and Co.

Expenses Increase

48 A major reason for increased expenses in 1976 was that many firms were building their capacity to handle larger volumes of transactions. The attempts to increase capacity had begun in 1975. Many major firms had been increasing their computer and communications capabilities in order to facilitate handling larger volumes of transactions and to put them in a better position to shift to a central market system.

49 Congress and the Securities and Exchange Commission were pushing for the development of a central market system, and this was likely to involve sophisticated electronic switching of orders between the various marketplaces and make the market a more efficient system. Firms with the most advanced computer and communications capabilities were projected to move into this market easily and with relatively low additional expense.

50 Another factor that increased expenses in 1976 was inflation. Inflation had remained at a level high enough to have a significant impact on costs. The percentage increases were especially high for postage and telephone services, two services which securities firms use very heavily.

Banks' Impact on the Brokerage Industry

51 Several banks had begun offering automatic investment services where particular stocks could be purchased on a monthly basis by the banks' checking-account customers. Banks were able to bunch orders together to take advantage of the lower commission rates available on large transactions. In September 1976, Chemical Bank took brokerage services one step farther. It offered retail brokerage rates well below the rates that individuals could get at brokerage houses. Chemical Bank could offer the discount rates because the bank got large discounts itself by placing the orders through Pershing and Co., a New York Stock Exchange member firm. On all but the smallest of orders,

the transaction fees from going through Chemical Bank were well below the prevailing retail commissions charged by brokers. Individuals making large or frequent trades would have quickly made up the $30 annual fee for access to Chemical's order desk. Chemical also offered safekeeping of the securities.

52 Chemical's plan was forecast to have a significant impact on the securities industry if it was profitable and if Congress did not act to keep them from continuing the plan. The Senate was investigating banks' securities activities and could possibly take action unfavorable to Chemical's service. The Securities Industry Association was also considering asking the Federal Reserve Board or state banking authorities to bar Chemical's brokerage activities. If Chemical could make profits on its brokerage service, and if the activities were not illegal, Chemical's lower rates would cause brokers to lower the rates they charged in order to remain competitive. Such actions would cut further into the profits of the brokerage industry.

The Brokerage Industry in 1977

53 The 12 large publicly held brokerage companies monitored by Standard & Poor's reported earnings of $60 million in the first half of 1977—down 54 percent from the record $130 million in 1976's first half. In the same period, total revenues declined only 2 percent from the first half of 1976.

54 Brokerage firms were relying less on securities commissions, although they remained the largest source of revenue, and more on diversified products and services. Firms were actively entering the insurance business, expanding foreign brokerage operations, developing new services, and intensifying marketing efforts. In the years 1972 through 1975, investment firms' securities commissions accounted for 52 percent of gross revenues. In 1976, they represented 46 percent, and in 1977, they were 44 percent of the total.

55 In May 1975, fixed commission rates were abandoned on all transactions, regardless of size. Rates did come down slightly but were expected to come under increased pressure for downward revision because of the proliferation of discount brokerage firms. The major area where competition had driven rates down was in institutional transactions, where rates had fallen 44 percent since April 1975. The impact of discounted commissions on revenues was reflected in the fact that while the dollar value of NYSE trades in 1977 declined 9.4 percent, commission revenues fell 17 percent. The problems of discounts were substantial for some firms. About one third of NYSE member firms lost money in 1977.

56 The decline in the number of brokerage firms continued in 1977. Since 1970, the number of NYSE member firms fell to 370 in 1977 from about 570. The expense of maintaining large research staffs and cutting commission rates had pared profits to the point that many firms had merged, cut back, diversified, or gone out of business. With the decline in the number of firms doing a public business, concentration in the securities industry was increasing. By 1977, the 25 largest firms had 65 percent of the industry's capital, 56 percent of commission revenues, and 64 percent of total revenues.

57 Trading profits continued to grow and account for 20 percent of total revenues in 1977. Trading profits were derived from brokers' market-making activities and from interest and dividends on securities held for trading. Because this source of income depended on the value of financial assets, it was a more volatile source of earnings

than commission revenues. Likewise, underwriting income was quite volatile, and this source of revenue fell 12 percent in 1977.

58 An increasingly important source of revenues, interest on margin borrowing, accounted for 10 percent of gross revenues in 1977, up from 8 percent in 1976. Such interest income was a relatively stable portion of earnings, tending to bolster profitability when other sources of earnings were down. In fact retail brokerage operations probably could not have been conducted profitably at 1977 rates were it not for margin lending.

59 In recent years, brokerage firms had noticed increased competition from banks. Several banks continued to offer automatic investment services, where certain stocks could be purchased monthly by checking-account customers. However, Chemical Bank, which had begun to offer brokerage services in 1976, dropped its program as unsuccessful. As of 1977, all bank brokerage services account for less than 1 percent of the total value of transactions on all stock exchanges. Bank expansion of brokerage services in the future was a genuine possibility, however, because of regulatory changes and access to customer's money.

Current Situation

60 1977 was a year of declining earnings and profits for Merrill Lynch. Markets were poor in each important area that the corporation served as broker or dealer. Total commission revenues from listed securities, options, over-the-counter, mutual funds and commodities were expected to drop from $442,947,000 to about $365 million—a decline of over 17 percent. Total principal transaction revenues were also down about 28 percent, falling from $261,285,000 to a projected $188 million. As a result of these declines, net income was expected to fall from $106 million in 1976 to about $44 million in 1977. Earnings had fallen to about $1.25 per share for 1977 as compared to $3.01 per share in 1976. (Statements of Merrill Lynch's financial position in December 1977 are presented in Appendixes A through E.) These declines occurred in a year marked by the uncertainty among both large and small investors. Despite moderate but steady growth in GNP as well as improvement in other leading economic indicators, investors seemed to focus on the negatives.

61 The Federal Reserve had been periodically stepping into the markets to tighten the money supply. Short-term and intermediate-term interest rates were increasing. As a result, trading activities, especially in the fixed income markets, were especially hard hit. Stocks had declined in attractiveness for investment purposes, because with the high interest rates, it was possible to get a good return on an investment by buying six-month certificates. Investors increasingly turned to high-yielding bonds or to holding capital assets for future investment.

62 Merrill Lynch's problems were compounded by lower commission rates. A new era of competition to lower commission rates charged to large investors had begun about the middle of 1975. Merrill Lynch had become involved in the scheme of reduced commissions for larger investors in hopes of attracting the larger accounts. This aggressive approach substantially increased the capital committed to handling large transactions. Merrill Lynch's new policy was to offer discounts to meet those offered by their competitors in order to gain orders and market share, as long as the business attracted by the discounted commissions remained profitable. The policy was one of the major reasons for the increase of Merrill Lynch's share of public New York Stock Exchange volume, which was reversing the downtrend of 1975 and 1976.

63 Merrill Lynch experienced increases in revenues in its other traditional areas. The corporation had maintained its position as the leading manager of corporate underwritings and had increased its penetration of the fee-based corporate finance business. Merrill Lynch also ranked first in municipal financing for the third straight year. On an international scale, the American dollar had declined in value against other major currencies. The weakening dollar, in combination with the U.S. securities markets, weakened the confidence of foreign investors and lessened the attractiveness of American securities.

Commercial Banking Activities

64 With its huge asset base and network of branch offices, Merrill Lynch was in a position to move into activities normally associated with commercial banks. The 1933 Glass-Steagall Act mandated the separation of investment and commercial banks in the United States.

International Banking

65 The Glass-Steagall Act had no effect on foreign bank operations since they fell outside U.S. jurisdiction. Merrill Lynch, in fact, already operated commercial banks in London and Panama that took deposits and made loans to overseas corporations. The total capital in these banks reached $50 million during 1977. Such growth indicated that commercial banking activities would offer tremendous financial clout for a financial services firm.

66 Consistent with its strategy to provide a full range of financial services to its customers, Merrill Lynch International wanted to increase its consumer banking overseas. However, any expansion into international banking would put the firm in direct competition with U.S. banks, foreign subsidiaries and such universal banks as Deutsche Bank and Union Bank of Switzerland.

Domestic Banking—the Cash Management Account

67 Merrill Lynch was considering a type of broker-bank plan that would integrate a wide variety of financial services and, hopefully, circumvent the restrictions of the Glass-Steagall Act. The proposed account, called a Cash Management Account (CMA), would offer a whole range of services such as bill paying, record keeping, checking, and credit transactions. The idea for the CMA was recommended by SRI International. Merrill Lynch itself had spent one and a half years developing the conceptual, legal, and computer systems details.

68 The account would allow Merrill Lynch customers to deposit money in a Merrill Lynch money market fund and draw on those funds with either a check or a VISA card. Any unused balances in the customer's brokerage account would be transferred into the money fund once a week and would earn dividends daily. Additionally, those customers with stocks and bonds would also be able to borrow up to 50 percent of the value of those securities on deposit. This ability to borrow against securities would be, in essence, a direct line of credit as well as overdraft protection for checking purposes. Each Cash Management Account customer's securities, including the money market fund shares, would be protected up to $300,000 through the Securities Investor

Protection Corporation and supplemental securities protection. The interest on margin loans would be in the range of 6 to 8 percent compared with the 6¾ percent prime rate at commercial banks. However, more pertinent to individuals, the CMA rates would be considerably lower than the 10 to 12 percent conventional automobile loans or the 12 to 18 percent rate on most bank card purchases. Borrowing would automatically be triggered only after all the investment funds had been utilized.

69 Merrill Lynch had contracted the services of City National Bank of Columbus, Ohio, to handle the processing of checks, credit card drafts, and record keeping. Merrill Lynch would effect payment for CMA holders, extend credit, and provide a consolidated account statement. Both Merrill Lynch and City National saw the system, in which all units would be linked electronically, as the first step in a nationwide system of electronic funds transfer.

70 Merrill Lynch considered its ability as a superior mass merchandiser to be a distinctive competency and an advantage for entering the highly competitive banking field. Also, its national network of offices would be of tremendous benefit in marketing the CMA. In advertising the CMA, Merrill Lynch considered a direct-mail and print campaign as most effective. If implemented, the CMA would first be tested in a few pilot cities around the country.

71 Internally, the firm appeared to have the administrative capability to handle a large volume of new inputs. Merrill Lynch's data entry operators had shown great flexibility and adaptability in handling new applications. There was also sufficient capacity available to handle new data with the present systems, as shown by the fact that Merrill Lynch processed work for other companies during its own low-volume periods and work gaps.

Legal Implications

72 There were a number of major legal problems that Merrill Lynch had been considering. The firm had its own and other lawyers working to make sure the new product would not transcend any legal boundaries, such as the Glass-Steagall Act. It had presented the idea to the Federal Reserve, the Justice Department, and selected members of Congress. The Fed said that the new account would not violate any of its rules but warned that it would closely monitor the impact of this and any similar programs. The Justice Department neither approved nor disapproved the idea. Other anticipated implications were the almost certain outcries from bankers that Merrill Lynch became chartered and regulated by the Federal Reserve System.

73 For several years, the issue of separating investment and commercial banks had been blurred. The 1975 Securities Act directed a review of the Glass-Steagall Act. If brought to fruition, the CMA would surely add pressure to redefine or alter such legislation. Meanwhile, banks had been participating in activities that brokers consider to be Glass-Steagall infractions. Such activities included (1) financial advice to customers on long-term credits, mergers, and acquisitions, (2) certain kinds of term loans, and (3) lining up insurance or pension fund money for private placements. The Federal Reserve Board had fully endorsed banks' private placement activities. In response, the brokers' trade group (the Securities Industry Association) denounced the Fed's stand and urged Congress to solve the problem. Also, Congress had been debating the related issues of (1) whether to give interest-bearing checking-account privileges to nonbank thrift institutions and (2) whether to allow interstate branching of banks.

74 In light of the banking-brokerage confrontation, however, Merrill Lynch viewed

the CMA move more as a threat to brokers than to large banks. Merrill Lynch was one of the very few brokerage houses large enough to invade the banking business. It had $632 million in capital; its next largest rival had only $167 million. However, while Merrill Lynch was huge in comparison to other brokers, it was small compared to the large money-center banks.

How Banking Activities Could Benefit Merrill Lynch

75 Along with Merrill Lynch's other attempts to diversify its financial products and services, the company's move into commercial banking would be an attempt to offset the decreasing profitability and the cyclicality of brokerage profits. In a way, all brokers were already in the banking business through the medium of margin credit. In August 1977, Merrill Lynch topped $2 billion in margin loans—a loan portfolio that only 30 commercial banks could match. These margin loans were very profitable; in fact, 10 percent of Merrill's 1976 revenues came from interest on margin balances.

76 Merrill Lynch had its eye on a much broader source of customers and money through international and CMA banking activities. The CMA would be a way to attract new accounts as well as to hold old accounts. The CMA would have a finely segmented target market—probably the young (ages 35 to 45) executive beginning to build a stock portfolio and used unsecured credit. These customers would add money to Merrill's cash reserves and would have been good present and future investing clients for Merrill's brokers.

77 Margin loans were more extensively used under the CMA concept. Merrill Lynch held billions of dollars of value in fully paid securities owned by customers which represented billions in potential low-interest borrowing power. Through CMAs, funds that had previously been idle in brokerage accounts could be put to work in an interest-earning fund. The CMA would, in essence, allow margin credit for purchases other than additional securities.

78 The movement into banking would have other effects on Merrill Lynch. First, commercial banking opened up huge possibilities in diversified financial services. Second, the movement into banking could give Merrill Lynch a reputation for cleverness that it lacked. In spite of Merrill's size and scope, it had an image problem. To most observers, it appeared as a giant who had succeeded not through talent but simply because it was so big. The firm led in most investment fields, but it did not have the classy image of a Morgan Stanley or a First Boston or a Salomon Brothers. Merrill Lynch's movement into banking offered it an opportunity to do something unique. The firm would have the chance to prove its innovativeness and to establish a unique competitive advantage.

Other Areas of Interest

79 In its effort to become a leader in virtually all areas of financial services, Merrill Lynch was considering many alternatives. It would probably undertake all of them, but the consideration was how soon it would choose to do so. For example, a system of real estate offices throughout the country was on Merrill's forward schedule, assuming its current venture into the employee relocation business worked well. It could also decide to expand its Personal Capital Planning Group, which provided financial planning for people with $30,000 or more in income, beyond its three test offices into

a national branch system. Alternatively, it could move immediately to expand and broaden the product lines of Family Life Insurance.

Criteria for Accepting a New Project

80 Whatever moves Merrill Lynch decided to make, they were to be the result of systematic planning. The company had repeatedly expressed the willingness to sacrifice the possibility of large immediate profits to avoid the probability of large future losses. Any new project had to offer $500,000 in aftertax earnings and to provide a 15 percent aftertax return on investment within a three-year period. Merrill Lynch, in all instances, sought to repeat the successful formula it had used in the past—start small, learn the language and problems of the business, groom it to fit into Merrill's system of controls, and then plow in capital and personnel to grow.

Appendix A

MERRILL LYNCH & CO.
Statement of Changes in Consolidated Financial Position
Years Ended December 30, 1977, and December 31, 1976
(in thousands of dollars)

	1977	*1976*
Sources of funds:		
Funds from operations:		
Net earnings	$ 43,947	$ 106,608
Noncash charges—depreciation and amortization	19,862	15,584
Total funds provided by operations	63,809	122,192
Increase in borrowings:		
Securities sold under agreements to repurchase	572,819	282,142
Bank loans	168,437	679,756
Commercial paper	239,081	215,070
Borrowing agreements with institutions	78,800	—
Intermediate term loans	102,500	—
Total increase in borrowings	1,161,637	1,176,968
Increase in net payables to brokers and dealers	5,436	54,579
Proceeds form issuance and sale of stock	10,082	11,073
Other, net	(15,062)	95,178
Total sources of funds	$1,225,902	$1,459,990
Uses of funds:		
Increase (decrease) in financial assets:		
Net securities inventory	$ 451,462	$ 815,544
Securities purchased under agreement to resell	233,984	(68,566)
Customer receivables, net	383,988	587,811
Residential properties under contract	74,179	—
Total increase in financed assets	1,133,613	1,334,789
Increase in deferred insurance policy acquisition costs	15,780	11,815
Purchase of office equipment and installations, net of retirements	29,337	18,366
Treasury stock purchased	10,019	24,685
Cash dividends	30,215	28,341
Decrease in income tax liability	8,037	40,507
Increase (decrease) in cash and securities on deposit	(1,099)	1,487
Total uses of funds	$1,225,902	$1,459,990

Source: Merrill Lynch & Co., Inc., 1977 Annual Report, p. 11.

Appendix B

MERRILL LYNCH & CO.
Statement of Changes in Consolidated Shareholders' Equity
Years Ended December 30, 1977, and December 31, 1976
(in thousands of dollars)

	Common stock	*Paid-in capital*	*Retained earnings*	*Treasury stock*
Balance, December 26, 1975:				
36,140,179 common shares issued and 571,904 shares in treasury	$48,187	$87,418	$440,330	$ (8,518)
Net earnings			106,608	
Cash dividends: Common stock, $80 per share			(28,341)	
Common stock sold to employees under stock option and stock purchase plans (587,235 shares held in treasury)		(233)		11,306
Treasury stock purchased (997,900 shares)				24,685)
Balance, December 31, 1976:	48,187	87,185	518,597	(21,897)
Net earnings			43,947	
Cash dividends: Common stock, $.86 per share			(30,215)	
Common stock sold to employees under stock option and stock purchase plans (726,782 shares held in treasury)		(5,558)		15,640
Treasury stock purchased (521,900 shares)				(10,019)
Balance, December 30, 1977:				
(36,140,179 common shares issued and 777,687 shares in treasury)	48,187	81,627	532,329	(16,276)

Source: Merrill Lynch & Co., Inc., 1977 Annual Report, p. 10.

Appendix C

MERRILL LYNCH & CO.
Consolidated Balance Sheet
December 30, 1977, and December 31, 1976
(in thousands of dollars)

	1977	*1976*
Assets		
Cash and securities on deposit:		
Cash (includes time deposits of $33,718 in 1977 and $54,582 in 1976)	$ 84,069	$ 88,406
Cash segregated in compliance with federal and other regulations	17,699	16,125
Securities on deposit in compliance with federal and other regulations, at market value	132,106	130,442
Total cash and securities on deposit	233,874	234,973
Receivables:		
Brokers and dealers	192,176	165,207
Customers (less allowance for doubtful accounts of $10,622 in 1977 and $13,528 in 1976)	2,908,989	2,363,833
Securities purchased under agreements to resell	1,156,477	932,493
Other	176,652	101,982
Total receivables	4,434,294	3,563,515
Securities inventory, at market value:		
Bankers' acceptances, certificates of deposit, and commercial paper	580,810	870,342
U.S. and Canadian governments	1,927,010	1,350,763
States and municipalities	210,891	135,318
Corporates	364,988	246,559
Total securities inventory	3,083,699	2,602,982
Other:		
Investment securities, principally bonds, at amortized cost (market value, $53,869 in 1977 and $41,837 in 1976)	55,524	41,653
Office equipment and installations (less accumulated depreciation and amortization of $57,444 in 1977 and $49,548 in 1976)	92,409	74,337
Residential properties under contract	74,179	—
Deferred properties policy acquisition costs	44,513	37,330
Other assets	76,107	60,797
Total other	342,732	214,117
Total assets	$8,094,599	$6,615,587
Liabilities and Shareholders' Equity		
Loans:		
Bank loans	$1,926,278	$1,757,841
Commercial paper	632,878	393,797
Borrowing agreements with institutions	78,800	—
Securities sold under agreements to repurchase	2,176,604	1,603,785
Intermediate-term loans	102,500	—
Total loans	4,917,060	3,755,423
Payables and accrued liabilities:		
Brokers and dealers	373,153	341,748
Customers	1,088,782	927,614
Drafts payable	238,022	206,976
Insurance policy benefits	33,456	30,268
Income taxes	53,811	61,848
Employee compensation and benefits	75,000	78,688
Other	214,256	156,013
Total payables and accrued liabilities	2,077,480	1,803,155

Appendix C *(concluded)*

	1977	*1976*
Commitments for securities sold but not yet purchased, at market value:		
U.S. and Canadian governments	317,894	341,421
Other	136,298	83,516
Total commitments	454,192	424,937
Shareholders' equity:		
Common stock, par value $1.33⅓ per share—authorized 60 million shares; issued 36,140,179 shares	48,187	48,187
Paid-in capital	81,627	87,185
Retained earnings	532,329	518,597
Total shareholders' equity	662,143	653,969
Less common stock in treasury, at cost—777,687 shares in 1977 and 982,569 shares in 1976	16,276	21,897
Total shareholders' equity less common stock	645,867	632,072
Total liabilities and shareholders' equity	$8,094,599	$6,615,587

Source: Merrill Lynch & Co., Inc., 1977 Annual Report, pp. 8, 9.

Appendix D

MERRILL LYNCH & CO.
Statement of Consolidated Earnings
Years Ended December 30, 1977, and December 31, 1976
(in thousands of dollars except per-share amounts)

	1977 (52 weeks)	*1976 (53 weeks)*
Revenues:		
Commissions	$ 366,138	$ 442,947
Interest	353,784	237,857
Principal transactions	188,464	261,285
Investment banking	120,091	115,295
Insurance	44,650	34,358
Other	51,089	33,187
Total revenues	1,124,216	1,124,929
Expenses:		
Employee compensation and benefits	436,079	431,029
Interest	312,769	202,703
Occupancy expense and equipment rental	70,375	64,459
Communications	60,516	54,684
Brokerage, clearing, and exchange fees	36,436	38,476
Advertising and market development	33,557	26,039
Office supplies and postage	24,268	21,953
Insurance policyholder benefits	15,532	14,517
Other operating expenses	63,402	64,616
Total expenses	1,052,934	918,476
Earnings before income taxes	71,282	206,453
Income taxes	27,335	99,845
Net earnings	$ 43,947	$ 106,608
Net earnings per common share	$ 1.25	$ 3.01

Source: Merrill Lynch & Co., Inc., 1977 Annual Report, p. 7.

Appendix E

MERRILL LYNCH & CO.
Five-Year Financial Summary
Year Ended Last Friday in December 1973–1977
(in thousands of dollars, except per-share amounts)

	1977 (52 weeks)		*1976 (53 weeks)*		*1975 (52 weeks)*		*1974 (52 weeks)*		*1973 (52 weeks)*		*Compound growth rate, percent (1973–77)*
Revenues:											
Commissions:											
Listed securities	$ 257,037	22.8%	$ 319,882	28.5%	$ 313,827	32.1%	$ 236,052	29.5%	$ 273,498	36.0%	(1.5)%
Options	44,977	4.0	59,948	5.3	38,891	4.0	8,681	1.1	2,279	0.3	110.8
Over-the-counter securities	16,831	1.5	17,883	1.6	11,796	1.2	8,259	1.0	13,117	1.7	6.4
Mutual funds	2,610	0.2	2,185	0.2	2,848	0.3	4,556	0.6	25,012	3.3	(43.2)
Commodities	44,683	4.0	43,049	3.8	37,408	3.8	34,572	4.3	42,739	5.6	1.1
Total commission revenues	366,138	32.5	442,947	39.4	404,770	41.4	292,120	36.5	356,645	46.9	0.7
Interest:											
Margin balances	145,895	13.0	112,896	10.0	99,551	10.2	141,220	17.6	141,916	18.7	0.7
Securities owned and deposits	207,889	18.5	124,961	11.1	105,824	10.8	89,501	11.2	44,442	5.8	47.1
Total interest revenues	353,784	31.5	237,857	21.1	205,375	21.0	230,721	28.8	186,358	24.5	17.4%
Principal transactions:											
Government and agency securities	56,693	5.0	122,968	10.9	93,023	9.5	78,048	9.8	45,780	6.0	5.5
Municipal securities	21,075	1.9	29,428	2.6	23,638	2.4	14,961	1.9	11,666	1.5	15.9
Corporate securities	96,067	8.6	90,510	8.0	49,421	5.0	41,944	5.2	39,201	5.2	25.1
Money market securities	14,629	1.3	18,379	1.7	21,178	2.2	23,557	2.9	8,955	1.2	13.0
Total principal transaction revenues	188,464	16.8	261,285	23.2	187,260	19.1	158,510	19.8	105,602	13.9	15.6
Investment banking											
Underwriting fees	47,366	4.2	39,298	3.5	44,583	4.5	23,738	3.0	22,741	3.0	20.1
Selling concessions	72,725	6.5	75,997	6.8	80,984	8.3	44,280	5.5	35,237	4.6	19.9
Total investment banking revenues	120,091	10.7	115,295	10.3	125,567	12.8	68,018	8.5	57,978	7.6	20.0
Insurance:											
Life	32,593	2.9	27,222	2.4	23,505	2.4	20,674	2.6	18,252	2.4	15.6
Accident and sickness	7,028	0.6	7,007	0.6	7,299	0.7	7,374	0.9	6,933	0.9	0.3
Other	5,029	0.5	59	—	31	—	—	—	—	—	—
Total insurance revenues	44,650	4.0	34,358	3.0	30,835	3.1	28,048	3.5	25,185	3.3	15.4
Other revenues	51,089	4.4	33,187	3.0	25,446	2.6	23,212	2.9	28,361	3.8	15.9
Total revenues	1,124,216	100.0	1,124,929	100.0	979,253	100.0	800,629	100.0	760,129	100.0	10.3

Expenses:											
Employee compensation and benefits	$ 436,079	41.4%	$ 431,029	46.9%	$ 370,170	47.3%	$ 308,430	42.3%	$ 312,572	45.4%	8.7%
Interest	312,769	29.7	202,703	22.1	158,585	20.3	194,029	26.6	148,553	21.6	20.5
Occupancy expense and equipment rental	70,375	6.7	64,459	7.0	60,828	7.8	57,980	7.0	55,840	8.1	5.9
Communications	60,516	5.7	54,684	6.0	45,694	5.8	41,491	5.7	41,418	6.0	9.9
Brokerage, clearing, and exchange fees	36,436	3.5	38,476	4.2	33,969	4.3	26,752	3.6	29,941	4.3	5.0
Advertising and market development	33,557	3.2	26,039	2.8	21,674	2.8	17,481	2.4	19,451	2.8	14.6
Office supplies and postage	24,268	2.3	21,953	2.4	17,799	2.3	15,730	2.2	14,251	2.1	14.2
Insurance policyholder benefits	15,532	1.5	14,517	1.6	13,927	1.8	12,916	1.8	11,434	1.7	8.0
Other operating expenses	63,402	6.0	64,616	7.0	59,575	7.5	54,419	7.5	55,020	8.0	3.6
Total expenses	1,052,934	100.0%	918,476	100.0%	782,221	100.0%	729,228	100.0%	688,480	100.0%	11.2
Earnings before income taxes	71,282		206,453		197,032		71,401		71,649		(0.1)
Income taxes	27,335		99,845		101,341		33,866		34,921		(5.9)
Net earnings	43,947		106,608		95,691		37,535		36,728		4.6
Preferred dividend requirement	—		—		5		202		202		—
Net earnings applicable to common stock	43,947		106,608		95,686		37,333		36,526		4.7
Average number of common shares outstanding	35,147,074		35,389,834		35,595,107		35,917,361		35,738,835		
Net earnings as a percent of revenues	3.9%		9.5%		9.8%		4.7%		4.8%		
Per common share data:											
Net earnings	$ 1.25		$ 3.01		$ 2.69		$ 1.04		$ 1.02		5.2
Cash dividends declared	.86		.80		.59		.56		.56		11.1
Shareholders' equity	18.26		17.98		15.95		13.92		13.45		7.9
Balance sheet data (at year-end):											
Total assets	$ 8,094,599		$ 6,615,587		$ 4,879,012		$ 4,124,554		$ 3,815,571		
Shareholders' equity	645,867		632,072		567,417		506,002		486,775		
Return on average shareholders' equity	6.9%		17.8%		17.8%		7.6%		7.7%		

Source: Merrill Lynch & Co., Inc., 1977, Annual Report, p. 6.

case 15
Merrill Lynch & Co. (B)

Introduction

1 Until 1940, Merrill Lynch was a midsized brokerage firm whose most noteworthy achievement was surviving the Depression. At that time, however, cofounder Charles E. Merrill became convinced that brokerage houses, which had catered to the elite, had ignored a huge potential market. Merrill thus renamed his stockbrokers "account executives" and built a vast system of retail branches to sell Wall Street to Main Street. The firm used its retail distribution muscle to leverage itself into the leadership position in institutional brokering, trading, and investment banking.

2 Merrill Lynch remained the leading brokerage firm on Wall Street through the 1970s. During that period, the firm evolved from a product-oriented partnership to a financial market-oriented diversified-services corporation. They also dealt successfully with extensive deregulation of the financial-services industry in the late 1970s and early 1980s.

3 The Merrill Lynch of 1984 emerged as a publicly owned, financial conglomerate with a market orientation targeted to four principal groups of customers: individuals, corporations, institutions, and governments.

An Industry of Dynamic Change

4 The development of the financial services industry was determined by a line of important deregulation milestones: the Federal Reserve Board's removal of interest-rate ceilings on banks' large certificates of deposit in 1970; the Securities and Exchange Commission's 1975 dictum to stop the fixing of brokerage commissions; the creation of six-month market-rate certificates of deposit for banks and thrifts in 1978; and landmark legislation in 1980 and 1982 that cleared the way for interest-bearing checking accounts nationwide and the removal of the remaining interest-rate ceilings on bank accounts. These deregulation milestones combined with product innovation, government economic policy, rapid inflation, and historically high interest rates to produce a turbulent industry environment.

5 With market positions no longer set by regulation and thrifts in 1978; and landmark legislation in 1980 and 1982 that cleared the way for interest-bearing checking accounts nationwide and the removal of the remaining interest-rate ceilings on bank accounts. These deregulation milestones combined with product innovation, government economic policy, rapid inflation, and historically high interest rates to produce a turbulent industry environment.

This case was prepared by Frank L. Winfrey and John A. Pearce II of the University of South Carolina.

5 With market positions no longer set by regulation and with savers free to choose from a selection of investments, the financial services industry rapidly took on the characteristics of an industry shaped by market forces.

6 The first such characteristic was consolidation of resources with companies trying to achieve economies of scale. Two methods used to achieve these economies were (1) merging with similar institutions (see Exhibit 1) and (2) developing new services suited to distribution through existing facilities. A striking example of consolidation was the 1981 acquisition of Dean Witter Reynolds by Sears, Roebuck & Company which combined with Sears's Allstate and Coldwell Banker subsidiaries to make Sears a retail financial supermarket. The creative development of Universal Life insurance by E. F. Hutton Life in 1980 was an example of a new service suited to distribution through existing facilities, since the offices of E. F. Hutton stockbrokers performed the function.

7 Specialization through the unbundling of services was a second new characteristic of the industry. For example, discount brokers emerged after the "unfixing" of brokerage commissions in 1975. Discounters offered a no-frills transaction service without advice, or a broad product line, to their customers. By forgoing research services, discount brokers routinely underpriced their full-service competitors, such as Merrill Lynch, by as much as 70 percent of the normal commission. In 1983, discount firms accounted for about 15 percent of the share volume generated by individual investors.

8 A third characteristic was a profit squeeze in the financial-services industry. Heightened competition exerted strong pressure on profit margins which led to an increased emphasis on each company's productivity. An example of the pressure on profit margins was the trimming of staff research positions among merged firms. Typically, when firms with research staffs merged, the new organization promptly cut back the equivalent of one staff, thus reducing costs and improving profit margins.

9 The consulting firm McKinsey and Company reported that the financial-services companies most likely to survive the 1980s would be either relatively large firms (assets in excess of $1.5 billion) with plenty of excess capital or relatively small firms (assets of less than $800 million) which would be able to move quickly into specialized markets.

10 On May 1, 1975, the Securities and Exchange Commission "unfixed" commission rates on stocks. Over the following nine years, the average commission paid by institutional customers declined by about 40 percent, which meant that firms in the industry

Exhibit 1

Mergers involving Wall Street firms, 1981–1982

Acquired company	*Acquiring company*	*Date*	*Price ($ millions)*
Bache	Prudential	June 1981	376
Shearson Loeb Rhoades	American Express	June 1981	1,038
Salomon Brothers	Phibro	October 1981	554
Dean Witter Reynolds	Sears, Roebuck	December 1981	607
Foster and Marshall	Shearson/AmEx	March 1982	75
Loewi	Kemper	May 1982	64
Robinson-Humphrey	Shearson/AmEx	June 1982	77

Source: "The Morning after at Philbro-Salomon," *Fortune*, January 10, 1983, p. 76.

had to attempt to extract maximum revenues from other parts of the business. The source of these revenues became the retail operations, which focused on the individual investors. The fervor to expand and to obtain retail business flourished in what became a highly competitive environment.

11 While the industry exhibited an increasing concentration of capital through merger activity, the capital devoted to the securities industry actually declined as many firms diversified to other interests, such as real estate, insurance, oil and gas investments, and employee-relocation services.

12 Survival for the major brokerage firms in the new environment seemed to require firms to be all things to all people. The traditional mandate to the brokers to sell stocks was supplanted by a new priority to capture assets. The idea was to get as much of the clients' funds as possible: the risk money, the savings money, the sheltered income, and the insurance premiums. Revenues from such nonequity products grew from about 15 percent to about 50 percent of firms' retail income from 1975 to 1984.

13 The retail broker was naturally the one elected to market the new products, and the broker was expected to introduce new products to existing and prospective clients. The strategy was intended to work to the advantage of the brokers whose income would not be exclusively tied to the Dow, given their involvement with a satchel of diversified products.

14 The trouble was that the product proliferation created too many products for the broker to understand expertly. To exacerbate the problem, there was an ever-widening array of options, commodities, financial futures, tax shelters, financial planning, life insurance, annuities, cash management accounts, and money market funds. Virtually every large brokerage house needed its own expensive and elaborate support system to help the increasingly less-authoritative brokers.

The New Face of the Competition

15 Merrill Lynch had long been the largest firm in the brokerage business in terms of assets, revenues, and range of activities. The financial-services industry transitions that occurred from 1975 through 1984 rapidly changed its preeminent position, making the firm one of the new pack (see Exhibits 2 and 3). The new entities Merrill Lynch faced matched its financial strength and scope of activity.

Sears, Roebuck & Company

16 In late 1981, Sears became a major force in the financial services industry. The giant retailer augmented its presence in insurance and consumer credit by acquiring Dean Witter Reynolds Organization Incorporated, the nation's fifth-largest investment firm, and Coldwell Banker and Company, the nation's largest real estate broker. These two firms added to Sears's already impressive stable of existing financial services—Allstate property, casualty, and life insurance; mortgage life insurance; 87 Allstate Savings and Loan Association branches in California (with $3 billion in assets); interest-bearing credit for some 25 million active users of Sears credit cards; automobile and boat installment loans; and commercial realty and store leasing.

17 The company's 831 retail stores, 2,388 catalog outlets, 1,950 stand-alone Allstate Insurance sales offices, 348 Dean Witter offices, 87 savings and loan branches in Califor-

Exhibit 2

How Merrill Lynch ranks against its rivals

```
     Sears
     ***
     ***
8—   ***
     ***
     ***
6—   ***
     ***  Citicorp
     ***  ***
     ***  ***
4—   ***
     ***  ***  Shearson/American Express
     ***  ***  ***
     ***  ***  ***
2—   ***  ***  ***  Merrill Lynch
     ***  ***  ***  ***
     ***  ***  ***  ***  E. F. Hutton
     ***  ***  ***  ***  ***  Paine Webber
0—   ***  ***  ***  ***  ***  ***

Shareholders' equity ($ billions)
```

```
     Sears
30—  ***
     /
     ***       Shearson/American Express
     ***  ***
8—   ***  ***
     ***  ***
     ***  ***
     ***  ***
6—   ***  ***
     ***  Citi-
          corp  Merrill Lynch
     ***  ***  ***  ***
     ***  ***  ***  ***
4—   ***  ***  ***  ***
     ***  ***  ***  ***
     ***  ***  ***  ***
     ***  ***  ***  ***
     ***  ***  ***  ***  E. F. Hutton
     ***  ***  ***  ***  ***  Paine Webber
     ***  ***  ***  ***  ***  ***
     ***  ***  ***  ***  ***  ***
     ***  ***  ***  ***  ***  ***

Revenues ($ billions)
```

(as of December 31, 1982)

Source: "Merrill Lynch's Big Dilemma," *Business Week*, January 16, 1984, p. 62.

nia, and several hundred real estate locations clearly offered the Sears organization enormous competitive potential on a distributional basis.

18 Sears's in-house data base on consumer credit, by far the biggest of its kind, became the nucleus for a carefully targeted selling of home loans or financial products to prequalified Sears customers. The data base, data processing, and telecommunications capabilities of the company were also upgraded to provide a convenient nationwide electronic payment system capable of providing complete financial transaction services.

BankAmerica Corporation

19 BankAmerica Corporation skirted the Glass-Steagall and Bank Holding Company Acts which barred banks from markets and products that included mutual funds, insurance and securities underwriting, and brokerage services when it purchased Charles Schwab and Company, the country's largest discount brokerage firm. Because Schwab served only as an executor of orders and neither bought stock for its own account nor underwrote stock issues, BankAmerica was able to conform to the letter of the law. In acquiring Schwab, BankAmerica obtained a highly automated brokerage firm plus some 220,000 investors for its customer base. Beyond that, the acquisition offered a way for Bank of America, the nation's second-largest bank, to provide brokerage service to its 4 million customers.

Exhibit 3

The score on the Big Five (as of September 30, 1981, $ millions)

	Shearson/ American Express	*Citicorp*	*Merrill Lynch*	*Prudential-Bache*	*Sears/ Dean Witter*
What they get:					
Revenues	$ 7,000	17,300	3,800	13,200	2,770
Net income	510	420	200	n/a	630
What they've got:					
Assets	23,700	121,700	15,700	67,500	32,700
What they do:					
Securities brokerage	**		**	**	**
Securities trading	**	**	**	**	**
Cash management services			**		**
Investment management	**	**	**	**	**
Commodities brokerage	**		**	**	**
Corporate underwriting					
United States	**		**	**	**
International	**	**	**	**	**
Commercial banking					
United States		**			
International	**	**	**		
Savings and loan operations					**
Small-loan offices		**			**
Credit cards, charge cards	**	**			**
Traveler's checks	**	**			
Foreign-exchange trading	**	**	**	**	**
Leasing	**	**	**	**	**
Data processing services	**	**	**	**	**
Property and casualty insurance	**			**	**
Life insurance, health insurance	**		**	**	**
Mortgage insurance					**
Mortgage banking	**	**	**		**
Real-estate development				**	**
Commercial real-estate brokerage			**		**
Residential real-estate brokerage			**		**
Executive-relocation services			**		**

n.a. = Not available.
Source: "The Fight for Financial Turf," *Fortune,* December 28, 1981, p. 57.

20 In early 1984, Bank of America announced it would rent branch space to Capital Holdings Group of Louisville, Kentucky. Capital was an insurance holding company that planned to sell automobile, homeowner, and life insurance from the branch locations. A Bank of America spokesperson said the arrangement was designed to give the bank a head start in the race of commercial banks to expand into other financial services such as the insurance business.

Shearson/American Express

21 American Express's acquisition of Shearson Loeb Rhoades linked the Number 1 company in one financial field with the Number 2 company in another financial field. American Express was a unique financial house whose 113-year history had revolved around money transfers, travel services, card services, insurance, and international banking. Shearson was a brokerage house which had been developed through a series of acquisitions of old-line brokerages. The merger created an entity that could offer a plethora of financial-services packages from the combination of the American Express credit-card operations with 11 million cardholders, Shearson's money market fund and securities operations, Shearson's mortgage banking operations, Warner/Amex Cable and Satellite Communications subsidiaries, American Express Fireman's Fund insurance, and American Express International Banking Corporation. Additionally, shortly after the merger, Shearson/American Express acquired the Boston Company, an investment management firm; Balcor, a packager of real estate investments; four regional securities brokerage firms; the Trade Development Bank of Geneva (one of Switzerland's five largest banks), an overseas banking firm catering to the owners of "flight capital" and other very wealthy individuals; and Investors Diversified Services of Minneapolis, a company that specialized in selling life insurance, annuities, and mutual funds to individuals, particularly middle Americans. The Shearson/American Express strategy was to use the company's various sales forces to promote products manufactured by Shearson—Fireman's Fund, the International group, and the Travel Related Services group—to targeted individuals (see Exhibit 4).

22 Shearson/American Express made a distinct effort to change the image of its sales force to adapt to the new competitive environment. The firm renamed its 4,500 stockbrokers "financial consultants" and outfitted each of them with a private office.

23 In April 1984, Shearson/American Express agreed to acquire Lehman Brothers Kuhn Loeb Incorporated. The purchase was an expedient way for Shearson to strengthen two of its weakest lines—investment banking and trading, particularly in fixed-income and equity securities. The company was renamed Shearson Lehman/American Express.

Citicorp

24 Citibank expanded its activities into the retail securities industry when it began to offer discount-brokerage services at its 275 New York City branches. Some 600 of the nation's more than 14,500 banks offered discount brokerage services by early 1984. The Citibank discount-brokerage accounts were handled by Q&R Clearing Corporation, a unit of Quick and Reilly Incorporated, the New York discount-brokerage concern. Although Citibank had been offering such services as a part of its "personal asset

Exhibit 4

Segments of the financial services retail market as determined by Shearson/American Express

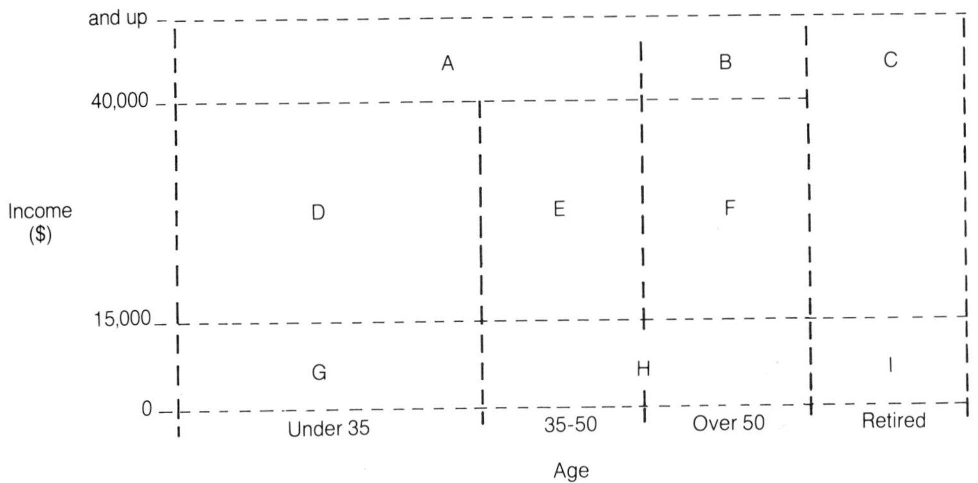

Key to the classification of investors:
A—Up and comers.
B—Affluent established.
C—Affluent retired.
D—Successful beginners.
E—Mainstream family.
F—Conservative core.
G—Young survivors.*
H—Older survivors.*
I—Retired survivors.*
* Denotes incomes below targeted levels.
Source: "Fire in the Belly at American Express," *Fortune*, November 28, 1983, p. 92.

account," Citibank's entrance into the brokerage business represented an expansion of financial-service activity by Citicorp, Citibank's parent.

25 As part of Citicorp's effort to develop a nationwide presence in the financial-services industry, the company purchased savings and loan associations in California, Illinois, and Florida and developed industrial banks, which offered commercial-banking services except checking accounts and trust services, in some 22 states.

26 Citicorp, the nation's largest bank holding company, pushed the state of New York unsuccessfully for changes in state banking laws to allow it to sell insurance. However, Citicorp did achieve a position in the travel and entertainment segment of the financial-services industry with its acquisition of the Diners Club credit-card operations. In late 1983, Citicorp purchased a maximum allowable 29.9 percent share of the London stockbrokerage firm Vickers da Costa (Holdings) PLC and approximately 75 percent of Vickers's overseas operations, which included branches in Hong Kong, Singapore, Tokyo, and New York.

27 These services, combined with its traditional banking services, strongly positioned Citicorp as major entrant in the financial-services industry of the 1980s.

E. F. Hutton

28 In its 1982 annual survey of the 1,000 leading U.S. companies, *Forbes* magazine ranked E. F. Hutton first in the brokerage group in return on equity, first in return on capital, and first in per share earnings growth. According to Lipper Analytical Associates, E. F. Hutton had the highest production per retail account executive in the industry. Besides its retail brokerage operations, Hutton was also active in tax-sheltered investments, life insurance, annuities, investment-management programs, and Hutton Credit company, which specialized in commercial paper. Still, E. F. Hutton chose to be viewed as one of the last basic securities business specialists. This was an image that Hutton management hoped would attract investors who felt stifled in the larger, less-entrepreneurial financial supermarkets.

29 E. F. Hutton was the first brokerage firm to enable its clients to electronically access their account information via personal computer or videotex. This "Huttonline" service allowed Hutton customers to tap into the CompuServe Network and retrieve any of their account information. The system also provided a broker-client electronic mail link so that each could leave messages to the other in the system. This helped to leverage both the customers' time and the brokers' time. The electronic system was seen as a major new way to hold down expenses and generate revenues.

Prudential/Bache

30 After the acquisition of Bache Halsey Stuart Shields by Prudential in 1981, the firm was renamed Prudential-Bache and reorganized into eight major operating groups structured around its various sales forces and lines of business. The firm offered more than 70 different investment products, including stocks, options, bonds, commodities, tax-favored investments, and insurance. A group of mutual funds was offered by the company through the investment management of Prudential, which represented a transfer of fund management resulting in a considerable savings to Prudential-Bache. The combination also produced several new investment products in areas such as real estate, options, and oil and gas investments, which were sold by both Prudential-Bache account executives and Prudential insurance agents licensed by the National Association of Securities Dealers.

31 Prudential, working through its Prudential Bank and Trust Company in Hapeville, Georgia, announced it would offer a credit card with a line of credit through one of the existing major credit-card networks.

Merrill Lynch

32 The 1983 earnings for Merrill Lynch rose more than 50 percent over the historically high levels of 1982 and 1981. However, this earnings pattern was threatened by competitive challenges resulting from the deregulated industry.

33 One of the essentials for competing in the new environment was a strong capital position. In 1973, Merrill Lynch's total stockholder equity was less than half a billion dollars, but by 1984, the company was above $2 billion. Merrill Lynch also continued to improve its return on equity in 1982 and 1983, though it lagged the industry average on this measure. Overall, it appeared that Merrill Lynch had the financial strength to compete on multiple fronts in the financial-services industry (see case appendixes).

34 Despite environmental transitions and increasingly direct competition from Sears,

Roebuck & Company, Shearson/American Express, Prudential-Bache, Citicorp, and other formidable companies, Merrill Lynch moved deftly to innovate services and to defend and expand its markets. By 1984, it, too, had formed a state-charted bank. Merrill Lynch formed the bank in New Jersey through a legal loophole in the federal definition of a bank by simply not offering a demand deposit service. The purpose of this new bank unit was to take consumer deposits, move into consumer lending, and offer unsecured lines of credit attached to VISA cards.

35 Merrill Lynch identified 38 products that affluent households purchased from 20 different financial-service vendors, such as lawyers, accountants, banks, finance companies, and real estate brokers. It then began packaging those services, creating total financial-care products such as the Cash Management Account (CMA).

36 The success of the Cash Management Account service was a star example of product innovation. The service went from 4,000 customers in 1978 to over 1 million customers in 1983. The significance of the product was magnified because it brought to Merrill Lynch a great many high-quality customers who had not previously done business with the firm.

37 Although Merrill Lynch's greatest strength was its retail system of 431 branch offices with 8,763 brokers, it had become a handicap as well. Because of its broad range of customer services, its compensation methods, and its full-service brokerage house culture, Merrill Lynch's approach remained very expensive at a time when discount brokering and other low-cost methods were gaining legitimacy and market share.

38 To counter the problem, Merrill Lynch began to convert its account executives into financial advisors. These advisors were seen as the hub of a network of salaried professionals and assistants specializing in insurance, lending, and tax matters. This new structure served a twofold purpose: (1) to upgrade, modernize, and reduce the labor intensiveness of internal communications and (2) to allow the company to gain control of the marketing and delivery function from its account executives. Customer communications and control of the client relationship were seen as a means for Merrill Lynch to gain the primary share of the profit derivable from a given product or service, thus permitting increased profitability for the firm.

The Potential for a Brokers' Mutiny

39 Merrill Lynch account executives shared four concerns with their counterparts in competing firms pertaining to the reorientation of the brokerage business:

40 An information overload developed as companies introduced new products and services. Brokers were expected to acquire a familiarity with the new products and new services in addition to their daily routine of 8 to 12 hours of selling, prospecting, environmental scanning, and transaction-related paperwork.

41 Many brokers maintained that their best clients resisted one-stop financial shopping, preferring instead to use specialists. Successful brokers did not want to dilute their image as brokers with their wealthy investor clients.

42 The new products and new services did not offer much, if any, return to the individual brokers. The commissions on selling insurance or annuities relative to selling equities did not warrant the effort and, thus, represented a significant opportunity cost to an individual broker. Some of the new services, such as cash management accounts, did not even offer commissions, while requiring account executive time.

43 The increased pressure by management to sell the new products and new services

made many brokers uneasy. Many felt that some of the new products ill-served certain investors. Those brokers recognized that the key to their long-run success rested in serving their clients well, not by pushing their firm's new products or services.

The Merrill Lynch Cash Management Account Financial Service

44 The Cash Management Account (CMA) financial service combined a brokerage account with other major financial services to simplify and organize most day-to-day money-transaction activities of participants. The CMA account was made available to investors who placed $20,000 or more in any combination of securities and cash in a Merrill Lynch brokerage account.

45 Idle cash in the securities account was invested automatically in shares of one of three no-load CMA money market funds (the CMA Money Fund, the CMA Government Securities Fund, or the CMA Tax-Exempt Fund), or the generated cash was deposited in an insured savings account. Dividends earned from any of the money funds were reinvested in the CMA account daily, and the interest on the savings account was compounded daily and credited monthly.

46 The CMA service provided investors with imprinted checks that could be used like bank checks to gain access to the assets in the account (both cash and securities). Additionally, a special VISA debit card issued through Bank One of Columbus provided the means to access a CMA account.

47 The program was set up so that a CMA account provided a line of credit backed by the assets in a hierarchy of cost of the asset, cash, money market funds, and then margin-loan (borrowing) power. These assets were accessible through either a VISA transaction or a CMA check.

48 The CMA program provided comprehensive monthly statements listing all transactions in the account chronologically. All securities transactions, money market fund earnings, interest on savings, and VISA and checking transactions were provided separately by category.

49 The innovative Merrill Lynch CMA account worried bankers and competing brokerage firms. The combination of a money fund with a debit card backed by a line of credit based on a customer's securities and funds on deposit proved to be an extremely popular product. Industry sources estimated that at least 6 million investors were prospective customers for these types of accounts, and it was reported that 1,000 new CMA accounts were being opened each day at Merrill Lynch. This phenomenal success prompted bankers and the other brokerage houses to start programs similar to the Merrill Lynch CMA account service.

50 Bache announced a similar product, the Bache Command Account, with an added feature of automatic insurance coverage on the account holder through its parent, Prudential Insurance Company of America.

51 Shearson/American Express introduced a Financial Management Account (FMA) which required a $25,000 cash or securities minimum. Shearson's FMA provided an American Express Gold Card to its participants, and its monthly statement also provided a summary of net worth for the current month and on a year-to-date basis for the customer.

52 Dean Witter's so-called Triple-A program allowed customers to draw on their investment accounts using checks or debit cards with any idle funds automatically swept into high-yield money-market funds.

53 Citibank offered a "personal asset account" encompassing the same combination of money funds, credit, and range of banking and investment services as their competitors.

54 Paine Webber had only some 35,000 clients with its version of the CMA, the "Resource Management Account," in early 1984, but the average balance in its customers' accounts was nearly twice the $70,000 to $80,000 average in the Merrill Lynch accounts.

55 The CMA account marked a change in fundamental focus for Merrill Lynch as the firm made an effort to increase its large-volume retail business and reduce its exposure to low-profit customers. The president of Merrill Lynch's Individual Services unit announced that the firm no longer desired to seek small accounts for its account executives. Such accounts were to be handled in the future by a clerk operating in a client services department at each branch. This move was designed to cut the cost of servicing individuals.

56 In some parts of the country, as many as 25 percent of the Merrill Lynch stockbrokers switched to competitor firms every year due to the increased pressure from the firm to be more productive. In response to this turnover problem, Merrill Lynch began to use litigation to prevent its brokers from walking away with clients, or at least, to force them to pay back the $16,000 to $18,000 cost of their training. It was a particularly active litigant because it was trying to change the dynamics of the relationship among the firm, the broker, and the customers. It wanted its customers to think of themselves as Merrill Lynch customers rather than as clients of a particular account executive. This was a large part of the rationale for the initiation of the CMA service—to develop customers who would stay with Merrill Lynch even if their broker account executive moved to another brokerage firm.

Additional New Products

57 Sophisticated investors were chased by a pride of brokerage house felines in the 1980s: CATS, LIONS, and TIGERS. These were acronyms for a successful variety of zero-coupon Treasury certificates Merrill Lynch and other firms packaged for Individual Retirement Accounts (IRAs). Merrill Lynch also introduced a new stock fund tied to the performance of the Standard & Poors 500 Stock Index which proved to be very successful.

58 In late 1983, Merrill Lynch expanded its consumer lending activities by the introduction of its Equity Access Account, a type of second mortgage which also proved to be very successful.

59 Merrill Lynch introduced the Capital Builder Account (CBA) in early 1984. The product was quickly dubbed the "Son of CMA," as it was basically a lower-priced and streamlined version of the CMA targeted at the more-modest investor, requiring a minimum investment of only $5,000, but it required customers to pay for each service above an allotted number of transactions.

Merrill Lynch Research

60 To provide professional, accurate, and timely research to its customers, Merrill Lynch assembled the largest research staff in the investment business. Merrill Lynch employed 94 equities analysts who covered 1,200 domestic firms, 200 foreign firms, and over 40 industries. Along with this vast breadth of coverage, the research staff was consistently rated as having the best analysts of the major brokerage firms.

61 Most of the men and women of Merrill Lynch's research division were finance-trained MBAs with operating experience from the industries they were assigned to cover. Merrill Lynch managed to attract and retain such talented analysts through a combination of factors: Merrill Lynch's prestigious research reputation, an attractive pay scale, extensive staff resources, and the computer-based opinion retrieval system (the QRQ System).

62 The Merrill Lynch QRQ System was an expanded equity data base which contained the detailed financial projections developed by the research analysts. This information was made available electronically to all branch offices at each account executive's desk. The data base contained current year, next year, and quarterly estimates of earnings; current and projected dividend rates; and the analysts' assessments of rates of growth in dividends and earnings projected five years into the future.

63 Besides providing fundamental equity analyses, Merrill Lynch's research effort employed 12 technical analysts who studied market data and produced technical market analyses, investment strategy advice, and fixed-income and government securities analyses.

The MRP Program (A Personnel Development Program)

64 The Merrill Lynch Management Readiness Program (MRP) was designed to respond to the need to identify talented employees and to prepare them for management positions. The first step in the program involved a selection process in which several levels of management participated in choosing candidates for the program.

65 The second step, the participant's seminar and program kickoff, was a highly interactive event. The employees studied themselves and the organization and began action planning. Each participant left the seminar with established career goals and a development plan detailing skill and knowledge areas necessary to achieve the goals. The participant's managers were given tools to help them and their subordinates define development goals and activities for the six-month program.

66 High-level managers served as mentors and were given development activities with four assigned proteges. They met monthly with the proteges and used whatever information and instructional approach they preferred.

67 In the final phase of the MRP, participants wrote a profile, or self-statement, that documented their goals and skills. The profiles were then presented to a wide range of high-level managers throughout the company to acquaint them with the potential management candidates. In its first two years of operation, more than 83 employees experienced some type of positive job change such as a promotion or special assignment.

The Perspective of Merrill Lynch's Management

68 In addresses to the Los Angeles Society of Securities Analysts and to the Twin Cities Society of Securities Analysts, Roger E. Birk, then president of Merrill Lynch, and Donald T. Regan, then chairman and chief executive officer of Merrill Lynch, outlined management's view of the firm's strengths and basic corporate objectives.

69 The two senior officers listed six major strengths:

1. Merrill Lynch's leadership in diverse market areas.
2. The firm's top credit ratings and financial strength.
3. A strong sales force backed by sophisticated staff and equipment.

4. Merrill Lynch's ability and willingness to adapt to new customer needs and attempts to provide better services.
5 The leadership, vision, and experience of the senior management group (which was relatively young and thus well positioned to offer long-term continuity).
6 Merrill Lynch's strong but flexible management-by-objectives (MBO) planning system.

70 The president and chairman listed three basic objectives for the company: (1) to improve profitability on a long-term sustainable basis; (2) to soften the cyclicality of earnings—both within their established operating areas and through the addition of new services; and (3) to make each cyclical peak higher than the preceding peak.

Future Directions

71 In 1984, Merrill Lynch was attempting to automate the delivery of its investment information. The firm bought a sizable interest in the cable television Financial News Network and had experimented with a two-way cable system that provided Merrill Lynch research through the Dow Jones News Retrieval System.

72 To expand its business information and business communications interests, Merrill Lynch announced that it planned to build a satellite communications center and office park on a 350-acre site on New York's Staten Island in conjunction with the Port Authority of New York and New Jersey.

73 In March 1984, Merrill Lynch announced a joint venture with International Business Machines Corporation (IBM) for the delivery of stock-quote and financial data to IBM desktop computers. The plan called for marketing the service to brokerage firms, banks, thrift institutions, real estate firms, and insurance companies. Merrill Lynch saw the financial information-services business as a means to cut its costs and generate revenue from existing operations such as its research and support units.

74 These attempts by Merrill Lynch to position itself as a technology leader in financial services were interpreted by analysts as strategies designed to reverse its recently eroding stature as the dominant force in the industry.

Appendix A

MERRILL LYNCH & CO.
Statements of Consolidated Earnings
Years Ended December 30, 1983, December 31, 1982, and December 25, 1981
(in thousands of dollars except per share amounts)

	1983 (52 weeks)	*1982 (53 weeks)*	*1981 (52 weeks)*
Revenues:			
Commissions	$1,523,291	$1,132,898	$ 928,645
Interest	1,792,478	1,943,980	1,835,471
Principal transactions	675,527	656,212	427,879
Investment banking	746,638	595,515	359,881
Real estate	392,035	245,051	167,759
Insurance	116,371	116,471	116,313
Other	440,566	336,074	202,234
Total revenues	5,686,906	5,026,201	4,038,182

Appendix A *(concluded)*

	1983 (52 weeks)	1982 (53 weeks)	1981 (52 weeks)
Expenses:			
Compensation and benefits	2,266,278	1,732,483	1,295,255
Interest	1,432,555	1,607,915	1,511,103
Occupancy and equipment rental	325,349	243,836	168,556
Communications	230,331	188,725	151,471
Advertising and market development	229,537	155,818	138,772
Brokerage, clearing, and exchange fees	143,824	121,645	93,578
Office supplies and postage	106,309	88,930	75,746
Insurance policyholder benefits	49,887	27,865	28,135
Other	356,514	303,739	242,151
Nonrecurring charges	153,500	—	—
Total expenses	5,294,084	4,470,956	3,704,767
Earnings before Income taxes	392,822	555,245	333,415
Income taxes	162,659	246,414	130,541
Net earnings	$ 230,163	$ 308,831	$ 202,874
Earnings per share:			
Primary	$ 2.68	$ 3.79	$ 2.57
Fully diluted	$ 2.59	$ 3.74	$ 2.57

Appendix B

MERRILL LYNCH & CO.
Consolidated Balance Sheets
December 30, 1983, and December 31, 1982
(in thousands of dollars, except per share amounts)

	1983	1982
Assets		
Cash and securities on deposit:		
Cash	$ 223,353	$ 311,939
Interest earning deposits	577,302	584,229
Cash segregated and securities on deposit for regulatory purposes	358,179	363,661
Total cash and securities on deposit	1,158,834	1,259,829
Receivables:		
Brokers and dealers	600,137	734,015
Securities borrowed	876,703	464,665
Customers (less reserve for doubtful accounts of $73,920 in 1983 and $79,304 in 1982)	6,061,184	4,777,978
Loans (less reserve for doubtful accounts of $16,925 in 1983 and $11,250 in 1982)	887,732	615,397
Resale agreements	5,975,094	4,361,346
Other	1,298,755	967,811
Total receivables	15,699,604	11,921,212
Securities inventory, at market value:		
Money market instruments	2,192,726	1,545,781
Governments and agencies	2,450,424	2,058,036
Corporates	1,320,529	963,401
Municipals	864,404	804,264
Total securities inventory	6,828,083	5,371,482

Appendix B *(concluded)*

	1983	*1982*
Other assets:		
Investment securities	462,373	624,749
Property, leasehold improvements, and equipment (less accumulated depreciation and amortization of $180,722 in 1983 and $155,755 in 1982)	615,699	443,738
Equity advances for residential properties	372,957	412,363
Deferred insurance policy acquisition costs	99,269	87,953
Other	902,264	575,913
Total other assets	2,452,562	2,144,716
Total assets	$26,139,084	$20,697,239
Liabilities and Stockholders' Equity		
Liabilities:		
Short-term borrowings:		
Bank loans	$ 1,033,777	$ 501,738
Commercial paper	4,890,164	2,684,387
Repurchase agreements	7,609,198	6,237,890
Demand and time deposits	869,814	1,004,933
Securities loaned	593,386	800,601
Total short-term borrowings	14,996,339	11,229,549
Long-term borrowings:	1,264,096	756,869
Total borrowings	16,260,435	11,986,418
Commitments for securities sold but not yet purchased, at market value:		
Governments and agencies	1,408,248	641,994
Corporates	536,934	585,572
Municipals	52,418	50,421
Total commitments for securities sold	1,997,600	1,277,987
Other liabilities:		
Brokers and dealers	394,777	541,576
Customers	3,168,070	3,123,700
Drafts	514,953	397,277
Insurance liabilities	129,537	84,937
Income taxes	143,275	295,594
Compensation and benefits	560,107	468,840
Other	1,082,311	1,088,028
Total other liabilities	5,993,030	5,999,952
Stockholders' equity:		
Common stock, par value $1.33⅓ per share; 200,000,000 shares authorized in 1983 and 1982; 89,970,834 shares issued in 1983, and 78,559,846 shares issued in 1982	119,960	104,746
Paid-in capital	419,551	112,191
Accumulated translation adjustment	(7,355)	(4,280)
Retained earnings	1,390,683	1,226,757
Total stockholders' equity	1,922,839	1,439,414
Less:		
Treasury stock, at cost; 442,089 shares in 1983 and 515,022 shares in 1982	9.314	6.532
Unamortized expense of restricted stock grants	25.506	—
Total	1,888,019	1,432,882
Total liabilities and stockholders' equity	$26,139,084	$20,697,239

Appendix C

MERRILL LYNCH & CO.
Statements of Changes in Consolidated Financial Position
Years Ended December 30, 1983, December 31, 1982, and December 25, 1981
(in thousands of dollars)

	1983	*1982*	*1981*
Source of funds:			
Net earnings	$ 230,163	$ 308,831	$ 202,874
Cash dividends	(66,284)	(52,232)	(45,480)
Earnings retained	163,879	257,599	157,394
Non-cash charges:			
Nonrecurring charges	153,500	—	—
Other	237,652	168,465	161,513
Increase (decrease) in:			
Commitments for securities sold but not yet purchased	719,613	46,362	443,480
Brokers and dealers payable	(146,799)	258,360	(80,742)
Customers payable	44,370	648,272	161,510
Drafts payable	117,676	(253,163)	340,526
Income taxes	(152,319)	143,873	(114,814)
Compensation and benefits	91,267	195,092	46,237
Other liabilities	(5,717)	203,028	269,326
Other, net	(349,580)	(149,359)	(165,254)
Funds provided before financings	873,542	1,518,529	1,219,176
Increase (decrease) in financings:			
Short-term:			
Bank loans	532,039	(495,259)	(351,332)
Commercial paper	2,205,777	836,966	753,966
Repurchase agreements	1,371,308	324,605	2,765,822
Demand and time deposits	(135,119)	300,253	(37,159)
Securities loaned	(207,215)	259,323	(93,175)
	3,766,790	1,225,888	3,038,122
Long-term:			
Senior debt	623,910	102,733	134,701
Subordinated debt	(116,683)	152,395	—
Issuance of common stock	97,850	—	—
Sale of common stock under employee stock plans and conversion of convertible subordinated debentures, net of treasury stock and restricted stock grants	196,436	15,443	44,468
	801,513	270,571	179,169
Funds provided from financings	4,568,303	1,496,459	3,217,291
Total funds provided to increase assets	$5,441,845	$3,014,988	$4,436,467
Increase (decrease) in assets:			
Cash and securities on deposit	$ (100,995)	$ 247,052	$ (239,262)
Brokers and dealers receivable	(133,878)	395,838	(188,207)
Securities borrowed	412,038	235,157	93,287
Customers receivable	1,283,206	102,575	(95,562)
Loans receivable	272,335	269,679	(35,541)
Resale agreements	1,613,748	(66,980)	2,081,264
Securities inventory	1,456,601	1,158,716	2,155,794
Other, net	638,790	672,951	664,694
Increase in assets	$5,441,845	$3,014,988	$4,436,467

Appendix D

MERRILL LYNCH & CO.
Five-Year Financial Summary
Year Ended Last Friday in December, 1979–1983
(in thousands of dollars except per share amounts)

	1983 (52 weeks)		*1982* (53 weeks)		*1981* (52 weeks)		*1980* (52 weeks)		*1979* (52 weeks)	
Revenues:										
Commissions:										
Listed securities	$ 852,920	15.0%	$ 650,385	12.9%	$ 554,512	13.7%	$ 630,876	20.9%	$ 421,887	20.6%
Options	166,712	2.9	167,487	3.3	125,564	3.1	141,960	4.7	80,023	3.9
Commodities	187,572	3.3	168,730	3.4	156,107	3.9	159,616	5.3	103,501	5.0
Over-the-counter securities	106,352	1.9	53,993	1.1	61,066	1.5	57,415	1.9	29,386	1.4
Mutual funds	126,730	2.2	46,595	.9	24,494	.6	22,309	.7	7,061	.4
Money market instruments	83,005	1.5	45,708	.9	6,902	.2	—	—	—	—
Total commissions	1,523,291	26.8	1,132,898	22.5	928,645	23.0	1,012,176	33.5	641,858	31.3
Interest:										
Margin loans	462,127	8.1	450,566	9.0	619,401	15.3	447,182	14.8	340,475	16.6
Securities owned and deposits	905,679	15.9	856,988	17.0	676,778	16.8	433,694	14.3	296,097	14.4
Resale agreements	424,672	7.5	636,426	12.7	539,292	13.3	249,999	8.3	178,177	8.7
Total interest	1,792,478	31.5	1,943,980	38.7	1,835,471	45.4	1,130,875	37.4	814,749	39.7
Principal transactions:										
Money market instruments	18,079	.3	23,163	.5	15,103	.4	12,263	.4	4,868	.2
Governments and agencies	45,710	.8	143,434	2.8	60,687	1.5	22,472	.7	17,387	.9
Corporates	399,430	7.0	289,308	5.8	223,285	5.5	210,205	7.0	174,136	8.5
Municipals	212,308	3.8	200,307	4.0	128,804	3.2	55,950	1.9	35,233	1.7
Total principal transactions	675,527	11.9	656,212	13.1	427,879	10.6	300,890	10.0	231,624	11.3
Investment banking:										
Underwriting and advisory fees	247,743	4.3	206,934	4.1	147,051	3.6	106,410	3.5	79,006	3.9
Selling concessions	498,895	8.8	388,581	7.7	212,830	5.3	172,768	5.7	83,647	4.1
Total investment banking	746,638	13.1	595,515	11.8	359,881	8.9	279,178	9.2	162,653	8.0
Real estate:										
Brokerage	272,980	4.8	160,397	3.2	100,555	2.5	39,940	1.3	8,586	.4
Relocation Fees	64,951	1.1	56,863	1.1	45,209	1.1	28,729	1.0	28,758	1.4
Other	54,104	1.0	27,791	.6	21,995	.6	17,698	.6	15,679	.8
Total real estate	392,035	6.9	245,051	4.9	167,759	4.2	86,367	2.9	53,023	2.6

Insurance:										
Life	60,895	1.1	55,992	1.1	52,514	1.3	47,325	1.6	42,780	2.1
Annuities	46,975	.8	52,616	1.0	37,352	.9	13,426	.4	6,561	.3
Mortgage guaranty	—	—	—	—	20,251	.5	23,237	.8	20,867	1.0
Other	8,501	.1	7,863	.2	6,196	.2	6,507	.2	6,800	.3
Total insurance	116,371	2.0	116,471	2.3	116,313	2.9	90,495	3.0	77,008	3.7
Other	440,566	7.8	336,074	6.7	202,234	5.0	122,492	4.0	71,081	3.4
Total revenues	5,686,906	100.0	5,026,201	100.0	4,038,182	100.0	3,022,473	100.0	2,051,996	100.0
Expenses:										
Compensation and benefits	2,266,278	39.8	1,732,483	34.5	1,295,255	32.1	1,079,283	35.7	736,728	35.9
Interest	1,432,555	25.2	1,607,915	32.0	1,511,103	37.4	879,002	29.1	638,498	31.1
Occupancy and equipment rental	325,349	5.7	243,836	4.8	168,556	4.2	123,817	4.1	100,671	4.9
Communications	230,331	4.1	188,725	3.8	151,471	3.7	113,610	3.8	90,025	4.4
Advertising and market development	229,537	4.0	155,818	3.1	138,772	3.4	101,185	3.3	60,006	2.9
Brokerage, clearing, and exchange fees	143,824	2.5	121,645	2.4	93,578	2.3	83,028	2.7	57,060	2.8
Office supplies and postage	106,309	1.9	88,930	1.8	75,746	1.9	53,752	1.8	40,014	2.0
Insurance policyholder benefits	49,887	.9	27,865	.6	28,135	.7	24,087	.8	19,554	1.0
Other	356,514	6.3	303,739	6.0	242,151	6.0	203,180	6.7	116,721	5.6
Nonrecurring charges	153,500	2.7	—	—	—	—	—	—	—	—
Total expenses	5,294,084	93.1	4,470,956	89.0	3,704,767	91.7	2,660,944	88.0	1,859,277	90.6
Earnings before income taxes	392,822	6.9	555,245	11.0	333,415	8.3	361,529	12.0	192,719	9.4
Income taxes	162,659	2.9	246,414	4.9	130,541	3.3	160,460	5.3	75,773	3.7
Net earnings	$ 230,163	4.0%	$ 308,831	6.1%	$ 202,874	5.0%	$ 201,069	6.7%	$ 116,946	5.7%
Earnings per share:										
Primary	$ 2.68		$ 3.79		$ 2.57		$ 2.72		$ 1.60	
Fully diluted	$ 2.69		$ 3.74		$ 2.57		$ 2.71		$ 1.60	
Average shares used in computing earnings per share:										
Primary	86,410,000		82,744,000		80,920,000		74,088,000		72,892,000	
Fully diluted	92,178,000		84,478,000		80,950,000		74,354,000		72,892,000	

Per share and share amounts have been restated to reflect the two-for-one common stock split that was distributed in June 1983.

case 16
Sambo's Restaurants

1 In the latter part of 1979, Sambo's, a family restaurant chain which, by anyone's standard, had a phenomenal growth story, found itself installing a new management team. The new executives were chosen by City Investing Corp., a large conglomerate, who had acquired a 16 percent interest in Sambo's after Sambo had slid into technical default on its long-term debt. With its investment in Sambo's, City Investing acquired a company facing numerous lawsuits from previous owners and managers as well as boycott threats from certain minority groups. The chain's name was still the target of activists as they proclaimed it was a racial slur against blacks due to the children's story "Little Black Sambo." Manager turnover was high, and profits were on a rapid decline.

2 Despite all these problems, the "Kings of Turnarounds" said the investment in Sambo's was a gift toward the future.

Trade of Business

3 Sambo's Restaurants, Inc., (see Exhibits 1 and 2) operates family-styled restaurants at affordable prices. Most of the restaurants have a standard decor, menus, and hours of operation (24 hours). As of January 1, 1981, Sambo's operated 1,118 restaurants in all but three states. Approximately 84 percent of these restaurants are operated under individual restaurant joint venture (IRJV) agreements. Sambo's is the managing agent in all cases and returns at least 50 percent interest in each of most cases.

4 As managing agent, the company provides the restaurants with most of the food and related products they use. The company charges the restaurants all of the actual expenses incurred at the restaurant level. The company also provides operational, accounting, advertising, and management-related services and charges each restaurant a proportionate share of these expenses based on sales.

5 In addition to their restaurant operations, Sambo's is involved in equipment leasing, real estate, insurance, and product distribution. Their primary purpose in having these supplemental operations is to complement their restaurant operations and create for themselves a competitive edge. These supplemental operations allow Sambo's to take advantage of substantial volume discounts and cost efficiencies.

The research and written case information were presented at a Case Research Symposium and were evaluated by the Case Research Association's Editorial Board. This case was prepared by A. J. Strickland and graduate research assistant Bob Louis, both of the University of Alabama.

Exhibit 1

Exhibit 2

Company Background

6 Founded in 1957 by Sam D. Battistone and F. Newell Bohnett, Sambo's began with one coffee shop on the beach in Santa Barbara, California. In 1967, Sam D. Battistone, Jr., at the age of 27, took charge of the small chain of restaurants. Under his management, within a mere five years, the fledgling chain of Sambo's blossomed from a privately held $3 million-a-year regional operation, primarily in California, to become a $68 million publicly held enterprise with units across the western United States.

7 At the age of 33, Sam D. Battistone, Jr., had what most men work for all their lives. As president of Sambo's Restaurants, Inc., he was successful and rich with almost $10 million in Sambo's stock. The May 1, 1976, issue of *Forbes* referred to him as a "prodigal son."

8 In 1973, the young Battistone left Sambo's to venture on his own. However, he was still active in the company—he was still a member of the board of directors and still managed the family's extensive California real estate holdings. On his own, he formed a new company, Invest West Sports, which soon owned, among other operations, 50 percent of a World Football League team, an interest in the New Orleans franchise of the National Basketball Association, and a rather large group of sports camps. Venturing on his own, though, wasn't as fruitful as the young Battistone had envisioned. By 1975, he was looking at million-dollar losses, rather than the million-dollar gains he had been accustomed to at the helm of Sambo's.

9 During Battistone's leave of absence, however, Sambo's continued to grow under his successor, Wayne Kees. By 1975, the chain had 526 restaurants with earnings increasing at the phenomenal rate of 46 percent *each year* since 1965. During 1975,

Exhibit 3

Growth of units

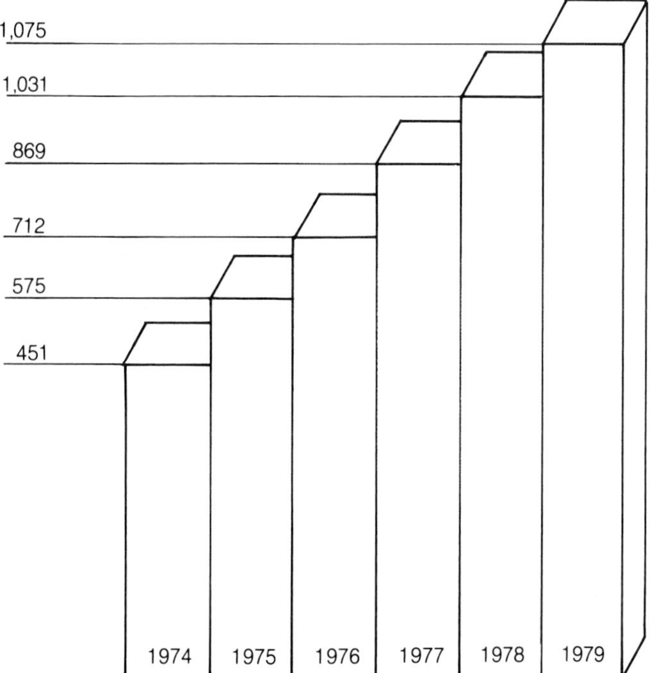

Number of Sambo's units open, 1974-1979

earnings were up over 37 percent to $17.6 million on a sales increase of $138 million. (See Exhibit 3.)

10 In January, 1976, Wayne Kees, at the age of 53, suddenly decided to retire at the same time Battistone returned to take over Sambo's active management. Company executives insisted it was only coincidental that Kees decided to retire at the same time Battistone was to return.

11 Battistone, upon returning to the presidency of Sambo's, commented to a *Forbes* writer, "When I left to do other things, that was something I had to do. I love the restaurant business. Those three years gave me a chance to look at Sambo's objectives of wanting to do in our segment of the industry what McDonald's did in theirs."

12 During 1976, Sambo's stock was listed on the New York Stock Exchange, and the chain had approximately 750 restaurant units located in 40 states. Although Sambo's was having remarkable earnings growth, Battistone was concerned about the level of traffic growth at the chain's units. Battistone commented:

> We have been a volume control oriented company all along. Since our founding, we always felt that the basic way to run a restaurant is to control food costs,

> and by the word-of-mouth advertising, you'll continue to grow. But we also realize that as you become larger and the competition becomes greater, you have to market your product. I like the opportunity of moving from a cost-controlled company to being a marketing one. The way we're organized, any additional volume we had really makes a difference because it comes right down to the bottom line. It's much better than being a volume-orientated company looking for controls.

13 In 1976, Battistone increased the marketing expenditure rate to 2.75 percent of gross revenues, up a full percentage point from the 1.75% being charged previously. In addition, he hired Arthur G. Gunther, a marketing expert from McDonald's, to help bolster Sambo's marketing effort. Battistone felt that the increased advertising would lead to an annual growth in the restaurants' sales volume of 5 percent.

14 As Sambo's continued to prosper, Battistone became more and more concerned about trying to maintain the impressive growth record they had experienced in the past. The earnings growth record served as a model for the entire restaurant industry.

Sambo's Fraction-of-the-Action Blueprint

15 Sambo's strategy for growth was concentration with limited backward vertical integration. Sambo's objective was straightforward—they simply wanted to be the nation's fastest-growing restaurant chain. The strategy for growth was developed by Battistone, Sr., and was termed *Fraction of the Action.*

16 In late 1957, with the opening of their second unit, the two cofounders sold 20 percent of the original Santa Barbara Sambo's to the first manager/partner for $20,000. They believed there must be a sharing of profits as an intrinsic feature of the organization if they were eventually to grow into a major chain. The first manager was also given the opportunity to invest again, this time in the new unit. This concept remained intact through the early years—the operating manager/partner purchasing 20 percent for $20,000, the corporation usually retaining 50 percent, and other managers and field supervisors having to purchase shares in the remaining 30 percent. This remaining 30 percent was put into a pool, which included similar 30 percent interests in the other restaurant, and then "investment units" from this pool were sold for $5,000 each.

17 The manager's 20 percent stake together with his investment units made him more than just an employee by giving him a share in the restaurant's profits. By 1974, the return on investments were averaging 50 percent a year. According to Wayne Kees, "Our boys know they can make it big and retire after a few years if they want. They promote themselves, each other, the chain, and they work like dogs." Kees cited four territorial managers, each with a salary of $850 per month, who were making more than $100,000 a year from their investments.

18 During 1976, the average store was showing a 66 percent profit. This percent of profit was unheard of in the restaurant business, but it was accomplished, in part, by Sambo's keeping the manager's salary very low. Battistone commented about the salaries:

> The original salary of a partner/manager was only $500 a month, and after 20 years, that salary was still only $750 a month. We eliminated entirely a

certain segment of the population from even wanting to come into our management because the salaries were so low.

19 A person who invests in his own business, who has a chance to participate in the profit of his own restaurant, who has his own capital involved, who can build an estate and invest in his own future is better off than a salaried or bonus person.

20 However, we also had to pay a livable wage along with those benefits for everyday living.

This unique management-incentive program virtually eliminated turnover. In addition, the program has received credit for holding marketing costs down to 1.75 percent of total sales, compared to 3 percent to 5 percent as an industry average. The 50 percent interest that Sambo's kept gave management control over its restaurants. No less important was the initial $20,000 from each manager and the $5,000 each investment unit generated. These contributions provided substantial capital for the company's expansion purposes.

21 The incentive plan, though, did have some drawbacks. The most important was the need to keep growing at an increasing rate, because unless more restaurants were added, there could be no investment units to reward managers. The growth situation was compounded because sales and profits tend to reach a certain level and then hold there. For Sambo's, each unit was expected to reach a net profit level of $50,000 a year and then remain at that level. (See Exhibit 4.)

Exhibit 4

SAMBO'S RESTAURANTS, INC.
Consolidated Statements of Earnings
For the Years Ended December 31, 1974–1977

	1977	*1976*	*1975*	*1974*
Revenues:				
Restaurant sales	$453,058,000	$348,443,000	$118,401,821	
Food and restaurant supply sales (non-owned)	19,299,000	19,344,000	11,957,804	$ 8,692,157
Sales of interests in restaurant joint ventures	15,962,000	7,700,000	6,460,000	5,092,000
Other income	3,434,000	4,831,000	2,124,042	2,845,190
Total revenues	491,753,000	380,318,000	138,943,667	100,871,721
Costs and expenses:				
Cost of sales:				
Restaurant sales	284,864,000	212,757,000		
Food and restaurant supply sales	18,453,000	18,571,000		
Operating, general, and administrative	111,608,000	81,968,000		
Minority interests in income-restaurant joint ventures	20,237,000	20,719,000		
Depreciation and amortization	12,527,000	7,625,000	4,753,383	3,414,359
Interests	4,388,000	722,000	655,059	320,225
Total expenses	452,077,000	342,362,000	108,263,089	77,333,669
Earnings before income taxes	39,676,000	37,956,000	30,680,578	23,538,052
Income taxes	15,330,000	14,890,000	13,040,000	10,692,000
Net earnings	$ 24,346,000	$ 23,066,000	$ 17,640,578	$ 12,846,052
Earnings per common share	$ 1.90	$ 1.80	$ 1.48	$ 1.09

22 One new restaurant manager made the following comment shortly after he left Sambo's: "They run a lot of people through this (hiring and training) program compared to the number they get out of it. They are getting a lot of cheap labor, if you ask me, and they seem to be looking for people with money to buy investment units, not people with management ability."

23 Restaurant managers are recruited from many occupations, from gas station operators to teachers. The majority of personnel recruited are, according to a Sambo's executive, willing to work hard to achieve a goal.

24 After a detailed training program covering everything from dishwashing to management, the new manager is ready to begin work in the field under the watchful eye of a veteran manager.

25 Each new manager tends to have a common style after completing the training program. Regardless of the manager's age, each seems to spend no more than 10 years managing a restaurant. The training classes also hear many stories about managers who worked for only a few years and then "retired" at $40,000 a year. This incentive made the promote-from-within policy work extremely well.

26 Obtaining the $20,000 down payment required to purchase the 20 percent interest seemed to deter some managers from starting up at Sambo's, but most banks were willing to loan the money, on an unsecured basis, since the rate-of-return-on-an-investment track record for Sambo's was so sound.

A Changing Course

27 1977 came and was projected to be another banner year for Sambo's. But instead of being a record-breaking year, 1977 proved to be one of the darkest periods for Sambo's. Top management and Battistone himself realized that Fraction-of-the-Action and the company's continued success were on a collision course. When Battistone, Sr., started the unique incentive plan, he misjudged how successful the plan would be. The continuance of capitalizing each store at $100,000 over the years resulted in a powerful leveraging situation, also partly brought on due to the unrealistic overhead charges that were being made. The result was that in 1976, the average store was showing a $66,000 profit or 66 percent return on investment. As the managers purchased additional investment units, they grew to expect the same 66 percent return. It was not long until top management realized it could not keep the high rate of return going in the future. Owen Johnson, senior vice president and treasurer, commented to Madelin Schnider in a leading trade journal: "It was unfair to employees, stockholders, and customers to offer this kind of motivation to managers. We were hesitant to tamper with something that was working, and yet, it was an unreasonable return on investment. It had to be changed." And change it did.

New Compensation Program

28 In August 1977, Sambo's introduced a new compensation package for managers that substantially changed the 20-year-old Fraction-of-the-Action program. The plan was to give Sambo's a leading edge for managerial talent in an industry where competition for such talent had heightened. The new plan was to provide more immediate

benefits for the restaurant managers and their families; retain the opportunity for ownership participation for the individual managers; and to be more consistent with the fair return to Sambo's shareholders. The program consisted of upgrading manager base salaries from the original $9,000 annual amount to a new range of $15,000 to $21,600 a year. Quarterly bonuses were also granted for superior profit performance. The combined salary and bonus packaged aids nearly doubled the direct compensation managers received under the old program.

29 The "new deal" also included greater life insurance coverage as well as extended medical coverage for all members of the managers' families.

30 The managers were still allowed to purchase interests in their restaurants, but some significant changes were made in the program. Under this new program, managers were entitled to purchase a 1 percent interest in their restaurants as well as the right to invest in units of other restaurants. The interest-purchasing price was increased from the old $1,000 per 1 percent of interest to $3,000 per percent of interest investment.

31 Managers who were employed at the time of the change were given the choice of continuing under the old plan or selling part of their interests back to the company and participate in the new compensation program. The new system was considered one of the best in the industry, but compared to the old program, it was not seen as desirable by many.

32 Nearly 250 managers left the company upon hearing the proposed changes. Management was concerned what effect such a large turnover rate among its managers might have on the company's operation. After much debate, they decided to keep the new program. The old program was seen as too risky, due to an informal investigation by the SEC into the income-recording procedures for the capital contributed by the managers in obtaining their interest shares. The SEC concluded the company could no longer record this cash flow as income if Sambo's wished to maintain the option to repurchase the interests of those managers who left. The ruling as well as the desire to make appropriate changes for the future led Sambo's to stay with the new program. The abandonment of the old plan, which had been the keystone of their growth success, led to a chain of events that was to plague the company for many years to come.

Effect of the Change

33 Fiscal year 1978 was looked upon with great enthusiasm by company officials. They felt the new compensation program would stop the manager turnover problem and get the company back on its path of profits, but the financial picture for 1978 would be dampened by rumors of pending mergers and litigation from former managers/investors in the old programs. To help combat the sluggishness of the firm's profits, Battistone formed an advisory board made up of selected unit managers and made several significant alterations to the company's operations.

34 Menu selection was greatly enlarged to better meet the wants and demands of the American public. Children's dishes and many regional specialty dishes were added to the menu. The changes were heavily promoted, mostly through the medium of television. Sambo's commercials were run in over 150 separate market areas covering

Exhibit 5

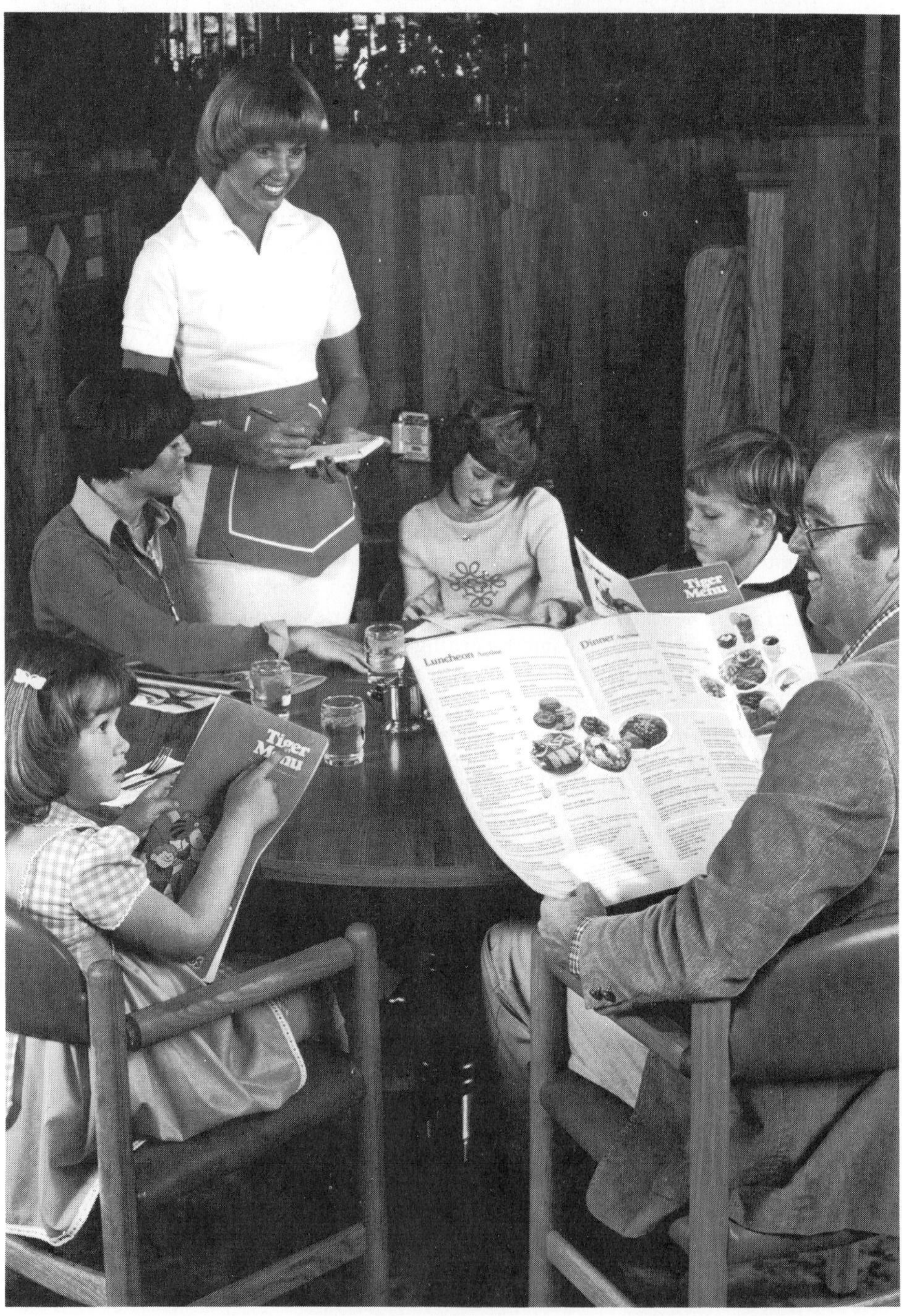

all the states in which the company operated. The Sambo's theme, "Just what the family ordered," was effectively distributed through all mass-media channels. The new expanded regular menu had over 180 separate items and an entire new dessert menu (see Exhibit 5).

35 Complementing the menu-expansion program, several of the Sambo's units underwent major renovation while others incorporated minor changes in an attempt to create a more-relaxed environment and dining pleasure. The more-extensive remodeling incorporated the latest design and decor concepts of Sambo's newest and most-successful restaurant. Such changes as new lighting, carpeting, and color schemes created a relaxing mood, while layout changes and installation of state-of-the-art equipment were aimed at increasing production efficiency to reduce operating costs. In 1978 alone, over $10 million was spent on leasehold improvements.

Worsening Conditions

36 Despite the valiant efforts put forth by the company's management, 1978 was a poor financial year with net earnings dropping more than $15 million from the previous year to a low of $7.56 million (see Exhibit 6). The manager-turnover problem was a major contributor to the poor financial showing. It was estimated that during the year, more than half of the company's restaurants were staffed by inexperienced managers, which led to a particularly high level of operating costs. The decision to retain a larger percentage ownership in new restaurants led to a rather drastic reduction in revenue and profits from sales of restaurant interests in the latter half of the year. Due to liquidity problems, the board of directors voted to not declare dividends in the first half of 1979 and to reevaluate the dividend policy at that time for future periods.

Litigation Proceedings

37 During 1978 and 1979, the number of legal proceedings against Sambo's rose significantly, most of them relating to the disposing of the Fraction-of-the-Action compensation program. Former restaurant managers contended that: (1) changes in the compensation program had adverse effects on the managers' retirement plans; (2) certain charges by the company to the restaurant joint ventures were excessive; (3) unreasonable restraints of trade were in effect under the company's distribution procedures; and (4) there were improper accountings by the company as to the financial interests of the subject restaurants.

38 In addition to these suits, pending legal action was evident in some states as to whether the company could continue to use its name in its restaurant business. Many racial advocates claimed the name was a direct racial slur against blacks. The company denied these allegations, claiming "Sambo's" was a combination of the names of its two founders, Sam Battistone, Sr., and F. Newell Bohnett. In the near future, the company would have to decide whether to "fight or switch" in its attempt to keep the name of Sambo's.

Exhibit 6

Sambo's stock price profile, 1971–1979 (SRI versus S&P 400)

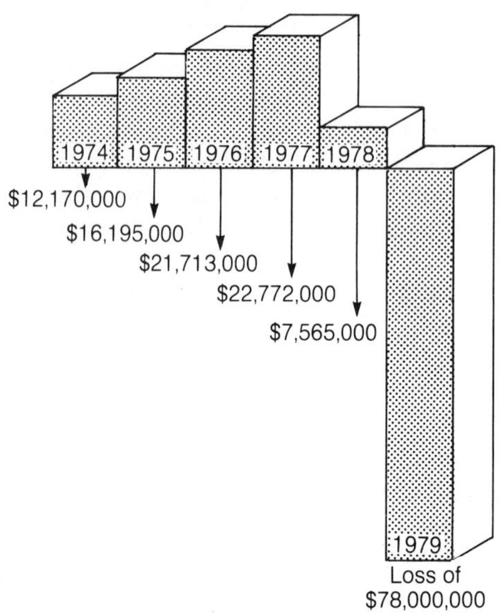

Sambo's stock price profile, 1971-1979
SRI vs S&P 400

S&P 400

Sambo's (SRI)

Stock prices ($)

140.0
120.0
100.0
80.0
60.0
40.0
20.0
0.0

1971 1972 1973 1974 1975 1976 1977 1978 1979

Prices over time period

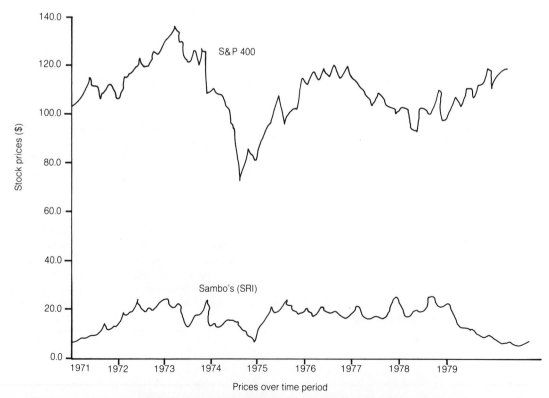

The diagram pictures prices paid for Sambo's stock over a nine-year period. Above, an older unit.

Troubles Lead to New Management

39 The first half of 1979 was disastrous for Sambo's as its losses were well over $20 million and its liquidity position was suspect at best. In June of 1979, the company was unable to meet the financial rate requirements and other conditions that were set forth in the long-term debt covenants. These long-term liabilities of approximately $100 million had to be reclassified as current liabilities. The default led to the unseating of Battistone as chief executive officer. His successor, Karl V. Willig, was named in July to succeed him, but Willig would hold the post only for a very brief time, just five months, before he, too, would be replaced.

40 In November 1979, Sambo's sold 593,875 shares of a new series of cumulative, convertible, voting preferred stock to GDV, Inc., an 80 percent owned subsidiary of City Investing Corp. The preferred stock represented an approximate ownership interest of 16 percent of the common stock outstanding. Along with the ownership interest came the right to name new management. City Investing installed the "Kings of Turnaround" as Sambos new management. This group of turnaround experts was spearheaded by Daniel E. Shanghnessy, who with his crew, had worked a managerial miracle while at Motel 6, a budget motel operation.

41 The new management team found a formidable task. The 1979 loss figure was $77.8 million which in Shanghnessy's words was "an abominable performance." Knowing that time is of utmost importance in turning the performance of a floundering company around, the new team embarked on a strategy to reduce company losses and get Sambo's back on their feet financially.

42 Key elements of their strategy included slashing general and administrative expenses; severely cutting marketing, training, and headquarters support personnel; revisions of menus to emphasize higher-margin items and to enable the units to increase their selling prices; and the development of local marketing programs to aid in increasing sales volume in low-volume restaurant units.

43 The administrative cuts led to the disappearance of district managers. In altering its structure to meet the new situation, the chain was divided up territorially with regional vice presidents responsible for groups of 100 or more restaurants. Disgusted unit managers left the chain and were replaced primarily by lower-paid high-school graduates. The estimated savings from the cost-cutting strategy amounted to approximately $40 million for 1980.

Further Alterations

44 In the early spring of 1980, Sambo's again revised their compensation program. The new package significantly reduced the amount of monetary compensation available to unit management. The plan, now based on sales volume rather than profit level, was again greeted unfavorably by managers.

45 In July, Sambo's received another cash infusion from City Investing, via its GDV, Inc., subsidiary, of just over $15 million in exchange for 1,034,483 shares of convertible, preferred stock. This investment raised GDV's interest level to approximately 34 percent.

46 Another cost-cutting procedure was instated in 1980 by Shanghnessy and his "cost bandits" as they raised the administrative overhead charge to the individual units from 1.6 percent to 5.1 percent of sales, an increase of nearly 225 percent, in an attempt to meet the family restaurant image that new management wished to commu-

nicate. Sambo's recruited the former advertising chief at Walt Disney Productions to lead its promotional efforts and hired a foreign-trained chef to aid in bringing its menu "alive."

Improving Results and Optimism

47 The results of Shanghnessy's first six months of 1980 were very commendable. The company reported a loss figure of only $7 million, and it estimated that the total loss for 1980 would be around only $12 million, compared to nearly $78 million in 1979. Though happy with the results of his efforts, Shanghnessy was concerned with overall sales volume, which had, for the first time, dipped below $500,000 on a unit basis. The industry norm at that time was nearly $640,000 per unit. Thus, Shanghnessy embarked on a profit analysis by unit to determine where the problem lay. As suspected, there were numerous poor-performing units, but in spite of this problem, Shanghnessy and his management team were optimistic of future operations. (See Exhibits 7 and 8.)

Exhibit 7

SAMBO'S RESTAURANTS, INC. AND SUBSIDIARIES
Consolidated Statements of Operations
For the Years Ended December 31, 1978–1979, and January 1, 1981
(in thousands of dollars)

	January 1, 1981	*December 31, 1979*	*December 31, 1978*
Revenues:			
Restaurant sales	$489,170	$543,817	$538,629
Food and restaurant supply sales		25,165	22,189
Sales of interests in restaurant joint ventures			13,209
Other income	927	5,411	3,416
Total revenues	490,097	574,393	577,443
Costs and expenses:			
Cost of sales:			
Restaurant sales	321,485	345,468	338,097
Food and restaurant supply sales		24,117	20,442
Operating	91,879	94,475	77,432
Selling, general, and administrative	31,121	105,967	69,950
Minority interests in income (losses) of restaurant joint ventures	(3,484)	6,601	12,054
Depreciation and amortization	31,485	30,352	25,617
Interest, net	29,232	31,981	24,544
Write-downs of assets and provisions for losses		35,211	
Total costs and expenses	501,718	674,172	568,136
Earnings (loss) before income taxes	(11,621)	(99,779)	9,307
Income taxes (credit)		(22,000)	1,742
Net earnings (loss)	$ (11,621)	$ (77,779)	$ 7,565
Earnings (loss) per common share	$ (1.05)	$ (6.06)	$0.59

Exhibit 8

Financial statements

SAMBO'S RESTAURANTS, INC.
Consolidated Balance Sheets
(in thousands of dollars)

	January 1, 1981	*December 31, 1979*
Assets		
Current assets:		
Cash, including temporary cash investments of $51,845 and $25,703	$ 49,204	$ 47,870
Accounts receivable, less allowance for doubtful accounts of $10,087 and $5,819	3,700	5,810
Refundable income tax		8,996
Inventories	19,623	18,495
Prepaid expenses and other	4,127	1,860
Total current assets	76,654	83,031
Property and equipment, partially pledged:		
Land	27,637	27,586
Buildings and improvements	47,992	53,890
Leasehold improvements	36,636	27,922
Furniture, fixtures, and equipment	166,854	162,591
	279,119	271,989
Less accumulated depreciation	84,514	64,798
Net property and equipment	194,605	207,191
Leased property under capital leases:		
Land	406	406
Buildings	198,718	187,786
Furniture, fixtures, and equipment	8,570	9,734
	207,694	197,926
Less accumulated amortization	46,998	37,623
Net leased property under capital leases	160,696	160,303
Other assets:		
Investments in repurchased restaurant joint venture interests, at cost, less accumulated amortization of $885 and $401	4,588	2,583
Deposits and miscellaneous assets	5,355	5,506
Total other assets	9,943	8,089
Total assets	$441,898	$458,614

Exhibit 8 *(continued)*

	January 1, 1981	*December 31, 1979*
Liabilities and Shareholders' Equity		
Current liabilities:		
Notes payable to banks		$ 17,846
Long-term debt reclassified		97,400
Accounts payable	$ 20,015	59,494
Accrued expenses	33,360	31,598
Current maturities of long-term debt and obligations under capital leases	12,933	6,963
Total current liabilities	66,308	213,301
Long-term debt	115,691	5,426
Obligations under capital leases	191,749	188,116
Deferred income taxes	1,389	1,389
Other long-term liabilities, commitments, and contingencies	13,000	
Shareholders' equity:		
Preferred stock	28,659	13,659
Common stock, issued and outstanding, 12,841,518 shares	7,063	7,063
Additional paid-in capital	28,931	28,931
Retained earnings (deficit)	(10,892)	729
Total shareholders' equity	53,761	50,382
Total liabilities and shareholders equity	$441,898	$458,614

Wall Street Reactions

48 Wall Street professionals recognized in 1980 that Sambo's was definitely a leading candidate for a turnaround from its problems and losses of the past few years. Their notion was heavily based on the fact that City Investing had a reputation of buying up companies that represented potential future improvement and gains as well as the fact that the management team installed by City Investing was notorious as cost-cutters and turnaround specialists. The public confidence in Sambo's also seemed to rise in 1980 as the market price of its common stock rose from a low of 3½ to approximately 8 by the latter part of the year. According to an investment analyst, Sambo's stock was an attractive speculation vehicle.

Exhibit 8 *(continued)*

SAMBO'S RESTAURANTS, INC.
Consolidated Statements of Changes in Financial Position
For the Years Ended December 31, 1978–1979, and January 1, 1982
(in thousands of dollars)

	January 1, 1981	*December 31, 1979*	*December 31, 1978*
Sources of working capital:			
Net earnings (loss)	$ (11,621)	$ (77,779)	$ 7,565
Items which do not use working capital:			
Depreciation and amortization of property and equipment	20,290	19,217	16,331
Net capitalized lease expense	3,542	3,327	1,257
Deferred income taxes		(9,201)	4,880
Write-downs of assets		29,184	
Other, net	575	1,692	1,790
Working capital provided by (used in) operations	12,786	(33,560)	31,823
Effect of debt restructuring	115,246		
Proceeds from sale of property and equipment	532	6,146	5,879
Proceeds from term loans			5,000
Proceeds from mortgage financing		876	5,822
Mortgage assumptions	2,547		
Net change in revolving credit loans		1,300	21,300
Proceeds from sale of preferred stock	15,000	13,659	
Other, net	16,119	7,313	(8,425)
Total sources	162,230	(4,266)	61,399
Applications of working capital:			
Reclassification of long-term debt		92,150	
New properties	2,814	15,879	79,205
Replacements and rehabilitations	11,784	10,295	6,000
Current installments of restructured debt	4,000		
Current installments and repayments of mortgage obligations	3,016	4,366	2,703
Cash dividends declared			7,705
Total applications	21,614	122,690	95,613
Increase (decrease) in working capital	$140,616	$(126,956)	$(34,214)
Changes in components of working capital:			
Increase (decrease) in current assets:			
Cash	$ 1,334	$ 36,709	$(32,434)
Accounts receivable	(2,110)	(5,056)	(4,344)
Refundable income taxes	(8,996)	(810)	9,096
Inventories	1,128	(14,796)	13,983
Prepaid expenses and other	2,267	183	18
(Increase) decrease in current liabilities:			
Notes payable	17,846	(5,846)	(8,725)
Long-term debt reclassified	97,400	(97,400)	
Accounts payable	39,479	(33,174)	(7,321)
Accrued expenses	(1,762)	(8,325)	(2,656)
Current maturities of long-term obligations	(5,970)	1,559	(1,831)
Increase (decrease) in working capital	$140,616	$(126,956)	$(34,214)

Exhibit 8 ***(concluded)***

SAMBO'S RESTAURANTS, INC.
Consolidated Statements of Shareholders' Equity
For the Years Ended December 31, 1978–79, and January 1, 1982
(in thousands of dollars)

	January 1, 1981	*December 31, 1979*	*December 31, 1989*
Preferred stock, no par value, authorized 2,000,000 shares:			
$1.84 cumulative convertible (on a four-for-one basis into common stock) voting; liquidation preference $23 per share; 593,875 shares issued (during fiscal 1979) and outstanding	$ 13,659	$13,659	
$1.45 cumulative convertible (on a four-for-one basis into common stock) voting; liquidation preference $14.50 per share; 1,034,483 shares issued (during fiscal 1980) and outstanding	15,000		
Total preferred stock at end of year	28,659	13,659	
Common Stock, no par value (stated value, $.55 a share); authorized 43,000,00 shares; issued and outstanding, 12,841,518 shares at beginning and end of each year	7,063	7,063	$ 7,063
Additional paid-in capital, balance at beginning and end of each year	28,931	28,931	28,931
Retained earnings (deficit):			
Balance at beginning of year	729	78,508	78,648
Net earnings (loss) for the year	$(11,621)	(77,779)	7,565
Cash dividends—$.60 per share			(7,705)
Balance at end of year (deficit)	(10,892)	729	78,508
Total shareholders' equity at end of year	$ 53,761	$50,382	$114,502

case 17
The Georgia-Pacific Comply Dilemma

The Problem

1 In 1979, management at Georgia-Pacific Corporation, a manufacturer of forest products, was considering the introduction of a new item into its product line. Called comply, it was a wood product substitute for plywood that utilized more of the tree than did traditional plywood products. Comply was, therefore, considered a more-efficient use of resources.

2 The efficient use of timber resources was a factor of growing importance for Georgia-Pacific. Studies had shown that demand for timber was increasing more rapidly than was the available supply. Although comply seemed to help alleviate the scarcity problem, it had only recently been developed. A complete study of comply, along with assessments of Georgia-Pacific's strengths and weaknesses, the wood products industry, and Georgia-Pacific's competitors, was necessary before a decision regarding full-scale production could be made.

The Company

3 Georgia-Pacific Corporation was founded in Atlanta, Georgia, in 1927 by Owen R. Cheatham for an investment of $12,000. In its early years, Georgia-Pacific grew steadily, becoming an industry giant through explosive expansion between 1955 and 1965. The company increased its size by seven times during that period.

4 The Federal Trade Commission considered the tremendous growth to have resulted from Georgia-Pacific illegally restraining competition within the softwood-plywood industry. Thus in 1972, Georgia-Pacific was forced to agree to the sale of 20 percent of its assets. These assets were used to form a new independent corporation, Louisiana-Pacific. At birth, Louisiana-Pacific was the sixth-largest domestic producer of lumber. The agreement also prohibited Georgia-Pacific from acquiring an interest in any softwood-plywood producer in the United States for 10 years and limited its purchases of timberland.

5 Despite this setback, Georgia-Pacific's management continued to pursue a policy of growth and diversification related to the core business of wood products, and it quickly grew as a truly diversified natural resources firm. Its holdings included gypsum,

---

This case was prepared by Professor John A. Pearce II of the University of South Carolina with the assistance of Alfred V. Brown, Margaret H. Brown, and Daniel D. McVicker. It has been accepted for publication in the *Journal of Management Case Studies*.

coal, natural gas, oil, and 6 million acres of timberlands—assets totaling more than $4.4 billion. The company diversified into three major areas: (1) building products, (2) pulp and paper, and (3) chemicals. Diversification did not slow the growth of the company's core business, wood products, which grew to include: plywood, particleboard, lumber, paper bags and sacks, corrugated packaging, facial and bathroom tissue, paper plates, check safety paper, and package labels.

6 By 1979, Georgia-Pacific had sales of more than $3.7 billion and had grown into the nation's 56th-largest industrial corporation with over 200 plants in the United States, Canada, Indonesia, Brazil, and the Philippines. It also had 151 building materials distribution centers across the United States, as well as numerous sales offices throughout the world. Through the strengths of its distribution system and material resources base, Georgia-Pacific had become the largest producer of forest products in the world. It ranked first in plywood production, third in lumber production, third in gypsum production, and eighth in paper production. It was also trying to become a dominant force in the chemical business.

7 Management saw the opportunity to enter the chemical business as a natural outgrowth of its manufacture of plywood, pulp, and paper products. Many chemicals were produced as by-products, and many more were used in the manufacturing processes. In 1959, Georgia-Pacific built its first resin plant to supply its building products manufacturing operations, and by 1975, the firm's chemical division supplied most of the major chemicals necessary for its building products and paper manufacturing operations. Production in excess of company needs (approximately two thirds of total production) was sold to outside customers. Chemicals manufactured included phenol, methanol, acetone, chlorine, caustic soda, polyvinyl chloride, household bleaches and detergents, swimming pool chemicals, alcohol, sulfuric acid, turpentine, and charcoal. Top management regarded its diversified product offering as one of the company's big strengths. Company sales by industry for the years 1975–79 are shown in Exhibit 1.

8 In its efforts to become a leader in the wood industry, Georgia-Pacific made several major decisions which seemed very risky at the time. In 1946, the company began manufacturing plywood in Washington. Plywood was a new product at that time, and industry competitors felt it lacked profit potential. Georgia-Pacific began manufacturing plywood from hardwoods in 1949 and, in 1963, was the first company to successfully produce plywood from southern pine trees. By the end of 1979, Georgia-Pacific was the largest manufacturer of plywood and plywood products in the world.

9 Another strategic decision which helped to strengthen Georgia-Pacific was its move into actual ownership of timber. The company purchased its first lumber company in Oregon in 1951 and, by 1979, controlled about 6 million acres of timberlands throughout the world. Within the company, this timber became known as "green gold." These vast timber holdings supplied the company's resource needs, eased the dependence on government and private landowners, and served as collateral for the firm's financial activities. The decision to purchase timberlands exemplified management's drive for self-sufficiency in the resources needed to operate. Although the company's forest resource base was among the largest in the industry, an active timber and forest acquisition program ensured its continued expansion. Top management considered timberland a sound investment because it made the company more self-sufficient and financially stronger since the timberholdings tended to appreciate in value.

10 Along with expansion of timberholdings came recognition of the need for the prudent

Exhibit 1

Sales by industry segment for the period 1975–1979

Sales (millions)	*1975*		*1976*		*1977*		*1978*		*1979*	
Building products:										
Plywood	$ 713	30%	$ 960	32%	$1,222	33%	1343	30%	1338	26%
Lumber	429	18	660	22	884	24	1178	27	1283	25
Gypsum	95	4	117	4	160	4	203	5	229	4
Other	191	8	244	7	275	8	393	9	478	9
Total	$1,428	60	$1,981	65	$2,541	69	$3,117	71	$3,328	64
Pulp, paper, and paperboard products	691	29	763	25	780	21	875	20	1,269	25
Chemicals	183	8	243	8	301	8	344	8	542	10
Other operations	57	3	51	2	53	2	67	1	68	1
Total sales	$2,359	100%	$3,038	100%	$3,675	100%	$4,403	100%	$5,207	100%

Source: Georgia-Pacific, 1981 Annual Report to Shareholders on Operating and Financial Results, p. 22; and Georgia-Pacific, 1977 Annual Report to Shareholders on Operating and Results, p. 29.

management and increased utilization of these valuable resources. The company continually looked for new products and better planting and harvesting techniques that would permit more efficient usage of its trees. The company's search for new and innovative products enabled it to be the first in the world to use redwood waste particles in the manufacture of paper. Productivity was also increased through company research in the development of faster-growing, more disease-resistant strains of trees which increased wood yielded per acre. By using wood residuals—such as bark and fine sawdust, which were otherwise economically unusable—to fire boilers in several of the company's plants, the company achieved nearly 50 percent energy self-sufficiency.

11 The corporation's marketing arm for most of its building products was its distribution division. Since competition was based primarily on service, particularly product availability, Georgia-Pacific believed its 151 distribution centers, strategically located to serve U.S. markets, gave it a favorable competitive position. These centers furnished plywood, lumber, gypsum, and other materials to building material dealers, industrial accounts, and major contractors, which helped make Georgia-Pacific a very efficient, high-volume commodity marketer. At the same time, these centers also enabled the company to keep a finger on the pulse of the marketplace. New products could be test-marketed easily by selection of individual distribution centers for new-product introduction. Exhibit 2 shows sales by distribution centers.

Exhibit 2

Dollar sales of Georgia-Pacific's distribution centers

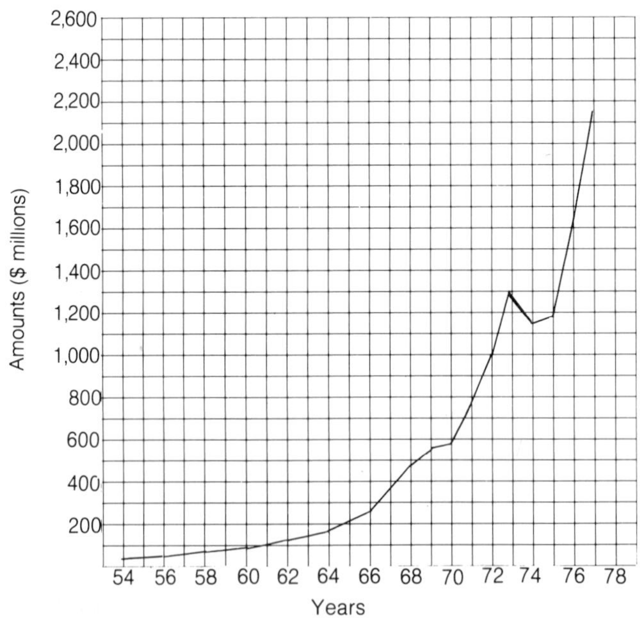

Source: John R. Ross, *Maverick—The Story of Georgia-Pacific Corporation*, 1980, p. 312.

12 From its beginning, Georgia-Pacific enjoyed a good working relationship with the financial community. When Owen Cheatham, the company's founder, needed money to begin his operation, he went to his lenders with a detailed plan and payout schedule. Over time, the firm continued to follow this same practice, which has contributed to its ability to tap financial markets for needed capital.

13 Growth and initiative on the part of management was encouraged by a highly decentralized structure that gave executives and plant managers individual responsibility and freedom to manage their operations in their own ways. Such a management structure also allowed for smooth transitions during management personnel turnover.

14 Georgia-Pacific showed remarkable growth in the 1970s. Their five-year goal to double earnings, begun in 1973, was achieved more than one year early, in 1976. In 1977, Robert Floweree, the chairman of the board, announced another five-year growth plan for the corporation. Sales goals for 1981 were set at $5.25 billion with earnings targeted to reach $430 million, or double the 1976 earnings level. The five-year plan included a $2 billion expenditure goal for plant and equipment. Exhibit 3 shows the breakdown of these expenditures for the years 1977 to 1979.

15 In looking ahead, Georgia-Pacific intended to continue to increase its timber base near its U.S. manufacturing operations, thereby ensuring supply and reducing transportation costs. Since three fourths of its products are sold in the Eastern states, the corporation decided to move its corporate headquarters from Portland, Oregon, to Atlanta, Georgia.

16 Operating profits, as defined by Georgia-Pacific, represented income from operations before corporate, general, and administrative expenses, interest income and expense, and income taxes. Exhibit 4 shows the operating profits by division for the years 1975–79.

17 Georgia-Pacific had consistently maintained a philosophy of growth and expansion.

Exhibit 3

Capital expenditures for 1977–1979 ($ millions)

	1977		*1978*		*1979*	
Property, plant, and equipment:						
Building products:						
New plants, distribution centers, and equipment	$70		$95		$115	
Replacement and modernization	60	$130	70	$165	90	$205
Pulp and paper:						
New plants and equipment	75		45		95	
Replacement and modernization	70	135	50	95	90	185
Chemicals:						
New plants and equipment	90		90		120	
Replacement and modernization	10	100	15	105	10	130
Total property, plant, and equipment		365		365		520
Natural resources:						
Timber and timberlands	75		95		260	
Natural gas and oil properties	10	85	20	115	35	295
Total capital expenditures		$450		$480		$815

Source: Georgia-Pacific, 1982 Annual Report to Shareholders on Operating and Financial Results, p. 21.

Exhibit 4

Operating profits for the period 1975–1979 ($ millions)

Operating profits	*1975*		*1976*		*1977*		*1978*		*1979*	
Building products	$97	34%	$190	47%	$347	69%	$434	73%	$329	52%
Pulp, paper, paperboard	123	42	113	28	50	10	61	10	154	24
Chemicals	60	21	91	22	96	19	87	15	137	22
Other operations	10	3	13	3	11	3	15	2	13	2
Total operating profits	$290	100%	$407	100%	$504	100%	$595	100%	$633	100%

Source: Georgia Pacific, 1981 Annual Report to Shareholders on Operating and Financial Results, p. 22; and Georgia-Pacific; 1977 Annual Report to Shareholders on Operating and Financial Results, p. 29.

The consolidated income statements (Exhibit 5) and balance sheets (Exhibit 6) show the company's performance.

The Industry

18 Georgia-Pacific was directly affected by a variety of economic conditions. Changes in the level of housing starts, commercial building activities, cost of money, inflation, energy shortages, and unemployment all had their impact on the sales and net income of the company.

19 Housing construction had historically been strongly influenced by changes in the nation's population, wealth, and wood prices, all of which affected demand for wood-based products such as housing, furniture, and paper. Exhibit 7 shows the U.S. population from 1920 to 1970, with projections to the year 2000.

20 According to the Department of Commerce, the demand for housing was expected to increase 15 percent annually by the year 2000. New residential construction and home remodeling accounted for about two thirds of all softwood plywood produced. Exhibit 8 shows softwood plywood production from 1970 to 1979. Softwood plywood, used most often in construction, was made from pine and fir trees; hardwood plywood, made from maple and gum trees, was mainly used for furniture making. About 20 percent of softwood plywood was used for nonresidential construction, with the remainder directed to industrial and miscellaneous markets. Exhibit 9 shows the cycles and trends of residential and nonresidential construction in the United States from 1969 to 1977.

21 Plywood had experienced strongly increased usage in residential construction during the 1970s, when the amount of plywood used for the average single-family home had approximately doubled.

22 Past studies have shown that price increases in timber products had relatively little effect on demand in the short run. However, in the long run, as price continued to rise, demand for timber products declined and the use of competitive materials increased.

23 In 1973, America experienced a lumber shortage, and as a result, the U.S. Forest Service conducted a study of the future supply and demand of timber products in the United States. This study reported that the demand for lumber, plywood, woodpulp, and other forest products was increasing more rapidly than the available timber supply,

Exhibit 5

GEORGIA-PACIFIC CORPORATION
Statements of Consolidated Net Income
For the Years Ended December 31, 1975–1979
(in thousands of dollars except per share data)

	1975	*1976*	*1977*	*1978*	*1979*
Net sales	$2,358,600	$3,038,000	$3,675,000	$4,403,000	$5,207,000
Costs and expenses:					
Cost of sales	1,798,900	2,331,900	2,920,000	3,410,000	4,100,000
Selling, general, and administrative	144,600	161,000	194,000	231,000	279,000
Depreciation and depletion	133,800	151,000	175,000	194,000	228,000
Interest expense	49,800	38,000	33,000	38,000	66,000
Provision for income taxes	83,500	141,000	191,000	228,000	208,000
Gross income	2,210,600	2,823,000	3,513,000	4,101,000	4,881,000
Net income	$ 148,000	$ 215,000	$ 262,000	$ 302,000	$ 326,000
Income per share of common stock:					
Primary	$ 1.60	$ 2.12	$ 2.54	$ 2.93	$ 3.11
Fully diluted	$ 1.53	$ 2.05	$ 2.47	$ 2.84	$ 3.02

Sources: Georgia-Pacific, 1981 Annual Report, p. 23; and Georgia Pacific, 1977 Annual Report to Shareholders on Operating Income and Financial Results, p. 31.

with much of the rise in demand resulting from the population growth. The problem of increased demand was compounded because the number of trees grown each year was decreasing. Commercial forests were shrinking at a rate of about 500,000 acres per year, while the demands for forest products and lands for recreation were expanding. Commercial forest land was that which had the capability of growing commercial quantities of timber suitable for harvest. Of the 500 million acres of commercial forest land in the United States, private citizens owned 59 percent, the government owned 27 percent, and the forest products industry owned 14 percent. Because of the declining timber supply, the United States would have to increase its reliance on wood imports. The U.S. Forest Service projected that by the year 2000, the softwood timber supply would fall short of demand by at least 2 billion board feet.

24 The 1973 Forest Service study also projected that the demand for plywood would increase more rapidly than the demand for lumber for the remainder of the century. While lumber use in housing was expected to increase 50 percent by the year 2000, plywood usage was expected to double. The use of plywood in nonresidential construction was also expected to double from 1970 levels of 17.8 billion square feet to 36.8 billion square feet by the year 2000.

25 One of the problems Georgia-Pacific and the forest products industry faced was the government's restriction of timber cutting in national forests. National forest lands contained 52 percent of the country's softwood timber, the type of timber from which most plywood was made. Despite this large inventory, the national forests supplied less than 30 percent of the nation's softwood timber requirements. The majority of

Exhibit 6

GEORGIA-PACIFIC CORPORATION
Consolidated Balance Sheets
For the Years Ended December 31, 1975–1979
(in thousands of dollars)

	1975	*1976*	*1977*	*1978*	*1979*
Assets					
Current assets:					
Cash	$ 31,800	$ 25,000	$ 11,000	$ 21,000	$ 22,000
Marketable securities	16,600	—	—	—	—
Receivables	250,000	295,000	256,000	418,000	502,000
Inventories*	376,700	423,000	449,000	496,000	585,000
Prepaid expenses	6,600	10,000	9,000	9,000	14,000
Total current assets	$681,700	$753,000	825,000	944,000	1,123,000
Natural resources, at cost less depletion:					
Timber and timberlands	319,900	331,000	385,000	453,000	683,000
Coal, minerals, natural gas, and oil	26,800	30,000	36,000	52,000	81,000
Total natural resources	346,700	361,000	421,000	505,000	764,000
Property, plant, and equipment:					
Land, buildings, machinery, and equipment at cost	2,049,900	2,285,000	2,657,000	2,988,000	3,476,000
Less: Reserves for depreciation	721,900	836,000	995,000	1,123,000	1,283,000
Total property, plant, and equipment	1,328,000	1,449,000	1,662,000	1,865,000	2,193,000
Noncurrent receivables and other assets	47,500	21,000	21,000	30,000	38,000
Total assets	$2,403,900	$2,584,000	$2,929,000	$3,344,000	$4,118,000

softwood timber was being supplied by the forest products industry lands, which contained only 17 percent of the nation's softwood timber. Although the United States had 70 million more acres of hardwood forest than softwood forest, much of this resource was relatively untapped.

26 Another problem that plagued the forest industry was the government's demand that it refrain from the practice of "clear-cutting"—harvesting all the trees from a given area at the same time. Clear-cutting offended environmentalists and violated provisions of the Organic Act of 1897.

27 However, in September 1976, Congress passed legislation to alleviate part of the timber-supply problem and improve the long-term outlook for timber production in this country. The National Forest Management Act amended the 1897 Organic Act and permitted a greater share of the nation's timber requirements to be harvested from the national forests. It also allowed clear-cutting and other modern forestry practices.

28 After passage of this act, environmentalists demanded that more national forest lands be included in the Wilderness System (established by Congress through the

Exhibit 6 *(concluded)*

	1975	*1976*	*1977*	*1978*	*1979*
Liabilities					
Current liabilities:					
Current portion of long term debt	$ 98,600	$ 36,900	$ 46,000	$ 60,000	$ 70,000
Accounts payable and accrued liabilities	130,100	206,700	254,000	321,000	400,000
Income taxes	25,600	67,200	65,000	28,000	32,000
	254,300	310,800	365,000	409,000	502,000
Commercial paper and other short-term notes supported by confirmed seasonal bank lines of credit	—	222,600	13,000	52,000	159,000
Total current liabilities	254,300	533,400	378,000	461,000	661,000
Long-term debt, excluding current portion	606,900	317,700	607,000	702,000	984,000
Convertible subordinated debentures:					
5¾% due 1994	75,000	—	—	—	—
5¼% due 1966	125,000	125,000	125,000	125,000	125,000
6⅛% due 2000	100,000	—	—	—	—
Deferred income taxes	215,000	250,000	280,000	325,000	380,000
Employee stock purchase plan	—	5,800	10,000	5,000	9,000
Redeemable preferred stock	—	—	—	—	165,000
Capital stock and surplus:					
Common stock	48,300	79,000	82,000	82,000	82,000
Paid-in surplus	701,300	905,700	1,021,000	1,023,000	1,023,000
Earned surplus	279,900	368,800	428,000	625,000	827,000
Less: common stock held in treasury, at cost	(1,800)	(1,400)	(2,000)	(4,000)	(138,000)
Total capital stocks and surplus	1,027,700	1,352,100	1,529,000	1,726,000	1,794,000
Total liabilities	$2,403,900	$2,584,000	$2,929,000	$3,344,000	$4,118,000

* Inventories recorded at the lower of cost or market.

Sources: Georgia-Pacific, 1976 Annual Report; Georgia-Pacific, 1977 Annual Report to Shareholders on Operating and Financial Results, pp. 32–33; Georgia-Pacific, 1978 Annual Report, pp. 30–31; Georgia-Pacific, 1980 Annual Report, pp. 34–35.

Wilderness Act of 1964). When land was protected, insect disease and fires were controlled. No roads could be built and no motor vehicles were allowed. In 1977, as a result of pressure from environmentalists, President Carter called for a study of 62 million acres of national forest land that had the potential to be set aside as wilderness. During the study period, which was expected to last for two years, no timber cutting would be permitted on that land. The forest industry was concerned that results of the study could strike an even harder blow to the nation's future timber supply.

29 Because fewer timberlands would be available for harvest, the cost of timber would increase, meaning that profits of fewer companies would keep pace with sales growth.

Exhibit 7

U.S. population 1920–1970, with projections to the year 2000

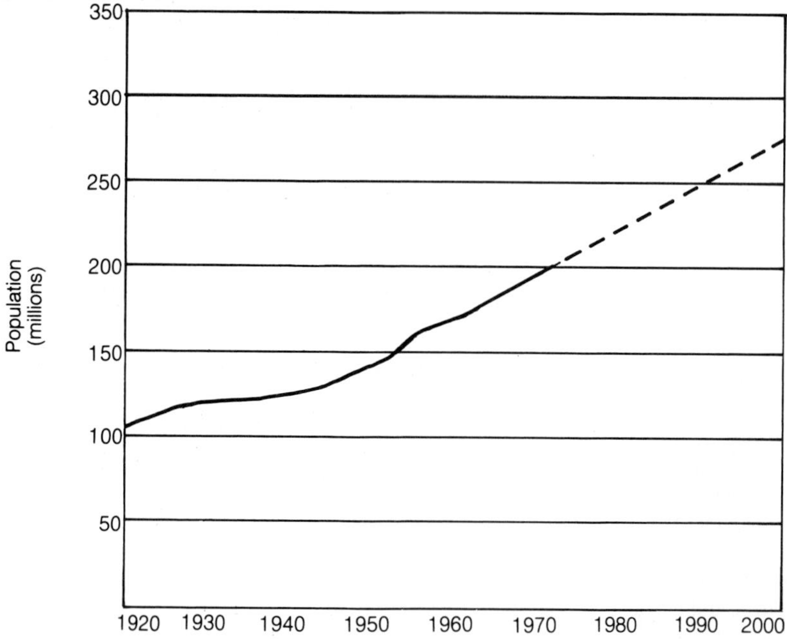

Source: U.S. Bureau of the Census.

Exhibit 8

U.S. softwood plywood production

Year	*Softwood plywood production (million square feet)*
1979	19,744
1978	19,492
1977	19,721
1976	17,841
1975	15,706
1974	15,306
1973	17,929
1972	17,843
1971	16,353
1970	14,149

Source: Department of Commerce, National Forest Products Association, Standard & Poor's Industry Surveys, 1981, p. B127.

Exhibit 9

Residential and nonresidential construction, seasonally adjusted (indexed, 1967 = 100)

Construction markets' cycles and trends, 1969 to 1977.
Source: *Cycles and Trends in Construction Markets,* 1977, p. 1.

Thus, Georgia-Pacific's management anticipated that timber ownership would become the critical determinant of a company's ability to grow with controlled manufacturing costs.

The Competitors

30 Since the early 1970s, Georgia-Pacific had taken many risks to get ahead. During that time, the company borrowed heavily from banks and insurance companies when the other companies were not doing so, using the money to finance the acquisitions which had always been a key element in its corporate growth strategy. By the mid-1970's, Georgia-Pacific's strategic risk-taking was paying off as the company began to capture market share from its major competitors.

Exhibit 10

Selective data on Georgia-Pacific's key competitors (in thousands of dollars)

	1975	*1976*	*1977*	*1978*	*1979*
Total sales:					
Boise Cascade	$1,458,050	$1,931,530	$2,315,780	$2,573,110	$2,916,610
Champion International	2,530,000	3,079,000	3,127,000	3,475,145	3,750,960
Weyerhauser	2,421,271	2,868,379	3,282,768	3,799,400	4,422,000
Softwood plywood sales:					
Boise Cascade	*	*	*	*	*
Champion International	315,000	450,000	496,000	647,159	636,958
Weyerhauser	238,000	362,000	453,539	555,000	599,000
Net income:					
Boise Cascade	63,890	100,830	115,610	132,800	174,920
Champion International	61,020	135,940	138,620	168,688	247,120
Weyerhauser	164,740	305,970	303,890	370,700	511,600
Total assets:					
Boise Cascade	1,569,324	1,731,242	1,799,048	1,981,947	2,309,057
Champion International	2,180,000	2,564,000	2,465,000	2,856,104	3,040,485
Weyerhauser	2,421,271	2,868,379	3,282,768	4,466,922	4,961,673
Stockholders' equity:					
Boise Cascade	866,241	945,371	959,088	1,058,397	1,178,400
Champion International	980,000	1,162,000	1,257,000	1,358,964	1,535,028
Weyerhauser	1,788,839	1,981,886	2,179,485	2,313,792	2,731,168

* Plywood sales dollars not provided.

Sources: Boise Cascade, 1977 Annual Report, p. 22; Boise Cascade, 1981 Annual Report, p. 32; Champion International, 1977 Annual Report, pp. 18, 42, 68–69; Champion International, 1981 Annual Report, p. 1; Weyerhauser, 1977 Annual Report, pp. 24–55; Weyerhauser, 1981 Annual Report, pp. 27, 32, 33, 52, 53.

31 Competition was intense in the plywood and wood product specialties markets, but although many competitors existed, Georgia-Pacific faced its main competition from three giants: Boise Cascade, Champion International, and Weyerhauser. Exhibit 10 contains selective data on these companies.

32 Each of these competitors had strategies and goals for their organizations, and it was necessary for Georgia-Pacific to analyze their strategies, goals, and product lines to ascertain where its competitors were headed.

33 Boise Cascade and Georgia-Pacific were involved in different product lines within the paper and wood industries. Boise Cascade placed its emphasis on paper manufacturing. Capital expenditures in this area stressed efficiency and flexibility to enable Boise Cascade to capitalize on the growing demand for its papers. The company also planned to grow as a converter and distributor of paper and wood products, and these operations were well positioned in favorable markets. Boise was a leading producer of composite cans, a product being marketed as a substitute for other types of packaging. It was a leader in distribution of office products, but with a market share of less than 3 percent, there was room for growth. The building materials distribution and manufactured housing operations were expected to grow along with the housing industry. Of all of Boise Cascade's divisions, only the wood products manufacturing was not expected to experience any significant growth since sufficient capacity existed within the indus-

try to handle demand for the foreseeable future. Instead, this company sought to increase efficiency in its wood products manufacturing.

34 Champion International changed its strategic objectives in the 1970s. Management wanted to withdraw from any nonforest products businesses, and in 1977, this objective was achieved along with expansion into the paper packaging business. Divisions included timberlands, building materials, paper, and paper packaging. The company planned to spend $1.9 billion for capital projects from 1978 to 1982, using this money for business preservation, expansion, maintenance of competitive cost-effective management, and profit improvement.

35 Weyerhauser, another Georgia-Pacific competitor, was the only large forest products company to have net self-sufficiency in its raw material supply. This gave it both a materials-cost advantage and more manufacturing flexibility than any of its competitors. Its timber stands appreciated each year at a higher rate than inflation. Weyerhauser, like Georgia-Pacific, used forestry programs to manage its lands for increased productivity. Weyerhauser believed that the future industry environment would require different product mixes and processes which would mean a change in raw materials. The firm believed that the industry's future leaders would be those who were in the forefront of the effort to increase timber growth and raw-material utilization, replace obsolete manufacturing processes, and reduce energy and chemical uses. Weyerhauser exported a large percentage of their goods. Their forests were located principally in the Pacific Northwest, which provided easy access to ports. In the short term, the company planned to reduce manufacturing costs and increase productivity through capital investment and efficient cost-effective management with emphasis on the Pacific Northwest operations.

The Strategic Decision—Comply

36 To meet the need for increased demand of wood products, the American Plywood Association and the U.S. Forest Service and Department of Housing and Urban Development initiated a research program to develop products that would utilize timber in a more efficient manner. About one third of the timber cut in U.S. forests was wasted in logging and milling operations. One result of the research was the development of comply, a name which stood for composite plywood. Comply was made by sandwiching a panel of oriented fiberwood flakes between sheets of pine veneer; heat, pressure, and a special glue were used to bond the panel to the sheets of pine veneer.

37 Comply was stronger than plywood for most uses and met the American Plywood Association's quality standards. Designed as a substitute for plywood, Comply looked and performed like plywood and would have the same market applications. However, comply could make use of more wood from each tree than conventional plywood. About 45 percent of a tree's wood volume could be used in making plywood, with the rest ending up as residue. Comply, on the other hand, could use all of the tree, except sawdust and bark. A comply plant would require half as many trees as raw materials for a plywood plant to produce an equivalent number of panels.

38 Other differences existed between comply and plywood production: much-smaller trees could be used in manufacturing comply, and sound portions of dead and damaged trees and wood residues, such as limbs and tree tops, could be used for the core. This was not feasible in plywood manufacturing. Whereas most plywood was made from softwood timber, a variety of tree species, including both hardwood and softwood,

Exhibit 11

Costs of a comply plant

Site	$ 470,000
Building	1,596,000
Machinery and equipment	14,597,000
Contingencies and escalations	1,477,000
Construction capital required	$18,140,000

Source: Norman Springate and Associates, 1977.

could be used for the core of comply. One negative quality of comply was that a panel was heavier than a plywood panel and, therefore, more difficult to handle on a construction site.

39 In 1977, as a result of the government's cooperative research on comply, Potlatch Corporation took the initiative and opened (in Idaho) the country's first factory for manufacturing comply. The executives at Georgia-Pacific were considering producing and marketing the new product, as were at least four other companies, but none of the companies had made a firm commitment. Georgia-Pacific, upon talking with Potlatch, found they would welcome Georgia-Pacific, or any other large company, into the market, recognizing it would speed the acceptance and use of comply by the building industry.

40 Potlatch claimed it had patented rights on comply production technology and would sell this technology to Georgia-Pacific at a cost of $250,000 for the first comply plant built and $100,000 for each additional plant built by Georgia-Pacific during the next 10 years. However, the legal staff of Georgia-Pacific determined the patents were not valid and such payments would not be required. Since the patents were invalid, Georgia-Pacific's management felt that if it decided to manufacture comply, a one-time payment of only $50,000 would be sufficient to secure a working relationship with Potlatch. This would allow Georgia-Pacific to consult Potlatch for working out bugs in the manufacturing system.

41 Before Georgia-Pacific would seriously consider comply as an alternative product, the cost of the resources necessary for its production had to be investigated, and in 1977, the company hired an outside consulting firm to conduct a feasibility study on comply and its related costs. Norman Springate and Associates looked at the require-

Exhibit 12

Estimated financial data if comply is produced (year 1)

Net sales to be generated	$14,572,000
Net profit before taxes	4,042,000
Net profit after taxes	2,021,000
Net cash flow	3,768,000
Investment credit	1,475,000

Source: Norman Springate and Associates, 1977.

Exhibit 13

Comparison of cost of plywood versus comply

	Comply panel	*Plywood panel*
Wood	$1.28	$1.74
Resin and wax	.70	.62
Labor	.84	.62
Overhead	1.19	1.24
Total	$4.01	$4.22

Source: Norman Springate and Associates, 1977.

ments for building a plant for comply manufacturing purposes. Exhibit 11 provides the result of this study on relevant start-up costs.

42 The consultant also conducted financial analyses to determine the type of revenue that would be generated with the comply plant. Exhibit 12 gives a brief summary of the estimated revenues.

43 Georgia-Pacific itself did a cost analysis of producing one piece of plywood versus one piece of comply of the same dimension (4 by 8 feet) in one of their existing factories. The results, as shown in Exhibit 13, demonstrated that production of comply would be less expensive than plywood. The company felt comply had the potential to command a premium price because its solid core resisted hole punctures and the sealed edges reduced expansion from water absorption. Also, comply, by its design, was stronger than an equivalent panel of plywood.

44 Georgia-Pacific was faced with the need to examine the diverse data it had available and to decide whether to proceed with the production of comply.

case 18
The Kevlar Decision at Du Pont

Introduction

1 In late 1978, the vice president for textile fibers at Du Pont proposed an increase in the annual output of Du Pont's aramid fiber, Kevlar. His plan called for an annual production of 45 million pounds by 1982—tripling the then current rate of 15 million pounds. The proposal called for expenditures of $250 million to expand the Richmond, Virginia, plant where Kevlar was produced and the La Place, Louisiana, facility that manufactured PPD, an essential ingredient in Kevlar.

2 In line with Du Pont company policy, the proposal went to the executive committee of the board of directors, headed by Irving Shapiro, chairman of the board. Shapiro and the other committee members were acutely aware that, if approved, the tripling of Kevlar capacity would represent the largest capital expenditure on a single product in company history. They also realized that the proposed expansion was only one of a number of options available to Du Pont in handling its newest miracle product. Other options were to discontinue production, to maintain current output, or to expand well beyond the proposed 45 million pounds per year level. In acting on the specific proposal, the committee would naturally review all these options in light of the general economic situation, the company's current goals and resources, the actual and potential demand for Kevlar in its various industrial markets, and the possible alternative uses of available resources. Moreover, in making its final decision, the committee would find it hard to ignore past problems in production and marketing Kevlar and the fiber's history of unprofitability.

The Du Pont Company

3 Founded in 1802 by French immigrants, E. I. du Pont de Nemours & Co., by the beginning of the 20th century, had grown to be the dominant American manufacturer of gunpowder and explosives. Profits from munitions sales during World War I increased the firm's capital from $83 million to $308 million and allowed an aggressive policy of diversification in the postwar era. In the 1920s, Du Pont entered the chemicals, plastics, paint, dye, textiles, and film businesses. By acquiring a controlling interest in General Motors, a market for many of its products was assured. Through a licensing

This case was prepared by Professors John A. Pearce II and Michael S. Smith of the University of South Carolina, with the assistance of Peter Davis, David Hastings, and David Johnson. It has been accepted for publication in the *Journal of Management Case Studies*.

agreement, it also became the North American producer of two French miracle products—rayon and cellophane. Most important of all, Du Pont began investing heavily in basic chemical research. This led to the introduction of a steady stream of proprietary (that is, patented and trademarked) products between 1930 and 1960—neoprene synthetic rubber, Lucite acrylic resin, nylon, Teflon, Orlon, and Dacron. Indeed, chemical research and product innovation became Du Pont's hallmarks. Increasingly, the company saw itself as a high-technology enterprise furnishing unique and innovative products to a variety of end-use manufacturers in diverse fields—textiles and apparel, tires and rubber, automobiles, aerospace, and so on. By the 1970s, Du Pont manufactured hundreds of products in four categories:

Chemicals: nonbranded commodity chemicals such as acids, methanol, and formaldehyde; special-purpose chemicals like Freon refrigerant and antiknock compounds for gasoline; pigments for paints, plastics, and so forth.

Plastics: Resins, elastomers, films.

Specialty products: herbicides, fungicides, and pesticides; explosives; paints and finishes; pharmaceuticals; clinical analyzers; firearms and ammunition (through its Remington subsidiary).

Fibers: apparel and carpet fibers; industrial fibers (especially for tire reinforcement); spunbonded fibers for packaging and carpet backing.

4 These products were manufactured and marketed internationally as well as domestically. Exhibit 1 shows the relative size of each product group. By the 1970s, Du Pont had distribution and/or production operations in 27 countries around the world. Most were wholly owned subsidiaries such as Du Pont de Nemours Deutschland Gmbh and Du Pont Taiwan Ltd. But they also included joint ventures such as Butachimie, formed in France with Rhone-Poulenc to produce adiponitrile (an ingredient in nylon). The newest cooperative undertaking was a synthetic fibers plant in Iran, which opened in 1978.

5 With growth, diversification, and multinationalization came organizational change. A centralized family firm before World War I, Du Pont pioneered the decentralized, multidivisional structure when it diversified in the 1920s. The basic unit in this structure was the industrial division, headed by a vice president/general manager who enjoyed broad latitude in purchasing, production, and other facets of operations. In 1978, there were nine industrial divisions: Biochemicals; Chemicals, Dyes and Pigments; Elastomers; Fabrics and Finishes; Petro-Chemicals; Photo Products; Plastics; Textile Fibers. All foreign operations, regardless of product type, were grouped in the International Division. These industrial divisions were, in turn, supported by various staff departments, the most important of which was the Central Research and Development Department.

6 After 50 years of relative decentralization, the board of directors, in 1978, endeavored to reduce the autonomy of the industrial departments and to reassert central authority, especially in planning and strategic management. Consequently, two committees of the board—the executive committee and the finance committee—took on increased power. The executive committee—consisting of the chairman of the board, the president, and four senior vice presidents—made companywide policy, supervised all operations, and reviewed all major departmental proposals (such as the Kevlar expansion).

Exhibit 1

Sales and net income by product groups ($ millions)

	Chemicals	*Plastics*	*Specialty products*	*Fibers*	*Total*
Sales:					
1973					
Amount	$1,077	$1,256	$1,348	$2,283	$ 5,964
Percent of total	18%	21%	23%	38%	100%
1974					
Amount	1,313	1,485	1,677	2,440	6,910
Percent of total	19%	22%	24%	35%	100%
1975					
Amount	1,381	1,397	1,887	2,557	7,222
Percent of total	19%	19%	26%	36%	100%
1976					
Amount	1,625	1,798	2,174	2,764	8,361
Percent of total	19%	22%	26%	33%	100%
1977					
Amount	1,752	2,070	2,518	3,095	9,435
Percent of total	18%	22%	17%	33%	100%
1978					
Amount	1,807	2,330	3,003	3,444	10,584
Percent of total	17%	22%	28%	33%	100%
Net income:					
1973					
Amount	107	124	112	243	586
Percent of total	18%	21%	19%	42%	100%
1974					
Amount	76	110	92	126	404
Percent of total	19%	27%	23%	31%	100%
1975					
Amount	102	26	138	6	272
Percent of total	38%	9%	51%	2%	100%
1976					
Amount	148	109	168	34	459
Percent of total	32%	24%	37%	7%	100%
1977					
Amount	132	151	202	60	545
Percent of total	24%	28%	37%	11%	100%
1978					
Amount	124	165	278	220	787
Percent of total	16%	21%	35%	28%	100%

Source: Du Pont, 1976 Annual Report, p. 23; Du Pont, 1978 Annual Report, p. 28.

The finance committee had authority to approve all large capital expenditures and new financing, which meant it would also act on the Kevlar proposal.

7 The finance committee also served as the last bastion of Du Pont family control of the company. By 1978, the family owned only 35 percent of the over 48 million shares of common stock outstanding. With the 1977 merger of Christiana Securities (the

family holding company) with the Du Pont Company itself, these shares were scattered among hundreds of individual family members. The board of directors—once dominated by Du Ponts—now consisted mostly of nonfamily company executives and outsiders. The last Du Pont chairman, Lammot du P. Copeland, Sr., stepped down in 1971. However, in the finance committee, with its extensive power over dividend policy and investment strategy, five of nine seats were held by Du Pont family members, and given the method of appointment to the committee (new members were chosen by the old ones), it was likely to stay that way.

Recent Strategy and Performance

8 In 1978, Du Pont was finally recovering from an unprecedented slump in profits that had been all the more serious because it was unanticipated. In 1973, the company had enjoyed record earnings of $586 million, which produced an all-time high EPS of $12.04. This resulted mainly from strong worldwide demand for the synthetic fibers of which Du Pont was the world's leading producer (42 percent of Du Pont's total profits in 1973 were generated in the fibers division). Seeing a worldwide shortage of synthetics and expecting consumption to rise 60 percent over the next five years, in 1974, Du Pont launched a capital investment program to expand fiber production capacity by one third. To finance this expansion, Du Pont incurred its first domestic long-term debt since the 1920s by borrowing $100 million in June 1974. This was followed with a record debt offering of $500 million in October 1974. Du Pont's debt-to-capital ratio, which stood at only 5.9 percent in 1973, rose steadily thereafter to a peak of 22.2 percent in 1976. At the same time, Du Pont eschewed backward integration into petroleum feedstocks, choosing instead to continue to purchase gas and oil from the major producers.

9 Continued reliance on petroleum producers proved to be precisely the wrong strategy for the mid-70s. In the wake of the Arab oil embargo, oil prices increased dramatically, and Du Pont's expenses for raw materials and energy jumped 80 percent in one year. Meanwhile, the general economic downturn reduced demand for synthetic fibers. Coupled with the ongoing expansion of productive capacity, the downturn made it impossible to recover increased costs by raising prices. As a result, income from fibers collapsed in 1974–75 and dragged down overall corporate profitability (see Exhibit 2). Instead of a 8–10 percent per year growth in EPS—a stated objective of the company in 1973, it declined from $12.04 in 1973 to $5.43 in 1975. Stock prices followed suit, declining some 40 percent in two years, as shown in Exhibit 3.

10 As stated repeatedly by Irving Shapiro, Du Pont's financial goal was to restore profitability to its 1965 level when return on equity exceeded 20 percent (in 1975, return on equity stood at 7.3 percent). One way to accomplish this goal was through backward integration into petroleum to assure supplies of feedstocks at reasonable prices. Between 1975 and 1977, Du Pont entered a joint venture with National Distillers and Chemicals Corp. to build a methanol plant in Texas, launched a refining venture with Atlantic-Richfield (ARCO later withdrew), and attempted but failed to take over Shenandoah Oil Corporation. In 1978, Du Pont joined with Conoco in a five-year venture to explore for natural gas, while continuing to purchase oil on the open market.

11 As of 1978, industry experts were predicting that crude oil prices would increase from $12.40 per barrel to $13.30 in January 1979 and to $14.50 by late 1979. With

Exhibit 2

Profitability (percent)

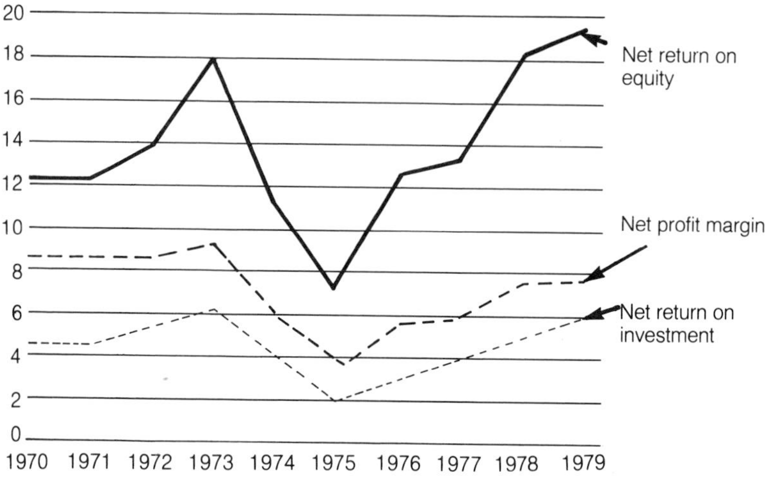

Source: Du Pont, 1979 Annual Report, pp. 27–28.

Exhibit 3

Du Pont financial overview ($ millions)

	1971	*1972*	*1973*	*1974*	*1975*	*1976*	*1977*	*1978*
Income statement:								
Sales	$4,371	4,948	5,964	6,910	7,222	8,361	9,435	10,584
Cost of goods sold	2,867	3,262	3,879	5,052	5,410	6,028	6,746	7,353
Earnings before taxes and minority interests	652	774	1,077	682	453	822	980	1,344
Net income	357	414	586	404	272	459	545	787
Per share data:								
Earnings	7.33	8.50	12.04	8.20	5.43	9.30	11.06	15.96
Prices: high	158	184	204	179	134	161	135	138
low	130	144	145	85	87	117	105	106
P/E ratio	22–18	22–17	17–12	22–10	25–16	17–13	12–10	9–6
Balance sheet:								
Return on assets	9.4%	10%	12.8%	7.4%	4.4%	6.8%	7.6%	10.1%
Return on equity	12.8%	13.7%	18.0%	11.4%	7.3%	12.1%	13.6%	18.0%
Long-term debt	$ 236	240	238	793	889	1282	1290	1099
Long-term debt as percent of capital	6.8%	6.6%	5.9%	16.3%	17.5%	22.2%	21.1%	17.2%

Source: *Standard & Poor's Stock Reports,* April 1980, p. 784.

the ending of price controls in 1979, domestic prices were expected to move to the world price level in the early 1980s. Slackening pressure from the Arab countries, increased domestic production, and development of offshore oil fields, especially in the North Sea, were expected to dampen upward pressure on prices in the 80s. Still, a price of $20 per barrel was forecast for the end of that decade.

12 In 1976, Du Pont's fiber division also made strategic changes in the area of research and development. Instead of emphasizing basic research and the development of entirely new businesses, Du Pont sought product and process innovation in support of existing businesses. Product diversification led to more intensive and efficient exploitation of proprietary technology. The portion of the R&D budget devoted to improving existing product lines and reducing costs in existing production increased from 66 percent to 75 percent of the total. Some 22 R&D adventures were dropped. Subsequent research focused on four areas: improvement of superior products (for example, better forms of nylon); discovery of new products from proprietary technology (for example, new uses of Kevlar); cost reduction by substituting cheaper materials in production; and cost reduction by new process technology. Overall, the research emphasis was on short-term payout.

13 Du Pont simultaneously reevaluated its position in the fibers industry and decided on a three-point plan to improve profitability: price increases (when market conditions permitted), better utilization of capacity, and product innovation. Forecasting it would take two years for demand to catch up with existing capacity, the company dropped any immediate plans for further plant expansion. The emphasis was to be on marketing premium or strong fibers instead of standard fibers, increased penetration of fast-growing markets (such as carpeting and the medical applications of spunbonded products), withdrawal from mature and/or marginal product markets (such as acetate yarns), and consolidation of production facilities. Du Pont hoped it could eventually reduce its dependence on the volatile, highly discretionary consumer markets in fibers (apparel and carpeting) and increase its share of the less-volatile industrial fibers market.

14 As these ideas were being implemented, Du Pont's performance improved markedly. In 1976–78, its income rose in all product divisions except chemicals. Most dramatic was the recovery of fibers income: from net earnings of only $6 million in 1975 (2 percent of total earnings) to $220 million in 1978 (28 percent of the total). This improvement stemmed from the rebound of the synthetic fibers industry as a whole. Du Pont's total annual earnings rose from $5.43 to $15.96 million in the same interval. Especially important in this recovery was the profitability of foreign operations. Foreign assets accounted for only 9.5 percent of the total sales in 1978, yet they produced 18 percent of total profits. Higher profits helped to lower the debt-to-capital ratio from its 1976 peak (22.2 percent) to 17.2 percent in 1978.

15 Du Pont's recovery, while clearly tied to the general economic upturn in 1976–78, seemed, nonetheless, to confirm the wisdom of the strategic decisions made in 1976. In 1978, Shapiro believed more strongly than ever that his profitability goal—20 percent return on equity—was achievable through continued emphasis on technological leadership and new-product development. As he told *Forbes* magazine (October 2, 1978), "Our gamble is that the highest R&D budget in the industry will create enough products to keep our momentum going; our greatest strength is that we can go worldwide every time we invent a new product."

16 Crucial to this strategy was the future performance of the fibers division. Shapiro saw this as the cash cow that would support investments in areas of higher long-term profit potential such as photo supplies, agricultural chemicals, and electronic instruments. And prospects for the short-term profitability of synthetic fibers were good. According to *Chemical and Engineering News* (December 4, 1978), unused capacity for fiber production in the United States in 1979 would be half of what it was in 1976, the result of a shift in women's fashions towards garments requiring more fabric and also the result of an increase in fiber exports and decrease in fiber imports rising from the weak position of the U.S. dollar against foreign currencies.

17 But continued improvement in fibers income was only half of the Du Pont strategy. The other half involved decisions on which technology to exploit vigorously and which to emphasize and on which products to develop, which to put on hold, and which to phase out. By 1978, Du Pont had plans to capitalize on proprietary technology in a number of areas. In chemicals, expansion of titanium dioxide production on the basis of Du Pont's new chloride process was underway. In the health-products field, Du Pont was following its successful automatic chemical analyzer with the CKMB isoenzyme analyzer for use in heart attack diagnosis. In agricultural products, a host of new fungicides and herbicides, such as Curzate and Lexone, were slated for introduction. Greatest hopes, however, were held for fiber products, particularly for Kevlar aramid.

Kevlar

18 Aramids were a whole new category of synthetic fibers resulting from Du Pont's basic research in polymer chemistry and fiber structures in the 1960s. In 1965, a Du Pont research scientist, Stephanie Kwolek, discovered a complex ethylene-based polymer which, when dissolved in a solvent and pushed through a spinneret, formed a thin but tenacious fiber that, pound for pound, was five times stronger than steel and extremely heat resistant. This was Kevlar.

19 Believing that Kevlar would revolutionize the fibers industry the way nylon did in the 1940s, Du Pont management immediately targeted it for commercial development. However, production problems delayed its introduction. In the early 70s, the solvent used in fabrication came under suspicion as a carcinogen, and a redesign of the production system was necessary so workers could be protected. Because this raised production costs, the price of Kevlar had to be pegged higher than originally projected. Increased costs created problems for Du Pont marketers searching for industrial applications in which Kevlar's "value-in-use" would be sufficiently high to warrant its substitution for competing materials, such as steel. One such application was found in the tire industry, where high-performance radial tires with belts of Kevlar were introduced in 1975. Within two years, demand for Kevlar among seven major tire manufacturers had risen enough to justify the initial expansion of output from 10 million to 15 million pounds per year. As it contemplated further expansion in 1978, Du Pont established a special marketing team to promote Kevlar in ballistic vests, ropes and cables, and marine and aerospace applications. At the same time, Du Pont set out to negotiate long-term contracts with its principal customers for Kevlar, especially the tire manufacturers.

The Financial Situation

20 At the end of 1978, Du Pont was in its strongest financial position in years. The heavy capital outlays dictated by the 1973 decision to expand production of synthetic fibers had peaked in 1975. Since then, capital expenditures had declined 27 percent, from $1,066 million to $780 million in 1977. At the same time, net income had risen 190 percent, from $272 to $787 million per year, and stockholders' equity had risen 26 percent, from $3.8 billion to $4.8 billion. A better financial outlook allowed Du Pont to fund 100 percent of its capital improvements internally and to reduce corporate indebtedness by $148.9 million in 1978, as seen in the 1978 Statement of Changes in Financial Position (see Exhibit 4). If the Kevlar expansion was approved, capital expenditures were expected to rise above $900 million in 1979 and above $1.3 billion in 1980. Other projects involving multimillion dollar investments in each of the next two or three years included the new titanium dioxide plant at De Lisle, Mississippi;

Exhibit 4

E. I. DU PONT DE NEMOURS & CO.
1978 Statement of Changes in Financial Position
($ millions)

	1978
Cash and marketable securities—beginning of year	$ 237.8
Sources of funds:	
Net income	787.0
Depreciation and obsolescence	776.0
Other noncash charges and credits—net	96.9
Funds provided by operations	1,659.9
Net proceeds from sale of News-Journal Company	44.3
Common stock issued in connection with compensation plans	19.5
Total sources of funds	1,723.7
Uses of funds:	
Dividends	358.4
Capital expenditures:	
Additions to plants and properties	714.2
Investment in affiliates	71.5
Reduction (increase) in borrowings:	
Short term	(29.0)
Long term	
Reductions	191.1
New borrowings	(13.2)
Reduction in capital lease obligations	12.8
Net increase in working capital—excluding cash, marketable securities, and short-term borrowings	338.8
Purchase of treasury stock	5.6
Increase (decrease) in other assets and investments	(14.8)
Miscellaneous—net	(1.9)
Total uses of funds	1,633.5
Cash and marketable securities—end of year	$ 328.0

Source: Du Pont, 1979 Annual Report, p. 39.

an adiponitrile plant at Victoria, Texas; improvements in neoprene production at Maydown, Northern Ireland; expansion of mylar production at Florence, South Carolina; and a methanol plant joint venture with National Distillers at Deer Park, Texas.

21 Despite rising costs, Du Pont expected to finance all these capital improvements internally. However, it also had access to external sources of capital. Reduction of outstanding debt in 1978 lowered Du Pont's debt-to-capital ratio from 21 percent (end of 1977) to 17 percent (end of 1978). At year's end, Du Pont had unused lines of bank credit totaling $1.4 billion, which provided for borrowing at the best available commercial rates—11.75 percent in December 1978 as compared to an average interest rate of 17.6 percent on all Du Pont debt. Funds might also be raised through sale of stock, although management considered this unlikely. Stock offerings had been extremely rare in recent company history. The market price of Du Pont common stock, while stable, remained substantially below the 1973 level. A 3-for-1 stock split, reducing par value of common stock from $5 to $1.66 and increasing outstanding shares to 145 million, was being planned for early 1979.

The Legal Environment

22 Perhaps more crucial for the Kevlar proposal than financial constraints were legal questions. Du Pont had patented Kevlar in 1968, which gave it exclusive production rights in the United States and most foreign locations until 1985. While patents on various components of the Kevlar production process might effectively extend Du Pont's legal monopoly in Kevlar beyond that date, the company had to deal with the possibility that competing products would enter the market within three years after the expansion of production at Richmond. Indeed, already in 1978, industrial intelligence indicated that Enka Ag, the West German fiber arm of the Dutch group, Akzo, was preparing to introduce a Kevlar-like aramid well before 1985. Du Pont's legal office was currently considering action for patent infringement. Such unexpected competition, of course, could severely depress prices and undercut the expected profitability of Kevlar production in the early 1980s.

23 Meanwhile, three other aspects of the legal environment required consideration: antitrust action, environmental regulation, and employee health and safety. Du Pont had a long history of antitrust litigation. In 1957, the Supreme Court had forced divestment of Du Pont's holdings in General Motors. In 1974, Du Pont and eight other companies pleaded no contest to charges of price fixing in the dye industry. And in 1978, the FTC had charged Du Pont with attempting to monopolize the $600 million titanium dioxide industry. Undoubtedly, the government would watch Du Pont closely for any signs it was trying to monopolize the aramid industry informally after the expiration of its Kevlar patent.

24 Du Pont also found potential legal problems in the area of environmental protection. Throughout the 1970s, the chemicals industry had been a target of investigation by the Environmental Protection Agency (EPA) and various consumer groups on questions of air and water pollution. Early in the decade, Du Pont had joined other major chemical firms in a suit to overturn the EPA's authority to regulate discharges into rivers, but in 1977, the Supreme Court ruled in the EPA's favor. In the same year, Du Pont suffered a major blow to its Freon market when the government banned fluorocarbons in aerosols because of the threat to the ozone layer of the atmosphere. As of 1978,

Du Pont had over $650 million invested in environmental control and an annual operating budget for pollution control of $236 million. It also faced possible bans on several of its pesticides and fungicides on the grounds they may be carcinogens.

25 The issue of carcinogenic effects of Du Pont's products was raised most often in the area of occupational safety. Reports of high incidences of cancer among Du Pont employees handling certain highly toxic products had more than once on short notice forced Du Pont to redesign production processes to reduce or eliminate worker exposure. Although Du Pont had already faced and overcome this problem relative to the manufacture of Kevlar, it was impossible to predict whether further problems of this sort would arise among those who handle Kevlar in its various end-use applications. Cancer detection research was still in its infancy, and carcinogenic effects are often not identified for some time after the introduction of a product or process. Du Pont would continue to face considerable risk in this area.

Markets

26 Du Pont viewed Kevlar as a specialty product capable of capturing a small share of several markets. As of 1978, these markets included tire reinforcement, aerospace, protective clothing, and marine and sporting equipment.

27 **The Tire Market.** First and foremost among the industrial applications of Kevlar was tire reinforcement, specifically belts for high-performance radial tires. In this market, its chief competitor was steel. Exhibit 5 shows that steel consumption in tire manufacture rose from 3 million pounds in 1970 to 175 million in 1978. *Chemical and Engineering News* predicted consumption would rise to 350 million pounds by 1983. If Kevlar could cut into steel's share of this market to any appreciable degree, it would enjoy enormous demand. Already, since 1975, use of Kevlar in radial tires had grown fivefold to an estimated 5 million pounds per year. Sales to tire manufacturers were expected to account for half of the $80 million in total Kevlar sales projected for 1979.

28 Kevlar faced several obstacles in competing with steel in the tire market. One obstacle was the image steel had built. Another was price. The form of Kevlar used in

Exhibit 5

Creative material consumption in tire manufacturing (millions of pounds)

	Steel	*Polyester*	*Nylon*	*Glass fiber*	*Aramid*	*Rayon*	*Total*
1970	3	150	265	35	—	86	539
1971	5	179	276	36	—	113	609
1972	24	222	291	37	—	94	668
1973	60	242	274	34	—	73	683
1974	97	232	287	26	—	58	700
1975	117	232	229	27	1	28	634
1976	132	236	206	26	2	18	620
1977	167	283	252	31	3	22	758
1978	175	265	250	34	5	29	758

Source: Rubber Manufacturers Association; *Chemical and Engineering News,* April 4, 1979, p. 10.

tire belts cost 4½ times what steel belts cost ($5.85 per pound for Kevlar versus $1.10 per pound for steel). On the other hand, Kevlar enjoyed certain advantages over steel. Tests had shown that, at speeds of 100 MPH or more, tires became hot and the tread expanded, pulling away from the steel belt and causing blowouts. Firestone's troubles with its Firestone 500 radial were apparently attributable to this weakness. Kevlar belts, however, had the capacity to expand slightly when heated, which would prevent such separation. Thus, Kevlar had a distinct advantage over steel for tires used in cars driven at high speeds (e.g., police cars) and on tractor-trailers. Also, because of its weight-to-strength advantage (pound for pound Kevlar is five times stronger than steel), Kevlar-reinforced tires were lighter than steel-belted tires. Kevlar-belted truck tires, for example, were 20 pounds lighter than steel-belted tires. With 18 tires on a standard truck rig, the use of Kevlar tires would result in a 360-pound weight reduction, allowing greater fuel efficiency in a period of rising fuel costs.

29 The future of Kevlar in tire applications depended not only on the substitution of Kevlar belts for steel belts in radial tires but also on the growth of radial tires' share of the new car and replacement markets. Overall figures for tire production appear in Exhibit 6. Of all original-equipment passenger tires sold in 1972, only 6 percent were radials; by 1977, 69 percent were radials, and this share was predicted to rise to 70 percent in 1978, 75 percent in 1979, and 80 percent by 1980. Meanwhile, the actual number of original-equipment radials sold would depend on new car production as well as on market share. Ford estimated that demand for domestic automobiles would decline by 3 to 4 percent in 1978.

30 As Exhibit 6 reveals, the largest segment of the passenger tire market—70 percent—was replacement tires. This segment was also important because it offered higher profit margins and was more clearly dominated by domestic manufacturers than the original-equipment market (only 12.6 million out of 129 million replacement tires sold in 1977 were foreign made). Because of growth in this market, total passenger tire sales were expected to rise to 193 million units in 1978. The truck and bus tire market was also expected to grow 3–4 percent in the coming year and shift increasingly to radials (in 1977, 25 percent of all truck tires sold were radials versus 2 percent in 1975). Quantitatively, truck tires could become Kevlar's biggest market since upwards of five pounds would be used in every belted radial truck tire.[1]

31 **The Aerospace Market.** Because of its strength-to-weight characteristics, Kevlar had also caught the eye of aerospace manufacturers. By 1978, it was being substituted for aluminum in wing-control surfaces and nonload-bearing parts of fuselages and for fiberglass in engine casings in aircraft (Douglas DC-10, Lockheed L-1011, and DeHaviland DHC-7). In these applications, Kevlar offered a 25–30 percent weight reduction over its competitors. This was crucial since it required three pounds of fuel to lift one pound of payload off the ground in most aircraft. Every pound taken off an airliner saved $300 in fuel costs over the life of the airplane—and this figure would increase as fuel costs rose. Weight reduction was even more crucial in missiles and spacecraft where the fuel-to-payload ratio approached 20 to 1 and where weight reduction might mean not only less fuel consumption but also larger payloads and

[1] Estimate based on the facts that a truck tire with a Kevlar belt weighs 20 pounds less than a steel-belted tire and that, in a given application, the amount of Kevlar required is only one fifth the amount of steel required.

Exhibit 6

Pneumatic casings (tires) (in thousands of units)

		Shipments								
		Passenger			Truck and bus			Tractor-implement		
Year	*Total production*	*Total**	*Original equipment*	*Replacement*	*Total**	*Original equipment*	*Replacement*	*Total**	*Original equipment*	*Replacement*
1977	231,638	189,552	55,668	129,283	37,031	10,330	25,912	5,048	1,887	2,972
1976	185,950	177,009	49,905	123,000	31,529	8,668	22,282	5,376	2,066	3,173
1975	186,704	167,625	39,375	122,956	28,655	8,077	19,751	5,291	1,929	3,189
1974	211,390	175,170	43,395	124,154	34,248	11,850	21,295	6,387	2,129	4,072

* Including exports.
Source: Rubber Manufacturers Association; *Standard & Poor's Industry Surveys,* July 1979, p. R204.

longer ranges. Already Kevlar was being used in some components of the Trident missile.

32 In 1978, Kevlar used by the aerospace market sold for an average price of $19 a pound (various forms of Kevlar ranged from $5 to $30), which was as much as 10 times as expensive as aluminum and fiberglass but well below a competing fiber composite, Boron, which cost $200 per pound. There was hope that by 1980, Kevlar components would be no more expensive than aluminum components because an automated production system was to replace the costly practice of manually building up components layer by layer.

33 The aircraft industry in which Du Pont was seeking new markets for Kevlar seemed headed for expansion in 1978. Among commercial airlines, equipment purchases normally followed a six- to eight-year cycle. The figures in Exhibit 7 indicate that the current cycle had bottomed out in 1976–77. Commercial aircraft deliveries for 1978 would total 284, 99 more than 1977, and total airline sales were predicted to rise from $3.6 billion in 1977 to $6.3 billion in 1982. Private aircraft sales were also expected to rise above the 18,225 domestic deliveries and 3,665 foreign deliveries in 1978.

34 The outlook for military aircraft and spacecraft was not as promising. Domestic orders were expected to suffer because of de-emphasis on space exploration, the success of the SALT II disarmament talks with the Russians, and President Carter's pledge to balance the budget by 1981. However, foreign military sales were expected to compensate somewhat for the domestic cutbacks, despite the Carter administration policy of limiting military exports. The Mid-East countries would continue to be a growth market for American military aircraft. Iran, for example, placed orders in 1978 for 160 F-16 fighters.

35 **Other Markets.** A small but dynamic market for Kevlar—accounting for about 10 percent of its sales—lay in protective clothing, especially bulletproof vests and coat linings. In this area, Kevlar's performance had been extraordinary. In tests and in actual incidents, lightweight vests made with Kevlar and weighing only 2½ pounds

Exhibit 7

Production of commercial transport aircraft (fixed wing, multiple engine)

Company and aircraft	*1973*	*1974*	*1975*	*1976*	*1977*	*1978*
Boeing:						
707	11	21	7	3	3	10
727	92	91	91	61	67	117
737	17	41	51	41	25	40
747	28	21	20	27	20	33
McDonnell Douglas:						
DC-9	21	48	35	44	16	22
DC-10	57	46	43	19	12	18
Lockheed:						
L-1011	39	41	25	16	11	8
L-100-30/C-130	29	23	43	27	31	36

Source: *Standard & Poor's Industry Surveys,* January 1979, p. A13.

had repeatedly prevented death or serious injury to persons shot at point-blank range. By early 1978, more than 23 percent of the 650,000 police officers in the United States were wearing Kevlar vests, including the entire New York City police force. This market was expected to grow. Also, in light of rising crime rates, domestic civilian sales of Kevlar-based protective clothing might also become significant. In 1978, Du Pont was supplying Kevlar to a number of manufacturers of such clothing, including Second Chance, Armor of America, and Burlington.

36 Du Pont also hoped to penetrate the recreational boat market (as a reinforcement in the hulls of sailcraft, canoes, and kayaks) and the sporting equipment market (skis, hockey sticks, tennis rackets, and fishing rods). Both markets had been growing rapidly in the late 1970s but faced an uncertain future as renewed inflation reduced disposable personal income and diverted spending away from leisure-time durable goods. Less-volatile markets for Kevlar appeared to lie in such industrial applications as high-pressure thermoplastic hydraulic hose and belting for various types of machinery. Unfortunately, the amount of Kevlar required in these diverse new markets remained almost impossible to estimate in 1978.

The Strategic Decision

37 Advocates of the further expansion of Kevlar production saw continuously growing demand for the fiber in a variety of markets in the 1980s and predicted that Kevlar would account for 10 percent of the profits of the Textile Fibers Division by the end of the decade. However, Irving Shapiro and the executive committee realized that such forecasts rested on a number of critical assumptions about general economic conditions, price differentials, market acceptance of Kevlar, and the behavior of competitors. These underlying assumptions would have to be scrutinized with utmost care before expansion could be approved. Shapiro and his colleagues remembered only too clearly the Corfam fiasco of the late 1960s in which Du Pont lost millions of dollars in all-out production of a leather substitute before demand had been suitably developed. More recently, they remembered the losses arising from overexpansion of synthetic fibers production on the basis of overly optimistic forecasts of consumer demand.

case 19
Swiss-tex

Introduction

1 Intex Products, Inc., was a closely held chemical company headquartered in Greenville, South Carolina. The company specialized in sales to the textile, transportation, and paper industries and enjoyed a 20 percent increase in sales in 1980 to $21 million. Richard Greer, president and chief executive officer, joined the family firm in 1970, immediately after earning a BBA from the University of South Carolina and an MBA from Harvard, and rose quickly through several positions in the company. As CEO, he had the enthusiastic support of the board of directors.

2 In 1974, Intex and the Fritz Nauer Company, a Swiss manufacturer of polyurethane foam (sponge) products with about $15 million in annual sales, entered into a 50-50 joint venture. The new company, called Swiss-tex, was formed to fabricate and market products using the Nauer foam in the United States. Swiss-tex started in a small way with about 3,000 square feet of space at the back of an Intex warehouse. Sales began slowly, but after 1977, they mushroomed so dramatically that for the fiscal year July 1978 through June 1979, sales were estimated to exceed $1.1 million.

3 It was during that year that Greer began to see a need for changes at Swiss-tex. He was both pleased and concerned with the company's performance. Net income was estimated to be 17 percent of sales, but at least as important to him, the high rate of growth was expected to continue. On the other hand, Swiss-tex was more than two months behind in filling orders, despite the fact that in 1978, the company had expanded its capacity to a 10,000-square-foot facility leased from Intex. The backlog appeared to have caused some loss of business from impatient customers. In addition, expensive logistical problems and high inventory costs were incurred in the handling and storage of the light-weight, but bulky, raw foam. More than 12,000 square feet of warehousing had been leased in several locations in Greenville solely for its storage.

Swiss-tex Foam Products

4 Greer believed that one of the principal reasons for Swiss-tex's rapid expansion was its unique product. Although some other U.S. companies made polyurethane foam—mainly for use in furniture padding, no other U.S. manufacturer had the special technology of the Fritz Nauer Company, from which Swiss-tex purchased 95 percent of its raw material. The Nauer foam products had a high tensile strength, could include

This case was prepared by Professors John A. Pearce II of the University of South Carolina and Benjamin M. Oviatt of Oklahoma State University. It has been accepted for publication in the *Journal of Management Case Studies.*

a marbled coloring effect and antibacterial properties, would never harden like cellulose sponges (the most popular raw material), and could be economically produced in either small or large quantities. Swiss-tex used these qualities in a wide variety of products, some of which are shown in Exhibit 1.

5 *Do-Gooders* were the general-purpose cleaning implements. This line included utility sponges, sponges with varying grades of a scouring surface laminated to one side, and one sponge mounted on a stick for cleaning glassware. Some of the scouring sponges were sculptured to form a hand grip. Sold mainly in grocery stores, this line seemed to have low buyer interest and had the company's lowest profit margin of products.

6 The *Anti-bact* sponges were among the company's fastest-growing products. Polyurethane sponges in the past had been a problem because of their tendency to allow bacterial growth, causing an unpleasant look and odor. The Nauer company developed a method to eliminate the problem by including bacteriostatic and fungostatic ingredients in its foam-pouring process. The personal care products all contained this ingredient as well as marbled colors. Some had a "loofah-like" scrubber laminated to the sponge. The profit margin on these products was moderate but satisfactory.

7 Sales of sponges and scrubbers to industrial, variety, and automotive-supply firms were also at important levels.

8 OEM (original equipment manufacturers) sales were projected to be about 50 percent of Swiss-tex's total in 1979–80. These were bulk sales of foam made for other manufacturers who used it in their own products. Packaging material was one such use. Swiss-tex foam had also become popular for products such as mop heads on self-wringing mops because the sponge did not harden to make compression difficult. This was a high profit margin area, and one customer might order $30–$50,000 worth of foam at one time. It was also a dangerous area. It made the company dependent on a product that provided no public brand name identification for Swiss-tex. Greer was concerned that the OEM line was pushing Swiss-tex to its manufacturing capacity, and he wanted the company to concentrate more on product lines that would establish a recognition factor while its product was still unique to the United States.

The Production Process

9 Production actually began in Switzerland. The Fritz Nauer Company poured the raw foam, sold it at cost to Swiss-tex, and shipped it to Greenville for fabrication into a usable product. At the Nauer facility, liquid foam was poured from a nozzle onto a long table. The foam rose rapidly and expanded like a loaf of bread to hold its shape. Expansion was so dramatic that the amount of foam produced, relative to the amount of raw materials used, ensured Nauer of significant excess capacity. The company's uniquely efficient process allowed the economical production of small quantities in several separate color runs. This was beyond the capability of U.S. foamers, who required a relatively long production run for economy.

10 After production, the foam bun, measuring 1-by-2-by-.5 meters, was mechanically compressed, vacuum packed, loaded onto a boat, shipped to Charleston, South Carolina, or Savannah, Georgia, and then trucked to Greenville. Upon arrival, most buns were stored in leased warehouses in their compressed state. Swiss-tex was forced to use these warehouses because of a shortage of storage space at their production facility (see Exhibit 2).

Exhibit 1

Promotional materials

Welcome the Do-Gooder family of sponges into your home. They're a hard-working bunch with some progressive new innovations for cleaning up lots of areas in your home. Each family member has his own special talent, but like all families, the members have common traits...traits which make them different than the cellulose sponges you're used to buying.

Do-Gooders are made of polyurethane, not cellulose. That means they'll never get hard. They'll stay flexible and absorbent wet or dry. And talk about tough. Do-Gooders even resist cracking, tearing and flaking. All they really need in order to last a good long time, is an occasional bath. Just rinse them clean after every use and periodically toss them in either your washing machine or your dishwasher. They'll come out clean and fresh, last a lot longer and do a lot gooder.

Now meet the members of the Do-Gooder family. Each one does every bit as much good as the next, but each does its good in different places.

Home 'n Car Clean-up.

This is the big daddy of them all. He was designed to do a superior job on the big jobs around your house. He's a thick husky fellow, but amazingly easy to handle. His sides are shaped to fit your hand so he can tackle the big jobs like your car, walls and floors without being cumbersome. One big swipe cleans a lot of dirty territory.

Tub 'n Tile non-scratch clean-up.

This is the two-faced member of the family who's especially designed for tub and sink clean-up in the bathroom. She has a scrubbing surface ideal for removing stubborn soap film from porcelain and tile, but she won't scratch or wear it away. In fact, she's safe to use on any "scratchable" surface...chrome fixtures, medicine cabinets and even mirrors. Once you've scrubbed with the non-scratch scrubbing side, you just turn her over to rinse and wipe with the sponge side. She's really two clean-ups in one.

Dish 'n Teflon® non-scratch clean-up.

This member of the family you'll want to get to know from all sides. Her non-scratch scrubbing side is especially designed to clean your dishes and Teflon®-coated cookware. In fact, she's safe to use on any washable surface...your refrigerator, stove top, range hood or any porcelain surface. Her opposite side is a flexible sponge for wiping and rinsing. And her other two sides are gently shaped with easy-to-grip grooves.

Pot 'n Pan Clean-up.

Here's the twin brother of Dish 'n Teflon®—only his job is to clean your pots and pans. His tough, heavy-duty scrubbing surface won't be gentle with baked-on, fried-on food. In fact, it's so tough it'll even take on barbecue grills and broilers. But like his sister, Pot 'n Pan clean-up has the same sturdy sponge side for wiping-up and the same easy-to-grip grooves in his sides.

Glass 'n Dish clean-up.

This gal is long and lean...perfect for fitting into and getting dirt out of glasses, jars, and bottles. She can get into those hard-to-get places and really get them clean...and save you from getting your hands dirty. You'll like her for regular dishes too. With her super sponge and dandy handle, she'll get you in and out of a lot of dirty spots.

Now that you've met the Do-Gooder family, welcome them into your home. Because there's a lot of good to be done around a home and these are the clean-ups who can do it gooder than any others.

11 The interior of the facility itself was arranged for maximum efficiency. When buns were brought to the building, they were unpacked in the staging area and then stacked in the center storage space which was capable of holding a one- or two-day supply of raw material. Before fabrication began, the hard unusable crust was cut off the bun and discarded. The processing began at a large vertical saw, a delicate instrument needing careful supervision and often watched by the plant manager. Some of the resulting slabs were then taken to the spray booth for lamination of a scouring or a loofah-like surface, then to the small vertical saw to be cut to finished size. Other slabs were taken directly to the small vertical saw. Scrap foam produced during fabrication was sold for pillow stuffing. Some products were then taken to the packaging

Exhibit 1 (*concluded*)

Luxurious Personal Care With a New, Hygienic Twist.

The Anti-bact process was developed to inhibit the spread of bacteria and fungi, that so often grows in a bath sponge. Anti-bact is manufactured by integrating active chemical agents into the cells of the sponge through an exclusive process developed in Switzerland. Your customers will be assured a fresh, mildew-free sponge with every use.
Our easily recognized marble colored Puffs are available in an assortment of popular colors.

A large masculine size sponge for invigorating showers or baths.
No. 0533

Our rounded sponge is ideal for face, neck, and other spot cleansing. Also a great size for the children's bath.
No. 0531

A special sponge to make that bath or shower a more relaxing occasion. It's convolute "loofah-like" scrubber provides finger massage as you bathe.
No. 0535

It's a unique, hand-sized sponge with a "loofah-like" scrubber for skin stimulation and removal of tough skin around ankles, knees, and elbows.
No. 0534

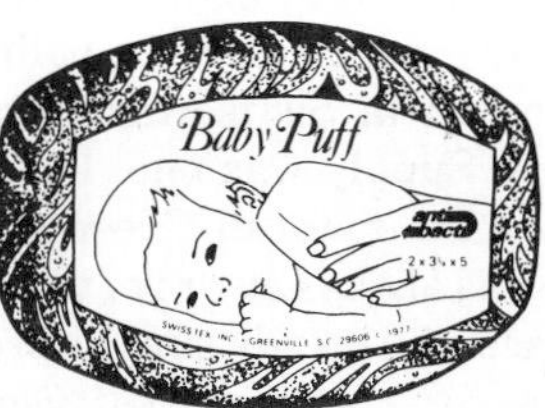

This sponge is perfectly shaped for cleansing of small areas. It's soft and gentle on baby's skin and easy to hold.
No. 0530

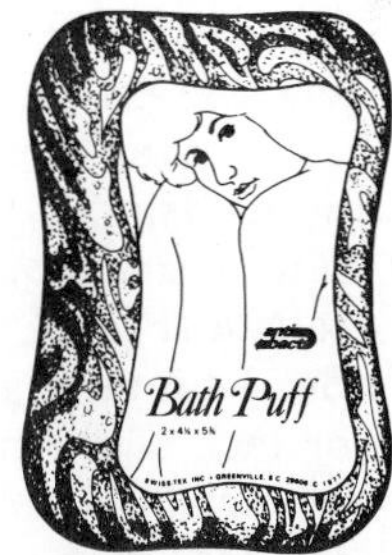

It's hand size shape makes it the perfect sponge for soft lathering and rinsing, promising a more pleasurable bath.
No. 0532

Exhibit 2

Swiss-Tex plant—1979

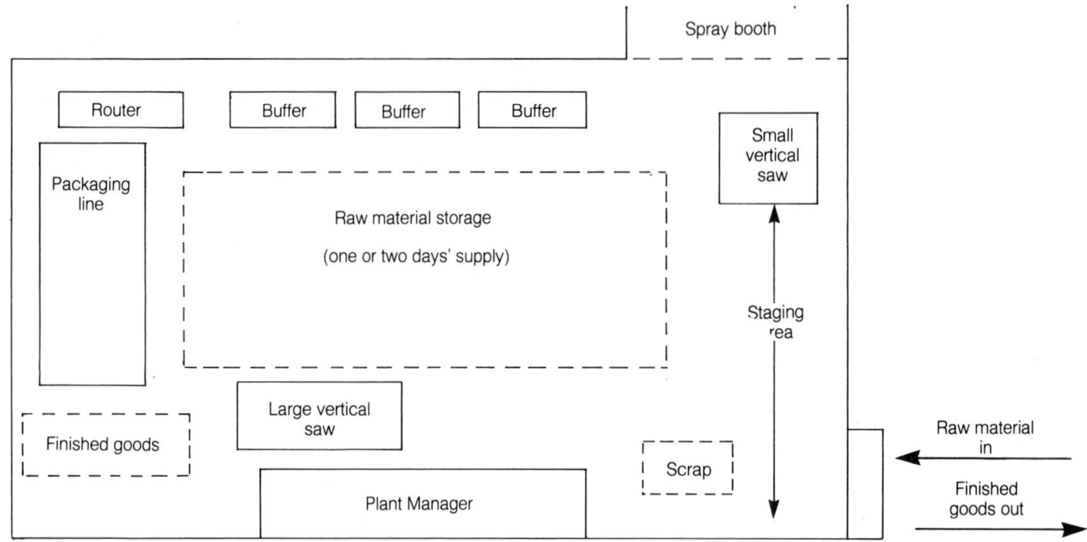

line, but many were specially shaped or rounded by the three buffing machines. The scouring sponges were sent to the router to have grooved cuts made to form a hand grip. After packaging, the finished goods were stored for a short time, then moved to the staging area for shipping.

12 Because of the two- to three-month backlog, the plant was only producing "to order." The largest orders were for mop heads and other OEM products requiring relatively simple processing and using about 20–25 buns in an eight-hour shift. Capacity, with a product mix dominated by OEM foam, appeared to be about $1.6 million in annual sales; break-even was estimated at $95,000 per month with a two-shift schedule.

13 Swiss-tex avoided many production risks, pollution problems, and technical problems by having the foam poured in Switzerland. But it assumed other risks common to international operations. Supply was one. Lead time was two months from an order to Nauer until receipt of the foam in Greenville. Transportation was expensive, and Swiss-tex management was always aware of uncontrollable hazards such as dock strikes or lack of shipping space. Although supply problems from Switzerland had not yet materialized, some Swiss-tex managers believed they were an inevitable part of being involved with a foreign partner.

14 One problem that had already been encountered was the currency exchange rate. At that time, the trend was for the U.S. dollar to lose value in relationship to the currencies of several industrialized countries. Swiss-tex would order from Nauer, then watch the order become more expensive as the value of the Swiss franc rose. When liquidity became sufficient, Swiss-tex began to prepay most invoices from Switzerland and, thus, had eliminated some of these extra costs. Yet changes in the value of the dollar continued to cause Swiss-tex problems in projecting costs.

15 There were also some problems inherent to the domestic manufacturing operation. The spray booth was a potential health hazard to employees, so a powerful ventilation system was required. The highest domestic production risk came from the fact that polyurethane was highly flammable and was considered to be in the same industrial risk category as oil. This caused their storage leases to be $2 per square foot per year, about 50 to 75 cents higher than less-risky goods stored in the Greenville area.

The Industry

16 The purpose behind the Swiss-tex venture was to combine Intex management and marketing expertise with Nauer's superior technology to bring a unique product to U.S. customers. After several years of success, there was still no U.S. company that could duplicate Swiss-tex products. The strength, color, antibacterial quality, and distinctive shapes and surfaces of their sponges, along with the flexible and efficient Swiss process, gave Swiss-tex superior competitive advantages. The product's only disadvantage, a minor one, seemed to be that it was somewhat less absorbent than cellulose.

17 Swiss-tex had sales in all areas east of the Mississippi River, and industrial sales had expanded to the West. It had always been a bit difficult to precisely define the company's markets because it actually competed against many products with similar purposes, but from different raw materials. Swiss-tex scouring sponges competed with SOS, Brillo, and many others. The personal care line competed with everything from loofahs, to wash cloths, to bars of soap.

18 The main competition, however, was from the standard American cellulose sponge of which Du Pont was the principal manufacturer. Greer had been told that this business had difficult pollution problems, that it was not profitable, and that Du Pont would prefer to get out of it.

19 Swiss-tex sales included one OEM customer with annual orders of $350,000. With orders of such size, Greer knew that competitors like Reeves Brothers Foam and Scott Foam (a division of Scott Paper), which required large production runs to achieve economy, might soon be attracted to pour Swiss-tex type foam. Intex attorneys advised Greer that patents could provide Swiss-tex with very little protection. Additionally, he was aware that another European manufacturer had technological expertise similar to Nauer's, although it temporarily lacked the capacity to export to the United States. The threat of the entrance of a competitor with great financial and marketing strength was of real concern to Swiss-tex management and to Greer.

The Proposal

20 The development of the long backlog on orders and the resulting loss of business provided a ready market for other manufacturers. Robert Graham, president and chief operating officer of Swiss-tex, approached Greer informally about a proposal to meet the increasing demand. Greer asked that Graham submit his ideas in writing with supporting figures as soon as possible so the planning staff at Intex could review the alternatives.

21 Graham's formal proposal appears as Appendix A. Basically, it included an increase of 42 percent for FY 79–80 and the same gross margin that was estimated for the

end of FY 78–79. Graham proposed construction of a new 90,000-square-foot facility on Intex property to be financed by 7.25 percent, 20-year, tax-free, industrial revenue bonds, plus equity supplied by Nauer and Intex.

22 The proposed site was on 10 acres of a 164-acre tract of land owned by Intex that had been purchased several years before for $3,000 per acre. At the time of the Swiss-tex formation, Intex had agreed with Nauer to sell land to Swiss-tex at the original cost if the sales were judged to warrant the construction of additional facilities for the subsidiary. The site had two major advantages: (1) It was only 15 minutes away from Intex headquarters, which handled all Swiss-tex accounting, payroll, and pension plans at cost, and (2) the additional acreage provided ample space for continued expansion, including the construction of a foam-pouring plant. Estimates indicated that with about $5 million in annual sales, foam pouring in the United States would be economical.

23 Scott Dales, Intex vice president of manufacturing, estimated that costs could be cut 20 percent by building a U.S. foam-production facility. Intex and Nauer had agreed in the beginning that, should domestic foaming become a reality, Nauer would thereafter earn royalties on all Swiss-tex sales.

24 An alternate proposal to Graham's was that Swiss-tex lease approximately 40,000 square feet. A third idea, supported by several Intex managers, was that Graham's proposal be cut to construction of a 40,000-square-foot facility. There was general agreement that 90,000 square feet was more than required at the time. Some felt that Graham's sales projections were too optimistic, that the market was soft, and that entrance of a large U.S. foamer into the market could be disastrous for Swiss-tex sales.

25 Greer reviewed the proposals and knew that little new information was likely to appear. His Swiss partner had deferred the judgment to Intex since Intex had superior knowledge of the U.S. market. So Greer called a meeting of the Intex planning staff to give the various proposals a final going over.

The Meeting

26 Intex officers attending were Scott Dales, vice president of manufacturing; George Phillips, vice president of finance; and Mike Byrd, vice president of marketing. Greer asked that Dales summarize the Swiss-tex need for additional space.

27 Dales began by noting that if Graham's sales projection held up, Swiss-tex's present production capacity would be at the theoretical limit by 1980. He stated that the purchase of two new saws would improve efficiency without adding any labor costs and that all labor increases would be proportional to sales. He felt that 40,000 square feet would be ample for the manufacturing process, for on-site storage, and for 3,000 square feet of office space. Especially important was the added storage capacity which would cut the risk of delays associated with the long lead times on orders from Switzerland. He estimated that production and storage economies alone would increase gross margins by 4 to 5 percent annually. He concluded from preliminary discussions with contractors that construction of a 40,000-square-foot facility made of prestressed concrete would take six months to complete and would cost approximately $830,000. According to Dales, Graham's proposal of a larger plant would require nearly the same construction time but would cost $1.5 million.

28 Dales was the principal exponent of a cautious approach. He said he could appreciate

both sides of the issue but generally favored the lease option. He estimated that 40,000 square feet could be leased for $2 per square foot per year with quite flexible terms. He expressed his concern about a more powerful competitor acquiring the technology, and he reminded everyone of the lucrative offers they already had for the Intex land.

29 "Furthermore," he said, "I'm of the opinion that 40,000 square feet is more than enough to satisfy our present needs. A 42 percent increase in sales in a single year is just too optimistic for me. We've never had such an increase. I think we'd be on more solid ground if we leased space until these sales actually materialized. And finally, I'm concerned that, with Graham's proposal, the net income-to-sales ratio would fall from over 17 percent to under 7 percent."

30 "Scott, I can appreciate your fears concerning Bob's sales projection," Greer interjected, "but my only concern about Swiss-tex's profitability is that it maintain an income high enough to meet its obligations to creditors. Although Swiss-tex is a joint venture, giving us less flexibility with its earnings than with those of Intex, I'm certain our partner in Switzerland understands that our objective is to help our company grow as rapidly as possible on a sound financial base. George, how is that base?"

31 "Well, quite good, I'd say. Swiss-tex has no long-term debt. ROI has been almost 20 percent, and growth has never been less than 15 percent per year and has approached 30 percent in the last year. But the most-attractive thing to me about Bob's plan is the 7.25 percent financing. Recent AAA taxable issues have been selling to yield more than 9.25 percent; so this is a bargain, even with the $200,000 equity required from each partner. Indications are that the bonds could be placed privately, with 'interest only' for the first two to three years, and amortized thereafter. If production efficiencies pan out, as Scott has indicated, Swiss-tex could qualify for a $200,000 investment tax credit, whether we buy or lease. But that's an estimate subject to error. I must say, I believe Scott is right about 40,000 square feet being enough for now, but excess capacity could be useful if the business really expands. Besides, Intex needs even more storage space than the 10,000 square feet that would be available after Swiss-tex moves out of our facilities. Swiss-tex could turn around and rent space to us in its new building at, say, $1.25 per square foot. And they could lease to others for even more. That's a good deal for them, since we've only been charging them 65 cents per square foot per year during all the time they've been in our facility. But, of course, the accuracy of the sales projection is the critical unknown."

32 "Thanks, George. You're right," agreed Greer. "What about it, Mike?"

33 "I know the projected increase in sales is high, but Graham's projections have, traditionally, been conservative. We should look even further down the road. My figures show that a new 40,000-square-foot plant would have a capacity of $7.3 million in sales with the present product mix, and with 90,000 square feet we could support a $25 million business. Graham's marketing people are excellent, and you can see the results. With a 90,000-square-foot facility, we could really push the branded products and expand to the West Coast.

34 "On the other hand, if a big foamer acquires technology similar to ours before we've completed our expansion and promotional efforts, they could really threaten our sales. We can't compete yet with an established national distribution channel and advertising blitz. And they might have the capability of undercutting our prices. I think the first thing we've got to decide is what the potential competitors are likely to do, and what we can do about them. Then we can compute the kind of productive expansion we can afford."

Conclusion

35 As Greer left the meeting, he considered the projected 42 percent sales increase. Graham was an experienced manager with sound business judgment, yet Greer knew that Graham wanted to build that new plant very much. Some might even see the proposal as self-serving, although Greer found it difficult to believe that Graham would distort such a report. Greer's position as CEO forced him to look at the proposal dispassionately. It would be necessary to consider not only competitors and financing but also the future risks of depending on a foreign supplier, the advantages and risks of a domestic foam plant in the future, and the ability of Swiss-tex to establish a good brand name image with customers.

36 He resolved to announce his recommendation to the board at their meeting in two weeks. He was sure the board would support his decision.

Appendix A

April 27, 1979

Memorandum

To: Mr. Richard Greer, President and Chief Executive Officer, Intex Products, Inc.

From: Mr. Robert Graham, President and Chief Operating Officer, Swiss-tex

Re: FY 79–80 projections including facility expansion

37 Attached are copies of the projected profit and loss statement (Table 1); sales and operating forecast by quarter (Table 2); cash flow analysis (Table 3); selling, general, and administrative expenses (Table 4); and the manufacturing expense budget (Table 5).

38 I am pleased to report we are projecting a net profit after taxes of $109,791 for fiscal 1979–80. This forecast includes the necessary amounts for relocation of our manufacturing facilities to our new manufacturing plant along with the associated charges for the construction and building of this new facility during the 1979–80 fiscal year.

39 Our projected sales forecast shows an increase of $468,139 or approximately 42 percent over the estimated sales for fiscal 1978–79. Based on the information available to us at the present time and the new business we have acquired during the past fiscal year, we feel this to be a realistic sales estimate. Our projected gross margin for the new fiscal year is based on the estimated gross margin for fiscal 1978–79 of approximately 41 percent. We have also forecasted our cost of goods sold at 60 percent of net sales for the new year.

40 Our analysis of our cash flow projections for the fiscal year indicate we will have a positive flow for the first two quarters, a negative flow for the second half of the year, and a positive cash flow of approximately $44,304 for the entire year.

41 Our selling, general, and administrative expenses have been budgeted at an increased level necessary for the level of sales we have forecasted for the new fiscal year. Appropriate amounts have again been included for the establishment of a retirement program for our executive and administrative people. The estab-

lishment of this program during the current year will eliminate the existing inequities with the retirement program covering our manufacturing personnel. I have budgeted an 8 percent increase in salaries for our executive and administrative people for the fiscal year. I personally consider this to be minimal and necessary to maintain the quality of our personnel in order to ensure our continued growth and future success.

42 We have budgeted a total of $46,900 for our marketing accounts. This money will be used in promoting our existing programs as well as establishing new product lines during the new year.

43 The increase in our manufacturing expenses reflects the overall increase in manufactured products we have experienced during the past year. I have also budgeted appropriate amounts for relocation expenses as well as depreciation expenses on our new manufacturing facility. As previously stated, we have budgeted our cost of goods sold at 60 percent of our net sales for the new fiscal year. We feel this is an ambitious goal for us, particularly in view of the additional expenses we will be incurring with the new manufacturing facility but feel the increased volume will allow us to absorb the additional expenses.

44 If we proceed soon with construction, we could be relocated during the third quarter of the 1979–80 fiscal year to the new plant site. Financing for the new facilities and equipment will be completed through the proceeds of an industrial revenue bond as well as the additional equity financing by the two shareholders. We will be considering the purchase of additional equipment as we deem it necessary and appropriate in order to maintain our manufacturing capabilities.

45 I will be pleased to answer any questions you may have concerning this budget.

RG/jyh

Attachments

Table 1

Forecast fiscal 1979–80

	Estimate 1978–1979	*Budget 1979–1980*	*Increase*
Gross sales	$1,113,861	$1,582,000	$468,139
Discounts and allowances	13,373	18,800	5,427
Net sales	1,100,488	1,563,200	462,712
Cost of goods sold	643,312	937,920	294,608
Rental income	—	16,072	16,072
Gross profit	457,176	641,352	184,176
Selling, general and administrative expenses	259,558	390,800	131,242
Rental income	—	595	595
Operating profit	197,618	251,147	53,529
Interest expense	608	70,313	69,705
Net profit before taxes	197,010	180,834	(16,176)
Taxes: state	4,700	10,850	6,150
federal	—	60,193	60,193
Net profit after taxes	$ 192,310	$ 109,791	$ (82,519)

Table 2

Sales and operating forecast (fiscal 1979–80)

	1st quarter	*2d quarter*	*3d quarter*	*4th quarter*	*Total*
Variety	$ 8,648	$ 9,059	$ 10,072	$ 14,221	$ 42,000
Institutional	56,623	59,318	65,945	93,114	275,000
Automotive	10,295	10,785	11,990	16,930	50,000
Do-Gooders	38,092	39,905	44,363	62,640	185,000
OEM	164,720	172,560	191,840	270,880	800,000
Personal care	45,298	47,454	52,756	74,492	220,000
Miscellaneous	2,059	2,157	2,398	3,386	10,000
Gross sales	325,735	341,238	379,364	535,663	1,582,000
Discounts and allowances	3,871	4,055	4,508	6,366	18,000
Net sales	321,864	337,183	374,856	529,297	1,563,200
Cost of goods sold	193,188	202,310	224,914	317,578	937,920
Rental income	—	—	6,429	9,643	16,072
Gross profit	128,746	134,873	156,371	221,362	641,352
Selling, general, and administrative expenses	80,466	84,296	93,714	132,324	390,800
Rental income	—	—	238	357	595
Operating profit	48,280	50,577	62,895	89,395	251,147
Interest expense	5,859	17,578	23,438	23,438	70,313
Net profit before taxes	42,421	32,999	39,457	65,957	180,834
Taxes	16,388	11,749	14,928	27,978	71,043
Net profit after taxes	$ 26,033	$ 21,250	$ 24,529	$ 37,979	$ 109,791

Table 3

Cash requirements

	1st quarter	*2d quarter*	*3d quarter*	*4th quarter*	*Total*
Profit before tax	$ 42,421	$ 32,999	$39,457	$65,957	$180,834
Provision for taxes	2,000	2,000	2,000	2,000	8,000
Cash depreciation	3,300	13,925	13,925	13,925	45,075
From operations	43,721	44,924	51,382	77,882	217,909
Receivables—end	140,054	146,019	209,156	283,605	283,605
Receivables—beginning	190,000	140,054	146,019	209,156	190,000
Receivable investment	(46,946)	5,965	63,137	74,449	93,605
Inventory investment	30,000	10,000	20,000	20,000	80,000
Additional cash required	$ (63,667)	$ (28,959)	$31,755	$16,567	$ (44,304)

Table 4

Selling, general and administrative expenses (fiscal 1979–1980)

		Estimate 1978–1979	*Budget 1979–1980*	*Increase*
700	Salaries—exempt	$ 74,620	$ 74,322	$ (298)
701	Salaries—hourly	-0-	25,458	25,458
711	Incentive pay	26,600	34,860	8,260
715	Commissions	28,496	40,468	11,972
718	Outside services	12,000	14,000	2,000
719	Legal, audit, and professional fees	2,300	3,600	1,300
725	Retirement	—	8,980	8,980
726	Payroll taxes	4,970	6,428	1,458
727	Group insurance, $750/person	2,830	3,750	920
728	Workman's compensation	135	175	40
730	General insurance	2,360	3,000	640
734	Taxes and licenses	700	800	100
740	Maintenance and repairs	825	1,000	175
741	Freight	38,800	60,000	21,200
753	Depreciation	150	1,311	1,161
760	Amortization	300	300	—
764	Telephone and telegraph	8,000	9,000	1,000
765	Postage	950	1,200	250
766	Office stationary	2,200	2,500	300
768	Dues and subscriptions	600	3,600	3,000
770	Provisions for bad debt	5,000	7,500	2,500
774	Personnel relations	150	200	50
776	Interviewing and hiring	4,400	500	(3,900)
777	Travel and entertainment	12,000	18,000	6,000
778	Supervisor and executive training	50	300	250
780	Trade shows	4,170	6,000	1,830
784	Collection expense	102	360	258
786	Expendable tools	50	1,200	1,150
787	Miscellaneous expense	50	788	738
788	Processing supplies	-0-	100	100
792	Gas, oil, and diesel fuel	2,500	3,600	1,100
793	Salesmen's samples	2,000	3,000	1,000
796	Rental—land and buildings	1,400	1,400	—
797	Rental—machinery and equipment	500	1,200	700
798	Rental—auto and trucks	2,600	5,000	2,400
801	Advertising—media	2,400	16,000	13,600
802	Advertising—design	—	4,000	4,000
803	Market research	—	3,000	3,000
804	Package design—labels	2,050	1,500	(550)
805	Package design—containers	—	1,500	1,500
806	Literature—purchases	—	3,000	3,000
807	Literature—design	—	1,500	1,500
810	Gratis goods	6,500	8,400	1,900
818	Promotion—premiums/gifts	—	2,000	2,000
819	Promotion—printed matter	6,800	5,000	(1,800)
820	Promotion—other	—	1,000	1,000
	Total	$259,558	$390,800	$131,242

Table 5

Manufacturing budget (fiscal 1979–1980)

		Estimate 1978–1979	*Budget 1979–1980*	*Increase*
700	Salaries and wages	$ 11,358	$ 24,024	$ 12,666
701	Manufacturing labor	69,912	122,973	53,061
718	Outside services	8,758	10,000	1,242
725	Retirement plan, 6% of $146,997	4,822	8,820	3,998
726	Payroll taxes, 7.9% of $146,997	5,913	11,613	5,700
727	Group Insurance, $750/per year, 17 people	6,731	12,750	6,019
728	Workman's compensation, $2.50/$100 of $146,997	1,349	3,675	2,326
730	General insurance	2,288	3,809	1,521
734	Taxes and licenses	7,816	8,400	584
740	Maintenance and repairs	2,097	2,400	303
753	Depreciation	13,337	45,075	31,738
764	Telephone, $90/quarter; fire alarm	205	360	155
767	Relocation expense	—	10,000	10,000
776	Interviewing and hiring	67	200	133
777	Travel	383	500	117
785	Uniform expense	175	200	25
786	Expendable tools	3,914	4,800	886
787	Miscellaneous expense	291	1,000	709
788	Processing supplies	402	600	198
789	Electricity	5,750	8,000	2,250
790	Water	600	600	—
791	Fuel	2,350	2,000	(350)
792	Gas, oil, and diesel fuel	325	360	35
796	Rental—land and buildings	20,322	13,200	(7,122)
797	Rental—machinery	207	240	33
798	Rental—truck and auto	1,686	360	(1,326)
	Total manufacturing expenses	$171,058	$295,959	$124,901

case 20
Marion Laboratories, Inc.

1 Michael E. Herman, senior vice president of finance for Marion Laboratories, had just received word that the board of directors was planning to meet in three days to review the company's portfolio of subsidiary investments. In particular, he and his senior financial analyst, Carl R. Mitchell, were to prepare an in-depth analysis of several of the subsidiaries so the board could be better positioned with respect to a subsidiary's compatability with Marion's overall strategic objectives. The analysis was part of a continuing process of self-assessment to assure future growth for the company. At the upcoming meeting, the board was interested in a review of Kalo Laboratories, Inc., a subsidiary that manufactured specialty agricultural chemicals.[1]

2 Kalo was profitable and in sound financial shape for the fiscal year just ended (see Exhibit 1). But Kalo, in the agricultural chemical industry, was unique for Marion, and Herman knew that Kalo's long-term status as a Marion subsidiary would depend on more than just profitability.

3 Marion's future had been the subject of careful study following the first two years of earnings decline in the company's history. In fiscal 1975, net earnings for the company were 12 percent lower than in 1974. In fiscal 1976 Marion faced a more-serious problem as earnings fell 30 percent below 1974 levels while sales decreased 4 percent and cost of goods sold rose by 12 percent above 1974 levels.

4 As a result of the interruption in the earnings' growth pattern, Marion sought to reexamine its corporate portfolio of investments. By fiscal year 1977, some results from the reappraisal were seen, as earnings rose 28 percent from the previous year. Although sales continued to climb, earnings had not yet recovered to the 1974 level by the end of fiscal year 1978. Marion's long-range planning was an attempt to define what the company was to become in the next 10-year period. Current subsidiaries and investments were analyzed within this 10-year framework. As part of this long-range planning, a statement of Marion's corporate mission was developed.

5 Statement of corporate mission:

1. Achieve a position of market leadership through marketing and distribution of consumable and personal products of a perceived differentiation to selected segments of the health care and related fields.

This case was prepared by Marilyn L. Taylor and Kenneth Beck of the University of Kansas. Reprinted with permission of the Case Research Association.

[1] Kalo Laboratories, Inc., was utilized as the case subject due to the singular nature of the segment information available in Marion Laboratories, Inc., SEC submissions and does not reflect Marion's intentions as to its investment in Kalo or any of its other subsidiary operations. Materials in this case were generally gathered from publicly available information.

Exhibit 1

MARION LABORATORIES, INC.
Sales Profits and Identifiable Assets by Industry Segments
For the Years Ended June 30, 1974–1978
(in thousands of dollars)

	1978	*1977*	*1976*	*1975*	*1974*
Sales to unaffiliated customers:					
Pharmaceutical and hospital products	$ 84,223	$ 72,299	$59,236	$64,613	$54,165
Specialty agricultural chemical products	9,302	5,227	2,880	4,522	4,044
Other health care segments	23,853	22,605	18,722	14,961	13,569
Consolidated net sales	$117,378	$100,131	$80,838	$84,096	$71,778
Operating profit:					
Pharmaceutical and hospital products	$ 27,900	$ 23,439	$18,941	$28,951	$25,089
Specialty agricultural chemical products	905	382	(328)	881	620
Other health care segments	929	1,251	(593)	686	871
Operating profit	29,734	25,072	18,020	30,518	26,580
Interest expense	(1,546)	(1,542)	(898)	(97)	(83)
Corporate expenses	(5,670)	(4,474)	(3,106)	(2,795)	(2,475)
Earnings before income taxes	$ 22,518	$ 19,056	$14,016	$27,626	$24,022
Identifiable assets:					
Pharmaceutical and hospital products	$ 75,209	$ 69,546	$60,376	$43,658	$35,103
Specialty agricultural chemical products	3,923	3,805	1,801	1,942	1,790
Other health care segments	14,635	14,875	13,902	14,229	12,217
Corporate	5,121	3,424	4,518	3,928	3,770
Discontinued operations	—	—	—	3,370	6,865
Consolidated assets	$ 98,888	$ 91,650	$80,597	$67,127	$59,745

Source: Marion Laboratories, 1978 Annual Report.

2. Achieve long-term profitable growth through the management of high risk relative to the external environment.
3. Achieve a professional, performance-oriented working environment that stimulates integrity, entrepreneurial spirit, productivity, and social responsibility.

6 In addition to these more-general goals, Marion also set a specific sales goal of $250 million. No time frame was established to achieve this goal as the major emphasis was to be placed on the stability and quality of sales.

7 Herman realized, however, that even though there was no written timetable for earnings growth, it was well understood that to meet stockholder expectations, the company must grow fairly rapidly.

8 On June 8, 1978, in a presentation before the Health Industry's Analyst Group, Fred Lyons, Marion's president and chief operating officer, emphasized Marion's commitment to growth. In his remarks he stated:

> We expect to grow over the next 10 years at a rate greater than the pharmaceutical industry average and at a rate greater than at least twice that of the real gross national product. Our target range is at least 10–15 percent compounded growth—shooting for the higher side of that, of course. Obviously, we intend to have a great deal of new business and new products added to our current operations to reach and exceed the $250 million level.
>
> Our licensing activities and R&D expenditures will be intensified. . . . At the same time, we'll introduce some selective in-house research business into Marion through the acquisition route. It is our intention to keep our balance sheet strong and maintain an A or better credit rating, to achieve a return on investment in the 12–15 percent range, and to produce a net aftertax compared to sales in the 8–12 percent range.

9 To finance this growth in sales, Marion was faced with a constant need for funds. Most of these funds in the past had come from the company's operations. To finance a $25 million expansion in its pharmaceutical facilities, the company, in fiscal year 1976, found it necessary to borrow $15 million in the form of unsecured senior notes due to mature on October 1, 1980, 1981, and 1982 with $5 million due on each of those dates.

10 In regard to possible future financing, Herman made the following comments before the Health Industry's Analyst Group: "Most of you realize that industrial companies have debt-to-equity ratio of 1:1, and if we desired to lever ourselves to that level, we could borrow $66 million. However, we would keep as a guideline the factor of always maintaining our A or better credit rating, so we would not leverage ourselves that far."

11 Although Marion was fairly light on debt, the potential for future borrowing was not unlimited. Besides maintaining an A credit rating, they felt a debt-to-equity ratio greater than 4:1 would be inconsistent with the pharmaceutical industry.

12 To analyze Kalo's future as well as the futures of the other nonpharmaceutical subsidiaries, Herman realized that he and his analysts would have to consider the impact of these financing constraints on Marion's future growth. With unlimited financing in the future, he would have only had to make a good investment decision. However, to balance the goals of a strong balance sheet and a high-growth rate, Herman was faced with making the optimal investment decision. It was with these constraints that Herman would eventually have to make his recommendation to the board of directors.

Company History

13 In 1979, Marion Laboratories, Inc., of Kansas City, Missouri, was a leading producer of ethical (prescription) pharmaceuticals for the treatment of cardiovascular and cerebral disorders (see Exhibit 2). Marion also owned subsidiaries that manufactured hospital supplies, proprietary (nonprescription) drugs, eyeglasses, optical accessories, electrical home stairway elevators, and specialty agricultural chemicals.

14 Marion Laboratories was founded in 1950 by Ewing Marion Kauffman. Prior to establishing his own company, Kauffman held a job in the field sales force of a Kansas City pharmaceutical company. After four years on the job, his sales efforts were so successful he was making more money in commissions than the company president's

Exhibit 2

Marion's major ethical pharmaceutical products

Product	*Product application*	*Estimated market size ($ millions)*	*Marion's product*	*Share of market*
Cerebral and peripheral vasodilators	Vascular relaxant to relieve constriction of arteries	90–100	Pavabid®	22%
Coronary vasodilators	Controlled release nitroglycerin for treatment of angina pectoris	90–100	Nitro-Bid®	12
Ethical and OTC plain antacids	Tablets for relief of heartburn	37	Gaviscon®	26
Andogens-estrogens	Product for treatment of calcium deficiencies	12	Os-Cal®	46
Topical burn anti-microbials	Ointment for prevention of infection in third-degree burns	8	Silvadene®	57
Urologic anti-spasmodics	Product for treatment of symptoms of neurogenic bladder	10	Ditropan®	10

Source: Smith, Barney, Harris, Upham and Co., research report, January 19, 1978.

salary. When the company cut his commission and reduced his sales territory, Kauffman quit to establish his own firm.

15 In its initial year of operation, the new company had sales of $36,000 and a net profit of $1,000. Its sole product was a tablet called Os-Vim, formulated to combat chronic fatigue. The company's three employees, counting Kauffman, worked from a 13- by 15-foot storeroom that served as manufacturing plant, sales office, warehouse, and headquarters.

16 From the company's inception, the major emphasis for Marion was on sales and marketing. Kauffman was successful in developing an aggressive, highly motivated sales force. During the mid-1960s, the company's sales effort was concentrated on developing Pavabid, introduced in 1962, into the leading product in the cerebral and peripheral vasodilator market.

17 While other drug companies were spending large amounts on research and development, hoping to discover new drugs, Marion concentrated on the sales effort, spending very little on basic research. Nearly all of its research expenditures were directed at improving its current products or further developing products licensed from other drug companies. This particular approach to product development was still being followed in 1979.

18 Beginning in the late 1960s, Marion decided to reduce its dependence on Pavabid which accounted for more than half of Marion's sales. In the pharmaceutical area, the company continued to minimize basic research and worked to develop new drug sources. Marion also began diversifying into the hospital and health products sector by acquiring existing firms in those areas. (See Exhibit 3 for a summary of Marion's

Exhibit 3

Summary of subsidiary acquisitions and divestitures

Name of subsidiary	*Type of product(s)*	*Date acquired*	*Date divested*
Marion Health and Safety	First aid and hospital products	1968	—
American Stair-Glide	Manufacturer of home stairway lifts and products to aid the handicapped	1968	—
Kalo Laboratories	Manufacturer of specialty agricultural chemicals	1968	—
Rose Manufacturing	Industrial fall protection devices	1969	Sold: 1978
Mi-Con Laboratories	Manufacturers of opthalmic solutions	1969	Merged into MH&S: 1973
Pioneer Laboratories	Manufacturer of sterile dressings	50% in 1970	Sold out: 1971
Signet Laboratories	Vitamin and food supplements	1971	Discontinued operations, selling some assets: 1975
Optico Laboratories	Eyeglasses, hard contact lenses, and related products	1973	—
Certified Laboratories	Manufacturer of IPC products	1969	Sold: 1978
IPC	Marketed IPC products	1969	Merged into Pharmaceutical Division, 1979
Marion International	Distributor of Pharmaceutical Products, Inc.	1971	—
Inco	Industrial creams	1972	Merged into MH&S: 1974
Occusafe	Consulting services; re: OSHA regulation and compliance	Incorporated: 1972	Discontinued operations: 1973
Nation Wide Chemical	Specialty ag-chem products	1973	Merged into Kalo
Marion Scientific	Manufacturer and distributor	Acquired by MH&S: 1973	—
Colloidal	Specialty agricultural products	1973	Merged into Kalo 1974
WBC	Holding company for IPC property	Incorporated: 1976	Sold: 1978
SRC	Specialty ag-chem products	1977	Merged into Kalo

acquisition and divestiture activities.) Taking advantage of the high market value of its common stock, the company acquired several subsidiaries engaged in businesses other than pharmaceuticals.[2]

Organization

19 Marion's operations in 1979 were divided into two separate groups—the Pharmaceutical Group and the Health Products Group (see Exhibit 4). The Pharmaceutical Group's operations were a continuation of the original ethical drug line of the company, and the Health Products Group was composed of subsidiaries purchased by Marion in the hospital and health-related fields.

20 Fred W. Lyons, 41, was president, chief executive officer, and member of the board of directors. As president, Lyons was responsible for the total operation and performance of the corporation. This responsibility included the company's pharmaceutical operating group as well as all subsidiary operations, corporate planning functions, and corporate supportive activities.

21 Lyons joined Marion in 1970 as vice president, general manager, and director. He came to Marion from a similar position with Corral Pharmaceuticals, Inc., a subsidiary of Alcon Laboratories, Inc. He was a registered pharmacist and had received an MBA (master of business administration) degree from Harvard University in 1959.

22 Also serving on the board of directors, as senior vice president and chief financial officer, was Michael E. Herman, 37, who had joined Marion from an investment banking firm of which he was a founding partner. Herman started with Marion as vice president of finance in 1974 and, in 1975, was named director of the company. His responsibilities were financial planning, financial control of operations, management information systems, treasury functions, product development, and strategic long-range planning. Herman was also chairman of the company's new business task force committee which was responsible for the financial review, planning, evaluation, and negotiation of acquisitions. He had a bachelor of science degree in metallurgical engineering from Rensselaer Polytechnic Institute and an MBA from the University of Chicago.

23 Gerald W. Holder, 48, was the senior vice president in charge of administrative functions for Marion. Holder was responsible for all corporate administrative functions, including Marion's legal, personnel, facilities and engineering services, public relations, and risk management staffs. He had joined the company in 1973, rising to the senior vice president level in March of 1978.

24 James E. McGraw, 46, was senior vice president of Marion Laboratories, Inc., and president of the company's Pharmaceutical Group. He was responsible for the manufacturing, marketing, quality control, and accounting functions within the two operating units of the Pharmaceutical Group: the Professional Products Division and the Consumer Products Division. McGraw had joined Marion in 1974 from a position as president of the General Diagnostics Division of Warner-Lambert Company.

25 Tom W. Olofson, 36, was a senior vice president and president of the Health Products Group. His responsibilities included financial and planning aspects for each of the subsidiaries in that group.

26 Within the described organization, Marion made some of its operating decisions in small-group or task-force settings that brought together corporate personnel from sev-

[2] Price-earnings ratios for Marion in 1968 and 1969 were 46 and 52, respectively.

Exhibit 4

Organization chart

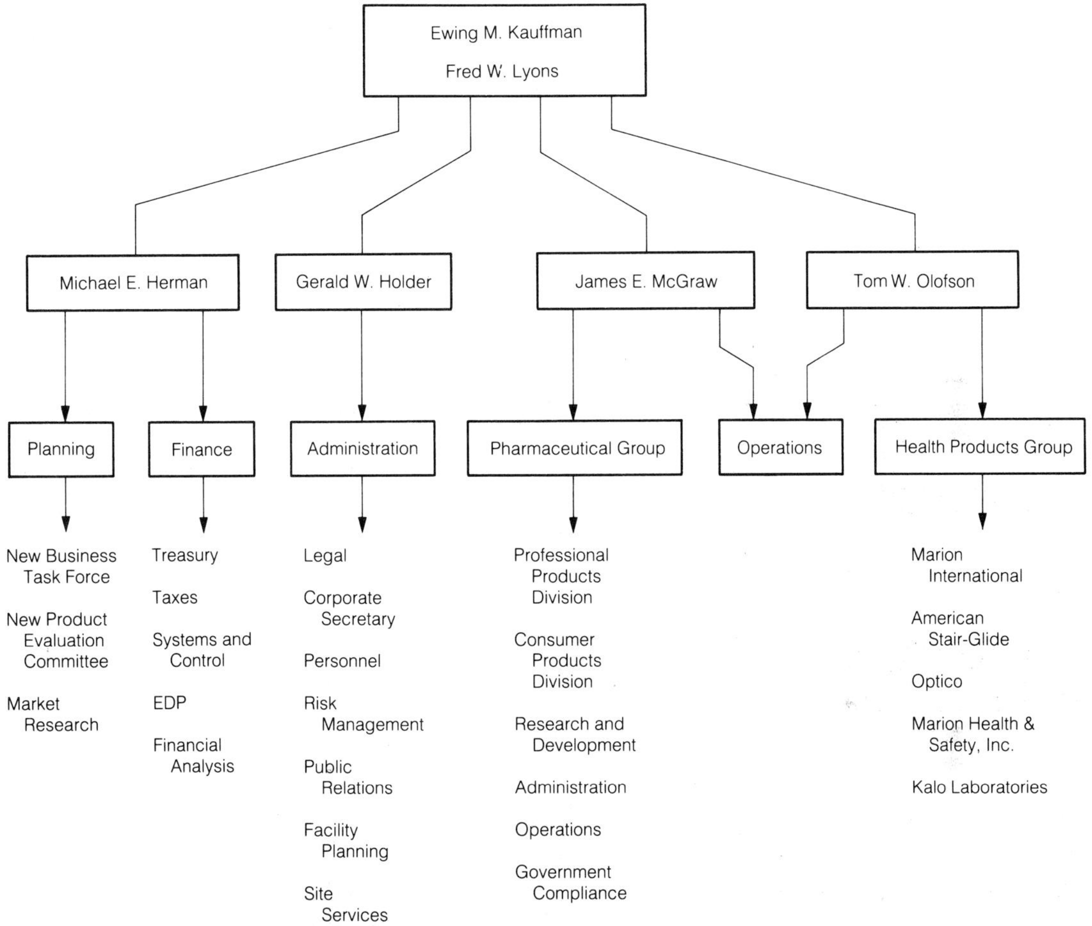

Organization chart was rendered by authors.

eral different disciplines. The process of approving certain capital expenditures was an example of the review and analysis process.

27 Marion had a formal capital expenditure review program for expenditure on depreciable assets in excess of $10,000. At the option of the group president, it could also be applied on expenditures less than $10,000, but in this case, only the group president was involved in the review process.

28 If the net present value of cash flows was positive, a person requesting funds was required to complete a form and submit it to a corporate planning group. This group consisted of corporate accounting and facilities planning personnel who, since the

company was operating with limited funds, decided which projects, based on financial and strategic considerations, should be forwarded to Fred Lyons for final approval or rejection. This process occurred after the planning period and prior to the purchase of the asset. The capital expenditure review program was used for expenditures in both the Pharmaceutical Group and the Health Products Group.

Pharmaceutical Group

29 Marion's ethical and over-the-counter drug operations were the major components of the Pharmaceutical Group, which was further divided into the Professional Products Division and the Consumer Products Division. The Pharmaceutical Group, which was responsible for research and development, administration, operations, and government compliance, was headed by James E. McGraw. Although Marion had been exclusively an ethical drug maker prior to diversification efforts, the company had recently increased its operations in the proprietary drug area.

30 In 1978, Marion formed the Consumer Products Division from what had been International Pharmaceutical Corp. (IPC) to market its growing nonprescription product line. This market area, previously untapped for Marion, was expected to be a major ingredient for near-term growth. To aid in the marketing of its nonprescription line, Marion hired a full-scale consumer advertising agency for the first time in the company's history.

31 Sales for the Consumer Products Division were boosted when, in fiscal 1978, Marion purchased the product Throat-Discs from Warner-Lambert's Parke-Davis Division. In addition, Marion also purchased two Parke-Davis ethical products, Ambenyl cough-cold products and a tablet for the treatment of thyroid disorders. Because of the timing of the acquisition, most of the sales and earnings were excluded from that year's earnings results. Sales for these three lines were expected to be nearly $8 million in 1979.

32 Marion's ethical pharmaceutical products were marketed by its Professional Products Division. The company sold its ethical products with a detail sales force of about 200 that called on physicians, pharmacists, and distributors within their assigned territories. The sales force was very productive by industry standards and was motivated by intensive training and supervision and an incentive compensation system. There was very little direct selling to doctors and pharmacists, the main purpose of the sales visits being promotion of Marion's products. In addition, Marion had an institutional sales force that sold directly to hospitals, institutions, and other large users.

33 In fiscal 1978, 80 percent of Marion's pharmaceutical products were distributed through 463 drug wholesalers. All orders for ethical drug products were filled from the Kansas City, Missouri, manufacturing plant. Marion's pharmaceutical distribution system is diagrammed in Exhibit 5.

34 During 1978, the company decided to use its improved liquidity position to aid its wholesale drug distributors. Many wholesalers used outside financing to purchase their inventory and were unable to maintain profit margins when interest rates rose. By extending credit on key products, Marion helped its distributors maintain higher inventories and gave the company a selling edge over competitors.

35 One of Marion's major goals for each of its products was for the product to hold a

Exhibit 5

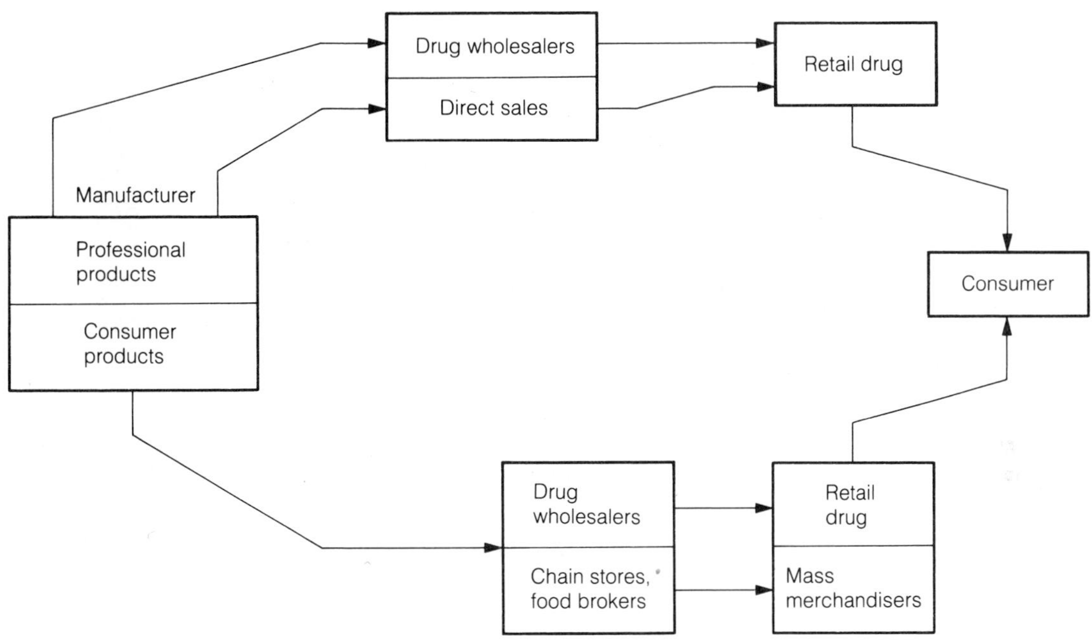

market leadership position in the particular area in which it competed. This goal had been accomplished for most of the company's leading products. (See Exhibit 2.)

36 Capturing a large share of a market had worked particularly well for Marion's leading product, Pavabid, which in 1978, accounted for 18 percent of the entire company's sales. Marion was decreasing its reliance on Pavabid (see Exhibit 6) which, since its introduction in 1962, had been the company's most-successful product. Through the 1960s, Pavabid had been responsible for almost all of Marion's growth. In recent years, as the product's market matured, sales growth had slowed, forcing the company to become less dependent on Pavabid. The decrease in sales of 3.9 percent in fiscal year 1976 was due primarily to previous overstocking of Pavabid and the subsequent inventory adjustments at the distributor level.

37 In April of 1976, the Food and Drug Administration (FDA) had requested that makers of papaverine hydrochloride (sold by Marion as Pavabid) submit test data to support the safety and efficacy of the drug. Many small manufacturers were not able to submit the data and dropped out of the market. Marion complied with the request and had not yet been notified by the FDA of the outcome of the review by early 1979. A negative action by the FDA was not expected, since it had taken so long for a decision and papaverine had been used safely for decades. However, if the FDA ruled that compounds such as Pavabid could not be marketed, either because they weren't safe or weren't effective, Marion would lose its leading product.

38 In August 1977, the FDA requested that manufacturers of coronary vasodilators, including nitroglycerin compounds like Marion's Nitro-Bid, submit test data to prove

Exhibit 6

Changing product mix

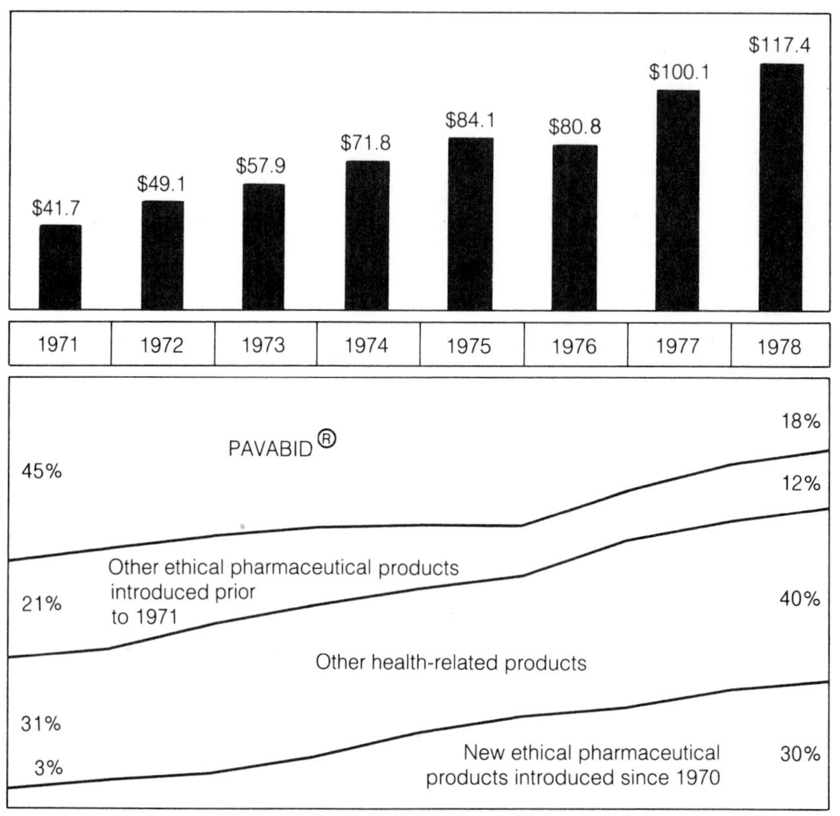

Source: Marion Laboratories, 1978 Annual Report.

product safety and efficacy. This review was the same process that Pavabid was subject to, and a negative ruling, although not expected, would adversely affect the company.

39 Proving its products to be safe and effective was only one area in which the company dealt with the FDA. Before any ethical drug product could be marketed in the United States, Marion had to have the approval of the FDA. The company was required to conduct extensive animal tests, file an investigational new-drug application, conduct three phases of clinical human tests, file a new drug application, and submit all its data to the FDA for final review. With the FDA's approval, the drug firm could begin marketing the drug.

40 The approval process from lab discovery and patent application to FDA approval took from 7 to 10 years. Often a company had only seven or eight years of patent

Exhibit 7

Selected ethical drug companies, 1977 (thousands of dollars)

	Net sales	*Cost of goods sold*	*R&D expenses*	*Net income**
Pfizer Inc.	$2,031,900	$978,057	$ 98,282	$174,410
Merck & Co.	1,724,410	662,703	144,898	290,750
Eli Lilly & Co.	1,518,012	571,737	124,608	218,684
Upjohn Inc.	1,134,325	—	102,256	91,521
SmithKline Corp.	780,337	299,338	61,777	89,271
G. D. Searle & Co.	749,583	345,224	52,645	(28,390)
Syntex Corp.	313,604	132,710	27,648	37,643
A. H. Robbins Co.	306,713	122,374	16,107	26,801
Rorer Group Inc.	186,020	59,606	5,174	18,143
Marion Laboratories	100,131	37,330	5,907	10,652

* Aftertax.
Source: *Drug and Cosmetic Industry,* June 1978.

protection left to market its discovery and recover the average $50 million it had taken to fully develop the drug.

41 To avoid the R&D expenses necessary to fully develop a new drug entity into a marketable product, Marion's source for new products was a process the company called search and development. Marion licensed the basic compound from other drug manufacturers large enough to afford the basic research needed to discover new drugs. Generally, the licensors, most notably Servier of France and Chugai of Japan, were companies lacking the resources or expertise necessary to obtain FDA approval and marketing rights in the United States. Marion's R&D effort then concentrated on developing a product with an already identified pharmacological action into a drug marketable in the United States. By developing existing drug entities, Marion was able to shorten the development time required to bring a new drug to market and at a cost lower than discovering its own drugs. This enabled Marion to compete in an industry dominated by companies many times its own size. (See Exhibits 7 and 8 for drug industry information.)

42 In addition to the FDA, the federal government was also affecting the drug industry with activities that promoted generic substitution. In early 1979, 40 states had generic substitution laws that allowed nonbranded drugs to be substituted for branded, and

Exhibit 8

Ethical drug industry composite statistics

	1978	*1977*	*1976*	*1975*
Sales ($ millions)	$12,450	$10,859	$10,033	$9,022
Operating margin (percent)	22.5%	22.2%	21.9%	22.1%
Income tax rate (percent)	36.5	36.4	36.2	36.7
Net profit margin (percent)	11.8	11.7	11.7	11.6
Earned on net worth (percent)	18.5	17.9	18.2	18.4

Source: Value Line Investment Survey.

often more expensive, drugs. The U.S. Department of Health, Education and Welfare and the Federal Trade Commission had also recently proposed a model state substitution law and a listing of medically equivalent drugs. The maximum allowable cost (MAC) guideline for reimbursement of Medicaid and Medicare prescriptions was the lowest price at which a generic version was available.

43 Generics accounted for 12 percent of new prescriptions being written and were likely to increase in relative importance. The industry was looking to its ability to develop new drugs to offset the expected shortfall in earnings expected in the 1980s due to loss of patent protection on many important drug compounds.

44 The effect that generic substitution laws would have on Marion was unclear. The company had always concentrated on products with a unique pharmacological action rather than those that were commodity in nature. Generic substitution required an equivalent drug be substituted for the brand name drug, and there were uncertainties about how equivalency would be defined.

45 Marion's pharmaceutical operations had not produced a major new product for several years. Products that were in various stages of development were diltiazen hydrochloride, an antianginal agent; sucralfate, a nonsystematic (doesn't enter the bloodstream) drug for the treatment of ulcers; and benflourex, a product that reduced cholesterol levels in the blood.

Health Products Group

46 Subsidiaries selling a wide range of products used in health care and related fields made up Marion's Health Products Group. The company had bought and sold several subsidiaries since beginning to diversify in 1968 (see Exhibit 3). By 1978, the group of subsidiaries was responsible for 39 percent of total company sales and 22 percent of earnings before taxes.

47 Several times after purchasing a company, Marion had decided to sell it or discontinue operations. The divestment decision in the past had been based on considerations such as a weak market position, low-growth position, excessive product liability, or a poor fit with the rest of Marion.

48 In his presentation before the Health Industry's Analyst Group, Fred Lyons noted the importance of a subsidiary fitting in with the rest of Marion when explaining the company's decision to sell Rose Manufacturing.

> You may have noticed that during this past year we determined through our strategic planning that Rose Manufacturing, in the fall-protection area of industrial safety, did not fit either our marketing base or our technology base. Therefore we made a decision to spin Rose off, and we successfully culminated its sale in November of 1977. Rose, like Signet Laboratories three years ago, just did not fit.

49 In adjusting its corporate profile, Marion was always searching for companies that provided good investment potential and we were consistent with the company's goals. To provide a framework within which to evaluate potential acquisitions and to avoid some of the mistakes made in past purchases, Marion developed a set of acquisition criteria to be applied to possible subsidiary investments.

Search criteria for acquisitions

Product area:	Health care
Market:	$100 million potential with 8 percent minimum growth rate
Net sales:	$3–$30 million
Tangible net worth:	Not less than $1 million
Return on investment:	Not less than 20 percent pretax
Method of payment:	Cash or stock

50 The board of directors made the ultimate decision on the acquisitions and divestment of Marion's subsidiaries. At the corporate level, Herman was responsible for evaluating changes in the corporate portfolio and, based on his analysis, making recommendations to the board. Since Herman was also on the board of directors, his recommendations were heavily weighted in the board's final decision.

51 In early 1979, Marion had four subsidiaries in its Health Products Group—Marion Health & Safety, Inc., Optico Industries, American Stair-Glide, and Kalo Laboratories. Following is a brief description of each:

52 *Martion Health & Safety, Inc.,* sold a broad line of hospital and industrial safety products through its Marion Scientific Corp. and Health and Safety Products Division. Recently introduced, Marion Scientific products (a consumer-oriented insect bite treatment and a device for transporting anaerobic cultures) showed good acceptance and growth in their respective markets. Distribution was generally through medical/surgical wholesalers and distributors who, in turn, resold to hospitals, medical laboratories, reference laboratories, and so forth. The Health and Safety Division manufactured and/or packaged primarily safety-related products (hearing protection, eye-wash, and so forth) and first-aid kits and kit products, such as wraps, adhesive bandages, and various over-the-counter products. Sale of these products was made to safety equipment wholesalers/distributors who resold to hospital, industry, institutions, and so on. Sales of Marion Health & Safety, Inc., were estimated by outside analysts to have increased about 17 percent, to a level estimated at $19 million. Pretax margins were about 10 percent in this industry. Marion Health & Safety, Inc., was headquartered in Rockford, Illinois.

53 *Optico Industries, Inc.,* participated in the wholesale and retail optical industry. Its main products were glass and plastic prescription eyeglass lenses and hard contact lenses. Outside analysts estimated this subsidiary recorded sales gains of about 26 percent for 1978 for sales estimated to be about $8 million. Optico had reduced profitability during 1978 due to expansion of its retail facilities. Pretax margins for 1978 were estimated at 6 percent, but this was expected to improve when the expansion program was completed. Optico's headquarters were located in Tempe, Arizona.

54 *American Stair-Glide Corp.* manufactured and marketed home stairway and porch lifts and other products to aid physically handicapped individuals. These products were principally sold to medical/surgical supply dealers for resale or rental to the consumer. In some instances, distribution was through elevator companies. Sales were estimated at about $5 million annually by outside analysts. This subsidiary was expected to grow slowly and steadily and it had a very stable historical earnings pattern. The trend for greater access to buildings for the handicapped was expected to impact favorably on this Grandview, Missouri-based subsidiary.

Exhibit 9

Kalo Laboratories sales and earnings information ($ millions)

	1978	*1977*	*1976*	*1975*	*1974*	*1973*
Sales	$ 9	$ 5	$ 2	$ 4	$ 3	$ 2
Cost of goods sold, (percent of sales)	43%	54%	61%	53%	55%	48%
Expenses:						
R&D expense	8	7	7	5	5	3
Marketing, selling, and general administrative expenses	37	31	42	23	24	27
Total expenses	45%	38%	49%	28%	29%	30%
Total assets	$ 5	$ 4	$ 2	$ 2	$ 2	$ 1
Total investments*	3	3	1	1	1	.5

* Includes Marion's equity in Kalo and funds lent on a long-term basis.
Based on authors' estimates.

55 *Kalo Laboratories, Inc.*, operated in the specialty agricultural chemical market and provided products to meet specialized user needs. In the past, Kalo had been successful in marketing its line of specialty products. (See Exhibit 9—Kalo's past earnings information.) In assessing Kalo's future, there were many risks to consider. These risks included competition from large chemical companies, governmental regulatory actions, and uncertain future product potentials.

Competition and Industry

56 The U.S. and Canadian agricultural chemical market was estimated to be $3.2 billion in 1978 and growing at more than 15 percent a year.[3] The industry was dominated by large chemical manufacturers including Dow Chemical, Du Pont, Stauffer Chemical, and Gulf Oil. The market was also shared by large ethical drug manufacturers including Eli Lilly, Pfizer, and Upjohn. (See Exhibit 10 for agriculture-related sales.) Economies of scale allowed the larger companies to produce large amounts of what might be perceived as a commodity product (herbicides, insecticides, and fungicides) at a much lower cost per unit than the smaller companies. Diversification of and within agricultural product lines assured the larger manufacturers even performance for their agricultural divisions as a whole.

57 Since smaller chemical companies like Kalo could not afford to produce large enough amounts of their products to match the efficiency and prices of the large companies, these firms concentrated on specialty markets with unique product needs. By identifying specialty chemical needs in the agricultural segment, Kalo was able to produce its products and develop markets that were very profitable but weren't large enough to attract the bigger firms.

[3] Du Pont, 1979 Annual Report; and Upjohn, 1979 Annual Report.

Exhibit 10

Total and agriculture-related sales, selected companies, 1979

	Total sales ($ millions)	Agriculture related	
		Sales ($ millions)	Earnings (before tax)
Eli Lilly	$2,520	$920*	28.6%
Pfizer	3,030	480*	9.8
Upjohn	1,755	280*	9.2
Marion (1978)	100	9	9.0

* Includes international sales.
Source: Value Line Investment Survey.

Products

58 Since the larger chemical companies dominated the large product segments, Kalo's products were designed to meet the specialized needs of its agricultural users. Kalo's product line was divided into four major classes—seed treatments, adjuvants, bactericides, and herbicides.

59 Seed treatments for soybeans accounted for the majority of Kalo's sales. One product in this area was Triple Noctin. Products in the seed treatment class were intended to act on soybean seeds to increase their viability once in the ground. Kalo manufactured seed treatments for soybeans only.

60 Adjuvants were chemicals that, when added to another agricultural product, increased the efficacy of the product or made it easier to use. For instance, Biofilmo prevented liquid fertilizer from foaming, making it easier to apply, and Hydro-Wet enhanced the soils' receptiveness to certain chemicals, which reduced runoff into surrounding areas.

61 The newest product for Kalo was the adjuvant Extend, a chemical compound added to fertilizer that made it bind chemically with the soil or the plant. The binding process helped retain the fertilizer where it was applied, making each application longer lasting and more effective. Extend was only recently introduced, and its success was difficult to assess at such an early stage. However, Kalo's management was planning to build a family of products around it. Sales projections showed Extend contributing between 60–70 percent of Kalo's future growth through 1987.

62 Bactericides and herbicides were the final two product classes at Kalo. Bactericides were applied to the soil to either inhibit or encourage the growth of selected bacteria. One product, Isobac, was used to control boll rot in cotton. Herbicides, mainly for broadleaf plants, were used to control or kill unwanted weeds, leaving the desirable crop unharmed.

63 In the past, Kalo had acquired several of its products by acquiring the company that manufactured them. When it purchased a going concern intact, Kalo was able to gain both the manufacturing facilities and an existing distribution system. In the future, Kalo expected to diversify its product line in a similar fashion. To enlarge its existing product lines, Kalo was planning to use both internal and contract R&D.

An example of enlarging the product family was the planned adaptation of its products to many different crop applications.

64 Because Kalo did not have a well-diversified product line, its operations were more cyclical than the overall agricultural sector. Two major factors beyond Kalo's control—the weather and spot prices for commodities—made its annual performance extremely unpredictable.

65 Kalo's operating results were seasonal as its products were primarily intended to be applied in the spring months. It was not unusual for the subsidiary to show a net loss from operations for the nine months from July until March and show a large profit in the three months of April, May, and June, when the products were being purchased for immediate application. If the spring months were particularly rainy, Kalo's profitability was adversely affected. Heavy farm equipment couldn't operate on wet fields without getting stuck, and application was impossible until the fields dried out. Once the fields were dry, Kalo's agricultural users often did not have time to apply the herbicides or other products even though it would have been economically advantageous to do so.

66 The other factor that affected the demand for Kalo's products was the spot pricing of commodities. The price of commodities relative to each other had a large effect on the total amount of each type of crop planted. Because the producer was free to switch crops yearly based on the spot prices, Kalo's demand for the upcoming planting season was uncertain and variable. Kalo was particularly vulnerable to swings in demand caused by the substitutability of crops since many of their products were applicable only to soybeans.

Distribution and Marketing

67 The end user of Kalo's products was usually the individual farmer. Kalo and the rest of the agricultural chemical industry had a distribution system like the one shown below.

Manufacturer → Wholesaler or super distributor → Retailer → Farmer

↓

Applicator
(if special
equipment needed)

68 Kalo promoted its products with a sales force of about 30. The main task of these salespeople was to call on and educate wholesalers/distributors on the advantages, unique qualities, and methods of selling Kalo's products. In addition, some end-user information was distributed to farmers, using pull advertising to create demand. A limited amount of promotion was done at agricultural shows and state fairs, but because of the expense involved, this type of promotion was not used often.

Kalo's Future

69 Sales forecasts prepared by the staff analysts for Herman looked very promising as they predicted sales gains of $4 to 6 million in each of the next nine years (see Exhibit

Exhibit 11

Kalo Laboratories sales forecast (current $ millions)

	1978	*1979*	*1980*	*1981*	*1982*	*1983*	*1984*	*1985*	*1986*	*1987*
Net sales	9	12	16	20	25	30	35	40	45	50

Based on casewriters' estimates.

11). There were, however, some important assumptions on which the forecasts were based.

70 As mentioned earlier, 60–70 percent of the forecasted growth was to come from a product family based on the new product, Extend. A great deal of uncertainty surrounded the product, however. Since it was new, the current success of Extend was difficult to measure, particularly in determining how current sales translated into future performance. If the market evaluation for Extend and related products was correct, and if a family of products could be developed around Extend, then the sales potential for the proposed product family was very promising, provided Kalo was able to exploit the available sales opportunities.

71 Additional growth projected in the sales forecasts was to come from existing products and undefined future products that were to be developed or acquired. Approximately 20 percent of the growth was to come from the existing products in the next four to five years. Ten to 20 percent of the growth in the later years of the forecast was expected to come from currently unknown products.

72 For Kalo to realize the forecasted growth, it was going to be necessary for Marion to provide financing, since it would be impossible for Kalo to generate all the required funds internally. Kalo had been a net user of cash, provided by Marion, since 1976. (See Exhibit 9 and Exhibit 12 for information about Marion's investment in Kalo.) Marion's management did not consider the amount of cash provided through the first part of 1979 to be excessive so long as Kalo maintained adequate profitability and steady growth rates. In addition to the long-term funds provided by Marion, Kalo also required short-term financing of inventory each year due to the seasonability of its sales.

Exhibit 12

KALO LABORATORIES
Balance Sheet
For June 30, 1978
($ millions)

Current assets	$2.5	Current liabilities	$1.4
Plant, property, and equipment (net)	1.9	Long-term debt	1.0
Other	.2	Capital	2.2
Total assets	$4.6	Total liabilities	$4.6

Based on casewriters' estimates.

Exhibit 13

MARION LABORATORIES, INC.
Consolidated Balance Sheet
For 1977 and 1978

	1978	*1977*
Assets		
Current assets:		
Cash	$ 381,116	$ 961,588
Short-term investments, at cost which approximates market	2,561,660	10,028,297
Accounts and notes receivable, less allowances for returns and doubtful accounts of $1,845,466 and $2,305,793	28,196,199	20,576,412
Inventories	19,640,945	15,568,170
Prepaid expenses	2,305,403	1,461,367
Deferred income tax benefits	757,585	895,110
Total current assets	53,842,908	49,490,944
Property, plant, and equipment, at cost:		
Land and land improvements	2,832,588	2,935,671
Buildings	24,458,746	25,224,652
Machinery and equipment	19,671,607	18,110,907
Aircraft and related equipment	1,670,904	1,670,904
Construction in progress	365,311	357,338
Total plant, property, and equipment	48,999,156	48,299,472
Less accumulated depreciation	10,725,533	8,585,190
Net property, plant, and equipment	38,273,623	39,714,282
Other assets:		
Intangible assets	4,774,055	2,042,762
Notes receivable (noncurrent)	890,692	11,589
Marketable equity securities, at market value	688,914	—
Deferred income tax benefits (noncurrent)	318,434	249,647
Miscellaneous	99,597	141,232
Total other assets	6,771,692	2,445,230
Total assets	$98,888,223	$91,650,456
Liabilities and Stockholders' Equity		
Current liabilities:		
Current maturities of long-term debt	$ 82,102	$ 95,004
Accounts payable, trade	3,979,341	4,224,105
Accrued profit-sharing expense	1,752,515	243,096
Other accrued expenses	3,864,168	3,008,238
Dividends payable	1,260,612	1,198,938
Income taxes payable	4,391,252	5,030,219
Total current liabilities	15,329,990	13,799,600
Long-term debt, excluding current maturities	15,580,072	15,661,399
Deferred income taxes payable	1,107,000	733,000
Deferred compensation	177,975	172,889
Stockholders' equity:		
Preferred stock of $1 par value per share: Authorized 250,000 shares; none issued	—	—
Common stock of $1 par value per share: Authorized 20 million shares; issued 8,703,346 shares	8,703,346	8,703,346
Paid-in capital	3,474,358	3,475,443
Retained earnings	58,358,925	51,604,550
	70,536,629	63,783,339
Less: 293,153 shares of common stock in treasury, at cost (189,500 shares in 1977)	3,819,243	2,499,771
Net unrealized loss on noncurrent marketable equity securities	24,200	—
Total stockholders' equity	66,693,186	61,283,568
Commitments and contingent liabilities	—	—
Total liabilities and stockholders' equity	$95,888,223	$91,650,456

Source: 1978 Marion Laboratories, 1978 Annual Report.

Exhibit 14

MARION LABORATORIES INC.
Ten-Year Financial Summary
(in thousands of dollars, except per share data)

	1978	*1977*	*1976*	*1975*	*1974*	*1973*	*1972*	*1971*	*1970*	*1969*
Sales:										
Net sales	$117,378	$100,131	$80,838	$84,096	$71,778	$57,937	$49,066	$41,492	$35,322	$30,188
Cost of sales	43,177	37,330	29,315	26,078	21,715	18,171	14,932	12,262	10,622	8,985
Gross profit	74,201	62,801	51,523	58,018	50,063	39,766	34,134	29,430	24,700	21,203
Operating expenses	51,718	43,397	37,292	31,699	26,991	21,155	19,164	17,181	13,828	12,453
Operating income	22,483	19,404	14,231	26,319	23,072	18,611	14,970	12,249	10,872	8,750
Other income	1,581	1,194	683	1,404	1,033	722	709	599	630	328
Interest expense	1,546	1,542	898	97	83	109	116	88	198	260
Earnings:										
Earnings from continuing operations before income taxes	22,518	19,056	14,016	27,626	24,022	19,224	15,563	12,760	11,403	8,818
Income taxes	10,804	8,404	5,628	13,295	11,791	9,297	7,730	6,364	5,899	4,493
Earnings from continuing operations	11,714	10,652	8,388	14,331	12,231	9,927	7,833	6,396	5,405	4,325
Earnings (loss) from discontinued operations	—	—	—	(3,617)	(120)	76	488	—	—	—
Net earnings	$ 11,714	$ 10,652	$ 8,388	$10,714	$12,111	$10,003	$ 8,321	$ 6,396*	$ 5,405	$ 4,325
Common share data:										
Earnings (loss) per common and common equivalent share:										
Continuing operations	$ 1.38	$ 1.23	$ .96	$ 1.65	$ 1.40	$ 1.14	$ .90	$ .76	$ .65	$ .52
Discontinued operations	—	—	—	(.42)	(.01)	.01	.06	—	—	—
Net earnings	$ 1.38	$ 1.23	$ .96	$ 1.23	$ 1.39	$ 1.15	$ .96	$ .76*	$ .65	$ .52
Cash dividends per common share	$ .59	$ .53	$ .52	$ .48	$ .28	$ .21	$ .20	$ .16	$ .12	$ .12
Stockholders' equity per common and common equivalent share	$ 7.87	$ 7.09	$ 6.63	$ 6.29	$ 5.52	$4.16	$ 3.16	$ 2.52	$ 2.01	$ 1.47
Weighted average number of outstanding common and common share equivalents	8,475	8,640	8,707	8,708	8,689	8,715	8,651	8,396	8,377	8,354

* Before extraordinary charge of $916,000, equal to 11 cents per common share resulting from the disposition of investment in affiliated companies.
Source: Marion Laboratories 1978 Annual Report.

Government Regulation

73 Another major uncertainty in Kalo's future was an unpredictable regulatory climate. Regulation of agricultural chemicals was under the jurisdiction of the Environmental Protection Agency (EPA), and compliance with the EPA was similar to compliance with the FDA. The process of developing and introducing a new chemical product took from 8 to 10 years, which including 2 to 5 years necessary to obtain EPA approval. The costs of developing and bringing a new product to market were generally from $5 to 10 million.

74 Once a product was on the market, the EPA had powers of recall similar to the FDA and could require the company to do additional research. The prospect of having a product removed from the market was an added element of risk for Kalo if any of its products were affected. No problems were expected for Kalo although several of the subsidiary's products (particularly its herbicides and bactericides) had a relatively high potential for environmental problems if not applied correctly.

The Decision

75 Herman knew that in making his recommendation, he would have to balance the immediate and long-term resource needs and goals of Marion. Although Kalo looked promising from the forecasts, there were many uncertainties surrounding the subsidiary's future to be considered.

76 Since Marion had no new drug products ready to be introduced soon, the company would have to rely on other areas of the company to reach its growth goals. Kalo was growing, but it was also requiring a constant input of funds from its parent.

77 One possibility for growth was to purchase another drug manufacturer and add its products to Marion's, taking advantage of any distribution synergies that might exist. To make such a purchase, the company would need more resources. To sell a subsidiary could provide needed resources, but to do so quickly, under less than optimum conditions, would surely result in a significantly lower price than could be realized under normal conditions. The income and cash flow impact of this approach would be undesirable.

78 With the board meeting so soon, Herman was faced with analyzing the complex situation quickly. In three days, he would have to make his recommendation to the board of directors.

case 21
Dr Pepper Company (revised)

1 "We all know it ain't over 'til the fat lady sings," Foots Clements quipped, after shareholders approved a private buy-out in February 1984 that ended Dr Pepper's 53 years as a public company. And sure enough, a rotund vocalist in an operatic silver toga, burst from a side door of the Fairmont Hotel ballroom in Dallas. After she sang "Auld Lang Syne," the Dr Pepper shareholders, many of them misty eyed, left the company's last public meeting.

2 America's most misunderstood soft drink, Dr Pepper, is into the soft-drink big time now. It is the nation's third largest soft-drink concern, accounting for approximately 10 percent of U.S. soft-drink sales in 1983. Even though Dr Pepper's market share declined 3 percent in 1982 and remained flat or, at best, up slightly in 1983, according to Emanuel Goldman, a partner of San Francisco-based Montgomery Securities, it is a company to be reckoned with in the soft-drink industry behind the leaders Coca-Cola and Pepsi-Cola, and 1982 marked the 25th consecutive year of increased sales and earnings (see Exhibit 1).

While its rapid national emergence is a relatively recent phenomenon, Dr Pepper's beginnings can be traced to 1885. The gradual evolution of Dr Pepper occurred as follows:

3 1885—Dr Pepper formula was perfected and introduced by Robert S. Lazenby, eminent beverage chemist in Waco, Texas. Drink was first served in Wade B. Morrison's old corner drugstore in Waco.

4 1890—Dr Pepper was being bottled at numerous points in Texas, and syrup was being hauled from Waco by Wells Fargo Express. The first corporate owner of the Dr Pepper formula and Dr Pepper trademarks was a Texas corporation, Artesian Manufacturing & Bottling Company of Waco. The present Dr Pepper Company emerged from consolidations of the Artesian corporation with several minor firms.

5 1921—J. B. O'Hara, young U.S. Army engineer from Duryea, Pennsylvania, was married to Lazenby's daughter and joined his father-in-law in the business. He later became president and chairman of the board and provided the spark that launched the company on its road to success. Lazenby and O'Hara moved the company from Waco to Dallas two years later and established a corporation under the laws of the state of Colorado on July 5.

6 1927—O'Hara discovered the findings of Dr. Walter Eddy, Ph.D., of Columbia University, which proved that sugar provided energy and that the average person experienced a letdown during the normal day at 10:30 A.M., 2:30 P.M., and 4:30 P.M. Thus, O'Hara

---

This case was prepared by George S. Vozikis and Timothy S. Mescon, both of the University of Miami, Florida.

Exhibit 1

Gross revenues, margin, and net income, 1968–1982

Year	*Gross revenues ($ millions)*	*Operating profit margin (percent)*	*Net income (in thousands of dollars)*
1968	$ 41.9	19.7%	$ 4,108
1969	49.5	19.1	4,642*
1970	57.4	17.7	5,629
1971	63.6	18.6	6,772
1972	77.4	19.0	8,102
1973	98.9	17.0	9,736
1974	128.3	13.5	9,902
1975	138.2	16.4	11,904
1976	151.8	18.4	15,530
1977	226.8	16.4	20,322
1978	271.0	15.1	23,565
1979	291.8	14.4	23,609
1980	339.5	14.2	26,933
1981	370.6	14.0	29,944
1982	516.1	7.6	12,474
1983	560.4	3.9†	21,600

* After 5-cents-a-share nonrecurring loss on cyclamates.
† Net income before extraordinary items as a percent of sales.

reasoned that Dr Pepper, because of its sugar content, would supply energy and, taken at 10, 2, and 4 o'clock, would enable a person to avoid these fatigue periods. So Dr Pepper's slogan, "Drink a Bite to Eat at 10, 2 and 4 o'clock" became famous and is still recognized as one of the most significant and valid soft-drink slogans ever.

7 1930—By 1930, Dr Pepper distribution had spread throughout the South and into the Midwest, and a few bottlers served the West Coast. There were approximately 400 bottlers distributing Dr Pepper. Some were relatively small but provided thorough distribution in many urban and rural areas.

8 1931—H. S. Billingsley joined the company as auditor. From secretary, he rose, in 1947, to vice president; in 1951, member of the board of directors; 1964, executive vice president; 1966, president and chief operating officer (CEO); 1967, president and chief executive officer; 1969, chairman of the board and chief executive officer; 1970, chairman of the board. He retired from the company in 1974 and served on the board of directors until 1975.

9 1940–45—O'Haro's theory that Dr Pepper provided energy proved to be a lifesaver during World War II, when sugar rationing threatened to curtail operations of the soft-drink industry. His theory, along with other evidence supplied by industry leaders, prompted the War Rationing Board to rescind an earlier ruling requiring sugar quotas for the manufacture of soft drinks.

10 1942—W. W. Clements joined the company as zone manager. He moved up to become vice president-marketing in 1957; executive vice president and member of the board

in 1967; president and chief operating officer in 1969; president and chief executive officer in 1970; chairman of the board, in 1974; and chairman of the board and chief executive officer in 1980.

11 1946—Dr Pepper Company stock was listed on the board of the New York Stock Exchange under the symbol DOC. This was an important milestone in the success of Dr Pepper and resulted in a broadened ownership of stock in the company.

12 1950—Although growth had been conservative through the years, it had been solid. Distribution gradually expanded with bottling plants serving wider areas. The number of plants had not increased, but the area served was greater. Growth in the company's structure became more pronounced, and Dr Pepper weathered a number of economic storms. A modernized logo design without the period after Dr was introduced for bottle crowns. Though the logo has evolved further, the period has never reappeared.

13 1956—Wesby R. Parker joined Dr Pepper Company. He was responsible for important changes including a management development program and the introduction of Hot Dr Pepper which shocked many people. Today, Hot Dr Pepper is recognized as a major asset to the company and the only carbonated soft drink that has had any success as a hot beverage.

14 1960—By now, Dr Pepper had become well established as the growth product in the industry and one of the major soft-drink brands in America. Its national distribution was better than 75 percent and gaining. Territory consolidation, plant mergers, and new franchises continued to expand product availability and improve Dr Pepper's market position. Advertising was spread nationwide to reach unfranchised areas for Dr Pepper's introduction.

15 1962—Diet Dr Pepper was introduced. Other diet soft drinks already were on the market—some with negative experience due to inferior taste. Extensive research had gone into Diet Dr Pepper to make sure it was right. The delay proved worthwhile. Diet Dr Pepper was considered more identical in taste to the original product than many other leading brands. It achieved wide popularity and contributed substantially to Dr Pepper's annual sales.

16 1963—A major roadblock to domestic franchise expansion was removed when a U.S. district court ruled that Dr Pepper was not a cola. Bottlers formerly restricted by agreements with cola franchisers from producing and selling two cola brands were able to join a growing network of Dr Pepper franchise operations with protected territories for manufacturing and distributing Dr Pepper products.

17 1970—Dr Pepper was introduced in the New York City market, largest soft-drink consuming area in the world, with some 18 million people. The drink was introduced by a Dr Pepper Company franchisee, the Coca-Cola Bottling Co. of New York, Inc. Dr Pepper introduced the "Misunderstood" ad campaign developed by Young & Rubicam.

18 1971—After extensive research, Sugar-Free Dr Pepper, formulated with saccharin as a sweetner, was introduced, replacing Diet Dr Pepper due to the FDA ban on cyclamates imposed in 1969. Sugar-Free Dr Pepper quickly grew in popularity to become the leading soft drink in many markets. Current logos and colors for Dr Pepper and Sugar-Free Dr Pepper were introduced.

19 1972—Growth continued at the rate of 15 percent per year as Dr Pepper became the fourth largest selling soft drink in America.

20 1973—Two important developments made 1973 a significant year in Dr Pepper's

progress; (1) Domestic franchising was virtually complete; less than one half of 1 percent remained unfranchised; and (2) Dr Pepper made its first major move into the international market with its introduction in Japan by the Tokyo Coca-Cola Bottling Co., Ltd. Negotiations with this company formed a joint-venture company, Dr Pepper Japan, Ltd.

21 1974—The "Most Original Soft Drink" advertising campaign was introduced to make new customers aware of Dr Pepper's unique taste.

22 1976—Domestic growth continued at a record-setting pace as Dr Pepper moved into Malta, Europe, and surveyed controlled foreign growth. Metric packaging was introduced by several bottlers. One- and two-liter returnable bottles were well accepted in the marketplace.

23 1977—Acquisition and development of major franchises in Houston, Texas, and southern California, as construction continued on a $21 million Dallas-Forth Worth production facility, laid the groundwork for increased corporate growth. John B. Connally was elected to the board of directors following the death of Jack Vaughn, a director since 1960. For the 20th consecutive year, sales and earnings reached all-time high levels at $226.8 million and $20.3 million, respectively.

24 1978—Record sales of $271 million produced record net earnings of $23.5 million and "Peppers" began popping up all over as Dr Pepper successfully introduced "Be a Pepper" advertising to receptive audiences. Dr Pepper Company concluded its arrangement with Dr Pepper Japan, Ltd., and set up Dr Pepper Japan Company to enable greater franchise opportunities in the Far East. Expansion into new international markets brought Dr Pepper to Jordan and Guatemala. San Diego assets of the southern California franchise were sold to an independent franchisee, and increased marketing efforts were realized for the company's largest subsidiary plant market covering the counties of Los Angeles, San Luis Obispo, Santa Barbara, and Ventura. This southern California territory encompasses a trade population of 9.5 million. Dr Pepper was made available in PET (polyethylene terephthalate) plastic, two-liter bottles. Governmental concern about the safety of saccharin developed into legislation, placing an 18-month moratorium on banning saccharin and requiring cautionary labeling on all products containing the artificial sweetner, including Sugar-Free Dr Pepper. Consumers perceived Sugar-Free Dr Pepper to satisfy a need for no-sugar diets and continued to purchase the product.

25 1980—Dr Pepper became the Number 3 selling soft drink in the United States as net sales of $333 million achieved another record. Charles L. Jarvie became the 10th and youngest (43) president of Dr Pepper Company in February. The board of directors also elected Jarvie chief operating officer and a member of the board. W. W. Clements remained chairman of the board and chief executive officer. "Be a Pepper" continued to gain national attention through advertising and promotion programs.

26 Purchase of the Dr Pepper Bottling Co. of Corpus Christi, Texas, made the Gulf Coast plant the company's sixth wholly owned subsidiary. In July 1980, then President Jimmy Carter signed into law the Soft Drink Interbrand Competition Act, thereby upholding the integrity of the industry's franchise system. Richard A. Zimmerman, president and CEO of Hershey Foods Corp., was elected to the board of directors. The expansion of international marketing took Dr Pepper to Sweden, Nigeria, and Chile.

27 1981—Dr Pepper acquired Soft Drinks, Inc., its licensed bottler in Albuquerque,

New Mexico. In September, Dr Pepper and Welch Foods, Inc., signed a definitive agreement for Dr Pepper's newly formed subsidiary, Premier Beverages, Inc., to acquire U.S. marketing rights to the Welch's line of carbonated soft drinks, with strawberry, orange, apple, grape, and root beer flavors, through a network of 226 licensed bottlers.

28 1982—Dr Pepper acquired the Canada Dry soft drink business unit, with the exception of the Canada Dry bottler in New York, from Norton Simon, Inc., for $143 million. This purchase was part of what Dr Pepper called its Cadillac strategy by which it hoped for aggressive sales of noncola drinks with strong brand names, according to Foots Clements. Norton Simon was also paid an extra $10 million for its agreement to stay out of the soft drink business for five years and $2 million for a two-year technical-assistance agreement. The purchase price was greater than Dr Pepper's net worth at the time of the acquisition, estimated at $116 million. In November, Charles L. Jarvie, chief operating officer, resigned and was replaced by Richard Q. Armstrong, who until then was president of Canada Dry.

29 1983—Dr Pepper introduced caffeine-free/sugar free Pepper Free in January, and in April a sugared version of Pepper Free followed. Canada Dry introduced a Canada Dry salt-free seltzer drink. Rita C. Clements, Dallas investor and former First Lady of Texas as the wife of Gov. William P. Clements, Jr., was elected as a new member in the board of directors. In September, Dr Pepper retained the investment banking firm of Lazard Freres & Co. to explore investment opportunities, including "a merger with or sale of assets to another company," according to W. W. Clements. In December, a $560 million acquisition offer from an investor group led by Castle & Cooke, Inc., a Honolulu-based food-products company, was received and translated to $24 per share. Earlier, a bid of $513 million or $22 a share had been received from Forstmann Little & Co., a New York investment firm.

30 1984—On February 28, Dr Pepper shareholders approved by a wide margin the $22-a-share merger proposal by Forstmann Little & Co. to take the company private with about 35 shareholders (see Exhibit 2). At the same time, W. W. Clements announced company plans to sell Canada Dry and an undetermined number of bottling plants. Richard Q. Armstrong resigned and was replaced by Joe K. Hughes.

Management

31 Dr Pepper is professionally managed and has some family control. Virginia Lazenby O'Hara, daughter of the founder, owns approximately 9 percent of the stock. Ms. O'Hara's late husband was president, then chairman, from 1933 to 1961. He was succeeded by Wesby R. Parker, who joined the firm after some years with General Foods. Three of Parker's top executives died in an airplane crash in 1964, and Parker died in 1967. He was succeeded by Hascal Billingsley. All these presidents came from the financial or operations function.

32 The current chairman, Woodrow Wilson Clements, is the first with a major background in marketing. Foots, as Clements likes to be called, studied at Howard College and graduated from the University of Alabama (1935), where he played football. He went from route salesman to sales manager of the Dr Pepper Company in 1942. He was successively district manager, sales promotion manager, assistant manager of the bottler service, and general sales manager, 1951–1957; vice president, marketing,

Exhibit 2

IMPORTANT MESSAGE TO THE SHAREHOLDERS OF DR PEPPER COMPANY

The Special Meeting of Shareholders of Dr Pepper Company will be held on February 28—only two weeks away. It is important that all shareholders sign and return their proxy cards immediately.

The Meeting has been called to vote upon the proposed merger of Dr Pepper Company with a privately held company newly formed by Forstmann Little & Co., and an affiliated partnership. If the proposed merger is approved, each Dr Pepper shareholder will receive $22 in cash per share. In addition, all shareholders who owned Dr Pepper on the dividend record date of February 10 will also receive a dividend of $.21 per share.

Your Board of Directors has carefully considered the terms and conditions of the proposed merger and unanimously recommends a vote FOR the proposed merger.

Approval of the merger requires the affirmative vote of two-thirds of the shares outstanding as of the Special Meeting record date—January 9, 1984. Regardless of the number of shares you own, every vote is important.

If you were a Dr Pepper shareholder on the January 9 record date, only you can vote the Dr Pepper proxy for your shares. If you do not vote, your inaction could hurt the chances of a successful vote on the merger and thereby deprive Dr Pepper shareholders of the opportunity to receive $22 cash for their shares.

As you know, there are no other merger or acquisition offers being made to Dr Pepper shareholders. This is the only offer being made and it is unanimously recommended by your Board of Directors. Our independent investment bankers, Lazard Frères & Co., and Blyth Eastman Paine Webber, Inc. have given their opinions that the terms of the merger and the price of $22 per share are fair from a financial point of view to the shareholders, respectively.

If your shares are held in the name of a brokerage firm, your broker can vote only upon receiving your specific instructions. Please sign and return your proxy card in the envelope provided by your broker. To ensure that your vote is counted, contact the party responsible for your account and instruct him or her to execute a proxy card on your behalf for the merger.

Thank you for your consideration and support.

Sincerely,

W. W. Clements

W. W. Clements
Chairman & Chief Executive Officer

If you have any questions about voting your shares, please call our proxy solicitor:

Toll-Free 800-221-3343
or
212-619-1100 (collect)

1957–1967; executive vice president and director, 1967–1969; president and chief operating officer, 1969; president and chairman, 1970.

33 Foots Clements reflects his rural Alabama upbringing in his folksy approach to employees and bottlers, and he relishes telling tales. Clements, a supersalesman who enjoys drinking the company product hot or cold, predicts that Dr Pepper will exceed the sales of Coca-Cola, probably within 20 years (see Exhibit 3).

34 In February 1980, Charles L. Jarvie was elected president, chief operating officer, and a director of Dr Pepper, succeeding W. W. Clements. In an inteview with *The Wall Street Journal* on February 27, 1980, Clements said that Jarvie was expected to take over the soft-drink operations of Dr Pepper and also help it find, evaluate, and operate its first food-industry acquisition. "I'm a salesman, not a buyer," Clements said. "I'm delighted to get rid of the day-to-day operating responsibilities." Clements's new role was that of CEO and chairman of the board, but he had not devoted much thought to retiring from work and the day-to-day responsibilities at Dr Pepper. In 1985, Dr Pepper will mark its 100th birthday, and Clements will mark his 50th year selling it, even though the company refused to hire him the first three times he applied for a job! A passion for work and patient determination has marked Clements's rise within the Dr Pepper ranks:

> I'm a very positive, hard-headed, determined individual inside, and I try to maintain a little different composure outside. But I just won't allow myself to accept any defeat as permanent."

35 In October 1980, Clements made another move to show his faith in long-time Peppers and to soften the blow to their morale from the arrival of an outsider, Charles Jarvie. He created a new senior vice president level and promoted three of his veteran executives to the new designation: John R. Albers, marketing; Alvin H. Lane, finance/secretary; and Richard D. O'Connor, corporate bottling plants.

36 In November 1982, Jarvie resigned under pressure. Insiders claimed he clashed with Clements over the company's mass-marketing strategy, especially after sales of

Exhibit 3

W.W. "Foots" Clements

Born: July 30, 1914, in North Port, Ala.

Occupation: Chairman and chief executive officer of Dr Pepper Co.

Favorite restaurants: Mr. Peppe, Pyramid Room, The Mansion, Jean-Claude, Il Sorrento. ("Being single, I have to eat out a lot.")

Clubs: Chaparral Club, City Club, Tower Club, Dallas Country Club.

Favorite music: Big bands, New Orleans jazz.

Dislikes: Golf ("It's frustrating, not relaxing"), Coke and Pepsi ("Just any kind of cola. They taste terrible.")

"I'm a very positive, hardheaded, determined individual inside, and I try to maintain a little different composure outside. But I just won't allow myself to accept any defeat as permanent."

Source: John Kirkpatrick, "W. W. Clements," *The Dallas Morning News,* July 18, 1982, p. 4E.

Dr Pepper fell 3 percent in 1982, costing it its third-place ranking. Clements said about Jarvie's resignation: "It was a brand new business for him. I would have been as lost in his business." (Jarvie had been hired from Procter & Gamble where he ran the food-products division.)

37 The new president, Richard Q. Armstrong, was known basically for his experience as a soft-drink "salesman" like Foots Clements. He maintained a close relationship with the bottlers while he was president of Canada Dry, something that Jarvie, with a reputation of being tough and decisive, never really accomplished.

38 Right after shareholders approved the Forstmann Little & Co. proposal to take the company private, Clements announced the resignation of Richard Armstrong, who "didn't have the Dr Pepper religion that we required." The new president and chief operating officer is Joe K. Hughes, 56 years old, who was executive vice president and had been associated with Dr Pepper for 15 years. "All our energies and resources will now be devoted to Dr Pepper," Clements said. "We're going to get lean and mean."

39 Dr Pepper, like many other private companies such as Hallmark Cards, United Parcel Service, and Cargill, will have a strengthened managerial hand and save at least $5 million, according to Clements, by not having to report to shareholders and the Securities and Exchange Commission. The last board of directors (before going private) consisted of the following individuals:

Board of directors

Richard Q. Armstrong, president and chief operating officer, Dr Pepper Company, Dallas, Texas

W. W. Clements, chairman of the board and chief executive officer, Dr Pepper Company, Dallas, Texas

Rita C. Clements, investor, Dallas, Texas

Edwin L. Cox, oil and gas producer, Dallas, Texas

Charles G. Cullum, chairman of the executive committee, the Cullum Companies, Inc. (supermarkets and drugstores), Dallas, Texas

Lamar Hunt, chairman of the board, Kansas City Chiefs Football Club, Kansas City, Missouri, and vice president, Hunt Energy Corporation, Dallas, Texas

Pat W. McNamara, Jr., Dr Pepper bottling companies, Lubbock and Plainview, Texas

William R. Robertson, Jr., chairman and chief executive officer, Robertson's Beverages, Inc. (soft-drink bottling plants), chairman and chief executive officer, North Carolina Television, Inc., Washington, North Carolina

A. F. (Pete) Sloan, president and chairman of the board, Lance, Inc. (snack food and bakery products), Charlotte, North Carolina

John P. Thompson, chairman of the board and chief executive officer, the Southland Corporation (retail food stores), Dallas, Texas

Richard A. Zimmerman, president and chief operating officer, Hershey Foods Corporation, Hershey, Pennsylvania

Marketing

40 Dr Pepper Company is the oldest major manufacturer of soft-drink concentrates and syrups in the United States. Founded in Waco, Texas, in 1885, Dr Pepper Company markets, sells, and distributes its concentrates, extracts, and fountain syrups principally to independent, licensed bottlers under the major brands of Dr Pepper, Canada Dry, and Welch's carbonated sodas.

41 Dr Pepper's business is seasonal, with the second and third calendar quarters accounting for the highest sales volume. It manufactures, markets, sells, and distrbutes soft-drink concentrates (the basic ingredient for soft drinks) and fountain syrups (concentrate with sweeteners and water added), principally to independent, licensed bottlers in the United States. It also bottles and distributes soft drinks through five wholly owned subsidiaries and cans soft drinks for sale to licensed bottlers.

42 Licensed bottlers add sweeteners and carbonated water to concentrates to produce finished soft drinks which are packaged under appropriate trademark and brand labels and, by right of authorized agreements, are sold in protected geographic territories. In the United States, Dr Pepper products are distributed by some 460 bottlers. There are 185 Canada Dry bottlers, and 240 bottlers sell Welch's products.

43 The company also bottles, cans, and distributes soft drinks through 10 wholly owned subsidiaries and packages soft drinks for sale to licensed bottlers. Fountain syrups are sold to bottlers, wholesale distributors for resale to fountain/food-service accounts, and directly to fountain accounts.

44 Dr Pepper, Canada Dry, and Welch's soft drinks comprise about 10 percent of the total industry share of volume. Each is a leader in its respective category, with Dr Pepper claiming a 92 percent share of the Pepper category. Canada Dry Ginger Ale is that category's leading seller, and Canada Dry Club Soda, Tonic, and Seltzer are Number 1 in their categories. Welch's Grape is the leader in that flavor segment.

45 When Dr Pepper Company acquired Canada Dry in February 1982, it also secured rights to Canada Dry's worldwide soft drink business. Canada Dry products are manufactured and sold by some 180 bottlers in more than 80 countries.

46 Since 1977, Dr Pepper has expanded and simplified its sales and marketing organization to make it more responsive to bottlers' needs and opportunities in the marketplace. To achieve this, Richard Q. Armstrong, Dr Pepper's former CEO, outlined the following actions in the company's 1982 Annual Report:

> First, we are budgeting realistically for continued discounting at intense competitive levels.
>
> Second, our base marketing support for all bottlers will be keyed to achievable business plans, carefully developed with our bottler-partners and geared to produce profitable results for both parties.
>
> Third, departments that were overstaffed or underutilized have undergone thorough reorganization that has resulted in a streamlined structure with a capacity to respond to bottler needs quickly and decisively.
>
> Fourth, our combined resources are being brought together at every level where we see greater strength through synergy. Yes, we remain committed to the separate sales and marketing of our product lines, but in 1983, we will experience significant savings through consolidated extract production, quality control, accounting, purchasing, and information systems.

In fact, by March 1, 1983, our extract consolidation project was virtually completed, resulting in a more-efficient production facility for manufacturing Canada Dry Ginger Ale extract and other concentrates. This plant is adjacent to the existing Dr Pepper concentrate facility at corporate headquarters in Dallas.

Competition

47 The soft-drink industry is highly competitive. The company competes not only directly for consumer acceptance but also for shelf space in supermarkets and for maximum marketing efforts by multibrand licensed bottlers. The company's soft-drink products compete with all liquid refreshments and with numerous nationally known producers of soft drinks including Coca-Cola, Pepsi-Cola, and 7up, several of which are extremely strong from the standpoint of personnel, products, and finances, as well as regional producers and private-label suppliers. Competition may take many forms, including pricing, packaging, and advertising campaigns. Furthermore, there have been, and probably will continue to be, soft drinks produced by other companies which attempt to simulate the unique flavor of Dr Pepper.

48 Dr Pepper accounts for 10 percent of U.S. soft-drink sales (including Canada Dry and Welch's). It still finds itself, however, in a market dominated by colas and entangled in a war for supermarket shelf space and market share. Ensuing price wars have forced the smaller company to curtail its effort to become a national brand and concentrate on protecting its prime market strongholds in the South and Southwest, where Dr Pepper's market share is between 20 and 25 percent. "We didn't have enough funds to move 200 million people," lamented Clements.

49 Lower volume performance and subsequent reduced profitability for Dr Pepper and Sugar-Free Dr Pepper in 1982 was attributable to a soft economy, heavy increases in marketing expenditures, and an extraordinary high level of competitive discounting. These efforts lowered the Dr Pepper and Sugar-Free Dr Pepper combined brands' market share from approximately 6.5 percent to 6 percent. Brand Dr Pepper shipped 6 percent less than in 1981, and Sugar-Free Dr Pepper was off about 3 percent, compared to the previous year.

50 Despite a sluggish economy and fierce competition from colas and flavors, Welch's for 1982 increased its sales revenue. Welch's Grape and Strawberry continued to represent more than 85 percent of total volume. Welch's Grape, the flavor most closely associated with the Welch's name for more than 100 years, represents 55 percent of total volume. Blind taste tests, conducted by Rawson Associates, Ltd. show that no other grape soda is preferred over Welch's. Single drink sales continued to be Welch's volume mainstay in 1982.

51 Canada Dry Ginger Ale, which represents approximately 45 percent of Canada Dry's total domestic volume, grew at a 5 percent rate and recorded the highest unit sales volume in the history of this flagship brand. Canada Dry Ginger Ale growth outpaced that of the ginger ale category and achieved a 34.4 percent share of the category within food stores, an increase of nearly one full share point versus the prior year. This strong sales performance further increased Canada Dry Ginger Ale's leadership position as America's largest-selling ginger ale.

52 Canada Dry Club Soda, America's number 1 sparkling water, increased its dominant share of the club-soda category by more than one full share point to a 33.4 percent

share. Canada Dry Seltzer in the salt-free segment of the sparkling-water category, was expanded into more than 50 percent of the United States during 1982. Canada Dry Seltzer captured more than a 10 percent share of this rapidly growing segment of the sparkling-water category.

53 Canada Dry Tonic Water achieved a strong sales performance in 1982 within the highly competitive tonic-water category, maintaining its firm position as America's largest-selling tonic water. As a group, Canada Dry's mainline products—Ginger Ale, Club Soda, Seltzer, and Tonic Water—generated a 4 percent unit volume sales gain.

54 Exhibit 4 presents the soft-drink market shares for the top-selling brands. A special report on how Americans quench their thirst was recently published by M. Shanken Communications. *Beverage Trends in America* was surveyed our drinking patterns and revealed some very interesting trends that prevail, especially regarding more concern with our health. This report was reproduced in *USA Today* on March 15, 1984, and presented in Exhibit 5.

Exhibit 4

Soft drink market shares, 1976–1981 (percent of market)

	1976	*1977*	*1978*	*1979*	*1980*	*1981*
Coca-Cola	24.3%	24.5%	24.3%	23.9%	24.3%	24.2%
Pepsi-Cola	17.0	17.2	17.6	17.9	17.9	18.3
7up	6.3	6.0	5.9	5.6	5.4	5.0
Dr Pepper	5.0	5.3	5.4	5.5	5.5	5.4

Source: Standard & Poor's Industry Surveys.

Fast-Food/Fountain, Vending

55 Dr Pepper is available in 35 percent of the total fast-food/fountain accounts, an increase from an estimated 30 percent availability in 1976. These accounts rely primarily on five-gallon tanks for receiving and dispensing fountain products to their customers. To improve Dr Pepper's availability in these accounts, the company has had a tank distribution program (TD system) since 1976.

56 Virtually all of the major franchisors currently offer incentives for purchases of vending machines. They generally take the form of percentage rebates on all machines over a minimum or a percentage of the price of the unit.

57 Dr Pepper has come up with a support program which not only offers the incentive but also assists the bottler/canner by providing financial assistance. By financing through Dr Pepper, the firm would save two ways. First, by combining all orders, Dr Pepper orders the vending machines in truck-load quantities.

58 Through arrangements made by Dr Pepper, the bottlers finance their purchases with a Dallas, Texas bank, and are contingently liable for repayment of these loans to the bank. In addition, Dr Pepper Company has continued its aggressive vendor refurbishment program, offering bottlers the opportunity to repaint and rework vendors already in the market. The program provides a fresh presentation of the Dr Pepper trademark, which was redesigned in 1981.

Exhibit 5

What we drink

Our drinking habits vary by region. Northeasterners and Westerners consume more alcohol per person than Southerners and those in the North Central region. Here's a regional look at U.S. beverage consumption.

North central

27 percent of U.S. population consumes 27.1 percent of total beverages

alcoholic	27.2%
nonalcoholic	27%

Northeast

22 percent of U.S. population consumes 21 percent of total beverages

alcoholic	26.3%
nonalcoholic	20.6%

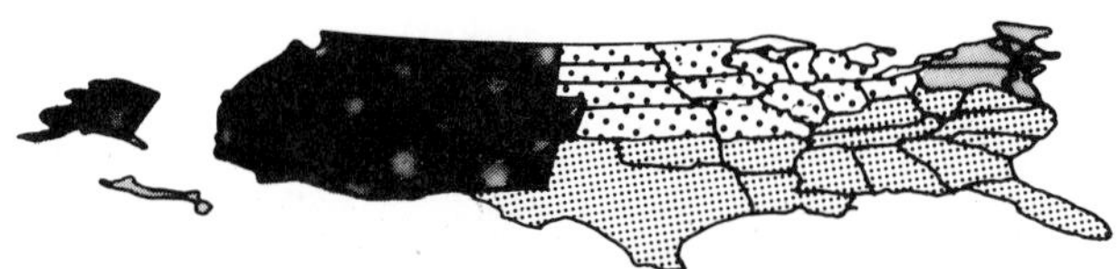

West

19 percent of U.S. population consumes 19.4 percent of total beverages

alcoholic	21.7%
nonalcoholic	19.3%

South

32 percent of U.S. population consumes 32.5 percent of total beverages

alcoholic	24.8%
nonalcoholic	33.1%

Source: National Family Opinion Inc.'s 1982 Share of Intake Panel (SIP) Study.

Exhibit 5 (*continued*)

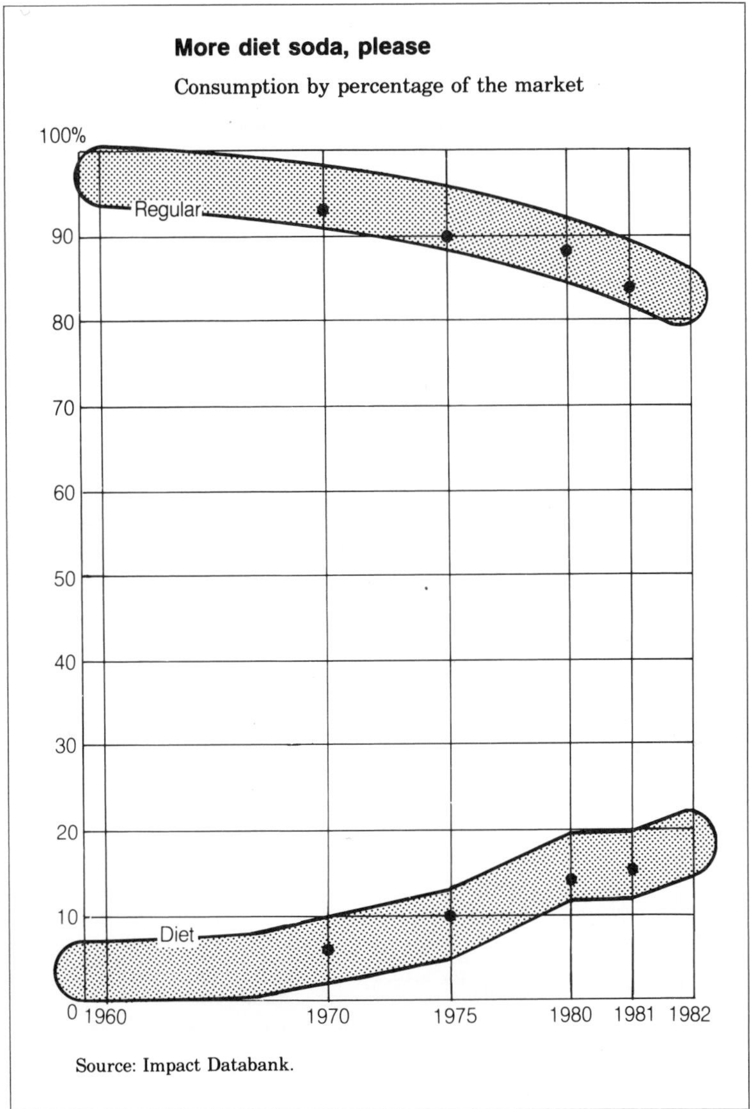

Source: Impact Databank.

Exhibit 5 (*concluded*)

Less water, more soda pop

Total consumption in gallons per person

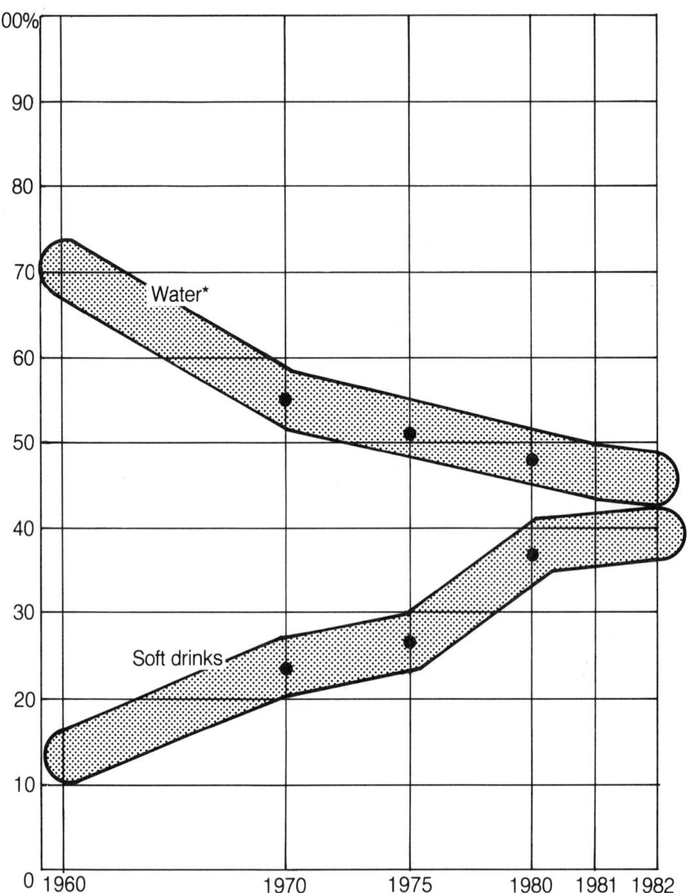

* Bottled and tap water.
Source: Impact Databank.

Nonalcoholic choices

	Total non-alcoholic consumption	*Soft drinks*	*Coffee*	*Milk*	*Fruit juice drinks*	*Tea*	*Other*
Male	52.8%	54.1%	51.9%	58.8%	51.9%	47.1%	48.1%
Female	47.2	45.9	48.1	41.2	48.1	52.9	51.9

Source: National Family Opinion Inc.'s 1982 Share of Intake Panel (SIP) Study.
By John Sherlock, *USA Today*.

Promotion/Advertising

59 The soft-drink industry is characterized by heavy advertising expenditures, and this is primarily how Coke and Pepsi wage their wars. Pepsi leads the way in advertising expenditures—$143,138,000 in 1981, compared to $117,968,000 for Coke. Dr Pepper takes a very distant third at $25,119,000 (Standard & Poor's Industry Surveys, 1982). Does this advertising work? Does a large advertising budget mean a large market share? It does. The two companies with the greatest advertising budgets also have the greatest market shares. However, it is interesting to note that despite a 40 percent increase in advertising expenditures in 1981, Dr Pepper actually lost .1 percent of its market share. Pepsi increased its market share by .4 percent in 1981 while Coke's dropped .1 percent. Yet, at the same time, Pepsi decreased its advertising by 5 percent and Coke increased its expenditures by 3 percent.

60 However, despite these findings, advertising in the soft-drink industry would seem to be successful in that the brand differentiation is small enough that something such as singing a particular product's jingle as one walks into the store could mean the difference between buying a Coke and a Pepsi. Studies call for a 4.5 percent growth in the industry over the next three years, with sales increasing from 76.9 billion units in 1982 to 87.8 billion units in 1985 (Standard & Poor's Industry Surveys, 1982).

61 Dr Pepper increased its $25 million advertising budget in 1982 by nearly 15 percent to $28 million. That year was also the end of the "Be a Pepper" campaign featuring lead "Pepper" David Naughton, whose commercials made Dr Pepper the Number 2 favorite commercial, behind Miller's Lite Beer. (See Exhibits 6 and 7.)

62 The 1982 campaign undertaken by the advertising company of Young and Rubicam moved to a new theme and a new song. "To be a Pepper, original like a Pepper, all you gotta do is taste," sang Ray Bolger, *The Wizard of Oz* scarecrow. Other spots featured Scott Baio, young star of the hit TV series, "Happy Days"; high-stepping Pepperettes who celebrated the great taste of Dr Pepper and a technical masterpiece, "Revolving Room." The rotating set in the latter spot enabled Fred Astaire to dance up the walls and on the ceiling in the 1950s film classic, *Top Hat.*

63 Sugar-Free Dr Pepper advertising incorporated a new theme line, "Oh, what a surprise . . . the taste is gonna open your eyes." Print became a more-important medium for Sugar-Free Dr Pepper with strong ad and coupon schedules in women's service magazines.

64 Five major promotions in 1982 were highlighted in the late-spring, high-level consumption period when one lucky Pepper won $1 million. "Be a Pepper Millionaire" ran from mid-May through June and is believed to have offered the largest single cash prize in soft-drink promotion history. Other promotions for 1982 included:

"Endless Summer" (Feb./March)—Coupon sweepstakes and refunds combined to offer five winner trips for two to Caribbean resorts.

"Test These Tastes" (March/April)—Teaming with sugar-free Velamints, this Sugar-Free Dr Pepper promotion featured an all-purpose sports bag.

"Be a Western Pepper" (July/Aug.)—Coupon supported western wear sweepstakes offered $50,000 in prizes. Top prize was a $10,000 western wardrobe and a trip to Dallas.

"New York New Year's Eve" (Oct./Nov.)—Top prize was a trip for two to New York City for New Year's Eve to appear on the "New Year's Rockin' Eve" TV

Exhibit 6

Exhibit 7

special with Dick Clark, $10,000 for a Big Apple shopping spree, and a year's supply of Dr Pepper.

65 On January 22, 1981, the following report appeared in *The Wall Street Journal:*

> Dr Pepper Co. filed suit in federal court against Sambo's Restaurants, Inc., and Bozell & Jacobs Inc., an advertising agency, claiming that Sambo's "dancing seniors" commercial is an imitation of its popular "Be a Pepper" commercial.
>
> The suit says the Sambo's commercial, produced by Bozell & Jacobs, is "designed to attract senior citizens into Sambo's restaurants" and uses a jingle, "parts of which are substantially similar to the jingle composed" by Dr Pepper. The suit says the Sambo's commercial even contains the phrase, "don't you want to be a senior, too?" Dr Pepper's commercial uses the phrase "wouldn't you like to be a Pepper, too?"
>
> Moreover, the suit claims, the format and theme of the Sambo's commercial, including the music and dancing, "are very similar" to Dr Pepper's commercial. The suit says the use of the commercial has hurt Dr Pepper because it attracts customers into Sambo's restaurants "more than one half of which don't serve Dr Pepper, but do serve soft drinks other than Dr Pepper."

This lawsuit indicates the importance that the company attaches to its award-winning national advertising theme conceived by Young & Rubicam, Inc., back in 1970. With the 1970 advertising campaign, Dr Pepper became "America's Most Misunderstood Soft Drink." And in many part of the country it was. Research showed that consumers thought since it was brown, it should taste like a cola or a root beer. Thus, the "Most Original Soft Drink Ever" campaign was developed and minimusical TV commercials told consumers "It's not a cola, it's something much, much, more."

66 Even though a federal judge in Dallas ruled in July 1981 that Sambo's Restaurants, Inc., could no longer use its "dancing seniors" television commercials because they infringed on the Dr Pepper Company's copyrighted advertising campaign, Clements decided in August 1982 to get away from the dancers because "everybody is copying us." In 1983, the company spent $28 million to promote Dr Pepper alone but planned only one national promotion and no network TV advertising. Instead, the money went to local ads and promotion in cooperation with bottlers. Although 90 percent of its $119 million marketing outlay went to the bottlers, the company found it was still vulnerable in markets where its minor role moved neither bottler nor consumers. The 1984 campaign is a $32 million effort with "Hold out for Dr Pepper" as a theme. It is based on surveys that convinced the firm that the market segment it seeks, the group of people which regard themselves as those who do not follow the trend, will grow from 30 percent of the population to 50 percent by 1990. So the "most misunderstood" soft drink has evolved into a soft drink that is "held out for the out-of-the-ordinary!"

Trademarks

67 The importance of Dr Pepper's trademark (Dr Pepper) to its business cannot be overemphasized. Trademarks are valid as long as they are used properly for identification purposes. Federal registrations of trademarks are protected for 20 years and can be renewed indefinitely as long as the trademarks are in lawful use. Dr Pepper's federal registration for Dr Pepper is valid and subsisting in the U.S. Patent Office.

68 The Dr Pepper trademark has long been identified with the numerals 10, 2, and 4. People frequently ask what they mean.

69 A Columbia University professor, Dr. Walter H. Eddy, conducting research into the human diet, discovered that three meals per day were insufficient to provide energy to keep an active person at top-level efficiency. He pinpointed three times during the day between meals when energy in the human body drops to its lowest ebb. These are 10 A.M., and 2 P.M., and 4 P.M.

70 In a book titled *The Liquid Bite,* he urged that around these periods each day a normal person should restore energy through food consumed in liquid form, such as in a pure, healthful soft drink like Dr Pepper. The sugar content in Dr Pepper supplies quick energy. Thus, the numerals 10, 2, and 4 were identified on the clock-shaped Dr Pepper trademark pointing up these specific hours as a reminder that Dr Pepper is not only a delightfully different soft drink but also a "Friendly Pepper-Upper" (see Exhibits 8 and 9).

Exhibit 8

Dr Pepper's 10–2–4 trademark

71 Other than its federal license agreements, Dr Pepper has no material, existing trademark license agreements permitting the use of its trademark in advertising. Generally, such agreements are nonexclusive, and the right to use a trademark terminates upon cancellation of the trademark license agreement.

International Operations

72 Dr Pepper's soft drinks are packaged and sold under the trademarks of Canada Dry, Dr Pepper, Mission, and Salute in more than 80 countries by more than 180 bottlers, distributors, or jobbers. The global map in Exhibit 10 illustrates availability of Dr Pepper products in the international marketplace, excluding the United States and Canada.

73 In 1982, against a depressed global economy and a 3 percent decrease in total soft-drink consumption, the international division again outperformed the industry by a

Exhibit 9

The original Dr Pepper trademark (1885)

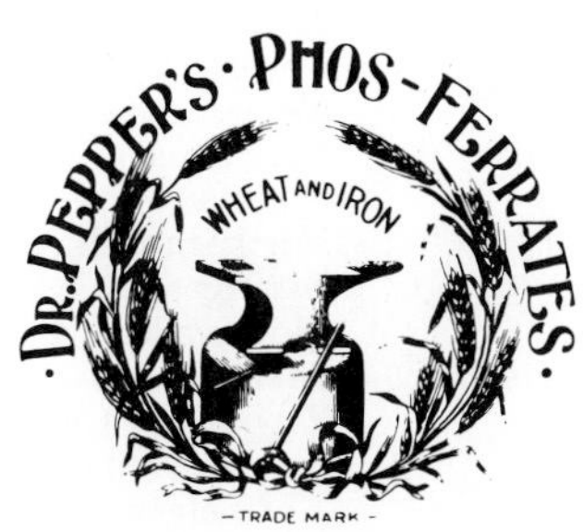

Exhibit 10

Dr Pepper's international distribution

Argentina
Aruba
Australia
Austria
Barbados
Bahrain
Belgium
Bermuda
Bolivia
Canary Islands
Chile
Columbia
Costa Rica
Curacao
Cyprus
Dominican Republic
Ecuador
Egypt Arab Republic
El Salvador
England
Finland
France
French Windward Islands
Greece
Guadeloupe
Guam
Guatemala
Haiti
Holland
Honduras
Hong Kong
Hungary
Iceland
Indonesia
Italy
Ivory Coast
Japan
Jordan
Kuwait
Lebanon
Malta
Mexico
Mozambique
Namibia
Netherland Antilles
Nicaragua
Nigeria
Northern Ireland
Norway
Okinawa-ken
Pakistan
Papua New Guinea
Peoples' Democratic Republic of Yemen
Peru
Puerto Rico
Qatar
Republic of Ireland
Republic of Panama
Republique Populaire Du Congo
Reunion Island
Saudia Arabia
Senegal
Sierra Leone
Singapore
South Africa
South Korea
Spain
Sweden
Switzerland
Syria
Tanzania
The Bahamas
Syrian Arab Republic
Thailand
Trinidad
Tunisia
United Arab Emirates
Virgin Islands
Venezuela
West Indies
Yemen Arab Republic
Yugoslavia
Zimbabwe

wide margin. Case sales increased by 5 percent, and operating profit (before corporate charges) rose by 22 percent compared to 1981. International trading problems created by intrinsically weak local economies are magnified by the strength of the dollar or more properly, the chronic weakness of many lcoal currencies. This is leading to increased restrictions on imports and limits the abilities of many U.S. companies to increase prices to offset the effects of cost inflation.

Regulations

74 Government decisions can have a profound impact on Dr Pepper Company and consumers. To keep management, employees, and shareholders apprised of new and on-going government and scientific matters, Bill Massmann is Dr Pepper Company's principal communicator with legislators, regulatory agencies, trade associations, and scientific groups. His major involvement in 1980 was with franchise legislation (a major bill was passed), the Food and Drug Administration's unsuccessful attempt to ban saccharin, and USDA's partial ban of soft drinks in schools. Massmann described his job in the following statement:

> The course of my job introduces new facets to old government issues and challenges of new problems. With firmly established products like Dr Pepper and Sugar-Free Dr Pepper, our company has a solid foundation for growth. Our growth objectives make everyone's job important. Because we are still a rather small and uncomplicated company, there is much sharing of information and ideas. This makes us able to react quickly to changing conditions—a definite advantage in future times of decision.

75 A few states have adopted statutes intended to reduce solid waste due to discarding of bottles, cans, and other packaging material. These statutes generally require purchasers of bottled or canned beverages to make deposits on soft-drink bottles or cans, or they impose a tax on packaging materials payable at the time the packaging material is sold by its manufacturer to the soft-drink producer. Such laws have tended to increase soft-drink prices in such states and, depending upon the degree of use by a particular bottler of containers affected by the statutes, may have an adverse impact on sales and profits of bottlers there. If these laws reduce soft-drink consumption, there would likely be a reduction in concentrate sales and profits.

76 On March 9, 1977, the U.S. Food & Drug Administration (FDA) stated it would issue a proposal to ban the use of saccharin in foods. The proposed ban was published on April 15, 1977, and could have taken effect as early as mid-July 1977. Subsequently, on November 23, 1977, the Saccharin Study and Labeling Act was signed into law. The act provided, among other things, that the FDA could not ban the use of saccharin in foods for an 18-month period, ending May 23, 1979. Since the expiration of the moratorium on the proposed ban on May 23, 1979, the president signed into law a bill extending until June 30, 1981, and on August 24, 1981, the president signed into law Senate Bill 1278 which extended the moratorium through August 1983. The moratorium is contingent upon the failure by the Secretary of Human Services to find that saccharin presents an unreasonable and substantial risk to the public health and safety, based upon data reported to him after the date of enactment of the bill.

77 Sugar-Free Dr Pepper utilizes saccharin and has become one of the leading low-calorie soft drinks in the United States, accounting for approximately 20 percent of

the company's domestic Dr Pepper unit volume. Sugar-Free Canada Dry products account for approximately 7 percent of the domestic Canada Dry business. Alternate low-calorie formulas such as aspartame, have been developed and are expected to raise the demand for diet drinks. Aspartame, a substance said to be 200 times sweeter than sugar, lacks the bitter taste and also apparently lacks the health risks associated with saccharin. In July 1983, Searle & Co. the manufacturer of aspartame, announced that the Food and Drug Administration approved its low-calorie sweetner sold under the brand names NutraSweet and Equal. NutraSweet is a food additive while Equal is a tabletop sweetner. Its base price is around $85 a pound, while saccharin sells for $4. Despite the price differential, Dr Pepper announced, in September 1983, that it planned to use aspartame to replace or supplement saccharin as a sweetening ingredient, joining the rest of the industry.

78 On another front, a nine-year-long struggle with the Federal Trade Commission (FTC) to preserve the integrity of the bottler franchise system reached a positive conclusion for Dr Pepper. In July 1980, President Carter signed into law the Soft Drink Interbrand Competition Act, thus ending a battle that began in 1971 when an FTC complaint questioned the validity of the system of protected bottler franchises. In July 1981, a Federal Trade Commission hearing dismissed antitrust complaints against five soft-drink manufacturers in light of the 1980 legislation. Crush, Dr Pepper, 7up, Royal Crown Cola, and Canada Dry had maintained that the franchise arrangement of giving licensed bottlers an exclusive right to sell a company's products in a particular area was not violating antitrust laws.

79 Another sensitive issue for the soft-drink industry, and Dr Pepper in particular, is a Food and Drug Administration warning to pregnant women to curb caffeine consumption. This warning stems from a study, completed in 1980, that possibly linked caffeine with birth defects. The economic impact of such an issue is enormous because caffeine is an ingredient in widely consumed products, including soft drinks (see Exhibit 11).

Exhibit 11

Caffeine count

Beverage	*Milligrams*
Coffee:	
1 cup	93–153
Tea:	
1 cup brewed 1 minute	28.0
1 cup brewed 3 minutes	44.0
Iced tea (12 oz. serving)	70.0
Chocolate (1 oz. serving)	5.0
Soft Drinks (12 oz. cans)	
Mountain Dew	54.0
Coca-Cola	45.6
Diet Coke	45.6
Dr Pepper	39.6
Pepsi-Cola	38.4

Source: *FDA Consumer,* American Dietetic Association, and *Beverage Industry.*

The FDA has proposed taking caffeine off its GRAS list (a list of additives generally recognized as safe) and putting it on an interim list for safety testing. The FDA also proposed, in 1981, that caffeine no longer be required in cola and pepper drinks. Unquestionably, caffeine is a potent drug. Once ingested, it travels quickly through the bloodstream, constricting some blood vessels and dilating others. It increases the metabolic rate by about 10 percent and steps up the output of stomach and urine. The lethal dose is about 10,000 milligrams or the equivalent of 100 cups of coffee in one sitting. Fortunately, caffeine is quickly metabolized, and the typical amount consumed at dinner time is almost gone from the bloodstream by the next morning.

80 In an attempt to reach health-conscious consumers, soft-drink makers jumped on the bandwagon that Royal Crown started with its highly successful no-caffeine diet RC 100 soft drink in 1980. Pepsi and Coca-Cola introduced caffeine-free colas in both diet and sugar versions. Dr Pepper introduced a caffeine-free Pepper-Free version in January 1983, and in May of the same year, a 99.9 percent caffeine-free Dr Pepper was introduced sweetened with sucrose and/or fructose. W. W. Clements claimed that "although research is more positive than ever before that no reasonable possibility exists that caffeine in soft drinks can be harmful, because it is perceived to be harmful by some, we need to give the public a choice."

81 On yet another front, a 1979 Food and Drug Administration nationwide survey found that Americans want food labels to list all ingredients, tell more about calories, sugar, cholesterol and fat, and be written in simpler language. Current rules require disclosure of ingredient and nutritional information on only some foods. Dr Pepper has taken the initiative in voluntarily disclosing the nutritional information of their products as evidenced by Exhibit 12, part of the company's promotional material.

82 Other governmental rulings that may have an effect on Dr Pepper's operations are those concerning the evaluation—by consumer panels set up by the FTC—of media messages to detect misleading advertising; a protectionist national sugar policy; and

Exhibit 12

Dr Pepper's nutritional information and ingredients (one serving—8 ounces/240 ml.)

	Dr Pepper	*Sugar-Free Dr Pepper*
Calories	96.0	2.0
Carbohydrates	24.8 grams	0.5 gram
Sodium*	18.4 mg	24.0 mg
Phosphorus*	26.4 mg	28.0 mg
Calcium*	6.4 mg	0
Potassium*	1.6 mg	0
Chloride*	11.2	9.6 mg
Saccharin	0	69.1 mg/0.29%
Caffeine	26.4 mg	26.4 mg

* The quantity of these elements may vary slightly due to variations in treated local water used to produce Dr Pepper.

Dr Pepper and Sugar-Free Dr Pepper contain no fat, protein, vitamins, or other minerals requiring disclosure by labeling regulations.

finally, a proposed ban in schools on premeal soft drinks (a ban advocated by the USDA).

83 On this last issue, president Clements made the following statement during the 1978 annual stockholders' meeting:

> We are interested in the health of children. We do not sell our product as a health product. We feel very strongly that our product and similar products are extremely important parts of the diet of Americans, and particularly the youth. It provides a balanced diet. We don't suggest that they drink it instead of milk.
>
> We are working very hard to try to educate people because there is less education on nutrition than there is on economics. The American people are ignorant, virtually, of economics and even less informed on nutrition. We are working hard to try to point out the facts and to provide Dr Pepper as a variety part of the diet, not as a replacement of anything in particular.

Operations

84 The principal administrative and manufacturing facilities of the company are located in Dallas, Texas, in buildings of approximately 298,000 square feet aggregate, situated on 27 acres of land (see Exhibit 13). Additionally, Dr Pepper has a manufacturing facility in Birmingham, Alabama, containing 31,000 square feet, which is situated

Exhibit 13

on less than one acre of land. The land and buildings are in good condition and contain the equipment necessary for the production of concentrate and syrups to meet the needs of its customers.

85 In 1978, Dr Pepper Metroplex Refreshment Company completed construction of its $21 million production and distribution facility in the Dallas suburb of Irving. The facility contains 440,000 square feet, of which 385,000 square feet are used for production and warehousing, 26,000 square feet, for office area, and 29,000 square feet, for maintenance and special events. It contains five high-speed bottling lines and one high-speed canning line. Production capability of the facility is 25 million cases annually. The Metroplex bottling company also occupies additional warehouse buildings. One, at the site of the Dallas manufacturing facility, has an area of 102,000 square feet. Two other warehouses of approximately 33,000 square feet and 67,000 square feet, each situated on approximately four acres of land, are located in other areas of Dallas and Fort Worth.

86 The San Antonio, Texas, bottling subsidiary owns 30,000 square feet of administrative-production-distribution facilities situated on four acres. In Waco, a 36,000-square-foot administrative-distribution facility located on four acres is owned by that subsidiary. Buildings and equipment owned by San Antonio and Waco are well maintained.

87 The company's Houston subsidiary performed a distribution function from two adjacent warehouses, 75,200 square feet and 72,500 square feet, respectively, both of which were occupied under short-term leases. A 21-acre site was purchased in Houston for an administrative-production-distribution facility. The 200,000-square-foot plant, opened in 1981, has one high-speed dual filler bottling line and one high-speed 72-valve canning line. Estimated investment of the Houston facility project was $18 million and was to be financed principally through internally generated funds.

88 The company has a bottling and canning facility located in Gardena, California, on approximately nine acres. This property houses its administrative, manufacturing, and warehousing operations within several buildings which total 135,700 square feet. This subsidiary has distribution warehouse operations located on approximately 2½- and 5-acre tracts in Fullerton and Sylmar, California, respectively, with floor space of 33,000 square feet and 25,000 square feet. The property and equipment, which are owned by the subsidiary, are in good condition. The company's bottling subsidiaries lease various warehouses for distribution purposes. A complete list of Dr Pepper's subsidiaries and manufacturing facilities is presented in Exhibit 14.

PRODUCTION

89 Dr Pepper Company has manufactured high-quality syrups and concentrates since 1885. Few companies in any food category have manufactured longer. The most unique taste in the soft-drink industry begins in the company's compounding lab and syrup-making facility in Dallas where fountain syrups and concentrates are made. After compounding, formula ingredients are blended to rigid specifications by syrup makers under conditions designed to assure a uniform and wholesome product.

90 Twenty-three flavors and other ingredients produce the inimitable taste of Dr Pepper. The formula is locked in two banks with access restricted to a handful of company officials, two at a time. In addition to the ingredients, the flavor depends on a complicated blending process that produces the aromatic Dr Pepper concentrate. The necessity of secrecy was recently stressed by Dr Pepper Company chairman, W. W. Clements: "Our greatest strength is the very unique and distinctive taste of Dr Pepper. After

Exhibit 14

Dr Pepper Company and Subsidiaries

	Name	*Location*	*State or Country of Incorporation*
1.	Parent:		
	Dr Pepper Company	Dallas, Texas	Colorado
2.	Subsidiaries:		
	Dr Pepper Metroplex Refreshment Company*	Irving, Texas	Texas
	Dr Pepper Bottling Company of Waco*	Waco, Texas	Colorado
	Dr Pepper Bottling Company of Corpus Christi*	Corpus Christi, Texas	Texas
	San Antonio Dr Pepper Bottling Company*	San Antonio, Texas	Colorado
	Dr Pepper Bottling Company of Houston, Inc.*	Houston, Texas	Texas
	Dr Pepper Bottling Company of Southern California*	Gardena, California	California
	National Drinks Bottling Company†	Gardena, California	California
	National Drinks Leasing Company†	Gardena, California	California
	Dr Pepper Japan Company*	Tokyo, Japan	Texas
	Dr Pepper Beverage Sales Company*	Dallas, Texas	Texas
	Southern California Packaging Company*	Gardena, California	Texas
	Dr Pepper International Sales Corp.*	Dallas, Texas	Texas
	Gulf Coast Dr Pepper Bottlers, Inc.*	Pensacola, Florida	Texas
	Dr Pepper Bottling Company of Albuquerque*	Albuquerque, New Mexico	Texas
	Premier Beverages, Inc.*	Dallas, Texas	Texas
	North Carolina Dr Pepper Bottlers, Inc.*	Washington, North Carolina	North Carolina
	Washington Can, Inc.‡	Washington, North Carolina	North Carolina
	Washington Shopping Center, Inc.‡	Washington, North Carolina	North Carolina
	Dr Pepper Finance N.V.*	Dallas, Texas	Netherlands Antilles
	Dr Pepper (Canada) Limited*	Toronto, Ontario	Canada
	Worldwide Beverages Limited§	County Kildare, Ireland	Ireland
	CDC Holdings, Inc.*	Dallas, Texas	Texas
	Soset, Inc.‖	New York, New York	Delaware
	Canada Dry Corporation‖	New York, New York	Delaware
	Canada Dry Services, Ltd.‖	New York, New York	Delaware
	Cott Incorporated‖	New York, New York	Delaware
	Mission Incorporated‖	New York, New York	Delaware
	No-Cal, Incorporated‖	New York, New York	Delaware
	G. B. Seeley's Sons, Inc.‖	New York, New York	Delaware
	Worldwide Beverages Australia, Limited‖	Edgecliff, N.S.W. Australia	Delaware
	Canada Dry Overseas, Ltd.‖	New York, New York	Delaware
	Canada Dry South East Asia, Ltd.‖	Bangkok, Thailand	Delaware
	Canada Dry Export Ltd.‖	New York, New York	Delaware
	Canada Dry Products Ltd.‖	Johannesburgh, South Africa	Delaware
	Canada Dry Worldwide, Inc.‖	Beirut, Lebanon	Delaware
	Spur Products, Inc.‖	New York, New York	Delaware
	Canada Dry Germany, Inc.‖	Munich, West Germany	Delaware
	Canada Dry International, Inc.‖	London, England	Delaware

* Wholly owned.
† Wholly owned by Dr Pepper Bottling Company of Southern California.
‡ Wholly owned by North Carolina Dr Pepper Bottlers, Inc.
§ Wholly owned by Dr Pepper (Canada) Limited.
‖ Wholly owned by CDC Holdings, Inc.

almost 100 years in the marketplace, it still has not been successfully copied or imitated."

91 The company is able to obtain all raw materials from more than one source and is currently not subject to loss of production if one supplier should cease operations. The price of certain raw materials, sugar and high-fructose corn sweeteners in particular, is determined by both domestic and world supply and demand and is, therefore, subject to fluctuation. The ability of Dr Pepper to pass on price increases of ingredients and materials to customers will depend on a variety of matters, including competitive factors, economic conditions, customer price resistance, and government regulations.

92 While Americans consume more sweeteners today than they did 20 years ago, they are consuming less refined sugar. Sugar has been replaced with low-calorie and corn sweeteners, particularly fructose. The average number of pounds of sweeteners each of us consumes in a year is presented in Exhibit 15.

93 Soft-drink companies have expressed differing opinions on the quality and taste of high-fructose corn syrup (HFCS), a less-expensive sweetener than the traditional sucrose. Because of such diverse views on the implementation of fructose as a total replacement of sucrose, major franchisors are using various amounts of HCFS in their sweetener formulations—and some use none at all.

94 Extensive consumer testing of high-fructose corn sweetener (HCFS 55 grade) led Dr Pepper to authorize bottlers to use the substance on a 100 percent sweetener basis in Dr Pepper. This provides substantial cost savings over sugar (sucrose) or blend usage and makes Dr Pepper a more profitable product, thus encouraging sales. Similar tests are now being conducted on an even more efficient fructose grade (HCFS 42) with good initial results.

Exhibit 15

Yearly U.S. consumption of sweeteners per person (pounds per year)

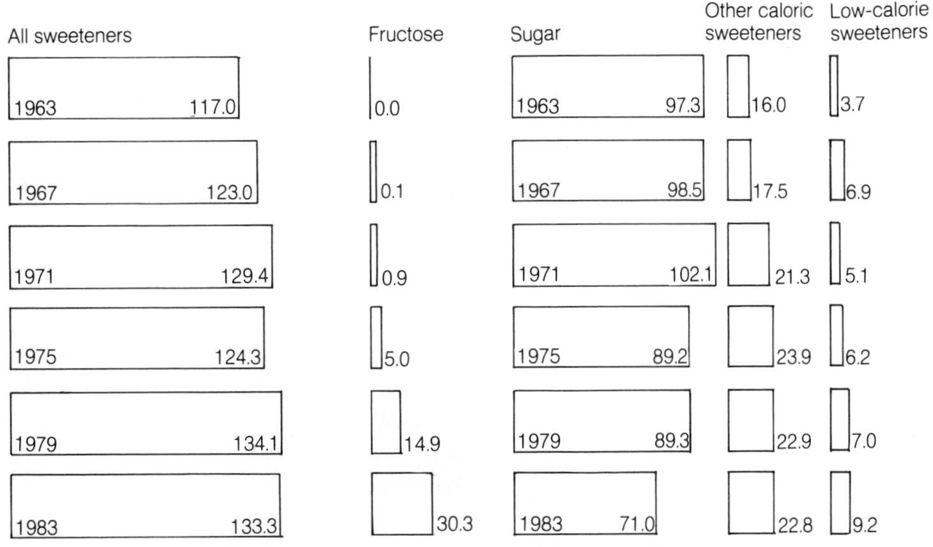

Source: U.S. Department of Agriculture and *USA Today,* March 15, 1984.

Packaging

95 Packaging has played an important role in expanding the availability of soft drinks. Cans are lightweight, do not break, help retain coolness, are especially adaptable for vending machines, and offer convenience for single servings. Bottles offer flexibility because of the range of sizes and are resealable and refillable (see Exhibit 16). The plastic bottle overcomes the glass bottle's disadvantages of weight and being breakable.

96 Coca-Cola took an early lead in plastic bottle development with the acrylonitrile (AN) bottle produced by Monsanto. But the FDA raised questions as to its safety, contending that acrylonitrile monomers can migrate from the bottle to the beverage. Monsanto maintains that no migration occurs under normal conditions of use, but Coca-Cola has discontinued use of the bottle until the matter is resolved.

97 About the time the safety question was raised for the AN bottle, PepsiCo announced the introduction of plastic bottles made from polyethylene terephthalate (PET) and manufactured by Amoco Chemical. The PET bottle is also produced by Goodyear Chemical, Hoover Ball & Bearing, and Owens-Illinois.

98 Sales of plastic beverage bottles, in their infancy in 1977, jumped to about 800 million units in 1978 and doubled in 1979, dominating the large-size, two-liter soft-drink market. In 1979, plastic began to penetrate the one-liter size market, even though that size in plastic costs 22 percent more than glass. The glass industry fought back and in 1979, introduced the so-called contour-pack: a six-pack of short glass bottles

Exhibit 16

held together by a plastic lid. The plastic industry's response in 1981 was a half-liter size (16.9 oz.) made out of the same polyethylene terephthalate (PET) as the successful two-liter bottle. The new machines that produce these bottles can produce them at a cost competitive to the 16-oz., nonreturnable glass bottles, which cost about 8.5 cents. To make things even more complicated, a new technology of continuous casting of aluminum sheets has made aluminum cans, which in 1980 cost about 9 cents, much less costly to produce. *Beverage Industry* predicted that plastic bottle containers will account for 27.5 percent of all soft-drink containers in 1985. In 1980, that percentage was 17.3 percent. Essentially, Dr Pepper's product line includes the sizes shown in Exhibit 17. In addition to the regular six-pack bottles or cans, Dr Pepper introduced, in 1979, a 12-pack can carton that appears to be an outstanding success. Bulk sales (including containers of over 32 ounces) are the most rapidly expanding package segments.

Exhibit 17

Packaging

Product	*Returnable glass bottles*	*Nonreturnable glass bottles*	*Cans*
Dr Pepper and Sugar-Free Dr Pepper	6 ounces	10 ounces	8 ounces
	10 ounces	16 ounces	12 ounces
	12 ounces	32 ounces	16 ounces
	16 ounces	1 liter	
	26 ounces	48 ounces	
	28 ounces	64 ounces	
	32 ounces	2 liters	
	1 liter		
	2 liters		
Salute (six flavors)	10 ounces	10 ounces	12 ounces
	16 ounces		
Waco (fountain syrup in six flavors)			

Managerial Incentive Programs

99 In recent years, Dr Pepper has had two plans that were created to motivate effective managerial performance: (1) a qualified stock-option plan[1] and (2) a long-term incentive compensation plan.

100 In 1976, Dr Pepper Company shareholders approved the adoption of the long-term incentive compensation plan which includes a long-term nonqualified stock-option plan and a contingent performance award plan for key managerial personnel. On April 15, 1980, the company established a cash incentive plan. The plans are administered by a committee of the board of directors whose members are neither officers, employees, nor participants under the plan.

101 Nonqualified stock options and/or performance awards can be granted each year

[1] A qualified pension plan is one that meets stringent IRS and ERISA regulations and provides tax advantages to both the company and employees. An unqualified plan does not acquire the same tax advantages but, as a result, is not subject to certain IRS restrictions.

beginning in 1976 and continuing through 1985. Cash incentive awards may be granted through 1990.

102 Contingent performance awards are to be earned over a five-year award period, and the cash portion is payable at the end of that period. A new five-year award period will begin each year through 1985. The cash incentive awards may be earned each year through 1985. The cash incentive awards may be earned over a three-year award period and are payable at the end of that period. The cash portion of performance awards and the cash incentive awards, which are being accrued over the award periods, may be adjusted based upon corporate performance goals attained for such periods.

103 Dr Pepper and its subsidiaries employed approximately 4,000 people as of December 31, 1982. The "Dr Pepper spirit" is the moving force of all these employees. Richard Q. Armstrong describe this important motivating force in the company's 1982 Annual Report:

> [M]ost important, there is a new spirit within your company that truly reflects our own positive attitude. Our people believe in themselves and the products they sell. They know that no other company in our industry enjoys the meaningful and lasting relationships with the bottler community that we enjoy. They know further that each of our products fills important segments of the market and that the growing independence of all bottlers, regardless of their main parent company affiliation, supports our strong case to fill these voids.

Finance and Accounting

104 Dr Pepper has experienced a steady increase in annual sales since 1976. Exhibit 18 provides a five-year summary of operations. In December 1981, Dr Pepper obtained a $120 million line of credit from several banks for the purpose of acquiring Canada Dry and for other corporate purposes. At December 31, 1982, the company had outstanding $93,150,000 of that line.

105 In 1983, management expected to utilize its line of credit for short-term borrowings to meet working capital requirements. In addition, the company had long-term debt of $32,807,000 and $4,838,000 of short-term notes payable outstanding. This total debt of $130,795,000 brings the company's year-end debt-to-equity ratio to .85:1.

106 On September 1, 1982, Dr Pepper improved its liquidity by selling 2.5 million shares of the company's common stock. Net proceeds of $33,893,000 were used to repay indebtedness incurred in financing the acquisition of Canada Dry.

107 Exhibits 19, 20, 21, and 22 provide information on Dr Pepper's balance sheet, changes in financial position, and income statement for the past years.

108 The increase in inventories and property, plant, and equipment for 1982, calculated on the current-cost method, exceeded amounts calculated by the constant-dollar method by $4,154,000. This indicates that during the current year, the specific price of these assets increased at a faster rate than the general rate of inflation as measured by CPI-U. Such amounts, commonly known as "holding gains or losses," are not included in net earnings nor available for distribution to stockholders.

109 The constant-dollar accounting method adjusts historical costs to dollars of equal purchasing power, as measured by the consumer price index for all urban consumers (CPI-U). The current-cost accounting method adjusts historical costs of specific assets

Exhibit 18

DR PEPPER COMPANY AND SUBSIDIARIES
Summary of Results of Operations and Financial Condition
For the Years Ended December 31, 1978–1982
(in thousands of dollars except per share amounts)

	1978	*1979*	*1980*	*1981*	*1982**
Operating results:					
Net sales	$275,279	$297,131	$339,547	$370,613	$516,136
Cost of sales	143,573	155,269	174,621	181,290	249,284
Gross profit	131,706	141,862	164,926	189,323	266,852
As a percent of net sales	47.8%	47.7%	48.6%	51.1%	51.7%
Administrative, marketing, and general expenses	$ 90,292	$ 99,416	$116,722	$137,541	$227,758
Operating profit	41,414	42,446	48,204	51,782	39,094
Other income (expense), net	1,508	1,442	2,055	1,396	(16,896)
Earnings before income taxes	42,922	43,888	50,259	53,178	22,198
As a percent of net sales	15.6%	14.8%	14.8%	14.3%	4.3%
Income taxes	$ 19,056	$ 19,924	$ 23,326	$ 23,234	$ 9,724
Effective tax rate	44.4%	45.4%	46.4%	43.7%	43.8%
Net earnings	$ 23,866	$ 23,964	$ 26,933	$ 29,944	$ 12,474
As a percent of net sales	8.7%	8.1%	7.9%	8.1%	2.4%
Balance sheet data:					
Current assets	$ 48,756	$ 56,777	$ 60,775	$ 65,083	$132,348
Current liabilities	16,544	21,036	30,178	29,794	71,848
Working capital	32,212	35,741	30,597	35,289	60,500
Current ratio	2.9:1	2.7:1	2.0:1	2.2:1	1.8:1
Property, plant, and equipment, net	50,538	58,373	74,174	85,736	132,061
Additions to property, plant, and equipment	20,776	16,149	24,987	23,278	64,757
Other assets	10,763	11,108	14,880	17,500	94,475
Total assets	110,057	126,258	149,829	168,319	358,884
Capitalization:					
Total debt	539	949	8,993	10,723	130,795
Deferred taxes and credits	3,572	4,757	5,661	6,356	8,374
Stockholders' equity	88,893	99,741	111,911	125,952	153,595
Total invested capital	93,004	105,447	126,565	143,031	292,764
Return on average stockholders' equity	28.7%	25.4%	25.5%	25.2%	9.2%
Return on average invested capital	27.5%	24.2%	23.4%	22.4%	8.0%
Per share of common stock data:					
Net earnings	$ 1.15	$ 1.16	$ 1.30	$ 1.45	$ .58
Dividends	.61	.67	.72	.78	.82
Book value	4.30	4.82	5.41	6.08	6.61
Weighted average shares outstanding	20,687	20,681	20,685	20,710	21,533
Number of employees	2,100	2,100	2,300	2,600	4,000

Note: 1981 and prior years have been restated to reflect the merger with Big Red Bottling Company of San Antonio, Inc., on July 23, 1982.

* The acquisition of the Canada Dry business had a significant impact on results and data reported for 1982 as compared to prior years.

Exhibit 19

DR PEPPER COMPANY AND SUBSIDIARIES
Consolidated Balance Sheet
December 31, 1982, and 1981

	1982	*1981*
Assets		
Current assets:		
Cash and temporary cash investments—1982, $7,648,000; 1981, $10,470,000	$ 14,493,000	$ 12,391,000
Accounts receivable—trade, less allowance—1982, $2,158,000; 1981, $752,000	63,394,000	29,186,000
Inventories	36,806,000	14,673,000
Federal income tax refund	3,871,000	—
Prepaid advertising and other assets	13,784,000	8,833,000
Total current assets	132,348,000	65,083,000
Notes receivable and investments	5,495,000	2,929,000
Property, plant, and equipment—net	132,061,000	85,736,000
Other assets—at unamortized cost or nominal value		
Excess cost over net assets of businesses acquired	10,787,000	5,530,000
Franchises, formulas, trademarks, and other	67,218,000	8,413,000
Covenants not to compete and consulting agreements	10,975,000	628,000
Total other assets	88,980,000	14,571,000
Total assets	$358,884,000	$168,319,000
Liabilities and Stockholders' Equity		
Current liabilities:		
Accounts payable	$ 47,642,000	$ 16,760,000
Accrued expenses	17,399,000	5,791,000
Current portion of long-term debt	890,000	943,000
Notes payable	4,838,000	3,563,000
Income taxes payable	1,079,000	2,737,000
Total current liabilities	71,848,000	29,794,000
Long-term debt, less current portion	125,067,000	6,217,000
Deferred income taxes	7,636,000	6,022,000
Other deferred credits	738,000	334,000
Stockholders' equity		
Preferred stock $1 par value. Authorized 4,000,000 shares; issued and outstanding, none	—	—
Common stock without par value. Authorized 50,000,000 shares; issued—1982, 23,242,086 shares; 1981–20,701,885 shares	14,657,000	13,939,000
Additional paid-in capital	33,518,000	—
Retained earnings	107,026,000	112,013,000
Foreign currency translation adjustment	(1,606,000)	—
Total stockholders' equity	153,595,000	125,952,000
Contingencies	—	—
Total liabilities and stockholders' equity	$358,884,000	$168,319,000

Exhibit 20

DR PEPPER COMPANY AND SUBSIDIARIES
Consolidated Statements of Changes in Financial Position
For the Years Ended December 31, 1980–1982

	1982	*1981*	*1980*
Sources of working capital:			
Net earnings	$ 12,474,000	$29,944,000	$26,933,000
Add items which do not affect working capital:			
Depreciation of property, plant, and equipment	18,432,000	11,716,000	9,186,000
Amortization of other assets	3,955,000	449,000	269,000
Deferred income taxes	1,614,000	628,000	857,000
Working capital provided by operations	36,475,000	42,737,000	37,245,000
Issuance of common stock under compensation plans	343,000	128,000	16,000
Increase in long-term debt	155,182,000	5,604,000	1,924,000
Proceeds from sale of common stock	33,893,000	—	—
Other	404,000	560,000	590,000
Total sources of working capital	226,297,000	49,029,000	39,775,000
Uses of working capital:			
Dividends on common stock	17,461,000	16,030,000	14,782,000
Additions to property, plant, and equipment	26,786,000	23,278,000	24,987,000
Acquisition of Canada Dry Corporation, less working capital acquired of $30,932,000:			
Property, plant, and equipment	37,971,000	—	—
Excess cost over net assets acquired	4,697,000	—	—
Franchises, trademarks, and other	58,200,000	—	—
Covenants not to compete and consulting agreements	12,000,000	—	—
Increase in notes receivable and investments	2,566,000	—	479,000
Reduction of long-term debt	36,332,000	1,467,000	569,000
Increase in other assets	3,467,000	3,563,000	4,104,000
Foreign currency translation adjustment	1,606,000	—	—
Total uses of working capital	201,086,000	44,338,000	44,921,000
Total increase (decrease) in working capital	$ 25,211,000	$ 4,691,000	$ (5,146,000)
Changes in components of working capital:			
Increase (decrease) in current assets:			
Cash	$ 2,102,000	$ (1,101,000)	$ 477,000
Accounts receivable	34,208,000	3,293,000	4,178,000
Inventories	22,133,000	998,000	(910,000)
Federal income tax refund	3,871,000	—	—
Prepaid advertising and other assets	4,951,000	1,117,000	254,000
	67,265,000	4,307,000	3,999,000
Increase (decrease) in current liabilities:			
Accounts payable	30,882,000	2,313,000	(1,083,000)
Accrued expenses	11,608,000	1,785,000	(394,000)
Notes payable and current portion of long-term debt	1,222,000	(2,407,000)	6,689,000
Income taxes payable	(1,658,000)	(2,075,000)	3,933,000
	42,054,000	(384,000)	9,145,000
Increase (decrease) in working capital	$ 25,211,000	$ 4,691,000	$ (5,146,000)

Exhibit 21

DR PEPPER COMPANY AND SUBSIDIARIES
Consolidated Statements of Earnings
For the Years Ended December 31, 1980–1982

	1982	*1981*	*1980*
Net sales	$516,136,000	$370,613,000	$339,547,000
Cost of sales	249,284,000	181,290,000	174,621,000
Gross profit	266,852,000	189,323,000	164,926,000
Administrative, marketing, and general expenses	227,758,000	137,541,000	116,722,000
Operating profit	39,094,000	51,782,000	48,204,000
Other income (expense):			
Interest expense	(18,423,000)	(519,000)	(433,000)
Other—net	1,527,000	1,915,000	2,488,000
Total other income (expense)	(16,896,000)	1,396,000	2,055,000
Earnings before income taxes	22,198,000	53,178,000	50,259,000
Income taxes	9,724,000	23,234,000	23,326,000
Net earnings	$ 12,474,000	$ 29,944,000	$ 26,933,000
Earnings per common and common share equivalent	$ .58	1.45	1.30

Exhibit 22

DR PEPPER AND SUBSIDIARIES
Earnings before Income Taxes and Income Tax Expense
For the Years Ended December 31, 1980–1982

	1982	*1981*	*1980*
Earnings before income taxes:			
United States	$19,095,000	$54,824,000	$52,707,000
Foreign	3,103,000	(1,646,000)	(2,448,000)
Total earnings before income taxes	$22,198,000	$53,178,999	$50,259,000
Income tax expense:			
United States federal:			
Current	$ 5,053,000	$20,480,000	$20,970,000
Deferred	1,614,000	628,000	857,000
State and local	1,443,000	2,126,000	1,499,000
Total United States	8,110,000	23,234,000	23,326,000
Foreign:			
Current:			
Canada	283,000	—	—
Other	1,331,000	—	—
Total foreign	1,614,000	—	—
Total income tax expense	$ 9,724,000	$23,234,000	$23,326,000

to the cost of purchasing or replacing them in the current year without regard to making improvements or installing different types of replacement assets.

110 The effects of inflation under the constant-dollar method were determined by adjusting the historical cost of inventories; property, plant, and equipment; cost of sales; and depreciation expense to average 1982 dollars using the CPI-U. With respect to the current-cost method, inventories were estimated based on quantities on hand at the end of 1982 and costs in effect, before applying LIFO reserves, during the fourth quarter of 1982. In estimating cost of goods sold under the current-cost method, inventories carried at LIFO were adjusted only to reflect LIFO layer liquidation, while cost of goods sold relating to all other inventories were adjusted to reflect approximate prices incurred during the fourth quarter of 1982. The current cost of property, plant, and equipment was estimated by adjusting historical cost by externally generated price indexes relevant to the assets of the company. Related depreciation was computed by adjusting historical cost depreciation by the same indexes. At December 31, 1982, the current cost of inventories, property, plant, and equipment, and net of accumulated depreciation was $215,039,000.

111 Inventories aggregating $12,482,000 in 1982 and $12,179,000 in 1981 are determined using the LIFO method. The excess of current cost over stated last-in, first-out cost was approximately $2,500,000 at December 31, 1982, and $2,423,000 at December 31, 1981. The LIFO method had the effect of reducing 1982 net earnings by $42,000, 1981 net earnings by $190,000 ($.01 per share), and 1980 net earnings by $691,000 ($.04 per share).

112 Property, plant, and equipment are stated at cost. For financial reporting purposes, depreciation is provided on the straight-line method over the estimated useful lives of the assets. Accelerated depreciation methods are generally used for income tax purposes.

113 Maintenance and repairs are charged to operations as incurred; renewals and betterments are capitalized and depreciated. The cost and accumulated depreciation of assets sold or disposed of are removed from the accounts. Resultant profit or loss on such transactions is credited or charged to earnings.

114 Interest cost incurred during the period of construction of plant and equipment is capitalized as part of the cost of such plant and equipment and is amortized over the depreciable life of the related assets. Total interest cost was $18,468,000 in 1982 and $957,000 in 1981; of these amounts, $45,000 and $438,000, respectively, have been capitalized. Interest capitalized in 1980 was nil.

115 Excess of cost over fair market value of net assets of acquired businesses and costs of franchises, formulas, trademarks, and other are being amortized on a straight-line basis over 40 years. Covenants not to compete and consulting agreements are being amortized on a straight-line basis over the lives of the covenants and agreements. Accumulated amortization of other assets was $5,088,000 and $1,133,000 at December 31, 1982, and 1981, respectively.

116 The aggregate maturities of long-term debt, excluding maturities under the revolving line of credit ($93,150,000 at December 31, 1982, which can be converted into a seven-year loan in 1984), as such maturities are not currently determinable, for the five years ending December 31, 1987, follow: 1983—$890,000, 1984—$745,000, 1985—$1,951,000, 1986—$746,000 and 1987—$663,000.

117 The weighted average short-term borrowings were $3,626,000 during 1982 ($3,831,000 in 1981 and $3,285,000 in 1980). The maximum balance included in these calculations

at any month-end was $4,838,000 during 1982 ($7,505,000 in 1981 and $6,508,000 in 1980). The weighted average effective interest rate for 1982 was 8.6 percent (10.8 percent for 1981 and 9.4 percent for 1980).

Epilogue

118 Dr Pepper ended 53 years as a public company in February 1984, when a fat lady sang, the shareholders approved a private buy-out, and Foots Clements shook hands with Theodore Forstmann of the Forstmann Little investment firm and senior Dr Pepper executives. The buy-out was an arduous experience, but Dr Pepper management has a stronger hand now in managing the company. Forstmann emphasized that nothing would be changed, except they would concentrate more on marketing Dr Pepper domestically, instead of venturing into other brands, such as Canada Dry. As Foots Clements put it: "All our energies and resources will now be devoted to Dr Pepper. We're going to get lean and mean!"

SECTION

Competitive Industry Analysis

case 22
Note on the Deregulated Airline Industry

Focus

1 The U.S. airline industry can be segmented into three groups: major, national, and regional airlines. Major carriers are defined by the Civil Aeronautics Board (CAB) as those carriers with more than $1 billion in revenues annually. National carriers are airlines that have annual revenues of $75 million to $1 billion. Regional airlines are those with revenues less than $75 million annually.

2 In 1984, there were 11 major carriers in the United States, 16 national carriers, and over 260 regional or commuter airlines. Exhibit 1 presents a listing of major and national airlines.

3 Major airlines' operations can be broken down into international and national operations, but this industry note will deal only with national operations since to include international factors would require the consideration of several additional complex issues such as exchange rate, political risk, and foreign governments' regulations.

4 Furthermore, only the passenger travel activity of the three groups will be considered. Other services offered by the carriers, such as airmail or air cargo, will not be discussed for two reasons. First, these other activities are not main generators of revenue, and second, there are other airlines which specialize in some of those services, and they have their own unique characteristics. Including an analysis of nonpassenger travel would not help in accomplishing the main purpose of this industry note, namely, to identify the broad framework of critical factors that impacted the airline industry.

5 Finally, data for the years 1979–1984 will be used to support the analysis, since these years reflect most, if not all, of the factors which affected the industry in its deregulation period.

This industry note was prepared by John A. Pearce II of the University of South Carolina with the assistance of Esam H. Kawther of King Abdul-Aziz University, Saudi Arabia.

Exhibit 1

Carrier grouping in 1984

Major carriers*

American Airlines	Republic Airlines
Continental Air Lines	Trans World
Delta Air Lines	United Airlines
Eastern Air Lines	USAir, Inc.
Northwest Airlines	Western Air Lines
Pan American World Airways	

National carriers

Air California	Ozark Air Lines
Air Florida System	Pacific-Southwest
Alaska Airlines	Piedmont Aviation
Aloha Airlines	Southwest Airlines
Capitol International Airways	Texas Air Corporation
Flying Tiger	Transamerica
Frontier Airlines	Wien
Hawaiian Airlines	World Airways

* Braniff International was dropped from the list in 1983.

Impact of Deregulation

The Pre-Deregulation Era

6 For 40 years, from 1938 until late 1978, all airline carriers were subject to CAB regulation, and four conditions characterized this pre-deregulation era:

1. Fares which were tightly controlled.
2. Competition which was restricted.
3. New service(s) which could be granted only if the carrier proved to the CAB that there was a public need.
4. Cost increases, such as in labor cost, which were passed by the carriers directly to the consumer.

7 As a result of these conditions, competition among the various carriers was concentrated on services and schedule convenience. Furthermore, competition between national and regional carriers was minimal because regional airlines were largely feeder airlines to the larger national carriers who would then provide the link that carried passengers to their final destinations.

The Deregulation Era

8 The passage of the Airline Deregulation Act in October 1978 set in motion a complete transformation of the U.S. airline industry. Among other changes, this act removed almost all market-entry barriers and fare control. Consequently, the industry became more susceptible to swings in the business cycle, leading the industry to a major shake-up, with various players and factors involved. The remainder of this industry

note will provide detailed information regarding those players and factors. The discussion will be presented in a manner which highlights the considerations that were critical to the airline industry.

Political and Legal Factors

9 Before the Airline Deregulation Act, the U.S. airline industry was treated as other important public utilities—such as electric and telephone services. This meant total regulation of fares, of markets, and, consequently, of competition. However, the deregulation act enabled airlines not only to set their own fares but it also allowed trunk carriers to eliminate services to marginally profitable markets. As a result, the route systems of all carriers were substantially restructured, and a number of new carriers entered the market. Specifically, prior to deregulation, the 11 major airlines shown in Exhibit 1, plus Braniff International, served 679 locations. At the end of 1981, these same carriers served 692 locations, but these locations represented the deletion of 132 cities and the addition of 145 others.

10 A company-specific illustration of the rerouting that took place involved Pan American World Airways. Between September 1980 and September 1982, its airlines operations lost over $906.9 million. Pan Am's stock went as low as $2.50 in 1982, bringing the company's market value to only $180 million—approximately the price of two new 747 airplanes. Edward Acker, the chairman of Pan Am, attributed the situation to several reasons, one of which was the disorganized, unprofitable domestic route system. Therefore, one of the first things he did when he took over the chairmanship in late 1981 was to rearrange Pan Am's domestic network to work mainly as a feeder system for the company's international flights from New York, Miami, Los Angeles, and San Francisco. By the second quarter of 1983, the company was again generating profits. This example also illustrates how major and national airlines exited from many short-haul, lighter-density routes during the years from 1979 to 1983. The decreased competition of major airlines created some attractive growth potential for the various regional airlines, and in response, several regional carriers not only added routes but also expanded former routes and acquired larger, longer-range aircraft. Some even arranged with major airlines to provide reciprocal traffic feed and to share facilities such as reservation systems and ticketing. For instance, Dolphin Airlines, a two-year-old carrier, signed agreements with Ozark, Delta, Republic, Northwest, and American Airlines which included joint and add-on fares. Specifically, American Airlines agreed to take a passenger into a Dolphin hub city, and Dolphin would carry that passenger anywhere on its Florida network for $19.

11 However, the U.S. government retained control over other important aspects of the airline industry. For instance, the Federal Aviation Administration (FAA) monitored the safety of the airplanes and controlled air traffic. This power was enhanced as a consequence of the illegal strike by members of the Professional Air Traffic Controllers Organization (PATCO) in August 1981. As a result of the subsequent firing of the strikers, the FAA was designated to hire and train new controllers and to allocate slots to airlines because of reduced traffic in airports.

12 To a lesser extent, government regulations affected the industry through a subsidy program. The government paid a number of carriers to provide services for communities too small to support profitable operations. From June 30, 1980, to June 30, 1982, the government paid a total subsidy of $181.6 million. Of this amount, approximately 37 percent went to major airlines; 47 percent, to the national airlines; and 16 percent,

to the regional airlines. Overall, subsidization accounted for 1 percent of the total revenue of all certified airlines.

Economic Factors

13 Bad economic conditions hurt the airline industry in many ways. For example, looking upstream in the industry, aircraft purchases represented multimillion-dollar capital outlays—amounts beyond airlines' cash capabilities. Attempts to enter money markets to borrow the necessary funds became extremely difficult and even unprofitable when interest rates were high. Delta Airlines can be a case study that reflects these problems. Until the end of 1981, Delta International was considered by many experts to be the world's most-profitable airline. But due to various factors, one of which was the general state of the economy, Delta's profits shrank from $146.5 million in 1981 to $20.8 million in 1982. Then, in its 1983 fiscal year, Delta reported a loss of $86.7 million, its first loss in 36 years. The 1980–1982 recession, combined with record high interest rates, forced Delta to delay the delivery of its new Boeing 757s and 767s.

14 Delta was not the only airline hurt by the recession. Most major carriers, as well as nationals and regionals, experienced sharp reversals of their profit trends. For instance, TWA fell from a $25.6 million profit in 1982 to a $16.2 million loss in 1983, while Eastern's deficit grew from $3 million to $33.7 million during the same period. Only United and American Airlines generated profits. United went from a $4.4 million loss to a $109.9 million profit. American Airlines enjoyed a jump from $466,000 to $34.4 million in profits, largely attributable to the selling of tax credits. An even worse pattern could be shown if the national and the approximately 260 regional airlines were included in the analysis. With few exceptions, (for example, Southwest) the recession forced small carriers to remain in the red because of low traffic and high interest rates. This led to a total of $1.3 billion in operating loss in the years 1980–82 for all airlines combined compared to an estimated profit of $200–$800 million in 1983.

15 When the U.S. economy started to improve, particularly in the second half of 1983, carriers began to realize some profits. For instance, the net income of Southwest Airlines for the first half of 1983 reached $13 million, up 30 percent over the same period in 1982. People Express showed a $4.2 million net profit in the second quarter of 1983, on top of an $3 million gain in the first quarter. Northwest Airlines, which had a net loss of $1.5 million in the last quarter of 1982, jumped to a $14.4 million net profit in the second quarter of 1983.

Price/Cost Structure

16 Profitability in the airline industry depended largely on a carrier's ability to control costs, particularly those for labor and fuel.

17 **1. Labor Cost.** Employee wages and salaries were among the largest controllable expenses faced by the airlines, particularly the major ones. Wages grew steadily during the period of government regulation, but the carriers passed down most of their costs to consumers. After deregulation, however, the pass-through technique could not be used since passengers had the option of using cheaper competitors. In 1984, Air Line Pilots Association (ALPA) members earned about $69,000 a year for about 50 hours

Exhibit 2

Labor costs as a share of total 1982 cost

Low-fare airlines

Muse Air	19%
People Express	20%
Southwest	27%

Major carriers

Continental	34%
Eastern	37%
Pan Am	34%
Republic	36%
TWA	35%
Western	34%

Adapted with modifications from: "Airlines in Turmoil," *Business Week,* October 10, 1983, p. 100.

of flight per month, and mechanics earned an average of $30,000 a year, plus fringe benefits. In contrast, the new, small, nonunionized airlines could hire unemployed pilots to fly 70 hours a month for approximately $30,000 a year. In fact, labor cost represented 33 to 37 percent of the total operating costs of the major airlines in 1982. On the other hand, nonunionized national and regional carriers enjoyed a substantial advantage over the majors by keeping their labor costs in the 19- to 27-percent range (see Exhibit 2).

18 This cost differential was perhaps the main reason that small airlines were able to offer and sustain low fares for a long period of time. The new airlines utilized their cost savings to promote their low-fare strategies. People Express, for example, succeeded in generating more than $2 million in profits during the first nine months of 1982, while Pan Am, Eastern, and TWA were all in the red. The key to People's success was a cost base which averaged 5.3 cents per seat-mile, compared to an 11-cent average for major airline competitors. This advantage enabled People Express

to offer a one-way ticket to Florida for only $69, thus luring passengers from Eastern, Delta, and others.

19 Another successful small airline was Southwest, which gained market share by controlling its costs while charging rock-bottom fares. Cost control at Southwest did not stop at labor costs. Its ticketing procedures were simplified, with 55 percent of its tickets sold through its cash registers, 15–18 percent through its vending machines, and the remaining 25 percent through travel agents. In contrast, travel agents sold 60 percent of Delta's tickets and 50 percent of USAir's tickets, while charging a 10 percent commission. Such cost savings provided Southwest and other similiar carriers an additional leverage against competition.

20 To compete with these nationals and regionals, larger carriers were pressed to cut labor costs, trim work rules, and increase workers' productivity. Republic Airlines, which lost $214 million from 1979 through 1981, bargained successfully for $73 million in 1982 temporary pay cuts and wage deferrals. In early 1983, Republic received an additional 15 percent pay cut for nine months, which translated to about $100 million in savings.

21 The threat of Pan Am's bankruptcy enabled it to obtain a 10 percent wage cut from its employees, saving approximately $110 million in 1983. In return, employees received stock-ownership and profit-sharing plans, which Pan Am's management counted on to boost employee morale as well as productivity. Pan Am also cut its work force by 5,000 workers down to a level of 25,000.

22 Western Airlines reached an agreement with its unionized labor in early 1983 to accept a 10 percent pay cut which translated to a $50 million savings. In exchange, the airline gave its workers 25 percent of the company stock. Even the financially strong United succeeded in persuading its pilots to not only defer two wage increases but also increase their flying time 15 percent. In return, the company provided a lifetime no-layoff guarantee.

23 These examples have one particular common and unique future—almost all the concessions were made in a relatively friendly and cooperative atmosphere. However, other airlines such as Continental Air Lines and, to a lesser extent, Eastern Airlines, took a confrontational approach. For example, despite an excellent route structure, strong marketing, and an efficient fleet, Eastern had serious liquidity problems resulting from high labor costs and an accelerated capital-spending program. As a result, Eastern's lenders disapproved the additional costs which would have been incurred from new contracts with IAM and the Transport Workers Union which represented Eastern's flight attendants. The company then appealed to its workers, asking for a 15 percent pay cut to save $300 million through 1985. Eastern added that if the employees refused the proposed cut, the carrier would either go out of business—as happened to Braniff in 1982—or would face reorganization under Chapter 11 of the bankruptcy laws—as Continental had done only a few weeks prior. Pressures and threats from both sides made the disruption of Eastern's services imminent, influencing travel agents to avoid bookings on the airline. However, only hours before the planned strike was to have taken place, an agreement was reached. Basically, it called for wage cuts and the formation of a team of outside consultants who would study Eastern's books and records to see whether they supported the company's claims of near-insolvency.

24 Perhaps the most dramatic example of the confrontational approach was provided by Continental Airlines. In 1982, the company asked for $90 million in permanent pay cuts and work-rule improvements from its pilots, and got them. Yet, Continental

continued to lose money at a potentially disastrous rate. Five contributing factors were known:

1. Price wars which were ravaging the industry.
2. A weak economy and accompanying low traffic levels, particularly at Continental's main hub in Houston.
3. The competition from Continental's low-cost rivals, such as Muse Air, Southwest Airlines, and People Express. (Refer again to Exhibit 2).
4. A poor marketing strategy.
5. Management instability.[1]

25 In combination, these factors led the company to report an $18 million loss in the second quarter of 1983, instead of an expected $10 million profit. Therefore, Continental asked its pilots and flight attendants to make up the difference. They declined. Consequently, on September 24, 1983, Continental asked for protection from its creditors under Chapter 11 of the Bankruptcy Code of 1978. An important aspect of this law was that it permitted the company to dismiss its union contracts. The financial impact was a 50 percent pay cut for pilots and flight attendants, shorter vacations, suspension of the pension plan, and tighter work rules designed to increase productivity. These cost savings enabled a redesign of Continental's marketing strategy. It offered a "price-slashed" fare of $99 between any two cities in the country. Continental claimed this fare would satisfy its cash needs if their planes could fill 40 percent of its seats. This meant the company had dropped its load factor from 65 to 40 percent, which enabled it to compete head-to-head against its low cost rivals.

26 2. **Fuel Cost.** Fuel costs were the second most important element, after labor expenses, in the cost structure of the airline industry. Fuel costs for a single airline were as high as 34 percent of operating expenses, as was the case with Pan Am. This high percentage resulted from two facts: (1) Most jets used by major carriers were not fuel efficient, and (2) fuel cost was itself very high. For example, in 1981, Pan Am's fuel cost was $1.15 per gallon. Fortunately, however, by the end of 1982, the glut of oil in world markets, record high inventories, and reduced industry demand started fuel prices on a downward trend. In 1982, Pan Am's fuel costs had dropped to 95 cents per gallon. Exhibit 3 displays trends in fuel consumption and revenues and illustrates the downward trend of fuel consumption for the years 1975 through 1982.

27 In the area of fuel costs, regional carriers again enjoyed an important advantage over the major airlines. The cost of fuel per gallon was essentially the same for all airlines, but the use of fuel-efficient airplanes that seated from 8 to 50 passengers on economical runs of up to 250 miles proved to be a successful weapon in the small airlines' efforts for survival and market share.

28 The basic-niche strategy used by regionals usually involved providing services between major cities and airports that were underused or ignored. For example, Atlantic Express realized that people from New York's Long Island found it extremely time consuming to commute through New York's airports. Therefore, in January 1983, Atlantic inaugurated service from Republic Airport in Farmingdale to several major cities, including Boston, Syracuse, New York, and Albany. In March 1983, Atlantic Express's load factor—defined as the percentage of filled seats on a given flight—

[1] "Airlines in Turmoil," *Business Week*, October 10, 1983, pp. 98–102.

Exhibit 3

Fuel consumption versus traffic for major carriers (monthly)

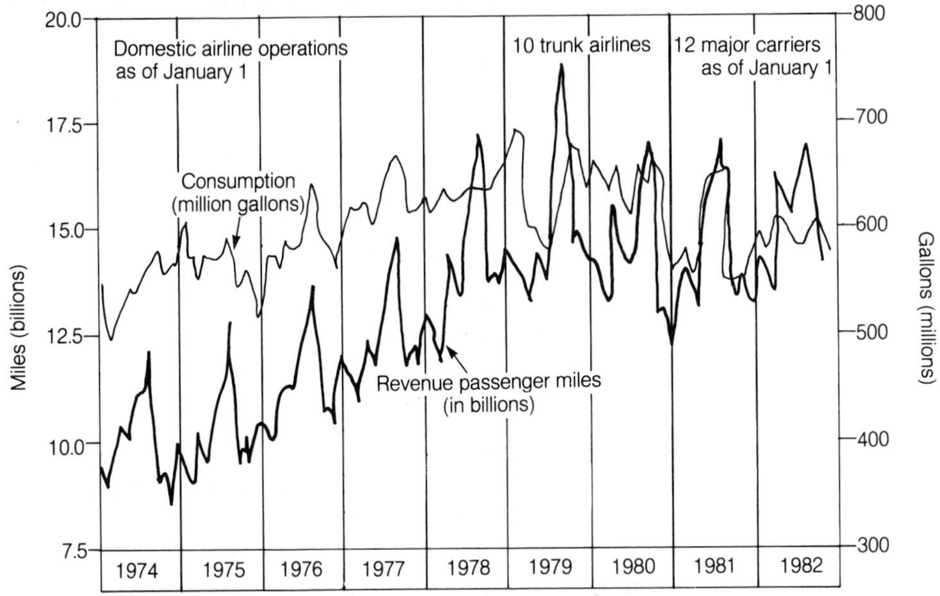

Source: Civil Aeronautics Board.

was only 10 percent. But by the end of July, its load factor reached 49 percent, its break-even point. For major carriers, a load factor of up to 60 percent was needed to break even because of higher fuel costs and less-fuel-efficient planes.

29 Perhaps an even more striking case was that of Waring Air. On December 1982, the company received certification from the FAA to begin business as a scheduled carrier. By the end of 1983, with only four, eight-seat planes, Waring had reached $770,000 in sales and a profit of $75,000. In most of its routes, only four passengers were required to reach the break-even point. However, no major airlines could obtain such results with their 90- to 150-seat aircraft.

30 In 1982, almost 20 million people flew with regionals whose aircrafts held fewer than 50 seats. In that same year, regional airlines served 817 airports in North America, compared to only 766 in 1981. In fact, about 65 percent of all airports in the United States were being serviced exclusively by regional carriers.

31 In response to such challenges, many major and national airlines tried to minimize the effects of their cost disadvantage. To reduce fuel costs, most large carriers decided to upgrade their fleets. Delta and Eastern Airlines, for example, retooled their fleets by purchasing Boeing 757s, the most-advanced and most-fuel-efficient jetliners in the world. Other national carriers, such as Southwest, emphasized the flexible, smaller, fuel-efficient Boeing 737–200, which became the world's best-selling airplane in 1980 and 1981, with orders of 106 and 129 planes, respectively.

32 As a result of such conservation steps, total fuel consumption for major airlines

declined 8 percent in 1982, following an increase of 5 percent in 1981 and far larger jumps in the two preceding years, as shown in Exhibit 3.

33 An issue related to fuel costs concerned what economists call the substitution effect. They argue that the consumer is only willing to pay a certain price for a certain good or service. Once the price exceeds that level, the consumer will attempt to substitute a less-expensive product (for example, margarine for butter, vinyl for leather). The phenomenon also operated in the airlines industry. Since many airline passengers were tourists, there was a time/cost trade-off involved in their decision to chose air travel over other methods of transportation. As fuel costs rose, the travel-time savings offered by air travel were increasingly offset by the dollar savings offered by substitute transportation modes. This specific condition seriously affected Delta Airlines. From June 1982 until June 1983, many of Delta's traditional Florida passengers choose to drive instead of fly. Since Florida travelers constituted 25 percent of Delta's passengers, the airline faced a serious problem. As a counterstrategy, Delta discounted approximately 90 percent of its Florida tickets, resulting in a very substantial decline in its 1982–1983 fiscal year profit margins.

Capacity Utilization

34 Idle capacity translates to lower income and eventually less profit or even loss. What made this issue especially complicated in the airline industry was that demand fluctuated around seasonal variations. For example, traffic evaporated as schools opened, while business travel was at its heaviest from October through May.

Exhibit 4

Airline traffic statistics

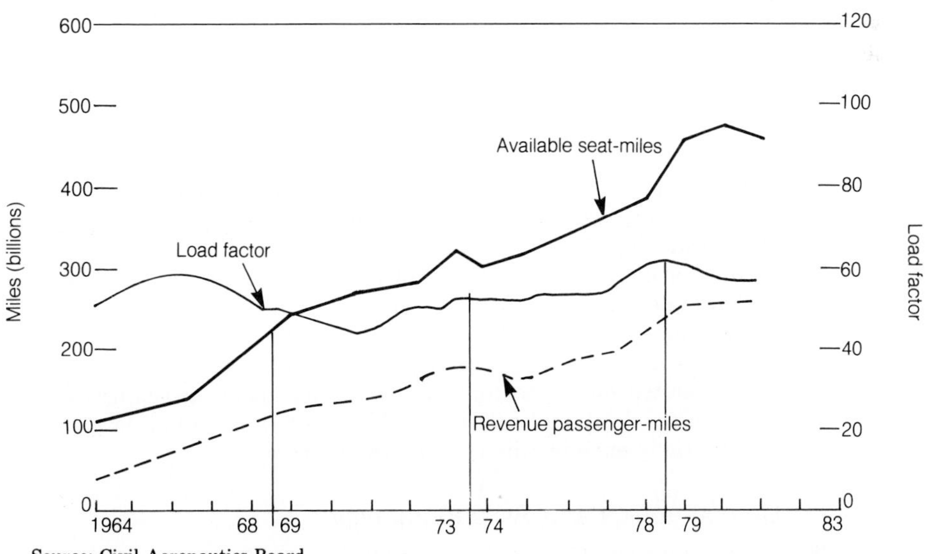

Source: Civil Aeronautics Board.

Exhibit 5

Airline market shares

Airline	*Share of total revenue passenger-miles*	*Share of total available seat-miles*
American	14.9%	13.8%
Continental	13.3	14.4
Delta	14.1	14.4
Eastern	4.8	5.1
Northwest	4.0	4.0
Pan Am	4.4	4.4
Republic	4.4	5.0
TWA	9.3	8.9
United	19.9	19.1
USAir	3.1	3.1
Western	4.2	4.1

Source: Adapted with modification from: Thomas Canning, "Air Transportation: Current Analysis," *Standard & Poor's Industry Survey* (October 1983), p. A60.

35 From 1979 to 1984, capacity in the airline industry, as measured by available seat-miles, rose faster than traffic demand. As seen in Exhibit 4, the industry experienced a fairly stable load factor, while available seat-miles were constantly increasing. As a result, the average certified carrier was losing money. In addition, the rising capacity had an important implication for the industry's future, namely, that even modest increases in rates might further depress demand.

36 A widely used measure of an airline's ability to effectively market its capacity was the ratio between the carrier's share of total revenue passenger-miles flown by its industry group and its share of domestic capacity—available seat-miles. A positive traffic/capacity relationship, meaning a greater share of traffic than capacity, indicated an above-average load factor and effective marketing of capacity. Exhibit 5 illustrates these relationships for the 11 major carriers in 1982. An important observation is that some of those carriers shown in Exhibit 5 had positive ratios and yet were losing money. The explanation was that it was not enough for airlines to utilize their available capacity. Rather, the prices they charged also had to be high enough to cover operating costs. In many cases, sufficient margins were not achieved as a consequence of high labor costs, high fuel costs, and fare wars.

37 Another measure that reflected the underutilization of airlines' capacities was the post-1978 decline in the share of domestic traffic transported by the U.S. major carriers. For instance, in June 1982, the major carriers accounted for 87 percent of the revenue passenger-miles for all CAB-certified airlines. Before deregulation, however, those carriers accounted for 95 percent of the revenue passenger-miles. This shift illustrates the success of national and regional carriers in obtaining larger market shares and also partially explains the occurrence of fare wars.

Demographics and Psychographics

38 During the late 1970s and early 1980s, the Sun-Belt states of Florida, Texas, Arizona, and California experienced the nation's greatest population growth, enabling further

penetration by carriers in these areas. In fact, between September 1978 and December 1981, the West and the South accounted for approximately 70 percent of the new stations added by both major and national airlines. This growth was more than twice that in the North Central and Northeast regions of the country during the same period. Houston, Orlando, Phoenix, Dallas/Fort Worth, and Las Vegas all showed substantial increases in the number of airlines and the number of flights serving their airports. Weekly departures from Orlando increased over 50 percent, while flights from Phoenix rose about 60 percent. Airlines which were either creating new hubs at those cities or connecting those cities to their existing hubs were United, American, Southwest, Pacific Southwest, Delta, and Dolphin Airlines.

39 A psychographic-related effect on the airline industry was the preference organizations had for holding their conferences in warm cities, particularly during fall and winter seasons. Such high-margin travel combined with normal business travel to account for 50 percent of all passenger-miles, prompting many airlines to undertake aggressive strategies designed to increase their direct sales to associations and corporate meeting planners. The rationale for these actions were twofold. First, airlines sought to eliminate their excess capacity. Second, they wished to reduce the commissions they paid to travel agents and meeting planners. Travel agents, who sold more than 65 percent of domestic air tickets, charged a 10 percent commission on each ticket they sold. When airlines could save this commission, they could be more flexible in offering discounts directly to associations and corporations. The potential importance of these actions is suggested by the statistics in 1982 which showed that U.S. organizations held about 10,000 conventions and 707,000 company meetings.

40 Finally, demographic and psychographic information, such as birth and death rates, styles of living, and educational patterns, were crucial to the planning process of all airlines. Exhibit 6 presents an example of how one such variable, disposable personal income could be used to improve carrier predictions of industry growth trends.

An Industry Overview of Competitive Strategies

41 The passage of the Airline Deregulation Act resulted in a massive restructuring of the industry. Increased competition and greater fare flexibility were some of the goals as well as the end results of the act. After historically controlling about 95 percent of the passenger travel business, major airlines experienced sharp (8 percent) declines in passenger-miles with accompanying declines in revenues and profits. New entrants enjoyed certain cost advantages over the major, well-established carriers attributable to the use of nonunion labor forces with much lower wage scales, greater flexibility in work rules, and more fuel-efficient aircraft that were much less expensive to operate.

42 Regional carriers also skillfully executed some innovative and well-planned strategies. For example, many relied on older airports, which offered ease of access because of their centralized locations. Regional airlines also attempted to select routes that did not put them in head-to-head competition with larger airlines. In fact, as discussed earlier, some regionals established cooperative agreements with major and national carriers, such as working as feeders or by providing the last portions of trips for their passengers.

43 In many respects, the operating strategies of the national carriers were similar to those of the majors. Both emphasized hub areas where they had strong competitive positions as a basis for extending their operations to other profitable locations. Piedmont's grand strategy, for example, was to connect medium-sized cities in the Southeast

Exhibit 6

Airline performance and disposable personal income

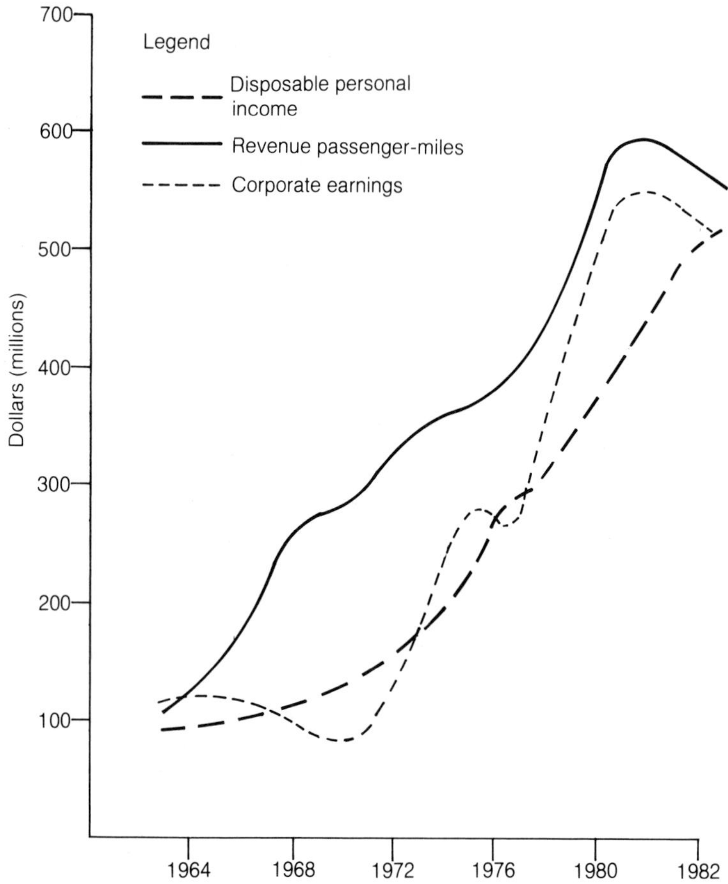

Source: Thomas Canning, "Air Transport: Current Analysis," *Standard & Poor's Industry Survey* (October 1983), p. A5.

with major cities in Florida, the Southwest, and the West. Piedmont's success with the strategy resulted in a fivefold growth in net income between 1979 and 1983.

44 In contrast, the main strategy of the major airlines following deregulation was the establishment of hub operations. To do so, feeder routes were designed to bring passengers to a central hub, where they could be transferred to other flights of the same carrier. Some airlines, United and Delta among them, established multiple hubs to capture or keep bigger shares of strategically located airports or cities.

45 With the major carriers, however, differences existed in the way they responded to deregulation and the new competitive environment. One clear contrast can be seen in the experience of USAir and Braniff. USAir followed a conservative path by adding

new stations gradually, by being very selective in its equipment purchases, and by stressing the suitability of its new planes to its primarily short-haul system. This well-planned growth raised the company's net income from $22 million in 1978 to $59.6 million in 1982.

46 In contrast, Braniff aggressively started 48 nonstop segments and entered 18 new cities in the United States after only two months of deregulation. As its financial position steadily deteriorated, Braniff took some desperate actions in 1981 and early 1982, trying to create turnaround momentum. Strategies included the sale of some of its fleet, the cancellation of new orders, the abandonment of unprofitable routes, and the restructuring of its debt with its creditors. Despite all of these actions, Braniff was forced to file for bankruptcy in May 1982. Following reorganization and after being acquired by Hyatt Corporation of Chicago, Braniff staged a downscaled comeback in early 1984.

Conclusion

47 As the first half-decade of the modern deregulated era drew to a close, several observations seemed relevant to strategic planning in the airline industry:

1. Demand was relatively and somewhat predictably seasonal.
2. Technological innovation offered increasing release from high fuel consumption. But new airplanes would require considerable capital expenditures.
3. With the industry life cycle in its maturity stage, the success of one airline seemed always to come at the expense of another.
4. Profitability depended largely on a carrier's ability to control costs, particularly those for labor and fuel.
5. Telecommunications technology increasingly threatened the industry as a substitute for business travel.
6. Mobility barriers were greatly diminished.
7. Low operating ratios, high contribution margins, and capital intensity all served as important, though partial, determinants of a carrier's profitability.

Recommended Reading

1. "Another Airline Price War Is In the Making." *Business Week,* October 3, 1983, pp. 46–47.
2. Dreyfack, Medeleine. "Airlines Battle for Survival." *Marketing & Media Decisions,* April 1983, pp. 119–26.
3. Farrell, Kevin. "New Airlines Go Regional." *Venture,* July 1983, p. 73.
4. Fenwick, Thomas. "Airlines." *U.S. Industrial Outlook,* 1983, pp. 44:6–44:8.
5. Kozicharow, Eugene. "Carriers Press to Cut Labor Costs." *Aviation Week & Space Technology,* August 29, 1983, pp. 29–31.
6. Ott, James, "Airlines Pursue Convention Market." *Aviation Week & Space Technology,* August 15, 1983, pp. 28–29.
7. ———. "Regional Carriers Facing Multiple Challenges," *Aviation Week & Space Technology,* January 17, 1983, pp. 28–29.

case 23 Braniff International Corporation (A)

1 Braniff International Corporation, incorporated in 1930 as Braniff Airways, Inc., carried passengers, freight, and mail in the southwest corner of the United States. In 1965, Greatamerica Corporation assumed control of Braniff by purchasing 52 percent of its stock, and as part of a reorganization plan, Harding Lawrence was named president. Lawrence, a former executive vice president for Continental Airlines, utilized an unusual promotional campaign which exhibited panache in a relatively conservative industry. Some of the promotional tactics for the Dallas-based airline, designed to increase exposure outside the southwest United States were:

1. Establishing VIP lounges in all major airports so business passengers traveling with Braniff would have a special place to relax before, between, or after flights.
2. Hiring fashion designer Pucci to design several different uniforms for the stewardesses.
3. Painting Braniff planes with bright colors such as blue, orange, and green.

2 Coupled with an attempt to overcome a bad on-time record, these highly visible maneuvers were very successful in achieving national recognition for Braniff and in helping to increase Braniff's passenger-load factor.

3 Braniff experienced rapid growth until late 1969, when its military charter collapsed and the Justice Department cited Braniff for antitrust activities. The company took a number of measures to effect its recovery. Though financially unable to purchase large, wide-body airplanes (747s), Braniff took advantage of the benefits which planned fleet standardization could provide. Use of a narrow selection of planes allowed Braniff to reduce costs in several ways—pilots and maintenance crews were trained for only one type of airplane, and parts could be interchanged among planes.

4 Since the proportion of business travelers was greater for Braniff (70 percent) than for the industry (60 percent), Braniff focused its turnaround measures on the business traveler, increasing the number of cities served and the number of flights to each city. The average daily usage per plane exceeded the industry average by 0.9 hours, and the time between major maintenance overhauls that kept the plane on the ground for several days was lengthened. Thus Braniff, in an attempt to boost profits, opted to increase productivity of the planes rather than increase fares.

5 The turnaround measures were successful, and Lawerence was applauded as one of the most-competent chief executive officers in the airline industry.

This case was prepared by Professors John A. Pearce II and Sandra J. Teel of the University of South Carolina with the assistance of Susan L. Martin and Kathy M. Smith. It has been accepted for publication in the *Journal of Management Case Studies*.

6 Braniff's response to problems encountered in the mid-1970s was equally successful. From 1975 to 1976, fuel prices increased 30 percent, and labor costs increased 17 percent. During negotiations for a new union contract, Braniff traded arbitration on unresolved issues for a union agreement not to strike. Rather than pulling back, Braniff forged ahead through route expansion and diversification.

7 These diversifications were either a complement to the airline or a means to maximize its strengths. Braniff International Hotels, Inc., as a service to Braniff passengers, provided private housing and dining facilities in Braniff's headquarters at Dallas-Fort Worth (DFW) airport as well as a hotel and discotheque in Austin, Texas. Braniff Realty Company provided fueling and tie-down services at Love Field in Dallas and owned six aircraft which it leased to Braniff.

8 To capitalize on existing strengths, Braniff Education Systems, Inc., (BES) was established. BES taught courses for the public on such topics as ticketing, reservations and sales, travel agency operations, and flight engineer training. The BIC Guardian Services, Inc., (BIC) was established shortly after airports increased security screening to prevent hijacking. BIC conducted security screening for several airports, including DFW.

9 In an attempt to improve productivity, interdepartmental competition was encouraged. Departments prepared progress reports that were first examined by management, then distributed to other departments for comparison. Fleet standardization continued as standard operating procedure for Braniff as did high-frequency flights. By the end of 1976, all parts of the Braniff operation were working well. Revenue per passenger-mile and the passenger load factor had increased over the previous year. Braniff was planning to expand its services to Europe. This expansion effort was supported by a strong financial picture with ample cash and a net working capital of $14.3 million.

International Operations

10 Braniff extended its service to international markets, beginning with flights to Central and South America. As early as 1952, Braniff was flying to Mexico, Panama, and most countries in South America where Lima served as the hub of its operations. Despite the 1975 discovery of payoffs by Braniff to Latin American travel agents to influence tickets sales, Braniff continued to cultivate this market, because load factors in Central and South America were higher than domestic load factors. In 1977, prior to its entry into the European market, Braniff's load factor for international operations was 56.6 percent versus 47 percent for domestic operations.

11 In late 1977, Braniff's scope of international operations was broadened to include transatlantic service to London. The new service, scheduled to begin March 1, 1978, was to be a daily round-trip service from DFW to Gatwick, requiring 18 operating hours out of every 24 for the "great 747 pumpkin." Lawrence, renowned for his policies of frequent and nondiscriminating service and fares for the southwestern transatlantic passenger, proposed low promotional fares that would rival any East Coast passenger rate. Experience gained from service to Honolulu evidenced the benefit of long in-flight engine utilization which caused less engine wearout than more frequent takeoff utilization (at full throttle).

12 Before Braniff could commence the London flights, a conflict arose between the CAB and the British Civil Aviation Authority (BCAA) over the proposed DFW/London fare. While awaiting the eventual settlement of the fare dispute, Braniff was already

planning and implementing its strategies for getting the new service underway. Briefly, some of its tactical moves were:

1. Arranging for an aircraft prior to final CAB approval.
2. Leasing as opposed to buying a ticket office in London.
3. Hiring and training British citizens as agents and clerks.
4. Delivering ticket stock to both British travel agents and wholesalers.
5. Training 10 extra 747 flight crews.

13 Braniff continued its expansion into European markets. In January 1979, it entered into an agreement with British Airways and Air France to provide a through service via Washington, D.C., to London and Paris. Braniff operated the Concorde from DFW to Washington, and the British and French airlines flew the transatlantic stretches. Under this arrangement, Braniff gained additional exposure to European markets through its inclusion in London and Paris airline traffic schedules.

14 In June 1979, Braniff further expanded its European connections by offering low-fare nonstop direct service from DFW and Boston to Paris, Frankfurt, Amsterdam, and Brussels. Further expansions in 1979 took Braniff to the Far Eastern market where it began service to Guam, Hong Kong, Korea, and Malaysia. Braniff anticipated adding Japan and the Philippines to round out its route structure.

Deregulation

15 Representing the first deregulation of an entire industry in decades, the Deregulation Act (October 24, 1978) was viewed as a possible precursor to anticipated relief for other "overregulated" U.S. industries. Under federal regulation, routes and fares had to be approved by the CAB, thereby limiting the factors of competition to such variables as scheduling and service. Deregulation was intended to return airlines to a market-controlled industry. According to the 1978 law, the CAB's authority over fares and rates would end by 1983, and by 1985, the agency itself would be abolished. In the years 1979 to 1981, each airline was permitted to claim one new route of its choice without the board's approval. At the same time, carriers were assured of more-speedy application and approval for new routes, acquisition of which required only a demonstration that a carrier was "fit, willing, and able" to serve the new route and that its operation would be consistent with, rather than required for, public convenience. Opposition to any new entry had to prove, at the very least, danger to the public welfare.

16 Although fares were still partially regulated in markets where an airline controlled less than 70 percent of the traffic, an airline could otherwise adjust its fare without CAB approval by:

1. A reduction of up to 70 percent from the standard industry fare.
2. An increase of up to 10 percent over the standard industry fare—the fare level in effect as of July 1, 1977, for each pair of points.

17 Unfortunately, the impact of deregulation was experienced during a rapid growth period for the airline industry. Cheaper fares and intense promotional campaigns had brought an increase in the number of routes available and the number of travelers. Simultaneously, spiraling fuel prices, recessionary trends, decreases in disposable in-

come and, thus, in the number of vacation travelers, and other limiting factors caused unanticipated and mounting problems for the airline industry. Deregulation was thus tested during an economic downswing.

Industry Response to Deregulation

18 The industry reaction to deregulation was slow and somewhat cautious, holding back and reassessing, "enhancing and integrating," and strengthening existing route structures. The trunk lines seemed to be searching only for profits as a means for determining scheduling strategies. Retrenchment had been difficult. The choice was between a reduction in the size of the fleet or in the size of the jet in order to transport fewer passengers yet serve more locations and increase the frequency of service. At the same time, the commuter lines had great expansion opportunities. Some carriers leaned either aggressively or defensively toward acquisition or merger to bolster their positions.

19 The changes in pricing due to deregulation were hailed as particularly helpful to the struggling industry. Prices continued to increase, but more slowly under competition than under artificial regulation. The new policy was more responsive since it allowed for quicker adjustments both upward (to pass on fuel-price increases) or downward (to attract new customers through discounting). Services could be reduced or even eliminated more quickly, and equipment could be used more productively through the flexibility afforded by the act.

20 While the airline industry as a whole had assumed a rather conservative position in response to deregulation, Braniff had responded quite differently. Dubbed as "sprinting strategy," Braniff's aggressive route expansion was met with near disbelief by the other trunk carriers. In October 1978, Braniff picked up 89 dormant routes. In December, they applied for 59 more but were able to activate only 32 (due to a CAB-established 45-day limitation on activation). With the end-of-the-year push, Braniff added 16 new cities to its schedule before Christmas, increasing its route-miles by 35 percent and its available seat-miles by 11 percent. In mid-January, Braniff applied for approximately one third of the dormant routes and, for the period January 1, 1979, to February 25, 1979, offered one-third-off discounts between new cities and other domestic points. On January 25, 1979, service was introduced for an additional 14 nonstop routes.

21 In conjunction with the route expansion, Braniff hired 627 pilots and undertook work on a $45 million expansion of its terminal facilities in the DFW airport. To be completed by 1988, the expansion was expected to increase simultaneous loading space accommodations from 24 to 47 aircraft.

Braniff's Operating Strategies

22 The deregulation strategy was based on Lawrence's faith in Braniff's flexibility, which he attributed to fleet standardization. Braniff's domestic fleet consisted almost exclusively of Boeing 727s—both the 727–100 series with a capacity of 100 passengers and the 727–200 series with a capacity of 130 passengers. The 727 had only three engines and substantial commonality of parts and subsystems between the 100 and 200 series.

Lawrence's claim, even as early as 1972, was that fully allocated operating costs per mile for the DC-10 were double those for the 727–200. The 727 could be operated twice as often with more seats available.

23 Frequency rather than capacity was the key to Braniff's scheduling success. The size of the Boeing 727 permitted multistops without creating bottlenecks, and yet it was cost efficient, particularly for the low-density markets in which Braniff operated. Because it was efficient and suitable for smaller airports, the 727 could also be used to develop new markets.

24 Braniff subscribed to high fleet utilization. Figures for 1977 show Braniff operated its carriers an average of 8.3 hours per day versus the industry average of 7.4 hours per day.

25 As a result of fleet standardization, small spare parts inventory, lower training costs for crews, and high fleet utilization, Braniff experienced lower-than-average direct operating costs, which meant earning a profit with a smaller percentage of seats filled. The low break-even load factor enabled Braniff to maintain its additional routes with low load factors that were sufficient to cover the additional operating expenses.

26 Like Delta, Braniff had developed a good hub-and-spoke system for feeding its routes, particularly in DFW and Denver. With good feeders into the hubs, Braniff increased its opportunities for picking up new or extended routes out of the hubs. Braniff's choice of low-density routes provided yet another competitive advantage.

27 These operating strategies seemed to have placed Braniff in a sound position for expanding its routes. Its adopted strategies for dealing with the expansion also seemed technically sound. For example, Braniff curtailed its training of other airline crews in Dallas and began training only its own crews. It provided only light service to new routes and scheduled new flights for off-peak hours to prevent disruption of existing flights until it could assess demand. Further, until permanent set-ups could be justified, Braniff leased counter and gate space and negotiated service agreements in newly entered airports.

28 Braniff's expansion was rapid, but it moves were not irrevocable. Braniff chose to enter markets quickly, make temporary arrangements, assess the demand, and adjust scheduling accordingly.

Financial and Other Relevant Data

29 Braniff was attracted by the potential profits to be realized as a result of deregulation and the apparent growth of the airline industry. Industry earnings were a record high in 1978 but fell in 1979 because of the weakening economy and the increased costs of both fuel and other operations. Airline traffic continued to grow with the help of new routes and promotional fares which reduced the passenger yield (the average fare collected per passenger-mile), but traffic gains were offset by this drop in passenger yield and the rising costs of operations.

30 Domestic traffic was up by 15 percent for the trunk lines (major carriers) in the first four months of 1979, and international traffic was up 21 percent. During the same period, the locals (regionals) also achieved a 33 percent gain in traffic. However, during the first quarter of 1979, the yield dropped 3.3 percent, and operating expenses increased 15.7 percent, resulting in an operating deficit of $13 million and an increase of only 12 percent in operating revenue. The net loss for the first quarter 1979 amounted

to $603,000 for the industry. In 1978, the industry had recorded $9.8 million in net income for the same period.

31 During 1979, the U.S. economy was unstable and was predicted to worsen in 1980. Gross national product (GNP) increased by only 3.3 percent in 1979 compared to a 3.9 percent gain in 1978. Real disposable personal income registered only half of its 1978 gain in 1979—2.3 percent versus 4.6 percent. Paralleling these declines was a growth drop in revenue passenger-miles, up only 5.8 percent in 1979, a minor gain when compared to the 15.9 percent increase of 1978. As a result, the depressed economy had heightened price consciousness so greatly that fare reductions were perceived as the only means to achieve traffic gains.

32 Braniff experienced a net *loss* of $44,330,000 in 1979 as compared to a net *gain* of $45,230,000 in 1978. Factors attributing to the loss were rapid expansion, the price of jet fuel, the increase in labor and other operating costs, and the state of the economy. In 1979, Braniff substantially increased its operation as a result of the deregulation of the airlines. A comparison of the 1978 and 1979 balance sheets (see Exhibit 1) shows that total assets increased from $855 million to $1.13 billion, an increase of 32.7 percent, while total liabilities increased from $605 million to $936 million, an increase of 54.72 percent. In contrast, the equity of the firm decreased 26 percent. Braniff was constantly increasing the size of its fleet, the size of the work force, and the number of its facilities during the year. The sixth-largest airline in number of enplaned passengers, Braniff planned an increase in fleet second only to United, the largest airline.

33 Braniff did, however, achieve a significant gain in revenue and airline traffic, and revenues reached a record high of $1.2 billion. Operating revenues were up 38.5 percent from 1978, and airline passenger traffic in revenue passenger-miles increased 39.7 percent while available seat-miles also were up 33.7 percent. Domestic traffic increased 32.3 percent, and international traffic was up 6.1 percent. Exhibit 2 compares the fluctuations in airline traffic and the revenue per ton-mile of Braniff to its major competitors.

34 However, these gains in revenues and traffic were counteracted by the explosive increase in operating expenses, especially the cost of jet fuel. The composition of Braniff's operating expenses is shown in Exhibit 3. Aircraft, fuel, oil, and taxes, along with labor costs, accounted for the bulk of expenses. Fuel alone increased 94.2 percent in 1979, and labor costs rose 34.2 percent. Braniff spent $409 million for fuel in 1979 in contrast to $210 million in 1978. The average price per gallon jumped from 40.2 cents to 78 cents. The increase in each operating expense can be seen in Exhibit 4, which compares the income statements for the years 1978–1979.

35 Exhibit 5 shows the significant difference in fuel-price increases and the airline-fare increases. Although CAB granted fare increases in 1979, the increases lagged behind in dollar value and time. The industry experienced a loss of approximately $470 million as a result of the lag, more than $60 million (12.76 percent) of which was experienced by Braniff.

36 As of December 31, 1979, Braniff had 30 million shares of 50 cents par value of authorized common stock issued and outstanding. Earnings per share were −$2.21 for the year, with the price of the stock fluctuating from $14⅜ to $6¾, as shown in Exhibit 6. The price-earnings ratio of 1978 was 2.0, but because of the loss in 1979, it was not meaningful for 1979. Also, Braniff had 5 million shares of preferred stock with none outstanding.

Exhibit 1

BRANIFF INTERNATIONAL CORPORATION AND SUBSIDIARIES
Consolidated Balance Sheet, December 31, 1978, and 1979
(in thousands of dollars)

	1979	*1978*
Assets		
Current assets:		
Cash	$ 32,007	$ 6,607
Marketable securities	1,486	6,558
Net accounts receivable	105,987	88,929
Receivables from airport authorities	2,821	11,180
Inventory	37,772	26,072
Other current assets	7,788	2,173
Total current assets	187,861	141,519
Equipment purchase deposits	30,391	67,355
Property and equipment, net	863,429	612,189
Other assets:		
Deferred charges	32,798	15,930
Long-term prepayments	18,450	15,911
Long-term receivables and investments	1,792	2,261
Total other assets	53,040	34,102
Total assets	$1,134,721	$855,165
Liabilities		
Current liabilities:		
Notes payable and current maturities of long-term debt	$ 23,393	$ 14,112
Accounts payable	118,420	56,605
Current liabilities under capital leases	10,558	7,997
Unearned revenues	19,822	11,231
Dividends payable	1,023	1,820
Accrued compensation and retirement benefits	26,791	27,926
Accrued vacation pay	21,677	15,741
Other current liabilities	31,466	20,111
Total current liabilities	253,150	155,543
Long-term debt:		
Senior debt	507,912	320,985
Subordinated debt	70,286	27,692
Total long-term debt	578,198	348,677
Other noncurrent liabilities:		
Capital leases	87,047	49,393
Other	3,335	3,145
Total other noncurrent liabilities	90,382	52,538
Deferred credits:		
Deferred federal income taxes	10,312	46,280
Other	4,062	1,976
Total deferred credits	14,374	48,256
Preferred stock:		
Authorized, 5,000,000 shares of $1.00 par value; none outstanding		
Common shareholders' equity		
Common stock; authorized, 30,000,000 shares of $0.50 par value; issued and outstanding: 1979, 20,019,045; 1978, 20,018,671	10,010	10,009
Paid-in capital	46,785	46,783
Retained earnings	141,822	193,359
Total common shareholders' equity	198,617	250,151
Total liabilities	$1,134,721	$855,165

Source: Braniff International Corporation, 1979 Annual Report.

Exhibit 2

Selected airline traffic and freight statistics, 1977–1979 (in thousands of miles)

	Revenue-miles			*Revenue passenger-miles*			*Total revenue ton-miles*		
	1977	*1978*	*1979*	*1977*	*1978*	*1979*	*1977*	*1978*	*1979*
Domestic:									
American	21,418	22,447	23,751	1,748,014	1,921,089	2,210,871	231,775	247,424	270,728
Braniff	8,362	9,452	9,762	490,646	643,986	631,821	58,061	73,351	72,148
Continental	6,814	7,970	8,316	570,448	666,205	622,543	80,135	91,749	84,587
Delta	18,827	20,363	20,515	1,575,288	1,909,226	1,862,276	182,601	214,903	209,996
Eastern	19,766	20,527	21,803	1,388,892	1,657,241	1,924,288	154,973	184,612	211,685
Trans World	17,077	16,320	15,228	1,270,707	1,309,958	1,188,124	156,769	155,451	139,650
United	30,963	35,574	35,174	2,613,138	3,274,376	3,673,152	327,619	398,024	432,030
International:									
American	2,418	2,477	2,631	234,315	293,612	330,749	36,054	38,526	41,514
Braniff	1,747	1,961	1,934	151,214	170,778	188,302	18,338	20,141	21,729
Continental	239	423	740	11,641	27,811	68,471	1,492	3,714	14,229
Delta	338	502	338	34,806	51,997	47,129	4,248	5,825	5,706
Eastern	2,031	2,401	2,689	251,636	308,271	367,853	34,470	38,631	45,149
Pan Am	10,424	10,386	9,955	1,386,225	1,565,124	1,542,800	244,107	251,816	248,872
Trans World	4,567	4,569	3,731	546,125	614,540	564,657	84,526	85,140	76,069

Source: *Aviation Week and Space Technology* 108 (February 6, 1978), p. 41; 110 (February 5, 1979), p. 33; 112 (February 18, 1980), p. 37.

Exhibit 3

Operating expense comparison, Braniff International Corporation, 1978–1979

	Composition (percent)		*Percent increases*	
	1979	*1978*	*1979 versus 1978*	*1978 versus 1977*
Aircraft fuel, oil, and taxes	29.8%	23.8%	94.2%	26.7%
Salaries, wages, related taxes, and employee benefits	29.3	33.9	34.2	19.3
Depreciation and capital lease amortization	4.9	6.6	16.5	8.9
Operating leases and rentals	3.4	2.7	93.8	47.9
Landing fees	2.2	2.6	33.0	7.6
Outside services and repairs	9.3	8.2	75.2	32.5
Materials and supplies	2.5	2.9	36.1	28.0
Traffic commissions	5.0	5.1	52.6	43.1
Passenger food service	4.4	4.4	56.1	38.4
Advertising and promotion	1.4	2.0	6.4	17.0
Communications	1.5	1.6	51.9	33.3
All other expenses	6.3	6.2	55.2	29.3
Total	100.0	100.0	55.3	24.4

Source: Braniff International Corporation, 1979 Annual Report.

Alternatives

37 Grumblings among the stockholders suggested that any action Braniff took to respond to third quarter 1979 losses would be closely inspected at the next stockholders' meeting. Meetings of top management to determine the course of action needed generated a wide variety of alternative viewpoints but coalesced around the following analysis.

38 Increases in fuel costs coupled with the sizable increase in routes were responsible for the strain on Braniff's budget. While it had no control over fuel costs, the number of routes could certainly be reduced. Obviously, the choice of routes to drop should depend on the route's profitability. Only months earlier, the Federal Aviation Authority (FAA) had proposed that Braniff be fined because of maintenance irregularities which the FAA attributed to rapid route expansion. Thus, another benefit of route reduction would be a return to standard maintenance of aircraft. Dropping some routes would also free aircraft that could then be sold to generate additional revenues to offset the increased fuel costs. This measure was seen as merely temporary since Braniff had no intention of halting its growth.

39 Braniff was reviewing its labor contracts in an attempt to secure an agreement for a wage cut. The exact size of the wage cut could only be determined through negotiations. However, as a sign of good faith, Lawrence offered to take double the wage cut other employees took.

40 A new promotional campaign was suggested as a measure for increasing the passenger load factor. An advertising campaign would focus on the services Braniff offered and on how their services differed from other airlines. Since their cash was already depleted, they planned to follow the lead of Pan Am and Continental to trade airline

Exhibit 4

BRANIFF INTERNATIONAL CORPORATION AND SUBSIDIARIES
Statement of Consolidated Income,
For the Periods Ending December 31, 1978, and 1979
(in thousands of dollars except per share amounts)

	1979	*1978*
Operating revenues:		
Airline:		
Passenger	$1,200,329	$845,353
Express, freight, and mail	84,559	68,080
Charter	15,226	18,843
Transport related	28,213	24,789
Other	8,039	8,238
Nonairline subsidiaries	9,909	6,805
Total operating revenues	1,346,275	972,108
Operating expenses:		
Airline:		
Flying and ground operations	546,841	382,277
Aircraft fuel, oil, and taxes	409,635	210,883
Maintenance	131,691	88,853
Nonairline subsidiaries	3,271	2,992
Sales and advertising	158,659	108,737
Depreciation* and amortization, less amounts charged to other accounts	75,343	60,980
General and administrative	41,273	37,227
Total operating expenses	1,384,713	891,949
Operating income (loss)	(38,438)	80,159
Nonoperating expenses (income):		
Interest expense	55,919	34,201
Interest capitalized	(6,265)	(4,992)
Interest income	(3,809)	(3,129)
Other—Net	(2,553)	(1,156)
Total nonoperating expenses	43,292	24,924
Income (loss) before income taxes	(81,730)	55,235
Provision (credit) for income taxes	(37,400)	10,005
Net income (loss)	$ (44,330)	$ 45,230
Earnings (loss) per common share	$(2.21)	$2.26
Weighted average number of common shares outstanding	20,019	20,016

* Depreciation was computed on the straight-line method.
Source: Braniff International Corporation, 1979 Annual Report.

tickets for advertising time and space. Since advertising alone was seen as insufficient to overcome the problems, part of the promotional campaign was to be some type of discounted fare program. One suggestion was a 10 percent reduction in fare between certain cities, provided the traveler used Braniff for the entire trip.

41 Braniff also considered increasing its fares by the maximum allowed by the deregulation act. This would boost revenues since ticket sales constituted the bulk of Braniff's revenues.

Exhibit 5

Fuel price increases versus airline fare increases, 1979 domestic operations

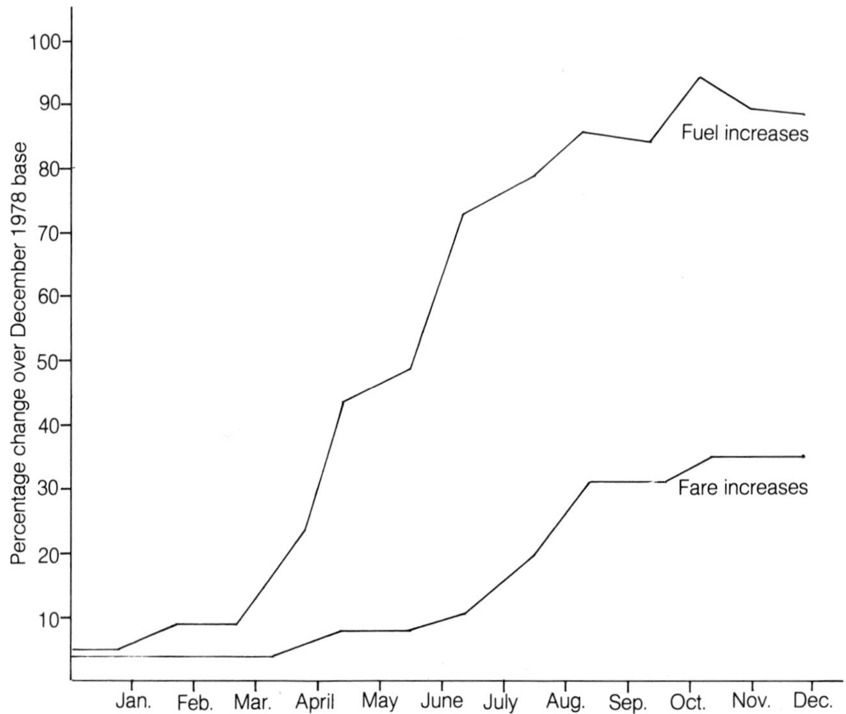

42 Long-term debtholders had become increasingly uneasy over Braniff's plight and had stipulated that Braniff could not secure any other senior long-term debt. Besides postponement of the payment of long-term debt, Braniff's only other options appeared to be the sale of preferred stock and short-term debt. The company considered selling 3.75 million shares of preferred stock in an attempt to generate $75 million to retire debt and finance aircraft. Braniff also had a verbal commitment for a $100 million loan (short term) at an interest rate of 1½ percent above prime.

43 Braniff continued to have many strong points, most notably its Latin American operations. Therefore, a merger with another airline was being considered. It was hoped that a merger would bolster domestic and European lines. One company seen as highly probable for a merger was Eastern Airlines, but Eastern had also been experiencing problems. Chief Executive Frank Borman had been credited with an Eastern turnaround since 1975 even though he had been unable to significantly reduce its debt load. Other problems associated with an Eastern-Braniff merger were that (1) both companies had very high debt-to-equity ratios, (2) restraint of trade questions would arise since virtually all of Latin American travel was controlled by Eastern

Exhibit 6

Common stock data, Braniff International Corporation, 1970–1979

	Per share data						
					Price		
Year Ending December 31	*Book value*	*Earnings*	*Dividends*	*Payout ratio*	*High*	*Low*	*P/E ratio*
1970	$ 4.14	$*d*0.13	$0.47⅞	NM	10⅔	5⅞	NM
1971	4.60	0.49‡	Nil	Nil	16½	7⅝	34–16
1972	5.44	0.85‡	Nil	Nil	19⅝	12⅞	23–15
1973*	6.61	1.15	Nil	Nil	16¼	8¼	14–7
1974*	7.77	1.30	0.15	11%	12½	4½	10–3
1975	8.37	1.02	0.20	20	9¼	5	9–5
1976	9.47	1.31	0.23	17	14¼	8¾	11–7
1977	11.00	1.82	0.28½	16	11⅛	7½	6–4
1978	12.50	2.26	0.34½	15	18⅝	8⅞	8–4
1979	9.92	*d*2.21	0.36	NM	14⅜	6¾	NM

Data as originally reported. Adjusted for stock divisions of 3 percent November 1972, 3 percent November 1971.

* Reflects accounting change.

† Before specific items of −0.22 in 1975, −0.03 in 1971.

‡ Fully diluted: 0.81 in 1972, 0.43 in 1971.

NM = Not meaningful.

d = Deficit.

Source: *Standard & Poor's Stock Reports: New York Stock Exchange, A–C, January 1981* 47, no. 231, sec. 6 (New York: Standard & Poor's, December 1).

and Braniff, and (3) both airlines had agreed to very costly contracts for new airplane deliveries. Nonetheless, the strength of Braniff's Latin American operations coupled with Eastern's domestic strength suggested a potentially good merger.

44 It was crucial that Braniff have a positive response to its problems in the short run since it was highly unlikely stockholders would allow the losses to continue without demanding some reorganization of top management.

case 24
Braniff International Corporation (B)

"We have our costs under control . . . and our economic picture will vastly improve from here on out." (H. L. Lawrence, February 29, 1980)

"Braniff is a financially sound company. Braniff isn't in financial trouble. Braniff isn't in a financial hole." (H. L. Lawrence, August 21, 1980)

"Braniff is on the right course and should do well. (H. L. Lawrence, December 31, 1980)

Problems of a Billion-Dollar Airline

1 Braniff International Chairman Harding L. Lawrence had a goal: to make Braniff a billion-dollar airline. When the deregulation of the airline industry first took effect in October 1978, Lawrence seized the opportunity to embark upon an ambitious growth strategy, and in just one year, Braniff expanded its passenger capacity by 37 percent to become the nation's sixth-largest airline. In that one year, 1979, Braniff was indeed the billion-dollar airline Lawrence had envisioned. Revenues rose by 65 percent from the beginning of the expansion to a total of $1.35 billion by year-end.

2 The expansion included the addition of 20 domestic destinations as well as service to Europe, Asia, and the Pacific. But such large-scale expansion proved costly for Braniff. Its operating expenses rose 55 percent in 1979 as compared with an average industry rise of 21 percent, and to service all its new routes, it borrowed heavily to acquire additional aircraft. At 2.9, Braniff had one of the highest debt-to-equity ratios in the industry. Beginning with the third quarter of 1979, net losses were reported for four consecutive quarters.

3 Braniff had originally undertaken its expansion strategy to protect itself against its larger competitors, especially American Airlines. Braniff's management anticipated that under deregulation, its competitors would drastically reduce fares, a move that would drive smaller airlines out of business. Braniff felt that increased size would be its best means of survival if such fare wars occurred. However, much of the expansion was based on second-choice routes that either no other carrier wanted because of low traffic or because a particular airline already was firmly entrenched.

4 Braniff was not alone in facing financial strain. The entire airline industry encountered sharply rising fuel costs coupled with a general slowdown in airline traffic because of an economic recession. It was not surprising, then, that the increased competition

---

This case was prepared by J. Kay Keels and John A. Pearce II of the University of South Carolina.

and fare wars Braniff feared became a reality. However, because of its expansion activities, Braniff was more exposed to these hardships than most of the major carriers in the industry.

5 By late 1980, Braniff's finances were in serious trouble. Planned stock offerings had to be cancelled due to its failure to meet earnings requirements; it was blocked from using its bank line of credit; and some of its creditors had placed it on a cash-only status. Braniff's shortage of cash was becoming desperate, and drastic measures were required.

6 Braniff began by cutting capacity by eliminating several of its less profitable routes, and by October 1980, capacity had been slashed by nearly one third from a year earlier. The flashy Concorde service from Dallas to London and Paris, several of the Pacific flights, and a number of domestic flights were all gone.

7 One fund-raising tactic employed by Braniff was that of selling aircraft. During 1980, more than 20 jets were sold, including 15 727-200s to American Airlines and a 747 jumbo jet to an Argentine firm.

8 A second measure used to help ease the cash shortage was borrowing from banks, insurance companies, and suppliers. To obtain these loans, Braniff was forced to take the drastic step of offering its planes and equipment as collateral.

9 Although strapped for cash, to remain competitive, Braniff was forced to engage in drastic fare cutting, and in some domestic markets, the cuts exceeded 80 percent.

10 In the last quarter of 1980, Lawrence appealed to Braniff employees to help the company ease its financial problems by accepting a 10 percent pay cut. As a show of sincerity, he pledged to cut his own $300,000 per year salary by 20 percent if the deal was accepted. This time the Lawrence confidence backfired. On one hand, the chairman was assuring the press that Braniff's financial condition was solid, while on the other hand, he was appealing to Braniff's employees because the firm's financial position was tenuous. The unions representing Braniff's employees cited Lawrence's duplicity as they rejected the pay-cut plan, even though some employees had already been laid off as a result of worsening financial conditions.

11 Merger talks were begun with Eastern Airlines late in 1980. Although a joint agreement might have helped pull the troubled Braniff through its financial troubles, Eastern itself was experiencing cash problems which ultimately ended the merger talks.

12 Overall, Lawrence's turnaround measures were viewed as too little too late. Under pressure from bankers and other lenders, Braniff's board solicited Lawrence's resignation on December 31, 1980.

13 On January 7, 1981, John J. Casey, formerly board vice chairman, was named president, chairman of the board, and chief executive officer. Among other problems, Casey inherited a long-term debt that had grown to over $600 million. Braniff's lenders took an active role in designing a new course for the airline by selecting a group of assistants for Casey who were known for their financial expertise.

14 Under Casey's direction, Braniff's operations were streamlined to emphasize three major areas: marketing—to plan and sell the product; operations—to produce and maintain the product; and finance—to analyze expenses and report on revenues. Management's immediate objectives were increased revenues and decreased expenses, and its initial strategies included reassigning resources to the most-profitable areas, eliminating nonprofitable operations, and selling additional aircraft.

15 Shortly after his election, Casey succeeded in rallying the company's employees to Braniff's cause. Effective March 1, 1981, all of the airline's unions approved an em-

ployee salary program whereby all employees' pay, including that of top management, was cut by 10 percent. These pay cuts were deemed voluntary contributions and were put into a special fund to help meet corporate cash requirements. Perhaps employees were convinced of Casey's commitment when he suspended his own $180,000 a year salary indefinitely.

16 However, a crisis arose simultaneously. Some $40 million in principal and interest on Braniff's long-term debt were due on March 1. Braniff sought a deferral until July 1, which its creditors reluctantly granted, contingent upon two factors: (1) the initiation of the employee salary program and (2) the company's development of a detailed operating plan for the remainder of the year.

17 To handle the debt-restructuring task, Casey brought in Howard P. Swanson as his top financial executive. Swanson was credited with having performed a similar task at Trans World Airlines.

18 Despite all these efforts, the question of Braniff's continued viability was raised by its auditors in the annual report issued at midyear 1981. Casey emphasized that the firm's continuation was at least partially dependent upon the continued deferral of debt payments.

19 Surprisingly, the deferral was again granted. This time Swanson was credited with convincing the airline's lenders to forgive interest payments on debt outstanding until February 1982. The once-critical July 1 deadline passed, and Braniff was still operating.

Changes in Market Strategy

20 Just before the final quarter of 1981, Braniff moved to strengthen its management. Howard Putnam, president and CEO of Southwest Airlines, was named president and chief operating officer of Braniff. The contrast between Southwest and Braniff was dramatic. For the previous six quarters, Southwest had posted the industry's highest margin of operating profit, while Braniff was the industry's biggest loser. The announcement of Putnam's appointment was viewed as a positive sign. Observers felt Putnam would not have accepted the job had he not believed a Braniff turnaround was possible.

21 Putnam first moved to completely revamp Braniff's fare structure. The new marketing strategy, called Texas Class, featured discounted single-class air service for a single price. The number of different fares charged by Braniff nationwide dropped from 582 to just 15. Under the system, the new fares undercut regular coach fares by an average of 45 percent, and were to be available every day for every seat of every Braniff flight. Putnam referred to the strategy as "getting back to basics." Braniff had been transformed from a conventional trunk airline into one that more nearly resembled a commuter airline. The success of the strategy was dependent upon the success of the new fare system in generating additional passenger traffic. Braniff was relying on its convenience and simplicity to appeal to travel agents and the general public.

22 One undesired effect of the Texas Class fare structure was retaliation by Braniff's competitors. American Airlines, Braniff's chief competitor, announced it would immediately meet Braniff's fares on every competing route. Braniff's fare strategy was revolutionary and risky. If it worked, Braniff would have effected a complete change in the structure of air travel prices. No longer would there be discounts and other fancy pricing tactics—just prices, some high and some low.

23 As a further attempt to make its resources more productive, Braniff scheduled its

planes to fly more hours every day. For example, late-night and early-morning departures were added to existing routes. In addition to their pay cuts, pilots agreed to fly 10 extra hours per month, half of them without pay. Layoffs continued to reduce the size of Braniff's work force.

24 As the February 1 deadline for debt payment approached, Braniff's only hope for survival was yet another extension. The company was broke, but it continued to operate. Although no major airline had ever failed, many observers questioned how much longer the carrier's creditors would support its operation since they held the liens on Braniff's planes.

25 The 37 creditors—22 banks, 15 insurance companies, and 2 suppliers—had to be convinced one more time. Braniff sought to have its debt commitments extended to October 1, 1982, and again to be forgiven the $40 million in interest payments.

26 Braniff's competitors, especially its chief rival, American Airlines, would benefit directly from the company's bankruptcy, and American had retaliated immediately in the fare wars even though it meant substantial losses. However, American was large and strong enough to withstand such losses in the short term while it knew Braniff was not. Further, American had added several directly competing routes in an attempt to defeat Braniff's strategy. Now there was evidence that American was urging Braniff's creditors to withdraw their support.

27 There was little incentive, however, for the creditors to let the troubled carrier fail. If Braniff were forced into bankruptcy, creditors would be left with their collateral—dozens of 727 jets for which there was almost no market because of the recession-induced U.S. travel slump. The alternative was for lenders to accept some equity and forgive some of the total long- and short-term private debt which at this point had reached $733.2 million.

28 Throughout this time period, Braniff continued its slimming and trimming tactics. Late in April 1982, the South American routes were leased to Eastern Airlines in a $30 million deal. Despite Braniff's precarious financial position, its officials were guardedly optimistic that the Eastern deal might lead the way toward generating sufficient revenues for survival.

29 Then, two weeks later, Braniff surprised the industry and some of its own executives. At midnight on May 12, 1982, Braniff suspended all flying operations. The reason for the abrupt cessation of service was not immediately clear, but it was suggested that one of Braniff's lenders had called in its portion of the debt. Braniff was one step away from bankruptcy.

30 Even as the announcements halting flights and telling workers to stay home were made, Braniff directors were meeting to decide whether to file under Chapter 11 or Chapter 7 of federal bankruptcy proceedings. Under Chapter 11, the company would be protected from its creditors while the court oversaw its reorganization plans. Chapter 7 would guide the liquidation of the company's assets.

31 A few hours later, Howard Putnam declared he had not taken the Braniff job in order to preside over its liquidation. Braniff was filing to reorganize under Chapter 11.

32 Bankruptcy experts were puzzled by the way Braniff had proceeded. Normally, a troubled firm will file under Chapter 11 in order to continue to operate while being protected from its creditors. Braniff, however, had first shut down its operations, then laid off its employees, and finally filed for reorganization. Despite the unorthodox procedure, Putnam insisted that the airline would resume operations—either under

its own name or under someone else's as a consequence of a merger. Putnam explained that the decision to cease operations was made because Braniff was simply out of cash. The next day, May 13, 1982, would have been a scheduled payday for Braniff employees, and Putnam indicated the company could not have met its payroll.

The Search for a Reorganization Plan

33 Braniff was allowed 120 days to file its reorganization plan with the courts. The firm's management quickly decided that its best hope lay in a joint venture. Throughout the remainder of 1982, Braniff engaged in merger talks with several airlines. As the filing deadline drew near, Braniff sought and obtained an extension on its filing date, and 1982 closed without a concrete decision.

34 Through the first quarter of 1983, Braniff's fate remained a question mark. Putnam negotiated with 16 airlines concerning the utilization of the company's aircraft, equipment, facilities, and personnel, but only Pacific Southwest Airlines presented a viable plan. Although major creditors and the bankruptcy court approved the pact, it was rejected by a U.S. appeals court, thereby terminating the Braniff-PSA talks.

35 With its last hope of a joint venture seemingly gone, Braniff's management turned its attention toward a reorganization plan that stopped just short of full liquidation. Under the plan, due to be submitted in federal bankruptcy court on April 4, 1983, the firm would divest itself of all its assets related to flying and would form a small business that would provide ground service and contract maintenance for other carriers. Braniff officials continued to believe that a live company in any form was better for creditors than a dead one. In Braniff's favor, the court deadline was postponed until April 18 due to a crowded court calendar.

The Hyatt Alternative

36 In the meantime, Braniff began talks with Hyatt Corporation, the Chicago-based hotel chain. Hyatt offered an investment proposal in return for an interest-bearing note and a majority of the voting stock in the reorganized company. Under the Hyatt plan, Braniff would resume flight operations.

37 The talks with Hyatt encountered some major obstacles, most notably the disapproval of Howard Putnam who considered the plan to be underfunded. Even after the original offer was raised considerably, Putnam still opposed it. As the April 18 deadline for filing reorganization plans drew near, no agreement had been reached. Braniff filed its original ground service proposal but with the stipulation that revised plan could be filed that could include resumption of flight operations. Clearly, the door was being left open for Hyatt to sweeten its offer. The talks continued.

38 Finally, in June 1983, Braniff and Hyatt agreed on a plan to put Braniff back in the air. Under the plan, Hyatt would ensure the new airline some $70 million in funding. In return, Hyatt would get 80 percent interest in the reorganized airline and more than $300 million in Braniff tax credits.

39 However, the agreement still faced numerous hurdles. First, there was an effort by American Airlines to squelch the deal. American knew Hyatt was having trouble convincing Braniff's creditors to accept its offer. So American attempted to sway the creditors by offering to buy Braniff's remaining fleet, thus effectively halting any plan that would put Braniff in the air again. Second, the environment was less than ideal

for a new entrant into an industry already plagued by overcapacity and revenue-draining fare wars. Third, the immediate problem was to get Braniff's major creditors to agree to the proposal. Many of them were skeptical and feared they might end up as two-time losers. Finally, the proposal required the approval of the bankruptcy court.

40 The major obstacle turned out to be the secured creditors' objections to the lease offer made to them by Hyatt. As holders of the liens on Braniff's planes, the creditors felt they could realize a larger yield by selling the aircraft. For weeks, Hyatt's Jay Pritzker, a principal in the firm, mediated between Braniff's management and its creditors, trying to secure agreement from the lenders.

41 After much negotition, an acceptable offer was tendered. The last major hurdle had been cleared. In September 1983, the Braniff reorganization plan was approved by a federal bankruptcy court, and the stage was finally set for Braniff to fly again.

42 Hyatt's plan for Braniff was ambitious, but it held many advantages. From the beginning, the plan had the support of Braniff's unsecured creditors and its employees. Most of its unions granted positive cost advantages in wage contract renegotiations, and these concessions alone gave Braniff the chance to operate as one of the lowest-cost carriers in the industry. In addition, many Braniff workers volunteered to work for free prior to the start-up date to get their jets back in the air. Some employees even came out of retirement to help.

43 Industry analysts believed Hyatt's toughest job would be to put together a capable management team. Though none of the top management of the "old Braniff" remained, good management was a Hyatt trademark. It had consistently been rated as one of the best-managed chains in the lodging industry. Perhaps Hyatt could bring from outside the industry what the airline lacked.

44 Braniff also had to win over doubting and somewhat disgruntled travelers and travel agents. When the airline had abruptly shut down in 1982, many of its passengers had been left stranded, holding worthless tickets. Competing airlines were reluctant to honor Braniff tickets since they knew they would be unable to collect from Braniff. Additionally, since travel agents sell more than 60 percent of all airline tickets, their acceptance was crucial.

45 Hyatt's strategy was aimed at getting travelers and agents to try the "new Braniff." Hyatt was confident their service was good enough to keep customers once it had them. To attract customers, a joint promotional campaign with the March of Dimes was initiated whereby a 5 percent savings on the ticket price would be donated to the March of Dimes. To build goodwill among travel agents, Braniff held elaborate receptions in many of the cities it served and also gave agents free tickets. An additional aid to booking travelers came as part of a lawsuit settlement against Braniff's old rival, American Airlines. Braniff was awarded the right to placement in American's computerized reservations system.

46 The new Braniff that began flight operations on March 1, 1984, was a sleeker, slimmer edition of the former major carrier. There would be no overseas flights and no first-class service. Instead, Braniff divided its passengers into business-traveler and leisure-traveler segments. Counting heavily on the business traveler, Braniff offered its "business cabin" area as a special attraction.

47 The new airline initially employed some 2,200 people to handle its flight schedules to 19 cities. The 30 727 planes that remained in Braniff's fleet featured the standard red, white, blue, and silver exterior but had a plush new look inside.

48 Despite the tenuous condition of the industry that had not fully recovered, despite the many months of management failure and employee unrest, despite the doubts of creditors, despite the obstacles posed in trying to win over a skeptical public, and despite the stiff competition Braniff faced on every one of its planned routes, the new Braniff proudly rolled down the runway once again. The optimism that prevailed against all the odds was evident in Braniff's March 1984 public announcement:

The new Braniff Only in America

This is the beginning of a modern American success story. Today, the first day of operation for the new Braniff, is proof to us that the system works.

We're not talking about business as usual here. The largest start-up in the history of aviation does not just happen. This is the result of twenty-two months of intensive work. Twenty-two months of searching for new solutions and new ideas. Twenty-two months of joint effort.

The new Braniff is a proud symbol for a new era of cooperation. The spirit of cooperation that exists between Braniff employees and our new management team is a signpost for the future.

We frankly admit that without the support, without the outstanding reasonableness of all Braniff people (who are now 65% more productive than their counterparts at other airlines), there would be no new Braniff.

We're confident that twelve months from today, our spirited service and redoubled efficiency will have earned and secured your continued patronage.

case 25
Southwest Airlines: Interstate Travel

1 "It's been a hectic few months," reflected Camille Keith (Southwest Airlines' Vice President of Public Relations), "but we're finally spreading love outside of Texas." While the urge to sit back and relax was very strong, she knew that the job of expanding air service to the three new markets had just begun. Was the introduction successfully launched? What did the new market customers think of Southwest? Was the advertising working?

2 Ms. Keith knew that marketing research held the answers to many of her questions, and that a thorough review of recent strategy was in order. Some information was already available, but some other would probably need to be collected. "Let's see where we stand," she commented to Tom Volz (Southwest's Vice President of Marketing and Sales).

3 "Fine!" replied Mr. Volz, "Let's get together first thing tomorrow morning."

4 "Tomorrow's meeting means a long today," thought Ms. Keith, as she began reviewing the background on the campaign planning. "Hold my calls and see if my other meeting this afternoon can be postponed," she called to her secretary.

The Company

5 Southwest Airlines began intrastate service in Texas on June 18, 1971, with three Boeing 737-200 aircraft, and a marketing strategy which highlighted several unique attributes:

1. Simplicity of operations (one type of aircraft, Dallas' Love Field headquarters, simplified passenger check-in and fare structure, and no food service)
2. High productivity (daily aircraft utilization of more than 11 hours and 10 minutes turnaround times between most flights)
3. Focus on passenger business (no large air freight and no U.S. mail)
4. Serving short-haul, mass transit commuter market (flight segments under two hours and fare structure competitive with bus and auto travel)

6 As of March 15, 1980, Southwest had grown to 1,600 employees, 31 aircraft, 1,852 total system-wide weekly flights, and an average load factor of 68.3 percent (based on 1979 figures and a 118 seat capacity). Exhibit 1 illustrates their growth in passenger boardings over the years in operation, and Exhibit 2 shows their operating statistics in relation to income.

Exhibit 1

Southwest Airlines passenger boardings

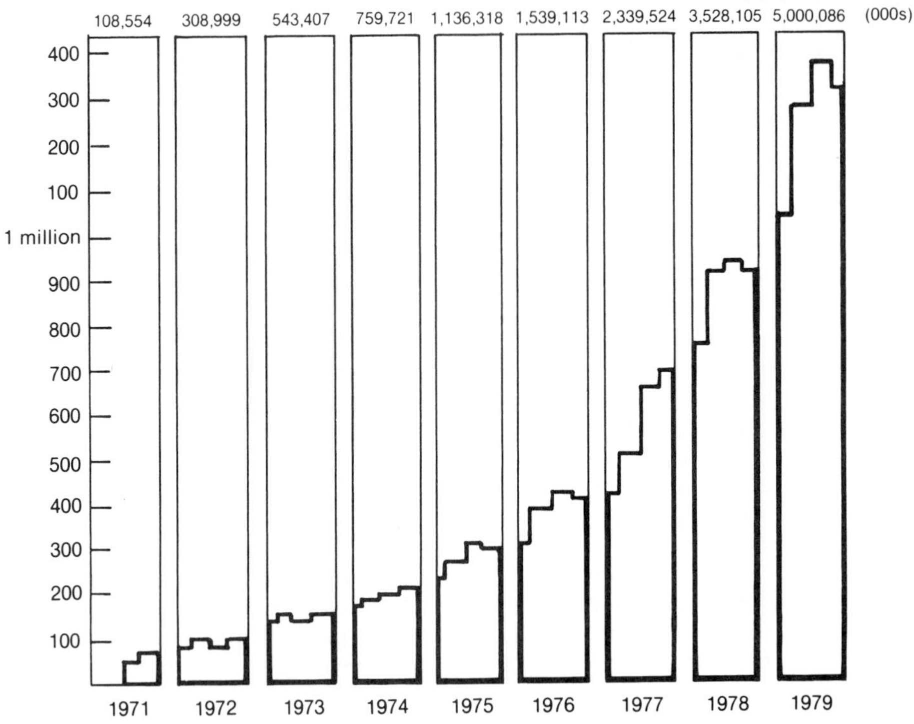

Source: Southwest Airlines Boarding Reports.

7 Between 1972 and 1979, the number of passengers carried grew at an annual rate of 48.9 percent. The reason for this growth, according to Southwest's management, was that they offered a good product in a receptive market at a fair price that the average person could afford.

8 In late 1978, Southwest Airlines served 11 major Texas cities as an intrastate carrier subject to the economic regulation of the Texas Aeronautics Commission. However, in December of that year, Southwest received their Certificate of Public Convenience and Necessity from the Civil Aeronautics Board, providing them the authority to extend their service beyond Texas. The first route outside Texas was to New Orleans almost immediately, and routes were added to Oklahoma City on April 1, to Tulsa on April 2, and to Albuquerque on April 3, 1980.

The Market

9 1979 was a year of considerable change within the airline industry. Deregulation had precipitated many fare reduction programs; however by the end of the year, the fuel crisis had seemingly reversed this policy, and fares had increased once again.

Exhibit 2

Southwest Airlines financial statements

Consolidated Balance Sheet
For the Years Ended March 31
($000)

Assets	*1980*	*1979*
Current:		
Cash and commercial paper	$ 8,936	$ 8,374
Accounts receivable	11,678	5,447
Other	1,590	1,058
Total current assets	22,204	14,879
Flight and ground equipment, at cost less reserves	169,507	112,763
Other noncurrent assets	877	366
Total assets	$192,588	$128,008
Liabilities and Net Worth		
Liabilities:		
Current:		
Accounts payable and accrued liabilities	$ 10,615	$ 6,287
Current maturities of long-term debt	4,720	1,750
Total current liabilities	15,335	8,037
Long-term debt less current maturities	98,487	63,250
Deferred federal income tax	14,186	10,398
Deferred other	942	387
Total liabilities	128,950	82,072
Net worth:		
Common stock and paid-in capital	15,828	14,448
Retained earings	47,810	31,488
Total net worth	63,638	45,936
Total liabilities and net worth	$192,588	$128,008
Share data:		
Common stock issued and outstanding (Note A) (000s)	4,567	4,500
Book value per share	$ 13.94	$ 10.21

Consolidated Statement of Income
Three Months Ended March 31
($000)

	1980	*1979*
Operating revenues:		
Passenger	$38,878	$24,732
Package express	1,116	799
Other	192	146
Total operating revenues	40,186	25,677
Operating expenses:		
Flight operations excluding fuel	3,470	2,453
Fuel and oil	12,631	5,286
Maintenance	2,383	1,521
Passenger services	1,654	1,173
Terminal operations	4,485	3,126
Promotion and sales	1,808	1,479
Insurance, taxes, and administrative	2,662	1,895
Depreciation	2,638	1,858
Employee profit sharing expense	923	688
Total operating expenses	32,654	19,479
Total operating income	7,532	6,198
Nonoperating expense (income):		
Interest and other income	(1,020)	(40)
Interest expense	2,459	1,813
	1,439	1,773
Income before federal income tax	6,093	4,425
Provision for federal income tax	1,784	1,097
Net income	$ 4,309	$ 3,328
Weighted average common and common equivalent shares outstanding (Note A) (000s)	4,544	4,500
Net income per share	$ .95	$ .74

Comparative Operating Statistics
Three Months Ended March 31

	1980	*1979*
Number of flights	18,833	15,935
Passengers carried	1,189,745	1,038,657
Passenger miles flown (000)	383,773	317,806
Passenger load factor	63.9%	67.9%
Operating revenues per flight	$2,134	$1,611
Operating expenses per flight	1,734	1,222
Operating income per flight	$ 400	$ 389

Note A: All share data adjusted to reflect the effect of the 3-for-2 stock split on February 23, 1979.

Basis of Presentation—The consolidated financial statements include the accounts of the Company and its wholly owned subsidiary Midway (Southwest) Airway Co. All significant intercompany accounts or transactions have been eliminated in consolidation. Certain reclassifications of amounts previously reported in the financial statements at March 31, 1979, have been made to conform to the presentation at March 31, 1980.

Exhibit 3

Southwest Airlines new markets

Oklahoma City, the capital of Oklahoma, is the largest municipality in the state with a population of 368,164 (1970 census). Located in Central Oklahoma on the North Canadian River, the city represents the state's financial, commercial, and industrial center built on rich oil and gas lands. Its industry includes meat packing, electronic components, production of transportation equipment, and oil field supplies. A frequent convention center, it has also grown into an aeronautical complex, housing Federal Aviation Administration facilities and Tinker Air Force Base. Additionally, a variety of tourist attractions such as the National Cowboy Hall of Fame and the Western Heritage Center are located in Oklahoma City, approximately 181 air miles from Dallas.

Tulsa, Oklahoma, a city of 330,350 (1970 census), has been dubbed "The Oil Capital of the World and is the western-most inland water port in the United States. Next to oil, aviation and aerospace industries are the next largest employers. A beautiful city of parks and old homes, Tulsa is also the home of the University of Tulsa and Oral Roberts University. Located at the base of the Ozark Mountains, the city is surrounded by lakes, and is a water sports haven. Tulsa is approximately 237 air miles from Dallas.

Albuquerque, New Mexico is the largest city in New Mexico with a population of 243,751 (1979 census). Located in North-Central New Mexico on the Upper Rio Grande, it is a fast-growing center of trade, small industry, federal agencies, and a famous health resort. Following World War II, growth accelerated rapidly due primarily to Sandia Corporation's nuclear weapons laboratory and Kirtland Air Force Base, a nuclear effects research laboratory and satellite tracking station. Albuquerque's manufacturing industry includes brick and tile, wood products, Indian jewelry, clothing, and business machines. Additionally, several railroad shops, lumber mills, and food processing plants are located there, as well as the University of New Mexico. Albuquerque is approximately 580 air miles from Dallas.

10 Fuel costs in 1978 averaged 37 cents per gallon, while 1979 saw an increase to 80 cents per gallon by the year's end. Southwest Airlines' management projected that fuel costs would exceed $1 per gallon in 1980, representing 40 percent of their budget for operating costs.

11 The deregulation trend, however, afforded Southwest the opportunity to expand service into new markets, and their business philosophy pointed to three cities with apparent growth potential. The Oklahoma City, Tulsa, and Albuquerque markets are described briefly in Exhibit 3. It was felt that expanding air service to these cities from their Dallas headquarters offered a profitable strategy to capitalize on the regulatory changes. Exhibit 4 illustrates the relative location of these new markets.

Marketing Research

12 The potential for expanding service appeared profitable given the trends evident in executive class boardings (see Exhibit 5), total passenger boardings (see Exhibit 6), the 1979 load factors (see Exhibit 7), and the projected growth (see Exhibit 8). To supplement these data, however, a research project was conducted in the fall of 1979. A random, systemwide survey of 7,900 Southwest Airlines' passengers was conducted on board flights to identify the frequency of flying and the attributes deemed important by these passengers.

13 Each respondent was asked how many round-trip flights he had taken on Southwest

Exhibit 4

Southwest Airlines air miles between new markets

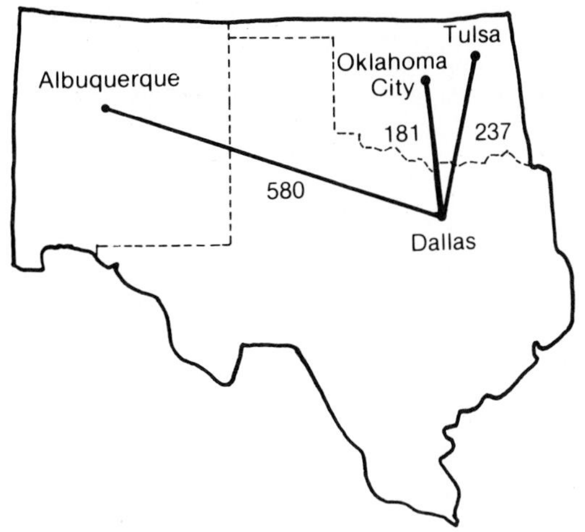

Exhibit 5

Southwest Airlines executive class boardings, 1979

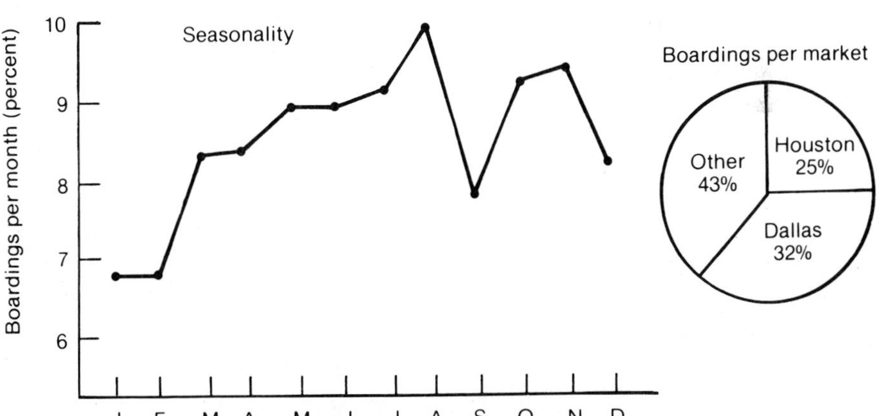

Exhibit 6

Southwest Airlines total passenger boardings, 1979

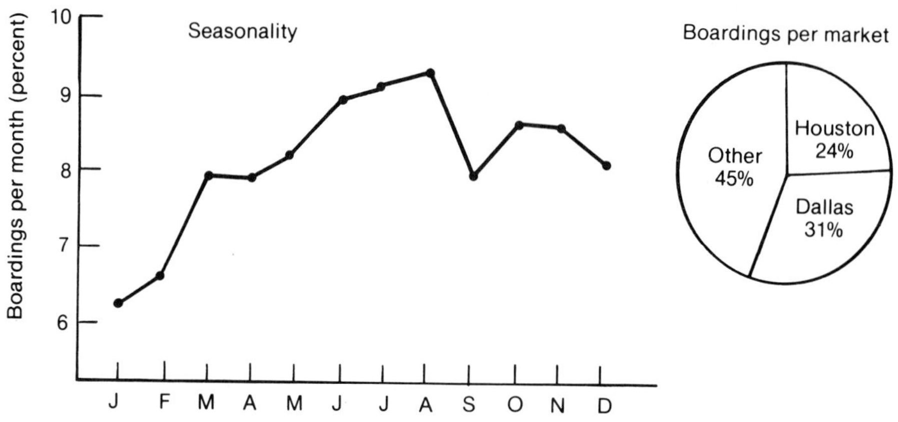

Exhibit 7

Southwest Airlines 1979 load factors

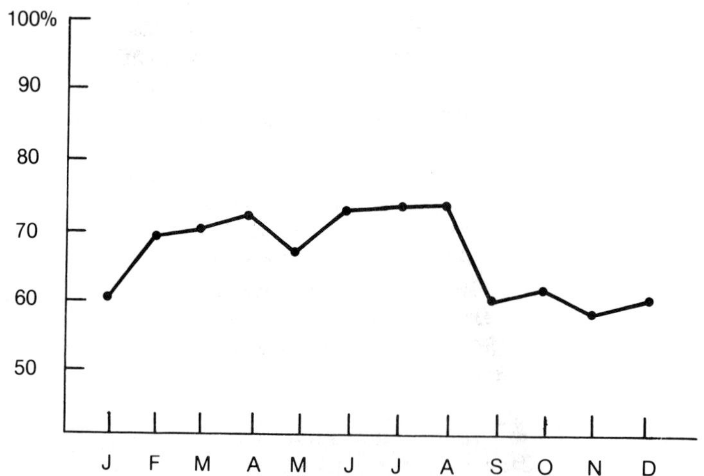

Exhibit 8

Southwest Airlines 1980 forecast

			Increase	
	1979	*1980*	*Number*	*Percent*
Total passenger boardings	5,000,000	7,000,000	2,000,000	40
Total trips	76,000	105,000	29,000	38
Available seat miles	2,500,000,000	3,500,000,000	1,000,000,000	40
Revenue passenger miles	1,500,000,000	2,500,000,000	1,000,000,000	67

during the past year. The results (shown below) indicated that 18.7 percent of the respondents accounted for 55 percent of the total trips.

No. of flights	*Percent of respondents*	*Percent of trips*
1–2	22.9%	3%
3–6	29.0	11
7–12	16.7	13
13–20	12.7	18
21–40	10.9	28
41+	7.8	27
	100.0%	100%

14 Respondents were also asked to evaluate various airline attributes in terms of importance, using a four-point rating scale (4 = very important; 1 = not important at all). As shown below, departing on time of schedule was rated as the most important attribute by the majority of those surveyed.

Attribute	*Rank*	*Percent of respondents rating important*
On-time departure	1	98.61
Frequency of scheduled departures	2	97.86
Friendly ground personnel	3	97.12
Convenient departure times	4	96.99
Courteous hostesses	5	95.51
Baggage handling	6	93.01
Lower fares	7	91.05

15 After assessing what passengers generally wanted in air service, respondents were also asked to indicate their particular likes and dislikes concerning Southwest Airlines. Low fares was the highest ranked positive attribute (see below).

Attribute	*Rank*
Low fares	1
Convenient airports	2
Pleasant hostesses	3
Convenient (in general)	4
On-time departure	5
Frequency of scheduled departures	6
Prompt and efficient service	7

16 In another independent survey, *Texas Business* polled their subscribers concerning airline service. The results of this survey coincidentally appeared in their February 1980 issue, just as Southwest Airlines was granted their three new interstate routes. The results (shown below) indicated Southwest was rated as "excellent" or "good" by over 90 percent of those 795 respondents.

	Meals	*Ticketing performance*	*Luggage handling*	*Hospitality*	*Overall performance*
Southwest	*	1	1	1	1
American	2	2	3	2	3
Delta	3	3	2	3	2
Continental	1	4	4	4	4
Braniff	4	7	7	6	7
Eastern	5	5	5	5	5
Texas Int'l.	6	6	5	7	6

* No meal service.
Source: Texas Business, February 1980.

Marketing Strategy

17 Besides maintaining a consistent growth pattern in previously established routes, Southwest Airlines management's highest priority in 1980 was the introduction of the new routes to Oklahoma City, Tulsa, and Albuquerque on April 1, 2, and 3 respectively. Service from Dallas' Love Field to these new markets was established as follows.

Market	*Schedule*
Oklahoma City	7 round-trips daily
Tulsa	7 round-trips daily
Albuquerque	4–5 round-trips daily

18 Passengers arriving from these cities to Dallas' Love Field could connect with flights to the rest of the Southwest Airlines' system from Love Field. Likewise, passengers from other destinations could travel to these new cities through a connection at Love Field. However, Southwest did not plan to have any direct flights from the new cities

Exhibit 9

Southwest Airlines 1978 origins and destinations report

From Oklahoma city	
150,000	Dallas/Ft. Worth
115,000	Houston
30,000	New Orleans
26,000	San Antonio
13,000	Midland/Odessa
12,000	Austin
10,000	El Paso
27,000	N/A
383,000	
From Tulsa	
160,000	Dallas/Ft. Worth
150,000	Houston
34,000	New Orleans
15,000	San Antonio
13,000	Midland/Odessa
9,000	Austin
3,000	Rio Grande Valley
29,000	N/A
413,000	
From Albuquerque	
108,000	Dallas/Ft. Worth
50,000	El Paso
40,000	Houston
20,000	San Antonio
11,000	New Orleans
11,000	Midland/Odessa
10,000	Lubbock
24,000	N/A
274,000	

to other Southwest Airlines' markets until passenger load factors to Dallas' Love Field were deemed successful.

19 To assist in the planning and development of these new routes. Southwest obtained a traffic history analysis of the 1978 origins and destinations (O&D) from each of the new markets. Dallas/Ft. Worth was the O&D leader from each of the new cities, with Houston ranking a strong second (particularly from Tulsa and Oklahoma City). The latter was hypothesized to be the result of petroleum-related industry traffic. Albuquerque, was marked not only by an increasingly growing business community (particularly in electronics) but also as a pleasure travel market. The New Mexico area was becoming a very popular ski market to Texans. Exhibit 9 illustrates the 1978 O&D's from each new market.

Advertising Strategy

20 The introduction of the new routes was supported by a heavy radio and newspaper advertising campaign created by the Bloom Agency, Southwest's advertising agency

Exhibit 10

Southwest Airlines print advertisement

THANKS TO YOU, WE'RE STILL IN LOVE.

On February 15, 1980, a compromise bill authorizing limited interstate service from Love Field was signed into law. The bill permits Southwest Airlines to use Love Field both for flights within Texas and to states bordering Texas. It also signals the end of a long and heated controversy over Love Field's use as a satellite airport.

We at Southwest have held fast in the belief that Love Field represents a valuable service to our passengers, both for intrastate and interstate travel. And hundreds of thousands of Texans feel the same way. The strength of those convictions was demonstrated when Love Field was threatened by a bill proposing total elimination of all interstate flights from Love.

Last November when the contents of that proposed bill became public, supporters of Southwest and of Love Field made their feelings known in editorials, letters, mailgrams, and over 160,000 signatures on petitions circulated by Southwest. One particularly heartwarming show of support was the response to our "Now is the time to fight for Love" ad asking for endorsement in the form of a mail-in coupon. We ran that ad only one time and received an overwhelming response of over 16,000 coupons.

These massive demonstrations of support by citizens throughout the state helped convince the U.S. Congress that Southwest Airlines and Love Field do indeed provide a valuable service to Texans.

The generous support of our passengers and friends was particularly meaningful to all of us here at Southwest. Not only because it aided in a compromise bill which permits our continued growth, but also because it shows that the service we provide is important to you. And we're reaffirming our service commitment by opening flights to Oklahoma City, Tulsa and Albuquerque in April.

In the meantime, we hope you'll accept a less tangible display of gratitude in the form of one simple statement: thank you.

Herbert D. Kelleher
Chairman of the Board

Howard D. Putnam
President and Chief Executive Officer

SOUTHWEST AIRLINES

of record. Two weeks before the inaugural flights, the campaign broke with small "teaser" advertisements in the new market newspapers. The advertisements contained headlines such as "Here Comes Love, Southwest Style" and listed a phone number to make reservations.

20 That same week also began 60-second radio spots, running primarily in the morning and late afternoon, designed to reach the businessman during drive time. It was felt by both Southwest's marketing team and the agency that businessmen represented the heaviest travelers and the appropriate target audience for these messages.

21 The week before the initial flights, the newspaper advertisements were stepped up to twice daily, and the radio schedule was doubled. Nearly every radio station in the new markets was running Southwest Airlines' spots. On Monday, March 31, just days before the inaugural flights, full-page advertisements appeared in addition to the teaser newspaper advertisements in each of the local markets.

22 Monday also marked the posting of 30 sheet outdoor posters with messages such as "Tightwads Rejoice" and "Big D, Little $" on the major arterials throughout the new market cities. The full-page advertisements ran once daily through each inaugural flight, and radio stations continued to broadcast "That's Love, Southwest Style." Exhibit 10 illustrates another print advertisement which appeared in *Southwest,* their in-flight publication.

23 On the day of each inaugural flight, Howard Putnam (President of Southwest Airlines) joined Tom Volz and Camille Keith to welcome new passengers personally, and later dignitaries at banquets held after each new route opening. Billboards proclaimed each city's welcome to Southwest, and four-color, double-truck newspaper advertisements announced that air service had officially begun.

24 The advertising blitz in those first three weeks was designed to reach approximately 90 percent of the households in each new market, and the combination of newspaper, radio, and outdoor advertising was meant to add breadth to the media coverage. Although no television or magazine advertising was conducted during this period, a number of news stories appeared, reflecting Southwest's public relations releases.

Effectiveness Research

25 While Southwest regularly conducts on-board passenger surveys, the occasion of these route extensions prompted them to supplement their research program. On-board surveys were administered randomly by flight attendants to new market customers one week after the expansion of service to garner some general feedback on how passengers in the new markets had heard about Southwest and the new routes. Further, there was some feeling at Southwest that the radio buy had been too wide, and they wanted to see if that was correct.

26 The results of the three surveys conducted by Southwest (see Exhibits 11, 12, and 13) were somewhat confusing to Ms. Keith as she reviewed them, along with a variety of other information, in preparation for her meeting the next morning. For example, how could television have ranked so highly in advertising recall when no television advertising had run? What explanations could be offered for the differential results obtained between the new market cities? What were the managerial implications of the survey results, and what action was next appropriate? Was more research needed? These were the types of questions which were bound to come up in the meeting, and she knew she had less than 24 hours to prepare the answers.

Exhibit 11

Southwest Airlines advertising recall study: Oklahoma City service

1. Where do you recall seeing or hearing the Southwest Airlines advertising of the new route service?

Newspaper	145	Billboard	29	Other	14
Radio	92	Magazine	16		
TV	43	Don't know	24		

2. In which newspaper(s) did you see this advertising?

Ft. Worth Star Telegram	6	*Daily Oklahoman*	69
Dallas Morning News	53	*Oklahoma Journal*	11
Dallas Times Herald	40	Other	12

3. On which radio station(s) do you recall hearing this advertising?

KBYE, Oklahoma	0	KXXY, Oklahoma	1	KNTU, Texas	0	Other	4
KEBC, Oklahoma	21	KZUE, Oklahoma	5	KOAX, Texas	3		
KFNB, Oklahoma	0	WKY, Oklahoma	5	KRLD, Texas	17		
KOCY, Oklahoma	7	KAAM, Texas	1	KVIL, Texas	9		
KOFM, Oklahoma	7	KBOX, Texas	3	WFAA, Texas	5		
KOMA, Oklahoma	7	KFJZ, Texas	2	WRR, Texas	2		
KTOK, Oklahoma	13	KLIF, Texas	8	KNUS, Texas	4		

4. On which television station(s) do you recall seeing this advertising?

KOCO, (Ch. 5) Oklahoma	19	KERA, (Ch. 13) Texas	3
KTVY, (Ch. 4) Oklahoma	15	KTVT, (Ch. 11) Texas	2
KWTV, (Ch. 9) Oklahoma	4	KXAS, (Ch. 5) Texas	6
KDFW, (Ch. 4) Texas	8	WFAA, (Ch. 8) Texas	11

5. Do you recall seeing or hearing NEWS coverage about the new routes? Where?

Newspapers	63	TV	35
Radio	43	Magazine	6

6. Did you hear about the new route service from a travel agency?

Yes	29
No	215

7. What in the advertising attracted you?

Convenience of SWA	132	Friendly service	59
Low fares	140	Close in airports	124
High frequency	78		

8. What is your occupation?

Professional/technical	118	Service workers	2
Managers/administrators	107	Student	5
Sales workers	37	Retired	3
Clerical workers	3	Unemployed	5
Craftsmen/foremen	1	No answer	1
Operatives	0		

9. Into which of the following age categories do you fall?

18–24	18	35–44	90	55–64	26
25–34	78	45–54	57	65 over	8

10. Into which of the following categories does your total yearly household income fall?

$10,000 and under	5	$20,000–$24,999	16
$10,000–$14,999	9	$25,000 over	210
$15,000–$19,999	57	No answer	26

11. How frequently do you fly?

Once a week or more	76
Two or three times a month	129
Seldom	73

Exhibit 12

Southwest Airlines advertising recall study: Tulsa service

1. Where do you recall seeing or hearing the southwest Airlines advertising of the new route service?

Newspaper	131	Billboard	40	Other	17
Radio	90	Magazine	16		
TV	51	Don't know	26		

2. In which newspaper(s) did you see this advertising:

Ft. Worth Star Telegram	8	*Tulsa Tribune*	53
Dallas Morning News	64	*Tulsa World*	82
Dallas Times Herald	32	Other	21

3. On which radio station(s) do you recall hearing this advertising?

KAKC, Oklahoma	7	KVOO, Oklahoma	13	KOAX, Texas	4
KCFO, Oklahoma	1	KXXO, Oklahoma	2	KRLD, Texas	10
KELI, Oklahoma	8	KAAM, Oklahoma	2	KVIL, Texas	8
KFMJ, Oklahoma	0	KBOK, Texas	7	WFAA, Texas	8
KMOD, Oklahoma	17	KFJZ, Texas	4	WRR, Texas	0
KRMG, Oklahoma	33	KLIF, Texas	2	KNUS, Texas	7
KTOW, Oklahoma	2	KNTU, Texas	1	Other	2

4. On which television station(s) do you recall seeing this advertising?

KOTV, (Ch. 6) Oklahoma	17	KERA, (Ch. 13) Texas	4
KTEW, (Ch. 2) Oklahoma	18	KTVT, (Ch. 11) Texas	5
KTUL, (Ch. 8) Oklahoma	21	KXAS, (Ch. 5) Texas	5
KDFW, (Ch. 4) Texas	14	WFAA, (Ch. 8) Texas	16

5. do you recall seeing or hearing NEWS coverage about the new routes? Where?

Newspapers	106	TV	58
Radio	56	Magazine	9

6. Did you hear about the new route service from a travel agency?

Yes	49
No	242

7. What in the advertising attracted you?

Convenience of SWA	127	Friendly service	82
Low fares	206	Close in airports	141
High frequency	84		

8. What is your occupation?

Professional/technical	112	Service workers	3
Managers/administrators	105	Student	4
Sales workers	49	Retired	6
Clerical workers	8	Unemployed	7
Craftsmen/foremen	4	No answer	7
Operatives	2		

9. Into which of the following age categories do you fall?

18–24	6	35–44	52	55–64	13
25–34	61	45–54	46	65 over	3

10. Into which of the following categories does your total yearly household income fall?

$10,000 and under	10	$20,000–$24,999	35
$10,000–$14,999	11	$25,000 over	239
$15,000–$19,999	13	No answer	13

11. How frequently do you fly?

Once a week or more	96
Two or three times a month	143
Seldom	94

Exhibit 13

Southwest Airlines advertising recall study: Albuquerque service

1. Where do you recall seeing or hearing the Southwest Airlines advertising of the new route service?

Newspaper	104	Billboard	24	Other	18
Radio	49	Magazine	13		
TV	29	Don't know	17		

2. In which newspaper(s) did you see this advertising?

Ft. Worth Star Telegram	7	*Albuquerque Journal*	36
Dallas Morning News	45	*Albuquerque Tribune*	9
Dallas Times Herald	36	Other	5

3. On which radio station(s) do you recall hearing this advertising?

KABQ, New Mexico		KRST, New Mexico	1	KNTU, Texas	
KDQQ, New Mexico	6	KZIA, New Mexico		KOAX, Texas	5
KJOY, New Mexico	9	KZZX, New Mexico	1	KRLD, Texas	14
KKIM, New Mexico	1	KAAM, Texas		KVIL, Texas	12
KOB, New Mexico	11	KBOX, Texas	2	WFAA, Texas	4
KPAR, New Mexico		KFJZ, Texas	1	WRR, Texas	
KQED, New Mexico	1	KLIF, Texas	6	KNUS, Texas	4
KRKE, New Mexico	4			Other	4

4. On which television station(s) do you recall seeing this advertising?

KGGM, (Ch. 13) New Mexico	7	KERA, (Ch. 13) Texas	3
KMXN, (Ch. 23) New Mexico		KTVT, (Ch. 11) Texas	1
KOAT, (Ch. 7) New Mexico	10	KXAS, (Ch. 5) Texas	14
KOB, (Ch. 4) New Mexico	6	WFAA, (Ch. 8) Texas	16
KDFW (Ch. 4) Texas	12		

5. Do you recall seeing or hearing NEWS coverage about the new routes? Where?

Newspapers	44	TV	28
Radio	32	Magazine	5

6. Did you hear about the new route service from a travel agency?

Yes	16
No	130

7. What in the advertising attracted you?

Convenience of SWA	72	Friendly service	50
Low fares	116	Close in airports	60
High frequency	23		

8. What is your occupation?

Professional/technical	75	Craftsmen/foremen	0	Retired	2
Managers/administrators	58	Operatives	3	Unemployed	3
Sales workers	18	Service workers	1	No answer	2
Clerical workers	3	Student	2	Other	1

9. Into which of the following age categories do you fall?

18–24	25	35–44	97	55–64	37
25–34	96	45–54	60	65 over	9

10. Into which of the following categories does your total yearly household income fall?

$10,000 and under	3	$20,000–$24,999	13
$10,000–$14,999	9	$25,000 over	131
$15,000–$19,999	22	No answer	10

11. How frequently do you fly?

Once a week or more	41
Two or three times a month	87
Seldom	53

case 26
Note on the U.S. Lodging Industry

1 In 1947, the City Hotel, the first building constructed in the United States specifically for hotel purposes, opened in New York City. Prior to this monumental occasion, travelers were obliged to stay in houses converted into any of a variety of roadside inns. The City Hotel, a 73-room structure, quickly became the focal point for all social activities in New York, a growing town of 30,000. Not to be outdone, the cities of Boston, Baltimore, and Philadelphia soon followed New York with their own lavish hotels.

2 From the late 1700s to Ellsworth M. Statler's 1907 sales promotion (A Room and a Bath for a Dollar and a Half), the lodging industry has come a very long way.

3 By early 1983, the industry boasted some amazing statistics (see Exhibit 1). From its modest beginnings about 200 years ago, it now includes some 56,410 establishments providing over 2.6 million rooms per day and employing over 1.2 million people. Almost 2 million rooms are less than 20 years old, and over 850,000 have been added since 1973. During the past 25 years, gross annual income for all U.S. lodging establishments has risen from under $3 billion to over $30 billion for 1983.

4 On a worldwide basis, the figures are even more staggering. Futurists predict that by the end of the century, as larger numbers of people pursue business and personal travel, the travel industry will have become the world's largest. Indeed, that may happen much sooner. "Tourism is second only to oil in total world trade receipts," says Lord Hirshfield, president of Laventhal & Horwath International. The U.S. tourism industry, the second largest U.S. retail industry, produced $191 billion in sales or 6 percent of the U.S. gross national product (GNP) in 1982 and accounts for 30 percent of the worldwide tourist industry. In 1980, 11 out of the 20 largest hotel organizations were U.S. companies.

Competitive Structure of the Industry

5 Back in the 50s and 60s, it was said that all the average hotel operator had to do was unlock the front door in the morning and make his bank deposit at night. As the nation's gas guzzlers took to the roads, developers discovered that even a simple roadside motel could be the next-best thing to a private mint. Unencumbered by long-

---

This revised edition of an earlier version of the lodging industry note was prepared by Richard Robinson, University of South Carolina; Tom Van Dyke, University of South Carolina; and Tim Mescon, University of Miami.

Exhibit 1

The commercial lodging industry (sic 7011), 1982

	Amount (1982)	*Annual increase since 1960*
Total revenue ($ millions):		
Current (1982) dollars	$ 29,300	9.5%
Current (1972) dollars*	11,563	3.1
Average daily:		
Rooms available	2,450,500.0	1.9
Total employment (peak)	1,181,900.0	3.4
Hours worked (millions)	1,743.6	2.3

* 1982 revenue expressed in terms of 1972 dollars.
Source: Laventhol and Horwath, CPAs.

term leases, hotel owners could raise the rates as often as they could get away with it. And the franchise field was wide open. Firms like Holiday Inns, Hilton, and Ramada spread their properties far and wide.

6 Times have changed. Roadside properties never really recovered from the oil woes of 1973. Hotel chain executives have turned to more-profitable locations that draw customers from more than one source, such as industrial parks, airports, and selected downtown locations, to minimize development risks. More companies are competing for fewer prime locations. At the same time, the larger companies are splitting their operations to increase market share. Holiday Inns, for example, is considering plans for budget, luxury, all-suite, and resort divisions. Marketing, once neglected, has become all-important, and competition among chains is keen. The risks are great, but some analysts still feel that the returns can be better than average if you're in the right place at the right time.[1]

Industry Capacity and Demand

7 There have been two major periods of growth in the number of guest rooms available in the United States. The first occurred in the years 1920–29 when nearly 500,000 rooms were added, increasing the available capacity to over 1.5 million guest rooms. The second period began in the late 1950s and, except for the years 1975–78 following the oil crisis, that growth has continued to over 2.6 million rooms available to U.S. lodging customers.

8 But the increase in capacity has not been matched by similar increases in demand (see Exhibit 2). Through July 1983, the lodging industry had completed 42 consecutive months of declining occupancy rates while adding rooms at an unprecedented rate.

[1] John Gamrecki, "Hotel/Motel: Lodging's Investment Potential," *Fact,* January 1984, p. 35. See Appendix A for a description of the differences between a service business and a manufacturing business.

Exhibit 2

Growth in capacity versus demand

	Average annual increase	
	Capacity	*Demand*
1960–1969	0.4%	0.7%
1970–1979	0.9	2.0
1980–1982	2.9	0.7

Note: CAPACITY = Number of rooms available daily. DEMAND = Number of rooms occupied daily.
Source: Laventhol and Horwath, CPAs.

Between 1969 and 1978, the industry added about 25,000 rooms a year, and since 1978, that rate has quadrupled to about 110,000 new rooms a year. Announced expansions shown in Exhibit 3 represent approximately 175,000 new rooms out of estimates ranging from 150,000 to 343,000 to be built in 1984.

9 Growth in demand (occupancy) has clearly not kept pace with growth in supply (number of rooms). Exhibit 4 shows that the nationwide occupancy trend has steadily declined since the late 1970s. The 1982 occupancy level was the industry's lowest since 1958. Exhibit 5 suggests that the occupancy decline was generally felt throughout almost every category and location of the industry.

10 This steady decline in occupancy has led to an increased reluctance to raise room rates, even where costs are increasing. As Exhibit 6 shows, room rates that typically increased over 15 percent in the late 1970s were increased by less than 4 percent in 1983. Some competitors are beginning to consider couponing and/or price cutting to build occupancy levels. Laventhol and Horwath, the lodging industry accounting firm, warns that substantial occupancy increases are necesssary when price-cutting tactics are used.

Participants and Segments

11 At least eight basic characteristics promote competition in an industry: (1) numerous competitors, (2) competitors of roughly equal size and power, (3) slow industry growth (causes fights to increase market share), (4) lack of differentiation in service, (5) high fixed costs, (6) perishability of the product, (7) high exit barriers, and (8) diverse rivals in strategies, origins, and personalities. The lodging industry exhibits most of these characteristics.

12 Exhibit 7 shows the top 25 U.S. lodging chains in 1977 and 1982. The number of competitors has rapidly increased, and they are becoming more equal in size. That the growth of the industry is projected to slow to 2 percent a year for the mid-1980s is evident by the growing capacity/occupancy gap. The basic service all lodging institutions offer is the rental of a room, though current organizations have ingeniously differentiated this basic concept, each seeking customers through numerous strategies.

Exhibit 3

Announced plans for 1984

Hotel or Motel	*Add properties*	*Drop properties*
Econo Lodges of America	80–110	
Super 8	50	
Thrifty Scot Motel	10	
Comfort Inns	60 30–40% will be new property	
Best Value Inns/Superior Motels	100	
Budget Host Inns	120	
Sundowner Motor Inns	150	
Magic Key Inns	45–50	
Friendship Inns International	48	
Travelodge	50 90% will be new	
Viscount	50	
Rodeway Inn International	45	12–15
Days Inn	4	
Quality Inn	55	
Quality Royales	10	
Ramada Inns, Inc.	60	
Ramada Hotels	30	
Ramada Renaissance	10	
Sheraton	24	10
Hilton	12–15	
Holiday Inns	35	
Holiday Inn Crowne Plaza	10	
Scottish Inn	30	
Red Carpet	30	
Master Host	17	
Best Western International	160	
Granada Royale Hometels	12	
Brock Residence Inns	250	
Quality Choice Suite	80	
Guest House Suites	3–5	
Embassy Suites Holiday Inn	4	

Sources: Joe Jancsarek, *"The Franchise Market, Great Choices from the Middle and Upscale Chains,"* Terry Breen, *"The Budget Chains,"* and Margaret Opsata, "The All-Suite Chains," *Hotel and Motel Management,* September 1983.

The average cost per room in buying a previously owned motel was $17,381 in 1982, while the per-room cost was as high as $275,000 for newly built, downtown luxury hotels. Traditionally, opportunities for converting a hotel or motel into another operation have been limited (high exit barriers). The service a hotel offers is very perishable—a room to use for 24 hours. And the loss of room sales for one period cannot be recovered because the hotel has only a fixed number of rooms to rent.

13 The lodging industry has evolved into three segments: budget, midprice, and upscale. A fourth type, suite hotels, has recently been introduced, and this segment will probably compete with upscale and midprice segments. The following information highlights the basic industry segmentation by the end of 1982:

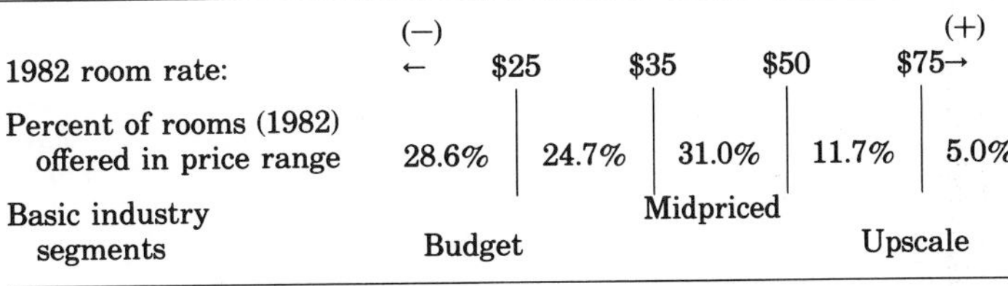

(–)
(+)
1982 room rate:
← $25
$35
$50
$75→
Percent of rooms (1982) offered in price range
28.6%
24.7%
31.0%
11.7%
5.0%
Basic industry segments
Budget
Midpriced
Upscale

Laventhol and Horwath, CPAs, 1982.

14 The budget lodging segment caters to clientele who do not desire the extras offered by most hotels and motels—restaurant, lounge, lobby areas, and meeting and convention services. Each chain may vary the cost-saving techniques it employs, but overall, each strategy is designed with a price-conscious guest in mind.

15 La Quinta is an example of a budget hotel. La Quinta Motor Inns, Inc., develops, owns, and operates motor inns designed primarily to serve business travelers. Its marketing concept is to provide guests with quality, comfortable accommodations, and essential services in convenient locations at a reasonable price. By offering only services and facilities most preferred by the business traveler and eliminating such nonessentials as banquet facilities, extensive public areas, and large meeting rooms, La Quinta can offer an alternative to the higher-priced convention or resort-oriented lodging establishments.

16 La Quinta Motor Inns are generally located on major traffic arteries near business districts, airports, medical complexes, universities, and industrial parks. Typically, a motor inn has from 106 to 138 rooms and features 24-hour front-desk and message service, color television with AM-FM radio, same-day laundry service, swimming pool, and food service provided by a free-standing restaurant operated by a national or regional chain. Other competitors in the budget segment include such firms as Days Inns, Motor 6, Red Roof Inns, Thrifty Scot, Comfort Inns, and Econo Lodges (see Exhibit

Exhibit 4

Percentage of occupancy, 1962–1981

Year	*A*	*B*	*C*
1962	64.2%	71.5%	67.5%
1967	68.0	74.7	73.1
1972	63.2	70.2	68.2
1977	69.8	71.1	70.2
1978	72.7	72.8	72.7
1979	73.2	71.8	72.8
1980	69.9	68.8	69.5
1981	67.2	68.4	67.6
1982	65.5	63.9	64.8

A—Downtown and resort hotels.
B—Roadside motels.
C—Combined hotels and motels.
Source: Pannell, Kerr, Forster, *Trends in the Hotel Industry*, 1983 U.S. edition.

Exhibit 5

Occupied by selected categories

	1982 (estimated)		1983 (estimated)	
	Occupancy (percent)	*Percent change from 1981*	*Occupancy (percent)*	*Percent change from 1982*
Total U.S.A.	64.6%	−4.6%	65.4%	−1.4%
Affiliation:				
Chain	65.8	−4.4	66.1	−1.8
Independent	60.1	−4.9	62.7	0.5
Location:				
Center city	62.7	−4.9	62.4	−1.9
Suburban	64.4	−6.5	63.5	−5.4
Highway	65.4	−3.7	66.3	0.3
Airport	68.3	−4.2	68.8	−2.4
Resort	64.9	−2.4	71.0	2.7
Size:				
Under 150 rooms	66.0	−5.0	63.5	−3.8
150 to 299 rooms	63.6	−4.5	65.7	−1.8
300 to 600 rooms	63.6	−5.6	63.8	−2.7
Over 600 rooms	65.6	−2.5	68.8	3.6
Region:				
Northeast	67.9	−4.0	66.1	0.6
Southeast	64.0	−2.6	75.1	9.0
North Central	60.0	−4.3	58.2	0.2
South Central	65.0	−7.3	61.2	−12.4
West	69.3	−4.0	68.4	−1.4
City:				
Boston	68.1	−6.1	64.3	−3.3
Cleveland	50.9	−5.7	51.0	0.6
Cincinnati	59.5	2.9	56.6	—
Dallas	64.2	−5.2	61.1	−10.0
Daytona Beach	66.2	0.1	74.9	0.8
Des Moines	52.9	2.7	52.2	1.8
Detroit	63.0	−5.1	64.8	0.3
Ft. Lauderdale	61.2	−7.3	65.3	−3.8
Houston	60.8	−10.3	54.6	−18.6
Indianapolis	58.6	−2.7	59.6	−2.9
Miami	57.2	−12.1	54.5	6.4
Minneapolis	58.6	−2.5	60.1	1.7
New Orleans	70.1	−5.5	64.7	−13.0
New York City	70.8	−3.2	70.6	3.8
Orlando	69.0	5.5	88.4	25.0
Philadelphia	62.1	1.0	63.6	4.1
Pittsburgh	52.4	−11.2	58.3	−9.9
Portland	53.9	−9.6	*	*
San Antonio	67.0	−9.0	70.5	−5.6
San Diego	71.7	−2.3	76.1	3.3
St. Louis	57.2	−1.2	58.3	2.2
Tampa Bay	59.2	−3.7	70.6	0.3
Tulsa	62.4	−16.8	51.9	−17.9
Washington, D.C.	62.7	−8.5	71.1	8.2

* Not available.

Source: Laventhol and Horwath, *Trend of Business in the Lodging Industry.*

Exhibit 6

Occupancy and room rates

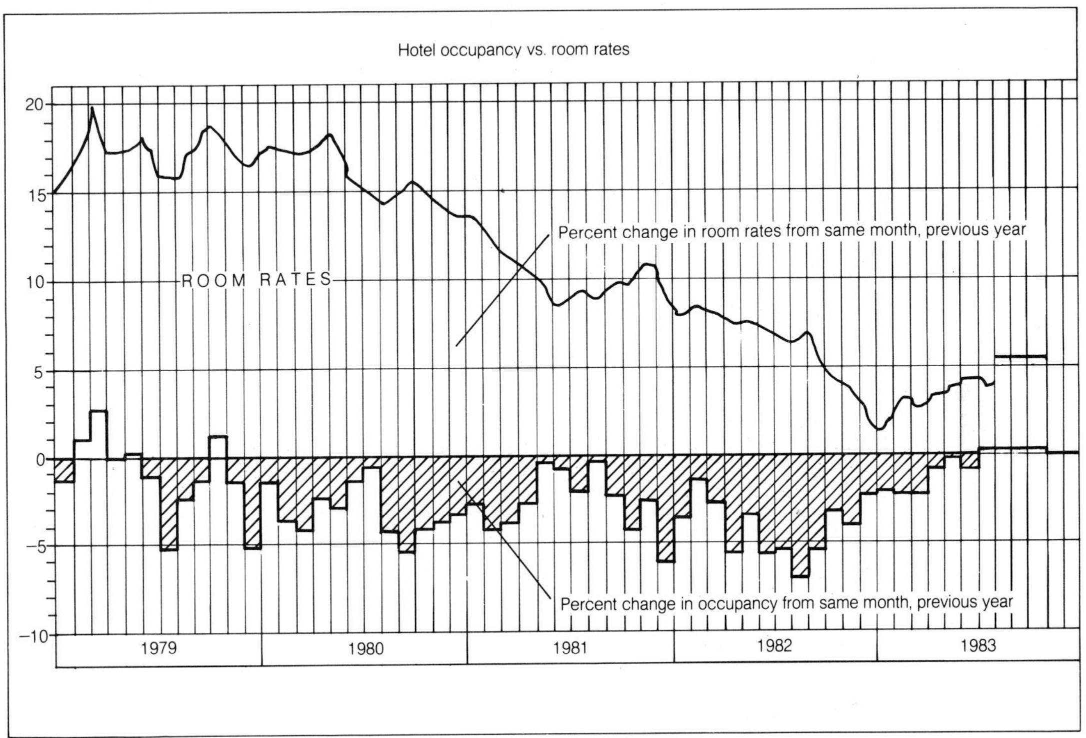

The price of rate cutting

Present occupancy level		Occupancy required to maintain current profitability when there is a room rate reduction of:			
		5%	*10%*	*15%*	*20%*
78%	....	82.2%	86.9%	82.2%	98.1%
76	....	80.1	84.7	89.8	95.6
74	....	78.0	82.5	87.5	93.1
72	....	75.9	80.2	85.1	90.0
70	....	73.8	76.0	82.7	88.1
68	....	71.7	75.8	80.4	85.6
66	....	69.6	73.5	78.0	83.0
64	....	67.5	71.3	75.6	80.5

Source: Laventhol & Horwath National Trend Reports.

Exhibit 7

Top 25 U.S. lodging chain, 1977 and 1982

Name of chain	U.S. properties			Status of properties			Average single rate	Average occupancy	Total properties U.S. and foreign	
	Number	Rooms	Company owned	Franchise or member	Management contract	Other			Number	Rooms
1982:										
Holiday Inns, Inc.	1,518	264,400	174	1,344	0	0	$41.78	69%	1,735	312,314
Best Western International	1,814	161,061	0	1,814	0	0	$48	70	2,925	219,100
Ramada Inns, Inc.	564	88,711	68	489	7	0	n.a.	n.a.	605	96,914
Sheraton Corporation	352	86,985	18	295	39	0	n.a.	n.a.	432	123,035
Hilton Hotels Corp.	239	84,661	17	188	51	0	67.15	66	239	84,661
Friendship Inns International	924	68,750	0	924	0	0	38.50	72	924	68,750
Howard Johnson Company	515	60,390	135	380	1	0	n.a.	n.a.	515	60,390
Quality Inns International	465	54,432	24	436	5	0	n.a.	n.a.	573	68,930
Marriott Corporation	109	47,155	27	25	57	0	n.a.	n.a.	118	50,495
Days Inns of America, Inc.	324	45,757	130	194	0	0	$30	68	325	45,880
Motel 6, Inc.	346	38,119	346	0	0	0	18.71	76	346	38,119
TraveLodge International, Inc.	509	37,557	30	251	0	262	n.a.	n.a.	543	40,004
Hyatt Hotels Corporation	70	37,500	n.a.	n.a.	n.a.	n.a.	n.a.	n.a.	70	37,500
Rodeway Inns International	147	18,139	5	147	6	0	n.a.	n.a.	152	18,600
La Quinta Motor Inns, Inc.	133	16,362	117	14	2	0	$35	71	133	16,362
Westin Hotels	23	15,132	n.a.	n.a.	n.a.	n.a.	n.a.	72	50	26,557
Magic Key Inns	374	14,052	0	377	0	0	$22	77	377	14,194
Downtowner/Passport International	85	14,000	0	85	0	0	n.a.	n.a.	85	14,000
Econo Lodges of America	185	13,460	20	166	0	0	24.68	70	186	13,500
Preferred Hotels Worldwide	30	10,510	0	30	0	0	n.a.	n.a.	54	16,375
Americana Hotel Corporation	32	10,073	28	4	0	0	n.a.	n.a.	36	11,579
Stouffer Hotels Corporation	25	10,000	12	0	13	0	n.a.	n.a.	25	10,000

Thunderbird/Red Lion Inns	51	10,000	51	0	0	0	n.a.	n.a.	51	10,000
Red Roof Inns	92	9,700	92	0	0	0	$20	80	92	9,700
Dunfey Hotels	26	9,575	19	0	9	0	62.48	66	28	10,929
1977:										
Holiday Inns, Inc.	1,527	244,316	233	1,273	13	—	$24.56	71.2%	1,724	284,306
Best Western, Inc.	1,600	127,733	—	1,600	—	—	24.71	71.0	2,155	148,823
Ramada Inns, Inc.	633	88,388	109	506	10	—	24.00	68.0	667	95,141
Friendship Inns	1,058	82,000	—	1,058	—	—	n.a.	n.a.	1,488	104,000
Budget Motels & Hotels	1,310	80,100	—	1,310	—	—	n.a.	n.a.	1,310	80,100
Sheraton Corporation	334	72,530	21	289	26	—	28.19	68.7	402	98,705
Hilton Hotels Corp.	177	64,113	18	129	30	—	37.90	70.0	177	64,113
Howard Johnson Company	525	58,246	134	391	—	—	n.a.	80	532	59,160
TIMOA, Inc.	315	46,475	—	315	—	—	n.a.	n.a.	315	46,475
Days Inns of America, Inc.	296	42,370	131	165	—	—	13.88	70.7	297	42,492
TraveLodge Int'l/Trusthouse Forte, Inc.	482	34,760	35	204	—	277*	n.a.	n.a.	516	37,240
Quality Inns	277	30,000	31	246	—	—	21.50	66.5	285	31,000
Hyatt Hotels Corp.	53	27,000	—	—	53	—	n.a.	n.a.	53	27,000
Motel 6, Inc.	242	24,090	242	—	—	—	9.45	n.a.	242	24,090
Marriott Hotels	51	20,925	35†	16	—	—	n.a.	n.a.	56	23,000
Red Carpet/Master Hosts	138	17,588	3	134	8	—	21.00	73.1	145	18,850
Rodeway Inns of America	141	17,450	—	141	—	—	20.00	70.0	145	18,000
Western Int'l Hotels	23	15,000	23†	—	—	—	n.a.	70.0	50	26,000
Hotel Systems of America	70	9,000	—	60	10	—	18.75	70.0	70	9,000
La Quinta Motor Inns, Inc.	71	8,195	56	15	—	—	17.50	90.0	71	8,195
American Travel Inns	125	7,500	—	125	—	—	n.a.	n.a.	125	7,500
Americana Hotels	12	7,270	n.a.	n.a.	n.a.	n.a.	n.a.	n.a.	12	7,270
Dunfey Family Hotels & Motor Inns	24	7,175	16	—	—	—	n.a.	n.a.	25	8,025
Radisson Hotel Corp.	19	6,990	7	—	12	—	28.42	60.0	20	7,105
Stouffer Hotels	20	6,954	9	7	4	—	35.00	72.0	20	6,954

n.a. = Not available. * Includes joint-venture properties. † Includes all corporate-managed properties, not necessarily owned by the chain.

Source: *Lodging Hospitality*.

7). Competitors in this segment have typically been regional operations like Days Inns in the east, La Quinta in Texas, and Motel 6 in the west.

17 The next segment is the midpriced hotel or motor lodge. They usually have a lobby with a public area and offer a restaurant and a lounge on the premises. Banquet and conference facilities may also be available. Midpriced lodging differs from budget lodging primarily in that it offers more service and gives more attention to customers.

18 Holiday Inns dominates this segment. Holiday Inns executives claim that "three out every four hotel customers are in this broad, midpriced segment." Ramada Inns, Sheraton, Best Western, Quality Inns, and Howard Johnsons are four chains seen as key midpriced competitors.

19 The final segment is the upscale hotel or motel which caters to status-conscious travelers. These operations usually offer more services such as doormen, valet service, bellboys, and so forth. The lobbies are usually very elaborate, and the properties usually offer elegant dining, a lounge, meeting rooms, and conference and banquet facilities. The rooms are usually more spacious and have better furniture and other amenities, such as shampoo, shower caps, fragrant soaps, and so on. The emphasis is on personalized service for all guests.

20 Hyatt Hotels, typically associated with the upscale lodging market, offer two types of lodging accommodations—the standard upscale rooms and the regency rooms. The hotels that offer regency accommodations are usually denoted by the title Hyatt Regency. Hyatt Regency properties offer both styles of accommodations but usually reserve the upper floor of the hotel for the regency club where guests are provided more services, such as a concierge, fresh flowers, and bathrobes in each room plus apples and cookies, as well as the traditional mint on the pillow at night. Hyatt growth has been exceptional in the past 10 years, tripling in size to 70 hotels in the United States and 42 hotels in foreign locations. In 1983, Hyatt was projected to reach $1.7 billion in worldwide sales.

21 Other firms traditionally focusing on this segment include Hilton, Marriott, Radisson, Dunfrey, Granada Royale, Westin, and numerous downtown or resort independents.

22 The suite segment is a new innovation in the lodging industry. The suite typically consists of a living room with sofa bed and a bedroom, each with its own television set and telephone and usually includes a kitchenette with a wet bar, range, and refrigerator. Suites do not provide bellmen, large meeting rooms, or standard room service. Some operators build restaurants and lounges with the suites and lease their management and operation to independent parties, while others choose instead to locate their properties close to other hotels and restaurants that do provide food and beverage. Because the suites have reduced the public area, they do not require as large a staff as for a typical hotel, and maintenance at a suite is usually less demanding than at a full-service hotel. Another benefit is that if the suite hotel concept does not work out, these facilities could easily be converted into condominiums or apartments.

23 Chains that exclusively catered to one segment of the lodging industry are now actively moving into other segments. By 1982, Holiday Inns had moved into the upscale and suite market with Crowne Plaza and Embassy Suite Hotels. In 1983, it acquired the (upscale) Granada Royale Hometel System (13 company-owned and 8 franchised units, each consisting of 250 suites offering one or two bedrooms and a sitting room) for $111 million. In early 1983, Holiday Inns was rumored to be ready to announce the development of a new national chain of budget hotels called Hampton Inn. Holiday

Inns previously had tried to enter the budget segment but found these properties cannibalized their regular trade. Quality Inns offers three types of facilities—Comfort Inn (budget), Quality Inns (midpriced), and Quality Royale (upscale). Hyatt offers the Hyatt and Hyatt Regency. Ramada has also followed suit by introducing Ramada Renaissance, Ramada Hotels, and Ramada Inns. Marriott has moved into midpriced market with the Marriott Courtyard.

24 Other lodging chains are trying to attract customers by urging new customer groups to patronize existing properties. Hyatt, for example, began to run advertisements emphasizing its friendly staff and a "We Wish You Were Here" slogan in mid-1982. The new $10.5 million campaign replaced ads showcasing the Chicago chain's splashy architecture. Thanks to the new ad campaign, Hyatt's occupancy rate jumped more than four percentage points to considerably higher than 70 percent. Hyatt presently is trying to broaden its clientele base. They have saturated all large U.S. cities with convention-size hotels and have to decided to build small projects in secondary cities. "We were appealing to the upper-class clientele, but we were missing out on the upper-middle sector of the market that should also be our customers," explains J. Patrick Foley, president of Hyatt Hotels. "We are trying to broaden our market base." Some industry analysts warn that Hyatt and other upscale hotel chains run the risk of diluting their reputations for quality that fueled earlier growth by trying to attract customers "a cut below" their traditional market.

25 Many analysts believe the lodging market has reached the saturation point or is nearing it very quickly, asserting the lodging industry is reaching the mature stage in its cycle. They point to the fact that many lodging firms (Holiday Inns, Howard Johnsons, and Days Inns) have begun discounting and couponing to attract customers—a move that has encouraged higher-end chains to drop their rates significantly. This has not only hurt profit margins but has also taken business from previously sound lower-end chains that suddenly found themselves offering less-elegant accommodations for the same price as the midpriced chains. The budget motels have recently initiated attempts to unite. *Hotel and Motel Management* reported in early 1983 that the nation's budget lodging chains are close to forming a trade organization to promote budget motels through advertising, market research, and public relation campaigns. The supporters of this idea include Super 8, Comfort Inns, Econo Lodges of America, Red Roof Inns, La Quinta, and Thrifty Scot.

26 The budget segment has been a profitable one as the following figures from *Business Week* (October 31, 1983) convey:

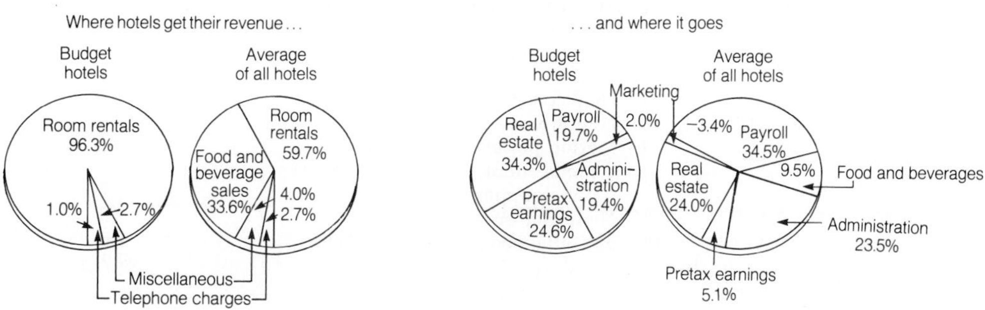

Pretax margins doubling Holiday Inns' current ones could attract the industry leader. "Holiday Inns has the resources to become a major factor in the budget category," warns Peggy P. Wilson, lodging analyst at Morgan, Keegan & Co., of Memphis. "Regionals such as Days Inns or La Quinta could start seeing a lot hotter competition." Daniel W. Daniele, an economy lodging expert at Laventhol & Horwath agrees: "The regionals are being pressed to expand their [service] areas before the big national chains move in a big way. Otherwise," says Daniele, "they'll be forced to remain just regionals."

Buyers of Lodging Services

27 Business travelers have traditionally accounted for almost 70 percent of the lodging industry's revenue. Of that 70 percent, no single entity is big enough within the business travelers to exert undue pressure on the lodging industry (see Exhibit 8). On a localized basis, however, specific business consumers may have bargaining power to encourage a lodging chain to offer lodging at reduced prices. While large national buyers don't exist, most companies or trade organizations often shop around for the best package deal for conventions and special prices for company travel.

28 Pleasure travelers are generally a very fragmented group that will offer no concentrated bargaining threat to the lodging industry. Travel agencies probably offer the most united organization in terms of purchasing pleasure travel services. But travel organizations and lodging organizations both have the same goal—to increase travel trade, with each organization complementing the other.

29 Demographic trends foretell major changes in buyer patterns which numerous analysts expect will benefit the lodging industry. By 1990, the most significant population change will be a 20 percent growth in the number of persons aged 25 to 44 (see Exhibit 9). This age group typically has spent the most on travel and lodging (over 62 percent of travel receipts in 1982). The World War II baby-boom infants have grown up and, on the whole, are better educated and more widely traveled than their parents. Since they are more comfortable traveling than their parents, they place a

Exhibit 8

Business customers (major purchasers of lodging)

Rank	*Industry*	*Percent of total*
1.	Wholesale trade	14.4%
2.	Finance, insurance, and real estate	7.2
3.	Miscellaneous professional services	7.0
4.	New construction	4.7
5.	Retail trade	3.8
6.	Health care services	3.4
7.	Food processors	3.2
8.	Motion picture production; amusement, recreation services, and commercial sports	2.7
9.	Nonprofit organizations	2.6
10.	Miscellaneous business services	2.6
		51.6%

Source: U.S. Department of Commerce.

Exhibit 9

How age mix will change

Population growth will be greatest in the 40–49 age class but impressive in the 30–39 and over-65 groups.

Age group	1980	1990	Change
Under age 20	70,525,000	73,972,000	Up 2.1%
Age 20-29	39,848,000	38,122,000	Down 4.3%
Age 30-39	31,275,000	40,175,000	Up 28.5%
Age 40-49	22,718,000	31,220,000	Up 37.4%
Age 50-64	32,885,000	32,198,000	Down 2.0%
Age 65 and over	24,927,000	29,824,000	Up 19.6%

Source: U.S. Department of Commerce.

School enrollments—a look ahead

With a surge in the kindergarten to 8th grade population, the family business is on its way back.

	1980	1990	Change
Preschool (age 3-4)	2,009,000	2,574,000*	Up 28.1%
Elementary (grades K-8)	29,796,000	33,871,000	Up 13.7%
High school	14,329,000	11,876,000	Down 17.1%
College	12,376,000	11,047,000	Down 10.7%

* Latest projection.

Changing work force

Women will have a great impact on the work force and hotel house count and consequently on hotel services.

	1970	1980	1990	Change
Big influx of women Women in civilian work force	31,520,000	44,000,000	54,300,000	Up 28% in 1980s
And nonwhites Nonwhites in civilian work force	9,197,000	12,500,000	15,600,000	Up 25% in 1980s
But slower growth among men Males in civilian work force	51,195,000	59,600,000	65,100,000	Up 9% in 1980s

Note: The proportion of women seeking work will rise from 51 percent in 1980 to 57 percent by 1990. But for men, the participation rate in the work force will fall slightly, to 76 percent—largely due to earlier retirements.

Age-group shifts, 1980–1990—projected change in population segments (based on population projection of 243.5,513,000 in 1980)

Most significant trend of the times for hotels is the growth of the middle-aged and retired markets.

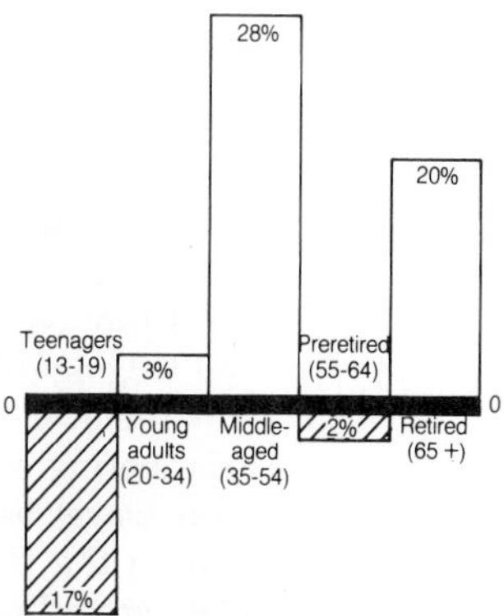

Source: *Lodging Magazine,* January 1984. Data gained from Census Bureau.

high priority on personal growth and experience outside the scope of everyday activity and regard travel as a necessity, not a luxury.

30 The 65-and-older group will increase by 20 percent by 1990 to 13 percent of the population. According to Dr. Frechtling of the U.S. Travel Data Center, "Senior citizens are becoming an increasingly affluent group tapping the resources of social security, pensions, and private savings. Also, they don't spend as much as younger families on home furnishing, appliances, and educations. Therefore, they find it easier to finance vacation trips and have more time to travel."

31 Women in the work force will increase by 23 percent to 55 million by 1990, whereas men are projected to increase by only 9 percent to 65 million. With the additional women in the work force will come an increase in two-income families, who will become an increasingly targeted market. James E. Durgin, president of Marriott's hotel division, reports that increasingly large numbers of working women, especially those with families, will be looking for vacations from both family and job responsibilities. Numerous chains anticipate that working couple getaways will prove even more popular in the future. "Due to the economy and increase of two-income families, the nature of both business and leisure trips will change" says Holiday Inns' Dan Philip. He notes, for example, both a discernible increase in business trips extended for several days for leisure and an increase in the number of spouses accompanying their husbands or wives on business trips.

32 The 1990s will bring an increase in the number of preschool and elementary school children and a decrease in the number of high school and college students. If the trend toward limiting the number of children in a family continues, some analysts feel this will translate into a resurgence of the family-vacation-type buyer.

Foreign Tourism's Growing Importance

33 In 1980, foreign tourism receipts accounted for an estimated $12 billion in U.S. export earnings, placing tourism as the fourth most important export earner in U.S. industry, exceeded only by chemicals, motor vehicles and parts, and grain and cereal preparations. The year 1980 marked the first year in which there were more tourists from overseas (8.1 million) coming to the United States than Americans visiting overseas (8 million).

34 Expenditures by foreign visitors in the United States have been growing faster than other measures of U.S. economic activity. Between 1970 and 1979, according to *Nation's Business*, these expenditures grew more than 250 percent, well ahead of the growth of the gross national product (up 141 percent) and U.S. personal consumption expenditures (up 144 percent). The majority of foreign tourism expenditures goes to food and lodging (62 percent), with travel a distant third.

35 While overseas visitors exceeded Americans going overseas in 1980, travel between neighboring countries (Canada and Mexico) kept the United States from a favorable total travel balance—22.8 million Americans abroad versus 22.2 million foreigners visiting the United States. Expenditures by foreign tourists in the United States in 1980, according to the U.S. Travel Service (USTS), were:

Mexico	$2.5 billion	West Germany	$500 million
Canada	2.4 billion	United Kingdom	470 million
Japan	775 million	France	215 million

Exhibit 10

Nationality of 1982 U.S. hotel guests

	All establishments	By area				
		North-east	South-east	North Central	South Central	West
U.S.	87.4%	89.0%	84.6%	94.3%	87.1%	79.7%
International	12.6	11.0	15.4	5.7	12.9	20.3
Total	100.0%	100.0%	100.0%	100.0%	100.0%	100.0%
Other nationalities—Ratio to total international:						
Canadian	31.8%	23.5%	32.7%	37.1%	20.4%	41.9%
Japanese	13.4	20.0	2.4	16.4	7.5	25.3
Mexican	12.5	3.0	4.1	6.5	34.3	8.7
British	8.8	11.7	14.1	7.7	5.6	5.5
South American	8.0	6.1	19.7	1.7	7.1	0.5

Source: Laventhol and Horwarth.

36 Tourists from abroad vary considerably in their travel and expenditure patterns. For example, USTS reports Canadians are strongly auto oriented and stay an average of nine days per visit, and less than 20 percent use the services of travel agencies; West Germans use travel agencies more and travel to more places, averaging 24-day visits; Japanese travel largely on all-inclusion tours, stay in first-class hotels, and frequent Hawaii, Guam, and the West Coast; Latin Americans emphasize shopping in their visits, spending about $3.7 billion each year.

37 Canada and Mexico have traditionally accounted for the largest number of foreign tourists. In 1980, Mexico overtook Canada as the leading source of tourist revenue, but by 1983, Canadians were again in the lead. This dominance was evident in every region except the South Central, where Mexican travelers were the primary source of foreign demand (see Exhibit 10). More than 1 million 1980 tourists were from Japan, which has ranked third since early 1972.

38 In 1982, Japanese replaced Mexicans as the second-largest group of international travelers to the United States, due to travel restrictions instituted by the Mexican government. U.S. hotels generally reported significant drops in the level of demand by Central and South American travelers.

39 Devaluation of the dollar in 1980, along with a lower rate of domestic inflation than that of many overseas countries, turned the United States into a vacation bargain, and expanded air routes made the United States more accessible.

40 Best Western, recognizing the bargain a 1980 devalued dollar generated for foreign tourists, led major U.S. chains in efforts to attract this growing market. They recruited over 852 new international affiliates in 18 countries, ostensibly to increase familiarity with its name. Best Western also changed its name (to Western International) and added international flavor with the familiar crown symbol.

41 J. W. Marriott, Jr., president of the Marriott Hotel chain, represented the predominant view within the industry. In a 1981 interview with *U.S. News & World Report*, Marriott was asked, "Has an influx of foreign visitors taxed hotel facilities in some key areas?" His response:

> Yes, but it's a key element in only a few cities. People coming to the United States from Europe want to see New York and they want to see Washington. If they have enough money, they may go someplace else—perhaps Disney World in Florida. Travelers coming from Asia generally go to Los Angeles, San Francisco, and Las Vegas—and maybe to Hawaii. But that's about the extent of it. Only a half-dozen cities are affected to any extent by pressures from overseas visitors.

Sensitivity to currency exchange rates may also be behind Marriott's cautious approach. Simply stated, a rise in the value of the dollar can send Americans abroad and slow the foreign traveler flow to the United States. By 1983, American citizens were taking advantage of the dollar's strength on the world currency market and traveling abroad in greater numbers than ever before. Devaluation of Mexico's peso made tourism there a particularly good value, and American travel to Europe was also at an all-time high. Unfortunately for domestic hoteliers, U.S. gateway markets are not benefiting. European, Canadian, and Mexican tourists were hard pressed to travel to the United States because of the higher rates they had to pay for U.S. goods and services—a problem aggravated by the lagging recoveries from the 1981–82 European and Canadian recessions.

42 A major problem in accommodating foreign travelers is the language barrier and other practices these travelers are accustomed to. J. S. Linen, president of American Express's travel division, offered the following observation:

> We, as a country, including the travel industry, have not been geared for anything other than English. We need to break the one-language barrier and develop multilingual servicing capabilities . . . from customs declaration forms to hotel menus and front-desk information. We need to replace English-only signs with symbols to identify common locations such as rest rooms, mail drops, dining rooms in hotels, and transportation facilities throughout the country.
>
> Most international travelers are used to changing currency with ease in banks and hotels abroad. By comparison, few U.S. banks and hotels have developed these relatively simple capabilities.
>
> Foreign visitors also face widespread problems with acceptance of prepaid hotel vouchers issued abroad, and few have any clear idea of how big this country is.
>
> The most significant segment of the international travel market is the pleasure traveler, and until these visitors can feel comfortable traveling in the United States, we're losing a valuable potential market.[2]

Multiuser, Big-City Location Boom

43 By early 1979, travelers in major urban markets like San Francisco, New York, Chicago, Denver, Kansas City, Miami, and Los Angeles were facing a 19th-century problem—a place to stay is hard to find. In 1978 alone, Holiday Inns refused more than 200 million guests for lack of space.

44 What was causing this growing discrepancy between supply and demand? Some of the reasons behind the shortage of hotel rooms in these metropolitan, multiuser areas

[2] *Nation's Business,* May 1981, p. 63.

were more and bigger conventions, increasing business travel, an influx of foreign visitors, and a general boost in travel, spurred by low-cost air fares. The director of franchise planning for Holiday Inns sees several underlying factors that will continue increased demand:

A steady increase in the number of families with incomes in excess of $20,000—a group that rents four times as many room-nights as those with lower incomes.

A predicted 50 percent rise in the number of individuals aged 35 to 49, the group with the greatest propensity for travel.

The growing independence of women, who are traveling more for business and pleasure and have more money to spend.

The declining birthrate, giving adults more time and money for trips.

Increasing worldwide use of air travel—which means multiuser, often metropolitan areas close to airports are where demand will grow, not roadside locations.[3]

45 Responding to these pressures, most major hotel chains set into motion major expansion plans for the metropolitan, multiuser markets. By early 1979, industry analysts were projecting a need for 145,000 new rooms *annually* over the next 20 years.

46 A major difficulty for hotel operators in these major metropolitan areas is the variance in peak occupancy. San Francisco, for example, has two peak periods. June through August brings hordes of tourists, while September and October fill hotels with conventions. New York, however, often remains sold out from September to May. Washington, D.C., peaks during March–May and October–November, with Monday through Thursday being consistently sold out while weekends incur heavy vacancy.

47 Even with the seasonal cycles, lodging industry participants and independent investors looked bullishly at major city markets as the decade of the 70s came to a close. However, by 1983, particularly with the impact of the 1981–82 recession on demand, several investors were much less optimistic about city center development. Occupancy levels, traditionally in the high 70s, were in the low 60s. Cities such as Dallas, Denver, and Atlanta were said to be hotel-saturated.

Suppliers to the Industry

48 A supplier group can exert significant bargaining power on an industry when it is concentrated (or dominated by a few companies), when its product is differentiated (or has high switching costs), when there are few substitutes for its product, when it poses a credible threat of integrating forward into the industry's business, or when the industry is not a customer of major importance to it.

49 The suppliers for the lodging industry present a large array of diverse products and services (see Exhibit 11). The following are goods a typical hotel needs on a recurring basis: food, cleaning supplies, linens, alcoholic beverages, and personal care items. Suppliers of these items are fragmented local or regional wholesalers. The only potentially concentrated group may be food wholesalers. Sysco and CFS Continental, the two largest firms in the market, have both been aggressively expanding via acquisition. Fleming has also made a significant inroad into this market with its acquisition of

[3] *Nation's Business,* June 1979, pp. 76–80.

Exhibit 11

Major suppliers of goods and services to the lodging industry

Rank	*Industry*	*Percent of total*
1.	Wholesale trade	23.0%
2.	Finance, Insurance, and real estate	17.7
3.	Government services	12.7
4.	Manufacturing—durable and nondurable goods	9.7
5.	Electric, gas, and sanitary services	8.7
6.	Miscellaneous business services	5.9
7.	Communications—telephone	5.4
8.	Maintenance and repair; construction	4.8
9.	Advertising services	3.6
10.	Personal services—Laundry and dry cleaning	2.5
		94.0%

Source: U.S. Department of Commerce.

White Swan, a large foodservice wholesaler in Texas. Together, these firms control less than 20 percent of the food wholesaling business nationwide.

50 In the durable goods area, hotels also have many suppliers. Durable goods purchased by hotels include kitchen equipment, tables and chairs, televisions, beds, desks, and dressers. The 1983 Foodservice Equipment Specialist Buyer Guide and Product Directory has a listing of almost 1,400 manufacturers of foodservice equipment, supplies, furnishings, and related products.

51 Financial resources are obviously a key resource for the lodging industry. Again, the group includes numerous suppliers with no single source being a major provider, although insurance companies have become increasingly active in ownership of hotel properties. Supplies of financial resources remain linked primarily to prevailing economic characteristics as shown in Exhibit 12.

Substitutes for Lodging Services

52 Substitute products or services threaten an industry when they are (1) subject to trends that will improve their price-performance trade-offs with traditional industry services or (2) when they are produced by industries earning high profits.

Currently no substitute service represents a major threat to the lodging industry. But the market does offer substitute products, each of which divert a small portion of the industry revenues.

53 On the business side of the industry, teleconferences offer an increasingly viable substitute for traditional lodging services. Using satellite communications equipment, business people in different cities can get together for meetings without leaving town, and several large corporations have invested in telecommunication equipment. The

Exhibit 12

Period	*Dates*	*Characteristics*	*Financing methods*	*Sources*	*Comments and problems*
1	January 1, 1976, to December 31, 1978	Inflation-fueled EXPANSION.	Permanent mortgages with no lender ownership. Limited partnerships (for equity).	Life insurance companies. Savings and loan associations. Savings banks. Pension funds (few). Industrial revenue bonds. Urban development assistant grants.	Investment in real estate considered an excellent hedge against inflation. Room rate increases more than offset higher costs of operation. Inflation forced costs of financial institutions above fixed-rate returns.
2	January 1, 1979, to June 30, 1981	Economic STAGFLATION. Rapidly increasing inflation.	Permanent mortgages with lender ownership. Convertible mortgages. *Participating mortgages.* Land purchase and leaseback with participating mortgages.	Life insurance companies (equity as well as debt financing). Pension funds. Commercial banks.	Life insurance companies shift investment strategies and channel a greater portion of their funds from securities to real estate. By late 1979, following an unexpected run on funds by consumers, traditional sources of debt financing for real estate development disappear. National life insurance companies make a concerted effort to attract, invest, and manage monies for pension funds.
3	July 1, 1981, to January 1983	RECESSION. Rate of inflation decreases dramatically. Interest rates remain high.	*Floating rate term* loans. *All equity.* Seller mortgages.	Life insurance companies (equity as well as debt financing). Pension funds. Commercial banks. Credit companies. Joint ventures. Limited partnerships. Sellers Industrial revenue bonds.	Real estate financing brought nearly to a standstill. Financial projections for proposed projects are revised downward and no longer produce the rates of return demanded by lenders and developers. Aggressive developers attempt to finance projects on a temporary basis, plan to move into more realistic long-term debt financing later.

Source: *Financing the Lodging Industry: Players and Techniques of the 1980s.* Laventhol and Horwath, 1982.

June 1981 deregulation of the communications industry enabled end-users to "resell" their services to end-users, changing the nature of communication in the hotel industry. For the first time, hotels can, in effect, go into the telecommunications business and recover the cost of providing long-distance telephone service. Since 1981, Holiday Inns, Hilton Hotels, Sheraton Corporation, Marriott Corporation, Hyatt Corporation, and Ramada Inns have introduced teleconferencing. Holiday Inns operate the largest privately owned network of satellite receivers, with 350 earth stations expected to be in use in 1983. How much teleconferencing will cannibalize the lodging industry is hard to discern, but major hotel chains appear to be hedging their bets.

54 The other substitutes are mostly directed at pleasure travel—time sharing, bed and breakfast (room rental), camping, and recreational vehicles. Several years ago, time sharing was sweeping the nation. People could invest their money in a permanent vacation site at the fraction of the cost, and time-sharing companies offered several sites where a person could vacation. The time-sharing idea, however, never really caught on.

55 Bed and breakfast, involving private homes that rent rooms to guests and provide a breakfast, has become very popular in Europe and in some large cities in the United States, but little threat is offered.

New Entrants and Barriers to Entry

56 New entrants may bring new capacity, the desire to gain market share, and often substantial resources when they enter an industry. Six major barriers to entry in most industries are economies of scale, product differentiation, capital requirements, cost disadvantages independent of size, access to distribution channels, and government policy. The three most important barriers to entry into the lodging industry are product differentiation, capital requirements, and economies of scale.

57 The past 20 years have witnessed a big change in the lodging industry. Each chain has increasingly targeted specific markets and sought to attract certain types of customers. Most chains have had some success in inducing chain loyalty. For example, Holiday Inns claims to be the preference of one out of every three travelers. While the exact level of chain loyalty is hard to determine, advertising, promotion, and experience with different chains have created a typical customer that is more knowledgeable about lodging services and capable of differentiating these services. Furthermore, a key aspect of lodging service is often the *location* of the facility. In many local markets, the choice locations (for example, close to airports, civic centers, and beaches) have been developed by existing chains. This fact clearly *differentiates* the locational aspect of the service existing properties offer in a particular, local market from what a potential entrant might *profitably* offer.

58 Though not as critical in the lodging industry as in other industries, capital requirements and economies of scale do play a role as lodging chains grow. New organizations that want to enter the lodging industry with a new concept face a large capital outlay. Current costs for a hotel range from $20,000 to $250,000 per room depending upon the building characteristics, amenities offered, and land costs. A rule of thumb in the industry is that room rates must be at least $1 for every $1,000 invested per room if the project is to be financially sound. Thus, where costs are high, the new hotel might have to charge rates above current area levels to cover its investment.

59 If an entrant seeks to build a strong industrywide position, time is required to develop and promote (and possibly franchise) the new concept. Economies of scale are important to support an effective reservation system, training capacities, and essential administrative overhead necessary to operate a multilocation business. Such concerns, however, do not inhibit the entrepreneur who seeks to enter only one local market.

60 Presently, there are three typical ways to enter the lodging industry. The first is as an independent operator. The independent operator is facing increasingly stiff competition from lodging chains (see Exhibit 13). The 1981–82 recession hurt the independent more than the chains. Hotel and motel construction typically is capital intensive, and bankers are increasingly encouraging potential builders to become associated with a lodging chain. "Conservative consumers, loath to spend their precious traveling dollars on unproven independents, increasingly are selecting brand-name hotels," says Daniel Lee, a stock analyst with Drexel Burnham Lambert. "A brand name is now vital," he says, "and travelers won't go out of their way to look for an independent. Chain advertising has done little to dispel consumer fears of independents and often deliberately fosters suspicion of unknowns."

61 The second alternative, which has been increasingly popular, is franchising. This route usually involves an initial fee, a royalty on revenues, and possibly additional fees such as advertising and reservation fees (see Appendix B). The franchisor usually stipulates building requirements and often provides designs. In return, the franchisor offers a name that provides differentiation from competitors, usually a nationwide reservation system, a sophisticated marketing program that would be out of the reach of most independents, and a framework of rules, regulations, and examples of how successful operations work. "Franchising provides a vital network of support to most hotel operators," says one hotel-chain executive. She estimates that independent hotel

Exhibit 13

Franchising and the motel industry

Factors	*Franchises**	*Reservation network†*	*Independents*
Percentage of growth since 1969	+223%	+188%	−59%
Percentage of motel industry			
1969	42	24	34
1978	62	32	6
1982	72	25	3
Properties with restaurants	93	78	44
Average number of rooms	102	84	25
Percentage of interstate motels			
1969	52%	30%	18%
1978	61	36	3
1982	63	33	1
Average occupancy rate:			
1978	72	68	52
1982	66	63	51

* For example, Holiday Inns, Days Inns.
† For example, Best Western.

operators stand a four-to-one chance of failing when compared with chain-affiliated operators. According to the U.S. Department of Commerce, 1982 saw a 3.5 percent increase in franchisee-owned properties over 1981, and 1983 estimates called for an additional increase of 3.3 percent.

62 A third, less capital intensive way of entering the lodging industry has been as a reservation network. Best Western is by far the most successful. Entering the industry in the late 1950s as a reservation service to independent hotel and motel operations, Best Western now leads Holiday Inns in the number of properties in its network. Quality Inns developed its industry position in a similar fashion. Rather than invest in brick and mortar, this approach simply creates and links a network of existing (or newly built) properties behind a highly promoted brand name backed up by a reservation system and some service standards. Many analysts do not think the industry could support more reservation-only entrants.

Lodging Industry Diversification

63 In an effort to broaden their earnings base, several major lodging participants began diversifying into related business areas in the late 1970s. Casino gaming has received the greatest attention in recent years. Since casinos often include hotel, food, and beverage facilities, several major lodging firms, including Holiday Inns, Hilton, Hyatt, and Ramada Inns, have moved into casino gaming. Gerald Hallier, chief operating officer of Ramada Inns, Inc., offers the following scenario:

> Even established companies that are doing well in Nevada, such as Del Webb, Caesars World, and Summa, don't have as good a chance as the big companies because they lack the base [from which] to expand. In the long run, it's the big companies like Holiday Inns, Ramada Inns. and Hilton which will do the best, because they have the muscle.[4]

64 Hallier's vision seems quite accurate as Holiday Inns, in just three years, had become the largest firm in casino gaming by mid-1981.

Exhibit 14 shows the rate of casino gaming growth since 1970. At a compounded annual rate of over 17 percent, casino gaming is quite attractive to established lodging firms with obviously related competencies. In the Las Vegas market alone, visitor spending tripled in eight years as shown in Exhibit 15. And after Atlantic City legalized gambling in May 1978, gross wins initially exceeded projections.

65 Aside from Nevada, where casino gambling has been sanctioned since the late 1940s, Atlantic City is the only other location in the United States to permit casinos. The attraction to Atlantic City is based primarily on its proximity to major East Coast population centers. While it is believed that this market is currently attracting patrons living within 75 miles of the city, there is a vast potential market of some 60 million living within a 300-mile radius. This compares with 16 million persons within the same distance of Las Vegas.

66 Historically, the gaming industry has been the ultimate growth business, with revenues increasing in each succeeding year. Although gains have moderated somewhat during economic contractions, gross revenues have continued to climb. Inflation does

---

[4] "Holiday Inns: Refining Its Focus to Food, Lodging—and More Casinos," *Business Week*, July 21, 1980, p. 104.

Exhibit 14

Domestic casino gaming ($ millions)

Year	Clark County (Las Vegas)	Washoe County (Reno/Tahoe)	Total Nevada	Atlantic City	Total United States
1980*	1,550	475	2,330	600	2,930
1979	1,424	423	2,120	325	2,445
1978	1,236	367	1,846	134	1,980
1977	1,016	280	1,519	—	1,519
1976	847	230	1,262	—	1,262
1975	770	193	1,126	—	1,126
1974	685	170	1,004	—	1,004
1973	586	159	858	—	858
1972	476	138	731	—	731
1971	399	133	633	—	633
1970	369	116	575	—	575

Source: Nevada State Gaming Control Board: Resorts International; and New Jersey Casino Control Commission.

not seem to have a significant negative impact on the earnings of gaming companies, since the amount of money wagered tends to rise with inflation. Some industry insiders believe that gambling increases during economic downturns because people are looking for ways to take their mind off their problems; the hope for a good winning streak can be a powerful inducement.

67 The expansion in Nevada and New Jersey underscores the seemingly insatiable demand for gambling in this country. It has been estimated that more than $100 billion is wagered annually; this figure includes illegal gambling. Most states now permit some form of wagering, such as bingo, horse and dog racing, lotteries, and

Exhibit 15

Las Vegas tourist activity: 1972–1979

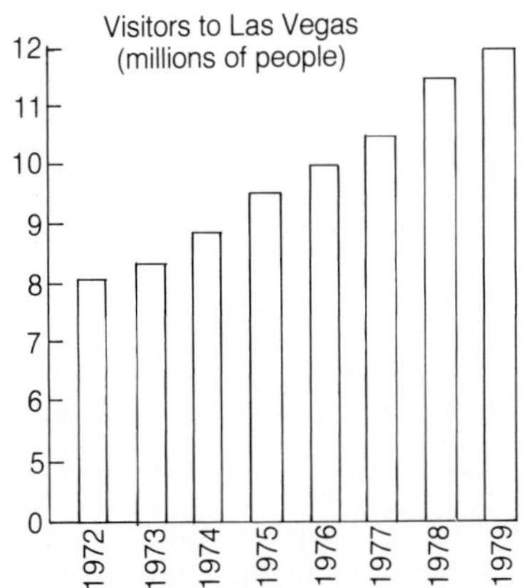

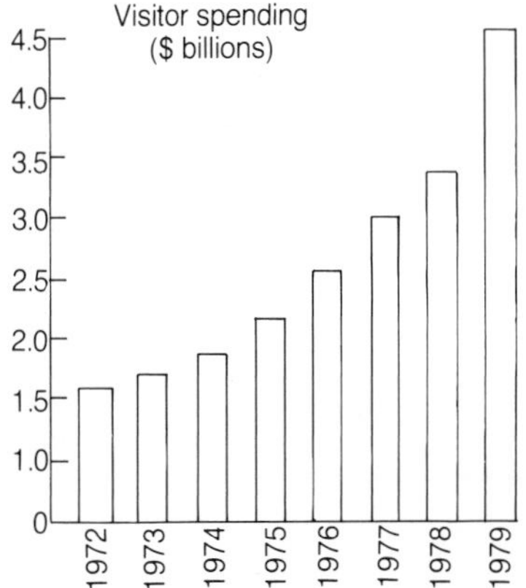

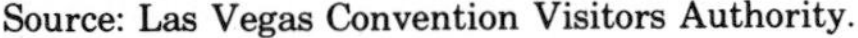

Source: Las Vegas Convention Visitors Authority.

jai alai. Some individuals feel that competition from private enterprise is the best method of eliminating the criminal element from gambling.

68 Legislatures have recognized the potential economic benefits that can be derived from the legalization of casino gaming. The fees and taxes generated by casinos would be welcome by most governmental units. Fees and taxes collected by Nevada in 1979 totaled $101.5 million, and the tax rate in New Jersey is currently 12 percent.

69 The New York State legislature recently approved eight different bills that would permit casino gaming. Since passage by two consecutive legislatures is required before a constitutional amendment can be put on the ballot for voter approval, this action gives the legislature another year to determine the form that casino gaming could take as well as where it would be located. The legalization of casino gaming in New York could significantly impact the growth of the Atlantic City market. This would be particularly true during winter months, when many residents would prefer to do their gambling closer to home. Other states assessing legalization include Massachusetts, Illinois, and Pennsylvania.

70 Another diversification area for lodging firms has been the family restaurant business. Both Holiday Inns and Days Inns initiated moves in this direction in late 1978. Holiday Inns acquired Perkins Cake and Steak, Inc., a 340-unit, midwestern restaurant chain. Days Inns initiated its own restaurant chain, DayBreak, on a limited basis. Marriott controls two restaurant chains—Hot Shoppe and Roy Rogers. Brock Hotels is developing Show Biz Pizza Place. While promising numerous lodging-related synergies, expansion of these ventures (and movement by other lodging firms) was virtually halted by the 1981–82 economic downturn.

For the Future

71 The recent explosion in the building and renovation of motels and hotels has been a source of concern and speculation by investors and industry experts. The 1982 American Hotel and Motel Association annual survey on construction and modernization estimated that 237,300 new hotel rooms would be built in 1982, with 366,300 more coming on line in 1983 and 343,500 more in 1984. For the same three-year period, the report stated that only 97,400 rooms will be removed. The report drew criticism from experts in the industry as being "too optimistic." The report also drew the attention of investors and financial advisors. *The Wall Street Journal,* in a 1983 "Heard on the Street" section, discussed hotel stock issues, the occupancy lags, and new construction:

> In a report reaching clients last week, Edward M. Tavlin, lodging analyst at Prescott, Ball & Turben, advises sale of the three stocks (Hilton, Marriott, and Holiday Inns). The industry has been hurt by the recession, he says, but earning problems of the leading hotel stocks aren't simply recession related. Mr. Tavlin worries most about the upper-middle to luxury end of the business, which is in the midst of a building binge. The American Hotel and Motel Association's recent survey on construction and modernization shows staggering estimates for new-room additions. The estimates, if correct, would result in a 76 percent increase in available rooms in this segment between 1982 and 1984. Analysts say that demand, meanwhile, will rise only about 2 percent a year for the next several years. Mr. Tavlin disputes the industry's figures but says that, even if

the estimates are reduced greatly, there will be many saturated markets in the next several years. This would lead, he feels, to a squeeze on profits and a disappointing recovery in national occupancy.

72 Selected business indicators important to the lodging industry suggest improved demand for the mid-1980s (see Exhibit 16). One disappointing trend between 1982 and 1983 is the continued decline in international air arrivals.

73 The lodging industry has been fortunate in the past in that government has not instituted prohibitive and restrictive laws or regulations, but the governmental influence is growing. Recently Congress passed a tax law requiring the lodging and foodservice industry to report employee tips to the Internal Revenue Service. The impact, though slight, does show government's growing awareness of the industry and its growing economic importance. An area of potential problems may be fire safety, especially with the rash of deadly hotel fires in 1982 and 1983. If the industry does not develop some self-regulations, the government may intervene.

74 The gasoline shortages of 1973–1974 and 1979 had a dramatic but short-lived impact on the lodging industry. The industry survived these crises but is more aware of the dependence on gasoline and natural resources. At present, 86 percent of vacationers and 66 percent of business travelers still use the automobile for transportation. Offering some stability, Saudi Arabia is committed to maintaining a worldwide oil price of

Exhibit 16

Selected business indicators

					Percent change from	
	Period	*(1983) Latest month*	*(1983) Previous month*	*(1982) Year ago month*	*Previous month*	*Year ago month*
Airline traffic (billion rev. pass. miles)	Nov.	15.5	16.6	14.5	–6.6	6.9
Highway traffic (billion vehicle miles)[1]	Oct.	37.8	37.5	35.9	0.8	5.3
Personal income ($ billion)[2]	Nov.	2,832.3	2,811.9	2,633.1	0.7	7.6
Unemployment rate (percent)[3]	Nov.	8.2	8.8	10.4	–6.8	–21.2
Number employed (millions)	Nov.	104.4	103.6	100.8	0.8	3.6
Short-term interest rate[4]	Nov.	11.0	11.0	12.0– 11.5	NM	NM
Long-term interest[5]	Nov.	9.79– 12.91	12.75– 9.79	9.96– 13.07	NM	NM
Consumer price index	Nov.	303.1	302.6	293.6	0.2	3.2
Consumer confidence index (1969–70—100)	Nov.	89.4	85.7	54.8	0.4	6.3
Hotel occupancy (percent)	Sept.	64.8	71.0	61.6	–8.7	5.2
Hotel room rate (national average $)	Sept.	53.20	51.27	51.75	3.8	2.8
Travel price index (100 = 1967)[6]	Sept.	355.0	354.7	345.2	0.1	2.8
Person trips (millions)[7]	Aug.	134.6	124.2	145.9	8.4	–7.7
International air arrivals[8]	June	710,310	667,330	972,737	6.4	–27.0

[1] Rural arterial roads.
[2] Seasonally adjusted, at annual rate.
[3] Seasonally adjusted.
[4] Prime rate.
[5] Corporate, Moody's Average.
[6] Calculated by the U.S. Travel Data Center, includes price of gasoline, common carrier transportation, lodging, foodservice, and amusement, and recreation.
[7] Recorded each time a person takes a trip 100 miles or more away from home, compiled by the U.S. Travel Data Center's National Travel Survey.
[8] Number of aliens arriving in the United States by air.
NM—Not meaningful.
All figures are subject to revision.
Source: The Conference Board, 1983.

Exhibit 17

Selected revenue and expense trends

	1963	*1968*	*1973*	*1978*	*1979*	*1980*	*1981*	*1982*
Ratios to total revenues:								
Revenues								
Rooms	50.4%	53.5%	54.1%	57.3%	59.2%	59.9%	60.4%	60.5%
Food	30.5	28.2	27.9	26.0	25.1	24.0	23.7	23.5
Beverages	11.5	11.1	11.0	9.6	9.4	9.1	9.0	8.9
Other revenues and income	7.6	7.2	7.0	7.1	6.3	7.0	6.9	7.1
Total operated departments' income	47.0	50.4	48.1	51.7	52.6	53.9	54.0	53.4
Income after property taxes and insurance*	22.0	25.9	21.1	23.9	25.5	25.8	25.2	23.6
Property taxes and insurance	4.1	4.3	4.6	3.8	3.2	3.0	3.1	2.9
Payroll and related costs	34.9	32.9	35.7	34.2	33.0	32.8	33.0	34.1
Dollars per available room:								
Total revenues	$6,961	$8,607	$10,278	$15,929	$17,678	$19,258	$20,853	$21,152
Income after property taxes and insurance*	1,534	2.231	2,164	3,811	4,516	4,962	5,261	4,989
Cost per dollar of sales:								
Food	34.8¢	33.6¢	35.6¢	33.8¢	34.7¢	33.7¢	33.1¢	32.8¢
Beverages	27.2	24.3	22.9	21.5	21.6	21.5	21.4	21.3
Combined food and beverages	32.7	31.0	31.9	30.4	31.0	30.3	29.7	29.5
Percentage of occupancy	67.8%	72.9%	69.2%	72.7%	72.8%	69.5%	67.5%	64.8%
Average room rate	$14.30	$17.41	$ 22.07	$ 34.69	$ 39.26	$ 45.38	$ 51.09	$ 54.80

* The income after property taxes and insurance is before deducting depreciation, rent, interest, amortization and income taxes.
Source: Pannel, Kerr, Foster, *Trends in the Hotel Industry,* 1983 U.S. edition.

$29 per barrel through 1987. While gasoline is not a current problem, one quarter of the U.S. interstate highway system is worn out according to *Lodging* magazine. They warn that one fifth of America's roads are unsafe and that estimates for repair run into the hundred of billions.

75 The lodging industry has become increasingly dependent on room revenue as its primary income source (see Exhibit 17). This dependence comes at a time when the industry's supply of rooms is rapidly expanding and guests are both more knowledgeable and apparently discerning (see Exhibit 18). Judging from the low 1982 occupancy rates shown in Exhibit 19, each type of location can expect to be patronized by a continually more aware and demanding customer base.

76 Tom Herring, incoming 1984 president of the American Hotel and Motel Association, gave a sense of future industry concerns in his January, 1984 inaugural remarks:

> 77 This industry is in a whole new set of circumstances, just as many industries seem to be—telecommunications, automobiles, and airlines among them. All are in transition. . . . As an industry, we have changed dramatically, reflecting the major changes in our society—the impact of the automobile, the airplane, and the construction of an interstate highway system which lets you drive from Laredo, Texas, to New York City without having to stop for a single red light. Ours has been a growth industry, and we don't want to change that. But change begets changes. And changes require adjustment and new ways of thinking.
>
> 78 Our rapid growth has made our industry the object of affection for new and influential forces. In the recent past, these external forces have begun to impact our business, and a number of new players are now seated at the table: we have real estate investment trusts, lenders of every kind, franchise salesmen, feasibility experts, real estate brokers, large developers who "use" hotel projects to anchor their enterprises, convention and visitor bureau staffs eager to build huge new centers, some feasibility firms who grind out "*Made to Order*" feasibility studies, market research firms with little insight into the operational side of the hotel industry, and government interference in the financing process.
>
> 79 Many hoteliers no longer are in ownership, and large financial institutions

Exhibit 18

Guest satisfaction by length of stay

	Length of stay, nights		
Feature	*One*	*Two*	*Three or more*
Cleanliness of room	80	77	63
Room size and furnishings	75	70	63
Helpfulness of employees	80	75	56
Front-desk service	95	75	63
Restaurant and food service	72	58	46
Room rates	53	54	47

Note: Sample of four types of hotels: executive, center city, airport, and budget. Guest satisfaction was measured as: Very satisfied = 100; Satisfied = 50; and Dissatisfied = 0.

Source: Adapted from "The Push Button Questionnaire: A New Tool for Measuring Customer Satisfaction," *Cornell HRA Quarterly Review*, February 1979, p. 76.

Exhibit 19

Market data

	Location				
	Center city	*Airport*	*Suburban*	*Highway*	*Resort*
Source of Business					
Domestic	90.0%	94.7%	95.3%	95.6%	85.6%
Foreign	10.0	5.3	4.7	4.4	14.4
Total	100.0%	100.0%	100.0%	100.0%	100.0%
Percentage of repeat Business	41.7%	57.3%	55.1%	46.9%	36.2%
Composition of market					
Government officials	4.3%	2.2%	4.1%	4.9%	1.0%
Businessmen	32.4	44.8	52.6	49.4	11.6
Tourists	28.7	33.1	21.9	28.8	56.9
Conference participants	27.7	17.0	17.6	10.6	27.3
Other	6.9	2.9	3.8	6.3	3.2
Total	100.0%	100.0%	100.0%	100.0%	100.0%
Percentage of advance reservations	83.6%	76.7%	79.4%	59.2%	87.2%
Rental revenue per room					
1982	$12,462	$10,444	$9,632	$9,264	$13,724
1970	5,134	4,910*	4,900*	4,837	5,749
Food revenue per room					
1982	4,422	3,386	3,218	2,457	6,230
1970	2,709	2,310*	2,250*	2,081	3,530
Beverage revenue per room					
1982	1,783	1,581	1,763	1,308	2,112
1970	1,144	950*	1,010*	803	1,280
1981 occupancy	67.0%	72.1%	70.7%	71.6%	64.2%
1982 occupancy	64.2%	66.0%	68.8%	66.0%	68.0%
1981 average rate	$ 48.48	$ 38.58	$38.38	$34.63	$ 51.37
1982 average rate	$ 56.12	$ 44.98	$38.09	$38.09	$ 55.62

* Estimated.
Source: Laventhol and Horwath.

now own many properties. In short, our industry has expanded so radically in the past decade and has been so heavily impacted by forces external to it, I fear we are in danger of forgetting what business we are in.

80 I hope to carry us back to our roots, to remember that we are innkeepers, in the traditional sense, and to reawaken our understanding and appreciation for the art of hoteling.

81 Our industry should be healthy, and in order to survive, it must grow. But that growth cannot be unrealistic and undisciplined. It must be responsible, based on sound business judgment and the best information available.

82 La Posada Hotels operates in South Texas close to the border in what has been called a depressed region. Even so, new hotels are being built today despite the fact that community occupancy rates are running about 44 percent. In some

instances, new hotel projects seem to be driven solely by the strong credit of the owner. In one case I know of, discussing the prospects for success of one new hotel, a banker recently said "well, the man is good for it."

83 I am not saying that anyone who wants to compete in the lodging industry shouldn't compete. In fact, competition keeps us healthy and strong. But I don't think it makes good sense to plan on a third- or fourth-generation ownership before a hotel becomes profitable.

84 I'm willing to compete with any hotel in my area or any other city where La Posada might operate. But I want to make certain that my business decisions about expansion and growth are always based on good, credible information and not just wishful thinking. Just because I have good credit doesn't mean that the world needs another hotel from Tom Herring.

Appendix A: Operating a Service Business

85 The lodging industry is considered part of a larger industry known as the service industry. A service organization differs in several ways from a manufacturing organization. To gain a better understanding of the companies competing in the lodging industry, this appendix provides a brief explanation of the service organization and the service delivery concept to aid the reader in developing an appreciation for the differences between service and manufacturing companies.

86 The U.S. government's Standard Industrial Classification (SIC) defines services as "establishments: primarily engaged in providing a wide variety of service for individuals, businesses, government establishments, and other organizations." It is an event or process produced and used within a short period of time. Services cannot generally be retained after they are produced, but the effect of the service may remain. Even though a service is intangible and perishable, in truth, most services involve purchase of certain goods. Each purchase involves a bundle of goods and/or services. "This bundle involves three distinct areas: (1) the physical items or facilitating goods, (2) the sensual benefit or explicit service, and (3) the psychological benefit or implicit service."[5] In this context, lodging operations offer a room, which in turn provides the guest with the physical items of a bed and bathing facilities. In the case of a restaurant or lounge on the premises, the physical item would be the food or drinks. The sensual benefits include items such as clean towels and sheets, the physical comforts the room offers, or the conveniences or amenities of a restaurant, lounge, swimming pool, sauna, and so on. The psychological benefits, though they vary dramatically, may include the friendliness of the staff and/or the status of the hotel, leaving the customer with a sense of well-being.

87 In the production of a service, the process not only creates the product but also simultaneously delivers it to the customer. Design of the service package and control of the design requires a greater understanding of the consumer psychology than for a manufactured good because of the intangible and often nonexplicit nature of the service. In a manufacturing operation, however, the customer is very rarely exposed to the production facility. Manufacturing firms do not usually fall prey to the critical eyes of the customers. In a restaurant, however, the customer physically resides at the production facility while the food is being prepared. Unlike the manufacturing

[5] W. Sasser, P. Olsen, and D. Wyckoff. *Management of Service Operations.* (Boston: Allyn & Bacon, 1978).

operation, the service organization requires the customer's presence at the production facility for delivery of service. The restaurant needs to not only produce the food but to also simultaneously coordinate the delivery of the food while it is hot. Restaurant operations, therefore, have concentrated on efficient service delivery systems.

88 In a service delivery system, the absence of inventory removes from the service manager an important buffer used by most manufacturing managers to handle fluctuations in demand. For example, a hotel or motel has a specific number of rooms it can rent. If the owners do not rent all the rooms for a particular evening, the potential revenue is lost and can never be recaptured. The same logic follows for a restaurant; it only has a specific number of seats and a staff that can serve only a limited number of people. The combination of perishability and wide swings in volume place heavy pressure on the marketing executives of service firms to develop and implement plans to alter the demand schedule for a firm's service to fit more closely to its physical capacity. If the marketing effort fails, the firm either has periods of idle capacity or periods of insufficient capacity or both.

89 Another characteristic of a service product is the heterogeneity of output produced by firms claiming to produce the same service. In a manufacturing firm, a certain number of products are sampled to ensure quality and consistency. Service firms, especially restaurants, do not have this opportunity. Restaurants must meet the customers' time constraints, and it is highly impractical to randomly sample customers' orders. The system is highly dependent on the cooks, waiters, and waitresses to produce a consistently high-quality product upon demand, which may vary from hectic rush-hour periods to extremely slow periods between meals. The service industry, therefore, has typically been a people-oriented business, relying on both the employees and the customers to create heterogeneity. In service organizations, employees continually interact with the customer. To a large extent, the service a customer receives and his or her impression of the organization depends upon the mood and attitude of the employee serving that particular customer. Service organizations spend a great deal of time and money creating an image for their particular organization. They promote this image through advertising but also depend on their employees to convey this image and to produce the desired product at the right time and place. Manufacturing firms, on the other hand, produce physical properties and are not generally dependent on employees to merchandise and sell the product.

90 The last difference between manufacturing and service firms is the limited geographic area from which service can draw customers. Manufacturing firms can benefit from enonomies of scale; they can build one central plant and distribute their product nationwide. Service organizations, however, can only attract customers within a reasonable driving or walking distance. To reproduce its concept, service organizations must diversify geographically—build firms in a variety of locations.

91 For the most part, a service organization depends on how the concepts of service and service delivery system are designed, implemented, and perpetuated. Service organizations are in the business of catering to the desires of their customers.

Appendix B

What it takes to join a chain

Name of chain	Franchise/membership requirements					Franchise/membership fees				
	Minimum of rooms	*Food facilities*	*Meeting space*	*Swimming pool*	*Laundry*	*Initial fee*	*Royalty*	*Advertising fee*	*Reservation fee*	*Other fees*
Best Value Inns/ Superior Motels Circle 401	25					50% of annual dues	None	None	None	Monthly dues: average of $.30/room/day
Best Western International Circle 402	None	°		°		$9,248 on 100 units	None	None	None	$24.071/year for 100 units
Brock Residence Inns Circle 403	64		°	°		$250/suite	3% suite gross	2.5% suite gross	None	None
Budget Host Inns Circle 404	None					$250	$300 for first 30 units. $5 each after 30.	$2/room/year	None	$150 inspection fee for non-AAA or Mobil rated applicants
Comfort Inns Circle 405	None			°		Conversions: $100/unit $9,850 minimum Construction: $100 unit $15,000 minimum	3% room gross	1% room gross	1% room gross + $.50/booked reservation through reservation system	Terminal: $125 plus local phone line costs and installation
Days Inns of America Circle 406	100	°	°	°		$15,000/100 rooms. $100 for rooms over 100. $5,000 for restaurant.	5% lodging 3% food, gas & gift	1%	$2.80/room/month + .8% gross lodging & $1.40/ reservation, less $1/reservation made at another Days Inn	.03% monthly gross lodging for education
Downtowner Motor Inns Circle 407	100	°		°		$50/room $5,000 minimum	2% room gross	1% room gross	$1.50/room/month	None
Econo Lodges of America Circle 408	50					Conversions: $5,000 Construction: $10,000	2% room gross	2% room gross	Included in advertising fee	None
Friendship Inns International Circle 409	None					$2,000 one-time cost	None	None	$2.45/confirmed reservation	$30/unit/year

Appendix B *(continued)*

Name of chain	Franchise/membership requirements					Franchise/membership fees				
	Minimum of rooms	Food facilities	Meeting space	Swimming pool	Laundry	Initial fee	Royalty	Advertising fee	Reservation fee	Other fees
Golden Tulip Hotels America . . . . Circle 410	None	°				$14,000 for 200-room hotel	$5,000 for 200-room hotel	$3/room/month up to 200 rooms Over 200, $1.50/room/month	$5/reservation	None
Granada Royale Hometels . . . . Circle 411	160	°	°	°	°	$50,000	4% suite gross	1% suite gross	1% suite gross	None
Hilton Inns . . . . Circle 412	100	°	°	°		$250/room/first 100 rooms Over 100, $150/room	5% room gross	None	$4.93/reservation	None
Holiday Inns . . . . Circle 413	100	°	°	°		$300/room $30,000 minimum	4% room gross	1.5% room gross but no less than $.08/room/night	1% room gross but no less than $.06/night	$3.50/room Holidex fee
Howard Johnson . . . . Circle 414	120	°	°	°		$20,000	5% room gross	1% room gross	1% room gross + $2/room/month	None
Knights Inn . . . . Circle 415	100	°	°	°		$100/room	3% room gross	None	None	4% + percentage of profit.
Magic Key Inns . . . . Circle 416	120					$500	$16.20/room/year, minimum of $243 and 60 units or $972 maximum	None	5% of earned income	None
Master Hosts Inns . . . . Circle 417	50	°	°	°		$50/room $5,000 minimum	2½% room gross	$.10/room/day	$1.50/room/month	None
Passport Inns . . . . Circle 418	30					$30/room $2,000 minimum	1½% room gross	.5% room gross	$1.50/room/month	None

Quality Inns . . . . Circle 419	None	◦	◦	◦		Conversions: $100/unit $9,850 minimum Construction: $100/unit $15,000 minimum	3% room gross	1% room gross	1% room gross + $.50/system reservation	Terminal: $125/month + phone line costs and installation
Quality Royale . . . . Circle 420	None	◦	◦	◦		Conversions: $100/unit $9,850 minimum construction: $100/unit $15,000 minimum	3% room gross	1% room gross	1% room gross + $.50/system reservation	Terminal: $125/month + phone line costs and installation
Ramada Inns . . . . Circle 421	100	◦	◦	◦		$20,000 on first 150 rooms $100/each additional room $50,000 maximum	3% room gross	3.5% room gross	Included in reservation fee	None
Red Carpet Inns . . . . Circle 422	50					$40/room $4,000 minimum	2% room gross	$10/room/month	$1.50/room/month	None
Rodeway Inns . . . . Circle 423	100	◦		◦	◦	Conversion: $7,500 Construction: $15,000	3% room gross	1% room gross	$3.75/room/month + .07 of 1% room gross	Sign lease or purchase
Scottish Inns . . . . Circle 424	None			◦		$30/room $2,000 minimum	1% room gross	1% room gross	$1.50/room/month	None
Sheraton Inns . . . . Circle 425	100	◦	◦	◦		Conversions: $15,000 Construction: $15,000 + $100/room over 150 rooms, $40,000 maximum	5% room gross	None	1.6% room gross, $6/room/month minimum, and $12.50/room/month minimum	None
Summitt Hotels . . . . Circle 426	None	◦	◦	◦	◦	$50,000	2% room gross	2½% room gross	Included in advertising fee	None
Super 8 Motels . . . . Circle 427	30				◦	$15,000	4% room gross	1% room gross	None	None
Thrifty Scot Motels . . . . . . Circle 428	60		◦		◦	None	5¾% room gross over $250/room	1¾% of total revenue	1% of total revenue	None
Travelodge . . . . Circle 429	100					$10,000 or $100/room, whichever is greater	2½% room gross	3½% room gross	None	None

Source: *Lodging* magazine, 1983.

case 27
Best Western International, Inc.

1 "If we ever committed ourselves to a single purpose, we would revolutionize the entire lodging industry." Commitment is certainly not lacking among the tier of top managers at Best Western International, Inc. Chief executive officer, Bob Hazard, embodies his statement. In a five-year period, Hazard has directed the metamorphosis of a once sleepy Phoenix, Arizona, based lodging referral network to a full-service chain. Today Best Western is the largest lodging chain in the world with more than 2,500 individually owned and operated inns, hotels, and resorts throughout the United States and in 18 foreign countries.

2 The strength of the Best Western operation has always centered on the independent unit owner. Best Western was founded in 1948 by M. K. Guertin, a California entrepreneur who was forever seeking novel ways to increase business at his motel. Guertin was convinced that many of his customers would appreciate referral suggestions for quality motels throughout California. Based on the potential of this premonition, Guertin set out to examine properties in the area that maintained high standards of comfort and examine properties in the area that maintained high standards of comfort and cleanliness at a reasonable price. From these humble beginnings, the loosely knit referral organization grew to nearly 500 properties by 1960.

3 In the early 60s, members of the network recognized that as their numbers grew, a more structured system of guidelines, a unified marketing effort, and improved quality control methods were required. Specific objectives and standards were established, and the group incorporated as Western Motels, Inc. This new direction proved quite successful. Notoriety of the network grew, and many property owners in the East sought membership in the organization. As the company grew, the members established guidelines for governance and elected a board of directors. In 1966, the highly successful referral organization decided to establish its headquarters in Phoenix, Arizona.

4 The bubble of success was nearly burst by infighting in the late 1960s and early 1970s that permeated the company. Rumors that the network would sell its name to Standard Oil of Indiana, accompanied with major disagreements on structure and direction, divided the membership.

5 In 1974, under the direction of Peter Wurst, a co-owner of seven Best Western properties, the organization emerged from its troublesome days with a new corporate mission.

6 In November 1974, Best Western's board of directors decided to drop the referral

This case was prepared by Professors Sheila A. Adams and Timothy S. Mescon of Arizona State University.

organization image, drop the word *motel* from its name, and begin competing directly with other full-service chains in the industry.

7 To direct this new effort, the board hired Bob Hazard, vice president of hotels at American Express. Hazard, in turn, brought in Gerald Petitt, a colleague at American Express, to handle operations of the newly revamped organization.

8 "Our member services are so comprehensive that we believe they can't be matched anywhere else in the industry." Hazard claims. "Best Western offers the independent property the advantages of a recognized brand name and international marketing identity without the loss of individuality or operational autonomy."

9 Hazard can offer quantitative support for his assertions. In 1978, the properties in the Best Western chain earned combined revenues of $1,133,572,000, an increase of $208,368,000 over 1977. Of greater importance, combined net profit before taxes for all Best Western properties increased 55 percent, from $110,975,000 in 1977 to $171,-697,000 in 1978.

10 In 1978, the board of directors approved a name change in articles of incorporation. The new corporation name, reflective of perceived future growth areas, is Best Western International, Inc.

Management at Best Western

11 Image at Best Western is a primary concern. Best Western 's new single-site multilevel headquarters consists of 65,000 square feet of space. The headquarters have an obvious southwestern tone with Spanish arches and tile roofs, open courtyards, and beamed ceilings (see Exhibit 1).

12 Hazard emphasizes the importance of a distinctive headquarters, stating:

> We are a marketing organization in the process of proving we are a first-class operation. When we opened here in January of 1978, we thought we would be comfortable in this working environment for 10 years, but out staff has grown very quickly. We will be adding a 67,000-square-foot expansion in the spring of 1980, including a new 10,000-foot reservation computer center.

Corporate Structure

13 Best Western International is an association of member firms and is organized on a nonprofit basis. (See Exhibit 2.) Should the company choose to terminate operations, all monies remaining after the liquidation of debts would be distributed to a nonprofit educational organization or charity.

14 The seven-member board of directors is elected from the seven geographical districts comprising the company's operating area (see Exhibit 3).

15 Directors are elected for a term of three years and serve without compensation. The maximum number of terms any individual may serve is two, whether or not they are consecutive. At the first regular annual meeting of the board, the directors name the officers of Best Western, including president, vice president, and secretary-treasurer. The executive vice president of the company (presently Bob Hazard) is named by the board and is the chief executive officer of the company (see Exhibit 4).

Exhibit 1

Present headquarters opened in January 1978

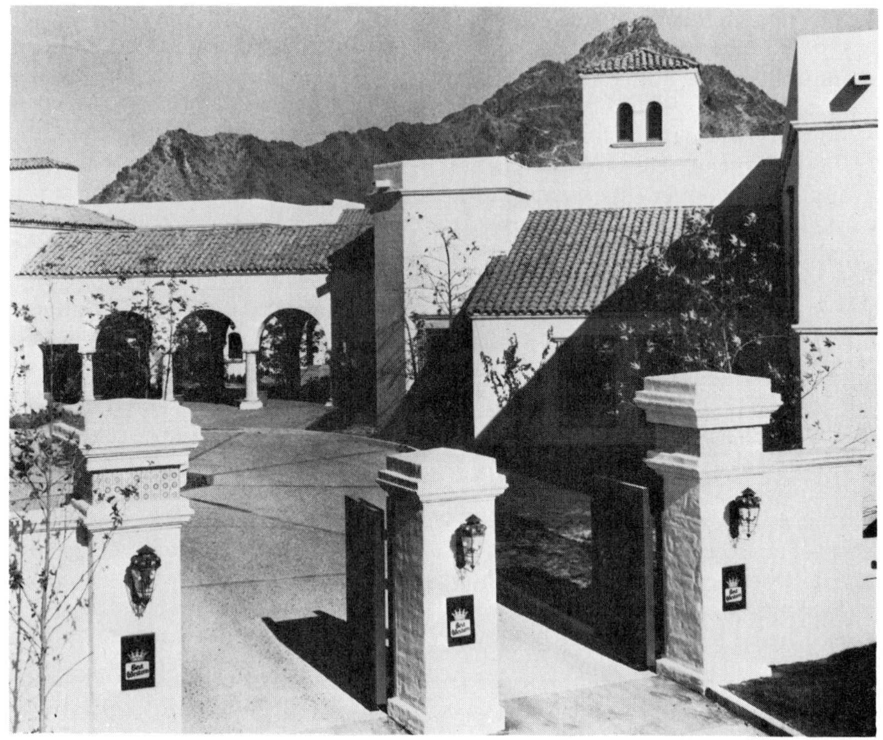

Management team

16 *Executive Vice President—Robert C. Hazard.* In July 1974, Bob Hazard resigned from the vice presidency with American Express Company and assumed the role of vice president marketing with Best Western International. In 1975, Hazard was promoted to executive vice president, and in 1978, he was named chief executive officer of the company.

17 A cum laude graduate (class of 1956) of Princeton University, Hazard proved to be the guiding force behind the recent growth and improvement of the Best Western network. Some of the accomplishments attributed to Hazard include:

- Guiding the expansion of the Best Western chain from 900 to more than 2,500 properties in all 50 states and 18 foreign countries.
- Adding 680 foreign affiliates to Best Western International.
- Instituting a demanding quality control program which in the past four years had forced 467 properties to sever their affiliation with Best Western.
- Introducing B-W Advertising, Inc., B-W Financial Services, Inc., and B-W Management Services, Inc.

Exhibit 2

Best Western Beach and Oceanaire Motel, Long Beach, California: first Western property

Exhibit 3

Governor regions

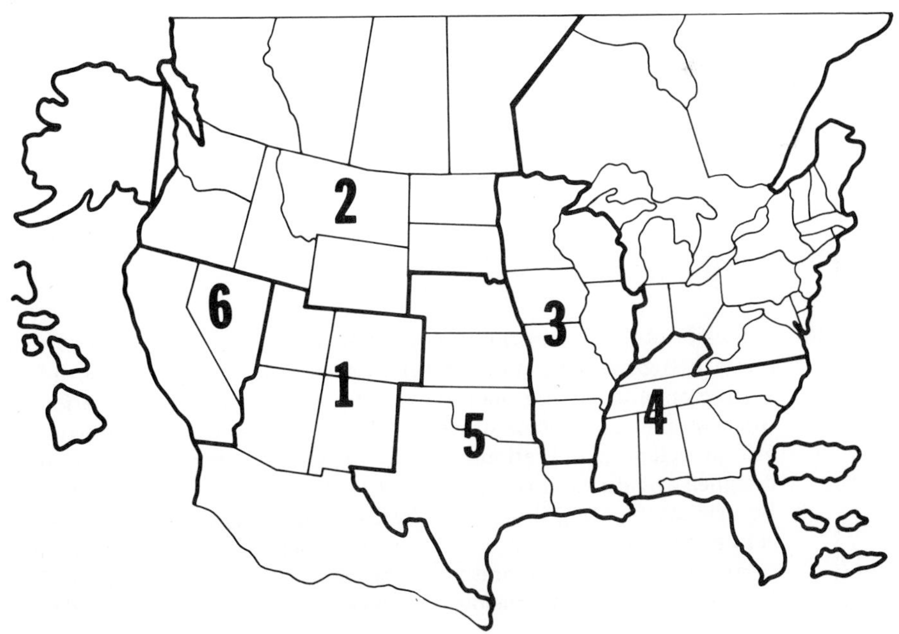

Exhibit 4

Best Western management staff

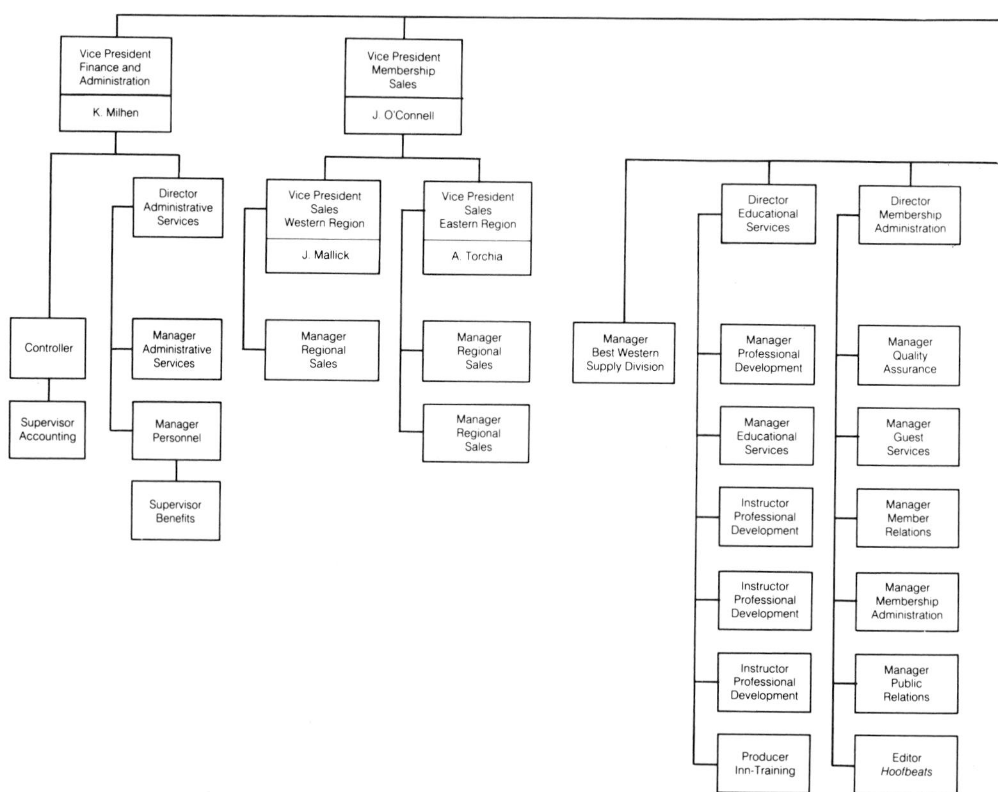

18 *Vice President, Operations—Gerald W. Petitt.* Petitt holds two undergraduate degrees in engineering and an MBA in marketing from Dartmouth College. Formerly a director of sales and operations with American Express, he joined Best Western International as director of reservations in 1974. He was subsequently promoted to vice president of operations, and in 1978, was named chief operating officer. Petitt designed and directed the opening of Best Western's market and reservations center. Besides coordinating this center, Petitt is also responsible for overseeing the membership services department, quality control inspection system, educational training department, corporate communications department, marketing research department, B-W wholesale supply division, and travel industry, marketing, and travel agent departments.

Exhibit 4 *(concluded)*

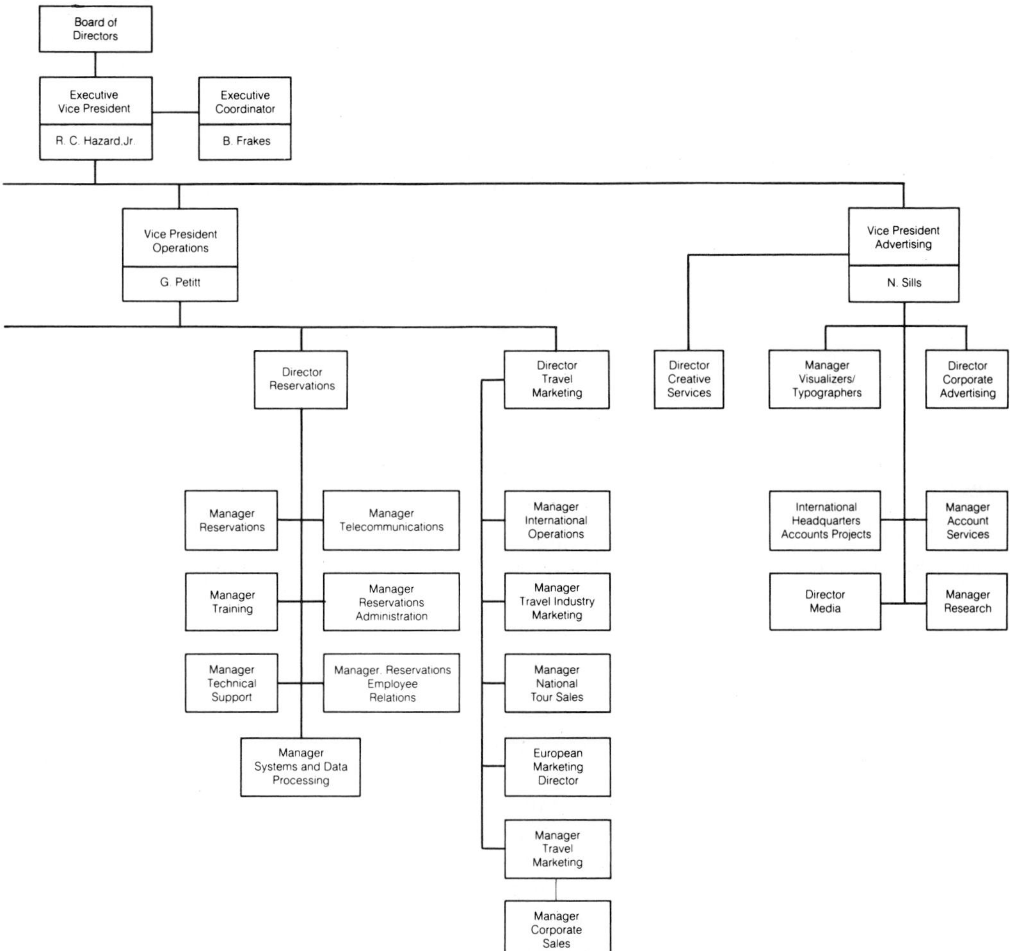

19 *Vice President, Finance and Administration—Kendall G. Milhon.* A certified public accountant and 1967 graduate of Washburn University in Topeka, Kansas, Milhon began his career with Best Western in 1976 when he assumed the role of corporate controller. In March of 1978, he was promoted to vice president of finance and administration. Milhon manages an accounting staff of 12 and an administrative staff of 15 and directs all of the corporate building maintenance and furniture acquisition operations. Additionally, he is directly responsible for managing Best Western's short-term cash investments and for the financial services division.

20 *Vice President, Advertising—Malcolm T. Sills.* Following his graduation from the University of Denver, Malcolm Sills went to work as an office boy with a local ad agency. He quickly rose through the ranks, first as an account executive, then as an

office manager, and finally as a vice president of a large Denver-based advertising agency. At this junction, Sills elected to implement an entrepreneurial dream and founded his own agency, Frye-Sills, Inc., in Denver. The agency was tremendously successful, but Sills longed for yet another challenge. In 1978, he accepted the position of vice president and general manager of advertising for Best Western International. Utilizing over 30 years of professional experience, Sills completely revamped Best Western's in-house advertising operation. He was responsible for innovating Best Western's "Media Trade Bank," a system that traded empty rooms for broadcast time and print space. This program matched the $3.5 million budget collected from member assessments and provided Best Western with $7 million worth of exposure in 1979.

21 *Vice President Membership Sales—John P. Matlick.* Matlick is also a relocated executive from American Express. He was formerly a regional sales director for the credit card and reservations division. In 1974, he was appointed western regional vice president for membership sales at Best Western and, in July of 1979, was promoted to head Best Western's domestic and international sales programs. Matlick developed and implemented a number of innovative marketing programs that doubled new revenues from $1 to $2 million annually.

Membership

22 As mentioned, Best Western is a nonprofit corporation owned by its members. Initial affiliation fee is set at a minimum of $2,805 (20 rooms or less) plus $25 for each additional room. Annual dues are $610 (up to 20 rooms) plus $21 per room up to 50. For properties with more than 50 rooms, the dues are $1,240 plus $7 per room over 50. Each unit owner contributes 8 cents per room per day for advertising and one half cent per room per day to support the professional development program.

23 Finally, reservation fees include 8 cents per room per day, plus 50 cents for each room booked through the reservation center. The new ST*R terminal is the only approved reservation system. This equipment is leased for $185 per month. Until this terminal is installed, the member must belong to the ST*RLINE toll-free telephone network. The cost for this service is $1 per room per month.

24 Simply, cost of membership for a 100-unit property with 70 percent occupancy charging $22 a room-night was $10,613 in 1977. This is about one third the amount required by Best Western's major competitors.

25 Each Best Western property is independently owned and operated. The properties range in size from 14 to 900 rooms. Collectively, Best Western offers 165,000 rooms in 1,500 cities worldwide. (See Exhibits 5 and 6.)

26 Applications for membership are forwarded to the board of directors. If the board approves, the applicant's initial membership is slated for a one-year probationary period. Memberships only apply to a single individual. If an individual owns multiple properties, he must prepare multiple applications for memberships.

Special Requirements

27 While Best Western prides itself on unifying a collection of fiercely independent owner/operators, the company does require certain consistencies in all its properties. Some of these include:

1. All incoming telephone calls must be answered using the name Best Western.
2. All new members are required to send a representative to orientation seminars.
3. All members must accept reservations from travel agents and pay a minimum of a 10 percent commission on the gross room rental.
4. All members must use in each room:
   a. Guest soap with the Best Western logo.
   b. Stationery with the Best Western logo.
   c. Book matches with the Best Western logo.
   d. Drinking glasses with the Best Western logo.
   e. Best Western logo door decals.
5. Additionally, all members must choose five of the following in-room items and five of the following public areas items:

In room (select any 5 items)

a.	Key tags.	*l.*	Sani bags.
b.	Phone decals	*m.*	Utility bag.
c.	Dial rings.	*n.*	Laundry bag.
d.	Waste baskets	*o.*	Shoe shine cloth.
e.	Ash trays.	*p.*	Paper hand towel.
f.	Ice tubs.	*q.*	Ice scraper.
g.	Plastic tray.	*r.*	Shoe horn.
h.	Stationery bag.	*s.*	Phone book cover.
i.	Shower curtain.	*t.*	Pens or pencils.
j.	Shower cap.	*u.*	Door message cards.
k.	Toilet seat bands.	*v.*	Room number decals.

Public areas—office, lobby, or restaurant (select any 5 items)

a.	Business cards.	*l.*	Welcome mat.
b.	Folios	*m.*	Cloth emblem.
c.	Statements.	*n.*	Mileage meter.
d.	Reservation forms.	*o.*	Restaurant checks.
e.	Purchase order forms.	*p.*	Bar checks.
f.	Post cards.	*q.*	Menu covers.
g.	Phone book cover.	*r.*	Place mats.
h.	Function binder.	*s.*	Napkins.
i.	Pens or pencils.	*t.*	Stapler.
j.	Name badges.	*u.*	Logo buttons.
k.	Travel guide holder.	*v.*	Best Western flag.

6. Finally, all Best Western properties are subject to inspection three times yearly.

28 Improved property quality control has been a major objective established by Hazard. "We have 14 inspectors that spend 365 days a year on the road. Each property is inspected on-site and judged according to our 1,000-point checklist. If a property scores 800 points or below, it is immediately placed on probation and given the choice to upgrade or be terminated." In the past four years, Best Western has cancelled 467 property memberships. During the same time period, the company received more than 11,000 membership inquiries and approved 882 new members.

Exhibit 5

Best Western Twin Peaks Motel, Ouray, Colorado

Exhibit 6

Best Western Posada Inn, San Diego, California

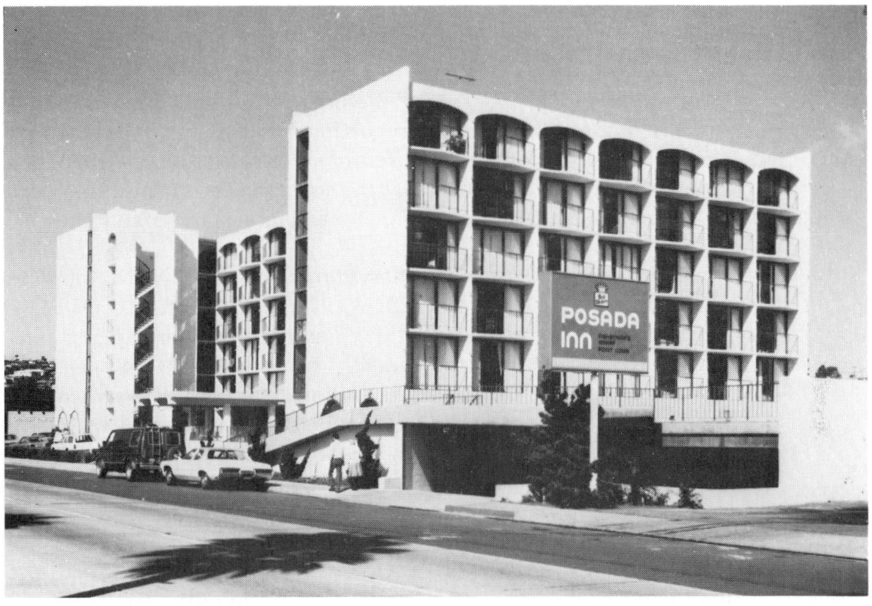

Company Services

29 Best Western provides a number of valuable services to its members. Some of the more notable of these support services include: (Many will be discussed at length in later sections.)

B-W Advertising, Inc.—provides a varied selection of advertising services to chain members and directs corporate advertising expenditures of $10 million. Also, this in-house agency coordinates the distribution of over 5 million copies of the Best Western Road Atlas and Travel Guide. This publication is designed to stimulate room sales and to generate repeat business.

B-W Insurance Agency—this agency, a wholly-owned subsidiary of Best Western, offers a variety of insurance packages to association members.

B-W Financial Services—provides financial assistance to all members for long-term permanent (mortgage) and interim (construction loans) financing.

Supply division—offers wholesale purchasing of furniture and supplies to Best Western members.

Reservations—the new ST*R system at Best Western reduces advance reservation time to approximately 30 seconds and is expected to quadruple bookings.

Identity—Best Western argues that the chain sign is a veritable people magnet. A 1976 survey conducted by the company indicates that 76 percent of the association's membership claim at least one fourth of their business can be credited to the sign.

Professional Institute—provides a number of training and development courses for all member motor inns, hotels, and resorts. It's easy to be the best—all you need is the best properties and the best-trained people in the hospitality industry.

Financial Performance

30 Revenues of $15,578,538 in 1978 were 105 percent higher than 1975. Reservations were providing an increasing proportion of revenues to the company. In 1976, reservations provided 33 percent of corporate revenues and, by 1978, this figure was up to 42 percent. Of note is the fact that the company received a lesser percentage of advertising payments, membership dues, monthly dues, and affiliation fees in 1978 compared to 1976.

31 In 1976, the Best Western reservation center received 2,450,974 calls that resulted in gross room sales of $47,494,026. In 1978, reservations received 4,034,934 calls producing $106,313,705.47 in sales. The 1977 annual membership cost of a 100-room property was $7,115. In 1979, this membership cost rose to $10,947 per year.

32 Accounts payable for the years ending 1977 and 1978 indicate $384,000 payable to Telemax Corporation. In 1969, Best Western contracted with Telemax to provide a central reservation system. In 1971, Telemax terminated the contract and filed for bankruptcy. Best Western insisted that Telemax did not perform under terms stipulated in the contract and suspended all payments to the company. The case is now currently in litigation, and the outcome is unknown.

33 Additionally, Best Western is currently involved in a lawsuit filed by an ex-association member, alleging that his contract was unduly terminated. The plaintiff in this case is asking for a damage settlement of $1 million. The company is also involved as defendant in a number of other claims of this nature but considers these to have little potential impact on the firm's financial performance. A review of some pertinent financial information is contained in Exhibits 7 and 8.

Marketing

34 Best Western Advertising Agency, created as a full-service agency in 1976, manages B-W's mulitmillion dollar corporate advertising program. With 1979 billings of $6.5 million, its principal goal is to build a favorable marketing image among its many publics. National media promotions attempt to sell B-W to tour brokers, bus associations, travel agents, corporate travel planners, and the traveling public among others. National and regional television, radio, magazines, newspapers, and outdoor advertising are all used to build awareness and preference for Best Western.

35 Beyond corporate advertising, the chain offers direct, personalized advertising assistance to all members. Each district has its own account executive who serves as a direct link to the advertising department at headquarters. Account executives work with individual properties to design local advertising and marketing campaigns utilizing radio and TV, newspapers, travel agent ads, billboards, Yellow Page ads, public relation promotions, brochures, menus, letterheads, and hundreds of related projects. The account executive may call on the expertise of media research specialists, copywriters, artists, and others at the headquarters agency. Although members are charged

Exhibit 7

BEST WESTERN INTERNATIONAL, INC.
Consolidated Statements of Revenue, Expenses, and Net Assets
For the Years Ended November 30, 1975–1978

	1978	*1977*	*1976*	*1975*
Revenues:				
Membership dues and affiliation fees	$ 4,459,060	$ 3,977,295	$3,426,995	$2,608,000
Reservations	6,528,293	4,440,956	3,159,545	2,572,433
Advertising	3,559,567	2,786,656	2,365,230	1,864,024
Purchasing commissions	386,531	289,658	305,805	358,438
Insurance commissions	38,512	85,811	62,266	—
Interest income	157,911	75,322	—	—
Other	448,664	318,040	194,856	187,909
Total revenues	15,578,538	11,973,738	9,514,697	7,590,894
Expenses:				
Advertising:				
Travel guide	1,313,110	1,056,174	914,018	993,818
Other advertising	2,686,552	1,575,427	1,523,699	1,361,757
Salaries, wages, and commissions	4,053,901	2,728,256	2,072,319	1,757,695
Payroll taxes and employee benefits	587,956	380,066	272,101	222,152
Telephone	2,240,401	1,844,600	1,428,756	1,251,660
Building and equipment rental	1,136,049	805,767	578,346	247,473
Depreciation and amortization	717,360	452,107	383,658	363,152
Travel	552,674	483,631	340,726	317,494
Postage and freight	181,960	186,727	264,477	265,716
Supplies	346,809	291,698	227,869	124,009
Professional fees	69,593	126,353	157,358	84,574
Bad debts	55,864	30,387	92,993	77,970
Directors' fees	78,800	60,428	57,200	53,444
Outside services	46,511	52,991	45,252	85,435
Maintenance	131,610	61,036	200,783	48,682
Interest	240,179	37,994	393,781	237,144
Other	761,156	537,630	205,277	20,050
Income tax expense (benefit)	(71,276)	551,817	—	—
Total expenses	15,129,209	11,263,089	9,158,613	7,512,225
Revenues in excess of expenses	449,329	710,649	356,084	78,669
Net assets at beginning of year	1,817,545	1,106,896	750,812	672,143
Net assets at end of year	$ 2,266,874	$ 1,817,545	$1,106,896	$ 750,812

for the service, rates are economical due to B-W's nonprofit status and group purchasing power.

36 One campaign undertaken by the association is the Media Trade Bank advertising program. In an effort to fill rooms during soft seasons and increase the efficiency of the advertising dollar, a system of exchanging unsold room-nights for advertising was devised. Each B-W property contributes room-nights equal to one half of 1 percent of the property's room-nights. This figure multiplied by the average room rate becomes the property's Media Trade Bank account, of which half is invested in corporate advertising and half in advertising the B-W property itself. Many regions vote to pool their Media Trade Bank budgets to sell the entire region with a high-impact cooperative program.

Exhibit 8

BEST WESTERN INTERNATIONAL, INC.
Consolidated Balance Sheets
For the Years Ended November 30, 1975–1978

	1978	*1977*	*1976*	*1975*
Assets				
Current assets:				
Cash	—	$ 256,000	$ 227,440	$ 547,114
Short-term investment, at cost which approximates market	784,478	—	—	—
Accounts and notes receivable (net of allowance for doubtful accounts of $85,000 in 1978, $41,000 in 1977, $40,000 in 1976, and $48,277 in 1975)	1,271,051	644,616	512,174	444,463
Prepaid expenses and other assets	37,638	45,504	20,091	29,771
Deferred travel guide costs	1,276,272	1,313,036	1,037,905	937,271
Refundable income taxes	165,157	—	11,250	—
Total current assets	3,534,596	2,259,156	1,808,860	1,958,619
Property and equipment, at cost:				
Land	813,675	813,675	813,675	—
Building	3,308,925	3,125,333	153,235	—
Signs	3,180,234	2,731,955	2,302,199	2,055,631
Furniture and equipment	1,362,579	1,094,701	409,021	324,236
Leasehold improvements	9,933	9,933	245,553	235,688
Land improvements	34,355	26,784	—	—
	8,709,701	7,802,381	3,923,623	2,615,555
Less accumulated depreciation and amortization	2,596,336	1,953,419	1,866,659	1,800,846
Total property and equipment	6,113,365	5,848,962	2,057,024	814,709
Other assets	11,547	24,169	26,165	4,584
Total assets	$9,659,508	$8,132,287	$3,892,049	$2,777,912
Liabilities and Net Assets				
Current liabilities:				
Bank overdraft	$ 406,391	—	—	—
Current installments of long-term debt	61,400	70,000	—	—
Current portion of obligation under capital lease	58,875	67,200	—	—
Accounts payable and accrued liabilities	2,461,196	2,038,947	$1,534,166	$ 999,805
Travel guide expenses payable	1,143,750	1,210,754	951,437	838,270
Income taxes payable	—	360,774	—	16,806
Deferred income taxes	256,244	284,166	214,486	112,959
Deposits—membership applications	105,398	99,767	31,291	13,645
Accrued interest	6,623	12,479	—	—
Deferred income	101,936	21,057	53,773	35,615
Total current liabilities	4,601,813	4,165,144	2,785,153	2,027,100
Long-term debt, less current installments	2,505,390	1,733,305	—	—
Obligations under capital lease, less current installments	210,045	329,219	—	—
Deposits	27,903	36,629	—	—
Deferred income taxes	47,483	50,445	—	—
	2,790,821	2,149,598	—	—
Net assets	2,266,874	1,817,545	1,106,896	750,812
Commitments and contingent liability				
Total liabilities and net assets	$9,659,508	$8,132,287	$3,892,049	$2,777,912

37 Media Trade Bank guests include a TV producer filming a special with crews staying in various locations while shooting, a network vice president on a business trip, and a group of announcers for professional rodeo. The program is expected to gain B-W upwards of $5 million in advertising annually.

38 Other marketing programs focus on special audiences; for example, a presentation at the American Bus Association (ABA) Marketplace included a corporate-sponsored breakfast for the ABA, a hospitality suite, prizes, and a series of B-W booths. A special program, Guestcheque, directed at the European market, makes it possible for members to attract European visitors and assure prompt payment in U.S. currency through a large U.S. bank.

Supply Division

39 A major benefit of Best Western membership is the buying power represented by the supply division. Through vendor contracts, the division offers brand-name products at member discounts. Commissions for Best Western from the sales (over $250,000 annually) help cover operating costs of headquarters thus keeping member fees and dues lower. Vendor contracts include agreements with Pepsi-Cola, Shasta, Columbia Match Company, Chevrolet, Farmer Bros. and Wechsler Coffee Companies, Fort Howard Paper Company, RCA Service Company, and Inn Keepers Supply Company. Inn Keepers Supply (IKS), the largest institutional supply company in the country, offers a comprehensive line of room furnishings and restaurant equipment as well as design services for lobby, guest rooms, and restaurant. The company also provides a variety of B-W logo items such as shower curtains, glasses, soap, ashtrays, and wastebaskets as well as a line of over 1,200 different hotel/motel forms, decals, menu covers, and so forth. Arrangements exist with a number of companies to provide specialty logo items including wooden signs, Kellogg breakfast menus, Rosemary Candy Company lollipops, and the ubiquitous T-shirt.

Reservations

40 B-W prides itself on having the finest modern equipment and the finest reservation staff in the industry. The brains of the property-to-property system are the more than 800 ST*R terminals installed at front desks of members all over the United States. The ST*R system has three components: a CRT display screen (cathode ray tube—similar to a television screen), a computerized keyboard for sending messages, and a hard-copy printer for receiving reservations and messages from other B-W properties and the reservation center in Phoenix. Using these terminals, members are urged to make their guests' following-night reservations at another Best Western property. If no rooms are available at the guest's first choice facility, ST*R automatically displays availabilities at the nearest alternate Best Westerns. The entire process can be completed in approximately 30 seconds, and the reservation information is transmitted instantaneously to the other property. (See Exhibit 9)

41 For members whose ST*R terminal is not yet installed, there is a toll-free ST*RLINE to the reservations center which also handles calls directly from the traveling public. Volume of calls to the reservations center increased by 1 million from 3.1 million in 1977 to 4.1 million in 1978 and was still going up rapidly in 1979. The same year showed a 35 percent increase in confirmed reservations and a 52 percent increase in

Exhibit 9

gross room sales dollars while the cost of the 3.9 million room-nights sold remained exactly the same as the year before. B-W officials attribute this remarkable record to the combination of new equipment which improved efficiency of operations and its well-trained staff.

42 Canadian Best Western members have their own reservations center with toll-free ST*RLINE funded, as is the U.S. line, by a $1 per room per month charge to members. As in the United States, members are urged to use the toll-free number exclusively for completely computerized and, in Canada, bilingual reservation capability.

43 Ted MacPherson, manager of B-W telecommunications department, describes ambitious plans for the future. "Telecommunications includes all means and methods of transmission of information such as telephone, telex, teletype, video, microwave, cable, and satellite. The possibilities of satellite transmission of information to members include in-room movies, cleaner data transmission, and a reduction in output errors as well as reduction of dependence on telephone lines. Additionally, we would like to expand the overall capabilities of Best Western utilizing advanced technology to improve efficiency in reservations and communications while minimizing costs."

Professional Institute

44 "In a labor-intensive business, the competitive edge between lodging chains for 'the best' is very thin. We need to develop our people's talents and promote and nurture

their dedication to excellence." With these words Gerald Petitt, operations vice president and chief operating officer for Best Western, explains the philosophy behind headquarters' extensive educational services. Each year, four regional conferences are scheduled as 2½-day educational and training sessions. Business spiced with recreation is provided at resort conference centers with facilities for an expected 500 attendees. In 1979, meetings were scheduled at Hilton Head, South Carolina; Colorado Springs; Monterey, California; and Lake of the Ozarks, Missouri. Each year's meeting focuses on one topic of particular interest to members. One year attention is devoted to housekeeping; another year, front desk or financial management will serve as the theme. Meetings are planned on a five-year cycle to facilitate members' plans and scheduling.

45 B-W's new headquarters in Phoenix, Arizona, serve as a focal point for an intensive, on-going member education program. George Ross, professional communicator, heads the educational services department which develops, supervises, and conducts the continuous training programs both in Phoenix and in numerous locations around the country.

Professional Development Program

46 This program is responsible for training new members and keeping B-W members abreast of innovations in the lodging industry. Four full-time instructors conduct programs designed to enhance service and cut costs for the member innkeeper. A professional development program catalog, distributed annually, provides a description of facilities available, a calendar of training sessions, and the location and course description for all programs, including remote sessions, round-up, area meetings, and orientation seminars. Courses offered include:

1. The management development course—designed for personnel directly involved with on-site management (for example, general manager, front desk manager, executive housekeeper, and so on).
2. Fundamentals of hotel/motel operations course—designed for the new owner who has never owned a property, has no experience in the industry.
3. Orientation seminar course—a mandatory program for all new B-W members.
4. Front office management course—designed to teach or reinforce basic skills for the general manager, front-office manager, and assistant.
5. Personnel management course—designed to help B-W operators deal more efficiently with their employees, with focus on government regulations, record keeping, and employment requirements.
6. Food and beverage management course—designed for personnel directly or indirectly involved in food and beverage operations (such as general manager, food and beverage manager, restaurant manager and assistant, and purchasing agent).

47 Attendance at courses is traditionally high. For example, the management development program drew 1,000 B-W owners and operators during 1978. A shortened, intensive version of the normally five-day course was taken to remote locations during 1979. To make attendance easier for more operating personnel, three-day sessions were held in Georgia, Minnesota, and West Virginia.

48 A section of headquarters, designated a learning laboratory with mock-ups of all room types found in the hospitality environment, doubles as a studio for production

Exhibit 10

A gracious Cotswold stone hotel set in 10 acres of garden woodland, the Best Western Hare and Hounds Hotel is convenient to Bristol, Gloucester, Cheltenham, and Bath. Guests at the hotel can choose from old world garden strolls, squash and tennis on the Hare and Hounds' own courts, or the warmth and charm of a log fire at any of the hotel's three pubs. It is one of 108 interchange hotels now affiliated with Best Western, the world's largest lodging chain.

of training films. Each B-W property maintains an inn-training film library designed to supplement each manager's on-site training efforts. New film strips are mailed regularly from headquarters as a reflection of B-W's belief that first-class facilities and service can only be accomplished through a comprehensive and professional training program.

49 The cost of attending programs is paid by all members through a monthly educational assessment. Individual students pay their own transportation, room and board, and a book and materials fee.

International Operations

50 In late October 1979, Best Western executives from around the world convened in London, England. Those present at the conference included the board of directors

from the United States, the chairman of each of the international affiliate organizations, and the chief executive officers and key personnel from each country. The meetings were called to set policies and determine expansion directions for the organization on a worldwide basis.

51 Bob Hazard notes, "Six years ago, Best Western had no international affiliates. Today, it has properties in 18 countries." Foreign affiliates include a 135-member hotel group in England-Scotland-Wales, 80 Best Westerns in New Zealand, as well as properties in Canada, Mexico, Australia, southern Africa, Ireland, France, Austria, Denmark, Sweden, Finland, Luxembourg, Andorra, and the Caribbean.

52 In an effort to increase Best Western's share of the international travel market, a new director of marketing for Europe was recently appointed. Brendan Ebbs, experienced in both the U.S. and European travel industry, intends to concentrate on three aspects of international operations. "My first priority is to channel visitors from Europe into Best Western properties in North America. Next, I'll be aiding Best Westerns on this side of the ocean by helping make sure that U.S. visitors stay in Best Western's European affiliates. And, of course, I'll be seeking new groups of quality European hotels to join Best Western."

Best Western International, Inc. (B): Update—1981

53 As it moves into the 1980s, Best Western has emerged as the most-aggressive suitor for Holiday Inns's share of the lodging industry market. In total number of sites, Best Western has surpassed Holiday Inns. By the end of 1980, Best Western had over 2,700 locations to Holiday Inns's 1,755 company-owned and franchised units. These were the only two U.S.-based lodging chains to top $1 billion in 1979 lodging sales. Best Western topped $1.5 billion in systemwide 1980 revenues. Exhibits 11, 12, and 13 provide updated information on Best Western's financial performance and position through November 30, 1979. Combined net profit before taxes for all Best Western properties rose from $30 million in 1975 to over $205 million in 1979.

Quality Control

54 Best Western has placed increasing emphasis on standardized quality control across its rapidly growing system. Claiming to have "the toughest quality control inspection system in the lodging industry," each Best Western property is visited twice a year by one of 14 full-time inspectors and rated in terms of facilities, maintenance, and cleanliness on a stringent 1,000-point rating system. More than 338 mismanaged or worn-out properties have been terminated in the last three years for failure to meet Best Western's increasingly tougher quality control standards.

55 As an indicator of its quality lodging emphasis, Best Western's goal is to have the top-rated property in every market area by 1989. Currently, Best Western has the top-rated property in 532 cities in the United States and Canada according to *Mobile Travel Guide.*

56 To further this commitment, B-W supply division (a wholly owned subsidiary) has established purchasing relationships with major manufacturers to supply Best Western affiliates with a wide variety of high-quality products at low prices (up to 30 percent discounts).

Future Business: The Foreign Traveler

57 As he looked toward the 1980s, Robert Hazard, Best Western's chief executive officer (CEO), sees the foreign traveler as the answer to gasoline shortages, prices, and other

This update was prepared by Richard Robinson, University of South Carolina.

Exhibit 11

BEST WESTERN INTERNATIONAL, INC., AND SUBSIDIARIES
Consolidated Statements of Revenues, Expenses and Net Assets
For the Years Ended November 30, 1978–1979

	1979	*1978*
Revenues:		
Membership dues and affiliation fees	$ 4,825,205	$ 4,459,060
Reservations	10,467,046	6,528,293
Advertising	3,960,314	3,559,567
Purchasing commissions	449,568	386,531
Insurance commissions	65,346	38,512
Interest income	318,048	157,911
Other	730,133	448,664
Total revenues	20,815,660	15,578,538
Expenses:		
Advertising:		
Travel guide	1,354,919	1,313,110
Other advertising	3,052,839	2,686,552
Salaries, wages, and commissions	5,138,152	4,053,901
Payroll taxes and employee benefits	912,733	587,956
Telephone	2,725,704	2,240,401
Building and equipment rental	2,592,042	1,136,049
Depreciation and amortization	801,278	717,360
Travel	771,817	552,674
Postage amd freight	202,997	181,960
Supplies	503,226	346,809
Professional fees	143,576	69,593
Bad debts	80,000	55,864
Directors' fees	95,025	78,800
Outside services	44,003	46,511
Maintenance	159,713	131,610
Interest	263,855	240,179
Other	867,180	761,156
Income tax expense (benefit)	263,299	(71,276)
Total expenses	19,972,358	15,129,209
	843,302	449,329
Revenues in excess of expenses		
Net assets at beginning of year	2,266,874	1,817,545
Net assets at end of year	$ 3,110,176	$ 2,266,874

threats to the U.S. lodging industry. When gasoline hits $2 a gallon, according to Hazard, auto driving will fall by 17 percent.[1] In a 1980 interview with *Forbes,* Hazard said: "We must move boldly and decisively before changing conditions drop our occupancy and profits."[2] Instead of following Holiday Inns into casino gambling, Hazard's answer has been to make a major effort to attract foreign travelers. He expects the

[1] Best Western's major competitor, Holiday Inns, flatly disagrees. Their research suggests no real change in highway auto travel at $2-a-gallon prices. Other studies, like the American Petroleum Institute agree with Best Western.

[2] "Somebody Must Be Wrong," *Forbes,* April 14, 1980, p. 86.

Exhibit 12

BEST WESTERN INTERNATIONAL, INC., AND SUBSIDIARIES
Consolidated Statement of Changes in Financial Position
For the Years Ended November 30, 1978–1979

	1979	*1978*
Financial resources were provided by:		
Revenues in excess of expenses	$ 843,302	$ 449,329
Items which do not use (provide) working capital:		
Depreciation and amortization	801,278	717,360
Provision for noncurrent deferred income taxes	247,555	(2,962)
Loss on retirement of property and equipment	2,006	11,695
Other	—	(6,587)
Working capital provided by operations	1,894,141	1,168,835
Proceeds from long-term borrowings	—	796,695
Proceeds from sale of property and equipment	46,648	—
Other	—	23,672
Total resources provided	1,940,789	1,989,202
Financial resources were used for:		
Purchase of property and equipment	1,005,251	1,004,508
Computer software development costs	544,196	—
Current installments and repayment of long-term debt	61,512	24,610
Current installments and repayment of obligations under capital lease	56,005	119,174
Other	46,461	2,139
Total resources used	1,713,425	1,150,431
Decrease in working capital deficit	$ 227,364	$ 838,771
Analysis of (increase) decrease in working capital deficit:		
Cash	$ —	$ 256,000
Short-term investments	(220,362)	(784,478)
Accounts and notes receivable	(534,170)	(626,435)
Prepaid and other expenses	(60,289)	7,866
Deferred travel guide costs	1,113,679	36,764
Refundable income taxes	165,157	(165,157)
Bank overdraft	(294,478)	406,391
Current obligation under capital lease	10,528	(8,325)
Current installments of long-term debt	5,600	(8,600)
Accounts payable and accrued liabilities	619,455	422,249
Travel guide payable	(1,143,750)	(67,004)
Income taxes payable	328,125	(360,774)
Deferred income taxes	(339,666)	(27,922)
Deposits—membership application	20,676	5,631
Accrued interest	18,210	(5,856)
Deferred income	83,921	80,879
Decrease in working capital deficit	$ (227,364)	$ (838,771)

devalued dollar to attract increased foreign tourism and foreign businesses that will replace declining American travelers' dollars.

58 By early 1980, Best Western had recruited 852 new international affiliates in 18 countries. In 1980, Best Western added over 320 international affiliates to that number, including 28 West German properties. At present, 35 percent of Best Western membership is international. Hazard felt international visitors more familiar with the Best

Exhibit 13

BEST WESTERN INTERNATIONAL, INC., AND SUBSIDIARIES
Consolidated Balance Sheets
For the Years Ended November 30, 1978–1979

	1979	*1978*
Assets		
Current assets:		
Short-term investments, at cost, which approximates market	$ 1,004,840	$ 784,478
Accounts receivable (net of allowance for doubtful accounts of $130,685 in 1979 and $85,000 in 1978)	1,805,221	1,271,051
Prepaid expense and other assets	97,927	37,638
Deferred travel guide costs	162,593	1,276,272
Refundable income taxes	—	165,157
Deferred income taxes	83,422	—
Total current assets	3,154,003	3,534,596
Property and equipment, at cost:		
Land	813,675	813,675
Building	3,461,062	3,308,925
Signs	3,570,290	3,180,234
Furniture and equipment	1,669,257	1,362,579
Leasehold improvement	4,659	9,933
Land improvements	34,355	34,355
Total property and equipment, at cost	9,553,298	8,709,701
Less accumulated depreciation and amortization	3,284,614	2,596,336
Net property and equipment	6,268,684	6,113,365
Deferred costs and other assets	598,799	11,547
Total assets	$10,021,486	$9,659,508
Liabilities and Net Assets		
Current liabilities:		
Bank overdraft	$ 111,913	$ 406,391
Current installments of long-term debt	67,000	61,400
Current obligation under capital lease	69,403	58,875
Accounts payable and accrued liabilities	3,080,651	2,461,196
Travel guide expense payable	—	1,143,750
Income taxes payable	328,125	—
Deferred income taxes	—	256,244
Deposits—membership applications	126,074	105,398
Accrued interest	24,833	6,623
Deferred income	185,857	101,936
Total current liabilities	3,993,856	4,601,813
Long-term debt, less current installments	2,443,878	2,505,390
Obligations under capital lease, less current installments	154,040	210,045
Deposits	24,498	27,903
Deferred income taxes	295,038	47,483
Net assets	3,110,176	2,266,874
Commitments and contingent liability	—	—
Total liabilities and net assets	$10,021,486	$9,659,508

Exhibit 14

Best Western directory symbols

English	Español	Deutsch	Français
Restaurant on premises or within 500 feet.	Restaurante en el establecimiento o a menos de 150 metros.	Restaurant direkt auf Best Western Grund oder in höchstens 150m Entfernung.	Restaurant dans l'établissement ou au plus à 150 mètres.
Cocktail lounge on premises or within 500 feet.	Bar salón en el establecimiento o a menos de 150 metros.	Cocktail Bar im Hause oder in höchstens 200m Entfernung.	Bar avec salon dans l'établissement ou au plus à 150 mètres.
Swimming pool.	Piscina.	Swimming pool.	Piscine.
Indoor swimming pool.	Piscina interior.	Swimming pool im Hause.	Piscine couverte.
Banquet/meeting facilities*	Salones para reuniones o banquetes*	Gesellschafts- und Konferenzräume*	Salons pour banquets ou réunions*
Children under 12 free in same room with parents*	Se admiten gratis los niños de hasta 12 años de edad que compartan la misma habitación con los padres.	Freie Übernachtung für Kinder unter 12 Jahren, die zusammen mit den Eltern schlafen*	Gratuit pour enfants au dessous de 12 ans partageant la chambre de leurs parents*
Facilities for handicapped.	Instalaciones especiales para inválidos.	Einrichtungen für Behinderte.	Installations spéciales pour handicapés.
Fly/Drive packages.	Excursiones combinados avión/automóvil.	Kombinierte Flug-Mietwagen Angebote.	Excursions avion/automobile.
Pets allowed.	Se permiten animales domésticos.	Tiere erlaubt.	Animaux domestiques autorisés.
Pets limited*	Número de animales permitidos.	Nicht alle Tiere erlaubt.	Nombre limité d'animaux.*
No pets allowed.	Se prohiben los animales.	Hunde verboten!	Les animaux ne sont pas permis.
Higher rates for special events or holidays.	Tarifas más altas en dias de fiesta o acontecimientos especiales.	Zuschläge bei besonderen Anlassen oder an Feiertagen.	Tarifs plus élevés les jours fériés ou pendant les périodes de vacances.
Senior Citizen rates*	Tarifas especiales para retirados.	Ermäßigungen für Senioren.	Tarifs spéciaux pour retraités*
Live entertainment.	Entretenimiento en vivo.	Live Unterhaltung.	Cabaret-attractions.
In-room movies available.	Peliculas disponibles en su propia habitación.	Kino.	Diffusion vidéo de films dans votre chambre.
Golf course nearby.	Campo de golf cercano.	Golfanlage in der Nähe.	Terrain de golf à proximité.
Tennis courts nearby.	Campo de tennis cercano.	Tennisanlage in der Nähe.	Terrain de tennis à proximité.
Sauna.	Sauna.	Sauna.	Sauna.
24-hour airport courtesy car service.	Servicio de automóvil para transporte al aeropuerto 24 horas al dia.	Auto Service zum Flughafen rund um die Uhr.	Voiture navette gratuite entre l'aéroport et l'hotel 24 heures sur 24.
Limited airport courtesy car service*	Limitaciones del transporte al aeropuerto*	Auto Service zum Flughafen, jedoch zeitlich begrenzt.	Limitation de la navette gratuite aéroport-hotel.
Horseback riding nearby*	Se puede montar a caballo cerca*	Reitmöglichkeiten in der Nähe*	Randonnée à cheval approximitée*
Fishing nearby*	Se puede pescar cerca*	Angelmöglichkeiten in der näheren Umgebung*	Pêche autoriser approximitée*
Skiing nearby*	Se puede esquiar cerca*	Gelegenheit zum Schilaufen in der Nähe*	Piste de ski approximitée*
Playground.	Campo de recreo.	Spielplatz.	Terrain de jeu.

*(Contact property for specific information.)

*(Póngase en contacto con el establecimiento correspondiente para obtener información más especifica.)

*(Setzen Sie sich mit Best Western in Verbindung zwecks näherer Informationen.)

*(Pour tout renseignement complémentaire, contacter l'établissement correspondant.)

Exhibit 15

Best Western membership concept: Annual fee comparison

Because Best Western is the only nonprofit hotel corporation in the world, its affiliates are provided with the most-effective marketing, operational, and training programs in the industry at a cost substantially below those of any other major chain.

Yet the decision to join the world's largest lodging chain should be based on more than just reduced affiliation expenditures. The true value of Best Western International cannot be measured in terms of decreased membership fees, but rather in its ability to generate substantial new business, increase profits for its affiliates, and allow complete operational independence.

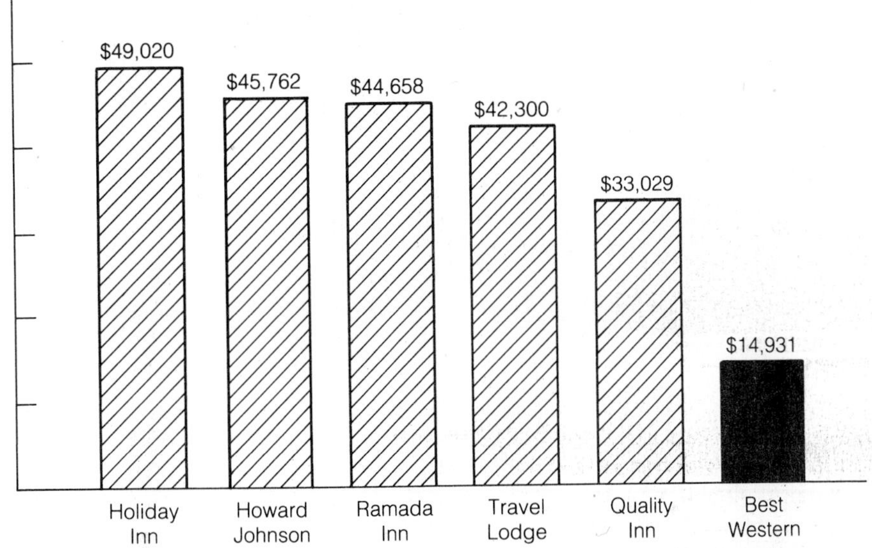

* Estimated costs for a 100-room hotel grossing $6,650 per room per year, based on latest available information.

Western name would more likely choose the U.S. Best Western properties. He feels Best Western's individualized properties will be an added advantage:

> Rooms appealing to foreigners are not those favored by Americans. Standardized packaging and cookie-cutter rooms will lose their appeal. They will be replaced by properties offering individual personality and atmosphere.[3]

59 As further evidence of this commitment to the foreign traveler, Best Western is the first lodging chain to provide multilingual directories, as shown in Exhibit 14.

The Future

60 Best Western is currently the fasters-growing chain in the lodging industry. Facing increasingly competitive conditions, Best Western feels its unique concept as a nonprofit association of independent lodging operators will lead it to the top (see Exhibit 15).

[3] Ibid.

61 In 1981, Best Western sought this goal with new leadership. Robert Hazard left Best Western to become CEO at Quality Inns. Rumors suggested the departure was prompted by a sizable offer from Quality Inns as well as increasing pressure from Best Western's independent membership for a greater voice in key decisions being made by Hazard.

case 28
Days Inns of America, Inc.

1 Cecil B. Day, a millionaire apartment developer from Atlanta, Georgia, sensed a void in the lodging industry while traveling with his family in New England in 1968 and in California in 1969. Full-service lodging facilities for the family with a limited travel budget did not exist. Day thought about Georgia and commented, "I realized that no one was looking out for the middle American, the guy with two, three, or four children traveling on a limited budget. Here was a need I was convinced we could fill. I noticed, too, that the budget chain, which had 31 units when I was on the West Coast a year before, now had 72."

2 By 1970, the full-service, economy concept of Days Inn became a reality with the opening of the first Days Inn in Savannah Beach, Georgia. It caught on quickly, and Days Inn soon became the fastest-growing chain in the world, doubling in size every six months. By 1978, it was ranked as the sixth-largest full-service lodging chain in North America.

3 By 1983, there were 322 Days Inns and Lodges in 31 states and Canada (see Exhibit 1), providing 45,416 rooms to their more than 25 million yearly guests.

4 The 322 Days Inn motels are 41 percent company-owned and 59 percent franchised.The revenue dollar in fiscal 1983 was divided as shown in Exhibit 2. Financial highlights are presented in Exhibit 3.

The Days Inns Concept

5 Cecil Day's "budget luxury" concept was a four-in-one economy facility, offering basic traveler services at reasonable prices. The four services—lodging, gasoline, restaurant, and gift shop—were to be of a streamlined, no-frills quality, oriented toward the budget-conscious traveling family. By eliminating unnecessary luxuries (like large lobbies and lounges) and achieving operational efficiencies (like one cashier station for restaurant, gift shop, gas, and lodging), DIA was able to offer standardized rooms similar to Holiday Inns, Ramada Inns, and Marriott at a 25 to 35 percent lower price. As they move into the 1980s, DIA has eliminated the phrase *budget luxury* from its vocabulary. But as the following excerpt from its 1983 annual report indicates, the underlying Days Inn concept remains unchanged:

> From its beginning, Days Inns has recognized that Americans want value for their dollar. The company's strategy has been to offer the traveling public

This case was developed by Richard Robinson and Patricia McDougall of the University of South Carolina.

Exhibit 1

Locations of Days Inns and Lodges: 1983

Open Days Inns and Lodges

Canada—1
Alabama—10
Arizona—1
Arkansas—3
California—5
Colorado—3
Connecticut—1
Florida 77
Georgia 46
Illinois—5
Indiana—11
Kansas—1
Kentucky—14
Louisiana—11
Maryland—5
Massachusetts—2
Michigan—4
Mississippi—5
Missouri—1
Nevada—1
New York 1
North Carolina—24
Ohio—14
Oklahoma—2
Pennsylvania—2
South Carolina—23
Tennessee—16
Texas—17
Virginia—17
West Virginia—2
Wyoming—1

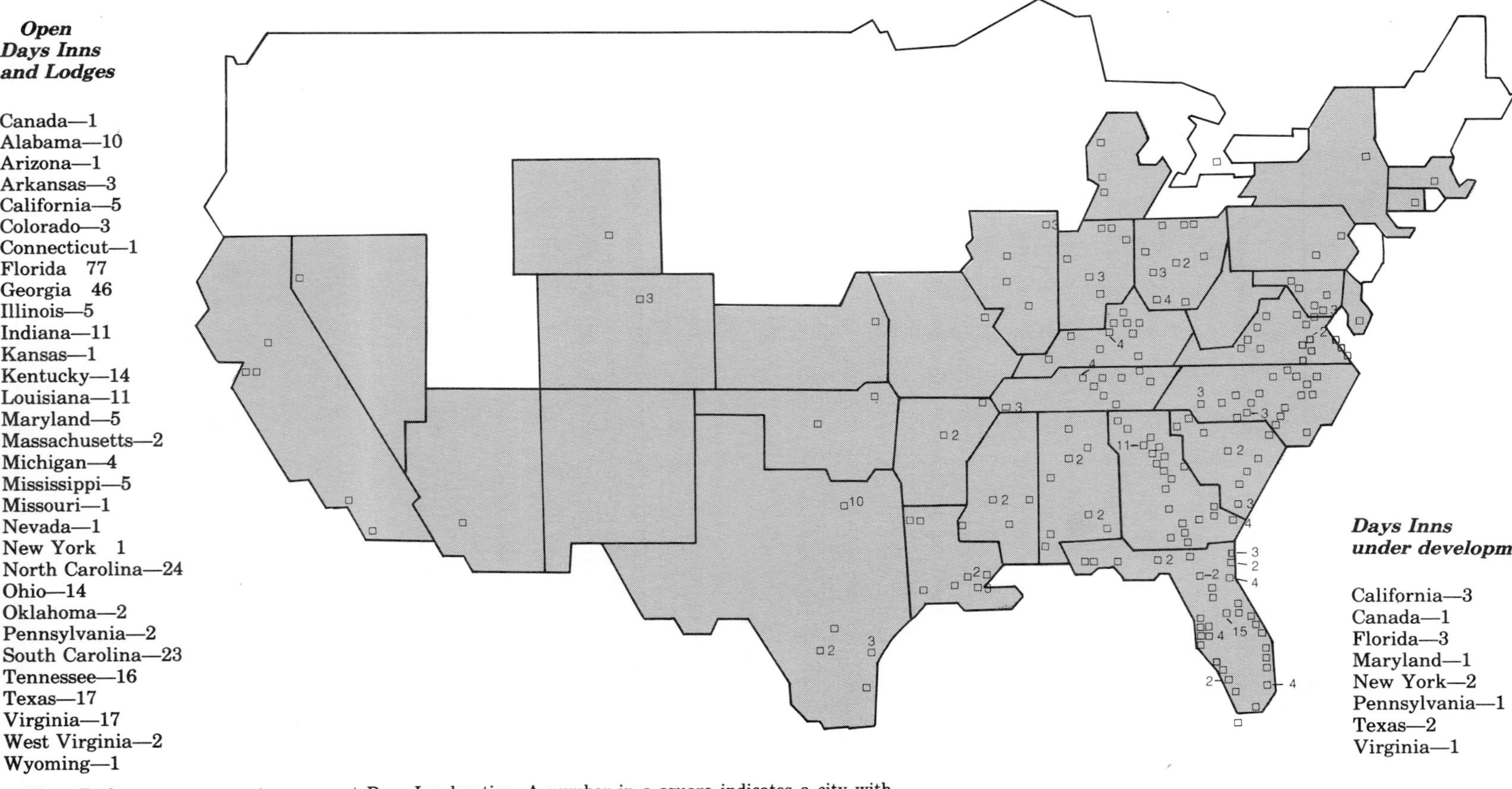

Days Inns under development

California—3
Canada—1
Florida—3
Maryland—1
New York—2
Pennsylvania—1
Texas—2
Virginia—1

Note: Each square represents a current Days Inn location. A number in a square indicates a city with more than one Days Inn (the number indicating how many in that city).

Exhibit 2

Revenue dollar, fiscal 1983

Lodging 62 percent	Food, gasoline, and novelties 27 percent	Franchise fees 3 percent	Rental 1 percent	Other 2 percent	Gains on sale of properties 4 percent

clean, comfortable rooms at an affordable price and accessories and amenities usually provided only by higher-priced competitors. That strategy, plus a determined quest for excellence in all areas of the business, has enabled Days Inns to achieve the goals it has set for itself in the past. Today Days Inns is becoming the new standard of American lodging.

6 Asked to define exactly what the Days Inn concept is, Richard Kessler, the youngest chief executive officer (CEO) in the lodging industry, said:

> Our intent is to serve the value-conscious traveler. Our properties do not have elaborate lobbies, cocktail lounges, or convention facilities. A typical Days Inn property includes a family restaurant, a gift shop, and a self-service gasoline facility. Each inn has a swimming pool, full-size rooms with complete bath, two double beds, telephone, and color television. We offer our guests one-stop convenience for food, gasoline, relaxation, and a good night's lodging. As we have developed, our strategy has evolved, but our basic concept is unchanged.

7 While DIA's concept remains unchanged, its market strategy has evolved considerably from what it was when Richard Kessler and Cecil Day built the first Days Inn in 1970 at Savannah Beach, Georgia.

8 Days Inn focused primarily on family travelers in its early development, building along interstate highways in the eastern United States. Later, DIA focused on destination locations (particularly Florida) that received customers from the eastern interstate network. But as DIA moves into the 1980s, its market strategy has taken a new focus to accommodate changing trends in traveler characteristics.

9 Exhibit 4 provides DIA's projections of the changing customer mix for the travel industry in the 1980s. DIA does not interpret this to mean a movement out of its role of serving the budget-conscious family, which Richard Kessler considers an important core constituency at Days Inns. Nonetheless, this changing customer mix has led DIA to link its future growth to the ability to cater to the changing customer segments. Commenting on the typical Days Inn customer in the 1980s, Kessler offered the following:

> Our guests are business men and women who pay their own expenses or travel on limited expense accounts. They are government employees and military per-

Exhibit 3

Financial highlights for the years ended September 30, 1979–1984

	Projected 1984	*1983*	*1982*	*1981*	*1980*	*1979*
Net revenue	$269,214,000	$233,552,000	$205,527,000	$188,983,000	$168,963,000	$151,179,000
Income before taxes	30,005,000	26,145,000	15,138,000	13,895,000	14,610,000	9,327,000
Net income	18,503,000	16,420,000	11,700,000	8,646,000	8,920,000	8,113,000
Stockholders' equity:						
Historical cost	74,697,000	56,194,000	39,939,000	21,062,000	12,710,000	1,288,000
Current value before potential costs on realization	—	367,822,000	277,290,000	203,335,000	164,448,000	146,869,000
Current value after potential costs on realization	—	257,069,000	195,011,000	134,281,000	108,082,000	85,208,000
Occupancy rate	70.0%	69.1%	65.7%	68.9%	70.3%	72.2%
Average room rate	$33.00	$30.06	$27.47	$24.09	$21.25	$18.48

Exhibit 3 *(concluded)*

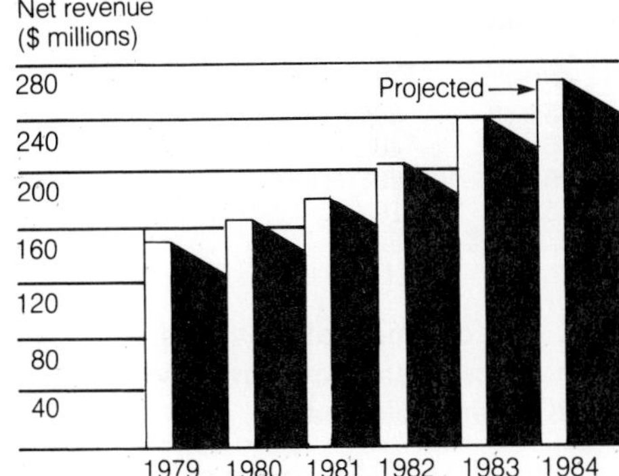

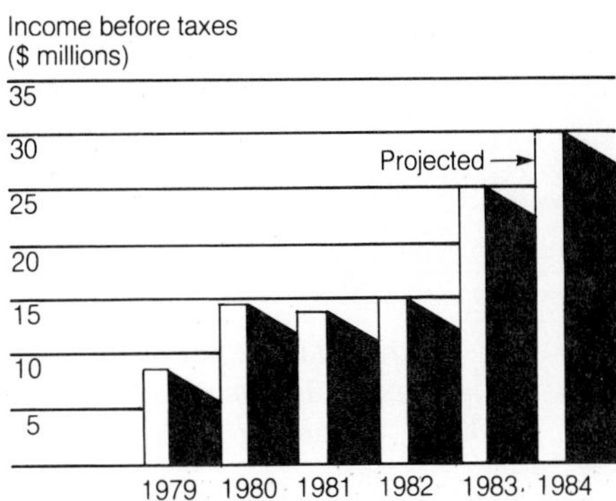

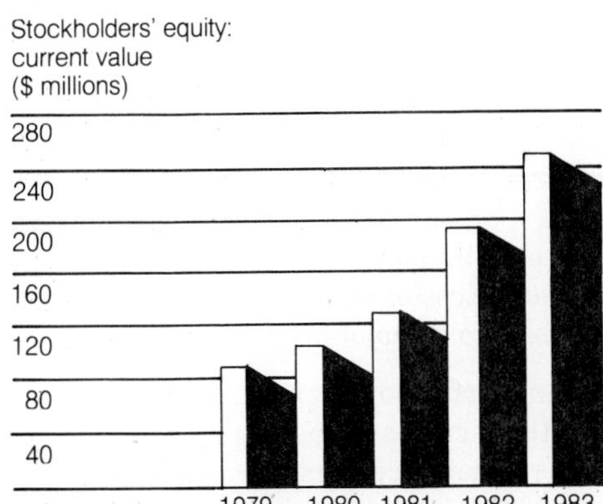

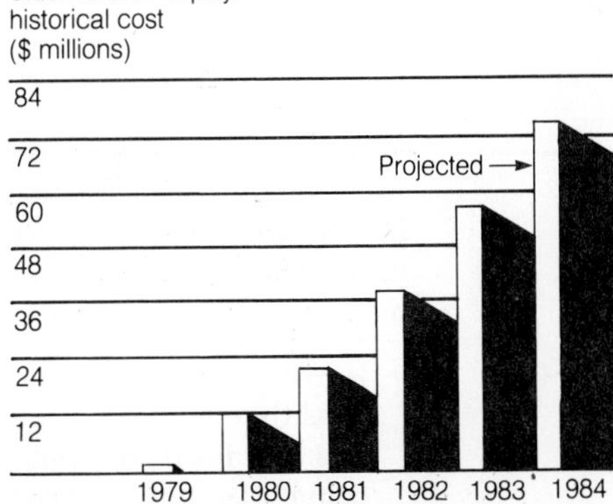

sonnel traveling on a per diem. They are vacationing families who want to minimize their lodging expense, younger adults raising families and purchasing homes, and senior citizens living on fixed incomes. The two latter groups, incidentally, will grow dramatically during the 1980s. The 35–44 age group will increase 51 percent in this decade and will take 44 percent more trips than the average of the general population. The 55-and-older population will increase by 13.6 percent.

10 Gradually DIA's customer base has expanded from families attracted to vacation locations like Walt Disney World and Epcot Center (where Days Inn hosts more visitors

Exhibit 4

Changing customer mix in the lodging industry (Days Inns estimates)

Market segment	*Now*	*Future*
Family	65%	30%
Business	15	40
Over 55	15	20
Government, military	5	10

than any other lodging chain), senior citizens, and commercial travelers. DIA has expanded its commercial market with suburban, airport, and downtown locations.

11 Referring to these market expansion moves, Kessler explained:

> In 1983 we opened 13 new hotels in locations selected to increase our service to the value-conscious traveler. Although remaining firmly committed to our traditional customer base of traveling families, senior citizens, military personnel, and government officials on a per diem, we are continuing to expand our commercial market. Because many commercial travelers utilize our facilities year-round, we are able to minimize the effects of travel cycles. We are working toward a customer mix divided evenly between commercial and vacation travelers.

12 Stressing the need for flexibility, DIA has diverted from its earlier strategy of excluding such facilities as meeting rooms to that of providing rooms and other facilities to accommodate small-to medium-sized business meetings and related social events at downtown and airport properties, as well as at some of the suburban locations.

13 DIA has altered its marketing strategy in terms of site location and geographic location. For the 1980s, DIA will concentrate almost exclusively on major cities adjacent to centers of transportation, government, military, or commercial activity. In addition, DIA will seek airport locations, says Richard Kessler, because of the airlines' increasing role in serving a more-transient America. Richard Kessler offered the following comments on DIA's move from an interstate emphasis to a major-city emphasis.

> We have completed building the base of our north-south network in the East. Less than 50 percent of our business today (1981) comes from interstate properties. Our future depends on suburban locations in major centers of transportation, commerce, and government. Although we consider downtown sites, we locate primarily in the suburbs because of the broader combined customer base of commercial and family travelers, because suburban properties generally have higher visibility and easier access, and because of high real estate appreciation.

14 Geographically, DIA will place major emphasis on westward expansion. In 1980, Days Inns opened its first Denver location, and seven western properties were opened by the end of 1983. The first California property was opened in 1981 in Sacramento. Kessler enthusiastically supports this westward expansion:

> The Denver-Rocky Mountains area is emerging as the energy center of the United States. In addition to its oil, it has become the focal point in the search for and production of alternate energy sources, encompassing the prospectors

Exhibit 5

New locations for fiscal 1984

Orlando Buena Vista	Monterey Seaside
Orlando International Drive	Miami Airport
Baltimore Inner Harbor	Bradenton
Corpus Christi	Amarillo
Santa Clara–San Jose	San Francisco Bay Bridge
Washington Springfield Mall	San Francisco Airport

and developers of oil shale, coal, uranium, and others. Denver is the location of the Solar Energy Research Institute as well, which will have a decided impact on the local economy. In addition, Denver is rebuilding into a major national business center. There is a tremendous influx of companies into the area. Colorado Springs has become a mecca for the electronics industry. Nine major electronics companies are there now, and four more are building facilities. The Rocky Mountains area is bursting with growth, and the potential for long-term real estate appreciation is excellent.

California offers everything that is called for in our strategic planning. It has a $16 billion tourist industry, an occupancy rate 9 percentage points higher than the national average, and a population of 20 million, which is nearly 10 percent of the U.S. population. Its economy of $315 billion is the ninth largest in the world, larger than that of Canada or Australia. It has 113 major military installations (more than any other state in the country), large government operations, great concentrations of higher education and high-technology industry. The population is very mobile. Twenty-five million people traveled through the state in 1979. We see very little competition in the California market that can match Days Inn motels in quality and price.

15 While DIA will look westward, key markets are still being developed east of the Mississippi. Shown in Exhibit 5 are the 12 new locations planned for 1984.

16 DIA has utilized a cluster concept, which involves developing a number of locations within a geographical region or along major highways. The practice maximizes operational synergism and efficiency; for example, it makes maximum use of advertising, ensures greater quality control, and encourages reciprocal business within the system. In an interview with *Business Week,* Kessler expressed the belief that by clustering, he could cut advertising and service costs and undercut competitors by 30 percent.[1]

17 Kessler has repeatedly said that he follows a "grow and plateau" formula in expanding the Days Inn network. From 1978 through 1980, DIA was at a plateau phase, adding a net increase of only nine locations, but 1981 appeared to signal the reemergence of a growth cycle. Tom Epps said, "DIA plans to add 12 or more properties for the next several years," suggesting Kessler is looking for a much-higher plateau.

18 Talking with *Lodging* magazine, Kessler summarized this new growth phase at Days Inns in simple terms: "We plan to go downtown. And to Washington, D.C. And out West—particularly to Texas, Colorado, and California."

---

[1] "Day's Inns: Looking for a Birth in a Crowded National Field," *Business Week,* October 31, 1983, p. 71.

Leadership at Days Inn

Cecil B. Day, Sr.—Founder

19 Born the son of a rural Georgia Baptist minister in 1934, Cecil Day grew up in Savannah and Macon, Georgia. As a high school student, he worked in his uncle's real estate office during the afternoons to help support his family after the death of his father. Day later worked full-time for a heating and air-conditioning company while attending Georgia Tech as a full-time student. After graduating in 1958, he soon became involved in the real estate business as a salesperson with an Atlanta-area realty company.

20 By 1962, Day had established his own realty company, Day Realty Associates, Inc., in Atlanta. In the year following its establishment, the company concentrated on building and operating apartments, amassing nearly 2,000 units, in addition to investing in other properties. In 1970, the company closed one of the largest sales ever in the southeastern real estate market—selling the majority of its apartment properties for over $13 million. The profits from that sale provided the financial base for the development and expansion of Days Inns.

21 Christian service was an important part of Cecil Day's life. He created a chaplain service as a corporate division of Days Inns of America, Inc. When a member of Gideons International complained to Day at a motel opening about guests stealing Bibles, Day responded, "Who needs a Bible more than a person who steals one?" Day started a program encouraging guests to take Bibles from Days Inns rooms, and by 1977, he had distributed over 1 million Bibles. Day's philosophy of combining sound business practices with Christian service is prominent throughout the company. Not only is Days Inns one of the few corporate tithers in history but it also extends personal chaplain services to guests and employees through its chaplain services division.

22 In December 1978, at age 44, Cecil Day died of cancer. In a statement to the *Atlanta Constitution,* Richard Kessler said:

> Day was an inspiration to all of us in the Day companies as a man of integrity, sincerity, and courage. We will continue to operate under the Christian principles Day established and maintain the corporate objectives he planned.

Richard C. Kessler, Chairman of the Board

23 With the loss of Cecil Day, it would not have been surprising to see the tightly held motel enterprise flounder as it readjusted to a leadership transition. Such occurrences are quite common in small- and medium-sized firms where the founder is a central driving force. At DIA, no such floundering occurred. Richard Kessler, who was appointed chief executive officer by Day in 1977 at the youthful age of 29, was well entrenched in the leadership of the DIA enterprise. As shown in the November 1979 interview with *The Atlanta Journal* (see Exhibit 6), Richard Kessler has been a key decision maker at Days Inns since it opened the first motel.

24 Top management at DIA has remained virtually unchanged since the mid-1970s. The one exception was the departure in 1980 of Doug McClain, vice president for operations, who left DIA to join a motel development group.

25 This departure led Kessler to reexamine the appropriateness of the management and organizational structure at DIA for the 1980s. This reexamination culminated in reorganizing DIA along what Kessler called the forum concept. DIA was organized in a matrix-type format with multiple management forums providing flexible yet tight management control of its rapidly growing and dispersed locations. Exhibit 7 provides a brief sketch of Kessler's forum organization. In this concept, the top management forum is composed of Kessler, Niemann, Burnette, Bush, and Prince. Additional forums are developed vertically along functionally specialized lines and horizontally along regional operating lines. This concept seeks to maintain tight control and expertise in DIA's strategic functional activities while maintaining integrated accountability and flexibility at regional operating levels.

Finance Division

26 Headed by Ken Niemann, the financial division anticipates a requirement of $80 million to finance its 1984 development program. In addition to corporate finance and accounting, Niemann's responsibilities include marketing, the Days Inn Reservation System, internal audit, and employee relations.

27 The marketing department encompasses a wide range of functions, including sales, general and outdoor advertising, public relations, and customer relations. Days Inns has been recognized as a marketing innovator in the motel industry. Current marketing programs—the Inn-Credible Card, Stay and Kids Eat Free, September Days Club, the Visit USA Voucher, and Dynamite Days—are discussed in a subsequent section. Some of the key parts of DIA's marketing strategy include the following:

28 **Pricing Strategy.** Days Inns' strategy has been to offer comfortable accommodations to the traveling public at economical rates. By streamlining operational costs, eliminating frills, and standardizing facilities, Days Inns is able to charge prices substantially below those of most competitors and to maintain a profitable, growing operation.

29 **Advertising.** Days Inns has followed a strategy of innovative advertising aimed at selected, budget-conscious market segments, such as families and retired people. Its billboard advertising is standardized by format and color scheme for all properties (company owned and franchises). A considerable amount of advertising is directed toward travel agents who receive a 10 percent or more commission for reservations. In 1983, approximately 14,000 travel agents participated in DIA's new Travel Agent Program, which generated more than $7.2 million in lodging revenues—almost double the anticipated amount.

30 **Days Inns Reservation System.** The computer center located at corporate headquarters in Atlanta is at the heart of the reservation center. Leading the industry in calls per room available, the reservation center generated over 30 percent of DIA's 1983 lodging sales.

Company officials hope to generate an additional 4,000 room nights per month with the recent association with American Airlines' SABRE system and Delta Airlines' DATAS II. A similar tie-in with United Airlines' APOLLO system will be completed in 1984.

Exhibit 6

The rise of Richard Kessler

Leaning forward on the couch of his expensively furnished office in the Day Building on Buford Highway, 33-year-old Richard C. Kessler says he can't think of any failures he's had while working for Days Inns of America.

"I don't think I've blown it anywhere along the way in the past eight years," he says.

As president and chairman of the board of the country's sixth-largest lodging chain, Kessler's self-confidence isn't surprising. He started working for Cecil B. Day, Sr., when Day founded Days Inns in 1970 and has never looked back.

Now running a 307-motel chain whose reservation system gets 4 million calls a year (fourth largest in the country) at what he says is the lowest cost per call in the industry, Kessler talked about his start with the company.

Before he graduated from Georgia Tech in 1970 with a master's degree in industrial engineering, Kessler interviewed with several real estate and development companies in Atlanta, but all would have put him in a very narrow, specialized job.

"I wanted to work quickly with a top person in the real estate business," Kessler says. He had talked with Day before entering Tech and talked to him again about finding a job.

In May 1970, Day met with Kessler at Savannah Beach, where they later built the first Days Inn. Kessler signed on as Day's personal assistant, and soon Kessler's father, a contractor, was knocking down the old Tybee Hotel to clear a site for the 60-room motel.

For most of the next two years, Kessler supervised the company's building program. While on a trip to Orlando, Florida, before Disney World opened, Kessler says he "felt the potential" for real estate growth in the area. When he returned to Atlanta, he told Day he should open a development office in Orlando.

"Fine," Day answered. "How would you like to go down there and run it?" he asked Kessler. Kessler agreed and spent the next three years in Florida. Those years included the gas shortage, recession, and depressed real estate market of 1973–74.

"Cecil called me one day in the summer of 1973 and said, 'Something's happening in this market. Let's reel in our horns and get prepared to weather an economic storm.' Three weeks later the oil embargo was announced," Kessler says.

Banks then cut off all funds to the motel business, Kessler says. "We had to make it with whatever cash we had in the system. I told my people, 'It is survival time. We are going to find out how strong we are.' "

Before the gas shortage, Kessler and Day had set up Day Realty of Orlando and Day Realty of Florida to build motels that Days Inns of America would lease or operate. To adjust for the recession, Kessler relieved the parent company of its leasing obligations and took over a 2,000-room operation.

"I wanted to put my fate in my own hands by actually running the motels," Kessler says. He owned 30 percent of the Florida company, and his financial prospects were tied heavily to the Florida operation.

Kessler, Day, and Days Inns all survived the recession. By 1975, however, Day was convinced he needed management help in Days Inns of America and called Kessler back to Atlanta to help out.

"Cecil called me and said he had a problem in Atlanta and that he needed help with it," Kessler says. Kessler insisted that he report directly to Day. Day doubled Kessler's salary, made him chief financial officer, in charge of everything except the chain's field operations, and promised him the company's presidency in 18 to 24 months if he did a good job.

"I knew that I could do it," Kessler says. "I always had it in mind that I would come back to Days Inns and run it."

Exhibit 6 *(concluded)*

> With a new controller, Kessler says he rebuilt the company's financial systems in a year and placed $8 million worth of permanent loans with banks to replace motel construction loans. Today Kessler is responsible for 307 Days Inns and Days Lodges (which offer one-bedroom apartment-like suites instead of simple rooms), of which 110 are owned and operated by the parent company. The rest are franchised.
>
> The privately held company is turning record profits, and Kessler says one of his most-satisfying successes is "seeing the teamwork at Days Inns come together in the last year." October is a traditional "down" month in the motel business, he says, but this October, the company showed pretax income of $546,000 despite a drop in occupancy rates. Last October 1978 was the first October that the company showed a profit, and it was only $111,000, so Kessler is convinced that better days are ahead for Days Inns.
>
> Although he believes gas prices will continue to rise to the world price of about $2 per gallon and that inflation will hover around 10 percent annually, Kessler says 1980 should be good for Days Inns.
>
> "Americans are going to travel," he says. "They may delay a trip, but they won't cancel it."
>
> Kessler's conversation about his 9½ years with Days Inns includes many stories that begin, "Cecil called me up and said . . ." Kessler explains: "I carried out his ideas. My job was to implement them."
>
> Day died of bone cancer in December 1978 at age 44, so Kessler has been on his own.
>
> Kessler owns 10 percent of the stock in Days Inns of America. About 81 percent is owned by a holding company Day formed in 1978, called the Cecil Day Co. Kessler also owns between 23 percent and 30 percent of eight realty companies associated with Days Inns.

Source: David B. Hilder, "The Rise of Richard Kessler," *The Atlanta Journal,* November 30, 1979.

31 **Employee Relations.** With regard to employee benefits, the 1977 annual report offered the following comment:

> Employee benefits historically have been a major Days Inns priority, and 1977 was our most-active year in implementing personnel programs. New direct-benefit packages include: longer vacations; additional holidays, including the employee's birthday; expanded life and health insurance; and a reimbursement policy to encourage continuing education.
>
> We introduced a series of programs designed to promote creative interaction between employees and management. Among these was a system to reward cost-saving suggestions by Days Inns personnel. We initiated a series of seminars with instruction tailored to job-related needs. To improve communication between the field and the home office, we held retreats and conferences for management at various levels and discussed common goals and problems.
>
> With the help of local merchants, we arranged discounts which entitle Days Inns employees to substantial savings on a variety of products. These discounts are administered by our newly created employee services branch.

32 Additional benefits include discounts (20 percent) on lodging and food at Days Inns properties throughout the system. The Day Cap Savings and Retirement was introduced

Exhibit 7

The forum concept at Days Inn

Board of Directors

Richard Kessler

	Ken Niemann Finance Chief Financial Officer	Roy Burnette Operations Chief Operating Officer	Bob Bush Administration Chief Administrative Officer	Thomas S. Prince Investments Chief Investment Officer
	Senior Executive Vice Presidents	Senior Executive Vice Presidents	Senior Executive Vice Presidents	Senior Executive Vice Presidents
Atlantic Region (Operations)	Financial Managers	Operations Managers	Administration Managers	Investments Managers
Florida Region (Operations)	Financial Managers	Operations Managers	Administration Managers	Investments Managers
Southwest Region (Operations)	Financial Managers	Operations Managers	Administration Managers	Investments Managers
Pacific Region (Operations)	Financial Managers	Operations Managers	Administration Managers	Investments Managers

in 1983, providing employees an opportunity to build a retirement fund with pretax dollars and receive matching contributions from the company.

Operations Division

33 To minimize costs, Days Inns were built using componentized wood-frame and masonry construction. Most rooms open to the outside, except in colder climates, where interior corridors are used. Most Days Inns facilities were built according to the same 122-unit plan, as shown in Exhibit 8.

34 All rooms are exactly alike, allowing for a considerable savings on furnishings by being able to buy in volume. Most Days Inns rooms are 12 feet by 24 feet and are furnished with two double beds, wall-to-wall carpeting, a color television, a direct-dial telephone, and individual heating and air-conditioning units. The bath room has a full tub, a shower, and a vanity area. (See the diagram of a typical room in Exhibit 9.) Rooms are designed to reduce cleaning time and to easily accommodate maintenance activity.

35 Considerable efficiencies are obtained in the design of the restaurant/registration building. The registration desk, restaurant cashier's area, and gift shop all share the same office in the restaurant building, cutting down on the number of employees required. There are no lobbies, no meeting or convention rooms, no cocktail lounges, no bellhops, and no room service. Laundry is done on the premises at most Days Inns.

36 While offering such efficiently streamlined facilities, most inns have a swimming pool, a children's playground, a coin-operated laundry for guest use, restaurants, and gift shops, and many newer properties have game rooms.

37 In the early 1970s, many Days Inns also offered Days Lodges facilities. Commenting on this, a Days Inns executive said:

> We discovered that many people are interested in staying at one location for several days to several weeks. So we created Days Lodges to pick up where Days Inns left off. It is one of the best values in the lodging industry.

38 Sleeping accommodations are similar to those of the inn rooms, but there is also a kitchen (completely furnished with utensils and dishes), a private patio, and a living-dining area. The price is slightly higher than the price of a Days Inn room, but a Lodge suite can accommodate up to six persons.

39 In implementing operations strategies, Chief Operations Officer Burnette summarizes the strategies as:

1. Recruit the best-qualified people available.
2. Train them extensively and keep them motivated.
3. Know each market in which the company operates.
4. Anticipate changes in consumer needs and demands as they occur.
5. Keep management's attention focused on the relationship between productivity, service, and controllable costs.

40 Training and motivation of employees is high priority at DIA. In 1983, more than 100 new managers were trained at the Day Learning Center in Atlanta, which was opened in 1977. According to the 1977 annual report:

> The concept has been a novel one: the conversion of a busy full-service property, with rooms, gift shop, restaurant, and gasoline facilities, into a training center.

Exhibit 8

A typical 122-unit Days Inn project

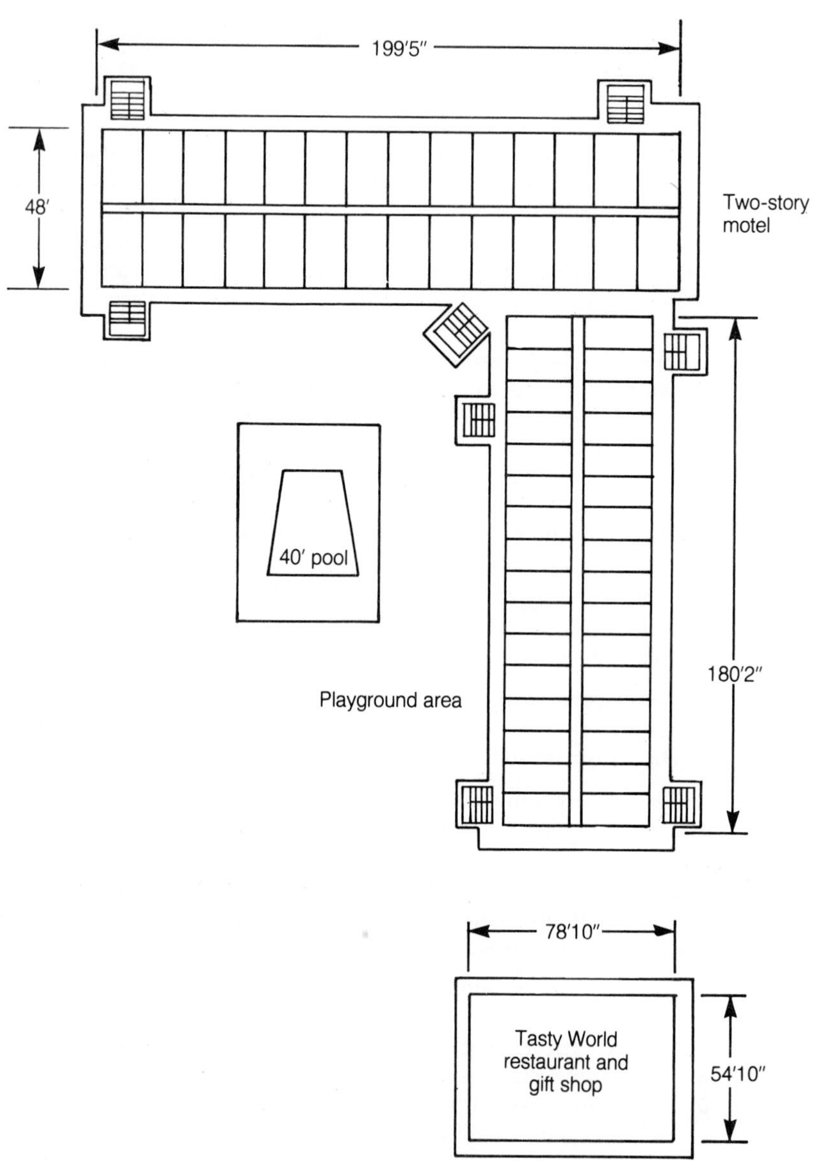

Exhibit 9

A Days Inn room

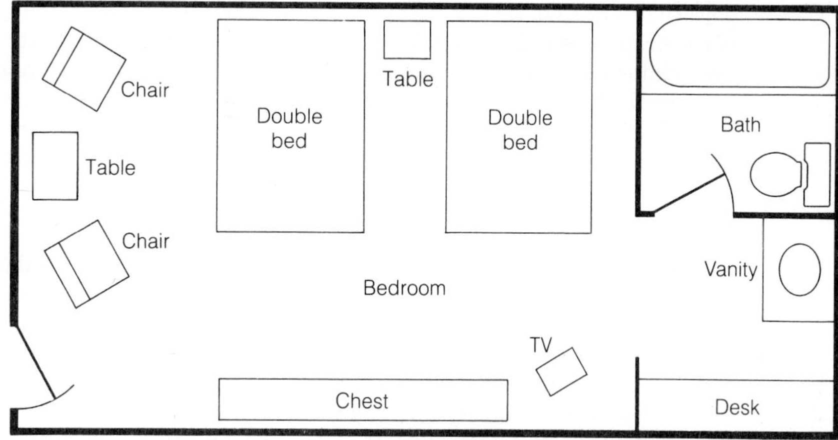

Thus, management candidates receive instruction, perform, and live in an actual working environment for three to six weeks. Candidates perform all operational tasks including cooking and serving food, busing tables, cleaning rooms, laundering, front-desk operations, and night auditing.

The concept has been expanded to make the property an experimental center for the testing of new products, techniques, and procedures. This action benefits the candidates directly, since they enter their first career assignments proficient in the applications of Days Inns' latest programs.

41 Days Inns has established a multilevel employee development program, which is coordinated by the training department. Essentially a career planning/development tool, the employee development program helps employees develop personal guidelines for more rewarding Days Inns careers. The program is aimed at all levels of employees. To identify and ensure top management resources for the future, the department has the franchise general managers' seminar program. This program provided continued training for the 75 general managers (through 1977) who elected to participate. The management training center offers continued updating and career development assistance for midlevel management. For new and lower-level employees, the training department provides career planning assistance (and guidelines) as well as continuous updating on future opportunities within Days Inns and suggestions for incremental career goals.

Investment Division

42 As chief investment officer, Tom Prince oversees the management of DIA's real estate assets from site selection for new development through divestiture of properties that no longer meet investment criteria.

43 Real estate investment and asset management receive close attention at DIA. Each property is continually evaluated as to its income-producing contribution, its real estate equity value, and any investment alternative.

44 Properties no longer fitting the company's strategic plan or not meeting performance objectives are sold, and the equity is reinvested in higher-yielding properties. Some of the properties which are sold because they have matured as a real estate investment are retained as franchise units, thereby generating additional franchise fees.

45 In fiscal 1982, four properties (three were retained as franchises) were sold, resulting in gains of over $7 million. Eight properties were sold for 159 percent of their estimated current value in fiscal 1983, producing about $10 million in pretax profits.

Administrative Division

46 Under the direction of Bob Bush, this division is responsible for design, construction, and franchising. Quality assistance and security are also coordinated through this division.

47 In addition to the 10 new Days Inns opened in 1983, renovation also began on 3 existing hotels purchased during the year and converted to Days Inns. Slated for an early 1984 opening is the new 260-room, $10 million Baltimore Inner Harbor Days Inn. As a joint effort between DIA, city government, and business leaders, the joint-use project includes a Days Inn Hotel, a major office building, and a public parking facility. With its location in a historic area, the hotel is designed to match the architecture of the area rather than conforming to the traditional Days Inn design.

48 At the end of 1983, franchise owners operated 190 Days Inn properties, accounting for 25,150 of the chain's 45,416 rooms.

49 Both franchise and company-owned properties must meet the same standards set by the company's Quality Assurance Program. Every three months, inspectors pay unannounced visits for an in-depth evaluation of each property. Coinciding with this plan was the creation of the 450 Club. Membership in this club is conferred upon owners where properties score at least 450 out of a possible 500 points on quality assurance evaluations for four consecutive quarters. Properties below acceptable levels that are not brought up to standard within a specific period of time are removed from the system.

50 A three-year program, beginning in 1983 to renovate all 60 corporate Tasty World restaurants, will require $3 million in construction funds. Franchise operations will begin a similar program in 1984.

Marketing Programs

51 **September Days Club.** If necessity is the mother of invention, the 1974 recession turned out to be about the best mother Days Inns could have asked for. The business slump of 1974 led Days Inns to create the September Days Club (SDC) as a way of "thanking the senior citizens who contributed so much to the success of the motel chain." *Lodging* magazine, the official publication of the American Hotel and Motel Association, offered this July 1977 observation of Days Inns' thankful gesture:

> What that meant in marketing language was to invite any of 44 million Americans over 55 to accept a free membership in a club entitling them to 10 percent discounts in food and lodging at 270 Days Inns across the United States.

52 Originally, this 10 percent discount applied to the month of September, a perennial low-occupancy month in the motel industry, but because of an overwhelming response, SDC was extended to a year-round program. The September Days Club is the first and only club in the lodging industry for persons 55 years of age and over, and it is also the only lodging industry club to offer discounts to senior citizens on food and gifts as well as lodging. Initially, membership was free, but now there is a charge of $10 per year (per individual or per couple), which entitles members to a quarterly magazine *(September Days)*, discounts on pharmaceuticals, meals, and gifts, and access to organized tours as well as the 10 percent Days Inn discount. This club has approximately 250,000 members, and members stay an average of five room nights per year.

53 *Lodging* offered the following observation on the program:

> Days Inns has done a brilliant job of tapping the biggest hotel/motel market in America and perceiving its special needs and dreams. It has provided one more proof that the markets are there—for innkeepers perceptive enough to identify them and aggressive enough to "reach out" for them. And, creative enough to cultivate them and make them grow.

54 **Inn-Credible Card.** Launched in 1982, the Inn-Credible Card offers business travelers a special discount, express check-in, complimentary morning coffee, check-cashing privileges, and a 9 P.M. room guarantee. In its first two years of operation, over 18,000 corporate applications were processed and 215,000 Inn-Credible cards were distributed.

55 **Stay and Kids Eat Free.** Children age 12 and under eat breakfast, lunch, or dinner free when accompanied by a registered adult guest at participating DIA restaurants.

56 **Visit USA Voucher.** Aimed at the $14 billion international travel market, the program entitles foreign guests to a discount on regular room rates. Days Inn has retained a firm in England to handle reservations from the United Kingdom.

57 **Dynamite Days.** DIA's newest program to boost occupancy and generate additional revenue awards guests coupons that can be redeemed for merchandise from a Dynamite Days catalog.

Financial Position

58 In fiscal 1983, DIA surpassed projections for revenues and profits, setting new records for both. By the end of 1983, the DIA system had 45,416 rooms with an average room rate of $30.06, up from 1982's $27.47 average room rate (see Exhibit 3).

59 Occupancy increased from 65.7 percent in 1982 to 69.1 percent in 1983. DIA management attributed the increased occupancy to new marketing programs, a resurgence in interstate travel attributable to an improved economy, and the opening of Epcot. Control of operating costs has allowed DIA to achieve a break-even occupancy rate of 50 percent, well below the industry average of 65 percent.

60 Exhibits 10 through 12 present recent financial data on Days Inn. Stockholder's equity was $56,194,000 on a historical cost basis and over $257 million based on current value in 1983.[2]

---

[2] DIA places major emphasis on the appreciation of its growing real estate investment (motel properties) as an important indicator of true corporate performance. Exhibit 13 illustrates this emphasis, providing DIA's annual consolidation of current values statement that is included in its annual reports.

Exhibit 10

DAYS INNS OF AMERICA, INC.
Consolidated Balance Sheets (Historical Cost) and Statements of Current Values
As of September 30, 1982–1983

	1983		1982	
	Statement of current values	*Balance sheet (historical cost)*	*Statement of current values*	*Balance sheet (historical cost)*
Assets				
Current assets:	$ 2,799,000	$ 2,799,000	$ 2,291,000	$ 2,291,000
Cash	2,799,000	2,799,000	2,291,000	2,291,000
Money market investments	20,555,000	20,555,000	9,509,000	9,509,000
Accounts and notes receivable, net of allowance for doubtful accounts of $602,000 and $688,000:				
Franchisees	2,079,000	2,079,000	1,310,000	1,310,000
Refundable income taxes	—	—	1,792,000	1,792,000
Other	6,383,000	6,454,000	4,870,000	4,979,000
Retail inventories and supplies	2,959,000	2,576,000	2,585,000	2,204,000
Prepaid expenses	3,663,000	3,663,000	1,492,000	1,492,000
Total current assets	38,438,000	38,126,000	23,849,000	23,577,000
Property and equipment	592,496,000	396,667,000	446,108,000	332,625,000
Less: Accumulated depreciation	—	(81,568,000)	—	(72,715,000)
Franchisee and other notes and accounts receivable, net of allowance for doubtful accounts of $314,000 in 1982	17,313,000	18,019,000	9,734,000	9,050,000
Franchise agreements	19,993,000	—	20,570,000	—
Deferred charges	7,578,000	7,578,000	6,663,000	6,553,000
Investee bond proceeds	22,203,000	22,203,000	28,359,000	28,359,000
Other assets	3,145,000	2,927,000	905,000	668,000
Total assets	$701,166,000	$403,952,000	$536,078,000	$328,117,000

Liabilities and Stockholders' Equity				
Current liabilities:				
Notes and bonds payable	$ 14,623,000	$ 13,547,000	$ 9,032,000	$ 11,728,000
Accounts payable	9,301,000	9,301,000	8,480,000	8,480,000
Accrued expenses and other liabilities	12,663,000	12,663,000	9,001,000	9,001,000
Income taxes payable	2,628,000	2,628,000	—	—
Current liabilities excluding deferred income taxes	39,215,000	38,139,000	26,513,000	29,209,000
Deferred income taxes	2,752,000	2,752,000	3,665,000	3,665,000
Total current liabilities	41,967,000	40,891,000	30,178,000	32,874,000
Notes and bonds payable, due after one year	269,590,000	291,124,000	221,508,000	248,704,000
Income taxes on realization of estimated current values	92,581,000	—	68,666,000	—
Real estate commissions on realization of estimated current values	18,172,000	—	13,613,000	—
Deferred income taxes	6,612,000	6,612,000	2,977,000	2,977,000
Deferred income and other liabilities	8,944,000	8,944,000	3,107,000	3,107,000
Minority interest in consolidated subsidiary companies	6,231,000	187,000	1,018,000	516,000
Stockholders' equity:				
Common stock $.10 par value—1,100,000 shares authorized, 386,805 shares issued	64,000	64,000	64,000	64,000
Capital surplus	8,818,000	8,818,000	8,642,000	8,642,000
Retained earnings	49,846,000	49,846,000	33,796,000	33,796,000
Treasury stock at cost—33,949 and 34,862 shares	(2,534,000)	(2,534,000)	(2,563,000)	(2,563,000)
Unrealized appreciation before estimated costs on realization of current values	311,628,000	—	237,351,000	—
Current value equity	367,822,000	—	277,290,000	—
Less: Potential costs on realization of current values:				
Income taxes	(92,581,000)	—	(68,666,000)	—
Real estate commissions	(18,172,000)	—	(13,613,000)	—
Total stockholders' equity	257,069,000	56,194,000	195,011,000	39,939,000
Total liabilities and stockholders' equity	$701,166,000	$403,952,000	$536,078,000	$328,177,000

Exhibit 11

DAYS INNS OF AMERICA, INC.
Consolidated Statements of Income
For the Years Ended September 30, 1982–1983

	1983	*1982*
Net revenue:		
Lodging	$145,185,000	$121,411,000
Food, gasoline, and novelties	63,198,000	62,648,000
Franchise fees	7,820,000	7,609,000
Rental income	1,771,000	2,006,000
Other income	5,675,000	4,164,000
Gains on sales of properties	9,903,000	7,689,000
Total revenue	233,552,000	205,527,000
Costs and expenses:		
Cost of food, gasoline and novelties	37,477,000	37,971,000
Selling, general, administrative, and operating expenses	127,199,000	114,846,000
Depreciation and amortization	18,695,000	16,496,000
Interest expense, net of interest income of $2,702,000 and $2,452,000	24,036,000	21,076,000
Total costs and expenses	207,407,000	190,389,000
Income before provision for income taxes and extraordinary item	26,145,000	15,138,000
Provision for income taxes	9,725,000	4,358,000
	16,420,000	10,780,000
Extraordinary item (tax benefit from utilization of loss carryforward)	—	920,000
Net income	$ 16,420,000	$ 11,700,000

61 During 1983, DIA added $62 million to the company's value, only 26 percent of which was in historical accounting net income. The balance, 74 percent, was in real estate and other asset appreciation.

62 To monitor its cash needs, DIA places major emphasis on financial forecasting. Exhibits 14 and 15 illustrate corporate-level forecasts for the next five years and forecasting accuracy for fiscal 1983. DIA carries such forecasting to the individual motel on a weekly basis.

63 Financing its ambitious growth plans for the 1980s will be a challenge for DIA. The 1983 annual report predicts an anticipated need of $80 million is fiscal 1984 to finance the company's development program. Over the next five years, the company forecasts the development of more than 80 properties, with approximately 12,000 rooms, emphasizing metropolitan locations near suburban shopping centers, office parks, commercial areas, airports, historic areas, and civic centers. The company's policy of retaining all equity in its real estate holdings will make this task even greater.

64 Land in the proposed sites is more expensive than the previously purchased interstate sites, in many instances forcing DIA to build high-rise structures. When asked about the rising real estate and construction costs in the major-city centers DIA has targeted, Kessler and Ken Niemann (chief financial officer) said:

Kessler: Right now, for example, we are financing some properties with industrial revenue bonds, through both private placements and public offerings, and we

Exhibit 12

DAYS INNS OF AMERICA, INC.
Consolidated Statements of Changes in Financial Position
For the Years Ended September 30, 1982–1983

	1983	*1982*
Financial resources were provided by:		
Operations:		
Net income before extraordinary item	$ 16,420,000	$ 10,780,000
Add income charges (credits) not affecting working capital:		
Depreciation and amortization	18,695,000	16,496,000
Deferred income taxes	3,635,000	5,044,000
Minority interest in net income of consolidated subsidiaries	(1,168,000)	(413,000)
Accumulated income tax prepayments	—	222,000
Gains on sales of properties, net of tax	(7,320,000)	5,890,000
Working capital provided by operations	30,262,000	26,239,000
Extraordinary item (tax benefit from utilization of loss carryforward)	—	920,000
Increases in notes and bonds payable	85,753,000	72,886,000
Decrease (increase) in invested bond proceeds	6,156,000	(8,753,000)
Proceeds on sales of properties, net of tax	10,196,000	9,214,000
Increase (decrease) in other liabilities	6,676,000	(272,000)
Disposal of property and equipment	1,255,000	511,000
Issuance of stock to acquire minority interests	266,000	8,437,000
Net acquisition of minority interest of subsidiary companies	—	370,000
Total working capital provided	140,564,000	109,732,000
Financial resources were used for:		
Acquisition of property and equipment	78,015,000	67,858,000
Reductions of notes payable	43,333,000	27,246,000
Net increase in receivables from franchisees and others and other assets	11,228,000	4,681,000
Cash dividends	370,000	351,000
Increase in deferred charges	1,025,000	3,548,000
Purchase of treasury stock, net	61,000	867,000
Minority interest in subsidiary dividend	—	42,000
Total working capital used	134,032,000	104,593,000
Increase in working capital	$ 6,532,000	$ 5,139,000
Analysis of changes in working capital		
Increase (decrease) in current assets:		
Cash	$ 508,000	$ (542,000)
Money market investments	11,046,000)	2,881,000
Accounts and notes receivable:		
Franchisees	632,000	67,000
Other	1,526,000	2,566,000
Refundable income taxes	(1,792,000)	1,792,000
Retail inventories and supplies	372,000	(425,000)
Prepaid expenses and other	2,257,000	411,000
(Increase) decrease in current liabilities:		
Notes and bonds payable	(1,819,000)	(3,226,000)
Accounts payable	(821,000)	228,000
Accrued expenses and other liabilities	(3,662,000)	(1,296,000)
Income taxes payable	(2,628,000)	694,000
Deferred income taxes	913,000	1,989,000
Increase in working capital	$ 6,532,000	$ 5,139,000

Exhibit 13

DAYS INNS OF AMERICA, INC.
Note to Consolidated Statements of Current Values
September 30, 1983 and 1982

The Consolidated Statements of Current Values are supplementary information which provide relevant information about the assets and liabilities of the Company which is not provided by traditional financial statements (historical cost basis). Although current values differ significantly from the historical cost amounts and are not required for presentation of financial position in conformity with generally accepted accounting principles. Management believes that such information is useful to the readers of its financial statements.

Unanticipated events and circumstances may occur after September 30, 1983, which may cause actual current values to vary substantially from the values estimated herein.

Management's estimates of current values were reviewed and analyzed by Landauer Associates, Inc., real estate consultants, whose letter of concurrence accompanies this Note.

The Consolidated Statements of Current Values are not intended to and do not represent the amount that could be realized from the sale of the Company; rather, the values estimated to be realizable in an orderly disposition of the Company's individual assets and liabilities under the willing buyer/willing seller concept. Under this approach, such estimated values are reduced by $110,753,000 in 1983 ($82,279,000 in 1982) for estimated income taxes and real estate commissions, which could be payable in such a disposition of the assets and liabilities. The values of the interests in the various properties is the estimated current investment which investors will make to purchase the Company's interest in each property's future cash flow.

Management's estimates of current value basis stockholders' equity of $257,069,000 and $195,011,000 at September 30, 1983 and 1982, respectively, are summarized as follows:

	1983		1982	
	Current values	*Historical cost basis*	*Current values*	*Historical cost basis*
Property and equipment interests:				
Motels and other facilities owned and operated	$441,365,000	$238,891,000	$290,054,000	$172,546,000
Motels leased from others	96,700,000	34,544,000	105,291,000	44,550,000
Motels owned and leased to others	2,306,000	1,633,000	1,763,000	1,003,000
Motels under construction	16,017,000	16,017,000	18,222,000	18,222,000
Office buildings, warehouse, and other	24,461,000	16,649,000	18,484,000	15,181,000
Inimproved land	11,647,000	7,365,000	12,294,000	8,408,000
	592,496,000	315,099,000	446,108,000	259,910,000
Franchise agreements	19,993,000	—	20,570,000	—
	612,489,000	—	466,678,000	—
Historical cost basis	(315,099,000)	$315,099,000	(259,910,000)	$259,910,000
Recognition of deferred gains on sales of properties	1,584,000		1,861,000	
Current value reduction in notes receivable	(2,361,000)		(1,286,000)	
Current value increase in inventories and supplies	383,000		381,000	
Current value reduction in notes and bonds payable	20,458,000		29,892,000	
Other	218,000		237,000	
Minority interest in unrealized appreciation	(6,044,000)		(502,000)	
Historical cost basis stockholders' equity	56,194,000		39,939,000	
Current value equity	367,822,000		277,290,000	
Less: Potential costs on realization of current values				
Real estate commissions	(18,172,000)		(13,613,000)	
Income taxes	(92,581,000)		(68,666,000)	
	(110,753,000)		(82,279,000)	
Current value basis stockholders' equity	$257,069,000		$195,011,000	

Exhibit 14

DAYS INNS OF AMERICA, INC.
Comparison of Actual to Forecasted Income and Stockholders' Equity
For the Year Ending September 30, 1983

	Actual	*Forecasted*	*Variance*
Net revenue:			
Lodging	$145,185,000	$143,556,000	$ 1,629,000
Food, gasoline, and novelties	63,198,000	63,800,000	(602,000)
Franchise fees	7,820,000	8,233,000	(413,000)
Rental income	1,771,000	2,231,000	(460,000)
Other income	5,675,000	5,811,000	(136,000)
Gains on sales of properties	9,903,000	—	9,903,000
Total revenue	233,552,000	223,631,000	9,921,000
Costs and expenses:			
Cost of food, gasoline, and novelties	37,477,000	37,767,000	290,000
Selling, general, administrative, and operating expenses	127,199,000	131,707,000	4,508,000
Depreciation and amortization	18,695,000	17,819,000	(876,000)
Interest expense, net of interest income	24,036,000	26,182,000	2,146,000
Total costs and expenses	207,407,000	213,475,000	6,068,000
Income before provision for income taxes	26,145,000	10,156,000	15,989,000
Provision for income taxes	9,725,000	3,859,000	(5,866,000)
Net income	$ 16,420,000	$ 6,297,000	$ 10,123,000
Stockholders' equity	$ 56,194,000	$ 46,444,000	$ 9,750,000
Occupancy			
Average room rate			
Number of company hotel/motel openings	13	8	5
Number of franchise hotel/motel openings	1	0	1
Number of company hotel/motel sales	7	0	7
Number of hotels/motels disfranchised	13	5	(8)
Total rooms at year end (operating and under construction	45,416	45,300	116

are pursuing additional IRB funding. We have just signed agreements with a consortium of banks for $30 million in revolving lines of credit. Ken Niemann, our chief financial officer, can give you details on that.

Niemann: We have a commitment for $30 million in interim financing. That means we do not have permanent financing arranged for a property before we build it. The banks will carry the loan, until we find a permanent lender for a period of 8–12 years. When we get the permanent financing and pay off the bank loan, that amount is added back to our line of credit. This gives us great flexibility, allowing us to purchase a site and begin development without the risk of losing a prime location while we are searching for permanent financing. It also lets us enter the permanent loan market at the most-advantageous time. But we will continue to seek long-term commitments from traditional sources such as savings

Exhibit 15

DAYS INNS OF AMERICA, INC.
Consolidated Statements of Forecasted Changes in Financial Position
For the Years Ended September 30, 1984–1988

	1984	*1985*	*1986*	*1987*	*1988*
Net revenue:					
Lodging	$170,714,000	$195,554,000	$223,925,000	$258,342,000	$300,425,000
Food, gasoline, and novelties	68,539,000	80,424,000	94,912,000	111,261,000	130,618,000
Franchise fees	7,976,000	9,424,000	10,811,000	12,161,000	13,362,000
Rental income	2,780,000	2,959,000	3,137,000	3,325,000	3,521,000
Other income	9,205,000	10,464,000	11,430,000	12,516,000	13,746,000
Gains on sales of properties	10,000,000	12,000,000	14,000,000	15,000,000	16,000,000
Total revenue	269,214,000	310,825,000	358,215,000	412,605,000	477,672,000
Costs and expenses:					
Cost of food, gasoline, and novelties	38,862,000	43,628,000	49,291,000	55,542,000	62,931,000
Selling, general, administrative, and operating expenses	151,172,000	176,219,000	204,085,000	236,297,000	274,839,000
Depreciation and amortization	20,501,000	22,311,000	24,802,000	27,983,000	31,945,000
Interest expense, net of interest income	28,674,000	33,271,000	38,296,000	44,475,000	51,911,000
Total costs and expenses	239,209,000	275,429,000	316,474,000	364,297,000	421,626,000
Income before provision for income taxes	30,005,000	35,396,000	41,741,000	48,308,000	56,046,000
Provision for income taxes	11,502,000	13,025,000	15,541,000	18,141,000	21,178,000
Net income	$ 18,503,000	$ 22,371,000	$ 26,200,000	$ 30,167,000	$ 34,868,000
Stockholders' equity	$ 74,697,000	$ 97,018,000	$123,218,000	$153,385,000	$188,253,000
Occupancy	70.0%	71.0%	72.0%	72.5%	73.0%
Average room rate	$33.00	$35.25	$37.00	$39.00	$41.50
Number of company hotel/motel openings	12	15	17	19	21
Number of franchise hotel/motel openings	9	8	8	8	8
Number of company hotel/motel sales	8	8	8	8	8
Number of hotels/motels disfranchised	6	4	4	4	4
Total rooms at year end (operating and under construction)	46,500	47,800	49,500	51,300	53,300

and loan associations, pension funds, and life insurance companies. We are currently in discussions with several sources that have the ability to finance a number of projects under a single commitment.

Competition

65 Having prospered as a regional, DIA now faces competition with other budget-motel chains as the company seeks to enter the national market. *Business Week* cites the bare-bones Motel 6 chain as the firmly entrenched leader in the West and points to La Quinta Motor Inns, Inc., which has already saturated Texas with properties aimed at traveling salespeople, as planning to expand in the same locales as targeted by Kessler.

66 National chains have responded to the budget-chain threat by seeking to broaden their market bases to attract the cost-conscious traveler. Holiday Inns and Quality Inns have both developed new budget-hotel chains to compete in this market.

67 When asked about major lodging chain movement into casino gaming, several executives responded that Days Inns "would never get into gambling or even add lounges to its motel facilities." One executive, Tom Eppes, elaborated on this stance:

> We're profiting from that (movement by Holiday Inns, Ramada Inns, Hilton, and so forth). As they move toward such "high-end entertainment," it leaves a good bit of their previous market behind. As they increase their gambling and entertainment-related emphasis, we increase our market share by providing the budget-conscious consumer with accommodations Holiday Inns and others can no longer afford to provide.

68 These executives perceive competitors' movement into high-end amenities as leaving behind families and business travelers who used to stay with Holiday Inns and similar firms. From Days Inns' perspective and market research, "these travelers don't want to cut travel but do want to economize while traveling." Eppes points to Holiday Inns' new Holidomes, a series of metropolitan properties with domed courtyards to provide recreational opportunities for exercise-conscious travelers, as an example of leaving the cost-conscious traveler behind. "Considering the energy costs and people costs in operating such a facility," he says, "there is no way they can profitably serve anyone but the high-end traveler."

69 With this type of movement by bigger competitors, Days Inns' executives see a vast U.S. market for the Days Inns concept. "California, the biggest-traveled state in the United States," says Eppes, "offers dozens of market opportunities for Days Inns locations." When asked about future plans for international expansion, Eppes summarized Days Inns focus for the 1980s:

> Eventually, we may develop internationally. We currently have our location in Ontario, Canada. But there are so many U.S. markets for the Days Inns concept, we will keep ourselves busy just keeping up with those for at least the next decade.

Days Inns in the 1980s

70 DIA's corporate objectives (see Exhibit 16) remain unchanged as the guiding force behind its mission for the 1980s.

Exhibit 16

Days Inns' mission and corporate objectives

Days Inns of America, Inc., is a privately held corporation committed to fulfilling its business responsibilities within the framework of Christian ethics. In doing so, the company intends to exert the kind of positive influence which strengthens the free enterprise system. In accomplishing this commitment, the company actively pursues the following primary objectives:

1. To maintain the health of the corporation and to ensure its continued existence and growth through superior performance.
2. To benefit society by improving the quality of life of both employees and customers, by promoting healthy family life, and by encouraging small business enterprise through franchising.
3. To earn fair and satisfactory profits by offering excellent hospitality services at a real value to the customer.
4. To develop and maintain an environment in which all employees can realize their highest business potential, achieve personal fulfillment, and find genuine enjoyment through positive accomplishments.
5. To create a business environment in which dedicated teamwork makes possible the economic prosperity and security of both company and employees.

71 For Richard Kessler, entering the 1980s was seen as a launching pad for the future. "We know where we are and where we are going," Kessler says. "We have the three basic components to make it in the 1980s. First of all, because Days Inns is a privately held company, we have the flexibility to make decisions not necessarily based on immediate profits."[3]

72 The second ingredient in the Days Inns formula is its character as an entrepreneurial company, which Kessler believes adds a dimension of interaction and excitement to the business.[4]

73 This excitement helps the company attract top-notch, creative people, Kessler's third component for success. Many of his executives have been with the company since the early 1970s and have since risen to top-management positions, with ownership interests in the company. A spirit of optimism and creativity surrounds the staff at the Days Inns headquarters in Atlanta. "People-wise, we're in the best shape we've ever been in," says Kessler. "We've been growing talent in a tree-farm environment. The people know how to operate."[5]

74 While a privately held corporation, DIA follows the unusual practice of providing annual reports similar to publicly held firms. This practice has intermittently fueled speculation that DIA is laying the groundwork for going public. With its ambitious growth plans, this would be a logical financing alternative. When asked in 1980 if he was considering taking Days Inns public, Kessler said:

[3] "Days Inns Rises to the Challenge in the 1980s," *Lodging Hospitality,* July 1980, p. 42.

[4] Ibid.

[5] Ibid.

> No, our ownership will remain with Cecil B. Day Companies and with those key executives whose motivation and dedication make the company successful. We see distinct advantages to being a private company, and we intend to remain one. Being private lets long-run decisions override short-term considerations. It relieves us of the pressure to show increased earnings each period. Such pressure often motivates the sale of valuable, appreciating assets in order to improve earnings. We think we are better able than a public company to create a good long-term strategic plan and to implement it in a cyclical marketplace.

75 In addition to upholding Cecil Day's desire to remain privately held, Kessler has continued a financial tradition he and Day started in 1970. DIA continues to tithe 10 percent of its profit after taxes to benefit religious and social projects.

76 The tradition of remaining a privately held firm may be coming to an end for DIA. In November 1983, Cecil Day's former wife, Deen Day Smith, chairman of the Cecil B. Day Companies, which has controlling interest in Days Inns of America, announced that her interest in the hotel-motel is for sale. Goldman, Sachs & Co. has been retained by Cecil B. Days Companies to screen offers and represent ownership in this issue. A tender offer for all Days Inn stock by a group of franchise owners who have retained Prudential Bache was announced in early 1984.

77 Speculation in the industry that the company will go public has been fueled by the ambitious expansion strategy Kessler has adopted for the company. Taking the company public may be necessary to generate the capital for expansion. Kessler commented in a 1983 *Business Week* interview that going public was a possibility to get more cash to build with. He estimated the company could have a market value of $450 million to $500 million. Kessler is estimated to own between 10 and 15 percent of the stock. *Business Week* analysts suggested Kessler may be forced to take this step to fund his "ambitious expansion strategy" which they estimate will cost $400 million over six years while its 1983 debt was already "six times equity."

case 29
Congress Motel and Brown's Overnite Trailer Park (A)

1 The lure of steady profits from a small motel operation has occasionally led people to enter the motel business when they found major highways being built adjacent to their land. Typically, these independent owner-operators constructed 20- to 30-room units, which are classified as mom-and-pop operations. Congress Motel is one such operation. Located outside of the city of Ashburn in southwest Georgia, it was built in 1966 by a local farmer on land he owned adjacent to the new interstate highway.

2 The completion of the interstate network in the 1960s and 1970s had a major impact on the motel industry. With the relative prosperity of the American public and their increasing leisure time, the United States witnessed a virtual explosion in the proliferation of motel chains. By franchising (Holiday Inns, Ramada Inns, Days Inns, and so forth) and systematic reservation networks (Best Western and Quality Inns, for example), standardized motel accommodations suddenly blanketed the interstate highway network. In 1975, Holiday Inns claimed that "a new Holiday Inn room was being built . . . every 15 minutes." With strong financial capacities, sophisticated reservation systems, large advertising budgets, and reasonably priced, quality accommodations, these motel chains created a challenging environment for the small, independent operations like Congress Motel.

The Browns

3 Calvin and Christine Brown had lived in southwestern Georgia since birth. Calvin Brown is 48 years old, and Christine Brown is 47; they married in 1948. Calvin Brown met Christine when she was visiting her grandparents who lived across the field from his father's farm.

4 Calvin completed high school in 1947 and received the American farmer's degree from a vocational program in Kansas City two years later. Christine Brown completed high school just prior to her marriage.

5 Brown had a farming operation for the 19 years prior to starting his motel in 1966. He still helps his father with a small farming effort and receives a $5000-per-year rental on a 20-acre peanut allotment in his name. Christine worked for five years as a nut sorter with a local peanut company prior to the birth of her first child in 1954. The Browns have two sons (aged 24 and 22) and one daughter (aged 14). Mrs. Brown maintains household responsibilities and also assists her husband in operating the motel office.

Exhibit 1

Congress Inn*

* The name was changed to Congress Motel in 1972.

6 In 1966, with Interstate 75 being built adjacent to some of his farmland, Brown chose to enter the motel business as an alternative to a lifetime of sporadic profitability as a family farmer. Interstate 75 promised to be a major tourist route to Florida, and motels were relatively scarce in the area. Brown sought to capitalize on the location of his farmland and reap the promise of steady profits with his own interstate motel. He also decided to construct a campsite adjacent to his new motel that could accommodate 28 recreational vehicles and numerous tent campers. Mr. Brown called the camping facility Brown's Overnite Trailer Park.

Location and Facilities

7 Congress Motel is part of the South I-75 travel industry from Macon, Georgia, to the Florida line. This area reflects the same pattern of franchise dominance as experienced nationwide.

8 The South I-75 travel industry will experience a greater traffic flow (an increase of approximately 32 percent), according to the Georgia Travel Bureau (see Exhibit 3).

9 Based on sampling procedures conducted by the Georgia welcome centers and information on the facilities available, Exhibit 4 offers some indications of motel and campground expectations in this South I-75 area. For example, the average motel occupancy should gradually increase, but its level in 1980 reflects an overbuilt South I-75 motel industry. On the other hand, campground construction is expected to double in an

Exhibit 2

Christine and Calvin Brown

Exhibit 3

Projected travel flow

	1976	*1980*	*1990*
Average daily volume (cars)	26,000	36,000	44,600
Average daily recreational/ vacation volume	8,840	12,240	14,960

Exhibit 4

Welcome center projections

	1980	*1990*
Number of motel rooms available	8,280	9,108
Number of cars desiring motels	6,487	7,779
Average occupancy rate at South I-75 motels	78.3%	85.4%
Number of campsites available	840	1,680
Number of vehicles desiring camping	1,469	2,244
Average occupancy rate at South I-75 campgrounds	175%	133%

Exhibit 5

South I-75 travelers

	1967	*1975*
A. Average number of days in Georgia:		
1–2	68%	51%
3 or more	32	49

	1964–1967	*1974–1975*	*1977–1978*
B. Type of accommodations desired:			
Motel	66.0%	53.0%	50.0%
Camping	1.8	10.5	12.8

C. Activities most frequently engaged in by frequently mentioned on surveys:
1. Going to scenic places.
2. Going on picnics.
3. Camping.
4. Fishing.

attempt to partially close a large gap, with demand (for camping facilities) exceeding supply.

10 Through the welcome centers' survey of travelers, some additional market information on South I-75 travelers is summarized in Exhibit 5. It suggests that South I-75 travelers are staying longer in Georgia, increasingly seeking to camp while traveling, and enjoying outdoor-oriented entertainment activities.

11 Congress Motel is located on the southeast corner of the I-75 exit just outside Ashburn, Georgia. A large lake at the front of the property abuts the northbound exit ramp and provides an attractive setting for a motel/campground facility. Exhibit 6 provides a diagram of the interchange and the location of competitors and other businesses.

12 The motel/campground is situated in full view of the northbound traveler—the traveler can see the property before reaching the exist. However, the southbound traveler cannot see the property until after passing the exit ramp. The front office is conveniently located to handle incoming traffic for both the motel and the campground.

13 The motel facility consists of 26 double-sized rooms built in the original (1966) brick structure. In 1967, Brown added two sets of four single units (portable trailers) to accommodate the high volume of single (business) traffic; they are attractively situated at the north and south ends of the original structure (see Exhibit 7). In July 1978, there was a $15,300 balance outstanding on an SBA loan for these two four-room units. All units have a TV, air conditioning, and adequate furnishings.

14 Attempting to offer recreational facilities comparable to those of the major motel chains, Congress Motel has a swimming pool, a miniature golf course, a large lake for fishing, and picnic tables along the lake. It does not, however, have a restaurant. A truck-stop restaurant was located across the street until 1975, when it closed for lack of business. The closest restaurant in 1977 was a popular, local country food restaurant two miles away.

Exhibit 6

Diagram of interchange

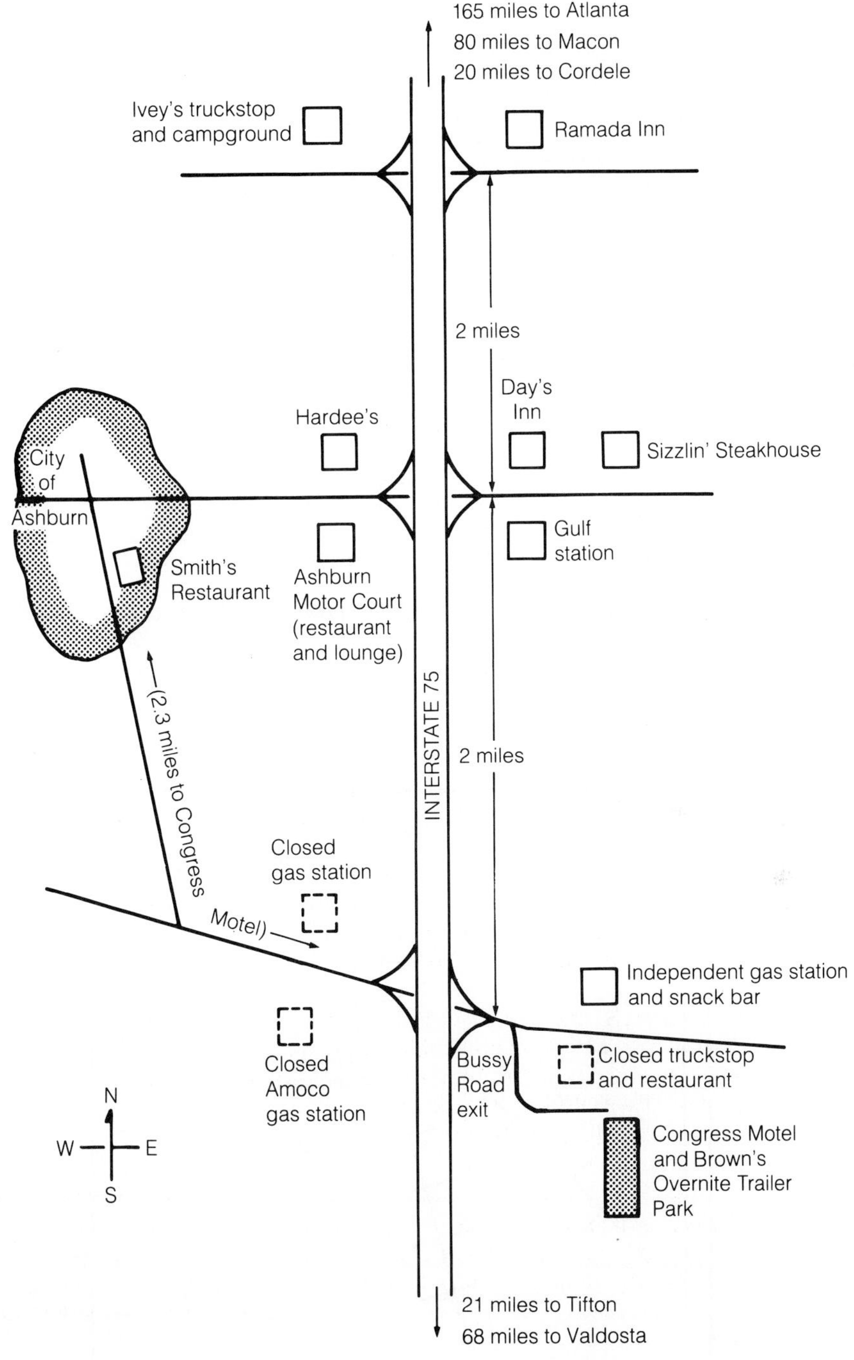

Exhibit 7

Diagram of buildings and campground

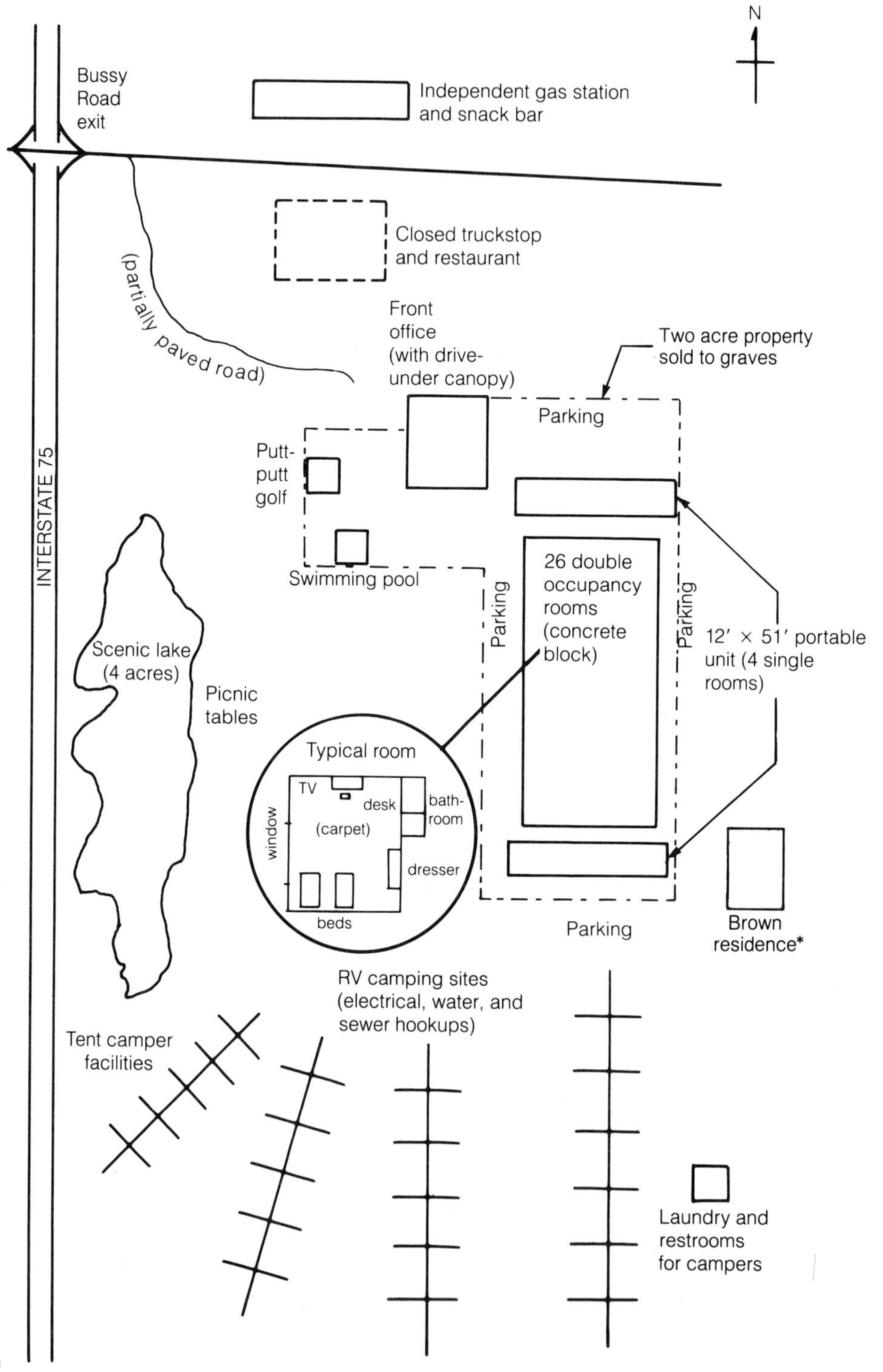

15 Concerning the lack of a restaurant, Brown said:

> We never put in a restaurant because of the overhead involved. There used to be a restaurant over there [gesturing to an abandoned gas/restaurant facility] where my guests could just walk over. They [the restaurant] left about three years ago and so have two of the three gas stations on this interchange. Now when my guests want to eat, I send them to Mrs. Smith's restaurant in Sycamore, about two miles down the road.

16 The campground facility was developed in 1966 on land owned by Brown adjacent to the motel facility. In addition to the recreational vehicle (RV) hookups, Brown constructed a shower/rest room/laundry facility for tent campers. Commenting on the campground facility, Brown said:

> When I opened the motel, it seemed easy to add some sites for trailer campers. My family, at one time, frequently took vacations using trailer camping. For the sites, I installed sewage disposal running to the same oxidation pond used by the motel. Altogether, adding camping sites cost me only one fourth (per site) what these campground chains pay for similar site development, and that doesn't include the fact that I own the land.

17 "The campground was named Brown's Overnite Trailer Park because it would attract truckers and trailer campers as well as let the trailer campers know that hookups were available," according to Brown. Brown further indicated that this name would "identify me personally to repeat customers" and that "it could easily be painted on present billboard runners."

Marketing Strategy

18 Motels located alongside interstate highways face a common, critical challenge—to get the interstate travelers' attention and encourage them to exit at the appropriate interchange and utilize the motel (or campground) facilities. The larger chains, with national advertising and name recognition, have a distinct advantage in this regard. To Brown, the key to his success in this regard centered around billboard signs, pricing strategy, and name (see Exhibit 8).

19 "I tried to advertise as much as I could on my signs and even repaint them myself, when I have time, to save money," offered Brown. Mr. Brown has 12 billboards, 6 north of the Bussy Road exit and 6 located south of that exit. All signs face I-75. Continuing, Brown noted that "the highest I pay for sign rent is $210 per year. I own the signs and rent the site. Nowadays, it costs $150 a month to rent a billboard on I-75. Most of the chains here have to pay that price and have only five or six signs." Shortly after opening his motel in the late 1960s, Mr. Brown reached agreement with several family friends, allowing him to build and place billboard signs on property they owned along I-75. These agreements have remained with only nominal increases in rental fees. Brown advertised the motel in AAA literature and by placing brochures in welcome center travel stands prior to 1974. In mid-1974, the brochures were discontinued to reduce costs. Also, AAA deleted Congress Motel from its listing in late 1973 due the presence of portable rooms on the premises. Mr. Brown advertises his campground in an annual RV directory distributed nationwide.

Exhibit 8

20 Congress Motel charges the second-lowest prices of any motel between Macon and Valdosta, Georgia (Florida line). The standard rates at Congress Motel are $8 for single occupancy and $10 for double occupancy. The only lower price is $7.88 for a single. The campground charges $3 per vehicle plus 25 cents for each person over two in the party. Brown has been contacted by several campground chains (KOA, Ponderosa); they want him to increase his rates, which are about $1 to $2.50 below competitors' rates. Brown advertises the motel prices on six of his billboard signs and the campground price on one of these signs. A welcome center survey indicated that the average expense for a party (one vehicle) on South I-75 for one day in a motel or campground (1975) was $11.27 for motel accommodations and $4.51 for camping accommodations. Commenting on his prices, Brown noted:

> Prices in this area are really quite low. But I'm still lower than anyone except La Quinta around Tifton [Georgia]. Even at my price, I only have to have about 55 percent average occupancy to break even.

21 Brown later indicated that he would keep his prices low for the foreseeable future. "That's my main advantage. I just can't seem to get enough people in here," added Brown. The average single-room rate for chain motels in the are are: Holiday Inn—$14.50, Ramada Inn—$13, Days Inn—$11.88, Ashburn Motor Court—$10.88. Commenting on competition along South I-75, Brown said:

> There have been a lot of motels built between Macon and Valdosta [Georgia] since I opened up. I've tried to keep my price low, but those Days Inns and some budget inns have really hurt. I still get some repeats from my snowbirds from up north and Canada, but I think a lot of folks just prefer to spend the extra dollars to have a restaurant and lounge to go. But a lot of other places are hurting. The Ashburn Motor Court up the road closed, but some Arabs bought them out and reopened it. A new Ramada Inn just north of me was built and never opened. The gas crisis just hurt me. The Amoco station and the Citgo station [on this interchange] closed, which stopped people getting off here. It's a dying interchange.

22 When the motel was opened in 1966, Brown paid $7,500 for a Congress Inn franchise and operated under that name for several years. In 1972, Brown ended his franchise agreement, feeling his business derived virtually no benefit from the 2 percent (of room revenue) franchise fee he was paying. The name was changed to Congress Motel at this time. According to Brown:

> I was throwing away money for hardly any services when I used "Congress Inn." So I just changed the "Inn" to "Motel" and quit paying. But I don't know. "Motel" seems to be out-of-date in this business. People think you're a run-down facility. And I'm beginning to think "Congress" hurts me too since it reminds people of Washington bureaucrats and Watergate. At least that's what my sign painter said.

23 Brown's camping facility seems to face an identity problem with the name Brown's Overnite Trailer Park. In the spring issue of *RV Magazine,* the trade magazine for the campground industry, an article discussed the trend toward standard use of *campground* as the word campers most frequently associated with a full-service facility. In pointing this out, Brown remarked:

> I think my name might cause people to think of a truck stop. I used to do a lot of business with truckers before the diesel station closed. But I've got all the basic hookups for RVs that the KOAs or Ponderosas have, yet I don't seem to be getting the business.

Financial Situation

24 Brown experienced impressive occupancy rates in the early years (see Exhibit 9) of operation but has seen those figures drop drastically since 1973. Commenting on this, Brown said:

> Business has really been down the last four years. The gas crisis of 1973 and 1974 really hurt us, and we haven't recovered yet. We've tried to keep our price very low ($8/single, $10/double) and cut costs by doing most of the work ourselves. I even do the painting on my billboards when I have time. We still have repeat customers, particularly older snowbirds from up north and Canada, but overall

Exhibit 9

Annual occupancy rates—motel

Year	*Average room revenue*	*Annual occupancy rate*	*Year*	*Average room revenue*	*Annual occupancy rate*
1966	$5.50	42.44%	1973	$7.15	57.42%
1967	5.60	59.09	1974	8.55	38.38
1968	5.78	75.29	1975	8.70	39.81
1969	6.01	66.03	1976	9.15	38.90
1970	6.40	66.65	1977	9.30	34.41
1971	6.40	79.22	1978	9.32	36.00*
1972	6.57	90.01			

* Estimate.

Exhibit 10

CONGRESS MOTEL
Income Statement
For the Years Ended December 31, 1966–1977

	1966	*1967*	*1968*	*1969*	*1970*
Income:					
Room rent	$ 10,225.00	$ 28,958.50	$36,563.00	$49,144.00	$52,940.00
Vending machine	117.27	684.78	887.04	1,019.15	1,063.00
Trailer park	—	2,535.30	3,468.75	5,682.00	6,071.80
Land rent	—	—	—	—	1,200.00
Sign rent	—	—	—	—	—
Miscellaneous income	—	20.20	—	—	171.58
Total income	10,342.27	32,198.78	40,918.79	55,845.15	61,447.18
Expenses:					
Labor	2,390.89	4,756.25	4,004.91	7,059.93	8,079.97
Payroll taxes	107.64	202.10	176.22	299.83	316.46
Linen	2,094.90	3,329.20	—	660.75	257.20
Utilities	1,050.28	4,028.62	4,570.56	4,719.82	5,659.40
Telephone	1,587.06	3,298.16	2,258.81	2,589.90	3,988.56
Supplies	1,217.97	2,360.05	5,231.19	4,106.92	4,774.30
Insurance	250.00	2,323.72	1,157.40	1,229.02	1,794.23
Advertising	831.18	1,903.94	1,325.76	750.81	—
Dues and subscriptions	24.00	—	15.00	—	—
Depreciation	6,004.27	11,268.15	11,022.32	17,174.22	18,236.50
Discounts	6.51	44.96	—	—	—
Interest	6,733.55	7,932.78	9,685.40	7,509.73	11,874.66
Professional service	500.00	240.00	359.50	750.00	—
Rent	—	1,800.00	—	—	—
Repairs	—	701.96	1,013.46	1,012.47	2,819.55
Taxes	—	1,027.78	—	41.15	1,258.44
Royalties	—	815.06	—	—	—
Bad checks	—	—	137.60	—	46.76
Drinks	—	560.22	717.58	—	—
Postage	—	—	21.48	109.36	53.70
Gas and oil	—	—	—	592.42	1,215.11
Sign rent	—	—	—	—	2,261.42
Lease	—	—	—	—	1,600.00
Theft	—	—	—	—	—
Miscellaneous expenses	—	—	516.32	—	177.03
Total expenses	22,799.15	46,592.95	42,183.51	48,606.33	64,413.29
Net income or (loss)	$(12,456.88)	$(14,394.17)	$ (1,264.72)	$ 7,238.82	$ (2,966.15)

occupancy is way down. The trailer park keeps a steady $7,000 to $9,000 business to help out. No doubt we're hurt by not having a restaurant, but I send some of my guests to a good local restaurant 2½ miles away. My banker thinks we have a poor image and need gimmicks, but I just don't know.

25 After reaching a high of $73,392 in 1972, Congress Motel's room revenue fell steadily to a nine-year low of $39,719 in 1977 (see Exhibit 10.) This decline occurred even though average rates per rented room steadily increased. With the exception of moder-

Exhibit 10 ***(concluded)***

1971	*1972*	*1973*	*1974*	*1975*	*1976*	*1977*
$62,919.00	$73,392.00	$50,829.00	$40,721.00	$42,966.00	$46,269.00	$39,719.00
1,099.29	1,506.77	556.69	714.03	1,411.55	1,425.92	1,079.54
6,197.00	8,186.75	7,218.25	6,778.75	7,828.65	9,100.09	10,050.25
2,600.00	1,663.61	1,875.00	2,755.00	3,000.00	4,200.00	—
—	—	180.00	195.00	195.00	210.00	210.00
101.10	831.46	1,364.09	1,945.84	307.81		(312.58)
72,916.39	85,580.59	62,023.03	53,110.01	55,708.01	61,205.01	50,746.21
8,996.98	9,495.01	7,603.85	7,649.25	7,636.87	8,561.08	7,141.51
428.43	689.11	559.53	474.23	347.31	453.93	377.69
503.60	—	—	—	—	—	—
5,473.98	7,162.84	7,016.87	7,436.03	8,515.53	9,041.32	10,448.30
3,960.43	4,542.37	4,481.58	2,799.13	706.91	778.09	749.03
6,278.57	8,248.67	5,961.13	5,500.97	5,799.46	5,607.13	5,563.92
1,903.47	3,020.27	3,034.23	3,160.70	3,735.82	4,639.79	4,508.67
2,302.26	2,500.01	1,055.88	1,348.16	1,445,48	146.31	548.39
—	379.00	368.00	322.80	—	25.00	15.06
16,807.53	15,027.76	15,594.78	15,047.61	9,990.94	8,263.42	6,949.89
—	—	—	—	—	—	—
8,458.11	8,803.66	7,382.52	10,111.02	11,315.10	10,727.39	8,649.63
600.00	600.00	611.75	396.50	720.00	720.00	1,037.50
—	1,800.00	—	—	—	—	—
2,270.01	3,063.32	4,359.33	2,552.23	2,003.70	2,780.44	2,318.56
3,079.56	82.29	1,907.21	1,510.26	3,356.99	1,780.86	1,838.44
—	—	—	—	—	—	—
—	—	—	—	—	—	—
—	—	—	378.25	—	—	—
80.87	177.70	—	31.00	—	33.00	—
1,066.77	866.76	1,218.90	883.79	848.74	1,393.00	1,210.04
—	—	—	—	—	—	—
—	—	—	—	—	—	—
—	110.00	—	—	—	—	—
—	91.40	106.18	196.19	196.41	—	11.87
62,210.57	66,660.17	61,261.74	59,798.22	56,619.22	55,929.43	51,368.44
$10,705.82	$18,920.42	$ 761.29	$ (6,688.21)	$ (911.21)	$ 5,275.58	$ (622.23)

ate declines in the period 1973–1974, trailer-park revenue has risen steadily since operations began in 1967 (see Exhibit 10).

26 Commenting on room revenue, Brown said:

> We were doing real good until the 1974 gas shortage. Since then, we've never really recovered, and things are really getting tight. I've had to get financing for everything I buy and take out several short-term loans to get over critical times (particularly May and September). In 1975, I got SBA [Small Business

Exhibit 11

CONGRESS MOTEL
Balance Sheet
For the Years Ended December 31, 1966–1977

	1966	*1967*	*1968*	*1969*	*1970*
Assets					
Cash on hand	$ 300.00	$ 300.00	$ 500.00	$ 100.00	$ 190.09
Franchise	7,500.00	7,500.00	7,500.00	7,500.00	7,500.00
Inventory—antiques	—	—	—	—	—
Land	90,000.00	90,000.00	110,000.00	112,720.71	112,720.71
Fixed assets	136,241.49	138,859.44	144,898.03	167,993.46	172,793.08
Accrued depreciation	(6,004.27)	(18,141.60)	(29,163.92)	(46,690.07)	(64,926.57)
Prepaid interest	1,529.32	842.30	—	—	—
Personal residence	—	—		13,893.10	13,893.10
Total assets	$229,566.54	$219,360.14	$233,734.11	$255,517.20	$242,170.41
Liabilities and Net Worth					
Bank overdraft	$ 1,586.83	$ 367.72	$ —	$ 913.78	$ —
Payroll taxes	89.46	58.87	104.41	—	134.46
Sales taxes	42.12	14.69	82.30	244.05	153.14
Notes and accounts payable	26,764.20	30,070.87	10,867.55	33,060.89	35,839.96
Mortgage payable	126,981.11	114,137.30	135,916.25	122,363.29	118,051.96
Total liabilities	155,463.72	144,639.53	146,970.51	159,612.01	155,628.68
Net worth					
Calvin Brown	74,102.82	74,720.61	86,763.60	103,611.45	94,473.04
Drawing	—	—	—	(7,706.20)	(7,931.31)
Total liabilities and capital	$229,566.54	$219,360.14	$233,734.11	$255,517.26	$242,170.41

Administration] to refinance my loans so that I would have longer to pay things off. But now I'm having trouble again.

27 In order to survive the economic conditions of 1973 and 1974, Brown substantially increased his debt (see Exhibit 11), using additional assets as collateral. In 1975, Brown was experiencing severe cash flow difficulties which caused problems in meeting obligations to the SBA. At that time, Brown had two SBA loans and several additional notes payable. The 1975 notes provided for 15 monthly payments totaling approximately $3,964; two additional notes represented a monthly obligation of another $275. These notes accounted for a total liability on August 31, 1975, of $126,720. In 1975, the SBA contracted with a CPA firm to develop a refinancing proposal for Congress Motel. The proposed refinancing program is shown in Exhibit 12. The CPA firm offered the following comments concerning the refinancing proposal:

The proposed refinancing program has been developed to help ease the cash flow situation for the current business. From our discussions with Brown, it

Exhibit 11 (*concluded*)

1971	*1972*	*1973*	*1974*	*1975*	*1976*	*1977*
1,051.39	$ 1,935.07	$ 169.59	$ 782.83	$ 868.71	$ 2,500.00	$ 76.20
7,500.00	7,500.00	7,500.00	7,500.00	7,500.00	7,500.00	7,500.00
—	—	—	3,500.00	2,500.00	—	—
112,720.71	112,720.71	110,000.00	117,515.00	117,515.00	117,515.00	117,097.50
172,905.47	184,175.57	190,033.71	190,033.71	190,033.71	189,793.60	191,170.07
(81,997.85)	(87,051.63)	(99,761.98)	(114,809.59)	(124,800.53)	(131,497.14)	(138,437.03)
—	—	668.67	6,428.31	7,655.96	6,688.12	5,761.28
13,893.10	13,893.10	13,893.10	13,893.10	—	13,893.10	13,893.10
$220,072.82	$233,174.82	$222,503.09	$224,843.36	$215,165.95	$206,372.68	$197,051.12
$ —	$ —	$ 228.81	$ —	$ —	$ 263.37	$ —
231.89	250.49	215.39	236.14	93.52	207.58	148.79
277.33	135.43	93.32	153.10	176.24	150.33	89.42
35,225.23	51,553.40	63,529.91	90,586.00	59,444.78	53,585.63	32,100.90
—	—	—	—	—	—	—
102,337.37	85,797.17	72,561.03	61,463.39	89,689.01	89,116.71	107,780.29
138,071.82	137,736.49	136,628.46	153,438.63	149,403.55	143,323.62	140,119.40
97,247.55	106,921.42	97,353.91	88,574.63	73,404.73	65,762.40	86,509.33
(9,246.55)	(11,483.04)	(11,479.28)	(16,169.99)	(6,642.33)	(2,713.34)	(9,577.61)
—	—	—	—	—	—	—
$226,072.82	$233,174.82	$222,503.09	$224,843.36	$215,165.95	$206,372.68	$197,051.12

appears reasonable that these businesses may be improved to the point where the cash inflow may improve and these businesses may become profitable again. Even though refinancing may cause additional expense due to penalties or a higher prevailing interest rate, we feel that it is necessary in order to reverse the cash flow.

Our overall approach was to select those notes which required a substantial monthly payment or which extended over 12 months. Four notes which expire by May 1976 have not been considered since they only represent a combined monthly obligation of $355.

The proposed plan will require monthly payments of approximately $2,400; however, this amount drops to $1,653 by June 1976 due to expiring notes. This program may be improved if any of the existing notes may be retired by selling the related collateralized assets. In addition, the note to the Tifton Federal Savings and Loan may be reduced by a release clause if any real estate lots were sold.

Exhibit 12

Proposed refinancing program—Congress Motel and Brown's Trailer Park

	Note payable, balance at August 31, 1975	Current plan		Proposed plan, monthly payments
		Monthly payments	Last payment	
SBA 1	$ 47,920[a]	$1,436		$ 574
SBA 2	8,620[b]	336		154
Ashburn Bank	8,320[c]	250		
	7,680[c]	273		225
	1,770[c]	220		
	131	68	October 1975	68
Citizens Bank	12,230[d]	240		
	2,136[d]	107		254
	6,044[d]	178		
	494[e]	123	December 1975	123
Ben Hill	1,270[f]	78		78
Edgar Brown (monthly provision)	1,200[f]	75		75
C & S Bank—Tifton	560[e]	62	May 1976	62
International Harvester	612[e]	102	February 1976	102
	938[e]	93		93
Safeco Insurance	1,194[g]	398	December 1975	398
Tifton Federal Savings and Loan (monthly provision—interest only)	25,600[h]	200		200
Total	$126,719	$4,239		$2,406

[a] Original, 1966—26-room motel facility, land, pool, office.
[b] On 34-space trailer park/campground and facilities.
[c] On two portable trailer units with four single (motel) rooms in each.
[d] On five acres of land—for operating capital.
[e] On equipment.
[f] Loan from friend—operating capital.
[g] Financed insurance premium.
[h] Loan on 43 house lots—operating capital.

Future Directions

29 The Browns are concerned about the future of their business. They see gas prices, chain motels, a dying interchange, and threatening highway beautification billboard laws as major clouds in their future.

30 Brown thinks that advertising gimmicks and a generous buyer are keys to future success. Otherwise, he foresees "hard, penny-pinching times ahead."

31 Sitting in an old reclining chair in the front office with his eyes fixed on the I-75 traffic, Brown commented:

> I know I've gotta do something. Right now it's like robbing Peter to pay Paul. That sign over there [pointing to a high-rise, red neon sign next to the interchange

> with the word *Motel* and an arrow] had the "Congress" blown off by a tornado in 1975. Maybe I should change my name, but then I'd have to replace the Motel part and that'd cost. I sometimes wish I could just sell this place. A lot of foreigners are buying up businesses and farms around here since it's close to Plains. One talked to me through a realtor; he was from Venezuela, but he would only put 20 percent down. Well, I've gotta do something. Maybe, since I'm close to Jimmy Carter territory, I should call it Carter Inn.

The refinancing plan was approved in September 1975.

28 Brown has two loans through a local bank which are guaranteed by the SBA (90 percent of the loan amount) through its small business loans guaranty program. "My banker has put me in touch with some people at the University of Georgia to try to develop some gimmicks to improve my occupancy," said Brown, "because he [the banker] knows it's hard for me to keep up with my SBA loan payments that are with his bank." Brown continued:

> We've considered changing the name and redoing the signs, but that might cost \$210 (minimum) per sign. One guy from SBA talked about that as well as working out something with a local restaurant, getting fishing poles for guests to use at my lake and free coffee. But all of that will cost money they will have to loan me, and I doubt they will. The SBA man did mention something about a holiday on my SBA (guaranteed) loan payments which would mean \$728 per month.
>
> I've done a lot to keep costs down. I do almost all my maintenance and yard work. I have cut down on the number of maids I use, and to save even more, I've left rooms uncleaned until all rooms are used up so that maids just come in every other day or so. I took telephones out of the rooms in 1974 because it was costing so much. I've dropped AAA and several other advertising programs. I've also put off repairs on some items such as TVs and air conditioners. Several items like sheets, bedspreads, and shower curtains could be replaced, but I've postponed that. Sometimes I think I would have been better off to have just kept my farm and made this a big trailer park—never built the motel, but I did pay off about \$100,000 of my SBA loan by 1972 when things were good.

case 30
Congress Motel (B)

1 Calvin Brown had a serious decision to make as he headed into the spring 1978 travel season. Congress Motel's 1977 performance had been the worst in almost 10 years. Room revenue had fallen from over $73,000 to under $40,000, even with room rates up over 50 percent during the same period. And the first four months of 1978 were virtually identical to 1977's low levels. Finding it increasingly difficult to keep Congress Motel current in its financial obligations, Brown pondered two choices:

1. Find a way to sell or get out of his business and start a new career.
2. Endure the stress of the current situation and try to stabilize and hopefully revitalize his motel/campground business.

2 At his banker's urging, Brown had been talking with consultants from the Small Business Development Center, College of Business Administration, University of Georgia, since October 1977. These consultants were assisting Brown in examining his Congress Motel dilemma through a systematic planning effort described in Exhibit 1. Below are excerpts from the consultants' report on the situation from their initial visit with Brown:

3 Congress Motel facing severe cash flow problems . . . mainly a decline in sales and low motel occupancy . . . Brown attributes problems to gas crisis of 1974 and growth in I-75 motel chains . . . very focused on monthly expenses . . . trying to do things like cut grass, paint billboards, and repair air conditioners to save money . . . little emphasis (by Brown) on dynamics of the south I-75 travel industry other than his immediate interchange . . . minimal attention to the campground's potential—no occupancy records kept . . . (Brown) hopes we (SBDC) can get him gimmicks to increase motel occupancy.[1]

4 With the help of the student consultants, Brown was encouraged to analyze his situation in a structured manner similar to the analysis phase in Exhibit 1. Exhibit 2 presents the results of this analysis. Brown (with the consultants' assistance) identified key strengths and weaknesses of his business. Data were sought indicating general or specific opportunities and threats within his relevant environment.

5 This analysis or general forecasting activity led to the development of a simple planning matrix shown in Exhibit 3. The purpose of the planning matrix was to focus Brown on developing specific actions or strategies that (1) maximized utilization of his strengths, (2) avoided basing strategies on critical weaknesses, (3) targeted potential

---

This case was prepared by Richard Robinson, University of South Carolina. In order to best utilize this case, you should first read and analyze the Congress Motel (A) case provided earlier in this book.

[1] University of Georgia SBDC. Athens, Georgia, case file no. 081, *Congress Motel.*

Exhibit 1

Crisis planning at Congress Motel

Phase I analysis	*Phase II alternative/choice*	*Phase III implement/monitor*
1. Internal focus—evaluation of firm's strengths and weaknesses in finance, marketing, facilities, location, management, services or product, pricing, costs, customer relations, image, etc. 2. External focus—evaluation of opportunities and threats in particular industry, regional market, sources of capital, economy, technology, and regulation. 3. Competition focus—evaluation of firm's comparative standing with direct competitors—comparison of strengths and weaknesses from above relative to specific competitors within identified external situation.	1. Identification of critical internal weaknesses or external threats that must be met before the other action can be taken. 2. Identification of unusual strengths or external opportunities that must quickly be exploited. 3. Brainstorming generation of ideas/actions that maximize internal strengths to meet external opportunities and minimize impact of internal weaknesses or external threats. 4. Move from general to specific very early in process. 5. Identify simple alternatives. 6. Choose actions.	1. Commit actions to priority and timetable. 2. Begin efforts toward most critical first. 3. Continue brainstorming discussion with key information sources—partner, banker, accountant, competitors, supplies, SBDC. 4. Identify effectiveness measures of individual actions—like occupancy rate. 5. Systematically monitor measures.

opportunities on which to focus his strengths, and (4) minimized the impact of major threats. The actions and strategies developed are shown inside the Exhibit 2 matrix.

6 This analysis provided the basis for Brown to decide whether he should try to get out of the business or endure and try to turn the business around. Brown and the student consultants surmised three options:

1. Continue to operate the business (or close it if occupancy drops below 30 percent) and put all of Brown's efforts into selling an ongoing concern or liquidating the property and equipment if initial buyers were scarce.
2. Continue to operate the business but cut overhead and excess operating capacity to a minimum.
3. Continue to operate the business by changing its image and placing future emphasis on the campground side of the operation.

7 Brown chose the third option. The first option was eliminated primarily because Brown had informally entertained buyer inquiries for several years, never receiving an offer sufficient enough for Brown "to get money out of the business." Gradual liquidation would be difficult to accomplish, and it was unlikely to generate the necessary revenue to pay off all loans and retain ownership of Brown's house—currently a part of the business's assets.

Exhibit 2

Phase I: Analysis

A. Internal focus:

1. Business names/image: *motel* conveys mom-and-pop image: *Overnite Trailer Park* conveys same; *Congress* not helpful in terms of anti-Washington atmosphere.
2. Prices: second-lowest motel price ($8 single) and *lowest* campground price within 150-mile radius.
3. Cash position: very poor/minimal working capital.
4. Billboards: cost—major advantage: own all boards; number of signs (12) a major advantage: sign copy—disadvantage: done by Brown to save money, and price advertised on only 4 out of 12.
5. Location: semidying interchange, 1 gas station, 2 miles to a restaurant, but quiet and serene.
6. No restaurant: too costly.
7. Condition of property: motel relatively new—1966; campground reasonably scenic—but laundry and showers need cleanup.
8. Extras: swimming pool, miniature golf, 3-acre lake, picnic tables.
9. Campground: 26 of the 34 spaces with water/electrical/sewage hookups, other 8 with water for tent campers: all paid for in 1967.
10. Breakeven point: motel—52% occupancy; campground—18% occupancy.

B. External focus:

	1976	*1980*	*1990*
1. South I-75 travel industry characteristics (Atlanta to Florida):*			
Average daily volume:			
Cars	26,000	36,000	44,600
Recreational/vacation	8,840	12,240	14,960
Number of motel rooms available		8,280	9,108
Number of cars desiring motels		6,487	7,779
Average occupancy rate—south I-75 motels		78%	85%
Number of campsites (RV) available		840	1,680
Number of vehicles desiring camping		1,469	2,244
Average potential occupancy rate—south I-75 campgrounds		175%	133%
	1967	***1975***	***1977***
Average number of days in Georgia:*			
1–2 days	68.0%	51.0%	50.0%
3 or more	32.0	49.0	50.0
Type accommodations desired:			
Motel	66.0	53.0	50.0
Campground	1.8	10.5	12.8

2. Name recognition according to trade magazines: *Inn* is more recognized as clean, safe, and desirable than *motel; campground* more recognized as RV area than any other.
3. SBA or bank loan availability; not much receptivity.
4. SBA loan repayment holidays; with good reason, SBA-guaranteed loan payment can be postponed for six months and renewed for subsequent six months.

* Available through state of Georgia welcome center surveys.

8 The second option was rejected, after lengthy consideration, because Brown was already operating with as little overhead as possible. In essence, this option had been Brown's strategy since 1974, and it had done little good.

9 To pursue the third option, Brown required more cash than the business was currently generating. Unfortunately, given the business's poor performance over the last four years, his banker refused to loan any additional money even when presented a thorough turnaround plan by Brown and the student consultants.

10 Brown and the SBDC consultants concluded that changing the name of his business was the critical component of a turnaround strategy. The name change, they concluded, had to use current terminology (*inn* and *campground*) to increase traveler interest and, at the same time, place greater emphasis on Brown's camping facilities. The camping facilities were his greatest strength in light of current market conditions.

11 After considering several names, Brown and the consultants decided on Lakeview Inn and Campground. This name, it was felt, communicated a scenic property that should attract the camping travelers' interest. But to implement this change required at least $210 per sign for Brown's 12 billboards and 2 on-site signs.[2] Furthermore, it would have to be done immediately so as not to confuse potential interstate customers.

12 Since the business itself would not generate the necessary $3,000 at current levels for at least one year, outside financing was critical. Brown and the student consultants determined that a SBA-loan holiday would be the only realistic means of providing the necessary working capital to rapidly redo the signs. With a reprieve on the two SBA loans, Brown would have an additional $748-per-month cash flow. The sign company that would paint the signs was amenable to a 90-day repayment schedule if Brown could arrange the SBA-loan holiday.

13 Exhibit 4 shows the priorities that were established to implement this turnaround strategy. With the help of his banker, the SBA-loan holiday was approved effective June 30, 1978. The billboard changes were completed in July 1978, as shown in Exhibit 5. The fourth and fifth priorities were implemented at the same time.

Five Years as Lakeview Inn and Campground

Campground

14 The remainder of 1978 showed a dramatic improvement in campground occupancy compared to Brown's estimates of occupancy for the same period the previous year (an estimated 300 percent improvement). Since 1978, campground revenue has maintained a consistent level as shown in Exhibit 6. Commenting in early 1984, Mr. Brown made this observation:

> The campground continued to do good, especially in March and April and during the fall. We're staying above $18,000 every year, and *repeat* business is always real good in the campground.

---

[2] This price was quoted for professional repainting as mentioned in the Congress Motel (A) case. While Brown had been repainting his signs to save money, it was deemed critical by the consultants that rebuilding the business's *image* necessitated professional repainting since Brown's only communication medium was highway billboards.

Exhibit 3

Phase II: Alternatives and key considerations

	Opportunities				
	Increased I-75 traffic volume	***Increased demand for camping***	***Lack of camping facilities available***	***Cost of competitors getting into camping business***	***Increased days in Georgia***
Strengths: Prices and low break-even point	Increase in number of budget-conscious travelers	*Key advantage:* Current prices of $3.25 per day for campsite can be raised by $1 and still be below south I-75 average			
Number (12) and costs of billboards	Repeat exposure	*Key advantage:* Ability to get good advertising exposure about campground for interstate traveler at minimal long-term costs to Brown			
RV campground facility paid for		Critical: Obvious strategic advantage matching unused strength with sizable market opportunity			
Extras: (Pool, miniature golf, lake, picnic)	Important to more travelers	*Advantage:* Attractive to camper families			
Weakness: Name and image—motel and trailer park	Need to improve for repeat business				
Billboard copy: Hand painted Wording Price and campground					Emphasize recreational extras
Cash position Lack of working capital					
No restaurant	More travelers not concerned, possibly	Often self-contained; don't need restaurant			Hurts likelihood of stayovers; must deal with somehow
Lost AAA listing	Same as above				

Exhibit 3 (*concluded*)

		Threats			
Cost of signs on I-75 south	***Possible SBA six-month loan repayment holiday***	***Over Competitive motel industry on I-75 south***	***Name recognition and image associated with*** **motel**	***Name recognition and image associated with*** **trailer park**	***SBA bank receptivity to additional loans or refinancing***
		Brown's break-even point offers strategic advantage			
Key advantages: Exploit use of all these (12 signs)					
		Critical: Place emphasis on campground facility and on motel price			
		Important: Chain-type extras at no extra cost—emphasis on signs			
	Critical: Source of working capital to change signs, image, and make improvements	*Important:* Target market family, budget-conscious, outdoor-ori- ented travelers	*Critical:* Change names to reflect current consumer preference for *Inn* and *Campground.* *Lakeview* projects image attractive to recreational vacationing traveler		
	Critical: Source of cash flow to change signs		*Critical:* Signs must be profes sional, simple, standardized with equal billing for camp ground to improve *image*		
	Critical: Allows $748/month additional cash flow to pay for changes				*Important:* Avoid wasting time along this route
		Distinct disadvantage: especially at motel. Try to make local discount arrangement			
					Sell portable rooms—get back AAA and reduced debt

Exhibit 4

Phase III: Strategic priorities in Congress Motel's turnaround strategy

First:	Cash flow—negotiate six-month SBA loan holiday with additional six-month option—necessary to generate cash flow to implement other actions—represents two SBA loans with $748 total monthly payment.
Second:	Change name to Lakeview Inn and Campground.
Third:	*Professional* repainting of all billboards using standardized copy and color scheme—emphasis on price, campground facilities, and extras—equal billing to campground.
Fourth:	Raise prices of campground facilities by $1 to coincide with name change.
Fifth:	Improvement of condition of motel/campground property—campground laundry and showers having first priority.
Sixth:	Consider alternative use of portable rooms which caused AAA rating loss.
Seventh:	Investigate arrangement with local country restaurant for discount arrangement for motel/campground guests.

15 Mr. Brown estimates that 50 to 60 percent of Lakeview's campground business is repeat business. Repeat business is predominantly older, often retired people from Canada and the Great Lakes region. "My snowbirds," as Brown affectionately calls this clientele, "come through in the fall on their way to Florida and stop back by in March and April on their return after spending the winter in Florida."

16 Campground competition has not changed since 1978. A campground (Arabia campground) adjacent to a major truck stop located 10 miles north of Mr. Brown's interchange remains his most-direct competitor. A second competitor, Ponderosa, is a franchise of the national chain of the same name. Located approximately 20 miles north

Exhibit 5

Picture of an interstate billboard

Before

After (July 1978)

Exhibit 6

LAKEVIEW INN AND CAMPGROUND
Income Statement
For the Years 1978–1983

	1983	*1982*	*1981*	*1980*	*1979*	*1978*
Income:						
Room rent	$38,073	$34,982	$39,105	$38,539	$38,255	$42,479
Campground rent	18,805	18,204	18,350	18,312	16,306	15,556
Sign rent	1,734	1,058	670	762	410	1,410
Putt-Putt	950	850	788	913	860	737
Vending machines	910	800	951	956	1,156	1,953
Miscellaneous income	1,636	798	1,725	878	—	613
Other income:						
Assets sold (less cost)		3,386	6,253	—	17,962	—
Produce sold (less cost)		—	1,338	608	1,142	—
Land rent	2,500	3,000	3,500	—	3,600	7,500
Total income	63,808	63,078	72,680	60,968	79,637	70,248
Expenses:						
Labor	6,352	6,368	7,830	7,487	7,365	8,570
Payroll taxes	383	404	493	551	542	603
Linen	—	—	—	—	—	—
Utilities	8,804	9,067	7,354	6,049	5,099	5,054
Telephone	—	—	879	994	905	746
Supplies	6,681	6,578	5,610	7,158	6,559	5,681
Insurance	4,567	4,177	3,822	3,723	2,863	4,645
Advertising and signs	2,384	1,226	2,046	1,893	1,795	1,919
Other expenses	293	209	456	101	8,532	265
Professional services	3,000	2,100	1,323	1,200	1,402	970
Repairs	4,912	3,479	3,637	3,254	3,640	6,020
Taxes	396	2,124	2,026	1,585	1,507	1,795
Gas and oil	2,476	3,119	707	1,925	1,681	1,127
Interest	7,215	6,140	6,427	11,643	13,100	6,055
Depreciation	5,859	6,015	6,475	7,460	8,900	9,561
Total expenses	53,324	51,006	49,085	55,023	63,890	53,011
Net income	$10,484	$12,072	$23,595	$ 5,945	$15,747	$17,237

of Lakeview Campground, the Ponderosa has had its problems. Talking with the casewriter in early 1984, Mr. Brown said, "the Ponderosa has gone bankrupt twice in the last three years." Continuing, he said, "Someone has just recently opened it again." Mr. Brown's campground rates rose from $4 per couple in 1978 to $4.50 (1980) to $5.50 in 1983. Set at $6 per couple in 1984, his rates have still remained substantially below those charged by the Arabia and Ponderosa campgrounds.[3] Ponderosa, for example, charged a $9 daily site rental charge plus additional hook-up fees for sewer and electrical service in 1984.

[3] Brown charged 25 cents per extra person for families larger than two people. In the summer, he charged campers 25 cents admission to the swimming pool at the adjacent motel.

Motel

17 In 1979, Brown was able to sell the eight portable motel rooms for $15,000.[4] The proceeds were used to pay off a smaller SBA loan—originally made for these units. In addition, Brown sold about $5,000 worth of equipment (TVs, beds, and so forth) associated with these eight portable rooms.

18 Except for the dip below $35,000 in 1982, annual motel revenue has hovered around $40,000 since 1978. Unfortunately, according to Brown, this revenue stability has been maintained through steadily increased rates. The average room rate in 1978 was $9.32 with an estimated occupancy around 36 percent for the 34 rooms. By 1980, the average rate was $12.52. Mr. Brown estimates that motel occupancy has fluctuated between 27 percent and 30 percent since 1980. Since the eight portable rooms were sold in 1979, these occupancy figures reflect only demand for the 26 original rooms. The average room rate was $12.52 in 1980. By the end of 1983, the single-occupancy room rate was $15.88. Commenting on his pricing strategy, Mr. Brown said, "I just raise the rate to keep from going in the hole. I'm still the lowest for a single—Days Inns is at $21.88, and Ashburn Motor Court is at $18.88, but price doesn't really seem to help. I rent just as many at $15 as I do at $10." Lakeview Inn's annual revenue since 1978 is shown in Exhibit 6, and the balance sheet for the same years is shown in Exhibit 7.

19 While no new motel competitors have entered Lakeview's market, at least three motels have changed ownership. Ashburn Motor Court, Days Inn, and Master Hosts have been acquired by Arab investors since 1980, according to Brown. One acquisition, Master Hosts, just north of Ashburn, Georgia, was formerly a Quality Inn before it went bankrupt. Commenting on the competitive situation, Brown observed "Every motel on the northbound side of I-75 within 20 miles of Ashburn is doing poorly." Brown offered the following fundamental reason:

20 This location is just too short a distance from Florida. A northbound traveler can leave from anywhere across the middle of the state of Florida and pass this area within one day. It didn't use to be that way—in 1972, we had over 90 percent occupancy. Back then, the cars seemed to back up more often and travel slower.

21 Brown says the lack of a reservation system is a major reason southbound traffic does not stop at Lakeview Inn. Most of his competitors are part of a national chain or a reservation network. Industrywide data supports his concern. Seventy-three percent of all room-nights at highway/roadside motels are arranged through advanced reservations according to industry experts. The figure is as high as 90 percent for airport locations. Brown has developed a brochure (see Exhibit 8) as one means to overcome the reservation system problem. He places it at the Georgia welcome center on I-75 just north of the Florida line.

Billboards

22 In 1980, Brown was notified by the Georgia Highway Department that all 12 of his interstate highway signs were in violation of current billboard laws. The violation

[4] The motel had 26 (predominantly with double beds) rooms in its original, concrete-block structure. Mr. Brown added two sets of four portable, single-occupancy rooms at either end of the original structure in response to the rapid increase in demand in the early 1970s. See the Congress Motel (A) case for greater detail).

Exhibit 7

LAKEVIEW INN AND CAMPGROUND
Balance Sheets
For the Years 1978–1983

	1983	*1982*	*1981*	*1980*	*1979*	*1978*
Assets						
Cash	$ 159	$ 256	$ 313	$ 443	$ 9	$ 189
Franchise	—	—	—	—	—	7,500
Land	169,253*	116,363	116,571	116,989	116,989	117,197
Personal residence	13,893	13,893	13,893	13,893	13,893	13,893
Fixed assets	187,085	186,617	185,448	183,677	183,443	195,441
Accrued depreciation	(167,338)	(161,479)	(155,464)	(148,989)	(141,528)	(148,009)
Prepaid interest	347	—	—	520	3,153	6,198
Total assets	$ 203,399	$ 155,649	$ 160,761	$ 166,533	$ 175,959	$ 192,409
Liabilities and Net Worth						
Liabilities:						
Sales tax payable	$ 104	$ 78	$ 87	$ 91	$ 78	$ 160
Payroll tax payable	186	158	202	204	148	284
Accounts payable	2,246	3,285	4,128	4,258	4,205	1,913
Notes and mortgage due (1 year)	84,419†	28,150	19,607	27,016	25,300	23,762
Notes and mortgage due (over 1 year)	40,884	44,851	56,041	67,470	82,531	100,725
Total liabilities	130,243	77,522	80,065	98,039	112,262	126,844
Net worth:						
Calvin Brown (capital)	78,128	80,695	68,490	63,697	65,565	56,931
Add: Net income	10,484	12,072	23,599	8,121	15,747	17,237
Add: Life insurance costed	—	—	—	10,000	—	—
Less: Drawings	14,396	14,640	11,393	13,324	17,616	8,603
Total net worth	74,216	78,127	80,696	68,494	63,696	65,565
Total liabilities and net worth	$ 203,399	$ 155,649	$ 160,761	$ 166,533	$ 175,959	$ 192,409

* Includes the farm land purchased in late 1983 by Mr. Brown, as mentioned in paragraph 28.

† Includes the refinancing of a $7,000 note at a local bank to $45,000 in order to purchase some farm land in late 1983.

Exhibit 8

Lakeview Inn brochure

Calvin G. Brown

invites you to come

and enjoy the quiet

qualities at his

LAKEVIEW INN
and
CAMPGROUND

The Lakeview
Personnel Will Give
You A Hearty

Y'ALL COME
SEE US Y'HEAR

Lakeview Inn

- *26 ROOMS AVAILABLE*
- *SOUTHERN ATMOSPHERE*
- *EASY ACCESS*
- *TV IN EVERY ROOM*
- *REASONABLE RATES*
- *HEAT & AIR CONDITIONING*
- *RESTAURANT 3 MILES*

"Your Comfort
Is Our Creed"

NEXT TIME YOU TRAVEL
YOU WILL REMEMBER LAKEVIEW

Lakeview

Set in the midst of South Georgias Pecan, Peanut and Agriculture Center - Places of interest within a few miles on every side.

Goldkist Peanut Plant - Ashburn
Georgia Agrirama - Tifton
Plains Ga. - Presidents Home - Americus
Okeefenokie Swamp - Waycross
Westville - 1800's Town - Westville, Ga.

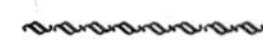

Enjoy The Southern

Way Of Life

- Beautiful Lakeview -

- Georgia Hospitality -

"At Its Very Best"

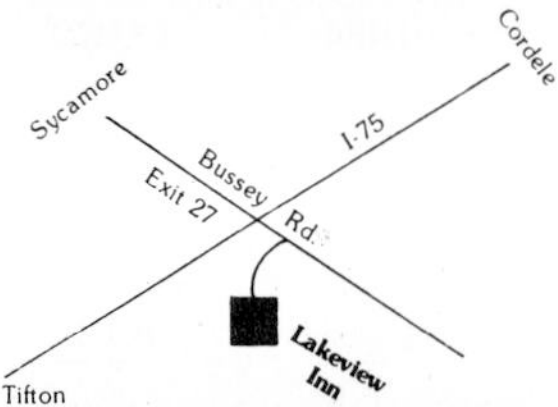

Lakeview

Inn

and

Campground

I-75 AT BUSSEY RD.
EXIT 27

SYCAMORE, GEORGIA

Big Accommodations
At
Reasonable Prices

A PLACE TO PUT YOU AT EASE

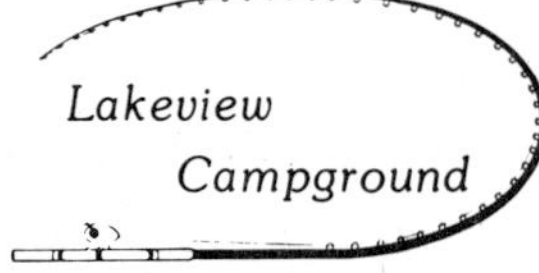

- FISHING · SHUFFLBOARD
- MINATURE GOLF
- SWIMMING POOL
- PLAYGROUND

- FOOD MART ADJACENT
- HOT SHOWERS
- LAUNDRY ROOM
- 34 PULL THRU SITES

CALL FOR RESERVATIONS

Lakeview Inn
And
Campground

Route 1
Sycamore, Georgia 31790

Phone (912) 567-3357

pertained to their distances from the interstate right-of-way (they were too close) and/ or the fact that each sign was in a noncommercial area. Brown appealed the highway department ruling and eventually was allowed to keep 10 signs if he paid a $50-per-year sign permit fee. While allowing him to keep 10 signs, the highway department would not grant Brown's request that it remove the trees planted on highway right-of-way in the early 1970s. By 1981, these trees had grown sufficiently high to effectively block the signs from the travelers' view. Brown actively pursued removal of these trees from 1981 to 1984 with no success. He offered the following comments on the billboard situation in mid-1984:

23 I've got two signs way down south you can still see pretty good. The one on the property here and one just north of this exit (for southbound traffic) are visible. But the others have trees completely blocking them out. It doesn't really matter in the long run because they're going to have standard expressway signs saying what's at each exit—those where you put your logo on it. It may take two to three years, but I think that is what will happen.

24 Mr. Brown was unsure if the new expressway signs would mean billboards located within 100 feet of commercial areas (acceptable under the current law) would have to come down—most major chains located signs in such areas. He hoped everyone would eventually take their signs down. Brown decided to have his signs repainted in early 1983 but doesn't feel occupancy was helped.

Bussey Road Interchange[5]

25 In 1980 and 1981, Brown was pleased to see the reopening of several businesses on his interchange. Down to just Lakeview Inn and a discount gas station in 1979, Texaco and Shell had reopened gas stations by 1981. Perhaps of greater importance to Brown, the truck stop and restaurant within walking distance of his motel reopened in 1981. Brown felt the restaurant was well received by his guests.

26 The 81–82 recession took its toll on these Bussey Road Exit businesses. By October 1983, the truck stop and restaurant had closed, and rumors were out that one of the major gas stations would again close. Reflecting his frustration in early 1984, Brown said:

> I've had a lot of people come in and register, and there wouldn't be one other person here. The people that had just registered would go around and get to studying about it (the lack of other guests) and then come back to the office wanting to get their money back. They say it's too desolate, and I have to give the money back. Then they may go up to Ashburn where it's more lit up.

Brown said the problem also happens with campground registrants, but on a much less frequent basis.

27 Brown is unaware of any plans to reopen the truck stop or restaurant. There is talk, according to Brown, of building a "Ford Theatre" in Ashburn (one exit north) to try and pull tourists into the greater Ashburn area.

28 Asked about the future, Brown had two basic observations:

[5] See Exhibits 6 and 7 in the Congress Motel (A) case for a diagram of the Bussey Road interchange.

> The traffic count is still okay, and I frequently get inquiries about buying this place. Just today, a doctor stopped in to see if I wanted to sell the place—he's the third person this week to ask that question. They must see this place as a real tax dodge. So far, no one has come through with an acceptable offer—I would need at least 25 percent down.
>
> I'm doing okay for now. The campground with my farmland rental takes care of my financial needs—I'm not hurting yet. In fact, I just bought my dad's farmland—he had filed bankruptcy, and I didn't want it to go out of the family. I borrowed the money at the bank and lease out the land to cover the payment.

Mr. Brown felt that since the land should always pay for itself (leasing for farming), he was not financially overextending himself. 1984 also meant that Brown had only four more years before all loans and mortgages on Lakeview Inn and Campground would be paid in full.

1984 Divestiture

29 Ed Graves approached Mr. Brown about buying Lakeview Inn in early 1984, and on January 16, 1984, a sale was closed whereby Mr. Graves acquired the motel and swimming pool from Mr. Brown for $135,000. Graves paid Brown $8,000 down and signed a 20-year note at 11 percent with Mr. Brown for the balance. Graves's payments for principal and interest was $1,398 per month. Brown called the arrangements a "wraparound deal" whereby Brown stays obligated on all SBA loans and keeps other obligations (utilities, insurance, sign rental, and so forth) in his name. In return, no warranty deed was issued to Graves. The property will be deeded once the $135,000 is paid. Graves is obligated to pay Brown, in addition to the $1,398 payment, the following amounts on a monthly basis:

$100 per month for rental of four signs (Graves must pay for upkeep).

$75 per month for water and sewage.

$300 per month for insurance.

Exhibit 9 shows exactly what Mr. Graves has contracted to buy. Brown retains control of the campground (7 acres and the lake) as well as 2½ acres of property adjacent to the motel. Graves bought 2 acres which is essentially the motel, its parking lot, and the swimming pool. Graves will collect campground fees for Mr. Brown and receive $1.00 per party for providing this service.

30 Brown retains ownership of his home adjacent to the motel and campground properties. His home is included as a business asset. Mr. and Mrs. Graves will live on the motel property in an efficiency apartment adjacent to the motel office.

31 Graves moved to Tampa, Florida, in 1982 after a career as a printer with a Dayton, Ohio, newspaper company ended in early retirement. (His job was eliminated when the company computerized printing operations.) Graves had no motel experience although Mrs. Graves had worked as a night auditor for a Tampa motel for the last year.

32 Shortly after acquiring the motel property, Graves had an unexpected appendectomy operation, but he was fully recovered by mid-March and looking forward to a good

Exhibit 9

Diagram of facilities and property sold to Graves

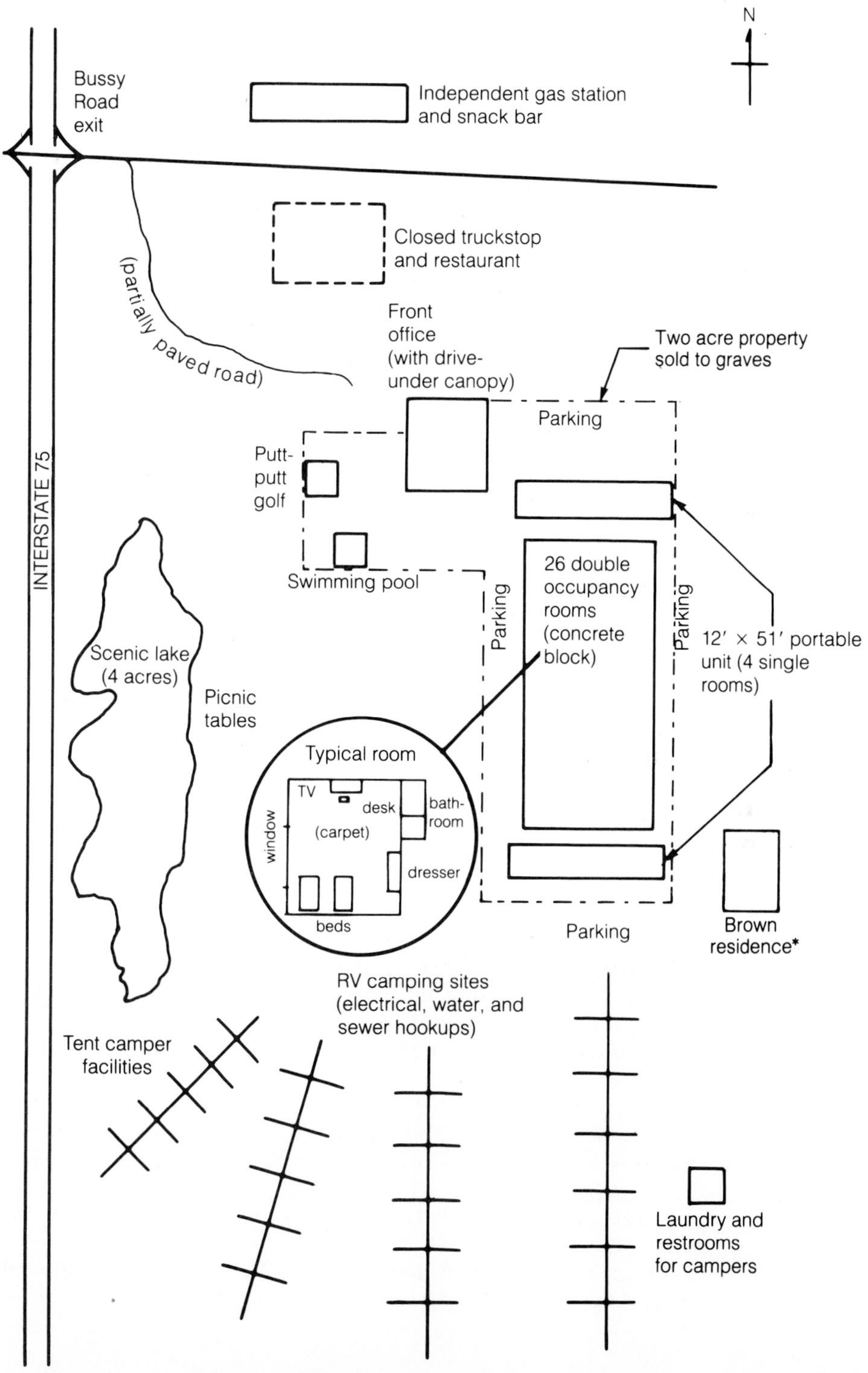

* Located about one fourth mile east of the motel property.

spring for his new motel property. Brown offered the following assessment of Graves's prospects:

> Mr. Graves is going to live in the office. He and Mrs. Graves will clean the rooms and do most of the work themselves. He can make it if he pinches pennies like I did for so long.

33 Brown regularly drops in on Graves to see how business is going and offer advice. Since he is still obligated on all loans, Brown takes advantage of his location (next door) to make sure the property is not becoming run down. Brown is relieved to be "out from under the 24-hour responsibility" and looks forward to 1988 when all SBA loans and mortgages will be paid in full. By the end of May 1984, he was impressed with how hard Mr. and Mrs. Graves seemed to be working. They had been able to keep up payments, and it did not appear to Mr. Brown that occupancy had improved significantly.

case 31
Note on the Grocery Industry

History

1 Prior to the 1920s, the grocery business was probably the least advanced of all retail industries. Separate stores existed for baked goods, meat, fish, and dry foods. It was not until the mid-1920s that the concept of a supermarket emerged so that customers could make all their purchases at one store. The pioneers of the industry included John Hartford of The Great Atlantic & Pacific Tea Company, Inc., Michael Cullen of King Kullen, Barney Kroger of The Great Western Tea Company, and Clarence Saunders of Piggly Wiggly.

2 The year 1932 saw the first time in the industry's history that profits were down. Throughout the Depression years of the 1930s, numerous supermarkets started and went bankrupt. Even then, however, the larger-volume stores were beginning to dominate the scene.

3 By 1939, the corner mom-and-pop grocery store was having difficulty maintaining competitive prices with the high-volume supermarkets. As a result, Congress passed a series of laws with the intent of keeping these larger stores from running the small, family-owned stores out of business.

4 In the 1940s, The Great Atlantic and Pacific Tea Company, Inc. (A&P) forged ahead as the nation's Number 1 food retailer. All chains, however, suffered stock shortages during the war years and had trouble attracting customers from any appreciable distance due to gas rationing. When the war ended grocery sales skyrocketed. Sales for 1947 increased 20 percent from the previous year. Inflation and low levels of unemployment also helped stimulate the demand for groceries.

5 With the 1950s came the introduction of frozen foods and nonfood items and the merging of many of the leading chains as industry consolidation occurred.

6 The early 1960s brought the emergence of the convenience store and the discount store. By 1965, standard supermarkets retaliated by issuing millions of stamps in an effort to boost sales. S&H Green Stamps and Top Value Stamps became a fixture in every family's repertoire of goods to help them stay within their budget. Food prices climbed dramatically in the late 1960s—enough that discounting became the major theme by the decade's end.

7 Rising costs and falling profit margins led to more food price increases in the 1970s. Meat prices climbed so fast that many shoppers began to remove it from their weekly

---

This case was written by William Reese and Larry D. Alexander of Virginia Polytechnic Institute and State University with the assistance of J. Kay Keels.

grocery lists. A new concept in store design also emerged. The larger-size superstore helped keep prices on food items in line through higher volume and the sale of more high-profit, nonfood items.

8 The late 1970s and early 1980s saw an increase in stores packaging foods in containers featuring their own labels to cut costs. Other retailers attempted more-drastic cost-cutting measures by opening no-frills warehouse stores where shoppers marked their own prices and bagged their own groceries but were compensated with lower prices.

9 In the mid-1980s, there seemed to be a pull on grocery stores from each end of the spectrum. On one end, the warehouse stores were trying to see how low they could cut costs by offering the customer only bare necessities. On the other end, the larger chains were offering more and more nonfood items in an effort to build volume with the attraction of one-stop shopping. Each store type seemed to satisfy important niches in the grocery industry.

National Supermarket Chains

10 National chains are perhaps the best-known representatives of the grocery industry. Exhibit 1 shows the top U.S. grocery chains, four of which are profiled in the following paragraphs.

Exhibit 1

Leading U.S. grocery chains, 1982

Chain	*Sales ($ billion)*	*Total number of stores*
Safeway Stores, Inc.	17.0	2,400 (1,888 U.S.)
The Kroger Co.	11.5	1,258
Lucky Stores, Inc.	7.5	1,576
Food store sales	5.0	541
American Stores Co.	7.5	1,100
Food stores		680
Winn-Dixie Stores, Inc.	7.0	1,220
The Great A&P Tea Co., Inc.	4.7	1,055
The Grand Union Co.	4.0	725
Albertson's, Inc.	3.5	412
Jewel Cos., Inc.	5.4	
Food stores	3.4	347
Supermarkets General Corp.	3.0	
Food stores	2.7	117
Dillon Cos., Inc.	3.0	485
Publix Supermarkets, Inc.	2.6	265
Vons Grocery Co.	2.4	167
Stop & Shop Cos., Inc.	2.2	
Food stores	1.3	125
Giant Food, Inc.	1.9	130
Ralphs Grocery Company	1.3	104
Waldbaum, Inc.	1.5	140

Sources: Newspaper Advertising Bureau; and Kenneth W. Clarfield and Jean Kozlowski, "Supermarkets and Grocery Chains," *Standard & Poor's Industry Surveys* (1983).

Kroger

11 In January 1983, Kroger became the industry leader in U.S. sales with its acquisition of the Dillon Company. Kroger reached this lofty position primarily through the aggressive store-building campaign it began in 1972 and through its substantial manufacturing capabilities.

12 The Kroger Company was founded in 1883 by Barney Kroger, starting as a single store in Cincinnati called The Great Western Tea Company. Barney Kroger headed the business himself until 1928. By then, the chain had spread to several other states and was one of the nation's 10 largest grocery chains.

13 When Kroger entered a second expansion phase in the 1970s, it did so with a clearer idea of what it wanted to accomplish. Because CEO James Herring felt that customers would respond to larger stores with a wider selection of nonfood items, Kroger became the first chain to open superstores. These superstores emphasized one-stop shopping by continually adding new services like delicatessens, wine shops, and floral centers.

14 Kroger stores were heavily concentrated in the midwestern and southeastern portions of the country. Unfortunately, since those areas were hit hard by the 1981–1983 recession, many Kroger stores did not experience the sales growth they had hoped for in the early 1980s.

15 All Kroger stores were unionized. This meant that the company was forced to pay a premium for its labor. Often, Kroger was the only unionized chain in many of its markets and was forced to make up for higher labor costs with higher store volume. So far, Kroger had been able to do so.

16 In addition to Kroger and Dillon food stores, Kroger owned and operated Super X drug stores, usually located next to Kroger stores. Kroger also operated Barney's warehouse store and Bi-Lo box stores, which were located in only the Cleveland, Ohio, area.

17 Traditionally, Kroger did not offer many of the promotional gimmicks that other chains did, but relied heavily on print advertising and the advertising of its private-label brands. In 1981, Kroger initiated cost-cutter brands, a generic labeling of national and Kroger-manufactured products which offered lower prices than most national brands.

Safeway

18 Although Kroger held the Number 1 spot in U.S. sales, Safeway stores sold the most groceries worldwide. With about one fourth of its sales outside the United States, Safeway was the only major U.S. chain to have moved significantly into foreign markets.

19 In the United States, Safeway stores were located in the far western states and in the area surrounding Washington, D.C. These locations proved especially beneficial during the 1981–83 recession, as they included some parts of the country hit least by the resulting unemployment. When high unemployment hit an area, people bought fewer of the high-margin items on which supermarkets had come to depend.

20 Safeway's 2,454 stores were located as follows: 1,919 in the United States, 294 in Canada, 98 in the United Kingdom, 28 in West Germany, and 115 in Australia. In addition to its supermarkets, Safeway operated a series of warehouse food stores called Food Barns and Liquor Barn discount liquor stores located in California and Arizona.

The 67 Liquor Barns together with the 700 Safeway stores that carried liquor made Safeway the world's largest retailer of alcoholic beverages.

21 During the mid-1970s, Safeway's management seemed to be led by the conservative influence of its legal department. According to current CEO Peter Magowan, "Safeway adopted the strictest possible interpretation of government antitrust and other regulations. Lawyers nixed plans to create health-food departments in stores because of possible legal hassles over insect infestation. They curtailed advertising of loss leaders because of possible legal exposure if stores ran out of items."[1] Wall Street also recognized the problem. In 1981, Safeway's stock was still selling at the same price for which it sold in 1964.

22 In 1980, Safeway attempted to turn things around by hiring 37-year-old Peter Magowan as chairman and chief executive officer. Magowan's father had guided the company during its growth years of 1955–69, and the company hoped that the son would be equally effective.

23 The younger Magowan immediately curtailed the heavy legal influence by putting retailers in control of the company. The company closed stores that were located too close to other Safeway stores and began opening 100 new superstores per year. These new stores were called superstores because their size was typically in the 40,000- to 60,000-square-foot range. Safeway also reorganized its organizational structure which, according to Magowan, had been "decentralized to a fault."

24 It appeared that Safeway was following Kroger's strategy of 10 years earlier. However, Safeway did take a different route with private-labeled products by concentrating on national brands rather than its own labels. In the early 1980s, Safeway started to regain some of the momentum it lost during the 1970s, and it appeared unlikely that another food chain would take over its Number 1 position in the near future.

Winn-Dixie

25 Winn-Dixie's 1,222 grocery stores, including 11 Buddies stores, were located only in the southeastern region of the United States. A third of them were located in Florida alone. The firm began in 1914 with a single store owned by William M. Davis. Davis was one of the first grocery merchants to employ the idea of cash-and-carry grocery stores. His four sons, two of whom were still with the company in the mid-1980s, helped him open 34 Table Supply Stores located in South Florida.

26 In 1944, the company negotiated several mergers that helped it become the fourth-largest food retailer in the country. The Table Supply chain's first merger resulted in the Winn & Lovett food stores. The Davis family located their new headquarters in Jacksonville.

27 After World War II ended, Winn & Lovett merged with or acquired Steiden stores in Kentucky, Margaret Ann stores in Florida, Wylie Company stores in Alabama, Penney stores in Mississippi, King stores in Georgia, and the Eden and Ballentine stores in South Carolina. In 1955, when it combined with Dixie Home stores in North and South Carolina, it changed its name to Winn-Dixie. Winn-Dixie went on to acquire the Ketner and Milner stores in North and South Carolina and the Hill stores in Louisiana and Alabama.

---

[1] "Safeway Stores: Back to Price Wars for a Company that Played It Too Safe," *Business Week,* April 5, 1982, pp. 108–9.

28 Through these acquisitions, Winn-Dixie gained many experienced grocery people, some of whom have become its top executives. In contrast, many of its competitors tended to promote managers and executives from only their base companies.

29 Winn-Dixie was slow to move toward the superstore concept. As a result, many markets were already saturated with regular grocery stores and superstores, and Winn-Dixie had trouble obtaining financing for its own new store construction. So the company changed its strategy in favor of remodeling its existing stores.

30 Winn-Dixie climbed to the Number 4 position in sales nationally despite the facts that it was located in a relatively small portion of the country and that it had been built from many small, diverse chains. The synergies resulting from its integration efforts contributed to Winn-Dixie's success.

The Great Atlantic & Pacific Tea Company, Inc. (A&P)

31 The Great Atlantic & Pacific Tea Company, Inc., was established in 1869 by George Hartford. A&P was the oldest chain in the industry, and for many years the firm dwarfed its competition. In the last decade, however, the company suffered substantial losses and was forced to close stores and moved out of entire cities. In 1981, the company declared a $231 million loss for the year. Since then, the company has made a desperate attempt to rescue itself from the brink of insolvency. But competition from larger chains has made A&P's recovery attempt difficult.

32 Though A&P continued to grow, it always seemed to be responding to strategy moves of competitors rather than initiating change itself. For example, A&P began building supermarkets in 1937 but only in response to King Kullen stores that had already proved to be so successful. The later addition of nonfood items, trading stamps, and the discount approach were all ideas that A&P picked up after someone else in the industry first introduced them.

33 In 1969, A&P's sales of $5.7 billion made it the world's largest food retailing firm. Stores seemed to be located everywhere, and weekly sales topped $100 million. So great was its size and power, A&P influenced all aspects of the food industry from farmers to food processors to wholesalers to competitors.

34 In the early 1970s though, Safeway and Kroger began challenging A&P's Number 1 ranking, and in 1972 Safeway passed A&P in total sales. Industry observers blamed A&P's decline on small, poorly located stores, insufficient service, and haphazard sales promotion. Even in the 1980s, A&P stores still had a dull, old-fashioned image which was reinforced by the fact that many of A&P's employees were old.

35 In the spring of 1972, A&P decided to take aggressive action to try and regain its place as the industry leader. It initiated a "Where Economy Originates" (WEO) campaign, a drastic price-slashing move designed to increase market share. The program seemed to be working at first, but the company couldn't maintain profitability with its low prices and consequently had to raise them again.

36 The price wars that the WEO campaign brought about left A&P badly bruised. While all of its attention was focused on prices, unfortunately, A&P paid little attention to its deteriorating stores. Throughout the late 1970s, sales and profits continued to decline.

37 In 1979, A&P began opening low-overhead Plus stores that carried only a limited assortment of items sold at discount. Unfortunately, these Plus stores were not success-

ful. By 1981, A&P had dropped to fifth place in grocery sales and was forced to discharge a third of its work force.

38 When things seemed darkest for A&P, a bit of good fortune occurred. A $250 million surplus was found in the company's pension fund. As of late 1982, A&P had not yet received the money, but chances looked good that the courts would turn it over to the firm in the next year or so.

39 In 1981, A&P pulled out of Philadelphia. But in 1982, it reopened 18 stores in the city with new labor union contracts. In exchange for getting their jobs back, union members gave back 25 percent of their wages and benefits, a $10 million savings for the company. However, employees gained the right to share in decisions with A&P managers. They would divide 1 percent of the stores' annual sales, but only if labor costs were 10 percent of sales or less. A&P's former Philadelphia labor cost average had been 15 percent. A&P made this arrangement in hopes that employees would be motivated to treat customers well so that they would remain loyal to A&P. For 1982, A&P posted $32 million in earnings. This was its first year in the black since 1977.

Regional Grocery Chains

Mick-or-Mack

40 Mick-or-Mack food stores were founded in 1927 by Norman MacVay, who ran the business until he died in 1975. In October of 1981, Peter McGoldrick and Conrad Stephanites jointly purchased the company, and in 1983 Stephanites became the chief executive officer.

41 There were only 13 Mick-or-Mack stores, most located in the Roanoke Valley of Virginia. Until August of 1983, two additional stores operated in the small Virginia towns of Blacksburg and Christiansburg. Since Mick-or-Mack was not publicly owned, it did not have to disclose figures on sales and earnings. However, a company spokesman reported that Mick-or-Mack stores averaged $4 million in sales annually. Stores averaged 21,000 square feet in size.

42 When Stephanites and McGoldrick bought the chain, it was not doing well and was not keeping up with new trends in the industry. According to CEO Conrad Stephanites, "Things that were taken for granted by a regional chain, we weren't even doing. We weren't open Sundays, we were still giving stamps, we were not aggressive in price, and our stores were blah. We were working from a base that was 10 years behind the times."[2]

43 Mick-or-Mack bought its groceries from a wholesaler because there was no advantage to operating its own warehouse to serve just 13 stores. The wholesaler that Mick-or-Mack used was Fleming Company, the Number 2 rated wholesaler in the United States.

44 Mick-or-Mack attempted to take advantage of its regional status by emphasizing

---

[2] Personal interview with Conrad Stephanites, president of Mick-or-Mack Stores, August 16, 1983, at company headquarters in Roanoke, Virginia.

to its customers that their food dollars were being recycled back into the local economy. The company further attempted to build up its local image by taking part in fund raising for charity events.

45 Mick-or-Mack did not carry as many private-label brands as did Kroger and Winn Dixie, its two biggest local competitors. Instead, it carried a wider assortment of national brands in an attempt to differentiate itself from its rivals.

46 In contrast to their national chain competitors, all Mick-or-Mack stores were nonunionized. In order to preserve this advantage, Mick-or-Mack management offered employees benefits that union contracts would be hard-pressed to match. One example was the Mick-or-Mack fun check. When taking a two-week paid vacation, an employee was paid for three weeks.

Fisher Foods

47 Fisher Foods was another example of a regional chain. It operated the Fazio's regional supermarket chain. As of 1983, there were 40 Fazio's in the Cleveland, Ohio, area and 17 located elsewhere in Ohio.

48 When it first started in 1908, the chain was known as Fisher Brothers Co. It changed its name to Fisher Foods in 1961. During the 1960s, Fisher was a growth-oriented company that did little wrong. It was known for its high-quality meats and other fine food and could afford to operate on a high margin. In 1968, Fisher acquired Dominick's Finer Foods. Dominick's had 71 supermarkets in the Chicago area, and these stores accounted for much of Fisher's income during the middle and late 1970s. In September 1981, Fisher Foods sold the Dominick's stores for $100 million, a figure which greatly exceeded its book value.

49 Fisher Foods' most publicized developments in the late 1970s came in the courtroom, rather than in the grocery aisles. Fazio's, along with two other Cleveland-area supermarket chains, was found guilty of fixing prices over two periods during 1976–78. The three chains were ordered to collectively pay a $2 million fine and to distribute $20 million in free groceries to area residents from 1982 to 1987. In 1982, Fisher Foods faced another lawsuit from May Co. for the sum of $180 million. May brought this suit because Fisher Foods discontinued a trading stamp program for which Fisher had contracted with May.

50 The Fazio's food stores experienced regular growth throughout most of the 1970s, reaching a peak in 1978. However, the company lost $5.3 million in 1979 on a no-frills warehouse venture. Since then, other problems have continued to mount.

51 Fazio's has always tried to project an image of a high-quality, premium-price supermarket. During the inflationary years of the 60s and early 70s, that strategy proved to be quite successful in the suburban areas of northeastern Ohio. Shoppers who wanted to get the best meats and the freshest produce shopped at Fazio's. The image did not appeal to everyone, but it attracted enough customers to allow the company to continue its expansion.

52 With the 1981–1983 recession and the resulting high levels of unemployment (14 percent in Cleveland), shoppers in Fazio's stores became willing to trade some quality for price. With Fazio's resulting drop in sales, losses from its warehouse store, and its legal problems, Fisher Foods experienced a loss for 1982. As a result, the company

tried to streamline operations in 1983 by selling nonvital assets to obtain cash needed to move into more favorable markets.

Convenience Stores

53 Convenience stores, typically smaller than grocery stores, carried fewer items, had higher prices, and tried to attract customers by quickly providing supplemental grocery items and extended shopping hours.

54 While large supermarkets targeted their marketing efforts toward women in the 18 to 49 age range, convenience-store customers were typically men from 18 to 35. Since working men had less free time, they used convenience stores as a way to quickly pick up a few needed items. However, as more women entered the work force, they also relied more on the nearby convenience store to supplement their shopping needs.

55 Convenience stores fared exceptionally well in low-income areas though area residents could least afford to pay the higher prices charged by convenience stores. Two reasons for this phenomenon were offered. First, many lower-income people did not own cars and the local convenience store was the closest grocery store to their homes. Second, most supermarket chains were reluctant to build stores in low-income, high-crime urban areas.

56 Grocery items in convenience stores were marked up as high as 30 percent over conventional grocery store prices. Health and beauty aids typically were marked up even higher. The exceptions were milk, bread, beer, and wine. Milk was often sold below cost in an effort to attract customers. Bread, beer, and wine were often priced fairly close to supermarket prices.

57 All the large convenience store chains and most of the small ones were members of the National Association of Convenience Stores. Promotional ideas, new products, and different strategies were openly discussed among representatives of competing chains at various workshops and conventions. In many ways, the association was more like a cooperative effort than firms competing ruthlessly against one another.

58 In the mid-1980s, two major threats faced the convenience stores. The biggest threat was the oil companies who were beginning to sell convenience items at their gas stations. Many stations had 15 to 20 gas pumps, which generated a large daily volume of customer traffic. Furthermore, gas stations got their customers in and out in just a few minutes, just as convenience stores did. When gas stations started selling milk, tobacco products, and bread, most of these customers were drawn away from the convenience stores.

59 The other major threat was large supermarkets that began staying open 24 hours a day. One of the big advantages enjoyed by convenience stores had been their extended hours. However, with the option of shopping late at night at either a convenience store or a supermarket, a customer often chose the lower-priced supermarket. At odd hours, either alternative could provide the same quick service.

60 Surveys showed that convenience stores attracted most customers from only a one-mile radius of the store. This meant it was essential that they be located near homes, apartments, or businesses. However, as more and more convenience store chains opened, it became apparent that the successful ones might be firms that would identify neglected products and untapped dimensions of customer service.

Southland Corp. (7-Eleven)

61 This modern-day American institution was originally named for its long hours of operation, 7 A.M. to 11 P.M. 7-Eleven's sales of $6.76 billion in 1982 made it the nation's 10th largest retailer and its leading convenience store.

62 Over 7,000 7-Eleven stores were located in 42 states, the District of Columbia, and five provinces of Canada and served almost 7 million customers every day. Forty percent of these stores were operated by franchisees and the remainder by managers hired by Southland.

63 7-Eleven stores benefited from putting gasoline pumps in front of its stores. Forty percent of the stores had self-service pumps as of 1983, and gas sales accounted for 26 percent of total store sales.

64 One of Southland's basic strategies with 7-Eleven was to make each store a clone of the rest. One company executive boasted that he could walk into most stores blindfolded and find any item requested.

65 Southland had always been an innovator with its 7-Eleven stores. It was the first grocery chain that had stores open 24 hours. More recently, Southland began opening stores in the inner city, an innovation some industry observers felt might also start a trend.

66 Southland's expansion plans involved opening about 400 new stores around the country each year. However, about 250 stores were closed each year. Though store sites were carefully selected and a net gain of 150 stores occurred each year, it was costly to close so many stores.

67 Southland described its 7-Eleven stores this way:

> Generally, the stores are open every day of the year and are located in neighborhood areas, on main thoroughfares, in shopping centers, or on other sites where they are easily accessible and have ample parking facilities for quick in-and-out shopping. The company emphasizes personal, courteous service and clean, modern stores. The stores attract early and late shoppers, weekend and holiday shoppers, and customers who may need only a few items at any one time and desire rapid service. Typical stores contain approximately 2,400 square feet, carry more than 3,000 items, and have distinctive and easily recognizable facades.[3]

To maintain a modern store appearance, older stores were remodeled by Southland. Most of the items carried were nationally or locally advertised brands. In addition, 7-Eleven stores carried a sizable portion of private-label products.

Silverwood Industries (Hop-In)

68 Silverwood Industries, which operated Hop-In Convenience Stores located in North Carolina, Tennessee, and Virginia, was founded in the mid-1960s by John Hudgins. Hop-In started as a single store in southwestern Virginia with Hudgins as the owner-operator. The number of Hop-In stores grew so rapidly in the 1970s and early 1980s that the company's logo of a rabbit seemed most appropriate.

---

[3] Southland Corporation, Form 10-K (Washington, D.C.: Securities & Exchange Commission, 1983), pp. 1–2.

69 This large regional convenience-store chain was acquired by Silverwood Industries, a publicly owned Canadian firm, in early 1982. Silverwood also owned 700 stores that made up the Max Convenience Stores chain. After this acquisition, Hop-In began to experience some growing pains. Twenty-six of the company's 160 stores were closed due to ongoing losses.

70 Many Hop-Ins had four gas pumps located outside the store. While little money was made on gas sales, it did help bring customers into the store. Hop-In marketing analyst Lara Nance commented, "Most gas customers only buy gas at the time of the sale; however, they will often return later to buy milk and bread. If they get in the habit of stopping at Hop-In to buy gas, they'll stop here on their way home to get some higher-margin food items."[4]

71 A typical Hop-In was 2,200 square feet and had sales of $312,000 per year. Those sales were achieved with very little advertising since it was not given a high priority at Hop-In. In fact, advertising was always the first thing to be cut when money was tight. With significantly fewer advertising dollars than 7-Eleven, Hop-In attempted to draw customers to its stores by offering coffee mugs and bunny bonus cards. Shoppers could collect stamps to get free coffee when they purchased gas. Both of these promotional gimmicks emphasized Hop-In's coffee, which the company felt was one of its biggest assets. They also tried to get businesspeople to stop at Hop-In for coffee on their way to work each day.

72 Since Hop-In did not issue franchises, all stores were run by a store manager and were coordinated out of the headquarters office. Although each Hop-In contained basically the same items on the same shelves, individual managers had requested that their stores be allowed to carry some different items. If the central office approved this request, store managers could modify their offerings to better serve their unique customer groups. This especially benefitted stores located in areas that served different ethnic groups with distinct food wants and needs.

Warehouse Stores

73 In industry surveys taken from 1978 through June 1983, the main reason customers selected or changed grocery stores was price. Good service, friendly employees, and clean stores were nice, but what the shoppers really wanted were low prices. In response, warehouse stores, a totally new type of grocery store, emerged to provide those lower prices.

74 Warehouse stores were quite different from traditional grocery stores. The food was usually stacked in boxes: there were no service clerks, and often customers had to price items themselves. The floors were often concrete instead of tile, and the building had a drab appearance. Some warehouse stores did not supply bags (or else you paid a few cents for each one you used), and there was no one to help carry the groceries out to the car. However, in exchange for these inconveniences, customers saved 10 to 30 percent over traditional supermarket prices on nearly every item in the store.

75 Different warehouse stores met with various levels of success. Some were owned by a major national chain with the warehouse stores operating under a different name.

[4] Personal interview with Lara Nance, marketing analyst for Hop-In Stores, August 16, 1983, in company headquarters in Roanoke, Virginia.

For example, Kroger ran both the Barney's warehouse store and the Bi-Lo stores, Grand Union operated Basics warehouse stores, and Safeway ran the Food Barn stores. These operations had all proven to be successful. On the other hand, A&P's Plus warehouse stores and Fisher Food's Warehouse stores both had to be closed at a financial loss.

76 Despite the setbacks experienced by some warehouse stores, the concept appeared to be firmly established in the industry. By 1983, there were 1,800 warehouse (or depot) stores which had captured 7.4 percent of all grocery sales in the United States. Customers remained loyal due to the warehouse's promise to keep prices down as much as possible. Ninety-two percent of the warehouse customers in one survey expressed satisfaction with their stores and rated them favorably on providing high-quality products, low prices, and product variety. Furthermore, when people were asked why they did not shop at a warehouse store, the Number 1 reason given was that there was no such store in their local area.

77 Warehouse-store operators cited a number of reasons for the format's popularity and success. First, such stores were less expensive to build than conventional grocery stores. Second, many stores generated more money per week than did regular grocery stores in the same location. Third, some customers perceived that warehouse stores had the freshest food because their high volume meant quick turnover.

78 Two independent warehouse stores had had been a part of that growing trend were the Warehouse of Groceries in Jeffersonville, Indiana, and Pick'N Save in Lake Geneva, Wisconsin. The owners of both stores credited their success to keeping prices down while still offering customers essentially what they looked for in a conventional supermarket.

79 One industry observer suggested two factors that kept customers from returning to warehouse stores. One was a dirty, dingy store. The other was a limited selection of products.

80 Pick 'N Save was one warehouse that avoided these two pitfalls. Its stores had a low ceiling, used bright lights, and had a tile floor. Its produce and meat departments were almost on a par with that of the average national chain's. However, cut boxes were stacked 10 feet high or on 86-inch-high warehouse racks to keep stocking costs down. Pick 'N Save's typical 10,000 store items made them comparable to many grocery stores, except their prices were lower.

Basics

81 Basics, a division of Grand Union, operated 19 stores in Florida, Maryland, Virginia, and New Jersey. Basics was a typical warehouse store except that its shelves stocked mostly national label brands, instead of the label of its parent company. Basics described its stores as follows:

82

> When customers enter a Basics, they immediately notice that, except for the main produce aisle, the rest of the store follows a different shopping pattern. Once inside the store, the customers are greeted by endless displays of garden-fresh produce. The produce line consists of some 165 items, as compared to a supermarket selection of about 300. At the tip of the produce aisle is the Basics deli, stocking all of the popular cold cuts. A special slicing machine cuts row after row of cold cuts, and they are bulk displayed. From the deli, the customers

> walk down a long aisle, spanning the width of the store, filled with fresh meat on one side and a wall of soda on the other. The abbreviated meat section contains all of the traditional favorites, like roasts, chicken, and steaks, but there is no service butcher. Many products are also sold in larger, family packs for added savings.[5]

In addition, Basics stores contained a dairy section, frozen foods, and some general merchandise.

Wholesalers

SuperValu

83 SuperValu, the nation's largest food wholesaler, engaged primarily in selling food and nonfood products on a wholesale basis to independently owned retail food supermarkets throughout most of the United States. About 85 percent of the SuperValu's sales and earnings were from wholesale groceries. Total sales for 1983 were $5.2 billion with net earnings of $68 million.

84 SuperValu operated 16 grocery warehouses and also owned and operated some 111 retail grocery stores. Although SuperValu was called a wholesaler, it saw itself in the retail grocery support business. It provided retail services to 2,345 retail grocery stores. Its services included advertising and sales promotion, consumer research, professional retail training programs, professional retail counseling, management assistance and development, contract negotiation assistance, retail accounting services, retail labor scheduling, merchandising services, insurance services, and tax counseling. In sum, SuperValu helped people operate better supermarkets. It also helped companies find new sites, design and equip new stores, display merchandise, train employees, and write advertisements.

85 SuperValu's success came partly from its ability to help independent retailers improve their bottom-line performance without burdening them with the overhead of a large corporation. Large chains were not as likely to use its services because they did most of these things themselves. Generally, the retailers SuperValu served had no national marketing plan, no single image, and no vertical integration. Still, these independents performed well, earning 1¼ percent to 3 percent net profit after taxes and after paying SuperValu. The average for the grocery industry as a whole was under 1 percent. SuperValu seemed to be in the business of helping independent grocery retailers prosper by beating the chains with its array of expert services.

Co-ops

86 Co-ops usually formed because a group of individuals wanted something that traditional grocery stores in their area did not offer, such as natural foods or low prices. These people opened their own store, operated it themselves, bought their own food, and sold it at their own established prices. Unfortunately, many co-ops lacked grocery

[5] Grand Union Company, "Grand Stand," March 1983, p. 4.

expertise and managerial ability, were under-capitalized, and had perpetual cash flow problems.

87 People who shopped at co-ops usually did so because they liked the atmosphere. Generally, co-ops were all self-serve, and customers made purchases in bulk quantities. Some co-op employees would provide free advice on the foods customers were purchasing. Co-ops usually seemed to be more concerned with what people bought than the dollar amount of their order. A customer shopping at a co-op often found no air conditioning, drab walls, and hand-printed promotional signs.

88 Supermarkets were not necessarily avoided by most co-op customers; most of them did some shopping there anyway. However, as supermarkets expanded to include nutrition and health-food centers, some of the co-ops' customers were drawn away. One Kroger store manager in a city of over a 100,000 people felt that there were over 900 people in that city alone who ate nothing but health foods. He felt that his store would do well if it put in a nutrition center to serve these and other health-conscious customers. The future of co-ops appeared promising. As people became more educated about food, many would be attracted to a co-op for at least part of their nutritional needs.

89 There were two national associations for co-ops—the Consumer Cooperative Alliance located in Ann Arbor, Michigan, and the Consumer League in the United States of America with headquarters in Washington, D.C. Unfortunately, neither association had active members who were willing to work cooperatively.

90 Co-ops seemed to meet the needs of a select group of people. While they did not pose a serious threat to the larger supermarkets, they definitely had carved out a niche in many communities. Approximately 15,000 food co-ops operated in the United States in 1983. Although they served a small percentage of the total public, their combined annual sales still amounted to billions of dollars.

The Roanoke Natural Food Cooperative

91 The Roanoke Natural Food Cooperative was started in 1973 by nine area individuals who felt that the traditional grocery stores in the area did not meet their needs. They formed a co-op which has grown into the largest one operating between Washington, D.C., and Atlanta. However, with gross sales of $400,000 per year and a store with only 3,000 square feet of space, the Roanoke co-op was only a bit larger than a convenience store. It was owned by its 950 shareholders and run by two full-time managers and volunteer workers. The full-time staff received a 32 percent discount on all co-op items in addition to their regular salary.

92 Volunteers who worked 30 or more hours per month at the co-op received a 31 percent discount on all purchases while those who worked less than 30 hours per month received an 18 percent discount, and those members who chose not to work in the store still were granted a discount of 7 percent. Nonmembers could also shop at the co-op but had to pay full price. Interestingly, 40 percent of the co-op's sales went to nonmembers.

93 The Roanoke co-op had a very simple strategy for setting prices—every item was marked up 47 percent over cost. This was to establish the nonmembers' price. The co-op did most of its business in natural foods but also sold books, crafts, and greeting cards. Many of these other items were marked up much more than 47 percent. The

foods sold often were not found in a typical grocery store, and customers had to weigh or measure items for themselves. Exotic teas and coffees, spices, nuts, jams, and a limited assortment of fresh produce lined the shelves. Natural junk food and ice cream were popular items.

94 Approximately 170 customers per day shopped at the Roanoke Natural Food Cooperative ranging in age from 17 to 75. Although some customers were people leading alternative lifestyles, others were doctors, lawyers, and businesspeople, all of whom were very concerned about what they ate.

95 The Roanoke co-op purchased its foods from a wide variety of suppliers. Most were large food suppliers on the East Coast. It took time for a co-op to locate good sources of supplies for nontraditional foods, because many of these suppliers did not advertise. All suppliers were carefully screened to ensure that only natural foods were sold in the co-op.

96 The Roanoke co-op advertising was limited compared to the supermarket chains, but occasionally ads with coupons were run in the local newspaper. When they had a fair amount of cash on hand, they sometimes promoted a sale on a local AM radio station. Most advertising, though, was done through word of mouth and specialized newsletters sent out by other organizations that were also interested in natural foods.

EXHIBIT 2

Key operating characteristics of profiled companies

Name	*Corporate headquarters*	*Primary region*	*Number of stores*	*1982 sales (in thousands of dollars)*	*1982 profits (in thousands of dollars)*	*Average size of stores (square feet)*	*Special ties*
Kroger	Cincinnati, Ohio	Midwest	1,200	$11,901,892	$143,758	36,000	Superstores
Safeway	Oakland, California	Far West	2,454	17,632,821	159,660	28,000	Stores in other Countries
A&P	Montvale, New Jersey	North	1,016	4,607,817	31,211	25,000	Struggling for survival
Winn-Dixie	Jacksonville, Florida	Southeast	1,222	6,764,472	103,513	27,000	Mergers
Mick-or-Mack	Roanoke, Virginia	Roanoke, Virginia	13	60,000	n.a.	21,000	A single-city chain
Fisher Foods	Cleveland, Ohio	Northeast Ohio	45	524,328	(176)	30,000	High price, high quality
7-Eleven	Dallas, Texas	United States	7,165	6,756,973	108,051	2,400	Identical stores
Hop-In	Roanoke, Virginia	Virginia, North Carolina, Tennessee	134	80,000	n.a.	2,200	Good coffee
SuperValu	Minneapolis, Minnesota	United States	16 warehouses	5,197,081	68,031	n.a.	Wholesalers
Roanoke Co-op	Roanoke, Virginia	Roanoke, Virginia	1	400	n.a.	3,000	Natural foods

n.a. = not available.

EXHIBIT 3

Sales and number of food stores, 1973–1982 ($millions)

	Chains		Independents		Convenience stores	
Year	*Sales*	*Units*	*Sales*	*Units*	*Sales*	*Units*
1982	125,582	18,330	111,318	104,970	15,100	38,700
1981	119,905	19,070	106,875	108,130	14,120	37,800
1980	108,115	18,700	105,285	112,600	12,400	35,800
1979	93,375	18,725	96,025	116,050	10,000	34,125
1978	84,280	19,350	88,670	117,650	8,710	32,500
1977	76,250	20,930	79,160	124,890	7,380	30,000
1976	71,340	21,550	74,340	134,750	8,300	27,400
1975	66,750	23,080	70,300	143,730	5,480	25,000
1974	61,240	24,190	842755	151,240	5,320	22,700
1973	52,975	25,025	55,805	154,235	4,350	20,300

Sources: *Progressive Grocer,* Kenneth W. Clarfield and Jean Kozlowski, "Supermarkets and Grocery Chains, *Standard & Poor's Industry Surveys* (1983).

97 Some of the key characteristics that distinguished these representative firms in the grocery industry are summarized in Exhibit 2. Exhibit 3 shows how the number of chains, independents, and convenience stores changed during the last 10 years. Exhibit 4 compares store types according to operating characteristics.

Trends in the Grocery Industry

Store Size and Type

98 The trend in stores has been toward two extremes—low cost and wide selection. The low-cost warehouse stores were beginning to offer some services in addition to lower prices. The superstores and combination stores (grocery and drug stores together or adjacent) continued to increase in size. They also offered more and more nonfood items. Exhibit 5 shows what customers felt was important in choosing a store.

99 *Progressive Grocer* magazine noted trends in store size and type in its 1983 "Annual Report on the Grocery Industry" as follows:

100 The variety of store formats also keeps expanding. Warehouse-style outlets, a concept reminiscent of the earliest supermarkets, have flourished recently and carved out substantial market shares in a number of areas. Subtypes ranging from basic bare bones to fashionably frugal are being developed. Hybrids, combining a warehouse core with specialty and boutique perimeters, have been successful.

101 Combination stores are growing in importance as the choice of customers who want one-stop shopping. Convenience stores, providing their own distinct service, now number 38,700 and are going strong. With sales in excess of $15 billion (not counting gasoline), their market share has reached 6 percent. But the star performers are superstores. These 30,000-square-feet and up heavyweights annu-

EXHIBIT 4

Characteristics of various store types

Estimated	*Limited assortment store*	*Warehouse store*	*Conventional supermarket*	*Superstore*	*Combination store*	*Convenience store*
Weekly volume	$65,000	$110,000	$100,000	$230,000 ($150,000 minimum)	$270,000 ($150,000 minimum)	Gas $15,000 No gas, $6,700
Selling area (square feet)	9,000	18,000	17,000	Minimum 30,000	Minimum 30,000	2,500
Checkouts	3	7+	7	9+	9+	1+
Employees equivalent	8	26	30	60	60	4
Full time	3	14	20	40	40	2
Part time	10	24	20	40	40	4
Gross margin (percent)	12	16	21	23	25	30
Number of items	Under 1,500	1,500–7,500+	8,000–12,000	15,000+	20,000+	3,100
Share of supermarket dollar sales (percent)	1.5	3.1	68.1	23.5	3.8	na
Percent of total supermarkets	2.7	3.3	80.3	12.0	1.7	na

n.a. = not applicable.

Source: *Progressive Grocer;* Kenneth W. Clarfield and Jean Kozlowski, "Supermarkets and Grocery Chains," *Standard & Poor's Industry Survey* (1983).

EXHIBIT 5

What's important in choosing a store?

1. Lowest possible prices	78.9 percent
2. Pleasant shopping experience/helpful personnel/good service	75.3 percent
3. One-stop shopping	72.1 percent
4. Prices marked on individual packages	70.0 percent
5. Store located nearby	68.3 percent
6. Selection or variety of store brands and lower-priced products	63.6 percent
7. Finish shopping as quickly as possible	54.4 percent
8. Open late hours	43.5 percent
9. Double coupons or other special incentives	41.7 percent
10. Special departments, such as deli or bakery	38.7 percent

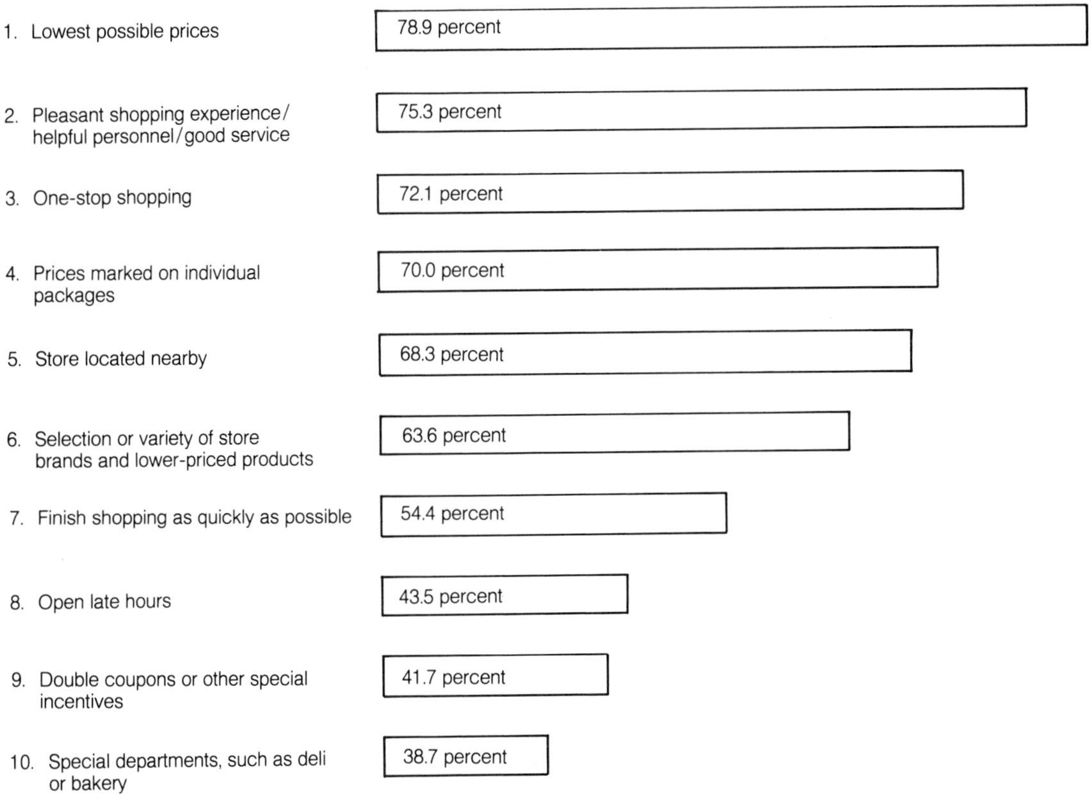

Note: Each factor was rated as not at all important, slightly important, of medium importance, very important, or extremely important. Answers were converted to scores on a 0-to-100 scale.

Source: Robert Dietrich et al., "What's Important in Choosing a Store," *Progressive Grocer,* October 1981, p. 52.

ally take a larger share of total sales and are judged by industry leaders to have the best prospects for future success. At present, 3,200 superstores account for an estimated 16.5 percent share of the market and 23 percent of supermarket sales.

102 Despite the proliferation of formats, the standard, conventional model still represents 79 percent of all supermarkets and checks out 47.2 percent of total volume (65.7 percent of sales by supermarkets). Its dominance is likely to decline, however. As the American public divides into more and more segments, each with specific buying motives, and as retailers increasingly adopt positioning strategies to attract those segments, undifferentiated stores will find it harder to compete.[6]

[6] Walter H. Heller, "50th Annual Report on the Grocery Industry," *Progressive Grocer,* April 1983, p. 56.

103 Exhibit 6 shows the number of each type of store in the United States over the last seven years. As can be seen by viewing the chart, the superstore was by far the most popular type, but the biggest advances over the past few years were made by warehouse stores.

104 Though warehouse stores were growing in sales and number of stores, superstores, which had only been in vogue since 1975, already outnumbered all other types. By 1981, 75 percent of all new grocery stores constructed in the United States were superstores.

105 A very definite trend for all segments of the industry was longer store hours to satisfy the growing need for more shopping time during evenings and early morning hours. The changing character of the work force justified the extended hours and thus made store operation more cost efficient.

Marketing

106 Over the years, the grocery industry has consistently used newspaper advertising more than any other media as is shown in Exhibit 7. However, large national chains found that television advertising reached more potential customers than did other media. Newspaper advertising was also beginning to decline in popularity due to large drops in the circulations of major newspapers in recent years.

EXHIBIT 6

Formats: Superstores still lead the pack

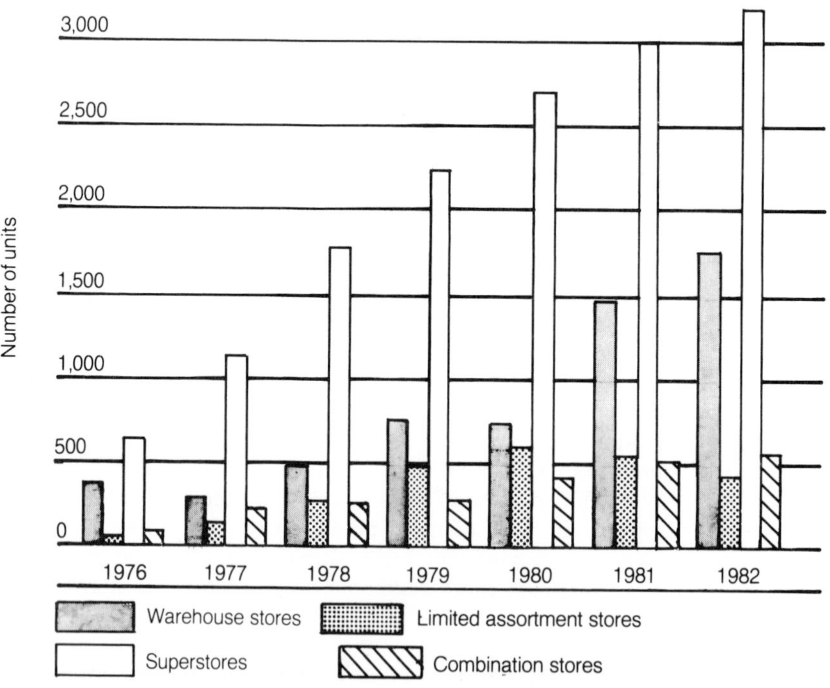

EXHIBIT 7

Newspapers slip a notch—percent share of advertising budget (independents)

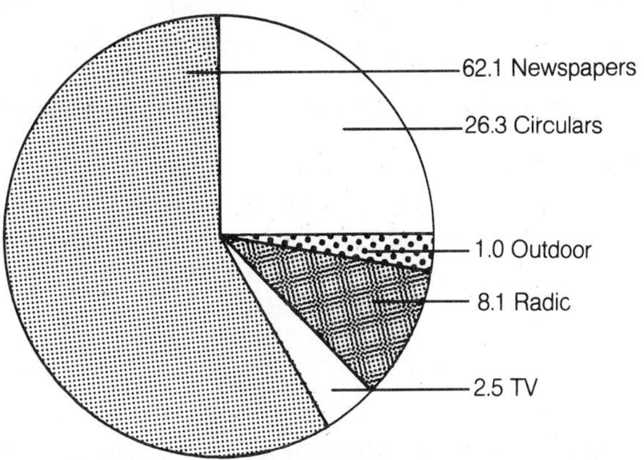

Newspapers are far and away the favorite advertising medium of independent operators, garnering 6 of 10 ad dollars from the 68 percent of operators who use them. Compared to the previous year, however, newspapers slipped 4 percent in share of budget and 2 percent in number of operators. The difference went mainly to circulars, which grew 4 percent in share of dollars while increasing 8 percent in number of operators using. Results vary by region, the West is the biggest user of newspapers and TV but the smallest user of circulars.

Source: Walter H. Heller. "50th Annual Report on the Grocery Industry," *Progressive Grocer,* April 1983.

107 Most of the space that food retailers bought in newspapers was devoted to coupons. Couponing emerged in earnest in the mid-1970s and continued in the 1980s as the most widely used food promotional advertising technique. In 1965, manufacturers distributed 10 billion coupons. In 1982, the figure had increased tenfold to 100 billion. The cost savings for customers who used them was significant. For example, the redeemed value of coupons in 1974 amounted to $220 million, which more than doubled to $550 million by 1979. Although coupons remained popular, other types of games and gimmicks seemed to be on their way out.

108 In the mid 1980s, stores also began emphasizing the size of the sale-per-customer-visit in contrast to earlier years when stores had focused their marketing efforts mostly on getting new customers into the store. With store loyalty on the decline, the concern was with maximizing the number of dollars customers spent once they were in the store.

Product Line

109 More and more shoppers bought house-label brands in the 1980s to save money, even though in the late 1970s, ultra-low-priced generic brands were not well-received.

Many grocers moved away from them since customers did not trust products that no one claimed. However, they were willing to purchase items with the store's name on it even if it was not a national brand.

110 With customers trading down to many private-label brands, stores increasingly relied on the sale of nonfood items to boost their overall profit margin to an acceptable level. In fact, Kroger and Safeway committed up to 50 percent of the sales space in new stores to nonfood items. Major types of nonfood purchases included housewares, pet supplies, greeting cards, and toys.

111 A major trend in the meat department is that beef consumption has gone down, while chicken sales have continued to grow. Some industry observers speculated that by 1985, chicken would be the primary meat item carried by grocery stores.

112 Other trends included more purchases of fresh produce, health foods, and ethnic items, particularly Hispanic foods.

Market Growth

113 The rapid growth rate that the grocery industry experienced during the late 1970s began to slow down significantly in the early 1980s. High unemployment, less inflation, and a slowdown in the population growth rate all were contributors.

114 While total supermarket sales for grocery items increased steadily during the 1970s, the early 1980s had zero real increases when adjusted for inflation. For 1981, real sales decreased 1.2 percent as compared to 1980. Because of the high interest rates accompanying the 1981–1983 recession only 270 new stores were built in all of 1982.

Innovation

115 The biggest innovation in the grocery industry in the early 1980s was the large-scale introduction of computer scanners. Approximately 23 percent of all supermarkets, some 6,500 stores, already were using optical scanners all by 1980. These computer-assisted devices allowed clerks to check out items more quickly, helped store managers analyze inventory, assisted in shelf-space allocation decisions, and analyzed the effectiveness of various promotional campaigns.

116 The potential uses of the scanner in the near future are promising. As one Kroger official put it:

> With hand-held micro computers in the aisle, minicomputers in the office, scanning at the front end, electronic ordering and invoicing in the warehouse, sophisticated analysis of item movement, computerized assistance on promotional decisions, and the availability of sensitive programs to fine tune shelf space allocation, the stage is set for extraordinary advances in operating and merchandising precision.[7]

Customer Profile

117 It was announced in July of 1983 that for the first time since 1978, low price had been dethroned as the main reason a customer changed or selected a food store. Accord-

[7] Ibid., p. 60.

ing to the Food Marketing Institute, the new Number 1 reason customers selected a store was because it had a quick checkout. The Number 2 reason was its national brand variety. Third was a tie between courteous employees and low prices.

118 Exhibit 8 shows a profile of grocery customers. Regular shoppers were classified according to sex, age, size of household, household income, and education. According to *Progressive Grocer,* the following generalizations could be made:

119 Conventional supermarkets have the oldest, poorest, least-educated customers, a fact which augurs poorly for their long-term prospects. The income patterns of superstore and economy format customers are quite similar, although the latter can claim an edge with better-educated households. In shopping behavior, those who regularly patronize economy format stores are the most compulsive or at least the best organized, reading ads, making lists, and clipping coupons. Shoppers of combination stores are the least likely to shop at drug and discount stores, presumably because their major needs are fulfilled via one stop shopping.

EXHIBIT 8

Who shopped where

	Type of store				
Regular shoppers	***Conventional***	***Superstore***	***Combination***	***Warehouse***	***Other***
Sex:					
Male	25%	33%	22%	13%	7% = 100%
Female	25	29	20	17	9
Age:					
Under 25	21	36	16	23	4
25 to 34	13	39	23	20	5
35 to 44	21	35	23	14	7
45 to 64	26	23	10	17	15
65 and over	45	21	18	9	7
Size of household:					
One	33	28	22	10	7
Two	26	29	21	13	11
Three	21	33	17	21	8
Four or more	23	29	19	20	9
Household income:					
Under $10,000	56	18	15	8	3
$10,000–$15,000	34	28	12	16	10
$15,000–$25,000	20	33	17	19	11
Over $25,000	10	35	27	18	10
Education:					
Less than high school graduate	57	18	5	12	8
High school graduate	25	33	16	16	10
Attended college	18	34	28	13	7
College graduate	10	27	29	22	12

Source: Robert Dietrich et al., "Customer Profiles—Who Shops Which Format," *Professive Grocer,* October 1981, pp. 48–49.

Exhibit 9

Percent who shop at two or more different-type stores

	Percent naming as regular store	*Percent naming as store also shopped in*	*Total shopping format*
Conventional supermarket	25.3	17.1	42.4%
Superstore	29.3	22.8	52.1
Combination store	20.0	19.1	39.1
Warehouse store	16.1	22.7	38.8
Other	4.2	12.3	16.5

120 The most clear-cut difference among the shopper segments is evidenced by the evaluation of the importance of price marking on individual packages, a practice revered by the older, more-conservative shoppers of conventional stores, but of little importance to shoppers of economy format stores [warehouse stores] who've learned to love the scanner and the precisely annotated register tape it produces.

121 Patrons of economy format stores aren't too satisfied about the store's ambience, its selection of national brands, or some of its departments, but these are the trade-offs they're willing to make for their very high satisfaction with the one thing they're really interested in, everyday [low] pricing.[8]

122 Exhibit 9 shows the results of a study of persons who shop in two or more different-type grocery stores. Men frequented grocery stores that were open late. Coupons generally didn't mean much to them nor did special prices. Warehouse-type stores were preferred more by people with incomes over $15,000 than those in worse economic situations. The more affluent shoppers appreciated a store with special service departments regardless of the prices charged. Few basic differences existed between working women and housewives as to store choice. However, working women did prefer a store that was open late hours. They also liked a complete store so they could avoid going to a second grocery store. On the other hand, housewives were more likely to be influenced by coupons. Younger shoppers liked stores that were open late hours, including convenience stores, and they were more receptive to new grocery innovations, such as generics or in-store drug services.

Threats to the Grocery Industry

123 Exhibit 10 summarizes how independents and chain grocery store managers rated various problems facing the grocery industry. Some of these threats are discussed below.

[8] Robert Dietrich et al., "Competitive Dynamics in the Marketplace," *Progressive Grocer,* October–December 1981, pp. 51–53.

Exhibit 10

Independent and chain grocery store managers ratings for key problems

Energy costs lead the problem parade

Independents	Problem	Chain managers
32	Energy costs	42
39	Local economic conditions	35
42	Cut-throat competition	44
48	Labor costs	37
51	Customer pilferage	50
43	Interest rates	50
43	Cash flow	37
57	Employee pilferage	53
50	Government regulations	9
59	Cost of goods	63
54	Vendor pilferage	48
49	Disinflation	49
29	Consumer activism	25

Percent who say major problem (shaded bar)

Percent who say moderate problem (white bar)

Legal/Political

124 Many grocery industry insiders agreed that the two biggest legal/political threats to stores were unit pricing and bottle bills. Many municipalities had passed ordinances that required all grocery stores to mark the sales price on every item in the store. Pressure for the passage of these laws came mostly from senior-citizen groups. Most stores practiced unit pricing, but with the increased use of scanning, there was a tremendous potential reduction in labor cost if hand-stamping every item could be avoided. Price changes could be facilitated by one simple change in the computer. Unfortunately, unit-pricing laws (which required putting the price on every store item) hindered stores from capitalizing on potential productivity increases offered by scanners.

125 Bottle-bill legislation, which was typically enacted at the state level, was designed to reduce highway litter. Proponents of these bills claimed that by placing a mandatory deposit on all beverage containers, people would be less likely to discard them improperly. Where such bills were in effect, merchants that sold cans and bottles served as a recycling center. The grocery industry opposed such bills because it felt that the inconvenience of recycling and paying deposits for disposable containers was an undue hardship.

Costs

126 There was a constant threat that costs would escalate faster than sales. The costs of operating a grocery store continued to rise and many people in the industry were concerned that there was no apparent way to contain these increases.

127 Energy and labor costs were the biggest problems. In 1982, energy costs rose 11 percent, and labor costs rose 6 percent. Exhibit 11 summarizes 1982 wage rates for key store jobs in various regions and for various store types.

Exhibit 11

Going wage rates—1982 (dollars per hour)

	Part-time clerk		*Full-time clerk*		*Journeyman meat cutter*	
	I	*C*	*I*	*C*	*I*	*C*
Sales volume:						
$2–$4 million	$3.99	$4.53	$4.79	$5.64	$ 7.91	$ 8.52
$4–$8 million	4.31	4.82	5.19	5.97	8.64	9.12
$8–$12 million	4.87	5.93	5.56	6.69	9.45	10.31
$12 million +	5.69	5.92	6.48	6.41	10.80	10.83
Region (Unweighted):						
North Atlantic	4.21	4.78	4.95	6.04	8.10	9.21
Great Lakes	4.08	5.56	4.96	6.05	8.99	10.69
Plains	4.05	4.66	5.13	6.35	8.71	11.00
South Atlantic	3.77	4.07	4.38	5.16	6.39	7.32
South Central	3.58	4.26	4.31	5.37	7.21	9.05
West	5.84	8.32	6.63	8.38	10.30	11.73
Format:						
Warehouse	4.59	4.93	5.39	5.97	9.00	9.90
Superstore/combo	4.98	5.86	5.60	6.48	9.63	10.89
Average supermarket	$4.21	$5.03	$5.03	$6.08	$ 8.35	$ 9.37

A very regular pattern can be observed in hourly wage rates. Chains average higher wages than independents due to higher organization of the labor force. For both groups the higher the store volume, the higher the wage rate. The West, as always, is far ahead as the region with highest labor costs for chain and independent alike. Lowest wage rates prevail in the South Atlantic for chains and in the South Central for independents. It should be noted that union wages are higher than the all-store averages. For instance, a full-time unionized independent clerk costs $1.58 an hour more than the average for both union and nonunion stores. A union independent journeyman meat cutter costs $2.55 per hour more than the average for independent union and nonunion stores combined.

I = independents; C = Chain.

128 Labor costs were highest for the largely unionized chains. In 1982, 54 percent of the clerks and 55 percent of the meat cutters in chains were unionized compared to only 17 percent and 22 percent, respectively, for independent stores. Smaller stores, regional chains, and stores located in the South all tended to be less unionized.

129 Federal legislation was proposed in 1983 which would make labor costs even more critical. This union-backed bill sought to mandate automatic yearly pay increases for workers to protect their real income from decreases due to inflation. In an industry that traditionally paid a fair share of its workers more than the minimum wage, such legislation would burden store owners with locked-in cost increases for labor.

130 Exhibit 12 shows grocery store costs as a percentage of sales over a five-year period. With costs increasing so rapidly, the key difference between successful and unsuccessful stores in the last half of the 1980s would be their ability to control costs.

The Economy

131 During 1983, recession, along with fiscal and monetary policies, produced a sharp drop in the inflation growth rate. Despite this, interest rates remained high, and real interest rates (difference between actual interest rates and the inflation rate) reached historic highs. Many grocery chains and independents found themselves burdened with high costs but were unable to raise their prices. Profitability was substantially threatened.

132 The economic situation just described is known as disinflation. It was a new situation for grocers. Store owners had been accustomed to high growth in sales and profits, largely due to inflation. Under the current situation, however, they did not have an extra 10 percent to 12 percent built into their figures.

133 Industry experts were divided in their opinion of how disinflation would affect the grocery industry. Surveys did show, however, that store managers felt the overall economic climate was their biggest worry, followed by energy costs.

Competition

134 Over the years, history has shown that supermarkets, as a group, had a tendency toward self-destruction. Price wars often resulted in store closings for the losers and huge losses for the winners. Industry price wars followed a predictable pattern. A recession slowed down inflation, which caused margins to be reduced; supermarkets attempted to attract their competitors' customers and steal market share; destructive price wars resulted as stores sought to protect their customer base and often, all grocery stores involved lost in the process.

135 The economic climate of the early 1980s seemed to be just right for price wars, but no major wars broke out during 1982 or 1983 since the major chains were showing uncharacteristic restraint. While no one in the industry wanted to take part in a price war, few avoided one if challenged. Kroger CEO Lyle Everingham explained why: "We intend to defend the customer base we worked so hard to get, and this has an effect on the behavior of the more reckless competitors in the marketplace."[9]

136 What made price wars an even more likely and deadly occurrence was the increasing lack of store loyalty among grocery shoppers. One recent study showed that 23 percent of over 800 shoppers interviewed had switched their regular supermarket in the past

[9] Jonathan Greenberg, "Supermarkets," *Forbes,* January 3, 1983, p. 204.

Exhibit 12

Percent various grocery store costs represented

Food chains—gross margin, expenses, earnings					
Item	*53 Chns. 1977–78*	*46 Chns. 1978–79*	*55 Chns. 1979–80*	*61 Chns. 1980–81*	*50 Chns. 1981–82*
	Percentage of Sales				
Gross margin	21.74	21.50	21.71	22.03	22.32
Expense					
Payroll	12.34	12.23	12.39	12.70	12.66
Supplies	1.03	0.99	1.08	1.07	1.07
Utilities	1.08	1.04	1.04	1.15	1.24
Communications	0.08	0.08	0.07	0.07	0.07
Travel	0.09	0.08	0.09	0.09	0.09
Services purchased	1.29	1.13	1.20	1.14	1.20
Promotional activities	0.40	0.31	0.35	0.32	0.41
Professional services	0.06	0.06	0.07	0.08	0.05
Donations	0.01	0.01	0.01	0.01	0.01
Insurance	0.90	0.88	0.85	0.90	1.02
Taxes and licenses (except on income)	1.00	0.90	0.98	0.94	1.04
Property rentals	1.25	1.13	1.18	1.12	1.20
Equipment rentals	0.18	0.14	0.14	0.17	0.14
Depreciation & amort.	0.69	0.81	0.79	0.88	0.87
Repairs	0.61	0.83	0.59	0.65	0.64
Unclassified	0.97	1.19	1.09	0.90	1.14
Total exp. bef. interest	21.40	20.57	20.84	21.16	21.60
Total interest	0.57	0.61	0.15	0.25	0.19
Total expense (including interest)	21.97	21.18	20.99	21.41	21.79
Net operating profit	d0.22	0.32	0.73	0.62	0.53
Other income or deductions					
Credit for imputed interest	0.41	0.42	0.41	...	...
Cash discounts earned	0.59	0.61	0.52	0.52	0.56
Other revenue, net[1]	0.06	0.34	0.14	0.31	0.34
Total net other inc.	1.07	1.37	0.66	0.84	0.91
Total net earnings before income taxes	0.84	1.70	1.89	1.46	1.44
Total income taxes	0.33	0.77	0.59	R0.57	0.56
Total net earnings After income taxes	0.51	0.93	0.80	R0.89	0.88
Earnings as % net worth Aftertax earnings	7.48	13.27	11.66	R12.55	11.53
Number of stockturns	12.43	13.54	12.77	13.42	13.59
Sales (in thousands of dollars)					
Avg., per store	4,535	5,852	5,864	6,937	8,216
Avg., per identical store	4,470	5,906	5,893	6,947	8,199

d-Deficit, R-Revised.
[1] Includes profit or loss on real estate.
Source: Cornell University.

Exhibit 13

Promotion techniques: Small supers, big effort (percent using)

		Total U.S.	*$2–$4 million*	*$4–$8 million*	*$8–$12 million*	*$12+ million*
Merchandise	Independent	50	50	53	41	38
(Dinnerware, etc.)	Chain	59	55	60	61	56
Bonus (2x) coupons	Independent	30	30	30	25	26
	Chain	32	30	32	31	35
Register tapes	Independent	19	17	24	16	19
	Chain	27	26	27	30	31
Games	Independent	24	28	19	12	7
	Chain	26	33	27	16	18
Saver plans	Independent	13	15	11	11	7
	Chain	16	23	14	12	12
Trading stamps	Independent	12	14	9	7	5
	Chain	15	21	15	11	9
Sweepstakes	Independent	8	9	7	10	5
	Chain	10	13	9	11	10
None of these	Independent	25	24	25	36	43
	Chain	22	24	21	22	23

About three of four independent managers/owners and chain managers make use of these seven promotional lures, but large variations exist, depending upon store volume. The lowest volume supermarkets, for example, use games, saver plans, and trading stamps at rates two to four times greater than some of the other stores. Note that the larger volume independent supers depend upon these seven techniques the least.

12 months. It appeared that the grocery industry's biggest threat was internal. In addition to price wars, a variety of promotional techniques was employed to attract customers. Exhibit 13 summarizes their frequency of use.

The Industry Outlook

137 Despite rising costs, a slowing population growth, and intense competition, industry insiders tended to be optimistic. Most felt that the supermarkets' future prospects looked very bright. The most important determinants would be the ability to adapt to a rapidly changing environment, to find ways to curtail cost increases, and to find creative ways to better satisfy various customer groups.

138 Some industry observers believed that major corporate chains would emphasize super and combination stores and concentrate their activities on markets with enough population density to support them. The smaller-sized regular grocery store would be operated typically by independents and located in outlying sections of big cities or in smaller-sized cities.

139 Conrad Stephanites, Mick-or-Mack's CEO, summed up the industry's future prospects by saying, "It is going to have problems, and there are going to be setbacks, but that has been inherent in this business since Day 1. It is a business that continually changes, but in some ways, some things never change. People still want clean stores, friendly service, fair prices, and personalized care."

case 32
Safeway Stores: World's Largest Food Retailer

Introduction

1 In 1982, after three years of below-average financial performance, Safeway Stores, Inc., sold its 70-store Nebraska-Iowa division. Company officials said they could not keep prices competitive because of the region's limited population growth and the influx of nonunionized stores. They gave similar reasons for moves out of the company's Memphis and southwest Missouri markets. Some industry experts interpreted these drastic cutbacks differently. They wondered if recent poor financial performances and dwindling market shares suggested that Safeway, the world's largest food retailer, was about to fall like the once-mighty A&P had fallen in years past.

2 The picture appeared somewhat brighter in 1983 as this Oakland, California, headquartered firm posted its first earnings increase in four years. Some of the credit for this improvement was due to a 3 percent real increase in sales and higher profit margins. However, a significant portion of the credit could also be attributed to revenues gained from the 1982 divestments, as well as lower first-in, first-out accounting changes. Had Safeway indeed reversed its four-year slide? Would this grocery giant continue to make other necessary improvements to retain its industry leadership? As one skeptical competitor noted, "Safeway is not driving a PT boat, but a battleship, and you just can't move that fast."[1]

History

3 Safeway had its beginnings in American Falls, Idaho, where a Baptist minister by the name of Skaggs built a tiny grocery store. His aim was to help poor local wheat farmers who were dependent on storekeepers offering credit at exorbitant interest rates. Skaggs's idea was to sell groceries for cash at a savings. He operated the store until 1915 when one of his six sons, Marion Barton "M. B." Skaggs purchased the company for $1,088.

4 M. B., who is generally recognized as Safeway's founder, decided that by accepting a small profit margin, he could build his one small store into a larger business. He

---

This case was prepared by Barbara Spencer of Virginia Polytechnic Institute and State University.

[1] "Safeway Stores: Back to Price Wars for a Company that Played It Too Safe," *Business Week*, April 5, 1982, p. 109.

reduced costs by buying directly from food manufacturers and eliminating as much wasted operating expense as possible. In less than 11 years, he expanded the organization to 428 retail units operating in 10 states. His motto, "Distribution without Waste," continued with the company through the 1970s.

5 In 1926, M. B. merged his stores with the Sam Seelig stores of Southern California and incorporated under the name of Safeway. He then embarked on a five-year period of rapid expansion, mainly through acquisitions. By 1931, the company was serving virtually the same geographical markets in the United States and Canada as it did later on in the 1970s and 1980s. Amazingly, Safeway operated the most stores in its entire history during 1931, when it had 3,527 outlets.

6 Skaggs, a practical businessman, also rapidly moved into warehousing. By 1925, he had established a wholesaling operation in the Pacific Northwest. By 1929, this operation had expanded to include branch warehouses in 20 cities throughout the western United States and Hawaii. Although Skaggs relinquished the presidency to Lingan A. Warren in 1931, Safeway continued to grow. By the mid-1930s, Safeway had 21 bakeries, 6 coffee-roasting plants, 3 meat-distributing plants, a milk condensery, a candy and syrup factory, a mayonnaise plant, and a produce-purchasing company.

7 While the total number of stores declined from its 1931 record high, the average number of square feet per store increased dramatically from around 1,000 square feet in 1926 to 3,000 square feet in the 1930s. It later increased to between 5,000 and 6,000 square feet in the early 1940s and up to 10,000 square feet by the end of that decade. This increase in store size corresponded to the shift from consumer walking to driving. As a side note, every new Safeway store came with a parking lot by 1938.

8 Under Warren, Safeway prospered throughout the 1930s and 1940s, but net income dropped from $14.7 million in 1950 to $7.3 million in 1952. Net income as a percent of sales fell from 1.2 percent in 1950 to 0.4 percent during this same period, even though sales increased by $429 million to $1.6 billion in 1952.

9 When Robert Magowan took over in 1955, he quickly turned the company around. Net income rose to $25.4 million in 1956, and net income as a percent of sales returned to its former level of 1.2 percent and continued to rise to 1.8 percent in 1966. Magowan remained a key force behind Safeway's strategic moves as chairman of the board from 1966 until his retirement in 1971. His staunchly conservative management style became a company trademark.

10 Magowan's successor, Quentin Reynolds, served as president from 1966 to 1971 and then as board chairman from 1971 to 1974. Like Magowan, Reynolds was an extremely successful corporate leader and had worked his way up through the ranks from his first position as a food clerk. During Reynolds's tenure as CEO, Safeway earned more money than any other food chain. During this period, first inflation and then price controls, instituted under President Nixon in the early 1970s, reduced supermarket profits to an average of less than a half a cent on a dollar of sales. Yet, Safeway earned at least three times as much as the industry average by making every penny count.

11 Safeway did several things during that period which really helped profitability. For example, instead of spending money on a glamorous corporate headquarters, the company's 250 corporate-level employees worked in an old converted warehouse. In addition, all bills were paid within 30 days to take advantage of discounts. Yet there was no skimping where customers were concerned. Rather, all stores were large and modern, offered unit pricing, and provided nutritional labeling.

12 During these same years, the company also experimented with nonfood discount stores. In some instances, these Super-S stores were located right next to its own supermarkets. Under the management of food executives, who were admittedly out of their league, these stores failed dismally causing Safeway to retreat rapidly back to the low-margin food business. Later on, when Safeway expanded its supermarkets to 25,000 square feet, only 1,000 square feet were devoted to higher-margin, nonfood items.

13 It was during Reynolds's tenure that a number of social issues exploded in the external environment. For example, minority civil rights concerns and consumerism reached peaks of activity in 1968. Riots erupted in Washington, D.C., and housewives boycotted supermarkets all across the country. Reynolds took several actions to respond to these problems. He joined the National Business Council for Consumer Affairs, improved the company's affirmative-action program, and established a program to develop minority business. He even initiated the innovative process of labeling ground beef according to its fat content, as opposed to the cut of beef from which it came, to avoid misleading customers.

14 While Reynolds was focusing on the external environment, President William Mitchell was in charge of internal operations. Mitchell, who joined Safeway in 1936 as a clerk in the accounting department, was extremely conservative and cautious. Some of his deliberateness was probably due to the variety of lawsuits against Safeway in the early 1970s.

15 Several of Safeway's lawsuits focused on store prices. In 1973, the Federal Trade Commission accused Safeway of advertising food at sales prices but actually selling it at regular prices. Safeway, Kroger, and several other chains were convicted of this charge in 1977. In 1974, the company was charged with employment discrimination against women and minorities in a $10 million class-action suit. During that same year, Safeway also was the Number 1 target of Cesar Chavez's United Farm Workers Union, which demanded the firm sell only produce with their union label. Also, in 1974, a U.S. Senate committee headed by Senator William Proximire found identical prices on 2,969 out of 3,959 items checked in the Kansas City stores of Safeway and A&P. Proxmire pointed out that Safeway made more profits than the rest of the industry but never offered lower prices than competitors. Moreover, his survey showed that Safeway had higher prices in 13 areas across the United States where it dominated the market. In 1975, several price-fixing charges were brought against Safeway, with the best known probably being the case in which 500 cattle feeders charged that Safeway, A&P, Kroger, American Stores, Jewel, Winn-Dixie, Food Fair, Grand Union, and Supermarket General conspired to pay low cattle prices to farmers but still charged high prices to consumers. This suit was later dismissed.

16 As a result, it was little wonder that President Mitchell increasingly surrounded himself with financial and legal executives. Under their influence, Safeway adopted the strictest possible interpretation of government antitrust and other regulations. Lawyers vetoed plans to create health food departments in stores because of potential legal hassles over insect infestations. They even curtailed advertising of loss leaders because of possible legal exposure if stores ran out of items.

17 In 1973, Safeway passed A&P and became the world's largest food chain in terms of sales, net income, market value of shares, and stockholders' equity. Because of this feat, Mitchell was honored as the most-outstanding chief executive officer in the grocery industry in 1975. It was at that point, paradoxically, that Safeway began

Exhibit 1

Safeway's market-share changes in key cities

Key cities	*1976*	*1981*	*Rank among competitors in 1981*
Baltimore	6%	8%	3
Dallas	31	28	1
Denver	42	39	2
Des Moines	15	13	3
Houston	12	16	2
Kansas City	25	20	2
Los Angeles	9	8	4
Phoenix	10	11	3
Portland	25	18	3
Salt Lake City	19	17	2
San Diego	20	19	1
San Francisco/Oakland	26	27	1
Seattle	30	35	1
Washington, D.C.	32	30	2

Source: Jeff Blyskal, "A&P West," *Forbes*, April 12, 1982, p. 62.

losing market share in key cities. Exhibit 1 shows how Safeway's market share and rank among competitors fared between 1976 and 1981 in 14 key cities.

18 With Mitchell planning to retire in 1980, the company named Dale Lynch, formerly head of Safeway's successful 253-store northwestern region, as president in late 1977. Earnings bounced back to $146 million in 1978, up 43 percent on a 12 percent increase in sales. However, in the first quarter of 1979, net income dropped 8 percent below the first quarter earnings of 1978, and the 57-year-old Lynch suffered a heart attack, which caused Mitchell to change his mind about promoting Lynch to chairman and CEO. Mitchell still insisted on retiring but submitted 10 names to the board of directors for consideration as a successor.

19 In a surprise move, the board selected Peter Magowan, the 37-year-old son of Robert Magowan, the former CEO, as the new chairman and chief executive officer. Despite concerns about nepotism and his young age, Magowan seemed to give the giant company a new life. Before coming to Safeway, the younger Magowan had earned a B.S. degree at Stanford and a master's degree at Oxford and had studied international relations at Johns Hopkins University. He started at Safeway as a real estate negotiator, managed a 15-store district in Houston, and held posts of increasing responsibility in both Safeway's U.S. and international divisions. Most recently, he had been vice president of Canadian and overseas subsidiaries.

20 Magowan's top priorities when he took office in January of 1980 were to regain market share, expand superstores and nonfood merchandising, and make Safeway the lowest-cost operator in the industry again. His task was a formidable one since earnings had slid since 1978, and Safeway's 10.6 percent return on equity was one third lower than the retail food industry average. Furthermore, its market share had fallen in 9 of 14 major cities.

21 Magowan immediately started making major changes. He soon added over 200 superstores with bakeries, delicatessens, natural food departments, cosmetic centers, and pharmacies. Superstores derived their name from their enormous size, usually above 30,000 square feet and many of these enormous one-stop shopping centers stocked more than 12,000 different items. In addition, Magowan moved Safeway into Liquor Barns, discount Food Barns, and gourmet food outlets. By 1981, it appeared that Safeway had stopped the erosion of sales and market share, but some industry observers questioned the company's ability to maintain these improvements.

Safeway's Operations in the 1980s

Marketing/Sales

22 Marketing at Safeway was headed up by John Prinster, senior vice president of marketing. Prinster, 52 years old, was appointed to this position in 1981.

23 Safeway stores offered customers a full line of food and nonfood products in large grocery store and superstore formats. Food items at a typical Safeway store included fresh fruits and vegetables, meats, poultry and fish, frozen foods, dairy products, baked goods, delicatessen and gourmet foods, dry goods, and other items. Nonfood items, which varied depending on the store size, often included soaps, health and cosmetic products, magazines and paperback books, paper products, hardware, electrical appliances, cameras and photography equipment, toys, garden supplies, auto accessories, and cigarettes.

24 Health and beauty aids were doing so well that they accounted for 40 percent of the nonfood sales. Furthermore, these products tended to be high-profit items. By 1982, Safeway also had pharmacies in 300 stores. Health and beauty aids sales were much higher in stores that also had a pharmacy.

25 New ways were constantly being used to appeal to customers and to make shopping enjoyable. Many stores soon housed video games, floral shops, wine and cheese shops, bakeries, and even live lobsters. Over 250 automatic teller machines were installed in stores in 1983, and the company began experimenting with computer sales, aluminum recycling, salad bars, and bulk items such as sugar, flour, and nuts.

26 The use of innovative store layout was also utilized to attract shoppers. For example, instead of the usual box shape, Safeway's 61,000-square-foot Arlington, Texas, superstore was constructed with broad sections meeting to form a wide-based *V* as shown in Exhibit 2. Within this *V*, an island contained many of the store's specialty items. Shelves were built lower than usual so that customers could always see the service island. Open around the clock, this new store held about 20,000 items, almost double the number for conventional stores.[2] Magowan chose Arlington for his first super, superstore because with the area's excellent competition, it provided a good test.

27 Safeway had long tailored its individual stores to local markets and continued this policy in the 1980s. Stores in affluent areas featured gourmet shops while those in ethnic neighborhoods offered freshly baked tortillas or tofu. Moreover, to meet the needs of today's health-conscious consumers, the company sold leaner beef cuts as well as more poultry and seafood. Produce sections tripled their offerings with over

[2] Manuel Schiffres and Joseph Benham, "As Supermarkets Get Even More Super," *U.S. News & World Report,* June 13, 1983, p. 66.

Exhibit 2

Floor layout for Safeway's 61,000-square-foot superstore—Arlington, Texas

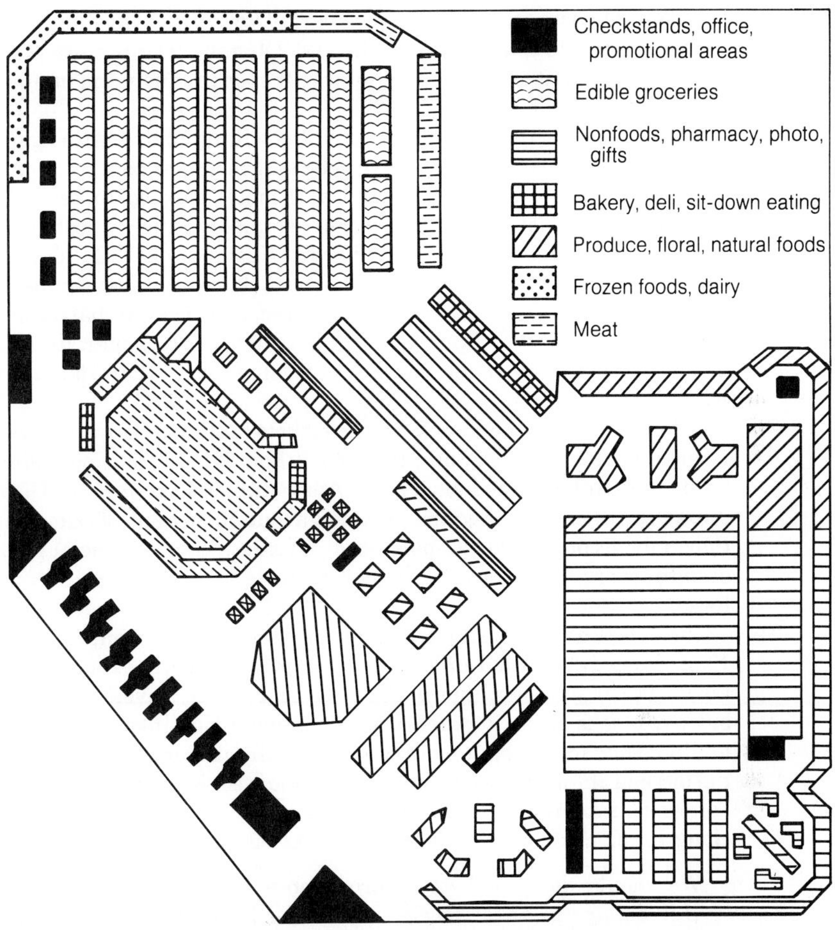

Source: Safeway Stores, Inc., Annual Report, 1982, p. 32.

180 different items. Low-sugar fruits and low-sodium vegetables appeared on shelves, and natural foods became one of the firm's biggest-selling items.

28 In 1982, the company began reducing its emphasis on private-label groceries. Private-label grocery products often were manufactured by the same firms that packaged various national brands, but then they put a different label on the package. Some private-label products were packaged by the grocery chains themselves, if they had vertically integrated backwards into such operations. While such house-label products were described as the downfall of A&P, other grocery chains had been helped by them. For example, Kroger grocery stores achieved a great deal of its profits from lower-priced private-label brands sitting right next to higher-priced national brands.

29 Safeway aggressively promoted its wares and took the lead in using magazine advertising while decreasing its emphasis on newspapers. They also used radio during weekday rush hours and television during evening prime time. For example, one television ad series showed customers interacting with Safeway employees and products as the background lyrics said, "Proud to be part of your life." This theme was further reflected in the company's sponsorship of the U.S. Olympic training site near Colorado Springs. In that capacity, it supplied the center with food products and financial backing through the end of 1984.

30 In the early 1980s, Safeway clearly was willing to do battle against the competition in important cities to protect its volume and customer base. This was clearly a changed policy from years past when Safeway's motto seemed to be to let the other chain initiate action. Not so any more. For example, Safeway lost up to as much as $50 million during the summer of 1981 in Washington, D.C., alone. That brutal price war saw initiator Giant Food equally hurt, but two other competitors were forced to vacate the nation's capitol. In another recent price-war battle in Denver, Safeway's actions caused Dillon Company, the city leader, to suffer its first profit decline in almost 20 years. No longer was Safeway going to let others damage its market position without a fight.

31 Safeway's development of foreign markets has led the industry. Safeway first entered foreign markets in 1962, and by 1982, it had 535 international stores: 294 in Canada, 98 in the United Kingdom, 115 in Australia, and 28 in West Germany. During that same year, these four regions provided about 50 percent of Safeway's profits, although they only accounted for 20 percent of its sales. These financial returns were achieved despite severe economic conditions in Canada and intense price competition in Australia.

32 The company's British operations registered a 4 percent increase in profits during 1982. Safeway's British unit then attempted to purchase a 98-store chain from Fitch Lovell PLC for $54 million in April of 1983. Fitch Lovell initially accepted the offer, but two weeks later, it reneged when Linfield Holdings Company offered them $59.3 million, thus initiating a bidding war. Finally in June of 1983, Safeway gave up when the bid had climbed to $70.3 million. Undaunted, Magowan expressed plans to continue Safeway's expansion in the United Kingdom. He was also looking at Japan, Taiwan, Hong Kong, Singapore, and Malaysia. As he put it:

> We should do a lot better abroad once those currencies stabilize against the U.S. dollar and those foreign economies begin picking up, because there's even greater growth potential in those markets than in the United States.[3]

33 Magowan formed an international-development division to more systematically develop foreign markets. John Kimball headed up this division and managed the directors of operations in Australia, Germany, and the United Kingdom. In addition, he helped set up a joint venture to run 13 stores in Mexico and 4 more in Saudi Arabia through a management contract. Other significant international activities thus far have included the signing of technical-assistance agreements to manage supermarkets in Kuwait and Oman and the signing of an import-export agreement with Allied Imports, a Japanese marketing group that would provide a market for the overseas distribution

[3] Mitchel Gordon, "Safeway Stores Again Poised for Back-to-Back Profit Records," *Barron's*, March 7, 1983, p. 47.

of Safeway's private-label items. In addition, the company acquired a 49 percent interest in a Mexican food retailer, partly to learn more about selling to the growing U.S. Hispanic market.

Manufacturing/Operations

34 Safeway had 2,454 stores at the start of 1983, 1,806 of which were conventional grocery stores averaging 24,000 square feet. However, Safeway also had approximately 500 superstores averaging 40,000 square feet in size. Finally, the firm had 81 Food Barn warehouse-type stores and 67 Liquor Barn discount liquor stores. Food Barns were primarily in Los Angeles, Kansas City, and Washington, D.C., whereas the Liquor Barns were all located in California and Arizona.

35 In addition, Safeway operated 55 fast-food outlets selling chicken and seafood, operated 8 food-variety combination stores, was involved in a joint venture for 3 egg-production facilities, owned 3 wholesale outlets in Mexico, owned 2 clothing stores, owned 55 percent of Holly Enterprises, and owned 49 percent of Casa Ley.

36 Out of its total of 2,454 stores, 1,919 were located in the United States—1,690 in 22 of the 24 states west of the Mississippi River and the remaining 229 in the Mid-Atlantic region. Safeway's heaviest concentration was along the West Coast and the western providences of Canada. Its biggest competitor, Kroger, on the other hand, was strongest in the mid-western states and the southeastern portions of the United States.

37 Safeway clearly excelled at replacing older stores in saturated areas with newer, more-modern outlets. As one frustrated competitor commented, Safeway hasn't even required its customers to change their habits. On some occasions, it has simply built the new store on part of the old parking lot and torn down the old building over a weekend. On Monday, there was a brand new store, but it was at the same old familiar place.

38 Safeway was late in spotting the trend toward superstores but then quickly became committed to the concept. It had no superstores as of the end of 1978. However, starting in 1979, the company added over 100 superstores per year, each averaging 40,000 square feet. These one-stop shopping superstores doubled Safeway's volume in more-profitable nonfood items in five years to well over 20 percent of total sales. Furthermore, most superstores were able to show a profit within one year.

39 The company had equipped 915 stores with computer-assisted power management systems by the end of 1982 to monitor and control all energy uses within the store. Safeway also developed a fuel-reduction program for its extensive truck fleet. In fact, Safeway's various energy-conservation programs had been so successful that the firm received an award from the Federal Energy Administration.

40 The company streamlined its manufacturing and processing facilities. In 1981 and 1982, for example, Safeway reduced the number of meat prefabricating plants from 11 to 3, discontinued several produce prepackaging operations, combined production of two biscuit plants into one facility, and reduced its nonstore work force by over 3,000 positions. Still, the extent of its manufacturing capabilities remained significant.

41 As of 1983, Safeway operated 105 manufacturing plants. They included 21 milk plants, 18 bakeries, 17 ice cream plants, 9 produce-prepackaging plants, 5 soft drink bottling plants, 5 egg-candling plants, 4 fruit and vegetable processing plants, 3 meat-processing plants, 3 fresh beef fabricating plants, 3 coffee and tea plants, 3 dressing

and salad oil plants, 2 jam and jelly plants, 2 household chemicals plants, 1 edible oil refinery, 1 spice plant, 1 dry pet food plant, and 7 other various plants. In all, approximately 12 percent of Safeway's employees were engaged in these various processing and distribution functions.

42 Each Safeway retail division, and the stores that comprised it, was supported by these modern distribution centers, which were actually a collection of specialized warehouses. Thus, groceries, meats, dairy products, frozen foods, and produce were all kept in separate warehouses depending on their maintenance needs. Safeway, which pioneered the distribution concept, had established a network of 29 distribution-warehouse centers by 1983.

43 A key function of the various distribution-warehouse centers was to receive thousands of items and then assemble them into truckloads that were sent out to the stores. The supporting fleet of vehicles needed to distribute supplies to its countless stores included 2,500 tractor-trailers plus 2,600 additional trailers, comprising the

Exhibit 3

SAFEWAY STORES, INCORPORATED, AND SUBSIDIARIES
Consolidated Balance Sheet
As of January 1, 1983, January 2, 1982, and January 3, 1981
(in thousands of dollars)

	1982	*1981*	*1980*
Assets			
Current assets:			
Cash	$ 63,808	$ 44,075	$ 115,758
Receivables	73,105	72,180	56,633
Merchandise inventories:			
FIFO cost	1,627,440	1,496,775	1,269,560
Less: LIFO reductions	289,450	276,339	256,093
	1,337,990	1,220,436	1,013,467
Prepaid expenses and other current assets	142,646	128,984	83,809
Total current assets	1,617,545	1,465,675	1,269,667
Other assets:			
Licenses, notes receivable, and investments	49,616	40,814	31,775
Deferred income tax charges	7,220	—	—
Excess costs of investment in subsidiaries over net assets at date of acquisition, less amortization	14,301	16,234	2,859
Total other assets	71,137	57,048	34,634
Property:			
Land	174,623	159,113	138,201
Buildings	279,736	232,139	176,631
Leasehold improvements	403,413	375,407	363,143
Fixtures and equipment	1,610,584	1,497,632	1,336,333
Transport equipment	165,761	155,189	161,763
Property under capital leases	1,140,436	1,187,204	1,217,075
	3,774,553	3,606,684	3,393,146
Less: Accumulated depreciation and amortization	1,572,602	1,477,092	1,363,906
Total property	2,201,951	2,129,592	2,029,240
Total assets	$3,890,633	$3,652,315	$3,333,541

Exhibit 3 (*concluded*)

Liabilities and Stockholders' Equity			
Current liabilities:			
Notes payable	$ 88,028	$ 141,208	$ 116,679
Current obligations under capital leases	45,564	46,384	44,855
Current maturities of notes and debentures	13,845	10,406	5,880
Accounts payable	948,632	868,143	726,429
Accrued salaries and wages	149,492	136,628	129,457
Other accrued expenses	142,603	128,075	102,074
Income taxes payable	11,257	21,912	30,108
Total current liabilities	1,399,421	1,352,756	1,155,482
Long-term debt:			
Obligations under capital leases	767,309	809,393	844,011
Notes and debentures	488,877	328,223	207,218
Total long-term debt	1,256,186	1,137,616	1,051,229
Deferred income taxes	—	5,102	1,529
Accrued claims and other liabilities	97,931	81,743	69,614
Commitments and contingencies			
Stockholders' equity:			
Common stock—$1.66⅔ par value Authorized 75,000,000 shares Outstanding 26,149,743, 26,115,917, and 26,115,917 shares	43,583	43,527	43,527
Additional paid-in capital	64,573	63,436	63,436
Cumulative translation adjustments	(96,042)	(66,414)	(45,441)
Retained earnings	1,124,981	1,034,549	994,165
Total stockholders' equity	1,137,095	1,075,098	1,055,687
Total liabilities and stockholders' equity	$3,890,633	$3,652,315	$3,333,541

Safeway Stores, Inc., Annual Report, 1982, pp. 22–23.

largest private trucking fleet in the country. Because of its tremendous size, management believed it stood to gain more than the competition from the Transportation Act of 1980, which permitted backhauling, longer trailers, and heavier payloads. To exploit this potential advantage, Safeway started examining trucking routes and store delivery schedules. It then announced plans to reduce fuel expenses and make maximum use of trailer space by combining deliveries and mixing loads as well as by vigorously pursuing backhaul opportunities. In this way, the expense of the return trip was covered, many times at a profit.

Finance/Accounting

44 Harry Sunderland, age 47, was the chief financial officer and treasurer for Safeway. He had been an officer with Safeway since 1972.

45 Several exhibits provided here review the company's financial performance. Exhibit 3 shows Safeway's balance sheet for calendar years 1980 through 1982. Exhibit 4 shows the consolidated statement of income and retained earnings for the same three years. For the year ending December 31, 1982, sales were $17.6 billion, and net income

Exhibit 4

SAFEWAY STORES, INCORPORATED AND SUBSIDIARIES
Consolidated Statement of Income and Retained Earnings
For the 52 Weeks Ended January 1, 1983, the 52 Weeks Ended January 2, 1982, and the 53 Weeks ended January 3, 1981
(in thousands of dollars)

	1982	*1981*	*1980*
Sales	$17,632,821	$16,580,318	$15,102,673
Cost of sales	13,628,052	12,945,923	11,816,733
Gross profit	4,004,769	3,634,395	3,285,940
Operating and administrative expenses	3,653,561	3,363,478	2,999,130
Operating profit	351,208	270,917	286,810
Interest expense	129,484	120,393	99,614
Other (income), net	(26,536)	(15,822)	(16,486)
Income before provision for income taxes	248,260	166,346	203,682
Provision for income taxes	88,600	58,062	74,544
Net income (per share: $6.11, $4.15 and $4.94)	159,660	108,284	129,138
Retained earnings at beginning of period	1,034,549	994,165	932,911
Cash dividends on common stock (per share: $2.65, $2.60, and $2.60)	(69,228)	(67,900)	(67,900)
Additions resulting from stock acquisitions	—	—	16
Retained earnings at end of period	1,124,981	$ 1,034,549	$ 994,165

Source: Safeway Stores, Inc., Annual Report, 1982, p. 21.

was $159,660,000. Exhibit 5 sheds some light on where the sales and profits came from by overviewing the financial performance of the stores by major geographical areas. Finally, Exhibit 6 provides a five-year summary of earnings, financial statistics, and other statistics.

46 Since overall statistics are sometimes hard to comprehend, one can consider what individual stores were expected to do. A conventional Safeway store did about $5 million in annual sales and was run by 65 people. Superstores, on the other hand, did between $10 and $15 million in sales and employed 120 to 150 people. Within each store, the goal was to be competitive with its pricing. That translated into being competitive with other stores offering comparable value on products of similar quality.

47 Arch competitor Kroger used 15 percent market share as a make-or-break point for each of its stores. If a store couldn't stay above that level, it was closed down. In contrast, under Magowan, Safeway had downplayed the importance of market share in favor of store volume. Magowan once stated that he would rather close down three stores with $100,000 weekly sales and open up one large store with a $250,000 weekly volume. He used this example to stress he was more interested in sales and profits in individual stores than in market share. Consequently, when Magowan closed stores, he did it more on the basis of low store volume.

48 The company has also taken care to cut its losses in cities or regions when necessary. One past example was its 1962 decision to abandon the large New York market. Due to excessive pilferage, unions, and a small market share, it was unable to turn a profit and sold all 163 stores. The most-recent divestiture decision was the closing of its 70-store Nebraska-Iowa division in 1982 which was mentioned earlier. However,

Exhibit 5

Financial information by geographic area (in thousands of dollars)

	1982	*1981*	*1980*
U.S. sales	$13,252,699	$12,491,852	$11,518,993
Gross profit	3,128,111	2,815,057	2,576,021
Operating and administrative expenses	2,921,505	2,688,571	2,424,175
Operating profit	206,606	126,486	151,846
Income before provision for income taxes	110,199	21,050	70,283
Provision for income taxes	34,090	(6,007)	18,735
Net income	76,109	27,057	51,548
Net working capital including merchandise inventories at FIFO cost	384,744	277,160	229,099
Less: LIFO reductions	289,450	276,339	256,093
Net working capital (deficit)	95,294	821	(26,994)
Total assets	2,838,616	2,675,569	2,461,407
Net assets	559,389	532,185	566,909
Cumulative translation adjustments	—	—	—
Canada sales	2,569,717	2,404,972	2,190,917
Gross profit	549,112	504,543	449,339
Operating and administrative expenses	452,170	410,701	357,894
Operating profit	96,942	93,842	91,445
Income before provision for income taxes	93,387	103,256	95,263
Provision for income taxes	41,902	47,011	42,761
Net income	51,485	56,245	52,502
Net working capital including merchandise inventories at FIFO cost	—	—	—
Less: LIFO reductions	—	—	—
Net working capital (deficit)	135,108	150,681	161,428
Total assets	619,486	578,281	518,702
Net assets	365,767	430,063	372,197
Cumulative translation adjustments	(54,219)	(40,362)	(41,806)
Overseas sales	1,810,405	1,683,494	1,392,763
Gross profit	327,546	314,795	260,580
Operating and administrative expenses	279,886	264,206	217,061
Operating profit	47,660	50,589	43,519
Income before provision for income taxes	44,674	42,040	38,136
Provision for income taxes	12,608	17,058	13,048
Net income	32,066	24,982	25,088
Net working capital including merchandise inventories at FIFO cost	—	—	—
Less: LIFO reductions	—	—	—
Net working capital (deficit)	(12,278)	(38,583)	(20,249)
Total assets	432,531	398,465	353,432
Net assets	211,939	112,850	116,581
Cumulative translation adjustments	(41,823)	(26,052)	(3,635)

Source: Safeway Stores, Inc., Annual Report, 1982, pp. 30–31.

Exhibit 6

Five-year summary of earnings, financial statistics, and other statistics

	1982	*1981*	*1980*	*1979*	*1978*
Earnings:					
Sales	$ 17.6B	$ 16.6B	$ 15.1B	$ 13.7B	$ 12.6B
Percent of annual increase	6.3%	9.8%	10.1%	9.3%	11.6%
Cost of sales	$ 13.6B	$ 12.9B	$ 11.8B	$ 10.8B	$ 9.8B
Gross profit	4.0B	3.6B	3.3B	2.9B	2.7B
Percent of sales	22.7%	21.9%	21.8%	21.3%	21.7%
Operating and administrative expenses	$ 3.7B	$ 3.4B	$ 3.0B	$ 2.6B	$ 2.4B
Percent of sales	20.7%	20.3%	19.9%	19.1%	18.9%
Operating profit	$351.2M	$270.9M	$286.8M	306.6M	352.9M
Interest expense	129.5M	120.4M	99.6M	91.3M	74.1M
Other income—net	(26.5M)	(15.8M)	(16.5M)	(13.9M)	(10.8M)
Income taxes	88.6M	58.1M	74.5M	81.5M	130.6M
Net income	159.7M	108.3M	129.1M	147.7M	159.0M
Cash dividend per share of common stock	2.65	2.60	2.60	2.60	2.30
Average shares of common stock outstanding	26.1B	26.1B	26.1B	26.1B	26.1B
Financial statistics:					
Working capital	218.1M	112.9M	114.2M	127.1M	211.6M
Addition to property	511.9M	518.3M	493.0M	435.9M	303.1M
Depreciation and amortization	242.4M	226.0M	204.5M	180.9M	162.9M
Total assets	3.9B	3.7B	3.3B	3.1B	2.8B
Long-term debt	1.3B	1.1B	1.1B	955.7M	880.7M
Equity of common stockholders	1.1B	1.1B	1.1B	994.4M	903.2M
Per share of common stock	43.48	41.17	40.42	38.08	34.61
Cash dividends on common stock	69.2M	67.9M	67.9M	67.9M	60.0M
Other statistics:					
Employees at end of year	156.5K	157.4K	150.0K	148.9K	144.2K
Stores opened during year	153.0	159.0	160.0	104	111.0
Stores closed during year	176.0	98.0	169.0	115	103.0
Total stores at end of year	2,454	2,477	2,416	2,425	2,436
Total store area at year-end (in square feet)	66.8M	65.5M	62.1M	59.5M	57.5M
Average annual sales per store	$ 7.2M	$ 6.7M	$ 6.1M	$ 5.6M	$ 5.1M

K = thousands, M = millions, B = billions.
Source: Safeway Stores, Inc., Annual Report 1982, p. 18.

65 of those stores were sold at a $6 million profit, generating sizable funds to invest in other areas with a greater potential return. The five remaining stores were transferred to another division.

49 When Magowan first took office in 1980, the company's stock price had not increased since 1964. Even in 1982, Standard & Poor's actually advised investors to avoid Safeway stock. Safeway's management responded and took several steps to increase its stock's

attractiveness. The quarterly dividend was increased to 70 cents per share of common stock starting with the fourth quarter of 1982. In early 1983, the board of directors declared a two-for-one stock split. A dividend reinvestment and stock purchase plan was approved allowing stockholders to buy more shares—at 5 percent below market price. In addition, Safeway filed a $200 million stock issuance with the SEC. The proceeds were to be used to reduce short-term debt and for general corporate purposes. As 1982 came to an end, Safeway's common stock had made progress on the New York Stock Exchange. It started the year at $26.50 and closed at an impressive $45.75. During that same year, the Dow Jones averages rose by only 19.6 percent.

Research and Development

50 True to its name, Safeway had traditionally followed the safe route of letting others take the risks and then trying to play catchup. However, under Magowan, the company attempted to become more innovative. Magowan tried out many new ideas, moved Safeway into new businesses, such as Liquor Barns and fast-food chains, and was even considering the company's potential to provide a complete customer financial network similar to that provided by Sears. By 1983, this new philosophy had resulted in only one major failure—in-store home repair centers, which were a complete flop.

51 Unlike Kroger, Safeway did not use a formal customer research department. In fact, the company did not spend anything on research and development activities from 1980 through 1982. Nor did it conduct customer research related to the development of new products or services or the improvement of existing products, services, or techniques. However, by 1983 the picture had changed. According to one Safeway executive, "In the past, we ran our business by giving the consumers what we thought they wanted. Now we've got to find out what they want and then develop the products."[4] Under this new philosophy, the chain began using its scanner checkout system to test the results of price and display changes and to help figure out shelf-space allocations. The marketing staff also started to monitor customer attitudes by providing check-cashing privileges and discounts to those who filled out questionnaires on a regular basis.

Human Resources/Personnel

52 This functional area was headed by John Repass, senior vice president of human resources. Aged 51, Repass had been in this present position since only 1979 but had been a company officer since 1973.

53 With over 156,000 full- and part-time employees, labor was among Safeway's biggest costs, particularly so since the company had always been one of the most-heavily unionized of all the retail food chains, with over 1,300 separate three-year contracts. It had paid higher-than-average wages for a long time; however, extended strikes still plagued the firm, sometimes resulting in temporarily shutting down stores in large regions. For example, a meat-cutters strike in 1973 forced the temporary closing of over 100 stores. In 1978, the Teamsters Union went out on strike for four months, which caused major disruptions of the company's northern California stores.

---

[4] "Safeway Jilts the Family of Four to Woo the Jogging Generation," *Business Week*, November 21, 1983, p. 99.

54 When the bulk of these union contracts were renegotiated in 1983, Safeway's management felt it had made considerable progress in achieving parity with competitors for labor costs. Working with union leadership, Safeway negotiated lower wage rates and got less-restricted work rules included in many contracts.

55 Safeway also beefed up its employee communication program to provide workers with greater understanding of the organization's promotion system and how their roles meshed with the rest of the operation. To this end, several policies were installed. Notices of job openings were distributed to all Safeway stores and put up on a bulletin board. Career counseling sessions were held to explain how to prepare for future job openings. Employees were advised about the growth plans of the company and the number of each type of jobs it would be needing in the future. Employees were encouraged to use the educational reimbursement plan to a greater extent. Local colleges were utilized to teach specialized skills and supervisory courses. Finally, divisional newsletters were used to publicize employees who had been promoted and to explain how they got their jobs.

56 With more than 2,000 stores, the need to promote employees into new positions of responsibility was a never-ending proposition for Safeway. In the late 1970s and early 1980s, Safeway felt it needed to train about 350 new store managers, 350 new meat department managers, 700 new assistant store managers, and 800 new produce managers. Furthermore, this had to be done each year during that period to satisfy the demand caused by retirements, promotions, transfers, resignations, and the opening of new stores.

57 Working on better ways to assess candidates for promotion, management developed a retail career development center program which put assistant store managers through simulated exercises resembling actual situations faced by store managers. This provided employees with a good understanding of their own strengths and weaknesses while the company got an objective evaluation of promotion candidates.

58 Paradoxically, at the uppermost levels of the organizational structure, Magowan no longer promoted almost exclusively from within. On many occasions, he hired outsiders skilled in running pharmacies, delicatessens, health food departments, liquor stores, and other nongrocery operations. This was clearly a departure from Safeway's past tradition of almost always promoting from within.

Management

59 Safeway had been decentralized to a fault under Mitchell. While leaving most merchandising decisions with local stores, Magowan tightened controls in certain areas. For example, he centralized the organization's purchasing and advertising departments as well as its processing of fresh meat. Moreover, he brought regional managers back to headquarters and fundamentally reorganized headquarters. He created an office of the chairman, which he ran along with four senior vice presidents whom he promoted to share this new office.

60 In addition to these moves, Magowan took the company away from the lawyers, who ruled during Mitchell's reign, and turned it over to executives with strong retail experience. He also brought in more young managers from the outside with fresh ideas to help turn the conservative Safeway around. Youth was clearly being emphasized. Safeway's 1982 annual report even profiled 17 key middle managers on the rise who ranged in age from 31 to 45.

79 Although union concessions had helped to alleviate the problem for some chains in the short run, the situation was expected to change. Since many unions had agreed to pay cuts to assist their companies during hard times, it was doubtful they would sit by idly when profits began to go up again. Moreover, some experts felt that labor unions would attempt to recoup the losses they suffered during those weak economy years of 1981–1983.

80 As for managerial pay, some experts feared that the U.S. Labor Department's Wage and Hour Division would adopt new white-collar salary test levels to determine who was exempt from overtime pay. If this legislative threat were to materialize, assistant store managers and supervisors who currently worked long hours, but were not paid for it, would acquire nonexempt jobs requiring overtime pay. This could mean that their salaries would increase by up to 50 percent.

81 Energy costs were a bigger problem than ever. Especially because of their refrigeration systems, supermarkets were large users of energy. During 1982 alone, energy costs for chains climbed by over 15 percent. Many stores installed glass doors on their refrigeration units to reduce these costs.

82 Finally, consumers were also becoming more vocal when confronted with defective merchandise or dissatisfied with it for any seeming reason. A defect was legally defined as anything wrong with a product which might cause harm. It could refer to something omitted from a product or something that should not be a part of it. This could include not only the product itself but also packaging, misleading or inadequate warnings, instructions, or other literature. For the grocery industry, there was an extra catch. Even though food products could be spoiled or impure through no fault of the manufacturer or seller, the law allowed courts to hold stores liable even though no fault or lapse of conduct on their part had taken place. Thus, supermarkets not only had to carefully monitor the products they sold but also had to prevent misuse or abuse of their products if at all possible.

83 Although it was still many years away, some industry executives saw a possible revolutionary change coming. Some added that they did not view it so much as a threat but rather as a technological change that they would have to adjust to. It seemed quite possible that some day customers might be able to order their groceries from a monitor in their home. Some cable networks already had established a television channel devoted to listing the prices of commodities at various local grocery stores, and viewers were able to compare prices without leaving their living rooms. It may not be too long before they would select grocery items with a keyboard attached to their television sets. The grocery store would then deliver the order later the same day.

The Future for Safeway

84 With its aggressive entrepreneurial chief executive officer, Safeway had come a long way from its former conservative posture. In 1983, it had adopted a more-innovative stance than ever before and was willing to try out new ideas, even before its competition did.

85 The company had chosen to continue expansion, both inside and outside of the country, despite its already gigantic size. It had also expanded the size of its new stores to well over 30,000 square feet in what seemed to be a response to a rather well-established industry trend.

61 Safeway was organized along both a functional and a geographic basis. It was functionally organized at the corporate level with vice presidents (or equivalents) heading up retail, supply, and a variety of corporate services, which included (1) personnel and public relations, (2) general counsel, (3) grocery merchandising, (4) advertising and market research, (5) treasurer, (6) controller, (7) management information and services group, and (8) real estate construction and engineering. All of these people reported directly to Dale Lynch, who was the president and chief operating officer. In turn, the 61-year-old Lynch reported to the 40-year-old Peter Magowan, chairman of the board and chief executive officer, who was clearly the firm's chief strategist.

62 Within the retail functional area, however, Safeway was organized according to regional locations. Among those people who reported to John Bell, the vice president regional manager—retail, were three U.S. regional managers. Vice President Bell also functioned as one regional manager and had 847 stores grouped under his 7 divisions. The Los Angeles division had 185 stores; Phoenix, 88; Richmond, 77; Sacramento, 92; San Diego, 52; San Francisco, 203; and the Washington, D.C. division, 150. A second U.S. regional manager, Fred MacRae, had responsibility for 497 stores grouped in six divisions. The Butte division had 28 stores; Denver, 146; Portland, 94; Salt Lake City, 59; Seattle, 129; and the Spokane division, 41. William Maloney, the third and final U.S. regional manager, had 575 stores under him. The Dallas division had 153 stores; El Paso, 54; Houston, 99; Kansas City, 79; Little Rock, 65; Oklahoma City, 68; and the Tulsa division, 57. Stores in Canada and overseas were similarly grouped and first reported to a division manager who in turn reported to a regional manager in that country or a major geographic region.

63 In 1982, Safeway's first strategic management program was established to help the company adapt to the changing environment. As spelled out in its 1982 annual report, the corporate mission included the following five elements:

1. To be a growing company.
2. To be a profitable company.
3. To be a worldwide company.
4. To be a retailer of groceries.
5. To be a retailer of related consumer goods and services.[5]

The External Environment

The Grocery Industry

64 The grocery industry has been described as dynamic, complex, and very competitive. Billion-dollar chains were operating on a bottom line of less than 1 percent profit. Thus, there was little room for error for the managers who made them run. In the 1980s, competitive pricing made already-slim margins even smaller.

65 With all this competition, it was not uncommon for supermarkets to engage in price wars in specific markets. Unfortunately for the stores, usually the only winner in these wars was the customer. These price wars took many forms. Sometimes the stores just lowered their prices. Other times, they offered double, triple, or even quadru-

[5] Safeway Stores, Inc., *Safeway Stores, Incorporated, Annual Report, 1982* (Oakland, California: Safeway Stores, Inc., 1982), p. 1.

ple savings on coupons. At still other times, gimmicks such as stamps, games, or giveaways were initiated. No matter what the method, the reason was always the same. One store or chain in an area decided it needed to improve its market share, so it offered an incentive to customers to shop there for a change. Since the larger volume could lead to greater revenues than the cost of the promotion, it seemed like a good idea. It made further sense since statistics showed that many of the shoppers stayed with the new store as regular customers, even after the promotion was over.

66 The extra volume had to come from somewhere, and it was usually from the other grocery stores in the area. Naturally, they had to lower their prices or offer some sort of promotion to protect their share, and another price war was on. One industry observer explained that chain promotions were very important to generate new customers and protect the ones a store already had.

67 One major trend in the 1980s was the sizable increase in the number of superstores, which represented a major shift in how a growing number of Americans did their grocery shopping. Their higher store profitability was often attributed to very high volume, many more high-margin food and nonfood items, and fixed and variable costs being spread over a larger volume.

68 Safeway's Chairman Peter Magowan accurately assessed the situation when he commented, "It's not going to be good enough to be just the best in running a conventional grocery store."[6] Not surprisingly, the majority of stores closed in the 1980s were conventional grocery stores, while, conversely, about 70 percent of the new stores opened were superstores. Furthermore, many existing stores were being rapidly converted to larger, superstore-type formats.

69 Interestingly, the industry trend toward superstores appeared to be incongruent with the traditional three premises of supermarket operation:

1. Convenience and fast service.
2. Mass merchandising of volume items.
3. High productivity and efficiency.

70 Anyone who had ever entered a supermarket knew that walking through one of them took time. Walking through a 30,000 or more square foot superstore obviously would take even more time. With the recent increases in energy and labor costs, it was questionable just how much money these stores actually saved. In fact, one study showed that as store size exceeded 27,000 square feet, productivity tended to decrease.

71 Despite these potential problems, customer acceptance of superstores was high. Consumers seemed to enjoy the easy access to a variety of competitively priced goods and services under one roof. It was even predicted that price wars would lessen in number and intensity as higher profits arrived all around.

Changing Demographics

72 One demographic change that Safeway and other grocery chains had to deal with was the reality that more women than ever before were in the labor force. Over half of all women aged 16 and over held jobs outside the home, and it was anticipated that another 7 million women would do so before the 1980s were over. While this meant that many women had more money for shopping, they also had less spare

[6] "Safeway Stores," p. 108.

time to do it in. In addition, more males began to share the grocery-sh Recent studies have confirmed that in households where both spouses male is twice as likely to share in the shopping. A second reason for th male shoppers was the growing number of single male households in the U including both young, single men and those who have been divorced.

73 Supermarkets needed to be aware of this demographic change becaus proached grocery shopping from a rather different perspective than did general, men considered the task to be a bother. Therefore, convenience was e instead of bargains. Clearly, they were willing to pay more to save time. In men were more loyal to particular brands; thus, they preferred shopping that offered a wide variety of major brands.

74 A second key demographic change was the shifting population among r the United States. The migration to the Sun Belt was increasing in the ear causing unprecedented population growth in Texas, Florida, California, an southern states. Furthermore, the ethnic makeup of the population itself was ch According to the 1980 census, about 12 percent of the U.S. population was bla 8 percent Hispanic. However, it was expected that the number of Hispanics surpass blacks by 1990. In fact, they were predicted to account for 50 percent of C nia's population by the year 2000.

75 A third key demographic change was that the population was getting older 25 to 44 age group was growing three and a half times faster than the total popula and the number of people over 65 was expected to reach 31 million by 1990. Al new baby boom was expected to peak between 1985 and 1989 with 4 million expe births per year.

76 This older population was more educated and more affluent than ever before. such, they demanded superior quality and a wide selection of items to choose fro Many of them were also very interested in health and nutrition and had chang their eating patterns. For this subgroup, their consumption of beef, whole milk, coffe and eggs had dropped while purchases of chicken, low-fat milk, and cheese had soared In addition, ethnic foods, wines, and easy-to-prepare foods were gaining increasing popularity among this older group.

Industry Threats and Problems

77 The industry's sales growth had increased in recent years, but at a decreasing rate. First, the economic downturn from 1981 to 1983 hurt even the strongest of retail chains. Second, grocery shoppers started purchasing cheaper-priced private-label brands and generics to a greater extent. Third, more grocery shoppers reduced their purchase of higher-margin, nonfood items when they went to the grocery store.

78 An increasingly major expense item for grocery stores was wages. In the late 1970s and early 1980s, wage increases outpaced increasing grocery sales. It was even worse for those chains that linked cost-of-living increases with rises in the consumer price index. When inflation finally began to slow down, unionized grocery stores were stuck with annual wage increases negotiated when inflation was increasing rapidly. This caused operating margins to further erode. Some grocery chains responded by closing their least-profitable stores, particularly in the depressed Midwest. These closings and the threat of additional closings elsewhere helped some grocery chains obtain wage and benefit concessions from their respective unions.

86 An industry report in 1982 concluded that perhaps the companies best positioned to emerge from the recession of the early 1980s would be the ones that carried a light debt load, sported a strong cash flow, and found the means to finance expansions internally.[7] Whether Safeway meets these goals may ultimately depend on its ability to react quickly given its size. The environment of the grocery industry was currently so dynamic that predictions as to what lay down the road were very tenuous. If interest rates did not rise again, if profit margins continued to grow through the continued expansion of superstores, if costly price wars could be avoided, if union negotiations continued to fare well, and if overseas currencies stabilized in the countries where the company did business, then Safeway would probably do well. But what if some of these assumptions did not hold true? What would lie ahead for Safeway then? Large battleships, like grocery giants such as Safeway, have lots of momentum once they get going, but how long does it take them to put on the brakes and change their basic direction?

[7] "Supermarkets and Grocery Chains—Disinflation Squeezing Retail Profits," *Standard & Poor's Industry Surveys* (New York: Standard & Poor's, 1982), p. R182.

case 33
The Southland Corporation

1 In 1978, the world's largest chain of convenience food stores was 7-Eleven markets, a division of the Southland Corporation. The 7-Eleven chain started from very humble beginnings in 1927 to surpass the $3 billion sales figure in 1978. Southland showed all indications of continuing its 15 percent annual growth rate and capitalizing on consumer acceptance of convenience shopping. As the president of a rival chain expressed it, "I think it has to be said that Southland is one of the great retailing stores of our time."

Company History

2 In 1924, Jodie Thompson wanted to get married, but his $40-a-week salary from a Dallas ice-making firm was not enough to support a wife and family. From working on the ice docks and overseeing sales that summer, Thompson came upon the solution—chilled watermelons. No one had ever tried to sell chilled watermelons (or any other retail item for that matter) off the ice docks in Texas. Thompson's boss was initially very skeptical but finally gave approval to try the idea. The venture was a success, and by the end of the summer, Thompson had made $2,300.

3 In the summer of 1927, one of the dock managers of the Southland Ice Co. found that he could do a much brisker business by staying open 16 hours a day, seven days a week. He also noted that late-hour ice customers often complained about there being no place to pick up a loaf of bread or a bottle of milk. The dock manager persuaded Thompson, who by then was secretary-treasurer and a director of Southland Ice Co., to finance an inventory of bread, milk, and eggs and stack them on the dock. The items sold well, and shortly thereafter, when Thompson became president, all the company's ice docks were stocked with grocery items, and the enterprising dock manager was assigned the task of finding new store sites. At the advice of a local advertising agency, Thompson named the stores 7-Eleven because they were open from 7 A.M. to 11 P.M.

4 By the mid-1950s, Southland had expanded to about 300 stores, mostly in Texas and Florida. As the United States became more urbanized, with many people commuting to work from the suburbs, Thompson and his two oldest sons believed that Southland could move into and redefine the niche once dominated by mom-and-pop corner grocery stores; they felt that selling customers convenience in the form of accessible hours,

This case was prepared by Dr. John Thiel and Jim Brown of the University of Tennessee.

handy locations, big parking lots, and well-selected merchandise would translate into a competitive edge and accelerate a shift of buyer patronage from the rapidly failing corner groceries to Southland's convenience food store concept. Southland's store expansion program began in earnest about 1960.

Southland's Current Business Structure

5 In 1978, Southland's business interests were organized into three major groups. The Stores Group was the world's largest operator and franchiser of convenience stores with 6,599 7-Eleven stores in 42 states, the District of Columbia, and 5 provinces of Canada. Its three distribution centers served 3,916 7-Eleven stores with approximately 50 percent of their merchandise needs. Food Centers, located at each distribution center, prepared a variety of sandwiches for distribution to 7-Eleven and other customers. Other retail operations included 109 Gristede's and Charles & Company food stores and sandwich shops in metropolitan New York, 383 R. S. McColl confectionery, tobacco, and news stores, and 7 7-Eleven units in the United Kingdom. Southland also had an equity interest in 5 Super Siete stores in Mexico and 23 Naroppet stores in Sweden. An additional 279 7-Eleven stores were operated by area licensees in the United States, 559 in Japan, 5 in Canada, and 12 in Australia.

6 The Dairies Group, another part of the Southland Corporation, was a major processor of dairy products which were distributed under 11 well-known regional brand names in 34 states and the District of Columbia.

7 The Special Operations Group included the Chemical, Reddy Ice, Hudgins Truck Rental, and Tidel Systems which manufactured money-handling devices for retail operations. In addition, Chief Auto Parts, a retail automobile supply chain of 119 stores in southern California, was added to the group in late 1978.

8 Exhibit 1 gives a breakdown of the sales revenues and operating profits of these three groups. Exhibit 2 provides a corporatewide financial summary, and Exhibit 3 is a condensed statement of consolidated earnings.

Customer Profile of Southland's 7-Eleven Stores

9 Approximately 5.4 million people patronized 7-Eleven stores daily in 1978. Based upon a study it conducted that year, Southland came up with a profile of its customers:

69.8 percent males.
80.2 percent in 18–49 age group.
80.9 percent live/work in area.
4.3 average trips a week.
30.1 percent shop weekends.
50.2 percent shop 1 P.M. to 10 P.M.
$1.54 average purchase.
822 customers daily per store.

On the average, the typical customer spent less than $2—and three to four minutes—at the store and often made at least one unplanned impulse purchase. Though these small unplanned purchases did not amount to much extra expense for the individual customer, they resulted in significant extra sales and profits to Southland, given that over 5 million customers a day were involved.

Exhibit 1

Revenues and operating profits by major business segment ($ millions)

	1978		1977		1976		1975		1974	
Revenues:										
Stores Group	$2,791.0	90%	$2,271.9	89%	$1,857.5	88%	$1,556.0	87%	$1,405.4	87%
Dairies Group	253.4	8	236.5	9	236.1	11	208.3	12	184.0	11
Special Operations Group	40.9	2	33.7	2	26.0	1	25.0	1	22.6	2
Corporate	4.8	—	3.3	—	2.4	—	1.5	—	2.2	—
Total	3,090.1	100	2,545.4	100	2,122.0	100	1,790.8	100	1,614.2	100
Operating profits:										
Stores Group	142.7	92	115.7	90	92.3	86	80.8	88	68.5	85
Dairies Group	6.7	4	6.0	5	8.6	8	10.1	11	8.1	10
Special Operations Group	6.0	4	6.7	5	6.4	6	.9	1	4.0	5
Total	155.4	100	128.4	100	107.3	100	91.8	100	80.6	100

Source: Company records.

Exhibit 2

Southland Corporation financial summary (in thousands of dollars)

	1978	*1977*	*1976*	*1975*	*1974*
Operations (Note 1):					
Total revenues	$ 3,090,094	$ 2,545,415	$ 2,122,023	$ 1,790,805	$ 1,614,188
Increase over prior year	21.40%	19.95%	18.50%	10.94%	15.47%
Net earnings	$ 57,097	$ 45,317	$ 37,849	$ 32,068	$ 27,167
Increase over prior year	25.99%	19.73%	18.03%	18.04%	25.85%
Per revenue dollar	1.85%	1.78%	1.78%	1.79%	1.68%
Return on beginning shareholders' equity	17.30%	15.62%	14.56%	13.72%	13.16%
Assets employed (Note 1):					
Working capital	$ 141,633	$ 136,693	$ 101,536	$ 80,196	$ 72,495
Current ratio	1.54	1.66	1.63	1.58	1.55
Property, plant, and equipment including capital leases (net)	677,284 $	$ 567,442	$ 506,190	$ 447,392	$ 406,486
Depreciation and amortization	67,724	61,735	55,029	47,974	43,078
Total assets	1,134,476	942,531	799,261	696,107	639,599
Capitalization (Note 1):					
Long-term debt	261,460 $	$ 195,520	$ 153,093	$ 119,911	$ 105,609
Capital lease obligations	211,342	192,547	178,556	163,380	155,918
Shareholders' equity	374,467	329,952	290,142	259,940	233,659
Total capitalization	847,269	718,019	621,791	543,231	495,186
Shareholders' equity to total capitalization	44.20%	45.95%	46.66%	47.85%	47.19%
Per share data (Notes 1 and 2):					
Primary earnings	$ 2.83	$ 2.26	$ 1.92	$ 1.63	$ 1.42
Earnings assuming full dilution	2.74	2.19	1.85	1.58	1.35
Cash dividends	.68	.55	.44	.36	.30
Shareholders' equity	18.55	16.48	14.68	13.23	12.21
Other data:					
Cash dividends	$ 13,627	$ 10,961	$ 8,660	$ 7,033	$ 5,834
Dividends as a percent of earnings (Note 1)	23.87%	24.19%	22.88%	21.93%	21.47%
Stock dividends	3%	3%	3%	3%	3%
Average shares outstanding (Note 3)	20,181,879	20,015,512	19,761,788	19,642,947	19,137,414
Average diluted shares (Note 3)	21,129,981	21,028,143	20,911,047	20,883,719	20,854,737
Market price range (Note 3)					
High	$ 33¾	$ 25⅞	$ 26⅛	$ 26¼	$ 18⅞
Low	21½	19¼	19⅛	14	11⅜
Year-end	26¾	24⅝	25½	20⅜	14¼
Number of shareholders	8,627	8,764	8,881	9,093	9,351
Number of employees	37,000	34,000	31,000	28,600	28,200

Notes:

(1) The years 1974 through 1977 have been restated for the change in the method of accounting for leases to comply with the provisions of *Statement of Financial Accounting Standards No. 13* which was adopted early in accordance with the requirements of the Securities and Exchange Commission.

(2) Based on average shares outstanding adjusted for stock dividends.

(3) Adjusted for stock dividends.

Source: Southland Cooperation, Annual Report, 1978.

Exhibit 3

THE SOUTHLAND CORPORATION
Consolidated Statement of Earnings
For the Years 1974–1978
(in thousands of dollars except per share data)

	1978	*1977*	*1976*	*1975*	*1974*
Revenues:					
Net sales	$3,076,532	$2,536,109	$2,115,769	$1,787,928	$1,609,257
Other income	13,562	9,306	6,254	2,877	4,931
Total revenues	3,090,094	2,545,415	2,122,023	1,790,805	1,614,188
Cost of sales and expenses:					
Cost of goods sold, including buying and occupancy expenses	2,311,024	1,903,791	1,577,141	1,323,799	1,184,835
Selling, general, and administrative expenses	619,519	510,337	435,687	374,234	348,797
Interest expense	15,804	13,540	9,707	7,936	8,674
Imputed interest expense on capital lease obligations	19,325	18,064	15,388	13,969	12,982
Contributions to employees savings and profit-sharing plan	11,714	9,726	8,346	6,995	5,899
Total cost of sales and expenses	2,977,386	2,455,458	2,046,269	1,726,933	1,561,187
Earnings before income taxes	112,708	89,957	75,754	63,872	53,001
Income taxes	55,611	44,640	37,905	31,804	25,834
Net earnings	$ 57,097	$ 45,317	$ 37,849	$ 32,068	$ 27,167
Per share:					
Primary earnings	$ 2.83	$ 2.26	$ 1.92	$ 1.63	$ 1.42
Earnings assuming full dilution	$ 2.74	$ 2.19	$ 1.85	$ 1.58	$ 1.35

Source: Southland Corporation, Annual Report, 1978.

10 According to a reporter for *The Wall Street Journal:*

> Southland's 7-Elevens are successors of the old-fashioned mom-and-pop grocery, but they prosper by catering to the modern urge for instant gratification. Their customers fill their pantries at the supermarket but dash instead to the closest 7-Eleven to fill their latest desire for, say, cigarettes or cold beer. Indeed, well over half the goods a 7-Eleven sells are consumed within 30 minutes.[1]

The same article quoted a 7-Eleven customer who lived in Dallas:

> I usually stop by on the way to work to get a roll, in the afternoon to pick up a TV dinner, and sometimes during the day to get a coke. I'm a bachelor and it's quick and convenient.

This view reflected management's own perceptions that Southland was really in the convenience business rather than in the retail grocery business.

[1] Gerald F. Seib, "Despite High Prices and Sparse Selection, 7-Eleven Stores Thrive," *The Wall Street Journal,* May 1, 1979, p. 1.

Store Growth and Locations

11 Southland's management looked upon convenience as "giving customers what they want, when they want it, where they want it." As a consequence, in 1978, 5,407 of Southland's 6,599 7-Elevens were open around the clock and 91 percent were open beyond the traditional 7 A.M. to 11 P.M. hours. Moreover, Southland emphasized easily accessible neighborhood locations and quick, friendly service; its product lines included popular fast-foods selections and, at 30 percent of its locations, self-service gasoline.

12 In recent years, Southland has opened about 500 new 7-Eleven stores per year. The net gain in stores has been smaller, however, because population shifts, changes in traffic patterns, lease expirations, and relocations to newly available and more desirable sites have resulted in some existing stores being closed. The number of store openings and closings since 1972 are shown in Exhibit 4.

13 Southland used a meticulous store site selection system; the primary criteria included such factors as (1) the traffic count in front of the site, (2) the ease with which passing cars could enter and leave the site, (3) the site's visibility from the street or road, (4) the number of people living within a one-mile radius, (5) the site's proximity to apartments, subdivisions, and high-traffic commercial establishments, (6) the adequacy of parking space, and (7) whether the site was a natural stopping-off point in the traffic flow by the site. To make sure its small 2,400-square-foot stores were readily seen from approaching traffic, they were carefully positioned in a heavy traffic area where they could be seen easily and were convenient to passers-by. Traffic patterns and flows were so crucial that stores had failed because a street was made one-way or because the opening of new streets and subdivisions had shifted traffic away from a site. Southland extensively studied potential sites and used a computer to estimate a proposed store's sales for its first five years.

14 John Thompson, Southland chairman, recently indicated that when a store starts looking like a loser, "We would rather close then and take our licks." The poor performers were identified by computerized analysis; by merely punching the store number into a computer terminal, executives could call up on a terminal display the store's current sales and earnings and tell how close it was to its budget. The company's management kept a close check on each store's operating performance.

15 In 1977, Southland started opening central-city stores. Located in high-density metropolitan residential areas, Southland saw them as filling a genuine need for walking customers. The company now has central-city stores in Philadelphia, Boston, San Fran-

Exhibit 4

	New stores opened	*Existing stores closed*	*Total 7-Eleven stores*
1972	424	83	4,455
1973	426	80	4,801
1974	n.a.	n.a.	5,171
1975	566	158	5,579
1976	528	154	5,953
1977	658	254	6,357
1978	550	308	6,599

n.a. = Not available.

cisco, and New York City; more are planned. According to Thompson, the central-city stores "open up a whole new market area we haven't yet been able to serve. We will attempt to build and merchandise stores according to their neighborhoods."

Product Lines and Merchandising

16 Southland continually experimented with the product mix offered in the stores. Some products, like the frozen concoction "Slurpee," became huge successes. Others, like 7-Eleven beer, flopped.

17 One Southland executive stated, "There's little risk involved in experimenting. We have a built-in market base of 5 million customers a day. Things that don't work out we can throw out after a week or two. Things that catch on in one store we can try nationwide. Our computers in Dallas can tell us overnight about any new market trends."[2] 7-Eleven stores carried 3,000 different items, about 23 percent of them Southland's own house brands. The larger percentage of brands available in a 7-Eleven store were nationally recognized brands; however, each item was located in a space predetermined by a Southland computer in Dallas. One Southland executive indicated:

> There is no room to store a lot of different brands of the same product. Our customers don't have time to make choices anyway. We usually put on our shelves only the top one or two sellers of every product line, and we put them in the area of the store where we think the customer would like to find them. It's all been researched and market tested. I can walk into most stores blindfolded and find any item you want.[3]

18 Through 1977, Southland's biggest selling item was tobacco—cigarettes primarily—followed closely by groceries, beer and wine, soft drinks, nonfood items such as magazines and Kleenex, and dairy products (see Exhibit 5). However, tobacco products dropped from number one in 1978, the change primarily due to increased gasoline sales. 7-Elevens have at times sold shotgun shells, television tubes, watermelons, and cancer insurance. Among the stores' best selling items today are fast-food sandwiches, disposable diapers, and *Playboy* magazines (of which 7-Elevens sell far more than any other retailer). In general, the items carried were products that would be needed on a fill-in basis or else bought on impulse.

19 By the end of 1978, self-service gasoline accounted for 60 percent of all gasoline sales in the United States and showed every indication of increasing beyond that figure, according to industry sources. In response to this demand, 7-Eleven provided self-service gasoline at 1,857 locations. A substantial increase in volume at existing units, as well as the addition of gasoline at 284 stores during 1978, resulted in a 70 percent gasoline sales increase for the year. The availability of gasoline also led to the generation of additional sales, as more than 30 percent of 7-Eleven's gasoline customers in 1978 purchased other merchandise.

20 One merchandising trend of particular import was that of adding higher-margin items to each store's product line to try to boost store profitability. Fast-food items like sandwiches, pizza, soup, coffee, fruit punch, and draft soda (like Slurpee) carried gross margins in the 40 percent range. Nonfood impulse items, which had margins

[2] "7-Eleven Creates a Mood of Convenience at a Price," *The Washington Star,* November 27, 1978.

[3] Ibid.

Exhibit 5

7-Eleven store sales by principal product category*

	1978	*1977*	*1976*	*1975*	*1974*
Groceries	13.4%	14.0%	14.6%	15.3%	17.1%
Gasoline	13.4	9.8	6.8	3.9	2.7
Tobacco products	12.9	14.2	14.7	15.6	15.7
Beer/wine	12.9	13.7	14.4	14.8	14.1
Soft drinks	10.9	11.0	10.7	11.5	11.5
Nonfoods	9.4	9.9	10.2	9.5	9.3
Dairy products	8.9	9.3	9.6	9.5	10.5
Other food items	5.5	4.7	4.7	4.2	3.9
Candy	4.7	5.0	5.4	5.7	5.3
Baked goods	4.6	5.0	5.3	5.7	5.9
Health/beauty aids	3.4	3.4	3.6	3.9	4.0
Total	100.0%	100.0%	100.0%	100.0%	100.0%

* The company does not record sales by product lines but estimates the percentage of convenience store sales by principal product category based upon total store purchases.
Source: Southland Corporation, Annual Report, 1978.

in the 35 percent range, were also being added. Both compared favorably with Southland's recent storewide margins of 25 percent to 27 percent. Southland's fast-food division, which in 1978 experienced a 30.5 percent sales gain, produced approximately 30 sandwiches marketed under the 7-Eleven and Landshire labels. These were distributed either fresh or flash-frozen for reheating in microwave or infrared ovens. The division in 1978 sold approximately 80 million sandwiches to 7-Eleven stores, other retailers, and institutional customers; it also furnished 7-Eleven stores with more than 1 million gallons of Slurpee syrup.

21 Southland's management was optimistic about the potential for increasing its share of the food-away-from-home market. Projections called for this segment to increase its share of the consumer's total food dollar owing to greater numbers of women entering the work force, higher family incomes, smaller families, and more single people—all of which acted to reinforce the lifestyle where a higher percent of disposable personal income would be spent for food prepared outside the home.

Pricing

22 According to Southland's marketing research director, people just about everywhere are willing to pay a little extra for the convenience a 7-Eleven offers—especially when the consumer is hit by an urge to buy. Most of the items in a 7-Eleven are therefore priced some 10 to 15 percent above the levels in most supermarkets. But, as shown in Exhibit 6, a few items, like milk, are priced more competitively.

23 As one 7-Eleven customer put it:

> There's a lot I don't like about 7-Eleven stores. They look tacky. They charge too much. They sell stuff that isn't good for you, and they always seem to be getting robbed. But yes, I do shop there. They're so convenient.[4]

[4] "Southland Is the Best Example I Know of Modern Capitalism," *The Washington Star,* November 26, 1978.

Exhibit 6

Sample comparisons of prices at 7-Eleven stores and Safeway supermarkets in 1978

Item	*7-Eleven*	*Safeway*
Cascade (20 oz.)	$ .98	$ .89
Shredded wheat (12 oz.)	.93	.75
Tuna (chunk light, 6 oz.)	1.19	.99
Campbell's chicken noodle soup	.36	.30
Jello instant pudding (4 oz.)	.40	.35
Log Cabin maple syrup (12 oz.)	1.15	.93
Hellman's mayonnaise (16 oz.)	1.23	.99
Franco-American spaghetti (14 oz.)	.39	.34
Domino sugar (5 lbs.)	1.59	1.49
Wesson oil (16 oz.)	1.19	.99
V-8 juice (46 oz.)	1.09	.85
Maxwell House instant coffee (6 oz.)	4.29	3.79
Kellogg's corn flakes (12 oz.)	.85	.69
Hydrox cream-filled cookies	1.19	1.09
6-pack of Budweiser (12 oz.)	2.33	1.99
6-pack of Schlitz Light	2.34	1.99
Gallo burgundy wine	2.23	1.99
6-pack of Pepsi (16 oz.)	2.02	1.89
7up (32 oz.)	.71	.63
Hostess cup cakes (2)	.35	.33
White bread (22 oz.)	.73	.40
Hostess powdered doughnuts (12)	.99	.99
Dozen eggs (grade A large)	.89	.79
Minute Maid orange juice (quart bottle)	.85	.75
Philadelphia cream cheese (3 oz.)	.43	.34
Salt (26 oz.)	.35	.30
Bayer aspirin (50 tablets)	1.19	.89
Heinz ketchup (14 oz.)	.79	.61
French's mustard (9 oz.)	.55	.43
Carton of Winston cigarettes	4.79	4.49
10 Briggs hot dogs	1.69	1.39
Half-gallon milk	.91	.91
Total (32 items)	$40.97	$35.55

Source: *The Washington Star,* November 26, 1978.

So far, though, no consumer activist groups had targeted 7-Eleven for either its high prices or its line of merchandise.

24 Southland seemed to have discovered, and was helping perpetuate, its own market segment—a world of customers caught in a time crisis, willing to pay extra to save themselves a few seconds waiting in line. A Wall Street analyst said:

> It is perplexing to us why Southland's revenue growth has accelerated when rising prices have stretched the consumer's budget to a considerable extent. Perhaps it is time rather than money which is the precious commodity to most Americans at present. The appeal of convenience stores has nothing to do with price. It has to do with people's lifestyles and their constant need for fill-ins.

The more tightly the pocketbook is pinched, the less frequently the housewife shops at her supermarket, and the more need she has for last minute fill-ins.[5]

Franchise Activities

25 Of the 6,599 7-Eleven stores operating at the end of 1978, 4,056 were company operated and 2,543 were franchised. The typical franchise agreement allowed for the company to lease the property and equipment to a franchisee in exchange for a fee of $10,000 plus roughly half the store's profits. Southland allowed new franchises a 120-day grace period to pull out of their contracts without losing their initial investments. Most of the franchisees were couples with children and the family typically worked in the store.

Southland's Advertising for 7-Elevens

26 In January 1978, Southland introduced its first prime-time network 7-Eleven commercial to the largest audience in television history prior to Super Bowl XII. Product awareness messages featuring Hot-to-Go coffee, Egg Hamlette, Chili Dog, Slurpee, or sunglasses reached 58 million households each broadcast week. In addition to the network television commercials, advertisements were aired on approximately 500 radio stations and published in more than 200 newspapers nationwide.

27 During 1978, broadcasts remained the company's major advertising vehicle with spot radio getting 30 percent, network television 35 percent, spot television 25 percent, newspapers 4 percent, and outdoor advertising 6 percent. Total television advertising increased 22 percent during the first half of 1978, compared with the same period in 1977.

28 7-Eleven stores are decidedly male oriented. However, due to the increased buying power of women in today's society, Southland's advertising had begun to be geared specifically toward women.

Distribution Centers

29 Southland's 7-Eleven stores were served by distribution centers in Florida, Virginia, and Texas that were specifically designed to meet the needs of 7-Eleven for a reliable and efficient source of supply, frequent delivery, and a high in-stock position. The system also enabled the stores to have the flexibility to respond quickly to customer preferences and seasonal changes in demand, as well as to implement promotional programs and introduce new products. The centers serviced 3,916 7-Eleven stores at the end of 1978.

30 Store stock lists, which are compiled and updated monthly by computer, were tailored to the merchandise specifications of each store, enabling personnel to easily determine their restocking needs. The store orders were then transmitted through a network of computer terminals located at 7-Eleven district offices and connected to the computer center in Dallas, which assimilated the orders and transmitted them to printing terminals at the appropriate distribution center. From these printed lists, the store orders were then picked and assembled for delivery. Custom-designed trucks with separate

[5] "7-Eleven Creates a Mood of Convenience."

compartments for dry, chilled, and frozen merchandise followed computer-planned routes to achieve maximum savings of energy and time.

31 Southland's concept of delivering prepriced merchandise in less-than-case-quantities eliminated overstocking, assured fresh merchandise on the store shelves at all times, promoted more-productive use of selling space, and improved store profitability. The importance of stores not having to order full cases of merchandise was highlighted by Southland's manager of information services: "Can you imagine how long it would take to sell 48 cans of tomato paste in a 7-Eleven? Now we can give them three cans and keep it fresh." During 1978, the computerized inventory control system enabled the stores to achieve an average inventory turnover of 23 times while maintaining a 99 percent order fill rate.

32 In many cases, store managers did not even bother to order groceries; that was done by warehouse employees whose only job was visiting each 7-Eleven twice a month to take inventory and order merchandise.[6] The computer then took over, sending hundreds of orders to a warehouse, deciding which orders to ship on what truck, and telling employees how to stack goods inside the truck to fill it to the brim. The trucks were able to begin delivering only hours after the warehouse got the order. Southland's computer also helped analyze the layout of merchandise in the store—by keeping track of what items sold well in which shelf locations.

Financing

33 The long-term policy of Southland was to finance expansion from retained earnings, although other methods of raising funds were used when necessary. In late 1978, the company offered $50 million of unsecured 9⅜ percent sinking fund debentures, due December 15, 2003. These debentures, as well as a 1977 8⅜ percent issue, were rated A by both Moody's and Standard & Poor's and were listed on the New York Stock Exchange.

34 In April 1978, the annual cash dividend rate was increased 20 percent to 72 cents per share. Cash dividends have been paid each year since 1957, and the annual rate has been raised seven times in the last eight years, providing shareholders an average compound growth rate of 20.7 percent. In addition, for the 13th consecutive year, a 3 percent stock dividend was distributed.

35 In recent years, Southland has been forced to increase its debt burden to finance corporate expansion—especially the growth in the number of 7-Eleven stores. To open a new store, Southland had to invest more than $180,000. This included land costs of about $50,000, a store building costing an average of $70,000, equipment installation of $46,000, and initial inventory costs of $18,000 to $25,000. In the case of franchised stores, Southland advanced most of the up-front investment, with the exception of the $10,000 franchise fee.

36 The capital costs of financing 400–500 new stores per year had exceeded Southland's retained earnings and internal cash flow capabilities during recent years; the resulting debt increases were in such an amount as to cause a steady decline in Southland's equity capitalization percentage (see Exhibit 2).

37 Although a 41-year-old Southland official expressed the view that the company would be adding a net of 300–400 stores per year for the rest of his lifetime, it was not

[6] Seib, "Despite High Prices."

clear that Southland could continue to finance such an ambitious store-expansion program without adversely affecting earnings. Higher site and construction costs and higher interest rates were becoming significant factors; so was the move to increase store size from 2,400 square feet to the 2,700- to 3,000-square-feet range. In 1977, Southland spent an estimated $75.3 million to open 658 stores; in 1978, the figure exceeded $95 million for 550 new stores.

38 Nor was it clear that such a rate of expansion was consistent with market opportunities. Already there were over 33,000 convenience food stores in the United States—approximately one for every 6,600 persons. Prime sites were becoming hard to find and were increasingly expensive. According to one industry trade publication, several factors were at work:

> Munford executives, like most in the business, have set their sights on prime corner locations with high visibility and heavy traffic counts. Because Munford is selecting former gas station sites for its new units, traffic counts have replaced household density, once the sacred cow of the industry's site selection procedure.
>
> In fact, one Majik Market is making $7,000 per week in food sales—the industry average is $5,257—without a house within a five-mile radius of the store.
>
> Secondary sites, mainly at the mouths of suburban subdivisions and in shopping malls, are a thing of the past. "The suburban, residential convenience store is doomed," explained Tom Ewens, vice president of real estate for Houston-based National Convenience Stores, Inc., "because the sales volume that those units produce simply can't keep pace with the costs of land, construction, and operation."
>
> But the recently sought-after, first-rate corner spots are getting harder for convenience store chains to find due, in part, to increased competition from other retailers for the same locations. As store sizes creep up to the 3,000-square-foot mark, and lot sizes expand to allow for increased gas and parking facilities, convenience stores are looking for roughly the same size lot that a fast-food unit, drug store, bank, or gas station might want. This means that the sector's traditional strength of flexibility in site selection is being somewhat impaired.
>
> And in some markets, notable parts of Arizona, Texas, and Florida, where convenience stores already account for 10–12 percent of grocery sales, there just aren't that many choice spots to be found.
>
> John C. Nichols II, senior vice president and chief financial officer of Convenient Industries of America, Inc., reveals that the Louisville, Kentucky-based operator of Convenient Food Marts is having to look at more sites today than in the past to find good ones, like its industry counterparts. Three years ago a site might have been selected from two or three. Now it's more likely that seven or eight are considered before a choice is made.
>
> What's happening is that convenience stores are pinning their hopes for higher sales volumes and profits on primary locations, while coping with higher real estate and operations costs than they faced at former sites.
>
> This means that convenience stores' profit and loss statements will likely get tighter and tighter, the line between a winning and losing location more thinly drawn.[7]

Exhibits 7 and 8 contain additional financial data on Southland.

[7] "What's Down the Road for Convenience Stores," *Chain Store Age Executive*, June 1979, pp. 23–24.

Exhibit 7

SOUTHLAND CORPORATION
Consolidated Balance Sheets
For the Years Ended December 31, 1977 and 1978

	1978	*1977*
Assets		
Current assets:		
Cash and short-term investments	$ 82,745,504	$ 65,903,801
Accounts and notes receivable	78,968,103	75,171,378
Inventories	161,254,967	126,913,578
Deposits and prepaid expenses	26,777,392	21,436,624
Investments in properties	55,857,419	53,319,492
Total current assets	405,603,385	342,744,873
Investments in affiliates	27,364,352	26,717,136
Property, plant, and equipment	479,554,364	389,251,583
Capital leases	197,730,040	178,190,671
Other assets	24,223,652	5,627,054
Total assets	$1,344,475,793	$942,531,317
Liabilities and Shareholders' Equity		
Current liabilities:		
Accounts payable and accrued expenses	$ 211,920,848	$168,894,391
Income taxes	18,636,987	15,481,417
Long-term debt due within one year	13,254,868	4,142,055
Capital lease obligation due within one year	20,157,217	17,533,856
Total current liabilities	263,969,920	206,051,719
Deferred credits	23,235,908	18,460,424
Long-term debt	261,460,472	195,520,000
Capital lease obligations	211,342,074	192,546,677
Committments for operating leases	—	—
Shareholders' equity:		
Common stock $1 par value, authorized 40 million shares, issued and outstanding 20,200,557 and 19,557,287 shares	202,006	195,573
Additional capital	242,339,882	223,499,443
Retained earnings	131,925,591	106,257,781
Total shareholders' equity	374,467,419	329,952,497
Total liabilities and shareholders' equity	$1,134,475,793	$942,531,317

Source: Southland Corporation, Annual Report, 1978.

Recent Trends in the Convenience Food Industry

39 In 1957, the industry consisted of 500 stores with an annual volume of $75 million. Ten years later, there were 8,000 convenience stores with combined sales of $1.3 billion. In 1978, the corresponding figures were some 33,000 stores and an annual sales volume of $8.7 billion. Average annual sales growth during the last five years was about 17 percent. Sales volumes in convenience food stores were approaching 5 percent of total U.S. grocery sales, up from 1.7 percent in 1967. Many industry sources predicted favorable sales growth for convenience food stores for the years ahead. Sales revenues

Exhibit 8

SOUTHLAND CORPORATION
Consolidated Statements of Changes in Financial Position
For the Years ended December 31, 1978 and 1977

	1978	*1977*
Sources of working capital:		
From operations:		
Net earnings	$ 57,097,109	$ 45,317,241
Expenses charged to earnings which did not require outlay of working capital:		
Depreciation and amortization	46,839,875	41,991,861
Amortization of capital leases	20,884,330	19,743,097
Deferred income taxes and other credits	6,552,597	3,415,874
Working capital provided from operations	131,373,911	110,468,073
Long-term debt	70,658,506	61,534,160
Capital lease obligations	41,907,748	37,409,857
Retirements and sales of property	13,555,200	12,774,857
Retirements and sales of capital leases	1,397,049	6,191,948
Issuance of common stock		
Conversion of notes	—	2,690,000
Acquisitions	—	2,310,000
Key employees incentive plan	470,992	462,278
Employee stock options	704,463	97,343
Total sources of working capital	260,067,869	233,938,516
Uses of working capital:		
Property, plant, and equipment	141,438,084	96,324,184
Capital leases	41,907,748	37,409,857
Reduction of capital lease obligations	23,112,351	23,419,196
Payment of long-term debt	4,718,034	16,862,491
Cash dividends	13,627,443	10,960,976
Net noncurrent assets of businesses purchased for stock and cash	29,180,394	9,111,552
Retirement of long-term debt upon conversion of notes	—	2,690,000
Investments in affiliates	647,216	1,061,359
Other	366,089	836,640
Cash paid in lieu of fractional shares on stock dividend	130,199	105,267
Total uses of working capital	255,127,558	198,781,522
Increase in working capital	$ 4,940,311	$ 35,156,994
Changes in working capital:		
Increases in current assets:		
Cash and short-term investments	$ 16,841,703	$ 39,504,544
Accounts and notes receivable	3,796,725	7,788,618
Inventories	34,341,389	21,884,637
Deposits and prepaid expenses	5,340,768	1,482,830
Investment in properties	2,537,927	9,342,429
Total changes in working capital	62,858,512	80,003,058
Increases (decreases) in current liabilities:		
Accounts payable and accrued expenses	43,026,457	38,624,253
Income taxes	3,155,570	4,442,417
Long-term debt due within one year	9,112,813	(611,614)
Capital lease obligations due within one year	2,623,361	2,391,008
Total increases in current liabilities	57,918,201	44,846,064
Increase in working capital	$ 4,940,311	$ 35,156,994

Source: Southland Corporation, Annual Report, 1978.

Exhibit 9

Breakdown of 1976 margins, expenses, and net profit for the representative convenience store*

Sales	100.0%
Cost of goods sold	71.2
Gross margin	28.8
Expenses:	
Employee wages	10.6
Employee benefits	1.9
Advertising and promotion	0.7
Property rentals	3.3
Utility expenses	3.2
Other expenses	5.7
Total expenses	25.4
Net profit before taxes	3.4

* Determined by trade sources from industrywide data.
Source: *Convenience Stores,* September–October 1977, p. 44.

were projected to increase at a 15 percent annual rate, and volume was expected to reach 8 percent of total grocery sales by 1980.

40 For the extra convenience and service they offered, convenience food stores took higher markups on the items they sold. Whereas conventional supermarkets had an average gross margin of 22.4 percent in 1978, the gross margins in convenience food stores were typically 28 to 30 percent. Exhibit 9 gives a breakdown of the 1976 gross margin, expenses, and net profits for the representative convenience food store.

41 Recently, industry observers had become concerned with the increased competition that supermarkets seemed to be initiating. Specifically, the trends of many supermarkets toward longer hours, Sunday openings, and express-lane checkouts had the potential of eroding the market shares of convenience food stores. In response, some convenience chains were keeping prices on selected high-volume items as close to those of supermarkets as possible. Munford's Majik Market stores, Southland's biggest competitor, recently adjusted the prices of some 25 of its best-selling items to be competitive with supermarket prices.

42 In addition to competition from supermarkets, competition from other retail sectors was emerging. Fast-food chains, liquor-delis, gas stations carrying food items, and discount and drug outlets with newly added food items were a new competitive threat. These types of firms were expected to expand their convenience food lines and to begin to carry high-traffic nonfood items. Furthermore, many of the drug stores were staying open longer hours and opting for locations with many of the same features of convenience stores.

7-Eleven's Competitors in Convenience Foods

43 7-Eleven in 1978 was more than seven times the size of Munford, its nearest competitor. (Munford is the only other convenience chain listed on the New York Stock Exchange.) In recent years, while 7-Eleven had been booming, Munford had been having more than its share of problems. While in the process of closing marginal and unprofitable units, earnings and sales for Munford suffered accordingly. In addition to their stores

Exhibit 10

Sales and earnings of convenience chains (in thousands of dollars)

	Sales			*Earnings*		
Company	*1978*	*1977*	*1976*	*1978*	*1977*	*1976*
Southland	$3,089,000	$2,544,414	$2,121,146	$57,000	$45,348	$40,277
Munford	378,950*	340,174	334,770	6.090	(770)	3,427
Circle K	363,783	302,603	262,362	8,196	6,912	5,122
National Convenience stores	263,705	233,208	212,606	5,011	3,536	2,652
Utotem group	221,423	206,041	192,499	9,658	8,788	8,822
Convenient Industries of America	177,732	146,598	123,368	1,148	896	857
Sunshine-Jr. stores	93,553	81,225	68,899	1,622	1,432	1,387
Shop & Go	82,729	70,136	60,780	2,271	1,655	1,650
Hop-In food stores	31,714	22,739	14,077	658	392	280
Lil' Champ	22,727	21.006	18,807	778	647	592
Grand total	$4,725,316	$3,968,144	$3,409,314	$92,432	$68,836	$65,066

Note: Includes sales and earnings from operations other than convenience stores where applicable.
* Estimated.
Source: *Progressive Grocer,* April 1978.

group, Munford experienced problems with Farmbest Foods, a dairy operation acquired in 1975. The Farmbest operation lost money in 1977 due to unsettled industry conditions in Florida and Alabama.

44 A new merchandising concept being tried by Munford, in order to catch up with the industry, was to join forces with major oil companies such as Texaco, Gulf, and Amoco by putting Munford's Majik Market convenience stores at existing gasoline station sites. The executives of Munford felt that there were many advantages for this concept, because they were convinced that the consumers were accepting the idea of buying gasoline at convenience stores very well.

45 Another competitive factor in the convenience store field was Circle K. For a period of four years through 1977, Circle K virtually halted its store expansion program in favor of remodeling and renovating older, existing stores. The Circle K chain, like Munford and others, entered the gasoline business, but with a basic difference from Munford, Circle K's strategy was to retain its recognition and image as convenience first and gasoline second. For this reason, Circle K chose to add gasoline pumps to their existing stores, not vice versa, as Munford did. Circle K planned to add 60 to 70 stores a year through the mid-1980s.

46 A third competitor of 7-Eleven was the National Convenience stores chain. In 1976, a young, dynamic man named Pete Van Horn became president of National Convenience. Not being fettered by the bonds of tradition in the industry, Van Horn slashed the number of stores, lowered personnel turnover, increased sales in remaining stores, and in general, put National Convenience on a sound footing. Van Horn was anxious to try out his ideas about store layout, merchandising, and expansion; his goal at the end of 1977 was to double earnings in the next four years.[8]

47 Exhibit 10 presents comparative sales and earnings for 10 leading convenience food chains. Exhibit 11 contains per-store sales and profit statistics for the 1974–1978 period.

[8] "The Convenience Stores," *Financial World,* November 1, 1977.

Exhibit 11

Average sales and profit statistics for top 10 publicly held convenience food store chains

	1978	*1977*	*1976*	*1975*	*1974*
Yearly sales per store	$274,115	$263,895	$240,828	$232,140	$213,800
Weekly sales per store	$5,257	$5,061	$4,606	$4,452	$4,110
Profit on pretax sales	3.65%	3.48%	3.64%	3.32%	3.39%
Profit on aftertax sales	1.98%	1.8%	1.92%	1.71%	1.77%
Yearly pretax profit per store	$10,026	$9,194	$8,762	$7,723	$7,240
Yearly aftertax profit per store	$5,431	$4,752	$4,523	$3,978	$3,780

Source: "Eighth Annual Dollars-per-Day Survey of Small Food Store Industry," *Chain Store Age Executive,* June 1979, p. 26.

Southland's Dairies and Special Operations Groups

48 Initially, the Dairies and Special Operations Groups were formed to vertically integrate their activities with 7-Eleven. The Dairies group processed and distributed milk, ice cream, yogurt, juices, eggnog, dips, and toppings; in 1978, it served 5,295 of Southland's convenience stores and supplied 66 percent of all the dairy products sold in all 7-Eleven stores. The group includes 28 processing plants and 86 distribution locations. However, more and more of the Dairies group sales volume was coming from outside Southland. In 1978, 65 percent of the unit's $400 million sales revenues were to food retailers such as Denny's and Wendy's. The expansion of sales to outside companies was being pursued through the development of new high-margin novelty items such as sundae-style yogurts, cheeses, and frozen dairy items like Big Deal, Gram Daddy, and Big Wheel.

49 A similar trend was evident in the Special Operations group. While this division supplied other Southland units with food ingredients, ice, Slurpee concentrate, preservatives, sanitizers, and cleaning agents, in 1978 a total of 72 percent of sales were to outside customers. In 1978, the chemicals unit was expanded by the acquisition of a New Jersey fine chemicals plant; this acquisition allowed Southland to market a broader line of products to customers in the agricultural and pharmaceutical industries. The division's Hudgins Truck Rental unit was expanding its efforts to provide full-maintenance truck leasing to national and regional customers as well as to Southland operations; in 1978, its outside sales were up 10 percent and accounted for 68 percent of revenues. In 1978, a new unit called Tidel Systems was added to the Special Operations group; it manufactured an innovative money-handling device designed to reduce losses from robberies and to increase store-site cash handling efficiency. While Southland planned to install the device at its 7-Eleven stores, there was an even greater potential for sales to other retailers, and a nationwide sales and maintenance organization was being assembled.

The Acquisition of Chief Auto Parts

50 In December 1978, at a cost of $20 million, Southland acquired the assets of Chief Auto Parts, a chain of 119 retail automobile supply stores in southern California. A

typical Chief store was 2,000 square feet in size, open seven days a week, and located in a neighborhood shopping center close to homes or businesses. The stores sold approximately 7,500 replacement parts and accessories and carried both national brands and private-label products. The average purchase was $5, and a large percentage of sales were on weekends when most do-it-yourselfers had time to service their cars. Chief also had a modern warehouse in Los Angeles from which it supplied its stores.

51 There was some thought that the Chief acquisition signaled a move by Southland to diversify into small-store-retailing, particularly those kinds of retail businesses which had operating characteristics similar to those of 7-Eleven stores.

Future Outlook

52 Southland management's view of the future for its 7-Eleven stores was exemplified by John Thompson, chairman:

> We believe that the growth opportunity in the convenience store area is great. I'm very bullish on the future. There are many parts in the United States that are not saturated with convenience stores, and I would say that Texas and Florida are the two most saturated areas. Even in those states we can go 20 to 40 more stores a year, depending on housing. But in the rest of the United States, there is relatively much less saturation, so that as far as we're concerned, we think we can build 500-plus stores a year for a long time. Why, the Northeast is a great area. We haven't really saturated that market at all. And the Midwest? Well, we've hardly gotten started there. And California? Well, sure, we have 900 stores in California, but you can build forever in that state. I guess you could say the future for us looks marvelous.[9]

However, in 1979, several industry observers were taking a more-cautious stance and asking if the industry was not on the verge of maturity.

[9] "Southland Is the Best Example."

Subject Index

T

U–V

W

Y–Z

This book has been set CAP in 10 and 9 point Century Schoolbook, leaded 2 points. Part numbers are 50 point Helvetica Bold and chapter numbers are 14 point Helvetica Light. Part and chapter titles are 24 point Century Schoolbook Bold. The size of the type page is 35 by 47 picas.

Case Index